Exploring the Bible

STEPHEN L. HARRIS

Professor Emeritus
California State University, Sacramento

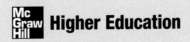

Boston   Burr Ridge, IL   Dubuque, IA   New York   San Francisco   St. Louis
Bangkok   Bogotá   Caracas   Kuala Lumpur   Lisbon   London   Madrid   Mexico City
Milan   Montreal   New Delhi   Santiago   Seoul   Singapore   Sydney   Taipei   Toronto

Mc Graw Hill Higher Education

Published by McGraw-Hill, an imprint of The McGraw-Hill Companies, Inc., 1221 Avenue of the Americas, New York. NY 10020. Copyright © 2010. All rights reserved, No part of this publication may be reproduced or distributed in any form or by any means, or stored in a database or retrieval system, without the prior written consent of The McGraw-Hill Companies, Inc., including but not limited to, in any network or other electronic storage or transmission, or broadcast for distance learning.

This book is printed on acid-free paper.

1 2 3 4 5 6 7 8 9 0 QPD/QPD 0 9

ISBN: 978-0-07-340736-4
MHID: 0-07-340736-4

Editor in Chief: *Michael Ryan*
Editorial Director: *Beth Mejia*
Sponsoring Editor: *Mark Georgiev*
Marketing Manager: *Pamela Cooper*
Production Editor: *David Blatty*

Manuscript Editor: *Thomas L. Briggs*
Design Manager and Cover Designer: *Cassandra Chu*
Production Supervisor: *Tandra Jorgensen*
Composition: *10/12 Adobe Caslon by Aptara, Inc.*
Printing: *45# New Era Matte, Quebecor World, Dubuque*

Cover: Building the Ark, 17th century painting on copper. © The Art Archive/Queretaro Museum Mexico/Gianni Dagli Orti

Library of Congress Cataloging-in-Publication Data

Harris, Stephen L., 1937–
   Exploring the Bible / Stephen L. Harris. — 1st ed.
     p. cm.
   Includes bibliographical references and index.
   ISBN-13: 978-0-07-340736-4 (alk. paper)
   ISBN-10: 0-07-340736-4 (alk. paper)
   1. Bible—Textbooks. I. Title.
   BS605.3.H37 2010
   220.6'1—dc22
                                    2009001856

TEXT CREDITS   Scripture quotations are from the New Revised Standard Version of the Bible, copyright © 1989 by the National Council of the Churches of Christ in the USA. Used by permission. All rights reserved.

PHOTO CREDITS   2.1, © Israel Museum, Jerusalem; 3.2, © British Museum, London/Bridgeman Art Library; 3.3, © Bildarchiv Preussischer Kulturbesitz/Art Resource, NY; 3.4, © The British Museum, London; 3.5, © Scala/Art Resource, NY; 3.6, 3.7, © Réunion des Musées Nationaux/Art Resource, NY; 3.8, © Egyptian Museum/PhotoEdit; 4.1, © R. Sheridan/ Ancient Art & Architecture Collection Ltd.; 4.2, Courtesy Nicolas Wyatt/ Edinburgh Ras Shamra Project/University of Edinburgh; 4.3, © Sandro Vannini/Corbis; 6.1, Courtesy of the Asian and Middle Eastern Division, The New York Public Library, Astor, Lenox and Tilden Foundations; 6.3, © Réunion des Musées Nationaux/Art Resource, NY; 9.1, Impression of Lachish, based on Assyrian wall reliefs, 1951, by Alan Sorrell, (1904–74)/British Museum, London, UK/The Bridgeman Art Library; 10.1, © Erich Lessing/ Art Resource, NY; 11.1, © Zev Radovan/www.BibleLandPictures.com; 13.3,13.4, © Erich Lessing/Art Resource, NY; 16.2, 17.2, © Oriental Institute Museum, University of Chicago; 17.3, © Zev Radovan/www.BibleLandPictures.com; 18.1, © Bible Lands Museum. Photo by David Harris; 18.2, © Bildarchiv Preussischer Kulturbesitz/Art Resource, NY; 21.1, © Erich Lessing/Art Resource, NY; 23.1, © The British Museum; 23.2, Courtesy of the University Museum, University of Pennsylvania, Neg. #S8-68052b; 23.3, Courtesy of the Bible Lands Museum Jerusalem. Photo Credit: M. Amar and M. Greyevsky; 26.2, © Erich Lessing/Art Resource, NY; 27.1, © Israel Museum/PhotoEdit; 28.1, The Metropolitan Museum of Art, Rogers Fund, 1980. (08.258.47). Photograph © 2000 The Metropolitan Museum of Art; 28.3, © Scala/Art Resource, NY; 28.4, © Bettmann/Corbis; 28.5, © Foto Marburg/Art Resource, NY; 28.6, © Museo Archeologico Nazionale, Taranto, Puglia, Italy/The Bridgeman Art Library International; 28.7, © Giraudon/Art Resource, NY; 28.8, © Bildarchiv Preussischer Kulturbesitz/Art Resource, NY; 29.1, © Richard T. Nowitz/Corbis; 29.2, © Richard T. Nowitz; 30.2, © Scala/Art Resource, NY; 30.3, © Erich Lessing/Art Resource, NY; 30.4, © Scala/Art Resource, NY; 30.5, © Zev Radovan/www. BibleLandPictures.com; 30.6, Samuel H. Kress Collection, Photograph © 2005 Board of Trustees, National Gallery of Art, Washington.; 31.2, © Metropolitan Museum of Art. Bequest of Mrs. H. O. Havemeyer, 1929. The H. O. Havemeyer Collection. 29.107.35; 31.3, © Photri; 31.4, © Scala/Art Resource, NY; 31.5, © Zev Radovan/www.BibleLandPictures.com; 32.1, © HIP/Scala/Art Resource, NY; 32.2, © Erich Lessing/ PhotoEdit; 32.3, © Erich Lessing/Art Resource, NY; 33.1, 33.3, 33.4, 34.1, © Scala/Art Resource, NY; 34.4, © AKG London; 34.6, © Eric & David Hosking/Corbis; 34.7, © Scala/Art Resource, NY; 35.2, © Alinari/Art Resource, NY; 35.3, © Erich Lessing/PhotoEdit; 35.6, Photo courtesy of the Rev. Dr. James E. Straukamp; 36.1, 37.2, © Erich Lessing/Art Resource, NY; 38.2, 38.3, 38.5, © Scala/Art Resource, NY

The Internet addresses listed in the text were accurate at the time of publication. The inclusion of a Web site does not indicate an endorsement by the authors or McGraw-Hill, and McGraw-Hill docs not guarantee the accuracy of the information presented at these sites.

www.mhhe.com

Table of Contents

Preface v

Part One **An Introduction to the Bible and the Biblical World** 1

CHAPTER 1 **The Bible: An Overview** 3

CHAPTER 2 **How the Bible Was Created: Transmission, Canonization, and Translation** 18

CHAPTER 3 **The Ancient Near East: The Environment That Produced the Bible** 31

Part Two **The Hebrew Bible/Old Testament** 51

CHAPTER 4 **The Five Books of Torah (Divine Teaching): Themes and Theories** 53

CHAPTER 5 **In the Beginning: The Book of Genesis** 67

CHAPTER 6 **Freedom and Responsibility: The Book of Exodus** 77

CHAPTER 7 **Law, Holiness, and Rebellion: The Books of Leviticus and Numbers** 88

CHAPTER 8 **A New Vision of Moses' Teaching: The Book of Deuteronomy** 94

CHAPTER 9 **The Story of Ancient Israel: How the Promised Land Was Gained and Lost** 101

CHAPTER 10 **Faith and War: The Book of Joshua** 106

CHAPTER 11 **Yahweh's Warriors: The Book of Judges** 114

CHAPTER 12 **The Rise of David and the Birth of a Kingdom: The Books of 1 and 2 Samuel** 121

CHAPTER 13 **From the Glory of Solomon to Exile in Babylon: The Books of 1 and 2 Kings** 129

CHAPTER 14 **Israel's Prophets: Proclaiming the Word of Yahweh** 144

CHAPTER 15 **Prophets to the Northern Kingdom: The Oracles of Amos and Hosea** 153

CHAPTER 16 **Prophets of the Assyrian Threat: The Oracles of Isaiah, Micah, Zephaniah, and Nahum** 158

CHAPTER 17 **Prophets of the Babylonian Crisis: The Oracles of Jeremiah, Habakkuk, and Obadiah** 168

CHAPTER 18 **Prophets in Exile: The Oracles of Ezekiel and Second Isaiah** 176

CHAPTER 19 **After the Exile—Israel's Last Prophets: The Oracles of Haggai, Zechariah, Third Isaiah, Joel, Malachi, and Jonah** 184

CHAPTER 20   **The Writings: Israel's Changing Life with God** 192

CHAPTER 21   **The Postexilic Readjustment: The Books of Ezra and Nehemiah** 196

CHAPTER 22   **Worshiping at the Second Temple: Hebrew Poetry and the Book of Psalms** 201

CHAPTER 23   **Israel's Wisdom Writers: The Books of Proverbs, Job, and Ecclesiastes** 208

CHAPTER 24   **Festival Scrolls: The Books of Ruth, Song of Songs, Lamentations, and Esther** 224

CHAPTER 25   **Reinterpreting Israel's History: The Books of 1 and 2 Chronicles** 233

CHAPTER 26   **Keeping God's Law in a Hostile World: Revolt of the Maccabees and the Book of Daniel** 238

CHAPTER 27   **The Second Canon: Books of the Apocrypha** 249

Part Three   **The New Testament** 263

CHAPTER 28   **The World in Which Christianity Originated: Roman Power, Greek Culture, and the Cult of Deified Rulers** 265

CHAPTER 29   **First-Century Judaism: Diversity, Messianic Expectations, and the Birth of Christianity** 282

CHAPTER 30   **Telling Jesus' Story: The Gospel of Mark** 291

CHAPTER 31   **The Synoptic Problem: The Gospel of Matthew and Its Relationship to the Gospels of Mark and Luke** 307

CHAPTER 32   **Jesus as a Savior for "All Nations": The Gospel of Luke** 325

CHAPTER 33   **Another Way of Telling Jesus' Story: The Gospel of John** 336

CHAPTER 34   **An Account of Early Christianity: The Book of Acts** 350

CHAPTER 35   **Paul and the Gentile Mission: Letters to Churches at Thessalonica, Corinth, Galatia, Rome, Philippi, and Colossae** 363

CHAPTER 36   **Continuing the Pauline Tradition: Second Thessalonians, Colossians, Ephesians, and the Pastoral Epistles** 391

CHAPTER 37   **General Letters on Faith and Behavior: Hebrews and the Catholic Epistles** 401

CHAPTER 38   **Continuing the Apocalyptic Hope: The Book of Revelation** 412

CHAPTER 39   **Our Judeo-Christian Heritage: The Biblical Concept of God** 424

Glossary 437

Index 464

Preface

Exploring the Bible is designed to help beginning students undertake their first systematic study of the Bible. Divided into three parts, the book opens with an overview of the Bible's contents, surveying the major themes of both the Old and New Testaments. Giving students a perspective from which to approach reading biblical literature, Part One shows how the biblical books were transmitted to us and how biblical writers commonly adopted and transformed older traditions of the ancient Near East as they portrayed Israel's special relationship with God. This section also introduces students to some of the important assumptions and methods of scholarly analysis of the biblical text.

Exploring the Bible incorporates the tools of current scholarship, but it focuses primarily on making clear the essential message of each individual biblical book. Part Two follows the three-part division that Jewish editors gave to the Hebrew Bible (Old Testament). Jewish scholars commonly refer to these three parts by the acronym *Tanakh*, which stands for *Torah* (divine teaching), *Nevi'im* (Prophets), and *Kethuvim* (Writings). In general, this tripartite division reflects the order of the Hebrew Bible's chronological growth and parallels the historical development of the Jewish community of faith.

Beginning with Genesis, we examine the Hebrew Bible (Tanakh) book by book, placing each document in its religious, literary, and historical context. After surveying scholarly theories about the composition of the Torah—also known as the Pentateuch—we examine biblical traditions about Israel's origins and the Israelites' Exodus from Egypt to the territory of Canaan (Palestine), which God had promised their ancestor Abraham. In studying the Tanakh's second part—the Nevi'im (Prophets)—we continue the national epic of Israel's history, from archaeological discoveries relating to Israel's emergence in Palestine, to the establishment of the kingdom of David and Solomon (c. 1000 BCE), to Assyria's destruction of Israel (721 BCE) and Babylon's conquest of Judah (587 BCE) (the books of Joshua through 2 Kings). In chronological order, we then survey the messages of Israel's individual prophets, which provide divine pronouncements (oracles) on the ethical causes for Israel's national rise and fall (the books of Isaiah, Jeremiah, Ezekiel, and the twelve "minor prophets").

In the third division of the Hebrew Bible (Old Testament)—the Kethuvim (Writings)—we study the characteristics of Hebrew poetry as developed in the worshiping community (the Book of Psalms) and Israel's wisdom literature, with special emphasis on the books of Job and Ecclesiastes. In his poetic theodicy, a literary attempt to account for God's permitting evil and undeserved suffering, the author of Job boldly challenges traditional biblical concepts of God. Deeply skeptical of attempts to discover divine purpose in the world, the writer of Ecclesiastes offers an ironic counterpoint to the theological certainties of the Torah and Prophets.

The Writings include works of enormous literary and intellectual diversity, ranging from gentle tales of love, such as Ruth; to anguished mournings over Israel's sufferings, such as Lamentations; to a revision of Israel's history from a priestly perspective, the books of Chronicles. Jewish editors made 2 Chronicles the last book of the Hebrew Bible, giving its final words—a decree by Cyrus the Great of Persia ordering Jews to return from exile to rebuild Jerusalem—a resonating significance. At the conclusion of the Tanakh, God is implicitly seen as operating invisibly behind the scenes, using an entirely human agency to restore his people to divine favor.

By contrast, the Book of Daniel offers bewildering images of cosmic violence, supernatural entities, and symbolic previews of the future course of history. To place Daniel's mystic visions in their religious and historical context, we explain the rise and nature of Israel's apocalyptic expectations, specifying the characteristics of apocalyptic thought and literature (Chapter 26). In Chapter 27, we survey deuterocanonical books, writings that appeared in Greek editions of the Hebrew Bible but were excluded from the Tanakh, such as 1 and 2 Maccabees, Tobit, and Judith. Known as the Apocrypha, the deuterocanonical books also include apocalyptic works, such as Baruch, and wisdom literature, such as the Wisdom of Solomon.

To begin Part Three—the New Testament—we provide a sociohistorical transition to the Greco-Roman world in which Christianity, the offspring of Israelite religion, originated. As clarifying background to the twenty-seven New Testament books, we discuss the political power of Rome, the pervasiveness of Greek language and thought, and the Roman Empire's cult of deified rulers. (Whereas the Old Testament was written in Hebrew, with some later books in Aramaic, a related tongue, the New Testament documents are entirely in Greek.) Chapter 29 presents the first-century-CE Palestinian environment in which Jesus of Nazareth and his followers proclaimed the dawning kingdom of God. It emphasizes the diversity of early Judaism, describing the distinctive beliefs of such groups as the Sadducees, Pharisees, and Essenes, presumed copyists of the Dead Sea Scrolls. The major differences between diverse first-century Jewish concepts of a national Messiah and early Christians' belief that Jesus was Israel's Messiah are carefully delineated. Beginning with Mark's story of Jesus, all four Gospels—as well as scholarly theories about the literary relationships among them—are thoroughly discussed. Each of the four Gospels is allowed to speak for itself, with no attempt to blur their distinctive portrayals of Jesus.

The Book of Acts' account of Christianity's growth from a Jewish messianic movement in Palestine to a largely Gentile (non-Jewish) faith established throughout the Roman Empire is followed by a presentation of Paul's unique contribution to the religion. Chapter 35 not only summarizes Paul's distinctive theological beliefs, ranging from his doctrine of justification by faith to his ideal of selfless love, but also analyzes each of the seven letters, including 1 and 2 Corinthians, Galatians, and Romans, that scholars regard as genuine Pauline. Chapter 36 discusses the six letters that the scholarly community believes were probably written by Paul's disciples.

After discussing Hebrews, the catholic epistles, and Revelation—like Daniel, an apocalyptic work—*Exploring the Bible* concludes with a discussion of the Bible's most important contribution to global religion—its composite portrayal of God. Reviewing crucial passages composed over a period of perhaps a thousand years, the final chapter analyzes biblical writers' sometimes ethically problematic attempts to describe or define the infinite complexity of ultimate Being.

From Genesis to Revelation, we examine the unfolding narrative of the divine–human relationship, as God—in an amazing variety of ways—interacts with humanity to accomplish his long-range purposes. In analyzing the biblical narratives of Israel's partnership with God and the teachings of Jesus and his followers, this text consistently highlights major events—as well as the theological meaning that biblical writers give them—to help students easily distinguish the Bible's most important ideas and themes, principles that inform the contemporary faiths of Judaism, Christianity and Islam.

Learning Aids

Exploring the Bible contains many aids to facilitate learning. Each chapter begins with a concise summary of key topics/themes. Further, important terms—persons, places, and concepts—are printed in **boldface,** listed alphabetically at end of each chapter, and then concisely defined in the extensive Glossary at the back of the book. To help students master the material, the presentation in each chapter is clear and direct, geared to the undergraduate with no previous exposure to the academic study of the Bible. At the end of every chapter are "Questions for Discussion and Review," calculated to stimulate individual thought as well as class discussions. Useful scholarly references are included in the "Recommended Reading," offering students sources for further research. Selected for their accessibility to beginning students, these listed resources, such as *The New Interpreter's Dictonary of the Bible,* are found in almost all college libraries.

Other pedagogical tools include numerous charts, tables, boxes, and maps. From tables listing books of the Old Testament found in Jewish, Protestant, Catholic, and Orthodox Bibles, to summaries of major events in biblical history, to parallels among the four Gospels, students will find helpful information at a glance. Boxes provide concise descriptions of topics that supplement the main text. They explain a wide range to topics: the primal watery abyss in Genesis; Egyptian myths anticipating biblical concepts of creation; the gender of God; archaeology and the origins of Israel; Gospel concepts of the afterlife; Jesus' final words; and milestones in the growth of Christianity.

While maps show the topography of the Promised Land and the location of important biblical cities and nations, the many illustrations depict important archaeological sites and artifacts, as well as later artistic renditions of biblical figures and events.

Acknowledgments

Among those who have helped make this text a reality, I would particularly like to thank the following reviewers whose practical advice serves to make this text more useful in the classroom:

Samuel D. Breslauer, University of Kansas

Paul Brians, Washington State University

Jeannie Constantinou, University of San Diego

Crerar Douglas, California State University, Northridge

Daniel Keith Falk, University of Oregon

Chris Frilingos, Michigan State University

Sandra Gravert, Appalachian State University

John K. Simmons, Western Illinois University

I would also like to thank the sponsoring editor, Mark Georgiev; the production editor, David Blatty, whose helpful attention is greatly appreciated; and Thomas Briggs, for his expert editing of the manuscript.

PART ONE

An Introduction to the Bible and the Biblical World

CHAPTER 1
The Bible   3

CHAPTER 2
How the Bible Was Created   18

CHAPTER 3
The Ancient Near East   31

CHAPTER I

The Bible

An Overview

Key Themes/Topics Divided into two main sections, the Old Testament and the New Testament, the Bible is a diverse anthology of documents composed over a span of about 1,100 years. Written in the Hebrew language (hence the name "Hebrew Bible"), the first section contains the story of ancient Israel, God's chosen people. The Hebrew Bible is also known as the Tanakh, an acronym based on the first letter of each of its three major parts: *Torah* (Law or Instruction), *Nevi'im* (Prophets), and *Kethuvim* (Writings). The Tanakh explores the partnership between God and Israel, with whom he concludes a series of covenants (pacts or agreements), including divine promises for a permanent homeland and other blessings. A collection of twenty-seven Greek books that the early Christian community added to a Greek edition of the Hebrew Bible, the New Testament focuses on the ministry of Jesus of Nazareth and the teachings of his followers, presented as the fulfillment of God's promises to Israel.

 ## Why Read the Bible?

Translated into hundreds of languages, the Bible is the world's most widely distributed book. In the United States, English-language editions top the best-seller lists every year. In 2005, for example, Americans bought at least 25 million copies of the Bible, more than twice as many as the year's next most popular book. According to recent polls, about 91 percent of Americans families own at least one Bible (the average number of Bibles per household is four), and almost half the American population reads the Bible at least once a week.

Globally, about 2 billion people—approximately a third of the world's population—are "people of the book," Jews and Christians who worship the biblical concept of God. In the Western Hemisphere, biblical ideas and principles continue to exert an enormous influence on people's thought and behavior. Even people who do not belong to a church or synagogue typically express biblical attitudes in forming their personal views of life. Even when unaware that they are doing so, many Americans judge their own and others' conduct according to biblical principles of social justice and ethical responsibility. From popular notions about angelic visitations to speculations about the time of Jesus' return to earth or the fate of people after they die, most Americans typically echo biblical ideas.

While almost every American family owns one or more Bibles, polls indicate that few in the United States are familiar with its contents. When asked to name the four **Gospels**—the four accounts of Jesus' life that form the first part of the New Testament—most Americans could not name even one. Only a small percentage could list more than two or three of the Ten Commandments, and fewer still knew where to find them in the Bible (Exodus 20 and Deuteronomy 5). Some college students thought that Moses was one of Jesus' twelve apostles. Even among people who regularly attend church,

3

pollsters found, the level of biblical knowledge is almost equally limited.

Religions claiming to base their teachings on the Bible are almost unbelievably diverse: There are three main branches of Judaism and, worldwide, 30,000 distinct Christian denominations, with more than 200 different denominations in North America alone. With so many different religious groups competing for people's allegiance, it is crucial to understand what the Bible is and how it acquired its present form.

This textbook has dual goals: to acquaint students with the Bible's principal themes and content and to familiarize readers with the work of contemporary biblical scholarship. For the past two centuries, since the scientific revolution, an international body of scholars—Jewish, Catholic, Protestant, and others—has labored to analyze the individual biblical books, trying to place them in their social and historical context and to understand each writer's individual message. As readers will discover, we are all the beneficiaries of this ongoing scholarly enterprise.

 ## A Brief Survey of the Bible's Contents

In studying the Bible systematically, readers quickly discover that it is not a single volume but a library of many different books, written over approximately eleven centuries. In fact, the English word *bible* comes from the Greek *biblia* (meaning "little books"), a term that accurately expresses its nature as a collection of many individual writings. Christianity's two main divisions—Catholic and Protestant—have slightly different editions of the Bible. Whereas Protestant bibles typically contain sixty-six books, Catholic bibles include several additional books in the Old Testament, commonly known as the **Apochrypha.** Catholics and Protestants thus have a somewhat different **canon**— the official list of documents that a religious community accepts as authoritative and binding. The Greek Orthodox Church has a canon similar to the Catholic, but with the addition of three more books (see Table 1.1). (For a discussion of the Apocrypha or "second canon," see Chapter 27.)

Viewed as a whole, the Bible is the story of God's complex relationship with humanity. The first book, Genesis, opens with an account of God's creation of the universe and of humans, whom he* fashions in his "im-

age" and "likeness." The final book, Revelation, closes with a re-creation, a "new heaven and a new earth" in which God and humankind at last dwell together in peace. Between Genesis and Revelation, which provide a clear-cut beginning and ending to the biblical story, lies a dazzling array of literary genres—from narratives about Israel's rise and fall, to legal regulations and statutes, to prophesy, to speculations about God's rule of the world, to both devotional and erotic poetry, to Gospels, to letters, and to bewildering visions of End time (see Box 1.1).

Known to Christians as the Old Testament, the Bible's first part is essentially the drama of God's long-term relationship with **Israel**, the people he chooses to be his special possession (see Box 1.2). The first eleven books, Genesis through 2 Kings, are an extended narrative of the God–Israel partnership as it developed over a course of perhaps 1,000 years. Often called the "national epic of Israel," this narrative beings with God's call to **Abraham,** regarded as Israel's chief ancestor; continues with God's rescue of Abraham's descendants, the Israelites, from slavery in Egypt; describes their occupation of **Canaan** (Palestine), the land God promised to Abraham's offspring; recounts Israel's growth as a monarchy under King David and his heirs; and concludes with a catastrophic event— the total destruction of the Davidic state and the deportation of its leading citizens to Babylon. (See the map of Israel and the ancient Near East in Figure 1.1.) This national disaster—which marked the destruction of the capital, **Jerusalem,** and the splendid Temple of Solomon, as well as the permanent overthrow of David's line of kings—marks a crucial turning point in biblical history. As we shall see, this historical event, which took place in 587 BCE,† preoccupied the minds of many biblical authors who, in different ways, struggled to understand God's purpose in allowing his human partner to suffer so severely. Before surveying some of these later biblical books, however, it is helpful to see how ancient editors arranged Israel's sacred writings.

---

*Although biblical writers consistently use the masculine pronoun ("he") for God, many scholars urge us to remember that by definition God transcends all human dimensions, including gender distinctions.

†BCE is an abbreviation for "before the Common Era," corresponding to BC ("before Christ"); CE refers to the "Common Era," a religiously neutral term many scholars use instead of "AD" (*anno domini*, Latin for "in the year of our Lord").

TABLE I.I Order of Books in the Old Testament (Tanakh)

HEBREW BIBLE (MASORETIC TEXT)	GREEK SEPTUAGINT BIBLE	ROMAN CATHOLIC AND GREEK ORTHODOX* OLD TESTAMENT	PROTESTANT OLD TESTAMENT
I. Torah (Pentateuch)	*Pentateuch*	*Pentateuch*	*Pentateuch*
Genesis	Genesis	Genesis	Genesis
Exodus	Exodus	Exodus	Exodus
Leviticus	Leviticus	Leviticus	Leviticus
Numbers	Numbers	Numbers	Numbers
Deuteronomy	Deuteronomy	Deuteronomy	Deuteronomy
II. Nevi'im (Prophets)			
(Former Prophets)	*Historical Books*	*Historical Books*	*Historical Books*
Joshua	Joshua	Josue (Joshua)	Joshua
Judges	Judges	Judges	Judges
	Ruth	Ruth	Ruth
1–2 Samuel	1–2 Regnorum (1–2 Samuel)	1–2 Kings (1–2 Samuel)	1–2 Samuel
1–2 Kings	3–4 Regnorum (1–2 Kings)	3–4 Kings (1–2 Kings)	1–2 Kings
	1–2 Paralipomenon (1–2 Chronicles)	1–2 Paralipomenon (1–2 Chronicles)	1–2 Chronicles
	1 Esdras	1 Esdras**	Ezra
	2 Esdras (Ezra–Nehemiah)	Ezra–Nehemiah (2 Esdras in orthodox canon)	Nehemiah
	Esther	Tobias (Tobit)†	Esther
	Judith	Judith†	
	Tobit	Esther (with additions)	
	1–4 Maccabees	1–2 Maccabees†	
		3 Maccabees**	
	Poetry and Wisdom	*Poetry and Wisdom*	*Poetry and Wisdom*
	Psalms	Job	Job
	Odes	Psalms (plus Ps. 151**)	Psalms
		Prayer of Manasseh**	
	Proverbs	Proverbs	Proverbs
	Ecclesiastes	Ecclesiastes	Ecclesiastes
	Song of Songs	Canticle of Canticles (Song of Songs)	Song of Songs
	Job		
	Wisdom of Solomon	Wisdom of Solomon†	
	Sirach (Ecclesiasticus)	Ecclesiasticus† (Ben Sirach)	
	Psalms of Solomon		

(continued)

*The Greek Orthodox Bible contains all the books included in Catholic editions, plus three additional books—Prayer of Manasseh, 1 Esdras, and 3 Maccabees—and an additional psalm, Ps. 151. The books in the Orthodox canon are marked with a double asterisk (**).

†Not in Jewish or most Protestant Bibles; considered deuterocanonical in Catholic and Orthodox Old Testaments.

TABLE I.I *(continued)*

HEBREW BIBLE (MASORETIC TEXT)	GREEK SEPTUAGINT BIBLE	ROMAN CATHOLIC AND GREEK ORTHODOX OLD TESTAMENT	PROTESTANT OLD TESTAMENT
(Latter Prophets)	*Prophetic Books*	*Prophetic Books*	*Prophetic Books*
Isaiah		Isaias (Isaiah)	Isaiah
Jeremiah		Jeremias (Jeremiah)	Jeremiah
		Lamentations	Lamentations
		Baruch (including the epistle of Jeremias)†	
Ezekiel		Ezechiel (Ezekiel)	Ezekiel
		Daniel (with additions: Prayer of Azariah and Song of the Three Young Men,† Susanna,† Bel and the Dragon†)	Daniel
Book of the Twelve			
Hosea	Hosea	Osee (Hosea)	Hosea
Amos	Amos	Joel	Joel
Micah	Micah	Amos	Amos
Joel	Joel	Abidas (Obadiah)	Obadiah
Obadiah	Obediah	Jonas (Jonah)	Jonah
Jonah		Micheas (Micah)	Micah
Nahum	Nahum	Nahum	Nahum
Habakkuk	Habakkuk	Habucuc (Habakkuk)	Habakkuk
Zephaniah	Zephaniah	Sophonias (Zephaniah)	Zephaniah
Haggai	Hagai	Aggeus (Haggai)	Haggai
Zechariah	Zechariah	Zacharias (Zechariah)	Zechariah
Malachi	Malachi	Malachias (Malachi)	Malachi
III. Kethuvim (Writings)			
	Isaiah		
Psalms	Jeremiah		
Job	Baruch		
Proverbs	Lamentations		
Ruth	Epistle of Jeremiah		
Song of Songs	Ezekiel		
Ecclesiastes	Susanna		
Lamentations	Daniel		
Esther	Bel and the Dragon		
Daniel			
Ezra-Nehemiah			
1–2 Chronicles			

*The Greek Orthodox Bible contains all the books included in Catholic editions, plus three additional books—Prayer of Manasseh, 1 Esdras, and 3 Maccabees—and an additional psalm, Ps. 151. The books in the Orthodox canon are marked with a double asterisk (**).

†Not in Jewish or most Protestant Bibles; considered deuterocanonical in Catholic and Orthodox Old Testaments.

BOX I.I **What to Look For in the Bible and Where to Find It**

As the West's single most influential literary work, the Bible shapes people's attitudes and beliefs in almost every sphere of life, even when many Westerners may not be aware that their thought processes are being influenced. From ideas about the origins of life and the nature of God to the ultimate destiny of humankind, the biblical text informs the worldview of 2 billion people, particularly in North America. The Bible's teaching in several key areas is summarized below.

TOPIC	BIBLICAL SOURCE
FROM THE HEBREW BIBLE (OLD TESTAMENT)	
Creation of the world	Genesis 1:1–2:4a (first version); Genesis 2:4b–2:25 (second version)
Alienation of God and humanity	Genesis 3:1–3:24 (Adam and Eve's expulsion from Eden)
The global flood	Genesis 6:5–8:2 (and origin of rainbow, Gen. 9:13–17)
God's promises to bless the world through Abraham	Genesis 12:1–3; 22:15–18
The ten plagues on Egypt	Exodus 6:28–12:42
Miraculous sea crossing	Exodus 14:1–15:21
The Ten Commandments	Exodus 20:1–17; Deuteronomy 5:6–21
Ratification of Mosaic Covenant between God and Israel	Exodus 24:1–18 (cf. Exod. 34:1–28)
Israel's conquest of Canaan (Palestine)	Joshua 1:1–24:33
God's promise to keep King David's descendants on Israel's throne "forever"	2 Samuel 7:8–17; also Psalms 89:19–37
Declaration that only Israel's God exists	Isaiah 40:10–28; 45:5–7; 46:8–11, etc.
What God requires	Micah 6:6–8
Moving beyond traditional concepts of God/the problem of evil	Job 1:1–19:29; 38:1–42:17
First promise of future life (resurrection)	Daniel 12:1–3
Human immortality	Wisdom of Solomon 3–9 (Apocrypha)
FROM THE NEW TESTAMENT	
Jesus' Sermon on the Mount	Matthew 5:1–7:28; cf. Luke 6:14–49
Accounts of Jesus' resurrection	1 Corinthians 15:3–7; Matthew 28:16–20; Luke 24:1–32; John 20:1–21; 24
Expectations of Jesus' imminent return	1 Thessalonians 4:13–5:11 (earliest Christian document); Matthew 24:1–25; 46; Mark 13:1–36; Luke 21:5–36
Jesus as Word of God incarnated as man	John 1:1–14
Emphasis on love, human and divine	1 Corinthians 13:1–13; Mark 12:28–31; John 3:16; 15:12–15
God is love	1 John 4:8, 16

 ## The Old Testament and the Hebrew Bible (the Tanakh)

Because it was composed in Hebrew, the language spoken in ancient Israel, many scholars prefer to call the Old Testament (the Jewish Scriptures) the **Hebrew Bible.** Today's biblical scholars also favor studying Israel's Scriptures in the three-part arrangement that ancient Jewish editors gave them: the Law (Hebrew, *Torah*), Prophets, and Writings. An acronym* derived

---

*Acronym: a word made up of the first letter or letters of a successive group of words.

BOX I.2   **Multiple Meanings of the Name "Israel"**

In the Hebrew Bible, the name "Israel" has several meanings. In most cases it is used to denote collectively the ancient Near Eastern people with whom God entered into a special partnership. Historically, it also refers to two different but related political entities: (1) the twelve-tribe United Kingdom of Israel, which was briefly unified under its first three kings, Saul, David, and Solomon (c. 1020–922 BCE), and (2) following Solomon's death (c. 922 BCE), the ten northern tribes that withdrew from the United Kingdom to form the separate nation of Israel. The smaller southern kingdom, with its capital at Jerusalem, was then named after its leading tribe, Judah. The term "Israel," however, continued to be used to describe collectively all of God's people from both the northern kingdom of Israel and the southern kingdom of Judah.

During the last five centuries BCE, when first Persia and then Greece controlled Judah's former territory (then called Judea), its inhabitants were commonly known as Jews (people of Judea).

---

from the initial consonants of the Hebrew Bible's three main divisions, **TaNaKh** refers to **Torah** (Hebrew for "Instruction" or "Teaching"), **Nevi'im** (Prophets), and **Kethuvim** (Writings) (see Box 1.3). Because it contains five separate books—Genesis, Exodus, Leviticus, Numbers, and Deuteronomy—the Torah is also known as the **Pentateuch** (from the Greek for "five scrolls"). Because **Moses,** Israel's first great leader and lawgiver, is the leading human figure in four Torah books (Exodus through Deuteronomy), this division is further known as the Mosaic Law or Books of Moses. (See Chapter 4 for a discussion of scholarly theories about the Torah's origin and authorship.)

The Tanakh's second part, the Nevi'im, is divided into two subsections. The first subunit, traditionally called the Former Prophets (Joshua, Judges, 1 and 2 Samuel, 1 and 2 Kings), opens with Israel's conquest of Canaan and ends with the loss of that land to Babylon's armies. According to biblical reckoning, this long narrative section covers a period of more than six centuries, from about 1200 BCE to 587 BCE, when Babylon demolished Jerusalem.

The second subunit of the Nevi'im, called the Latter Prophets, does not continue the narratives of Israel's history during the exile in Babylon or of its eventual return to rebuild Jerusalem and its Temple. Instead, this subsection consists of the fifteen prophetic books, from the "Major Prophets"—Isaiah, Jeremiah, and Ezekiel—to the twelve "Minor Prophets," including Amos, Hosea, Micah, and Malachi. Although these books include some editorial commentary, they consist primarily of prophetic **oracles,** pronouncements believed to be divinely inspired and that prophets typically delivered as "the word of the LORD." Rather than predictions of events in the distant future, most of the prophets' oracles address specific political or social crises in Israel's national history. Biblical prophets were most active during two extremely critical periods. Amos, Hosea, Isaiah, and Micah prophesied during the eighth and seventh centuries BCE, when Assyria, an aggressive Near Eastern military power, threatened to destroy Israel. During the late seventh and early sixth centuries BCE, when the Babylonian menace loomed, Habakkuk, Jeremiah, and Ezekiel warned of Jerusalem's imminent destruction (see Chapter 16). As arranged in the Hebrew Bible (Tanakh), the prophetic works immediately follow the historical narratives about Israel's rise and fall. The prophets' warnings typically highlight moral issues, such as the people's breaking their pledge to worship Israel's God alone, that, according to many biblical authors, led to Babylon's overthrow of the Israelite nation.

The Tanakh's third and final division, the Kethuvim (Writings), contains the most diverse material, ranging from volumes of poetry, such as Psalms, Song of Songs, and Lamentations; to short stories, such as Ruth and Esther; historical narratives, such as Ezra and Nehemiah; books of wisdom, such as Proverbs, Job, and Ecclesiastes; and visionary speculations about God's future intervention in world history in the Book of Daniel. Although Daniel appears among the prophets in the Christian canon, it is so different from most prophetic writings that Jewish editors did not include it with traditional books of prophecy (see Chapter 26).

Jewish scholars closed the Kethuvim—and hence the Hebrew Bible (Tanakh) itself—with 1 and 2 Chronicles, a late retelling of Israel's history from the time of its early kings to the end of the Babylonian exile. Although Ezra and Nehemiah relate events that occurred later than

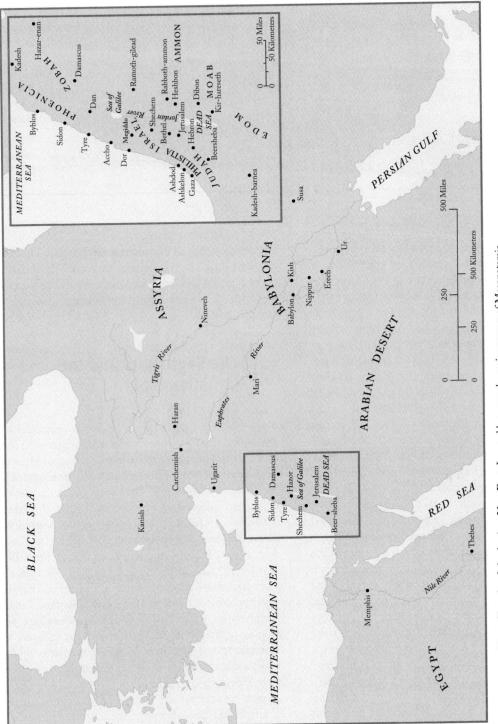

FIGURE I.I Map of Israel and the Ancient Near East. Located between the major powers of Mesopotamia (Assyria and Babylon) and Egypt, the kingdom of Israel was repeatedly devastated by the military invasions of its stronger neighbors, events that loom large in the biblical narratives. The inset shows Israel as it appeared between about 921 and 721 BCE, when it was divided into the southern kingdom of Judah and the northern kingdom of Israel. The northern state of Israel ceased to exist when the Assyrians destroyed it in 721 BCE. The smaller state of Judah, with its capital at Jerusalem, however, was partly restored about fifty years after the Babylonians destroyed it in 587 BCE.

BOX 1.3   Tanakh—The Three-Part Hebrew Bible

A comparatively recent term for the Jewish Scriptures, Tanakh is an acronym composed of the first letters of the three major divisions of the Hebrew Bible. Vowel sounds are inserted between the consonants.

T Torah (Mosaic Instruction)

- Genesis, Exodus, Leviticus, Numbers, Deuteronomy

N Nevi'im (Prophets)

- The Former Prophets: Joshua, Judges, 1 and 2 Samuel, and 1 and 2 Kings

- The Latter Prophets (compiled in the individual prophets' names): Isaiah, Jeremiah, Ezekiel, and the Scroll of the Twelve (Hosea, Amos, Micah, Joel, etc.)

K Kethuvim (Writings)

- Psalms
- Job, Proverbs (Wisdom books)
- Festival scrolls: Ruth, Song of Songs, Ecclesiastes, Lamentations, and Esther
- Daniel (an apocalypse)
- Ezra–Nehemiah, 1 and 2 Chronicles (historical narratives)

---

those covered in the books of Chronicles, editors deliberately assigned Chronicles the important end position in the canonical Hebrew Bible. At the end of Chronicles, **Cyrus the Great** (reigned 558–530 BCE), emperor of Persia and conqueror of Babylon (539 BCE), issues an order encouraging Jewish exiles to return from Babylon to Jerusalem. The returning exiles have a major purpose—to rebuild the Jerusalem Temple that the Babylonians tore down and thus restore the formal worship of Israel's God. By according Chronicles the final word in the biblical record of Israel's long partnership with God, the Tanakh offers its readers an open invitation to journey back to their homeland where God is again present in his favored sanctuary. Whatever the future may bring, the Jewish Bible concludes with a strong reaffirmation of the enduring bond linking God to his chosen people.

In general, this textbook will follow the order of books given in the Tanakh, respecting the three-part division of Israel's Scriptures that apparently was already in place by the second century BCE. In his preface to the Greek edition of the Wisdom of Jesus Son of Sirach (also called Ecclesiasticus), the translator refers to the "Law [Torah]," the "Prophecies [Nevi'im]," and "the rest of the books," probably an allusion to the Writings (Kethuvim). According to the Gospel of Luke, Jesus and his followers—all Jews of the first century CE—were also familiar with the Hebrew Bible's tripartite structure: The risen Jesus speaks of "the law of Moses [Torah], the prophets [Nevi'im], and the Psalms" (Luke 24:44). As the first book in the Writings, Psalms may have stood for the Tanakh's entire third section. Approaching the Hebrew Bible according to the Tanakh's arrangement, in the order in which Jesus and his contemporaries

apparently knew it, has distinct advantages. The three divisions reflect not only the approximate chronological order in which the books were written but also the order in which they subsequently were added to the canon (see Chapter 2).

The Septuagint and the Christian Bible

If the Hebrew Bible of Jesus's day was organized in a three-part structure, how is it that Christians have an Old Testament with a different ordering of the contents, one that ends with the prophetic books instead of the books of Chronicles? The answer lies in the fact that Christians adopted a different edition of the Israel's Scriptures, a Greek version known as the **Septuagint.** About 250 BCE, Greek-speaking Jews living in Alexandria, Egypt, began a translation of the Hebrew Bible into Greek. According to legend, seventy-two scholars from Jerusalem, working in pairs, labored seventy-two days to produce a definitive Greek edition of the Tanakh. Popularly known as the "work of the seventy." the Septuagint (abbreviated **LXX**) rendered the Hebrew and Aramaic texts (some later books were written in Aramaic, a tongue commonly spoken after the exiles' return from Babylon) into **koinē,** the "common" Greek then spoken throughout the eastern Mediterranean region. Contrary to legend, however, the project of producing a Greek version of the Bible was accomplished by scholars in Alexandria, not Jerusalem, and extended over a long span of time. After the Torah was translated, the books of the Prophets and Writings were gradually added during the last centuries BCE. In fact, the Septuagint edition eventually included about fourteen late books or parts of books, such as Tobit, Judith, Additions to Daniel, and the Wisdom of Solomon (included in the Apocrypha), that Jewish editors did not admit to the Hebrew canon.

Because Greek was the language most widely spoken among early Christians, most New Testament authors—who wrote entirely in Greek—not only quoted passages from the Septuagint but also effectively regarded it as the church's primary Bible. As a result of adopting this Greek version of the Jewish Scripture, the early church also apparently followed the Septuagint's arrangement of contents. The difference between the Tanakh's ordering and that of the early church is important, for it reflects significant differences in the religious meaning of the biblical collection for Jews and Christians. Most Christian Bibles divided the Old Testament into four sections, grouping books according to their literary genre (category), regardless of their original function or date of composition. The four-part Old Testament follows the same order as the Tanakh for the first five books (the Pentateuch or Torah). In its second unit, however, the Christian arrangement shows several changes, placing the Book of Ruth between Judges and 1 Samuel (Ruth is set at the time of the Judges), and following the books of Kings with the much later 1 and 2 Chronicles, Ezra, Nehemiah, and Esther (this section also includes 1 and 2 Maccabees in Catholic editions and 3 Maccabees as well in Greek Orthodox Bibles). The Old Testament's third division features works of poetry and wisdom, from Job to the Song of Solomon.

It is in making the Prophets the Old Testament's fourth and final unit, however, that Christian editors most significantly revised the meaning of the Hebrew Bible. The Old Testament closes, not with 2 Chronicles' clarion call for Jews to return to Jerusalem, but with Malachi's prophecy about an unnamed future "messenger" and the sudden reappearance of the prophet Elijah. Carried to heaven in a fiery chariot, Elijah was expected to return to earth during the "last days" (Mal. 3:1, 22–24; cf. 2 Kings 1–2). By placing the Prophets (Nevi'im) as the final word of the Old Testament—the climax of God's revelation to Israel—Christian editors emphasized the supreme importance of prophetic statements about a royal descendant of King David—the "anointed one" **(Messiah)**—who would eventually appear to restore David's kingdom. When "Messiah" was translated into Greek, it

became *Christos*, from which the English "Christ" is derived.

In the Christian view, Israel's prophetic oracles served mainly to foretell events in the life of **Jesus** of Nazareth, who they believed was David's ultimate heir. Israelite prophetic writings thus form a natural literary bridge to the New Testament accounts of Jesus' ministry, the Gospels. According to the Gospel authors' interpretation, Malachi's unidentified "messenger" or "herald" was Jesus' immediate forerunner, John the Baptist, whom the first three Gospel authors identify as the returned Elijah (Matt. 11:10–14; Mark 9:11–13; Luke 7:27–28). All four of the Gospel writers repeatedly quote passages from the Torah, Prophets, and Psalms to prove that Jesus—in spite of his dying a publicly shameful death usually reserved for slaves and criminals—was in truth Israel's royal Messiah. The Christian canonical order of books, and the New Testament authors' use of them, effectively transforms the Jewish Scriptures into a proto-Christian document. From this perspective, the chief purpose of the Old Testament was to prepare for and foretell the career of Jesus and the birth of Christianity. (For a list of the New Testament books, see Box 1.4.)

The New Testament

Authors of the Hebrew Bible are concerned with Israel as a whole, the people with whom God has a long and often troubled relationship. In the New Testament, however, the writers focus on a single Israelite—Jesus—presenting him as God's son, the promised deliverer of Israel whose sacrificial death somehow reconciles humanity to God. The structure of the New Testament canon emphasizes Jesus' centrality: The first four books, the Gospels, are biographies of Jesus, and the fifth, the Book of Acts, is a narrative describing how Jesus' early followers spread a proclamation about Jesus as world savior from Jerusalem to Greece to Rome. After the Gospels and Acts are thirteen letters ascribed to **Paul,** early Christianity's most prominent missionary, who was the first to interpret the theological significance of Jesus' death, resurrection, and ascension to heaven. (From the Greek words *theos*," "God," and *logos*, "reason," theology is the study of concepts about God's nature and intentions toward humankind.) Written between about 50 and 60 CE, Paul's letters are the earliest surviving Christian documents. Historically, Paul's most important contribution

---

BOX 1.4   **Contents of the New Testament**

A collection of Greek books that Christian editors added to the Septuagint, a Greek edition of the Hebrew Bible (Old Testament), the New Testament includes twenty-seven different writings. Although Paul's letters (composed between about 50 and 60 CE) are the earliest surviving Christian documents, editors placed the Gospels first in the New Testament canon, followed by the Book of Acts, two collections of letters (those ascribed to Paul and those attributed to leaders of the Jerusalem church). The New Testament closes with an apocalyptic vision of future history, the Book of Revelation.

The Gospels:

> According to Matthew
>
> According to Mark
>
> According to Luke
>
> According to John

An account of early Christianity's geographical expansion and numerical growth:

> The Book of Acts

A collection of Paul's letters and letters ascribed to Paul:

> Romans
>
> 1 Corinthians
>
> 2 Corinthians
>
> Galatians

Ephesians

Philippians

Colossians

1 Thessalonians

2 Thessalonians

1 Timothy

2 Timothy

Titus

Philemon

A collection of general letters and other documents, most ascribed to leaders of the early Jerusalem church:

> Hebrews
>
> James
>
> 1 Peter
>
> 2 Peter
>
> 1 John
>
> 2 John
>
> 3 John
>
> Jude

An apocalyptic vision of heaven and future history:

> The Book of Revelation

---

to the Jesus movement was his firm insistence that **"Gentiles"**—a term that includes all non-Jewish peoples—be accepted into the church (Greek, *ekklesia*) on an equal footing with Jews, biological descendants of Abraham (see Chapter 35). The New Testament's fourth section consists of the Book of Hebrews and a second collection of letters, most attributed to leaders in the Jerusalem church, Peter, James, and John. Like Paul's letters, these writings are largely meditations on Jesus' universal significance and the proper modes of behavior for those who believe in him. As noted above, the canon ends with Revelation, an English title translating the Greek *apokalypsis* (meaning a "disclosure" or "uncovering"), a symbolic "unveiling" of the invisible spirit world and the events of End time. (For helpful scholarly references in Bible study, see Box 1.5.)

Encountering God

In the history of world religion, the Bible's most far-reaching contribution is its complex portrait of God. Throughout the Old and New Testaments, God is both the invisible, unknowable source of all that exists and also intimately involved in human affairs. The biblical God is *transcendent,* a supernatural being of unlimited power whom even the highest heavens cannot contain (1 Kings 8:27). But he is also *immanent,* a God who descends to earth, apparently in human form, to break bread with his friend Abraham under shady oak trees (Gen. 18:1–33) and who "speaks to Moses face to face, as one speaks to a friend" (Exod. 33:11; cf. Exod. 24:9–11; Deut. 34:10). Unique among gods of the ancient world, he refuses to share his worship with other

---

BOX 1.5 **Tools for Studying the Bible**

Several one-volume Bible dictionaries offer concise alphabetized essays on important topics:

Achtemeier, Paul J., ed. *The HarperCollins Bible Dictionary*, rev. ed. San Francisco: HarperOne, 1996. Contains scholarly, reliable, and accessible entries.

Brown, R. E.; Fitzmeyer, J. A.; and Murphy, R. E. *The New Jerome Biblical Commentary*. Englewood Cliffs, NJ: Prentice-Hall, 1990. Although slightly dated, provides excellent discussions of all canonical books by leading Catholic scholars.

Evans, Craig A., and Porter, Stanley E., eds. *Dictionary of New Testament Background*. Downers Grove, IL: InterVarsity Press, 2000. Concise essays by generally conservative scholars.

Freedman, David Noel; Myers, Allen C.; and Beck, Astrid B., eds. *Eerdmans Dictionary of the Bible*. Grand Rapids, MI: Eerdmans, 2000. Current and scholarly, an excellent resource.

For geographical and historical background to both the Old and New Testaments, see the following:

Aharoni, Yohanan; Avi-Yonah, Michael; Rainey, A. F.; and Safrai, Ze'ev, eds. *The Carta Bible Atlas*, 4th ed.

Jerusalem: Carta, 2002. Includes information on archaeological excavations.

Metzger, Bruce M., and Coogan, Michael D., eds. *The Oxford Companion to the Bible*. New York: Oxford University Press, 1993. Interpretive mini-essays on alphabetized topics.

Multivolume Bible aids include the following:

Freedman, D. N., ed. *The Anchor Bible Dictionary*, Vols. 1–6. New York: Doubleday, 1992. Somewhat dated, but still a major resource.

Keck, Leander, ed. *The New Interpreter's Bible*. Nashville, TN: Abingdon Press, 1994–. A multivolume series featuring complete biblical texts (Genesis through Revelation) with parallel NIV and NRSV translations; includes extensive scholarly commentary.

Sakenfeld, Katharine D., ed. *The New Interpreter's Dictionary of the Bible*. Vol. 1, A–C, 2006; Vol. 2, D–H, 2007; Vol. 3, I–Ma, 2008. Nashville, TN: Abingdon Press. Excellent scholarly discussions, with additional volumes scheduled for publication in the near future.

---

gods and forbids humans to make images of him (Exod. 20:1–6). First revealed as "the God of Israel," he eventually becomes known as the *only* God. Toward the end of the Babylonian exile, a prophet scholars call Second Isaiah confidently declares that no other gods exist:

> I am the LORD, and there is no other;
> besides me there is no god . . .
> I form light and create darkness,
> I make weal and create woe;
> I the LORD do all these things.

(Isa. 45:5, 7; cf. Isa. 46:9)

The prophet also reminds us that God differs qualitatively from the humans who worship him:

> For my thoughts are not your thoughts,
> nor are your ways my ways, says the LORD.
> For as the heavens are higher than the earth,
> so are my ways higher than your ways
> and my thoughts than your thoughts.

(Isa. 55:8–9)

The Hebrew Bible's portrayals of God, which profoundly influenced the concepts of divinity depicted in both the New Testament and the Quran (Koran), the holy book of Islam, are amazingly diverse. Different biblical authors not only present God in a wide variety of roles and images, ranging from warrior and judge to tender parent and nursing mother, but also show the Deity engaged in an astonishing array of paradoxical actions. God (in Hebrew **El** [singular] or **Elohim** [plural]) first appears in the opening chapters of Genesis. By the power of his word alone, Elohim creates the universe, transforming a dark, watery **chaos** (the disorganized matter preceding creation) into an orderly **cosmos** (harmonious system) in which life can flourish. A few chapters later, however, God is "sorry" that he created humanity and abruptly returns the world to its precreation state of turbulent sea, drowning the entire human race except for a single family (see Chapter 39).

The tension between God's will to create and to destroy, to bless and to curse, established in the first eight chapters of Genesis, suggests his ambivalent attitude toward humankind. Demanding that the rational creatures whom he fashioned as "images" of himself offer total obedience, God manifests a distinctly humanlike disappointment and anger when humans resist his authority. Balanced against his righteous determination to punish disobedience, however, is God's *hesed*, a Hebrew word meaning "steadfast love," toward those who honor him. Far from the emotionally aloof center of cosmic reason that some philosophers assume, the biblical God is a multifaceted personality capable of strong passions. He is a being who loves and hates, who generously saves his favorites and ruthlessly exterminates his enemies.

In one of the Bible's most crucial passages, God reveals his personal name to Moses. As a disembodied voice issuing from a burning bush, God informs Moses that he is "the God of your father, the God of Abraham, the God of Isaac, and the God of Jacob," Israel's most prominent forebears (Exod. 3:6). Moses then asks who this ancestral God (Hebrew, *Elohim*) may be, for "Elohim"—the plural form of "El" (God)—is a generic term for divine beings and may apply to any number of ancient Near Eastern deities.* The voice replies:

> I AM who I AM . . . Thus you shall say to the Israelites, "I AM has sent me to you." The LORD [Yahweh], the God of your ancestors, . . . has sent me to you. This is my name forever; and this is my title for all generations.
>
> (Exod. 3:14–15)

Although most English translations blandly render the divine name as "the LORD," this practice obscures the importance of God's self-disclosure to Moses. In the ancient world, personal names had real meaning. When Israel's God confides his name to Moses, he simultaneously reveals much about his nature and purpose. Appearing almost 7,000 times in the Hebrew Bible (in every book except Ecclesiastes and Esther), the divine name is represented by four consonants, which are commonly given in English as YHWH. These four letters of God's name are called by the Greek term **Tetragrammaton.** According to one widely accepted theory, the name derives from the Hebrew verb "to be" or "to cause to be" ("create"). As God explains to Moses, "I AM who I AM," or, in another rendering, "I Shall Be What I Shall Be." God is here speaking in the first person; in the third-person singular, the phrase becomes **"Yahweh"** ("He Is"). The meaning of Yahweh's name is thus closely tied to the Bible's view of God as the Lord of history, the eternal Being who has long-range plans for humanity and who also takes decisive action to bring them into existence. In Exodus 3 he commissions Moses to confront Egypt's

ruler, demanding that Pharaoh release the enslaved Israelites, out of whom Yahweh plans to create a people "for his name."

Because biblical Hebrew is written almost entirely in consonants, readers must supply the vowel sounds, including those of the divine name. Although we do not know exactly how the four consonants were pronounced, many scholars agree that the name should be vocalized as "Yah´-weh," as it is rendered in some modern translations, such as the Anchor Bible and the New Jerusalem Bible. Late in biblical history, reverence for God's sacred personal name and anxiety about profaning it through unworthy usage prompted Jewish religious authorities to use **Adonai** (Hebrew, "Lord") when reading aloud passages containing the Tetragrammaton. Most modern English translations print LORD in small capitals wherever YHWH appears in the biblical text. The name of many biblical characters incorporate the divine name, including Joshua ("Yahweh Saves") and Jesus, a Greco-Roman form of the same Hebrew name. In the New Testament, "Jesus" is rendered *Iesous,* a Greek sounding of the Hebrew name *Jehsua,* a later version of *Jehoshua* or *Joshua.* Like the Joshua who led his fellow Israelites into the Promised Land, Jesus' name affirms that "Yahweh Saves." In this text, we will use "Yahweh" when referring to Israel's God.

Yahweh—Lord of the Covenant

In both the Old and New Testaments, God's preferred means of establishing relationships with individuals or groups is through a **covenant** (Hebrew, *berith*). A common practice for making alliances in the ancient Near East, *covenant* means "agreement," "pact," "vow," "treaty," or even "contract." The first two parts of the Tanakh (Torah and Nevi'im) are largely structured around four covenants that Yahweh concludes with selected partners or recipients. Each covenant is named after the person for or through whom it is negotiated: Noah, Abraham, Moses, and David. In the Gospels, Jesus—on the evening before his crucifixion—makes a fifth or "new" covenant with his disciples (Matt. 26:27–28).

The Covenant with Noah

Unlike the other three Old Testament covenants, which deal exclusively with Israel, Yahweh's first covenant is concluded with all humankind. Immediately after the global Flood, God categorically promises Noah that he will never again destroy (almost all) humanity (Gen. 8:21), at least not by drowning them (Gen. 9:11–15).

*Not only the Egyptians and Babylonians but also all of the nations bordering Israel had personal names for their patron gods. Moab's god was named Chemosh; Edom's was Milcom. Canaanites worshipped El and his son Baal, the storm god.

Yahweh reminds himself to keep this vow by summoning a rainbow to follow rainstorms. In the **Noachan Covenant**, God encompasses all forms of life as equally sacred, emphasizing the interrelatedness of humans, animals, birds, and the earth itself. A bond "between God and every living creature," this covenant is universal and "everlasting" (Gen. 9:1–17).

The Covenant with Abraham

In contrast to the universality of the pact through Noah, the **Abrahamic Covenant** expresses God's commitment to a single individual and his biological descendants. Fundamental to Israel's understanding of its special bond to Yahweh, the covenant with Abraham entails a series of explicit promises in which God swears to make Abraham's progeny into a mighty nation, to create from them a line of kings, to give them the land of Canaan "forever," and through them to bless "all the families of the earth." (Provisions of the Abrahamic Covenant appear in four different versions of Yahweh's promises: Gen. 12:1–2; 15:1–21; 17:1–27; and 22:15–18.) Descended from Abraham's son Isaac and grandson Jacob, Israel saw itself as heir of God's promises to this ancestor, whom Genesis portrays as a model of faith and submission. Israel's possession of Canaan, its homeland, is thus seen as a divine right, a unilateral land grant from the Deity.

The Covenant Made Through Moses

Whereas the Abrahamic Covenant largely consists of divine promises made without imposing specific conditions on the covenant bearer, the covenant formulated at Mount Sinai through Moses is explicitly *conditional* on the people's faithfulness to Yahweh and to his legal requirements. At Mount Sinai (also called Horeb), Yahweh announces that he is a "jealous God" who will not tolerate Israel's veneration of any rival power (Exod. 20). Named for its human mediator, the **Mosaic Covenant** involves pledges from both God and Israel and makes clear that the people's future welfare depends entirely on their collective obedience. *If* the people keep their vow to obey all the approximately 600 laws and statutes delivered at Sinai, *then* Yahweh will be their champion, fight their battles, give them material prosperity, and guarantee their permanent settlement of Canaan.

Conversely, if the Israelites fail to honor God alone—rejecting all other deities—he will abandon them to their enemies. Thus, in describing the origin of Israel's covenant relationship with God, the biblical authors establish the terms by which they will narrate and interpret Israel's later history. Israel's historical experiences—its early military victories and political success under leaders such as King David—result from fidelity to Mosaic principles. By contrast, Israel's eventual fate—defeat by Babylon and loss of the promised homeland—are the consequences of its failure in covenant obedience. Editors of the historical narrative that begins in Genesis 12 and extends through 2 Kings, Israel's national epic, foreshadow Israel's tragic destiny by inserting dire warnings of the divine curses that will afflict Israel for betraying its bond to Yahweh:

> The LORD will send upon you disaster, panic and frustration in everything you attempt to do, until you are destroyed and perish quickly, on account of the evil of your deeds, because you have forsaken me. The LORD will make the pestilence cling to you until it has consumed you off the land you are entering to possess. The LORD will afflict you with consumption, fever, . . . with fiery heat and drought, and with blight and mildew; . . . The sky over your head shall be bronze, and the earth under you iron. . . .

(Deut. 28:20–23)

Like a rejected spouse, Yahweh will turn his original loving commitment into a burning desire for vengeance on the former beloved:

> And just as the LORD took delight in making you prosperous and numerous, so the LORD will take delight in bringing you to ruin and destruction; . . . The LORD will scatter you among all peoples, from one end of the earth to the other; and there you shall serve other gods . . . you shall offer yourselves for sale to your enemies as male and female slaves, but there will be no buyer.

(Deut. 28:63–64, 68; cf. 2 Kings 24–25)

As readers of the Torah and Prophets will discover, the key to understanding the Bible's sometimes complex narratives and legal provisions is the biblical writers' belief that Israel's tragic fate stems directly from its covenant breaking. The upholder of cosmic justice, Yahweh cannot tolerate his partner's infidelity and righteously punishes it by allowing foreign nations to destroy his people. A twenty-first-century historian is likely to interpret Israel's sequential domination by other nations—Assyria, Babylon, Persia, Greece, and Rome—as the inevitable outworking of imperial aggression in which powerful empires naturally conquer weaker states such as Israel and its neighbors. To both Old and New Testament authors, however, the real meaning of Israel's sufferings lies in its ethical failure to obey God.

The Covenant with David

Yahweh makes his fourth and final Old Testament covenant with King David, to whom he promises a line of royal descendants who will occupy Israel's throne "forever" (2 Sam. 7:11–17; Ps. 89:19–37). Whereas the Mosaic Covenant is concluded with Israel as a whole, the **Davidic Covenant** is restricted to a single elite family and, like the Abrahamic Covenant, is entirely *unconditional*. Yahweh states that he will punish disobedient kings, but he will not overthrow the Davidic dynasty as he overthrew the kingship of David's predecessor, Saul. As we shall discover, the contrast between God's ironclad pledges to Abraham and David on the one hand and the highly conditional nature of the Mosaic Covenant on the other generates considerable tension in the Hebrew Bible. In the New Testament, when Israel has been reduced to a tiny province in the Roman Empire, the issue of God's vow to David—and its implications for Jesus as "king of the Jews"—remains a major political and theological concern (Matt. 27:27–29, 42; John 19:14–22).

A Fifth Covenant?

Only once in the Hebrew Bible does a writer predict that Yahweh will someday inaugurate a new covenant with Israel. In a famous passage describing the future restoration of Jerusalem, the prophet Jeremiah states:

> The days are coming, says the LORD [Yahweh], when I will make a new covenant with the house of Israel and the house of Judah. It will not be like the covenant I made with their ancestors when I took them by the hand to bring them out of the land of Egypt—a covenant that they broke, though I was their husband, says the LORD: this is the covenant that I will make with the house of Israel after those days, says the LORD. I will put my law within them, and I will write it on their hearts; and I will be their God, and they shall be my people.
>
> (Jer. 31:31–33)

Besides reaching out to his people's "hearts," Yahweh will touch their minds: Instead of having to learn his teachings, Israelites, by divine grace, will spontaneously be filled with knowledge of their God. Graciousness will replace divine anger as God allows himself to forgive and forget his people's errors (Jer. 31:34; cf. Deut. 30:6; Ezek. 11:19–20).

For Christians, fulfillment of Jeremiah's prophecy of a new covenant takes place at the final meal Jesus hosts for his disciples (the "Last Supper"), when he inaugurates a "covenant" (a term almost synonymous with "testament") with his friends. According to Matthew's Gospel account, Jesus "took the cup and gave it to them [the disciples], saying Drink ye all of it. For this is my blood of the new testament" (Matt. 26:27–28, King James Version). The adjective "new," not present in the early Gospel manuscripts, was added later to emphasize the change in God's relationship with humankind (cf. Mark 14:24; 1 Cor. 11:25). Most contemporary English translations, including the New Revised Standard Version, the New Jerusalem Bible, and the Revised English Bible, omit the interpolated "new" and use "covenant" instead of "testament" in this passage.

Believing themselves to be the people of the "new covenant" that Jesus introduced the night before his death, Christians eventually called their collection of sacred writings the New Testament. Although the Hebrew Bible (Tanakh) became known as the Old Testament (cf. 2 Cor. 3:14; Gal. 3:15–18), many scholars suggest that it is more appropriate to call it the *First Testament*—the original covenant by which Yahweh irrevocably bound himself to Abraham's descendants. Because Christians believe that the ancient Tanakh promises made to Israel were fulfilled in Jesus and his followers (all members of the Jewish community), they saw the international Christian movement as a continuation—and extension—of Yahweh's partnership with Israel. In a speech ascribed to **Peter,** Jesus' chief disciple, the Book of Acts asserts that now God has expanded his covenant to embrace all people:

> Then Peter began to speak to them [an ethnically mixed group of Jews and Gentiles]. I truly understand that God shows no partiality, but in every nation anyone who fears him and does what is right is acceptable to him.
>
> (Acts 10:34–35).

From the Christian perspective, all people of faith, whatever their national origins, become Abraham's descendants (Gal. 3:6–9). By embracing both Jews and non-Jews in a covenant relationship, Israel's God at last fulfills the ancient promise to Abraham, that through him "all the families of the earth shall be blessed" (Gen. 12:3).

QUESTIONS FOR DISCUSSION AND REVIEW

1. What does the word *bible* literally mean, and how does this definition express the nature of the Bible as an anthology of religious literature?

2. The Christian Bible is divided into two major sections, the Old and New Testaments. Why is the first section also called the Hebrew Bible or Tanakh? Name

and describe the three parts into which Jewish editors divided the Tanakh.

3. In the long narrative about God's special partnership with Israel (Genesis through 2 Kings), list some of the major events. How does the story end? What kinds of books follow the introductory narrative section?

4. What are the Apocrypha or deuterocanonical books?

5. Define and discuss some of the various names and titles of the biblical God. What is the biblical God's personal name? How does God relate to humanity in general and to Israel in particular? Describe the four different covenants in the Hebrew Bible/Tanakh. What kind of divine promises do they contain?

6. Who is the chief figure of the New Testament? Why do Christians believe that God made a fifth covenant through him? How does the arrangement of books in Christian editions of the Old Testament (as opposed to the Tanakh's three-part order) give an anticipatory "Christian perspective" to Israel's Scriptures?

Terms and Concepts to Remember

chaos/cosmos	Jesus of Nazareth
covenant	Kethuvim (Writings)
Noachan Covenant	Moses
Abrahamic Covenant	Nevi'im (Prophets)
Mosaic Covenant	oracles
Davidic Covenant	Paul
deuterocanonical books/	Pentateuch
Apocrypha	Scripture
El/Elohim	Septuagint
Hebrew Bible/Old	Tanakh
Testament	Tetragrammaton/YHWH
Israel	Torah
Jerusalem	Yahweh

Recommended Reading

Alter, Robert, and Kermode, Frank, eds. *The Literary Guide to the Bible*. Cambridge, MA: Belknap Press, 1987. Scholarly essays on the Bible as literature, discussing the content and style of each major biblical book.

Armstrong, Karen. *The Bible: A Biography*. New York: Atlantic Monthly Press, 2007. A brief, clearly written history of the Bible's growth and influence, and the changing methods of its interpretation.

Goldingay, John. "Covenant, OT and NT." In K. D. Sakenfeld, ed., *The New Interpreter's Dictionary of the Bible*, Vol. 1, pp. 767–778. Nashville, TN: Abingdon Press, 2006. Concisely surveys the covenant concept in both Old and New Testaments.

Metzger, Bruce M., and Murphy, Roland E., eds. *The New Oxford Annotated Bible, with the Apocryphal/Deuterocanonical Books* (New Revised Standard Version). New York: Oxford University Press, 1991. The version quoted in this text; includes helpful scholarly essays on biblical composition and history, as well as informative footnotes on virtually every page.

Newsom, Carol A., and Ringe, Sharon H., eds. *The Women's Bible Commentary—Expanded*. Louisville, KY: Westminster John Knox, 1998. Offers illuminating views of biblical texts from feminist commentators.

Schippe, Cullen, and Stetson, Chuck. *The Bible and Its Influence, Student Text* (Bible Literacy Project). New York/Fairfield, VA: BLP Publishing, 2005. Surveys the Bible's influence on art, music, and literature. Recommended for its lavish illustrations, but largely ignores contemporary scholarship.

CHAPTER 2

How the Bible Was Created
Transmission, Canonization, and Translation

Key Topics/Themes Because no original texts by any biblical author have survived, we must rely on copies of manuscripts made many centuries after the works were first composed. Before the Dead Sea Scrolls were discovered, beginning in 1947, the oldest copies of the Hebrew Bible were the series of manuscripts edited by medieval Jewish scholars, the *Masoretes* (transmitters). Known as the Masoretic Text (MT), it is the edition upon which most contemporary editions of the Old Testament (Hebrew Bible) are based. Dating from about 250 BCE to about 68 CE, some of the Dead Sea Scrolls, mostly in fragmental form, are about a thousand years older the the Masoretic Text. Written in Greek between about 50 and 140 CE, the twenty-seven books of the New Testament were later attached to a Greek edition of the Hebrew Bible, the Septuagint. In the early fifth century CE, a Christian scholar, Jerome, translated both the Hebrew Bible and the New Testament into Latin, creating the Vulgate Bible. Another millennium passed before the Bible was translated into English.

 Transmission of the Biblical Texts

The origins of the Bible are shrouded in mystery. In most cases, we do not know where or when individual books were written, what the names of their authors were, or in what social and historical circumstances they were composed. To find partial answers to these questions, scholars must carefully examine ancient manuscript copies of each book, searching for internal clues to the book's compositional history. Before ancient Israelite **scribes** (persons who knew how to read and write) committed them to writing, most traditions about Israel's past existed only in oral form. Passed on by word of mouth from one generation to the next, Israel's oral traditions were apparently very fluid, producing many variations in tales about its distant ancestors and early history. In both Old and New Testament times, the ancient world was largely an oral culture in which the few written texts repeatedly interacted with a larger environment of oral storytelling. During the centuries before Israel's written documents were regarded as sacred, scribes apparently felt free to revise them, incorporating additional oral traditions

and offering new insights into Israel's ever-changing historical circumstances. (For scholarly theories about the multiple authorship and scribal editing of the Torah, see Chapter 4.) With a few exceptions, such as the letters of Paul, the Bible we read today is the product of largely anonymous poets, lawmakers, and storytellers who give little information about when, why, or for whom they wrote.

Scholars' efforts to understand the long and complex literary processes by which the Bible attained its present form are complicated by the fact that we do not possess a single document from the hand of its original author. As scholars who specialize in analyzing ancient biblical texts realize, we have only copies of copies of copies, many of which show signs of repeated scribal revision. After centuries of copying, for example, none of the 5,000 extant manuscripts of New Testament books are exactly alike. Most differences involve minor errors in spelling or phrasing, but some discrepancies, particularly in theologically sensitive passages, are substantial (see Box 2.1, and Bart Ehrman in "Recommended Reading"). Prior to the fourth century CE, when the Roman emperor Constantine officially recognized Christianity as a legal religion and provided the church

18

BOX 2.1 Copyists' Changes to New Testament Manuscripts

No two ancient Greek manuscripts of New Testament books are exactly alike. Although most differences in the texts were probably caused by unintentional errors in copying, some textual variations seem to result from deliberate changes, many of which may have been motivated by theological considerations. A few of the oldest manuscripts, including the Codex Sinaiticus, do not contain the phrase "son of God" in Mark 1.1, leading some scholars to think that the phrase was inserted at the beginning of the Gospel to refute a belief that Jesus became God's adopted son at his baptism. Another possible intentional change, made for the same purpose, may appear in Luke's account of Jesus' baptism. Some early manuscripts have God declare, "You are my son; *this day* have I begotten you," a quotation from Psalm 2 (Luke 3:22, emphasis added). Most modern translations use an alternative phrasing that avoids the adoption issue, having God say, "You are my son, the Beloved; with you I am well pleased."

Similar concerns about a religiously correct understanding of Jesus' origins apparently influenced manuscript changes in Luke's story of the youthful Jesus' being left behind in the Temple. Mary's words to the child— "Look, your father and I have been searching for you in great anxiety"—were, in some manuscripts, changed to "*we* have been searching for you" (Luke 2:48, emphasis added). The copyist's change avoided any implication that Joseph was Jesus' real father. A theological belief that Jesus was omniscient (all-knowing) may have prompted a scribe to delete a reference to "the Son" from some copies of Matthew's statement that "But about that day and hour [of the End] no-one knows, neither the angels of heaven, nor the Son, but only the Father" (Matt. 24:36).

Perhaps the most notable scribal insertion into a New Testament text appears in very late manuscripts of 1 John 5:7–8, where a copyist inserted the Bible's only explicit reference to the Christian doctrine of the Trinity. The added passage asserts that God exists in three persons and that "these three are one." This trinitarian statement occurs in no manuscript dating prior to the fourteenth century.

Some scholars argue that theological controversies over such issues as Jesus' divinity and equality with God prompted some copyists to change manuscripts so that they conformed to the orthodox (theologically correct) position.

---

with government support, no complete editions of the New Testament survive. The oldest extant copies of the New Testament as a whole are the Codex Sinaiticus and the Codex Vaticanus. Before the fourth century CE, mere fragments of books survive, the oldest preserving a few lines from the Gospel of John, dated at about 125–150 CE. Only by carefully comparing hundreds of different manuscript fragments can scholars hope to produce a version of the text that seems to reflect the author's original intent.

The Masoretic Text

Until 1947, when the Dead Sea Scrolls were discovered (see below), the oldest surviving edition of the Hebrew Bible was the **Masoretic Text** (abbreviated **MT**)—the text on which most contemporary translations of the Old Testament are based. The MT takes its name from *Masorah* (Hebrew, "transmission"), a term referring to a school of medieval Jewish scholars (Masoretes) who, during the ninth and tenth centuries CE, produced a series of Hebrew Bible manuscripts. Two representative examples of the Masoretic tradition, the Aleppo Codex

and the Leningrad Codex, are among the most important manuscripts. Noted for their scrupulous care in copying each letter of the text, the Masoretic scholars also added vowel sounds and accent marks to the consonants of the Hebrew script.

The Dead Sea Scrolls

Until about sixty years ago, most scholars assumed that the Masoretic Text represented a single authoritative textual tradition going back to biblical times (see Box 2.2). Attempts to look beyond the MT to earlier phases of the texts' transmission were unsuccessful. Beginning in 1947, however, the situation changed dramatically. According to one tradition, a Bedouin shepherd boy, who had been idly throwing stones into the mouth of a cave near the northwestern shore of the Dead Sea, heard a sound like shattering pottery. When he climbed into the cave to investigate, he found pottery jars full of ancient manuscripts, now world famous as the **Dead Sea Scrolls.** Over the ensuing decades, additional manuscript discoveries in eleven different caves near the archaeological site of

---

BOX 2.2   From Scroll to Codex

For the first thousand years of its literary development, the Bible existed only as a slowly growing accumulation of individual manuscripts, each with its own compositional history. Biblical books were typically written on papyrus, paperlike sheets made from the papyrus plant, and then rolled around a small wooden stick to form a **scroll.** To accommodate longer books, such as each of the Pentateuch's five volumes or the "major" prophets (Isaiah, Jeremiah, and Ezekiel), strips of papyrus about nine or ten inches long and five or six inches wide were stitched or glued together, forming scrolls up to twenty-five to thirty feet long.

The papyrus scrolls, whose manufacture probably originated in Egypt around 3000 BCE, were gradually replaced by more durable material, such as parchment, which is made from the dried and treated skins of sheep, calves, or goats. Vellum, a finer grade of parchment, was formed from the tanned hides of kids and calves. In prophetic books, scrolls figure prominently, from the visions of Ezekiel to those of Revelation (Ezek. 2:8–3:3; Rev. 5:1–14; 10:1–11).

Although the sticks around which papyrus or parchment sheets were rolled were commonly fitted with handles, the process of unwinding a long scroll to find a particular passage made their use slow and cumbersome. The task of finding specific texts was particularly difficult in ancient times, when Hebrew manuscripts were written without vowels, capitalization, punctuation, or even spaces between words and sentences. It was not until the European Middle Ages that scholars, for greater ease of reference, divided biblical books into chapters and verses.

Because of the scroll's limitations, during Roman times, businessmen pioneered the use of the **codex,** a forerunner of the modern book in which individual papyrus or parchment leaves were sewn together to form a series of easily turned pages featuring a continuous text. Christians quickly adopted the codex for their sacred writings. The great fourth-century codex editions of the New Testament were copied in uncial characters, large or capital letters written in continuous script without spaces between words. Of particular value is the Codex Sinaiticus, a mid-fourth-century manuscript discovered in the 1800s in the monastery of Saint Catherine at the foot of Mount Sinai. Besides the entire New Testament (including books not now in the canon), the Sinaiticus also contains much of the Greek Old Testament. Additional pages of the Codex Sinaiticus were discovered as late as 1975.

Qumran have yielded more than 220 biblical manuscripts, mostly in small fragments, although a few, such as a scroll of Isaiah, are complete (see Figure 2.1). Dating from about 250 BCE to 68 CE, the Dead Sea Scrolls found near Qumran have provided scholars with copies of biblical books up to 1,000 years older than the MT. Scholars thus far have identified fragmental copies of every book in the Hebrew Bible except Esther. In addition, numerous fragments of noncanonical writings, such as the Book of Enoch, have been found preserved among Tanakh material, raising questions about the accepted contents of the Hebrew Bible during the last centuries BCE. (A discussion of the Essenes, a monastic Jewish group that most scholars believe produced the Dead Sea Scrolls, as well as an extensive collection of their own sectarian literature, appears in Chapter 29.)

Perhaps the most important archaeological find of the twentieth century, the Dead Sea Scrolls have revolutionized our understanding of the history of the biblical texts. Although some manuscripts, such as the Isaiah scroll, are extremely close to the MT version, many others show significant differences, including variations not only in phrasing but also in content. Some biblical books, such as 1 Samuel, contain sentences and even whole paragraphs absent in the medieval texts. One version of Jeremiah is considerably shorter than the MT edition, while a collection of the Psalms includes poems not present in the MT. Apparently, as late as the first century CE, Jewish scholars had not yet agreed upon a universally accepted text of the Hebrew Bible. The extensive variation in different textual traditions among the Dead Sea Scrolls makes us aware that the biblical text remained fluid and subject to scribal changes well into the early Christian period.

The Dead Sea Scrolls have enabled scholars to make numerous corrections in the biblical texts. By comparing the same passage in the Dead Sea Scrolls and the Septuagint edition, for example, translators of the New Revised Standard Version (NRSV) could render more clearly a controversial statement in Deuteronomy that

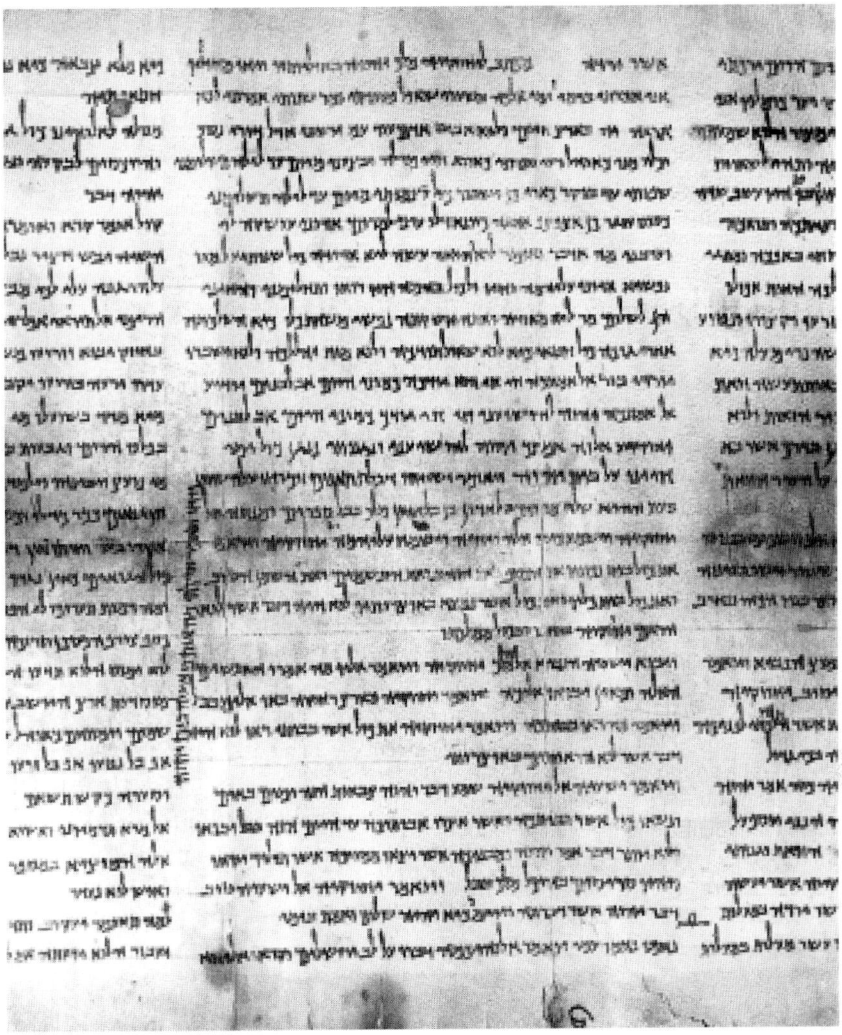

FIGURE 2.1 This passage is from one of the Dead Sea Scrolls, which were placed in clay jars and hidden in caves near the Dead Sea. The Essene library from the Qumran monastery includes the oldest surviving copies of the Hebrew Bible (Old Testament).

describes how various gods were assigned the supervision of different nations:

> When the Most High apportioned the nations, when he divided humankind, he fixed the boundaries of the peoples according to the number of the gods; the LORD's [Yahweh's] own portion was his people, Jacob [Israel] his allotted share.

(Deut. 32:8–9)

Copyists of the Masoretic Text, apparently troubled by the passage's reference to multiple "gods," changed the text to read "according to the sons of Israel." Although some recent English Bibles, such as the New International Version (NIV), retain the MT rendering, many scholars believe that the NRSV's translation is correct.

(It also accords with the concept of a "spirit prince" presiding over each individual nation in the Book of Daniel; cf. Dan. 10:13; 10:20–11:1; 12:1.)

Whereas the Masoretic scholars of the Middle Ages were exceptionally careful in copying biblical manuscripts—allegedly counting every letter in every line and then starting afresh if any errors were detected—some of the Dead Sea copyists were less exacting. A comparatively short fragment of Jeremiah manifests an unusual number of scribal corrections. After the first scribe copying Jeremiah 7:28–9:2 had omitted a lengthy passage (Jer. 7:30–8:3), a second copyist showed great ingenuity in trying to restore the missing text. Although he managed to insert part of the omitted section (Jer. 7:30–32) into the space between Jeremiah 7:29 and 8:4, he was forced to copy another part (7:32–8:3a) perpendicular to the left margin of the main text and to write verse 8:3b upside down at the bottom of the page (see Vanderkam and Flint in "Recommended Reading").

In contrast to the scrolls discovered near Qumran, a second, slightly younger group of manuscripts found along the Dead Sea to the south manifests a closer resemblance to the Masoretic Texts. Written in the late first and early second centuries CE—after the Romans had destroyed Jerusalem and the Jewish state in 70 CE—these manuscripts seem to reflect a new stage of textual transmission. According to many scholars, these younger manuscripts suggest that, at some point after the first Roman destruction of Jerusalem (Roman armies burned and razed it a second time in 135 CE), Jewish scribes succeeded in producing a somewhat more standardized edition of the biblical text, a forerunner of the medieval MT. Scholars caution, however, that the exact recording of Israel's Scriptures remained in flux for an extended period.

The Canon of the Hebrew Bible

At no time during the lengthy period of the Bible's formation—for either the Old or New Testament—did a religious council, either Jewish or Christian, explicitly determine its contents. The Hebrew Bible grew by slow degrees, with new documents added as Israel's writers, over many generations, meditated upon and interpreted the covenant community's political and spiritual experiences. Growth of the Christian canon was a similarly gradual process (see below).

After the Jewish exiles' return from Babylon to Jerusalem—a process that continued for more than a century following the Persian emperor Cyrus's decree in 538 BCE—Israel's legal and prophetic writings became not only more venerable but also more important in defining Jewish identity. Living under Persian domination, with little self-government or political power, the repatriated exiles looked increasingly to their Mosaic and other ancient traditions to explain who they were and what they must do as the people of Yahweh. According to the Book of Ezra, which describes conditions in postexilic Judah, the Persian emperor Artaxerxes ordered that "the laws of [Israel's] God" were to become the laws of Judah. The threat of political force backed up the emperor's decree: "All who will not obey the law of your God and the law of the king, let judgment be strictly executed on them, whether for death or for banishment or for confiscation of their goods or for imprisonment" (Ezra 7:25–26). We do not know the contents of the "book of the law of Moses"

that Ezra brought with him from Babylon, but some scholars believe that, under the authority of the Persian empire, Ezra produced a version of the Torah similar to what we have today. Whatever stage the Torah had reached in Ezra's time, the Pentateuch was the first part of the Hebrew Bible eventually to achieve canonical status.

Although not all scholars agree, many believe that the second main division of the Tanakh, the Prophets (Nevi'im), was generally accepted by about 200 BCE, at least by some influential groups within the Jewish community. As noted in Chapter 1, the earliest reference to all three parts of the Tanakh as authoritative appears in the preface to the Wisdom of Jesus Son of Sirach (Ecclesiasticus), in which the author's grandson and translator mentions "the Law [Torah] and the Prophets [Nevi'im] and the other books of our ancestors." Written in Egypt about 132 BCE, the preface's allusion to the "other books" probably refers to the Writings [Kethuvim], the last division of the Hebrew Bible to be canonized. Although some of the Writings, such as the Psalms, had been used in Israelite worship for generations, this part of the Hebrew Bible may have remained open-ended well into the early centuries CE, with some Jewish groups, such as those living in Alexandria, Egypt, accepting books that ultimately were not admitted to the Tanakh.

At one time, scholars believed that, following the Roman destruction of the Jewish state in 70 CE, a group of distinguished **rabbis** (Hebrew, "teachers") assembled at the coastal town of Jamnia (Yavneh) to consolidate and unify postwar Judaism. According to this tradition, the Academy of Jamnia (c. 90 CE) formally closed the canon, deciding exactly which books constituted Israel's genuine Scriptures. Scholars, however, no longer believe that the Jamnia rabbis acted to close the canon; some even doubt that such a rabbinical assembly took place. It now appears that defining the precise limits of canon, especially the Writings, may have been a function of the scribes who, in the late first and early second centuries CE, created a standard biblical text, forerunner of the later Masoretic Text. This standardization of the biblical manuscripts apparently occurred during the period between the two Jewish uprisings against Rome (66–73 CE and 132–135 CE). (For further discussion of the Old Testament canon, see Trebolle and Sanders in "Recommended Reading.")

The Canon of the New Testament

Like the formation of the Old Testament canon, the process by which the twenty-seven New Testament books became recognized as Christian Scripture took place gradually over an extended time. As with the Tanakh, the ultimate selection of books to include depended largely on their general familiarity and usefulness in regulating central beliefs and practices in the community of faith. For the first four centuries CE, worshipers attending services at churches in different parts of the Roman Empire likely would have found a startling variety of writings that individual congregations considered sacred. Whereas collections of Paul's letters and one or more of the four approved Gospels were widely used, many churches rejected such familiar books as Revelation, James, and 2 Peter. Along with the Gospels, Acts, and Paul's letters, some groups—while rejecting documents that would later become canonical—accepted works totally unfamiliar to modern readers, such as the Epistle of Barnabas, 1 Clement, the Apocalypse of Peter, and the Shepherd of Hermas.

Although most of the books eventually included in the New Testament were composed between about 50 CE (for 1 Thessalonians, Paul's earliest extant letter) and about 130–140 CE (for 2 Peter, probably the last written canonical document), it was not until late in the fourth century CE that a list of books appeared that corresponds exactly to the twenty-seven we know today. In 367 CE, Athanasius, then bishop of Alexandria, made the list part of his Easter Letter. Even after Athanasius issued his definitive tally, however, numerous churches continued to use New Testament collections that differed significantly from one another.

The Process of Growth

Perhaps the first step in creating the New Testament took place toward the end of the first century CE, when one or more of Paul's admirers searched the archives of various Pauline churches for surviving copies of his correspondence, gathering them into a single unit. This anonymous Pauline disciple began an anthology of early Christian literature to which the Gospels, Acts, and other documents gradually were added, eventually forming the New Testament.

By the time that 2 Peter was composed (early to mid-second century CE; see Chapter 37), Paul's letters had been recognized as Scripture, at least in some circles (2 Pet. 3:15–16). In the meantime, a large number of Gospels, all claiming to represent Jesus' authentic teachings, had been written. Well into the second century, most churches apparently recognized only the one Gospel known to their local group. The oldest extant reference to any of our canonical Gospels as "Scripture" occurs in a book called 2 Clement, ascribed to Clement, an early bishop of Rome. The quotation "I have come to

call not the righteous but sinners" matches a saying found in both Matthew (9:13) and Mark (2:17). Perhaps a few decades after Clement, Justin Martyr, a church leader executed in Rome in the 160s CE, cited the "memoirs of the Apostles" or "Gospels" as though they had attained an authority equal to that of the Hebrew Bible.

By the end of the second century CE, the international church had reached a compromise between the single Gospel championed by some of the oldest individual churches and the many different Gospels then in circulation. In accepting the present four, the Christian communities rejected numerous others, such as the Gospels attributed to Peter or to Thomas, consigning them to disuse and ultimate oblivion. Although many fragments of these rejected Gospels were known to modern scholars, the first complete copy of a noncanonical Gospel was not discovered until 1945, when the Gospel of Thomas was found at Nag Hammadi, Egypt. Of Thomas's 114 sayings ascribed to the risen Jesus, scholars believe that some may represent an earlier form of Jesus' authentic teachings that parallel versions included in the canonical Gospels.

The Gospel of Judas

Much to scholars' surprise, yet another ancient Gospel recovered from the Egyptian desert came to light in the early twenty-first century. First published in English in 2006, the Gospel of Judas portrays Jesus' betrayer in a radically different way from the canonical Gospels, making him the only disciple to perceive that Jesus belongs to the world of pure spirit. Composed originally in Greek about 140–160 CE and translated into Coptic (a form of the Egyptian language written in Greek letters) about 290–300 CE, the Gospel of Judas illustrates one of the many varieties of Christianly that prevailed during the early centuries CE. Like many of the noncanonical Gospels, the Judas document advocates a form of Christian Gnosticism (see below).

The Muratorian Canon

Whereas a compilation of Paul's letters, four Gospels, and Acts was generally accepted by the end of the second century, many other New Testament books—notably, Hebrews, Revelation, and the seven brief documents known as the catholic epistles—took an additional two or three hundred years to find widespread recognition. The **Muratorian Canon,** which scholars once dated to the late second or early third century CE but now think was probably assembled in the fourth century, is typical of the mixed bag of canonical and noncanonical books found in different church catalogues. Containing twenty-four books, the Muratorian Canon includes the four Gospels, Acts, thirteen letters ascribed to Paul (but not Hebrews), Jude, 1 and 2 (but not 3) John, the Wisdom of Solomon, Revelation, and the Apocalypse of Peter. The Muratorian list excludes five books that finally achieved canonical status, but it includes a Greek Wisdom book that was ultimately assigned to the Old Testament Apocrypha and an "apostolic" vision of hell that was not included in any canon.

Writing in the fourth century CE, the church historian Eusebius observed that, even after Constantine had legalized Christianity, the New Testament canon was not yet fixed. In describing the church's current opinions of a given book's authenticity, Eusebius divided contenders for official canonization into three categories. The universally "acknowledged" works number twenty-one, including the four Gospels, Acts, Paul's letters, and some of the catholic epistles. The "disputed" books, accepted by some churches but not others, include six that eventually entered the canon: Revelation, James, Jude, 2 Peter, and 2 and 3 John. Five other candidates for official inclusion failed to make the cut: the Acts of Paul, the Shepherd of Hermas, the Apocalypse of Peter, the Epistle of Barnabas, and the Didache, a fascinating collection of first-century Christian rituals and moral teachings. Eusebius's "rejected" books are Gospels ascribed to Peter, Thomas, and Matthias and the acts attributed to Andrew, John, and other apostles. In general, the canonization process, in which dozens of early Christian writings competed for inclusion, involved decisions on which books to leave out.

Marcion and Gnosticism

Marcion's Disputed Role Until recently, many scholars thought that the concept of fashioning a Christian scripture distinct from the Old Testament received its initial stimulus from the proposals of **Marcion.** A wealthy Greek shipbuilder who settled in Rome, Marcion (c. 140 CE) was a radical Christian advocate of Paul's doctrine of salvation by faith (see Chapter 35). Apparently influenced by Gnosticism (see below), Marcion insisted that Christians should reject the entire Hebrew Bible and replace it with a carefully edited version of Luke's Gospel and Paul's letters, the sole Christian writings he deemed worthy of belief. According to this older view, church leaders began to see the importance of defining a New Testament canon only after Marcion had proposed his severely abbreviated list of acceptable writings. In Marcion's day, the Bible that

Christians used consisted primarily of the Septuagint edition of the Hebrew Scriptures (which included the Apocrypha) and—at least in some locations—one or more Gospels and the anthologized Pauline letters. When Marcion demanded that Christians dispense with the entire Old Testament, which, he asserted, presented a violent and savage image of God, the church responded by affirming the indispensable authority of the Hebrew Bible, thereby assuring that Christianity would be firmly rooted in the religion of ancient Israel. It also began to emphasize the importance of writings other than a single Gospel and Paul's letters.

Gnosticism Marcion was at least partially influenced by a movement then widespread within the early church called **Gnosticism.** Taking its name from the Greek word *gnosis,* meaning "knowledge," Gnosticism is a general label applied to an extremely diverse set of beliefs and practices. Because the church later declared the Gnostic view of Christianity heretical (guilty of false teaching), most of our information about the movement derives from church writings attacking it.

In general, Gnosticism expresses a strongly mystical attitude toward human existence, emphasizing that an enlightened believer in Jesus achieves salvation through obtaining a spiritual understanding of heavenly truths denied the average person. Following Plato's duality of body and soul, Gnostics taught that reality consists of two distinct modes of being: (1) an invisible realm of pure spirit that is intrinsically good and to which the human soul belongs, and (2) an inferior physical world to which the desire-filled and corruptible body belongs. A "Higher God" is the source of ultimate truth, the unseen generator of the spirit world who sent Jesus Christ into the material world to impart a saving awareness of an immortal divine nature dwelling in human beings. In contrast, Yahweh, the Old Testament Deity, was a malignant power responsible for making the inherently corrupt world of matter.

Focusing on the insights of a spiritual elite, Gnosticism became a major source of dissension with the Christian community during the first three centuries of its existence. The Gnostics produced numerous influential writings, including several Gospels interpreting the teachings of Jesus, all of which the church eventually condemned. (For possible Gnostic elements in John's Gospel and the letters of John, see Chapters 33 and 37.)

Although Marcion's challenge to define a uniquely Christian scripture undoubtedly had its effect, most scholars now believe that the development of the New Testament canon resulted from a broader set of social and historical circumstances. Noting that Paul's letters had already been collected before Marcion appeared, scholars also point out that by 140 CE individual Gospels were being used in various churches, though few groups were probably then familiar with all four. These documents were regularly and extensively employed in worship services and in teaching converts. Read aloud in churches from Palestine and Egypt to Italy and Gaul (France), some books proved their long-term usefulness in maintaining a connection with Christianity's beginnings.

In general, it seems that the New Testament canon evolved to serve related purposes. First, canonization of specific texts clarified within the Christian community what beliefs church leaders considered true and acceptable. Questioners like Marcion and his Gnostic associates could thus be confronted with an officially sanctioned list of books that largely defined the faith. Second, the canon provided a unifying force for churches dispersed throughout the Roman Empire, imparting a firm written authority for universal belief and behavior.

The Latin Vulgate

Although canons at individual churches differed even after Athanasius's Easter Letter list (367 CE), a major development at the end of the fourth century was perhaps conclusive in permanently establishing the New Testament contents—Jerome's translation of the Bible, both Old and New Testaments, into Latin. Known as the **Vulgate** because it renders Scripture into the "vulgar" ("common") Latin of the western Roman Empire, this landmark work, produced between about 385 and 405 CE, remains the official Bible of the Roman Catholic Church. Its translator, Jerome, one of the great scholars and theologians of the period, followed Athanasius's canon and included all seven catholic epistles, as well as the controversial Hebrews and Revelation. Jerome's translation excluded other "disputed" Christian writings, however, rejecting the Epistle of Barnabas and the Apocalypse of Peter. Once regarded as virtually equal to what we think of as "genuine" New Testament works, these texts were henceforth relegated to obscurity. (For a list of abbreviations of biblical books, see Box 2.3.)

English Translations

Following the collapse of the western Roman Empire during the fifth century CE, literacy in Europe gradually declined. Accordingly, no major translation to rival the Latin Vulgate was published for nearly a thousand years. Prior to the Protestant Reformation in the early sixteenth century, most translators merely rendered Jerome's Latin version into some modern European language.

Not until the 1500s CE were translations again made directly from the Hebrew, Aramaic, and Greek texts.

Although none of his work has survived, the first person credited with translating the Bible into his native English was the Venerable Bede, a Benedictine monk and historian of Anglo-Saxon England. In the 730s CE, Bede rendered part of the Latin Vulgate into Old English. During the tenth and eleventh centuries, a few other biblical books, such as the Psalms, also appeared in English, but an English version of the entire Bible was not available until the late fourteenth century. To make Scripture more accessible to the English public, John Wycliffe, an English priest, translated both the Old and New Testaments, completing the project about 1384. Fearing the effect that hearing the Bible read in their own language might have on the untutored population, however, the English church in 1408 condemned Wycliffe's version and forbade any future translation.

Two historical events ensured that the Bible would soon find a large reading public in English. The first was Johannes Gutenberg's invention of movable type in 1455, a revolutionary advance in technology that made it possible to print books relatively quickly, rather than having to copy them laboriously by hand. The second was a new religious movement known as the Protestant Reformation, begun in Germany in 1517. In that year, a German monk named Martin Luther vigorously protested practices within the Catholic Church and promoted a widespread study of Scripture. Luther's German translation of the Bible (1522–1534) was the first version in a modern European language based not on Jerome's Vulgate but directly on the Hebrew and Greek texts.

The first English translator to work directly from Hebrew and Greek manuscripts was William Tyndale. Under the threat of church persecution, Tyndale fled to Germany, where his translation of the New Testament was published in 1525 (revised 1534). Official hostility to his work prevented him from completing his translation of the Old Testament, however, and in 1538, he was betrayed, tried for heresy (false teaching), and burned alive at the stake.

Although the Anglican Church under Henry VIII forbade the reading of Wycliffe's or Tyndale's translation, it nevertheless permitted free distribution of the first printed English Bible—the Coverdale Bible (1535), which relied heavily on Tyndale's work. Matthew's Bible (1527), containing additional sections of Tyndale's Old Testament, was revised by Coverdale, and the result was called the Great Bible (1539). The Bishop's Bible (1568) was a revision of the Great Bible, and the King James Version was commissioned as a scholarly revision of the Bishop's Bible. The Geneva Bible (1560), which

BOX 2.3   **Abbreviations of Books of the Bible, in Alphabetical Order**

THE HEBREW BIBLE (TANAKH OR OLD TESTAMENT)		DEUTEROCANONICAL (APOCRYPHAL) BOOKS	
Amos	Amos	Add. to Dan.	Additions to Daniel
1 Chron.	1 Chronicles	Add. to Esther	Additions to Esther
2 Chron.	2 Chronicles	Bar.	Baruch (includes Letter of Jeremiah)
Dan.	Daniel	Ecclus.	Ecclesiasticus (Wisdom of Jesus Son of Sirach)
Deut.	Deuteronomy		
Eccles.	Ecclesiastes	1 Esd.	1 Esdras
Esther	Esther	2 Esd.	2 Esdras
Exod.	Exodus	Jth.	Judith
Ezek.	Ezekiel	1 Macc.	1 Maccabees
Ezra	Ezra	2 Macc.	2 Maccabees
Gen.	Genesis	Tob.	Tobit
Hab.	Habakkuk	Wisd. of Sol.	Wisdom of Solomon
Hag.	Haggai		
Hos.	Hosea		

OTHER ABBREVIATIONS

THE HEBREW BIBLE (continued)		OTHER ABBREVIATIONS	
Isa.	Isaiah		
Jer.	Jeremiah	BCE	Before the Common Era; dates correspond to dates B.C.
Job	Job		
Joel	Joel	CE	Common Era; dates correspond to dates A.D.
Jonah	Jonah		
Josh.	Joshua	JB	The Jerusalem Bible
Judg.	Judges	KJV	The King James Version of the Bible, also called the Authorized Version (AV)
1 Kings	1 Kings		
2 Kings	2 Kings		
Lam.	Lamentations	NAB	The New American Bible
Lev.	Leviticus	NEB	The New English Bible
Mal.	Malachi	NIV	The New International Version of the Bible
Mic.	Micah		
Nah.	Nahum	NJB	The New Jerusalem Bible
Neh.	Nehemiah	NKJV	The New King James Version of the Bible
Num.	Numbers		
Obad.	Obadiah	NRSV	The New Revised Standard Version of the Bible
Prov.	Proverbs		
Ps. (pl., Pss.)	Psalms	NT	The New Testament
Ruth	Ruth	OT	The Old Testament
1 Sam.	1 Samuel	RSV	The Revised Standard Version of the Bible
2 Sam.	2 Samuel		
Song	Song of Songs	SV	The Scholars Version of the Bible
Zech.	Zechariah		
Zeph.	Zephaniah		

English Puritans had produced in Switzerland, also significantly influenced the King James Bible.

The King James Bible (Authorized Version)

By far the most popular English Bible of all time, the King James edition was commissioned by James I, son of Mary, Queen of Scots. James appointed fifty-four scholars to compile a new version of the Bishop's Bible for official use in the Anglican Church. After seven years' labor, during which the oldest manuscripts then available were diligently consulted, the king's scholars produced in 1611 England's officially Authorized Version. With its rhythmic prose and colorful imagery, the King James Bible remains unsurpassed in literary excellence. Its rich style has had a pervasive influence on subsequent English culture, with its phrasing of the Scriptures remarkably memorable and quotable.

Despite its wonderful poetic qualities, however, the King James Version has serious drawbacks as a text for studying the Bible. For many readers, the very attributes that contribute to its linguistic elegance—the archaic diction, elaborate sentence structure, and Renaissance vocabulary—tend to obscure the explicit meaning of the text. Translated by scholars who grew up on the then-contemporary poetry of Edmund Spenser and William Shakespeare, the King James text presents real problems of comprehensibility to the average American reader. Students who have difficulty understanding *Hamlet* or *King Lear* cannot expect to follow Paul's sometimes complex arguments when they are phrased in a style that has been largely obsolete for centuries. Even more important for serious Bible students, its translators lacked access to ancient manuscripts that have since been discovered, including the Dead Sea Scrolls, and to recent linguistic studies that have greatly increased our understanding of Hebrew and Greek language and thought.

Some Modern English and American Translations

Realizing that the English language changes over time and that words lose their original meanings and take on new connotations, Bible scholars have repeatedly updated and reedited the King James text. The first Revised Version of the King James Bible was published in England between 1881 and 1885; a slightly modified text of this edition, the American Standard Revised Version, was issued in 1901. Using the (then) latest studies in archaeology and linguistics, the Revised Standard Version (RSV) appeared between 1946 and 1952. Because contemporary scholarship continues to advance its understanding of biblical languages and textual history, an updated edition, the New Revised Standard (NRSV), with the Apocrypha, was published in 1991. Unless otherwise indicated, this textbook uses the NRSV for all quotations from both the Old and New Testaments.

Readers can now choose from a wide selection of modern translations, most of which incorporate the benefits of expert scholarship that draws on interdisciplinary fields of linguistic, historical, and literary studies. The Jewish Publication Society has a fluent edition of the Tanakh (Hebrew Bible), issued in 1985. Published in 1989, the New Jerusalem Bible transliterates several Hebrew terms for God—notably, the personal name Yahweh and the title El Shaddai—into the English text. The New English Bible (NEB) (1970, 1976), the product of an international committee of Catholic, Jewish, and Protestant scholars, was further refined and reissued as the Revised English Bible (1989).

The widely used New International Version (NIV), completed in the 1970s, reflects an Evangelical Protestant viewpoint. A Catholic translation, the New American Bible (NAB) (1970), is also highly readable. The multivolume Doubleday Anchor Bible is an excellent study aid. A cooperative effort by Jewish, Catholic, and Protestant scholars, each volume in the series is the work of an individual translator, who provides extensive historical commentary. Many of these comparatively recent translations are available in paperback editions, which typically contain extensive scholarly footnotes, maps, and interpretive material. Except for the Jewish edition of the Tanakh and the NIV, all of these Bible editions include the Apocrypha, books that reflect the growth of religious ideas in Judaism in the centuries immediately preceding the rise of Christianity.

Some translations favored by many students need to be used with caution. Whereas the Good News Bible offers a fluent paraphrase of the original languages in highly informal English, many scholars thinks that the Living Bible strays so far from the original texts as to be unreliable and misleading. Some doctrinally oriented versions, such as the New World Translation, published by the Watchtower Society (Jehovah's Witnesses), consistently tend to render theologically sensitive passages in a way that supports their distinctive beliefs.

◇ | Reading the Bible Analytically

The variety of literary forms found in the Bible—genealogies, legal instructions, prophetic oracles, historical narratives, devotional lyrics, erotic poetry, proverbs,

Gospels, letters, parables, short stories, essays of skeptical wisdom, and mystical visions of the future—is matched by the diversity of its religious thought. The Bible's overarching themes concern the nature of God and his relationship to humanity, but these themes are not expressed in a single monolithic viewpoint. Contributors to the biblical literature were many, and they wrote from an enormous range of personal, historical, and theological perspectives. Even in a single book, such as the Psalms, for example, we find a wide spectrum of religious feeling, extending from praises of God's grandeur to heartfelt questioning of the Deity's fidelity to his word. The affirmation of divine goodness in Psalm 118 and the celebration of Yahweh's glorious creation in Psalm 19 contrast markedly with the complaints about the sufferings the faithful endure in Psalm 44 (especially vv. 19–22). In Psalm 89, the poet even suggests that God has broken his sworn oath to David (Ps. 89:20–45).

For many contemporary readers, the extraordinarily diverse responses of different biblical writers to lived experience, from thanksgiving for God's generosity to bewilderment at his apparent failure to validate ethical behavior in human society (Eccles. 4:1–3), are one of the Bible's greatest strengths. Instead of promoting a doctrinally rigid view of the divine–human relationship, such as those that some religious institutions adopt, different biblical authors offer a wide range of religious perceptions and possibilities.

The rich diversity of voices speaking to us in both the Hebrew Bible and the New Testament has enormous value. To grasp the importance of this diversity, it is necessary to let each individual biblical writer speak for himself, without trying to force one author's statements to conform to those of another. Only by recognizing the multiplicity of viewpoints raised in Scripture will we begin to appreciate its power to illuminate the many dimensions and varieties of religious experience.

After the Enlightenment: New Ways of Understanding

In the decades preceding America's Declaration of Independence from England, European and American scientists and other scholars began to forge new tools to clear away long-held misconceptions about both the natural and the social worlds. Known as the Age of Enlightenment, this creative period inspired thinkers to challenge virtually all forms of traditional authority. In physics, the work of Isaac Newton and other mathematicians revolutionized our understanding of the physical universe. In the political arena, leading thinkers boldly rejected the claim that monarchs ruled by divine right,

triggering the American and French revolutions. In the social world, Enlightenment principles eventually led to radical changes in long-accepted institutions and practices, such as human slavery, exploitative child labor, and the subjugation of women. Religious claims, including authoritarian uses of the Bible, were similarly challenged. Since the eighteenth-century Enlightenment, an international community of scholars—Jewish, Catholic, Protestant, and others—has developed innovative methods to analyze the nature and growth of the biblical documents. Ranging from archaeologists, anthropologists, and historians to textual experts, linguists, and literary critics, this cosmopolitan body of scholars has provided us with an increasingly precise and well-documented study of the biblical literature and the environment out of which it grew. Virtually every textbook used in universities and seminaries today, including this one, draws heavily on the work of these scholars. (At the end of each chapter in this text, readers will find a list of helpful scholarly publications in the "Recommended Reading.")

In Chapter 4, we survey some of the principal scholarly theories about the Torah's authorship and dates of composition; in Chapter 31, we investigate the literary relationship of the first three Gospels (Matthew, Mark, and Luke). Here we will briefly clarify the concept of "biblical criticism." For some people, the term *criticism* may awaken negative feelings, perhaps implying fault-finding or a derogatory judgment. In biblical studies, however, it is a positive means of illuminating scriptural texts more accurately and objectively. The word *criticism* derives from the Greek *krino*, which means "to judge" or "to discern," to exercise rational analysis in evaluating something. In the field of art and literature, it involves the ability to recognize artistic worth and to distinguish the relative merits or defects in a given work. In biblical studies, various critical methods are used, ranging from techniques for investigating the oral traditions that preceded the written documents to literary interpretation of their final form, content, and structure.

For hundreds of millions of believers, the Bible embodies their most deeply held convictions and spiritual aspirations. Because of this emotional identification with the biblical message, trying to approach the Bible objectively is difficult. To some readers, the rigorous application of dispassionate logic to documents thought to reveal the divine will seems inappropriate. For many people, however, spirituality, reverence for concepts of divinity, love of the biblical tradition, and critical study are not incompatible. From this perspective, thinking analytically about religious texts and the cultural environments that helped shape them is both a tribute to the texts' intrinsic value and a means of understanding them more fully. Although scholarship cannot investigate the world of the spirit or the elusive dimension of religious transcendence that biblical authors explore, it offers enormous help in explaining the means—cultural, social, historical, and literary—by which ancient writers convey to us the insights of faith.

Reading the Bible from Different Social Viewpoints

In recent years, scholars have become increasingly aware that the meaning of any book—including the Bible—is to a large extent dependent on the reader's individual experience and viewpoint. In the United States, this is particularly true when readers belong to social groups such as ethnic or other minorities that the dominant culture commonly undervalues or marginalizes. Viewing biblical stories from a specific social location—such as the African American, Hispanic American, Asian American, Native American, or feminist community—is likely to give these stories a meaning that is distinctly different from that the male Caucasian majority perceives. When an African American whose forebears were plantation slaves reads the New Testament admonition for servants to submit cheerfully to their masters, no matter how abusive (1 Pet. 2:18–20; Col. 3:22; Eph. 6:5), the command is likely to resonate differently for her than it will for the descendants of white slave owners. Similarly, when a Native American reads Deuteronomy's order for the invading Israelites to kill, without exception, all the native inhabitants of Canaan (the territory God promised to Israel), the biblical command has an ominous ring (Deut. 7:2–4; cf. Josh. 10:30–40). Historically, many European settlers applied Deuteronomy's genocidal order to the indigenous populations of North America, exploiting a religious justification for the extermination of native peoples as American pioneers claimed their land.

As feminist critics have pointed out, women of all nationalities may read the Bible from a perspective fundamentally different from that of most men. Paul's flat refusal to permit a woman to teach in his churches (1 Cor. 14:34–35) or the Pastor's insistence that the first woman must be blamed for humanity's downward spiral into sin and death (1 Tim. 2:13–14) may spark feelings of incredulity or resentment unknown to the men reading the same passages. But, as feminist scholars have also observed, the same apostle who allegedly forbade women to address the congregation also recognized the role of women prophets (1 Cor. 11:5) and women as church officeholders, as well as "fellow workers" in the Christian fold (Rom. 16:1–5). Some scholars believe that the restrictions imposed on women in 1 Corinthians 14 result from a later copyist's attempt to make Paul's instructions conform to the antifeminist passages in a later (non-Pauline) letter (1 Tim. 3:11; see Chapter 36).

At his most insightful, Paul endorses a vision of radical equality—legal, ethnic, social, and sexual: "There is no such thing as Jew and Greek, slave and freeman, male and female; for you are all one person in Christ Jesus" (Gal. 3:28). For most societies, Paul's goal is an ideal yet to be realized. Most religious groups seem content to accept his more conventional statements regulating the social/sexual hierarchy. Both male and female scholars have come increasingly to see, however, that not only Paul but also much of our biblical heritage contains elements that are strangely blended: Material that is at once regarded as severely limited by its origin in intensely traditional ancient Near Eastern and Mediterranean societies appears alongside material that seems to transcend its culture-bound limitations to express universal principles of divine love. The Torah thus combines regulations perpetuating slavery and the oppression of women with commands to treat all people humanely. Embedded amid the ritual minutiae of Leviticus is the directive "you shall love your neighbor as yourself" (Lev. 19:18), a decree that Jesus of Nazareth singled out as second in importance only to the requirement to love God with one's whole being (Mark 12:28–31).

 ## A Canon Within the Canon

The challenge to discern, among many competing texts, the Bible's most enduring values will shape our journey as we thread through the complexities of biblical authors' diverse teachings. After surveying both Old and New Testaments, many readers discover that some biblical voices speak far more persuasively than others. "What does the LORD [Yahweh] require of you," asked the prophet Micah, "but to do justice, and to love kindness, and to walk humbly with your God?" (Mic. 6:8). In the Sermon on the Mount, Jesus offers an equally concise summary of biblical faith: "In everything do to others as you would have them do to you; for this is the [meaning of] the law and the prophets" (Matt. 7:12). When evaluating the biblical legacy, many readers, almost instinctively, gravitate toward its universal and abiding messages. Like

Martin Luther, they find a "canon within the canon," passages in which they can glimpse invaluable links in the divine–human bond. Intellectually and spiritually, the Hebrew and Christian Scriptures offer a unique avenue to exploring the ethical fountainhead of Western civilization.

QUESTIONS FOR DISCUSSION AND REVIEW

1. Do we possess any original manuscripts by biblical authors? What difficulties arise when there is a large chronological gap between the time of a book's composition and the date of the oldest surviving copies of the work? How do scholars go about trying to establish an authentic biblical text that may represent the original writer's intent?

2. What is the Masoretic Text (MT)? When was it produced, and what relationship does it have to modern English editions of the Hebrew Bible (Old Testament)?

3. Discuss the nature and importance of the Dead Sea Scrolls. When and where were they discovered, and what do they tell us about the copying and transmission of biblical documents?

4. Define the term *canon*. By what process was the canon of the three major divisions of the Hebrew Bible determined? How and when did Christians develop the present canon of the New Testament? Why did Christians feel a need to canonize their own Scriptures?

5. Discuss the historical significance of the Septuagint edition of the Hebrew Bible. Describe the work of Jerome in producing a new Latin translation of the Bible, the Vulgate.

6. What revolutionary events of the late fifteenth and sixteenth centuries contributed to the translating of the Bible into modern languages? What role did Martin Luther play?

7. Who were John Wycliffe and William Tyndale? Describe their contributions to creating a Bible in English. How did contemporary church authorities respond to their work?

8. What is the King James Bible (Authorized Version), and under what circumstances was it produced? Why are many later translations more reliable than the King James? List some important contemporary English editions of the Bible, such as the New Revised Standard Version used in this textbook.

9. In what ways did the Enlightenment, with its emphasis on rationality and scientific analysis, affect our interpretations of the Bible? How may a person's gender, ethnic background, and social location influence his or her response to a particular biblical text? How does the Bible's tolerance of human slavery affect your understanding of its ethical authority?

Terms and Concepts to Remember

codex
Dead Sea Scrolls
Gnosticism
Marcion
Masoretic Text (MT)
Muratorian Canon
rabbis
scroll
Vulgate Bible

Recommended Reading

Daniell, David. *The Bible in English: Its History and Influence.* New Haven, CT: Yale University Press, 2003. A scholarly survey of the Bible's pervasive impact on Anglo-American culture.

Ehrman, Bart. *Misquoting Jesus: The Story Behind Who Changed the Bible and Why.* San Francisco: HarperOne, 2005. A textual scholar examines examination by a textual scholar of the ways in which copyists changed biblical passages to reflect orthodox (correct) church teachings.

McDonald, Lee M. "Canon of the New Testament." In K. D. Sakenfeld, ed. *The New Interpreter's Dictionary of the Bible,* Vol. 1, pp. 536–547. Nashville, TN: Abingdon Press, 2006. A helpful overview of canonization process.

Metzger, Bruce M., and Ehrman, Bart D. *The Text of the New Testament: Its Transmission, Corruption, and Restoration,* 4th ed. New York: Oxford UP. Explains textual problems with which scholars deal.

Sanders, James. *From Sacred Story to Sacred Text: Canon in Paradigm.* Minneapolis: Fortress Press, 1986. An influential study.

Trebolle, Julio. "Canon of the Old Testament." In K. D. Sakenfeld, ed. *The New Interpreter's Dictionary of the Bible,* Vol. 1, pp. 548–563. Nashville, TN: Abingdon Press, 2006. Another helpful overview of the canonization process.

Vanderkam, James, and Flint, Peter. *The Meaning of the Dead Sea Scrolls: Their Significance for Understanding the Bible, Judaism, Jesus, and Christianity.* San Francisco: Harper San Francisco, 2002. An authoritative analysis of the scrolls and the light they have thrown on the origins of rabbinical Judaism and early Christianity.

CHAPTER 3

The Ancient Near East
The Environment That Produced the Bible

Key Topics/Themes Archaeological evidence indicates that humans have inhabited the Near East for tens of thousands of years, but it was not until about 3200 BCE that the first large urban centers were built. In southern Mesopotamia, the Sumerians erected the first cities, invented the wheel, devised a system of writing, and produced a written literature about the gods, the creation of the world, and the afterlife that offers many parallels to the biblical texts. Whereas Sumerian and later Babylonian city-states typically remained comparatively small and independent, the Egyptians created the first unified national state in the mid-third millennium BCE. For most of its history, Israel—located geographically between powerful empires in Egypt and Mesopotamia—was dominated politically by a succession of Egyptian, Assyrian, Babylonian, Persian, and Greek invaders. Historical events recounted in the Hebrew Bible can be understood only in their ancient Near Eastern context.

The Bible and the Ancient Near East

According to the Book of Joshua, God himself emphasizes the strong connection between Israel and the older cultures of the ancient Near East: "Thus says the LORD [Yahweh], the God of Israel: Long ago your ancestors—Terah and his sons Abraham and Nahor—lived beyond the Euphrates and served other gods" (Josh. 24:2). Asking that the Israelites now abandon "the gods that your ancestors served beyond the River and in Egypt"—and which some were then still worshipping—Yahweh again commands his people to honor him alone (Josh. 24:14–15, 23; cf. Exod. 20:2–3). Fully aware that Israel had imported religious traditions from both Egypt and lands "beyond the Euphrates," several biblical authors highlight the tension between Yahweh's demand for exclusive devotion and Israel's Near Eastern heritage, with its multiplicity of gods and myths about the world's creation and a great prehistoric flood.

The region "beyond the River" to which Joshua refers is **Mesopotamia,** an area at the head of the Persian Gulf in what is now southern Iraq (see Figure 3.1). Meaning "the land between the rivers"—a name the Greeks assigned it—Mesopotamia is a flat, swampy territory lying between the Tigris and Euphrates, two of the four rivers that traditionally bordered Eden (Gen. 2:10–14). In the long narrative from Genesis 12 through 2 Kings 25, Israel's story begins and ends in Mesopotamia. According to Genesis, Abraham was born in Ur, one of the area's oldest cities, and then moved to Haran in northwest Mesopotamia. When God summoned him, he and his family then traveled through Canaan to Egypt and back again, their itinerary encompassing virtually the entire geographical extent of the biblical world (Gen. 11:26–13:1). At the conclusion of 2 Kings, Abraham's Israelite descendants have come full circle, with exiles from Judah forcibly transported to Babylon, capital of a new Mesopotamian empire. Significantly, it is from Babylon that the priest-scribe Ezra later brings an edition of the Torah back to Jerusalem, where he introduces "the book of the law of Moses" to a crowd of returned exiles (Ezra 7; Neh. 8).

Given the dual traditions that Israel's ancestors originated in Mesopotamia—and that at least part of the Mosaic law code was developed there—we are not surprised to find many biblical texts reflecting a definite Mesopotamian influence. From a belief that the

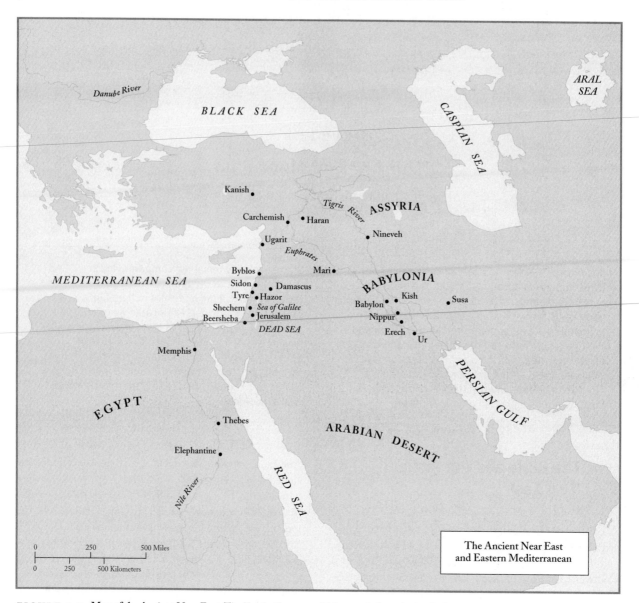

FIGURE 3.1 Map of the Ancient Near East. The Fertile Crescent, which extends from the head of the Persian Gulf northwestward through Syria and then southwestward through Canaan into Egypt, was the location of the world's oldest urban civilizations. In Genesis, the itinerary of Abraham's travels—from Ur on the southern Euphrates River of Haran in northern Mesopotamia and thence into Canaan and Egypt—marks the boundaries of the biblical world.

precreation world was an abyss of boundless water, to the story of a single household surviving a global flood, to concepts of a gloomy subterranean Underworld, biblical writers commonly echo ancient Mesopotamian traditions (see the discussion of the two Genesis creation accounts in Chapter 5). While freely borrowing from the oral and written traditions of ancient Mesopotamia and Egypt, however, the Bible's authors consistently transform them into something startlingly new. Whereas all other peoples in antiquity, including Egyptians and

Babylonians, practiced **polytheism** (belief in many gods), ancient Israel eventually began a religious revolution by embracing **monotheism** (belief in only one God). By making Israel's God the sole ruler of the universe, biblical authors extensively revised traditions inherited from other cultures, giving to Yahweh both the creative and destructive qualities of Mesopotamian gods. In our survey of ancient Near Eastern history and culture, we will focus on practices and beliefs that anticipate concepts presented in the Hebrew Bible.

A Prologue to the Biblical World

For many thousands of years before Israel came into existence, the **Fertile Crescent**—a strip of arable land curving from the head of the Persian Gulf northwestward to Syria and then southward through Canaan into Egypt—was studded with tiny villages and other settlements. Sites of prehistoric settlements abound from central Anatolia (modern Turkey), to Syria–Palestine, to Mesopotamia. At **Jericho,** famous for its walls that reputedly tumbled before the blast of Joshua's trumpets, archaeologists have discovered evidence of human habitation dating back to 9000 BCE. Lying six miles west of the Jordan River, north of the Dead Sea, Jericho is the world's oldest known walled town. Archaeologists have uncovered the ruins of a circular stone tower thirty feet high, as well as plastered, painted skulls with eyes made from seashells. Like other figurines from the Stone Age, these depictions of the human face probably had a religious meaning now impossible to know.

Repeatedly abandoned and then resettled over many millennia, Jericho's ruins now form a high mound of rubble called a **tel** (see Figure 10.2). Composed of numerous layers of debris, each representing a different period of settlement, tels mark the sites of ancient cities throughout the Near East.

Sumer: Cradle of Near Eastern Civilization

Shortly after 3500 BCE, a people called the **Sumerians** founded the earliest true cities, such as Ur, Abraham's birthplace, and Uruk, home to **Gilgamesh,** the first hero of Western literature. Remarkably innovative, the Sumerians constructed elaborate irrigation systems, erected monumental temples to their gods, and devised the first law codes to protect property and foster social order. By inventing the wheel (fourth millennium BCE), they made possible increased travel, trade, and economic prosperity. At an early date, Sumerian merchants exported goods to Egypt, which was simultaneously developing a highly sophisticated civilization in northeast Africa along the banks of the Nile River.

About 3200 BCE, the Sumerians devised a system of writing—known as **cuneiform**—that used wedge-shaped symbols inscribed with a sharp metal instrument on clay tablets. When dried or baked, these inscribed tablets proved almost indestructible, surviving to the present in many tens of thousands (see Figure 3.2). Although cuneiform writing was invented primarily to record tax lists, inventories, and various business transactions, it was also used to record topics ranging from magical spells to

FIGURE 3.2 Inscribed with cuneiform script, this clay tablet preserves part of an ancient Babylonian creation epic, the *Enuma Elish,* which depicts the primal universe as a vast watery chaos, as does Genesis (1:1–2, 6–9). For a striking parallel between Mesopotamian law and that contained in Israel's Torah, see Figures 3.6 and 3.7, which show the Babylonian king Hammurabi receiving a law code from the sun god Shamash.

mythical tales of gods and heroes. Some cuneiform literature foreshadows themes found in the Hebrew Bible, including traditions about the gods meeting together in a divine council or creating the world in six stages of separation and division (see Boxes 3.2 and 5.1).

Sumer's lasting contributions to later cultures range from the fields of religion and literature to those of mathematics and architecture. Fashioning a numerical system based on the sky god Anu, head of their pantheon (official roster of gods), the Sumerians introduced the practices of dividing the hour into sixty minutes and the circle into 360 degrees. Although less well known today than Egypt's pyramids, Sumerian building projects were no less impressive. Because the flood-prone, swampy plain they occupied lacked the granite and limestone that Egyptian builders used, the Sumerians mass-produced clay bricks, typically baked and glazed, with which they constructed massive walls around their cities. They also erected large temple complexes honoring their

FIGURE 3.3 The model of Marduk's sanctuary, with its towering ziggurat, emphasizes the god's role as Babylon's divine patron. These artificial mountains served as pedestals to which gods could descend to earth, treading the sacred stairways linking the human and divine worlds. Jacob's dream at Bethel (Gen. 28:10–17) envisions a similar "gateway to heaven."

city's patron deity. Their most distinctive architectural form was the **ziggurat,** a great square tower with multiple levels that dominated the city's skyline (see Figure 3.3). At the top level stood a chapel or shrine believed to house the god, such as Anu, to whom the tower was dedicated. With broad staircases connecting its several levels, the ziggurat functioned like the spire of a Christian church, a visible link symbolically connecting humans on earth with invisible gods inhabiting the sky.

The importance of the ziggurat, and the sacred urban site on which it stood, is expressed in Mesopotamian place names. *Babylon,* which eventually became the region's greatest city, means the "gate of the god," indicating its status as the holy place of **Marduk,** king of the Babylonian gods and creator of the world. The significance of Marduk's ziggurat in Babylon is suggested by its name, *Etemenanki,* which translates as the "house that is the foundation of heaven and earth."

When Jacob, Abraham's grandson, dreams of a vast ramp or "ladder" by which supernatural beings ascend to or descend from heaven, his vision conveys the ziggurat's religious function, providing a sacred zone at which the divine and human realms intersect. Setting up a stone pillar to commemorate his vision of the spirit world, Jacob exclaims

that Bethel, the "House of God" where he slept and where Yahweh appeared to him, is nothing less than the "gate of heaven" (Gen. 28:10–19), his personal Babylon. Jacob's perception of the ziggurat's purpose reflects a greater understanding of Mesopotamian religion than found in the equally famous story of the Tower of Babel (Gen. 11). In the Babel episode, the author presents building the tower as humanity's prideful attempt to "reach heaven," whereas the Mesopotamian ziggurat actually served as a pedestal by which the gods could step down to earth.

The Akkadian Invasion and the Formation of the First Empire

About 2500 BCE, Sumer was invaded by a Semitic people known as the **Akkadians.** Adopting the older Sumerian culture, including its cuneiform script, which they used to write down their own language, the Akkadians established the world's first empire. Sargon I of Akkad (ruled c. 2334–2279 BCE) rose from obscurity to become the earliest ruler to forge a union of previously independent city-states, including Ur. (For parallels between Sargon's story and that of Moses, see Chapter 6.) Sargon's most effective successor, his grandson Naram-Sin, proclaimed himself "king of the four quarters of the earth," indicating that he may have extended his rule over most of Mesopotamia. Among Naram-Sin's many exploits was his destruction of **Ebla,** a major city in northern Syria. In 1975, archaeologists excavating Ebla's royal archives uncovered an extensive library written in cuneiform. Dating to the twenty-third century BCE, Ebla's collection of hymns, proverbs, myths, and rituals offers a fascinating glimpse into northwest Mesopotamian culture that flourished centuries before Abraham. Shortly after Ebla's discovery, a few scholars made sweeping claims about its supposed connection to the Hebrew Bible. One proposed that Ebla's pantheon included a deity named Ya, an abbreviated form of Yahweh, and that a king called Ebrum may have been a forefather of Abraham. The majority of scholars, however, have since rejected such claims as premature and unverifiable. Although further study is necessary before Ebla's possible relevance to biblical traditions is understood, some early findings may be significant. One personal name appearing in the clay tablets—*Ishra-il*—seems too similar to *Israel* to be merely coincidental. Genesis states that Jacob had his name changed to Israel after wrestling with a mysterious night visitor at Peniel. The Ebla text suggests, however, that the name existed long before it was bestowed on the forefather of Israel's twelve tribes.

After dominating Mesopotamia for two centuries, Sargon's empire fell to a new invader, the Amorites (or "Westerners"), who swept through many parts of the Fertile Crescent. Merely raiding and looting in some areas, the Amorites settled in others, building new towns in northern and western Canaan, where their descendants were still living when the Israelites entered the area. They also founded or greatly expanded two important city-states in Mesopotamia—Mari on the middle Euphrates and Babylon on the river's southern segment. Located near the modern border of Syria and Iraq, the Mari sites have yielded more than 20,000 clay tablets approximately 4,000

years old. Some of these cuneiform texts contain information about Bronze Age social customs that historians formerly hoped would provide background for the Genesis stories about Abraham, Isaac, and Jacob. Unfortunately, these tablets, like those found at Nuzi, a comparable archaeological site on the upper Tigris River, do not offer any information about legal and marital practices of the mid-second millennium BCE that would help illuminate biblical texts. Despite alleged parallels to the domestic lives of Abraham and Sarah or of Jacob and his family, continued study of these cuneiform documents indicates that the social mores they reflect are not those of the Genesis narratives. Although archaeologists can unearth material remains of vanished civilizations approximately the same age as that of characters in Genesis, they have not been able to verify the historical existence of Israel's ancestors.

The Epic of Gilgamesh

In addition to countless legal and commercial records, archaeologists have also discovered important works of Mesopotamian literature that contain many similarities to parts of the Hebrew Bible. About 150 years ago, archaeologists uncovered the cuneiform library of the Assyrian emperor Ashurbanipal IV (ruled 668–627 BCE). Ashurbanipal was one of the last powerful rulers of imperial **Assyria,** a warlike nation that dominated the Near East from the eleventh to the seventh centuries BCE. (See Table 3.1 for a list of major events in biblical history). In the ruins of Ashurbanipal's palace at Nineveh, capital of the Assyrian Empire, excavators found a large collection of ancient literary documents, including the most complete known copy of the *Epic of Gilgamesh*. Although the Sumerians had composed stories about Gilgamesh, a legendary ruler of Uruk, as early as the second millennium BCE, the Assyrian version found in Ashurbanipal's royal

TABLE 3.1 Some Major Events in Biblical History

APPROXIMATE DATE	EVENT	BIBLICAL REFERENCE
1250 BCE	Moses leads Israelite slaves from Egypt and establishes worship of Yahweh at Mount Sinai/Horeb (according to biblical tradition)	Exodus 13–34
1200 BCE	Israelite tribes settle in Palestine's central hill; worship of Yahweh competes with cult of Baal	Joshua 1–24; Judges 1–21
1000 BCE	David becomes king of united Israel	2 Samuel 2–21
950 BCE	David's son Solomon builds Yahweh's Temple in Jerusalem	1 Kings 3–11

(continued)

TABLE 3.1 *(continued)*

APPROXIMATE DATE	EVENT	BIBLICAL REFERENCE
922 BCE	After Solomon's death, Israel splits into two rival kingdoms: Israel (north) and Judah (south)	1 Kings 12–13
860–840 BCE	The prophets Elijah and Elisha denounce Baal and promote exclusive worship of Yahweh	1 Kings 17–22
750 BCE	The prophets Amos and Hosea condemn Israel's exploitation of the poor and predict disaster	Amos 1–9 Hosea 1–14
722/721 BCE	Assyrian armies destroy Samaria, capital of Israel, sending refugees south to Jerusalem	2 Kings 17–20; Isaiah 36–37
701 BCE	Assyria devastates Judah, but Jerusalem escapes capture	2 Kings 19; Isaiah 37
621 BCE	Priests find early edition of Deuteronomy during Temple repairs; King Josiah's reforms centralize Yahweh's worship in Jerusalem	2 Kings 22–23
600–587 BCE	Jeremiah advocates submission to Babylon	Jeremiah 1–36
587 BCE	Nebuchadnezzar's Babylonian armies destroy Jerusalem and Solomon's Temple, ending David's line of kings	2 Kings 24; Psalms 74, 89
587–538 BCE	Babylonian exile begins Jewish Diaspora (scattering of Jews abroad); Jewish scribes and priests edit Mosaic traditions and accounts of national history	
539 BCE and after	After Cyrus of Persia conquers Babylon, some upper-class Jews return from exile to Jerusalem; Haggai and Zechariah urge rebuilding of Temple	Ezra 1–7; Haggai 2
538–330 BCE	Persia controls partly restored Judean state	
515 BCE	The Second Temple is built on site of Solomon's sanctuary	
445 BCE	The priest-scribe Ezra brings edition of Torah from Babylon and pursues reforms in Jerusalem	Ezra 7; Nehemiah 8
336–323 BCE	Alexander the Great conquers most of known world, bringing Greek culture and ideas to Near East	1 Maccabees 1
167–164 BCE	The Greek Syrian king Antiochus IV attempts to force Jews to abandon Mosaic traditions, triggering Maccabean Revolt and composition of Daniel	2 Maccabees 4; Daniel 1–12
63 BCE	The Roman general Pompey incorporates Judea into Roman Empire	
27–30 CE	Jesus of Nazareth proclaims imminent arrival of God's kingdom; the Roman governor Pontius Pilate orders him crucified; Jesus' disciples proclaim that he rose from dead and will return soon to impose universal rule	Mark, Matthew, Luke, and John
35–62 CE	Paul, a Diaspora Jew, experiences vision of risen Jesus and founds series of Gentile churches in Asia Minor and Greece	Galatians 1–2; 1 Corinthians 15
66–73 CE	Palestinian Jews revolt against Rome; Roman armies destroy Jerusalem and the Temple (70 CE); The first narrative of Jesus' life, the Gospel of Mark, is written	
80–90 CE	The Gospels of Matthew and Luke appear	
90–100 CE	The Gospel of John is composed	
313 CE	The emperor Constantine issues edict legitimizing Christianity, orders official copies of New Testament	

BOX 3.1 The Gilgamesh Flood Story and Biblical Parallels

When archaeologists discovered the ancient Gilgamesh epic, with its account of a global flood, they recognized many parallels between it and the Genesis flood story. In the Gilgamesh account, Enlil, a fierce god of wind and storm, persuades the other gods to reduce the noisy human population by drowning them in a mighty flood. Only Ea, god of wisdom, has compassion for humanity and warns Utnapishtim (the Babylonian counterpart of Noah) to build a boat, into which he brings his family and servants, as well as animals, birds, and other creatures to populate the postflood world. As Ea instructs him, Utnapishtim's job is to "leave possessions, search out living things, and save lives."

As "everything light turned to darkness," for six days howling winds and drenching rains "overwhelmed the land," turning "all mankind . . . to clay." By the seventh day, when the tempest finally ceases, floodwaters extend from horizon to horizon, showing no sign of life anywhere. After the waters begin to recede and the survivors' boat has "come to rest on Mount Nimush," Utnapistim—like Noah—sends out birds to see if they can find dry land. The first two birds, a dove and a swallow, soon return to the boat, but a raven released later finds food to eat and does not come back. (Compare Noah's release of a raven and dove from the ark in Genesis 7:8–11.)

As soon as Utnapishtim can leave his boat, he offers a sacrifice, burning the animal so that the gods above might smell "the pleasant fragrance." (In Genesis 8:21, God also enjoys "the pleasing odor" of Noah's postflood burnt offering.) Crowding "like flies" over the smoking meat, the gods finally realize that human worship is indispensable to their welfare and apparently resolve not to wipe out humanity again. When Ishtar, goddess of love and war, joins the other gods at the feast, she flings her jeweled necklace into the air (where it forms a rainbow). Like Yahweh in Genesis, she resolves never to "forget" the flood disaster, when the gods foolishly eliminated almost all their worshipers.

As scholars have noted, when Israel's writers incorporated their version of a prehistoric deluge into the Hebrew Bible, they created an ethical tension in their portrayal of God. In Genesis 1, God first appears as the originator of light, methodically transforming the darkness of primal chaos into a life-filled cosmos in which light and dark alternate. Surveying his completed work, God pronounces the world, including the humans made in "his image," "very good" (Gen. 1:31). Only six chapters later, however, Yahweh reverses his earlier evaluation of humanity: "And the LORD was sorry that he had made humankind on the earth, and it grieved him to his heart." Repelled by human "wickedness," God proceeds to "blot out . . . the humans I have created—people together with animals and creeping things and birds of the air, for I am sorry that I have made them" (Gen. 6:6–8). Only Noah and his immediate family are spared.

By assigning a single God the triple roles of creator, destroyer, and compassionate preserver of a few flood survivors, the Genesis authors combine conflicting traditions about the gods that Israel inherited from older Near Eastern cultures. In Mesopotamian myth, different gods play different roles in stories about creation and the global flood. In the *Enuma Elish*, one god—Marduk—subdues the forces of chaos and creates the world from Tiamat's watery corpse. Marduk then delegates the task of creating humankind to his father Ea, god of wisdom. Another tradition, found in the Atrahasis epic, states that a mother goddess, Nintu-Mami, is the divine potter who shapes humans out of clay. In Mesopotamian tradition, however, none of these creator gods is responsible for drowning all humanity in a global deluge. According to the Gilgamesh epic, it is Enlil, the ill-tempered god of storm and wind, who takes the part of destroyer and brings about the flood. The role of humanity's preserver goes to kindly Ea, who makes possible the survival of a few people to replenish the earth. In adapting Mesopotamian lore to fit their emerging monotheism, the Genesis writers assigned the actions of three different gods—Marduk, Enlil, and Ea—to a single divinity, Yahweh.

As a result of this merging of formerly separate divine personalities, the biblical God often manifests seemingly contradictory qualities. Thus, he is sometimes represented as having to change his mind about his own creative work, feeling "sorry" that he had made a flawed humanity. (See also Exodus 32:14 for another incident in which "the LORD changed his mind.") Israelite monotheism eventually ascribed all things to the one God—light and dark, mercy and judgment, peace and violence, life and death—creating a portrayal of God that incorporates cosmic opposites, as well as an ethical paradox (Isa. 45:5–7).

library has greater significance to biblical scholars. On the eleventh of twelve clay tablets on which the poem is inscribed, the royal scribes (professional copyists) who translated and edited the work inserted into the hero's adventures a long narrative about a global deluge. Apparently borrowed from a previously separate flood myth featuring Atrahasis, another Mesopotamian hero, the Gilgamesh version of the deluge contains remarkably close parallels to the Genesis flood story (Gen. 6–8) (see Box 3.1 for a summary of the Mesopotamian flood narrative).

BOX 3.2 The Divine Council

A belief that the gods who governed the world regularly met to discuss their plans for humanity is found throughout ancient Near Eastern literature, including the Bible. Apparently modeled on the practice of kings and emperors holding conferences with high-ranking advisors, the concept of a celestial assembly plays a prominent role in both Canaanite and Mesopotamian religion. In the Gilgamesh epic, the high gods meet to hear Ishtar's request to punish the hero who rejected her advances, a conference that results in the decision to torment Gilgamesh through the death of his beloved friend Enkidu. In the *Enuma Elish,* the gods, threatened by Tiamat, dragon of primal chaos, hold council to confer supreme kingship on the young warrior-god Marduk. In the Atrahasis epic, the gods meet after the world flood to debate other, less extreme means of limiting human population growth, such as war, plague, famine, and the assaults of wild beasts.

In the Hebrew Bible, Yahweh is portrayed as leader of the divine council, a heavenly assembly of deities. In contrast to older Near Eastern portrayals of divine council members, biblical texts emphasize the unique ethical character of Israel's God, particularly his concern for humanity's poor and downtrodden. According to Psalm 82, God implicitly contrasts his passion for justice with the other gods' misguided support of social and economic oppression:

> GOD has taken his place in the divine council,
> in the midst of the gods he holds judgment:
> "How long will you [the other gods] judge unjustly
> and show partiality to the wicked?
> Give justice to the weak and the orphan;
> maintain the right of the lowly and the destitute.
> Rescue the weak and needy;
> deliver them from the hand of the wicked."

(Ps. 82:1–4)

Because his fellow divinities lack the biblical God's insight and compassion, "they have neither knowledge nor understanding," causing them to blunder about "in [moral] darkness,"

undermining the "foundations" of justice on which the universe is based (Ps. 82:5). Without capacity for ethical growth, the rival deities are doomed to extinction, a prediction that forms the poem's climax:

> I [Yahweh] say, "You are gods, children of the Most
> High [Elyon], all of you;
> nevertheless, you shall die like mortals, and fall like
> any prince."

(Ps. 82:7)

The notion that a god can die may startle contemporary readers, but in the ancient world, defeated gods could indeed cease to exist. In the *Enuma Elish,* Marduk kills both the primal goddess Tiamat and her divine consort, Kingu.

Psalm 89 praises Yahweh as supreme among the "assembly of holy ones," members of the heavenly council. Underscoring God's unique "faithfulness," the psalmist asks:

> For who in the skies can be compared to the LORD
> [Yahweh]?
> Who among the heavenly beings is like the LORD,
> a God found in the council of the holy ones,
> great and awesome above all that are around him?

(Ps. 89:6–7)

Another glimpse of the divine council appears in 1 Kings 22, where Yahweh is shown seated on his throne and surrounded by "all the host of heaven"—divine courtiers and soldiers who form his invisible armies. God's purpose in calling this assembly is to fashion a strategy by which Ahab, king of Israel, can be lured into fighting a battle in which he will be killed. After council members offer contradictory suggestions, one "spirit" volunteers to perform the deception:

> "How?" the LORD [Yahweh] asked him. He replied, "I will go and be a lying spirit in the mouth of his prophets." Then the LORD said, "You are to entice him; and you shall succeed; go out and do it."

(I Kings 22:19–22)

Discovery of the Gilgamesh flood story made scholars aware, for the first time, that the Genesis authors apparently had drawn on an older Mesopotamian tradition in composing the biblical text. Widely distributed throughout the ancient Near East, tablets containing all or parts of the Gilgamesh epic have been found in numerous ancient libraries, including one at Megiddo

in Israel. The hero is even mentioned by name in the Dead Sea Scrolls, Jewish documents dating from about 200 BCE to 68 CE (see Chapter 2).

Gilgamesh's story has two distinct parts. In the first, he strongly bonds with a wild man, Enkidu, whom the gods created out of clay to be his life-partner. After the two friends slay monsters—such as the fiery Humbaba

Utilizing this "lying spirit," God then lures Ahab to his death.

The book of Job describes two parallel meetings of the heavenly council. In the first scene, Yahweh summons all the "sons of God" or "sons of the gods" (the Hebrew phrase *bene ha elohim* permits either translation) before his throne, among whom is the "Satan [Adversary]." In Job, the "Satan" is primarily a servant, a regular member of the divine court whose job, like that of the secret police of an ancient Near Eastern emperor, involves his patrolling the earth to identify potentially disloyal subjects. After drawing his faithful worshiper Job to the Satan's attention, Yahweh allows his agent to strip Job of all his possessions and to kill all his children. When the divine "sons" are again assembled in the heavenly throne room, Yahweh reproves Satan for turning him against Job "without cause," but he also allows the Satan to destroy the man's health, afflicting him with a loathsome skin disease (see Chapter 23).

Empowered by his great wisdom and ethical superiority, Yahweh is seen as reigning over the other council members, the unnamed "sons of the gods" or "[military] host of heaven." Ultimately reduced to a dependent status as Yahweh's servants, these heavenly beings become Yahweh's divine messengers (the meaning of the English word *angel*), running errands and conveying orders to human subjects. It is presumably these members of his heavenly court whom God addresses at creation when he proposes: "Let *us* make humankind in *our* image, according to *our* likeness" (Gen. 1:26, emphasis added). God's associates in creation are also identified as the "morning stars" and "heavenly beings" who joyfully acclaim the universe's birth (Job 38:7). In Genesis 2, Yahweh similarly evokes his divine council members when he says that "the man [after eating forbidden fruit] has become like one of *us*" and must be prevented from tasting the "tree of life," lest he acquire godlike immortality (Gen. 3:22) (see Figure 3.4).

FIGURE 3.4 The scene depicted on this Mesopotamian cylinder seal (c. 2200 to 2100 BCE) shows a seated god facing a female worshiper, also seated, with a stylized palm tree between them. Although nineteenth-century interpreters were wrong in labeling the figures "Adam and Eve," the seal's association of male deity, a "tree of life" with the woman's arm extended towards it, and the iconic presence of serpents vividly evokes images from the Genesis story of Eden.

and the fierce "bull of heaven," a personification of drought and earthquake—Gilgamesh commits a grave offense by rejecting the sexual advances of **Ishtar,** beautiful goddess of love and war and the divine patron of his city, Uruk. After the deeply offended Ishtar persuades the heavenly council to punish Gilgamesh by afflicting Enkidu with a fatal disease, Gilgamesh, overwhelmed by grief, experiences a crisis that changes his life. (See Box 3.2 for a discussion of biblical concepts of the divine council.) Horrified by his first personal encounter with death, Gilgamesh determines, through sheer force of will, to find a way to escape human mortality.

In the epic's second part, Gilgamesh leaves Uruk and begins a long, dangerous quest to find everlasting life. Leaving the known world behind, he crosses the "waters of death" and journeys through a region of total darkness to find the remote island dwelling of his ancestor, Utnapishtim. Like the biblical Noah, Utnapishtim is the only man (along with his family and servants) to have survived the great flood. He is also the only one to whom the gods have granted immortality. After enduring many hardships, Gilgamesh arrives exhausted at Utnapishtim's "faraway" paradise. Scoffing at his descendant's ambition to live forever, Utnapishtim reminds Gilgamesh that his host's possession of eternal life stems from unique, unrepeatable circumstances: being selected by the wise divinity Ea to build an ark, take aboard pairs of animals, and thus survive a watery cataclysm that wipes out the rest of humanity. In pity at Gilgamesh's despair, Utnapishtim's wife persuades her husband to reveal that a plant capable of miraculously restoring youth grows at the bottom of the sea. After risking his life to obtain the rejuvenating plant, Gilgamesh begins his perilous return to Uruk, only to have the plant stolen from him and eaten by a snake. The serpent is thus able to shed its skin, apparently renewing its life, whereas mortal humans tragically lack the ability to recapture lost youth.

On his journey to Utnapishtim's island, Gilgamesh meets Siduri, a wise barmaid and minor goddess, who tells him that he will never find the everlasting life he seeks, reminding him that the gods reserve it exclusively for themselves. Instead of wearing himself out trying to be a god, she says, he must accept the ordinary consolations of humanity's mortal state:

> As for you, Gilgamesh, fill your belly with good things; day and night, night and day, dance and be merry, feast and rejoice. Let your clothes be fresh, bathe yourself in water, cherish the little child that holds your hand, and make your wife happy in your embrace, for this too is the lot of man.

Siduri's advice is repeated almost exactly in the Book of Ecclesiastes, where the author laments the unacceptable fact that all human effort ends in death, and is thus "vanity and a chasing after wind." Life's only comfort lies in the enjoyment of commonplace pleasures that God concedes to mortals:

> Go, eat your bread with enjoyment, and drink your wine with a merry heart; for God has long ago approved what you do. Let your garments always be white; and do not let oil be lacking on your head. Enjoy life with the wife whom you love, all the days of your vain life that are given you under the sun.

(Eccles. 9:7–9)

Ecclesiastes' emphasis on human mortality reflects the Bible's general agreement with ancient Mesopotamian beliefs about the gods' prerogatives: Divine beings do not share their immortality with humankind. In Genesis 3, Yahweh posts a cherub wielding a fiery sword to keep the first humans from eating of the "tree of life" that grows in Eden, the "garden of God" (see Figure 3.5). Humanity is barred from tasting the tree's fruit, lest they imitate divinity and "live forever" (Gen. 3:22–24).

The Mesopotamian Underworld

Many readers are surprised to learn how relatively little either the Old or New Testament has to say about the condition of souls after death (for a notable exception, see the discussion of Paul's letters to the Corinthians in Chapter 35). Generally, most Hebrew Bible writers either ignore the subject or adopt the prevailing Mesopotamian view that all the dead, good and bad alike, descend permanently into a gloomy subterranean realm where they lead an impoverished and shadowy postmortem existence. Reflecting their Mesopotamian heritage, Tanakh authors do not offer even the most faithful Israelites the hope of immortality in heaven. Unlike the Egyptians, who took extraordinary pains to preserve their dead in richly decorated tombs in the expectation of a joyous afterlife, the ancient Israelites looked forward to no comparable reward. Israelite writers portray **Sheol,** the biblical Underworld for which every deceased person is destined, as a dark and dusty region of perpetual silence, virtually identical to that which the ghost of Enkidu describes to his surviving friend Gilgamesh. (For a discussion of biblical texts describing Sheol, see Box 23.1.)

In the canonical Hebrew Bible, only two persons—the Genesis figure Enoch (Gen. 5:21–24) and the prophet Elijah (2 Kings 2:1–12)—are, apparently without experiencing death, taken bodily up to heaven. No biblical prophet or wisdom writer proposes a similar fate for anyone else. Not until the second century BCE, when the apocalyptic Book of Daniel was composed, does a Tanakh author explicitly state that the dead will be physically resurrected to a future life of honor or disgrace (Dan. 12:3). By the time Daniel was written, Israelite society had been extensively exposed to concepts of the afterlife envisioned in both Persian religion and Greek philosophy (see Chapter 28 for a discussion of Greek beliefs about the immortality of the soul). For

FIGURE 3.5 This Assyrian figure—with a bull's body, eagle's wings, and human face—resembles the biblical cherubim (Ezek. 1:4–28; 10:1–22), such as Yahweh appoints to guard the entrance of Eden (Gen. 3:23–24).

New Testament writers, the resurrection of Jesus opened the way for his followers to exchange their human mortality for life everlasting (cf. 1 Cor. 15).

 The Law Code of Hammurabi

The city of Babylon, which plays a pivotal role in biblical history, first achieved prominence when the Amorites founded a dynasty there. In the reign of **Hammurabi** (also spelled Hammurapi), sixth king of the Amorite line, the city became the center of a new Mesopotamian empire. Uniting all Mesopotamian city-states under his rule, Hammurabi (reigned 1792–1750 BCE) created a broad dominion that rivaled that of Sargon I. An effective general and capable administrator, Hammurabi is best remembered for publishing a collection of laws known as the **Code of Hammurabi.** Scholars have divided the code into 282 separate units, which are inscribed on a stone slab nearly eight feet tall (see Figure 3.6). At the top of the stone column, a sculptor carved a portrait of the sun god Shamash bestowing the law code on Hammurabi, exactly as Exodus describes Yahweh giving his laws to Moses on Mount Sinai (see Figure 3.7).

Hammurabi's laws are expressed in the same literary structure and, in some instances, have the same content

FIGURE 3.6 The legacy of Babylon's first important king, the stele of Hammurabi—a basalt slab nearly eight feet tall—records an ancient Sumero–Babylonian legal code that contains statutes resembling laws found in the Mosaic Torah. Erected in the eighteenth century BCE, it reflects legal principles common to ancient Mesopotamia, the original home of the Israelite ancestors.

as the Mosaic statutes (see Box 3.3 for some examples). Both the Hammurabic and Mosaic codes employ the same legal procedures or formats (also known as "case law"): *If* such and such happens, *then* such and such will be the punishment. Part of the Mosaic legislation is also codified in a manner resembling the older Babylonian model, as in the section of Exodus known as the Book of the Covenant (cf. Exod. 20:22–23, 33; 24:7). Babylonian, Egyptian, and Israelite legal traditions commonly reflect similar concepts of justice, including protection of society's poor and powerless members. Both the Hammurabic and Mosaic laws refer specifically to "widows

FIGURE 3.7 In the ancient Near East, law codes—which kings and other leaders imposed on their people—were commonly ascribed to the nation's gods. In this scene from the top of the stele of Hammurabi, Hammurabi receives legal commands from the enthroned sun god Shamash, just as Moses is represented as receiving Torah laws from Yahweh 500 years later.

BOX 3.3 **Law of Hammurabi and Laws in the Mosaic Torah**

Code of Hammurabi

(Law 117) If an obligation came due against a seignior and he sold (the services of) his wife, his son, or his daughter, or he has been bound over to service, they shall work (in) the house of their purchaser or oblige for three years, with their freedom reestablished in the fourth year. (cf. Exod. 21:2–11; Deut. 15:12–18)

(Law 129) If the wife of a seignior has been caught while lying with another man, they shall bind them and throw them into the water. If the husband of the woman wishes to spare his wife, then the king in turn may spare his subject. (cf. Deut. 22:22)

(Law 130) If a seignior bound the (bethrothed) wife of a(nother) seignior, who had had no intercourse with a male and was still living in her father's house, and he has lain in her bosom and they have caught him, that seignor shall be put to death, while that woman shall go free. (cf. Deut. 22:23–27)

(Law 132) If the finger was pointed at the wife of a seignior because of another man, but she has not been caught while lying with the other man, she shall throw herself into the river for the sake of her husband. (cf. Num. 5:11–31)

[Incest Statutes 154–158; cf. Lev. 18:6–18; 20:10–21; Deut. 27:20, 22f]

Hammurabi's Laws of Retaliation (*Lex Talionis*)

(196) If a son has struck his father, they shall cut off his hand.

(196) If a seignior has destroyed the eye of a member of the aristocracy, they shall destroy his eye.

(197) If he has broken another seignior's bone, they shall break his bone.

(198) If he has destroyed the eye of a commoner or broken the bone of a commoner, he shall pay one mina of silver.

(199) If he has destroyed the eye of a seignior's slave or broken the bone of a seignior's slave, he shall pay one-half his value.

(200) If a seignior has knocked out a tooth of a seignior of his own rank, they shall knock out his tooth.

(201) If he has knocked out a commoner's tooth, he shall pay one-third mina of silver.

(202) If a seignior has struck the cheek of a seignior who is superior to him, he shall be beaten sixty (times) with an ox-tail whip in the assembly. (cf. Exod. 21:23–25; Lev. 24:19f; Deut. 19:21)

Ends with blessings and curses. (cf. Deut. 28)

---

and orphans" as representing a class of people who need to be shielded from exploitation.

Hammurabi declares that his purpose is to "promote the welfare of the people, . . . to cause justice to prevail in the land, to destroy the wicked and the evil, that the strong might not oppress the weak." As in earlier Mesopotamian law codes, however, Hammurabi's system did not offer equal protection to people belonging to different social classes. In general, the nobility fared far better than the classes beneath them. Whereas an aristocrat was allowed to pay a fine for manslaughter, a slave was automatically condemned to death. Merely injuring a person who stood higher in the social scale brought more severe penalties than did murdering a slave.

Both Mesopotamian and biblical laws imposed the death penalty for numerous offenses, and both allowed physical mutilation of the condemned. Judges and executioners were to "show no pity" when killing or mutilating offenders (Deut. 19:21). Known as the ***lex talionis,*** this law of retaliation—inflicting the same kind of injury that has been inflicted on a victim—was central

to the Israelite sense of justice. Biblical writers considered the *lex talionis* so important that they proclaimed it in three of the five books of the Torah (Exod. 21:23–25; Lev. 24:19–20; Deut. 19:21).

Although this principle of retaliation seems inhumane to most twenty-first-century readers, in both the Mosaic and Hammurabic codes, the *lex talionis* served to limit the degree of vengeance to which a wronged party was legally entitled: Injured persons could not take an aggressor's life but could only inflict wounds precisely equivalent to those that they had received. Both codes agreed, however, that upper-class offenders could escape physical punishment by paying for injuries inflicted on social inferiors. According to Babylonian law, a nobleman who blinded or knocked out the tooth of a commoner had to pay a fine. And if he seriously harmed another nobleman's slave, he had to pay one-half of the slave's value (Hammurabi, secs. 199, 201, etc.).

While making similar distinctions between persons of different social rank, such as owners and their slaves, the Mosaic code introduced a more humane element. Thus, a master who injured his slave had to set that slave free:

> When a slaveowner strikes the eye of a male or female slave, destroying it, the owner shall let the slave go, a free person, to compensate for the eye. If the owner knocks out a tooth of a male or female slave, the slave shall be let go, a free person, to compensate for the tooth.
>
> (Exod. 21:26–27)

Although slaves were regarded as physical property throughout the ancient world, the biblical provision was almost revolutionary in recognizing the slaves' humanity and in granting the right to freedom in compensation for injury.

In his Sermon on the Mount, Jesus offers the New Testament's most explicit judgment of the *lex talionis,* which he rejects and replaces with a new principle of nonviolence:

> "You have heard that it was said, 'An eye for an eye and a tooth for a tooth.' But I say to you, Do not resist an evildoer. But if anyone strikes you on the right cheek, turn the other also; . . . and if anyone forces you to go one mile, go also the second mile. Give to everyone who begs from you, and do not refuse anyone who wants to borrow from you."
>
> (Matt. 5:38–42)

While insisting that Jesus came to uphold the Mosaic legal system (Matt. 5:17–20), the author of Matthew's Gospel—the only Gospel writer to include this repudiation of the *lex talionis*—simultaneously urges Jesus' followers to practice a "higher righteousness." By "turning the other cheek," Jesus' disciples observe the principle behind the *lex talionis*—rejecting the claim to vengeance and thus ending the cycle of retaliation that poisons interpersonal relationships and destroys the peace of entire societies.

Egypt: The First National State

The name **Egypt** derives from a Greek word meaning the "Temple of Ptah," the term by which the Egyptians identified their country. The "temple" or holy dwelling place of Ptah, the Egyptian creator god, was the narrow strip of fertile land bordering the Nile River. Beyond this narrow cultivated zone, watered by annual floodings of the Nile, stretched vast, inhospitable deserts that effectively isolated Egypt from its African neighbors. Whereas the broad plains of Mesopotamia were easily—and frequently—invaded by foreign armies, Egypt's unique geographical features allowed it to develop independently of most foreign influence. Bordered on the east and west by arid wastes and on the south by a rugged terrain through which the Nile flowed in impassable cataracts, ancient Egypt enjoyed a largely uninterrupted period of stability and nation building.

From Kingdom to Empire

Beginning as a coalition of small political districts called *nomes,* Egypt first evolved into two distinct kingdoms known as Upper Egypt and Lower Egypt. About 3100 BCE, the two kingdoms were merged under the rule of Narmer, king of Upper (southern) Egypt. Historians divide subsequent ancient Egyptian history into three major periods: (1) the Old Kingdom, or Pyramid Age (Third to Sixth Dynasties, c. 2686–2160 BCE); (2) the Middle Kingdom, or Feudal Age (Eleventh and Twelfth Dynasties, c. 2030–1720 BCE); and (3) the New Kingdom or Empire (Eighteenth to Twentieth Dynasties, c. 1570–1075 BCE). Under the empire, New Kingdom pharaohs such as Thutmose I extended Egypt's dominion northeastward into Canaan (Palestine). About 1490 BCE, Egyptian forces defeated a coalition of more than one hundred rulers of Syrian and Canaanite city-states at the Battle of Megiddo, a site that in later history marked several decisive Israelite defeats. Regarded as of crucial significance in biblical history, this geographical site—*Har-Megiddo* (Armageddon)—lent its name as the place where cosmic good and evil would ultimately fight their climactic battle (Rev. 16:16).

Until the end of the New Kingdom, Egypt maintained a line of military fortresses in Canaan, guarding against invasions from Mesopotamia or Asia Minor (modern Turkey). The later New Kingdom, however, witnessed a gradual decline in power, as Egypt was plagued by internal divisions, economic difficulties, and increasing foreign aggression. During the Late Dynastic Period (Twenty-first to Thirty-first Dynasties, eleventh to fourth centuries BCE), first Assyrian and then Persian armies invaded and occupied the country. The end of native Egyptian rule arrived with Alexander the Great in 332 BCE. A dynasty founded by Alexander's successor, Ptolemy I, lasted for 300 years, eclipsed only when Rome incorporated Egypt into its empire in 30 BCE. (For a survey Israel's history during the Greek and Roman periods, see Chapters 26 and 28.)

Egypt's Enduring Legacy

The Egyptian system of writing, which featured pictorial characters—**hieroglyphics**—developed about the same time as, or shortly after, the invention of cuneiform script in Mesopotamia. The Egyptians also made spectacular advances in mathematics and astronomy, devising a calendar based on the solar year of 365 days. This calendar features twelve months of thirty days each, to which five festival days were added to round out the year. The familiar practice of dividing the day into twenty-four hours and beginning a new day at midnight is also an inheritance from ancient Egypt.

Egypt's numerous gifts to the modern world include the science of geometry. Devising methods to compute the areas and volumes of abstract geometrical forms, Egyptian architects applied these skills to build the world's first large-scale structures in stone. An edifice of massive grandeur, the multitiered Step Pyramid was constructed for King Zoser (Djoser) about 2650 BCE. Erected shortly afterwards, the enormous pyramids at Giza still tower hundreds of feet above the Nile Valley, the sole survivors among the ancient world's Seven Wonders.

Egypt's great pyramids and colossal sphinx at al-Jizah were already many centuries old when Abraham's grandson Jacob and eleven of his sons, driven by famine in Canaan, sought refuge in the prosperous Nile region. Because the Nile supplied Egypt's extensive irrigation system even in many drought years when crops in neighboring states failed, Ptah's land attracted many nomadic peoples hoping to secure Egyptian grain. According to Genesis, Israel's ancestors—the twelve sons of Jacob (Israel)—were among the many who settled temporarily in the delta region.

One popular theory holds that Semitic nomads were welcome in Egypt at the time Israelite tribes entered because Egypt was then ruled by foreigners known as the **Hyksos.** Although native Egyptians rarely surrendered control of their country, in the seventeenth century BCE, the Semitic Hyksos infiltrated the population, eventually taking over Pharaoh's throne. In 1560 BCE, an Egyptian revolt expelled the Hyksos rulers and established the Eighteenth Dynasty (see Chapter 6). This native royal line included some of Egypt's most famous rulers, including Queen Hatshepsut, the only female pharaoh, and Amenhotep IV.

Amenhotep IV, who changed his name to **Akhenaton** (ruled 1364–1347 BCE), scandalized the Egyptian priesthood by ordering that only a single deity, the sun god Aton, be universally honored. Some historians believe that Akhenaton established the world's first monotheism; most, however, think that his cult of Aton was really an example of **henotheism**—worship of a single god while admitting the existence of other deities. Although Akhenaton's religious experiment

was brief—his youthful successor, Tutankhamen, revoked his reforms—it may have set a precedent that indirectly influenced the biblical concept of Yahweh's "jealousy." The revolutionary belief that a single god could require his people to worship no other gods is the cornerstone of the Mosaic tradition (Exod. 20:2–6; Deut. 5:6–10).

Correspondence preserved in the ruined archives of Tel el Amarna, the site to which Akhenaton moved his capital, gives a vivid picture of Egypt during the dominion of Aton. The **Amarna Age,** the period of Akhenaton's reign, and the exclusive cult of the sun god Aton were largely forgotten by 1306 BCE, when Ramses I founded a new royal dynasty, the nineteenth. Under **Rameses II** (ruled 1290–1224 BCE), the Egyptian Empire reached its height. Many historians believe that Rameses II was the pharaoh before whom Moses appeared and whom Yahweh humiliated in the Exodus. Rameses made a habit of recording his military defeats, as well as his genuine victories, as complete triumphs. If a band of Hebrew slaves did escape from Egypt during his long reign, it is not likely that Rameses' court scribes would have seen fit to mention it.

Slightly later Egyptian records do, however, acknowledge the existence of Israel. The earliest known reference to Israel as a distinct people appears on a victory inscription of **Merneptah,** Rameses' son and successor. Merneptah boasts of his conquests in Canaan, claiming to have laid Israel waste, indicating that the Israelites were already established in the area near the close of the thirteenth century BCE (see Figure 3.8).

One of archaeology's most justly famous artifacts, the **Rosetta Stone** is a flat slab of basalt inscribed with the same message in three different scripts—Greek, hieroglyphic, and demotic (a simplified form of ancient Egyptian writing). In the 1820s, a French scholar, Jean-François Champollion, deciphered the inscriptions and thereby discovered the key to reading Egyptian hieroglyphics. Champollion's breakthrough allowed scholars for the first time to understand previously inaccessible works of Egyptian literature. Scholars have since translated many Egyptian documents related to the biblical text, finding several parallels to the Book of Proverbs, Job, and other examples of wisdom writing (see Chapter 23).

Similarities Between Egyptian and Israelite Traditions

In translating a wealth of Egyptian inscriptions and documents, scholars found striking similarities between some Egyptian beliefs and customs and those of ancient

FIGURE 3.8 The stele of Merneptah (ruled c. 1224–1211 BCE), son of and successor to Rameses II, contains the first extrabiblical reference to Israel's existence. Advertising his victories over various Canaaite states, Merneptah claims that he has so devastated Israel that its "seed [offspring] is not," a conventional military boast. A double figure of the god Amon appears at top center, with Pharaoh Merneptah (also in double representation) standing on either side of the deity.

Israel. Moses' name, like those of many subsequent Israelite priests, is Egyptian. Derived from the Egyptian verb *msw* (to be born) or the noun *mesu* (son), the same root appears in such Egyptian names as Thutmose and Ahmose.

Some scholars believe that Egyptian ethical and religious themes, such as the concept of Maat—which encompasses such principles as "truth," "justice," and "right conduct"—helped shape biblical views of Yahweh's righteousness. Another possible connection between the Egyptian and Israelite religions involves the way in which the two peoples housed their gods. In Egypt, statues of the gods—visible symbols of the deities' invisible presence—were hidden away in windowless sanctuaries. Because the statues were protected from public gaze by massive stone walls, the gods' "holiness" (separation from common life) was enhanced by

elements of secrecy and mystery. Only official priests and Pharaoh himself were allowed into the inner room that contained the sacred images. In Israel, King Solomon built a similar kind of Temple to house the Ark of the Covenant, in which Yahweh's *kavod* (glory) was invisibly enthroned. In some biblical writers' judgment, however, Solomon allied himself too closely with Egypt, marrying a pharaoh's daughter and erecting shrines to the gods of his many foreign wives in the Temple precincts (I Kings 9:16–18, 21; 11:1–8). Even after Solomon's time, Temple rituals continued to resemble those of Egypt: Only the hereditary high priest was permitted to enter the sanctuary's innermost chamber, the Holy of Holies that sheltered Yahweh's unseen presence. (Box 3.4 offers an account of possible links between Egyptian myths and biblical concepts of creation.)

Perhaps Egypt's most lasting contribution to biblical religion was the ritual practice of **circumcision**—the surgical removal of the foreskin (prepuce) from the penis. Circumcision was a physically distinguishing mark on all Israelite males. According to the Greek historian Herodotus, this originally Egyptian practice spread to a few other nations, whereas the majority of men "leave their private parts as nature made them" (*The Histories*, Book 2, 37). In listing nations that practice circumcision, Jeremiah places Egypt first, followed by Judah and its immediate neighbors, Edom, Ammon, and Moab (Jer. 9:25–26). In ancient Israel (as in contemporary Judaism), all male infants, when eight days old, routinely had the foreskin amputated (Gen. 17:12). This ancient Egyptian rite, in fact, is interpreted as the indelible "sign" of God's covenant with Abraham and all his descendants: "My Covenant shall be marked on your bodies as a Covenant in perpetuity" (Gen. 17:9–14).

 # Israel's Geographical Location— A Key to Its History

In many ways, Israel's destiny was shaped by its geography. Situated at the eastern shore of the Mediterranean Sea, on a land bridge between Mesopotamia and Egypt, Israel saw its territory conquered again and again by the superior military might of its imperial neighbors. According to the biblical record, Israel enjoyed national unity and political independence only briefly, during the reigns of its first three kings, Saul, David, and Solomon. This interval of Israelite autonomy, in the late eleventh through the mid-tenth centuries BCE, coincided with a period when the Mesopotamian and Egyptian states were relatively weak. Thereafter, a succession of aggressive

---

BOX 3.4 Egyptian Myths Anticipating Biblical Concepts of Creation

Two creation stories from ancient Egypt foreshadow elements that later appear in the Bible. In the first account, associated with Heliopolis (City of the Sun), the sun god Atum is the creator. Like Genesis 1, the Heliopolis account postulates a precreation expanse of water, called Nu, that had to be separated and divided during the process of forming the world. Embodying the life-giving energy of the sun, Atum encompassed within himself the totality of everything that exists. After rising from the limitless waters of Nu, Atum stood on a primeval mound (signifying the primeval earth) and produced, from his body, the gods Shu and Tefnut (representing air and moisture, respectively), as well as Geb (the male principle, earth) and Nut (the female principle, sky).

From Atum also came the gods who symbolized the divinely ordered structure of Egyptian society: Osiris, lord of the Underworld; his wife Isis, signifying the royal throne; Seth, Osiris's destructive brother, a personification of chaos; Nephthys, sister of Isis and wife of Seth; and Horus, son of Osiris and Isis, who represented the power of the reigning pharaoh.

In a rival creation myth, the priests of Ptah (after whom Egypt, the "Temple of Ptah," is named) made their patron god literally think and speak the world into being. During the thirteenth century BCE, Ptah's priests at Memphis insisted that Ptah was superior to all other gods, including Aton. According to a later version of the myth, inscribed on stone by order of Pharaoh Shabaka about 700 BCE, Ptah gave birth to all things, including the gods, by his "heart" and "tongue." Because many ancient languages, including biblical Hebrew, had few abstract terms, they commonly used the word for "heart" to mean "mind" or "consciousness." Ptah thus created by forming mental images of the universe and then commanding them to exist, fashioning the world by the power of his spoken word. In Genesis 1, God follows the same procedure. The concept of a divine utterance or word (Greek, *logos*) as the means by which all creation exists (and which Greek philosophers later elaborated on) found its ultimate expression in the opening hymn to the Logos (Word) in John's Gospel, where the writer identifies it with the prehuman Jesus, God's creative agent (John 1:1–5; see Chapter 33).

---

empires—the Assyrian, the Babylonian, the Persian, the Macedonian Greek, and, finally, the Roman—controlled the land Yahweh had promised to Abraham's descendants.

Had Israel been placed in a less vulnerable position, far from the crossroads of international commerce and imperialism, it might have escaped the devastation and exile that were its fate. Largely because of its geographical location, however, Israel endured a series of military defeats and foreign occupations that helped shape a biblical worldview that emphasizes national suffering and divine judgment.

The Geography of Palestine

This comparatively narrow strip of land, approximately 150 miles long and 70 miles wide, is slightly smaller than the state of New Jersey. Biblical writers refer to it as the "land of Yahweh," the "land of Israel," and the "good land," but most call it the "land of Canaan." Greek geographers assigned the name **Palestine** to the entire country, naming it after the **Philistines** who settled on the Mediterranean coast at about the same time that the earliest Israelites occupied the area's hilly interior, and it is the Greek name that most commonly prevails today.

Geographically, Palestine is divided into four distinct regions, each with its own climate and topographical peculiarities (see Figure 3.9). Moving from west to east, the first region one encounters is the coastal plain, a narrow belt, 20 to 30 miles wide, bordering the Mediterranean. This is the part that most visitors would have seen as they traveled along the "way of the sea" (Isa. 9:1), one of the two principal highways that traversed ancient Israel. (The other, known as the "King's Highway" [Num. 21:22], branches off toward Mesopotamia.) Although under Egyptian control during the time of the Exodus, the coastal region was later partly occupied by the **Philistines,** Israel's chief enemies during the period of the Judges. The second major region, an inland strip running roughly north-south, is an undulating limestone ridge of low mountains and small intervening valleys. Much less fertile than the coastal plain, this central hill country was the site of the earliest known Israelite settlements, primarily consisting of small farms and villages of a few hundred people (see Box 10.1). Extending northward from the Valley of Beersheba to the mountains of Lebanon, this linear ridge is broken in the north by the broad plain of Megiddo, which the New Testament Book of Revelation identifies as the future site of Armageddon (Rev. 16:16).

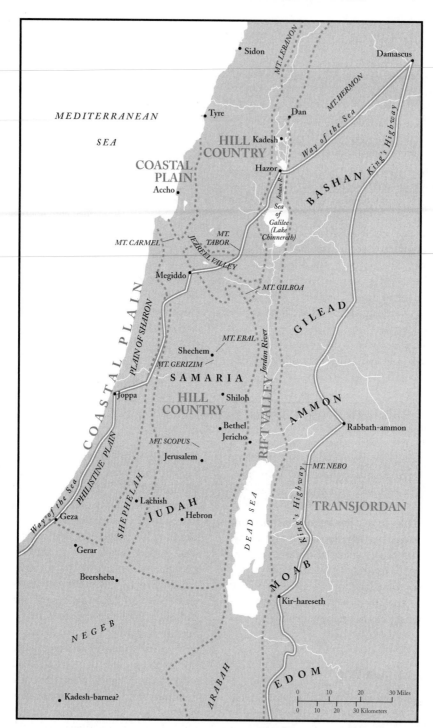

FIGURE 3.9 Map Showing Four Main Geographical Regions of Palestine (Canaan). From west (left) to east (right), the major regions include (1) a narrow coastal plain through which the "Way of the Sea" passes, leading northward along the Mediterranean coastline through Megiddo and Hazor to Damascus, capital of Syria; (2) a broad north-south trending limestone upland consisting of low mountains and generally narrow valleys (the central hill country); (3) a long rift valley through which the Jordan River flows southward from the Sea of Galilee to the Dead Sea; and (4) the Transjordan, a rugged, arid terrain cut by deep canyons and traversed by the "King's Highway," a branch of which eventually extends northeastward toward Mesopotamia (modern Iraq).

Megiddo's level fields join the Valley of Jezreel to the east, near Mount Gilboa, forming an east-west-trending greenbelt, the most fertile part of the country. Rising to elevations of more than 3,000 feet, these uplands drop steeply as one travels eastward into the next geographical zone, a deep rift valley that runs north-south through the entire region. Flowing from the Sea of Galilee in the north section of the valley, the **Jordan River** travels 65 miles southward to the Dead Sea, a large saltwater lake that lies 1,290 feet below sea level, the lowest point on the earth's land surface. Paralleling the Jordan on both sides is a lush band of vegetation; around the Dead Sea, however, nothing grows, making it a striking image of utter desolation.

Located east of the Jordan River, the fourth general region, **Transjordan,** is an arid mountainous terrain cut by deep canyons that flood during heavy seasonal rains. Extending from the plains of southern Syria east of Galilee to the Brook Zered at the southern end of the Dead Sea, Transjordan averages about 1,500 feet above sea level, although many individual peaks rise to twice that height.

Palestine's division into four discrete regions had several consequences for the people who inhabited the area. In terms of Israel's socioeconomic development, geographical differences and topographical barriers meant that people living in a particular region were commonly isolated from inhabitants of adjacent but dissimilar regions. Farmers cultivated the fertile plains, small valleys, and terraced hillsides, growing wheat, barley, olives, and grapes. On nearby stony ridges, shepherds pastured sheep or goats that grazed on scattered tufts of grass. By contrast, Israel's cities, most located in the central hill country, were trade centers open to considerable cultural exchange with itinerant traders from Egypt, Mesopotamia, Syria, Phoenicia, and other affluent urban civilizations.

Tensions Between the North and South

Following King Solomon's death in 922 BCE, the ten tribes occupying Israel's northern territories withdrew from their short-lived union with the tribes of Judah and Benjamin in the south. Although the more powerful and prosperous northern state of Israel endured many changes in rulership during its two centuries of existence, only a single dynasty—that of David—governed the poorer southern state of Judah. According to 2 Kings, when Assyrian forces destroyed Israel and its capital, Samaria, in 722/721 BCE, the Assyrians deported many Israelites and replaced them with foreign settlers. In the view of Judean scribes who produced the official history of this period, not only were the northern Israelites unfaithful to Yahweh, but their descendants practiced an unaccept-

able form of the Yahwist religion (2 Kings 17). Possessing their own edition of the Torah (but not the Prophets or Writings), this group—known as the **Samaritans**—occupied the area between Judah and Galilee. By New Testament times, Torah-observant Jews of Judea (the territory around Jerusalem) had come to regard the Samaritans as little better than a foreign cult. In the Gospel of John, Jesus' opponents accuse him of behaving like a hated Samaritan (John 8:48; cf. John 4).

The ancient tension between Israel's northern and southern regions reappears in the Gospel of Mark. In Mark (as well as Matthew and Luke), Jesus devotes most of his ministry to preaching in the northern area of Galilee, where he recruits his disciples and performs most of his miracles. Only after he travels south to Judea and Jerusalem does he meet with a fatal opposition, the official rejection that leads to his crucifixion. (For Mark's use of a north-south polarity in structuring Jesus' story, see Chapter 30.)

QUESTIONS FOR DISCUSSION AND REVIEW

1. Describe the Fertile Crescent and the region of Mesopotamia. What are some important Sumerian contributions to civilization? Explain the importance of cuneiform script.

2. Summarize the story of Gilgamesh and its relevance to the Bible. How does the flood account in Gilgamesh anticipate that in Genesis 6–8? In what ways does the Mesopotamian Underworld resemble the biblical concept of Sheol, abode of the dead?

3. List some of the parallels between Hammurabi's legal code and some laws found in the Mosaic Covenant. How do you explain the resemblances between Mesopotamian and biblical legal material?

4. Define the ancient Near Eastern concept of the divine council. How do biblical writers portray Israel's God, Yahweh, as presiding over this assembly of heavenly beings?

5. From what god is the name *Egypt* derived? Describe some of the achievements of this first nation-state. What religious changes did Akhenaton introduce? What is the importance of the Merneptah stele?

6. Describe the major geographical divisions of Palestine. How did sociopolitical tensions between the northern and southern regions affect Israelite history?

Terms and Concepts to Remember

Akhenaton (Amenhotep IV)	*lex talionis* (law of retaliation)
Akkad/Akkadians	Marduk
Amarna Age	Merneptah, stele of
circumcision	monotheism
cuneiform	polytheism
Egypt	Palestine
Fertile Crescent	Philistines
flood, Babylonian	Rameses II
Gilgamesh, Epic of	Rosetta Stone
henotheism	Samaritans
hieroglyphics	Sargon I
Ishtar	Sumer/Sumerians
Hammurabi, Code of	tel
Jericho	Transjordan
Jordan River	ziggurat

Recommended Reading

Dalley, Stephanie. *Myths from Mesopotamia: Creation, the Flood, Gilgamesh, and Others.* New York: Oxford UP, 1989. Careful translations of influential texts from Sumer, Assyria, and Babylon.

Matthews, Victor H., and Benjamin, Don C. *Old Testament Parallels: Laws and Stories from the Ancient Near East,* 3rd ed., New York: Panlist Press, 2007. Shows Egyptian and Mesopotamian sources or correspondences for individual books of the Bible.

Parker, Simon B. "The Ancient Near Eastern Literary Background of the Old Testament." In *The New Interpreter's Bible,* Vol. 1, pp. 228–243. Nashville, TN: Abingdon Press, 1994. A reliable and readable overview.

Pritchard, James B., ed. *Ancient Near Eastern Texts Relating to the Old Testament,* 3rd ed. Princeton, NJ: Princeton UP, 1969. Translations of relevant Egyptian, Babylonian, Canaanite, and other ancient literatures—the standard work.

Roberts, J. J. M. "Assyria and Babylonia." In K. D. Sakenfeld, ed., *The New Interpreter's Dictionary of the Bible,* Vol. 1, pp. 311–336. Nashville, TN: Abingdon Press, 2006. An informative survey of the chief Mesopotamian empires that dominated Israel.

Walton John H. *Ancient Near Eastern Thought and the Old Testament: Introducing the Conceptual World of the Hebrew Bible.* Grand Rapids, MI: Baker Academic, 2006. Places biblical writings in the context of their cultural environment.

PART TWO

The Hebrew Bible/ Old Testament

CHAPTER 4
The Five Books of Torah (Divine Instruction) 53

CHAPTER 5
In the Beginning 67

CHAPTER 6
Freedom and Responsibility 77

CHAPTER 7
Law, Holiness, and Rebellion 88

CHAPTER 8
A New Vision of Moses' Teaching 94

CHAPTER 9
The Story of Ancient Israel 101

CHAPTER 10
Faith and War 106

CHAPTER 11
Yahweh's Warriors 114

CHAPTER 12
The Rise of David and the Birth of a Kingdom 121

CHAPTER 13
From the Glory of Solomon to the Exile in Babylon 129

CHAPTER 14
Israel's Prophets 144

CHAPTER 15
Prophets to the Northern Kingdom 153

CHAPTER 16
Prophets of the Assyrian Threat 158

CHAPTER 17
Prophets of the Babylonian Crisis 168

CHAPTER 18
Prophets in Exile 176

CHAPTER 19
After the Exile—Israel's Last Prophets 184

CHAPTER 20
The Writings 192

CHAPTER 21
The Postexilic Readjustment 196

CHAPTER 22
Worshiping at the Second Temple 201

CHAPTER 23
Israel's Wisdom Writers 208

CHAPTER 24
Festival Scrolls 224

CHAPTER 25
Reinterpreting Israel's History 233

CHAPTER 26
Keeping God's Law in a Hostile World 238

CHAPTER 27
The Second Canon 249

CHAPTER 4

The Five Books of Torah (Divine Instruction)
Themes and Theories

Key Topics/Themes Presenting human history as a progressive revelation of the divine will, the Torah emphasizes both the promises of future benefits that Yahweh makes to Israel's ancestors—Abraham, Isaac, and Jacob—and the covenant obligations laid on their descendants—the Israelites—to worship Yahweh exclusively and to obey all his laws. Containing a diverse mixture of narrative, genealogy, poetry, law, folklore, and legend, the Tanakh's first five books are at least partly unified by an emphasis on Yahweh's covenant relationship with his people and on an accompanying theme of promises that are only partly fulfilled.

Although Jewish and Christian tradition ascribe all five books to Moses, almost all contemporary scholars agree that they are not the work of a single author, such as Moses, but the product of a long and complex process of oral transmission, multiple authorship, and extensive editing and revision over many different periods of Israel's history. A long-dominant theory of composition—known as the documentary hypothesis—asserts that the five books (Pentateuch) contain four main literary sources produced during four different historical eras. According to this theory, the four sources—J, E, D, and P—were eventually combined by redactors (editors) working after the Babylonian exile. Recent challenges to the documentary hypothesis abound, but scholars still identify distinct strands woven together in the Pentateuch, particularly J (the Yahwist), P (the priestly writer[s]), and D (the Deuteronomist).

 ## An Overview of the Torah

The first division of the three-part Hebrew Bible, the five books of Torah—called the **Pentateuch** (meaning "five scrolls")—opens with accounts of God's creating the world (Gen. 1–11) but quickly shifts emphasis to focus on the creation of Israel. Beginning with the call of Abraham in Genesis 12, the Torah narrates the story of Israel's origins and its transformation from a band of slaves into a "holy nation" dedicated to Yahweh's service. Virtually all events in Israel's story, including its escape from Egyptian bondage and miraculous deliverance at a chaotic sea, are merely prelude to the grand culmination—Yahweh's appearance at Mount Sinai/ Horeb. For observant Jews, the heart and soul of Torah (divine instruction) lie in the laws, statutes, ordinances, rituals, and precepts that Yahweh transmits through

Moses to the Israelites, prescribing a way of life that qualitatively distinguishes them from all other people. Most of the second half of Exodus, all of Leviticus, and the first part of Numbers (the second, third, and fourth Torah books) are devoted to enumerating Yahweh's specific instructions at Sinai. Prescribing a generally different program of legislation, Deuteronomy (the fifth book) is set "on the plains of Moab," where the Israelites are gathered to enter Canaan from the east and where this "Second Law" takes the form of Moses' three final speeches to his people.

Near the end of Deuteronomy, Yahweh asks Israel to choose between faithfulness to him, which will bring abundant life and prosperity to the nation, and the worship of other gods, which will bring not only suffering and death but also national destruction (Deut. 27–30). Israel's response to Yahweh's challenge determines its subsequent history, particularly its ultimate defeat and exile. Deuteronomy thus sets the tone and establishes the standards of covenant loyalty that the narrative books that follow it present. The books of Joshua through 2 Kings illustrate the disastrous consequences of Israel's covenant breaking and, from the viewpoint of their author/editors, explain the justice of Yahweh's allowing Babylon to conquer his people, burn the Jerusalem Temple where he had placed his "name," and bring a permanent end to the royal dynasty of David (587 BCE).

Scholars recognize that behind the written Torah lie countless generations of oral tradition during which stories of Yahweh's saving acts were passed on only by word of mouth. Moses' final speech appeals to the peoples' collective memory:

> Remember the days of old,
> consider the years long past,
> ask your father and he will inform you,
> your elders and they will tell you.

(Deut. 32:7)

Although scholars do not agree on when Israel's tales of "years long past" were finally preserved in writing, many of these ancient oral traditions were eventually incorporated into the Torah (see below).

Major Themes of the Pentateuch

Although they worked with diverse materials dating from different periods in Israel's history, the Pentateuch's final editors carefully arranged their various sources, both oral and written, to highlight the historical development of Yahweh's unique partnership with Israel. Two themes in particular help to unify the Pentateuch's rich collection of ancestral stories, genealogy, law, and poetry: (1) Yahweh's promises to Abraham, Isaac, and Jacob, and (2) Yahweh's ongoing relationship with their descendants, the Israelites. The divine promises—grouped together in Genesis 12–50—and Yahweh's binding demands upon his people—specified in the Torah's extensive legal requirements—shape not only the Pentateuch's general structure but also the historical narratives that follow (Joshua through 2 Kings; see Chapters 10–13). Encompassing both the divine promise of blessing and the fearful threat of future loss, the Torah books prepare readers for the account of Israel's bittersweet historical experience to come.

By emphasizing Israel's repeated violations of its covenant obligations, such as the rebellious worship of a

FIGURE 4.1 This ancient Mesopotamian relief shows a storm god standing on a bull pedestal, as well as a depiction of the sacred tree. Symbols of male strength and virility, figures of bulls were commonly used in art to symbolize a divine being, who was imagined as invisibly present, standing on the bull's back. Whereas Mosaic Law prohibited making images of Yahweh (Exod. 20:1–4), some Israelite leaders used bull statues or "golden calves" to represent Israel's God (1 Kings 12; cf. Exod. 32).

golden calf (Exod. 32), the Torah narrative underscores Israel's repeated disloyalties, insults to Yahweh that will eventually cause him to abandon them to their enemies (see Figure 4.1). Viewing their nation's past from the perspective of the Babylonian exile, Torah editors also envision a restoration of the divine–human relationship expressed in a return to the land promised to Abraham (Deut. 30). In predicting Israel's future restoration, God makes his most astonishing promise: He will give the Israelites the ability to trust and worship him alone, effecting an inner change that empowers the people to love him with all their "hearts . . . and souls" (Deut. 30:4–6).

Divine Promises

Before examining the complex nature of Yahweh's bond to Israel, we will survey six aspects of the vows that Yahweh makes to Israel's ancestors. Although the partial fulfillment of these vows serves to tie together the ancestral stories of Genesis with some of the later Torah narratives, as well as the historical books that follow, it is important to remember that not all versions of the divine promises contain all six of the provisions. Because different sources now embedded in the Torah had their individual tradition of the divine oaths, no two of them are precisely alike. (For a more complete discussion of Torah themes, see the work by David Clines in "Recommended Reading.")

A Son and Descendants The promise of a son occurs only in Genesis 18, where Yahweh appears to Abraham to predict Isaac's birth. However, it is usually linked with the more general promise of Abraham's descendants, who are to be as innumerable as the "stars of heaven" or the "sands of the sea." Abraham will become the father of a "multitude of nations"—including Israel through Isaac, and, according to another tradition, the Arab peoples through Ishmael—as well as a line of kings, the royal dynasty that David founds many centuries later. In Genesis, which is deeply concerned with issues of fertility and reproduction, the divine guarantee of progeny is countered by repeated threats to its fulfillment. Not only are Sarah, Abraham's wife, and Rachel, Jacob's favorite wife, unable to bear children for most of their lives, but in three separate incidents, foreign rulers unwittingly threaten the promised succession by taking the ancestors' wives into their harems. In addition, Yahweh himself seems to counteract the promise of a son by demanding that Abraham sacrifice the boy Isaac.

Divine Presence Yahweh's pledge to be an invisible companion to his favored covenant bearers figures most prominently in the Jacob story, in which God states that he will accompany Jacob on his many journeys (Gen. 26:3, 24; 28:15; 31:3). The theme of divine presence reappears as a major feature of Yahweh's intimate relationship with Moses (Exod. 3–4) and is also the force that guides and protects Israel on its perilous trek through the Sinai wilderness. Demonstrating the crucial importance of housing the divine presence in Israel's midst, detailed instructions for constructing the Tabernacle (the portable tent in which the implements of Yahweh's worship were carried) and Ark of the Covenant (the wooden chest containing the Ten Commandments) take up almost eleven chapters in Exodus (Exod. 25–31; 35–40). Interestingly, it is David with whom the divine presence is said to figure most prominently (2 Sam. 5:1–10) and who eventually takes charge of the Ark. David's heir, Solomon, later builds the Temple in Jerusalem, a sanctuary in which the Ark, signifying the divine presence, is later placed (1 Kings 8).

Land The theme of descendants and nationhood is closely linked to the promise of land, the territory of Canaan that Yahweh swears to give Abraham and his offspring (Gen. 12:1–8; 13:14–17; 15:7–21). Yahweh repeats this pledge to Jacob and his sons (Gen. 26:3–4; 28:4; 35:12; 50:24), but it is fulfilled only in the United Kingdom of David and Solomon (1 Kings 4:21). The entire narrative sequence of Genesis through 2 Kings, in fact, is largely a theological claim for Israel's divinely

granted right to wrest the land from its native inhabitants, the Canaanites, balanced by a theological argument explaining why Israel ultimately lost its possession of the land (Deut. 28–30; Lev. 26).

Universal Blessing Whereas the promise of land relates specifically to Israel's identity as a national state, Yahweh's assurance of blessing to Abraham and his descendants sounds a more universal theme. At the outset of his personal relationship with Abraham, Yahweh state that not only Abraham's heirs but "all the tribes [families] of the earth will bless themselves by you" (Gen. 12:3). The promise of a divine blessing that will ultimately include all peoples emphasizes the importance of Israel's mission as conveyer of God's favor to humankind (Gen. 18:18; 22:18, etc.).

Covenant As noted in Chapter 1, God's preferred means of defining his special relationship with Israel is through a series of covenants contracting him to remain Israel's patron God forever. Whereas God's pledge to Noah (Gen. 9) is made with all humanity, the various covenants with Abraham (Gen. 12; 15; 17; 22) relate exclusively to the chosen people. In Genesis 17, a passage that brings together almost all elements of the divine promises, God links the assurance of countless descendants, divine presence, land, kingship, and blessing, combining all these elements in a "Covenant in perpetuity, to be your God and the God of your descendants after you" (17:4–10). In making this covenant (*berit*), a term repeated thirteen times in twenty-two verses, God emphasizes that he solemnly binds himself to Abraham's progeny not only in the present but also in the future, perpetuating the God–Israel association for all time to come (see Chapter 5).

The Complex Nature of Yahweh's Bond to Israel

At the close of Deuteronomy, Moses is said to have composed a song that includes a tradition about how Yahweh came to be Israel's God. Evoking images of the heavenly council at which all the divine beings assemble to administer earthly affairs (see Box 3.2), Moses states that when the "Most High [Elyon]," head of the divine pantheon, assigned the various nations their patron deities—"according to the number of the gods"—Yahweh's "portion" and "allotted share" was Israel (Deut. 32:8–9; see Figure 4.2). Israel's assignment to Yahweh proves a difficult match for both parties, partly because

FIGURE 4.2   This statuette of bronze covered with gold depicts El, who was regarded as an embodiment of divine wisdom and compassion, qualities also ascribed to Yahweh.

Yahweh's ethical character differs so radically from that of the other gods.

Besides his sense of justice and compassion, Yahweh has other character traits that set him apart from the gods of Egypt, Canaan, and Mesopotamia. After guiding Israel to Sinai/Horeb and binding the people to him in a covenant of mutual loyalty, he reveals an attitude toward human worship that differs sharply from that of other divinities. The need for absolute commitment to him alone is an intrinsic component of the divine personality, "because the LORD [Yahweh], whose name is Jealous, is a jealous God" (Exod. 34:14). In the symbolic marriage between Yahweh and Israel, absolute faithfulness is essential; serving "gods whom he had not allotted to them," honoring other members of the divine council, will destroy the partnership (Deut. 29:26; cf. Hos. 1–3).

Yahweh's graciousness in liberating the Israelites from slavery and nurturing them as they journey through the wilderness contrasts painfully with his impatience and anger when the people repeatedly fail to show gratitude for his generosity. At the very moment when Yahweh is conveying his commandments to Moses atop Mount Sinai/Horeb, the people below hold a riotous celebration worshiping the notorious "golden calf," a flagrant breach of loyalty that brings Yahweh close to severing the covenant relationship altogether (Exod. 32).

Following their infidelity at Sinai, the Israelites consistently show a puzzling inability to worship Yahweh with the single-mindedness he requires. Although Yahweh leads them to oases of fresh water, feeds them with **manna** (a grainlike substance described as falling daily from heaven), sends flocks of birds to supply them with meat, and keeps their clothes from wearing out, the people respond only with "murmuring" and rebellion against Moses. When they reach the borders of the Promised Land and dispatch spies to investigate its inhabitants' potential resistance to their invasion, they listen only to the negative reports, demonstrating a total lack of faith in Yahweh's power to grant them military victory. In Numbers, their defeatist attitude contrasts markedly with Moses' praise of Yahweh as an invincible "warrior" after his triumph over the Egyptian army (Num. 14; cf. Exod. 15). Instead of increasing their devotion, the Israelites' forty years of companionship with Yahweh has a paradoxical result: The closeness and accessibility of God seems to diminish the people's capacity to revere and obey him.

Despite Yahweh's daily presence, manifest in formations of cloud and fire, the partnership between God and the people repeatedly threatens to unravel. Whereas Yahweh alternates between tender concern and destructive anger, the people's response fluctuates between fear of the divine presence and an odd collective amnesia that seems to keep them from remembering Yahweh's saving deeds in Egypt and at the miraculous sea crossing. Near the end of Deuteronomy, as the people make their final approach to Canaan's frontier, Moses concisely summarizes the Torah's portrait of the divine–human relationship. In this estimate, Yahweh the "Rock" is without fault whereas the human partner is deeply flawed:

> The Rock, his work is perfect, and all his ways are just.
> A faithful God, without deceit, just and upright is he;
> yet his degenerate children have dealt falsely with him,
> a perverse and crooked generation.
> Do you thus repay the LORD, O foolish and senseless
>   people?

(Deut. 32:4–6)

In thus describing the unequal union between the perfect Yahweh and a morally defective Israel, the Torah unequivocally pins the responsibility for the quality of Israel's future—prosperity or adversity—on the people themselves. In the account of Israel's historical experience in Canaan that ensues, the nation's sufferings derive not from Yahweh's unwillingness or inability to protect his people, but from his righteous anger at their faithlessness.

Some Literary Forms in the Pentateuch

Although the Torah is primarily regarded as sacred teaching, an account of Yahweh's unique relationship with Israel over space and time, it is also a composite document blending together several distinct categories of literature. Among the literary forms it contains are narrative, genealogy, etiology (a subgenre of narrative), itinerary, and detailed legal codes.

Narratives

Much of the Torah is devoted to Yahweh's laws and ordinances, but stories are an equally important part of God's teaching to Israel. Genesis, most of Exodus, and much of Numbers consist of **narrative**—an account of characters and events arranged in sequential order to illustrate a major theme or concept. Following a generally chronological development—from the creation of the world to the creation of Israel—the Torah contains all the elements typical of a story. These include setting (from Mesopotamia, to Canaan, to Egypt), characters (from Adam and Eve, to Abraham and Sarah, to Moses, Aaron, and their sister, the prophet Miriam), conflict (from the sibling rivalry of Cain and Abel to Yahweh's battle with Egypt's Pharaoh and his sometimes antagonistic relationship with his human partner, Israel), and plot (various promises to Abraham advancing through a series of loosely connected incidents until their partial culmination in the formation of Israel, a step-by-step unfolding of God's long-range historical plan).

Overlap Among Narratives Although editors divided the Torah into five individual books, each occupying a separate scroll, there is considerable overlap among them, with narratives and legal material carrying over from one volume to the next. The first continuous narrative, from Genesis 1:1 through Exodus 19:3, moves from God's creation of the universe to his assembling of the Israelites at the foot of Mount Sinai/Horeb. This narrative sequence includes a large chronological gap between the descent of Jacob's twelve sons into Egypt, which concludes Genesis, and the description of their descendants' Egyptian enslavement, which opens Exodus. Nevertheless, the entire Genesis–Exodus account functions as a coherent literary whole.

The second major section of the Pentateuch, Exodus 19:4 through all of Leviticus to Numbers 10:10, subordinates narrative to large blocks of ethical, ritual,

and legal material defining the terms of Yahweh's contract with Israel. With Exodus 19, narrative movement comes to an almost complete halt as Yahweh issues orders to prepare the people ritually for his appearance among them. In Exodus 20, Yahweh personally delivers the Ten Commandments (also known as the Decalogue, or "Ten Words") to a terrified audience. In the flow of hundreds of statutes and ordinances that follow the Decalogue, the law-giving is interrupted only occasionally by fragments of narrative, such as Exodus 24, which describes the formal ratification of the Mosaic Covenant, and Exodus 32–34, which relates the golden calf incident, Moses' furious smashing of the two tablets on which the Decalogue is inscribed, and Yahweh's graciousness in providing their replacement. Anchored at a single location—Sinai/Horeb—from Exodus 19 through Numbers 10, the law-giving takes up an entire year. It begins with the ritually purified Israelites vowing to obey Yahweh's laws—most of which they have not yet heard—and ends with their leaving the "mountain of God" to head toward Canaan.

The third part of the Torah, also a mixture of narrative and legal instruction (Num. 10:10–Deut. 34:12), covers Israel's forty-year journey through the desert, where Yahweh continues to deliver still more laws at the Tabernacle, the portable tent at which his "glory" is invisibly enshrined. It closes at the border between Moab and Canaan, where Moses gives three farewell speeches—which comprise the fifth Torah volume, Deuteronomy—in which he reviews Israel's experience with Yahweh up to that moment. Deuteronomy, which seems to embody a law code differing in many respects from those contained in Exodus–Leviticus–Numbers—closes with an account of Moses' death, the last event recorded in the Torah (Deut. 34).

The Narrative Voices As in other surviving ancient Near Eastern literature, such as the *Epic of Gilgamesh* and the *Enuma Elish*, the Torah has a narrator, the unidentified person who tells the story. In fact, as a result of the multiple traditions that have been woven into the Pentateuch, it has multiple narrative voices, each of which assumes absolute knowledge of the subject related. Speaking in the third person, the narrators presume to report the precise events of creation, a global flood, the origins of different national and ethnic groups, and other events of the remote past. Like the different poets who contributed to the composite *Epic of Gilgamesh*, the Torah authors commonly advance the narrative through dialogue, recounting long conversations between two characters even when no third party was present to witness the exchange. Examples include the debates between Yahweh and Abraham over the ethical issue of Yahweh's destroying Sodom (Gen. 18) and between Moses and Yahweh over the Deity's proposal to exterminate Israel (Exod. 32; Num. 14).

As many Near Eastern texts demonstrate, it was common literary practice for ancient writers to create speeches for both long-dead heroes and their gods, such as Gilgamesh's dialogue with his divine patron Shamash in the bejeweled "garden of the gods." Torah writers thus present much of Yahweh's self-revelation on Sinai/Horeb through private conversations with Moses (Exod. 3–4; 24; 32–34). Other Tanakh writers compose scenes set entirely in heaven, at which divine beings speak among themselves, such as the portrayal of Yahweh's celestial court in Job (Job 1–2; cf. 1 Kings 22:18–28 and Zech 3). The custom of fashioning dialogue for gods, prevalent in Mesopotamian and Egyptian literature, is also well illustrated in Homer's *Iliad* and *Odyssey,* epic poems perhaps contemporaneous with some parts of the Torah, in which Zeus and his fellow Olympians meet in council to discuss their plans for humankind.

Genealogies

The use of **genealogies,** a literary genre, to bind together individual narrative units and provide continuity seems to have been a common practice of Israel's priests. Because membership in Israel's priesthood was hereditary, passed from father to son, priests kept careful records of lines of descent that would validate a person's claim to priestly rank. Priestly writers seem to have been responsible for most of the Torah's genealogies. In Genesis, they used a rigid formula that lists a male figure's age at the time he fathered his first son, the number of years he lived after his firstborn, his age at the time of his death, and the fact that "he died" (see Gen. 5). Emphasizing the importance of male offspring, the priestly genealogists trace an unbroken line of descent from Adam to Abraham (Gen. 10–11). A variation of the genealogical lists occurs in Genesis 49, where Jacob, in the form of prophecy, pronounces moral judgments on his twelve sons. Another extensive genealogy occupies the opening chapters of Numbers, along with lists of priestly functions.

Etiologies

Some Torah passages take the form of **etiologies**—a particular kind of narrative that explains the cause or origin of some natural phenomenon, social custom, or religious ritual. Genesis features several etiological anecdotes, such as the folktale in which Lot's wife is changed into a pillar of salt, presumably to account for the unusual salt formations bordering the Dead Sea. The story of Jacob's wrestling all night with a mysterious visitor is also given an etiological emphasis, according to which the Israelites do not eat part of an animal's hip "because [the wrestler] had struck Jacob in the socket of the hip on the sciatic nerve" (Gen. 32:22–32). Genesis also includes two different etiological accounts explaining how Jacob's name was changed to "Israel" (32:26–30; 35:9–15) as well as two accounts of how Bethel (meaning "House of God") received its name (28:10–19; 35:6–7, 14–15).

Itineraries

A literary category that characterizes nomadic societies, the **itinerary**—accounts of a people's movements from one geographical area to another—may represent one of the Torah's oldest traditions. The Genesis account of Abraham's migration from Mesopotamia to Canaan traces a route marked by conventions of the genre, noting the place of departure, the destination, and specific place names, such as oases or campsites, along the way, as well as other distinctive geographical features. Related to the itinerary genre, the journey motif dominates much of the Torah's narrative action. Abraham, Jacob, Joseph, Moses, and the people of Israel are almost constantly on the move, traveling to or from the Promised Land. While Exodus recounts the Israelites' journey from Egypt to meet Yahweh at Sinai/Horeb, Numbers underscores their subsequent forty-year trek through an arid wilderness. The metaphor of homeless wanderers ever seeking a permanent resting place characterizes the Torah story of Israel's early life.

Who Wrote the "Books of Moses"?

Traditional View of Authorship

The ancient tradition that Moses composed the Pentateuch is based partly on a few scattered passages in which Yahweh orders Moses to write down some of God's specific instructions. According to Exodus 17:14, Yahweh tells Moses to "write [about the defeat of Amalek, a local king] as a reminder in a book." After receiving from Yahweh a list of legal ordinances, known as the **Book of the Covenant** (Exod. 21–23), Moses "wrote down all the words of the LORD" (Exod. 24:4). He also commits to writing the ritual laws revealed in Exodus (34:27–28) and Israel's travel itinerary during its journey from Egypt through the Sinai wilderness (Num. 33:2). In all of these texts, Moses is shown as recording specific events and individual legal codes, not the whole Pentateuch.

In Deuteronomy, however, Moses is pictured as compiling the entire law code contained in that book (Deut. 31:9), as well as lyrics to a "song" he taught Israel (Deut. 31:19, 22). In fact, Deuteronomy claims that Moses was responsible for the "words of the law [*torah*] to the very end (31:24), composing "this book of the law [Deuteronomy]," which he then entrusts to Israel's priests for safekeeping (31:9, 24–26). Most scholars believe that this legal work is the same "book of the law [*torah*]" found during repairs on the Jerusalem Temple during the late seventh century BCE, more than 600 years after the period when Moses supposedly lived (2 Kings 22:8–23:3). A validation of the sweeping religious reforms by King Josiah (ruled 640–609 BCE), this early edition of Deuteronomy (perhaps consisting of Chs. 12–26) probably stood alone, at the head of an early version of the historical books that follow it and that were influenced by its distinctive theology. In time, it was expanded and subsequently added to the scrolls of Genesis through Numbers, becoming the fifth book of Torah.

Problems with Mosaic Authorship

In contrast to traditional views, most contemporary scholars are convinced that, in its present form, the Pentateuch could not have derived from Moses. Even casual readers commonly notice numerous repetitions, contradictions, and discrepancies that point to the composite nature of the Pentateuch. If Moses is the presumed author, why is he always referred to in the *third person,* as an author writing *about* him would do? If Moses is truly "very humble, more so than anyone else on the face of the earth," as Numbers 12:3 describes him, would he plausibly make such an immodest evaluation of personal humility? Readers also note Deuteronomy's many repetitions of the phrase "until this day," a clear indication that the writer was looking back from his time to that of a distant past (Deut. 3:14; 34:6, etc.).

Deuteronomy's account of Moses' death might be seen as a postscript by a later hand, were it not written in exactly the same style as other parts of the book—and in language virtually identical to that in the historical books (Joshua through 2 Kings) that follow (see Chapters 10–13). Frequent anachronisms—the placing of persons or events out of their proper chronological order—also indicate post-Mosaic authorship. Many statements in Genesis, such as "At that time Canaanites were in the land" (Gen. 12:6; 13:7), refer to a period long after Moses' time, when the Israelites had finally expelled or assimilated Canaan's original inhabitants. References to territories east of the Jordan River as lying "beyond the Jordan" presuppose a vantage point on the west (Israelite) side of the river, but Israel's tribes did not occupy this western territory until much later (Gen. 50:10; cf. Num. 21:1). Other anachronisms, such as the Genesis list of Edom's kings who ruled "before any king reigned over the Israelites" (36:31), demonstrate that the author lived after Israel's monarchy had been established, centuries after Moses' day.

Even when studying the Pentateuch for the first time, readers are commonly struck by the great number of duplications—passages in which the same story, or a close variant, is told a second time. The phenomenon of duplication, present throughout both narrative and legal sections of the Pentateuch, begins with two different versions of creation. In Genesis 1, which has a lofty, majestic style, Elohim (God) creates all life forms, beginning with plants and animals and culminating with human beings, male and female, made simultaneously in his own image. Beginning in Genesis 2:4b, which has a more vivid, earthly style, it is "Yahweh Elohim" (Yahweh God) who fashions the first man and, only after creating a series of animals—none of which proves a suitable mate for *adam* (humankind)—models the first woman from *adam*'s rib. Whereas biblical editors sometimes placed two different accounts of the same event side by side, as they did with Genesis's two creation stories, other times they interwove two originally separate narratives. In Genesis 6–8, editors combined two narratives of a global deluge—Noah's Flood—that can easily be disentangled to produce two parallel flood stories that are fully complete in themselves. (In Box 4.1, the priestly version—in which the Flood lasts more than a year—appears in **boldface** while the older, Yahwist version—in which the deluge takes place in only forty days—is set in roman type. When the two accounts are read separately, virtually all the contradictions of the composite version disappear.)

Besides incorporating two different versions of Jacob's name-change to Israel (Gen. 32:22–32 and 35:9–15), Genesis includes not two but three different accounts in which the beauty of Israelite women attracts foreign rulers who take them from their husbands, only to have Yahweh inflict punishment on the offender. First, an unidentified Egyptian pharaoh takes Sarah from Abraham, who had represented his wife as merely his sister (Gen. 12:10–20); then, when Abraham again says that Sarah is only a sister, a Canaanite king, Abimelech, claims her (Gen. 20:1–18). In a third variation on this theme, it is Isaac, son of Abraham, who deceives Abimelech—now called a "Philistine" ruler—by misrepresenting his wife, Rebekah, as his sister (Gen. 26:1–14). In each incident,

BOX 4.1 **Two Versions of the Flood Story**

The present text of Genesis relating the story of a universal deluge combines two Flood accounts, attributed, respectively, to the Yahwist writer (J) and the priestly writer (P). Each of the two accounts stands alone as a complete and independent narrative in this translation from the Jerusalem Bible. (In this version, the translator uses the divine name Yahweh.)

The Flood—Genesis 6:5–8:22

(Priestly text in **boldface** capitals and small caps, J text in regular type)

GENESIS 6

5 And Yahweh saw that the evil of humans was great in the earth, and all the inclination of the thoughts of their heart was only evil all the day.

6 And Yahweh regretted that he had made humans in the earth, and he was grieved to his heart.

7 And Yahweh said, "I shall wipe out the humans which I have created from the face of the earth, from human to beast to creeping thing to bird of the heavens, for I regret that I have made them."

8 But Noah found favor in Yahweh's eyes.

9 **THESE ARE THE GENERATIONS OF NOAH: NOAH WAS A RIGHTEOUS MAN, PERFECT IN HIS GENERATIONS. NOAH WALKED WITH GOD.**

10 **AND NOAH SIRED THREE SONS: SHEM, HAM, AND JAPHETH.**

11 **AND THE EARTH WAS CORRUPTED BEFORE GOD, AND THE EARTH WAS FILLED WITH VIOLENCE.**

12 **AND GOD SAW THE EARTH, AND HERE IT WAS CORRUPTED, FOR ALL FLESH HAD CORRUPTED ITS WAY ON THE EARTH.**

13 **AND GOD SAID TO NOAH, "THE END OF ALL FLESH HAS COME BEFORE ME, FOR THE EARTH IS FILLED WITH VIOLENCE BECAUSE OF THEM, AND HERE I AM GOING TO DESTROY THEM WITH THE EARTH.**

14 **MAKE YOURSELF AN ARK OF GOPHER WOOD, MAKE ROOMS WITH THE ARK, AND PITCH IT OUTSIDE AND INSIDE WITH PITCH.**

15 **AND THIS IS HOW YOU SHALL MAKE IT: THREE HUNDRED CUBITS THE LENGTH OF THE ARK, FIFTY CUBITS ITS WIDTH, AND THIRTY CUBITS ITS HEIGHT.**

16 **YOU SHALL MAKE A WINDOW FOR THE ARK, AND YOU SHALL FINISH IT TO A CUBIT FROM THE TOP, AND YOU SHALL MAKE AN ENTRANCE TO THE ARK IN ITS SIDE. YOU SHALL MAKE LOWER, SECOND, AND THIRD STORIES FOR IT.**

17 **AND HERE I AM BRINGING THE FLOOD, WATER OVER THE EARTH, TO DESTROY ALL FLESH IN WHICH IS THE BREATH OF LIFE FROM UNDER THE HEAVENS. EVERYTHING WHICH IS ON THE LAND WILL DIE.**

18 **AND I SHALL ESTABLISH MY COVENANT WITH YOU. AND YOU SHALL COME TO THE ARK, YOU AND YOUR SONS AND YOUR WIFE AND YOUR SONS' WIVES WITH YOU.**

19 **AND OF ALL THE LIVING, OF ALL FLESH, YOU SHALL BRING TWO TO THE ARK TO KEEP ALIVE WITH YOU, THEY SHALL BE MALE AND FEMALE.**

20 **OF THE BIRDS ACCORDING TO THEIR KIND, AND OF THE BEASTS ACCORDING TO THEIR KIND, AND OF ALL THE CREEPING THINGS OF THE EARTH ACCORDING TO THEIR KIND, TWO OF EACH WILL COME TO YOU TO KEEP ALIVE.**

21 **AND YOU, TAKE FOR YOURSELF OF ALL FOOD WHICH WILL BE EATEN AND GATHER IT TO YOU, AND IT WILL BE FOR YOU AND FOR THEM FOR FOOD."**

22 **AND NOAH DID ACCORDING TO ALL THAT GOD COMMANDED HIM—SO HE DID.**

GENESIS 7

1 And Yahweh said to Noah, "Come, you and all your household, to the ark, for I have seen you as righteous before me in this generation.

2 Of all the clean beasts, take yourself seven pairs, man and his woman; and of the beasts which are not clean, two, man and his woman.

3 Also of the birds of the heavens seven pairs, male and female, to keep alive seed on the face of the earth.

4 For in seven more days I shall rain on the earth forty days and forty nights, and I shall wipe out all the substance that I have made from upon the face of the earth."

5 And Noah did according to all that Yahweh had commanded him.

6 **AND NOAH WAS SIX HUNDRED YEARS OLD, AND THE FLOOD WAS ON THE EARTH.**

7 And Noah and his sons and his wife and his sons' wives with him came to the ark from before the waters of the flood.

8 **OF THE CLEAN BEASTS AND OF THE BEASTS WHICH WERE NOT CLEAN, AND OF THE BIRDS AND OF ALL THOSE WHICH CREEP UPON THE EARTH,**

9 **TWO OF EACH CAME TO NOAH TO THE ARK, MALE AND FEMALE, AS GOD HAD COMMANDED NOAH.**

10 And seven days later the waters of the flood were on the earth.

11 **IN THE SIX HUNDREDTH YEAR OF NOAH'S LIFE, IN THE SECOND MONTH, IN THE SEVENTEENTH DAY OF THE MONTH, ON THIS DAY ALL THE FOUNTAINS OF THE GREAT DEEP WERE BROKEN UP, AND THE WINDOWS OF THE HEAVENS WERE OPENED.**

12 And there was rain on the earth, forty days and forty nights.

13 **IN THIS VERY DAY, NOAH AND SHEM, HAM, AND JAPHETH, THE SONS OF NOAH, AND NOAH'S WIFE AND HIS SONS' THREE WIVES WITH THEM CAME TO THE ARK.**

14 THEY AND ALL THE LIVING THINGS ACCORDING TO THEIR KIND, AND ALL THE BEASTS ACCORDING TO THEIR KIND, AND ALL THE CREEPING THINGS THAT CREEP ON THE EARTH ACCORDING TO THEIR KIND, AND ALL THE BIRDS ACCORDING TO THEIR KIND, AND EVERY WINGED BIRD.

15 AND THEY CAME TO NOAH TO THE ARK, TWO OF EACH, OF ALL FLESH IN WHICH IS THE BREATH OF LIFE.

16 AND THOSE WHICH CAME WERE MALE AND FEMALE SOME OF ALL FLESH CAME, AS GOD HAD COMMANDED HIM. And Yahweh closed it for him.

17 And the flood was on the earth for forty days and forty nights, and the waters multiplied and raised the ark, and it was lifted from the earth.

18 And the waters grew strong and multiplied greatly on the earth, and the ark went on the surface of waters.

19 And the waters grew very very strong on the earth, and they covered all the high mountains that are under all the heavens.

20 Fifteen cubits above, the waters grew stronger, and they covered the mountains.

21 AND ALL FLESH, THOSE THAT CREEP ON THE EARTH, THE BIRDS, THE BEASTS, AND THE WILD ANIMALS, AND ALL THE SWARMING THINGS THAT SWARM ON THE EARTH, AND ALL THE HUMANS EXPIRED.

22 Everything that had the breathing spirit of life in its nostrils, everything that was on the dry ground, died.

23 And he wiped out all the substance that was on the face of the earth, from the human to beast, to creeping thing, and to bird of the heavens, and they were wiped out from the earth, and only Noah and those who were with him in the ark were left.

24 AND THE WATERS GREW STRONG ON THE EARTH A HUNDRED FIFTY DAYS.

GENESIS 8

1 AND GOD REMEMBERED NOAH AND ALL THE LIVING, AND THE BEASTS THAT WERE WITH HIM IN THE ARK, AND GOD PASSED A WIND OVER THE EARTH, AND THE WATERS WERE DECREASED.

2 AND THE FOUNTAINS OF THE DEEP AND THE WINDOWS OF THE HEAVENS WERE SHUT, and the rain was restrained from the heavens.

3 And the waters receded from the earth continually, AND THE WATERS WERE ABATED AT THE END OF A HUNDRED FIFTY DAYS.

4 AND THE ARK RESTED, IN THE SEVENTH MONTH, IN THE SEVENTEENTH DAY OF THE MONTH, ON THE MOUNTAINS OF ARARAT.

5 AND THE WATERS CONTINUED RECEDING UNTIL THE TENTH MONTH; IN THE TENTH MONTH, ON THE FIRST OF THE MONTH, THE TOPS OF THE MOUNTAINS APPEARED.

6 And it was at the end of forty days, and Noah opened the window of the ark which he had made.

7 AND HE SENT OUT A RAVEN, AND IT WENT BACK AND FORTH UNTIL THE WATERS DRIED UP FROM THE EARTH.

8 And he sent out a dove from him to see whether the waters had eased from the face of the earth.

9 And the dove did not find a resting place for its foot, and it returned to him to the ark, for waters were on the face of the earth, and he put out his hand and took it and brought it to him to the ark.

10 And he waited seven more days, and he again sent out a dove from the ark.

11 And the dove came to him at evening time, and here was an olive leaf torn off in its mouth, and Noah knew that the waters had eased from the earth.

12 And he waited seven more days, and he sent out a dove, and it did not return to him ever again.

13 AND IT WAS IN THE SIX HUNDRED AND FIRST YEAR, IN THE FIRST MONTH, ON THE FIRST OF THE MONTH, THE WATERS DRIED FROM THE EARTH. And Noah turned back the covering of the ark and looked, and here the face of the earth had dried.

14 AND IN THE SECOND MONTH, ON THE TWENTY SEVENTH DAY OF THE MONTH, THE EARTH DRIED UP.

15 AND GOD SPOKE TO NOAH, SAYING,

16 "GO OUT FROM THE ARK, YOU AND YOUR WIFE AND YOUR SONS' WIVES WITH YOU.

17 ALL THE LIVING THINGS THAT ARE WITH YOU, OF ALL FLESH, OF THE BIRDS, AND OF THE BEASTS, AND OF ALL THE CREEPING THINGS THAT CREEP ON THE EARTH, THAT GO OUT WITH YOU, SHALL SWARM IN THE EARTH AND BE FRUITFUL, AND MULTIPLY IN THE EARTH."

18 AND NOAH AND HIS SONS AND HIS WIFE AND HIS SONS' WIVES WENT OUT.

19 ALL THE LIVING THINGS, ALL THE CREEPING THINGS AND ALL THE BIRDS, ALL THAT CREEP ON THE EARTH, BY THEIR FAMILIES, THEY WENT OUT OF THE ARK.

20 And Noah built an altar to Yahweh, and he took some of each of the clean beasts and of each of the clean birds, and he offered sacrifices on the altar.

21 And Yahweh smelled the pleasant smell, and Yahweh said to his heart, "I shall not again curse the ground on man's account, for the inclination of the human heart is evil from their youth, and I shall not again strike all the living as I have done.

22 All the rest of the days of the earth, seed and harvest, and cold and heat, and summer and winter, and day and night shall not cease."

Reprinted with the permission of Simon & Schuster from *Who Wrote the Bible?* by Richard Friedman. Copyright © 1987 by Richard Friedman.

the **patriarch** (term describing a venerable male family head or tribal founder or leader) receives a rich reward in cattle or other livestock for his deception.

As in the Flood story, the Exodus narrative of the Israelites' rescue at a chaotic sea blends together two (or three) once-separate traditions that now appear as a single account (Exod. 14–15; see Chapter 6). Exodus also includes two distinct versions of Yahweh's revelation to Moses of his sacred name. In the first, God states that he was formerly known as the "God [Elohim] of your fathers" (Exod. 3:6) but now reveals his hitherto unknown personal name, Yahweh. In the second, God tells Moses that he was formerly known to Israel's ancestors not as Elohim, but as El Shaddai:

> I am the Lord [Yahweh]. I appeared to Abraham, Isaac, and Jacob as God Almighty [El Shaddai, which may mean "God of the (cosmic) mountain"], but by my name The Lord [Yahweh] I did not make myself known to them.

(Exod. 6:3)

The Deity's declaration that he had not revealed his sacred name, Yahweh, before confiding it to Moses contrasts sharply with another Pentateuch tradition that Yahweh's name was known and used even before the Flood. Beginning in Genesis 2.4b, when "the Lord God [Yahweh Elohim] made the earth and the heavens," one literary strand that appears intermittently throughout the first four Torah books consistently identifies God as Yahweh. According to this writer, "people began to invoke the name of the Lord [Yahweh]" during the time of Enosh, grandson of Adam (Gen. 4:26). Most scholars believe that these conflicting claims about when Yahweh first disclosed his name offer important clues to the different sources and authorship of the Pentateuch.

 # The Documentary Hypothesis

For more than 200 years, an international body of scholars has tried to explain the contradictions, duplications, anachronisms, and other discrepancies found throughout the Torah. Although an increasing number of scholars have recently challenged the theory (see below), the **documentary hypothesis,** originally proposed during the mid-nineteenth century, is still the place where the majority of scholars begin an investigation of the Torah's sources and literary development. Even scholars who have abandoned the theory generally use its well-known division of the present Torah into separate sources, whether oral or written.

According to the documentary hypothesis, the Torah is a literary patchwork in which at least four originally separate written documents—dating from four different periods of Israelite history—were stitched together to create the present text. The interweaving of four once-independent strands explains both the repetitions and the contradictions in the Torah we have today (see Table 4.1).

J, the Yahwist Source

In the documentary theory, the oldest source is called **J** because its author typically uses the name *Yahweh* (German, *Jahweh*) for God. The **Yahwist** writer, also known as J, is the first to compose a continuous narrative of Israel's origins. J's work incorporates ancient oral traditions about Israel's prehistory and tales of the ancestral fathers and mothers. Identifying God as Yahweh from the beginning of his account, J opens his narrative with the second creation story (Gen. 2:4b–25) and the etiology of humanity's loss of Eden (Gen. 3:1–24), as well as one version of the deluge story (see Box 4.1). Highlighting the important role of women such as Sarah, Rebekah, Leah, and Rachel in the drama of Israel's ancestors, J recounts the wanderings of the patriarchs, their descent into Egypt, Yahweh's intervention to release the Israelites from Egyptian bondage, and the forging of the Yahweh–Israel covenant at Sinai, which is consistently J's name for the "mountain of God" (see Figure 4.3). Some scholars believe that J's extended narrative—parts of which are found embedded in Genesis, Exodus, and Numbers—also included the story of Israel's conquest of Canaan. Other scholars, such as Richard Friedman, argue that J also composed a narrative of David's rise to power as king of Israel, an account that forms the basis for much of 2 Samuel and 1 Kings 1–2.

Although most scholars recognize the existence of the J strand in the Pentateuch, controversy rages over the time of its composition. According to the classic view of the documentary hypothesis, J's narrative was produced, at least in part, as a justification for or validation of the Davidic monarchy, which, according to biblical reckoning, was established about 1000 BCE. After Davidic rulers had transformed Israel's formerly competing tribes into a fragile political unity—with both kings and priests recently centered at the new capital of Jerusalem—the Yahwist author composed a literary affirmation of the new order, perhaps in the late tenth century BCE. J's work, from the call of Abraham to the conquest of Canaan and the rise of Davidic kings, presumably functioned as a foundation document illustrating that Israel's social, political, and

TABLE 4.1 Four Hypothetical Sources of the Pentateuch

Although scholars have recently challenged the documentary hypothesis, most agree that the Torah contains at least four main sources, although some of these may have been oral traditions that scribes successively added to the texts.

SOURCE	CHARACTERISTICS
J (Yahwist)	Uses the personal name *Yahweh* for Israel's God Portrays God as having humanlike characteristics and behaviors Features a vivid, concrete style and a dramatic storyline, beginning with creation (Gen. 2:4b) and extending at least to the conclusion of the Mosaic Covenant at Sinai Has a strong orientation toward the traditions of Judah, setting many Genesis tales in that region
E (Elohist)	Uses the generic plural *Elohim* for Israel's God Features a less picturesque style and a less humanlike view of the Deity Begins the narrative with Abraham and concludes with the Israelites at the "mountain of God," which E calls Horeb Has a strong orientation toward the northern kingdom of Israel (the chief tribe of which was Ephraim), where most of his Genesis stories are set
D (Deuteronomist)	Emphasizes the conditional nature of the Mosaic Covenant and interprets Israel's military/political defeats as a direct result of the people's failure to worship Yahweh alone Features a more elaborate rhetorical style than J or E Reflects policies of Josiah's religious reforms (c. 621 BCE) Insists that only one central sanctuary is acceptable to Yahweh Has a strong influence on the writing of Joshua through 2 Kings, the Deuteronomistic History (DH)
P (priestly)	Focuses on priestly interests, particularly legalistic and ritual aspects of Israel's religious practices Features a precise, pedantic style, meticulously listing genealogies, censuses, dates, and instructions for the Tabernacle cult Is thought to have been added to the older JE epic during and after the Babylonian exile (after 587 BCE) Shows a strong resemblance to the concepts that the exilic priest-prophet Ezekiel expressed

religious institutions were the outworking of Yahweh's historical purpose.

Certainly, the J material integrated into the Torah focuses on **Judah,** the name of both the tribe to which David belonged and the southern territory over which he and his heirs ruled. To emphasize the importance of Judah in Israel's past, J associates many of the ancestors with geographical sites that are also significant to Judah's royal dynasty. Thus, in J's account, Abraham dwells in Hebron (also called Mamre) (Gen. 13:18; 18:1), the location of Judah's first capital city, where David's reign was first acclaimed (2 Sam. 2–5). J's description of the boundaries of the land that Yahweh promised to Abraham's progeny (Gen. 15:18) corresponds to the political frontiers of the Davidic kingdom (cf. 1 Kings 4:21). Because J emphasizes Judah's central role in Israel's story, he is regarded as a native of Judah, perhaps a member of the royal court living at Jerusalem, giving J's alphabetic

symbol a double meaning. (For more recent speculations about J's era, see below.)

E, the Elohist Source

According to the documentary hypothesis, the Pentateuch's second-oldest narrative strand—which many scholars now think was oral rather than a written document—is that designated as **E,** the **Elohist** tradition, so named because this source characteristically uses Elohim rather than Yahweh as the preferred title for God. Of the four hypothetical Pentateuchal sources, E is the least well preserved, although extended Elohist passages have been identified in Genesis and Exodus. Beginning with tales of Abraham and his descendants, E survives only in disconnected fragments interspersed with J and later material. In Genesis, E contributes mainly to stories of sibling conflict, such as the rivalry

FIGURE 4.3 The facial expression on this statuette of an ancient Egyptian scribe reveals the intelligence and consciousness of power characteristic of the literate professional class that controlled the preservation and interpretation of Egypt's history. In common with its Near Eastern neighbors, Israel developed a scribal class associated with the royal court that played a major role in creating the Bible.

between Jacob and Esau, as well as that between Joseph and his brothers. In Exodus, E provides accounts of Jethro, Moses' father-in-law; the first revelation of Yahweh's name to Moses; and Israel's encounters with God on his sacred mountain. Most of the E material parallels narratives from J and other contributors, adding traditions, such as Abraham's near-sacrifice of his son Isaac, to the end of the Abraham cycle (Gen. 20–22).

Although many scholars view E not as a formerly separate narrative but only as supplemental oral material added to enrich J's narrative, E includes some important variations in the biblical tradition. Whereas J specifies Mount Sinai as the sacred locale of Yahweh's covenant making, E names Horeb (as does Deuteronomy). J refers to Palestine's inhabitants as Canaanites, whereas E labels them Amorites. J identifies Moses' father-in-law as Ruel or Hobab, whereas E knows him as Jethro, priest of Midian.

In J's view, people worshiped Yahweh almost from the beginning of human history (Gen. 4:26), but E states that Yahweh kept his name secret until Moses' time (Exod. 3:15). Whereas J's portrait of God is strongly anthropomorphic (human in behavior and perhaps even appearance [Gen. 3:8–9]), E paints a

somewhat more abstract and remote Deity. J describes Yahweh strolling through Eden to enjoy a cooling breeze, dining with Abraham under the oaks of Mamre, personally wrestling with Jacob, and appearing directly to Moses. In contrast, E tends to present God as transcendent, typically employing an angelic go-between when speaking to Abraham or Moses. Whereas J sets many of the ancestral tales in Judah's territory, E prefers geographical sites connected with the northern tribes, the most prominent of which was **Ephraim,** thus also giving E's symbol a twofold significance.

The JE Epic

Elohist material, whether oral or written, may have been integrated with J traditions after 721 BCE, when the northern kingdom of Israel fell to the Assyrians. Israelite refugees fleeing south into Judah may have brought Elohist stories with them to Jerusalem, where they were used to enrich the J narratives. According to some scholars, the integrated JE narratives may first have been committed to writing during the reign of Hezekiah (715–687 BCE), the king of Judah who apparently offered protection to the refugees from Israel. As the archaeological record suggests, only in the seventh century BCE did Jerusalem become a city large enough plausibly to support a literate elite, which may have included court scribes who crystalized previously oral traditions into writing.

D, the Deuteronomist Source

The third principal source of the Pentateuch is known as **D,** the **Deuteronomist.** Scholarly opinion is now divided over the extent to which the Deuteronomist's influence is present in the five Torah books. Following the classic documentary hypothesis, many scholars believe that, whereas J and E passages appear throughout Genesis, Exodus, and Numbers, D's work is largely confined to the Book of Deuteronomy. Conversely, a smaller body of scholars recently has proposed that D is the dominant influence in the Pentateuch, with some maintaining that the core of Deuteronomy (Chs. 12–26) may be the oldest part of the Torah, to which JE material was later added as an extended introduction. These scholars argue that a large number of Deuteronomy-influenced passages were interpolated into the JE material of Genesis, Exodus, and Numbers.

While differing about the relative ages and literary relationship of JE and D, most scholars agree that Deuteronomy, or at least its central section, was the "book of the law [*torah*]" discovered in 621 BCE during repairs to the Jerusalem Temple. Discovery of this allegedly Mosaic document helped fuel or validate a major reform of Israelite religion initiated by King Josiah, who zealously followed Deuteronomy's command to centralize Judah's worship "at the place [Yahweh] will choose to set his name there and give it a home" (Deut. 12:4–6). Acting on Deuteronomy's declaration that Yahweh will accept sacrifices only at the "place" designated—assumed to be Jerusalem—Josiah systematically destroyed all other altars and shrines, including those at Bethel and other sanctuaries associated with the Genesis patriarchs (2 Kings 22:3–23:25; cf. 2 Chron. 34–35). Josiah's other reforms, such as the celebration of a national Passover feast, also echo policies advocated only in Deuteronomy.

P, the Priestly Source

The fourth and final contribution to the Torah, according to the documentary hypothesis, was the work of **priestly** writers who lived during and after the Babylonian exile (from 587 to perhaps as late as the fourth century BCE). Given the scholarly designation of **P**, this literary strand in the Pentateuch represents the concerns of a postexilic school of priestly authors/editors who labored to collect, preserve, and edit Israel's religious heritage. The P school assembled several originally separate legal codes, encompassing hundreds of laws, statutes, and ordinances, and inserted them at various points in the JE narrative of old Israel. Extensively revising the older material, the priestly editors compiled the vast body of legal material that extends from Exodus 35, through Leviticus, to Numbers 10. Although the priestly contribution emphasizes purity laws, sacrificial rituals, genealogies, and the elaborate details of formal worship, it also includes significant additions to the JE narrative. In addition to inserting a priestly version of the Abrahamic Covenant that prescribes circumcision (Gen. 17), P scribes blended their tradition of the Flood story with that of J, producing a considerably expanded (and self-contradictory) account of a global deluge (see Box 4.1). They also prefaced the Torah collection with a new creation account (Gen. 1) and concluded it with a narrative of Moses' death (Deut. 24), thus giving the entire Torah a priestly framework. (Table 4.1 summarizes the documentary hypothesis.)

Some Recent Challenges to the Documentary Hypothesis

Although many leading scholars still champion the documentary hypothesis, and many universities and seminaries continue to teach it as the standard model of

biblical criticism, over the past few decades, a growing minority of scholars has challenged its assumptions, particularly its claim that the Pentateuch incorporates four originally complete and independent documents (J, E, D, and P). Like any theory, the documentary hypothesis is useful only as long as it can successfully account for all the available facts, such as the repetitions, anachronisms, and innumerable inconsistencies found in the Torah. Recent critics of the theory—which in its original form proposed that the Torah consists of an interweaving of four distinct and complete documents—have emphasized the fragmentary nature of the supposed E document. Many argue that both E and P represent only intermittent editorial insertions into the Torah and that they never existed as separate, coherent written sources.

Other scholars suggest that the individual cycles of Genesis stories—about Abraham, Jacob, and Joseph—emerged independently of each other and were not linked together to form a chronological narrative until long after their (oral) composition. These scholars point out that most of the tales of Abraham, Isaac, and Jacob consist of a loosely connected series of incidents that have little in common with each other except that they all happened to a particular patriarch. By contrast, the Joseph story is a carefully structured unity—all of its parts subordinated to a well-developed plot. At some point in their development, biblical scribes put these individual tales in chronological sequence, adding only a few verbal connectives to stitch them together.

Scholars have long recognized the signs of oral composition behind the biblical stories, oral traditions that were passed down through many generations before finding written form in the Torah. Indeed, many advocates of the documentary hypothesis acknowledged the presence of diverse oral traditions underlying the four written sources. Recently, noting that ancient societies commonly used an interplay of oral and written traditions—written forms did not immediately replace circulating oral versions of the same tale—some scholars have insisted that the biblical texts betray too many characteristics of oral performance to be considered as literary compositions in the way the documentary hypothesis assumed.

In recent decades, scholars have proposed many alternatives to the documentary model, although none has yet won general acceptance. The most severe disagreements tend to focus on the issues of time and place of composition, particularly whether specific texts were composed before, during, or long after the Babylonian exile. The general trend among critics of the standard model is to place written composition of the Torah ever later in Israel's history, during the Persian or even the Hellenistic period.

QUESTIONS FOR DISCUSSION AND REVIEW

1. Define the term *Pentateuch,* and list the books it contains.

2. Describe some major themes of the Pentateuch and their function in helping to bind together the five books of Torah. How do the divine promises in Genesis 12–50 serve to unify the Torah's diverse material?

3. Except for Genesis, the Torah's narratives are commonly interrupted by large blocks of legal material. How are these two different literary genres—story and law codes—related to each other in the Pentateuch?

4. In Genesis, Yahweh makes a series of unconditional promises to Israel's ancestors; in Exodus and Deuteronomy, the Israelites make vows to worship Yahweh alone. How do the forms and conditions of these two sets of promises differ?

5. How well do you think that the Pentateuch's theme of divine promises—which are deferred to the indefinite future—serves to strengthen the divine–human bond? Explain your answer.

6. According to tradition, who was the Pentateuch's sole author? What difficulties in the Torah text lead scholars to question traditional beliefs about authorship?

7. Explain the documentary hypothesis and its view of the Pentateuch as a composite work in which four distinct oral and/or literary sources are combined. Identify the four main sources, giving their names and chief characteristics.

8. Describe some of the recent scholarly challenges to the documentary theory, including a renewed emphasis on oral composition and an increasingly late date for the time when the texts were finally crystalized in writing.

Terms and Concepts to Remember

Book of the Covenant	literary genres (categories)
documentary hypothesis	etiology
J (Yahwist)	genealogy
E (Elohist)	itinerary
D (Deuteronomist)	narrative
P (priestly writer(s))	manna
Ephraim	patriarch
Judah	Pentateuch
	Yahweh's bond to Israel

Recommended Reading

Blenkinsopp, Joseph. "Introduction to the Pentateuch." In *The New Interpreter's Bible,* Vol. 1, pp. 305–318. Nashville, TN: Abingdon Press, 1994. A good introduction to the Torah's multiple sources and themes.

Clines, David J. A. *The Themes of the Pentateuch,* 2nd ed. Supplement Series 10. Sheffield, England: JSOT Press, 1997. Surveys literary themes that help unify diverse Torah narratives.

Dorsey, David A. *The Literary Structure of the Old Testament: A Commentary on Genesis–Malachi.* Grand Rapids, MI: Baker Books, 1999. A detailed analysis of thematic continuities, organization, and literary units in each book of the Hebrew Bible; for more advanced students.

Dundes, Alan. *Holy Writ as Oral Lit: The Bible as Folklore.* New York: Rowman & Littlefield, 1999. Explains duplications in biblical narratives as typical of orally transmitted folktales.

Friedman, Richard E. *The Bible with Sources Revealed: A New View into the Five Books of Moses.* San Francisco: HarperOne, 2003. A forceful argument favoring the documentary hypothesis, with a new translation of the Torah featuring the four main sources printed in different colors.

———. *Who Wrote the Bible?* New York: Harper & Row, 1987. An excellent introduction to scholarly theories about biblical composition.

Niditch, Susan. *Oral World and Written Word: Ancient Israelite Literature.* Louisville, KY: Westminster John Knox Press, 1996. Examines the relationship between Israel's oral traditions and the biblical texts derived from them.

———. *A Prelude to Biblical Folklore: Underdogs and Tricksters.* Chicago: U of Illinois P, 1987, 2000. Analyzes oral characteristics of Genesis tales.

Schniedwind, William M. *How the Bible Became a Book.* Cambridge: Cambridge UP, 2004. Using archaeological evidence about the growth of literacy in Israel, concludes that the first extended biblical narratives probably originated in the eighth and seventh centuries BCE, during the reigns of Hezekiah and Josiah.

Van der Toorn, Karel. *Scribal Culture and the Making of the Hebrew Bible.* Cambridge, MA: Harvard UP, 2007. Placing Israel in the context of ancient Near Eastern scribal culture, argues that Israelite scribes of court and temple composed, revised and edited the biblical texts over many generations.

CHAPTER 5

In the Beginning
The Book of Genesis

Key Topics/Themes Opening with a stately narrative extolling God's creative majesty, Genesis introduces themes that will dominate much of the Hebrew Bible. In the first of three parts into which the book is traditionally divided (Chs. 1–11), emphasis falls on issues of human rebellion and divine punishment for disobedience. After expelling the first human couple from Eden, their paradise home, and witnessing humanity's downward spiral into violence, God almost completely annihilates the human race in a global deluge. (Only Noah and his family survive the catastrophe.) God then permanently divides the post-Flood population by erecting language barriers among peoples and scattering them over the face of the earth. In the second section, however—a cycle of stories about Israel's ancestors (Chs. 12–36)—God actively seeks to repair the broken bond between himself and humankind. Appearing to Abraham, progenitor of the future Israelite nation, God makes a series of promises for land, descendants, and universal blessing. In the third section (Chs. 37–50), the story of Joseph and his brothers, God uses the rivalry among Abraham's great-grandsons to further his plan for Israelite nationhood. Genesis ends with Abraham's descendants still few in number and settled in Egypt, far from their promised homeland in Canaan.

The first book of the Torah, Genesis serves as a prologue to the story of Israel's formation, the initial installment in an almost unbroken narrative that extends from Genesis 12 through 2 Kings. Sometimes called the "national epic of Israel," this long narrative traces the story of Israel from its beginning, when God promised Abraham to give his descendants a homeland "forever" (Gen. 12:1–3); through God's rescue of those descendants (the Israelites) from slavery in Egypt, the giving of his torah (divine teachings) at Mount Sinai, the military conquest of Canaan, and the birth of a united monarchy under Kings David and Solomon; to the nation's gradual decline and disastrous fall to Babylon in 587 BCE. A story that begins with hope inspired by divine promises thus ends in calamity, a crushing reversal that biblical writers unequivocally attribute to Israel's disobedience, its collective failure to honor Yahweh alone and faithfully keep his covenant.

The Primeval History

Although most of the biblical narrative focuses on God's special relationship with Israel, Genesis begins with accounts of creation and human origins, giving a universal perspective to the tales of Israel's ancestors that follow. In Genesis 1, God (Elohim) appears as a *transcendent* Being, unlimited by space or time, who speaks the world into existence. By the power of his word alone, God transforms the "deep," a dark, watery **chaos,** into a **cosmos,** an orderly system characterized by predictability and harmony. The chaotic "deep" (Hebrew, *tehom*) refers to the ancient Near Eastern concept of an undifferentiated sea that existed before divine action brought the world into being (see Box 5.1). Working with this primordial substance, God employs a six-step process by which the watery abyss is illuminated, divided, and shaped into a structured environment that will support life (see Figure 5.1).

BOX 5.1   Why So Much Water?

In Genesis 1, the precreation world consists of a boundless watery abyss, the raw material out of which God fashions the universe. After creating light, God then splits the chaotic waters of the primal "deep" (Hebrew, *tehom*) into two parts, dividing "the waters from the waters" by constructing a lofty "dome" or vault that separates "the waters that were under the dome from the waters that were above the dome" (Gen. 1:6–7). The open space between the earth's surface waters and those suspended above the "dome" or sky provides room for all the life forms that God then proceeds to create. "Gathered together in one place," earth's seas thus surround the "dry land" that animals and humans are to inhabit.

When God later decides to reverse the creative process in a global deluge, he reunites the bodies of water he had previously separated, opening both "the fountains of the great deep" and "the windows of the heavens" (Gen. 7:11). By merging the waters above and below the sky-dome, he temporarily returns the world to its primal state of watery chaos, destroying almost all of the life forms he had created.

The belief that water was the primary substance out of which divine powers made the world was widespread in the ancient Near East, including Mesopotamia, Egypt, and Israel. The Babylonian creation epic, the *Enuma Elish*, depicts the precreation chaos of limitless water as the deities Apsu (personification of sweet or potable water) and Tiamat (embodiment of saltwater). Tiamat's name, in fact, is closely related to the Hebrew *tehom*, the "deep," abysmal waters that

the biblical God molded into a cosmos, an ordered harmonious system in which life can flourish.

An Egyptian creation account associated with Heliopolis (meaning "City of the Sun") similarly postulates a primordial expanse of water, called Nu, that had to be separated and divided during the process of forming the world. According to the Heliopolis tradition, the sun god Atum arose out of Nu, standing on a primeval mound, a prototype of the inhabitable earth, encircled by endless ocean. Atum, who in his divine being encompassed the totality of everything that exists, became the source of all other gods, including Geb (the earth) and Nut (the sky). Even after Atum created an orderly world, Egyptians apparently feared an eventual return of the original watery chaos. In Egyptian cosmology (views about the universe's nature and purpose), the primal waters continue to surround the world, separated from it by the vault of the sky (Nut) and confined to subterranean regions by the overlying earth (Geb). A similar concept appears in biblical references to the mysterious "waters beneath the earth," the underground remnant of primeval sea on which the dry land is precariously balanced (Exod. 20:4).

Although biblical authors adopted prevailing traditions about cosmic waters, they radically transformed older Egyptian and Mesopotamian creation accounts, stripping them of polytheistic elements. While retaining concepts of a primal sea—as well as themes of creation through division and separation—Hebrew writers revolutionized these inherited motifs to exalt a single, omnipotent Creator, the God of Israel.

After creating light on day one (the first stage), God proceeds on the next three days to create the regions or environments that will provide the place or sphere for the objects and creatures he fashions on days four, five, and six. Thus the "dome" or sky-vault that he makes on day two—which separates "the waters that were under the dome from the waters that were above the dome"—becomes the space in which he will set the astronomical "lights" (sun, moon, and stars) on day four, as well as the region in which birds, created on day five, will fly. Similarly, the fashioning of "dry land" and plant life on day three provides the terrestrial environment that land animals and humans, created on day six, will occupy. In this carefully arranged design, each category of created object or life form has its own proper sphere.

The appearance of humanity, male and female together, *both* in the divine "likeness" and "image" (cf. Gen. 9:6), marks the climax of Genesis's first version of

creation. Pronouncing his creative labors "very good," God then "rests" on the seventh day. God's day of postcreation repose is later cited as the rationale for Israel's institution of the **Sabbath,** the seventh day of the week on which all work ceases (cf. Exod. 20:8–11; Deuteronomy, however, gives a different justification of the Sabbath, declaring it an opportunity to remember Israel's escape from forced labor in Egypt [5:12–15]).

A Second Version of Creation

Whereas Genesis 1 offers an elevated, transcendent, and highly structured view of creation, Genesis 2 gives a decidedly down-to-earth account, portraying a humanlike deity and a humanity (in Hebrew, *adam*) composed of dust (*admah*). Beginning in Genesis 2:4b, the narrator repeatedly uses God's personal name, Yahweh, and depicts him in terms analogous to human roles or

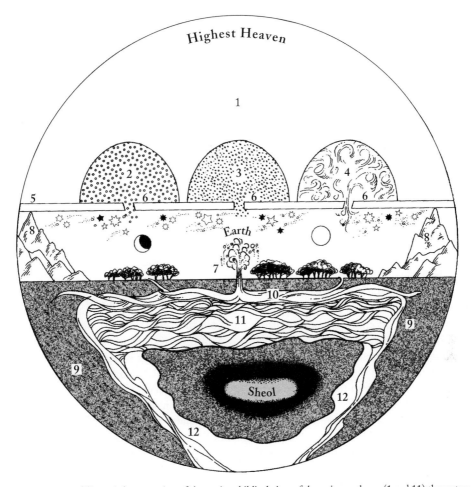

FIGURE 5.1 The artist's re-creation of the ancient biblical view of the universe shows (1 and 11) the waters above and below the earth; (2, 3, and 4) chambers or storehouses of hail, rain, and snow; (5 and 6) the firmament with its openings or sluices; (7) fountains of the deep; (8) the mountain pillars on which the firmament rests; (9) the pillars of the earth; (10) the navel of the earth; and (12) the watery abyss. Sheol, abode of the dead, is the dark cavern at the center of the lower hemisphere.

occupations, such as potter, gardener, and landowner. Whereas the first version of creation shows the cosmos emerging amid an oceanic abyss, surrounded by water, the second pictures the precreation world as a rainless, arid desert, watered only by subterranean springs.

Genesis 2 also gives a different order to creation. Whereas Genesis 1 states that God (Elohim) creates men and women simultaneously, at the end of a long sequence, the second account shows Yahweh shaping the first human (*adam*) out of dusty soil *before* he has created vegetation, animals, or a female of the human species. In the first account, humanity is imprinted with the divine image; in the second, the earthling is molded from ordinary clay, which is then animated by Yahweh's "breath." After sculpting the earthling, a mortal duality of earth and divine energy, Yahweh then plants a garden "in Eden," where he causes vegetation to grow, including a tree of life

and a tree of knowledge. (The term *adam* here means "earthling" or "humankind"; it is not used as the first man's personal name until later in the narrative.)

After placing the earthling alone in Eden, as sub-gardener and caretaker, Yahweh apparently notices that total solitude is "not good" for him. Resolving to "make him a helper as his partner," Yahweh next creates a variety of animals and birds, bringing them to the earthling to name. As if expecting the earthling to select a mate from this menagerie, Yahweh parades all his nonhuman species past the mortal, who can find no suitable companion among them (2:20). Perceiving that the human is qualitatively different from the other creatures he has made, Yahweh then puts *adam* to sleep, removing part of his body (the famous rib) and using it to construct the first woman. The woman's appearance—she is not called **Eve** until Genesis 3:20—inspired the first poetry:

Adam (now separated from his female component) rejoices that she is "bone of my bones and flesh of my flesh" (2:23; cf. Gen. 29:14, where Laban uses the same poetic phrase to describe his blood kinship to Jacob).

Adam, Eve, and the Serpent

In Genesis 3, the narrator uses an **etiology,** a tale that explains the origin of some phenomenon, to describe the source of humanity's alienation from God. This etiological story of the first human couple's loss of their paradise home uses one of the staples of global folklore, a talking animal. (The only other speaking animal in the Hebrew Bible appears in the tale of Balaam's donkey [Num. 22–24].) Although the Genesis serpent is commonly identified with Satan, neither the author nor any other Old Testament writer does so. In the Eden story, the serpent is not called "evil," but merely "subtle" or "crafty," possessing a skeptical intelligence that questions the way Yahweh runs things. It knows what God knows, that eating from the tree of knowledge will impart a new awareness of "good and evil," giving humans a godlike perspective (3:1–17). In fact, Yahweh confirms that the forbidden fruit has (magically) transformed humans into "one of us" (spirit members of God's heavenly council; see Box 3.2), which prompts him to keep the pair from acquiring another prerogative of godhood, immortality (3:22).

To prevent their eating from the "tree of life" and living "forever," Yahweh evicts Adam and Eve from Eden, putting the source of divinity permanently out of reach. The way back to their garden home is barred by **cherubim** who wield flaming swords (3:22–24). Common in Mesopotamian art, statues of cherubim—winged figures with animal bodies and human faces—typically guard the entrances to temples and royal palaces; in Exodus 25–31, Yahweh orders that images of them be placed on either side of the Ark of the Covenant, the rectangular wooden chest symbolizing his celestial throne and its guardians.

Throughout both the Old and New Testaments, God consistently opposes human wrongdoing, both through direct punishment and through lingering consequences to the guilty parties. When Adam and Eve disobey his direct command to avoid the tree of knowledge, God's response is swift and severe: The "crafty" serpent is stripped of its limbs and reduced to an object of human fear (3:5, 14–15). Yahweh intensifies the woman's pain in childbirth and consigns her to domination by her husband—a reflection of women's subordination to men in Israel's patriarchal society, but not part of the original divine plan. For the man, Yahweh blights the soil, condemning his male descendants to the exhausting labor that peasant farmers endure trying to wrest a living from arid Near Eastern fields.

The cost of knowledge without divine permission or guidance also includes a terrifying awareness of human mortality, and Yahweh reminds the pair that they must return to the soil from which they were formed. As the serpent had stated, they do not die in the same "day" that they disobeyed—Adam lives on for nearly 1,000 years—but the huge gulf between mortal humanity and immortal divinity is clearly drawn. Although Israel's neighbors, particularly the civilizations of Egypt and Greece, developed elaborate traditions about the fate of the human soul after death, the Hebrew Bible says little on the subject. It is not until the Book of Daniel (probably second century BCE) that a biblical writer explicitly introduces ideas about a future life (Dan. 12:1–3).

The Consequences of Human Frailty

Cain and Abel Despite the severity of his judgments, Yahweh is capable of surprising tenderness and concern for the earthlings who failed to trust his governance. Before driving Adam and Eve out into the harsh world of adult experience, God makes clothes of animal skins to cover their nakedness. After the exile from Eden, his presence abides with the couple, enabling them to fulfill the earlier command to bear children. Eve's first son, **Cain,** is born "with the help of the LORD [Yahweh]" (4:2). Even while bearing sons and daughters, Adam and Eve soon learn the inescapable consequences of their disobedience, which introduces violent crime into the world.

Introducing a theme of rivalry between brothers that disrupts family relationships throughout the Genesis narrative (and resurfaces in stories about King David's sons in 2 Samuel), the narrator shows Cain bitterly envious of his younger brother, **Abel.** When Yahweh prefers the animal sacrifice of Abel, a shepherd, to the grain offerings of Cain, a farmer, Cain reacts against this divine favoritism by killing his brother. Despite the seriousness of the crime—the first taking of a human life—Yahweh treats Cain with leniency, imprinting him with a "mark" that prevents other people (of unexplained origin) from punishing the murderer (4:13–15). Once the shedding of human blood has begun, however, humanity's condition deteriorates rapidly. The list of Cain's descendants culminates in Lamech, who savagely boasts that he avenges every wrong "seventy-seven-fold" (4:17–24), establishing a culture of violence that eventually leads to humanity's near-destruction.

The Flood In the Genesis account of the global **Flood,** God's response to human "wickedness" includes a profound sorrow: God feels "grieved . . . to his heart"

(6:5–6). "Sorry that he had made humankind," Yahweh resolves to wipe his failed experiment from the face of the earth. He thus reverses the separation of waters he had performed in Genesis 1, opening the "windows of the heavens" to release waters stored above the sky "dome" and causing subterranean "fountains of the great deep [primal abyss]" to "burst forth" (6:11). Drawing on Mesopotamian lore concerning a prehistoric deluge (compare Boxes 3.1 and 5.1), the Genesis authors/editors reproduce elements from the Atrahasis and Gilgamesh traditions, including a divine decision to spare a single human family. Like the flood-surviving ancestor of Gilgamesh, Utnapishtim, Noah is instructed to build an ark (rectangular boat) and stock it with all kinds of birds and animals. Unlike his aggressive contemporaries, Noah has "walked with God" (6:9; cf. 5:22), which results in his preservation, along with that of his wife; his three sons, Ham, Shem, and Japheth; and their wives.

Emphasizing that in God's purpose even global disaster involves a creative and saving element, Genesis 9 presents the post-Flood world as a new beginning for humanity. After repeating the command to "be fruitful" and repopulate the earth (9:7; cf. 1:28), God institutes the first of four biblical covenants. The covenant with Noah and his descendants is universal, encompassing the entire world population. Described as "everlasting," it includes affirmation of the sacredness of life, both human and animal, and a divine promise never again to drown the earth (9:1–11). Like the later agreements made through Abraham and Moses, the pact with Noah has a "sign"—a rainbow as a visible symbol of God's reconciliation with humankind.

The primeval history concludes by tracing the genealogies of Noah's sons— **Ham, Shem, and Japheth**— who represent the three principal branches of the human family known in biblical times (Gen. 10–11). From Shem come the Semitic peoples, among them the Babylonians, Assyrians, Arabs, and Israelites. Ham was the **eponymous** (name-giving) ancestor of the Egyptians and their political dependents, then including the Canaanites, while Japheth was the supposed progenitor of the Aegean Sea peoples, including the Greeks.

The Tower of Babel Amid the lengthy genealogies— often called the "table of nations"—editors inserted a story about the Tower of Babel. An etiological account explaining the great diversity of languages spoken in different geographical areas, this episode contains themes of human ambition and divine retribution that echo the Eden story. When humanity, united in language and purpose, attempts to build a tower "with its top in the heavens" and thus "make a name for [themselves],"

Yahweh realizes that "nothing that [humans] propose to do now will be impossible for them." After overthrowing the tower, Yahweh "confuses" human speech so that different groups can no longer understand each other and scatters a linguistically divided humanity throughout the earth (11:1–9). In so doing, God in effect establishes a globally diverse, multicultural society.

A Prologue to Israel: Stories of Israel's Ancestors

After surveying the human race as a whole, the Genesis account narrows to focus on the ancestors of a single nation, Israel. The remainder of Genesis (Chs. 12–50) is devoted to relating the stories of Abraham and Sarah, progenitors of the future Israel, and their colorful descendants through four turbulent generations. Opening with God's call to Abraham in **Haran**, a major city in northwestern Mesopotamia, the action then shifts all over the map of the Fertile Crescent, from the Euphrates River southwestward to the Nile in Egypt. The journeys of Abraham and his progeny, in fact, outline the geographical contours of the biblical world (see Figure 3.1).

The story of Abraham (Gen. 12–25) introduces a positive new phase in the divine–human relationship. After the Flood, Yahweh is apparently resigned to the inevitability of human wrongdoing (8:21–22) and prepared to display great flexibility in dealing with human frailty. According to biblical tradition, neither Abraham nor his father, Terah, was originally a worshiper of Yahweh. As natives of Ur, one of Mesopotamia's oldest cities, they naturally "served other gods" (Josh. 24:2; cf. Gen. 11:26–31). Yahweh's reason for uniquely honoring Abraham, the product of a polytheistic society, is not explicitly stated, but this can be partly inferred from Abraham's behavior. In Genesis 12, when Yahweh suddenly breaks into Abraham's consciousness, ordering him to abandon his home in Haran, where Terah had settled his family, and journey to an unspecified destination, Abraham immediately obeys. Whenever God speaks, Abraham *listens,* in the biblical sense of the verb—paying full attention to the divine summons and displaying an exemplary trust in the divine call. As Genesis 15 expresses it, Abraham "believed" Yahweh's promises, "and the LORD reckoned it to him as righteousness" (15:6).

The Abrahamic Covenant

To suggest the nature of divine–human interaction in Genesis, the narrator typically describes a **theophany**—a visible, audible, or otherwise perceptible appearance of God on earth. God's purpose in most of the Genesis theophanies is to "cut a covenant," voluntarily to initiate a binding partnership with Abraham and his descendants. In a strange and awesome visitation, Yahweh appears to Abraham at night and strides between two halves of a slaughtered animal, his action a covenant-making ceremony in which God implicitly invokes a curse on himself if he should break his word (15:1–18; cf. Jer. 34:18–20 for a similar ritual). Genesis gives four different versions of the Abrahamic Covenant (12:2–3; 15:1–21; 17:1–22; 22:15–18), a solemn contractual agreement by which Yahweh pledges to give Abraham's progeny, the Israelites, life-sustaining blessings, both material and spiritual. These promised benefits include a guarantee that Abraham's descendants will become as innumerable as the "stars of heaven" or the "sands of the sea"; a vow that God will be an abiding presence with his people; an oath to grant Abraham's heirs the entire territory of Canaan; the creation of a special covenant bond with Yahweh; the establishment of a future line of kings; and the eventual expansion of divine favor so that "all the tribes [families] of the earth will bless themselves by [Abraham]" (12:3). The promise of universal blessing highlights the importance of Israel's mission as specially chosen conveyer of Yahweh's goodwill to humankind.

As the rainbow's appearance following a storm represents God's covenant with Noah, so his pledges to Abraham have a visible sign, **circumcision.** Genesis 17 presents the ritual of circumcision, the surgical removal of the foreskin of the penis, as part of the Abrahamic Covenant. Other biblical passages, however, suggest that this requirement for all Israelite males was introduced at a much later date. Although incorporated into the Mosaic Torah (Lev. 12:1–5; cf. Exod. 12:44, 48), the practice of circumcision appears not to have been widespread in early Israel: Moses apparently is unaware that Yahweh requires circumcision, a lapse for which God threatens to kill him (Exod. 4:22–24). This puzzling episode may have served an etiological purpose, underscoring the need for all men in the covenant community to be circumcised. Another tradition, preserved in Joshua 5, offers a different account of Israelites' initiating the circumcision ritual. Before invading Canaan, Joshua orders his troops to submit to mass circumcision (Josh. 5:2–7), a rite with which they were apparently unfamiliar.

Abraham's Two Sons At age eighty-six, eleven years after he first receives Yahweh's promise to give him a son, Abraham finally has a child, **Ishmael**—not by his official wife, Sarah, but by **Hagar,** Sarah's Egyptian slave.

Another thirteen years pass, and Abraham is ninety-nine before Yahweh appears again, this time to dine with him under the oak trees of Mamre (near modern Hebron). When Sarah, long past the age of childbearing, overhears Yahweh's announcement that within a year she and Abraham will produce a son, she bursts out laughing—a response that gives their son **Isaac** his name (meaning, "he laughs") (18:1–12).

In the first of several biblical examples of men daring to debate God over the justice of his actions, Abraham questions Yahweh's intentions toward the "wicked" cities of Sodom and Gomorrah: "Shall not the Judge of all the earth do what is just?" Submitting to his covenant partner's persistent questioning, Yahweh finally declares that he will not destroy the cities if even ten righteous people can be found in them (18:16–35). In the end, Yahweh incinerates five cities located near the Dead Sea, but only after rescuing Abraham's nephew **Lot** and his two daughters.

The Binding of Isaac Most of God's appearances to Abraham involve divine blessings, but Yahweh's sudden demand that Abraham offer the teenage Isaac as a human sacrifice is a startling exception. Abraham's willingness to kill Isaac without pleading for the boy as he did for the people of Sodom and his silence in the face of this horrific command have long troubled Bible readers. With his knife poised to cut his son's throat, Abraham is stopped by the intervention of an angel, who directs him to spare Isaac and offer instead a ram caught in a nearby thornbush. Gratified by Abraham's total obedience, Yahweh reaffirms his covenant vows, repeating an earlier promise that his covenant partner will be a source of universal blessing (22:15–18).

The Genesis narrator interprets Yahweh's demand for human sacrifice as merely a test of Abraham's godly devotion. But the episode raises disturbing questions about both the nature of the biblical God and the character of Israelite religion. Although Israel's prophets vigorously denounce the practice of child sacrifice (cf. Jer. 19:5–6), some Torah statutes indicate that it was not unknown in the covenant community. According to Exodus, Yahweh commands his people: "The first-born of your sons you shall give [sacrifice] to me. You shall do the same with your oxen and with your sheep: seven days it shall remain with its mother; on the eighth day you shall give it to me" (Exod. 22:29b–30). A similar ordinance appears in Exodus 13:2: "Consecrate all the first-born to me; whatever is the first to open the womb among the Israelites, of human beings and animals, is mine." Another statute permits Israelites to "redeem" their sons by offering an animal substitute (Exod. 34:20), but—in a seldom-discussed passage—the prophet Ezekiel reveals that Yahweh did demand the sacrifice of male first-borns as recompense for Israel's collective disobedience:

> Moreover, I gave them statutes that were not good and ordinances by which they could not live. I defiled them through their very gifts, in their offering up all their firstborn in order that I might horrify them, so that they might know that I am the LORD.

(Ezek. 20:24-25)

In giving Israel commands "that were not good" and laws "by which they could not live," Yahweh intends to "horrify" his people, as if inviting them to question the ethical validity of religious demands, even when they purport to come from God. In the story of Isaac's near-sacrifice, Abraham is willing to give Yahweh what he asks for—the life of his son—but he also listens to a second—a higher—command to spare the boy and offer a ram in his place. Abraham thus proves decisively that he possesses the spiritual discernment to distinguish between good and evil (see also Micah 6:6 and Jud. 11:29–40).

The Story of Jacob and His Family

Isaac and Rebekah After devoting a dozen chapters to Abraham and Sarah, Genesis passes briefly over the career of Isaac, who emerges as an essentially passive figure. At his most memorable moments, Isaac is shown either as a hapless youth stretched out on a sacrificial altar (Ch. 22) or as an old man prone on his bed (Ch. 27), the victim of a deceitful conspiracy by his wife and younger son. A more decisive character, Isaac's wife **Rebekah** plays a major role in shaping Israel's destiny. Privately informed that Yahweh prefers her younger son **Jacob** (who is also her personal favorite) to his older twin **Esau** (the firstborn), she not only initiates the plot to deceive Isaac into blessing Jacob rather than Esau but also arranges for Jacob to escape his brother's vengeance by sending him from Canaan to live with her relatives in Mesopotamia.

Jacob A spiritual cousin of the quick-witted Greek hero Odysseus (Ulysses), Jacob is sometimes regarded as primarily a trickster. His function in the Genesis narrative, however, is far more complex than that dismissive label implies. Jacob's strengths and weaknesses, and his dynamic relationship to God, are presented as a paradigm for the character of Israel, the nation named after him (see below). In the totality of his story, which extends from prenatal struggles with Esau in Rebekah's womb (25:21–28) to deathbed evaluations of his twelve sons more than a century later (Ch. 49), Jacob undergoes a variety of powerful, life-changing experiences. As a young man, he shrewdly exploits his older brother's demand for instant gratification, persuading Esau to sell him his birthright for a pot of stew (25:29–31). He then completes the theft of Esau's inheritance, his legal right as firstborn, by taking over his brother's identity, lying to his nearly blind father, and deceiving Isaac into conferring the paternal blessing on him (Ch. 27).

After Rebekah learns that Esau plans to kill his usurping brother and sends Jacob fleeing northward to Mesopotamia, Yahweh begins a series of encounters with the fugitive that culminates in his bestowing a significant new identity upon Jacob. God first appears to him at an ancient sanctuary, where Jacob stops overnight on his way to Haran. Sleeping outdoors with a stone for his pillow, he dreams of a "ladder," a ramp reaching from earth to heaven on which angels ascend and descend (as Mesopotamian deities invisibly tread the ceremonial stairway of a Babylonian ziggurat). Yahweh also appears in the dream and restates the familiar Abrahamic promises, adding a vow to accompany Jacob on his journey. Although impressed by this night vision, Jacob hesitates to commit himself to Yahweh on the basis of a mere dream. After renaming the site **Bethel** (meaning "house of El"), Jacob boldly adds his own terms to the covenant promises Yahweh has just enunciated: "*If* God will be with me and will keep me [safe] . . . and will give me bread to eat and clothing to wear, . . . so that I come again to my father's house in peace, *then* the LORD [Yahweh] shall be my God . . ." Casting his covenant stipulations in the same "if . . . then" formula typical of the later Mosaic Law, Jacob informs the Deity that allegiance to him will depend on how effectively divine promises are translated into the realities of food and security (28:18–22).

The Theophany at Peniel (Penuel)

Despite conflict with his uncle Laban, whose daughters **Leah** and **Rachel** he marries, Jacob's twenty-year sojourn in Mesopotamia is productive in almost every sense. Not only does he acquire great wealth in the form of sheep, goats, and cattle, he also fathers eleven sons (some by his wives' maids) and a daughter, **Dinah.** (A twelfth son, Benjamin, is later born to Rachel.) Traveling back to Canaan to meet his estranged brother, Jacob has a second nocturnal revelation, this time at Peniel by the river Jabbok, a tributary of the Jordan. Alone in the dark and terrified of the next day's reunion with Esau, whose vengeance he has good reason to fear, Jacob suddenly finds himself attacked by an unknown "man." Wrestling all night, the two opponents are so evenly matched that neither can defeat the other. Only in the predawn light does Jacob recognize his mysterious assailant's identity, suddenly realizing that "I have seen God face to face" (32:30). Although a variant account of Jacob's encounter refers to his opponent as an "angel" (Hos. 12:4), one of the traditions incorporated into this passage implies that Jacob's adversary is God himself. If so, the Deity apparently assumes human form (and therefore limited human strength) for this physical struggle with Jacob. When Jacob refuses to release him, the divine attacker bestows both blessing and a name change—henceforth Jacob is Israel, the one who has "striven with God and with humans, and [has] prevailed." Instead of being Jacob (meaning "supplanter" [cf. Gen. 25:26; 27:36]), the trickster who stole Esau's legal rights, he is now Israel, signaling a new identity as one who effectively struggles with both God and mortals—and survives. Although modern scholars think that *Israel* probably means "God [El] rules," the Genesis writer's interpretation is highly appropriate to the biblical portrayal of Israel as a nation locked in a complex (and sometimes adversarial) relationship with God. To commemorate his encounter, Jacob renames the site Peniel (Penuel), which means the "Face of El [God]" (32:22–32).

After his reconciliation with Esau, Jacob makes another pilgrimage to Bethel, where God again appears, this time identifying himself as El Shaddai and renewing his covenant vow, adding that Jacob's descendants will include kings (35:1–14). In this second version of Jacob's name-change to Israel, Jacob again sets up a stone pillar, again anoints it with oil, and again changes the site's name from Luz to Bethel (Ch. 35; cf. Ch. 32). Although in Chapter 37 the narrative shifts from Jacob's adventures to concentrate on the conflict among his sons, Jacob once more takes center stage near the end of Genesis, when the dying patriarch offers an extensive catalogue of "blessings" (including some severe condemnations) for each of his twelve male offspring (Ch. 49). After his death, he is buried near Abraham's grave in Canaan.

The Story of Joseph and His Brothers

Although the final section of Genesis (Chs. 37–50) focuses on the story of **Joseph,** the book's editors title it "the story of the family of Jacob" (37:2). This editorial emphasis on Jacob/Israel's family as a group highlights the narrative's larger purpose—the transition from God's relationship with individual ancestors, such as Abraham and Jacob, to Yahweh's evolving partnership with a whole people. As the nucleus of a future nation, Jacob's twelve sons, with their wives and children, now form a corporate body, a development shown in Chapter 49, where Jacob describes each of his sons as distinctive tribal entities. "All these [Jacob's sons]," the narrator points out "are the twelve tribes of Israel" (49:28). This passage prepares readers for the emergence of Israelite nationhood described in the next book of the Torah, Exodus.

Whereas the tales of Abraham, Isaac, and Jacob are highly episodic—consisting of loosely connected narrative units bound together only by the theme of repeated divine promises—the Joseph story forms a coherent literary whole. (Only Chapter 38 interrupts the action with the interpolated story of Tamar posing as a prostitute to claim her legal right to a child from Jacob's son **Judah**). Often called a short story or novella, the self-contained Joseph section has a unified plot recounting Joseph's rise from kidnap victim, slave, and prisoner to a powerful position at the Egyptian royal court. Although Joseph's success story occupies the narrative foreground, God operates invisibly behind the scenes, using Joseph as his instrument who will eventually reconcile Jacob's quarreling sons, forging them into a united people. In this section, God appears only once, and not to Joseph but to Jacob, in a "night vision" (46:2–4; cf. 48:3–4). Instead of direct theophanies, Joseph receives only dreams—and a divinely granted ability to interpret them.

As a longer and more structured narrative than those found earlier in Genesis, the Joseph saga resembles other short stories found in the Hebrew Bible, such as Ruth and Esther. Like the major characters in Esther and the title hero of Daniel, Joseph is an essentially solitary member of the covenant community living in a foreign land, where he succeeds spectacularly because, as the narrator points out, "God is with him."

In the opening scenes of conflict between brothers, reminiscent of that between Cain and Abel or Jacob and Esau, Joseph is introduced as Jacob's favorite son. Decked out in his father's gift of an elaborate garment, he alienates his siblings by telling them two dreams, in both of which his entire family bows down to him. His jealous brothers then conspire to sell Joseph into slavery, after which he is taken to Egypt, where he works for Potiphar, an important official at Pharaoh's court. At this point, biblical tradition apparently draws on an ancient Egyptian tale about a virtuous young man who resists the attempts of his brother's wife to seduce him and who, after many misadventures, subsequently rises to become Egypt's crown prince (see James Pritchard's "The Tale of Two Brothers" in the "Recommended Reading"). Although he rejects the sexual advances of Potiphar's wife,

Joseph—like the hero of the Egyptian legend—is falsely accused of betraying his master and thrown into prison.

When Joseph's skill in making sense of dreams brings him to Pharaoh's attention, the lad correctly interprets the Egyptian ruler's dreams about seven starving cows eating seven fat cows as predicting seven future years of abundant harvests followed by seven years of crop failure and famine. Emphasizing that this foreknowledge is possible only because God chooses to reveal his intentions, Joseph is appointed Pharaoh's chief administrator. During the years of prosperity, Joseph governs Egypt shrewdly, filling its warehouses with surplus grain. When famine strikes, he controls the nation's food supply, exchanging grain and seed for the people's money, livestock, and land, all of which then become Pharaoh's property. By famine's end, the Egyptian population—excepting the priestly class, which retains its economic independence—has been reduced to mere "slaves," landless peasants toiling for Pharaoh, who is now Egypt's sole landowner (Chs. 41, 47).

Because famine conditions extend northward to Canaan, Jacob's ten oldest sons are forced to travel to Egypt to seek grain. (Jacob's twelfth son, Benjamin, stays home with his father.) After their arrival in Egypt, Joseph's brothers fall under his power, fulfilling Joseph's adolescent dreams of being exalted above his older siblings (Chs. 42–45; cf. 37:2–11). Only after putting his brothers, now needy and dependent, through prolonged anxiety and humiliation does Joseph—with impressive self-dramatization—reveal his identity, graciously forgiving their earlier treachery. Although the Joseph story reaches its climax in the brothers' recognition of Joseph's high status and their total dependence on his mercy, the story's final goal is not realized until Jacob is also brought into Egypt and the entire family, now reconciled and reunited, is welcomed as Pharaoh's honored foreign guests (Ch. 50).

In a final speech, Joseph tells his brothers that, although they "intended to do harm," God "intended it for good" (50:20), seizing on the brothers' jealousy and its consequences (Joseph's abduction to Egypt) as a means to benefit both Israelites and Egyptians. By Genesis's conclusion, Yahweh's vow to bless all earth's families through Abraham's descendants (12:1–3) is already being fulfilled. Joseph's deathbed request that his bones eventually be taken for reburial in Canaan also points toward future fulfillment of the divine plan, indicating that Israel's stay in Egypt will be only an extended detour in the long pilgrimage toward the Promised Land (50:24–26; cf. Exod. 13:19).

QUESTIONS FOR DISCUSSION AND REVIEW

1. Describe the differences between the two different creation accounts (Gen. 1:1–2:4a and 2:4b–2:25). How do you explain the significance of the fact that the first account calls God *Elohim,* whereas in the second he is called *Yahweh Elohim* (LORD God)?

2. Why does Yahweh decide to destroy all living things in a flood, and what resources does he draw on to do it? Why does God spare Noah and his family? Define the post-Flood covenant with Noah.

3. List the divine promises included in the covenant with Abraham and his descendants. What parts of this pact are fulfilled in Genesis, and which remain to be implemented?

4. Why does God ask Abraham to sacrifice his son Isaac? Why does Abraham obey the command for human sacrifice? How do you explain the ethical issues in this narrative (Gen. 22)?

5. Paint a verbal portrait of Jacob. Why do readers commonly label him a trickster? How does God relate to Jacob in unusual ways, including sending him dreams and wrestling with him during a night visitation? How does he become the ancestor of the twelve tribes of Israel?

6. Summarize the story of Joseph and his brothers. In what ways does Joseph's personal biography relate to the divine will in bringing Jacob's family to Egypt? Why does the author emphasize Joseph's importance to Egypt's ruler?

7. What parallels to Mesopotamian tradition do you find in Genesis? How do the Genesis authors transform ancient myths, particularly those of creation and the Flood, to exalt the God of Israel? Do you see the Genesis narratives as trying to give scientific explanations for the universe or to show that Yahweh Elohim is superior to all other creator/destroyer gods?

Terms and Concepts to Remember

Abraham/Abrahamic Covenant	Dinah
Adam	eponymous
Bethel	etiology
Cain and Abel	Esau
chaos/cosmos	Eve
cherubim	Flood
circumcision	Hagar
	Ham, Shem, Japheth

Haran   Leah
Isaac   Noah
Ishmael   Rachel
Jacob   Rebekah
Joseph   Sabbath
Judah   theophany

Recommended Reading

Alter, Robert. *Genesis: Translation and Commentary.* New York: W. W. Norton & Co., 1997. A fresh translation with literary interpretation.

Fretheim, Terence E. "The Book of Genesis." In *The New Interpreter's Bible,* Vol. 1, pp. 321–674. Nashville, TN: Abingdon Press, 1994. Offers extensive scholarly commentary on the Genesis text.

Jeansonne, Sharon P. *The Women of Genesis: From Sarah to Potiphar's Wife.* Minneapolis: Fortress Press, 1990. Examines Genesis narratives from a feminist perspective.

Levenson, Jon D. *Creation and the Persistence of Evil: The Jewish Drama of Divine Omnipotence.* San Francisco: Harper & Row, 1988. An important examination of biblical themes and their ethical/theological implications.

———. *The Death and Resurrection of the Beloved Son: The Transformation of Child Sacrifice in Judaism and Christianity.* New Haven, CT: Yale University Press, 1993. A candid examination of the theological concept of human sacrifice in the Tanakh and the New Testament.

O'Connor, Kathleen M. "Genesis, Book of." In K. D. Sakenfeld, ed., *The New Interpreter's Dictionary of the Bible,* Vol. 2, pp. 539–555. Nashville, TN: Abingdon Press, 2007. An excellent survey of the book's narrative flow and theological significance.

Pritchard, James B., ed. *Ancient Near Eastern Texts Relating to the Old Testament,* 3rd ed., Princeton, NJ: Princeton UP, 1969. Contains "The Story of Two Brothers," which an Israelite author adapted for the Joseph story in Genesis.

Scullion, John J. "Genesis, The Narrative of." In D. N. Freedman, ed., *The Anchor Bible Dictionary,* Vol. 2, pp. 941–962. New York: Doubleday, 1992.

CHAPTER 6

Freedom and Responsibility
The Book of Exodus

Key Topics/Themes In Exodus, God's promises to Abraham for numerous descendants, the divine presence, and a special relationship begin to be fulfilled. The families of Jacob and his twelve sons—numbering only seventy members—who had settled in Egypt at the conclusion of Genesis have, after many generations, become a populous community and a perceived threat to Egypt's ruler. After a long silence, Yahweh at last "remembers" his vow to Abraham and commissions Moses to lead the Israelites from Egyptian oppression to freedom as the "people of God." Divided into two main sections, the deliverance from Egypt and journey to Sinai/Horeb (Chs. 1–18), and the revelation of God's teaching at Sinai (Chs. 19–40), Exodus balances the initial theme of liberation from human tyranny with its later emphasis on Israel's ethical and legal responsibilities to its divine liberator. In the *torah* (instruction) that he communicates through Moses at Sinai, Yahweh introduces an entirely new dimension into his relationship with Abraham's progeny: Israel must obey a vast body of legal and ritual regulations if it is to benefit from God's patronage, its strict obedience a condition of divine favor. Major highlights include the story of Moses (Chs. 2–6); Yahweh's war against Pharaoh and the institution of the Passover (Chs. 7–13); the miraculous sea crossing and desert journey to Sinai/Horeb (Chs. 14–18); the Sinai theophany, golden calf episode, and ratification of the Mosaic Covenant (Chs. 19–24, 32–34); and instructions for the Tabernacle cult (Chs. 25–31, 35–40).

With the possible exception of Deuteronomy, Exodus expresses the core of Israelite faith more than any other book in the Hebrew Bible. In this dramatic account of Israel's escape from Egyptian bondage and sudden emergence as a society ruled directly by God—a **theocracy**—Exodus explicitly defines the nature of Yahweh's relationship to his chosen people. The narrative traces the Israelites' journey from the rigidly structured nation of Egypt, where Pharaoh reigns as a god-king, to an uninhabited desert, where Yahweh reveals that he alone is Israel's ruler. Descending to the summit of Mount Sinai/Horeb like a lightning bolt from heaven, Yahweh discloses to an awestruck people that he has rescued them from Pharaoh's control and given them freedom for one purpose: to worship and obey him. Unlike the Abrahamic Covenant, which makes few specific demands on the human partner, the pact that Yahweh concludes with Israel at Sinai

is bilateral—the people must swear to observe a large body of law or he will reject them. Whereas the benefits promised to Abraham's descendants are *unconditional*, God's pact with Israel is explicitly *conditional* on the people's unwavering obedience.

Although the Mosaic *torah* regulates a variety of Israel's activities—including formal worship, sacrifice, civil order, some property rights, and human slavery—it does not govern every aspect of life in the covenant community (there are laws regulating divorce, for example, but none covering marriage). Despite its omissions, the *torah* serves effectively to define the ethical and religious bonds linking Israel to its divine protector. Because observance of *mitzvoth* (Hebrew, "divine commandments") is designed to permeate and shape many aspects of the Israelites' daily existence, it functions as a constant reminder of their obligations to Yahweh.

◇ Israel in Egypt

While in Egypt, the Israelites become so numerous "that the land was filled with them" (Exod. 1:7), creating a population boom of foreign immigrants that alarms Egyptian authorities and results in the Israelites' enslavement. The blessings of fertility, so prominent in Genesis's alternating tales of barrenness and childbearing, unexpectedly bring Israel into conflict with a new Egyptian ruling family, a pharaoh "who did not know Joseph [and his contribution to Egyptian well-being]" (1:8). Although the narrative states that Israel's sojourn in Egypt lasted 430 years (12:40), other passages imply that it was much shorter (only four generations according to 5:16–20), a time span that many historians regard as more likely.

To date, historians and archaeologists have not been able to verify any of the events described in Exodus. No known Egyptian records refer to the plagues that allegedly devastated Egypt, the flight of Hebrew slaves, or the drowning of an Egyptian army. Nor do Egypt's many surviving archives mention the biblical Moses (who bears an Egyptian name) or the contest between his God, Yahweh, and Pharaoh, who was believed to embody Horus, a form of the sun god. The earliest Egyptian reference to Israel, Pharaoh Merneptah's victory monument, dates from the late thirteenth century BCE, when the Israelites were described as a people already living in Canaan (see Chapter 3).

The fact that Exodus identifies neither the pharaoh who oppressed Israel nor the one whom Moses confronted creates a problem in dating the events it relates. Although the total lack of references to specific historical figures increases the difficulty in establishing a reliable historical context for the Exodus, many scholars believe that the most probable setting for the story was Egypt's Nineteenth Dynasty (c. 1306–1200 BCE). Many historians favor this period because the radical changes in Egyptian political leadership that had preceded the Eighteenth and Nineteenth Dynasties provide a credible background to events described in Exodus 1 (see Figure 6.1). This shift in Egypt's rulers helps to explain the government's changed attitude toward the Hebrews (a term biblical writers commonly use for Israelites before their establishment in Canaan). For most of its long history, Egypt was ruled by native kings, but between about 1750 and 1550 BCE, the succession of Egyptian pharaohs was interrupted when non-Egyptian rulers dominated northern Egypt. Known as the **Hyksos** (an Egyptian term for "foreign princes"), this Semitic group is thought to have infiltrated Egypt from Syria and/or Canaan, roughly the

FIGURE 6.1 This Egyptian tomb painting depicts slaves making bricks for the building enterprises of an Eighteenth Dynasty pharaoh. Although the work pictured is almost identical to that ascribed to Hebrew slaves in the Book of Exodus, archaeologists—despite Egypt's wealth of extant inscriptions, archival records, and other artifacts—have been unable to find any physical evidence corroborating the Hebrews' presence there.

same region in which the Israelite ancestors had lived. It was probably a Hyksos pharaoh who, sharing many of the same social customs as the Hebrews, welcomed Joseph and his family to Egypt. Resentful of these foreign rulers, however, native Egyptian leaders drove the Hyksos out of Egypt in about 1550 BCE, reestablishing Egyptian control of the state and (perhaps) adopting a hostile policy toward remaining immigrants from Canaan. If this theoretical reconstruction of events is correct, the pharaoh who enslaved the Israelites was probably Seti (Sesthos) I (ruled c. 1305–1290 BCE) and Moses' royal antagonist was most likely **Rameses II** (ruled c. 1290–1224 BCE).

Yahweh and Moses

Yahweh's Preeminent Servant   No figure looms larger in Israel's story than Moses, the man whom tradition credits with founding the Yahwist faith. Moses' agency both in forming the Israelite nation and in transmitting Yahweh's laws to the covenant people is regarded as so crucial that later writers who contributed to the different oral and literary traditions embedded in the present text of Exodus describe him in a dazzling variety of roles—lawgiver, prophet, judge, and even military leader. Described as initially reluctant to take on the tasks that Yahweh assigns him (Exod. 4:10–17), Moses becomes not only God's chief instrument in creating Israel but also God's intimate confidant, speaking with Yahweh "face to face, as one speaks to a friend" (Exod. 33:11; cf. Deut. 34:10–11). Whereas Yahweh may commune indirectly with others by vision or dream, with Moses he speaks "plainly and not in riddles," even permitting him to see "the form of the Lord" (Num. 12:8). So prestigious is Moses' reputation as a legislator that all of Israel's laws, even those that clearly date from much later periods, are assigned Mosaic origins and thus given his unimpeachable authority. As Yahweh himself describes Moses' role, this exceedingly meek man (Num. 12:3) with a serious speech impediment (Exod. 4:10–11) acts "as a god for Pharaoh" (Exod. 7:1), a human vehicle for conveying divine power.

"Never again," states Deuteronomy, "has there arisen such a prophet in Israel like Moses, whom the Lord knew face to face" (34:10). While affirming Moses' unparalleled contribution to forging Israel's bond with Yahweh, however, biblical writers are careful to subordinate him to the God he serves. Rather than a hero in his own right, such as Gilgamesh, Moses is always Yahweh's obedient spokesman. Yet, for all his loyal service, Moses is not allowed to enter the Promised Land. Although his fatal error is not specified, some commentators assume that it is Moses' failure to give Yahweh full credit when he causes water to gush from a rock (Num. 20:10). Considering Moses' self-sacrificing commitment to Yahweh and his people—including his refusal to accept God's offer to make the family of Moses, and not Israel, his chosen nation (Num. 14:12)—Yahweh's verdict may seem unduly harsh. For the Torah writers, however, Moses is both a model of humble service *and* a demonstration that even the greatest of human beings cannot measure up to Yahweh's standard of perfect righteousness.

Moses' Infancy and Flight from Egypt to Midian

Scholars recognize that the account of Moses' infancy—particularly his rescue from a near-death experience—contains legendary material. In Near Eastern lore, the closest parallel to the baby Moses' exposure on the Nile is the Akkadian tale about the infant Sargon I, who, like the endangered Hebrew child, is cast adrift on a great river. After Sargon's mother places him in a pitch-sealed basket to float down the Euphrates River, he is rescued not by a princess but by an ordinary gardener, who subsequently raises the boy as his own. From such humble origins, Sargon rises to become ruler of the first Mesopotamian empire (see Chapter 3). This story of an infant who narrowly escapes death and later becomes a national hero—a common motif in world myth—is a variation on another biblical theme, that of the "barren wife" who, after many childless years, finally bears a son

chosen to lead Israel. Among these late-born but crucially important male children are Isaac, Jacob, Joseph, Samson, Samuel, and John the Baptist.

As a man of forty, Moses experiences the first of two radical changes in his life, one that foreshadows a recurring theme in the Torah narrative—his fellow Israelites' failure to value Moses' leadership. Having killed an Egyptian he found beating a Hebrew, Moses is forced to flee his native country when another Hebrew threateningly alludes to the crime. Instead of gratitude for Moses' championing the Hebrew cause against Egyptian oppression, the Hebrew displays only hostility to Moses.

After leaving Egypt, Moses settles in **Midian,** a desert region south of **Edom,** a country bordering the future state of Israel. Living as a shepherd, Moses marries the daughter of a local priest, named **Jethro** in one tradition incorporated into Exodus and **Ruel** in another. While tending sheep on the "mountain of God" in Midianite territory, Moses experiences the second great transition in his life course.

Two Revelations of the Divine Name

Although they derive from formerly separate traditions, Exodus's two accounts of the revelation of the divine name (see Chapter 1) have similar purposes: to demonstrate that El, Elohim, or El Shaddai—forms of the Deity that the Genesis ancestors worshiped—is really the same God as Yahweh, the divinity who now speaks to Moses from a burning bush. Contrary to the Genesis tradition that people invoked Yahweh's name even before the Flood (Gen. 4:26), the two different Exodus accounts insist that the divine name, Yahweh, was not known until God revealed it to Moses (Exod. 3:13–15; 6:2–4). Both of these narratives emphasize that El, head of the Canaanite pantheon, and Yahweh, Israel's divine patron, are one and the same.

The First Theophany The first disclosure of God's personal name occurs at the flaming bush on "the mountain of God," called Sinai in the Yahwist tradition and Horeb in Elohist passages and throughout the Book of Deuteronomy. Speaking from the midst of fire—the transforming element that symbolizes divinity—a voice informs Moses that he is the "God [Elohim]" of Abraham, Isaac, and Jacob who is about to redeem his people from Egyptian bondage (Exod. 3:7–8). For the sake of his "name," Yahweh will intervene on the stage of international politics, causing the "nations" to speak of his saving actions (3:1–16; cf. 32:11–14; Num. 14:19–21). (For a discussion of the significance of Yahweh's name, see Chapter 1.)

The Second Theophany In Exodus 6, Yahweh appears a second time to Moses, again insisting that the personal name he reveals was unknown to Moses' ancestors. In the priestly version of God's self-disclosure, Yahweh states:

> I am Yahweh. To Abraham and Isaac and Jacob I appeared as El Shaddai. I did not make myself known to them by my name Yahweh . . .
>
> (Exod. 1:1–8, Jerusalem Bible)

In both revelations of the sacred name (Exod. 3 and 6), the narrators associate Yahweh with a specific geographical locale—the "mountain of God" near Midian. (Passages in Deuteronomy, the Book of Judges and the prophet Habakkuk also link Yahweh to this region; see Deut. 33:2; Judg.4:4–5; and Hab. 3:3–7.) Although some traditions seem to limit Yahweh's geographical origins, the God will soon demonstrate his power over a broad area of the Near East: from Egypt, where he will humble Pharaoh, to Palestine, where he will inspire Israelite warriors to drive out the native inhabitants.

Yahweh's War Against Pharaoh

The Ten Plagues The Hebrews in Egypt at first openly doubt Moses' authority to lead them, a response that anticipates their future complaints and rebellions in the wilderness. Pharaoh also refuses to recognize the authority of Moses or his God, claiming that he knows nothing of Yahweh. But, as God had already informed Moses, Yahweh is prepared to deal with Pharaoh's stubbornness, inflicting a series of plagues calculated to break Egyptian resistance to his will. Beginning with a bloody pollution of the Nile and other Egyptian waters, the plagues gradually increase in severity. Swarms of frogs, then mosquitoes, and then gadflies afflict the Egyptians, demonstrating Yahweh's control of nature. Pharaoh begs Moses to end the plagues, promising to free Israel, but he then treacherously goes back on his word after the pests disappear.

The narrative attributes Pharaoh's stubbornness to Yahweh, who resolves to "harden" Pharaoh's heart, even before the ruler has an opportunity to make up his own mind (Exod. 4:21–23; cf. 7:3; 10:1, 20, 27; 14:8; a few other passages state that Pharaoh hardened his own heart). God's apparent interference with Pharaoh's free will may distress modern readers, but in the Exodus tradition, resistance was necessary to Yahweh's purpose. Pharaoh *had* to be uncooperative in order for Yahweh's power to be revealed (9:15–16; 10:1–2). If

Egypt had meekly submitted to Moses' request, there would have been no awesome plagues, no "signs and wonders" demonstrating the supremacy of Israel's God. In biblical portrayals, God is characteristically shown as focused on his public reputation, maneuvering people and events to maximize international recognition of his power—to "make [his] name resound through all the earth" (9:16).

When Pharaoh refuses to honor the God of his slaves, Yahweh intensifies the plagues' deadliness. From diseases of livestock, to devastating storms, to invasions of locusts, Egypt staggers beneath Yahweh's wrath. In the ninth plague, darkness shrouds the entire nation except where the Hebrews live, a frightening return to the primal darkness that engulfed the earth before God caused light to exist. A study of sources, combined in Exodus, shows that whereas the Yahwist cites only eight plagues, the priestly strand added two others—the infestation of gnats (8:16–19) and the affliction of boils on humans and animals (9:8–12)—making up the familiar ten. Another tradition, preserved in Psalm 105, reports only seven plagues and lists them in a different order, placing the plague of darkness first (Ps. 105:26–38; cf. Ps. 78:43–51).

Death of the Firstborn In visiting his final plague on the Egyptians, Yahweh employs a supernatural agent, the Angel of Death, which apparently represents a lethal aspect of the Deity. According to Exodus 12:39, Yahweh himself carries out the death sentences on all of Egypt's firstborn males, "from the firstborn of Pharaoh who sat on his throne to the firstborn of the prisoner who was in the dungeon." Today's readers may object to a notion of divine executions of innocent persons, such as the children of Pharaoh's prisoners, who had nothing to do with their ruler's policies. But the Exodus narrator is primarily concerned with the *thoroughness* of Yahweh's actions, which include all classes of Egyptian society. No one, guilty or innocent, is allowed to escape the divine judgment on the group to which he belongs.

The Passover To make sure that the Angel of Death distinguishes between Egyptian and Israelite households and spares the latter, the Israelites are told to sacrifice a goat or lamb and to smear its blood on their doorposts, prompting the divine executioner to "pass over" their dwellings. According to the priestly account in Exodus 12, the feast of **Passover** was initiated during the Hebrews' last night in Egypt when, shadowed by the dread angel's wings, they gathered safely inside their blood-marked houses to eat unleavened bread, bitter herbs, and the sacrificed lamb. In this section, the eating of unleavened bread is explained in terms of the haste with which the Israelites had to flee—they had no time to allow yeast to leaven the bread. A major annual observance in both ancient Israel and contemporary Judaism, the Passover ceremony is described in several Torah passages (Lev. 23:5–8; Num. 28:16–25). Whereas Exodus depicts Passover as a private family meal, with neither altar nor officiating priest, Deuteronomy transforms it into a public national festival. According to Deuteronomistic law, all Israelites must leave their homes and travel to Jerusalem to observe Passover (Deut. 16:1–8), an ordinance reflecting King Josiah's late-seventh-century BCE centralization of Yahweh's worship at the royal capital (2 Kings 23).

 ## The Escape from Egypt

For the ultimate demonstration of Yahweh's might, Pharaoh is prompted to lead his army in pursuit of the Israelites. Trapped between Egyptian charioteers and an impassable sea, the Israelites seem doomed to a humiliating return to slavery. At this crucial moment, however, Yahweh intervenes to deliver his people in an act that forever after would be remembered as the pivotal event in the story of Israel's salvation. The two chief sources of the present text, the Yahwist and the priestly, agree on the miraculous character of Israel's deliverance but present distinctly different versions of what happened. According to J's tradition, the Israelites remained quietly on the shore while Yahweh employed a strong east wind that blew "all night," driving back the sea and leaving its bed dry. In the morning, after the wind presumably has died down and the waters have flowed back to their normal depth, Yahweh causes the Egyptian troops to panic and dash headlong into the sea; in effect, "the LORD tossed the Egyptians into the sea" (Exod. 14:13–14, 24, 25b, 27). In J's account, only the Egyptians enter the sea; the Israelites merely "keep still" and watch their former oppressors drown. J's story roughly approximates the version preserved in the "Song of the Sea," an ancient poem that praises Yahweh as triumphant warrior: "Horse and rider he has thrown into the sea . . . Pharaoh's chariots and his army, he cast into the sea" (15:1, 4).

The priestly additions to J's narrative greatly intensify the miraculous element. Here, when Moses stretches out his hand, the sea literally parts, enabling the Israelites to walk across the seafloor between two standing walls of water. When Moses raises his hand a second time, the walls of water collapse: "The waters returned and covered the chariots and the chariot drivers, the entire army of Pharaoh that had followed them into the sea" (Exod. 14:15–18, 21–23, 28).

A fragment from another tradition suggests a more mundane turn of events, stating that Yahweh "clogged [the Egyptians'] chariot wheels so that they turned with difficulty." When the Egyptians realize that Israel's God is successfully opposing them, they lose courage and give up the pursuit (14:25). Although all traditions evoke a spectacularly well-timed rescue from Egyptian pursuers, the composite accounts' many discrepancies are almost impossible to reconcile.

In Hebrew, the location of Israel's dramatic sea rescue is called *yam suf,* which the Septuagint edition translates as the "Red Sea," a custom followed by the Vulgate and most English editions of the Hebrew Bible. With few sites mentioned in the Exodus narratives positively identified, neither the route the Israelites took from Egypt nor the body of water they encountered is known. Because *suf* commonly means "reed," as it does in the story of the infant Moses being discovered among the reeds of the Nile (Exod. 2:3–5), the Jerusalem Bible renders the phrase as "Reed Sea" or "Sea of Reeds," indicating that the body of water may have been a large marsh or lake, perhaps the swampy region north of the Gulf of Suez. Other suggestions for the geographical location of the *yam suf* include Lake Sirbonis (Lake Bardawil) or a southern extension of the present Lake Menzaleh. In the absence of any archaeological evidence identifying the Israelites' itinerary from Egypt to the Sinai wilderness, scholars have suggested several possible routes. One plausible reconstruction of Israel's path across the Sinai Peninsula appears in Figure 6.2. An alternate route, favored by some early Jewish and Arabic traditions, places the "mountain of God," the goal of the Israelites' exodus from Egypt, near Edom or Midian, desert regions southeast of Canaan.

A brief statement ending the *yam suf* account emphasizes its theological meaning. After they witness the drowning of Pharaoh's army, the Israelites—for the first time—unanimously acknowledge both Yahweh's saving power and the importance of Moses: "Israel saw the great work that the LORD [Yahweh] did against the Egyptians. So the people feared the LORD and believed in the LORD and in his servant Moses" (14:31). Whatever the historical facts underlying the *yam suf* tradition, biblical writers consistently used it for the dual purpose of testifying to Yahweh's redemptive acts and to the origin of Israel's faith.

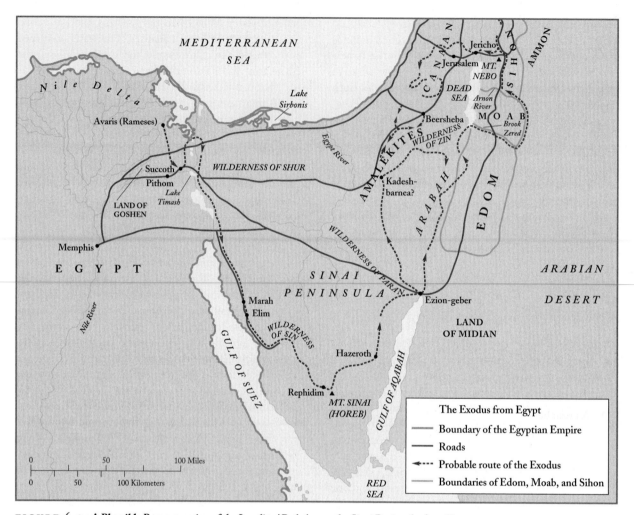

FIGURE 6.2 A Plausible Reconstruction of the Israelites' Path Across the Sinai Peninsula, from Egypt to the Promised Land. Although this map places Sinai/Horeb on the southern Sinai Peninsula, many historians believe that the sacred mountain was located in Midian, home of the priest Jethro, Moses' father-in-law.

 ## The Theophany at Sinai/Horeb

In Exodus 19, the long narrative that began with the call of Abraham (Gen. 12) reaches its culmination. As Abraham's descendants, now said to number 600,000 men, plus women and children (Exod. 12:37), assemble at the foot of Mount Sinai/Horeb, the Pentateuch's literary character undergoes a marked change. Instead of narrative, which makes up most of Genesis 1 through Exodus 19, the Torah henceforth consists primarily of Yahweh's laying down the terms of the covenant between him and Israel. A few narrative passages appear amid the legal material, particularly Exodus 24 and 32–34. But the Pentateuch's entire central section—Exodus

20:1 to Numbers 10—is devoted to the enumeration of Yahweh's detailed requirements for his people, who are to be a "priestly kingdom and a holy nation" (Exod. 19:6; see Box 6.1). The people remain camped at the "mountain of God" for more than a year while Yahweh's teaching (*torah*, with a small "t") is transmitted in discrete stages through Moses.

The Ten Commandments

God's instructions for Israel, the observance of which will identify the nation as truly his people, begin with the famous **Ten Commandments.** Also called the **Decalogue** (literally, "ten words"), this part of the Torah has the distinction of being the only legal passage in the Hebrew

---

BOX 6.1 The Mosaic Covenant

The central expression of Yahweh's partnership with Israel, the Mosaic Covenant, consists of two unequal parts: (1) a long list of God's ethical, legal, and ritual requirements and (2) a brief statement in which Israel agrees to obey those requirements. The first part includes the more than 600 laws and statutes contained in the books of Exodus, Leviticus, Numbers, and Deuteronomy. The people's formal response to keep God's commands—most of which they have not yet heard—is summarized in one brief passage (Exod. 24:3–8).

A study of ancient Near Eastern political documents leads scholars to believe that the Mosaic Covenant is modeled, at least in part, on formal treaties or alliances concluded between a major power and a lesser state. Known as the *suzerain treaty*, this form of agreement called for the suzerain—or great king—to aid or protect a less powerful vassal, who in turn pledged an oath of loyalty to his overlord. In the treaty concluded at Mount Sinai/Horeb, the sovereign Yahweh dictates the terms of the agreement, to which the inferior party, Israel, must agree. Assyrian and Hittite treaties from the first millennium BCE typically included the following provisions:

1. A preamble
2. An account of historical circumstances leading to the treaty
3. Stipulations and requirements
4. Arrangements for public reading of the text and for its safekeeping in a god's shrine
5. A list of divine witnesses to the treaty
6. A vivid list of blessings for abiding by its terms and of curses for violating them

All of these treaty provisions are found in the Torah, although they appear in widely scattered fragments throughout the biblical text.

After Yahweh arrives at Sinai/Horeb to initiate his treaty with Israel, he speaks directly to the people, reducing the traditional preamble and historical summary to a brief statement identifying himself as the divine suzerain and giving the reason for his vassal's submission to him: "I am the LORD [Yahweh] your God, who brought you out of the land of Egypt, out of the house of slavery" (Exod. 20:1–2). In fact, Yahweh's terse statement summarizes the entire Exodus narrative up to that point, with the Torah story of Israel's deliverance from Egyptian bondage functioning as an elaborate preamble to the Sinai treaty making.

Only one small part of Yahweh's covenant laws—the Ten Commandments and the Book of the Covenant (Exod. 20–22)—is given before Israel's ratification of the treaty takes place (Exod. 24). Moses then performs a binding ritual, slaughtering sacrificial animals and casting part of the blood on an altar representing Yahweh, thus sealing the treaty. After Moses reads from the Book of the Covenant and the people again vow to uphold all its requirements, he sprinkles the Israelites with the rest of the sacrificial blood, thereby confirming the people's commitment to their supreme Lord.

Although Moses calls on no divine witnesses to the covenant, the twelve stone pillars he sets up to represent the twelve tribes of Israel (Exod. 24:4) may have served that function. When Moses' successor, Joshua, conducts a similar covenant ritual, he erects a memorial stone that "has heard all the words of the LORD" spoken to the Israelites and will be a "witness" against them if they default (Josh. 24:27). In Deuteronomy, Moses calls on "heaven and earth" to testify against Israel if the people break their vows, invoking the whole cosmos as a sign of the seriousness of Israel's promise (Deut. 30:19). Observing the custom of recording and safeguarding Near Eastern treaties, both Moses and Joshua are shown preparing written documents that are then deposited in a shrine (Exod. 24:27; Josh. 24:25–26).

The blessings that will issue from keeping the covenant and the curses that will result from violating it are vividly described in Deuteronomy 28–30 (cf. Lev. 26). Yahweh's threat to trap covenant breakers in a harsh world in which the heavens are like "brass" and the earth is like "iron" (Deut. 28:23; Lev. 26:19) uses the same metallic imagery found in other Near Eastern treaty curses, including those appearing in a treaty that Esar-haddon, king of Assyria, concluded in 677 BCE.

Bible that Yahweh speaks directly to the people and that he himself writes down—on tablets of stone (Exod. 20:1; 24:12). Israel's first obligation is to worship Yahweh alone. The supreme command to "have no other gods before [Yahweh]" (20:3) does not deny that rival gods exist, only that Israel may not honor them. Although later biblical writers, such as the prophet scholars call Second Isaiah, categorically declared that only Israel's God truly existed (see Chapter 18), many other passages indicate that the early Israelite religion was not yet fully monotheistic, but henotheistic. **Henotheism**—allegiance to one god while conceding that others also exist—characterizes many biblical texts scattered throughout the canon. As Moses' song at the Sea of Reeds asks:

> Who is like you, O LORD [Yahweh], *among the gods?*
>
> (Exod. 15:11, emphasis added)

Israel's God is "incomparable" in his justice and saving power, but he is not the only deity in the universe. In Israel's eyes, he is simply far superior to the others: "For the LORD is a great God, and a great king above all gods" (Ps. 95:3); he is "exalted far above all gods" (Ps. 97:9). At meetings of the divine council, "the assembly of the holy ones," Yahweh reigns supreme over lesser deities:

> For who in the skies can be compared to the LORD [Yahweh]?
> Who among the heavenly beings is like the LORD,
> God feared in the council of the holy ones,
> great and awesome above all that are around him?
>
> (Ps. 89:5–7)

Israel is also to make no images of Yahweh. Attempts to liken God to "anything" that lives in the three-tier universe—"in heaven above, on the earth beneath, or in the waters under the earth [subterranean remnants of the primeval watery abyss]" are denounced as "idolatry" and expressly forbidden (Exod. 20:4–6). By refusing to associate God with any visible object or phenomenon, even by analogy, the command not only frees Israel's concept of God from any aspect of nature but also emphasizes his transcendence, his utter freedom from cosmic limits.

Nor is Yahweh's sacred name to be used unworthily, as in false oaths or for magical purposes. (In the ancient world, knowledge of a deity's "hidden" or self-defining name was thought to give persons who mastered it the ability to exert magical control.)

As the first Genesis creation account presents God's rest day—the **Sabbath**—as divinely instituted, so the Decalogue insists that Israel scrupulously observe the week's seventh day as a memorial, remembering that after completing his six-day creation, Elohim desisted from labor (Gen. 2:2–3). All levels of Israelite society, including women, children, and slaves, are routinely to be granted this respite from work (Exod. 20:8–10; cf. Deut. 5:12–15, which gives a different justification for the Sabbath).

The tenth commandment, not to "covet," or persist in desiring to possess property or persons that are not rightfully one's own, goes beyond outward behavior. By forbidding the Israelites to "covet" what belongs to others, God requires them to reject feelings of envy that may lead not only to chronic discontent but also to

harmful action. The other commandments—to honor one's parents and refrain from antisocial acts such as murder, theft, adultery, and perjury—are paralleled in the legislation of other Near Eastern societies. Israel's resolve to recognize only one God, who permits no image of his divinity, however, is unique in the ancient world (but see Box 6.2).

The Book of the Covenant

The collection of statutes and ordinances that immediately follows the Decalogue (Exod. 20:18–23:33) is known as the **Book of the Covenant.** Although the laws in this section presuppose a settled agricultural way of life in Canaan, they may be among the oldest legislation in the Pentateuch. After the Decalogue's revolutionary commitment to worshiping a single God and total rejection of images, however, this section's laws validating and regulating human slavery may come as a shock. Considering that the Torah narratives have just recounted Israel's liberation from bondage, it may seem inconsistent that Yahweh's law provides for Israelites to enslave their fellow citizens. Accepting the widespread practice of selling people to pay off debt, the Book of the Covenant reflects the social norms of antiquity, safeguarding the rights of property owners (21:1–11; cf. Deut. 15:12–18). Because neither the Hebrew Bible nor the New Testament condemns the owning, buying, or selling of human beings, many Western slaveholders later argued that the biblical God condoned the institution of slavery, a position bitterly contested before, during (and even after) the American Civil War.

The Golden Calf

The Exodus narrative, interrupted by a long block of priestly material (Chs. 25–31), resumes in Chapter 32. While Moses spends forty days atop Sinai, listening to Yahweh's extensive instructions for building the Tabernacle and receiving the Decalogue that God's "finger" has inscribed on two stone tables, the Israelites below begin to rebel. Feeling abandoned, the people urge Aaron, Moses' brother and Israel's High Priest, to make them a **golden calf,** which they immediately identify as the "gods [plural] . . . who brought [them] out of Egypt" (32:1–6). Informing Moses that he has observed the Israelites' lapse into idolatry and that he plans to wipe them out, Yahweh offers to replace Israel with Moses and his family. After persuading God to "change his mind" for the sake of his reputation among the Egyptians, Moses descends from the mountain, smashes the two tablets God had inscribed (32:7–20), and orders the Levites (members

---

BOX 6.2 Was God "Seen" at Mount Sinai?

The use of multiple sources, whether oral or written, in the Exodus account of Yahweh's appearances on Mount Sinai/Horeb has resulted in the interweaving of radically contrasting ideas about God's physical visibility. According to Exodus 33:20, Yahweh informs Moses that he is forbidden to see God's "face," because "no one shall see me and live." A few verses earlier, however, we are told that Yahweh "used to speak to Moses face to face, as one speaks to a friend" (33:11). Presuming a completely spiritual and transcendent Deity, traditional religion usually emphasizes the first statement: Mortals cannot survive an unmediated experience of divinity. The anthropomorphic concept of a deity who can be visible to human eyes, which is also embraced by the canonical texts, is typically denied or explained away.

The God who insists that his face not be seen remains essentially hidden during the disclosure of his "glory" to Moses. Placing Moses in a rocky cleft and shielding him with his "hand," Yahweh projects his "goodness" as if it were a separate entity passing across the mountaintop. When God finally moves the hand obstructing Moses' vision, it is only to allow the prophet a glimpse of his "back," which is not described. This account of the Sinai theophany is paradoxically almost as much a concealment as a revelation, serving to deepen the divine mystery (Exod. 33:17–25).

By contrast, a different tradition embedded in Exodus indicates that mortals could look directly at God and survive. In Exodus 24, Moses, Aaron, and seventy Israelite "elders" climb Sinai to enjoy a meal with God, an event that may have been based on the ancient Near Eastern custom of holding banquets to celebrate a powerful tribal chieftain's acceptance of lesser clans into a status of kinship. According to this passage, Moses and the elders "saw the God of Israel," who did not strike down his guests but permitted them to "eat and drink" as they "beheld" their divine host (24:9–11). Remaining firmly in the flesh, they consume material food even while basking in the divine presence, as a group repeating the experience of Abraham, who dined with God under the oak trees near Hebron (Gen. 18).

The Torah's inclusion of both anthropomorphic imagery in which God may be visible to human eyes (as J and other traditions say he was to Abraham, Jacob, and Moses) and its seemingly contradictory proclamation that Israel's God does not appear in physical form conveys both the transcendence and immanence of the biblical Deity. The mystery of an unknowable Spirit who can create the universe and also stoop to break bread with his mortal creation is maintained.

---

of his own tribe) to slaughter the golden calf worshipers. Again climbing Sinai/Horeb (he makes at least eight ascents in Exodus) to confer with God, Moses receives a second set of tablets, symbolizing Yahweh's reconciliation with a repentant Israel (Chs. 33–34).

The golden calf episode, which most scholars believe was a later addition to the Exodus narrative, seems to reflect events in Israelite history long after Moses' time. The idolaters' cry, "These are your gods, O Israel, that brought you [from] Egypt," corresponds almost word for word with a phrase in 1 Kings, where King Jeroboam sets up two "golden calves" as objects of worship and credits them with Israel's escape from slavery (compare Exod. 32:4, 7 with 1 Kings 12:28). By inserting a story about Israel abandoning Yahweh at Sinai to honor a golden calf, the Exodus redactors make the point that such acts not only violate the covenant with God but also will trigger divine wrath leading to national disaster, a lesson well known to the book's postexilic audience.

Although both Exodus and Kings portray "calf worship" as disloyalty to Yahweh, it was not necessarily an abandonment of Yahweh. Archaeological finds, including the El texts from Ugarit, indicate that Near Eastern gods commonly were envisioned as standing invisibly on the backs of calves, bulls, or other powerful animals (see Figure 6.3). The calf figures were merely pedestals for the divine presence.

The Tabernacle

Most of the legal/ritual material occupying the last half of Exodus is devoted to provisions for providing Yahweh with a shelter as he accompanies the Israelites on the long journey from Sinai/Horeb to Canaan. By far the longest Torah passages dedicated to a single topic, Exodus 25–31 contains specific instructions for building the **Tabernacle,** the portable tent-shrine that God will symbolically inhabit. Exodus 35–40 then records the Tabernacle's actual construction. Skilled artisans undertake

FIGURE 6.3 Hadad, Syrian god of storm, strides atop a bull in this basaltic stele. Grasping lightning bolts in each hand, Hadad invisibly rides an animal symbolizing power and terror. Because Canaanite artists commonly show El, father of the gods, also standing on a bull, many scholars believe that the notorious golden calf that Moses' brother Aaron manufactured and the two calf sculptures that Jeroboam set up in Israel were intended not as rivals to Yahweh, but only as pedestals on which the Deity could be invisibly enthroned (Exod. 32:1–35; 2 Kings 12:26–33).

the project from the inside out, first building the Ark of the Covenant, a rectangular chest, plated in gold leaf, on which Yahweh's "glory" will rest. Two golden statues of cherubim, token representations of the divine members of Yahweh's heavenly court who guard his throne, are placed at each end of the ark. Their wings outstretched, they shelter the *kapporeth*, or "ark cover" (later called the "mercy seat"), the place where God is invisibly enthroned and from which he will henceforth issue his commands to Moses (Exod. 37; cf. 25). After fashioning images of the divine council, the craftsmen then construct the other instruments of Yahweh's official **cult**—the authorized rituals, sacrifices, and other practices involved in the Deity's formal worship. These objects include a golden candleholder (the menorah), an altar, and numerous utensils used in the killing, skinning, and burning of sacrificial animals.

Exodus reaches its climactic moment when Yahweh, shrouded in cloud, enters the completed Tabernacle, filling it with his "glory." Stipulating that Israel will not take a single step toward its promised destination unless the "cloud" lifts from Yahweh's tent-shrine as a sign that the day's travels are to begin, Exodus concludes with an affirmation that the covenant people are at last being led directly by God himself. "For the cloud of the LORD was on the Tabernacle by day, and the fire was in the cloud by night, before the eyes of all the house of Israel at each stage of their journey" (40:38). For the first time since he strolled through Eden, Yahweh will again dwell intimately with mortals, assuming the challenge of shaping Israel in his image.

QUESTIONS FOR DISCUSSION AND REVIEW

1. According to Exodus, how did Abraham's descendants become enslaved in Egypt? Explain the possible role of Hyksos rulers—and their expulsion from Egypt—in the reversal of the Israelites' fortunes in Egypt.

2. Describe the role of Moses in rescuing the Israelites from Egyptian slavery. How did Moses come to live in Midian and associate with Jethro/Ruel, a local priest?

3. Discuss the two different accounts in which God reveals his personal name to Moses (Exod. 3–4 and 6). What is Yahweh's relationship to El/Elohim and/or El Shaddai, the names by which Israel's distant ancestors worshiped God? How do the Exodus traditions about revelation of the divine name relate to the Yahwist's use of the name throughout Genesis?

4. Describe the plagues that Yahweh inflicts upon Egypt, including the death of male Egyptian firstborn and its connection with the Israelite Passover observance.

5. What is the *yam suf,* and what is its significance to Yahweh's relationship to Israel? Explain the ways that two different source traditions now embedded in Exodus describe the event.

6. Summarize the covenant (pact or agreement) between Yahweh and the Israelites, describing its basic terms. List the Ten Commandments (Decalogue) and analyze their meaning. Describe some additional laws in the Book of the Covenant. What does the law say about human slavery?

7. How does the Mosaic Covenant differ from the earlier covenants made through Noah and Abraham? How much of the covenant's success depends upon the Israelites' behavior? Explain your answer.

8. Why do the Israelites worship a "golden calf"? What does this lapse demonstrate about their ability to keep Yahweh's covenant demands? What does Moses say to persuade a "jealous" God not to wipe faithless Israel off the face of the earth?

9. Explain the function of the Tabernacle and the Ark of the Covenant it contained. What natural phenomena reflect the presence of presence of Yahweh's "glory" as he personally dwells among his covenant people?

Terms and Concepts to Remember

Ark of the Covenant	Passover
golden calf	plagues on Egypt
historical evidence for the Exodus	Rameses II
	Sabbath
Hyksos	Tabernacle
Jethro/Ruel	Ten Commandments
literary sources of Exodus	(Decalogue)
Midian	theocracy
Mosaic Covenant	*yam suf*

Recommended Reading

Brueggerman, Walter. "The Book of Exodus." In *The New Interpreter's Bible*, Vol. 1, pp. 677–981. Nashville, TN: Abingdon Press, 1994. Contains extensive scholarly interpretation of the Exodus account by a leading theologian.

Clifford, Richard J. "Exodus." in R. E. Brown et al., eds. *The New Jerome Biblical Commentary*, 2nd ed., pp. 40–60. Englewood Cliffs, NJ: Prentice-Hall, 1990. A good introduction to the Exodus tradition.

Coogan, Michael D., ed. *The Oxford History of the Biblical World.* New York: Oxford UP, 1998. Discusses the theory that Yahweh's worship originated in Midian, where the "mountain of God" was located.

Cross, Frank Moore. *From Epic to Canon: History and Literature in Ancient Israel.* Baltimore: Johns Hopkins UP, 1998. Includes an essay on the concept of covenants between Yahweh and Israel.

Goldingay, John. "Covenant, OT and NT." In K. D. Sakenfeld, ed. *The New Interpreter's Dictionary of the Bible*, Vol. 1, pp. 767–778. Nashville, TN: Abingdon Press, 2006. Compares covenants with Abraham, Moses, and David.

Hoffmeier, James K. *Ancient Israel in Sinai: The Evidence for the Authenticity of the Wilderness Tradition.* New York: Oxford UP, 2005. Argues for a nucleus of historical fact behind the biblical account of Israel's desert wanderings.

———. *Israel in Egypt: The Evidence for the Authenticity of the Exodus Tradition.* New York: Oxford UP, 1997. Concludes that archaeological evidence is compatible with the biblical story of the Exodus.

Johnstone, William. "Exodus, Book of." In K. D. Sakenfeld, ed., *The New Interpreter's Dictionary of the Bible*, Vol. 2, pp. 371–380. Nashville, TN: Abingdon Press, 2007. Concisely discusses the content, structure, historical background, and theological importance of the Exodus account.

Mendenhall, George E. *Law and Covenant in Israel and the Ancient Near East.* Pittsburgh: Biblical Colloquium, 1955. An influential study of parallels between ancient treaty documents and the expression of Israel's covenant traditions.

CHAPTER 7

Law, Holiness, and Rebellion

The Books of Leviticus and Numbers

Key Topics/Themes Because Yahweh's "glory" is enshrined in the Tabernacle, placing God's "holiness" in their midst, the Israelites must be instructed in law and ceremony that will make them as "holy" as the Lord with whom they journey. Consisting almost entirely of legal and ritual material, Leviticus is a priestly composition designed to transform the covenant people into "a kingdom of priests" whose diet, clothing, festivals, and rituals distinguish them from all other nations. Besides emphasizing ritual "purity" and offering detailed regulations on how to maintain—or restore—a ritually "clean" state, Leviticus is distinguished by its "Holiness Code" (Chs. 17–26) and its instructions for observing

Yom Kippur, the Day of Atonement (Ch. 16). The Book of Numbers follows with a genealogy of Israel's tribes and offers an idealized organization built around Yahweh's presence (Chs. 1–10). Intermixing narrative and legal material, Numbers provides a partial account of Israel's forty-year desert wanderings and describes its itinerary from Sinai/Horeb to the Moab–Canaan border. The narration focuses on issues of leadership and obedience as the people complain about their hardships and rebel against Moses. For their failure to trust Yahweh's ability to grant them victory over the Canaanites, God condemns the entire older generation—including Moses, Aaron, and Miriam—to die in the wilderness.

 The Book of Leviticus

Priestly Functions and Concerns

Placed at the exact center of the five Torah books—a position implying its centrality to Israelite religion—Leviticus focuses almost exclusively on priestly functions and concerns. Taking its name from Greek and Latin translations of the Hebrew Bible—the Septuagint and Vulgate editions, respectively—Leviticus is typically viewed as an instructional manual for priests. The Levites for whom the book is named are referred to in only one passage (Lev. 25:32–34), but because every member of the priestly caste was presumably also a member of the Levite tribe, the title is not inappropriate.

As the contents make clear, the priestly author's primary concern is not for the Levite tribe as a whole, but only for those descended from Aaron, Israel's first High Priest. Aaron's descendants, from whom Israel's High Priest and the chief priests were to be selected, had a solemn twofold duty: (1) to preside over Yahweh's

sanctuary, with its elaborate system of animal sacrifices, and (2) to serve as models of ethical and ritual behavior pleasing to Israel's God. Not only must priests officiating at the Tabernacle maintain a state of ritual purity, they also must teach ordinary Israelites how to observe purity laws regulating what they eat and wear, with whom and what they physically come into contact, and with whom they may or may not have sexual relations. In Leviticus, "holiness" is both a physical state and a set of ethical behaviors. Most important, it is a distinctive quality of God that the Israelites must imitate:

> You are to make yourselves holy and keep yourselves holy, because I [Yahweh] am holy.

(Lev. 11:44)

From the perspective of Israel's priests, the world is divided into two mutually exclusive areas or dimensions, the sacred and the profane, or, in Leviticus' terms, the "holy" and the "common." To be "holy" is to be separated from or "set apart" from objects, actions, or relationships that the priestly system views as profane.

Because God's presence there renders the Tabernacle earth's most holy and sacred location, nothing profane or "unclean" may be allowed to approach it. Leviticus's opening section (Chs. 1–7) thus presents regulations for offering sacrifices, a means by which individual guilt and sin can be cleansed, a process necessary to restore harmony after wrongdoing has disrupted the divinely instituted order and to bring persons to a morally and ritually acceptable condition. Providing guidelines for ordinary Israelites on how to make proper sacrifices of animals or grain, this section covers procedures appropriate for the High Priest (4:3–12), the community (4:13–26), and the individual (4:27–35; 5:1–13).

The second section (Chs. 8–10) describes the exacting ceremonies for installing Aaronite priests. The third section (Chs. 11–15), which outlines rules for distinguishing "clean" from "unclean" foods and practices, also defines ritual defilements and the rites to effect their proper cleansing. Because Israel's priests see their environment in terms of polar opposites—"holy" and "pure" versus profane or "unclean"—with strictly defined boundaries that must not be crossed, they were deeply concerned about keeping different kinds of things from being mixed together. Priestly edicts thus forbid weaving wool and linen into a single garment or boiling a kid (young goat) in its mother's milk.

The priestly belief that everything must be of a single kind or nature also appears in the statutes for treating skin disorders. When a priest finds a man with a mottled skin, partly flaky and white with leprosy and partly of normal color and texture, he must pronounce him "unclean" (13:9–11). But if the disease spreads over the entire body so that the skin is uniformly leprous, the priest may judge the man "clean": "Since it has all turned white, he is clean" (13:12–17). It is not the disfiguring disease, or the possibility that it may infect others, that contaminates; it is the leper's displaying at the same time two different conditions that belong in separate categories.

The priestly list of sexual taboos reveals a similar abhorrence toward the mixing of kinds. Thus a man may not have intercourse with a menstruating woman because life-giving semen should not mix with a flow of blood, which is associated with death. Even when a woman is not menstruating, any sexual contact renders both partners "unclean" because the bodily fluids produced during intercourse have trespassed their natural boundaries within the body (15:16–24).

Women's biological functions are regarded as essentially "unclean." Merely touching an object previously used by a menstruating woman contaminates a person (15:19–32). Because giving birth releases blood, a woman who delivers a male child is considered unclean for seven days, and for another thirty-three days, she cannot participate in the social or religious life of the community. If she delivers a female baby, the period of her ritual uncleanness is doubled to fourteen days, and she is barred from normal activities for sixty-six days (12:1–8).

Leviticus lists many other sexual prohibitions that forbid a variety of erotic combinations, ranging from taking both a woman and her sister into a man's harem (18:18), to making love to a menstruating wife (18:19), to lying "with a male as with a woman" (18:22), all of which violate the priestly concept of acceptable boundaries. Leviticus also forbids marriage with a brother's wife, although Deuteronomy states that an Israelite should be encouraged to marry his brother's widow, a view that plays a major role in the Book of Ruth (Deut. 25:5–10).

Rituals of Atonement

Chapter 16 describes one of Israel's most significant ceremonies, the **scapegoat** offering. Every year, on the **Day of Atonement (Yom Kippur),** the High Priest is instructed to prepare two goats for sacrifice. At the Tent of Meeting (commonly identified with the Tabernacle), the priest draws lots for the goats, slaughtering one as a blood sacrifice to Yahweh and keeping the other alive as a symbolic bearer of the people's collective sins. Ritually laying hands on the live goat, the priest transfers the nation's guilt to the animal, which, figuratively laden with Israel's misdeeds, is then led out of the camp "to **Azazel,**" a desert deity or demon. The scapegoat thus removes the punishable object of Yahweh's wrath from the community and transfers it to the uninhabited wilderness.

The term *scapegoat* has come to refer to any innocent person who suffers for the crimes of others; its fullest expression in the Hebrew Bible is found in the Book of Isaiah, where Yahweh's " suffering servant," a guiltless man, bears the sins of his people and, by so doing, wins forgiveness for them:

> But he was wounded for our transgressions, crushed for
>   our iniquities;
> upon him was the punishment that made us whole, and
>   by his bruises we are healed.

(Isa. 53:5)

By taking away the people's collective offenses, the scapegoat ceremony places them "at one" with their God, effecting a reconciliation that restores the bond between Yahweh and the Israelites. Through such priestly rituals, the participants are cleansed or spiritually re-created and brought closer to the divine image in which humanity was originally formed.

The Holiness Code

With their repeated refrain "I am the Lord [Yahweh]," Chapters 17–26 form a distinctive body of material known as the **Holiness Code.** Covering a wide variety of topics, ranging from human sins and cleansing formulas to seasonal festivals, this portion of Leviticus emphasizes that Yahweh is the source of holiness and that Israel must observe specific procedures to acquire a holiness appropriate to his covenant partner. Despite the code's focus on ritual, it is important to remember that the priestly writers presuppose worshipers' ethical integrity—ceremony and sacrifice are no substitute for responsible behavior (cf. Mic. 6:6–8).

Amid the detailed instructions for making burnt offerings*, readers will find in Leviticus passages of striking ethical and psychological value: "You shall not be partial to the poor or defer to the great: with justice you shall judge your neighbor . . . You shall not take vengeance or bear a grudge against any of your people, but you shall love your neighbor as yourself: I am the Lord" (19:15, 18). Besides containing the Torah's only command to love one's neighbor as a religious duty, Leviticus also enjoins the Israelites to treat strangers and foreign residents with compassion, remembering that they themselves were once outsiders in a strange land (19:34).

The Holiness Code concludes by placing Israel's legal requirements in the general context of its obligations to Yahweh. In a passage similar to the lists of blessings and curses found in Deuteronomy 28–30, editors warn of the dire consequences to follow if Israel breaks its covenant vows. National security, divine protection, military victory, and economic prosperity are guaranteed if Israel keeps all Torah commands. Conversely, if Israel proves disloyal, it will suffer drought, famine, disease, poverty, military defeat, and total ruin (26:3–43).

This "predictive" passage, so similar to Deuteronomy's catalogue of disasters leading to exile, suggests that it was written during or after the Babylonian captivity (587–538 BCE). In fact, the priestly authors portray Yahweh as promising to "remember" his exiled people and restore them to Canaan (26:40–45). Noting similarities between the Holiness Code and legal material in the Book of Ezekiel, composed by a priest-prophet exiled in Babylon, some scholars believe that much of Leviticus dates from the time of Ezekiel or later. Other scholars date the Levitical rituals governing sacrifices to

late in the Second Temple period. (Returned Jewish exiles rebuilt the Jerusalem Temple, which the Babylonians had destroyed, about 515 BCE, when sacrificial rituals were resumed at Yahweh's altar and continued until the Second Temple's destruction in 70 CE.) The prophet Jeremiah, a contemporary of Ezekiel, categorically denies that any of the sacrificial practices observed in his day actually originated during the Mosaic era. According to Jeremiah, Yahweh "did not speak to them [the Exodus generation] concerning burnt offerings and sacrifices," implying that such elaborate ceremonies were a later priestly innovation (Jer. 7:22).

The Book of Numbers

Although Numbers—which mixes genealogies, laws, rituals, legends, poetry, and narrative—appears disorganized to most readers, the book has some thematic coherence. Numbers takes its title from its Greek name, *Arithmoi,* and Latin title, *Numeri,* referring to the census or "numbering" of the people described in the first four chapters. The Hebrew name, *Bamidbar,* means "in the wilderness," and better describes the book's contents—Israel's forty-year desert journey from Sinai/Horeb to the borders of Canaan. The combined elements of numbering and wilderness travel suggest part of Numbers' meaning. Israel's male population is counted twice: at the beginning of the book while the people are still receiving Yahweh's laws and again years later after the older generation has perished (Num. 1–4; 26). Although the first census lists men of military age as totaling 603,550 (1:46), scholars suggest that this unlikely figure can be interpreted more reasonably. Some propose that the word for "thousand" (Hebrew, *elef*) also refers to a military unit of no more than ten men, thus reducing the total number to 6,000-odd Israelite soldiers. The second census, near the end of the book, produces a total almost exactly the same as the first—601,730 potential fighters—and may be interpreted in the same way.

Perhaps the most significant aspect of the census taking is its exclusion of the Levite tribe, which now appears as a separate priestly caste with considerable religious and political power. Aaron's son Eleazar has inherited his father's role as High Priest (4:16)—two of his brothers, after offering "unholy fire before the Lord," had been "consumed" by Yahweh's "fire" (Lev. 10:2)—and he now controls the Tabernacle. In contrast to the earlier, seemingly egalitarian, declaration at Sinai that all Israelites were to form a "kingdom of priests"

---

*After Roman armies destroyed the Jerusalem Temple in 70 CE, all sacrifices prescribed in the Torah necessarily ceased; in Judaism, priestly ritual was replaced by prayer, humanitarian deeds, and other actions of enduring value.

(Exod. 19:6), Numbers assigns to the **Aaronite** males alone the privilege of direct access to the Tabernacle and, by implication, to God.

Rebellions in the Desert

Issues of authority—particularly quarrels about who can legitimately claim to represent Yahweh among the people—drive much of Numbers' narrative action. When the Israelites renew their now-familiar complaint about the monotonous diet of manna that God miraculously provides (cf. Exod. 16:14–15), Moses seems to reach the limit of his patience, informing Yahweh that the burden of leadership is too great for him to bear. Displeased at Moses' apparent weakness, God responds by "taking back" a portion of the prophetic spirit he had earlier conferred on Moses alone, transferring it to seventy tribal elders, and then punishing the remainder of the people with a plague.

Perhaps encouraged by the extension of Yahweh's spirit to a larger group, Moses' brother Aaron and sister Miriam question his authority and criticize his decision to marry a Cushite wife (presumably Zipporah, whom Exodus identifies as a Midianite). God upholds Moses' role as his sole intermediary—"with him I speak face to face, openly and not in riddles" (Num. 12:8)—and even afflicts Miriam with a leprosy-like condition. The equally guilty Aaron, as he had in the golden calf episode, goes unpunished. After Miriam spends a week in exile outside the Israelite camp, Moses intervenes on her behalf, and she, her health regained, is restored to fellowship. Although Numbers recognizes only Moses as Israel's leader, another tradition, preserved in the Book of Micah, indicates that God authorized a trio of leaders, including Miriam and her two brothers (Mic. 6:4).

A more threatening rebellion against Moses quickly surfaces when **Korah,** a Levite, and three prominent members from the tribe of Reuben, along with 250 other "leaders of the congregation, . . . well-known men," demand that Moses share his authority with other qualified leaders. Citing a covenant ideal— that all Israelites are spiritually equal—the rebels remind Moses that "Every member of the community is holy and the LORD is among them all" (16:3). Despite their plausible arguments, Yahweh rejects the rebel position in spectacular fashion: The earth suddenly yawns open to swallow Korah and his associates, including their wives, children, and possessions. Fire from heaven then incinerates the 250 men who had supported Korah's attempt to institute a more broadly based government for Israel (16:28–35). Yahweh's violent overthrow of the rebels raises unsettling questions about one of Israel's cornerstone institutions. By the time of the early monarchy (after 1000 BCE), political and prophetic authority have already begun to diverge from each other. Eventually, many Israelite prophets will become either independent of or antagonistic to the "anointed" king, in effect rejecting the rule of a single ruler and the concept of theocratic elitism that Numbers endorses.

Even more disturbing is Yahweh's reaction when a posse of spies brings back a negative report about Israel's chances of success in invading Canaan. Representing each of the twelve tribes, a dozen spies are sent into southern Canaan to check out the degree of resistance they are likely to encounter. Not only is the conclusion they reach—"we are not able to go up against this people, for they are stronger than we" (13:31)—a blow to Moses' credibility, it is also an insult to the concept of Yahweh as warrior. Only two spies, **Caleb** and **Joshua** (earlier identified as Moses' loyal assistant), have enough faith and courage to urge an immediate invasion of Canaan. And they alone of their generation are allowed to survive the subsequent forty years of wandering in the wilderness. Outraged at his people's lack of trust in his military powers, Yahweh again threatens to destroy the entire nation, exterminating every man, woman, and child he had brought out of Egypt. Eliminating Israel altogether, Yahweh will make only Moses and his family God's chosen people.

As he had following the golden calf episode, Moses again acts as intercessor between his faithless people and their wrathful God. Pleading with Yahweh to change his mind, Moses reminds God that "if you kill this people all at one time, then the nations who have heard about you will say, 'It is because the LORD [Yahweh] was unable to bring this people into the land he swore to give them that he has slaughtered them in the wilderness'" (Num. 14:15–16). God must recall his oath to Abraham and his public reputation, as well as his earlier words to Moses on Sinai/Horeb:

> The LORD [Yahweh] is slow to anger, and abounding in steadfast love, forgiving iniquity and transgression . . . .
>
> (Num. 14:18; cf. Exod. 32:11–13)

In the "greatness of [his] steadfast love," Yahweh controls his anger and decides not to destroy Israel "all at one time." His forgiveness, however, is limited. God does not summon an Angel of Death to slay the entire population, but he decrees that no Israelite over the age of twenty will live to enter Canaan. For every day that the spies reconnoiter the area, the Israelites must wander a year, until their "dead bodies shall fall in [the] wilderness" (14:29, 34).

Balaam's Blessing

The story of **Balaam**, a Canaanite prophet whom King
Balak of Moab hires to curse Israel because he does not
want them marching through his territory, is the longest
continuous narrative section in Numbers. Besides its use
of folklore—a talking donkey that can see spirit beings
invisible to human eyes—the Balaam incident is inter-
esting because it assumes that the curses of a genuine
prophet can indeed interfere with Israel's plans to attack
Canaan. This nationalistic tale has an ironic twist: Although Balaam earnestly tries to earn his fee by invoking the customary curses, Yahweh turns the curses into
blessings, making the Canaanite prophet a voice speaking Yahweh's own message. In its present form, the
Balaam episode seems to combine, rather confusingly,
two distinct versions of the story. In the first tradition
(23:7–21), Balaam agrees to accompany a delegation
from Balak only after God has explicitly ordered him to
go and "do only what I tell you." In the second tradition
(23:22–35), God is shown as being angry with Balaam
for agreeing to Balak's request, and so, before Balaam is
allowed to proceed, he must be humbled. When his
long-suffering donkey suddenly speaks in a human
voice, Balaam—typical of figures in folklore—shows
not the slightest surprise and willingly accepts the beast's
rebuke. Only then does he see what his animal sees, an
angel with a drawn sword standing in his path. Once
again, Balaam is instructed to journey on and speak only
those words that God permits him.

The three prophetic speeches that follow are poems
of praise— "how goodly are your tents, O Jacob" (24:5)—
and, in general, serve to celebrate Israel's special relationship with God. It is little wonder, then, that Balak feels
cheated and parts in anger from Balaam. More intriguing than this slightly comic outcome of Balaam's
commission is a poetic reference to a mysterious figure
whom Balaam envisions in the distant future:

> I see him, but not now; I behold him, but not near;
> a star shall come forth out of Jacob, a comet arise from
>   Israel,
> He shall smite the squadrons of Moab,
> and beat down all the sons of strife.
>
> (Num. 24:17)

Scholars commonly assume that this unnamed future
conqueror of Moab is King David and so view this
passage as an example of prophecy after the fact. The
intrusion of what appears to be material from the post-
Davidic period offers one possible clue to the editorial
process by which the narrative acquired its present form.
By including in Balaam's speech a prediction about the

Davidic monarchy, the editors make Israel's future triumph over Moab seem inevitable (see Chapter 11).

Balaam's veiled prophecy about a future Israelite
king is followed by yet another account of Israel's rebel-
liousness and disloyalty, the incident of Baal-peor
(Num. 25). The son of El and god of storm and life-
giving rain, **Baal** was worshiped throughout Canaan,
and in the historical narratives that follow the Pentateuch, he is Yahweh's chief rival for Israel's allegiance.
In this episode, two different acts of disobedience to
God—intermarriage (with either Moabite or Midianite women) and religious disloyalty—are correlated,
suggesting that marrying foreign women invariably
leads to covenant breaking. The plague, which Yahweh
visits on the Israelites for their **apostasy**—the act of
abandoning or rejecting a previously held religious
commitment—ends only when a priest, zealous for
Yahweh, murders two conspicuous offenders. Phinhas,
Aaron's grandson, drives a spear through the entrails
of both an Israelite man and the Midianite woman
he has taken into his family tent (25:6–8). Why the
Midianites—who were earlier shown to be supporters
of Moses and the worship of Yahweh (Exod. 18)—have
suddenly become a threat to Israel's survival is never
explained. Nor is it clear why the Midianites are lumped
together with the Moabites, or why marriage with a
Midianite warrants the death penalty. Up to this point
in the Pentateuch, attitudes toward marriage outside of
one's ethnic community have been ambivalent, even
contradictory. Thus it comes as a surprise that the linking of an Israelite man with a Midianite woman was
done in "open defiance of Moses and all the community
of Israel" (25:6). After all, had not Moses himself earlier taken a Midianite bride, Zipporah, whose father,
Jethro, praised Yahweh and counseled Moses in setting
up Israel's judicial system (Exod. 18:1–25)? When
Aaron and Miriam rebuke him for marrying a foreigner
(Num. 12), God vindicates Moses and punishes his
sister. Moreover, if intermarriage under any condition
was unacceptable to God, then Moses' provision for
sparing the lives of Midianite virgins, who then become
eligible to enter Israelite harems, becomes completely
illogical. This double standard toward intermarriage
persists throughout biblical history, with texts as
diverse as the books of Ezra, Nehemiah, Malachi, and
Ruth taking different positions on the issue.

Numbers' Conception of God

Israel's concept of God, which developed slowly over
many centuries, was eventually universalized in later
Judaism, Christianity, and Islam. In Numbers, however,

Israel's God is narrowly defined as the patron deity of a single people who shows little regard for other peoples or nations. But at times even God's commitment to Israel conflicts with other aspects of his volatile personality. Not only does Yahweh demand exclusive devotion and total obedience from his covenant partner, but he is ready to use extreme violence when Israel disappoints him. Upon learning of Israel's cowardice and unfaithfulness (Num. 13), God's first response is to exterminate the Israelites altogether. He is dissuaded from this course only when Moses reminds him (as he had earlier, in Exod. 32:11–12) that the surrounding peoples are likely to attribute his action to an inability to make good on his covenant promises. In effect, Moses appeals to God's vanity, his concern for his public image (Num. 14). As it turns out, God's eagerness to wipe out the Midianites is even keener than his desire for vengeance against disloyal Israelites (Num. 25).

Contemporary readers may have difficulty accepting a notion of God that includes intolerance and lethal violence. Different layers of tradition incorporated into the Torah narratives, of course, preserve different stages of Israel's understanding of Yahweh, from the **anthropomorphism** of a fully embodied God in parts of Exodus (24:9–11; 33:1–23) to the exalted, transcendent Creator of Genesis 1. Because Israel's worship of Yahweh evolved in close competition with the cults of Baal and other Near Eastern deities, it is not surprising to find, in its earlier stages, portrayals of God that are neither ethically well developed nor entirely stripped of mythological associations.

QUESTIONS FOR DISCUSSION AND REVIEW

1. Why do the priestly writers in Leviticus make distinctions between the sacred and the profane, the "clean" and the "unclean"? What is the most sacred place or object in the Israelite community? What is required of people who would approach this sacred space?

2. Describe the scapegoat ceremony in Leviticus 16, and explain its connection with the Day of Atonement. How are the Israelites' collective sins effectively separated from the people and the space they inhabit?

3. For what purpose does Balak, king of Moab, hire Balaam? Does the story imply that Balaam, a Canaanite prophet, can really communicate with Israel's God?

4. Discuss the common theme that runs through the various episodes in which some Israelite leaders challenge Moses' authority. What position does Yahweh take in each episode? Of those guilty of rebellion, why are Miriam, Korah, and 250 other Israelite leaders punished, but not Aaron? Do the priestly writers seem to show special favoritism toward Israel's first High Priest?

5. If all the Israelites collectively form a "kingdom of priests, a holy nation," as Exodus declares, why does Yahweh support only one man as Israel's leader and only the priestly caste as guardians of his sanctuary?

Terms and Concepts to Remember

Aaronite	Holiness Code
anthropomorphism	Joshua
Azazel	Korah
Balaam	manna
Caleb	Midianites
Day of Atonement (Yom Kippur)	scapegoat

Recommended Reading

Cross, Frank M., ed. "The Priestly Houses of Early Israel." In *Canaanite Myth and Hebrew Epic: Essays in the History and the Religion of Israel*, pp. 293–325. Cambridge, MA: Harvard UP, 1973. An indispensable resource for understanding how Israel's priests edited legal and ritual material.

Douglas, Mary. *Leviticus as Literature.* New York: Oxford UP, 1999. An insightful interpretation.

———. *Purity and Danger.* London: Thames & Hudson, 1966. A standard reference for interpreting Israel's ritual purity laws.

Dozeman, Thomas B. "The Book of Numbers." In *The New Interpreter's Bible*, Vol. 2, pp. 3–268. Nashville, TN: Abingdon Press, 1998. Provides extensive scholarly commentary.

Kaiser, Walter C., Jr. "The Book of Leviticus." In *The New Interpreter's Bible*, Vol. 1, pp. 985–1191. Nashville, TN: Abingdon Press, 1994. A complete text, with scholarly analysis and interpretative reflection.

Milgrom, Jacob. "Numbers, Book of." In D. N. Freedman, ed., *The Anchor Bible Dictionary*, Vol. 4, pp. 1146–1155. New York: Doubleday, 1992. A scholarly analysis.

CHAPTER 8

A New Vision of Moses' Teaching
The Book of Deuteronomy

Key Topics/Themes When Greek-speaking Jews translated the fifth and final Torah book into Greek in the third century BCE, they referred to it as the *Deuteronomion,* meaning "Second Law." This title is based on the assumption that when God instructs Moses to "prepare a copy of this Torah" (Deut. 17:18), "Torah" includes all of the laws contained in the Pentateuch's first four books as well. In fact, Deuteronomy is much more than a repetition of earlier teachings and legal material: In many respects, it represents a departure from, rather than a summation of, traditions in Exodus through Numbers. Cast in the form of Moses' three farewell speeches to a new generation of Israelites poised to enter Canaan, Deuteronomy has two main purposes: (1) to present a distinct set of ethical and religious standards Israel must meet if it is to enjoy fulfillment of the divine promises, and (2) to make a powerful statement about the causes of Israel's historical rise and fall as Yahweh's covenant people. In his first discourse, Moses reviews Israel's experience with God from Mount Horeb (Sinai in Exodus) through the wilderness (Chs. 1–4). In his much longer second speech, Moses presents an extensive law code distinct from that in Exodus–Numbers, providing a restatement of the Ten Commandments and a vivid description of the horrors that await Israel if the nation proves unfaithful (Chs. 5–28). His brief third speech, which also emphasizes the "two ways" of obedient life or disobedient destruction (Chs. 29–30), is followed by collections of ancient poetry about Yahweh and the Twelve Tribes (Chs. 32–33). The book ends with a brief account of Moses' death (Ch. 34).

Deuteronomy's View of History

Although it opens with a review of Israel's past association with Yahweh, the Book of Deuteronomy looks forward as well as back, anticipating the major themes of the historical writings that follow it. Collectively, the books from Deuteronomy through Joshua, Judges, Samuel, and Kings are known as the **Deuteronomistic History,** primarily because each of these books, in its own way, embodies one central historical thesis that we first encounter in the pages of Deuteronomy:

> If you will only obey the LORD your God, by diligently observing all his commandments that I am commanding you today, the LORD your God will set you high above the nations of the earth; . . . the LORD will make you the head, and not the tail; you shall be only at the top, and not at the bottom—if you obey. . . . But if you will not obey the LORD . . . then

all these curses shall come upon you and overtake you: . . . The LORD will cause you to be defeated before your enemies, . . . You shall become an object of horror to all the kingdoms of the earth.

(Deut. 28:1, 13, 15, 25)

As the prologue to the Deuteronomistic History (Joshua through Kings), Deuteronomy provides the interpretative framework for the narrative books that follow, showing in advance the inevitable and tragic consequences that will befall Israel for its infidelity to Yahweh. For the authors of both Deuteronomy and the Deuteronomistic History, the only measure of Israel's success—and the only guarantee of its continued existence—is obedience to God and commitment to the covenant and its laws. Yet this is the one requirement that Israel and its leaders seem unable to keep.

The book's Hebrew name *Eleh Hadevarim* (These Are the Words [of Moses]) is more appropriate than

94

the Greek title, with its implication that Deuteronomy is a supplementary "Second Law." Unlike the other books of Torah, in which Yahweh directs his words to Moses, who then transmits them to the people, Deuteronomy shows Moses speaking directly—and in his own words—to the Israelites, who have assembled on the plains of Moab, east of the Jordan River, just prior to their invasion of Canaan. The book takes the form of three farewell sermons that Moses delivers shortly before his death. Whereas Exodus portrays Moses as so inarticulate that he needs Aaron to speak for him (Exod. 4:10–12), Deuteronomy portrays him as stunningly eloquent.

Aware that he will not live to enter the Promised Land and that this occasion marks his last opportunity to emphasize the importance of loyalty to Yahweh, Moses begins with a brief summary of the Exodus and of the conflicts between God and his people in the wilderness (1:6–4:40) By focusing on the struggles that characterize the divine–human relationship, Moses tries to prepare the Israelites for the conquest of Canaan under the leadership of his successor, Joshua. And by insisting that nothing may be added to or taken away from the "statutes and ordinances" he has placed in the text (4:2), the authors/editors of Deuteronomy attempt to end the process they have followed in revising and updating earlier law codes.

 ## King Josiah and the Discovery of the Book of the Law

Biblical historians agree that the "book of the law" (literally, "book of instruction," or *sefer ha-torah* in Hebrew) that was found in 621 BCE when King Josiah was conducting Temple repairs (2 Kings 23:3–10) was none other than Deuteronomy, or some significant portion thereof. Josiah (ruled 640–609 BCE) is so clearly impressed by the dire warnings of this newly discovered book that it is tempting to imagine him reading Deuteronomy 28 with growing anxiety over its terrifying predictions of national disaster. Josiah's determination to reform Israel's religious life suggests that, if Deuteronomy was not already written or edited in the seventh century BCE, then, at the very least, its major themes of disobedience leading to Israel's destruction began to influence some leaders and prophets (including Jeremiah) at that time. Certainly, Josiah's campaign to destroy rural altars and shrines located throughout the region and to focus the nation's religious observances on the Temple in Jerusalem suggests the effects of Deuteronomy 12:14, which orders that all worship be centered at one (unnamed) shrine.

Moreover, the involvement of Shaphan, Josiah's court secretary, in the discovery and preservation of this scroll may well provide a clue to the identity of a Deuteronomistic "circle" responsible for advancing religious reforms. According to the Book of Jeremiah, the family of Shaphan was sympathetic to the prophet, who began to prophesy during Josiah's reign, and to Jeremiah's view of *torah* observance (Jer. 29:3; 36:10; cf. 2 Kings 22:3, 9, 12). One likely scenario, then, locates support for a rewriting of earlier law codes among the administrative elite of Josiah's court. Some court officials may have seen the decline in the power of the Assyrians, who had politically dominated the covenant people for more than a century, as an opportunity to advance a more rigorous and uncompromising form of Yahweh's worship at the highest levels of Judean society. Josiah's attempt to reconquer parts of the northern kingdom of Israel, which the Assyrians had previously controlled, indicates that Judean leaders took advantage of the power vacuum occasioned by Assyria's growing weakness (2 Kings 23).

Yet, in spite of Deuteronomy's obvious connection to the southern kingdom of Judah, many scholars believe that some of the traditions that found their way into this book had their origin among the northern tribes of Israel. After Assyrian armies destroyed Samaria, capital of the northern kingdom, in 721 BCE, northern priests and scribes probably fled south, bringing with them a collective memory of covenant renewal ceremonies, like those that Joshua held at the northern shrine of Shechem (cf. Deut. 27 and Josh. 24). According to this theory, northern covenant traditions were then merged with southern ceremonies enacted at Jerusalem. Josiah's reformist agenda would have provided the ideal climate for the editing and promotion (if not the actual composition) of the Book of Deuteronomy as we know it. At this point in the process of composition and/or editing, a specifically Judean perspective probably was introduced into the evolving text of Deuteronomy. Certainly, a southern audience would have found the idea of total triumph over its enemies—and those include its Canaanite neighbors (Deut. 11:24)—and a systematic refocusing of national religious life on Jerusalem particularly appealing in the wake of Assyria's near-destruction of Judah during the reign of Hezekiah.

Deuteronomy's composite text probably received yet another layer of expanded commentary and legislation after the fall of Jerusalem and the upper classes' exile to Babylon in 587 BCE. Revealing an awareness that both the northern kingdom of Israel and the southern realm of Judah already had suffered destruction and exile, a postexilic writer reflected on the covenant people's hardships, as well as their prospects for a return to the land:

> When all these things have happened to you, the blessing and the curse of which I have offered you the choice, if you take them to heart there among all the nations to which I have banished you, if you and your children turn back to him and obey him heart and soul in all that I command you this day, then the LORD your God will restore your fortunes . . . The LORD your God will bring you into the land which your forefathers occupied, and you will occupy it again.
>
> (Deut. 30:1–5)

Yahweh thus challenges the generation of exiles to succeed where their ancestors had failed. By making a concerted effort to observe the terms of covenant, the exiles may reoccupy their ancestral land, a prediction of Israel's future that found confirmation in the partial return of Judean exiles after 538 BCE, when the Persian conqueror of Babylon, Cyrus the Great, gave them permission to go back to their homeland. The final revisions of Deuteronomy, then, probably took place during the late sixth century BCE, or possibly during the century that followed.

However Deuteronomy may have come into existence, its authors and editors—whom scholars call the **Deuteronomists**—were determined to bring Moses before readers in a more memorable way than ever before. In Deuteronomy, Moses is not merely the covenant mediator between Yahweh and the people, the agent who transmits God's laws from atop Mount Sinai. He is also the divinely inspired guide who foretells Israel's long-term future and who provides the means—covenant obedience—that can reconcile them to God and restore their national fortunes. The Deuteronomists' Moses uses his last breath to hammer home the central themes of covenant theology and the meaning of Israel's rise, fall, and ultimate restoration as Yahweh's covenant partner—as the Deuteronomist school understood it.

For the Deuteronomists, Israel's relationship with God was based on reciprocal love and on a profound and unchanging commitment to fulfill all of the commandments contained in the Deuteronomistic code. As scholars have noted, this relationship closely resembles that of a powerful Near Eastern king to his vassals, who have sworn absolute loyalty to him. In both language and structure, Deuteronomy typically sounds like a diplomatic treaty between a great and a lesser power. The difference here, of course, is that the "king" in this case is the Creator of the universe, and the Deuteronomistic editors (perhaps influenced by the exilic prophet known as Second Isaiah; see Chapter 18) include declarations of unequivocal monotheism: "This day, then, be sure

and take to heart that the LORD [Yahweh] is God in heaven above and on earth below; there is no other" (4:39). In its emphasis on sincerity and conscientiousness in the service of this one God, Deuteronomy sets a higher, more rigorous standard of covenant loyalty, with even more drastic penalties for disobedience that earlier Torah texts had imagined.

◇ | Moses' Second Speech

Moses' three speeches are unequal in length, with the first a brief summation of the Exodus experience (1:6–4:44) and the third a short conclusion in which Moses binds the people and their tribal leaders to an oath of loyalty to Yahweh (Chs. 29–30). Forming the bulk of Deuteronomy, Moses' second speech (Chs. 5–28) lays out expanded versions of the Decalogue and of statutes found elsewhere in the Pentateuch. Many of the legal changes introduced in this core segment of the book reflect a heightened sense of moral urgency and of devotion to Yahweh. Overall, this section shows a marked tendency toward revisionism, a tendency that may well echo the themes of Josiah's reformation.

A Revised Ten Commandments

Perhaps the most obvious difference between traditions contained in previous Torah books and those in Deuteronomy appears in the Deuteronomistic version of the Decalogue. In Exodus 20, the Israelites are commanded to observe the Sabbath because "in six days the LORD made heaven and earth, the sea, and all that is in them, and on the seventh day he rested. Therefore the LORD blessed the Sabbath day and declared it holy" (20:11). The clear motive for halting all work on the Sabbath, then, is the desire to honor and to imitate Yahweh. As God rested from his labors on the seventh day of creation, so must Israel. Deuteronomy 5, however, offers a totally different rationale for Sabbath observance:

> Remember that you were slaves in Egypt and the LORD your God brought you out with a strong hand and an outstretched arm, and for that reason the LORD your God commanded you to keep the Sabbath day." (5:15)

In this explanation, the focus shifts away from the creation myth to the Exodus story, from an event out of time to a recent moment in history—and with that shift comes a new emphasis on what the Israelites can learn from their experience of slavery. In fact, references to the Exodus pervade Deuteronomy, and not just for the purpose of providing an historical backdrop for Moses' speeches. The Deuteronomists' view of the desert experience is as often symbolic as it is literal: The liberation from Egypt was accomplished so that Israel might serve Yahweh by faithfully observing his commandments. Their God-given freedom is therefore the freedom to choose a life in conformity to God's will.

Slaves and Other Marginalized Groups

Not surprisingly, the most dramatic changes that the Deuteronomists tried to bring about are found in laws affecting parts of Israelite society that were politically powerless or economically exploited. Deuteronomy's statutes regarding slavery attempt to improve the social status of Israelite slaves. In Exodus 21, the Covenant Code distinguishes between the treatment given male and female slaves, allowing male slaves to go free after six years of indentured service, while retaining the female slave who has submitted (by force?) to sexual intercourse with her master or his sons (Exod. 21:2–11). By contrast, Deuteronomy 15 gives the female slave the same privilege of freedom allowed her male counterparts (15:12–17). Most important, Deuteronomy urges masters against setting a slave free with no means of support:

> But when you set him free, do not let him go empty-handed. Give to him lavishly from your flock, from your threshing-floor and from your wine-press. Be generous to him because the LORD your God has blessed you . . . Remember that you were slaves in Egypt and the LORD your God redeemed you. (15:13–15)

The purpose of such legislation, clearly, was to break the cycle of poverty that led the poor to seek slavery as an alternative to starvation. An even more dramatic shift in the Deuteronomistic perception and treatment of slaves, however, occurs in a later chapter (23:15–16), where the Israelites are told (contrary to prevailing Mesopotamian law) that they are *not* to return a runaway slave to his master. In fact, the escaped slave should be allowed to settle wherever he wishes. No such provision exists anywhere else in the Pentateuch, and one can only wonder what would have happed if a general slave uprising had led to a mass flight of slaves seeking refuge in a different tribal territory. Still, no provision for a general manumission (legal freeing) of slaves appears in Deuteronomy, and the "right of escape" that this particular statute confirms is nowhere reconciled with the older and more generally acknowledged right to "own" other human beings as personal property. Nor do any New Testament writers criticize slavery as an institution or urge Christians to free enslaved fellow-believers (see the discussion of Paul's letter to Philemon in Chapter 35).

Besides slaves, the Deuteronomistic agenda shows concern for other marginalized groups, including widows, orphans, and resident aliens. Several times in the course of explaining the application of a specific statute, the Deuteronomistic writers show Moses reminding his audience that kindness toward the most vulnerable in their society is a mark of their obedience to God's will (see, e.g., 25:17–18). Nor is it enough, the Deuteronomists insist, simply to conform outwardly to a divine commandment: For the covenant to be truly fulfilled, the "heart and soul" must be engaged in the service of Yahweh's law. Nowhere is this ideal more eloquently stated that in the often-quoted passage in Chapter 6, a proclamation of faith known in Hebrew as the **Shema:**

> Hear, O Israel: The LORD [Yahweh] is our God, the LORD alone. You shall love the LORD your God with all your heart, and with all your soul, and with all your might. Keep these words that I am commanding you today in your heart. Recite them to your children and talk about them when you are at home and when you are away, when you lie down and when you rise. Bind them as a sign on your hand, fix them as an emblem on your forehead, and write them on the doorposts of your house and on your gates. (6:4–9)

In time, this command would become one of the central prayers of Jewish worship, so well known by Jesus' generation that he could quote verse 5 with every expectation that his audience would know exactly which portion of Deuteronomy he was quoting (cf. Mark 12:28–34; Matt. 22:36).

Covenant Renewal and National Restoration

The belief that Yahweh can be obeyed only by internalizing the precepts of Torah and by the constant application of the mind and will in God's service is found throughout Deuteronomy. The Israelites are told to heighten their ethical sensitivity by "circumcising" the "foreskin" of their hearts (10:16); they are not to "live by bread alone" but to nourish themselves through "every word that comes from the mouth of the LORD" (8:3). Such cultivating of spiritual awareness, of course, carries with it a higher level of anxiety lest the covenant partnership be broken. The **Deuteronomistic view of history** that emerges from this book places responsibility for the shattering of that relationship, and for all the suffering that follows, squarely on the shoulders of the Israelites. In Chapters 28–30, Moses is represented as reminding the Israelites that they have a choice between obedience to Yahweh—which brings military success and economic prosperity—or disobedience—which brings calamity and loss of the land. If the Book of Deuteronomy is, as most scholars assume, a seventh-century-BCE work significantly revised during the heartbreak of exile, then the so-called Deuteronomistic view is an interpretation of Israel's political collapse viewed after the fact, a retrospective lesson in the cost of covenant breaking. Determined to blame Israel's national misfortunes not on Yahweh's failure to defend his people but on the Israelites' own moral failings, the Deuteronomistic editors insist that whereas Yahweh was faithful to his promise, Israel was not.

But the Deuteronomistic writers see Yahweh's relationship with Israel as more than a failed experiment. Although God severely punishes the Israelites for their crimes and apostasy, he is also willing to forgive them if they approach him with a contrite heart:

> When all these things have happened to you, the blessings and the curses, . . . if you call them to mind among all the nations where the LORD your God has driven you, and return to the LORD your God, and you and your children obey him with all your heart and with all your soul, . . . then the LORD your God will restore your fortunes and have compassion on you, gathering you again from all the peoples. . . . Even if you are exiled to the ends of the world, from there the LORD your God will gather you, and from there he will bring you back . . . into the land that your ancestors possessed. (30:1–5)

For prophets of the late seventh and sixth centuries BCE, when Israel groaned under the weight of Babylon's domination, the promise of national restoration and covenant renewal offered both consolation and an affirmation that Yahweh is a God whose capacity for forgiveness is at least as great as his need to punish (see Ezek. 36:22–28). It is hardly surprising, then, to find these same sentiments expressed in a contemporary text like Deuteronomy. To enforce this lesson, and to underscore the concept that Yahweh indeed controls the events of history, the Deuteronomistic writers present two seemingly contradictory viewpoints, each linked to God's dual nature:

> It was not because you were more numerous than any other people that the LORD set his heart on you and chose you . . . It was because the LORD loved you and kept the oath that he swore to your ancestors, that the LORD has brought you out with a mighty hand and redeemed you from slavery . . . Know therefore that the LORD your God is God, the faithful God who maintains covenant loyalty with those who love him and keep his commandments, to a thousand

generations, and who repays in their own person those who reject him. (7:7–10)

This "theology of grace," as it is sometimes called, thus presents the covenant as an unearned gift, bestowed upon a possibly undeserving but nevertheless obligated Israel, from whom the Promised Land can be taken just as swiftly as it was given, and to whom it may yet be given back again.

A More Transcendent Deity

The Deuteronomist's view of God and his bond with Israel also differs significantly from that expressed in the first four Torah books. Modifying the J source's more anthropomorphic portrayal of Yahweh, Deuteronomy's authors emphasize God's transcendent, spiritual nature. He is a God who cannot be seen. Deuteronomy's Moses twice insists that the Israelites saw nothing during the theophany at Mount Horeb (Deuteronomy's characteristic name for Sinai): "Then Yahweh spoke to you from the midst of the fire, you heard the sound of words but saw no shape, there was only a voice" (4:12). This assertion contrasts with the Exodus tradition that Israel's "seventy elders" gazed on God as they shared a meal with him at Sinai (Exod. 24:18). Yahweh's invisibility, in fact, becomes the rationale for banning all physical representations of the divine: "Since you saw no shape on that day at Horeb . . . see that you do not [make] for yourselves a carved image in the shape of anything at all: whether it be in the likeness of man or of a woman" (4:15–17). In the Deuteronomist's eyes, Israel's distinctiveness among the nations is to be defined not only by its festivals, dietary laws, and ethical code but also by its refusal to associate Yahweh with any physical form.

Deuteronomy's view of the Tabernacle also differs from other traditions in the Pentateuch. In Exodus, Yahweh's "glory" literally inhabits the portable shrine during Israel's desert wanderings, his presence visibly manifested by a pillar of fire by night and a column of smoke by day (Exod. 40:34–38). In Deuteronomy, however, the writers make no comparable claim, stating only that God's "dwelling-place" is simply the site where his "name" resides (12:11). As for the Tabernacle's Ark of the Covenant, where priestly writers portray God's "glory" enthroned, the Deuteronomist presents it as simply a receptacle for the tablets of the Decalogue. This "name theology," as some scholars categorize it, finds even fuller expression in the Deuteronomistic History that follows. In 1 Kings 8:27, when Solomon dedicates the Jerusalem Temple to Yahweh, he explicitly declares that no earthly structure can possibly "contain"

Israel's God. The sanctuary is sacred only because Yahweh's "name" hallows it.

While emphasizing Yahweh's invisibility and transcendence, the Deuteronomist also ignores priestly traditions that suggest a more anthropomorphic concept of God. No longer do we read that God inhales a "pleasing odor" of animal sacrifice—a persistent image in the priestly texts (Gen. 8:20–21; Lev. 1:9, 13, 17)—nor do we encounter even the slightest suggestion that Yahweh somehow needs the sacrifices that Israel was commanded to offer him. Instead, it is the poor who must be fed, and along with the resident foreigners, they have become as much the beneficiaries of the tithing system as the Levites once were (Deut. 14:28–29; 26:12–13).

War, Conquest, and Genocide

In envisioning Israel's military conquest of Canaan, the Deuteronomist prescribes a series of policies that are potentially contradictory—and most of which are likely to shock contemporary readers. When the Israelite armies approach towns that are "very far from [their settlements]," they are first to offer "terms of peace"; if the townspeople accept these terms, they are not to be killed but instead subjected to perpetual "forced labor" (20:10–11). If they resist, however, all their men must be put "to the sword" and the "women, children, and livestock" taken as a reward of victory (20:13–15). For Canaanites occupying the areas that Yahweh has sworn to give Israel, however, the policy is total genocide—the deliberate extermination of entire populations. Yahweh's reason for ordering the slaughter of every Canaanite man, woman, and child is that their culture—particularly their worship of Baal—will become an apparently irresistible temptation to the covenant people:

> You must not let anything that breathes remain alive.
> You shall annihilate them . . . just as the LORD your
> God has commanded, so that they may not teach you
> to do all the abhorrent things that they do for their
> gods, and you thus sin against the LORD your God.
> (20:16–18)

All Canaanites are thus placed "under the ban"—the ancient practice of *herem*—a policy of holy war in which the enemy is dedicated to the attackers' God and, in effect, sacrificed to him (7:2–4).

Deuteronomy, however, offers a few exceptions to the policy of destroying everything associated with the Canaanites. When an Israelite soldier sees among the enemy captives "a beautiful woman whom [he] desires[s]," he may take her home and marry her. Giving a humane twist to this provision, the statute prescribes that if she

does not fully please him, he is not allowed to sell her into slavery but must set her free instead (21:10–14).

The Deuteronomist's concern for Israel's religious purity goes far beyond the elimination of Canaanite influence, extending even to Israelite intrafamily relationships. If an Israelite's wife, son, daughter, brother, or friend suggests worshiping any god other than Yahweh, the Israelite must not shield that person, but is obligated to report the offender to community leaders and then take the lead in stoning him or her to death without "pity or compassion" (13:6–10). Besides informing on family members suspected of being apostate, Israelites are commanded to facilitate the execution of disobedient children. The parents of a "stubborn and rebellious son who will not obey his father and mother" must denounce their child before "elders" at the town gate, after which the male citizens kill the boy by stoning. According to the Deuteronomist, such drastic measures are necessary to "purge the evil from your midst," causing "all Israel [to] hear and be afraid" (21:18–21). Where threats against Israel's status as a "holy nation" are involved, the Decalogue's prohibition against killing apparently does not apply (Deut. 5:17; cf. Exod. 20:13; Gen. 9:5–6).

Prophecy

No less perplexing is the Deuteronomist's position on prophecy, and the means by which any prophetic claimant can be judged authentic or false. Deuteronomy offers two "tests" by which any prophetic utterance can be verified: a pragmatic test and a dogmatic test. The latter can be found in Chapter 13, where the people are told to disregard a "prophetic" prediction—*even if it comes true*—when the prophet's intent is to lure people into honoring other gods. What matters, then, is not the prophet's accuracy but the religious content of his message. In Chapter 18, however, the Deuteronomist insists that the final test of a prophet's credibility is the accuracy of his predictions: "When the word spoken by the prophet in the name of the LORD is not fulfilled and does not come true, it is not a word spoken by the LORD" (18:22). But whichever standard of prophetic trustworthiness the Israelites finally adopt, they are at the same time assured that Yahweh "will raise up a prophet from among you like [Moses]" (18:15). Perhaps familiar with the great prophets of the eighth and seventh centuries BCE, the Deuteronomist reassures his audience that prophecy will continue to be one of the defining institutions of Israelite religious culture, even though Moses, the greatest of prophets, has departed the scene.

The Death of Moses

Moses' departure from Israel's midst is almost as sudden and mysterious as his entrance. Further, the narrator's inability to locate Moses' burial place ensures that, like the prophet Elijah's famous ascent to heaven (2 Kings 2:9–12), his death will inspire subsequent generations to speculate about its significance. Some later traditions, preserved in the New Testament letter of Jude, claimed that the devil appeared to claim Moses' body, but that the archangel Michael—identified as the spirit "prince" who serves as Israel's heavenly guardian (Dan. 10:13, 21; 12:1)—prevented him from doing so (Jude v. 9). Although the manner of Moses' death and his lack of a marked grave gave rise to supernatural explanations, the author of Deuteronomy 34 (thought to be a priestly scribe) creates a final image of the dying Moses that is painfully memorable. The man who had served God faithfully for eighty years, repeatedly placing Israel's welfare above his own, is allowed only to glimpse the Promised Land from afar, knowing that God will not permit him to set foot upon its sacred soil.

Before his death, Moses is assigned a final task: to bless the assembled tribes and, in a sense, to foretell their destinies. Although often compared, Moses' tribal blessings and those of Jacob in Genesis 49 reveal significant differences. In Jacob's deathbed speech, two tribes clearly dominate the rest and so receive the lion's share of the patriarch's favor: Judah and Joseph. In addition, Jacob curses Simeon and Levi for their warlike behavior and predicts their decline (Gen. 49:5–7). Deuteronomy 33 offers a very different scenario with the elevation of Levi to priestly status and the disappearance of Simeon altogether. Perhaps the most remarkable shift in this tribal hierarchy is the diminishing of Judah, whose precarious situation is barely alluded to in Moses' prayerful wish that Yahweh help defend Judah in its struggle with its "adversaries" (Deut. 33:7). The variable tribal fortunes to which these two overlapping yet discordant traditions attest, as well as the uncertain destiny of the emergent nation of Israel, will become the focal point of the next segment of the Tanakh, the Prophets (Nevi'im).

QUESTIONS FOR DISCUSSION AND REVIEW

1. In what ways is Deuteronomy different from the first four books of the Pentateuch? How does it portray Moses differently? How do many of its individual laws differ from similar statutes in other Torah books?

2. Why do scholars believe that Deuteronomy was the scroll (or "book of instruction") discovered during Temple repairs in the reign of Josiah? Given the book's emphasis on a central sanctuary, how would you connect it to Josiah's campaign to destroy all rival shrines outside of Jerusalem?

3. Define the Deuteronomistic view of history. Why is the importance of Israel's faithfulness to its covenant obligations so important to this view? Cite the list of blessings and curses from Deuteronomy 28–29 in your answer.

4. If you agree or disagree with Deuteronomy's mandate to destroy all Canaanites, explain the political or ethical reasons for your position.

5. Why do you suppose that the Pentateuch ends with Israel still outside the Promised Land and with Moses dying before he can experience the fulfillment of Yahweh's promises? Why do biblical narratives repeatedly emphasize the theme of *deferred realization* of divine promises? According to Proverbs 13:12, "Hope deferred makes the heart sick, but a desire fulfilled is a tree of life." Do Yahweh's delays in implementing his promises have an adverse effect on the well-being of his people? Explain.

Terms and Concepts to Remember

Deuteronomistic view of history
Deuteronomist
Deuteronomistic History
herem
"name theology"
Shema

Recommended Reading

Clements, Ronald E. "The Book of Deuteronomy." In *The New Interpreter's Bible*, Vol. 2, pp. 271–538. Nashville, TN: Abingdon Press, 1998. The full text, with commentary.

McBride, S. Dean. "Deuteronomy, Book of." In K. D. Sakenfeld, ed., *The New Interpreter's Dictionary of the Bible*, Vol. 2, pp. 108–117. Nashville, TN: Abingdon Press, 2007. Discusses the book's historical background, structure, content, and theological meaning.

Nelson, Richard D. *Deuteronomy: A Commentary*. Louisville, KY: Westminster John Knox, 2002. A thorough discussion.

Tigay, Jeffrey A. *Deuteronomy: The JPS Torah Commentary*. Philadelphia: Jewish Publication Society, 1996. A scholarly Jewish reading of the fifth Torah book.

Weinfeld, Moshe. "Deuteronomy, Book of." In D. N. Freedman, ed., *The Anchor Bible Dictionary*, Vol. 2, pp. 168–183. New York: Doubleday, 1992. Discusses the origin and content of the Torah's fifth book.

CHAPTER 9

The Story of Ancient Israel

How the Promised Land Was Gained and Lost

Key Topics/Themes An extended narrative of Israel's history, the books of Joshua through 2 Kings begin the second major portion of the Hebrew Bible, the Prophets (Hebrew, *Nevi'im*). Traditionally known as the Former Prophets, this opening section traces Israel's historical experience from Joshua's conquest of Canaan (c. 1200 BCE, according to biblical reckoning) to the immediate aftermath of Babylon's destruction of the Judean state (587 BCE). The second half of this Tanakh division, traditionally called the Latter Prophets, consists of fifteen separate collections of prophets whose utterances were gathered together under their individual names, such as Isaiah, Jeremiah, Ezekiel, Amos, Hosea, and Micah. The rationale for referring to this entire collection of narrative and prophetic oracles as the "Prophets" seems to derive from the view that all of Israel's history is to be understood in the light of prophetic *torah*—that whatever happened to Israel historically was a direct result of the community's covenant with Yahweh and of its repeated violations of that covenant. So understood, Israel's history becomes something more than the story of the rise and fall of a relatively short-lived and politically insignificant Near Eastern state. Both the Former and the Latter Prophets proclaim a theological interpretation of historical events according to which the judgment of God can finally be seen to prevail over Israel's stubbornness and disloyalty. This convergence of history and prophecy is what gives the Tanakh's second part its internal coherence and allows us to view its diverse writings through a single interpretive lens.

The Deuteronomistic Theory of History

Scholars refer to the Former Prophets (Joshua through 2 Kings) as the Deuteronomistic History (DH) because these theologically oriented narratives rigorously interpret Israel's historical experience according to rules laid down in the Book of Deuteronomy. As noted previously, Deuteronomy's philosophy of history is inflexible: When Israel worships Yahweh alone and faithfully obeys all his instructions, the nation will win all its battles and enjoy material prosperity. But if the people—or their individual leaders—mix Yahweh's cult with Canaanite elements, particularly the cult of Baal, the nation will suffer military defeat, financial ruin, and eventual enslavement to foreign invaders. Chapters 28–30 of Deuteronomy lay out this scenario in painful detail, no doubt reflecting the sense of collective shame and abandonment felt by Israelite exiles living in Babylon after 587 BCE. By projecting the belief that they had only themselves to blame for the loss of their homeland, dating back to the era of their beginnings as a nation, Judean priests and scribes were able to impose on their national history a single, consistent understanding of the catastrophe. Most important, in spite of national humiliation, this Deuteronomistic interpretation helped to ensure the survival of Israel's concept of God. Yahweh had not broken his promises or proved incapable of protecting his covenant partner from more powerful neighbors; the people suffered because they had disregarded their obligations to honor Yahweh alone. (Box 9.1 summarizes major events in the DH.)

BOX 9.1   Major Events in the Deuteronomistic History

Interpreting Israel's story strictly according to Deuteronomy's theory of history, the Deuteronomistic authors/editors emphasize the theological meaning of seven crucial periods or events:

- Joshua's conquest of Canaan: An obedient Israel wins all its battles (Joshua).
- Period of the judges (leadership by charismatic warriors): Worshiping Yahweh alone brings victory over Israel's enemies, while disobedience brings defeat (Judges).
- The Philistine crisis and birth of the monarchy: Philistine armies threaten to overrun Israel, triggering a crisis that leads to tribal unification and establishment of a twelve-tribe monarchy under Saul, David, and Solomon (1 and 2 Samuel).

- Withdrawal of the ten northern tribes: Following Solomon's death in 922 BCE, the nation divides into two independent units—the northern kingdom of Israel and the southern kingdom of Judah, with its capital at Jerusalem (1 Kings).
- The parallel stories of the divided kingdom: While Davidic kings continue to rule over Judah, the northern state of Israel is eventually destroyed by Assyria in 721 BCE (1–2 Kings).
- King Josiah's religious reforms in Judah following 621 BCE: Assyria's decline allows Josiah to reconquer part of Israel's territories (2 Kings).
- Babylon destroys Judah: Babylonian armies burn Jerusalem and the Temple, taking upper-class Judeans into exile (587 BCE) (2 Kings).

Two Editions of the Deuteronomistic History (DH)

Scholars differ widely over who may have written the DH, with some favoring a single author, such as Jeremiah's secretary Baruch, and others preferring to speak of a school or circle of priestly writers. Most scholars agree, however, that the canonical narratives represent at least two distinct stages of composition and revision. Scribes at the court of King Josiah (ruled 640–609 BCE) may have produced the first version to accompany (and presumably validate) Josiah's ambitious religious reforms and military campaigns. Clearly, the Deuteronomistic author saw in Josiah the very model of a righteous king, praising him in terms accorded no other Davidic ruler. Not only did Josiah do "what was right in the sight of the LORD," he "turned to the LORD with all his heart, with all his soul, and with all his might, according to all the law of Moses" (2 Kings 22:2; 23:25). Using language that explicitly echoes the Book of Deuteronomy (cf. Deut. 6:4–6), the author suggests a direct connection between Josiah's reformist agenda and the composition of the DH as its official manifesto. As noted previously, discovery of a scroll in the Temple that scholars believe to be an early version of Deuteronomy serves to reinforce the belief that the period of Josiah's reign over Judah was the culmination of Israel's Mosaic heritage.

In its original form, the DH had a remarkable literary symmetry. The first edition began with an account of Joshua's stunning military and religious exploits and ended in 2 Kings with a summary of Josiah's religious reforms and partial reconquest of the Promised Land. Backed by Yahweh's invisible armies, Joshua successfully led Israel in a holy war, capturing Canaanite strongholds and overthrowing Canaanite shrines. At the conclusion of the narrative, Josiah performs similar feats, leading Judah's troops into northern territories that had been previously lost to Assyria and systematically demolishing illicit places of worship throughout his kingdom (cf. Josh. 1–11; 2 Kings 23). Both men are portrayed as national heroes who exemplify Deuteronomistic faithfulness in action. Joshua's gathering together of the tribes for a solemn covenant renewal ceremony—witnessed by a stone monument that Joshua sets up to commemorate the event (Josh. 24)—is almost exactly paralleled when Josiah stands "beside a [Temple] pillar and [makes] a covenant before the LORD." In both cases, the covenant terms are read aloud to the people, who then swear to uphold them (Josh. 24:24–28; 2 Kings 23:3).

Probably written to help promote Josiah's crusade to honor Yahweh alone, this first version of the DH could give Israel's story a happy outcome, including the complete fulfillment of all the divine promises. Although the 600-year-long period from Joshua to Josiah had witnessed many reversals, attributed to the people's covenant breaking, in the long run Yahweh and his people finally were united under a king who "walked in the way of his father David"—an earthly agent through whom God could rule effectively. Adopting the Deuteronomistic law code as his country's constitution, Josiah presided zealously over a Judean theocracy.

After Josiah's early death (609 BCE) and Judah's subsequent fall to Babylon, however, the Deuteronomistic author(s) had to revise this neatly symmetrical presentation of Israel's history. Josiah's reign could no longer be seen as the climactic fulfillment of the covenant people's relationship with Yahweh, for this glorious moment was soon followed by national calamity (2 Kings 25). Viewing Israel's history from the perspective of exile in Babylon, the Deuteronomistic editors found a way to explain their nation's collapse and the permanent overthrow of the Davidic dynasty, which Yahweh had promised would govern his people forever (2 Sam. 7). It was one of Josiah's predecessors, King Manasseh, who was responsible for the catastrophe. Immediately following the passage extolling Josiah's life-giving reforms, the editor(s) inserted this critical warning:

> Still the LORD did not turn from the fierceness of his great wrath, by which his anger was kindled against Judah, because of all the provocations with which Manasseh had provoked him. The LORD said, "I will removed Judah also out of my sight, as I have removed Israel; and I will reject this city that I have chosen, Jerusalem, and the house [Temple] of which I said, My name shall be there."

(2 Kings 23:26–27; cf. 24:3–4)

The fathers' sins would be visited upon their great-grandchildren, because "the LORD was not willing to pardon" (2 Kings 24:4).

Revised during the Babylonian exile to reflect a devastating historical reality, the books of Joshua through Kings now present Israel's history according to a single principle—the fatal consequences of disobedience to Yahweh. As the Deuteronomistic historian(s) saw it, the nation's survival was *always conditional* on the people's strict adherence to covenant laws. Josiah's heroic efforts were ultimately futile, primarily because too many other kings, most notably Manasseh, had flagrantly violated Torah commands. In the Deuteronomistic view, these ancient failures perfectly account for every lost battle, foreign invasion, drought, crop failure, famine, plague, or political humiliation. All historical figures and events in the Former Prophets are subordinated to that conviction. By scattering brief references to the coming national defeat and exile throughout the revised Joshua–Kings narrative, the postexilic editors transformed the DH. Into the description of Solomon's inaugurating Yahweh's splendid Temple, for example, the editors insert a passage stating that the newly built sanctuary is destined to "become a heap of ruins" (1 Kings 9:7–8; cf. Deut. 4:26–27; 28:36, 63–64; Josh. 23:16; 1 Kings 11:35–36; 15:3–4; 2 Kings 8:18–19;

20:16–19, etc.). With such dark foreshadowings, the DH editors give Israel's story a tragic inevitability.

 ## Major Events and Their Meaning

By selecting those traditions that best conformed to his interpretation of events, the Deuteronomistic author (or the Deuteronomistic school) was able to subdivide Israel's history into essentially four distinct periods: (1) the era of Moses and the Exodus (Deuteronomy), (2) the conquest of Canaan (Joshua), (3) the period of tribal disunity (Judges), and (4) the story of the monarchy (the books of Samuel and Kings). This schematic arrangement of Israel's past allowed the Deuteronomistic writer(s) to review the history of Israel's covenant relation in precise Deuteronomistic terms. What emerges from this overview is a portrayal of Israel's response to Yahweh that is at once linear and cyclical in nature. Seen in long perspective, Israel moves almost inexorably toward its collective tragedy as king after king displays indifference toward or contempt for Yahweh's teaching, whether revealed at Sinai/Horeb to Moses or through a succession of prophets from Samuel to Isaiah to Jeremiah.

This downhill slide toward apostasy, however, is interrupted occasionally when a judge or a king appears who is obedient to Yahweh's will and who leads Israel toward repentance—a cyclical return to divine favor that causes a temporary delay in divine judgment. In the books of Samuel, King David, in spite of his checkered past, becomes the supreme example of such a leader. As long as David serves Yahweh faithfully, David and his people prosper, conquering their enemies and moving closer to the ideal of a holy nation that God had summoned them to become. Later, King **Hezekiah** (ruled 715–687 BCE) embodies many of the same religious strengths, purging Judah of its Canaanite religious symbols and practices (2 Kings 18) and placing his trust in Yahweh's appointed prophet, Isaiah (see Chapters 16 and 18). Hezekiah's devotion is sufficient to prevent Assyria from conquering Jerusalem—it had already destroyed the northern kingdom—but the kings who follow Hezekiah are just as corrupt as their predecessors (see Figure 9.1). Yahweh withholds his punishment, but only for a time.

Under Josiah's program of national religious renewal, it looked as if God and people would be reconciled at last, but when Pharaoh Necho invades Israel, the Egyptian ruler kills Josiah in battle (609 BCE) (2 Kings 23:29–30). According to Deuteronomy's moral formula—which equates loyalty to Yahweh with good

FIGURE 9.1   Like many cities throughout Canaan, Lachish was attacked repeatedly by invading armies. This Assyrian bas-relief from the royal palace at Nineveh realistically portrays the armies of Sennacherib laying siege to Lachish (701 BCE). Although Lachish, along with forty-six other Judean towns, was totally demolished (2 Kings 23:18), Jerusalem miraculously survived the Assyrian invasion. Note the assault ramp built against Lachish's gates and the civilian inhabitants fleeing by a side exit (right), while three naked captives are impaled on pointed wooden stakes (lower center).

fortune—the righteous Josiah's premature death is incomprehensible, and the Deuteronomistic writer(s) do not attempt to explain it. Faced with an historical event that sharply contradicted Deuteronomy's basic moral assumptions, DH editors simply fall back on Manasseh's shortcomings, which were too grave for Yahweh to excuse. Committed to a single theological view, the Deuteronomistic writer(s) did not see the world of international politics as a modern historian might view it. From the Deuteronomistic perspective, the aggressive Near Eastern empires that repeatedly invaded Israel's territory during the eighth and sixth centuries BCE were not the inevitable result of imperialist expansionism but simply the means that Yahweh used to punish his people. Assyria and Babylon were, unknown to their rulers, the instruments of divine wrath. (Apparently recognizing the moral inconsistency involved in Josiah's early death, the author of Chronicles later produced a revisionist explanation for this discordant event [2 Chron. 35:20–37]; see Chapter 25.)

Sources of the History

Whether one regards the Deuteronomistic History as the work of a single late-seventh-century-BCE writer—later revised by a postexilic editor—or of a school of authors/editors, this account clearly draws its information from a variety of sources. From the rich lore of Israel's traditions, both oral and written, the DH compiler may have tapped the following hypothetical sources:

- Stories about the Ark of the Covenant (1 Sam. 2:12–17, 22–25; 4:1–7:1).

- A narrative cycle about Saul, the first king of a united Israel (1 Sam. 9:1–10:16; 10:27–11:15; 13:2–7, 15-23; 14:1–46)

- An admiring account of David's rise to power and displacement of Saul (1 Sam. 18–20)

- A Court History (also known as the Succession Narrative) relating stories about David's reign and Solomon's accession to power (2 Sam. 9–24 and 1 Kings 1–2).

- Oral traditions about the prophets Elijah and Elisha (1 Kings 17–2 Kings 9)

- Royal archives containing accounts of the kings of Judah and Israel (1 Chron. 29:29–30).

In addition to these proposed sources, the DH text itself specifically refers to older written documents, such as the Book of Jashar (Josh. 10:13; 2 Sam. 1:18). Now lost, this volume seems to have been a collection of narrative poems about the conquest and the early monarchy. The Deuteronomistic editors also cite royal archives that recorded the deeds of Israelite and Judean leaders, including the Book of the Acts of Solomon (1 Kings 11:41), the Book of the Annals of the Kings of Judah (1 Kings 14:29), and the Book of the Annals of the Kings of Israel (1 Kings 14:19). These court records may have provided more extensive coverage of the various rulers' economic, political, and military accomplishments than the Deuteronomistic compilers cared to preserve. Unfortunately, none of these sources has survived.

QUESTIONS FOR DISCUSSION AND REVIEW

1. The term *Former Prophets* refers to what portion of the Hebrew Bible? What kinds of books are found among the Former Prophets?

2. Why do biblical scholars use the term *Deuteronomistic History* to refer to the books from Joshua to Kings? What interpretation of Israel's history do these books offer?

3. Why do many scholars think that the Deuteronomistic History probably was written during Josiah's reign and then revised after the covenant people had been exiled to Babylon? Why did Yahweh allow Josiah's religious reforms to be cut short and then abandon his people to their Babylonian conquerors?

4. Why would postexilic readers of the Deuteronomistic History have felt a sense of both historical closure and promise from reading these narratives? How could the Deuteronomistic theory of history give Israel both a sense of deserved failure and a future hope in the people's relationship with Yahweh?

Terms and Concepts to Remember

Canaan, conquest and
  loss of
Deuteronomistic History

Hezekiah
Josiah

Recommended Reading

Doorly, William J. *Obsession with Justice: The Story of the Deuteronomists.* New York: Paulist Press, 1994. An informative treatment.

McKenzie, Steven L. "Deuteronomistic History." In K. D. Sakenfeld, ed., *The New Interpreter's Dictionary of the Bible,* Vol. 2, pp. 106–108. Nashville, TN: Abingdon Press, 2007. Briefly reviews current theories about the composition and editing of the DH, Joshua through 2 Kings.

Miscall, Peter D. "Introduction to Narrative Literature." In *The New Interpreter's Bible,* Vol. 2, pp. 539–552. Nashville, TN: Abingdon Press, 1998. Outlines the structure and literary components of the Deuteronomistic History.

Noth, Martin. *The Deuteronomistic History* (JSOT Supplement). Sheffield, England: Sheffield Academic Press, 1990. Carefully demonstrates how the principles of Deuteronomy were rigorously applied to the historical narratives of Joshua through 2 Kings; a standard work.

CHAPTER 10

Faith and War

The Book of Joshua

Key Topics/Themes An idealized account of Israel's conquest of Canaan, the Book of Joshua illustrates Deuteronomistic faith in action: The Israelites' military victories are a direct result of their obedience to the covenant requirements spelled out in Deuteronomy. After an introduction emphasizing the link between *torah* observance and military achievement (Ch. 1), the book describes a rapid series of successful attacks on Canaanite centers (Chs. 2–12). The second half of the book lists the apportioning of land among the twelve tribes (Chs. 13–22), concluding with Joshua's farewell speech and an intertribal covenant renewal ceremony (Chs. 23–24).

Joshua, the Bible's sixth book and the first unit of the Deuteronomistic History, vividly dramatizes Deuteronomy's assertion that perfect loyalty to Yahweh's covenant will guarantee Israel possession of its Promised Land. Portraying Yahweh as a divine warrior who invisibly leads his people to military triumph, the first part of the narrative focuses on battle scenes that show faithful Israelite soldiers as an invincible force. The famous capture of Jericho, in which the city's defensive walls miraculously crumble before the blast of Israelite trumpets, demonstrates the irresistible power of a God-directed conquest. Because God himself fights for them, the invaders win every battle and capture every Canaanite city they attack—with one instructive exception. Israel's initial assault on the town of Ai fails but, as we later discover, only because one man—Achan—disobeyed Yahweh's orders and thereby brought defeat upon the Israelite army (see below).

The Conquest of Canaan as Covenant Fulfillment

Joshua as Another Moses

The author underscores his conviction that God will overthrow all enemies of an obedient Israel by describing a

theophany intended to parallel Exodus's story of Moses at the burning bush. When Joshua beholds a supernatural figure (either Yahweh or his angel) standing before him and holding "a drawn sword in his hand" (5:13–15), he is told to remove his sandals, because the divine presence makes "holy" the ground on which he stands (5:13–15; cf. Exod. 3:5, where the same phrasing is used). As Yahweh humiliated Egypt's pharaoh, so this mysterious "commander of the army of the LORD" will ensure the Canaanites' defeat, no matter how well fortified their strongholds. Like Moses, too, Joshua leads the people through parted waters—this time the Jordan River, which is held back at flood tide to permit Israel's crossing. Instead of Moses' staff, however, it is the Ark of the Covenant, carried by priests, that effects the miracle (Chs. 3–4). Joshua also resembles the great lawgiver in adding to the Book of the Covenant, in proclaiming Yahweh's commandments, and in presiding over a reenactment at Shechem of the pact that binds Israel to God (4:1–9; 23–24).

As with Moses, God is in almost continuous dialogue with Joshua, assuring him that, if he is "resolute" in his devotion to *torah* principles, every promise made to him will be fulfilled. What follows, then, is a series of conquest stories in which God's initial vow to Joshua—"every place where you set your foot is yours" (1:3)—is realized step by step. Whatever the historical reality behind Israel's occupation of Canaanite territory may have been (see Box 10.1), the author of Joshua has no doubt that the conquest was both swift and divinely ordained:

> Thus the LORD gave Israel all the land which he had sworn to give their forefathers; they occupied it and settled in it. The LORD gave them security on every side as he had sworn to their forefathers. Of all their enemies not a man could withstand them; the LORD delivered all their enemies into their hands. (21:43–44)

The narrator does admit to some exceptions to the general rule of successful conquest—the city of Jerusalem, for example, remains in Canaanite hands (15:63)—but the overall impression given is that Joshua's invasion ran quickly and smoothly to its foreordained conclusion. By the end of his campaign, it seems as if all the tribes and the individual clans that composed them had established themselves in a defensible territory. (In the Book of Judges, however, which historians believe paints a more realistic picture of early Israel, the Israelites possess only part of Canaan and live constantly under threat of attack from their Canaanite neighbors.)

Holy War

The extent to which God is prepared to go in supporting Israelite armies is illustrated by two of the best-known conquest narratives: the destruction of **Jericho** (see Figure 10.1) and the defeat of the Amorites at **Gibeon.** At Jericho, the Israelites do not even bother to lay siege to the city walls. Instead, seven priests march in front of the Ark, making a circuit of the city on seven successive days, blowing ram's horns as they march. On the seventh day, this ceremony is repeated seven times, culminating in a collective shout by the Israelite soldiers, whereupon the walls of Jericho collapse (Josh. 6:2–20). In an even more extravagantly supernatural way, the battle for Gibeon is won when Joshua commands the sun and moon to "stand still" (10:12–13) until the Israelites have had time to pursue and kill their opponents. That "the LORD fought for Israel" (10:14) is evident not only from the completeness of the victory but also from the fact that "not a man of the Israelites suffered so much as a scratch on his tongue" (10:21). As in the Exodus account of Israel's defeat of the Amalekites (Exod. 17:8–16), divine intercession or the supernatural empowerment of a leader, or both, are the defining elements of military victory. Such is the concept of "holy war" that Israel and its neighbors evidently embraced, and however ethically questionable this concept may seem to many contemporary readers, it represents an important aspect of Israel's claim that Yahweh—a warrior—was also the Lord of history.

The idea of holy war, as presented in Joshua and other Deuteronomistic writings, carries with it both a

FIGURE IO.I This photo shows several Neolithic (New Stone Age) features of the ancient town of Jericho, including a moat, circular tower, and stone fortifications. Although one of the World's oldest inhabited towns, Jericho was apparently abandoned during the late Bronze Age, the time of Joshua's supposed invasion. If any town occupied the site then, it was small and unfortified; archaeologists have been unable to find any trace of it.

BOX 10.1 Archaeology and the Origins of Israel

At one time, it appeared as if archaeology might verify the biblical account of ancient Israel's creation—that in the late thirteenth century BCE Joshua led Israelite armies into Canaan from east of the Jordan River, violently overthrowing Canaanite strongholds from Jericho to Hazor. From the 1930s through the 1950s, some leading American archaeologists, such as William F. Albright and Nelson Glueck, arguing from then-available evidence, suggested that biblical traditions of Joshua's conquest were probably historical. As the science of archaeology developed, however, vastly improved techniques for identifying and dating the material remains of past human activities have led most contemporary archaeologists to radically different conclusions about ancient Israel's likely origins. Improvements in radiocarbon dating of organic substances, such as wood and textiles, and the use of dendrochronology (counting of tree rings) to calculate increasingly precise dates of particular artifacts have caused most scientists to abandon the notion that the earliest Israelites were foreign invaders who staged a rapid and complete military occupation of Canaan. As a result of more sophisticated methodology and greater precision in dating, late-twentieth- and early-twenty-first-century archaeologists were forced to reevaluate their predecessors' work.

After excavating hundreds of sites, archaeologists were able to find little support for the biblical version of Israel's presence in Canaan. Although a few Canaanite cities, such as Hazor (located directly north of the Sea of Galilee), were sacked and burned during the late thirteenth century BCE, the supposed time of Joshua's assault, archaeologists have uncovered no physical evidence to identify the attackers as Israelites. Indeed, cities such as Jericho and Ai, which figure so prominently in the Book of Joshua, were apparently

unoccupied during the late Bronze Age when Israelite armies allegedly destroyed them. *Ai*, in fact, means "ruin" and, in Joshua's time, had not been populated for centuries.

Although a few scholars disagree (see below), since the 1970s, archaeologists, both American and Israeli, have reached a consensus: The earliest Israelites were not outsiders from Egypt but displaced native Canaanites. Archaeological digs at more than 300 sites dating to the early Iron Age (c. 1200–1100 BCE) have uncovered innumerable artifacts documenting ancient Israel's close connection to older Canaanite culture. The oldest Israelite settlements—and their places of worship—differ little from those of their Canaanite predecessors. Whereas the Philistines, a seafaring people who entered Palestine shortly after the Israelites supposedly arrived from Egypt, brought with them an easily recognizable style of pottery, art, and architecture, the early Israelite settlements reveal no comparable distinctiveness in their material culture. Even their large storage jars that feature a reinforcing band around the neck (known as "collar-rim" jars), which archaeologists once thought were unique to Israelite settlements, turn out to be Canaanite in origin (see Figure 10.2).

Extensive surveys of all known archaeological sites reveal this sequence of events: During the twelfth and eleventh centuries BCE, a rapid growth of new settlements in Canaan's previously little-populated central hill country suggests the appearance of what some archaeologists call "proto-Israel." Of the more than 300 early Israelite sites archaeologists have identified and analyzed, including both farms and villages, virtually all display an unbroken continuity with traditional Canaanite culture. One possible scenario suggests that as large Canaanite cities in the fertile coastlands underwent

rationalization for the mass slaughter of Israel's enemies and a rigorous code of military etiquette that places under a sacred *herem* (ban) all persons and valued objects associated with the enemy. When they capture Jericho, the Israelites—following the divinely mandated *herem*—systematically kill "all in the city, both men and women, young and old, oxen, sheep, and donkeys" (6:21). Pursuing a policy of genocide, Joshua's troops treat all Canaanites as if they were sacrifices to Yahweh, destroy-

ing "all that breathed, as the LORD God of Israel commanded" (10:40; cf. 10:30–33, 39; 11:11–14). God, in fact, is portrayed as inspiring Canaanite leaders to resist Joshua's armies, "so that they would come against Israel in battle, in order that they might be utterly destroyed, and might receive no mercy, but be exterminated, just as the LORD had commanded Moses" (11:20).

The Israelites' failure to capture **Ai,** which immediately follows their spectacular success at Jericho,

FIGURE 10.2 High, isolated mounds that dot the Palestinian landscape, tels represent sites of long-term human occupation, with a series of towns built successively atop the ruins of their predecessors. At most excavated sites, Israelite settlements superimposed upon older Canaanite towns show marked continuity with Canaanite culture, including styles of pottery and architecture.

socioeconomic collapse—part of the widespread upheavals that afflicted the Aegean and eastern Mediterranean region at the end of the Bronze Age and in the early Iron Age—Canaanite agricultural workers escaping the oppression of urban landowners fled to the central hill country. There they could start new lives beyond the reach of Canaan's tyrannical elite. Whether the newcomers were previously pastoral nomads or sedentary farmers fleeing urban despotism, they were, as most archaeologists agree, indigenous Canaanites, not foreign invaders (see Finkelstein and Silberman, and Dever in "Recommended Reading").

Despite archaeologists' general agreement that early Israel formed a continuum with older Canaanite culture, a few scholars insist that the earliest Israelites were in fact invaders from regions east of the Jordan River. Anson Rainey of Tel Aviv University argues that the early Israelites represented a southern extension of Aramean tribes that surged into Mesopotamia and North Syria (the ancient name of which was Aram). Rainey and others suggest that the proto-Israelite branch of migrating Arameans moved into Palestine's hilly terrain, settling and adopting local customs, including Canaanite pottery styles. To support his theory, Rainey cites several biblical passages, including Deuteronomy's famous credo: "A wandering Aramean was my ancestor [Jacob, whose name was changed to Israel]" (Deut. 26:5). Other scholars find more significant hints about Israel's Canaanite origins outside the Deuteronomistic texts. The prophet Ezekiel, for example, tells Israel:

> Canaan is the land of your ancestry and there you were born; an Amorite was your father and a Hittite your mother. . . . Then I [Yahweh] came by and saw you kicking helplessly in your own blood, and bade you live. (Ezek. 16:3–6)

Whatever light future archaeological discoveries may shed on Israel's historical origins, at present archaeology can offer little evidence to confirm the account of Joshua's conquest of Canaan.

makes abundantly clear how severe divine judgment can be when the rule of *herem* is ignored. When Joshua discovers that Achan had taken a shawl and some silver and gold as booty, he decrees that the man, as well as his entire family and domestic animals, be placed under *herem* and stoned to death, thereby removing the stain of covenant disobedience from the rest of the Israelite nation. That this rule could be relaxed, however, is apparent in two incidents. First, when the Gibeonites convince Israelite leaders that they have come from a distant land and so do not fall under the lethal category of "neighbors" (9:3–27), they are spared. Then, when Joshua captures and burns Hazor, identified as the major city in Canaan, they massacre the entire population but keep its livestock and other wealth for their own use (11:14).

The notion that Yahweh is prepared to destroy all of Israel's enemies and, ultimately, all of the world's great empires for the benefit of his chosen people is deeply embedded in texts that visualize Yahweh as a warrior-god (Exod. 15:3). And this notion lives on in the pages of later prophetic and apocalyptic literature (see the discussion of Daniel in Chapter 26). In Joshua, this idea assumes particularly graphic form in the battle for Gibeon, where Yahweh appears to fight alongside Israelite armies, hurling down huge hailstones that crush the opposing forces (10:11). Even the "Anakim," described in the Book of Numbers as "giants" who so intimidate the Israelite spies that they feel like "grasshoppers" (13:33), are either driven out of the land or killed, as Yahweh finally makes good on his Genesis promise to set aside the land of Canaan as Israel's inheritance (Josh. 11:22–23).

◇ | The Land That Israel Inherited

Fundamental to the biblical understanding of the relationship of Israel to the land it occupied was the belief that the land, with all its potential goodness, was a "gift" from Yahweh. Equally important, that gift was part of Yahweh's covenant and, like that agreement, was given on condition of service and loyalty. The Hebrew term most often used to define the nature of Yahweh's land grant is *nahalah*, meaning either "portion" or "inheritance." Whichever specific meaning one assigns to this word, it clearly presupposes that the Israelites did not "win" Canaan through their armed strength. Rather, it was bestowed upon them as an expression of Yahweh's generosity and in remembrance of God's oaths to Israel's ancestors. What follows from this conviction was the often-repeated assumption that Israel would continue to reside in the land "flowing with milk and honey" (Exod. 3:8) only as long as Yahweh permitted it. As the supreme landowner, Yahweh—if offended by his tenants' behavior—could take away their land as quickly and easily as he had given it in the first place.

> Do not say to yourself, "My power and the might of my own hand have gotten me this wealth." But remember the LORD your God, for it is he who gives you power to get wealth, so that he may confirm his covenant that he swore to your ancestors, as he is doing today. If you do forget the LORD your God and follow other gods to serve and worship them, I solemnly warn you today that you shall surely perish, because you would not obey the voice of the LORD your God.
>
> (Deut. 8:17–19)

Echoing the Deuteronomistic view, Israel's prophets of the eighth through the sixth centuries BCE consistently argue that if Yahweh can "summon" his people out of Egypt, he can just as surely send them back again as punishment:

> When Israel was a child, I loved him,
> and out of Egypt I called my son.
> The more I called them, the more they went from me;
> they kept sacrificing to the Baals,
> and offering incense to idols . . .
> They shall return to the land of Egypt,
> and Assyria shall be their king,
> because they have refused to return to me.
>
> (Hos.11:1–5)

Possession of the land, like nationhood itself, is therefore contingent (as are all things) upon divine judgment. Given the generally tragic course of Israel's history, biblical authors could interpret its loss of both land and nationhood only in terms of Deuteronomistic principles, with their strict logic of moral cause and historical effect.

Yet, for all the disastrous consequences of its covenant disobedience, Israel—and its God—does not regard defeat and exile as a permanent condition. As prophets from Amos to Malachi assure the covenant people, Yahweh will not entirely abandon them. The exile will not last forever, and at least a "remnant" of exiles will return to rebuild war-ravaged Judah. In a memorably poignant image, Jeremiah compares the land of Israel to Jacob's wife Rachel, who longs for the return of her exiled "children":

> A voice is heard in Raman, lamentation and bitter weeping.
> Rachel is weeping for her children;
> she refuses to be comforted for her children, because they are no more.
> Thus says the LORD:
> Keep your voice from weeping, and your eyes from tears; . . .
> they shall come back from the land of the enemy;
> there is hope for your future, says the LORD:
> your children shall come back to their own country.
>
> (Jer. 31:15–17)

What is sometimes called the "territorial dimension" of the covenant—the belief that Israel's attachment to the land is as enduring as God's love—is the theological assumption that stands behind this passage and many others like it. It may appear contradictory for any prophet to argue that, on the one hand, Israel has no entitlement or "right of possession" to the land

and that, because of its sins, it will be driven from its land, while, on the other, to proclaim that Judah will be restored both to its land and to God's favor. But this is exactly the prophetic message regarding the exile and all that follows from it. In combining two apparently opposing points of view, biblical prophets express their conviction that God's covenant with Israel is, at heart, a relationship of unconditional (and therefore redemptive) love.

Joshua's Covenant Renewal Ceremony

One of the most important sections of the Deuteronomistic History, Chapter 24 of Joshua offers a dramatic presentation of covenant values, as well as tantalizing clues about early Israel's ethnically and religiously mixed population (see Box 10.1). A careful reading of this crucial passage shows that the Israelite tribes who assemble at **Shechem** to renew their covenant vows to Yahweh consist of a varied population with different cultural and religious backgrounds. Rather than a unified group of recently liberated Egyptian slaves, the crowd at Shechem includes peoples of both Mesopotamian and Canaanite origins. Joshua begins his speech, modeled on Moses' farewell address in Deuteronomy, by observing that "long ago your ancestors . . . lived beyond the Euphrates and served other gods." He then asks his hearers to reject both the ancestral gods of Mesopotamia and the Canaanite deities they presently worship, "the gods of the Amorites in whose land you are [now] living" (24:14–15). When the crowd swears that they will "serve the Lord [Yahweh], for he is our God," Joshua questions their ability to do so. His audience of mixed ethnic groups has not fully understood the implications of Yahweh's "jealousy": An oath to worship Yahweh means that they cannot also honor Canaanite or other deities, for if they combine Yahweh's cult with that of Baal, God will destroy them (24:19–22). That the assembly at Shechem includes Canaanite groups—people who had not experienced the Exodus or previously been part of the Mosaic arrangement—is strongly indicated when Joshua orders the people to "put away the foreign gods that are among you and incline your hearts to the Lord, the God of Israel" (24:23). Joshua's plea would be unnecessary to a people who had journeyed with Yahweh for forty years through the wilderness. But it is understandable when

applied to groups previously unfamiliar with Yahweh's demands for exclusive devotion. (See Box 10.2 for three theories about Israel's origins.) Not only are the new recruits to the religion of Yahweh "witnesses" against themselves if they fail to live up to their commitment, but a more enduring "witness" is also invoked—the stone that Joshua erects to testify "against [them]: for it has heard all the words of the Lord that he spoke" (24:27–28). Regardless of their ethnic roots, the entire company is henceforth obligated to revere Yahweh alone.

The site of Joshua's covenant ceremony is significant. Shechem was an ancient Canaanite cult center of Baal Berith (literally, "Lord of the Covenant"); it was also a site near which Jacob had built an altar to El, the high God of Canaan with whom Yahweh was identified (cf. Judg. 9:1–6, 37; 10:47; Gen. 35:1–15). It thus had important associations with both native-born Canaanites and Israel's forebears. The fact that the Joshua narrative shows the Israelites occupying this area without having to fight for it suggests that the native inhabitants were already well disposed to the newcomers. Apparently, they were ready to merge with them and accept their God, whom they could envision as another manifestation of El, high God of Canaan as well as of Israel (Gen. 33:20).

In the opinion of many scholars, early Israel encompassed a variety of ethnic groups that achieved a tentative unity under the banner of worshiping Yahweh alone. If some indigenous Canaanite groups, as the prophet Ezekiel suggests (Ezek. 16:3–6), joined a band of escaped slaves from Egypt, they apparently agreed to embrace the Exodus story as their own, becoming by adoption children of Abraham and followers of the Mosaic tradition. In this case, the Exodus–Conquest story provided a unifying national theme that forcefully expressed a composite Israel's collective partnership with God.

Although Joshua preserves hints that Israel's occupation of Canaan involved both migrants from Egypt and some elements of the native Canaanite population, its primary function in the Deuteronomistic History is to emphasize that a covenant people faithful to their divine warrior will reap the rewards of Yahweh's promises to Abraham. Continued possession of the Promised Land, as Joshua's final warnings at Shechem make clear, depends entirely on the people's resolve to resist the temptations posed by Baal and other Canaanite gods and to honor Yahweh exclusively. All the discrete groups making up Israel were to echo Joshua's famous vow: "As for me and my household, we will serve the Lord" (24:15).

BOX 10.2 Three Models for the Origins of Israel

A lack of archaeological evidence to support the Book of Joshua's claim that Israelites invading from Egypt rapidly conquered and displaced native Canaanites during the late thirteenth century BCE has given rise to alternative theories about Israel's origins. Drawing on both biblical texts and archaeological discoveries, scholars have proposed three main theories, none of which has won general acceptance.

The Conquest Model

According to the first of these three hypothetical reconstructions of Israel's beginnings, the traditions about Israel's exodus from Egypt and military invasion of Canaan contain an element of authentic historical memory. As proof that a band of Israelites *did* invade Canaan, the proponents of this model point to the fact that sites such as Hazor and Debir seem to have undergone destruction at the end of the Bronze Age, although admittedly no evidence connects these destructions to the Israelites. They also note that the Merneptah inscription acknowledges that Israel was already present in Canaan by the late thirteenth century BCE (see Chapter 3). Critics of this theory, however, cite the total absence of archaeological proof for the Israelites' presence in Egypt, their journey through the Sinai desert, or their conquest of Palestine.

The Infiltration Model

Noting the sudden growth of small villages and farm communities in Canaan's previously unoccupied central hill country during the early Iron Age, advocates of the infiltration model argue that these newly established settlements represent Israel's earliest presence in the region. Rather than entering Canaan as violent warriors, these "proto-Israelites" immigrated gradually and peacefully, engaging primarily in pastoral and agricultural occupations. Although some immigrants may have come from Egypt, as a group they readily assimilated Canaanite culture, adopting Canaanite words such as *El* and *Elohim* when referring to their God. This theory not only explains the enduring popularity of Canaanite gods—Baal and Asherah—among the Israelite masses, it also helps to account for Israel's political disunity and its tribal leaders' deep distrust toward the monarchy (Judges and 1 Samuel). If the immigrants were largely unrelated, they probably felt no inclination to unite under the leader from a single dominant tribe, such as David's tribe of Judah.

The Social Revolution Model

By contrast, the third—"revolutionary"—model assumes that the people who became the Israelites were native Canaanites (a view generally supported by archaeological findings), some of whom rebelled against an exploitative urban elite, overthrowing their former rulers and establishing a society that valued relative freedom and independence. The rebels were composed of various indigenous Canaanite peoples who shared a common dislike of the aristocracy that governed the area during a period of declining Egyptian influence. Some of these Canaanite revolutionaries are allegedly referred to in the Amarna letters (correspondence that Canaanite rulers sent to Egypt's pharaoh) as *Hapiru*, whom the Egyptians regarded as bandits but sometimes employed as hired soldiers. It was these rebel city-dwellers and peasants who attacked several Canaanite cities, such as Hazor, undermining the ruling classes from within as well as without. The social revolution model explains the undeniable similarity between early Israelite and Canaanite culture, as well as the Israelite tribes' enduring suspicion of kingship. Additionally, the weakening of Egyptian control over Canaan following the death of Rameses III in the mid-twelfth century BCE would have made it easier for a peasant revolt to succeed, particularly if the trigger for that uprising was the introduction of a new religious movement, that of Yahweh. The social revolution theory, however, fails to explain why successful rebels decided to cast themselves as former Egyptian slaves or why they adopted the worship of Yahweh, a "jealous God," who absolutely refused to share his cult with any Canaanite deity.

Many scholars believe that none of these theories adequately addresses the complexity of Israel's historical origins. Not only is the available evidence too inconclusive to verify any of the three proposals, we also know little about the ethnic composition and civilization of Canaan's diverse peoples, let alone about the nomadic tribes who wandered in and out of the region. There remains a huge gap between Merneptah's brief reference to Israel in the late thirteenth century BCE and the much later inscriptions alluding to Israel's kings in the ninth century BCE. For almost 400 years, the archaeological record is virtually silent, leaving only the biblical texts from which to construct tentative theories about Israel's origins.

QUESTIONS FOR DISCUSSION AND REVIEW

1. How does the Book of Joshua equate fidelity to Yahweh with military and political success? In what specific incidents, such as the capture of Jericho and the failed assault on Ai, does the book illustrate the Deuteronomistic thesis?

2. In Joshua's idealized account of the Israelites' conquest of Canaan, in what ways does Yahweh function as divine warrior?

3. Define the concept of "holy war," and the use of *herem* in Joshua. What reasons do Deuteronomy and the Deuteronomistic History give to justify God's command to slaughter the entire population of Canaan? What do you think of this principle?

Terms and Concepts to Remember

Ai	Jericho
Book of Jashar	Palestine
Gibeon	Rahab
herem	Shechem

Recommended Reading

Coote, Robert B. "The Book of Joshua." In *The New Interpreter's Bible*, Vol. 2, pp. 555–719. Nashville, TN: Abingdon Press, 1998. A good analysis of the parallel stories of Joshua and Josiah.

Dever, William G. *Who Were the Early Israelites and Where Did They Come From?* Grand Rapids, MI: Eerdmans, 2003. Cites archaeological evidence for Israel's origins as an indigenous Canaanite people.

Finkelstein, Israel, and Silberman, Neil A. *The Bible Unearthed: Archaeology's New Vision of Ancient Israel and the Origins of Its Sacred Texts.* New York: Simon & Schuster, 2001. Points out the lack of archaeological evidence to support biblical accounts of Israel's ancestors, the Exodus, or the conquest of Canaan.

Gottwald, Norman K. *The Tribes of Yahweh: A Sociology of the Religion of Liberated Israel, 1250–1050 BCE.* Maryknoll, NY: Orbis Books, 1979. A groundbreaking argument for Israel's indigenous Canaanite origins as revolutionaries overthrowing urban elites.

Laughlin, John C. H. "Archaeology." In K. D. Sakenfeld, ed. *The New Interpreter's Dictionary of the Bible*, Vol. 1, pp. 232–247. Nashville, TN: Abingdon Press, 2006. A concise introductory survey of archaeological excavations in areas related to the Bible.

McDermott, John J. *What Are They Saying About the Formation of Israel?* Mahwah, NJ: Paulist Press, 1998. Surveys current theories about Israel's origins.

Meyers, Carol. "Early Israel and the Rise of the Israelite Monarchy." In L. G. Perdue, ed., *The Blackwell Companion to the Hebrew Bible*, pp. 61–86. Malden, MA: Blackwell, 2001, 2005. Surveys current archaeological and critical evaluations of Israel's origins.

Stager, Lawrence E. "Forging an Identity: The Emergence of Ancient Israel." In M. D. Coogan, ed., *The Oxford History of the Biblical World*, pp. 123–175. New York: Oxford UP, 1998. Surveys archaeological and textual evidence regarding Israelite origins and self-identity.

CHAPTER 11

Yahweh's Warriors
The Book of Judges

Key Topics/Themes Whereas the Book of Joshua indicates that the Israelites quickly and triumphantly occupied most of Canaan, the Book of Judges offers a more sober, and perhaps more realistic, view of Israel's tenuous hold on its Promised Land. A transitional account surveying the chaotic period between Joshua's death and the formation of Israel's monarchy (c. 1200–1020 BCE, according to biblical calculation), Judges emphasizes a strictly Deuteronomistic interpretation of Israel's history. When Israelites mix Yahweh's worship with Canaanite cults, their enemies conquer them. However, when the people repent and call on Yahweh's help, he inspires a "judge" (Hebrew, *shofet*) to lead Israelite armies victoriously against their oppressors, giving them temporary peace. Called to provide a military solution to repeated crises, the judges are not legal figures but charismatic ("spirit-filled") warriors whose job is to keep Israel from losing the limited parts of Canaan it already occupies. Without a central government, and threatened on all sides by stronger neighbors, such as the Philistines, the fiercely independent tribes drift toward a state of political and moral anarchy, as shown by the concluding account of tribal war against Benjamin. As the narrator bleakly comments, "In those days there was no king in Israel, and every man did what was right in his own eyes" (21:25).

Major and Minor Judges

Viewed structurally, the Book of Judges has six developed narratives, each recounting the exploits of a particular figure, such as Deborah, Gideon, or Samson. These are the "major" judges, as distinct from the "minor" figures, who are often little more than names on a page. The total number of judges, however, is twelve, which suggests that the Deuteronomistic author(s) wished to make these individual figures representative of Israel's twelve-tribe confederacy, imposing a tentative unity on a thoroughly disunited society that engaged in more or less constant local warfare.

Almost all of the major judges are politically "unattached" warriors who serve no one but themselves and Yahweh. Except for leading a few tribes into battle, they are not associated with tribal governance or with any intertribal organization. Gideon, in fact, does not appear to have been anything but a farmer when he was drafted into Yahweh's service. To make matters worse (from the

Yahwist standpoint), Gideon and his family seem to have been followers of Baal—hence his "other" name, *Jerubbaal*, meaning "let Baal plead" (see Figure 11.1).

Without a strong king who could unite the often uncooperative tribes (Deborah bitterly complains that only a few tribes will fight against a common enemy), Israel was forced repeatedly to defend its territorial claims in a series of inconclusive battles against its neighbors, including the bordering states of Edom, Moab, Philistia, and Ammon. Lacking a central sanctuary or an organized priesthood to enforce Yahweh's worship, the people behave as if Yahweh's *torah* was largely unknown to them (see Box 11.1). Seemingly ignorant of Yahweh's "jealousy," many Israelites apparently see no conflict in mixing his worship with that of rival gods, particularly the Canaanite Baal. According to the Deuteronomistic narrator, this **syncretism**—blending elements of different religions to create a new faith—explains Israel's inability to possess all of Canaan. It also allows the author to impose on this book a thematic unity and give the narrative a cyclical pattern: A fall from faith brings

FIGURE II.I This model shows a typical Israelite four-room house. With its four enclosed rooms arranged around a central courtyard, which was shared with domestic animals and where most of the household work was done, this pillared structure had a flat roof that offered its occupants a place to sleep on hot summer nights.

suffering, followed by repentance and restoration. When a righteous judge leads the people into worshiping Yahweh exclusively, the whole community prospers, winning all its battles against invading troops. After the loyal judge dies, however, the Israelites soon "prostitute themselves to Baal," arousing Yahweh's anger and causing him to abandon them to their enemies. In their anguish, the people then cry out to Yahweh, who is "moved to pity" and raises up a new judge to overthrow Israel's oppressors. After a generation of peace, the people typically backslide, and the whole cycle begins anew. This theory of history, with its theology of victory and defeat—the controlling thesis of the Deuteronomistic History (DH)—is clearly set forth in Judges 2:11–23. This crucial passage ends with a theological explanation of Israel's military failure to expel the Canaanites and to possess the land they claimed by divine right:

> Then the Israelites did what was wrong in the eyes of the LORD, and worshipped the Baals, and they abandoned the LORD, the God of their ancestors who had brought them out of the land of Egypt; they followed other gods, from among the gods of the peoples who were all around them, and bowed down to them; . . . So the anger of the LORD was kindled against Israel, and he gave them over to plunderers who plundered them; . . . Then the LORD raised up judges, who delivered them out of the power of those who plundered them. Yet they did not listen even to their judges; for they lusted after other gods and bowed down to them. . . . Whenever the LORD raised up

judges for them, the LORD was with that judge, and he delivered them from the hand of their enemies all the days of the judge. . . . But whenever the judge died, they would relapse and behave worse than their ancestors, following other gods.

(Judg. 2:11–19)

From a Cyclic Return to a Downward Spiral

Although tales about the various judges may seem to be placed in random order, the narrator subtly arranges his individual stories to illustrate a general theme. In the first part of the book, the author emphasizes the cyclic fall-from-and-return-to divine favor, but in the second half, he moves to a darker, less hopeful presentation of Israel's deteriorating condition. The transition from narratives in which judges bring Israel back to Yahweh to those reflecting a seemingly unstoppable downward spiral toward social chaos is the passage reporting on Abimelech's attempt to make himself king at Shechem (Ch. 9). After this tale of royal ambition ending in bloody conflict, Israelite leadership seems ever more deeply flawed. Jephthah, who follows Abimelech, commits human sacrifice and Samson, who never leads even a single clan to fight for Israel, is almost totally absorbed in his own erotic pursuits. The DH editors save their

BOX 11.1 Judges' Picture of the Emergence of Yahweh's Worship in Canaan

As the Book of Judges presents it, the Israelites' faith in Yahweh struggles against the seemingly irresistible temptation to combine his worship with that of Baal and other Canaanite gods. The Torah's portrayal of Yahweh's "jealousy"—his demand for exclusive devotion—seems not to have penetrated the people's consciousness, leaving them open to their Canaanite neighbors' religious influence. Judges' description of a religiously weak and confused Israel is difficult to reconcile with the nation's "official" history presented in Exodus through Joshua. In the Deuteronomistic version of Israel's past, the Israelites had possessed the complete Torah—and therefore knew their God's precise requirements, as well as the spectacular miracles he had performed on their behalf—ever since their encounter with Yahweh at Sinai/Horeb, making their repeated falls into apostasy inexcusable. In the Deuteronomistic Histroy, the people are shown as either willfully rebellious or massively indifferent to Yahweh's teaching, even though Joshua 24 states that all the tribes gathered at Shechem had unanimously sworn to abide by "the book of the law of God" (Josh. 24:24–26).

In contrast to Joshua, with its idealized version of Israel's invasion of Canaan, the Book of Judges shows not only how little of the land the tribes actually possessed but also how little they seem to know of Yahweh and the Mosaic *torah*. Judges preserves brief but important glimpses of early Israel's religious practices, indicating that instead of having been imported complete and ready-made into Canaan, the religion of Yahweh emerged slowly and painfully in a thoroughly Canaanite context. Contrary to the later official record, many biblical scholars believe that the cult of Israel's God probably evolved in a lengthy and complex process of syncretism, the blending together of different religious traditions to create a new religion.

Honoring Other Gods

Joshua notes that even after the Israelites had supposedly lived for two generations under the Mosaic Covenant, the people still honored Egyptian and Mesopotamian gods (Josh. 24:14). Judges adds that in Canaan the people worshiped a diverse array of gods: Baal, his female consort Astarte, and deities from almost every neighboring culture, including those of Moab, Ammon, Syria, Phoenicia, and Philistia (10:6). One of Judges' most prominent leaders,

Gideon, also bears the name Jerubbaal, a name extolling Baal's role as his worshiper's defender. After Yahweh appears to him, however, Gideon tears down Baal's altar and constructs a new shrine to Yahweh on the spot (6:25–32), an action by which Yahweh not only replaces a rival deity but also incorporates his attributes and powers. Foreshadowing this syncretism, Genesis states that when Abraham arrived at Salem, an ancient Canaanite shrine thought to be the future site of Jerusalem, he borrowed the titles of the Canaanite *El Elyon* (God Most High) for his divine patron, Yahweh (Gen. 14:17–22). At Shechem, where Joshua ratified Yahweh's covenant, Jacob centuries earlier had built an altar there and "called it El-Elohe-Israel [God the God of Israel]" (Gen. 33:20). According to Judges 9, a temple to "El-berith [El of the Covenant]" stood at Shechem during the time of Gideon's son Abimelech (Judg. 9:46); it is the same shrine referred to in Judges 9:4 as the "temple of Baal-berith [Baal of the Covenant]." Yahweh, eventually known as "Lord of the Covenant," is thus preceded by older Canaanite divinities who once held the same title. As archaeological discoveries of Israelite places of worship show them to be virtually identical to older Canaanite shrines, so the Judges narrative allows us to see that Yahweh's worship apparently emerged gradually in life-and-death competition with the cults of Baal and other Canaanite deities.

Judges also preserves a tradition that Yahweh was somehow associated with Edom (also called Seir), a nation reportedly descended from Jacob's twin brother Esau (Gen. 36:1). According to the Song of Deborah and Barak,

> Lord, when you went out from Seir, when you marched
>   from the region of Edom,
> the earth trembled, and the heavens poured, the clouds
>   poured water.
> The mountains quaked before the Lord, the one of Sinai,
> before the Lord, the God of Israel.

(Judg. 5:4–5)

In this passage, perhaps one of the oldest texts in the Bible, the poet attributes to Yahweh the turbulent qualities of Hadad, a storm god widely known in Canaan by his most common title *Baal* (Lord). Many scholars believe that the concept of the biblical Deity developed, at least in part, through the assimilation of traits and functions of older Near Eastern divinities, an historical process evident in Judges.

worst example of social degradation for the important end position, concluding their review of the nation's early history with an extended tale of gang rape, mutilation, murder, and savage intertribal warfare.

The Book of Judges' final verdict on the events described—perhaps added by a later editor—implies that the lack of a king, who presumably could have enforced laws of social order and covenant loyalty, accounted for Israel's decline into anarchy (21:25). Yet the story of Abimelech, who tried and ingloriously failed to establish an Israelite monarchy, leaves readers in doubt that a king is the answer to Israel's woes.

Ehud

The narrator begins his survey of prominent judges with **Ehud,** a left-handed Benjaminite, who, acting alone, succeeds in murdering Eglon, the king of Moab. Interestingly, we are told that Yahweh had "strengthened" the Moabite ruler to dominate the Israelites for eighteen years, to punish them for faithlessness (3:12). In a scene combining carnage with comedy, Ehud—claiming that he has "a word from God" for the king (3:20)—deceives Eglon into granting him a private interview. Unexpectedly drawing his hidden sword (presumably from his right side, where no one would expect to find it), Ehud plunges the blade into Eglon, who was so obese that the entire sword and hilt disappeared as "the fat closed over the blade." After Ehud escapes through a side window, the king's retainers speculate that their monarch, who has remained unusually quiet in his upper room, must be answering the call of nature. Ehud then raises an army from the northern tribe of Ephraim, which kills 10,000 Moabite warriors—vulnerable now that their leader is dead—and breaks Moab's hold on Israel so that the land "had rest eighty years" (3:12–30).

Deborah and Barak

In the story of **Deborah** and **Jael,** a similar act of politically motivated murder is celebrated as an execution of divine judgment. Of all the judges, Deborah is the closest to a figure of conventional religious authority. She functions not only as a judge, dispensing justice under her palm tree, but also as a "prophetess" (Hebrew, *isha n'viah*). When Barak, the general called upon to fight against Jabin, a local Canaanite prince, wants to know the best time to attack, he must rely on Deborah to set the date, for only she can discern Yahweh's plans (4:4–16)

Israel's God not only communicates through Deborah, but also employs another woman, **Jael,** who is married to a Kenite, to accomplish what Barak and other male soldiers cannot do. When **Sisera,** Jabin's army commander, flees from Barak and eludes capture, Jael lures him into her tent, where she hides and feeds him. While Sisera, having accepted the sacred protection of hospitality, sleeps, Jael drives a tent peg through the skull of her too-trusting guest. This act of treachery is hailed throughout Israel, proof that Yahweh could recruit a most unexpected warrior—a "mere" woman—to bring down his people's enemies. Emphasizing the humiliation a male warrior would feel at being slain by a woman, the narrator later quotes Abimelech, who lay dying from wounds incurred when a woman standing atop a tower threw a millstone at his head. Abimelech orders his armor-bearer to stab him "so people will not say about me, 'A woman killed him'" (9:52–54).

Jael's heroic deed is related twice, first in prose (4:17–22) and again in a long poem ascribed to Deborah and Barak, which not only praises Jael as "most blessed of women" (5:24) but also raises the overthrow of Jabin and Sisera to the level of a cosmic event:

> The stars fought from heaven,
> from their courses they fought against Sisera. (5:20)

Gideon and Abimelech

One of the more appealing judges, the humble **Gideon** is presented in stark contrast to his son, **Abimelech,** the only Israelite leader who proudly aspires to be king. Underscoring one of the book's persistent themes—that Yahweh must work with deeply flawed human material—Gideon is depicted as peculiarly unsuited to become Yahweh's chosen deliverer: He comes from a family of devoted Baal worshipers. His given name, Jerubbaal, means "let Baal plead" or "Baal defend him," although the text gives a different interpretation of the name (6:32). When Yahweh's messenger (or perhaps God himself) suddenly appears to inform Gideon that "the LORD is with you, mighty warrior," the devotee of Baal is skeptical. If Yahweh is really on their side, why has Israel been reduced to a state of utter poverty and famine by invading Midianite hordes, who have stripped the country bare, leaving the people nothing to live on? When the angel insists that Gideon is nonetheless Yahweh's choice to rescue Israel from Midianite oppression, Gideon responds in the conventional manner of a prophet resisting his call, emphasizing his unimportance and inadequacy. Only after Yahweh miraculously sets an altar afire does Gideon acknowledge God's presence, erecting an altar to Israel's divine warrior. At Yahweh's direction, under cover of darkness, he also tears down Baal's local altar, building a shrine to Yahweh on the site, much to the displeasure of his neighbors (6:11–32).

After Yahweh empowers Gideon with his spirit, God orders him to reduce the size of his Israelite army from a reported 22,000 to a small band of 300 men. The reason for this drastic cutback, Yahweh explains, is to make sure that the coming victory over Midian is publicly recognized as entirely God's work; otherwise, Israel "might take credit away from me" (7:2).

Abimelech's Ruinous Experiment

Following Gideon's military successes, the people invite him to be their king and establish a hereditary monarchy in which his sons would automatically succeed him—an offer he firmly rejects, declaring that in Israel "only the LORD will rule over you" (8:22–24; cf. 1 Sam. 8:4–22). Gideon's refusal to assume permanent power because God alone is Israel's true ruler is not merely an act of heroic self-denial but also a model for the Israelite theocracy. When Gideon's son Abimelech later accepts an offer of local kingship at Shechem, the ancient Canaanite sanctuary where Joshua had assembled the tribes in a covenant renewal ceremony, his behavior illustrates the potential evils of monarchy. Beginning his reign by slaughtering his seventy brothers, potential rivals to the throne, Abimelech is soon perceived as an object lesson in tyranny, a threat to Israel's traditional freedoms.

In a dramatic scene, Jotham, Gideon's only surviving legitimate son (Abimelech is the offspring of a slave girl), stands atop Mount Gerizim and graphically warns the citizens of Shechem about the evil that Abimelech's rule will bring upon them. As Jotham predicts, within three years, Abimelech's oppressive policies cause the men of Shechem to revolt, setting off a fiery chain of events that ends with Shechem's destruction and Abimelech's death at the hands of a woman (9:22–57). From the narrator's viewpoint, this attempt at kingship, in which thousands lost their lives, not only demonstrates the pitfalls of royal despotism but also anticipates the violent excesses of some later Israelite kings.

Jephthah and His Unnamed Daughter

Judges' account of Abimelech's destruction is a turning point in the narrative. Instead of reporting a cyclic process of sin, punishment, and redemption, the narrator now shows Israel plunging into a quagmire of political instability and violence. The son of Gideon and a prostitute whom his father's family has disinherited, **Jephthah** is one of the most morally equivocal judges. Possessed by "the spirit of the LORD," Jephthah vows that if God will grant him victory over the Ammonites, he will sacrifice as a burnt offering the first person he meets after returning home from battle. Ironically, this person turns out to be his virgin daughter, who, "with timbrels and dancing," has come to congratulate him on his triumph. After granting his "only child" an interval to prepare herself, Jephthah, as the narrator coolly phrases it, "did with her according to the vow he had made." The writers/editors do not condemn the implied human sacrifice. Rather, they cite the tale as an etiology explaining the ritual custom of Israelite women who annually lamented the horrific fate of Jephthah's daughter (11:29–40).

Samson and Delilah

Unlike any other figure in Judges, Samson—strongman and fabled lover—seems strangely detached from his fellow Israelites. He neither leads armies nor champions Yahweh's cause against Baal, but instead appears to live only for himself, pursuing his troubled relationships with women and fighting mainly for personal reasons. Even his most famous action—single-handedly pulling down the temple of **Dagon,** a Philistine god—appears motivated as much by a desire for personal revenge as by devotion to Yahweh (16:28). Nonetheless, Samson's career well demonstrates the author's view that God is able to use even the most unlikely human agent to accomplish his purpose, the death and humiliation of the Philistines (16:30–31).

The Deuteronomistic writer indicates Samson's importance in God's plan for defending Israel not only by giving his story more space than that allotted to any other judge (Chs. 13–16) but also by implying that Samson's role was divinely ordained. An angel twice foretells his birth to a childless couple, who are instructed to dedicate their son as a Nazarite. As visible signs of their consecration to Yahweh, **Nazarites** were to abstain from wine or other alcoholic drinks, eat only ritually "clean" foods, and leave their hair uncut. A man of driving passions as well as superhuman physical strength, Samson hardly fits the Nazarite ideal. His battles with the Philistines are less the result of a divine calling than the often accidental by-product of his amatory adventures. A seafaring people who then occupied the southwest coast of Canaan, the **Philistines** had already mastered the techniques of manufacturing iron weapons and horse-drawn war chariots, skills the Israelites apparently lacked. By introducing the Philistines as Israel's most dangerous enemy, the narrator prepares for the story of David that follows in the books of Samuel. Resembling Samson in his passionate nature, David will complete the judges' work by permanently eliminating the Philistine threat.

It is Samson's sexual affairs with women, both wives and prostitutes, rather than a wish to advance Israel's cause, that typically involve him in violent confrontations with the Philistines (15:1; 16:1). The hero's most celebrated entanglement is with **Delilah,** whom the Philistines bribe to betray her hitherto invulnerable lover. Breaking his Nazirite vow by revealing the secret of his strength, Samson, shorn of his hair, is captured, blinded, and enslaved at a Philistine mill. Only when his hair begins to grow again does Yahweh's spirit empower Samson to exact a final vengeance on his tormentors. In destroying Dagon's temple, along with 3,000 of the god's Philistine worshipers, the blinded hero surpasses his previous deeds: "So those he killed at his death were more than those he had killed during his life" (16:30).

Some commentators regard Samson, whose name in Hebrew, *Shimshon,* means "little sun," as a mythical figure whom early storytellers transformed into an Israelite champion. Certainly, if Samson is an historical character, his fellow Israelites do not see him as Yahweh's chosen instrument against the Philistines (15:9–20). In the Deuteronomistic History, however, he functions as a colorful example of Yahweh's ability to utilize even the most flawed character in accomplishing his purpose. When Samson crushes Dagon's worshipers—who are shown attributing Samson's imprisonment to their God's power—he proves himself, like Jael, an unexpectedly effective warrior against Israel's oppressors. Despite his spectacularly destructive final act, however, Samson does little to aid his fellow tribesmen during the long twenty years he had allegedly "judged Israel" (16:31).

 ## The War Against Benjamin

The Deuteronomistic editors reserved the most savage episode in Judges for the conclusion. Chapters 19–21 describe the Benjaminites' rape and murder of a Levite priest's woman companion, whose corpse the Levite cuts into eleven pieces, sending the eleven body parts to eleven tribes and asking them to avenge the crime by declaring holy war on the Benjaminites. Whereas Deborah had complained about the tribes' failure to unite, in this case, all eleven tribes cooperate to wipe out a fellow tribe of Israel. With Benjamin reduced to a mere remnant of its former size, the other tribes belatedly realize that they have almost exterminated an important part of Israel. Attempting to get around their vow never to marry their own daughters to any Benjaminite, the eleven tribes encourage the few surviving men of Benjamin to kidnap the women of **Shiloh.** In this way, the nearly extinct Benjaminites can recruit wives from

fellow Israelites without the other tribes' breaking their sworn oaths. Like the story of Abimelech, this narrative may serve as a criticism of the monarchy: Israel's first king, **Saul,** was both a failure and a Benjaminite, the leader of a supposedly tainted group.

After describing the social and moral turmoil afflicting early Israel, Judges' editor(s) pens a final ambiguous comment: "In those days there was no king in Israel; all the people did what was right in their own eyes" (21:25). Israel's early tribal experience gave the people little to choose from: Spirit-empowered leaders, no matter how temporarily successful, provided no lasting peace, and Abimelech's failed experiment in kingship boded ill for a future monarchy.

QUESTIONS FOR DISCUSSION AND REVIEW

1. Why does the author of Judges present Israel's early history as a repeated cycle of apostasy, punishment, and restoration? What function does the role of "judges"—military deliverers—play in this cycle? Why do the Israelite tribes repeatedly fall under the domination of neighboring kings and require rescuing from a series of oppressors?

2. How do the careers of individual judges—such as Ehud, Deborah, Barak, Gideon, and Jephthah—illustrate the Deuteronomistic theory of history? How does Samson differ from the usual kind of "judge"?

3. Discuss the significance of women in the Book of Judges, including the stories of Deborah, Jael, and Delilah, as well as unnamed women, such as Samson's mother and the Levite concubine who was raped, killed, and dismembered.

4. What conclusions does the Deuteronomistic author of Judges apparently draw from the repeated failures of Israel's tribal leaders to ensure either Israel's self-preservation or its fulfillment of covenant obligations? Why is teaching of Mosaic Law absent from the Judges narrative?

Terms and Concepts to Remember

Abimelech	Jephthah
Barak	judge
Dagon	Nazirites
Deborah	Philistines
Delilah	Samson
Ehud	Shiloh
Gideon	Sisera
Jael	syncretism

Recommended Reading

Dearman, J. Andrew. "Canaan, Caanites." In K. D. Sakenfeld, ed., *The New Interpreter's Dictionary of the Bible*, Vol. 1, pp. 532–535. Nashville, TN: Abingdon Press, 2006 Includes discussion of Canaanite religious cults completing with Israel's worship of Yahewh.

Hacket, Jo Ann. "There Was No King in Israel: The Era of the Judges." In M. D. Coogan, ed. *The Oxford History of the Biblical World*, pp. 132–164. New York: Oxford UP, 1998. A perceptive essay on the social forces operating during the period of the judges.

Matthews, Victor H. "Judges, Book of." In K. D. Sakenfeld, ed., *The New Interpreter's Dictionary of the Bible*, Vol. 3, pp. 446–457. Nashville, TN: Abingdon Press, 2008. Analyzes the sociological setting of the period and the ethical character of individual war leaders.

Olson, Dennis T. "The Book of Judges." In *The New Interpreter's Bible*, Vol. 2, pp. 723–888. Includes detailed commentary placing the tribes of early Israel in their Canaanite context.

Van Der Toorn, Karl. "Baal" and "Baals." In K. D. Sakenfeld, ed., *The New Interpreter's Dictionary of the Bible*, Vol. 1, pp. 367–370. Nashville, TN: Abingdon Press, 2006. Summarizes myths connected with Yahweh's chief rival in Israelite reliogion.

Webb, Barry G. *The Book of Judges: An Integrated Reading.* Sheffield, England: JSOT Press, 1987. A helpful resource.

CHAPTER 12

The Rise of David and the Birth of a Kingdom
The Books of 1 and 2 Samuel

Key Topics/Themes Although named for Samuel, a prophet and priest who is also the last of Israel's judges, the books of Samuel are really the story of David's rise to power as the ruler of the United Kingdom of Israel. Presenting David's triumph as the fulfillment of Yahweh's vow to bring from Abraham a line of kings, the narrative incorporates several different sources, including one favorable to the new institution of monarchy and another strongly opposing it. The first Book of Samuel begins by narrating the career of Samuel (Chs. 1–12) and then interweaves narratives about the tragic reign of Saul, Israel's first king, with accounts of David's God-directed ascent to Israel's throne (Chs. 13–31).

Second Samuel focuses entirely on David's reign, recounting his military victories, including the capture of Jerusalem, which he makes his new capital, and the establishment of a royal covenant in which Yahweh promises that David's heirs will rule over Israel forever (Chs. 1–7). David's fortunes abruptly decline, however, after his adulterous affair with Bathsheba and his plot to kill her husband, Uriah (Chs. 11–12). Although Yahweh does not desert him, David's crimes result in severe consequences, particularly in the form of domestic treachery and public rebellion (Chs. 13–20). An appendix of stories about David not integrated into the main narrative closes the book (Chs. 21–24).

The canonical books we know today as 1 Samuel and 2 Samuel were originally one long and unbroken narrative tracing the rise of the monarchy in the late eleventh century BCE. The separation of this narrative into two distinct books probably occurred when the scroll was translated from Hebrew, which was originally written without vowels, to Greek, which employs both consonants and vowels. Apparently finding it impractical to put the entire narrative on a single scroll, editors of the Greek Septuagint decided to divide the narrative into two volumes, ending the first with the death of Saul. A coherent narrative unit, the two volumes present one overarching theme—the rise of **David** from obscure shepherd boy to king of "all Israel." As the figure of Moses dominates four books of Torah, so that of David overshadows this literary account of Israel's political growth from a weak group of loosely confederated tribes to a powerful, united monarchy.

David, in fact, is the pivotal character in the Deuteronomistic History (DH): His appearance as Yahweh's divinely appointed ruler occupies the two central books. The first two volumes, Joshua and Judges, act as a prologue to David's story, highlighting the chaotic conditions that prevailed "when there was no king in Israel," before David arrived to rescue the covenant people from their own disorganization. The last two books, 1 and 2 Kings, evaluate the reigns of David's successors, most of whom compare unfavorably to their forefather David, the man "after God's own heart." In vowing to maintain David's heirs on the royal throne forever (2 Sam. 7), Yahweh binds himself to David and his descendants as to no other Israelite group, guaranteeing that Davidic hopes are inevitably part of Israel's future history. (New Testament writers, who typically portray Jesus as David's ultimate successor, emphasize Jesus' biological descent from David [Matt. 1:1–17; Luke 3:23–32; Rom. 1:3–4, etc.].)

The Book of 1 Samuel

The Role of Samuel

Although both books bear his name, **Samuel** dominates only the first twelve chapters of 1 Samuel and does not appear at all in 2 Samuel. In fact, as soon as David appears on the scene midway through the first book, he quickly overshadows all other characters, including his older rival, King Saul. Still, Samuel is a major player in the founding of Israel's monarchy, and he serves as a perfect transition from the era of the judges to the era of the kings. Perhaps the only biblical figure to play three roles simultaneously—those of prophet, judge, and priest—Samuel resembles the court prophets, such as Nathan, who come after him. He is also closely associated with the monarchy as an institution and with the two young kings he helps to place on Israel's throne. Ironically, Samuel's view of the monarchy is distinctly unfavorable. In fact, Yahweh privately informs him that the people's desire for a king is actually a rejection of God himself, no matter how dysfunctional the old judicial system has proven to be. Nonetheless, Yahweh instructs Samuel to warn the people of how they will be cruelly exploited when they appoint a king to rule over them:

> These will be the ways of the king who will reign over you: he will take your sons and appoint them to his chariots and his horsemen, and to run before his chariots. . . . He will take your daughters to be perfumers, cooks, and bakers. He will take the best of your fields, vineyards, and olive orchards, and give them to his courtiers. He will take one tenth of your grain and your vineyards and give it to his officers and his courtiers. He will take your male and female slaves, and the best of your cattle and donkeys, and put them to his work. He will take one-tenth of your flocks, and you shall be his slaves.
>
> (1 Sam. 8:11–17)

Yet, for all his opposition to establishing a monarchy, Samuel is instrumental in providing a religious basis for kingship by the very act of anointing Israel's first two kings. Like priests, kings receive their authority from God and so must be consecrated to him, symbolized by the **anointing** ritual, which consists of pouring holy oil over their heads. For all his disapproval of the institution, it is Samuel who first selects and anoints Saul, and then—while Saul is still reigning—secretly anoints David, thus ensuring the monarchy's continued existence. Samuel's reluctance to endorse the monarchy wholeheartedly, while at the same time acting to validate the authority of Israel's first two kings, seems typical of the mixed feelings the narrator displays throughout the books of Samuel. Some scholars regard the detailed catalogue of David's moral failings in 2 Samuel as an implicit indictment of the royal office he occupies, a position that leads to an abuse of power and that causes Yahweh to afflict David's people with plague and political turmoil. By contrast, the author of 1 Chronicles, who offers a revised version of David's reign, carefully erases all references to David's misdeeds. Instead, the Chronicler presents him chiefly as a priestlike leader whose life work is to prepare for building the Jerusalem Temple (1 Chron. 11–29).

Hannah's Prayer

At the opening of 1 Samuel, the author introduces a crucial Deuteronomistic theme—the absolute necessity for Israel's leaders to obey Yahweh's commands, and the terrible consequences that follow when they do not. This theological perspective appears first when **Hannah** offers a prayer of thanksgiving for the birth of her only child, Samuel. Declaring that Yahweh exercises total control over human lives, awarding success to the humbly obedient and a painful downfall to the arrogant, Hannah's words lay down the ethical standard that will determine the fate of Israelite rulers:

> The bows of the mighty are broken,
> but the feeble gird on strength. . . .
> The LORD kills and brings to life;
> he brings down to Sheol* and raises up.
> The LORD makes poor and makes rich;
> he brings low, he also exults . . .
> The LORD will judge the ends of the earth;
> he will give strength to his king,
> and exalt the power of his anointed.
>
> (1 Sam. 2:4, 6–8, 10)

Supporting the weak and overthrowing the strong who grow proud or oppressive, Yahweh initiates unexpected reversals of fortune among Israel's leadership. In addition to exalting Samuel while removing **Eli** and his sons from priestly office at Shiloh, Yahweh brings about Saul's ruin even as he raises David from obscurity to wealth and power. When David, in turn, grows overconfident and abuses his kingly authority by treacherously arranging for the death of Uriah, husband of the woman he covets, Yahweh punishes his favorite by creating for David the same kind of trouble that the king had inflicted on

---

*Sheol: the underground abode of the dead, where both good and wicked are housed in gloomy desolation (see Box 23.1).

others. Distorted images of their father—ambitious, lustful, opportunistic—David's sons Ammon and Absalom wreak havoc within the royal household. As if reenacting his father's undermining of Saul, Absalom captures the people's affection and temporarily drives David from power, causing him to experience what Saul must have felt when displaced by a younger rival. As Hannah had correctly observed, when dealing with Israel's God, even kings must expect their political successes and failures to correlate precisely with their degree of loyalty to Yahweh's covenant.

Samuel, Saul, and the Philistine Crisis

Despite the diversity of oral and written sources it uses, 1 Samuel is a skillfully constructed work of literature, binding diverse traditions with the same theme of **divine election** that motivates the action in Genesis and Exodus. As Yahweh suddenly, with no reasons given, calls selected individuals such as Abraham, Jacob, Joseph, and Moses to perform special tasks, so he chooses Samuel from before birth to serve him. The stories of the principal characters, each of whom is divinely elected in turn, are intricately interwoven. When Eli, a well-meaning but ineffectual High Priest who acts as Samuel's mentor, declines into impotence, God elevates Samuel to a position of moral leadership, ensuring that the cult rituals at the Ark of the Covenant will be properly maintained. As Samuel replaces Eli, so he prepares **Saul,** who first appears in Chapter 8, to take over Israel's government. Saul no sooner ascends the throne, than Samuel breaks with him, becoming his chief critic. David's appearance on the political stage introduces a new conflict, the jealous competition between King Saul and his successor—a rivalry that ends with Saul's death (Chs. 13–17, 31).

The Philistine Crisis The first seven chapters, describing Samuel's career, also paint a grim picture of Israel's political and religious situation, which is now even more desperate than that portrayed in Judges. Eli is feeble, and his sons are corrupt; the Philistines inflict a humiliating defeat on the Israelite armies and capture the Ark of the Covenant, the portable wooden shrine on which Yahweh is invisibly enthroned. Israel's loss of its most sacred possession is a crushing blow to national prestige, but its captors receive no benefits. The Philistines immediately are afflicted with a strange plague of tumors (some translations render them as "hemorrhoids"), which they ascribe to the Ark's supernatural powers. Although a twenty-year peace ensues following the Ark's return to Israel, continued Philistine aggression denies the Israelites any security.

Samuel and Saul Pressured by the Philistines and other enemies, many Israelites may have doubted their nation's continued existence. Some may have recognized that the old tribal confederacy, which lacked central leadership and was splintered by tribal rivalries, was no match for a tightly organized aggressor headed by a warrior-king. With Israel's future uncertain, some tribal leaders seem to have decided that national survival required the political unity that only an able king could give. When the elders petition Samuel to appoint a king, however, the narrator gives them no higher motive than a conformist desire to "be like other nations" (8:19).

The scribes and editors who produced the books of Samuel repeatedly draw on strikingly different traditions about the events they narrate, so it is not surprising that we have two versions of Samuel's anointing Saul as king—as well as two versions of how David became part of Saul's court. In the first version, God tells Samuel that he has already selected "a man from the land of Benjamin" to be king, even identifying his choice when Samuel comes upon a young man searching for his lost donkeys. After inviting Saul to feast at his house, Samuel privately anoints him as Israel's first king (9:14–10:8). In the second account, Samuel summons "all the tribes of Israel" together at Mizpah and casts lots to identify Yahweh's choice as king. Standing "head and shoulders" above other men, Saul is publicly identified as "the one whom the LORD has chosen. There is no one like him among all the people" (10:17–27). Both of these accounts depict Saul in a favorable light, suggesting to many scholars that one of the DH sources was a biography of Saul that emphasized his kingly qualities. According to this view, the final portrait of Saul that we now have in 1 Samuel—which shows him rapidly deteriorating into violent paranoia—is an unflattering revision of an older account. Scribes who supported David and his dynasty later redrew Saul's portrait, making him the neurotic failure he had to be for David justly to replace him.

Samuel's choice of Saul to lead the nation out of its social confusion and military weakness is logical. Tall, handsome, and brave, Saul belonged to a tribe so small and insignificant that his election does not arouse tribal jealousies. The incidents over which Samuel withdraws his support (in David's favor) illustrate, even after pro-Davidic editing, how impossible was Saul's historical position. When the prophet-priest fails to appear to offer the sacrifices necessary before going into battle, and when soldiers are deserting in droves, Saul tries to save the situation by performing the ritual himself—only to have Samuel furiously denounce him for taking over priestly duties (13:8–15). Although the narrator

---

implies that Samuel is justified in forbidding kings to take on priestly tasks, in 2 Samuel and 1 Kings, both David and Solomon routinely offer sacrifices at Yahweh's shrines (cf. 1 Kings 8:62–65). The decisive break occurs when Saul, perhaps feeling pity for a fellow ruler, spares the life of Agag, an **Amalekite** king who had been placed under the ban (*herem*), to be killed in Yahweh's name. Announcing that God has rejected Saul for disobedience, Samuel proceeds to butcher Agag as an offering "before the LORD in Gilgal" (15:10–33). Withdrawing the support of Israel's religious leadership, Samuel not only abandons Saul but also ensures his political downfall. Depicted as suffering from epilepsy and extreme depression, Saul rapidly loses control of events, particularly when the Philistines launch a new attack.

The Rise of David   At this critical moment, the narrative's real hero appears, a charismatic youth destined to replace Saul as king and to found a dynasty that will endure for more than four centuries. The writer's use of multiple sources is apparent in the two different versions of David's introduction to Saul's court. In the first account, David is presented as "a man of valor, a warrior," who is also a musician, a harpist whom Saul employs to drive out an "evil spirit" that God sends to torment him (16:14–23). In the second version, David is introduced as a stranger to Saul (17:55–56), and he is not a valiant soldier but "just a boy" who volunteers to fight the Philistine champion **Goliath** in single combat. Otherwise unarmed, David fells the "uncircumcised" Goliath with a stone from his slingshot (17:4–54). Countless generations have thrilled to the story of an adolescent youth overpowering a heavily armed giant with his simple homemade weapon, but in fact, David may have had little to do with Goliath's death. Portrayed as a God-empowered leader who would transform Israel from a faltering confederacy into a powerful, if short-lived Near Eastern mini-empire, David is credited with several legendary feats, some of which may have been accomplished by his associates. An appendix to 2 Samuel states that the Philistine warrior was slain by one of David's soldiers: "Elhanan son of Jaareoregim, the Bethlehemite, killed Goliath the Gittite, the shaft of whose spear was like a weaver's beam" (2 Sam. 21:19).

In general, biblical authors are concerned less with historical accuracy than with theological significance. As Yahweh's chosen one—Samuel secretly anoints him even before he joins Saul's retinue (16:1–13)—David acts as God's representative. When the DH writer portrays him as an inexperienced shepherd boy who overcomes a seemingly invincible giant, the purpose is to demonstrate that Yahweh can use weak human vessels to accomplish great deeds. David's speech to Goliath makes clear that slaying Israel's enemies is Yahweh's work, for which no human being can take credit:

> You come against me with sword and spear and javelin; but I come to you in the name of the LORD of hosts, the God of the armies of Israel, whom you have defied. This very day the LORD will deliver you into my hand, and I will strike you down and cut off your head; . . . so that all the earth may know that there is a God in Israel and that all this assembly may know that the LORD does not save by sword and spear; for the battle is the LORD's and he will give you into our hand. (17:45–47)

Further evidence that David enjoys divine favor appears when Saul's son Jonathan declares his love for the victorious youth. As the king's presumed heir, **Jonathan** should be David's chief rival. Instead, he works to promote David's advancement, stripping off his armor and giving it to his friend—an act that foreshadows David's taking his place as Saul's successor (18:1–5). Jonathan's sister **Michal** also becomes devoted to David, who, by marrying the king's daughter, further cements his ties to the royal family. If David's winning over his children does not arouse Saul's suspicions, the song that Israelite women sing in David's praise may have. Hailing David as a warrior superior to their king, the women indiscreetly portray him as a potential danger to Saul:

> Saul has killed his thousands,
> and David his tens of thousands. (18:7)

The king determines to eliminate his rival by having him lead assaults on the Philistines.

Blessed with an ability to command personal loyalty, David uses the affections of Jonathan and Michal, both of whom prefer to help him rather than their father, to derail Saul's attempts to murder him. When forced to flee Israel and take refuge among the Philistines, David even wins the friendship of the Philistine ruler, on whom he also practices his abundant powers of deception (Chs. 19–23). An outlaw and guerrilla fighter, David survives by his wits, eluding capture and twice refusing to kill Saul when he has the opportunity to do so. His restraint pays off, for when the Philistines eliminate Saul and Jonathan at the Battle of **Gilboa,** the way is open for David to ascend the throne (Chs. 24–31).

To heighten the contrast between Saul, whom God has abandoned and whom he afflicts with "evil spirits," and David, whose ambitions God crowns with success, the narrator portrays Saul as alienated from all positive divine communication. Driven by fear and despair, Saul consults a spirit medium, the infamous "woman of Endor," who conjures up the ghost or "shade" of Samuel. Rather than encouragement, however, Samuel has only curses for Saul: God has torn the kingdom from him and given it to David—and Saul is doomed to die the next day at Gilboa (28:3–25). Although active at various times in Israel's history, spirit mediums were outlawed (Deut. 18:10–11; Lev. 19:31), and consulting them was considered akin to idolatry. Eventually, biblical writers would reduce Saul's entire career to a description of his suicide after the Battle of Gilboa, a defeat blamed on his forbidden visit to the woman at Endor (1 Chron. 10:1–14).

The Book of 2 Samuel

David's Lament for Jonathan and Saul

The opening chapter of 2 Samuel, which continues uninterrupted the story of David's rise to Israel's throne, highlights two contradictory aspects of David's character that help make his personality so fascinating. In the beautiful poem lamenting the deaths of Saul and his son, David expresses an apparently genuine grief, especially for Jonathan, whose "love to [him] was wonderful, passing the love of women" (2 Sam. 1:19–27). In the preceding prose section, however, David behaves in a way that blends a public display of passionate grief with ruthless ambition. When the Philistines eliminate both Saul and his heir—the chief obstacles to David's advancement—David punishes the men responsible for advancing his cause, acquiring a public reputation for piously mourning fallen enemies. By executing the Amalekite who claims to have slain the former king, David not only absolves himself of any responsibility for Saul's death but also proclaims the life of Yahweh's anointed ruler to be sacred—a policy necessary to protect his own anointed status (1:1–16).

Acknowledged king of Judah, his own tribe, David has yet to become ruler of the northern ten tribes, who accept Saul's son **Ishbaal** (also called Ishbosheth) as their rightful monarch. After two chieftains from Benjamin (Saul's tribe) murder Ishbaal, bringing his head to David, the Judean king explicitly refers to his treatment of the Amalekite messenger, immediately sentencing both of his would-be benefactors to death (4:1–12). In each case, David quickly silences anyone who helps to clear the way to the throne, lest people suspect that he had somehow influenced them to act on his behalf. Although he owes much of his success to **Joab,** commander of his army, David repeatedly condemns his general for killing the king's opponents (3:22–39), particularly for Joab's removal of David's traitorous son **Absalom** (18:9–19:9).

Closely examining David's political motives and policies, the historian Baruch Halpern concludes that David was probably responsible for most of the violent actions that swept opponents from his path (see *David's Secret Demons* in "Recommended Reading").

After Ishbaal's murder, David, who has reigned over Judah at **Hebron** for seven years, is acclaimed king of all twelve tribes (5:1–5). Freed from pursuing intertribal warfare with the House of Saul, David now undertakes military campaigns—most led by the ruthlessly efficient Joab—that significantly expand Israel's borders. One of David's first exploits is to capture the Jebusite town of Jerusalem, which Joshua and his successors had been unable to conquer (Judg. 1:21). On the border between the territories of Judah and Benjamin, this ancient Canaanite sanctuary (cf. Gen. 14:18–24) was an ideal administrative site. By bringing the Ark of the Covenant to Jerusalem, David makes his capital the religious as well as political center of the newly united nation (2 Sam. 6).

Shrewdly drawing on the military and executive abilities of loyal followers like Joab, Abishai, and Elhanan (21:15–22), David quickly drives back the Philistines and the Ammonites, and forces neighboring states like Edom, Moab, and Damascus to pay him tribute. The text implies that at its greatest extent David's kingdom stretches from the frontiers of Egypt in the south to the Euphrates River in the northeast, although "the river" marking Israel's northern border is not named (see Figure 12.1). Scholars such as Baruch Halpern suspect that later editors exaggerated the dimensions of David's territorial conquests to make them fit the outline of the Promised Land given to Abraham in Genesis 15:18.

As the books of Samuel present it, a single man—whom Yahweh adopts as his son and whose political success is divinely ordained—rapidly transforms the fortunes of the nation, triggering a cultural revolution that affects almost every aspect of Israelite life. Commercial treaties with **Hiram of Tyre** and other trading peoples stimulate a flow of wealth and cosmopolitan influences into Israel such as it had never known before (Chs. 5 and 8). Not surprisingly, in ages to come, when the covenant people had fallen far short of the splendors that 2 Samuel describes, popular memories concerning this "lion of Judah" would shape the people's hopes for a new deliverer like David. Yahweh's Anointed (Hebrew, *mashiah*, "messiah")—a term applied to all Davidic kings—was to resemble David, beloved of God, a conquering hero and a political savior of his people (see the section "Israel's Messiah: A Jewish-Christian Debate," in Chapter 29).

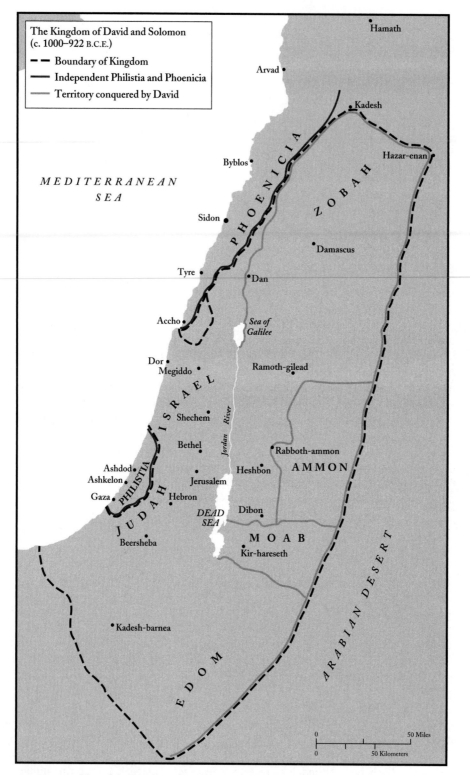

FIGURE 12.1 Map of the Kingdom of David and Solomon (c. 1000–922 BCE). At its height, the Davidic kingdom incorporated the territories of several neighboring states, including Edom, Moab, and Ammon.

The Davidic Covenant

In 2 Samuel 7, David offers, through his court prophet **Nathan,** to build a permanent sanctuary for the Ark, only to receive a polite refusal from Yahweh, coupled with an extraordinary promise:

> The LORD [Yahweh] has told you that he would build up your royal house. When your life ends and you rest with your forefathers, I will set up one of your family, one of your own children, to succeed you and I will establish his kingdom. It is he who shall build a house in honor of my name, and I will establish his royal throne forever. I will be his father, and he shall be my son. . . . Your family shall be established and your kingdom shall stand for all time in my sight, and your throne shall be established forever.

(2 Sam. 7:11–16)

Yahweh's pledge to establish David's line on Israel's throne "forever" is known as the Royal or **Davidic Covenant.** Like the vow to Abraham, this covenant—in stark contrast to the Mosaic pact—is *unconditional,* representing God's absolute attachment to an individual and his descendants. The difference here, of course, is that divine protection is given to a ruling family, and Yahweh is identified as the ruler's "father," an image repeated in the Psalm literature as well (Pss. 2; 89). As a "foundation myth," the Davidic Covenant confers a degree of legitimacy and permanence on the Davidic line that no other ruling family can claim. Whereas the highly conditional Mosaic Covenant is made with the Israelite people as a whole, the unconditional promise to David is restricted to the male heirs of a single family, who, according to God's explicit word, are guaranteed permanent dominion over the covenant community. Although Deuteronomistic writers—responding to Babylon's destruction of Jerusalem in 587 BCE—will eventually modify the terms of this covenant, making it dependent on individual rulers' obedience (cf. 1 Kings 9:1–9), biblical editors allowed the divine promise to stand uncontested in 2 Samuel 7 (cf. 2 Sam. 23:5). In Psalms 89, which renders Yahweh's sworn oath to David in poetic form, God's vow is also absolute, with no hint that it depended on human faithfulness.

David and Bathsheba

David's star continues to rise unimpeded—"the LORD gave victory to David wherever he went" (8:7, 13–15)—until he commits a fatal error, involving himself in a sordid affair of adultery and murder. When David abuses his kingly authority by seducing the already married Bathsheba and then plotting the death of Uriah, her husband, he reveals a depth of selfishness and amorality that raises questions about his fundamental character. To his credit, David sees immediately how appalling his conduct has been when Nathan, employing a parable, accuses him of having stolen Bathsheba (2 Sam. 12:1–7). Far from defending his conduct, David accepts his guilt and then does penance for his sins, but his repentance comes too late to avoid divine punishment. In general, Yahweh's anger falls on David's children, who, one after another, commit crimes of violence and disloyalty that mimic their father's misdeeds.

After David's firstborn son, Ammon, rapes his half-sister, **Tamar,** her full-brother, **Absalom** avenges (his) honor by killing the rapist. The assault of brother against brother echoes that of Cain and Abel, as well as the recent fratricidal civil wars that divided the houses of Saul and David (2–4). When Absalom, whose good looks and gift for attracting followers are a mocking image of the young David, leads a rebellion against his father, the aging king is forced to abandon his capital and seek refuge east of the Jordan River. Once again coming to his master's rescue, Joab disobeys David's instructions by killing Absalom, thus ending a major threat to David's crown. David's extravagant grief over his son's death disgusts the army commander, who rightly accuses the king of unwisely showing "love of those who hate you and . . . hatred of those who love you" (19:1–8).

Absalom's rebellion reveals a widespread dissatisfaction with David's rule, particularly among the northern tribes, whose battle cry is "What share have we in David? We have no lot in the son of Jesse. Away to your homes, O Israel" (2 Sam. 20:1). Although the loyalty of figures like Joab and the counselor Hushai prevents David from losing both his throne and his life, unhappiness with the Davidic dynasty persists through the next generation and resurfaces after Solomon's death (1 Kings 12–13). It is Solomon's heir (and David's grandson), Rehoboam, who will witness the permanent consequences of this tribal discontent, when the ten northern tribes reject the Davidic monarchy to form a separate nation of Israel.

Appendices

A collection of supplementary documents that have not been integrated into the main narrative forms the conclusion of 2 Samuel. These documents preserve six incidents, of which the theologically most significant are the first and last additions. In the first (2 Sam. 21), a three-year famine, conveniently interpreted as a sign of divine anger against Saul's family, gives David an excuse

---

to eliminate Saul's seven surviving sons. As potential causes of future rebellion, Saul's sons are turned over to their old enemies, the Gibeonites, for impalement.

The last supplement (2 Sam. 24) presents Yahweh inspiring David to take a census of the people, after which God punishes David's action by sending a plague that kills 70,000 Israelites. (Later biblical writers, apparently noting the moral illogic of such divine behavior, revise the story to make "Satan"—not Yahweh—the motivator of the census, a highly unpopular move because numbering of the population was done primarily for purposes of taxation and military recruitment [see 1 Chron. 21].) On the advice of the prophet Gad, David buys a Jebusite property used for threshing wheat, builds an altar there, and offers sacrifice to Yahweh. Perhaps because it is made at the future site of the Jerusalem Temple, David's sacrifice halts the Angel of Death in his tracks, thus ending the plague. This final narrative is consistent with 2 Samuel's portrayal of David's contradictory character: David is both the cause of his people's troubles and the instrument of its cure.

QUESTIONS FOR DISCUSSION AND REVIEW

1. According to 1 Samuel, what was the national crisis that brought about the formation of the Israelite monarchy? How does the story of the Philistines' capture of the Ark of the Covenant illustrate Israel's dire circumstances?

2. Summarize the opposing views of monarchy that we find in 1 Samuel. In what ways does Hannah's prayer at the beginning of the book introduce themes involving Yahweh's control of the rise and fall of Israel's leaders? How do Saul's fall and David's rise demonstrate the accuracy of Hannah's statements?

3. Summarize the terms of the Davidic Covenant. In what ways does it resemble the covenant with Abraham but differ essentially from the covenant mediated through Moses? How do God's promises to David make him and his male heirs different from all other members of the covenant community?

4. Consider the pattern of David's life and his reign. At what point do things begin to go very badly for him, and why?

Terms and Concepts to Remember

Absalom	Joab
Bathsheba	Jonathan
David/Davidic Covenant	Michal
Eli	Nathan
Gilboa, Battle of	Samuel
Goliath	Saul
Hannah	Tamar
Hebron	Uriah
Hiram of Tyre	

Recommended Reading

Alter, Robert. *The David Story: A Translation with Commentary of 1 and 2 Samuel.* New York: Norton, 2000. A fresh version of the Samuel narratives with helpful background explanations.

Birch, Bruce C. "The First and Second Books of Samuel." In *The New Interpreter's Bible*, Vol. 2, pp. 949–1383. Nashville, TN: Abingdon Press, 1998. Includes the complete texts, plus thorough annotation and interpretation.

Cross, Frank M., ed. "The Ideologies of Kingship in the Epic of the Empire: Conditional Covenant and Eternal Decree." In *Canaanite Myth and Hebrew Epic: Essays in the History of the Religion of Israel.* Cambridge, MA: Harvard UP, 1973. An important analysis of Israel's understanding of the Davidic Covenant.

Finkelstein, Israel, and Silberman, Neil. *David and Solomon: In Search of the Bible's Sacred Kings and the Roots of the Western Tradition* (reprint ed.). New York: Free Press (Simon & Schuster), 2007. Analyzes archaeological findings for evidence of Davidic kingdom.

Halpern, Baruch. *David's Secret Demons.* Grand Rapids, MI: Eerdmans, 2001. A controversial biography analyzing David's character and conduct.

McKenzie, Steven L. "David." In K. D. Sakenfeld, ed., *The New Interpreter's Dictionary of the Bible*, Vol. 2, pp. 27–39. Nashville, TN: Abingdon Press, 2007. Surveys critical theories about David's historicity, character, and accomplishments.

Meyers, Carol. "Kinship and Kingship: The Early Monarchy." In M. D. Coogan, ed., *The Oxford History of the Biblical World.* New York: Oxford UP, 1998. An informative essay.

CHAPTER 13

From the Glory of Solomon to the Exile in Babylon
The Books of 1 and 2 Kings

Key Topics/Themes Although divided into two volumes, the books of Kings form an unbroken narrative. It begins with the death of David and succession of Solomon, continues with the division of Israel into two rival kingdoms—the larger northern realm of Israel and the smaller southern state of Judah—and culminates with Assyria's destruction of Israel (721 BCE) and Babylon's destruction of Judah (587 BCE). Giving unequal coverage to the various kings of Israel and Judah, the two books contain three major parts: (1) the reign of Solomon (1 Kings 1–11), (2) the breakup of the Solomonic kingdom and an interweaving history of rulers in Judah and Israel (1 Kings 12–2 Kings 17), and (3) after Assyria eliminates Israel, an account of Judah until the Babylonian exile (2 Kings 18–25). Consistently applying Deuteronomistic principles to this theologically oriented narrative, the authors/editors ascribe the political and military defeat of both Israel and Judah to their rulers' collective failure to worship Yahweh alone, at the single place he had chosen, the Jerusalem Temple.

As the final—and longest—segment of the Deuteronomistic History (DH), the two books of Kings span a period of approximately 400 years. The narrative takes us from the glory days of King Solomon's reign over a united, prosperous Israel in the mid-tenth century BCE to one of his royal descendants' humiliating captivity in Babylon four centuries later. The last-recorded event in 2 Kings, the release of Judah's deposed ruler, **Jehoiachin,** from a Babylonian prison, took place about 562 BCE and thus provides the earliest possible date for the composition or final editing of the book in its present form. Written from the perspective of the Babylonian exile, the canonical edition of 1 and 2 Kings presents the national cataclysm as tragic and complete, the inevitable result of Israel's covenant breaking.

 Two Editions of the Deuteronomistic History

Many scholars believe that, before the present edition of Kings was produced, an earlier and much more optimistic version of the work existed, one that culminated in an enthusiastic description of the reforms of King **Josiah** (ruled 640–609 BCE). According to this view, the first edition was composed at the height of Josiah's triumphant religious and military campaigns, when he used his power to enforce centralization of Judah's national worship at the Jerusalem sanctuary and to reconquer part of the northern territories that Assyria had previously occupied (see Chapter 9). The early version thus portrayed Josiah's reign as the joyous fulfillment of Torah promises for land, blessing, and divinely favored kings. Unlike most of the other rulers mentioned, Josiah receives only praise from the DH writer, who declares that he pleased Yahweh more than any other ruler since David (2 Kings 22:2). In fact, the text describes Josiah as the perfect example of Deuteronomy's foremost command:

> Before him there was no king like him, who turned to the LORD [Yahweh] with all his heart, with all his soul, and with all his might, according to the law [*torah*] of Moses; nor did any like him arise after him.

(2 Kings 23:25; cf. Deut. 6:4–5)

As explained in Chapter 9, the original DH began with Joshua's divinely supported conquest of Canaan and probably ended with an account of Josiah's divinely

129

favored reconquest of many of the same territories. Unfortunately, Josiah's early death (609 BCE) and Judah's subsequent fall to Babylon (587 BCE) demanded a reinterpretation of Israel's history. Besides adding the final narrative about Judah's last kings and the people's exile to Babylon, the postexilic editors made brief insertions into the older narrative, foreshadowing Judah's downfall.

 ## A Narrow Standard of Judgment

With the notable exceptions of David and Josiah, the Deuteronomistic criteria for evaluating the effectiveness of a given king have almost nothing to do with his military victories or his economic policies. In the DH view, it does not matter whether a king is successful in extending the nation's territory, imposing its rule over neighboring kingdoms such as Edom and Moab, bringing the nation economic prosperity, or even promoting social justice for the poor and defenseless (the last a major concern of Israel's prophets). The narrator's judgment focuses almost exclusively on the issue of centralizing Yahweh's worship at "the place that the LORD your God will choose as his habitation to put his name there" (Deut. 12:5). Although the place is not specified in Deuteronomy, the authors/editors assume it to be Jerusalem, site of Solomon's Temple. Because DH writers regard all other sanctuaries—including ancient shrines at Bethel and Shechem where Abraham, Jacob, and Joshua offered sacrifices—as illegitimate, any ruler who does not vigorously enforce the centralization of Yahweh's cult at Jerusalem is consistently condemned. Although Israel had worshiped Yahweh at "high places" (altars built in various cities as well as on rural hilltops) from time immemorial, the Deuteronomistic standard requires their total destruction. The few kings of Judah, such as Hezekiah and Josiah, who campaign to eliminate all shrines outside Jerusalem are the only rulers to win DH approval. Not one of the northern kings receives a passing grade.

When the Davidic kingdom splits into two separate nations after Solomon's death, rulers of the northern state do not wish their subjects to worship only at the southern capital, Jerusalem. According to 1 Kings 12, the first northern king, **Jeroboam I** (ruled 922–901 BCE) establishes rival sanctuaries at either end of his domain, in the north at Dan and in the south at Bethel. This "sin of Jeroboam"—erecting golden calves on which Yahweh was thought to be invisibly enthroned at the two border sanctuaries—automatically prevents any northern ruler from pleasing God. A contemporary historian might point out that Judah's policy of centralizing royal, political, and religious functions at its own capital—and denouncing as apostate all who choose to worship elsewhere—shows considerable self-interest. However, in the DH view, Jerusalem is the *only* place where Yahweh will accept the sacrifices mandated by Mosaic Law.

The Book of 1 Kings

The Reign of Solomon

Given the vast importance that the DH author(s) accords the Jerusalem Temple, it is not surprising that the books of Kings devote more space to describing the reign of **Solomon,** the Temple's builder, than to any other king (1 Kings 1–11). First Kings opens with an account of King David's last days and the court intrigues, led by the prophet Nathan and David's wife Bathsheba, to have her son, Solomon, rather than David's oldest son, **Adonijah,** succeed to the throne. (Many scholars believe that the story of Solomon's succession is probably based on the same Court History that underlies 2 Samuel 9–20.) Even on his deathbed, David behaves like a typical Near Eastern monarch, reminding Solomon that, although he has promised to spare surviving enemies who participated in Absalom's revolt, his successor is bound by no such vow. Taking his father's hint, Solomon begins his reign by murdering not only Adonijah but also David's loyal general Joab and numerous others who might threaten the security of his crown. In a special blessing, Yahweh then grants him a "wise and discerning mind" (1 Kings 3:4–15), so that he soon earns international fame for the astuteness of his policies.

Israel's Prosperity Although the final verdict on Solomon's long reign is decidedly critical (1 Kings 11), most of the narrative expresses strong admiration for his material accomplishments, particularly his wealth and extensive building programs. Solomon's largest project is the royal palace, which includes a special mansion for his most important wife, the daughter of an unnamed pharaoh, with whom he forms a political alliance. Covering 11,250 square feet, the palace is much larger than the Temple (2,700 square feet), almost as if the sanctuary—on which the narrative focuses—were a religious extension of royal power (cf. 6:2; 7:2). Built to house the Ark of the Covenant, on which Yahweh's "glory" is enshrined, the Temple is a largely windowless rectangular edifice whose floor plan resembles that of other sanctuaries that archaeologists have recently excavated in Syria and Phoenicia (see Figure 13.1). According to 1 Kings 8, Phoenician architects, designers, and artisans played a

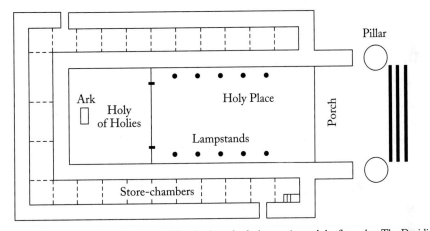

FIGURE 13.1 This reconstruction of Solomon's Temple shows both the exterior and the floor plan. The Davidic kings and their court theologians insisted that Jerusalem's royal sanctuary was the only place on earth at which Yahweh would accept sacrificial offerings, thus compelling Israelites to travel to the national capital to fulfill their Torah obligations.

major role in constructing the Temple. Hiram, a Phoenician king who was one of Solomon's chief partners in international trade, supplied both materials and skilled craftsmen. Despite his large income from commercial enterprises and increasingly heavy taxation of Israel's citizens, however, Solomon is forced to give twenty Galilean villages to Hiram to pay off his debts (9:10–14).

Dedication of the Temple The first king to be raised in an urban palace rather than in rural villages and pastures, Solomon assumes more of the trappings of royal privilege than his two predecessors. The extent to which royal power has increased since the days of King Saul is evident in Solomon's assumption of priestly duties in dedicating the Jerusalem Temple. Whereas Samuel publicly withdrew support from Saul when the king offered sacrifices, in the Temple ceremony, Solomon, apparently without opposition, takes over priestly functions, not only consecrating the sanctuary but also presiding over both animal and grain sacrifices. (1 Kings 8:62–65; cf. 1 Sam. 13:8–15). In the minds of many Israelites, particularly in the north, the Jerusalem Temple may have seemed too much like a dynastically controlled royal chapel (cf. 1 Kings 12).

In describing the Temple's dedication, the narrator draws a fine distinction between the older Tabernacle theology and the later Deuteronomistic concept of Yahweh's connection with the Jerusalem sanctuary. In Exodus, Yahweh appears to take up residence in his tent-shrine, his "glory" encamped among the Israelites (Exod. 40:34–38). In contrast to Exodus's sense of divine immanence—reenforced in 1 Samuel when the young Samuel experiences Yahweh literally standing and speaking to him in the Tabernacle (1 Sam. 3:10)—the DH insists that a transcendent Yahweh places only his "name" in the Temple. Although both the Exodus writer and the Deuteronomistic historian employ the same symbol of divine presence—a "cloud" that envelops both Tabernacle and Temple as a sign of Yahweh's acceptance—the Deuteronomistic author makes clear that no earthly shrine can hold the Deity. The long prayer of consecration ascribed to Solomon, a thoroughly Deuteronomistic composition, emphasizes that although Yahweh accepts the Temple, in reality "the highest heavens can not contain [him], much less the house that [Solomon] has built" (1 Kings 8:27). At the very moment that witnesses the fulfillment of Genesis's promise of the divine presence—or at least Yahweh's "name" abiding with Israel—the postexilic editor inserts an ominous reminder that Yahweh's future support depends on Israel's *torah* observance. Yahweh warns Solomon that his oath to preserve the Davidic line depends on wholehearted obedience to covenant laws. Describing an appearance to Solomon immediately after the Temple's dedication, the editor shows Yahweh explicitly informing the king that the "house" he has just sanctified with his presence will become a "heap of ruins," the condition to which Babylonian armies had reduced it at the time the book was edited (1 Kings 9:8–9; cf. 25:8–17).

After the generally positive evaluation of Solomon's accomplishments—his extraordinary riches, wisdom, fame, and diplomatic successes (1 Kings 10)—the editor's final verdict on the king seems almost out of place. A radical change of attitude toward Solomon marks Chapter 11, in which the narrator (a later editor?) severely criticizes him for marrying foreign wives and permitting them to continue worshiping their national gods. Solomon is said to have married 700 princesses and taken an additional 300 concubines (women who occupy a recognized status but who lack the position of a legal wife), for many of whom he erected altars to their native deities in the Temple precincts.

Breakup of Israel   Although the DH judges Solomon primarily from a religious viewpoint, the king's economic policies probably played a more important role in the breakup of Israel that followed his death. Ignoring the old system of tribal lands, Solomon divided the country into twelve new administrative districts, with each obligated to provide supplies for the royal court one month of every year. Even more unpopular was Solomon's practice of compelling Israelite citizens to work on his building projects, possibly using forced

Israelite labor to construct the Temple (1 Kings 4:7–19; 5:13–18; cf. 9:15–22). In thus portraying the negative aspects of Solomon's reign, the DH implicitly asks readers to remember Samuel's impassioned warning about the disadvantages of establishing a monarchy (1 Sam. 8:10–18). Indeed, the author of Deuteronomy 17 may well have based his description of kingly misbehavior on Solomon's practices, noting that a ruler should not "acquire many wives for himself, or else his heart will turn away" (Deut. 17:14–20).

Despite his failure to follow Yahweh as his father, David, had done, Solomon is allowed to die peacefully (c. 922 BCE). Yahweh declares, however, that he intends to strip Solomon's heir of the largest part of the kingdom. The territory of Judah, however, the nucleus of the Davidic realm, is to remain under his successors' control so that "David may always have a lamp before me in Jerusalem, the city where I have chosen to put my name" (1 Kings 11:12–13, 35–36; cf. assurances given to later Davidic rulers in 1 Kings 15:3–4; 2 Kings 8:18–19).

The Divided Kingdom

Jeroboam's Revolt   Rehoboam (ruled 922–915 BCE), Solomon's successor, foolishly refuses to lighten the crushing burden of taxes and forced labor that Solomon imposed on the people. Rehoboam's arrogant rejection of the northern tribes' plea for a more humane administration sparks a widespread revolt against the House of David. The ten northern tribes withdraw from the United Kingdom to form their own independent state—**Israel**—repudiating any tie to the Davidic line:

> What share do we have in David?
> We have no inheritance in the son of Jesse!

> (1 Kings 12:16; cf. 2 Sam. 20:1)

The uneasy alliance that Saul and David forged between the southern and northern tribes, with their different religious and political cultures, thus proves to be fragile and temporary. Only the southern tribes of Judah and Benjamin remain loyal to the Davidic dynasty and its sanctuary at Jerusalem. Although much smaller and poorer than its northern rival, as a political state **Judah** will survive Israel by more than a century, permitting Tanakh writers to interpret the subsequent history of the divided kingdom from an exclusively Judean viewpoint.

After Israel's secession, Kings records the history of a divided people, alternately describing individual reigns in Israel and then those in Judah (1 Kings 12–2 Kings 17; see Table 13.1). The Deuteronomistic narrator fits the reports on all rulers into a rigid formula.

TABLE 13.1 **Events and Rulers in the Divided Kingdom**

APPROXIMATE DATE BCE	MESOPOTAMIA AND EGYPT	ISRAEL	JUDAH	HEBREW PROPHETS
	Twenty-second Dynasty of Egypt (935–725)		Rehoboam (922–915)	
		Jeroboam I (922–901)	Abijah (915–913)	
	Pharaoh Shishak invades Palestine (c. 918)		Asa (913–873)	
900		Nadab (901–900)		
		Baasha (900–877)		
		Elah (877–876)		
		Zimri (876)		
		Omri (876–869)	Jehoshaphat (873–849)	
	Shalmaneser III (859–825) of Assyria	Ahab (869–850)		Elijah (Israel)
850		Ahaziah (850–849)	Jehoram (849–842)	
	Battle of Qarqar (853)	Jehoram (849–842)	Ahaziah (842)	Elisha (Israel)
	Hazael of Syria (842–806)	Jehu's revolt (842)	Athaliah (842–837)	
800		Jehu (842–815)	Joash (837–800)	
		Jehoahaz (815–801)	Amaziah (800–783)	
		Jehoash (801–786)		Amos (Israel)
		Jeroboam II (786–746)	Uzziah (Azariah) (783–742)	Hosea (Israel)
750	Tiglath-pileser III of Assyria (745–727)	Zechariah (746–745)		
		Shallum (745)	Jotham (742–735)	
		Menahem (745–738)		
		Pekahiah (738–737)	Ahaz (735–715)	Isaiah (Judah)
	Shalmaneser V (726–722)	Pekah (737–732)		
		Hoshea (732–724)		Micah (Judah)
	Twenty-fourth Egyptian Dynasty (725–709)			
725		Fall of Israel (722/721)	Hezekiah (715–687)	
	Sargon II of Assyria (721–705)			
	Twenty-fifth Egyptian Dynasty (716–663)			
700	Sennacherib (704–681)			
	Assyrian invasion of Judah (701)			
			Manasseh (687–642)	
	Esarhaddon of Assyria (681–669)			
	Ashurbanipal (668–627)			
650	Twenty-sixth Egyptian Dynasty (664–525)		Amon (642–640)	

(continued)

TABLE 13.1 *(continued)*

APPROXIMATE DATE BCE	MESOPOTAMIA AND EGYPT	ISRAEL	JUDAH	HEBREW PROPHETS
			Josiah (640–609) Deuteronomistic reforms (621 and following)	Jeremiah Zephaniah
				Nahum
600	Fall of Nineveh (612) Pharaoh Necho (610–594) Battle of Carchemish (605) Growth of Neo-Babylonian Empire under Nebuchadnezzar (605–562)		Jehoahaz (609) Jehoiakim (609–598/597) Jehoiachin (598/597) First Babylonian sack of Jerusalem (598/597)	Habakkuk
			Zedekiah (597–587) Fall of Jerusalem (587) Babylonian captivity (587–538)	Ezekiel Jeremiah

Source: In general, this table follows the dates derived from W. F. Albright, *Bulletin of the American School of Oriental Research.* 100 (December 1945), and adopted by John Bright, *A History of Israel* (Philadelphia: Westminster Press, 1972), pp. 480–481.

Every introduction to the kings of Israel includes a statement relating the Israelite monarch's dates to those of contemporary kings in Judah; the name of the capital city; the length of the reign; and a stereotypical condemnation of the king, invariably asserting that "He did what was evil in the sight of the LORD"— always because he did not support the Jerusalem sanctuary and instead encouraged Yahweh's worship at shrines in his northern territories. In introducing Judean rulers, the narrator follows a similar pattern, connecting the ascension of a Judean monarch with the then-reigning king of Israel, giving the king's age when he came to the throne and the name of the queen mother, and measuring his performance against that of David. Like the universally condemned kings of Israel, the majority of Judean rulers are similarly dismissed for doing "evil" and for being disloyal to Yahweh and the Jerusalem cult.

In the description of Jeroboam's revolt against the Davidic dynasty, the rebel is at first portrayed as potentially a champion of Yahweh, rescuing Israel from Solomon's practice of tolerating worship of foreign gods. As the prophet Ahijah reveals, **Jeroboam**—a former member of Solomon's court, now a rebel who has the support of Egypt's Pharaoh Shishak—is Yahweh's choice to lead the northern tribes back to covenant loyalty (1 Kings 11:26–40). As the first ruler of the northern kingdom, however, Jeroboam proves a great disappointment, primarily for establishing centers of Yahweh's worship outside of Jerusalem (1 Kings 12–13). Jeroboam's unpardonable "sin," giving royal support to rival shrines at Dan and Bethel, is continued by all of Israel's subsequent rulers, a policy that earns all of them a negative rating (see Figure 6.3). Although the DH accords him only a few lines, **Omri** (ruled 876–869 BCE), Israel's sixth king, was so effective that, long after his dynasty had fallen, the emperors of Assyria still referred to Israel as the "land of Omri."

Elijah and King Ahab

Considerably more space is allotted to the misdeeds of Omri's successor, King **Ahab** (ruled 869–850 BCE), who takes a Phoenician princess, the infamous **Jezebel,** as his queen. A native of Tyre, one of Phoenicia's most important port cities, and a devout worshiper of Baal, Jezebel is depicted as corrupting her husband's entire country. Ahab's tolerance of his wife's Baal worship brings him into confrontation with the most formidable prophet that Israel has yet produced, **Elijah** the Tishbite. In one of the Bible's most dramatic scenes, Elijah stages a public contest between Yahweh and Baal on Mount Carmel near the Mediterranean coast. When the priests of Baal—despite their shouts and self-mutilations—fail to draw a response from Baal, Elijah sarcastically mocks their antics, suggesting that their god is either asleep, on a trip, or (in some translations) answering the call of nature. By contrast, Elijah's God responds immediately to his prophet's call, sending fire from heaven that consumes not only a sacrificial bull but also the stones of the altar itself. The narrative reaches a climax, not in Elijah's mass slaughter of Baal's defeated priests, but in the ending of the long drought that Yahweh had sent to punish Israel's apostasy. When Elijah's assistant sees a small cloud, "no bigger than a man's hand" rising out of the distant sea, we know that a rainstorm will arrive to end the drought—and, most importantly, that it is Yahweh and not Baal who controls rain and all other forces of nature (1 Kings 18).

Furious that Elijah has killed her prophets, Jezebel resolves to kill Elijah as well, causing him to flee into the desert. Believing that he alone remains faithful to Yahweh, Elijah retreats to the traditional site where his faith was born, Mount Horeb (Sinai). Hidden in the same rocky cleft that once sheltered Moses, Elijah, too, encounters his God—not in wind, fire, earthquake, or other spectacular phenomena, but in a "sound of sheer silence" (1 Kings 19:11–12). Yahweh then commissions Elijah to return to the political arena, appointing new leaders who will presumably carry out the divine will more effectively than Ahab. Although God instructs Elijah to anoint Hazael king of Syria, Jehu king of Israel, and Elisha as the prophet who will replace him, Elijah lives long enough only to appoint his successor, to whom he passes on his prophetic mantle.

Illustrating the need to overthrow Ahab's administration, the narrative shifts to describe Jezebel's unjust prosecution of **Naboth,** whose choice vineyard Ahab covets. Determined to secure the vineyard for her husband, Jezebel persuades two elders falsely to accuse Naboth of apostasy, for which he is stoned to death (1 Kings 21). When Elijah denounces Jezebel's abuse of the Mosaic Law—which prescribes the death penalty on the testimony of two witnesses—Ahab repents and Yahweh decides to delay his punishment. The king, however, is soon killed in the Battle of Ramoth-Gilead (1 Kings 22). Elijah eventually receives the most spectacular validation given to any Israelite prophet—a public ascent to heaven (see below). (Figure 13.2 shows the kingdoms of Israel and Judah in Elijah's time.)

The Book of 2 Kings

The Elijah–Elisha Cycle

Because the two parts of Kings are really a single book, the account of Israelite and Judean rulers continues uninterrupted in 2 Kings. Preparing readers for the coming destruction of the northern kingdom, reported in 2 Kings 17, this section opens with an episode illustrating Yahweh's ongoing conflict with the Omrid dynasty. When King Ahaziah, who lies dying after falling from an upper story of his residence, sends to inquire of "Baalzebub, the god of Ekron" about his chances of recovery, Elijah intercepts the king's messenger and predicts Ahaziah's certain death. "Is it because there is no God in Israel," Elijah demands, "that you are going to inquire of Baal-zebub," a derisive term meaning "lord of the flies" that biblical writers commonly use for Baal. But when Ahaziah sends a captain and fifty men to bring Elijah to him, the prophet has Yahweh consume them with fire from heaven, a fate that also befalls a second contingent of soldiers. Although a third group persuades Elijah to descend from his hilltop retreat and visit the king, the prophet's message does not change, and Ahaziah dies for his disloyalty—the same fate the entire nation will soon experience (2 Kings 1:2–17).

Even when Israelite kings reject Baal in favor of Yahweh, however, the Deuteronomistic narrator still judges them adversely. After Jehoram, one of Ahab's sons, inherits the throne, he separates himself from his parents' Baalism, tearing down "the pillar of Baal that his father had made." Nonetheless, the author condemns him for doing "evil" because he "clung to the sin of Jeroboam," maintaining Yahweh's altars at Dan and Bethel (3:1–3).

Chapters 2–8 continue the Elijah–Elisha cycle, interweaving folk legends about the prophets' miracles with archival material about royal treaties, battles, and political intrigues. Elijah's prophetic career reaches a memorable climax when a "chariot of fire" pulled by fiery horses carries him, as in a "whirlwind," to heaven. The only other figure in the Hebrew Bible besides Enoch (Gen. 5:21) to be "taken" by God and thus to escape ordinary death, Elijah became the object of later prophetic speculation—that he will return to earth before God's final judgment (2 Kings 2; cf. Mal. 4:5–6).

Inheriting both Elijah's spirit and his prophetic mantle, Elisha continues his mentor's work, performing even more miraculous acts that mark him as a "man of God." Although some of Elisha's miracles, such as his parting waters to cross a river dry-shod or resuscitating the only son of a hospitable woman, are virtual duplications of Elijah's activities, others are unique to him.

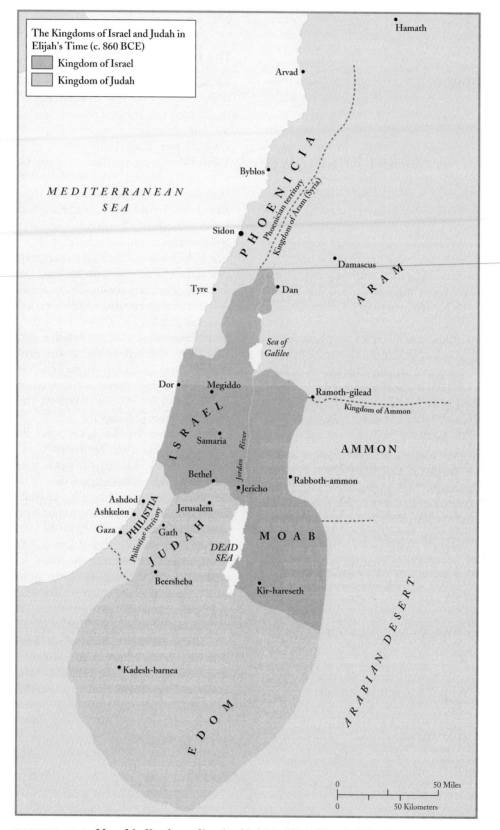

FIGURE 13.2   Map of the Kingdoms of Israel and Judah in Elijah's Time (c. 860 BCE).

Elisha causes an iron ax head to float on water, turns poisoned soup edible, multiplies barley loaves to feed 100 men, and cleanses a Syrian leper; he also foretells droughts, famines, military victories, and royal deaths.

Jehu's Bloody Purges

A political kingmaker as well as a prophet, Elisha secretly sends a messenger to anoint a new Israelite monarch—**Jehu,** a former captain of Ahab's guard. Supported by the army, Jehu (ruled 842–815 BCE) then plunges the nation into a bloodbath (2 Kings 9–10). Citing Elijah's curse on Ahab's dynasty, Jehu massacres all of Ahab's surviving sons, grandsons, friends, priests, and administrators, totally wiping out the royal family and its supporters. His treatment of Jezebel is particularly savage: Upon invading her palace, Jehu incites her servants to throw the queen from an upper window to a courtyard below, where dogs then eat her corpse. With Jehonadab, who shares his zeal for Yahweh, Jehu then assembles all known Baal worshipers in the great temple Ahab had built in **Samaria,** the capital city, and orders eighty executioners to butcher them all. Baal's shrine is torn down and the site turned into a public latrine.

For all his Yahwist fanaticism, however, Jehu does not entirely win the Deuteronomistic writer's approval. In neglecting to remove Jeroboam's golden calves from Bethel and Dan—thereby acknowledging the supremacy of the Jerusalem Temple—Jehu is judged not to have served Yahweh wholeheartedly. Nor was Jehu an effective king. His purges and massacres may have pleased some Yahwists, but he so drained the nation's supply of qualified leaders that Israel rapidly lost territory on every side. When Jehu died after a reign of twenty-eight years (of which only the violent first year is described in Kings), he left Israel politically weak, without allies, and considerably smaller in size than it had been under Omri and Ahab (2 Kings 10:32–35).

Jehu's low international status is graphically displayed on the Black Obelisk, a stone monument erected by Shalmaneser III (ruled 859–825 BCE), head of the Assyrian Empire (see Figure 13.3). The obelisk is

FIGURE 13.3 This panel of the Black Obelisk shows Jehu, king of Israel, groveling before the Assyrian emperor Shalmaneser III, to whom he pays tribute. The Deuteronomistic writers describe Jehu's revolt against Ahab's dynasty (842 BCE) as a Yahwist-inspired movement (2 Kings 9:1–10:36). However, as a result of Jehu's butchery of Israel's former ruling class, the nation was fatally weakened and eventually destroyed. Ironically, the Black Obelisk identifies Jehu as "son of Omri," founder of the royal line that the Yahwist usurper exterminated.

inscribed with five scenes depicting representatives of five different Near Eastern nations—including Israel—bringing tribute to the Assyrian emperor. One panel shows Jehu, or his ambassador, forehead to the ground, groveling before his foreign master. A roughly contemporary inscription on another monument, the Moabite Stone, celebrates Moab's liberation from Israel (see Figure 13.4) Omri, whose military successes the DH author studiously ignores, had previously conquered

FIGURE 13.4 The enormously important Moabite Stone, found in 1868, records the victories of Mesha, king of Moab, over the northern state of Israel (ninth century BCE). Grateful to Chemosh, the Moabite national god, for liberating him from the Israelite domination imposed by Omri and Ahab, Mesha articulates a Canaanite mirror image of the Deuteronomistic philosophy of history: "As for Omri, king of Israel, he humbled Moab many years, for Chemosh was angry at his land. And his son followed him and he also said, 'I will humble Moab.' In my time he spoke (thus), but I have triumphed over him and over his house, while Israel hath perished for ever!"

Moab, which then broke free of Israel's "oppression" after Jehu's excesses had weakened his country militarily and politically. Perhaps the most significant aspect of the Moabite Stone inscription is the revelation that in the mid-ninth century BCE Moab had developed a theology of history similar to that expressed in the books of Deuteronomy and Kings. As the Deuteronomistic historian attributes all of Israel's political and economic misfortunes to Yahweh's wrath, so the Moabites ascribed their earlier defeat by Israel to the anger of **Chemosh,** their national god, who first punished his people by—and then redeemed them from—Israelite domination. Ironically, Moab's ability to free itself from Israel is a consequence of Jehu's violent promotion of Yahweh's worship.

Although Elisha prophesies that a confederation of the rulers of Israel, Judah, and Edom will conquer "every fortified city" of Moab, the expedition fails. According to 2 Kings 3, when Moab's King Mesha, desperate to end the coalition's siege of his city, sacrifices his first-born son, such "wrath" ensues (from Chemosh?) that the Israelite attackers give up and withdraw (3:4–27).

An indirect result of Jehu's extermination of both Israelite and Judean kings was the elevation of a queen to Judah's throne, her reign the only interruption of the Davidic line in its entire history. A daughter of Omri (or perhaps of Ahab and Jezebel), **Athaliah** (ruled 842–837 BCE) was the wife of Jehoram, king of Judah. (Their son Ahaziah is not to be confused with the Israelite king of the same name whose death Elijah had predicted.) When Jehu murdered both Jehoram and Ahaziah (his heir) about 842 BCE, Athaliah seized control of Judah. Emulating Jehu's example, Queen Athaliah ordered the execution of all of Ahaziah's male offspring (her grandsons), rival heirs to the crown. Only one prince escaped; the chief priest, Jehoiada, secretly hid Ahaziah's infant son, Jehoash (also called Joash), in the Jerusalem Temple.

After Athaliah reigned successfully for six years, the priest Jehoiada masterminded a palace revolt in which Athaliah was murdered and the seven-year-old Jehoash placed on the throne. According to the Deuteronomistic narrator, Jehoash distinguished his long reign (837–800 BCE) by doing "what was right in the sight of the LORD" (2 Kings 12:2). Nevertheless, perhaps because he allowed his subjects to continue sacrificing to Yahweh outside Jerusalem, Jehoash's administration endured various humiliations, including having to turn over the entire national treasury to King Hazael of Syria to keep him from invading Judah. Despite the author's qualified approval, Jehoash, like his grandmother, came to a violent end, murdered by conspirators (12:17–20).

The Assyrian Invasion and Fall of Samaria

Although the northern kingdom enjoyed renewed prosperity under such kings as **Jeroboam II** (ruled 786–746 BCE), revolution and violent changes of rulership continued to destabilize Israel (see Figure 13.5). As Israel declined politically, a new threat appeared: After centuries of relative inactivity, **Assyria** began a period of vigorous military expansion, swallowing up lesser kingdoms and peoples as its armies marched from Mesopotamia to Egypt. As its power and territorial acquisitions increased, so did Assyria's ability to command tribute from weaker states. When Israel's last king, Hoshea (ruled 732–724 BCE), hoping for Egyptian help, stopped payments to Assyria, Assyrian armies laid siege to Samaria, which **Sargon II** captured and destroyed in 722/721 BCE. Because it was Assyria's policy to deport defeated populations to discourage rebellions, thousands of Israel's leading citizens were forcibly relocated elsewhere in the Assyrian Empire, and foreigners were moved into former Israelite territory.

According to the Deuteronomistic commentary in 2 Kings 17, Israel's fall resulted from its repeated offenses to Yahweh, its toleration of Baal cults, and its worship at unauthorized "high places." Yahweh remained concerned about this portion of the Promised Land, however, for, displeased with the new settlers, he afflicted the region with a "plague" of lions. Recognizing that the "god of the land" required appropriate worship, Assyrian rulers dispatched a previously exiled priest of Yahweh to teach the inhabitants how to sacrifice to Yahweh properly, ending the lion attacks. Because Israel's story is told from a distinctively Judean viewpoint, the writer's account of the ten "lost" tribes and the origin of the area's non-Israelite population is not, in the opinion of most scholars, historically reliable. Although an ethnically mixed group—known as **Samaritans** (after Israel's former capital of Samaria)—supplanted the older tribal units, they continued to worship Yahweh. Deuteronomistic prejudice against the Samaritans, who maintained sanctuaries competing with that in Jerusalem, colors the biblical account of their origins. Some New Testament authors portray the Samaritans in a kinder light, with Jesus making a "good Samaritan" the moral hero of a famous parable (Luke 10:29–37).

Judah Alone

Assyria and Hezekiah Although Judah escapes the northern kingdom's fate, Assyrian aggression remains a long-term threat to its continued existence. For more than a century, the rulers of Judah are forced to pay heavy tribute to Assyrian overlords. **Hezekiah** (ruled 715–687 BCE), the most notable king of the Assyrian period, alternates between submission and outright rebellion, a policy that yields mixed results (2 Kings 18–20). The narrator praises Hezekiah for his vigorous enforcement of Deuteronomistic principles, abolishing the "high places" and centralizing national worship at the Jerusalem Temple. Asserting Judean freedom from Assyrian influence, Hezekiah destroys the shrines of Canaanite and others gods that had been allowed to coexist with Yahweh's cult. Cutting down the poles and sacred pillars—symbols of the tree of life associated with the Canaanite goddess Asherah (whom some scholars believe was once revered alongside Yahweh, perhaps as his divine consort)—Hezekiah leads a religious reform anticipating that of Josiah. He even destroys the bronze serpent, called Nehushtan, that Moses reputedly had fashioned in the desert to cure people bitten by poisonous snakes (Num. 21:9). As a symbol of healing, the bronze image apparently had become an object of veneration—and hence a threat to Yahwist purity. No icon or relic, even one associated with Moses, can be allowed to deflect worship from Yahweh alone.

Although the narrative compares Hezekiah to King David in his faithfulness to Yahweh (2 Kings 18:3–8), the generally favorable DH attitude toward his reign also includes an element of ambivalence. The text states that Yahweh accompanied Hezekiah so that "wherever he went, he prospered" and seems to approve of the king's revolt against Judah's Assyrian oppressors. At the same time, Hezekiah's success is perilously close to failure. His refusal to pay Assyria tribute incites **Sennacherib** (ruled 704–681 BCE) to invade Judah in 701 BCE, capture most of its important towns, and levy a ruinously heavy fine on the nation. Hezekiah is forced to strip the Temple of its decorations and treasure, paying Sennacherib enormous sums of silver and gold, and then to submit again to the Assyrian yoke. Although one of Hezekiah's leading advisors, the prophet Isaiah, correctly forecasts that Jerusalem will survive the Assyrian siege unscathed, the king ends his twenty-nine-year reign impoverished and ruling over only a scrap of his former domain.

Jerusalem's Deliverance Assyrian and biblical accounts of Sennacherib's invasion of Judah differ strikingly, causing some historians to suppose that they refer to two separate campaigns. According to Assyrian records carved on a hexagonal prism, Sennacherib made Hezekiah "a prisoner in Jerusalem, his royal residence, like a bird in a cage"—though the prism says nothing of Assyria's failure to capture the city. According to 2 Kings

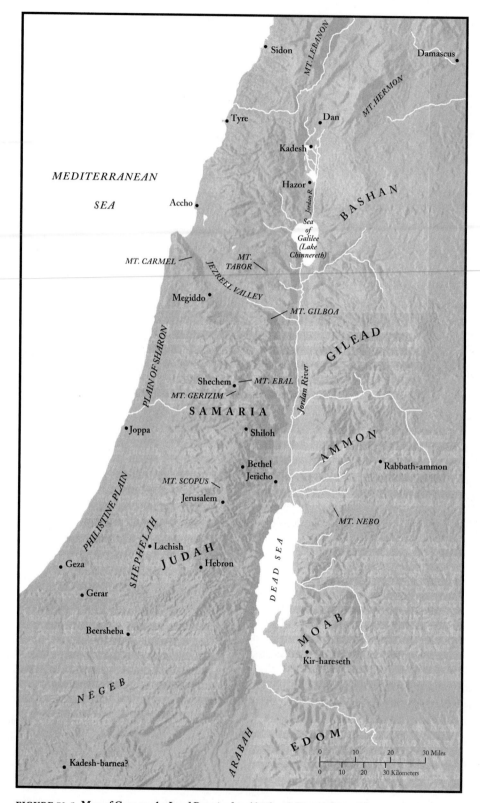

FIGURE 13.5 Map of Canaan, the Land Promised to Abraham's Descendants. The map shows the areas occupied by Judah and Samaria after the fall of the northern kingdom of Israel in the late eighth century BCE.

and an almost identical account in Isaiah 36–37, Jerusalem's escape is attributed to divine intervention. In a single night, Yahweh's Angel of Death strikes down 185,000 Assyrian soldiers, forcing Sennacherib to lift his siege and return to Nineveh, his capital. The biblical version has some indirect confirmation from nonbiblical sources, including the Greek historian Herodotus, who states that swarms of mice chewed through the soldiers' bowstrings (*Histories*, Bk. 2, 141). Some commentators interpret Herodotus's comments as referring to a rodent-carried outbreak of bubonic plague that killed Assyrian troops. After the Assyrian war machine's initial success in laying waste to most of Judah and slaying thousands of its inhabitants, the invaders' final victory had seemed inevitable, making their sudden withdrawal from Jerusalem appear a miracle. Jerusalem's deliverance may have contributed to a popular belief that the holy city would never fall into enemy hands—a view that the prophet Jeremiah would later attack (Jer. 7, 26).

Second Kings 20 relates an incident that evidently took place before Sennacherib's invasion, when Hezekiah still possessed great wealth. Attempting to recruit Babylon as an ally against Assyria, Hezekiah foolishly takes the Babylonian ambassador on a tour of his richly furnished palace and overflowing treasury, displaying all of Judah's economic resources to the foreigner's gaze. Appalled at the king's bad judgment, Isaiah prophesies that the country's entire wealth will be swept away to Babylon—a direct reference to Nebuchadnezzar's capture of Jerusalem more than a century later. Probably added during the postexilic DH revisions, this passage depicts a morally ambivalent Hezekiah. When Isaiah informs him that the disaster still lies in the future, the king finds the news "good," because "there will be peace and security in [his] day" (2 Kings 20:12–19).

Manasseh's Reign Whereas Hezekiah is judged favorably, the Deuteronomistic editors regard his son **Manasseh** (ruled 687–642 BCE) as the worst of all Judah's kings. Hezekiah swept away the "high places" throughout Judah, but Manasseh not only rebuilds them but also erects altars to foreign gods in the Temple itself. Reversing his father's Yahwist reforms, Manasseh commits virtually every covenant violation ever made by any king of Israel or Judah, promoting rampant Baal worship, black magic, and human sacrifice. His offenses include setting up a "carved image of Asherah," perhaps conceived as Yahweh's female companion, in the Jerusalem sanctuary. Charged with worse crimes than those of the Canaanites whom Israel had driven out, Manasseh nonetheless—according to the DH—reigns for "fifty-five years," longer than any other Davidic ruler (2 Kings 21:1).

The Book of Chronicles, written at least two centuries after the DH, adds a surprising conclusion to Manasseh's story, one not even hinted at in 2 Kings. According to 2 Chronicles, Manasseh is taken captive to Babylon, where he undergoes a sudden conversion to Yahwism, repenting his former misdeeds. Moved by his prayer, Yahweh permits Manasseh's restoration to Judah's throne, after which the humbled king conducts a religious reform anticipating that of Josiah. (The author of Chronicles cites the "records of the seers" as the source of this remarkable tale [2 Chron. 33:11–20]; see Chapter 25.) If the Deuteronomistic editors knew about a tradition in which Manasseh was transformed into an ardent Yahwist reformer, they found no place for a repentant Manasseh in their theology of history. The sorcerer-king is singled out as the primary cause of Judah's destruction, and his character is allowed no redeeming qualities (2 Kings 21:10–17; 23:26–27).

Josiah: The Deuteronomistic Hero

With the ascension of **Josiah**, Manasseh's grandson, Judah enters a new era in the development of Yahwistic faith. Reviving the policies of his ancestor Hezekiah, Josiah (ruled 640–609 BCE) fulfills both the letter and the spirit of Deuteronomy's commands to honor one God and sacrifice to him at one sanctuary only. Although some of its legal traditions may have been compiled in the northern kingdom several generations earlier, Deuteronomy (or at least its nucleus, Chs. 12–26 and 28) became Josiah's chief instrument in revitalizing Judah's national faith. Found during Temple repairs—renovations that probably involved removing Manasseh's Baalistic shrines and images—Deuteronomy brought an updated version of the Mosaic inheritance to general public notice. The narrator indicates that both king and people were previously unfamiliar with Deuteronomy's statutes and penalties and notes that holding a Passover ceremony, so important in the Pentateuch, is now considered something new. According to 2 Kings 23, no comparable Passover celebration was previously observed, during either the period of the judges or that of the monarchy (23:21–23).

Taking advantage of Assyria's rapid decline in the late seventh century BCE, Josiah extends his reforms into the former northern kingdom, tearing down altars and tomb monuments throughout the countryside. His campaign of national renewal is cut short, however, when Egypt's Pharaoh **Necho II** (ruled 610–595 BCE) invades the region on his way to aid the last remnants of Assyrian leadership in northern Syria. Whereas Necho wanted a weakened Assyria to survive as a buffer state between Egypt and the newly revived empire of Babylon, Josiah may have hoped to rid Judah of all foreign occupation, or, failing that, to support Babylon against Assyria. Attempting to intercept Necho's army, Josiah is killed at the Battle of Megiddo, thus bringing his Deuteronomistic reforms to a premature end and leaving Judah in the hands of weak or incompetent successors.

The Last Days of Judah

In 612 BCE, Assyria's capital, Nineveh, falls to the combined forces of the Babylonians and the Medes, a people who inhabited an area in what is now Iran. Although Pharaoh Necho rushes into the power vacuum that Assyria's collapse opens in the Near East, the Egyptians are soon defeated by **Nebuchadnezzar,** king of Babylon, at the Battle of Carchemish (605 BCE). The tiny state of Judah now must submit to the Babylonian yoke; its last kings are merely Nebuchadnezzar's tribute-paying vassals.

Josiah's son, **Jehoiakim** (ruled 609–598 BCE), whom Nebuchadnezzar placed on Judah's throne, unwisely rebels but dies before the Babylonians can retaliate, leaving his son and successor, Jehoiachin, to suffer the consequences of the revolt. In 598/597 BCE, Jehoiachin and his family are taken as prisoners to Babylon, the Temple is stripped of its treasures, and 10,000 members of Judah's ruling classes are deported to Mesopotamia (2 Kings 24). Nebuchadnezzar then appoints Jehoiachin's uncle **Zedekiah** (ruled 597–587 BCE) king in his place.

When Zedekiah, too, rebels against Babylon, Nebuchadnezzar besieges and destroys Jerusalem and its Temple. Without comment, the last verses of 2 Kings 25 briefly describe the holy city's devastation: The Babylonians tear down the city walls, shatter the Temple's bronze pillars and set the structure afire, loot and burn surrounding villages, and drive out much of the remaining population, leaving only the poorest citizens behind. Nebuchadnezzar appoints a Judean leader, Gedaliah, governor of the ruined city, but even that token of survival is lost when Judean nationalists murder Gedaliah. Fearing Babylonian retaliation, many of the remaining peasants flee to Egypt.

Has Yahweh Abandoned His People?

The flight of Jerusalem's impoverished inhabitants to Egypt brings the biblical story of Israel full cycle, back to the conditions under which their pre-Mosaic ancestors lived, as strangers in a foreign land. Trying to find moral sense in the national catastrophe, the Deuteronomistic editors blame the victims: The covenant community deserved to suffer because it broke faith with Yahweh. Apostate rulers like Manasseh led the way, but the people, mixing Yahweh's worship with that of Baal, Asherah, and other Canaanite gods, sinned so deeply that a righteous God could not refrain from punishing them. Prophetic witnesses to the disaster who were also influenced by the Deuteronomistic view of history, such as Jeremiah, similarly attributed Judah's fall to its covenant violations (see the discussion of Jeremiah's warnings in Chapter 17). Amid Jeremiah's fiery denunciations of the covenant community's failures, however, it is easy to overlook a significant glimpse of Yahweh's inner response to the national catastrophe. So great was his people's suffering under the Babylonian yoke that Yahweh confided to the prophet that he regretted bringing about Jerusalem's fall. As if only when directly witnessing the extent of his human partner's misery does God fully realize the consequences of his judgment: "I am sorry," he tells Jeremiah, "for the disaster that I have brought on you" (Jer. 42:10). God's brief apology for his actions is never repeated in either the Old or New Testaments.

Striving to understand God's intentions in having abandoned them to their enemies, Judean exiles in Babylon reworked Israel's ancient oral and written traditions about Abraham and his descendants to produce the remarkable epic of Israel's creation, growth, and death, Genesis through 2 Kings. In the crisis of God's apparent absence from his people, editors appended to Deuteronomy Yahweh's ominous warning, foreshadowing their suffering in exile: "I will hide my face from them; I will see what their end will be" (Deut. 32:20). The same editors, however, also included assurances that Yahweh would someday overthrow Israel's oppressors, restore their prosperity, and reaffirm the covenant partnership (Deut. 33:26–29; cf. Deut. 30:1–10), predicting a future return from exile to the Promised Land (see Chapters 18, 19, and 23).

QUESTIONS FOR DISCUSSION AND REVIEW

1. Explain why many scholars think that there were two editions of the Deuteronomistic History. What events during the reign of Josiah would seem to be a fulfillment of the ancient promises to Israel and stimulate the composition of an optimistic history of the covenant people? What events after Josiah's death necessitated a revision of the earlier edition of the DH? How did the DH editors account for the end of Judah's story?

2. Describe the accomplishments of Solomon's reign. In what ways was the Temple closely linked to the Davidic monarchy? What specifically Deuteronomistic ideas appear in the account of Solomon's dedication of the sanctuary (1 Kings 8)?

3. After Solomon's death, why did Israel split into two different kingdoms? What was the "sin of Jeroboam," and how did his installation of rival shrines in the northern kingdom influence the DH authors' judgment of the northern rulers?

4. Outline the conflicts between Israel's rulers, such as Ahab and Jezebel, and the prophets Elijah and Elisha. How was the rivalry between worshipers of Yahweh and those of Baal involved in Jehu's overthrown of the royal dynasty of Omri and Ahab? Who was Naboth, and how were Torah laws used against an innocent man?

5. How did Jehu's bloody purge of Ahab's family and Baal worshipers affect Israel politically? Did Jehu's massacres cause Yahweh to make Israel prosper? How did Jehu's actions help to bring a non-Davidic queen to Judah's throne?

6. Describe the fall of the northern kingdom and the Assyrian threat to Judah and Jerusalem. How did Hezekiah respond to Assyria's invasion of his territory? How did Jerusalem escape the fate of Samaria?

7. Contrast the policies of Manasseh and Josiah. Which king ruled longer, and which was cut down in his prime? Do the respective fates of Manasseh and Josiah illustrate the theory of history formulated in Deuteronomy? Explain your answer.

8. What happened to Judah and Jerusalem in 587 BCE? What issues about the partnership between Yahweh and his people did this event raise?

9. According to the DH, why did Yahweh abandon his people to the Babylonians? What king do the DH editors single out as having special responsibility for Judah's destruction?

Terms and Concepts to Remember

Adonaijah	Josiah
Ahab	Judah
Assyria	Manasseh
Athaliah	Naboth
Chemosh	Nebuchadnezzar
division of Israel and Judah	Necho II
Elijah and Elisha	Omri
Hezekiah	Rehoboam
Israel	Samaria
Jehoash	Samaritans
Jehoiakim	Sargon II
Jehu	Sennacherib
Jeroboam I	Solomon
Jeroboam II	two editions of Deuteronomistic History
Jezebel	Zedekiah

Recommended Reading

Cross, Frank M., ed. "The Themes of the Book of Kings and the Structure of the Deuteronomic History." In *Canaanite Myth and Hebrew Epic: Essays in the History and the Religion of Israel.* Cambridge, MA: Harvard UP, 1973. An important study.

Friedman, Richard E. *Who Wrote the Bible?* San Francisco: HarperOne, 1987. Shows clearly how scribes, after Jerusalem's fall, provided a revised edition of Kings to explain the national disaster.

Grabbe, Lester L., ed. *Good Kings and Bad Kings.* (Library of the Hebrew Bible/Old Testament Studies 393). London: T. & T. Clark, 2005. A collection of scholarly essays debating the historicity of the Kings account in the light of the archaeological record.

McKenzie, Steven. "Kings, First and Second Books of," In K. D. Sakenfeld, ed., *The New Interpreter's Dictionary of the Bible*, Vol. 3, pp. 523–532. Nashville, TN: Abingdon Press, 2008. A thoughtful examination of the books' compositional history, historicity, and theology.

Seow, Choon-Leong. "The First and Second Books of Kings." In *The New Interpreter's Bible*, Vol. 3, pp. 3–296. Nashville, TN: Abingdon Press, 1999. A helpful introductory analysis of the text, with historical and theological discussions.

CHAPTER 14

Israel's Prophets
Proclaiming the Word of Yahweh

Key Topics/Themes Known traditionally as the Latter Prophets, the collections of prophetic speeches compiled under the names of fifteen individual prophets complete the second major division of the Hebrew Bible, the Nevi'im (Prophets). The *navi*—the most commonly used Hebrew word to designate a "messenger" of Yahweh—is one who is called by God or who speaks on God's behalf. Collectively, these prophetic oracles (pronouncements believed to be divinely inspired) provide theological insights into God's relationship with the covenant people, particularly during times of crisis. Responding to specific social and political emergencies facing Israel, such as military threats from Assyria or Babylon, the prophets' words help to explain why Yahweh used these foreign empires as his "instruments" to punish his people for their disloyalty. The prophetic messages span a period of three centuries, from about 750 BCE to the fifth century BCE, when the institution of prophecy rapidly declined.

 The Prophets: An Overview

In the books of Samuel and Kings, the authors present Israel's history as a tragic failure. Despite enjoying the benefit of a special partnership with God—and the revelation of his instructions (*torah*) through Moses—the covenant people seem incapable of honoring their part of the covenant relationship. In the collections of prophetic speeches that follow the Deuteronomistic History in the Hebrew Bible, readers discover the specific reasons that Yahweh permitted the aggressive powers of Mesopotamia—first Assyria and then Babylon—to overwhelm his chosen people. In the mid-eighth century BCE, the prophets Amos and Hosea—the first to have their messages collected together under their individual names—warn inhabitants of the northern kingdom that their failure to worship Yahweh exclusively will lead to the nation's destruction. After Assyria destroys Israel (722 BCE) and threatens to engulf little Judah as well, prophets such as Micah and Isaiah of Jerusalem inform their fellow Judeans

that—unless they learn to behave justly and worship Yahweh alone—they too will suffer their God's wrath. When Babylon replaces Assyria as master of the ancient Near East in 605 BCE, Yahweh summons a new generation of prophets—including Habakkuk, Jeremiah, and Ezekiel—to warn that the ruling classes' misconduct, particularly their exploitation of the poor and their faithlessness to Yahweh, will bring national catastrophe. Two of Yahweh's spokespersons, Jeremiah and Ezekiel, live to witness their worst premonitions confirmed, when Nebuchadnezzar of Babylon burns Jerusalem and demolishes Solomon's Temple in 587 BCE.

Whereas the epic story of Israel's rise and fall is written mainly in prose, the prophets' speeches are mostly expressed in poetry, rhythmic language brimming with vivid metaphors and figures of speech. The books of Isaiah and Jeremiah, for example, contain some of the Bible's most memorable passages, including God's promises to bring universal peace (Isa. 2:2–4), to create a "new heaven and a new earth" (Isa. 65:16), and to establish a "new covenant" with his people (Jer. 31:31).

Isaiah also envisions an heir of David who will rule over Israel with perfect justice:

> For a child has been born for us, a son given to us;
> authority rests upon his shoulders;
> and he is named
> Wonderful Counselor, Mighty God,
> Everlasting Father, Prince of Peace. . . .
> and there shall be endless peace
> for the throne of David and his kingdom.
> He will establish and uphold it
> with justice and with righteousness
> from this time onward and forevermore.

(Isa. 9:6–7)

Although they freely criticize individual kings, many of the prophets associated with Judah's royal court—as was Isaiah of Jerusalem—regard the Davidic dynasty as God's instrument of earthly rule. Long after Babylonian armies had permanently abolished the Davidic throne, Isaiah's words would be reinterpreted as Yahweh's promise to restore David's crown. A descendant of David, it was thought, would eventually appear to reign gloriously, to save Israel from its enemies, and to reestablish a Davidic kingdom. A political figure, the promised one would be, like David, God's "anointed" (Hebrew, *mashiah*; English, "messiah"). Although the Hebrew Bible does not use the term in a technical sense—as in "*the* Messiah"—belief that a future "son of David" would someday arrive to vindicate Yahweh's oath to David (cf. 2 Sam. 7) sustained many Judeans during centuries of political oppression by foreign powers—from Babylon to Persia to Greece to Rome. By the first century CE, when Roman legions controlled the Promised Land, a small group of Israelites had come to believe that Jesus of Nazareth was David's long-awaited heir (see Chapters 28 and 29).

Careful study of Israel's prophetic literature reveals that most of the prophets' utterances relate specifically to events of their own time. Rather than predict events in the distant future, the prophets tend to address social and political crises—such as imminent military threats from Assyria or Babylon—that directly affected their contemporaries. The prophets' main function was to perceive and then announce Yahweh's will in an immediate circumstance, in terms comprehensible or at least relevant to their original audience. By illuminating God's intentions in the present, the prophets strove to bring Yahweh's people back into harmony with their covenant obligations or, failing that, to specify the punishments for disobedience.

◇ Biblical Portrayals of the Prophet

The Hebrew word for prophet, ***navi (nabi),*** means "one who is called" or "one who announces." (The plural form is *nevi'im,* which is also the title of the second section of the Tanakh.) Its Greek equivalent, *prophetes,* from which our English word is derived, means "a person speaking for God," one chosen to proclaim Yahweh's message, and includes both men and women. Prophetic announcements are commonly called **oracles,** statements revealing the divine will or purpose.

The prophetic calling included several notable women, the first of whom was Moses' sister Miriam (Exod. 15:20–21; Num. 12:2). In the period of the judges, Deborah was both a tribal leader and a prophet (Judg. 4:4). When priests discovered the lost manuscript of Deuteronomy during Josiah's reign, they brought the document to Huldah, "the prophetess," for interpretation and advice (2 Kings 22:14). The prophetess Noadiah was one of Nehemiah's prominent opponents in postexilic Jerusalem (Neh. 6:14; see also Isa. 8:2). Although comparatively rare in male-dominated Israelite society, women continued to play prophetic roles well into New Testament times (Luke 2:36; Rev. 2:20).

In the Pentateuch, Moses is presented as the ideal kind of prophet. Though Genesis refers to both Abraham and Joseph as "prophets," and God summons them to uphold covenant relationships, it is Moses who performs nearly all of the functions prophetic personalities were expected to carry out. To begin with, he personally receives Yahweh's direct communications:

> When there are prophets among you [Israel],
> I the LORD make myself known to them in visions;
> I speak to them in dreams.
> Not so with my servant Moses; . . .
> With him I speak face to face—clearly, not in riddles.

(Num. 12:6–8)

Moses, moreover, witnesses a theophany at Sinai/Horeb that the assembled Israelite masses can only dimly perceive: To them, Yahweh speaks in thunder; with Moses, he uses intelligible speech. As a sign of their particular intimacy, Yahweh allows Moses to glimpse either his "back" (Exod. 33:23) or his "face" (Exod. 33:11). There are limits to this intimacy, however, and at the risk of self-contradiction, the author-editor of Exodus concludes Chapter 33 with the observation that Yahweh's face "shall not be seen"—not even by Moses. Nevertheless, Moses is given the unique privilege of revealing Yahweh's teachings to the world in the form of legal and ethical-theological proclamations. Moses, however, is not only the human voice of divine revelation but also (at least within the tradition of Deuteronomy) the exemplary servant of Yahweh whose entire adult life is dedicated to God's service. At his death, the Deuteronomistic writer can exclaim: "Never since has there arisen a prophet in Israel like Moses" (Deut. 34:10).

Samuel and His Successors

Active in the late eighth century BCE, Hosea—one of the few prophets even to mention Moses or his role as lawgiver—recalls that it was

> By a prophet the LORD [Yahweh] brought
> Israel from Egypt,
> and by a prophet he was guarded. . . .

(Hos. 12:13)

The "classical" prophets whose words were compiled in writing under their names seem, strangely, to have forgotten Moses' contribution, rarely mentioning him or his *torah* in their pronouncements. In fact, prophecy as a social institution, and certainly as a literary tradition, seems to develop along with the monarchy, and as the monarchy comes to an end, so does prophecy (or at least those prophetic writings considered suitable for canonization). The reasons for prophecy's "decline" are subject to debate, but the connection between the monarchies of Judah and of Israel and the prophetic class, in both the northern and southern kingdoms, is often very close and politically charged. Samuel's dual role in the formation of the monarchy—he is both bitterly opposed to it (1 Sam. 8:4–22) and instrumental in the election of Saul and David to the throne—is often duplicated in later centuries by prophets who are sometimes supportive and at other times contemptuous of the king. Whatever their respective attitudes toward a particular monarch, the prophets are seldom reluctant to intervene in the political intrigues that surround the royal court. Nathan, for example, first announces that God has adopted David as his "son," promising an eternal dynasty, and then denounces David over his killing of Uriah (2 Sam. 12). Later, Nathan urges Bathsheba to demand that David appoint Solomon as his successor. In the next generation, the prophet Ahijah takes an even more direct role in the disputes between Solomon and northern tribal leaders when he invites Jeroboam to rebel against his royal patron and become king of a breakaway northern kingdom (1 Kings 11:26–40).

Elijah and Opposition to Established Authority

Perhaps the boldest attempt that any prophet makes in opposing his legitimate monarch is Elijah's confrontation with Ahab and Jezebel. In Elijah's prophetic career, we find a pattern of personal revelation, spiritual proclamation, and political engagement that become standard for many of the prophets who succeed him. Like Moses, Elijah is privileged to experience Yahweh directly in the form of a theophany on Sinai/Horeb (1 Kings 19); like Nathan, he is divinely instructed to defy his king—in this case, to denounce Ahab's crimes against Naboth (1 Kings 21). Elijah's greatest challenge, however, occurs when he attacks the priests of Baal on Mount Carmel (1 Kings 18). By first exposing Baalism as a fraud and then leading a massacre of its priests, Elijah not only places the demands of Yahweh above the prerogatives of the king but also explicitly denies the moral authority of Ahab's reign. As Nathan did, Elijah places the prophet above the king in Israel's spiritual life. When Ahab complains about another prophet, Micaiah, because "he prophesies no good for me; never anything but evil," he seems to feel betrayed, evidently assuming that a court prophet should support his patron (1 Kings 22:8). Elijah's and Micaiah's defiance of established authority in the service of God becomes a familiar pattern by the eighth and seventh centuries BCE: Amos rebukes both a king and his priest (Amos 7:10–17), and Jeremiah levels a death sentence against both a doomed priesthood and an equally doomed king (Jer. 7, 38). Although several prophets come from priestly families, as a group they keep their distance from both the Temple and the royal court, asserting an independence that reflects their self-perception as Yahweh's servants alone. (Box 14.1 discusses the succession of prophets.)

 ## Forms and Characteristics of Prophecy

Ecstatic Prophecy

Israelite prophets exhibit a range of behaviors and personality traits that distinguish them from priests, wisdom teachers, and other spiritual leaders of Israelite society. At one end of the prophetic spectrum is the **ecstatic prophet,** whose frenzied gestures were understood to result from divine possession. Saul exhibits this type of behavior twice in his career when, filled with the *ruah Elohim* (spirit of God), he strips off his clothes and falls to the ground, lying naked for a day and a night (1 Sam. 19:18–24). As with the later cults of Dionysus and Orpheus in ancient Greece, such emotional seizures were commonly introduced through music or dance. According to 1 Samuel 10, Yahweh's spirit possessed Saul while a wandering prophetic band played "harp, tambourine, flute, and lyre" (1 Sam. 10:5–13). When he wished to make contact with Yahweh, Elisha summoned a musician, and "while the musician was playing, the power of the Lord came on him" (2 Kings 3:15). Anthropologists sometimes describe such behavior as part of an **incubation ritual,** in which a prophet enters a state of altered consciousness by lying on an animal skin or on the ground, awaiting some revelation from the gods. In Saul's case, such behavior seems sudden and inexplicable—hence the proverb "Is Saul *also* among the prophets?" (1 Sam. 10:12). For the priests of Baal whom Elijah challenges, ecstatic and even self-mutilating actions are perfectly conventional ways of summoning Baal to their aid:

> Then they cried aloud, and, as was their custom, they cut themselves with swords and lances until the blood gushed out over them. As midday passed, they raved on until the time of the offering of the oblation, but there was no voice, no answer, no response.
>
> (1 Kings 18:28–29)

Whereas the priests of Baal fail miserably to obtain supernatural aid, Elijah succeeds brilliantly, eliciting a spectacular display of divine fire and the ending of a seven-year drought.

While forbidden to perform self-mutilation like the servants of Baal, even Yahweh's prophets were noted for their strange, even bizarre, behavior. Naked except for a loincloth, Isaiah paraded through Jerusalem's streets to illustrate the city's imminent humiliation and ruin. Jeremiah wore a yoke first of wood and then of iron, symbols of the Babylonian oppression (Jer. 27). Ezekiel carried the prophets' symbolic acts to an even greater extreme, cooking his food over a fire of human dung (Ezek. 4:12–15), refusing to mourn for his dead wife (Ezek. 24:15–27), and lying bound like a prisoner for 190 days on one side and then 40 days on the other (Ezek. 4:4–8). By dramatizing their messages through unconventional, even outrageous, conduct, the prophets publicly acted out their visions. Long before their oracles were written down, the *nevi'im* made prophecy dramatic performance—vivid displays of ecstatic passion that could not fail to attract onlookers' attention.

Divination

Another form of prophecy common in the ancient world—**divination**—also seems to have had its counterpart in Israel, in spite of Balaam's assertion to the contrary ("surely there is no divination in Israel" [Num. 23:23]). A practice that seeks to foresee future events or to discover God's otherwise hidden intentions, divination was apparently common among Israel's priesthood. When David cannot decide whether to pursue the Amalekites who have raided the village of Ziklag, he summons the priest Abiathar and "consults" the **ephod,** fully expecting a prophetic (directive) response (1 Sam. 23:6, 9; 30:7–8). A decorated garment worn by priests, the ephod apparently contained pockets in which objects for the casting of lots—perhaps the **urim** and the **thummim**—were kept. What these mysterious objects were, or even looked like (they may have been inscribed stones that were thrown like dice), is unknown, but they clearly were used in the divination process. The precise routine for this form of priestly divination is also unknown, but it seems that the ritual could produce only "yes" or "no" responses. Such casting of lots was used for the distribution of tribal lands (Num. 27:55–56) and for the selection of Israel's first king (1 Sam. 10:20–21; cf. 1 Sam. 14:41; Ezra 2:63).

In Israel, prophetic divination focused primarily on determining Yahweh's will for the near future, especially in calculating the potential for success or failure in military or political ventures. Deuteronomy 18:22 explicitly indicates that the hearers of a prophetic message would still be around to judge the outcome: "If a prophet speaks in the name of the Lord but the thing does not take place or prove true, it is a word that the Lord has not spoken." Jeremiah's contemporaries certainly assumed as much when they imprisoned him for predicting that Babylon would soon destroy Judah (Jer. 26). Ironically, they later turned to Jeremiah when the disaster he had foreseen was about to overtake them (Jer. 37). Both Isaiah and Ezekiel offered counsel to their fellow Judeans, who asked for a glimpse of the immediate future from a "seer" (*roeh* in Hebrew literally means "one who sees" or who possesses second sight). The clear assumption is that a true prophet can forewarn his audience of coming events because Yahweh allows his spokespersons to see beyond the immediate present. It is this talent that enables Samuel to tell Saul that his lost donkeys have already been found (1 Sam. 9:20) or that empowers Isaiah to predict, at the request of King Ahaz, that Judah's local enemies will be crushed by the Assyrian army (Isa. 7:14–17).

The Order of the Prophets' Appearances

Like other contributors to the Hebrew Bible, the prophets whose oracles became part of the canon appeared largely in response to urgent political or ethical crises that troubled the covenant community. Biblical editors placed anthologies of the prophets' oracles immediately after the Deuteronomistic History, thus highlighting the prophetic role in the courses of events that lead to the destruction of both Israel and Judah. As a group, the prophets bear witness to the covenant people's repeated failures to heed Yahweh's warnings about the dire consequences of their covenant breaking. Most of the prophets belong to one of three critical periods, in each of which Israel faced a military or spiritual crisis that threatened its existence: (1) the Assyrian threat (eighth century BCE), (2) the Babylonian invasion (early sixth century BCE), and (3) the restructuring of Judah after the Babylonian exile (late sixth and fifth centuries BCE).

The Assyrian Crisis (Eighth Century BCE)

Amos A Judean called to prophesy in the northern kingdom of Israel about 750 BCE, Amos accuses wealthy landowners of exploiting the poor and of ignoring God's concern for society's have-nots. Apparently reversing popular expectations—that the future "Day of Yahweh" would overthrow other nations while vindicating Israel—Amos declares that God will punish Israel along with other societies that foster social and economic injustice.

Hosea A native of Israel, Hosea compares his nation's worship of Baal to the breaking of a marriage bond with Yahweh. Although, like Amos, Hosea argues that economic inequality between rich and poor will bring divine punishment, he also emphasizes Yahweh's *hesed* (steadfast love),

likening God's love for Israel to that of a devoted father for his disobedient son.

Isaiah of Jerusalem A prophet intimately associated with the Jerusalem Temple and the Davidic royal family, Isaiah echoes the northern prophets in denouncing the ruling class's callous disregard for the poor. Active during the time of the Assyrian invasion of Judah (701 BCE), he counsels Judean kings to place their complete trust in God's power to protect the holy city. He also predicts that an heir of David will establish universal peace and justice.

Micah Unlike his contemporary, Isaiah, Micah is a rural villager who condemns rich urban landowners who "skin" and "devour" the peasant farmers. Criticizing the Jerusalem kings who permit such practices, Micah declares that the city and the Temple will be destroyed (Mic. 3:9–12).

The Decline of Assyria and the Rise of Babylon (Late Seventh and Early Sixth Centuries BCE)

Zephaniah Compiled during Josiah's reign (640–609 BCE), the oracles of Zephaniah begin by announcing that Yahweh plans to destroy all life on earth and end with the good news that God has repealed his judgment, restoring Judah to his favor. (The change of message may have resulted from Josiah's religious reforms.)

Nahum Shortly before Nineveh's fall (612 BCE), Nahum rejoices over Assyria's collapse.

Habakkuk Faced with Babylon's imminent conquest of Judah, Habakkuk wonders about Yahweh's fairness, concluding that the righteous person must have faith in God's ultimate justice.

Shifts in Prophetic Focus and Influence

For all their skill in "divining" God's will in particular circumstances, Israel's prophets were primarily neither fortune-tellers nor dream interpreters, the two most common offices that court prophets held in the ancient world. With the obvious exception of Joseph and Daniel, Israelite prophets do not hire themselves out to foreign kings as persons skilled in **oneiromancy** (the interpretation of dreams) or any other form of divination. The essential task of an Israelite prophet

was to be a truth-teller by declaring the word and will of Yahweh to his contemporaries. And the principal "truth" that the prophets were commisioned to proclaim was the true nature of the covenant relationship. As the prophets interpreted that relationship, Israel was bound, intimately and reciprocally, to Yahweh through a network of conditional and unconditional promises, past associations, and future expectations. Like a husband or a father—and prophets freely apply both metaphors to characterize God's feelings for Israel—Yahweh expects that some measure of loyalty and obedience will follow from his self-revelation to Israel. When Israel is neither loyal nor obedient, the

The Babylonian Exile and Promised Restoration of Judah (Sixth Century BCE)

Jeremiah Active during the reigns of Judah's last kings (Josiah to Zedekiah, c. 626–587 BCE), Jeremiah argues that Babylon is God's instrument of justice used to punish Judah for its sins. Presenting Judah's fate as a result of covenant breaking, Jeremiah then envisions a future covenant between Yahweh and his people, a bond that will not be broken (Jer. 31:31). Unlike Isaiah, who also advised Judean rulers during foreign invasions, Jeremiah sees little merit in the Temple or the Davidic dynasty.

Obadiah Obadiah condemns the neighboring state of Edom for joining the Babylonians in looting Judah (587 BCE).

Ezekiel A priest and mystic exiled in Babylon during Judah's last years (after 597 BCE), Ezekiel envisions Yahweh, too holy to remain dwelling in a polluted sanctuary, as abandoning the Jerusalem Temple. Ezekiel's denunciations of Judean sins are balanced by his visions of Judah's future restoration to renewed life with Yahweh at a gloriously restored holy city.

Second Isaiah Living among the Judean exiles in Babylon during Cyrus the Great's rise to power (c. 540 BCE), this unnamed prophet (known as Second Isaiah) explicitly advocates monotheism, declaring that Yahweh is the only God (Isa. 40–55). He also promises that Yahweh will stage a "new exodus," leading his people back from exile to a splendidly rebuilt Judah. Second Isaiah's four Servant Songs depict the redemptive role of Yahweh's chosen agent, Israel.

After the Exile: An Incomplete Restoration (Late Sixth and Fifth Centuries BCE)

Haggai Under Zerubbabel, a Davidic descendant whom the Persians appointed governor of the partly restored postexilic community, Haggai promises that Yahweh will cause the wealth of nations to flow into Jerusalem—if the Judeans will obediently rebuild the Temple.

Zechariah A contemporary of Haggai (c. 520 BCE), Zechariah produces a series of mystic visions involving the rebuilt Temple, the High Priest Joshua, the Davidic governor Zerubbabel, and Yahweh's future intentions for the covenant people. A later hand added Chapters 9–12.

Third Isaiah The third section of Isaiah (Chs. 56-66) includes oracles from almost the whole period of Israelite prophecy, including the work of a postexilic prophet referred to as Third Isaiah, who is sharply critical of the imperfectly restored Judah's religious failures.

Joel Of uncertain date, the collection ascribed to Joel contains a series of apocalyptic visions that depict plagues and other sufferings signaling the fierce Day of Yahweh. Calling his listeners to repentance, Joel foresees a climactic outpouring of the divine spirit upon all humanity.

Malachi This anonymous prophet (the book's title means "my messenger") also predicts a coming judgment on the terrifying day of Yahweh's visitation. Promising that an unidentified agent will appear to purify the Temple cult, Malachi ends by announcing the reappearance of the ninth-century-BCE prophet Elijah.

Jonah A humorous tale about a narrow-minded prophet who anticipates (and resents) his God's compassion for Gentiles, this prose work differs in form and content from all other books of prophetic literature. Highlighting Yahweh's decision to spare Nineveh, Assyria's hated capital, Jonah seems to offer an implied criticism of traditional Israelite prophecy, which tended to emphasize Yahweh's harsh judgments on both Israel and its enemies.

---

response in a complex mixture of divine sorrow and anger, followed by rejection:

> You have played the whore with many lovers;
> and would you return to me?
> says the LORD [Yahweh].
> Look up to the bare heights, and see!
> Where have you not been lain with? . . .
> You have polluted the land with your whoring
> and wickedness.
> Therefore the showers have been withheld,
> and the spring rain has not come;
> yet you have the forehead of a whore,
> you refuse to be ashamed.

> Have you not just now called to me,
> "My father, you are the friend of my youth—
> will he be angry forever,
> will he be indignant to the end?"

(Jer. 3:1–5)

This bittersweet message of love and anger is what the prophets themselves refer to as the "burden" of prophecy, especially for those active just before or during the Babylonian exile. Although the possibility of Israel's reconciliation to Yahweh is never ruled out during the 300 years of preexilic prophetic activity, the prevailing view in the canonical literature is that Israel has rejected every opportunity for genuine repentance and must therefore suffer divine punishment—the loss of its land and political independence.

This "reading" of Israel's history is, of course, identical with the interpretation of Israel's fate in the concluding chapters of Deuteronomy and throughout the Deuteronomistic History. As noted previously, the Former and Latter Prophets essentially agree on the meaning and causes of the exile. Some prophets emphasize that Yahweh's wrath will not last forever and that he will return a "remnant" of Judean exiles to their land (Amos 9:9–15; Jer. 30:1–22), but the preexilic prophets consistently insist that Israel has violated the covenant relationship and must bear the painful consequences.

This severe view undergoes a marked shift in both emphasis and perspective, however, in prophetic literature composed late in and after the exile. Even though the anonymous prophet known as Second Isaiah (responsible for Isa. 40–55) is not willing to forget Israel's sins, he is determined to proclaim that God has forgiven them:

> Comfort, O comfort my people, says your God.
> Speak tenderly to Jerusalem, and cry to her
> that she has served her term, that her penalty is paid,
> that she has received from the LORD's hand double
> for all her sins.

(Isa. 40:1–2)

Even more important than the lifting of divine judgment or a promised return to Judah (for exiles willing to heed the prophetic call to leave Babylon) is the prospect of a more glorious future than Israel has ever known:

> For I am about to create new heavens and a new
>   earth;
> the former things shall not be remembered or come
>   to mind.
> But be glad and rejoice forever
> in what I am creating; . . .
> The wolf and the lamb shall feed together,
> the lion shall eat straw like the ox;
> but the serpent—its food shall be dust!
> They shall not hurt or destroy
> on all my holy mountain,
> says the LORD [Yahweh].

(Isa. 65:17–18, 25)

This vision of human and cosmic renewal marks a clear departure from earlier prophetic traditions, and the more postexilic writers stress the novelty of this "new world order," the more radical their break with the past comes to seem. For writers who embrace the view that Yahweh is prepared to transform the entire universe,

both Israel and the peoples of the world are about to witness a fundamental change in the nature of reality. Human history as it has been previously experienced will come to an end with a divinely managed return to the state of the universe at the beginning of creation, when all things (humanity included) were pronounced "very good" (Gen. 1:31). That not all postexilic prophets subscribe to this visionary forecast is clear from the books of Malachi and Haggai, who fret, as their preexilic predecessors did, over Israel's shortcomings (Hag. 2:10–19; Mal. 1–2). Nevertheless, the promise of a divinely transformed cosmos and the possibility of a renewed covenant relationship inspire most of the prophetic writers of this period. Prophetic anticipations of this theme are present in Jeremiah 31 and Ezekiel 37, as visions of spiritual and national rebirth; such visions will become more intense and more urgent as Judah's returning exiles find that their restoration is only partial and incomplete.

As postexilic Judah endures centuries of foreign domination—with neither Davidic king nor political freedom—new voices are raised proclaiming new revelations of Yahweh's intentions, visions that are strikingly different from the traditional prophetic oracles of the preexilic era. The authors of Zechariah and, particularly, Daniel represent a radical change of emphasis, writing of Yahweh's imminent intervention to overthrow existing kings and empires and establish a supernaturally imposed kingdom (cf. Dan. 2:44). The only complete **apocalypse** (meaning "unveiling" or "revelation") in the Hebrew Bible, Daniel marks a new style of discourse, presenting its view of Yahweh's intentions in an array of bewildering images and mysterious symbols (presumably understood by a few who were spiritually "wise"). Daniel is so different from traditional prophetic books, in fact, that Jewish editors did not include it among the Prophets but instead placed it among the "Writings," the third and final section of the Tanakh. (For a discussion of **apocalyptic literature,** which includes both Daniel and many non-canonical works such as 1 and 2 Enoch, as well as the New Testament Book of Revelation, see Chapter 26.)

As we have seen, Israelite prophecy begins as an open proclamation of Yahweh's judgment of Israel and the world; its primary focus is on ethical, social, and political emergencies that the covenant people face. But as it draws toward its canonical end, prophetic writing becomes increasingly remote from the unfolding historical crises that motivated the classical prophets. In its apocalyptic form, prophecy refocuses on mystical speculations about God's future "End of history," expressing itself through sometimes grotesque symbols of beasts and metal statues (Dan. 2 and 7–8). The growing popularity of apocalyptic literature in the postexilic period signals, therefore, not only a growing disenchantment with history but perhaps also a growing disbelief in the prophet as an effective spokesperson for Yahweh. As priests such as Ezra, who brought a version of the Pentateuch from Babylon to Jerusalem, insisted that the returned exiles' main duty was to observe the Mosaic *torah*, priestly teaching apparently triumphed over prophetic pronouncements (see Chapters 21, 25, and 26).

The gradual formation of the biblical canon and the growing conviction among postexilic Jews that prophecy had come to an end are perhaps related movements. With the cessation of direct communications from God, the process of transcribing divine oracles must also come to a close, and with it the centuries-long epic of Israel's engagement with Yahweh. Paradoxically, the decline of prophecy seems to be linked, in part, to the very process of compiling the biblical canon. Other forces, cultural and political, were also at work undermining the authority of prophetic personalities or limiting the impact of their oracles. Even within the context of canonical prophetic literature, one can begin to find a corrosive skepticism directed at prophecy as such, and not simply at the credibility of a particular would-be prophet:

> Mortal, what is this proverb of yours about the land of Israel, which says, "The days are prolonged, and every vision comes to nothing"?

(Ezek. 12:22)

Ezekiel's response to this display of disbelief in the value of prophetic discourse is to denounce false prophets and to accuse Israel of faithlessness and rebellion. But the anxiety lurking behind this "proverb" clearly indicates an emerging culture of doubt. Even late prophets whose messages were subsequently added to the canon—the postexilic Haggai and Malachi—find it necessary to remind their audiences both that Yahweh still dwells among them (Haggai 2:4–5) and that indifference to God's word and insincerity of worship can only deepen divine alienation from Israel. However compelling the Deuteronomistic reading of Israel's fate must have seemed to Israel's prophets and editors of the biblical texts, it does not appear to have gained universal acceptance. Writing a few centuries BCE, the author of Ecclesiastes observes:

> Then I saw all the work of God, that no one can find out what is happening under the sun. However much they may toil in seeking, they will not find it out; even though those who are wise claim to know, they cannot find it out.

(Eccles. 8:17)

In the light of Judah's postexilic disappointments and the failure of Isaiah's visions of future glory, some later biblical writers openly doubted the prophets' claims to know the mind of God or his specific plans for the world.

But the turn away from prophecy may also reflect a shift in the center of both secular and religious authority. During the Persian period (539–332 BCE), after the monarchy had been replaced by a priestly theocracy, figures such as Ezra, the priest who brought from Babylon an authoritative edition of the Torah, assumed leadership of the covenant community (Ezra 7:1–29; 10:1–17; Neh. 8:1–18). Once the priesthood becomes the repository of Israel's collective memory and the principal interpreter of its covenant and epic history, both the conscience and historical consciousness of the nation is now in priestly hands. It will remain there until the rise of freelance interpreters of Torah later known as rabbis (teachers). In such a culture, the prophet begins to seem to many an unnecessary messenger from Yahweh. The priest, whom Malachi describes as a "messenger of the LORD of Hosts" (Mal. 2:7), gradually assumes the prophet's teaching and censoring functions.

QUESTIONS FOR DISCUSSION AND REVIEW

1. What role does the prophet play in the culture of ancient Israel? From whom does the prophet derive his or her authority? How is Moses a literary model for later prophets?

2. Why would kings like David, Solomon, and Ahab maintain court prophets? What function would they perform?

3. How does ecstatic prophecy differ from divination? What implements might a diviner employ to discover Yahweh's will in a particular matter?

4. Most biblical prophets appear during a specific military/political emergency in Israel's history. How do threats from Assyria and Babylon provoke prophetic responses?

5. Describe the shift in focus in postexilic prophecy. Which new themes do later prophetic writers emphasize, and how does that reflect Israel's new political situation?

6. What is the primary responsibility of an Israelite prophet? What do prophets mean when they speak of the "burden" of prophecy?

7. How do the teachings of the prophets relate to the central themes of the Deuteronomistic History? To what extent is prophecy in Israel an outgrowth of the thinking behind the DH?

Terms and Concepts to Remember

divination	oneiromancy
ecstatic prophecy	*roeh*
ephod	*ruah Elohim*
incubation ritual	*urim* and *thummim*
navi/nevi'im	

Recommended Reading

Barton, John. "Prophecy (Postexilic Hebrew)." In D. N. Freedman, ed., *The Anchor Bible Dictionary*, Vol. 5, pp. 489–495. New York: Doubleday, 1992. Examines prophecy after the Babylonian exile and Judah's partial restoration.

Blenkinsopp, Joseph. *A History of Prophecy in Israel*. Louisville, KY: Westminster John Knox Press, 1996. Surveys the course of Israelite prophecy.

Chisholm, Robert B., Jr. *Handbook of the Prophets: Isaiah, Jeremiah, Lamentations, Ezekiel, Daniel, Minor Prophets*. Grand Rapids, MI: Baker Academic, 2001. An accessible introduction.

Miller, John W. *Meet the Prophets: A Beginner's Guide to the Books of the Biblical Prophets*. New York: Paulist Press, 1987. A good place to start.

Peterson, David L. "Introduction to Prophetic Literature." In *The New Interpreter's Bible*, Vol. 6, pp. 1–23. Nashville, TN: Abingdon Press, 2001. Surveys typical themes and ethical issues of Israel's prophets.

Schmitt, John J. "Prophecy (Preexilic Hebrew)." In D. N. Freedman, ed., *The Anchor Bible Dictionary*, Vol. 5, pp. 482–489. New York: Doubleday, 1992. Examines prophets of the eighth through sixth centuries BCE.

Wilson, Robert R. *Prophecy and Society in Ancient Israel*. Philadelphia: Fortress Press, 1980. A helpful introduction.

CHAPTER 15

Prophets to the Northern Kingdom
The Oracles of Amos and Hosea

Key Topics/Themes Active in the northern kingdom during the eighth century BCE, Amos and Hosea were the earliest prophets to have their speeches preserved in book form. The growing power and presence of the Assyrian Empire loom in the background as the two prophets announce Yahweh's impending punishment of Israel's sins. Both prophets emphasize the people's apostasy and their leaders' corruption, greed, and exploitation of the poor. Providing a unique view of Israelite society and religion, Hosea uses the metaphor of an unhappy marriage to depict Israel's broken relationship with Yahweh.

Both Amos and Hosea begin their ministry during the reign of Jeroboam II (786–746 BCE), a reign notable for its length, relative peacefulness, and general prosperity. What Amos finds in the northern kingdom, however, is wealth in the hands of a few and poverty for the many. He also finds a spirit of moral indifference among the nation's political and social leaders, the class responsible for the economic inequalities he denounces. Beyond these common failures of social conscience, Hosea sees something even more serious—an appalling lack of commitment to Yahweh and to the covenant. Israel's disloyalty, manifest in a seemingly incurable attraction to foreign gods, expresses itself in two not unrelated ways: (1) a chilling absence of sympathy for the poor and (2) an equally absent understanding that Yahweh demands exclusive devotion. This double failure, as surely as Assyria's imperial ambitions, will cause tragedy for the Israelites in general and for the northern kingdom in particular. The inevitable doom that the two prophets see hanging over Israel reaches fulfillment when Assyrian troops overrun the country, destroying its capital, Samaria, in 722/721 BCE. As a state, the northern kingdom is literally erased from the map of the Near East, never to rise again.

The Book of Amos

Although placed third among the Minor Prophets (the twelve comparatively short books that follow the larger volumes of Isaiah, Jeremiah, and Ezekiel in the Tanakh), **Amos** was the first prophet to have his words recorded in book form. He was also the first to introduce major themes that would thereafter become staples of Israelite prophecy. Active during the reigns of Jeroboam II of Israel and Uzziah of Judah (783–742 BCE), Amos was an older contemporary of Hosea and Isaiah of Jerusalem. As if to place his career in a context of natural violence, his ministry is dated "two years before the earthquake," a geological event severe enough to shatter the northern town of Hazor and to be remembered centuries later in the writings of Flavius Josephus, the first-century-CE Jewish historian. A native of Judah from the small town of Tekoa, located about twelve miles south of Jerusalem, Amos is described as a shepherd, a herdsman, and a "dresser of sycamore trees." A man who labored among cattle and orchards, Amos insists that he is "no prophet, nor a prophet's son" (7:14). Amos's vigorous denial that he is "a prophet's son" is probably intended to distinguish him—an ordinary man whom Yahweh has summoned to deliver his message—from Israel's community or guild of professional prophets, most of whom were associated with particular shrines or a royal court. Belonging to neither a prophetic guild nor a band of court prophets where he would be expected to support a king's policies, Amos emphasizes his independence—and his direct personal relationship with Yahweh:

> . . . and the LORD [Yahweh] took me from following the flock, and the LORD said to me, "Go, prophesy to my people Israel."

> (Amos 7:15)

Yahweh's Demand for Economic Justice

The first cluster of oracles, presented in a bold, abrupt style, contains harsh criticism of Israel's various neighbors—Syria, Philistia, Tyre, Edom, and Moab—that Amos blasts for their inhumane treatment of conquered peoples. Then, unexpectedly switching targets, Amos suddenly attacks his Israelite audience, accusing its leaders of behaving no better than greedy foreign princes. His point is that Yahweh not only refuses to tolerate cruelty among the people whom he rescued from Egypt but also requires higher standards of ethical behavior from Israel than from those who do not enjoy Yahweh's special guidance.

Foremost among Israel's crimes was its shameful treatment of the poor and weak (see Box 16.1). Although the nation under Jeroboam had grown rich and comfortable, the wealthy had taken advantage of their economic power to crowd the poor from their land:

> Because they sell the righteous for silver,
> and the needy for a pair of sandals—
> they who trample the head of the poor into the dust
>   of the earth,
> and push the afflicted out of the way.

> (Amos 2:2–7)

Amos saw that behind the national prosperity and private luxury was a callous indifference to human suffering, which was no less a sin than sacrificing to idols. He was the first prophet to argue that social justice is as necessary a part of religion as worshiping one God only (8:4–8).

As archaeological digs at Samaria have demonstrated, Amos's description of (presumably aristocratic) women lying on beds of ivory (6:4) is not exaggerated. Nor is it likely that much of the wealth newly gained from trade and commerce trickled down to the lower classes. In fact, Amos aims his most stinging barbs at

Israelites who callously ignore the plight of those denied benefits from the nation's wealth:

> Ah, you that turn justice to wormwood,
> and bring righteousness to the ground!. . .
> Therefore because you trample on the poor
> and take from them levies of grain,
> you have built houses of hewn stone,
> but you shall not live in them;
> you have planted pleasant vineyards,
> but you shall not drink their wine.

> (Amos 5:7–11)

What particularly disgusts Amos is the smug attitude of the ruling classes, of those who live "at ease in Zion" (6:1), convinced that their conduct is irreproachable. For Amos, the moral contradiction of such behavior is that the very people who ignore the social demands of covenant law—the need to care for the poor, the fatherless, and the widowed—imagine that they are completely devoted to Yahweh. Amos observes, mockingly, how zealously the privileged classes of Israel bring sacrifices to the northern shrines at Bethel and Gilgal (4:4), but to no avail, because they have turned their backs on the poor whom God entrusted to their care. Sounding a theme that many prophets after him will echo, Amos (speaking for Yahweh) rejects the insincerity of Israel's worship:

> I hate, I despise your festivals,
> and I take no delight in your solemn assemblies.
> even though you offer me your burnt offerings
> and grain offerings,
> I will not accept them. . . .
> Take away from me the noise of your songs;
> I will not listen to the melody of your harps.

> (Amos 5:21–23)

Instead of elaborate ceremony, Yahweh desires "justice" and "righteousness like an ever-flowing stream" (5:24). No outward show of piety can substitute for true compliance with covenant ethics. The loss of Israel's wealth and power, which Amos foresees amid the splendor of northern cities, will soon follow. In his condemnation of the north, Amos leaves only the faintest hope that "the God of hosts will be gracious to the remnant of Joseph [the northern tribes]" (5:15).

The Terrible "Day of Yahweh"

Amos introduces another significant prophetic theme regarding Israel's future. Prior to his time, the **Day of Yahweh** apparently was thought to be a time of rejoicing, an era when God would overthrow all Israel's enemies and shower blessings on his people. Blasting such complacent assumptions, Amos reverses popular expectations by proclaiming the Day of Yahweh to be a Day of Judgment, a period of darkness and grief for sinful Israel (5:18–20). This pronouncement so upsets Amos's audience that Amaziah, the priest of Bethel, forbids the prophet to speak and expels him from the sanctuary (7:10–1). This does not, however, prevent Amos from continuing his forecast of doom. Israel, he says, is like a "basket of summer fruit, ripe for destruction" (8:1–4), and none will escape the day of wrath:

> Though they dig into Sheol [the underground abode
>   of the dead],
> from there shall my hand take them;
> though they climb up to heaven,
> from there I will bring them down.

(Amos 9:2)

Amos saw Yahweh as directing the fate of all nations, and not Israel alone. He had brought the Philistines from Crete just as he had brought Israel from Egypt; they and the Ethiopians were all the same to him (9:7–8). As the God who created the starry constellations of Pleiades and Orion, Yahweh is a cosmic, not a national, deity. Assyria, then just beginning its imperial expansion, was also under Yahweh's jurisdiction and would be the chosen instrument to punish Israel.

Amos embodies this message in a series of gloomy oracles and visions of judgment through which he conveys the certainty of Israel's destruction. Comparing Israel both to Sodom and Gomorrah and to Egypt (4:10–11), Amos recalls all of the punishments to which Yahweh has subjected Israel in the past, hoping for a collective change of heart. The time has passed, however, for repairing the broken covenant, and what lies ahead is only the spectacle of devastation and the death of the nation:

> On that day, says the LORD God,
> I will make the sun go down at noon,
> and darken the earth in broad daylight.
> I will turn your feasts into mourning,
> and all your songs into lamentation;
> I will bring sackcloth on all loins,
> and baldness on every head;
> I will make it like the mourning for an only son,
> and the end of it like a bitter day.

(Amos 8:9–10)

Each of Amos's visions reinforces his judgment, as he foresees Israel enduring a plague of locusts (7:1–3), then suffering devastation by fire (7:4–6), and finally being measured against a plumb (vertical) line (7:7–9) that shows the extent to which the covenant people fail to "measure up."

So unrelieved is Amos's pessimistic outlook for the northern kingdom that a later hand added a brief epilogue predicting Israel's future restoration:

> For lo, I will command and shake the house of Israel
>   among the nations. . . .
> On that day I will raise up the booth of David that
>   has fallen,
> and repair its breaches, and raise up its ruins,
> and rebuild it as in the days of old . . .

(Amos 9:9–11)

This promised reconciliation with Yahweh, focusing as it does on the Davidic monarchy, suggests not only a southern, Judean origin for these verses but also a postexilic date of composition. (In this passage, the Davidic throne already is "fallen," and his former capital already lies in ruins.) Reediting of Amos's oracles to the northern tribes by a later Judean scribe is not surprising. Many prophetic books show similar signs of postexilic revision, with scribes typically adding assurances of future restoration to balance the prophets' gloomy oracles of judgment.

The Book of Hosea

Traditionally placed first among the Minor Prophets, **Hosea** was a contemporary of Amos and the only native son of Israel whose work was preserved in the biblical canon. Unlike Amos, however, Hosea mixes his forecasts of divine punishment with passages expressing Yahweh's grief for his people's imminent destruction. Portraying a God who experiences conflicting emotions—anger and wounded love—at his people's apostasy, Hosea began his career about 747 BCE, during the reign of Jeroboam II, and continued prophesying into the reign of Israel's last king, Hoshea (732–724 BCE). After the northern kingdom's fall, Israelite refugees probably carried Hosea's oracles south to Judah, where Judean scribes reedited them. Even casual readers can see in the book's postscript—"Those who are wise understand these things; those who are discerning know them" (14:9)—the hand of a later editor. This redactor, writing after Judah's exile, urges his readers (using the words of then-contemporary wisdom teachers) to reflect on all this eighth-century-BCE prophet has revealed.

Hosea's Disastrous Marriage

From the viewpoint of both Amos and Hosea, Israel's last days are marked by social, religious, and moral decay, a perception reflected in their pronouncements. In

Hosea's case, the prophet cites his unhappy marriage to a woman named **Gomer,** who repeatedly betrays him with other lovers, as symptomatic of the entire nation's faithlessness. God's first words to the prophet are startlingly crude: "Go, take for yourself a wife of whoredom and have children of whoredom, for the land commits great whoredom by forsaking the LORD" (1:2). Following the divine command, Hosea dutifully marries Gomer, "the daughter of Diblaim," who seems incapable of keeping her wedding vows. Scholars are divided on whether to regard Gomer as a historical figure—a disloyal wife who causes her devoted husband endless pain and humiliation—or as a literary creation intended to illustrate how Yahweh (Israel's spiritual "husband") feels about his covenant partner's betrayal of their sacred bond. Even if the story of this dysfunctional marriage, the subject of the book's first three chapters, actually reflects Hosea's domestic arrangement, its primary intent is to express the flawed relationship between Yahweh and Israel.

It is to a culture that treats Yahweh as if he were merely one of a "host" of deities that Hosea turns, pleading on his God's behalf—and speaking in his voice—that they address him as "my husband" (Hebrew, *ish*) rather than "my Baal" (*ba'ali*) (2:16). This play on words has both a linguistic and a theological meaning. The word *ba'al* can mean nothing more than "lord and master;" in a male-dominated society like ancient Israel's, women commonly addressed their husbands as "my *ba'al*." The very same word capitalized, however, can also be understood to refer to the Canaanite fertility god **Baal,** and it is precisely this potential confusion of usage that goes to the heart of Israel's spiritual dilemma. Like his ninth-century-BCE predecessor Elijah, Hosea calls upon his fellow Israelites to renounce Baal and the calf god of Samaria (possibly a representation of the Canaanite El), as well as any other deity to whom they have attributed their good harvests and collective safety. It is to Yahweh alone that they can turn, because, whatever Israel may think, he is the sole source of fertility and of life itself:

> She did not know that it was I who gave her the grain, the wine, and the oil, and who lavished upon her silver and gold that they used for Baal.

(Hos. 3:8)

Israel's failure to know on whom its good fortunes really depend leads to its "divorce" and all the misfortunes that follow. In what is perhaps the most-often-quoted passage in this book, Hosea warns his audience that because they have "sowed the wind" they will inevitably "reap the whirlwind" (8:7). That Hosea holds the king

and the priesthood largely responsible for Israel's apostasy is clear from his repeated condemnations of both (4:6–9; 5:1–2; 6:9–10). The priests are particularly to blame for Israel's failure to "know" who Yahweh really is and what he demands: "My people are destroyed for lack of knowledge," God declares (4:6). The class privileged to teach Yahweh's "law" has proven too corrupt and too greedy to save the people in their care.

Nevertheless—and here Hosea departs most dramatically from Amos—Yahweh can neither forget nor deny the love he once felt for Israel—*and still feels.* God's longing to be reconciled to his people is just as strong as his determination to punish this "whoring" generation. Offering a rare description of God's conflicted mental state, Hosea shows Yahweh shifting from anger to sorrow to hope:

> How can I give you up, Ephraim [the most important northern tribe]?
> How can I hand you over, O Israel? . . .
> My heart recoils within me;
> my compassion grows warm and tender.
> I will not execute my fierce anger;
> I will not again destroy Ephraim;
> for I am God and no mortal,
> the Holy One in your midst,
> and I will not come in wrath.

(Hos. 11:8–9)

These are not divine mood swings, however, but rather an expression of divine **hesed,** of an inexhaustible love. More than any other prophet of his time, Hosea preserves a tradition that defines the covenant as everlasting and, to that extent, as unconditional. In a moving counterpoint to the failed marriage theme that runs throughout his book, Hosea portrays Yahweh as offering to marry Israel again and forever, only this time "in righteousness and in justice, in steadfast love, and in mercy" (2:19). In fact, it is on this note that the book concludes. Recalling the Exodus as a time of divine nurturing and trust—as well as rebellion (11:1–11)—Hosea presents Yahweh as a father unable to cast aside a beloved but badly behaved son. Hosea's emphasis on Yahweh's capacity for enduring love and forgiveness, and his resolve to renew a relationship that seemed beyond repair, strikes a chord that many later prophets will replay.

QUESTIONS FOR DISCUSSION AND REVIEW

1. According to Amos and Hosea, what are Israel's principal crimes? Does Israel's covenant with Yahweh entitle it to special consideration, or will it be judged just as severely as other nations?

2. Describe the Day of Yahweh. In what ways does Amos's understanding of this concept apparently differ from popular expectations of his day?

3. Why does Hosea use the example of his marriage to parallel the relationship of Yahweh and Israel? How does the idea of "steadfast love" (*hesed*) relate to this metaphor?

4. How can both Amos and Hosea speak of God's rejection and destruction of Israel in one breath and then hold out the hope of reconciliation in the next? Does this apparent inconsistency suggest a basic uncertainty surrounding God's nature? If he lived to witness Assyria's destruction of Israel in 722 BCE, how would Hosea reconcile his understanding of God's expressions of love for Israel with the fact that he abandoned the people to their enemies?

Terms and Concepts to Remember

Amos	Gomer
Baal	*hesed*
Day of Yahweh	Hosea

Recommended Reading

Birch, Bruce C. "Hosea, Book of." In K. D. Sakenfeld, ed., *The New Interpreter's Dictionary of the Bible*, Vol. 2, pp. 894–900. Nashville, TN: Abingdon Press, 2007. Sensitively examines the issue of Hosea's relationship with his unfaithful wife and its analogy to Israel's broken covenant with Yahweh.

Brenner, Athalya, ed. *A Feminist Companion to the Latter Prophets*. Sheffield, England: Sheffield Press, 1995. Prophetic oracles from women's perspectives.

Gowan, Donald E. "The Book of Amos." In *The New Interpreter's Bible*, Vol. 7, pp. 339–431. Nashville, TN: Abingdon Press, 1996. A helpful introduction.

King, Philip. *Amos, Hosea, Micah: An Archaeological Commentary*. Minneapolis: Westminster John Knox Press, 1988. Uses archaeological finds to examine the material culture of the eighth century BCE and illuminate the prophets' social criticism.

Premnath, Devadasan. "Amos, Book of." In K. D. Sakenfeld, ed., *The New Interpreter's Dictionary of the Bible*, Vol. 1, pp. 135–141. Nashville, TN: Abingdon Press, 2006. A concise analysis of Amos' major themes.

Yee, Gale A. "The Book of Hosea." In *The New Interpreter's Bible*, Vol. 7, pp. 197–297. Nashville, TN: Abingdon Press, 1996. A complete text with interpretive notes.

CHAPTER 16

Prophets of the Assyrian Threat
The Oracles of Isaiah, Micah, Zephaniah, and Nahum

Key Topics/Themes As Assyrian armies marched throughout the Near East, threatening to swallow up the covenant community, two eighth-century-BCE prophets—Isaiah of Jerusalem and his contemporary Micah—interpreted the meaning of international events for Yahweh's people. Isaiah's oracles are embedded in Chapters 1–39 of the book bearing his name. (The remaining chapters, 40–66, contain the work of two later prophets influenced by his thought.) Zephaniah, who lived during King Josiah's reign, when Assyria was in decline, first predicted global destruction and then, perhaps responding to Josiah's reforms, proclaimed that Yahweh had pardoned Judah. Late in Josiah's reign, Nahum rejoiced over Assyria's final collapse and the fall of Nineveh, its capital.

The brutal fact of Assyrian aggression—and the danger it posed to Yahweh's people—forms the historical background to the oracles of four Judean prophets—Isaiah, Micah, Zephaniah, and Nahum. After centuries of relative weakness, during the reign of Tiglath-pileser III (745–727 BCE), a newly energized Assyria began a series of military conquests, rapidly subjugating much of the Near East (see Figure 16.1). In addition to seizing the throne of Babylon, Tiglath-pileser subdued Syria and Palestine, forcing small states such as Israel and Judah to pay enormous sums in tribute (2 Kings 15:19–20). When Israel unwisely rebelled against Assyrian oppression, Shalmaneser V (ruled 726–722 BCE) laid siege to Samaria, the Israelite capital. Shalmaneser's successor, Sargon II (ruled 721–705 BCE), captured Samaria, destroying the city and deporting many of the northern kingdom's inhabitants to Mesopotamia (2 Kings 17; see Chapters 3 and 13). Weary of paying tribute to Assyria, under King Hezekiah, Judah also rebelled, inciting Sennacherib (ruled 704–781 BCE) to launch a frightening assault on Jerusalem. The prophet Isaiah's advice to Hezekiah during the prolonged Assyrian threat to Judah's center of worship forms an important part of his message.

 The Book of Isaiah

Standing first among the prophetic books, Isaiah contains some of the most famous passages in the Hebrew Bible, including visions of a future world peace in which all of creation, both human and animal, is subject to Yahweh's rule. Although traditionally regarded as the work of a single prophet, contemporary scholars believe that the Book of Isaiah is an anthology of prophetic literature that spans almost the entire era of Israelite prophecy, from the mid-eighth to the early fifth centuries BCE. Most scholars divide the book into three different parts, each representing a different historical period and a different author.

The first thirty-nine chapters of Isaiah contain the oldest material, oracles by **Isaiah of Jerusalem,** the historical prophet for whom the entire collection is named. Isaiah was active between about 742 and 701 BCE, a turbulent era that witnessed Assyria's destruction of Israel and the engulfment of Judah as well. Most of Isaiah's genuine speeches, embedded amid later prophetic and editorial additions, contain advice to Davidic kings during the Assyrian emergency, as well as

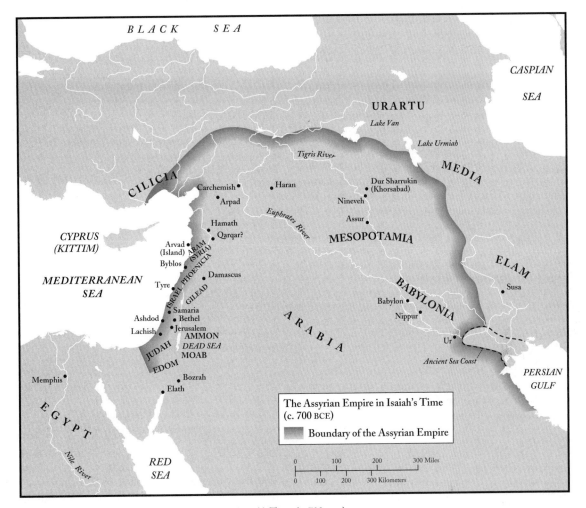

FIGURE 16.1 Map of the Assyrian Empire in Isaiah's Time (c. 700 BCE).

warnings of judgment against Judah for its sins. By contrast, oracles throughout the book's second section (Chs. 40–55) state that the time of judgment is past and that Yahweh is about to redeem his people. After Chapter 39, Isaiah is never again mentioned by name, Davidic kings are no longer in view, and Assyria disappears from the prophet's oracles, replaced by frequent references to Babylon. In this section, an unnamed prophet speaks words of comfort and encouragement to Judean exiles in Babylon, who, he says, are about to be released by **Cyrus,** emperor of Persia. The book's abrupt change of setting and tone, from the Assyrian crisis to the Babylonian captivity and from oracles of doom to oracles of hope, as well as differences in literary style, vocabulary, and theology, indicate a change of author, whom scholars call **Second Isaiah.** The book's final ten chapters, encompassing a variety of oracles from almost the whole range of biblical prophecy, are thought to

include passages from another anonymous prophet, **Third Isaiah,** who lived in Judah after the exiles' return from Babylon.

A Chorus of Three Prophetic Voices

Scholars have long wondered what principle guided ancient biblical editors when they combined the work of three different prophets from three different periods of Israel's history onto a single scroll. Some recent commentators suggest that the editors wished to illustrate the entire spectrum of Israelite prophecy in a book that they placed at the head of the prophetic collection. In its edited form, the Book of Isaiah represents and incorporates the three principal themes or concerns of Israel's prophets: warnings of divine judgment, promises of forgiveness and reconciliation, and responsibilities of restoration (see Clifford in "Recommended Reading").

Whereas the historical prophet, Isaiah of Jerusalem, warned the people of impending punishment for their social injustice and disloyalty to God, Second Isaiah proclaimed that the people's suffering was complete and their release from Babylon imminent. Third Isaiah then reminded the returned exiles of the ethical and religious obligations inherent in their restoration and reconciliation with Yahweh. The book as a whole thus served as a pattern or model for future generations, illustrating the nature and consequences of covenant breaking, as well as the willingness of Israel's God to save and redeem a repentant people. (Because this text discusses the prophets in their presumed chronological order, commentary on Second and Third Isaiah appears in Chapters 18 and 19, respectively.)

Isaiah of Jerusalem (Isaiah 1–39)

According to the book's opening verse, Isaiah of Jerusalem served as prophet and counselor to three Judean kings—Jotham, Ahaz, and Hezekiah. Beginning about 742 BCE, shortly after King Uzziah's death and the ascension of Jotham, Isaiah's career continued until at least 701 BCE, and perhaps as late as 687 BCE—a span of forty to fifty-five years. In Chapter 6, which most scholars think represents Isaiah's call to prophesy, he describes a mystical experience in the Jerusalem Temple that seems to have shaped both his concept of divine holiness and his sense of mission to the Judean people. Suddenly transported to God's throne room in heaven (which the earthly Temple symbolized), Isaiah beholds Yahweh presiding over the divine council. Israel's God is surrounded by myriads (tens of thousands) of **seraphim,** fiery creatures equipped with three sets of wings. Overwhelmed by the seraphim's praise of divine holiness and by a corresponding awareness of his own imperfection, Isaiah feels his lips symbolically cleansed by a burning coal, which qualifies him to speak Yahweh's words to Judah. Drawing on his later experience of his fellow Judeans' stubborn refusal to heed his message, however, Isaiah presents his inability to persuade his hearers to change their ways as predestined (determined beforehand by God) (Isa. 6:1–13). Some scholars have questioned whether this passage shows Isaiah's initial call to a prophetic vocation, but most regard it as representing Isaiah's sense of his divine commission.

The Structure of Isaiah's Oracles   Although editors did not arrange Isaiah's pronouncements either by topic or in the order in which they were given, scholars have found that various clusters of oracles relate to three principal crises of Isaiah's lifetime. The first set concerns the

Syro-Ephraimite War (735–734 BCE); the second, Hezekiah's temptation to ally Judah with Egypt (c. 711 BCE); and the third, the Assyrian invasion of Judah (701 BCE). In their present form, Chapters 1–39 contain both Isaiah's authentic sayings and material later added to expand and update his message. This section is commonly divided into six parts:

1. Prophetic accusations of wrongdoing in Judah and Jerusalem, interspersed with visions of universal peace under a Davidic ruler (Chs. 1–12)

2. Oracles of judgment against foreign nations (Chs. 13–23)

3. Apocalyptic visions of cosmic judgment and restoration (Chs. 24–27), a section known as the Little Apocalypse (probably dating to the fifth century BCE or later)

4. Denunciations of Judah and Jerusalem (Chs. 28–33) (probably delivered during the Assyrian invasion, when Isaiah saw Assyrian armies as the instrument of divine punishment on his people)

5. Additional oracles of judgment and blessing (Chs. 34–35) (probably added during the postexilic period)

6. Prose excerpts from 2 Kings showing Isaiah's interactions with King Hezekiah (Chs. 36–39), serving as a bridge to the much later oracles of Second Isaiah

Two Possible Fates   A preface to the whole collection of oracles ascribed to Isaiah of Jerusalem, the opening chapter surveys most of the book's major themes. Like most Israelite prophets, Isaiah ranges between pronouncements of utter doom and proclamations of glorious future blessings. For Isaiah, the opposite poles of destruction and salvation are not contradictory; rather, they represent two different possible fates for the covenant community. If Judah's leaders persist in exploiting the poor and governing unjustly, they are doomed (see Box 16.1). But if they obey Yahweh by placing human welfare above profit, they will prosper (Isa. 1:17; cf. 3:13–15; 5:8–20; 10:1–4). The quality of Judah's future depends on the ruling class's willingness to show compassion and promote social justice:

> If you are willing and obedient,
> you shall eat the good of the land;
> but if you refuse and rebel,
> you shall be devoured by the sword.

> (Isa. 1:19–20)

The nation's destiny is not fixed because, if the people change their behavior, Yahweh is willing to forgive, informing wrongdoers that, though their "sins are like scarlet, they shall be like snow" (1:18).

As if to illustrate the universal benefits of transforming Judah into a just society, later editors follow Yahweh's plea for compassion with one of Isaiah's most optimistic oracles—a vision of global peace with an exalted Jerusalem as the center of the new world order (Isa. 2:1–4). As **Zion,** the Jerusalem hill on which Solomon's Temple stood, becomes the new holy mountain, Yahweh extends his "instruction" (and covenant?) to encompass all peoples. Now inscribed on the United Nations Plaza in New York City, Isaiah's promise that all nations will convert their "swords" or other weapons of war into "plowshares [a plow's metal blade]," instruments of peace, expresses a long-held and as-yet unrealized ideal in Western culture.

In considering the standard by which Isaiah judges the ruling class's abuse of power, it is important to note that Isaiah never refers explicitly to the Mosaic Covenant. Instead of appealing to the Sinai/Horeb tradition, as Amos and Hosea occasionally do, Isaiah emphasizes Yahweh's special relationship with the Davidic dynasty in Jerusalem. This reliance on the Davidic royal line and the sanctity of the Davidic capital may explain why Isaiah regards every threat to Jerusalem and its anointed kings as an opportunity for the nation to show its absolute trust in Yahweh's sworn oath to preserve and protect David's heirs. The prophet repeatedly urges Judah's rulers to remain "quiet" in the face of military threats, avoiding foreign alliances and relying exclusively on Yahweh's promise to David (cf. 2 Sam. 7:11–17). Alluding to his pact with the Davidic dynasty, God promises that "I will defend this city to save it, for my own sake and for the sake of my servant David" (Isa. 37:35). Isaiah further assures his audience that "The LORD of hosts, like a bird hovering over its young, will be a shield over Jerusalem" (31:5).

The Syro-Ephraimite Crisis Isaiah's advice during the Syro-Ephraimite War in the mid-730s BCE illustrates his policy of absolute trust in Yahweh's commitment to David's city. As scholars reconstruct events, various small states—led by "Aram" (Syria) and "Ephraim" (Israel)—apparently formed a coalition to resist Assyrian expansion into the region. When the kings of Syria and Israel besieged Jerusalem to force King Ahaz of Judah (ruled c. 735–715 BCE) to join their alliance, Isaiah counseled a passive reliance on Yahweh to keep his vow to David and deliver the holy city (Isa. 7).

Ignoring Isaiah's advice, Ahaz negotiated with Assyria, and, thanks to Assyrian influence, the Syro-Ephraimite siege of Jerusalem was lifted. In saving his capital from the armies of neighboring Syrian and Israelite

kings, however, Ahaz played into Assyrian hands, so that Judah was quickly reduced to the level of a vassal state in the Assyrian Empire. Viewing Ahaz's policy as a betrayal of Yahweh, Isaiah then announces that Assyria will soon become the "rod" of God's anger to punish Judah for the king's lack of faith (7:18–25; 10:5–6, 28–32). Should Assyria exceed its mandate to chastise his people, however, Yahweh in turn will destroy it (10:7–19).

As a pledge that Yahweh will rescue his people from the Syro-Ephraimite crisis, Isaiah states that a young woman, perhaps Ahaz's wife, will conceive and bear a son, whose name, **Immanuel**—"God [El] is with us"— signifies that Yahweh is present to protect his people (7:13–15). By the time child is old enough to make wise decisions, Isaiah states, both Syria and Israel will have collapsed, ending their threat to Judah. Because both Damascus and Samaria, the respective capitals of these two neighboring states, were destroyed by Assyria within the next several years, Isaiah's confidence was vindicated by the event.

The heir born to Ahaz and his queen was Hezekiah, whose ascension to Judah's throne was perhaps the occasion for Isaiah's celebrated poem about an heir of David, which provides the text for a joyful chorus in Handel's *Messiah:*

> For a child has been born for us,
> a son given to us. . . .
> His authority shall grow continually,
> and there shall be endless peace for the throne
> of David and his kingdom.
>
> (Isa. 9:7)

Although Assyria crushed Syria, Israel, and other nearby states, Isaiah's coronation hymn for the new Davidic ruler predicts a flourishing Judah, secure because of God's pact with David (9:2–21). So forceful is Isaiah's Immanuel prophecy, with its optimism for Judah's divinely appointed monarchy, that—after the Davidic throne had been abolished—later generations viewed it as a messianic prediction. A term meaning "anointed" and applied to all Davidic kings, messiah later became identified with a future Davidic ruler who would restore the Davidic kingdom and vindicate Yahweh's people in the eyes of their national enemies. New Testament writers regard Jesus of Nazareth as the royal figure whom Isaiah foretold, although the historical Jesus did not reestablish the Davidic monarchy or free the covenant community from its political oppressors.

Hezekiah's Alliance with Egypt The prophet's attention was drawn from a future peaceable kingdom to more mundane political concerns in 711 BCE, when the Assyrians attacked the city of Ashdod, located near Judah's southwest border. This time, Egypt attempted to form a defensive alliance of Canaanite states to protect its own frontier. To pressure King Hezekiah not to join the Egyptian coalition, Isaiah paraded almost naked through Jerusalem's streets for three years, graphically illustrating the public humiliations of defeat and slavery that would result from relying on Egypt instead of Yahweh to save them from the Assyrians (Isa. 20). Depending on this unreliable nation, Isaiah says, is like leaning on a sharp broken reed that pierces the hand of the one who grasps it (36:6). Although Hezekiah did not at first commit Judah to Egypt's protection, he eventually joined Egypt in an anti-Assyrian coalition. This "unholy" alliance sparks some of Isaiah's harshest condemnations of Judah's king, courtiers, and other national leaders (Isa. 28–31). Later editors, however, inserted a passage into this section asserting that even Egypt will learn to "know" and worship Yahweh (19:19–22). Perhaps more surprising, these added verses predict that Egypt and Assyria will join forces with Israel to form a trio of Near Eastern powers that, together, will be a "blessing in the midst of the earth" (19:23–24).

Assyria's Assault on Jerusalem In 701 BCE, the Assyrians made their predictably violent response to Hezekiah's flirtation with Egypt. Sweeping down from the north, **Sennacherib** (ruled 704–681 BCE), one of Assyria's most formidable warrior-kings, cut off Judah's communication with Egypt and laid siege to Jerusalem—exactly as Isaiah feared (29:1–4). Although Hezekiah at first follows Isaiah's advice not to surrender, the Assyrians' capture and burning of all forty-six fortified cities in Judah leaves Jerusalem, now a solitary oasis in a desert of total devastation, completely vulnerable. The horrors of the Assyrian invasion are vividly depicted in artwork adorning Sennacherib's palace in Nineveh. One low-relief sculpture shows Assyrian troops attacking Lachish, one of Judah's largest walled cities, with Assyrian soldiers impaling captives on wooden stakes (See Figure 9.1). Sennacherib spares Jerusalem, but Hezekiah is compelled to pay a staggering price for his resistance—"three hundred talents [about ten tons] of silver and thirty talents [one ton] of gold" (2 Kings 18:14–16). This huge payoff for Jerusalem's deliverance is not mentioned in the version of 2 Kings that concludes the collection of First Isaiah's oracles (compare Isa. 36–39 with 2 Kings 18:13–20:19). His attempts at independence having failed, an impoverished Hezekiah has to give up large parts of his kingdom to Assyria and resume his role as Assyrian vassal.

A fortunate archaeological discovery provides us with an Assyrian inscription of Sennacherib's military victories in Palestine that, not surprisingly, differs from the biblical account of Jerusalem's deliverance. In

Sennacherib's report, he boasts that he sealed Hezekiah in his capital "like a bird in a cage" (see Figure 16.2). By contrast, the Isaiah–2 Kings narratives state that the Assyrian army withdrew from Jerusalem because

FIGURE 16.2 The cuneiform inscription on this hexagonal prism proclaims Sennacherib's military triumphs over Palestinian states and their Egyptian allies. Sennacherib, emperor of Assyria (704–681 BCE), boasts that his armies overwhelmed Judah, his siege of Jerusalem trapping King Hezekiah (715–687 BCE) "like a bird in a cage." Accounts of Sennacherib's invasion and Jerusalem's deliverance appear in 2 Kings 18:13–19:37 and Isaiah 36:1–37:38

Yahweh's angel slew 185,000 troops in a single night. Some scholars suggest that the two accounts refer to two different invasions, one in 701 BCE and a second some time later. Whether there were one or two Assyrian attempts to capture Jerusalem, for Isaiah, the significant fact was that David's city escaped the devastation inflicted on all other Judean towns, suggesting that Judah's capital, where Yahweh had placed his "name," enjoyed divine protection (Isa. 31:5; 37:35).

In addition to Isaiah's authentic oracles, Chapters 1–39 also contain a variety of passages that reflect later prophetic developments. One section, known as the Little Apocalypse (Isa. 24–27), probably dates from a period after the exile when Judah was a small part of the Persian Empire. Presenting visions of a future world judgment, this literary unit emphasizes Yahweh's universal rulership and includes passages that apparently express new beliefs about resurrection to a future life (25:7; 26:19–21). Most scholars, however, believe that these verses do not refer to an individual's posthumous fate but rather, like Ezekiel's famous vision of the "valley of dry bones," symbolically portray the "resurrection" or rebirth of the covenant community (cf. Ezek. 37). Allusions to Babylon's fall, such as the poem in Isaiah 14, are also postexilic and were probably composed by members of a prophetic school that preserved and edited the work of Isaiah of Jerusalem.

 ## The Book of Micah

The fourth and last of the eighth-century-BCE prophets, **Micah** was a younger contemporary of Isaiah of Jerusalem. Active between about 740 and 700 BCE, he directed his earliest prophecies against Israel's religious sins, predicting the northern kingdom's fall to Assyria (1:2–7). Unlike Isaiah, who may have belonged to Judah's aristocracy, Micah was a native of Moresheth, a village in the foothills southwest of Jerusalem. A man of the people, Micah takes a country-dweller's dim view of urban life and what he sees as its deplorable corruption. Viewing the city as a stronghold of the exploitative ruling classes, a tainted environment that will doom Jerusalem as it did Samaria, Micah denounces the greed and tyranny of merchants and landowners (2:1–5, 6–11; 3:1–4; 6:9–14). From his rural perspective, the prophet condemns not only the acquisitiveness of the rich who gobble up the property of poor farmers but the entire urban establishment, including its corrupt princes, judges, and priests. Micah has a special contempt for false prophets whose oracles for hire

support the privileged classes (3:9–12; cf. 7:1–4; see also Box 16.1).

Whereas Isaiah criticized the policies of individual kings while supporting the institutions of the Davidic dynasty and Temple cult, Micah shows them little respect. He scornfully denies that the sanctuary's presence in Jerusalem will protect the capital from harm and predicts that both city and Temple will be reduced to rubble (3:1–3, 9–12). (Micah's prediction was later cited at the trial of Jeremiah, a prophet who lived to see his oracles of Jerusalem's desolation fulfilled [Jer. 26:18].) Rebuking the Jerusalem nobility and priesthood (6:1–2, 9–16), Micah also denounces the professional seers who offer deceptive forecasts of comfort and who fear to tell the people unwelcome truths (3:5–8). He even rejects the belief that Israel's God requires animal or any other formal sacrifice. In the book's most celebrated passage, he—or a later disciple—argues that Yahweh asks only for acts of justice and love and for people to walk humbly in the divine presence (6:6–8). For many commentators, Micah presents a classic statement of the insight of the prophet warring against the ritualism of the priest.

Although they were both active during the reign of Hezekiah, neither Isaiah nor Micah mentions the other's work, perhaps because of the differences in their respective backgrounds and attitudes toward Judah's defining institutions of monarchy and Temple. According to many scholars, Micah's original oracles about Judah were largely negative, but later editors added several optimistic passages predicting Judah's future glory (4:1–5:15; 7:8–20). One oracle of world peace is expressed in almost exactly the same words as that of Isaiah, giving a very un-Micah kind of approval to the centrality of Jerusalem and its sanctuary in the divine plan (4:1–4; cf. Isa. 2:2–4). The references to Davidic promises and to a faithful remnant returning to Judah after exile, at which time all citizens will sit under their vines and fig trees in prosperous tranquility (Mic. 2:12; 4:4–8), also seems to have been inserted into Micah's work by later hands. The famous prophecy that Bethlehem one day will become the birthplace of a ruler whose "origin is from of old, from ancient days"—generally viewed as a messianic oracle—is also considered a later scribal addition.

Although in its present form Micah seems to include oracles composed after the prophet's lifetime, the book nonetheless represents the typical prophetic paradox in which Yahweh inspires words of both severe judgment and redeeming hope. In compiling prophetic sayings, later editors commonly attached words of encouragement even to the most harsh prophecies, concluding such works as Amos, Hosea, and Micah with visions of

---

BOX 16.1   Prophetic Concern for the Poor and Powerless

As the God of justice and *hesed* (steadfast love), Yahweh demanded that his people form a just society that actively practiced love of one's neighbor (Lev. 19:18). Although biblical writers portray Canaan as a land of abundance, "flowing with milk and honey," not all Israelites benefited equally from the land's resources. The Torah accordingly made specific provisions for the poor, insisting that they were entitled to the same legal rights as the rich (Deut. 16:19), a contrast to other Near Eastern law codes that applied different legal standards to nobles and to peasants. The Torah also required that no interest be charged for loans made to the poor (Lev. 23:35–37) and that their debts be canceled every seventh year (Deut. 15:1–2). In addition, landowners were not to cut the wheat growing in the corners of their fields, leaving it for the poor to harvest, a statute that plays a major role in the Book of Ruth (see Chapter 24).

Exploiting the Poor

Despite these Torah requirements and the social customs they reflect, some of Israel's ruling class found ways to increase their wealth by exploiting the poor, a practice that the prophets denounce as hateful to Yahweh. Although commonly overlooked today, one of the major reasons the prophets give for Yahweh's anger against Israel is economic injustice—the painfully unequal distribution of material possessions in

Israelite society. Eighth-century-BCE prophets, such as Amos, Micah, and Isaiah of Jerusalem, repeatedly point out that God is the champion of the poor and defenseless, and that he condemns the ruling classes' attempts to gain riches at the expense of the poor. Amos, the first prophet to have his oracles collected in written form, is also the first known to declare that Yahweh regards social justice as an indispensable aspect of faithfulness to him (Amos 8:4–8; cf. 2:6–7; 4:1–2; 6:4–6).

Isaiah's Warnings to Jerusalem's Elite

Particularly during times of drought, crop failure, and famine, the poor, who had little reserve to live on, were often forced to sell their farms and fields to wealthy landowners, a situation that Isaiah of Jerusalem finds intolerable:

> Woe to those who add house to house
> and join field to field
> until everything belongs to them
> and they are the sole inhabitants of the land.

(Isa. 5:8)

This policy of buying up others' property (ancestral land was regarded as Yahweh's heritage and was to be kept in the family) deeply offended Israel's God, who regards such greed as acts of theft:

---

future reconciliation and peace (cf. Amos 9:11–15; Hos. 14:2–10; Mic. 7:8–20). Despite Micah's sweeping attacks on Judah's leading authorities, his speeches were preserved on a scroll and housed in the Jerusalem Temple, a structure whose ruin he foretold (cf. Jer. 26:16–18).

 ## The Book of Zephaniah

The Day of Yahweh

In the work of **Zephaniah,** we return to themes first sounded by Amos—but now greatly intensified. Amos startled his listeners by announcing that the Day of Yahweh would be catastrophic for Israel, a time of darkness and suffering, but Zephaniah expands the idea of negative judgment to a cosmic level in which Yahweh exterminates *all* life on earth:

> I will utterly sweep away everything
> from the face of the earth, says the LORD.
> I will sweep away humans and animals,
> I will sweep away the birds of the air
> and the fish of the sea. . . .
> I will cut off humanity from the face of the earth.

(Zeph. 1:2–3)

Reversing his life-giving activity in Genesis, Yahweh will annihilate all creation, from nonhuman species to great kings, so that "their blood shall be poured out like dust and their flesh like dung" (1:14–17). On the day of his "jealousy," Yahweh will consume the earth, reducing it to a sterile wasteland (1:18). Zephaniah's declaration of God's resolve to kill every living thing contrasts markedly with Yahweh's post-Flood statement in Genesis that he will "never again curse the ground because of humankind . . . nor will [he] ever again destroy every living creature as [he had] done" (Gen. 8:21).

You [rich landowners] are the one who
destroys the vineyard [Israel]
and conceal what you have stolen from the poor.
by what right do you crush my people
and grind the faces of the poor?

(Isa. 3:15)

And when legislators pass laws favoring the interests of the rich over the have-nots, Yahweh is outraged:

Woe to the legislators of infamous laws,
to those who issue tyrannical decrees,
who refuse justice to the unfortunate
and cheat the poor among my people of their rights,
who make widows their prey
and rob the orphan.
What will you do on the day of punishment . . . ?

(Isa. 10:1–2)

The "infamous laws" to which Isaiah refers may be some that were eventually included in the Torah, particularly those that permitted destitute persons to sell themselves and/or their families into slavery in order to pay off debts (cf. Exod. 21:1–11; Lev. 25:39; Deut. 15:16–17; 2 Kings 4:1). Although in some cases slave owners were compelled to free native-born Israelites after six years, the masters nonetheless exercised the legal right to control their labor during that period.

Micah's Warnings

Micah, a rural contemporary of Isaiah of Jerusalem, accuses the wealthy, who "have the [political and economic] strength" to do so, of plotting not only to confiscate debtors' property but also to enslave the former owners:

Woe to those who plot evil,
who lie in bed planning mischief!
No sooner is it dawn than they do it
—their hands have the strength for it.
Seizing the fields that they covet,
and take over the houses as well,
owner and house they confiscate together,
taking both man and inheritance.

(Mic. 2:1–2)

Comparing greedy leaders, "who should know what is right," to cannibals, Micah shows them metaphorically devouring human flesh, tearing off their victims' skin and crushing their bones (Mic. 3:1–3).

In the prophetic view, Israel was called to maintain high standards of social justice, which precluded acquiring wealth through the misfortunes of others. Economic exploitation of the poor and vulnerable insulted the God who placed society's most defenseless under his special care.

Although we do not know what specific conditions triggered the prophet's vision of God's extreme violence, he was active during the reign of King Josiah (640–609 BCE), perhaps before the king initiated his Deuteronomistic reforms. The Judah that Zephaniah denounces so harshly was probably a society still under Manasseh's lingering influence, so tainted by the ruler's idolatries that Yahweh's wrath was considered as unavoidable as it was extreme. Apparently, Zephaniah was the first prophet (of whom we have any record) to speak out after the long silence that Manasseh and his immediate successor, Amon, presumably imposed on prophetic voices advocating that Yahweh alone was to be worshiped.

After categorically asserting that Yahweh will spare nothing that lives, Zephaniah concedes that a few humble people who keep the commandments may "perhaps . . . be hidden on the day of the LORD's wrath" (2:3). In fact, Chapter 2 implies the survival of a faithful remnant, for after neighboring nations—Moab, Ammon, and Philistia—have been destroyed, Judean survivors will take over their land (2:6–7, 9–10).

Curses and Promises

In Chapter 3, Zephaniah attacks the "soiled, defiled" leaders of Jerusalem, calling them "even wolves" who prey on the poor and who have learned nothing from the examples of other cities that Yahweh has demolished. As a result of their refusal to learn from God's earlier judgments, Yahweh will assemble the nations to pour out his fury on Judah (3:8). After describing a bleak future for humanity, however, Zephaniah concludes by offering an unexpected ray of hope. In a series of brief oracles, he predicts that Gentile nations will come to worship Yahweh (3:9–10; cf. Isa. 2:1–4; Mic. 4:1–5), that a repentant Israel will again seek its God (3:11–13), and that scattered exiles will be freed from their oppressors (3:19–20).

An unexpectedly joyous oracle may represent Zephaniah's response to the beginning of Josiah's reforms, which move Yahweh to avert his anger:

> Sing aloud, O daughter Zion;
> shout, O Israel!
> Rejoice and exult with all your heart,
> O daughter Jerusalem!
> The LORD has taken away the judgments against you,
> he has turned away your enemies.
> The king of Israel, the LORD, is in your midst;
> you shall fear disaster no more.
>
> (Zeph. 3:14–15)

Zephaniah's sudden optimism about Judah's future may express a belief that Josiah's cleansing of the Temple and his reintroduction of the Passover and other Mosaic observances have restored God's presence to the community. Josiah's military successes—God is now seen as a "warrior who gives victory" (3:17)—may have indicated to the prophet that Yahweh had changed his mind about destroying a nation stained by Manasseh's sins. In any case, Zephaniah's image of Yahweh happily joining in the musical chorus of national festivals (3:17) represents a striking shift in his vision.

The Book of Nahum

Of **Nahum**'s personal life or theological beliefs, we know nothing except that his message is unlike that of any other known biblical prophet. He neither laments his people's sins nor prophesies their punishment. Instead, his short book is composed of three poems rejoicing over the ruin of Nineveh, capital of the Assyrian Empire. His gloating, unrelieved by compassion, contrasts with the merciful attitude toward Nineveh's citizens expressed in the Book of Jonah (see Chapter 19).

The Fall of Nineveh

Nahum probably delivered his oracles about 612 BCE, either while the combined army of Medes and Babylonians was besieging the Assyrian capital or shortly after the city's capture. A major historical event, the fall of Nineveh to a Medo-Babylonian coalition permanently ended Assyrian domination of the Near East. Nahum was not alone in celebrating Assyria's collapse, for the empire that had destroyed Israel and humiliated Judah was notorious for its widespread cruelties. Assyrian armies routinely deported entire populations, tortured and mutilated captives, and chained prisoners with metal hooks in their jaws.

Nahum sees Nineveh's downfall as evidence of Yahweh's vengeance on Assyrian excess (1:2–3). Although Yahweh employed Assyria as his corrective "rod" or "club" to punish Judah and other states, the Assyrian leaders behaved with such arrogant savagery that they earned divine retribution. Using vivid poetic images, Nahum describes armed legions marching against Nineveh and plundering its treasures (Nah. 2). The numbering of Assyria's many crimes is equally eloquent (Nah. 3).

In one respect, however, Nahum resembles typical Israelite prophecy: the author interprets Nineveh's fate as part of Yahweh's intention to improve the condition of his covenant people. Released from Assyrian bondage, both Judah and a restored Israel will now enjoy a new era of freedom and security (2:2), "for never again shall the wicked invade you" (1:15). Despite his assurances of future security, however, only three years after Nahum's prophecy, Pharaoh Necho II invades Judah, killing King Josiah at Megiddo (2 Kings 23:29–35). Egypt largely controls Judah's affairs until about 605 BCE, when the Babylonians defeat Egyptian forces at the Battle of Carchemish and assume jurisdiction over Palestine, reducing Judah once again to vassal status.

QUESTIONS FOR DISCUSSION AND REVIEW

1. In what different ways do the prophets active during the eighth century BCE respond to the threat of Assyrian invasion? For what specific economic, ethical, and religious sins do prophets such as Amos, Isaiah, and Micah condemn the covenant people? In what ways have Yahweh's covenant partners failed to live up to their high calling?

2. Why do most scholars believe that the Book of Isaiah shows the work of at least three different prophets who lived at different periods of Judah's history? What differences in political setting do you see between Isaiah 1–39 and Isaiah 40–55?

3. When faced with Assyrian invasion, how does Isaiah of Jerusalem advise Judean kings? Describe Isaiah's many visions of a future universal peace under the rule of a Davidic descendant.

4. What happened to the northern kingdom in 722/721 BCE? What happened during Sennacherib's siege of Jerusalem in 701 BCE, vindicating Isaiah's plea to trust in Yahweh alone?

5. Read Micah 6:6–8 and interpret its meaning for an audience in ancient Judah.

6. Summarize Zephaniah's vision of the Day of Yahweh. According to Zephaniah, what is God's intention toward the earth's entire population? Why does God then change his mind? How may Josiah's reforms of Judah's national religion have affected Zephaniah's understanding of Yahweh's intentions?

7. Why have the prophetic oracles predicting the destruction of Israel, Judah, Assyria, and Babylon been fulfilled—but not those envisioning a time of universal world peace and prosperity?

Terms and Concepts to Remember

Ahaz and the Syro-
  Ephraimite crisis
Assyrian crisis
Immanuel
Isaiah of Jerusalem
Isaiah's visions of
  universal peace
Little Apocalypse

messiah
Micah's oracles on
  exploiting the poor
Nahum on Nineveh
Sennacherib
seraphim
Zephaniah's vision of the
  Day of Yahweh

Recommended Reading

Clifford, Richard J. "Isaiah, Book of," In K. D. Sakenfeld, ed., *The New Interpreter's Dictionary of the Bible*, Vol. 3, pp. 75–91. Nashville, TN: Abingdon, Press. Views Isaiah as a compilation of prophetic oracles spanning more than three centuries.

Isaiah of Jerusalem (Isaiah 1–39)

Blenkinsopp, Joseph, ed. *Isaiah 1–39: A New Translation and Commentary* (Anchor Bible, Vol. 19). New York: Doubleday, 2000. A scholarly analysis of Isaiah's oracles.

Childs, Brevard S. *Isaiah* (Old Testament Library). Louisville, KY: Westminster John Knox, 2000. An important study.

Hayes, John H., and Irvine, Stuart A. *Isaiah the Eighth-Century Prophet*. Nashville, TN: Abingdon Press, 1987. Places Isaiah in the context of the Assyrian threat.

Millar, William R. "Isaiah, Book of (Chaps. 24-27)." In D. N. Freedman, ed., *The Anchor Bible Dictionary*, Vol. 3, pp. 488–490. New York: Doubleday, 1992. Discusses the apocalyptic passages incorporated into the Isaiah collection.

Tucker, Gene M. "The Book of Isaiah 1–39." In *The New Interpreter's Bible*, Vol. 6, pp. 27–305. Nashville, TN: Abingdon Press, 2001. The full text with detailed commentary.

Micah

Anderson, Francis I., and Freedman, D. N., eds. *Micah: A New Translation and Commentary* (Anchor Bible, Vol. 24E). New York: Doubleday, 2000. A fresh translation with interpretative notes.

Simundson, Daniel J. "The Book of Micah." In *The New Interpreter's Bible*, Vol. 7, pp. 533–589. Nashville, TN: Abingdon Press, 1996. A helpful textual interpretation.

Wolff, Hans W. *Micah: A Commentary*. Minneapolis: Augsburg Fortress, 1990. A valuable resource.

Zephaniah

Achtemeir, Elizabeth. *Nahum-Micah: Interpretation*. Atlanta: John Knox Press, 1996. Includes commentary on Zephaniah.

Bennett, Robert A. "The Book of Zephaniah." In *The New Interpreter's Bible*, Vol. 7, pp. 659–704. Nashville, TN: Abingdon Press, 1996. Includes commentary.

Szeles, M. E. *Habakkuk and Zephaniah: Wrath and Mercy*. Grand Rapids, MI: Eerdmans, 1987. An informative study.

Nahum

Baker, David W. *Nahum, Habakkuk, and Zephaniah*. Downers Grove, IL: InterVarsity Press, 1988. A useful resource.

Garcia-Treto, Francisco O. "The Book of Nahum." In *The New Interpreter's Bible*, Vol. 7, pp. 592–619. Nashville, TN: Abingdon Press, 1996. A useful commentary.

CHAPTER 17

Prophets of the Babylonian Crisis
The Oracles of Jeremiah, Habakkuk, and Obadiah

Key Topics/Themes As witnesses to the last decades of Judah's collective existence and to the early decades of the Babylonian exile that followed, Habakkuk, Jeremiah, and Obadiah offer us an extraordinary lens through which to view the tragic end of Israel's experiment with nationhood. Jeremiah's prophetic career extends from the reign of Josiah to the first years after Jerusalem's fall to Babylon (c. 623–582 BCE).

During that time, Jeremiah repeatedly suffers public rejection and official persecution for urging Judah's last kings to submit willingly to Babylonian rule, thereby sparing the nation from total destruction. Of Habakkuk and Obadiah, we know little, except that they appear to be Jeremiah's near-contemporaries and their oracles resonate with the same anxiety over Judah's fate.

The Book of Jeremiah

More than any earlier prophet (even Elijah), **Jeremiah** becomes an object of public scorn for his apparent "disloyalty" in proclaiming that the Babylonians are nothing less than Yahweh's instrument of judgment, sent to punish Judah for its covenant breaking. At the risk of his life, Jeremiah attempts to convince both king and commoner that the only realistic course of action open to Judah is submission to **Nebuchadnezzar**, king of Babylon and new master of the Near East (see Figure 17.1). In spite of complaining that God has unfairly compelled him to deliver a deeply unpopular message, Jeremiah boldly urges Jerusalem's leaders to renew their commitment to Yahweh. In graphic detail, he also specifies the disastrous consequences if they continue to alienate their covenant partner.

The Structure of Jeremiah

Like the books of Isaiah and Ezekiel, Jeremiah is a composite work that can be broken down into four distinct parts: (1) oracles delivered during the reigns of Josiah, Jehoiakim and Zedekiah (c. 623–587 BCE) (Jer. 1–25), (2) biographical narratives combined with prophecies of

redemption and restoration (Jer. 26–45), (3) prophecies directed against the "nations" (Jer. 46–51), and (4) a concluding historical postscript taken largely from 2 Kings 24–25 (Jer. 52). Jeremiah 36 offers a clue about how this material may first have been gathered, and by whom, for in this chapter God instructs Jeremiah to

> take a scroll and write on it every word that I have spoken to you about Jerusalem and Judah and all the nations, from the day I first spoke to you in the reign of Josiah down to the present day.

(Jer. 36:2)

The "present day" is the fourth year of Jehoiakim's reign, about 605 BCE, but the actual writing of this scroll is done by a scribe, "**Baruch** son of Neriah," who served Jeremiah as both disciple and private secretary. (Like virtually all authors in the ancient world, Jeremiah dictated his thoughts to a scribe, who wrote them down on a papyrus scroll.) Scholars suggest that this scroll consisted largely of the material now found in Chapters 1–25, which then became the nucleus of a much larger collection of writings, some attributed to Jeremiah himself and some contributed by Baruch and later postexilic editors. This complex process of composition may account for the book's puzzling organization, for

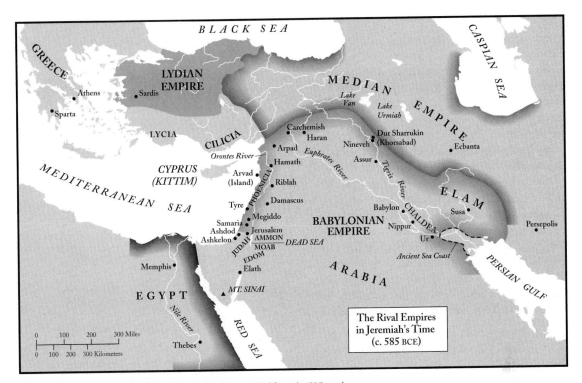

FIGURE 17.1   Map of the Rival Empires in Jeremiah's Time (c. 585 BCE).

material commonly appears out of chronological order and without any apparent transition from one group of writings to another. What holds the whole book together, however, is Jeremiah's focus on the catastrophe of Judah's destruction, the most important turning point in Israel's national history. As in Isaiah and other prophetic books, Jeremiah's oracles range from deepest pessimism to visions of a bright but distant future. In what may be an early pronouncement, Jeremiah declares that God already has decided to abandon Judah to the Babylonians:

> Thus will I shatter this people and this city as one shatters an earthen vessel so that it cannot be mended, and the dead shall be buried in Topheth because there is no room elsewhere to bury them.

(Jer. 19:11)

On other occasions, the prophet is more optimistic:

> . . . I am with you, says the LORD to save you;
> I will make an end of all the nations
> amongst which I scattered you, but of you I will not
>   make an end.

(Jer. 30:11)

In still other speeches, the prophet pleads desperately for the people to repent, for Yahweh is still willing to forgive:

> I will not be angry forever.
> Only acknowledge your guilt,

> that you have rebelled against the LORD your God,
> and scattered your favors among
> strangers [rival gods] under every green tree,
> and have not obeyed my voice, says the LORD,
> for I am your master;
> I will take you . . . I will give you shepherds after my
>   own heart,
> who will feed you with knowledge and understanding.

(Jer. 3:13–15)

What must the people of Jerusalem do to have Yahweh protect them as he had from Assyrian invaders? Jeremiah's answer is simple: They must behave in a manner worthy of their divine covenant partner, treating others with justice and compassion and demonstrating loyalty to Yahweh alone:

> For if you truly amend your ways and your doings, if you truly act justly with one another, and if you do not oppress the alien [resident immigrant], the orphan, and the widow, or shed innocent blood in this place, and if you do not go after other gods to your own hurt, then I will dwell with you in this place, in the land that I gave of old to your ancestors forever and ever.

(Jer. 7:5–7)

Whereas most of the poetic oracles in Jeremiah's first twenty-five chapters emphasize the certainty of

Yahweh's punishment if Judah fails to reform, the later prose narratives describe the terrible aftermath of Nebuchadnezzar's capture of Jerusalem. In Chapters 39–44, which refer to Jeremiah in the third person, a scribe (perhaps Baruch) describes in painful detail the horrors and sufferings that accompanied Jerusalem's fall. Writing with the vividness of an eyewitness, the narrator describes Babylonian armies slaughtering Jerusalem's citizens, looting Yahweh's Temple, burning the holy city, and forcing the survivors, bound in chains, to march hundreds of miles to Babylon (see Figure 17.2).

In fact, Yahweh himself seems appalled by the extreme measures he has taken to punish Judah, speaking as if he had not been able to visualize beforehand the harsh reality of his people's suffering. Urging a group of survivors to remain amid Judah's desolation (and not flee to Egypt, where they hoped to be safe from Nebuchadnezzar's anger), Yahweh admits that he may have made a mistake in smiting the people so severely:

> If you will only remain in the land, I will build you up and not pull you down; . . . for I am sorry for this disaster that I have brought upon you.

(Jer. 42:10)

FIGURE 17.2 An artist's reconstruction of Babylon at the time of King Nebuchadnezzar (605–562 BCE), founder of the Neo-Babylonian Empire and conqueror of Judah (587 BCE), illustrates the city's massive fortifications. During their captivity in Babylon, Judah's former ruling classes reedited and/or produced much of the literature that now forms the Hebrew Bible. The towering ziggurat at the left, an artificial mountain crowned with a chapel to the Babylonian gods, is characteristic of Mesopotamian religious architecture; its predecessors at Ur and elsewhere may have inspired the Tower of Babel legend (Gen. 11).

As God once regretted that he had created humankind (Gen. 6:6–8), so he is now "sorry" to have caused his human partners such extreme pain. Jeremiah's brief disclosure that Yahweh is capable of viewing his judgments as excessive is not repeated by other biblical writers, who assume that God is beyond self-doubt.

As he delivers oracles that mix doom and hope for the covenant community, Jeremiah also offers conflicting messages about Babylon. After Nebuchadnezzar takes hundreds of Judean aristocrats and artisans to Mesopotamia in the "first deportation" of 598/597 BCE, Jeremiah tells the exiles not to expect a speedy return to their homeland. Instead, they should settle down and take advantage of whatever opportunities their new home provides:

> Build houses and live in them; plant gardens and eat what they produce. Take wives and have sons and daughters; take wives for your sons, and give your daughters in marriage . . . and do not decrease.

(Jer. 29:5–6)

Indeed, Jeremiah instructs the deported Judeans to "seek the welfare of the city where I have sent you into exile, and pray to the LORD on its behalf, for in its welfare you will find your welfare" (Jer. 29:7).

Although Jeremiah is sure that Babylon is God's "rod of correction" to punish sinful Israel, he—or a later scribe—also condemns the Babylonians for their atrocities and predicts Babylon's ultimate fall:

> Then after seventy years are completed, I will punish the king of Babylon and that nation, the land of the Chaldeans, for their iniquity, says the LORD, making the land an everlasting waste. I will bring upon that land all the words that I have uttered against it, everything written in this book, which Jeremiah prophesied against all the nations . . . I will repay them according to their deeds [against Judah].

(Jer. 25:12–14)

Of all Jeremiah's oracles "against the nations," by far the most extensive are the passages proclaiming Yahweh's "wrath" against Babylon, predicting its fall to invaders from the "north" who will utterly demolish the city (Jer. 50:1–51:58):

> . . . and Babylon shall become a heap of ruins,
> a den of jackals,
> an object of horror and of hissing, without inhabitant.

(Jer. 51:37)

Although scribal additions to the Book of Jeremiah do not mention him, Cyrus of Persia would capture Babylon in 539 BCE, allowing the captive Judeans to return to their homeland. So important was Cyrus's role in accomplishing Judah's partial restoration that Second Isaiah calls him Yahweh's "messiah" (Isa. 45:1–4).

Jeremiah's "Confessions"

Judging by the long passages in which Jeremiah complains about Yahweh's forcing him to deliver so many negative oracles about his own people—sections known as the prophet's "confessions"—readers may think that they are being offered a glimpse into the prophet's individual psychology. Recently, however, scholars have pointed out that Jeremiah's complaints are less personal than conventional. Very similar passages appear throughout the prophetic literature and in narratives about Moses. Like Moses, Jeremiah protests that he is not qualified to act as God's agent (Exod. 3; Jer. 1:6–10), and like Elijah, he is a solitary figure who risks his life to carry Yahweh's message (Jer. 26:7–15; 38:4–13). Some of Jeremiah's speeches parallel the later wisdom books: Like Job, he curses the day he was born (Job 3:3; Jer. 20:17–18), and like the author of Ecclesiastes, he wishes that he had never been born rather than witness the sorrow he is compelled to behold (Eccles. 4:3; Jer. 20:17–18). He experiences prophecy as a "writhing of the bowels" and a "throbbing" of the heart (4:19). Jeremiah even accuses God of having deceived him and then alienating him from his countrymen (Jer. 20:7–10). To complete his misery, Yahweh forbids him to marry or to enter either a house of mourning or of feasting (16:1–9), thus blocking him from a normal life of social interaction. Even the men of his native village, Anathoth, threaten to kill him if he continues to prophesy (Jer. 11:21).

When he persists in urging Judean kings to submit to Babylonian domination, Jeremiah's fellow citizens shun him as "unpatriotic," even traitorous. From the perspective of many Judeans, Jeremiah's "defeatist" policy seemed to betray Judah to a hated oppressor. Despite attempts to kill him, however, a few friends and supporters keep Jeremiah alive throughout his long ordeal. Politically influential admirers from the Shaphan family (Jer. 26:4) arrange Jeremiah's release from prison, and when—during Nebuchadnezzar's siege of Jerusalem—he is cast into a muddy well to die, a sympathetic Ethiopian, Ebed-Melech, rescues him (Jer. 38:7–13; 39:15–18).

In a secret interview with Zedekiah, last of the Davidic kings to rule over the covenant people, Jeremiah begs the king to act boldly, to ignore his counselors' mistaken will to resist. By throwing open Jerusalem's gates to Nebuchadnezzar, Zedekiah can spare his people the agonies of slaughter and destruction after the city's inevitable fall. The prophet's recommendations are not based on political expedience, a policy of survival at all costs. Instead, Jeremiah offers the king and nation a religious challenge—to place their *trust* entirely in Yahweh's power to save. But Zedekiah, who is as weak and indecisive as Josiah had been zealous and resolute, fails to accept Yahweh's offer of safely (38:14–28). Perhaps fearing that he will be overthrown by Judah's die-hard patriots, Zedekiah apparently prefers to listen to prophets who deliver a more encouraging message.

Ten years earlier, after Nebuchadnezzar had first captured Jerusalem and deported many of its leading citizens to Mesopotamia (598/597 BCE), a prophet named **Hananiah** had optimistically promised deliverance from Babylon. Furious at Hananiah's "false" interpretation of Yahweh's will, Jeremiah walked the streets of Jerusalem wearing a wooden yoke, the symbol of coming slavery. After Hananiah angrily smashed the wooden yoke, Jeremiah returned wearing one of iron (Jer. 27–28). To Judah's ruling elite, Hananiah may well have seemed the true prophet, perhaps because, a century earlier, Isaiah had similarly predicted that Yahweh would protect his holy city:

> Like birds hovering overhead, so the LORD of hosts
> will protect Jerusalem;
> he will protect and deliver it,
> he will spare and rescue it.

(Isa. 31:5)

By contrast, Jeremiah vigorously opposes the notion that Yahweh will again spare Jerusalem or its Temple, where he had placed his "name." In two of his most provocative speeches, the prophet insists that the presence of Yahweh's sanctuary can do nothing to protect the city (Jer. 7 and 26). Shortly before Jerusalem's fall in 587 BCE, however, Jeremiah makes a rare gesture of faith in the future. As his world is disintegrating around him, he buys a field in Anathoth to demonstrate his belief that landownership in Judah will someday again be profitable (Jer. 32).

Jeremiah in Egypt

Having learned of Jeremiah's policy of submission, the Babylonian generals offer to take him to Babylon along with other prominent Judeans, but the prophet prefers to remain among the poor in the ruined city. After a group of Judean nationalists treacherously murder Gedaliah, a Judean whom Nebuchadnezzar had appointed governor, Jeremiah declares that Yahweh wishes them to remain in Judah, which he is now "sorry" he has destroyed. Fearing Babylonian retaliation for Gedaliah's murder, a band of survivors force Jeremiah to flee with them to Egypt. There, Jeremiah

FIGURE 17.3 Found by the hundreds throughout the countryside, these crudely modeled terra cotta figurines—dating from the eighth through the sixth centuries BCE—spark heated debate about their religious significance. Described as "prayers in clay," they may represent the women who used them as votive objects, visible petitions to Israel's God in matters of fertility, conception, and childbirth. Some archaeologists, however, regard them as images of the goddess Asherah, to whom Israelite women may have appealed as Yahweh's divine consort.

resumes his predictions of disaster for the exiles who disobeyed his oracle to remain in Judah, where they hoped (in vain, it turns out) to live beyond Nebuchadnezzar's reach. In Egypt, some Judean women declare that their misfortunes were the consequence of neglecting not Yahweh but rather the "queen of heaven" (possibly the Canaanite Asherah, or the Mesopotamian goddess Ishtar), for whom they baked cakes (Jer. 44:17–18; see Figure 17.3). Jeremiah's scorching reply is a restatement of the Deuteronomistic principle of cumulative guilt and accountability:

> The LORD [Yahweh] did not forget those sacrifices which you and your father, your kings and princes and the people of the land burnt in the cities of Judah and in the streets of Jerusalem, and they mounted up in his mind until he could no longer tolerate them. . . . This calamity has come upon you because you burnt these sacrifices and sinned against the LORD and did not obey the LORD or conform to his laws, statutes, and teachings.
>
> (Jer. 44:21–23)

The Book of Consolation

Perhaps the most famously influential passages in the Book of Jeremiah—which may have been added to the text after Judean exiles had returned from Babylon to Jerusalem—appear in Chapters 30 and 31. Commonly known as the "Book of Consolation," this section speaks of a time when the old covenant that Yahweh had made through Moses would be replaced by a new and better covenant:

> The days are surely coming, says the LORD, when I will make a new covenant with the house of Israel and the house of Judah. It will not be like the covenant that I made with their ancestors when I took them by the hand to bring them out of the land of Egypt—a covenant that they broke, though I was their husband, says the LORD. But this is the covenant I will make with the house of Israel . . . I will put my law within them, and I will write it on their hearts; and I will be their God, and they shall be my people.
>
> (Jer. 31:13–33)

This new covenant inscribed on human hearts would not be a short-lived reform, like that of King Josiah, but an everlasting bond between Yahweh and his people. A few other oracles contained in the book are equally optimistic about Israel's future with one foretelling a restored Davidic king who will "deal wisely" and "execute justice and righteousness in the land," so that "Israel will live in safety" (Jer. 23:5–6).

The Book of Habakkuk

Along with Nahum and Obadiah, the Book of Habak-kuk is one of the Tanakh's shortest books—and also one of the most puzzling. Unlike most collections of prophetic oracles, it has no superscription identifying the prophet or the reign during which he preached. References to the **Chaldeans** (the Babylonians)— "that fierce and impetuous nation"—would seem to place this book within the time span of Jeremiah, or at least within the political context of the late seventh century BCE. Beyond that, nothing is known about either the prophet or the length of his prophetic ministry. Curiously, **Habakkuk** is identified in the opening verse of the first chapter as a *navi,* or "prophet," a title that no other preexilic prophet seems to have claimed for himself. This fact leads some scholars to speculate that he may have been a "professional" seer or had had some association with the Temple cult. What is clear, however, is that he (or his editor) understood his oracle to be a *massa,* or "burden," a term that Ezekiel also employs to signify any prophetic speech that seeks to explain and justify Yahweh's actions to an uncomprehending audience.

Divine Justice and the Babylonian Threat

Habakkuk begins with a complaint that is also a lament, as the prophet struggles with the problem of divine justice and undeserved suffering. Like the author of Job, he tries to reconcile the biblical concept of a thoroughly "righteous" God with the reality of a world in which even people who try to behave justly are subject to excessive violence and wickedness. The Deuteronomistic response to such a crisis of faith invariably focuses on Israel's sins; whatever calamity overtakes the nation is seen as just punishment for covenant breaking. Habakkuk, however, takes a less dogmatic position, lamenting both the "wicked" who "surround the righteous" (Hab. 1:4) and the Babylonian armies that appear to be the instruments of divine judgment (cf. Jer. 21:4–7). Unlike Abraham's conversation with Yahweh over the fate of Sodom and Gomorrah (Gen. 18), Habakkuk's dialogue with God leads to no final affirmation that God's affliction of Judah is just. Instead, at the conclusion of Chapter 1, we are left with the prophet's bewilderment at God's "silence" in the face of Babylonian cruelty.

Chapter 2 takes a very different approach, presenting a minor **theodicy,** a literary attempt to justify God's ethical behavior, particularly his "delay" in administering clear-cut justice that supports the cause of the righteous and punishes wrongdoers. While awaiting Yahweh's response to his questions, Habakkuk declares that he "will stand at my watchpost," like a soldier standing guard on a city wall. When Yahweh does answer the prophet, he tells him to "write the vision; make it plain on tablets" so that others may read it (2:1–3). Yahweh's reply is essentially an assurance that, in good time, the "plunderer" of nations (presumably Babylon), will itself be plundered by the very peoples it has victimized. In the meantime, the prophet's assignment is to counsel patience and to live in faithful adherence to the very covenant that Yahweh only *seems* to have forgotten about but that he is sure to honor. The proud may swagger and the foolish may turn to idols, but the "cup" of divine judgment is "in the LORD's right hand" (Hab. 2:16), and the cruel invader will eventually be forced to drink from it. At present, Habakkuk is told, the "world" is to remain silent, secure in the conviction that Yahweh "is in his holy temple" (2:20).

A Psalm of Yahweh's Triumph

Chapter 3 appears to be separate literary unit, a poem that resembles many of the psalms. It even uses the musical term *selah,* a word used throughout the Book of Psalms and commonly understood to be a signal to the Temple orchestra. Although this lyric identifies itself as a "prayer," it is actually a celebration of divine victory over foes human and supernatural. Yahweh is described as angrily striding from the east amid storm clouds and lightning—a mighty warrior thundering along in horse-drawn chariots, flashing his arrows, and hurling his spear:

> Was your wrath against the rivers, O LORD?
> or your rage against the sea,
> when you drove your horses,
> your chariots to victory?
> You brandished your naked bow,
> sated were the arrows at your command.
> You split the earth with rivers,
> The mountains saw you, and writhed . . .

(Hab. 3:8–10)

The God depicted in these verses is clearly willing and able to execute immediate vengeance on Israel's oppressors. For he "came forth to save [his] people, to save your anointed [the Davidic king]" (2:12–13). With this anthropomorphic vision of Yahweh's military strength, the poet implicitly answers Habakkuk's cry about "how long" God will allow other nations to trample his heritage. The poem also moves Habakkuk's theodicy toward a mythological level, a cosmic struggle in which Yahweh emerges, at last, as the master of his universe as well as Lord of history. At a critical moment, then, in the life cycle of biblical faith, Habakkuk declares that no matter how many rivals—human or heavenly—Yahweh may face, he will defeat them, and humankind will eventually behold the execution of his divine plan.

The Book of Obadiah

Consisting of only one chapter, the Book of Obadiah is the shortest book of the Hebrew Bible, and it reflects conditions in Judah some time after the Babylonians had destroyed Jerusalem. The book focuses on two main issues: (1) the neighboring kingdom of **Edom** and its role in Judah's defeat, and (2) God's punishment of both Edom and the "nations" on the Day of Yahweh. About **Obadiah**—whose name means "Yahweh's servant"—we know virtually nothing, except that, like his predecessor Nahum, he looks forward to the utter destruction and humiliation of Israel's enemies.

According to Genesis, Edom was founded by Esau, Jacob's (Israel's) twin brother, and thus had a close kinship to Israel (Gen. 25:30; 36:1). When Babylonian troops looted and burned Jerusalem, however, the Edomites apparently joined them in plundering their "brother" nation:

> You should not have joined in the gloating over
> Judah's disaster
> on the day of his calamity.
> You should not have looted his goods
> on the day of his calamity.

(Obad. 1:13)

Other biblical writers of this period express equal bitterness over Edom's behavior (Ezek. 25:12–14; Lam. 4:21). The poet of Psalm 137 seems to link Edom with Babylon as Judah's destroyer, blessing a future avenger who will "take your little ones and dash them against the rock!" (Ps. 137:9). Obadiah is no less eager for vengeance and foresees a time when Edom's former allies will turn upon the country and devastate it, after which "Mount Zion [Jerusalem]" will occupy "Mount Esau" (v. 20).

Judah's revenge on Edom, however, marks only the beginning of a divine conquest, which all Israel's neighbors will witness on the Day of Yahweh:

> For the day of the LORD is near against all the nations.
> as you have done, it shall be done to you;
> your deeds shall return on your own head . . .
> and the house of Jacob shall take
> possession of those who
> dispossessed them.

(Obad 1:15, 17)

At that "day" of national vindication, "the house of Jacob shall be a fire, and the house of Joseph a flame" (v. 18), consuming everything in its path. When the smoke clears from this cosmic firestorm, Israel will possess even more territory than was taken from it by Nebuchadnezzar (vv. 17–21). Like other biblical writers, however, Obadiah sees Israel's future triumphs as part of the divine plan, for in reality, Israel's expanded "kingdom shall be the LORD's" (v. 21).

QUESTIONS FOR DISCUSSION AND REVIEW

1. What view of the Babylonian invasion of Judah do Jeremiah and Habakkuk share? In what ways do their explanations of the national disaster differ? Which prophet's message is closer to the Deuteronomistic theory of history?

2. Why is Jeremiah accused of being "unpatriotic" and "defeatist"? What does he advise King Zedekiah to do? After Nebuchadnezzar's armies breach Jerusalem's walls, what happens to Zedekiah, the last of David's "sons" to sit on Judah's throne?

3. Why does Isaiah predict that God will spare Jerusalem from the Assyrian threat? A century later, why does Jeremiah insist that Yahweh is using Babylon as his "instrument" to destroy Judah? Why has God changed his intentions toward the covenant people?

4. What hope for the more distant future do Jeremiah, Habakkuk, and Obadiah hold out to their contemporaries? How will Yahweh eventually deal with the nations that attack and plunder his people? What plan does Yahweh have to introduce a "new covenant" bond with Abraham's descendants?

Terms and Concepts to Remember

Baruch	Nebuchadnezzar
Chaldeans	Obadiah
Edom	Queen of Heaven
Habakkuk	theodicy
Jeremiah	Zedekiah

Recommended Reading

Brueggerman, Walter. *A Commentary on Jeremiah: Exile and Homecoming.* Grand Rapids, MI: Eerdmans, 1998. Places Jeremiah in the Babylonian crisis and its aftermath.
———. *The Theology of the Book of Jeremiah* (Old Testament Theology). Cambridge: Cambridge UP, 2006. Focuses on the prophet's perception of God's continuing activity in the world.

Ludrom, Jack R. *Jeremiah: A New Translation with Introduction and Commentary*, 3 vols. Garden City, NY: Doubleday, 1999 and 2004. An in-depth analysis.

Miller, Patrick D. "The Book of Jeremiah." In *The New Interpreter's Bible*, Vol. 6, pp. 555–926. Nashville, TN: Abingdon Press, 2001. The full text, with interpretative commentary.

Stillman, Louis. "Jeremiah, Book of." In K. D. Sakenfeld, ed., *The New Interpreter's Dictionary of the Bible*, Vol. 3, pp. 220–235. Nashville, TN: Abingdon Press, 2008. A helpful summary of the book's structure, major themes, and historical context.

Zimmerli, Walther, and Hanson, K. C. *The Fiery Throne: The Prophets and Old Testament Theology.* (Fortress Classics in Biblical Studies). Minneapolis: Augsburg Fortress, 2003. A scholarly analysis focusing on Jeremiah and Ezekiel; for more advanced students.

Habakkuk

Anderson, Francis I. *Habakkuk: A New Translation with Introduction and Commentary* (Anchor Bible, Vol. 25). New York: Doubleday, 2001. A scholarly investigation.

Gowan, Donald E. "Habakkuk, Book of." In K. D. Sakenfeld, ed., *The New Interpreter's Dictionary of the Bible*, Vol. 2, pp. 705–709. Nashveille, TN: Abingdon Press, 2007. An accessible introduction.

Hiebert, Theodore. "The Book of Habakkuk." In *The New Interpreter's Bible*, Vol. 7, pp. 623–655. Nashville, TN: Abingdon Press, 1996. The full text, with scholarly interpretation.

Obadiah

Pagan, Samuel. "The Book of Obadiah." In *The New Interpreter's Bible*, Vol. 7, pp. 435–459. Nashville, TN: Abingdon Press, 1996. The complete text, with commentary.

CHAPTER 18

Prophets in Exile

The Oracles of Ezekiel and Second Isaiah

Key Topics/Themes Ezekiel and the unnamed prophet scholars call Second Isaiah speak to an audience of Judeans exiled in Babylon. Whereas Ezekiel, who is both priest and prophet, initially focuses on Judah's sins and its pollution of Yahweh's sanctuary, after Judah's fall, he begins to predict a future time of restoration and a gloriously rebuilt Temple. By contrast, Second Isaiah (or Deutero-Isaiah) delivers enthusiastic oracles of encouragement to a group of exiles who soon will experience a wonderful "second exodus," journeying from Babylon back to Judah. Yahweh has selected a "messiah" to liberate his people, Cyrus the Great of Persia, who conquers Babylon in 539 BCE and permits captive Jews to return to their homeland. The first canonical prophet to declare that Yahweh is the only God, Second Isaiah also portrays Israel as God's "servant" who will bring "light" to other nations.

 ## The Book of Ezekiel

Taken to Mesopotamia during Nebuchadnezzar's first deportation of Judean leaders in 597 BCE, **Ezekiel** begins prophesying about four years later, while the kingdom of Judah still stood. Far from his homeland, Ezekiel lives in a community of exiled Jews on the "river Chebar," a large irrigation canal near the Euphrates River. Like Jeremiah, his older contemporary, Ezekiel warns his people that Yahweh, disgusted by the "abominations" committed in his sanctuary and in the streets of Jerusalem, is about to abandon his people. He also agrees that Babylon is God's chosen "instrument" to accomplish Judah's deserved punishment. Unlike Jeremiah, however, Ezekiel is given to strange, even bewildering visions, four of which dominate the structure of the book named for him. In Chapters 1–3, "the heavens were opened" and the prophet "sees" Yahweh enthroned on a heavenly chariot with wheels of fire, surrounded by grotesque beings who are part human, part animal, and part bird. In Chapters 8–10, Ezekiel—although located in Mesopotamia—sees Yahweh departing Jerusalem "by the east gate" and heading northeast toward Babylon. The vision's emphasis on Yahweh's mobility expresses

Ezekiel's belief that henceforth God will be present with the exiles, not with the Judeans remaining in Judah. In his most famous vision, celebrated in a popular spiritual, he beholds a "valley of dry bones," disjointed skeletons that suddenly are reassembled, reclothed in flesh, and revived to live again (Ch. 37). In the book's final chapters, Ezekiel sees Yahweh eventually returning to Jerusalem to occupy a magnificently rebuilt Temple, from which healing freshwater streams flow to water life-giving trees (Chs. 40–48). The writing style and imagery that Ezekiel employs to convey his visions resemble that of no other prophet; the book is brimming with metaphors and symbols that typically defy literal translation. No prophet has given a more vividly personal account of the impact that prophecy had on his mind and body:

> The hand of the LORD came upon me there, and he said to me, Rise up; go out into the plain, and there I will speak to you. So I rose and went out into the plain; the glory of the LORD was there, like the glory which I had seen by the river Kebar [a canal near Babylon], and I threw myself down on my face. Then a spirit came into me and stood me on my feet, and spoke to me: Go, he said, and shut yourself up in your house. You shall be tied and bound with ropes, man, so that you cannot go out among the people.

I will fasten your tongue to the roof of your mouth
and you will be unable to speak; . . . But when I have
something to say to you, I will give you back the
power of speech.

(Ezek. 3:22–27)

Whether Ezekiel was literally rendered mute and tied
up in his house is debatable, but this passage clearly
functions as a metaphor of Judah's condition shortly
before its fall, hemmed in on all sides by Babylonian
armies and cut off from communication with God.

Visions of the Throne Chariot

Ezekiel says that his initial visions took place during the
fifth year of deposed King Jehoiachin's imprisonment in
Babylon (c. 593 BCE), when, in a trancelike state, he
beholds God amid his heavenly court. Ezekiel's vision
begins with a storm wind and clouds of fire, out of which
emerge four winged creatures possessing both human
and animal features. In shape and appearance, the creatures resemble the cherubim, supernatural figures that
guard Yahweh's presence at the Ark of the Covenant
(Exod.25:18–20; 37:6–9; 1 Kings 6:23–28).

With their animal bodies, human faces, and eagles'
wings, the cherubim also resemble mythological figures
popular in Mesopotamian art, images with which Ezekiel
was probably familiar (see Figure 18.1). If so, they may
represent Babylonian divinities whom Yahweh has sub-
jugated to pull his throne-chariot. (Psalm 18:10 depicts
God riding on a cherub with "the wings of the wind.")
In describing his vision of the divine throne, Ezekiel
finds that human vocabulary is inadequate; he can only
invoke comparisons to sparkling jewels, glowing metals,
and the colorful radiance of the rainbow:

> About the dome over their heads [of the cherubim]
> there was something like a throne, in appearance like
> sapphire; and seated above the likeness of a throne
> was something that seemed like a human form.
> Upward from what appeared like the loins I saw
> something like gleaming amber, something that
> looked like fire enclosed all around; and downward
> from what looked like the loins I saw something
> that looked like fire, and there was a splendor all
> around. Like the bow in a cloud on a rainy day, such
> was the appearance of the splendor all around.

(Ezek. 1:26–28)

In careful phrasing ("something that looked like . . . "),
Ezekiel makes clear that his images are several stages
removed from the heavenly realities he struggles to
describe: "This was the appearance of the likeness of the
glory of the LORD" (1:28). He cannot portray Yahweh

FIGURE 18.1 Carved on an ivory plaque five by six inches in
diameter, this cherub figure resembles the "living creatures"
Ezekiel saw in his vision of Yahweh's heavenly throne. A
hybrid creature associated with Mesopotamian religion, the
cherub commonly has a human face (symbolizing intelligence),
the body of a bull or lion (representing strength), and the wings
of an eagle (indicating its supernatural swiftness as the god's
emissary). Yahweh's cherub guards the tree of life (Gen. 3:24),
and a pair of cherubim extend their wings over the Ark of the
Covenant, figuratively sheltering God's throne (Exod. 37:6-9;
Ps. 99:1). In Ezekiel's vision, cherubim with four faces, grotesque beasts far removed from the chubby infants of popular
tradition, draw Yahweh's heavenly chariot (Ezek. 1, 10).

himself, only what appeared to him as a resemblance of
a divine splendor that belongs to God. As Moses beheld
God's **kavod,** commonly translated as "glory" or "splendor," so Ezekiel can see not the Deity himself but only
the dazzling beauty that radiates from him.

After eating a scroll (representing Yahweh's message to Judah) that tastes like honey, Ezekiel is
appointed watchman over the House of Israel, earning
his own salvation by warning others of the impending
judgment (2:8–3:21). Those who heed the warning
will be spared the catastrophe; those who ignore it will
suffer destruction. Ezekiel here sounds the note of
free will and individual responsibility that recurs
throughout the book.

The unequal relationship between the immortal God and his human prophet is emphasized more than ninety times throughout the book, with Yahweh repeatedly addressing Ezekiel as "mortal." Many older versions of the Bible, such as the King James, literally translate the phrase "son of man," but the New Revised Standard Version's use of "mortal" correctly highlights the difference between eternal Yahweh and his fallible agent. Only in the Book of Daniel, produced long after Ezekiel's time, does the term "son of man"—or "one like a human being" seem to acquire an apocalyptic meaning (cf. Dan. 7:13).

Prophecy as Performance Art

In the first of many fantastic actions that Ezekiel performs to dramatize parts of his message, the prophet begins his ministry by being struck dumb and hence unable to voice his warning (3:22–27). He cooks his food over human waste to foreshadow how people trapped during Nebuchadnezzar's siege will be forced to eat "unclean food." When his wife dies, he neither weeps nor mourns, his lack of normal feeling intended to show that God will not mourn the loss of his Temple (4:9–17; 24:15–27).

Ezekiel's public displays sometimes border on the abnormal. Tightly bound in ropes, he lies down on one side for 190 days to symbolize the duration—each day for a year—of the northern kingdom's exile. Then he lies on his other side for another forty days to indicate the length of Judah's captivity (4:1–8). Finally, he shaves off his beard and the hair on his head, burning a third of the hair, striking another third with a sword, and scattering the last third to the winds, retaining only a few strands, which he binds up in his robe. This demonstration serves to inform the people that a third of them will die of famine and disease, a third will die by violence, and the remaining third will become captives in Babylon. The few stray hairs that he keeps represent those whom God will allow to escape (Ch. 5).

Yahweh's Abandonment of Jerusalem

Chapters 8–11 form a unity describing the pollution of the Temple and the departure of Yahweh's "glory" from Jerusalem. Ezekiel feels himself lifted by the hair and carried from Mesopotamia to Jerusalem, where he observes the "loathsome" idols with which disloyal priests have profaned God's holy place. Near the sanctuary, women weep for Tammuz, a Babylonian fertility god whose annual death and rebirth symbolized the cycle of the seasons. As Judean "elders" burn incense to hideous reptilian images, Yahweh sends an angelic scribe to record these "abominations" and to mark the foreheads of people who reject this perversion of God's worship. Those who remain unmarked, who accept the practices contaminating the Temple, are to be slain by six divine executioners. At this point, Ezekiel beholds Yahweh's "glory" leaving Jerusalem and traveling to the east, presumably to the exiled Judeans in Babylon.

Revision of a Torah Principle

In Chapter 18, Ezekiel—assuming the role of a lawgiver—boldly rejects an ancient Mosaic tradition to announce a new principle of divine justice. Whereas the Mosaic *torah* stated that God will punish the father's sins in his descendants—even to the fourth generation (Exod. 20:5)—Ezekiel promotes a new concept of ethical responsibility. Citing an old proverb that when fathers eat sour grapes the children's teeth are set on edge, Ezekiel declares that Yahweh will no longer punish the people collectively for their ancestors' wrongdoing:

> As I live, says the Lord GOD, this proverb shall no more be used by you in Israel. Know that all lives are mine; the life of the parent as well as the life of the child is mine: it is only the person who sins that shall die.

(Ezek. 18:3–4)

Although commonly interpreted as a pronouncement of *individual* accountability, most scholars believe that Ezekiel's statement refers to the fact that henceforth God will judge each generation on its own merits. The generation whose sins brought about Judah's destruction has been succeeded by a new generation that has the power to choose a better fate:

> Cast away all the transgressions that you have committed against me, and get yourselves a new spirit! Why will you die, O house of Israel? For I have no pleasure in the death of anyone, says the Lord GOD. Turn, then, and live.

(Ezek. 18:31–32)

Oracles Against Foreign Nations

As in the books of Isaiah and Jeremiah, prophetic oracles against foreign states are gathered together in a distinct unit (Chs. 25–32). Here Ezekiel delivers a series of stinging pronouncements against Israel's neighbors, especially those who profit economically or politically from Judah's sufferings. The oracles against Tyre, which take up three full chapters, are particularly harsh. A port city internationally famous for its wealth and far-flung trade network, **Tyre** occupied an island about half a mile off the Mediterranean coast, a natural setting that made it difficult for foreign invaders to capture. According to Ezekiel, Tyrian merchants had rejoiced when Babylonian armies first sacked Jerusalem in 598/597 BCE and thus weakened an important commercial rival. For this act, God resolves to destroy the city (26:1–6). Yahweh announces: "I will bring against Tyre from the north King Nebuchadnezzar of Babylon, king of kings, together with horses, chariots, cavalry, and a great and powerful army" (26:7). Nebuchadnezzar, Ezekiel states, will overthrow Tyre's defenses and enter the city as a conqueror, seizing its fabled treasures (26:11–12).

After describing in detail Tyre's luxury trade (27:10–25), Ezekiel devotes a long passage to denouncing the pride of Tyre's king, whose economic shrewdness and riches are rendered in mythic images of the original paradise:

> You were the signet of perfection,
> full of wisdom and perfect in beauty.
> You were in Eden, the garden of God;
> every precious stone was your covering, . . .
> Your heart was proud because of your beauty;
> you corrupted your wisdom
> for the sake of your splendor.
> I cast you to the ground. . . .
>
> (Ezek. 28:12–13, 17)

Even after a military siege that lasted for thirteen years, however, Nebuchadnezzar's troops were neither able to seize Tyre nor to dethrone its king. The city was eventually destroyed, reduced, in Ezekiel's phrase, to "a bare rock, . . . a place for spreading [fishermen's] nets" (26:5, 14). Tyre, however, did not fall until two and a half centuries after Nebuchadnezzar's time, when Alexander the Great captured the city and razed it.

Ezekiel was apparently undaunted by the failure of his prediction that Nebuchadnezzar's "horses" would "trample all [Tyre's] streets" (26:11). Either the prophet—or a later editor—then declares that Yahweh will compensate the Babylonian ruler for his wasted efforts by delivering Egypt's even greater riches into his hands (29:1–32:32). Because Egypt's pharaoh had not helped to rescue Judah from Babylon's oppression (29:6–10), and because Nebuchadnezzar had derived nothing from his long labor attacking Tyre, Yahweh resolved to "give the land of Egypt to King Nebuchadnezzar . . . and he shall carry off its wealth" (29:18–20). While weakening Pharaoh's "arm," and strengthening that of Nebuchadnezzar, Yahweh orders Babylonian armies to turn Egypt into a desert and to slaughter its entire population so that the land will be drenched in "flowing blood up to the mountains" (32:6, 12–16).

After scattering Egypt's population among foreign nations for "forty years," Yahweh will then return the exiles to a permanently weakened Egypt. Although he had defeated Egypt's Pharaoh Necho at the Battle of Carchemish (605 BCE), neither Nebuchadnezzar nor his successors succeeded in occupying the country or evicting the Egyptians from their land.

Ezekiel's Visions of Future Restoration

In Ezekiel 33, which is pivotal, the text briefly describes Jerusalem's fall and the miserable fate of those remaining amid the ruins. After this event, the prophet abandons his visions of judgment and focuses on Israel's future restoration. In Chapters 33–39, he predicts that God himself will become Israel's "shepherd" and rule the restored nation directly, or that he will appoint a descendant of David to guide the covenant people, who will then live in perfect security (Ch. 34; cf. 37:24–27).

Perhaps the most influential of Ezekiel's visions occurs in Chapter 37. Beholding a long valley littered with human bones, he hears a voice ask, "Mortal, can these bones live?" Miraculously, the fragmented skeletons reassemble themselves and are again clothed in flesh. Yahweh directs the winds to breathe life into them, and their resurrection is complete. In reading this section, it is important to remember that in this famous vision Ezekiel experiences a preview of Israel's rebirth: In 587 BCE, the nation had perished, but now Yahweh was raising it to renewed life. It was not until the Book of Daniel was composed four centuries later that a biblical writer explicitly described a belief in the **resurrection** of individual humans (Dan. 12:1–3).

In the next chapters, Ezekiel deals with future threats to Israel. Once the nation was restored to life, what was to prevent it from being overrun by superpowers even greater than Assyria or Babylon? To assure his audience that Yahweh will protect Israel's future security, the prophet introduces the strange account of **Gog** and **Magog,** unidentified aggressors who symbolize potential enemies (Chs. 38–39). In this vision, Ezekiel sees Jerusalem's would-be attackers destroyed when Yahweh directly intervenes to rescue his people. Foreseeing a violent and bloody deliverance, Ezekiel states that Israel's slain enemies are so numerous that it takes seven months to bury their corpses.

God's violent intervention is performed not only for Israel's sake but also for the public vindication of Yahweh's reputation. Like his previous humiliation of Egypt's pharaoh (Exod. 9:15-16), Yahweh's slaughter of Gog's armies serves to enhance God's international stature. When the Babylonians—worshipers of

FIGURE 18.2 Israel's national epic begins with Abraham's birth in the ancient Mesopotamian city of Ur (Gen. 12) and concludes with the last surviving Davidic King, Jehoiachin, a prisoner in the region's most powerful city, Babylon (2 Kings 25). The story of Yahweh's covenant people is thus given a Mesopotamian framework, suggesting the area's historical and cultural importance in the biblical worldview. This scale model of Babylon's central avenue and the blue-tiled Ishtar Gate (*top right*) shows the processional route along which the statue of Marduk, the Babylonian creator god, was carried during the city's annual New Year's festival and when the Babylonian creation epic was publicly recited.

Marduk—had conquered his people, to many it probably looked as if Yahweh, too, had suffered defeat (see Figure 18.2). To restore his prestige, Yahweh resolves to act resolutely in the future. Chapter 39 closes with his promise to return to Jerusalem all members of the covenant community who are currently scattered among foreign countries. This restoration will compel foreign leaders to "know that I am the LORD [Israel's] God." This refrain—that God's future acts of restoration will cause the nations to "know" that he reigns supreme—occurs about sixty times in Ezekiel's writing. Yahweh also vows "never again [to] hide [his] face from them" (39:28–29).

Future Israel

The book's final section (Chs. 40–48) offers a kind of blueprint for a future Israelite theocracy, when Yahweh will rule his people directly. In describing the gloriously rebuilt Temple, Ezekiel provides the detailed measurements, room by room and court by court, of an eternal sanctuary. He then envisions Yahweh's return to his favored dwelling place:

> And there the glory of the God of Israel was coming from the east; the sound was like the sound of mighty waters, and the earth shone with his glory. . . . As the glory of the LORD entered the temple by the gate facing east, . . . and the glory of the LORD filled the temple.

(Ezek. 43:1–6)

The prophet's visions have thus come full circle, from beholding Yahweh deserting the doomed sanctuary to beholding Yahweh's "glory" returning to a greater Temple.

Ezekiel's special priestly concerns significantly shape this vision. The idealized new Temple was to be administered not by the Levites in general, but by descendants of the priest **Zadok,** whose name means "righteous." (Zadok has served as high priest under both David and Solomon.) Levites may serve as attendants, but only Zadok's heirs are to enjoy full priestly authority. After listing regulations and ritual details of Temple worship, Ezekiel (or the disciples who compiled his work) paints a final vision of a crystal-clear stream issuing from beneath the sanctuary, a river whose waters transform the sterile Dead Sea basin into lush greenery suggestive of the Garden of Eden (47:1–12). Once restored to God's favor, Israel will enjoy a paradise existence that will realize, at last, God's vision for humanity.

 ## The Oracles of Second Isaiah (Isaiah 40–55)

In contrast to Isaiah of Jerusalem, Jeremiah, and Ezekiel, the anonymous prophet whom scholars call Second Isaiah focuses on messages of hope and consolation. One of the Hebrew Bible's greatest poets, Second Isaiah addresses his fellow exiles during the last years of the Babylonian captivity (c. 540 BCE). Announcing that Judah's time of punishment is fulfilled, he proclaims that Yahweh has fully pardoned his people and now plans to grant them their freedom. Yahweh will guide them on a "new exodus" out of Babylon and back to the Promised Land.

In shaping the Book of Isaiah into its present form, editors inserted a prose passage from the Book of 2 Kings to mark the transition from the oracles of Isaiah of Jerusalem to those of the unnamed successor. In Chapter 39, the inserted prose section ends with Isaiah warning King Hezekiah that all his wealth will one day be "carried to Babylon" and that his descendants will be servants "in the palace of the king of Babylon" (Isa. 39:5–7). From this point on, neither the name of Isaiah nor the Assyrian threat that preoccupied him is mentioned. From Chapter 40 on, all references to the Near Eastern political scene concern not Assyria but Babylon, which is already about to fall, and the rise of a new dominant power, that of the Medes and Persians.

Cyrus of Persia

Second Isaiah urges the unhappy exiles to see these international developments as evidence of Yahweh's hand at work, a revelation that Israel's God remains in full control of human history. Yahweh's purpose in the changing political scene is to deliver his captive people, for which task he has chosen **Cyrus the Great,** king of Persia. Although Cyrus, whose armies were then sweeping through the Near East, does not "know" Yahweh, the Persian leader is nonetheless God's chosen agent to restore Israel. After Cyrus wins a series of astonishing victories, he makes himself master of Media (549 BCE)

and Lydia (546 BCE). Viewing Cyrus's triumphs as proof of divine action, Second Isaiah declares that Cyrus is the "shepherd" who fulfills God's purpose in returning the exiles to their land (44:28–45:6; cf. 41:1–9, 25–29; 48:12–16, 20–22). Unlike Isaiah of Jerusalem, the exilic prophet does not look to a Davidic heir to rescue the covenant community; instead, he declares that Cyrus is Yahweh's "anointed," his "messiah" (45:1).

Because Second Isaiah refers to Babylon's fall to Cyrus as imminent but not yet accomplished (Isa. 47), his oracles were probably delivered shortly before 539 BCE, when Cyrus captured the city. A year after Cyrus took Babylon, the prophet's optimistic view of him as a liberator was vindicated by the Persian king's policy encouraging all groups imprisoned in Babylon to return their respective homelands. Although Second Isaiah regards Cyrus's liberation of exiles as if it were directed exclusively to the Judean community, the Persian emperor apparently pursued a general policy of returning virtually all exiled peoples to their native regions to restore local shrines. (The various gods whose sanctuaries were rebuilt presumably would be grateful to Cyrus and support his reign.) In spite of the Judean prophet's claims, Cyrus did not ascribe his conquests to Yahweh. According to the Cyrus Cylinder, an artifact inscribed with an account of Babylon's capture, Cyrus officially attributed his success to Marduk, chief god of the Babylonian pantheon. In this account, Marduk favored Cyrus because Babylonian rulers had neglected his worship, which the Persian liberator would revive.

Judah's All-Powerful God

Although he views a single group—Judean exiles—as occupying the center stage of world history, Second Isaiah, more than any previous prophet, emphasizes the universality of Judah's God. The prophet portrays Yahweh as without beginning or ending—or without divine rivals. Other gods simply do not exist: "They are all a delusion, their works are nothing; their images are empty wind" (41:29). Even Marduk (also called Bel) and his divine son, Nebo, supposedly responsible for Babylon's political dominance, are powerless before Yahweh:

> . . . for I am God and there is no other;
> I am God, and there is no one like me,
> declaring the end from the beginning,
> and from ancient times things not yet done . . .

(Isa. 46:9–10)

For Second Isaiah, God's will is irresistible, shaping human history in unforeseen ways to achieve his people's salvation. Because he is all-powerful and all-wise, Yahweh alone can predict the covenant community's restoration and guarantee its future reality:

> Who has announced from of old the things to come?
> Let them tell us what is yet to be.
> Do not fear, or be afraid;
> have I not told you from of old and declared it?
> You are my witnesses!
> Is there any god besides me?
> There is no other rock; I know not one.

(Isa. 44:7–8)

To the poet, Yahweh is both transcendent and immanent: From his heavenly perspective, mighty nations and empires are insignificant, no more than "a drop from a bucket" (41:15). Although he effortlessly commands the countless stars of heaven (representing the members of his celestial council), he also reaches out to touch human lives on earth. Invisibly arranging historical events for his people's benefit, Yahweh inspires the frightened and exhausted exiles to trust in the coming restoration of Judah. He will give them "wings like eagles" for their journey home (40:25–31).

In creating the covenant community anew, Yahweh extends to his people as a whole his promise to David, embracing all the faithful in his "everlasting covenant" (55:3–5). Summoning the Judean captives to a new role on the world stage, God will make them "a light to the nations" (42:6) and witnesses to his glory (43:10). In Second Isaiah's vision, God is about to fulfill the ancient promise to Abraham that his descendants ultimately will be a source of universal blessing. For exiles unable to grasp the magnitude of God's pardon and redemption, Yahweh reminds him that his plan for Israel exceeds the limits of human imagination:

> For my thoughts are not your thoughts,
> nor are your ways my ways, says the LORD.
> For as the heavens are higher than the earth,
> so are my ways higher than your ways
> and my thoughts than your thoughts.

(Isa. 55:8–9)

The Servant Songs

Unique to Second Isaiah is a series of poems known as the Servant Songs (42:1–4; 43:8–13; 49:1–6; 50:4–9; 52:13–53:12). In most of the songs, Israel is explicitly identified as God's "servant" (cf. 44:1–2; 49:3), a people commissioned to represent Yahweh in the world. In one of the songs, however, the poet seems to describe an individual rather than the people as a whole (52:13–53:12), portraying him as one "despised and rejected of

men: a man of sorrows and acquainted with grief" (53:3, King James Version). Known as the Suffering Servant, the unidentified figure in this poem is misunderstood, grouped with sinners, and condemned to an agonizing, humiliating defeat. Many scholars think that his poem voices a new development in biblical attitudes toward the meaning of suffering. Traditional views, such as those of most Israelite prophets and the Deuteronomistic writers, held that Israel's misfortunes resulted from its sinful disobedience. In Second Isaiah's poem, however, the afflicted person, though guiltless, willingly accepts the punishment for others' wrongdoing, enduring pain on their behalf:

> Surely he has borne our infirmities and carries our
>   diseases;
> yet we accounted him stricken, struck down by God,
>   and afflicted.
> But he was wounded for our transgressions,
> crushed for our iniquities;
> upon him was the punishment that made us
> whole, and by his bruises we are healed.

(Isa. 53:4–5)

Speculations about the identity of the Suffering Servant abound, ranging from the covenant people collectively to a single person who represents Israel, perhaps the prophet himself. The belief that sin and its penalty can be transferred from the community as a whole to a sacrificial object also appears in Leviticus 16. This passage prescribes an annual ritual in which the priest transmits the people's sins to a sacrificial goat, which is then sent away to die in the desert. Some scholars believe that this **scapegoat** ceremony may have given rise to a reevaluation of the meaning of suffering in which individual victims bear the consequences of communal guilt.

Although the early Christian movement identified the Suffering Servant with Jesus of Nazareth (cf. Acts 8:29–35), most scholars now look for an interpretation that respects the integrity of the Hebrew Bible. As noted previously, some commentators think that the one who suffered undeservedly was the prophet himself. Certainly, by preaching that Cyrus of Persia was God's instrument in overthrowing Babylon, the prophet invited retaliation from the Babylonian authorities. Members of his own community who had accepted a permanent exile and followed Jeremiah's advice to support Babylon's government may also have feared that Second Isaiah's pro-Cyrus message would damage their situation. Other biblical literature dealing with the exile suggests that cooperation with Babylon was encouraged: Jeremiah had urged submission to Babylonian rule (Jer. 29:3–10), and Daniel, though written later, similarly shows Judean leaders serving honorably at the Babylonian court (Dan. 1–5). To some exiles, Second Isaiah's political oracles were perhaps seen as a threat to their community's welfare. The persecution, imprisonment, and possible death of the anonymous servant—followed, after Cyrus's defeat of Babylon, by public vindication—may reflect the prophet's personal experiences. His disciples, who collected his oracles and preserved his teaching, may have interpreted his prophetic career as a story of unmerited sufferings followed by triumph.

Insisting that Yahweh alone is God, Second Isaiah proclaims an absolute **monotheism,** perhaps the first canonical prophet to do so. He also promotes a radical understanding of contemporary politics: The decline of Babylon and the rise of Persia under Cyrus are concrete evidence that only Yahweh controls history. Viewing the imminent return to Judah as a new exodus, the prophet defined the covenant community's new task as witnessing to Yahweh's incomparable power, wisdom, and saving purpose. God has now appointed Israel to bring "light" to a woefully dark world.

QUESTIONS FOR DISCUSSION AND REVIEW

1. When the heavens open to Ezekiel, what vision of God does he see? After the fall of Jerusalem, how does Ezekiel prepare his people for the future? What is the significance of his vision of the "valley of dry bones"?

2. How does Ezekiel's view of the Temple differ from that of Jeremiah or Isaiah of Jerusalem? In Ezekiel's view of Jerusalem's restoration, what role does the Temple play?

3. Why do scholars believe that the prophetic oracles contained in Isaiah 40–55 originated with a speaker different from Isaiah of Jerusalem? What Near Eastern power threatens Jerusalem in the first part of Isaiah's book? How have Judah's historical and political circumstances changed after Chapter 39? Why is Second Isaiah's message often called a "book of consolation"?

4. To what historical figure does Second Isaiah look for the release of his people? How would the conquests of this foreign leader be meaningful to an audience of Judean exiles in Babylon but not to Judeans living in Jerusalem in the eighth century BCE, the time of Isaiah of Jerusalem?

5. How does Second Isaiah advance the concept of monotheism? What specific passages declare that Yahweh alone is God of the universe?

6. Describe the "Servant Songs." How do you go about trying to identify the "Suffering Servant" of Isaiah 53? How do New Testament writers interpret this passage?

Terms and Concepts to Remember

Cyrus the Great
Ezekiel
Gog and Magog
kavod
monotheism
scapegoat
Second Isaiah (Deutero-Isaiah)
Servant Songs
Zadok's descendants

Recommended Reading

Ezekiel

Boadt, Lawrence. "Ezekiel, Book of." In D. N. Freedman, ed., *The Anchor Bible Dictionary*, Vol. 2, pp. 711–722. New York: Doubleday, 1992. The biblical text, with extensive scholarly interpretation.

Darr, Katheryn P. "The Book of Ezekiel." In *The New Interpreter's Bible*, Vol. 6, pp. 1075–1607. Nashville, TN: Abingdon Press, 2001. A thorough analysis of Ezekiel in its sociohistorical context.

Greenberg, Moshe. *Ezekiel: A New Translation with Introduction and Commentary*, 2 vols. Garden City, NY: Doubleday, 1983 and 1997. A thorough analysis of the text.

Klein, Ralph W. "Exile." In K. D. Sakenfeld, ed., *The New Interpreter's Dictionary of the Bible*, Vol. 2, pp. 367–370. Nashville, TN: Abingdon Press, 2007. Explains the circumstances of Ezekiel's deportation in 597 BCE.

Odell, Margaret. "Ezekiel, Book of." In K. D. Sakenfeld, ed., *The New Interpreter's Dictionary of the Bible*, Vol. 2, pp. 387–396. Nashville, TN: Abingdon Press, 2007. Places the prophet's oracles and visions in their historical Mesopotamian context.

Second Isaiah (Isaiah 40–55)

Blenkinsopp, Joseph. *Isaiah 40–55: A New Translation with Introduction and Commentary*. New York: Doubleday, 2002. Provides detailed interpretation of the Servant passages.

Childs, Brevard S. *Isaiah* (Old Testament Library). Louisville, KY: Westminster John Knox Press, 2000. Places the message of Second Isaiah in historical continuity with the oracles of Isaiah of Jerusalem.

Gottwald, Norman K. *The Hebrew Bible: A Socio-Literary Introduction*. Philadelphia: Fortress Press, 1985. Includes an insightful analysis of Second Isaiah's sociopolitical circumstances among the Judean exiles in Babylon.

Seitz, Christopher R. "The Book of Isaiah 40–66." In *The New Interpreter's Bible*, Vol. 6, pp. 309–552. Nashville, TN: Abingdon Press, 2001. A sensitive review of the oracles of Second and Third Isaiah.

CHAPTER 19

After the Exile—Israel's Last Prophets

The Oracles of Haggai, Zechariah, Third Isaiah, Joel, Malachi, and Jonah

---

Key Topics/Themes Writing when Judah was a small part of the vast Persian Empire, the last of Israel's canonical prophets struggled to interpret Yahweh's will for the imperfectly restored covenant community. While Haggai and Zechariah urge the returned exiles to rebuild the Temple, Third Isaiah and Joel criticize Judeans for their religious failures and also predict both judgment and future glory. Malachi foresees the return of Elijah and a future messenger of the covenant. Setting his story in the days of Assyria, Jonah offers a slyly humorous story about Yahweh's universality and compassion.

With Cyrus's conquest of Babylon in 539 BCE, the political situation in Judah quickly changed for the better. Cyrus's policy of restoring national shrines that the Babylonians had destroyed encouraged the Judean exiles to return home and rebuild Yahweh's Temple. No longer a kingdom, Judah became a small province in the Persian Empire. Granted some measure of self-government, Judah had a two-person leadership consisting of a Persian-appointed governor and a High Priest. Interestingly, the Persians selected Zerubbabel, Jehoiachin's grandson, to be Judah's governor in about 520 BCE.

Once in Jerusalem, however, **Zerubbabel** and the High Priest, **Joshua,** became the focal point of prophetic expectations. Both Haggai and Zechariah, postexilic prophets who campaigned for a rapid rebuilding of the Temple, apparently viewed Zerubbabel as a potential restorer of the Davidic dynasty. Whatever the prophets' hopes may have been, Zerubbabel quickly disappeared from the political scene, and the Persians remained firmly in control until the late fourth century BCE, when Alexander the Great overthrew Persia and established a vast, Greek-speaking empire (c. 332 BCE). Nevertheless, the belief that Yahweh had chosen Zerubbabel as his "signet ring" (Hag. 2:23), through which to accomplish wonders, certainly motivated the prophets of this generation to reflect on their changing relationship with Yahweh.

Accompanying this spirit of renewal, however, were deep political and social divisions between the group of returned exiles and the rest of Judah's population, many of whom had remained on the land while the ruling elite were led off to Babylon. As the books of Ezra and Nehemiah show, Jerusalem's postexilic religious leaders insisted that only the returnees from Babylon should govern the restored Judean community (see Chapter 21).

The Book of Haggai

A careful reading of the two books shows that Haggai and Zechariah are closely connected. Both works appear to have been written shortly before the completion and rededication of the Jerusalem Temple in about 515 BCE. In fact, many scholars view the two volumes as a composite work, overlapping in both content and date of composition. **Haggai** seems to address his message chiefly to Zerubbabel and Joshua, the men God has charged to hasten the rebuilding of his "house" (known as the **Second Temple**). Indeed, Haggai criticizes both the Judeans in general and the two leaders in particular for their lack of zeal in restoring Yahweh's official worship. Haggai even blames the community's poverty on the fact that many have rebuilt their own houses while Yahweh's "house" still "lies in ruins" (Hag. 1:8–10).

In this prophetic logic, Haggai follows the Deuteronomistic thesis, whereby Yahweh gives all rewards and punishments according to the community's collective obedience and service to its God. Whatever disappointment and poverty the returnees have experienced trying to wrest a living from their farms can therefore be attributed to denying Yahweh the honor he regards as his due. Any hope of an improvement in their living conditions, Haggai observes, will depend on the community's willingness to heed his message. The returned Judeans therefore must overcome the apathy or indifference that has kept them from completing Yahweh's earthly abode.

In the second and final chapter of his short book, Haggai shifts gears to emphasize the rewards that will follow the completion of Yahweh's "house," envisioning an apocalyptic upheaval that will trigger an influx of unimagined riches:

> Once again, in a little while, I will shake the heavens and the earth and the sea and the dry land; and I will shake all the nations, so that the treasure of all nations shall come, and I will fill this house with splendor, says the LORD of hosts.

(Hag. 2:6–7)

Reassuring his audience that the divine *kavod* (glory) will return to Judah and the new Temple, Haggai orders that the people first purify themselves, lest the sacrifices they offer become impure as well. Only after they have paid proper respect to Yahweh, precisely following priestly rituals, can they expect to enjoy the fruits of the earth.

Intensifying his apocalyptic imagery, Haggai concludes by prophesying the imminent overthrow of "the kingdoms of the nations"—after which Zerubbabel will apparently become Yahweh's "chosen" agent to rule his people (2:20–23). If the Persians viewed Zerubbabel as the focus of a prophet-inspired revolt, as this passage suggests, it explains why this descendant of David apparently did not continue as governor.

 ## The Book of Zechariah

The longest volume in the collection of twelve Minor Prophets, the Book of Zechariah dates, at least in part, from the same period as the Book of Haggai (c. 520–518 BCE). Displaying even more apocalyptic fervor than Haggai, Zechariah's sometimes obscure message implies that Yahweh—at long last—will now accomplish his long-term plan for Israel, though "not by might, nor

by power, but by my spirit, says the LORD of Hosts" (Zech. 3:6). Contemporary scholars believe that Zechariah's authentic oracles are contained in the book's first eight chapters. Chapters 9–14, commonly known as Second Zechariah, seem to be the work of other seers, perhaps a school of prophets influenced by his strongly apocalyptic style.

The historical Zechariah, who appears to have come from a priestly family, lived in a community in which poverty and insecurity had taken the place of the glorious future that Second Isaiah had so eloquently foretold. Although Zechariah emphasized the necessity of rebuilding the Temple to receive Yahweh's favor and material blessings, he also directed his message to the returned Judeans who felt deep disappointment at the failure of prophetic oracles promising peace and prosperity. In a series of eight visions—which are interpreted by an angelic figure—Zechariah addresses the people's anxiety about what Yahweh intends to do with them. Hopes that Zerubbabel would mount the throne of David are dashed when Darius, then emperor of Persia, puts down a budding revolt and consolidates his power. After Zerubbabel can no longer be viewed as the hoped-for restorer of the Davidic monarchy, Zechariah turns his attention to the prospects of Joshua, the High Priest, to whom he speaks about Yahweh's "servant the Branch," presumably another Davidic heir (3:8–10).

Particularly striking is Zechariah's vision of Joshua standing before Yahweh's heavenly council. When "Satan" (humanity's adversary), who is part of the celestial court (cf. Job 1–2), accuses the High Priest (who represents the returned exiles) of unworthiness, Yahweh's angel removes Joshua's dirty garments (symbolic of the community's sins) and reclothes him in splendid robes. This change of clothing shows that Yahweh has forgiven his people's collective misdeeds and that the period of national mourning is over. If the Judean community henceforth keeps God's commandments, it will prosper. Zechariah's mystical experience thus offers hope that Yahweh is at last taking action to improve the condition of his humiliated and foreign-dominated nation (Zech. 3:1–10).

A vision in Chapter 6 similarly emphasizes Joshua's messianic role as "the Branch," the person chosen to rebuild the sanctuary, wear a royal crown, and "sit and rule on his throne." Because this passage refers to cooperation between a royal monarch and priest, scholars believe that the prophecy originally applied to Zerubbabel, a descendant of David (Zech. 6:9–15; cf. references to Zerubbabel in 4:1–10). After hopes that Zerubbabel would reestablish the Davidic monarchy came to nothing, however, editors apparently substituted Joshua's name for that of the former governor. Although plans for restoring the kingship had become both futile and dangerous, it was still possible to view the High Priest as Yahweh's anointed and spiritual leader of the Jewish state.

Chapters 7 and 8, respectively, survey the ethical meaning of Israel's rise and fall as a nation and promise the people ultimate redemption though a messiah whose rule will transform the whole earth into a paradise. This section concludes with the prediction that not only will powerful nations come to Jerusalem to worship Yahweh, but ten foreigners will cling to a single Jew, begging him to teach them Yahweh's law. With its emphasis on Zion (or Jerusalem) as the spiritual center of the universe, this section echoes ideas first expressed in Isaiah 2 and 9.

Second Zechariah

The second part of Zechariah contains a wide variety of oracles, visions, and pronouncements, some of which seem to be as late as the Hellenistic (Greek) period in the fourth century BCE. This section, with its fantastic images and typically obscure style, appears to be the work of several different apocalyptic writers. In some ways, it resembles the apocalyptic predictions editors inserted into the Book of Isaiah (Isa. 24–27). Three distinct themes dominate Chapters 9–14: (1) Yahweh will punish Judah's neighbors at the same time that he gathers the remnant of his people back to Zion; (2) the nations will make war against Judah and Jerusalem; and (3) God himself will intervene on Judah's behalf, destroying its enemies and asserting himself as the "king over all the earth" (14:9).

Historically, this section of Zechariah had considerable influence on early Christian thought. Zechariah 9:9 declares that Jerusalem's king will come to the city "humble and riding on a donkey, on a colt, the foal of a donkey." The author of Matthew's Gospel, perhaps misunderstanding the poet's use of parallelism here, depicts Jesus as riding on two different animals at once (Matt. 21:1–7). Zechariah also mentions "thirty shekels of silver" (the price of a slave) (Zech. 11:13–14), the sum for which Judas betrays his Master. A particularly obscure oracle pictures Jerusalem as mourning "one whom they have pierced" (12:10), in a passage in which Yahweh also promises that "the house of David shall be like God" (12:8) leading victorious armies. Equally murky is the reference to striking a shepherd and scattering his sheep (13:7), which follows an apparent declaration that the gift of prophecy has been taken from Israel (13:2–6).

As in Ezekiel's vision of Gog and Magog (Ezek. 38–39), Zechariah 14 focuses on **eschatology** (Greek, "last things), visions of the final battle between good and evil that climaxes human history. For this cosmic confrontation, Yahweh will gather all nations to Jerusalem. The enemy will then plunder the city and slaughter nearly all its inhabitants. But at the last desperate moment, Yahweh himself will appear, striding from the Mount of Olives—which will be split by gigantic earthquakes—to fight for Israel.

Terror and slaughter, in both the natural and supernatural realms, will be followed by cosmic renewal. Yahweh now will transform the earth and its climate. Cold and frost will cease, streams will issue from Jerusalem, mountains will disappear, and all Palestine will become a plain—a highly desirable change for farmers and shepherds. Meanwhile, non-Jewish nations will suffer a plague that rots their eyes in their sockets and incites them to attack one another irrationally. Populations that survive this catastrophe will then make pilgrimages to Jerusalem, now physically elevated above all other cities, to worship at Yahweh's Temple. God's universal rule at last will be established.

The Oracles of Third Isaiah (Isaiah 56–66)

Second Isaiah had inspired his fellow exiles in Babylon with oracles of comfort, proclaiming a splendid future for a restored Judah and Jerusalem (Isa. 40–55; see Chapter 18). After Cyrus the Great's decree of 538 BCE paved the way for all peoples displaced by Babylonian conquerors to return to their respective homelands, a band of Judean exiles trudged back to Judah, now subject to Persian overlords. Instead of reentering the restored paradise that Second Isaiah had envisioned, however, the refugees found only ruin and devastation, with both the holy city and its sanctuary still heaps of rubble. With Judean cities "a wilderness" and Jerusalem "a desolation" (Isa. 64:10–11), the returned exiles suffered from extreme disappointment, poverty, and deprivation. Assuming Second Isaiah's role as a prophetic comforter, the anonymous seer whom scholars name Third Isaiah defines his mission as offering similar reassurance:

> The spirit of the LORD God is upon me,
> because the LORD has anointed me,
> he has sent me to bring good news to the oppressed.

(Isa. 61:1)

Third Isaiah describes his audience as consisting of "prisoners," "the brokenhearted," and "those who mourn in Zion [Jerusalem's sacred hill on which Solomon's Temple had stood]" (61:1–3). Proclaiming both "the year of the LORD's favor" and divine "vengeance" on Judah's oppressors, the prophet declares that the covenant community will rise from its ashes:

> They [the returned exiles] shall build up the
>   ancient ruins,
> they shall raise up the former devastations;
> they shall repair the ruined cities.

(Isa. 61:4)

As Isaiah of Jerusalem two centuries earlier had denounced the upper classes for defrauding the poor, Third Isaiah emphasizes that Judah's future prosperity depends not on reviving cultic sacrifices, but on caring for "the hungry," "the naked," and "the homeless poor" (58:7). Only then will the restored community become the world's "light," a beacon of social and economic justice that his exilic predecessor had foretold (58:10; cf. 42:6). Instead of an arid desert, Judah will then become "like a watered garden," a veritable Eden in which God could dwell (58:11, 14).

Expanding on Second Isaiah's message about God's omnipotence and universality, Third Isaiah declares that the covenant arrangement now embraces whole classes of people who previously were excluded. From now on, foreigners (perhaps those who had joined the Judean exiles in returning from Babylon) and "eunuchs" (male officials at Near Eastern courts were routinely castrated) will be part of the covenant community. Foreigners and eunuchs who "hold fast [the] covenant" are now authorized to serve at the sanctuary, for the new Temple will be "a house of prayer for all peoples" (56:1–8; cf. 66:18–23). Whoever rejects idols to worship Yahweh "shall possess the land and inherit [God's] holy mountain," their voluntary commitment to Israel's LORD making them heirs to all the divine promises (57:13).

Unlike his contemporaries Haggai and Zechariah, Third Isaiah neither raises expectations for a revival of the Davidic monarchy nor argues that renewed prosperity depends on rebuilding the Temple. Indeed, the prophet asserts that Yahweh's "house" is virtually irrelevant to the Deity, for whom all "heaven" is a "throne" and the earth merely a "footstool":

> What is the house that you would build for me,
> and what is my resting place?

(Isa. 66:1)

While regarding Temple reconstruction as relatively unimportant, Third Isaiah does agree with Haggai's

prediction that God will validate his people by showering them with foreign riches. The prophet directly addresses the anxieties of an impoverished society struggling to survive when he vows that Yahweh will soon flood Judah with "the wealth of the nations" (61:6). As in the days of Solomon, a flourishing international trade will attract foreign investment to Jerusalem, "so that nations shall bring you their wealth, with their kings led in procession. . . . The glory of Lebanon shall come to you" (60:6–13).

Some of Third Isaiah's predictions about the distant future resemble the eschatology of Zechariah. Looking beyond the bleak present to "new heavens and a new earth," a global paradise in which humans and animals will dwell peacefully together, the prophet embraces all humanity in his vision of cosmic harmony (65:17–25; 66:22–23). Such prophetic expectations of a divinely renewed creation persisted into the Greco-Roman period, when both Jewish and Christian writers composed apocalypses imagining the imminent fulfillment of the Book of Isaiah's hopes for a God-ruled future (see Chapter 38; cf. Rev. 21:1–4 and 2 Pet. 3:13).

The Book of Joel

Traditionally placed after Hosea as the second book of the Minor Prophets, the Book of Joel presents a double challenge to readers. First, the book gives no information about when **Joel** lived or taught, nor can we be sure that the entire work, short as it is, is the product of a single author. Structurally, Joel seems to divide itself into two parts. In the first section (1:1–2:17), the prophet describes a terrifying plague of locusts that are devouring the land; in the second (2:18–3:21), he foresees a time of judgment and redemption, when not only the locusts but Judah's regional enemies will be gone. Most scholars think that Joel belongs to the postexilic prophets. The economic hardships he mentions, the lack of any reference to a king, and the prominence of the priesthood in his thought—all suggest the social and political conditions of Judah in the late sixth or early fifth century BCE. Some scholars, however, point to Joel's image of an approaching army as referring to an imminent Babylonian invasion, suggesting that he prophesied before the exile.

Devastation and Redemption

Scholars who regard the book as a unity see the locust plague of the first chapter as a prologue to the message of deliverance that emerges in Chapters 2 and 3. Echoing the classical prophets of the eighth and seventh centuries BCE, Joel urges his audience to repent their sins and to return to God, who, he assures them, is "slow to anger, and abounding in steadfast love" (2:13). The benefits of such repentance, he says, will be the removal of the "northern army" that threatens Jerusalem and the restoration of the land's fertility. No longer will Israel have to fear either natural disasters or human malice, once Yahweh is to be found in the "midst" of his people.

Alternating between visions of cosmic terror and universal renewal, Joel foresees two completely different fates assigned to Israel and to its enemies. When Judah is restored, Joel proclaims, the "mountains shall drip sweet wine, the hills shall flow with milk" (3:18). As for Egypt, Edom, Tyre, Sidon, and Philistia, the Day of Yahweh will be a display of horrific doom:

> I will show portents in the heavens and on earth, blood and fire and columns of smoke. The sun shall be turned to darkness, and the moon to blood, before the great and terrible day of the LORD comes.

(Joel 2:30)

Reassuming his role as warrior-god, Yahweh himself will take blood vengeance for all the cruelties that its neighbors have inflicted on Israel. All nations will be summoned to the "valley of Jehoshaphat" to be tried before the court of divine justice. This "valley" appears to be an imaginary spot—or, more precisely, a metaphor for "standing in judgment." In Hebrew, the name *Jehoshaphat* literally means "Yahweh has judged," and it expresses Joel's understanding of what the Day of Yahweh represents. It is a time when God punishes Israel's enemies and rewards his faithful worshipers; it is also a definitive turning point in the history of Yahweh's covenant relationship with Israel. At last, the promise that Israel will become a holy nation is about to be realized. But instead of becoming a "kingdom of priests," it is now destined to become a nation of prophets:

> I will pour out my spirit on all flesh;
> your sons and your daughters shall prophesy,
> your old men shall dream dreams,
> and your young men shall see visions.
> Even on the male and female slaves,
> in those days, I will pour out
> my spirit.

(Joel 2:28)

Unlike Isaiah, however, Joel does not envision a universal sharing of divine gifts or a gathering of all peoples on the Temple mount. In a deliberate reversal of Isaiah's oracle, Joel mockingly urges the nations to "beat your plowshares into swords" (3:10), because Israel's vindication demands their destruction. In sharp contrast to most canonical prophets, Joel does not dwell on Israel's sinful past or present. Nor does he predict that either the locusts or the invading army will be more than a quickly passing threat. Instead, Joel emphasizes Yahweh's determination to honor his covenant pledge to preserve and defend Israel against its many foes. He repeatedly refers to Israel's validation as one of Yahweh's principal goals in global judgment. The prophet's scarcely concealed nationalism is as marked in Joel as it is in Nahum, intensified by the addition of apocalyptic themes. For Joel, as for many later apocalyptic writers, Israel's triumphal restoration and the world's End are indivisibly linked. Confidently, he predicts that Yahweh will always protect his holy city:

> But Judah shall be inhabited forever,
> and Jerusalem to all generations.
> I will avenge their blood, . . .
> for the LORD dwells in Zion.

(Joel 3:20–21)

Understandably, later Jewish and Christian writers frequently quote Joel's oracles about final judgment and his anointing the faithful with his divine spirit. The noncanonical Book of Enoch reflects Joel's ideas and imagery, as do the New Testament Gospels, which cite Joel's references to astronomical phenomena as events heralding Jesus' Second Coming (see Mark 13:24–25; Matt. 24:29; Luke 21:11, 25). The author of Acts, however, suggests that Joel's prophecy in 2:28–29 was fulfilled in the first century CE, when the Holy Spirit empowered the early Christian community at Pentecost (Acts 2:1–4, 7–21).

The Book of Malachi

Placed last on the scroll of the Twelve (Minor) Prophets, the short Book of **Malachi**—titled an "oracle" in the first verse—reflects conditions in Judah a few generations after the return from exile. Active at some time between the rededication of the Second Temple in 515 BCE and about 450 BCE, the prophet presents many of his oracles in the form of a fictional conversation between God and members of the partly restored Judean community. In these debates, which focus mainly on the sacrificial cult at the rebuilt sanctuary, God complains that people and priests insult him by offering defective animals. (Covenant law requires perfect, unblemished sacrifices [Lev. 22:17–25; Deut. 15:21].) In contrast to Gentiles (non-Judeans), whom he claims provide a "pure offering" as they worship Israel's God, Yahweh laments that his own people sacrifice only "blind," "lame," or "sick" creatures (Mal. 1:6–14).

The book's title, *Malachi*, means "my messenger" and is probably not the name of the prophet, an anonymous figure about whom no information is given. The title may have been taken from 3:1, a verse in which Yahweh announces that he is sending "my messenger" to "prepare the way" for God's imminent appearance at the Temple. This divine visitation, the author states, will expose Judah's inferior sacrificial system like a "refiner's fire," separating dross from gold (3:1–4). Although emphasizing that Yahweh arrives to cleanse the offensive rituals at the Second Temple, the author—whom we call Malachi to avoid confusion—broadens his charge to include the people's ethical obligations to their fellow Judeans. Those who take economic advantage of alien residents, "widows," and "orphans" or who "oppress the hired workers in their wages" risk divine judgment (3:5).

Returning to cultic matters, Malachi accuses the people of "robbing God" for not paying their tithes (one-tenth of their incomes) to maintain the Temple and its priesthood. If they are faithful in this, he promises, they again will receive divine favor, with Judah changing into "a land of delight" (3:8–12). In a frequently cited passage, Malachi appears to condemn divorce, perhaps in response to the policies of Ezra and Nehemiah, postexilic leaders who forced Judean men to cast off their foreign wives (3:13–16; cf. Ezra 10:3, 44; Neh. 13:23–29; see Chapter 21).

Responding to those who question God's justice (3:17), Malachi declares that Yahweh will intervene to champion the righteous and punish the wicked in a fiery day of judgment. Compiling a "book of remembrance" containing the names of those who revere him, Yahweh will spare them "on the day" that he acts (3:16–18). Although divine fire will consume evildoers, the faithful will behold "the sun of righteousness" rising "with healing in its wings," causing them to leap joyfully "like calves" over the ashes to which the wicked have been reduced. As a forerunner of this "great and terrible day of the LORD"—an eschatological image borrowed from Amos—Yahweh will send his messenger, who in a later verse is identified as the prophet Elijah (4:5).

In editing this collection of anonymous oracles, scribes added two passages to form a brief appendix: a command to observe all the Mosaic "statutes and ordinances" (4:4) and the identification of Elijah. In both Protestant and Catholic editions of the Bible, Malachi appears as the last book of the Old Testament, making its concluding references to Moses and Elijah a thematically effective transition to the New Testament. The prediction that Elijah—who had been carried to heaven, apparently without dying—would return to reconcile "parents to their children" resurfaces in the Gospels, in which John the Baptist is named as the promised harbinger of Jesus (cf. Mark 9:11–12; Matt. 17:9–13).

The Book of Jonah

In both literary form and content, the Book of Jonah differs strikingly from other prophetic works in the Hebrew Bible. Rather than a collection of oracles that address an ethical issue or political emergency, Jonah is a brief narrative relating the misadventures of a prophet who has trouble understanding his God. Set at the time when Assyria dominated the Near East, the story takes the name of its title character from a prophet who lived during the reign of Jeroboam II, an Israelite king who ruled during the eighth century BCE (2 Kings 14:25). Most scholars believe, however, that the book was composed during the postexilic period, when skepticism about prophetic predictions marked the end of Israelite prophecy.

In most prophetic writings, the prophet is described as overcoming his initial resistance to Yahweh's call and then delivering his oracles as divinely commanded. By contrast, **Jonah** is not only reluctant but deliberately disobedient when God summons him to warn the inhabitants of Nineveh, capital of the Assyrian Empire, of impending judgment. When ordered to preach in Nineveh, Jonah—perhaps suspecting that Yahweh's compassion may lead him to spare that hated city—heads in the opposite direction. Aboard a foreign ship sailing to Tarshish (probably Spain) in the remote western Mediterranean, Jonah falls asleep during a raging storm that God has sent to halt his prophet's escape.

Although they are Gentiles (non-Jews) who worship foreign gods, the sailors on Jonah's ship are portrayed as just and reasonable men, open to hearing the word of Israel's God. Casting lots, they learn that Jonah is the cause of the storm that threatens to capsize them, but they are too humane to throw the Israelite jinx overboard. Only after begging Yahweh's forgiveness do they hurl Jonah into the sea, where God has arranged for a large fish to swallow him.

Chapter 2 consists largely of Jonah's desperate prayer from the belly of the sea creature. In this poetic passage, Jonah, begging God to rescue him, likens his predicament to being plunged into the original watery chaos that preceded creation and to the helpless state of the dead in Sheol. Yahweh then orders the fish to spew Jonah out, depositing him onshore.

The author's repeated use of exaggeration and his description of totally improbable events suggest his humorous intent. After Jonah's "resurrection" from the fishy grave, the prophet again hears Yahweh's voice commanding him to go to Nineveh, described as so gigantic a metropolis that it takes three days to walk across it. Announcing his message as brutally as possible in a single sentence—"Forty days more, and Nineveh shall be overthrown!"—Jonah is unpleasantly surprised at the people's reaction. The entire Assyrian population, from the king on down, immediately repents. Even the animals wear sackcloth, a garment of mourning and humiliation, as if they, too, hope that Yahweh will change his mind and spare their city. Approving of the Assyrians' united response, Yahweh rewards them by deciding not to destroy their capital city.

Furious at such divine softheartedness, Jonah disapprovingly quotes the Exodus passage that describes Yahweh as "a gracious God and merciful, slow to anger, and abounding in steadfast love" (Jon. 4:2–3; cf. Exod. 34:6–7; Num. 14:17–19). As Jonah implies, it is one thing for Israel's God to manifest *hesed* (steadfast love) to his own people, but quite another for him to bestow it on a Gentile nation that does not worship him. Feeling betrayed because Yahweh did not validate his preaching by producing a spectacular catastrophe, Jonah asks to die. Yahweh has but one question for him: "Is it right for you to be angry?" (4:5).

While Jonah sulks by himself outside Nineveh's gates, Yahweh attempts to teach his prophet a lesson that might bring him closer to the divine perspective. First causing a leafy bush to grow, providing shade "to save him from his discomfort," Yahweh then sends a worm to kill the plant. Smoldering with resentment, the prophet again asks to die, his death wish contrasting sharply with God's concern for human life (4:6–8).

The book ends with a conversation in which Jonah and his God discuss the meaning of the plant's short life. How, Yahweh asks, can the prophet regret the death of a mere bush and not understand Yahweh's concern for the 120,000 humans living in Nineveh, people who "do not know their right hand from their left, and also many animals?" (4:9–11). The prophet who has learned that nowhere on land or sea can he escape Yahweh's reach is now also asked to think about the implications of Yahweh's universality. As Amos and Second Isaiah recognized, Israel enjoys a special relationship with God but does not have exclusive claim to divine care. The same God who created Israel also directs the destinies of other nations (Amos 9:7; Isa. 42:4–6; 45:1–6). The author does not reveal whether Jonah was able to embrace this larger perspective, leaving the question for readers to ponder.

QUESTIONS FOR DISCUSSION AND REVIEW

1. Haggai and Zechariah were active during the late sixth century BCE when a Judean "remnant" had returned from Babylon to Jerusalem. Although their prophetic oracles were revised by later editors, it is still possible to see that both prophets apparently hoped for a restoration of Davidic rule. Who was Zerubbabel, and what was his expected role in a restoration of the monarchy? What role did Joshua the High Priest play?

2. What benefits did Haggai and Zechariah promise the returned exiles when they completed rebuilding Yahweh's Temple in Jerusalem?

3. How does the work of "Second Zechariah" differ in form and content from the message of the historical prophet? Describe his eschatology.

4. The reality of life under Persian domination in a partly restored Judah contrasted painfully with earlier prophetic expectations, such as those of Second Isaiah. How do you connect postexilic disappointments in the present with Third Isaiah's visions of a future "new heavens and a new earth"?

5. How does Joel envision the coming "Day of Yahweh"? In what different ways will Yahweh's intervention in earthly affairs change things for Israel—and for its enemies?

6. What new twist does Malachi give expectations about the "Day of Yahweh"? How does this involve the return of Elijah? Who is the "messenger of the covenant"?

7. How does Jonah react when Yahweh commands him to prophesy divine judgment on Nineveh? Why does he try to run away? In what ways are his anxieties about Yahweh's mercy, even to Gentiles, justified?

8. The Israelite institution of prophecy began shortly after the creation of the Davidic monarchy and ended a generation or two after its destruction. What reasons can you give for the cessation of prophecy in the postexilic covenant community?

Terms and Concepts to Remember

Elijah, return of
eschatology
Haggai
Joel's visions of cosmic
   destruction
Joel's visions of divine
   inspiration
Jonah's disappointment in
   Nineveh's repentance
Joshua the High Priest
Judea, province of

Malachi's "messenger
   of the covenant"
"new heavens and a new
   earth"
Second Temple
Second Zechariah,
   eschatology of
Third Isaiah
Yahweh's wrath and mercy
Zechariah
Zerubbabel

Recommended Reading

Haggai and Zechariah

Boda, Mark J. H. "Haggai, Book of." In K. D. Sakenfeld, ed., *The New Interpreter's Dictionary of the Bible,* Vol. 2, pp. 715–718. Nashville, TN: Abingdon Press, 2007. A concise review of the book's theological content and historical circumstances.

March, W. Eugene. "The Book of Haggai." In *The New Interpreter's Bible,* Vol. 7, pp. 707–732. Nashville, TN: Abingdon Press, 1996. The full text, with detailed commentary.

Ollenburger, Ben C. "The Book of Zechariah." In *The New Interpreter's Bible,* Vol. 7, pp. 735–840. Nashville, TN: Abingdon Press, 1996. Examines both the historical prophet and later apocalyptic additions to his oracles.

Joel

Achtemeir, Elizabeth. "The Book of Joel." In *The New Interpreter's Bible,* Vol. 7, pp. 301–336. Nashville, TN: Abingdon Press, 1996. The complete text, with annotations.

Nogalski, James D. "Joel, Book of." In K. D. Sakenfeld, ed., *The New Interpreter's Dictionary of the Bible,* Vol, 3, pp. 339–343. Nashville, TN: Abingdon Press, 2008. Examines Joel's date, process of composition, and theological significance.

Third Isaiah (Isaiah 56–66)

Hanson, P. D. *Isaiah 40–66.* Louisville, KY: Westminster John Knox Press, 1995. (See also Christopher R. Seitz for Second Isaiah, "Recommended Reading," Chapter 18.)

Malachi

Ogden, Graham S., and Deutsch, Richard R. *Joel and Malachi: A Promise of Hope, a Call to Obedience.* Grand Rapids, MI: Eerdmans, 1987.

Roncace, Mark "Malachi, Book of." In K. D. Sakenfeld, ed., *The New Interpreter's Dictionary of the Bible,* Vol. 3, pp. 772–777. Nashville, TN: Abingdon Press, 2008. Analyzes questions of authorship, date, and religious message.

Schuller, Eileen M. "The Book of Malachi." In *The New Interpreter's Bible,* Vol. 7, pp. 843–877. Nashville, TN: Abingdon Press, 1996.

Jonah

Trible, Phyllis. "The Book of Jonah." In *The New Interpreter's Bible,* Vol. 7, pp. 463–529. Nashville, TN: Abingdon Press, 1996. A perceptive reading of Jonah's paradoxical view of Israelite prophesy.

———. "Jonah, Book of." In K. D. Sakenfeld, ed., *The New Interpreter's Dictionary of the Bible,* Vol. 3, pp. 375–379. Nashville, TN: Abingdon Press, 2008, Examines Jonah's satirical and theological purpose.

CHAPTER 20

The Writings
Israel's Changing Life with God

Key Topics/Themes The third major division of the Hebrew Bible, the Writings (Kethuvim), was the last to be adopted into the canon. As diverse in content as they are in literary form, the Writings include works ranging from devotional poetry (Psalms), to books of practical and speculative wisdom (Proverbs, Job, and Ecclesiastes), to theological histories reinterpreting Israel's past (1 and 2 Chronicles). Although some books in the Writings, such as the Psalms, contain preexilic material, most of the documents (such as Ezra and Nehemiah) reflect the difficulties of Judah's painful readjustment to life after the exile, when the covenant community was subject to Persian domination.

After the Exile: A Reinterpretation of Judah's Religious Mission

After the Babylonian exile, nothing in the covenant community was ever the same again. Although successive waves of Judean exiles returned to Jerusalem following Cyrus's defeat of Babylon (after 538 BCE), Judah's restoration was only partial. Despite the hopeful prophecies of Haggai and Zechariah (see Chapter 19), neither the Davidic dynasty nor the former state of Judah was restored. Nor, even after the Temple was rebuilt, did the promised "wealth of the nations" flow in to strengthen the impoverished community (cf. Haggai 2:7–9). Known then as the province of Judah (Ezra 5:8)—later called **Judea**—and restricted to a small territory surrounding Jerusalem, the Judean homeland was reduced to a small subunit of the Persian Empire. Except for a brief interval when the Maccabees (Hasmoneans) ruled (142–63 BCE), the Judean people never again enjoyed political independence (see Chapters 21 and 26). Persian administrators, following a policy of promoting local religions in the Persian Empire, supported the reestablishment of Yahweh's cult at the Second Temple, but the harsh reality of postexilic life seemed a mockery of Second

Isaiah's visions of a glorious future. Only a tiny scrap of the land promised to Abraham's descendants was still theirs, and an increasingly large number of Yahweh's people were living far from their homeland in the **Diaspora,** the scattering of Jews abroad in **Gentile** (non-Jewish) nations.

In contrast to the optimistic visions of Second Isaiah, Haggai, and Zechariah, the author of Nehemiah clearly expresses a sense of disappointment in Judah's imperfect restoration:

> Here we are, slaves to this day—slaves in the land you gave to our ancestors to enjoy its fruit and its good gifts. Its rich yield goes to the kings [Persian rulers] whom you have set over us because of our sins, they have power also over our bodies and over our livestock at their pleasure, and we are in great distress.
>
> (Neh. 9:36–37)

The Postexilic Community

Although Persia did not grant the province of Judea political autonomy or allow Davidic heirs to reestablish the throne, it actively encouraged Judah's religious functions. Persian officials significantly influenced the future course of Judaism by ordering an official edition of the Mosaic Torah (Ezra 7:1–26) and by making at least some funds available for reconstructing the Jerusalem sanctuary (Ezra 6:1–15). Instead of being ruled by Davidic kings who strove to make their nation a political force in the Near East, the former subjects of a monarchy now found themselves in a **theocracy,** a "God-ruled" society led by priests. The covenant community's historical transition from an independent kingdom aspiring to play a role in international politics to a people stripped of political influence and subservient to Persian authority also marks a change in the Judeans' understanding of their relationship with Yahweh. No longer governed by divinely appointed kings or involved in the political arena, Judah refocused its energies on its religious mission and priestly responsibilities.

Many of the books included in the Writings illustrate the postexilic community's focus on priestly concerns, particularly Yahweh's formal worship at the Second Temple. In editing this third and final section of the Tanakh, Jewish editors placed the Psalms, a collection of hymns and other songs performed at the Second Temple, as the first book in the Writings. The books of Chronicles, which reinterpret the role of Davidic kings to portray them as enthusiastic supporters of priestly Temple rituals, are given the climactic end position. In this arrangement, the Writings—and the Hebrew Bible as a whole—conclude with the proclamation of Cyrus, king of Persia, who invites Jews from throughout his empire to return to Jerusalem and support Yahweh's sanctuary (2 Chron. 36:22–23).

Between Psalms and Chronicles, which bracket the Writings, editors assembled a richly diverse anthology of sacred literature that differs significantly from other parts of the Hebrew Bible. This diversity in thought and theology contrasts sharply with the relative consistency found in the two earlier parts of the Tanakh. Although derived from many different sources, the material in the Torah is thematically bound together by Yahweh's series of promises to Israel's ancestors and by the provisions of the Mosaic Covenant. The theologically oriented narratives of Joshua through Kings (the Former Prophets) are unified by the authors/editors' controlling intent to show that Israel's tragic history was governed by a single principle, the consequences of disobedience to God's instructions. Even the fifteen books of the Latter Prophets, for all their varied responses to changing political and religious conditions over a period of more than three centuries, form a comparatively unified tradition. In general, the Tanakh's first two divisions unanimously support the Deuteronomistic theory of history, with its rigorous insistence that faithfulness to Yahweh brings national prosperity, whereas disloyalty brings disaster on the entire community. The Writings, however, present a surprisingly wide range of viewpoints, most of them free of Deuteronomistic thought. Books such as Job, Ecclesiastes, and Ruth express ideas sometimes at odds with old assumptions about God and his people that the Torah and Prophets commonly take for granted.

A Brief Survey of the Writings

Placed first in the Writings, Psalms is a compilation of devotional poetry that sets the tone for this part of the Tanakh, which as a whole explores the morally complex nature of the divine–human relationship after the exile. The 150 lyrics in this book show a broad range of religious feeling, from exulting praise of God to bitter complaints about his treatment of Israel. Many were probably composed during the period of the monarchy or sung at the coronation of Davidic kings. Others, however, reflect the postexilic situation, expressing bewilderment and disappointment at Yahweh's apparent failure to honor his promises to David or to provide the national blessings listed in Genesis and Deuteronomy. Raising issues of divine justice that are addressed throughout the Writings, several psalmists confront the painful contrast between the ancient promises and the bleak historical reality. Psalm 89 asks why Yahweh had broken his word to David, to whom God had sworn:

> I will not violate my covenant, or alter the word
> that went forth from my lips.
> Once and for all I have sworn by my holiness:
> I will not lie to David.
> His line shall continue forever,
> and his throne endure before me like the sun . . .

(Ps. 89:34–36; cf. 2 Sam. 7:11–17)

Babylon's overthrow of the Davidic line—never to be restored—appears to contradict God's oath:

> But now you have spurned and rejected him [David
> and his heirs];
> you are full of wrath against your anointed.
> You have renounced the covenant with your servant;
> you have defiled his crown in the dust.

(Ps. 89:38–39)

Yahweh's apparent rejection of the Davidic Covenant, which brought into question the trustworthiness of God's promises, was not the only theological issue that troubled the postexilic Judean community. In striving to understand their God's intentions, devout Judeans confronted another paradox: The more faithful they were to Yahweh, worshiping him exclusively, the more they suffered from injustice and foreign oppression. As the poet of Psalm 44 observes, God's promise to protect those loyal to him—the major premise of Deuteronomy—was not fulfilled in Judah's actual historical experience. In contrast to ancient traditions about Yahweh's saving acts in the remote past, the postexilic God seems indifferent to the massacres and other violence inflicted on his people:

> You have made us [the covenant people] like sheep
>   for slaughter,
> and have scattered us among the nations.
> You have sold your people for a trifle,
> demanding no high price for them.

(Ps. 44:11–12)

Questioning the Deuteronomistic assumption that suffering results from sin, the psalmist insists that his community has kept its Torah obligations:

> All this has come upon us,
> yet we have not forgotten you,
> or been false to your covenant.
> Our heart has not turned back,
> nor have our steps departed from your way,
> yet you have broken us . . .

(Ps. 44:17–19)

Ironically, it is *because* of their commitment to Yahweh that his worshipers suffer:

> *Because of you* we are being killed all day long,
> and counted as sheep for the slaughter.
> Rouse yourself! Why do you sleep, O LORD?
> Awake, do not cast us off forever!
> Why do you hide your face?

(Ps. 44:22–24; emphasis added)

Although the covenant people survived their many afflictions, Yahweh's refusal to come to their aid as he had in the days of Moses or David deeply perplexed many postexilic biblical writers. Why had God so mysteriously "hidden his face"? Why did he seem "asleep," indifferent to his people's sufferings?

Given no answer to the problem of Yahweh's "silence," the psalmists as a group focused on the people's obligations as a worshiping community. Priestly leaders also emphasized the importance of **liturgy,** a body of ceremonial rites performed in public worship (see Chapter 22). The author of 1 and 2 Chronicles devotes considerable space to Temple rituals, describing the duties of singers, priests, Levites, and others in carrying out the sacrifices and other formal practices of Yahweh's cult. In editing the Hebrew Bible, priestly scribes gathered five short books—Ruth, Song of Songs,

Ecclesiastes, Lamentations, and Esther—together to form a small anthology within the Writings. Known as the **Megillot,** or Festival Scrolls, this collection is designed to serve a liturgical purpose. At each of the five principal festivals or days of mourning in the Jewish religious calendar, one of the five documents was read aloud (see Chapter 24). The content of these five works is extremely diverse: Ruth is a gentle love story; Esther, a secular tale justifying Jewish military self-defense; Ecclesiastes, a skeptical meditation on self-contradictory aspects of wisdom and human inability to understand God's purposes; Lamentations, an agonizing reflection on Yahweh's abandonment of Jerusalem; and Song of Songs, a poem celebrating erotic love. All were used to serve the postexilic community's determination to serve Yahweh alone.

The historical narratives of Ezra and Nehemiah, which describe sociopolitical conditions in Judea under Persian domination, emphasize both a reorganization of postexilic society and the importance of teaching *torah* requirements to a depressed population. Both books focus on preserving the covenant community as a worshiping body while subject to foreign control (see Chapter 21). Jewish editors also placed the Book of Daniel among the Writings (although it usually appears among the Prophets in Christian Bibles). Completely unlike anything else in either prophetic, historical, or wisdom literature, Daniel is an **apocalypse,** a "revelation" or "unveiling" of unseen realities in the spirit world and of future events. Scholars believe that Daniel was composed during the mid-second century BCE, a time when foreign rulers briefly tried to force Judeans to give up their Mosaic traditions and adopt Greek religious and social customs (see Chapter 26). Probably the last-written book in the Hebrew Bible, Daniel also deals with issues of keeping Jewish identify and *torah* obligations in the Diaspora, when pressures on Jews to conform to foreign cultures were widespread.

Whereas many books in the Writings are closely associated with Second Temple rituals and/or maintenance of Jewish worship in the Diaspora, other texts explore major issues involving the nature of God and his governance of the universe. Known as wisdom literature, this branch of biblical writing addresses both practical and speculative (theoretical and philosophical) issues. The compilation of largely conventional observations in Proverbs offers commonsense advice on the value of behaving prudently, serving God, and cultivating the good life. In contrast, Job, a book of speculative wisdom, radically departs from most biblical portraits of God, challenging conventional piety to reconcile Yahweh's presumed goodness with the widespread phenomenon of human suffering. As a theodicy, Job raises ethical and theological questions that no religious thinker has yet satisfactorily resolved (see Chapter 23). (Two later Wisdom books, The Wisdom of Jesus Son of Sirach and the Wisdom of Solomon, are discussed with the deuterocanonical works in Chapter 27.)

With a few exceptions, this text discusses the Writings in the canonical order of the Hebrew Bible, beginning with Psalms and ending with 1 and 2 Chronicles. For coherence, however, the wisdom books, including Ecclesiastes, are covered together, with the practical counsel of Proverbs discussed before Job's profound exploration of cosmic justice and the problem of evil. A special case, Daniel is examined in the context of the Maccabean Revolt and the apocalyptic movement (see Chapter 26).

QUESTIONS FOR DISCUSSION AND REVIEW

1. What different categories of literature appear in the third major division of the Hebrew Bible, the Writings. In what ways—subject matter, themes, and theological concerns—do these books typically differ from the Torah and the Prophets?

2. To what new foreign power was the covenant community subjected after Judean exiles returned from Babylon to Jerusalem? How do some passages in the Writings challenge Yahweh for failing to keep his promises to David? Describe the crisis of faith that resulted from the incompleteness of the postexilic restoration.

3. How did Judah's leaders handle the shift in historical circumstances when the covenant community was no longer ruled by a Davidic monarch but became a society led by priests? Which books of the Writings reflect this change?

4. In the Torah, we read of Yahweh's direct intervention in history to rescue his people from Egypt, give them his teachings at Sinai/Horeb, and then use military force to settle them in Canaan. When Second Isaiah predicted that there would be a "new exodus" after Cyrus the Great released Judean captives from Babylon, why did Yahweh not again act decisively to restore his people in a free and independent kingdom? Although the returned exiles obediently rebuilt the Jerusalem Temple and strove to keep Torah regulations, why did God leave them in poverty, dominated by a new foreign empire?

Terms and Concepts to Remember

apocalypse
complaints about Yahweh's inaction
Diaspora
Gentile
Judea, province of
liturgy (in Second Temple)
Megallot/Festival Scrolls
partial postexilic restoration
practical wisdom
priestly theocracy
speculative wisdom

Recommended Reading

Albertz, Rainier. *A History of Israelite Religion in the Old Testament Period*, Vol. 2, *From the Exile to the Maccabees*. Louisville, KY: Westminster John Knox Press, 1994. Traces social and theological developments manifest in documents composed after the exile.

Birch, Bruce C.; Brueggeman, Walter; Fretheim, T. E.; and Petersen, D. L., eds. *A Theological Introduction to the Old Testament*. Nashville, TN: Abingdon Press, 1999. Includes a chapter on postexilic books reflecting multiple crises in Judea's partly restored community.

Collins, John J. "Introduction to Early Jewish Religion." In *The New Interpreter's Bible*, Vol. 1, pp. 284–291. Examines postexilic issues, including the Diaspora and the growth of apocalyptic expectations.

Morgan, D. F. *Between Text and Community: The "Writings" in Canonical Interpretation*. Minneapolis: Augsburg Fortress, 1990. Examines the various canonical books addressing diverse needs of the postexilic community.

CHAPTER 21

The Postexilic Readjustment
The Books of Ezra and Nehemiah

Key Topics/Themes Having lost both political independence and divinely appointed kings, Judean leaders, newly returned from the Babylonian exile, faced enormous difficulties in restructuring the covenant community. The books of Ezra and Nehemiah record the far-reaching changes in social policy and self-perception that characterize the postexilic period, when no significant action could be undertaken without express approval of the Persian government. Persian court officials commission Ezra, a priest and scribe, to return to Jerusalem to teach the Judeans the Mosaic Torah, an edition of which he brings from the community of Babylonian exiles (Ezra 7:12–26). Like Zerubbabel and the High Priest Joshua before them, Ezra and Nehemiah (a Persian-appointed governor of Judea) insist that only the returned exiles form the true Israel and refuse to allow descendants of Judeans who did not go into exile to participate in rebuilding Jerusalem or administering Temple worship. Struggling to maintain Jewish identity without political self-rule, Ezra and Nehemiah vigorously oppose intermarriage with non-Jews, forcing Judean men to divorce their foreign-born wives.

The Book of Ezra

Contemporary scholars generally agree that the books of Ezra and Nehemiah were originally a single volume bearing the name *Ezra* and were only later subdivided into two separate works. Scholars disagree, however, on precisely when these books were written and on their literary relationship to 1 and 2 Chronicles, which are also strongly oriented to priestly concerns. Because the two books describe events spanning the period between about 538 BCE to 400 BCE, it is probably safe to assume that they were written and edited shortly after the latter date, perhaps the early fourth century BCE when Persia still controlled Judea (see Figure 21.1).

Both **Ezra** and **Nehemiah** offer us a theological interpretation of political decisions made in both Persia and Judea. Persian emperors pursued a policy designed to ensure the stability of Persia's far-flung empire (see Figure 21.2), and it seems they regarded both Nehemiah and Ezra as politically reliable figures who could effectively manage the Judean community of returned

exiles. From a Persian viewpoint, uncertainty over the territorial ambitions of Greece and Egypt, as well as the geographical importance of Palestine in the Persian Empire, helped to make the missions of Ezra and Nehemiah diplomatically desirable.

Rebuilding the Temple

The Book of Ezra opens by quoting a royal edict that Cyrus the Great reportedly issued in 538 BCE, permitting Judean exiles living in Babylon to return to Judah for the purpose of rebuilding their ruined Temple. Although no copy of this edict has ever been found, it is certainly consistent with Cyrus's (and later Persian) policy of allowing subject peoples to manage their internal affairs and to worship their national gods. To that end, returning Judeans are given back the sacred vessels that Nebuchadnezzar had looted from the Temple, and under the leadership of one Sheshbazzar, a prince of the exiled royal family, more than 42,000 Judeans make the journey.

By the third chapter, however, Sheshbazzar disappears from the narrative and Zerubbabel, a

FIGURE 21.1 This bas-relief depicts a Persian satrap, or governor. The Persians divided their enormous empire into twenty administrative units called satrapies, each locally autonomous but ruled by the emperor's appointed governor. As the books of Ezra, Nehemiah, and Esther reveal, some upper-class Jews, including those from priestly families, rose to influential positions within the Persian administration. Because the Persians did not permit the restoration of the Davidic royal line, many priests assumed leadership roles in postexilic Judah.

descendant of David, takes over as governor, aided by Joshua the High Priest. As in the books of Haggai and Zechariah, Zerubbabel and Joshua lead in rebuilding the Temple, though not without conflict. Opposition to the rebuilding project comes from two sources: (1) native Israelites of mixed descent, later known as Samaritans, whose offer to help rebuild the sanctuary Zerubbabel and Joshua bluntly reject, and (2) the governor of the province "Beyond the River," an official named Tattenai. Tattenai, who may have viewed a restored Judean Temple (and, still later, rebuilt city walls) as the first stage of a potential political rebellion, challenges the legality of the entire project. This opposition backfires, however, when the new Persian king, **Darius,** orders a search of the royal archives and finds that Cyrus himself had authorized the rebuilding. In a plot twist that writers about Diaspora matters are particularly fond of, Darius not only allows the project to continue but also decrees that Tattenai and his subjects pay for it. The emperor even threatens to punish anyone who impedes the reconstruction effort. As in the Book of Esther, which is set at the Persian court, the Jews' "adversaries" are defeated, and political intrigue becomes the instrument through which God's purposes are accomplished.

Ezra's Mission

When Ezra appears in the narrative (c. 458 BCE), he comes equipped with at least two main goals. King **Artaxerxes** has sent him with a tribute of silver and gold for "the God of Israel, whose dwelling is in Jerusalem" (Ezra 7:15), and with the understanding that he is to reestablish not only the sacrificial system at the newly restored Temple but also a judicial system that will ensure obedience to the laws of Yahweh and of Persia. Ezra, however, has something else in mind. On learning that intermarriage with the surrounding peoples became commonplace during the exile, he openly mourns and denounces the "faithlessness" of the native-born Israelite population. When Israelite men come to him for guidance, he orders them to make a collective confession of sin and to divorce their foreign wives.

However disturbing Ezra's demand may seem to modern religious and social sensibilities, it is not inconsistent with earlier Torah traditions. Deuteronomy's code is particularly stern on this point, defending the ban on intermarriage on specifically religious grounds:

> Do not intermarry with them, giving your daughters to their sons or taking their daughters for your sons, for that would turn away your children from following

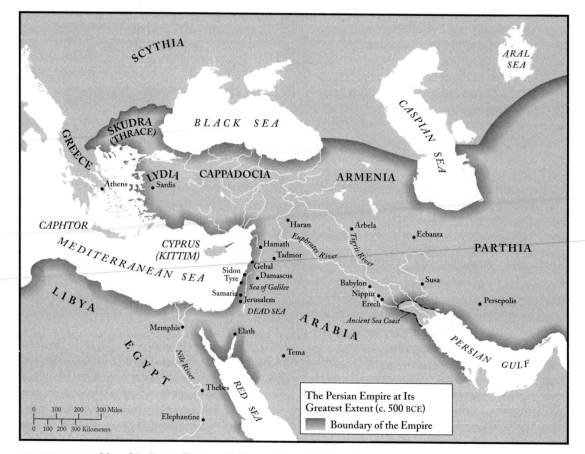

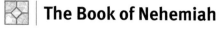

FIGURE 21.2   **Map of the Persian Empire at Its Greatest Extent (c. 500 BCE).**

me, to serve other gods. Then the anger of the LORD would be kindled against you; and he would destroy you quickly.

(Deut. 7:3)

Although some other biblical texts, notably the Book of Ruth, take a much more favorable view of intermarriage, the link between intermarriage and apostasy is commonly emphasized in Deuteronomistic literature. Solomon's unacceptable toleration of foreign cults, for example, is blamed on his love of "foreign women" (1 Kings 11:1–8). To preserve the integrity of the covenant community, Ezra and Nehemiah both insist that intermarriage is yet another expression of Israel's "broken faith" with Yahweh. As a scribe, priest, and teacher of *torah*, Ezra feels compelled not only to reestablish the sacrificial cult but also to mend the covenant relationship, which, as prophets before him had often observed, must be an exclusive one. To underscore the importance of taking partners only within the Judean community, the book ends with a list of men guilty of religiously unacceptable marriages.

The Book of Nehemiah

Originally combined with Ezra, the Book of Nehemiah enlarges our picture of conditions in postexilic Judah and Jerusalem. The account—written in the first person and resembling a personal memoir—opens with a description of Nehemiah's grief when he learns of the miserable conditions in Jerusalem. As an official cupbearer to Emperor Artaxerxes I in Susa, the Persian capital, Nehemiah sheds tears that draw the king's attention. Weeping over reports of the city's poverty and ruin, Nehemiah persuades Artaxerxes (ruled 464–423 BCE) to commission his return to Jerusalem to rebuild the city. Further, the emperor gives Nehemiah both an armed guard and an official letter to guarantee his safe passage back to Judah, as well as instructions to the region's governors to provide him with materials for the rebuilding of the Temple fortress gates and the city walls. But, as in the time of Zerubbabel, Nehemiah's plans for restoration are opposed by the very authorities who are supposed to assist him. (Reconstructing

Jerusalem's defensive walls would naturally increase the city's apparent independence, which Judah's enemies could interpret as resistance to Persian rule.)

Despite strong opposition from Sanballat, the governor in Samaria, and other rival officials, Nehemiah arms his builders with both tools and military weapons, and the city's walls are reconstructed in record time. After Artaxerxes finally appoints Nehemiah governor with a mandate to defend Jerusalem and to lighten the burdens of the common people, he institutes significant economic reforms, such as canceling debts and freeing slaves.

Ezra as Proclaimer of the Torah

At this point in the narrative (Neh. 8:1), Ezra makes his appearance, bringing with him the "book of the law of Moses, which the Lord had given to Israel." Exactly what this "book" contained cannot be determined from the passages that follow, but scholars have long assumed that Ezra's scroll included some portion, if not the whole, of our present Pentateuch. As scholars have long recognized, Ezra's return with Torah scrolls indicates that Mosaic traditions had been compiled and edited during the Babylonian exile. A large crowd gathers in a Jerusalem square to hear Ezra read aloud from his documents, which likely included extensive material judging by the seven days of public readings that Ezra performs. Apparently using a Hebrew text, which most of his postexilic audience did not understand, Ezra then rephrases it in Aramaic, the language most Judeans then spoke, "so that the people understood the reading" (Neh. 8:8). Instructing the people in Mosaic tradition, Ezra urges them to observe the festival of Sukkoth (or Tabernacles), a joyous harvest celebration commemorating the time when Israelites dwelt in huts or "booths" while traveling through the wilderness. In important respects, this scene resembles the covenant renewal ceremonies that Joshua and Josiah had previously led (cf. Josh. 24; 2 Kings 23).

Ezra then delivers a long speech summarizing Israel's history with God, emphasizing Yahweh's patience with his people's many apostasies. He concludes by describing Judah's unhappy present, when the Persians claim not only the land's produce but also the "bodies" of Yahweh's covenant people, reducing them to the status of virtual slaves.

In both Nehemiah and the book that bears his own name, Ezra is far more than a priest, scribe, or even bearer of the Mosaic Torah. He is the one figure from this period who *could* have influenced not only the interpretation of the biblical text but the actual composition as well. As some scholars suggest, Ezra may have been the principal editor responsible for weaving together all the sources of the Torah into a continuous narrative. This view of Ezra's key role is supported by his stature in later Jewish tradition, which sees him as the bearer of the "oral law" of Moses, an oral tradition supplementing that of the written text. In fact, the apocryphal Book of 2 Esdras (the Greek version of Ezra's name) portrays Ezra as a lawgiver second only to Moses himself. In 2 Esdras 14, God inspires Ezra to write ninety-four sacred books. Of these, twenty-four are canonical Scripture—the published Hebrew Bible—and the remaining seventy are reserved for the "wise," who alone can understand them. This passage implies that Ezra replaced the Hebrew Scriptures that the Babylonians had allegedly destroyed. The extrabiblical books are presumably those of the Deuterocanon (the Apocrypha), including apocalyptic works such as 2 Esdras itself.

Clearly, the author of Ezra-Nehemiah regards Ezra as an indispensable link between the pre- and postexilic scribal community. He bears not only the literal artifacts of Israel's covenant with Yahweh but also the interpretive authority that earlier generations vested in the prophets. Ezra's proclamation of the Mosaic Torah, with the full backing of the Persian state, defines Judah as a fundamentally religious community. From this moment in history, the people of Judea—whether in exile or in their native land—can quite legitimately be described as the "people of the book."

Less clear is Ezra's historical connection with Nehemiah and his religious reforms. After delivering his speech on Israel's covenant relationship with Yahweh, Ezra abruptly disappears from Nehemiah's account. In Nehemiah 13, when reading from the "book of Moses" resumes, it is not Ezra but Nehemiah who denounces Judeans who have violated covenant law by marrying women from neighboring counties, such as Ammon and Moab. It is almost as if Ezra's campaign against intermarriage, presumably years earlier, had never taken place. More likely, an overlap in traditions made it possible for editors to attribute essentially the same action or policy to these two different figures.

After being called back to Artaxerxes' court for a time, Nehemiah returns to Judah only to find that the people have, yet again, reverted to type and forgotten their covenant responsibilities. Nehemiah acts swiftly to end widespread neglect of the Sabbath and the equally common practice of intermarriage. In true Deuteronomistic fashion, he reminds his fellow Judeans of the terrible consequences of *torah* disobedience that have already befallen them. Nehemiah then proceeds to "cleanse" Judah of "everything foreign" (13:30) and to reestablish the covenant-centered society Judah was always intended to be. In theory at least, Nehemiah's promotion of a priestly theocracy would reverse the downward spiral of Israel's history. Although the exiles' restoration to their homeland had not brought fulfillment of Second Isaiah's joyous visions of national and world redemption, still Jeremiah's promise of return—"I will bring them back to this place, and I will settle them in safety" (Jer. 32:37)—has at last come to pass.

QUESTIONS FOR DISCUSSION AND REVIEW

1. Which figure in Persian history made it possible for the Judeans exiled in Babylon to return to their homeland? What was Persian policy toward Judea thereafter? What were its benefits and disadvantages for the Judeans?

2. Why do Ezra and Nehemiah pressure Israelite men to divorce their non-Israelite wives? How would the author of the Book of Ruth have responded to this demand?

3. In the books of Ezra and Nehemiah, we witness Ezra, a priest, scribe, and interpreter of Israel's past, proclaiming—with the backing of the Persian government—his edition of the Mosaic Torah. Explain how we are thus observing a profound shift toward the postexilic community's becoming a *torah*-centered society, a shift of religious authority from prophets who orally deliver Yahweh's words to priests who interpret a written Torah.

Terms and Concepts to Remember

Artaxerxes	Esdras
Cyrus	Samaritan
Diaspora	theocracy

Recommended Reading

Blenkinsopp, Joseph. *Ezra–Nehemiah: A Commentary*. Philadelphia: Westminster Press, 1988.

Klein, Ralph W. "The Books of Ezra and Nehemiah." In *The New Interpreter's Bible*, Vol. 3, pp. 661–851. Nashville, TN: Abingdon Press, 1999. Explains the postexilic Judeans' difficult situation under foreign domination.

———. "Ezra and Nehemiah, Books of." In K. D. Sakenfeld, ed., *The New Interpreter's Dictionary of the Bible*, Vol. 2, pp. 398–404. Nashville, TN: Abingdon Press, 2007. A concise introduction to the literary, historical, and religious issues that these two books present.

CHAPTER 22

Worshiping at the Second Temple
Hebrew Poetry and the Book of Psalms

Key Topics/Themes A major component of the Writings, Hebrew poetry typically uses the techniques of metaphor and parallelism to convey its meaning. An anthology of devotional lyrics, the Book of Psalms encompasses a broad range of responses to Israel's ever-changing historical experience, particularly the extended theological crisis that followed Babylon's destruction of Judah in 587 BCE. The collection of 150 poems, traditionally divided into five separate books, represents a variety of poetic forms that are generally classified according to their literary form and/or content, such as songs of praise, lament, and thanksgiving.

Hebrew Poetry

Approximately one-third of the Hebrew Bible is written in poetry. The Pentateuch and the Deuteronomistic History contain numerous short poems, ranging from Adam's heart-felt verse about Eve's creation (Gen. 2:23), to Miriam's song at the Reed Sea (Exod. 15:21), to Deborah's victory hymn (Judg. 5:1–31), to David's lament over Jonathan's death (2 Sam. 1:19–27). Poems are also scattered intermittently throughout the prose narratives in Genesis through 2 Kings. And many books in the Latter Prophets and the Writings are composed almost entirely in poetry, including not only the oracles of Isaiah, Jeremiah, Ezekiel, and the Twelve but also Psalms, Proverbs, Lamentations, and Job.

Simile, Metaphor, and Allegory

Like those of other cultures, Hebrew poets use a variety of rhetorical devices to achieve their effect. In the Song of Songs, two lovers are shown joyfully comparing each other's bodies to luscious fruits, domestic and wild animals, and even topographical features, celebrating in sometimes comical or even almost grotesque imagery their own delight in sexual love. Employing a series of **similes**—comparisons using "as" or "like"—the speaker admires his beloved's luxuriant hair and complete set of dazzling white teeth:

> Your hair is like a flock of goats,
> moving down the slopes of Gilead.
> your teeth are like a flock of shorn ewes
> that have come up from the washing,
> all of which bear twins,
> and not one of them is bereaved.

(Song of Sol. 4:1-2)

The poetic complaints in Lamentations also evoke strong emotions, but these are feelings of pain and sorrow at the desolation of Jerusalem. Here, the poet uses a **metaphor,** an implied comparison that portrays the city as a captive woman, dirty and dressed in rags:

> Her uncleanness was in her skirts;
> she took no thought of her future;
> her downfall was appalling,
> with none to comfort her.

(Lam. 1:9)

Mixing prose passages with short poems, Ecclesiastes offers an emotionally detached contrast to Lamentations' passionate grief, citing traditional—and sometime contradictory—examples of proverbial wisdom in poetic couplets. Yet the author concludes his skeptical comments with a singularly haunting poem that implicitly compares the body of a dying man to an old house. Creating a poetic **allegory**—a narrative in which one object or action functions as a symbol of something else—the author depicts the weakness and failing senses of extreme age as an old, crumbling house:

> . . . in the day when . . . the women who grind cease working because they are few, and those who look through the windows see dimly; when the doors on the street are shut, and the sound of the grinding is low . . .
>
> (Eccles. 12:3–4)

Unable to chew, see, or hear, the aged person prepares for his "eternal home," the grave.

Parallelism

In contrast to English poetry and that of other Western nations, Hebrew poetry does not use rhyme or regular meter, although many lines have a strongly rhythmic quality. Instead, the biblical poetic line is notable for its brevity, repetition of key words or phrases, vivid imagery, and, above all, various kinds of parallelism. The most characteristic feature of Hebrew poetry, **parallelism** involves expressing similar ideas in similar verbal structures. In *synonymous* parallelism, an idea presented in the first line is repeated in slightly different words in the second, a device the psalmists frequently employ:

> The heavens are telling the glory of God,
> and the firmament proclaims his handiwork. (Ps. 19:1)
>
> Praise the LORD, all you nations!
> Extol him, all you peoples! (Ps. 117:1)
>
> For who is God except the LORD [Yahweh]?
> And who is a rock besides our God? (Ps. 18:31)

In one of the many variations of synonymous parallelism, the second line offers a specific example to illustrate the general statement made in the first. In Psalm 106, the poet cites a notorious instance in which the Israelites proved ungrateful to the God who had rescued them from Egypt:

> Our ancestors, when they were in Egypt,
> did not consider your wonderful works;
> they did not remember the abundance of your
>   steadfast love,
> but rebelled against the Most High at the Red Sea.
>
> (Ps. 106:7)

A set of two couplets from the same poem emphasizes related aspects of Israel's deliverance by repeating the first statement in parallel but slightly different form:

> He rebuked the Red Sea, and it became dry;
> he led them through the deep as through a desert.
> So he saved them from the hand of the foe,
> and delivered them from the hand of the enemy.
>
> (Ps. 106:9–10)

In *antithetical* parallelism, one line makes a statement, and the next line expresses its opposite. Proverbs offers many examples of this form:

> A wise child makes a glad father,
> but a foolish child is a mother's grief. (Prov. 10:1)
>
> A slack hand causes poverty,
> but the hand of the diligent makes rich. (Prov. 10:4)
>
> The clever see danger and hide;
> but the simple go on, and suffer for it. (Prov. 22:3)

Symbolic or *formal* parallelism is not, strictly speaking, parallelism at all. In this poetic form, the first line expresses a thought, the second adds a new idea, and the third completes the statement. David's lament over the fallen Saul and Jonathan illustrates this pattern:

> I am distressed for you, my brother Jonathan;
> greatly beloved were you to me,
> your love to me was wonderful,
> passing the love of women.
>
> (2 Sam. 1:26)

Personification

In some poetic books, such as Proverbs, the author employs **personification,** the giving of human attributes to an idea or abstract concept, such as wisdom. Proverbs depicts divine Wisdom, God's primary attribute, as a woman who roams city streets, imploring foolish young men to listen to her and avoid her opposite, the "loose woman," whose ways lead to death (Prov. 8:1–11; cf. 1:20–33; 2:16–22; 5:3–23). In Proverbs 8, the writer personifies Lady Wisdom as God's firstborn, not only giving her cosmic stature but also making her the mediator between the human and divine realms:

> Before the mountains had been shaped,
> before the hills, I was brought forth . . .
> When he established the heavens,
> I was there . . .
> then I was beside him, like a master worker,
> and I was daily his delight . . .
>
> (Prov. 8:25, 27, 30)

Existing before the created world, Lady Wisdom serves as a witness to the stages by which the cosmos developed, her balanced phrases offering firsthand testimony to

God's creative activity. With its rhythmic repetitiveness, concrete images, and varieties of parallelism, biblical poetry awakens the imagination and stirs the feelings, inspiring readers to wonder and reflect.

The Book of Psalms

For many readers, the Book of Psalms contains the finest examples of Hebrew poetry. Consisting of 150 individual lyrics composed at different times over a span of perhaps six centuries, this poetic collection expresses virtually the full range of Israelite religious experience. From the heights of spiritual ecstasy to the depths of despair, Israel's poets respond in amazingly diverse ways to the ever-changing historical circumstances that affected their relationship to Yahweh. In the Torah and through the prophets, Israel's God speaks to his covenant people; in the Psalms, the community replies to God, exulting in his glorious presence or grieving over his mysterious absences from Israel's communal life.

A distinguishing feature of this collection is its emphasis on the Davidic monarchy. Both the poets who created the individual psalms and the editors who later compiled and edited them (the redactors) were profoundly attached to the House of David. Whereas some of the older psalms were written to commemorate events when David's descendants still ruled Israel—such as the coronation and enthronement of kings—others were composed long after the Babylonians had brought a permanent end to the monarchy. Like Isaiah of Jerusalem, the prophet who emphasized Yahweh's special relationship to David's royal line, many of the preexilic psalmists celebrated the close link between Israel's God and his anointed rulers. After the exile, some poets continued to evoke hopes connected with the Davidic Covenant, although they most typically emphasized the kingship of Israel's true ruler, Yahweh.

Despite their thematic association with the Davidic monarchy, the psalms are as diverse in religious feeling as they are in historical origin. Ranging from declarations of complete trust and confidence in divine protection (Pss. 23 and 91) to sorrowful complaints about God's apparent failure to shield his people from disaster (Pss. 44 and 89 [quoted in Chapter 20]), the psalms explore both the heights and the depths of Israel's troubled partnership with Yahweh.

The book's title comes from the Greek *psalmoi,* which refers to instrumental music and, by extension, the words accompanying the music. In translating the psalms, the editors of the Septuagint used *psalmoi* to render the Hebrew title *Tehillim,* which means "praises." Although each psalm has its own compositional history, as a collection, the psalms represent the lyrics performed—to the accompaniment of pipes, trumpets, flutes, harps, cymbals, tambourines, and other musical instruments—at the Second Temple as part of Yahweh's worship.

"Davidic" Authorship

The tradition that David composed the psalms probably owes much to his popular reputation as a musician and poet (1 Sam. 16:23; Amos 6:5). Phrases such as "of David" that later editors attached to particular psalms may mean only that the psalm thus marked is "in the manner of David" or that it concerns one of David's royal successors. (Grammatically, this phrase, in Hebrew, may also indicate that a particular poem was written *for* a Davidic prince.) Besides associating many psalms with Israel's idealized king, editors noted that other poets also contributed to the anthology: Psalm 72 is attributed to Solomon, Psalm 90 to Moses, and various others to Asaph and the sons of Korah. Numerous psalms are clearly post-Davidic, such as Psalm 72, which laments the destruction of the Jerusalem Temple, and Psalm 137, which describes conditions during the Babylonian exile. Of the 150 psalms, 116 have titles or superscriptions indicating authorship, setting, or directions to the Temple musicians. All such notations are probably later scribal additions to the texts.

Categories of Psalms

Early in the twentieth century, Hermann Gunkel pioneered modern techniques of analyzing the psalms critically, classifying them according to their literary form, presumed liturgical function, or topical content. As Gunkel found, different psalms take different forms, in part depending on the occasion for which they were composed, such as royal coronations or weddings, laments for personal or national suffering, petitions for divine help, and songs of thanksgiving for help received. Although scholars now recognize that many psalms combine different literary categories— such as mixing lament with praise and expressions of trust—and that some are too distinctively individual to be labeled at all, Gunkel's basic classifications remain useful.

Hymns or Songs of Praise In composing songs of praise, the poet typically cites specific reasons for which God deserves Israel's worship: his creation of the world and his saving actions in Israel's history. Psalm 8 honors

God for establishing an orderly universe, fashioning humanity in his divine image, and placing human beings, who are only a "little lower than God," at the apex of his earthly hierarchy:

> You have given them [humanity] dominion
> over the work of your hands;
> you have put all things under their feet.

(Ps. 8:6)

Psalm 104, which seems to be a Hebrew poet's revision of a much older Egyptian hymn to the solar deity that Pharaoh Akhenaton worshiped, pays tribute to Yahweh's strength and creative wisdom:

> You stretch out the heavens like a tent,
> you set the beams of your chambers on the waters,
> you make the clouds your chariot,
> you ride on the wings of the wind, . . .

(Ps. 104:2–3)

Although they were composed at different times, both Genesis 1 and Psalm 104 picture God as subduing "the deep," the primal chaotic waters (104:5). Other psalms, however, evoke ancient myths in which Yahweh had to fight primordial "dragons," monsters of chaos such as Leviathan:

> You divided the sea by your might;
> you broke the heads of the dragons in the waters.
> You crushed the heads of Leviathan;
> you gave him as food for the creatures of the
>   wilderness . . .
> you dried up ever-flowing streams [waters of the abyss].

(Ps. 74:12–15; cf. Isa 27:1)

Echoing Baal's mythical battle against Yamm (the all-encompassing sea) and Marduk's violent splitting in two of Tiamat, the primal sea, Psalm 89 shows Yahweh conquering Rahab, a personification of watery chaos:

> You rule the raging of the sea;
> when its waves rise, you still them.
> You crushed Rahab like a carcass;
> you scattered your enemies with your mighty arm.

(Ps. 89:9–10)

In addition to his acts of creative power, God is to be praised for his faithfulness in guiding and directing Israel's history. Psalm 78 surveys Yahweh's mighty deeds in rescuing Israel from Egypt, nurturing his people in the Sinai wilderness, and choosing David to shepherd the covenant community. In those ancient days, the poet recalls, Yahweh aroused himself from sleep to fight for Israel:

> Then the LORD awoke as from sleep,
> like a warrior shouting because of wine.
> He put his adversaries to rout . . .

(Ps. 78:65–66)

Psalm 105 similarly reviews Israel's distant past, when Yahweh made his promises to Abraham and Jacob, brought plagues upon his people's Egyptian oppressors, and turned the Canaanites' territory over to Israelite tribes.

A subset of the psalms of praise, known as the "Songs of Zion," centers on Jerusalem, the city made holy by God's invisibly dwelling in the Temple that stood on **Zion.** A prominent hill in Jerusalem that the psalmists endow with the qualities of Eden, Zion was traditionally the original site of God's earthly visitations (Pss. 46, 48, 84, 87, 122). Two of these psalms (46 and 48) seem to reflect a belief in Zion's invincibility, a confidence that it could never be conquered because Yahweh had placed his "name" there. Whereas Isaiah of Jerusalem supported this view of Zion, Jeremiah definitely did not, predicting that it would be overrun by Babylonian armies (see Chapter 17).

Psalms of Thanksgiving   Psalms of thanksgiving are typically prayers offered in gratitude for God's having saved or delivered the psalmist from danger (Pss. 18, 30, 40, 66, 116, 118). They commonly begin with expressions of praise, describe the situation that formerly threatened or troubled the poet—such as life-threatening illness, dangers of war, or the plots of enemies—and gratefully acknowledge God as the source of deliverance. In Psalm 30, the poet compares his former suffering to a descent into Sheol, the Underworld housing the dead:

> O LORD [Yahweh], you brought my soul from Sheol,
>   restored me to life from among those gone down to
>   the pit.

(Ps. 30:3)

In his distress, the poet reminds God that he will gain nothing by allowing his servant to die, for Sheol's eternally silent inhabitants can offer him no worship:

> To you, O LORD, I cried, . . .
> "What profit is there in my death,
> if I go down to the pit?
> Will the dust praise you?
> Will it tell of your faithfulness?"

(Ps. 30:8–9)

Now that Yahweh has rescued the poet from death, turning his "mourning into dancing," his worshiper can rejoin the living to praise God at his Temple. (For a description of Sheol, see Box 23.1.)

Laments Poems that emphasize sorrow, grief, mourning, or regret are classified as laments or complaints and feature both individual and communal psalms. Some individual laments, such as Psalm 55, are personal petitions that first praise God and then ask for rescue from the psalmists' enemies or for vengeance on them. Although many laments are concerned with forgiveness of personal sins (Pss. 38, 51), some are genuine complaints, implying that God has been unaccountably slow to redress injustice (Pss. 10, 58, 59).

Psalm 22, which opens with the plaintive cry "My God, my God, why have you forsaken me?" is a mixed genre, combining lament with praise. Following graphic descriptions of the poet's suffering, the psalm introduces a petition begging for God's help (22:1–21). Although the poem begins in bleak despair, after the petition (22:19–21), it changes abruptly to an exulting hymn of praise that culminates in a confident declaration of Yahweh's sovereignty (22:22–29). In the last two lines, the poet declares that both he and "a people yet unborn" will "proclaim [God's] deliverance," ensuring a continuity of worship into the far-distant future (22:30–31). With its striking contrast between the poet's initial grief and his later resolve to praise Yahweh, this lament, moving from sorrow to joy, illustrates an important theme in the Psalms. Although Yahweh's people may endure almost unbearable pain, their God remains present with them, an everlasting source of spiritual renewal. Redemption, in fact, is found in the midst of suffering. (Two Gospel writers show Jesus quoting the first line of Psalm 22 as his last words [see Chapter 30].)

Several communal laments focus on the Babylonian conquest that stripped Israel of its essential identity and institutions, including land, kingship, and sanctuary. Gunkel observed that many of these collective laments follow a structural pattern, typically beginning with an invocation that addresses God. Psalm 74, a communal dirge lamenting the Temple's destruction, asks the Deity if this national calamity means that he has permanently severed his covenant ties:

> O God, why do you cast us off forever?
> Why does your anger smoke against the sheep of
>   your pasture?

(Ps. 74:1)

In the second part, the complaint, the psalm specifies the reasons for the lament. In Psalm 74, God is invited to inspect the pitiful ruin of his holy place:

> Pick your steps over these endless ruins:
> the enemy have sacked everything in the sanctuary.
> They roared where your assemblies used to take
>   place, . . .
> Axes deep in the wood, hacking at the panels,
> they battered them down with mallet and hatchet;
> then, God, setting fire to your sanctuary,
> they profanely razed the house of your name to the
>   ground.

(Ps. 74:3–4, 6–7)

The poem next opposes the lament with a confession of trust, asserting the poet's reliance on God. After citing Yahweh's mythic battle against Leviathan, recalling his primordial triumphs, Psalm 74 affirms God's continuing mastery of creation, manifest in earth's seasonal cycles:

> Yours is the day, yours also the night;
> you established the luminaries and the sun.
> You have fixed all the bounds of the earth;
> you made summer and winter.

(Ps. 74:16–17)

The expression of confidence in Yahweh's ability to act is followed by a petition in which God is asked to take action to remedy the problem. Urging God not to "forget" his worshipers, the poet asks him to "remember" both the invaders who publicly defiled his holy place and the covenant people who depend on his vindication:

> Remember this, O LORD, how the enemy scoffs,
> and an impious people reviles your name.
> Do not deliver the soul of your dove to the wild
>   animals; . . .
> Have regard for your covenant, . . .
> Rise up, O God, plead your cause. . . .

(Ps. 74:18, 20, 22)

Although absent in two of the greatest communal laments, Psalms 44 and 74, some complaints close with a statement of thanksgiving in which the poet vows to proclaim what God has accomplished in the past.

Psalm 44, which also displays Gunkel's pattern of lament, contrasts the mighty deeds Yahweh performed in the remote past—actions the current generation has only heard about—with the misery the people experience in the present. This lament is particularly noteworthy for its rejection of the traditional Deuteronomistic view that only disobedience will bring disaster to the covenant community. The psalmist flatly states that the people (at least in his day) have remained faithful to their covenant vows and that they suffer simply because they keep Yahweh as their God. After describing the slaughters and humiliations their enemies regularly inflict on the faithful, the poet declares:

> All this has come upon us, yet we have not
> forgotten you,
> or been false to your covenant.
> Our heart has not turned back,
> nor have our steps departed from your way;
> yet you have broken us . . .
> Because of you we are being killed all day long,
> and accounted as sheep for the slaughter.

(Ps. 44:17–19, 22)

These communal laments, including the second half of Psalm 89, which implies that God has broken his sworn oath, collectively advance a persistent theme: God takes no action in the present and seems to have forgotten his ancient promises. In preparing their final edition of Book of Psalms, editors intermixed these laments with royal psalms—songs focusing on the Davidic kings—and enthronement psalms—lyrics praising Yahweh as Israel's eternal ruler. This juxtaposition of negative and positive theological confessions effectively mirrors the community's collective sorrows and joys as it struggles to find God in both darkness and light.

Royal Psalms Classified by their content rather than their literary form, royal psalms deal with events and issues involving Davidic kings. Scattered throughout the entire collection, royal psalms vary widely in subject and mood, ranging from the celebration of a royal wedding (Ps. 45) or the coronation of a new ruler (Pss. 2, 72, and perhaps 110) to laments over God's apparent failure to honor his pledge to David. As noted in Chapter 20, Psalm 89 first reviews God's unconditional terms of the Davidic Covenant and then contrasts the divine oaths with the historical fact that the dynasty has been overthrown. The first two psalms serve as a general introduction to the whole book, raising the issue of divinely ordained kingship. Psalm 2 opens by describing a revolt against "the LORD [Yahweh] and his anointed," directly associating the rule of God with political submission to his earthly representative, Israel's king. As previously explained, each Davidic ruler is Yahweh's **anointed**—a priest has rubbed holy oil on the king's head at the time of his installation in office. Historically, the psalm's allusion to rebellious kings probably refers to princes of neighboring states, such as Edom or Moab, who attempted to break free from Israel's domination after the death of a Davidic ruler and before his successor could consolidate his position. Viewed as part of the collection as a whole, however, this psalm also presents an important theological concept: Davidic monarchs may have been God's agents for governing his people, but Yahweh himself is Israel's real king. An assertion that Yahweh rules the world, with or without Davidic kings and despite apparently unending human oppositions, is perhaps Psalms' most significant message.

In Psalm 110, Yahweh addresses the king as "my lord," vowing to subdue his enemies and shatter all opposition. Surprisingly, the psalmist announces that Israel's anointed sovereign is also a priest:

> The LORD [Yahweh] has sworn and will not change
> his mind,
> "you [the king] are a priest forever
> according to the order of Melchizedek."

(Ps. 110:4)

This passage is unique in connecting a ruler with the mysterious figure of Melchizedek, the king-priest of Salem to whom Abraham paid tithes (Gen. 14:17–20). As many scholars have noted, the poet's attempt to present the king as both monarch and priest suggests that this particular psalm was composed, not for a Davidic king, but for one of the Hasmoneans. After the Maccabean Revolt (second century BCE), the Hasmoneans—a Levite family—founded a non-Davidic dynasty that ruled Judea from about 142 to 63 BCE. Although they were not descendants of Aaron, founder of Israel's priestly class, the Hasmoneans took over the office of High Priest, as well as that of king (see Chapters 26 and 27). They may have tried to legitimize their holding both offices by claiming descent from the king-priest Melchizedek. If this theory is correct, psalms that eventually became part of the canon were still being composed in the late second or early first century BCE.

Enthronement Psalms Although the Davidic dynasty ceased to rule in 587 BCE, hope remained, at least in some circles, that Yahweh would someday remember his vow and appoint a descendant of David to lead his people. The explicit, unequivocal language of the Davidic Covenant assured that in some future generation God would at last "remember" his word. In the meantime, the covenant community emphasized that Yahweh still reigned, over the "nations" as well as Judah. The enthronement psalms (93, 95–99) extol Yahweh as supreme monarch—"a great King above all gods" (95:3). "Exalted far above all gods," he is "most high over all the earth" (97:9). His ceaseless reign is evident not only in the mystery and beauty of nature (93:3–4; 96:6) but also in his "righteousness" and "truth" (96:13). Divine rule is perhaps most evident in Yahweh's strengthening presence among believers (97:10–12). Despite human

The Book of Proverbs

Whereas examples of speculative wisdom, such as Job and Ecclesiastes, deal with inquiries into the nature of God and the purpose of human life, the Book of Proverbs is devoted to practical wisdom, guiding readers to find their proper place in Israel's social and religious order. *Proverb* translates from the Hebrew term *mashal*, which means a "statement of truth" or "standard of appropriate behavior." The biblical proverb, based on observation and experience rather than divine revelation, typically gives advice on how to apply wisdom to everyday life, particularly in acquiring the correct social attitudes and behaviors that foster prosperity and respect. Many are purely material in tone:

> The wealth of the rich is their fortress;
> the poverty of the poor is their ruin.

(Prov. 10:15)

We are here given an obvious fact of life: Riches give security, and poverty the opposite.

For all the book's assurances that a good life will be Yahweh's reward to the wise, some proverbs are realistic enough to recognize that prosperity is never universal and that happiness is only a relative good. One saying even cautions that ambition for material gain may have too high a cost:

> Better is a dry morsel with quiet
> than a house full of feasting
> with strife.

(Prov. 17:1)

Agur, one of the few authors identified in the collection, resembles a Greek philosopher in counseling a "golden mean" between the unrestrained pursuit of wealth and the poverty that leads to crime:

> . . . Give me neither poverty nor riches;
> feed me with the food that I need,
> or I shall be full, and deny you,
> and say, "Who is the LORD?"
> or I shall be poor, and steal,
> and profane the name of my God.

(Prov. 30:8–9)

Agur's recognition that religious attitudes and behaviors are partly shaped by economic circumstances is rare in biblical literature, occurring only in wisdom writings.

Like much wisdom literature, Proverbs is not distinctively Israelite; most of its admonitions could apply

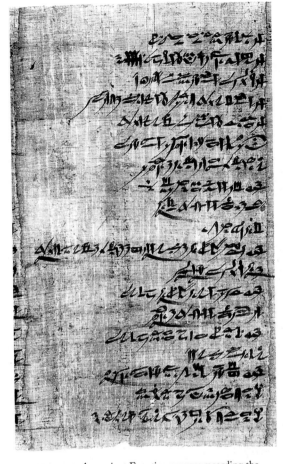

FIGURE 23.1 An ancient Egyptian papyrus recording the Wisdom of Amenemope (c. 1200 BCE) contains sage advice that was later incorporated in the Book of Proverbs (22:17–24:22). The wisdom movement permeated virtually the entire ancient Near East, creating an international legacy shared by Egypt, Mesopotamia, and Israel.

equally well in a society totally different from Israel's theocracy:

> Those who are kind reward themselves,
> but the cruel do themselves harm

(Prov. 11:17)

It is not surprising, then, that scholars have found close parallels to biblical proverbs in writings from Mesopotamia and Egypt. Indeed, a whole passage from the wisdom book of the Egyptian sage Amenemope was reprinted almost word for word in Proverbs 22:17–24:22 (see Figure 23.1). Scholars now realize that proverbs and other wisdom writings were produced in many different Near Eastern cultures and that Israel's sages in some cases borrowed from older literary collections.

King Solomon's Influence

Because King Solomon, who was credited with more than 3,000 proverbs (1 Kings 4:29–33), traditionally has been associated with the production of wise sayings, the superscription ascribing Proverbs to Solomon (Prov. 1:1) may mean no more than that these proverbs are written in the manner of Solomon. In fact, the book itself reveals something of the diversity of its sources by citing the wisdom teachers Agur (Prov. 30:1–14) and Lemuel (Prov. 31:1–9), about whom we know nothing apart from their sayings in the collection. Like the Psalms, Proverbs probably grew from many sources over a span of centuries.

Highlighting the transmission of knowledge from generation to generation, the Book of Proverbs commonly presents traditional wisdom as parental advice:

> Hear, my child, your father's instruction,
> and do not reject your mother's teachings . . .

> (Prov. 1:8)

The book's underlying assumption is that the younger generation has much to learn from the collective experience of earlier generations. This view of the superior wisdom of the elders is typical of most traditional cultures, and it would have appealed to teachers connected to Israel's most honored institutions—the royal court and the Temple. It is not unlikely, therefore, that some of the earliest wisdom teachers served as royal counselors or scribes whose task it was to train young men as scholars or diplomats, to prepare them for taking their elders' place in Israel's court bureaucracy.

The Value of Wisdom

A major motive of wisdom writers-as-parents is to teach young men the folly of acting on impulse (particularly sexual impulses) and the need for diligence and proper ambition. Admonitions to work hard and not be idle— "Go to the ant, you lazybones, consider its ways, and be wise" (Prov. 6:6)—are typically coupled with warnings against bad companions and seductive women. Although most of this advice is intended for young males, some is directed at young women as well. Proverbs' concluding chapter features an acrostic poem (in which every line in the Hebrew text begins with a different letter of the Hebrew alphabet in alphabetical order) that describes the character and duties of the ideal wife and mother. Her life obviously revolves around the home, and her sterling qualities are intended to enhance both the wealth and the well-being of her husband:

> A capable wife who can find?
> She is more precious than jewels. . . .

> She seeks wool and flax,
> and works with willing hands. . . .
> She considers a field and buys it;
> with the fruit of her hands
> she plants a vineyard. . . .
> She looks well to the ways of her household,
> and does not eat the bread of idleness.

> (Prov. 31:10–27)

Clearly the portrait of an energetic housewife in a well-to-do family, this description expresses Proverbs' conservative ideal that values a stable domestic arrangement governed by prudence and productive labor.

Heavenly Wisdom

A totally different portrayal of feminine wisdom appears in Proverbs 8, where a poet describes Yahweh's heavenly companion, commonly known as "Lady Wisdom." Whereas Folly (lack of knowledge or common sense) is likened to a prostitute who corrupts young men, Wisdom is personified as a noble woman who seeks to save youths from their own inexperience and bad judgment. This divinely created Wisdom first appears in Proverbs 1, where she is shown calling from the streets and housetops, promising rich treasure to those not too ignorant to value her. The writer's praise of Wisdom reaches a climax when she reveals her heavenly origin and cosmic role as the first element of God's creation:

> The LORD created me at the
> beginning of his work,
> the first of his acts of long ago . . .
> Before the mountains had been shaped,
> before the hills, I was brought forth—
> when he had not yet made earth
> and fields,
> or the world's first bits of soil.
> When he established the heavens, I
> was there,
> when he drew a circle on the face of the deep,
> when he made firm the skies above, . . .
> then I was beside him, like a master worker . . .

> (Prov. 8:22–30)

As the "beginning" of God's creative work, Wisdom is honored as if she were both the eldest and most influential advisor in Yahweh's heavenly council (see Chapter 39). Despite portraying her as though she were a celestial being distinct from God, however, the poet clearly intends to depict Wisdom primarily as a personification of a divine quality, an attribute of Yahweh by which he wisely shaped the cosmos and through which he communicates to humans. Later Jewish and

Christian thinkers, however, interpreted Wisdom's role quite differently. Philo Judaeus, a Jewish scholar living in Alexandria, Egypt, during the first century CE, identified biblical Wisdom with the Greek philosophic concept of the Logos (Word), by which God created the universe. (Whereas "Logos" is masculine in Greek, both the Hebrew [*Hochmah*] and Greek [*Sophia*] terms for "wisdom" are feminine, a factor that may have influenced Philo's patriarchal thinking.) In the Gospel of John, the author identifies Jesus of Nazareth with the divine Logos (Word), the agent through whom God fashioned the world (John 1:1–14; see Chapter 33).

The Book of Job

Whereas the Book of Proverbs assumes that wisdom lies in bringing one's life into harmony with Yahweh's orderly universe, the Book of Job radically attacks comfortable religious assumptions about divine order. A bold challenge to traditional views of God, Job dramatizes the plight of an innocent man whose intellectual honesty prevents him from portraying himself as sinful in order to validate conventional ideas about divine justice. Asserting his right to be heard, Job demands that God, who is both Accuser and Judge, appear in court to offer evidence that would justify treating a righteous person as if he were a criminal (see Figure 23.2). Cosmic in scope, Job ranges throughout the traditional three-story universe, from sessions of the divine council in heaven, to images of an earthly courtroom where God is figuratively placed on trail, to descriptions of Sheol, the underground place of the dead (see Figure 5.1). The book's climax occurs when Yahweh appears to Job in a storm, delivering two long speeches in which he chillingly describes the nature of his universe.

Issues of the Postexilic Age Although scholars do not agree on when Job was written, the general time of its composition can be inferred from the theological issues it confronts. The oldest surviving reference to the title character was recorded during the Babylonian exile, when Ezekiel mentioned three ancient figures who were considered models of righteousness: Noah, Danel (probably not the biblical Daniel), and Job (Ezek. 14:14, 20). Although Ezekiel says nothing specific about Job, he may have had in mind a tradition about Job's patience while suffering, a theme emphasized in the canonical book's first two chapters (Job 1:22; 2:9–10). In its questioning of God's right to prosecute a person of unusual goodness "for no reason" (2:3), however, the book is far more than a conventional

FIGURE 23.2 The cuneiform script on this clay tablet narrates a Sumerian variation of the Job story. Like the Book of Job, this text records the humiliating ordeals of a righteous man who nonetheless clings to his faith and is at last delivered from his undeserved sufferings. The problem of evil, with its conflict between the concept of a benign God and the fact of unmerited human pain, was a perplexing theme explored in Egyptian, Babylonian, and Israelite literature.

lesson about loyalty under severe testing. The Tanakh's most fully developed **theodicy**—a literary attempt to reconcile beliefs about divine goodness with the prevalence of evil—Job seems to express the deepest concerns of the postexilic era, when old assumptions about rewards for faithfulness and penalties for wrongdoing had lost much of their former authority.

For Job's author, previous attempts to explain his community's suffering and the justice of God were insufficient. In dealing with the crisis of their nation's destruction, the Deuteronomistic editors attributed both Israel's fall and Judah's destruction to their failure to obey Yah-weh's commands. According to the Deuteronomistic theory of history, the covenant people were a collective entity, a corporate body that prospered or suffered to-gether, not only for their own actions but also for those of their ancestors. Thus Judah was destroyed because Yahweh found the sins of King Manasseh to be unfor-givable (2 Kings 23:26–27; see Chapter 13). While in exile, Ezekiel proposes a variation on the old principle of collective community responsibility: Henceforth, Yah-weh will deal with his people in a new way, judging each generation according to its individual merits, rather than making it pay for the past sins of its ancestors or the fu-ture errors of its descendants (Ezek. 18). Declaring that Yahweh takes no "pleasure in the death of anyone" but wishes all to live, Ezekiel states that God will look favor-ably on new generations who turn from their parents' misdeeds to follow Torah commands. While stating that God will, after the exile, judge each generation individu-ally, Ezekiel nonetheless insists on preserving the old Deuteronomistic formula that equates good conduct with divine blessings. Despite his revision of the Mosaic principle, Ezekiel clearly presupposes that Yahweh will favor the good and condemn only the wicked. Because it is unthinkable that God behaves unjustly, all individuals must deserve whatever evils befall them.

As we have seen, the Book of Proverbs endorses this view: God's world manifests an intrinsic moral or-der in which all thoughts and actions have predictable consequences. Proper "awe" of Yahweh and diligent, prudent behavior will result in prosperity and honor, whereas disloyalty to God will ultimately bring failure and shame. Like the Deuteronomistic writers, the au-thors of practical wisdom assume a cosmic system of ethical cause and effect that justly determines the degree of good or evil present in human lives.

In times of peace and relative social stability, this philosophy seemed to work. Many of Israel's sages, who presumably were examplars of the policies they preached, taught their students that *torah*-keeping, honesty, and hard work almost invariably translate into economic suc-cess and public reputation. After Babylon's destruction of Judah, however, when thousands of *torah*-abiding people permanently lost family, health, land, and posses-sions, confidence that righteous behavior could ensure a good life was less easy to entertain. Widespread injustice turned the Deuteronomistic thesis on its head—foreign overlords cruelly exploited even the most obedient of Yahweh's servants (Ps. 44). Observing this moral disor-der, Job's author could accept neither Deuteronomy's simplistic theories nor Ezekiel's implication that human misery always derives from sin. Combining traditional

reverence for Yahweh with an acutely critical intelligence, Job's author demands moral logic and protests against discredited notions that equate good conduct with good fortune. Creatively expanding on ancient traditions about Job, the writer—in some of the Hebrew Bible's greatest poetry—forcefully illustrates his conviction that old theological claims about divine justice were woefully inadequate to explain the apparently random and arbitrary nature of human pain.

The Prose Prologue: Yahweh and the Divine Council

An Innocent Victim The prologue (Job 1–2) presents Job as a thoroughly admirable and godly person who in no way deserves the torments inflicted on him. Described as "blameless and upright, one who feared God and turned away from evil," he is exactly the kind of man to whom Proverbs promises a good life (Job 1:1; 1:8; 2:3; cf. Prov. 1: 33; 2:20–22; 3:1–10, 16–18, etc.) So careful is Job about not offending God that he offers sacrifices for his children in case they, even in thought, have sinned. No wonder Yahweh declares that "there is no one like [Job] on the earth" (Job 1:8). Although Job's "friends" will vigorously dispute it, seeking to justify their concept of God by making Job guilty, Job's innocence is abso-lutely essential to the book's theological meaning. Com-mending Job's moral excellence, Yahweh himself regards the man as faultless (1:8; 2:3; cf. 42:7). The friends' at-tempt to uncover some secret flaw in Job's character or behavior—an effort in which many modern commenta-tors have joined—is misguided, distracting attention from the real issue: the inadequacy of conventional ideas about God and the divine–human relationship.

Although Job's ethical superiority separates him from most people, he is also a universal type, the person of goodwill found throughout history. He is a model of humanity created in God's image. For this reason, the writer makes him not an Israelite but a native of Uz (a region south of Edom) who lived long before Israel's birth. Although not a member of the covenant community, Job endeavors to please God in every aspect of his life. Like the authors of many canonical proverbs, he assumes that God administers a just universe, rewarding good conduct and punishing bad. While still honoring his commitment to Yahweh, however, Job is suddenly plunged into moral chaos, forcing readers to confront the mystery of God's refusal to banish evil from his world.

Yahweh's Heavenly Court Job's troubles begin in heaven, where Yahweh has called an assembly of divine beings—the *bene ha elohim* (literally, "sons of the

BOX 23.2 Evolution of the Satan Concept

The biblical concept of Satan developed gradually over time. In the Book of Job, he is one of the "sons of God" who appear in the divine throne room, a regular member of the heavenly council who persuades Yahweh to test Job's loyalty to God. Serving as Yahweh's prosecuting attorney, Satan is a mere servant who can do nothing without God's express permission. The Hebrew text identifies him as "*the* Satan," using the definite article to emphasize his function—the term *Satan* means "Adversary" (Job 1–2). At this point in his historical development, the Satan has an adversarial relationship only with humankind, not with God.

According to historians of religion—scholars who analyze the growth of religious ideas and beliefs—the concept of Satan gradually evolved from the negative qualities once attributed to God. In this view, the Satan figure is essentially the "dark side," or psychological "shadow," of Yahweh's ethically ambivalent character. Tracing in chronological order the biblical references to Satan provides evidence that the violent and destructive traits formerly considered part of the divine nature were eventually ascribed to the Satan. The tension between contrasting aspects of the biblical God—who is both creator of light and life and a sometimes vindictive destroyer—is thus partly resolved. God can be seen as all-good and all-loving, while the Satan becomes responsible for all the world's evils.

Commonly overlooked biblical texts show Yahweh behaving in ways that later characterize his adversary. According to 1 Samuel, after selecting Saul as Israel's first king, God later sends an "evil spirit" to torment him (1 Sam. 16:14–23). God also commissions a "lying spirit" from his heavenly court to lead Ahab to his doom (1 Kings 22:18–28). Given some of the heavenly courtiers' willingness to lie, deceive, or torment,

albeit on his own orders, it is not surprising that Yahweh is reluctant to trust them:

> Even in his [heavenly] servants he puts no trust,
> and his angels he charges with error.

(Job 4:18)

A clear example of Satan's taking on the more sinister aspects of Yahweh's character occurs in the two accounts of King David's census. In the first version, Yahweh puts it into David's head to sin by taking a census of Israel—always hated by the people because it was done for purposes of taxation and military conscription. David's census-taking angers God, who then punishes not the king who ordered it but the people at large, sending a plague that kills thousands of Israelites (2 Sam. 24:1–25). In the second version, written hundreds of years later, it is not Yahweh who inspires David's census but the Satan; Yahweh merely punishes it (2 Chron. 21:1–30). The centuries that elapsed between the two parallel accounts witnessed a significant change in Israel's theological viewpoint. It was no longer possible to see Yahweh as both the *cause* of sin *and* the one who punished. The contradictory actions that the author of Samuel had ascribed to God the Chronicler now separates, assigning the cause of David's guilt to the Satan.

Whereas Tanakh authors give the Satan figure little space and scant respect, some New Testament writers enlarge his role in trying to disrupt the divine–human relationship. The Gospel accounts of both Matthew and Luke dramatize Satan's attempt to corrupt even the Son of God (Matt. 4: 1–11; Luke 4:1–13). Christian tradition also links the Hebrew concept of "Satan" to the non-Hebrew concept of "devil" (Greek, *diablos*), a term meaning "accuser" or "slanderer." In Revelation 12, the author equates Satan with the devil and with the serpent who tempted Eve (Rev. 12:12; cf. Gen. 3). (See Chapter 39.)

---

gods")—which includes "the Satan," a member of the divine council who serves as God's prosecuting attorney. At this point in Satan's historical evolution, *Satan* is not a proper name (the Hebrew text uses the definite article, for "the Satan"), nor is he Yahweh's enemy. Instead, "the Satan" (whose name means "Adversary") functions as Yahweh's servant, a supernatural agent whose task is to seek out and expose any disloyalty in God's human subjects (see Box 23.2). When Yahweh brings Job to his attention, the Satan suggests that Job will not remain loyal if deprived of children, property, and reputation. For reasons known only to himself, Yahweh accepts this

challenge, withdrawing the protective "fence" with which he had previously shielded Job from misfortune.

Stripped of divine protection, Job immediately experiences the power of chaos—the sudden injection of violent change into his formerly stable environment. Attacking nomads sweep away his flocks and herds; the "fire of God" consumes his sheep and shepherds; and a fierce wind crushes the house where his children are feasting, killing them all. Robbed of everything he holds dear by chaotic forces of earth, air, and sky, Job still blesses Yahweh's name (1:1–2:21). As if tempting God to doubt further the integrity of his human creation, the

Satan next persuades Yahweh to infect his faithful worshiper with a painful and disfiguring disease. Although Yahweh protests that such persecution is unjustified—his agent has "incited" God against Job "for no reason" (2:3)—he permits the Satan to do his worst, stipulating only that Job remain alive. In contrast to Yahweh, who yields to pressure from the Satan, Job rejects his wife's despairing plea to "curse God and die."

The Central Poetic Drama

Job's Lament In Chapter 3, the actions shifts from the heavenly court to Job's dungheap. In a long monologue, Job prays to have the process of creation reversed, asking for a return to the primal darkness that shrouded everything before God created light (cf. Gen. 1:1–2). If light and life are mere vehicles for pain, it is better not to exist or, once born, to sink quickly into the oblivion of Sheol, the dark subterranean realm where the human dead remain in eternal nothingness (cf. Eccles. 9:5, 10; see also Box 23.1). Job's agony is intensified by God's silence, the total absence of any communication that would give his misery ethical meaning. His reference to **Leviathan,** the mythical Dragon of Chaos—symbol of darkness and disorder that Yahweh subdued (but did not eliminate) during creation—expresses Job's direct experience of chaotic evil. It also anticipates the imagery in Yahweh's final speeches at the end of the drama, when God depicts himself as the proud owner of this monster (Job 3:8; 26:10–14; 41:1–34).

The Central Debate After delivering his anticreation monologue, Job is joined by three friends—**Eliphaz, Bildad,** and **Zophar**—with whom he will explore the nature of God and divine justice. As their speeches reveal, all three friends uncritically endorse the religious theories contained in Proverbs and the Deuteronomistic writings. Throughout the book, the three do not move from their initial position—that Job's present sufferings must result from some vile but unknown sin. Advocating long-accepted views of God, they argue—with increasing hostility—that Job must be guilty because God is just. An unmistakable sign of divine judgment, Job's misery confirms his error.

The book's central section is organized as a series of debates between Job and his three accusing friends. In three cycles of dialogue, each friend gives a speech, and Job, in turn, replies. In the last cycle, Job offers a final statement in which he reviews his life for any deed that might have offended God (Job 29–31). As the debates grow more heated, Job's early patience gives way to a realization of two unorthodox truths: (1) His humanity entitles him to innate moral rights, which God has

violated; and (2) if he is innocent and God is truly all-powerful, then the Deity must be responsible for the evil that he and all other people endure.

In Chapters 9 and 10, Job asks God to appear before him in human form so that their conflict can be settled in terms of legal justice. Even while demanding that God present evidence to prove Job's alleged wrongdoing, Job realizes that he has no chance to argue his cause before the Almighty. Anticipating Yahweh's climactic discourse, Job describes God's control of nature, the irresistible force that reduces all mortals to insignificance. Furthermore, Job recognizes that the power that afflicts him is the same power that will judge him:

> Though I am innocent, I cannot answer him;
> I must appeal for mercy to my accuser.
> If I summoned him [to a courtroom] and he
>   answered me,
> I do not believe that he would listen to my voice.
> For he crushes me with a tempest,
> and multiplies my wounds without cause; . . .
> If it is a contest of strength, he is the strong one!
> If it is a matter of justice, who can summon him?

(Job 9:15–19)

Acknowledging God's power, Job can only conclude that, in practice, Yahweh makes no effort to distinguish between the innocent and the guilty:

> It is all one; therefore I say
> he destroys both the blameless and the wicked.
> When disaster brings sudden death,
> he mocks at the calamity of the innocent.
> The earth is given into the hands of the wicked;
> he covers the eyes of the judges—
> if it is not he, who then is it?

(Job 9:22–24)

With courage born of his realization that good people can be more compassionate and ethically sensitive than the biblical God appears to be, Job suggests that God, who seems to revel in exercising his strength, also must learn what it means to be human, to experience the universe from the human perspective:

> I will say to God, Do not condemn me;
> let me know why you contend against me.
> Does it seem good to you to oppress,
> to despise the work of your hands
> and favor the schemes of the wicked?
> *Do you have eyes of flesh?*
> *Do you see as humans see?*
> *Are your days like the days of mortals,*
> or your years like human years,
> that you seek out my iniquity and search for my sin,

although *you know that I am not guilty,*
and there is no one to deliver out of your hand?

(Job 10:2–7; emphasis added)

Reversing the traditional wisdom that asks us to look at things from God's viewpoint, Job asks that God develop greater empathy for the human condition. To understand his human creation, God must experience his imperfect world as mortals do, without divine prerogatives of omniscience (complete knowledge), immortality, and immunity to pain.

In the final speech by one of Job's "false comforters," Bildad attacks the notion that any human can deserve God's favor, classing all mortals as mere "maggots" and "worms" (25:6; cf. similar views expressed by Eliphaz in 4:17–21 and 15:14–16 and by Zophar in 11:5–12). This attempt to justify undeserved suffering by reducing humanity to moral baseness—an assumption to which Job also refers (9:2; 12:9; 14:4)—is sometimes used to defend conventional beliefs about divine justice. The friends' emphasis on humankind's inborn depravity culminates historically in the later Christian doctrine of **original sin**, which asserts that all humans inherit from Adam an inescapable tendency to sin, resulting in their blanket condemnation by a righteous Deity. Job's author, however, makes no reference to the Genesis story about the first couple's disobedience or its alleged consequences for humanity. When Yahweh later appears to Job, he categorically rejects the friends' arguments and makes no allusion to humankind's supposedly innate sinfulness (42:7).

Elihu's Interruption Between Job's final challenge to God (Job 29–31) and God's appearance in the whirlwind that logically follows it (Job 38:41), editors inserted a lengthy speech by **Elihu,** a character whom the text has not previously introduced. Perhaps scandalized by Job's unorthodox questioning, the writer of Elihu's discourse attacks Job for refusing to make things easy by simply confessing his sins (perhaps including self-righteousness) and thereby restoring the comforting view of God's perfect justice. Rehashing the three friends' arguments, Elihu adds little to the discussion, although he claims to resolve the problem that Job's case presents. Full of self-confidence, Elihu presumes to speak "on God's behalf":

I will bring my knowledge from far away,
and ascribe righteousness to my Maker.
For truly my words are not false;
one who is perfect in knowledge is with you.

(Job 36:3–4)

After six chapters of Elihu's empty rhetoric, readers may well feel that the opening question in Yahweh's first speech applies to him rather than to Job: "Who is this that darkens counsel by words without knowledge?"

Yahweh's Revelation of His Universe

As Job foresaw in Chapter 9, when God at last appears, it is not in human form to explain why he subverts his assumed principles of justice by allowing the wicked to thrive and the good to suffer. Indeed, Yahweh appears in a superhuman display of power, celebrating his own strength and creative intelligence and refusing to answer any of Job's anguished questions. Speaking from the whirlwind as if to express the amoral energy of the natural world he has created, Yahweh emphasizes the enormous gap between divinity and humanity. In his first speech (38:1–39:30), God parades images of cosmic grandeur before Job's dazzled eyes. With grim humor, he demands that Job inform God about the miracle of creation, astronomical phenomena, and the curious habits of wildlife. He invites Job to share his creative pride in the world of animal violence, such as the fearless warhorse that delights in battle (39:19–25). In his final horrific example, Yahweh describes the eagle or vulture whose "young ones suck up blood," feasting on the bodies of the dying, indifferent to their pain (39:27–30).

Looking for the bread of understanding, Job is handed a scorpion (cf. Matt 7:9), a catalogue of impersonal natural wonders, and a pitiless survey of nature "red in tooth and claw." When Yahweh asks if Job, now deluged with examples of the savage and inexplicable, is ready to give up, Job merely replies that he will speak no more. Is Job's retreat into silence before God's self-revelation an act of reverent submission, or does it represent the numbness of moral shock?

Apparently unsatisfied with Job's wordless response, Yahweh then launches into a second long discourse, in which he strikes at Job's deepest fear: that in the absence of a comprehensible divine ethic, humanity will have to create—out of emptiness—its own meaning of life. When Yahweh asks, "Will you even put me in the wrong? Will you condemn me that you may be justified?" (40:8), Job's response must be no, for he has no wish to justify himself at God's expense. He merely asks Yahweh to administer the cosmos according to ethical principles that will encourage good conduct in human life. As he earlier observed, Yahweh's tolerance of the present system appears to support "the wicked," who too often triumph over their moral betters.

Yahweh next invites Job to examine the divine regulation of human society, asking him if he can duplicate the divine thunder that (when it chooses) can destroy the wicked (40:9–14). But Yahweh does not linger over his strangely inconsistent enforcement of justice in human affairs. Instead, he demands that Job consider the significance of two frightening monsters—Behemoth and Leviathan—that seem totally alien to human life. "The first of the great acts of God," **Behemoth** is a creature so powerful, so grotesque, and so removed from any possible relation to normal human experience that God's admiration for the monster compels Job to realize that the world is not a place designed primarily for humanity's benefit. When Yahweh equates Behemoth and humankind, telling Job, "I made [it] just as I made you" (40:15), he reveals a universe that is God-centered, a creation in which humans and dangerous beasts coexist, both the offspring of God. (This view contrasts markedly with that in Genesis 1:26–31, in which humanity, the pinnacle of creation, is divinely authorized to hold all other life forms in submission.)

Scholars formerly thought that Behemoth and Leviathan were, respectively, the hippopotamus and the crocodile. However, with the discovery of Ugaritic texts referring to Baal's defeat of Lothan, the primeval sea dragon, we now know that Leviathan is a mythological beast symbolizing the chaos that existed before creation—and that periodically asserts itself, threatening to unravel the world order. The Canaanite Lothan and Hebrew Leviathan are variant forms of **Rahab,** another version of the chaotic dragon that Yahweh subdued when imposing order on the cosmos (Ps. 89:9–10).

In Job, Yahweh describes Leviathan in mythic terms, as a dragon belching fire and smoke (41:18–20), at whose approach even "the gods are afraid" and thrown into a frenzy (41:25). Yet, terrifying as it is, Yahweh delights in the brute:

> On earth it has no equal, a creature without fear.
> It surveys everything that is lofty; it is king over
> all that are proud.

(Job 41:33–34)

Yahweh's reference to Leviathan's supremacy among the "proud" recalls his earlier declaration that he can overthrow the "proud" and the "wicked" who oppress others (40:9–14), although he chooses to do so only intermittently. As he tolerates the monster of chaos, amoral energy that has not been assimilated into the cosmic order, he apparently also incorporates arbitrary violence and unmerited suffering into his cosmic system.

Hearing Yahweh's description of Leviathan's role in the world, Job withdraws his questions about divine justice (42:2–3). The universe is as it is, an unfolding process in which light and dark, gentle and savage, and good and evil are intrinsic components. Leviathan, the dragon that can suddenly rear its head to shatter the peace of both nature and humanity, is perhaps a manifestation of the same mysterious disruptive force that Yahweh has made part of the cosmic whole (see Figure 23.3). Absolute sovereign, Yahweh is unlimited

FIGURE 23.3 Dating from the Sumerian Early Dynastic period (c. 2800-2600 BCE), this plaque is believed to show the Sumerian god Ninurta, a divine warrior and son of Enlil, who functions as a cosmic savior by defeating the primal monster of chaos. Biblical writers preserved aspects of this conflict myth in references to Yahweh's struggles with Leviathan, another name for the primeval serpent (cf. Ps. 74:12-17; Job 3:8; 26:13; 41:1–34; Isa. 27:1). The mythical dragon rears his seven heads again in the New Testament Book of Revelation, where, identified with Satan and the devil, he is cast from heaven by the archangel Michael (Rev. 12:3, 9; 13:1; 17:3).

by merely human concepts of right and wrong, a view of divine autonomy that Second Isaiah also expresses:

> I am the LORD, and there is no other.
> I form light and create darkness,
> I make weal and create woe;
> I the LORD do all these things.

(Isa. 45:6–7)

In surveying his universe, Yahweh assigns no role to the Satan, either as an agent who tests the loyalty of humankind or as a theoretical source of cosmic evil and rebellion. For the author of Job, as well as Second Isaiah, Yahweh's unity and omnipotence leave no room for any competing supernatural entity.

After disclosing the divine paradox that embraces polar opposites of light and dark, Yahweh asks Job to intercede for his three friends, because Eliphaz, Bildad, and Zophar "have not spoken of me what is right, as my servant Job has" (Job 42:7). Whereas the three friends defended a traditional concept of God, Job dared to point out the perplexing disconnection between standard notions of divine justice and the facts of real life, whereby people do not always receive what they ethically deserve. After experiencing God directly in the whirlwind, the uncontrollable power of nature, Job falls silent. He abandons his attempt to find moral logic in God's administration of the world, for Yahweh has revealed himself to be far more concerned with the complex phenomena of the universe he has created than with resolving issues of good and evil that trouble humans.

After accepting Job's intercession for his friends, however, Yahweh restores all of Job's possessions twice over, again placing his worshiper in the secure and prosperous state he inhabited before God removed the "fence" that shielded Job from harm. Although Job is given ten more children, they are not the same children he lost as a result of the controversy between Yahweh and his heavenly prosecutor. Dispenser of both "weal" and "woe," Yahweh governs a world in which—contrary to conventional wisdom—humans often find it agonizingly difficult to distinguish random chance from divine providence.

 ## The Book of Ecclesiastes

In the Book of Job, we are invited to share Job's pain and to question commonly accepted ideas about God's purpose in permitting good to go unrewarded and evil to flourish. The book asks readers to respond emotionally to Job's anguish as he contemplates Yahweh's ultimate responsibility for cosmic violence and unmerited suffering. By contrast, the author of Ecclesiastes adopts an emotionally neutral position of ironic detachment. From his ivory-tower perspective, he coolly surveys the moral uncertainties of a world dominated by unpredictability and random injustice. An aloof observer of human folly, he derives a certain dry amusement from the human predicament. He is puzzled by Yahweh's apparent unwillingness to enforce ethical principles in human society, but he simply concludes that God chooses to operate with no coherent mortal plan—at least not one that human beings can perceive (8:14, 16–17).

An element of Proverbs' practical wisdom also characterizes the work. Having experienced much, the author has found that there is "nothing new under the sun," nothing that has not been seen, said, or felt a thousand times before. He therefore advises his readers not to be taken in by the world's sham innovations. True wisdom lies in observing everything, knowing how little has genuine value, and refusing to become committed to the hopeless pursuits of wealth, power, fame or other goals to which most people blindly devote their lives.

Although the first verse attributes the book's authorship to "the son of David, King in Jerusalem" (presumably Solomon), most scholars regards this as merely a literary device that offers the writer an elevated position from which imaginatively to experience everything enjoyed by Israel's wealthiest and wisest monarch (1:1–2:12). Implied references to Solomon, however, are soon dropped.

In the Hebrew text, the author is most frequently referred to as **Koheleth** (Qoheleth), which the New Revised Standard Version translates as "Teacher." When translating the Tanakh into Greek, the Septuagint editors rendered *Koheleth* as "Ecclesiastes," deriving it from the Greek word "assembly" (*ekklesia*—the same term used for "church" in the New Testament). Various English translations use such words as *teacher, speaker,* or *preacher* to approximate what the name *Koheleth* may have meant. Exactly who or what Koheleth may have been or whom he "assembled" around him remains unclear, but the usual view today is that he was a *hakham,* or wisdom teacher. As a recognized sage, Koheleth may have assembled a circle of student-disciples around him, some of whom may have collected and edited his sayings. The book's epilogue (12:9–14) contains several editorial reactions to Koheleth's unorthodox teaching, possibly penned by his disciples.

Because the text refers to no historical events or rulers, scholars must try to date the work through its use of language and its apparent familiarity with various strands of Greek philosophy. After Alexander the Great incorporated Palestine into his empire (c. 332 BCE), Greek ideas began to influence many

Jewish thinkers, and Koheleth's sayings seem to reflect an awareness of both Stoic and Epicurean views (for a discussion of Greek culture and its impact on Judaism, see Chapter 28). Besides echoing Greek concepts, the text also uses both Persian loan words (words borrowed from the Persian language) and Aramaic verb forms, all indicating a date long after the return from exile. Many scholars conclude, then, that the book was probably composed during the late fourth or early third century BCE.

The Limits of Human Understanding and the Futility of Human Effort

Central to Koheleth's view of the human predicament is his conviction that, no matter how great the effort, human wisdom cannot discover a coherent meaning in life:

> When I applied my mind to know wisdom, and to see the business that is done on earth, how one's eyes see sleep neither day nor night, then I saw all the work of God, that no one can find out what is happening under the sun.

(Eccles. 8:16–17)

The Book of Ecclesiastes presents most of Koheleth's principal ideas in the first two chapters. The remaining ten mainly illustrate and elaborate on his basic perception that the rewards of humanity's customary labors are either short-lived or nonexistent. The book opens with a description of the eternal cycle of nature, in which all things—sun, rivers, seas—are seen as moving in endless circles and eventually returning to their starting point, only to begin the same cycle again. It is merely society's poor memory that causes people to imagine that anything new ever occurs. Individual observers are not around long enough to recognize that in the long view, all that is repeats itself without essential change.

Aware that knowledge is a burden—because wisdom makes it impossible to be optimistic about life—Koheleth nonetheless decides to sample the various pursuits that most people think are valuable. He first tries pleasure, a deliberate savoring of "folly":

> I searched with my mind how to cheer my body with wine—my mind still guiding me with wisdom—and how to lay hold on folly, until I might see what was good for mortals to do under heaven during the few days of their life. I made great works; I build houses and planted vineyards for myself; I made myself gardens and parks, and planted in them all kinds of fruit trees. . . . Whatever my eyes desired I did not keep from them; I kept my heart from no pleasure, for my heart found pleasure in all my toil. Then I considered

all that my hands had done and the toil I had spent in doing it, and again, all was vanity and a chasing after wind, and there was nothing to be gained under the sun.

(Eccles. 2:3–11)

At various points in his meditations, Koheleth offers several reasons for his conclusion that all human effort is "vanity." No matter how much he achieves in life, Koheleth—like all other humans—must ultimately die, leaving everything to someone else, perhaps an unworthy heir who will waste it all. Regardless of his successor's conduct, time itself will erase whatever he builds or creates. No matter how hard he labors or how wisely he plans, life can never compensate him for the toil and sacrifice expended to achieve his goals. Finally, death will inevitably frustrate all his intentions and hopes.

The Finality of Death   Lurking behind the author's pessimism is a conviction that death is the absolute end to life, that there is no consciousness beyond the grave. All people, righteous and wicked alike, will descend to Sheol without reaping either rewards or punishments in an afterlife. No other biblical writer, in fact, is as direct and positive in asserting that death equals annihilation. God, Koheleth argues, does not even distinguish between human and animal lives, let alone between virtue and sin:

> For the fate of humans and the fate of animals is the same; as one dies, so dies the other. They all have the same breath, and human have no advantage over the animals; for all is vanity. All go to one place [Sheol]; all are from the dust, and all turn to dust again. Who knows whether the human spirit goes upward and the spirit of animals goes downward to the earth?

(Eccles. 3:19–21)

God's existence is not to be doubted, but the Deity's presence in heaven has no direct bearing on earthly lives. Although God "will bring every deed into judgment" (12:14), that judgment is never connected to events in Sheol, the permanent grave for all humanity:

> The living know that they will die, but the dead know nothing; they have no more reward, and even the memory of them is lost. Their love and their hate and their envy have already perished; never again will they have any share in all that happens under the sun . . .

(Eccles. 9:5–6)

Unlike Daniel and the author of the Wisdom of Solomon, Koheleth foresees no afterlife in which God's grand designs will be made clear:

Whatever your hand finds to do, do with your might; for there is no work or thought or knowledge or wisdom in Sheol, to which you are going.

(Eccles. 9:10)

At his most despairing, Koheleth even questions the value of life itself:

Again, I saw all the oppressions that are practiced under the sun. Look, the tears of the oppressed—with no one to comfort them! On the side of their oppressors there was power—with no one to comfort them. And I thought the dead, who have already died, more fortunate than the living, who are still alive; but better than both is the one who has not yet been, and who has not seen the evil deeds that are done under the sun.

(Eccles. 4:1–3)

Nonexistence is thus preferable to a life in which we witness God's failure to act: If God permits "oppressors" to crush the weak and provides no "comfort" for the afflicted, it is better not to be born.

Try as he might, Koheleth can find no ethical design in the way God has organized the world:

And I saw that under the sun the race is not to the swift, nor the battle to the strong, nor bread to the wise, nor riches to the intelligent, nor favor to the skillful; but time and chance happen to them all.

(Eccles. 9:11)

It is difficult to imagine a statement more at variance with Israel's prophets or Deuteronomistic historians.

Given death's finality and life's random unpredictability, Koheleth advises people to seize whatever enjoyments they can from their fleeting existence:

Go eat your bread with enjoyment, and drink your wine with a merry heart; for God has long ago approved what you do. Let your garments [worn at festivals] always be white; do not let oil be lacking on your head. Enjoy life with the wife whom you love, all the days of your vain life that are given you under the sun, . . .

(Eccles. 9:7–9)

In dispensing this counsel, Koheleth taps the deepest roots of Near Eastern wisdom, paraphrasing Siduri's advice in the *Epic of Gilgamesh* (see Chapter 3). His advice also echoes the more recent (but equally materialistic) philosophy of Epicurus, which held that humans are only a chance collection of atoms that dissolve at death. According to the Epicurean view, human consciousness or "soul" is as physical as the body and, like the body, perishes utterly. Even if the gods exist, they are not interested in human affairs, which, as Koheleth agreed, are governed mainly by arbitrary chance. Some of Koheleth's other statements are typical of Stoicism, another Greco-Roman philosophy that influenced several biblical writers, including the author of the deuterocanonical Wisdom of Solomon. Stoic teaching, which emphasized self-discipline and logical thought, urged people to bring their lives into harmony with the divine principles ruling the universe (see Chapter 28). Ecclesiastes 3, which states that "for everything there is a season, and a time for every matter under heaven," seems to imply that a providence—a cosmic power guiding human destiny—directs all things. As an Israelite, the writer probably regarded Israel's God as the enforcer of the cosmic cycle of birth, growth, decline, and death. But Koheleth's God apparently is interested only in enforcing natural laws, not in giving meaning or order to human society.

Contradictory Wisdom The author's love of paradox puzzles some readers: Koheleth seldom makes a statement that he does not somewhere else contradict. Advising us to savor life and to drink wine with a joyful heart (9:7), he also states that it is better to frequent the house of mourning than the house of feasting (7:3). The day of death is better than the day of birth (7:1), but he would rather be a "living dog" than a "dead lion" (9:4). Many readers may miss the impact of this statement, for "dog" was a common Israelite name for non-Israelites, and "lion" can refer to a Davidic king, suggesting that a healthy person outside the covenant community is better off than a (deceased) anointed of Yahweh. The "righteous and the wise" are "in the hand of God" (9:1) but their end is no different from that of the "wicked" (9:2). It is as much a mistake to behave too wisely or righteously (7:16) as to be excessively wicked (7:17).

For many readers, these paradoxical views are among the book's chief strengths: The writer does not contradict himself, but simply asserts that life is too complex for absolute certainties. Just as there is a time to live and a time to die, so there are occasions when radically different attitudes and behaviors are appropriate. Koheleth refuses to confine himself to any single philosophical position. Whereas many Greek thinkers made logical consistency the test of truth, Ecclesiastes' author recognizes the irrational elements in life and refuses to omit observable variety in the interests of theoretical consistency. In a world where God does not seem to rule—and it is significant that Yahweh, the Lord of history, is not mentioned by name anywhere in the book—illogic and absurdity must be acknowledged. Unlike Israel's prophets, who confidently proclaimed Yahweh's oracles, Koheleth declares that God has so obscured his purposes—and life's meaning—that even the wise cannot discover it (8:17). The "work of God" is ultimately unknowable (11:5; cf. 3:9–11).

Postscripts

The book closes with a beautiful allegory in which human old age is compared to a decayed, crumbling house (12:1–8). Later writers added a series of brief comments. In the first, a disciple praises Koheleth for his wisdom and for writing "words of truth plainly" (12:9–10). Another comment, perhaps by a different hand, observes that "the sayings of the wise are like goads," as sharp as "nails" to prick or awaken disciples to a heightened awareness. A later, less admiring editor warns readers that "of making books there is no end" and that studying works like that of Koheleth is "a weariness of the flesh" (12:12). The final editorial observation—"Fear God, and keep his commandments; for that is the whole duty of everyone" (12:13)—may have been responsible for the book's eventual admission into the biblical canon. For some readers, the presence of this orthodox advice—at "the end of the matter"—at least partly redeems Koheleth's deeply skeptical, religiously uncommitted work.

QUESTIONS FOR DISCUSSION AND REVIEW

1. Describe the principal differences between the more "conventional" or "practical" wisdom books like Proverbs and the "critical" or "speculative" wisdom books like Job and Ecclesiastes. In what ways do these books differ from other parts of the Hebrew Bible?

2. The Bible's most profound exploration of divine justice and the problem of evil, the Book of Job asks us to reevaluate conventional notions about God and his relationship to humanity. In confronting the fact that many good people suffer undeservedly, why is it necessary—in terms of the book's theological purpose—to understand that Job is innocent of wrongdoing and that Yahweh afflicts him "for no reason"? When God appears in the whirlwind discussing Leviathan and Behemoth as his admirable creations, what does his speech show about Yahweh's attitude toward violent or amoral elements in his cosmos? According to Job's author, is God both all-good and all-powerful? From

God's perspective, how do we define "good"? Support your answers by citing specific passages from the biblical text.

3. In responding to the same theological and ethical problems that Job addresses, how does the author of Ecclesiastes deal with the problem of evil and injustice? Why does the "Teacher" (Koheleth) find it impossible to discern God's purpose in the world? Lacking certain knowledge of the divine will, how should humans behave in daily life?

4. Whereas the counsels of Proverbs generally support the moral law of actions and consequences found in the Deuteronomistic history, the books of Job and Ecclesiastes do not. Why do you suppose that biblical editors decided to include these two "unorthodox" books in the canon? How would you define the religious "advantage" in including a variety of theological outlooks in the canon?

Terms and Concepts to Remember

Behemoth	nature of Yahweh's
bene ha elohim	universe
Bildad	original sin
devil	proverbs
Elihu	Rahab
Eliphaz	Satan, the
Epic of Gilgamesh	Sheol
Koheleth	theodicy
Leviathan	wisdom literature
mashal	Zophar

Recommended Reading

Wisdom (General)

Bergant, Dianne. *Israel's Wisdom Literature: A Liberation-Critical Reading.* Minneapolis: Fortress Press, 1997. An innovative study.

Clifford, Richard J. "Introduction to Wisdom Literature." In *The New Interpreter's Bible*, Vol. 5, pp. 1–16. Nashville, TN: Abingdon Press, 1997. A concise survey.

Crenshaw, James L. *Old Testament Wisdom: An Introduction*, rev. ed. Louisville, KY: Westminster John Knox Press, 1998. A standard work.

Proverbs

Scott, R. B. Y. *Proverbs, Ecclesiastes* (Anchor Bible, Vol. 18). Garden City, NY: Doubleday, 1965. A scholarly translation with critical interpretation.

Van Leeuwen, Raymond C. "The Book of Proverbs." In *The New Interpreter's Bible*, Vol. 5, pp. 19–264. The full text, with extensive commentary.

Job

Balentine, Samuel E. "Job, Book of." In K. D. Sakenfeld, ed., *The New Interpreter's Dictionary of the Bible*, Vol. 3, pp. 319–336. Nashville, TN: Abingdon Press, 2008. A thoughtful essay on the theological implications of Job's encounter with God.

Crenshaw, James L., ed. *Theodicy in the Old Testament*. Philadelphia: Fortress Press, 1983. Wrestles with the problem of evil in human experience.

Habel, Norman C. *The Book of Job* (The Cambridge Bible Commentary). New York: Cambridge UP, 1975. Offers New English Bible text and perceptive analysis.

Mitchell, Stephen. *The Book of Job*. San Francisco: North Point Press, 1987. An informal translation with nontechnical commentary.

Newsom, Carol A. "Job, Book of." In *The New Interpreter's Bible*, Vol. 4, pp. 317–637. Nashville, TN: Abingdon Press, 1996. Covers theological interpretation.

Pope, Marvin H. *Job* (Anchor Bible). Garden City, NY: Doubleday, 1965. A forceful translation with many useful notes.

Ecclesiastes

Crenshaw, James L. *Ecclesiastes*. Philadelphia: Fortress Press, 1997. A standard work.

Gianto, Augustinus. "Ecclesiastes, Book of." In K. D. Sakenfeld, ed., *The New Interpreter's Dictionary of the Bible*, Vol. 2, pp. 178–185. Nashville, TN: Abingdon Press, 2007. An informative overview of this perplexing document.

Towner, W. Sibley. "The Book of Ecclesiastes." In *The New Interpreter's Bible*, Vol. 4, pp. 267–360. The complete text, with scholarly commentary.

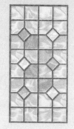

CHAPTER 24

Festival Scrolls

The Books of Ruth, Song of Songs, Lamentations, and Esther

Key Topics/Themes In the Hebrew Bible (Tanakh), five short books are grouped together as a discrete literary unit among the Writings. Known as the Megillot, all five books—Ruth, Song of Songs, Ecclesiastes, Lamentations, and Esther—have in common the fact that each is associated with a particular event of the Jewish religious calendar (see Table 24.1). The practice of reading these books at an annual religious ceremony may date back to the late Second Temple era (first century BCE), which could explain why these works are grouped together in the Masoretic Text (see Chapter 2). Apart from their liturgical function, however, these documents have little else in common. Ruth is a short story whose heroine is a non-Israelite, a young Moabite widow who migrates to Bethlehem and becomes an ancestress of King David. Whereas Song of Songs consists of lyrics celebrating erotic love, Lamentations is a collection of poems lamenting Babylon's destruction of Jerusalem. As for Esther, it is a tale of intrigue, courage, and revenge set at the Persian court of Xerxes I (ruled 486–465 BCE). Diverse in theme and in tone, these books appeal to a variety of human emotions—anxiety, skepticism, grief, and love—and do so within literary genres that set them apart from the rest of the Hebrew canon. (Because it is part of Israel's wisdom tradition, Ecclesiastes, one of the Megillot, is discussed along with Proverbs and Job in Chapter 23.)

The Book of Ruth

Except for the Book of Esther, the Book of Ruth is the only canonical work in the Hebrew Bible whose principal figure is a woman. In fact, two women characters—**Naomi** and her daughter-in-law **Ruth**—occupy the central position in the narrative, and the relationships they create, with each other and with God, are unique in biblical literature. Its importance recognized even in antiquity, the Book of Ruth was read at the Feast of Pentecost (Hebrew, *Shavuoth*) and was placed first among the Megillot. In the Septuagint, however, Ruth was inserted between the books of Judges and 1 Samuel, presumably because its story is set in the time of the Judges, and that is where it appears in most English Bibles today.

The Historical Setting: A Question of Intermarriage

Setting the story of Ruth and Naomi within the historical era of the Judges may be puzzling to many contemporary readers, because nothing in this book reflects the violence or political turmoil of that period. The author portrays relations between Moab and Judah as peaceful enough for an Israelite family to pass back and forth between Bethlehem and the Moabite midlands without hindrance or even so much as a hint of ethnic or religious hostility. Although the book repeatedly refers to Ruth as the "Moabitess," no one in Bethlehem seems to care that she is a foreigner or to object, later, when she marries **Boaz**, a native-born Israelite. Such generosity of spirit contrasts sharply with the Deuteronomistic tradition, which portrays the Moabite

TABLE 24.1 **The Megillot and Associated Festivals**

BOOK	FESTIVAL
Ruth	**Pentecost**—a late-spring harvest festival
Song of Songs	**Passover**—the annual holiday that commemorates the end of slavery for the Israelites in Egypt
Ecclesiastes	**Feast of Tabernacles,** or Feast of Booths—the autumn agricultural feast of thanksgiving
Lamentations	**Fast of the Ninth of Av** (July–August)—a day of mourning for the destruction of the Jerusalem Temple by the Babylonians in 587 BCE and the Romans in 70 CE
Esther	**Feast of Purim,** or Festival of Lots (February–March)—the celebration of Jewish deliverance from Persian attack

and Ammonite peoples as both inhospitable and totally unacceptable as marriage partners:

> No Ammonite or Moabite shall be admitted to the assembly of the LORD. Even to the tenth generation, none of their descendants shall be admitted to the assembly of the LORD, because they did not meet you with food and water on your journey out of Egypt, and because they hired against you Balaam son of Peor . . . to curse you. You shall never promote their welfare or their prosperity as long as you live.

(Deut. 23:3–6)

This negative assessment of the Moabites is even more striking in the books of Ezra and Nehemiah, where Judean men are roundly condemned for taking foreign wives or ordered to divorce them (Ezra 9–10; Neh. 13:23–27). These postexilic writers, eager to preserve Judean identity, regarded such intermarriage as an act of treachery against Yahweh or as the gateway to apostasy. Moreover, regional conflict between Israelites and Moabites, like that alluded to in Judges 3, would have made such a union highly unlikely. That King David is identified as a descendant of such a union suggests that, for the unknown author of Ruth, the issue of intermarriage was far from being a closed issue. Clearly, the author's intent is to elevate the stature of at least one Moabite woman until she ranks as an equal to "Rachel and Leah who together built up the House of Israel" (Ruth 4:11).

Ruth, Naomi, and Boaz

What is even more remarkable about this narrative is its focus on the lives of two obscure women who, beset by misfortune, cling together for mutual support and hope. Indeed, Ruth's profession of loyalty to Naomi has become a classic expression of love and devotion between two people:

> "Do not press me to leave you
> or to turn back from following you!
> Where you go, I will go;
> where you lodge, I will lodge;
> your people shall be my people
> and your God my God.
> Where you die, I will die—
> There I will be buried.
> May the LORD do thus and so to me,
> and more as well,
> if even death parts me from you!"

(Ruth 1:16–17)

As for Ruth's future husband, the wealthy landowner Boaz, his goodness and generosity are no less extraordinary than Ruth's. From their first encounter, he displays the virtues of a *torah*-observant Israelite man. Following the divine commandment to leave a portion of his fields or vineyards for the poor to harvest (Deut. 24:19–21), he offers to have Ruth gather grain from his fields, and from no others, and then orders his workers to leave her alone. When Boaz later discovers Ruth lying by his feet while he sleeps on the threshing floor, he responds with something more than generosity as she informs him that he is a near-kinsman and therefore eligible to marry her. His willingness to honor her request probably reflects his romantic interest in the young woman, but it also shows his appreciation of her discreet behavior: She has sought refuge under the "wings" of the Lord God of Israel (Ruth 2:12).

Boaz's conduct embodies two of the book's main themes: (1) that rewards will come, sooner or later, to those who commit themselves to Yahweh's providence, and (2) the importance of *hesed,* or loving kindness in all relationships, whether human or divine. In Boaz's view, Yahweh has placed Ruth in his care, and he would fail in his devotion to the God of Israel if he turned her away or denied the affection he feels for her. Human passion thus becomes an extension of providential care, and

Boaz serves as a moral agent through whom divine love can be realized. This is particularly true in light of the obligation laid upon the near-kinsman (the *goel* or "redeemer" in Hebrew), by Deuteronomy, a provision known as the Levirate law:

> When brothers reside together, and one of them dies and has no son, the wife of the deceased shall not be married outside the family to a stranger. Her husband's brother shall go to her, taking her in marriage, and performing the duty of a husband's brother to her, and the firstborn whom she bears shall succeed to the name of the deceased brother, so that his name may not be blotted out in Israel. But if the man has no desire to marry his brother's widow, then his brother's widow shall go up to the elders at the gate. . . . Then the elders of his town shall summon him and speak to him. If he persists, saying, "I have no desire to marry her," then his brother's wife shall go to him in the presence of the elders, pull his sandal off his foot, spit in his face, and declare, "This is what is done to the man who does not build up his brother's house." Throughout Israel his family shall be known as "the house of him whose sandal was pulled off."
>
> (Deut. 25:5–10; cf. Lev. 18:16 and 20:21, which seems to forbid marrying a brother's wife or widow)

As a potential "redeemer," Boaz can act responsibly *and* follow the dictates of his heart. Or he can behave as selfishly as the even nearer kinsman who refuses to marry Ruth, even when the prospect of inheriting her first husband's property is offered him. In this gentle tale, nothing is said about Ruth spitting in anyone's face or removing his sandal as a sign of disgrace. But this nameless relative serves, nevertheless, as an effective foil to Boaz, who gladly performs his duty to God and to the widow with whom he has fallen in love. Nor does the narrator see a problem with the overlapping of motivation. Boaz is allowed to act out of both self-interest and devotion to *torah* without having personal desire undermine or compromise obedience to the law.

That the fruit of this union pleases Yahweh is clear by the story's end. Boaz has fulfilled his Levirate obligations and found the perfect wife, while Naomi's bitterness vanishes when a grandson is born—to whom neighbor women refer as Naomi's son. The proof that God approves this marriage comes at the very conclusion of the narrative, when the narrator clarifies exactly who Ruth is: She is the great-grandmother of King David, and therefore the source, along with Boaz, of Israel's God-appointed dynasty. That a Moabite woman could be the forbear of Israel's most glorious king suggests that the author did not share the suspicion of foreign women or hostility toward intermarriage that Ezra and

Nehemiah so ardently advocated. The fruitful marriage of Moabite and Israelite is also a reminder of the prophetic tradition in which non-Israelites would one day be included among Yahweh's people. For many scholars, the book promotes an important theological insight—that Israel's God is universal and that he benevolently and indirectly draws human beings closer to him and leads them toward their own happiness.

Structure and Language

Viewed as a literary composition, the Book of Ruth shows numerous signs of artful arrangement and subtle use of language. The author's choice of names for his characters, for example, helps to reveal their essential qualities even before readers see them in action. Naomi's two sons are called Mahlon (meaning "illness") and Chilion (meaning "cessation"), so it hardly comes as a surprise when we learn, shortly after they are introduced to us, that they have died an early death. As for Naomi—whose name means "pleasantness"—she calls attention to the irony of that name when, as a poor widow, she returns to her hometown of Bethlehem:

> "Do not call me Naomi," she said, "call me Mara [meaning "bitterness"], for it is a bitter lot that the Almighty has sent me. I went away full, and the LORD has brought me back empty."
>
> (Ruth 1:20–21)

Similarly, Boaz's name—which means "strength"—has significance appropriate to his character, for his most obvious trait is integrity. Even the name of the town from which Elimelech (Naomi's husband) and his family depart for Moab, and to which Naomi and Ruth return years later, has thematic meaning: "Bethlehem" literally means "House of Bread," a fitting name for a story that begins with a famine and ends at harvesttime.

The book's structure is as artful as its language. Divided into two roughly symmetrical parts, the story first focuses on the struggles that Naomi and Ruth endure on their journey from Moab to Bethlehem and their adjustment to life there. The book's second part focuses on the unfolding relationship of Ruth and Boaz and its happy consummation. The unstated premise of both parts of this narrative is that, although Yahweh has taken away, he can also restore. What Naomi and Ruth lost in Moab, they regain in Judah through the *hesed* of Israel's God and through their mutual devotion.

Each of the book's two parts contains three scenes in which three interwoven lives are shown moving from famine to feasting, from death to life, from widowhood to marriage, and finally from bitterness to joy. Within this framework, major characters are portrayed with extraordinary economy; with just a few deft strokes the narrator makes us understand both Naomi's despair over the loss of her husband and sons and her determination to see her daughter-in-law Ruth succeed where she has failed.

Authorship and Date

Despite their general agreement on the book's literary excellence, scholars are divided on questions of authorship and date of composition. Scholars who focus on the theme of intermarriage and Ruth's status as an ethnic outsider tend to favor a postexilic date, seeing the book as a protest against religious authorities, such as Ezra and Nehemiah, who categorically forbid the taking of foreign wives. To support their view that Ruth is a relatively late work, they cite the presence of Aramaic words, departures from the Deuteronomistic tradition, and the general absence of social or historical realism, all of which suggest that the author lived so long after the period of the judges that he could paint an idealistic picture of that primitive era.

Scholars favoring an earlier, preexilic date of composition speculate that, long before the story was committed to writing, it existed as an oral folktale, thus giving credibility to an ancient tradition that Samuel was Ruth's author. In fact, if we compare the account of Hannah's conception of Samuel, which opens the Book of 1 Samuel, to the narrative describing Obed's birth in Ruth, we can see why tradition linked the two figures. Editors of the Septuagint thus chose to place the story of Ruth's child just before the story of Hannah's famous son. Both women are compensated—by Yahweh—for the barrenness and suffering in their lives, and each in her way serves as a model of trust in God's goodness.

The Song of Songs

Referred to variously as the Song of Songs, the Song of Solomon, and Canticles, this collection of love poems is the only example of erotic poetry in the Hebrew Bible. Similar anthologies of love poetry are found in the literatures of Babylon and Egypt, and numerous parallels have been drawn between specific images in the biblical Song and similar Egyptian and Babylonian poetic traditions. Like other Near Eastern love poets, the author of the Song of Songs celebrates both the exaltation and the anguish of sexual longing and fulfillment, invokes the beauty of nature, and tactfully avoids the subject of marriage. And like its Near Eastern counterparts, the Song seems to have been written as a secular entertainment.

No scholarly agreement exists today over why or when the Song of Songs was written or how it made its way into the biblical canon. Though traditionally ascribed to King Solomon (as are Proverbs and Ecclesiastes), the opening verse—"The Song of Songs, which is Solomon's"—could just as well have been translated "which is *for* Solomon." In any event, scholars tend to regard this statement as nothing more than a literary convention, linking Solomon—famous for his 1,000 wives and concubines and therefore presumably knowledgeable about the delights of carnal love—with this poem. Similarly, references to a "king" or to Solomon himself (Song 8:11) are thought to reflect a tradition of erotic lyrics associated with the Solomonic court or harem. Apart from this tradition, scholars can find nothing in the text that points to either author or time of composition. As a result, theories abound about what the Songs of Songs really means and how it found a place in Jewish Scripture.

A Celebration of Erotic Love

Read simply as an anthology of love lyrics, the Song of Songs can be seen as an honest celebration of what Proverbs 30:19 calls "the way of a man with a girl." Not only does the Song exalt sexual desire, but it draws a varied portrait of young lovers caught up in the sometimes painful longing for the beloved:

> You have ravished my heart, my sister, my bride,
> you have ravished my heart
> with a glance of your eyes,
> with one jewel of your necklace.

(Song 4:9)

Some commentators claim to have found traces of a courtship narrative, binding together the seemingly disconnected verses of this book in the framework of lovers' exchanging compliments and vows. Others regard the book as an anthology of poems highlighting the variations in lovers' shifting moods as a series of implied dialogues in which lover and beloved express their mutual admiration and desire. Many of the poems seem to involve secrecy, absence, or separation, which may explain why the love affair is so rarely consummated. But no reasons are ever given about why the lovers cannot express their love openly or resolve their longing for one another in marriage.

As if intoxicated by emotion, the poet pours forth torrents of images that compare the human body—both male and female—to fruits, flowers, animals (both domestic and wild), and even topographical features. Containing numerous terms, including geographical place-names, that appear nowhere else in Scripture, the lyrics place the loves in lush, scented environments where passion can flourish unrestrained. All of nature, rich in nourishment and sensation, provides metaphors for the lovers' intensely focused enjoyment of each others' bodies:

> How beautiful you are, my love,
> how very beautiful!
> Your eyes are doves
> behind your veil.
> Your hair is like a flock of goats,
> moving down the slopes of Gilead.
> Your teeth are like a flock of shorn ewes
> that have come up from the washing,
> all of which bear twins,
> and not one among them is bereaved.
> Your lips are like a crimson thread
> and your mouth is lovely.

(Song 4:1–3)

As in later Arabic love poetry, this catalogue of sensual images drawn from nature represents a highly stylized poetic convention. The poet's goal is not to provide a realistic physical portrait of his beloved, but to magnify her value by showing that she combines in herself all of the splendors of the natural world. When the poet states that "your neck is like the tower of David" (4:4), his comparison does not imply that the young woman's anatomy has an architectural rigidity, but instead serves to show his verbal command of a highly artificial poetic tradition. The Song's similes and metaphors thus have an imaginative boldness that is almost theatrical.

Gender and Courtship

From a contemporary feminist viewpoint, perhaps the Song of Songs' most outstanding quality is the presence of a female voice. The Song of Songs is the only book in the Hebrew Bible that focuses on the feelings of a woman in love and allows her more than equal time to express those feelings with startling honesty:

> My beloved thrust his hand into the opening,
> and my inmost being yearned for him.
> I arose to open to my beloved,
> and my hands dripped with myrrh . . .

(Song 5:4–5)

Because the poet frequently presents erotic feeling from a woman's rather than a man's perspective, some commentators suggest that the author may have been a woman. If so, she shrewdly sought to pass off her work as the youthful utterances of King Solomon, whose many wives made him seem a romantic figure to later

generations. Although the poems are anonymous, they do preserve a woman's voice—strong, passionate even, and self-conscious—that is heard for the first and last time in biblical literature.

Traditional Interpretations

Puzzled or embarrassed by the poet's enjoyment of physical love, many commentators have labeled the work an allegory—a fictional narrative in which characters, objects, and actions symbolize some higher truth. To Jews, the Song of Songs became an allegory of Yahweh's love for Israel. To Christians, it became an expression of Christ's love for his "bride," the church. Both of these figurative interpretations draw on a recurrent biblical image of the covenant relationship, the marriage metaphor, in which Yahweh is the "husband" to Israel's "wife." According to the prophet Hosea, God instructs Israel to call Yahweh "my husband" and to abandon her other lovers (Hos. 2:16). Similar statements appear in Jeremiah (2:2; 3:1–2), Isaiah (1:21), and Ezekiel (16:8–43; 23:1–45). At the very least, such marital imagery applied to the Yahweh–Israel relationship suggests multiple levels of meaning in the prophetic texts—in this case, a partly hidden metaphor of God's courtship of Israel and the complex emotional, psychological, and physical nature of their partnership. Most scholars believe that both Jewish and Christian commentators resorted to an allegorical method of interpretation to silence those who read the Song of Songs literally—as a frank affirmation of the human capacity for sexual pleasure.

 ## The Book of Lamentations

Whereas the Song of Songs is performed at Passover to celebrate God's redeeming love for Israel, Lamentations is the work that is chanted in sorrow when Jews gather each year to mourn the destruction of Jerusalem. According to tradition, the city fell to the Babylonians on August 9, 587 BCE, and again on the same day and month to the Romans in 70 CE., a national disaster commemorated at the solemn Fast of the Ninth of Av (see Table 24.1). The five poems in this little book vividly express the people's collective grief for the loss of their holy city and Temple. Whereas the prophetic books record public pronouncements of doom against the Judean capital, Lamentations (particularly Chs. 2 and 4) embodies the private anguish of individuals who personally experienced the fulfillment of Yahweh's harsh judgment.

The name "Lamentations" derives from the Greek *Threnoi* and the Latin *Threni*, both of which are translations of the Hebrew title *Qinoth*, meaning "dirges" (songs or poems of grief). The more common Hebrew name, however, is *Eikhah*, referring to the opening phrase "How lonely sits the city" (1:1). Although Lamentations appears immediately after the Book of Jeremiah in most English editions of the Old Testament, in the Hebrew Tanakh, it is placed among the Writings as one of the Megillot (Festival Scrolls).

Probably because Jeremiah is the great prophet of Jerusalem's doom (see Chapter 17), a relatively late tradition attributes Lamentations to him. The book itself does not mention the writer, and many scholars believe that it is the product of two or three anonymous poets, at least one of whom may have been an eyewitness to the horrors of the famine, starvation, and slaughter the poems describe. The oldest passages appear in Chapters 2 and 4, which were probably written shortly after Nebuchadnezzar's armies besieged and destroyed Jerusalem. Chapters 1 and 3 were composed somewhat later, perhaps in the fifth century BCE, and Chapter 5 during the postexilic period. Carefully structured, the first four poems are **acrostics:** Each has twenty-two verses, one for each of the twenty-two letters of the Hebrew alphabet, in which the first word of each verse begins with a different letter of the alphabet in sequential order. Chapter 5 also has twenty-two verses, but these are not arranged alphabetically.

From such artful wordplay, it is apparent that Lamentations is not a spontaneous outpouring of emotion, although the poets' feelings run deep and many passages are extremely moving. In Chapter 2, the poet emphasizes both the totality of Jerusalem's ruin and the dehumanization of its population, which hunger has driven to cannibalism:

> Look, O Lord, and consider!
> To whom have you done this?
> Should women eat their offspring,
> the children they have borne?
> Should priest and prophet be killed
> in the sanctuary of the Lord?

(Lam. 2:20)

"Slaughtering [Judah's inhabitants] without mercy," Yahweh has given his enemies reason to rejoice, while his people are subjected to intolerable conditions (2:21–22).

Adhering to the Deuteronomistic assumption, the poems of Chapters 1, 2, and 4 agree that Jerusalem's fall resulted from the people's sins, particularly those of the priests and prophets who had falsely promised

deliverance (4:13). Considering the thoroughness and long duration of the covenant community's devastation, however, the poets question Yahweh's intentions toward his worshipers. Will the severity of the people's suffering at last move God to show pity?

In the Book of Jeremiah, God briefly expresses regret for having so cruelly punished his people (Jer. 42:10), but Lamentations includes no divine apology for the extent of Judah's misery. Instead, the author of Chapter 5—writing long after some exiles had returned to a ruined homeland—can only wonder aloud at Yahweh's treatment of the covenant people, particularly his failure to restore them to his favor completely. Still under a foreign yoke, the people are enslaved in their own homeland, relentlessly exploited by taskmasters as harsh as those in Egypt. Facing the unresolved conflict between prophetic promises and historical reality, the poet asks if God has permanently abandoned his worshipers and begs for a *genuine* restoration:

> Why have you forgotten us completely?
> why have you forsaken us these many days?
> restore us to yourself, O Lord . . .
> renew our days as of old—
> unless you have utterly rejected us . . .

(Lam. 5:20–21)

The Book of Esther

In Lamentations, Jewish poets mourn for Jerusalem's desolation and for Yahweh's strange refusal to restore the returned exiles to freedom and national prosperity. In the Book of Esther, which was recited annually at the Festival of Purim, the anonymous author does not plead for God's help in Israel's restoration, but instead creates a short story in which Jewish exiles living abroad take action to ensure their own survival. The only book in the Hebrew Bible that does not even mention God, Esther at first glance appears to be an entirely secular tale, one in which human characters seem to act on their own initiative and without specific divine guidance. On closer inspection, however, Esther may represent a fresh and subtle way of representing God's hidden influence on human history. Like Ruth, the only other canonical book named for a woman, Esther does not show Yahweh directly intervening in human affairs—as he commonly does in the Pentateuch and the Prophets. Instead, Esther focuses on human actions and human motives that readers are free to interpret as somehow fulfilling the divine will. In the Hebrew edition of this book, the writer never refers to Israel's traditional institutions—the

Temple, priesthood, homeland, or Davidic dynasty, or even the Mosaic *torah*. Canonical Esther deals only with the issue of Jewish ethnic identity, dramatizing both the political opportunities and the dangers of Jews living in the Diaspora, subject to the prejudices or whims of foreign rulers.

By contrast, the Greek edition of Esther more than makes up for the Hebrew version's lack of religious content. Known as the Additions to Esther, the Greek Septuagint text includes long prayers, passages emphasizing that both **Esther** and her adopted father **Mordecai** faithfully observed Torah-mandated dietary laws, and other distinctive Jewish customs. In the Additions, Esther becomes a completely devout Jewish woman who loathes being married to **Ahasuerus** (probably **Xerxes I**), the emperor of Persia, and hates sharing both his bed and his banquets, where the food does not meet Levitical standards.

An Exciting Melodrama

The Hebrew author of this short story, apparently unconcerned about either dietary restrictions or foreign marriage, creates an exciting melodrama in which court intrigue rather than *torah* loyalty drives the plot. When Ahasuerus divorces Queen Vashti for her refusal to exhibit herself before his male courtiers, Mordecai, a loyal member of the royal bureaucracy, maneuvers events so that his beautiful cousin Esther, whom he has adopted (Esther 2:7), becomes queen. In the meantime, Mordecai has discovered a conspiracy against the emperor's life but is able to send a warning in time so that the conspirators are discovered and executed. Although Mordecai's deed is recorded in the Persian court annals, Ahasuerus does not know that he owes his life to a Jewish subject. The revelation of Mordecai's service to the state is delayed until this information can help trigger a dramatic reversal in the storyline.

Haman, whom the emperor has promoted to chief administrator at the court, becomes furious when Mordecai refuses to bow down before him and resolves not only to murder the Jew but also to exterminate his entire race. Telling Ahasuerus that a people who "do not keep the king's laws" (and are therefore potentially dangerous) are settled throughout the empire, Haman persuades Ahasuerus to eliminate this threat to national stability by ordering the execution of all Jews and the confiscation of their property. Haman casts lots (*purim*, hence the name of the festival) to determine the date of the massacre, which is to be the thirteenth day of the month of Adar (February–March) (3:7).

Esther's Heroism Following Mordecai's instructions, Esther has hitherto kept her Jewish identity a secret, but now he asks the young queen to risk her life by appearing unbidden before the emperor to plead for her people. For security reasons, all who enter the emperor's presence must do so by invitation only; persons who intrude uninvited are immediately put to death, a fact that Esther points out to her adoptive father. In Mordecai's speech persuading Esther to intervene with Ahasuerus, the author offers a rare hint that a higher power may be at work to save the Jews from destruction: "For if you [Esther] keep silence at such a time as this, relief and deliverance will rise from another quarter. Who knows? Perhaps you have come to royal dignity for just such a time as this" (4:14). Although who or what "another quarter" may be is never defined, many commentators see in this statement—as in Ahasuerus's easily manipulated character—evidence of divine Providence at work.

The unexpected events that follow Esther's courageous appeal to the king tend to confirm a providential interpretation. As Haman erects a lofty gallows on which to hang Mordecai, Ahasuerus—suffering from insomnia (divinely induced?)—orders recent court records read aloud to him and learns that Mordecai had saved his life. Haman is then duped into suggesting high honors for the emperor's rescuer, after which Esther reveals Haman's evil plot, which was intended to destroy her, a Jew, and Mordecai, to whom Ahasuerus owes his life. Dramatic justice is served when Haman is hanged on the gallows he had built for Mordecai. At Esther's suggestion, Haman's ten sons are hanged with him, bringing a permanent end to his family's advancement at court.

The Feast of Purim Unfortunately, the Jews living in the Persian Empire are still in danger from Ahasuerus's first decree, for Persian custom apparently assumes that all of the king's laws are just and cannot be revoked. Ahasuerus does, however, issue a second edict instructing Jews to fortify and defend themselves, which they do with spectacular success (Esther 8). Chapter 9 recounts how the Jews slew all who would have murdered them, after which they hold a joyous victory celebration, the Feast of Purim. Ironically, their triumph falls on the very day that Haman had selected for their mass slaughter.

History into Fiction

As a work of historical imagination, Esther interweaves some reliable information about the Persian Empire during the fifth century BCE with an ingenious tale of imminent catastrophe and redemption. Scholars believe that the author may have adapted the historical background from Herodotus's *History* (fifth century BCE) and other books that included detailed accounts of Persian culture and court customs. Attempts to verify specific events in the story, however, have been unsuccessful. We have no historical record of a Persian queen named Vashti, nor of any queen of Jewish descent named Esther. The Persian Empire consisted of 20, not 127, provinces, and it does not appear that any Persian monarch ever gave orders to kill all his Jewish subjects or to allow them, in turn, to massacre their would-be murderers. Indeed, the number of Persians allegedly killed while attacking the Jewish community is so large—75,000 according to Esther 9:16—that it seems unlikely that any contemporary or later Persian historian would have neglected to mention it. As for Esther being raised to the rank of queen, historians note that Persian kings typically married members of the Persian nobility. (It is possible that secondary wives in the emperor's large harem were non-Persians.) Esther's age is also problematic: The text indicates that Mordecai was among the exiles whom Nebuchadnezzar deported to Babylon during the reign of Jehoiachin (called "Jeconiah" here), which would have made him more than 100 years old during Xerxes' day. Esther could not have been much younger and therefore not likely to have dazzled the king with her beauty (2:6).

Although many scholars regard the name "Esther" as a variant of "Ishtar," the Babylonian goddess of love and war, others conclude that it is derived from the Persian word for "star." Mordecai, however, clearly takes his name from "Marduk," the head of the Babylonian pantheon, suggesting to some commentators a mythic background to this story in which Mordecai defeats a powerful opponent, as Marduk conquered the dragon Tiamat. (For discussions of Babylonian myth, see Chapters 3 and 5.) The fact that Yahweh is never referred to, or cited as the source of the Jews' deliverance, tends to reinforce the impression that the book's origins may be found outside Israelite religion or tradition. At the end of the book, an editor refers to the "annals of the kings of Media and Persia" (10:2), a document that no other ancient historian mentions. If this "lost" archive once existed, it suggests the presence of other, non-Israelite sources for the narrative that we can no longer access today.

Survival in the Diaspora

Although the Book of Esther has none of the supernatural or apocalyptic elements that dominate the Book of Daniel, it shares with Daniel a deep concern for the survival of Jewish communities living in the Diaspora, where enemies of the Jews can persuade foreign rulers to persecute them. No evidence exists that any Persian monarch ordered the execution of his Jewish subjects—or commanded them to kill his non-Jewish citizens—but both Daniel and Esther express deep anxiety about the welfare and security of Jews living far from the Judean homeland. During the long period of Persian domination of the Near East (from 539 BCE, when Cyrus of Persia captured Babylon, to about 332 BCE, when Alexander the Great conquered the Persian Empire), relations between Jews and their foreign rulers may have been uneasy, but they were generally peaceful. The situation changed abruptly during the second century BCE, when a successor of Alexander—Antiochus IV of Syria—make a concerted effort to destroy the Jewish religion in order to assimilate this resistant people into the Greek culture of his kingdom. The books of 1 and 2 Maccabees, part of the deuterocanon, offer a graphic account of Antiochus's savage persecutions of Jews who refuse to disobey the Mosaic *torah*—and of the successful rebellion against Antiochus's troops that temporarily created a politically independent Jewish state for the first time since Nebuchadnezzar's armies ravaged Jerusalem in 587 BCE. (For discussions of the Maccabean Revolt and its connection with the apocalyptic visions in Daniel, see Chapter 26.)

QUESTIONS FOR DISCUSSION AND REVIEW

1. Define the Megillot, and describe the diverse forms of literature it contains. What do these books have in common, and why were they grouped together as a unit in the Hebrew Bible (Tanakh)?

2. How do Ruth and Esther display initiative in a world dominated by men? Are their actions truly heroic or merely resourceful?

3. Why was a collection of erotic poetry—the Song of Songs—accepted into the biblical canon? How have interpreters tried to "spiritualize" the book?

4. What kind of audience would have found a Diaspora short story like Esther inspiring, or a group of love poems like the Song of Songs entertaining? How could erotic lyrics be fitted to the celebration of Passover? Would the same audience have found Lamentations equally entertaining?

Terms and Concepts to Remember

acrostics	Haman
Ahasuerus (Xerxes I)	Megillot (Festival Scrolls)
Boaz	Mordecai
Diaspora	Naomi
Esther	Passover
Fast of the Ninth of Av	Pentecost (Shavuoth)
Feast of Tabernacles (Feast of Booths)	Purim
	Ruth

Recommended Reading

Ruth

Brenner, Athalya, ed. *A Feminist Companion to Ruth.* Sheffield, England: Sheffield Academic Press, 1993. Essays expressing women's perspectives on Ruth's story.

Robertson-Farmer, Kathleen A. "The Book of Ruth." In *The New Interpreter's Bible,* Vol. 2, pp. 891–946. Nashville, TN: Abingdon Press, 1998. The full text, with enlightening discussion.

Song of Songs

Bloch, Ariel, and Bloch, Chana. *The Song of Songs: The World's First Great Love Poem* (Modern Library Classics). New York: Modern Library, 2006. A detailed analysis.

Nelson, James, and Longfellow, Sandra P., eds. *Sexuality and the Sacred: Sources for Theological Reflection.* Louisville, KY: Westminster John Knox, 1994. A collection of essays representing contemporary Christian views on human sexuality.

Weems, Renita J. "The Song of Songs." In *The New Interpreter's Bible,* Vol. 5, pp. 363–434. Nashville, TN: Abingdon Press, 1997. A helpful introduction, with detailed explanations of poetic metaphors.

Lamentations

O'Connor, Kathleen M. "The Book of Lamentations." In *The New Interpreter's Bible,* Vol. 6, pp. 1013–1072. The full text, with solid interpretation.

Provan, Iain W. *Lamentations* (New Century Bible Commentary). Grand Rapids, MI: Eerdmans, 1991. An informative treatment of the poems and their setting.

Esther

Berlin, Adele. *Esther: JPS Bible Commentary.* Philadelphia: Jewish Publication Society, 2001. Examines the book from a scholarly Jewish perspective.

Crawford, Sidnie White. "The Book of Esther." In *The New Interpreter's Bible,* Vol. 2, pp. 855–972. The biblical text, with scholarly analysis that includes a feminist reading.

Day, Linda. "Esther, Book of." In K. D. Sakenfeld, ed., *The New Interpreter's Dictionary of the Bible* Vol. 2, pp. 317–320. Nashville, TN: Abingdon Press, 2007. A brief introduction.

Moore, Carey. *Esther* (Anchor Bible). Garden City, NY: Doubleday, 1975. A recent translation with commentary.

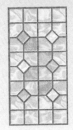

CHAPTER 25

Reinterpreting Israel's History
The Books of 1 and 2 Chronicles

Key Topics/Themes Because the restoration of Judah following the return from exile was only partial and incomplete—the Davidic monarchy was not restored, and Judah remained under foreign control—it became desirable to reevaluate Israel's past in terms of what the covenant community had actually become in the postexilic era. Based largely on 1 and 2 Kings, the books of Chronicles retell Israel's history from a priestly viewpoint, portraying the Davidic monarchs as primarily forerunners of the priestly aristocracy that administered the Second Temple.

 ## The Chronicler: A Priestly Revisionist

Recognizing that Yahweh, Lord of history, had drastically changed the direction of Israel's historical development, postexilic writers undertook the necessary task of reinterpreting the covenant community's past to depict it as a prologue to their unexpectedly diminished present. A century or two after the exiles' return from Babylon to Judea, an anonymous scribe known as the **Chronicler** again surveyed Israelite history, this time focusing on the center of national worship, the Jerusalem Temple. For the Chronicler, Israel's destiny was not necessarily to exercise political power on the world stage. Rather, it was to promote Yahweh's cult with ethical and ritual purity—a revisionist view that historical events seem to validate. Most of the promises made to Israel's ancestors in Genesis, particularly those for a secure homeland and a line of kings, no longer seemed attainable. Yahweh had permanently removed both the Davidic monarchy and Judah's political freedom. Almost all that remained was a belief in the divine presence, symbolized by the Holy of Holies in the rebuilt Temple.

Authorship

Because of their generally consistent priestly orientation, the four books of 1 and 2 Chronicles, Ezra, and Nehemiah were, in the past, commonly assigned to the same writer. Recently, however, many scholars have disputed the claim that the same person—the Chronicler—was responsible for all four narratives, pointing to differences in attitude and theology that distinguish Ezra and Nehemiah from the two books of Chronicles. Some scholars argue that the same priestly editor produced the final version of all four volumes, preserving older material that differed from his viewpoint and adding commentary to impart thematic unity. A majority of scholars, however, have concluded that the author of Chronicles was different from that of Ezra-Nehemiah. The prominence he gives to the Levites in their role as Temple singers and functionaries strongly suggests that he belonged to that group.

Sources and Themes

From the standpoint of biblical history writing, perhaps the most important aspect of Chronicles is the way in which its author freely changes older historical traditions in order to advance his theological understanding of God's purpose for Israel. Because 1 and 2 Chronicles are among the few documents for which we have canonical sources—the books are largely rewrites of 1 and 2 Samuel and 2 Kings—it is possible to see how the author changes his sources to make his theological points. While relying on the Deuteronomistic History (DH) for his narrative structure, the Chronicler consistently omits DH material that does not fit his religious agenda and adds information (from unknown sources) that emphasizes his priestly concerns. The author retains the DH view that Israel suffers because of its sins, but he produces new portraits of Israel's most prominent kings. In particular, he radically transforms the DH portrayals of David and Solomon, presenting them as priest-kings whose main concern was always the building, furnishing, and maintenance of the Jerusalem Temple. David is no longer an ambitious military leader whose heroic exploits elevate him to Israel's throne, where he creates a powerful if short-lived kingdom. Under the Chronicler's retouching of David's portrait, the king becomes not a warrior but a religious figure with the mentality and preoccupations of a priest. The stream of Israel's history thus flows, not toward the goal of political success and status in the international arena, but toward the properly regulated liturgy at the Jerusalem sanctuary—a religious mission that could be carried out regardless of Judea's postexilic lack of political autonomy (2 Chron. 35:16–19; 36:22–23).

The Chronicler draws mainly from Deuteronomistic narratives, although he also borrows genealogical lists from the Pentateuch and passages from various psalms to fill out his account. In addition to his canonical sources, the writer refers to otherwise unknown documents, such as the "records of the seer Samuel, . . . the records of the prophet Nathan, and . . . the records of the seer Gad" (1 Chron. 29:29–30; see also references to Solomon's archives [2 Chron. 9:29] and those of Hezekiah [2 Chron. 32:32]). The Chronicler may have used some historically reliable material not included in the Deuteronomistic History. It is now impossible, however, to verify the historicity of his extensive additions, such as descriptions of Hezekiah's sweeping religious reforms (2 Chron. 29–31) or of "wicked" Manasseh's unexpected change of character, a reversal not even hinted at in 2 Kings. According to the Chronicler, Manasseh—whose religious apostasy the DH specifically blames for Judah's fall to Babylon (2 Kings 23:26–27)—is himself deported to Babylon, where he sincerely repents of his sins. After being restored to his throne in Jerusalem (how is not explained), he initiates a program of religious purification anticipating that of Josiah (2 Chron. 33). As many commentators have observed, Manasseh's personal history—a cycle of sin, punishment, conversion, and restoration—exactly parallels what happened to Judah. In the Chronicler's hands, Manasseh comes to embody the covenant people's collective experience, that of a sinner redeemed by suffering and repentance.

The two books of Chronicles were originally one volume, until the Septuagint editors divided the work into two scrolls titled *Paralipomenon*, meaning "what was omitted"—that is, information not previously included in the books of Samuel and Kings. When translating the Vulgate, Jerome called the work *Chronicon*, the Latin name from which the English title is taken. This closely approximates the Hebrew title, *Dibre Hayamim*, which means "annals" (literally, "the book of acts of days").

The Book of 1 Chronicles

First Chronicles devotes the first nine chapters to a survey of world history—in the form of an extensive genealogy that begins with Adam and ends with a list of prominent Judeans (particularly Levites) who returned from the Babylonian captivity to Jerusalem (1:1–9:34). The narrative proper opens with a negative judgment of Saul's reign, here reduced to a brief account of the king's visit to the spirit medium of Endor and his ensuing suicide at the Battle of Gilboa (cf. 1 Sam. 28). This episode serves to contrast Saul's military and religious failures with the glorious successes of his divinely approved successor, David. The book's remaining twenty chapters are largely an uncritical celebration of David's accomplishments, illustrating the principle that faithfulness to Yahweh brings divine favor and national success.

David: An Idealized Priest-King

The author portrays David not as a warrior-poet and administrative leader (as he is in 1 and 2 Samuel) but exclusively as a devout worshiper of Yahweh. The Chronicler's David devotes most of his energies, not to waging war to defeat the Philistines and increase Israel's territories, but to supervising elaborate preparations for the Temple that his heir, Solomon, will later build in Jerusalem. This David eagerly contributes his wealth to gather construction materials for the sanctuary and to recruit the artisans and musicians necessary for its construction and liturgy. Transforming David into the perfect example of a priest-king, the author carefully omits any reference to David's wrongdoing, such as his committing adultery with Bathsheba and plotting to kill Uriah. In reshaping David's career, the Chronicler introduces a number of significant changes in the Deuteronomistic sources; his revisions include the following:

- Making Saul's failure as king a divine judgment caused by his visit to the medium at Endor, a betrayal of loyalty to Yahweh

- Having David proclaimed king over all Israel at Hebron (12:23–40), whereas Samuel states that only the tribe of Judah acknowledged him there (cf. 2 Sam. 2)

- Inserting a long prayer that David gives when he brings the Ark of the Covenant to Jerusalem, thus clothing the monarch in priestly robes (16:7–36)

- Insisting that David contributed enormous sums of gold toward building the Temple, thereby providing a good example to later Judeans (22:14–16; 28:14–19)

- Stating that David was responsible for assigning the Levites—cantors, gatekeepers, and bakers—their Temple duties, thus making a direct connection between the Davidic monarchy and the later Temple liturgy

- Asserting that David determined the plans, furnishings, and functions of the Temple and that Solomon merely carried them out (28:1–31)

- Removing all references to David's misdeeds, including his adultery with Bathsheba and responsibility for Uriah's murder

- Attributing to David a final speech in which he urges generous financial support for the construction and upkeep of the Temple (29:1–10)

- Implying that David transferred the reins of power to Solomon while he was still alive and that Solomon ascended the throne without opposition (29:22–28)

- Substituting "Satan" for "Yahweh" as the source of David's decision to take a census of the people, thereby removing from God the moral responsibility for this act (21:1; cf. 2 Sam. 24:1)

In depicting David as a priest-king whose reign is significant primarily because he uses his power to bring the Ark of the Covenant to Jerusalem and to promote construction of Yahweh's sanctuary there, the Chronicler asks his readers to remember David as an unblemished worshiper of Israel's God. He thus not only omits any reference to the king's driving ambition, his adulteries, or his sometimes treacherous politics but also deletes from the record such violent actions as David's ruthless elimination of Saul's heirs (his potential rivals). He includes no account of Absalom's revolt against his father or of

other rebellions and palace intrigues that shadowed the later years of David's reign. Further, the author allows Solomon to mount Israel's throne without having to shed a brother's blood (1 Chron. 29:22–28). Writing centuries after Nebuchadnezzar had brought the Davidic line of kings to an end, the Chronicler creates memories of an ideal David, a God-directed ruler who can serve as the model for a future heir who might, at some unknown time, reestablish David's throne. For the Chronicler, David becomes the prototype of Israel's Messiah, the anointed king who will ultimately restore Israel, fulfilling all the divine promises.

 ## The Book of 2 Chronicles

In his second volume, the Chronicler further develops his thesis that, from its inception, the Davidic dynasty's chief purpose was to promote Yahweh's worship at the Jerusalem sanctuary according to precise *torah* rituals. His description of the reigns of Judean kings serves mainly to show that royal failure to enforce correct worship at the Temple led to the monarchy's overthrow. In addition to demonstrating that too many kings were faithless to their covenant obligations and/or lacked the proper zeal for maintaining Yahweh's shrine, the author accuses the people as a whole of the apostasy that caused the nation's downfall (cf. 2 Chron. 36:14). By contrast, the Deuteronomistic History places responsibility for Judah's collapse squarely on Manasseh's shoulders (2 Kings 23:26–27; 24:3–4). By making the entire community responsible for Judah's destruction, the Chronicler apparently hoped to teach postexilic Judeans a lesson: To ensure their continued survival, they must wholeheartedly support national worship at the Second Temple.

Second Chronicles covers the four centuries from Solomon's ascension to Israel's throne to Cyrus the Great's proclamation encouraging exiled Judeans to return to Jerusalem (c. 922–538 BCE). Although the Chronicler includes a description of the conflict between Solomon's heir Rehoboam and the rebel Jeroboam that led to the division between Israel and Judah, he does not—unlike 2 Kings—offer a parallel account of the two kingdoms' monarchies. By the author's time, Judeans probably did not expect a reunion of the two nations, making the history of the northern kingdom seem irrelevant. Focusing on Judah's story, the Chronicler has little to say about Israel, referring to it only when its actions concern Judean affairs. Even so, the author still entertains the concept of an ideally united Israel, the special people of God.

From Solomon to Hezekiah

The book opens by enthusiastically describing the splendors of Solomon's legendary wealth and the king's monumental building projects, particularly the construction, ceremonial dedication, and divine consecration of the Temple. As he idealized David, so the author portrays Solomon in a consistently positive light, retaining nothing of 2 Kings' criticism of the king's later years (2 Chron 1–9; cf. 2 Kings 11). The Chronicler does, however, reproduce Kings' account of the confrontation between Rehoboam and the rebellious northern tribes that withdrew from the Davidic realm when the new king refused to change his tyrannical policies. To emphasize the link between the king's loyalty to Yahweh and his political fortunes, the writer creates an expanded narrative about Pharaoh Shishak's invasion of Judah and looting of the Temple treasury, humiliating consequences of Rehoboam's having "abandoned the law of the LORD" (2 Chron. 12:1–2).

After the split between Judah and Israel, the Chronicler rapidly scans the line of Davidic rulers, pausing to elaborate on the reigns of four kings whose religious policies he approves—Asa, Jehoshaphat, Hezekiah, and Josiah. Expansively rewriting Kings' story of Hezekiah, the author devotes four chapters (29–32) to the king's religious reforms, presenting them in a way that foreshadows Josiah's later and more thorough centralization of worship at the Jerusalem Temple. Portrayed as a zealous enforcer of the "one God, one sanctuary" ideal, Hezekiah makes a clean sweep of all rival shrines outside the capital, smashing their sacred objects. Chronicles also depicts Hezekiah as conducting extensive Temple renovations and instituting a nationwide Passover celebration, even sending messengers to the northern tribal territories (by then under Assyrian occupation), inviting all to participate in the Jerusalem rites (Ch. 30). Using phrases almost identical to those the DH applied to Josiah, the Chronicler states that "since the time of Solomon . . . there had been nothing like this in Jerusalem" (30:26; cf. 35:18 and 2 Kings 23:22–23). In praising the thoroughness of Hezekiah's actions, the author makes Josiah's later accomplishments seem less outstanding, a device that prepares readers for the author's strangely judgmental view of Josiah's behavior when the king battles against another invading Egyptian pharaoh (see below).

Manasseh's Sins and Repentance

Between the reforming programs of Hezekiah and Josiah came the reign of **Manasseh,** whose forty-five years on the throne exceeded those of any other ruler of Judah or Israel. The Chronicler agrees with the DH on Manasseh's "abominable" crimes, which include burning his son as a religious sacrifice, but then adds that this practitioner of "evil" underwent a remarkable conversion, an event about which 2 Kings is entirely silent. According to 2 Chronicles 33, after the Assyrians imprison Manasseh in Babylon, the former practitioner of black magic suddenly turns to Yahweh, who pardons the repentant king and restores him to his royal honors in Jerusalem. Why the Assyrians removed Manasseh in the first place or then decided to reinstall him as Judah's king the narrator does not explain. Instead of clarifying the political situation, the Chronicler adds a lengthy description of Manasseh's religious reforms, in which the king clears the temple of shrines to foreign gods he had previously installed there and elaborately rebuilds Yahweh's altar (all of which is absent from the DH). The author even claims that a copy of the prayer by which Manasseh persuades Yahweh to rescue him from Babylon is preserved in the "annals of the seers" (or, in some manuscripts, the "annals of Hozai" (2 Chron. 33:19). Although a document called the Prayer of Manasseh is included in the Apocrypha, scholars agree that it is not the same work to which the Chronicler refers.

Perhaps the most striking change that the Chronicler makes to his description of Judah's last kings is his reinterpretation of the circumstances surrounding King Josiah's death. After following 2 Kings' account of Josiah's sweeping religious reforms—and significantly expanding on the narrative of Josiah's Passover observances in Jerusalem—the writer inserts an episode featuring a dramatic confrontation between Josiah and Pharaoh Necho. Leading Egyptian armies through Judah's territory on his way to rescuing the last remnants of Assyria's army at Carchemish, Necho is—astoundingly—portrayed as a prophet of Yahweh. According to the Chronicler, Necho sends messengers to warn Josiah that the pharaoh is actually carrying out God's orders. Understandably skeptical that Necho speaks "from the mouth of God," Josiah intercepts the pharaoh's troops, is shot by archers, and, fatally wounded, is brought back to Jerusalem to die (2 Chron. 35:20–24). The Chronicler seems unable to accept the fact that the Davidic monarch most conspicuously effective in reestablishing Yahweh's worship was not allowed to continue his good works, but was struck down in his prime while defending his homeland. In his revisions, the author provides a reason for Josiah's untimely death—he failed to recognize the foreign invader as Yahweh's oracle!

Whereas the Deuteronomistic historian praises Josiah as faultless and blames Manasseh's sins for Judah's fall to Babylon (2 Kings 23:24–28), the Chronicler, strangely, reverses that judgment. He depicts a repentant Manasseh who dies in God's favor and a disobedient Josiah who fails to hear Yahweh's voice in an unlikely—and biblically unprecedented—source. Adhering to Deuteronomy's theory of history even while freely rewriting the Deuteronomistic narratives, the Chronicler insists on an inflexible law of crime and punishment.

The Placement of Chronicles in the Canon

Although the events that 2 Chronicles narrates took place before those recorded in Ezra and Nehemiah, editors chose to accord the books of Chronicles the climactic position in the Hebrew Bible. In this arranging the postexilic historical narratives out of chronological sequence, the editors had Cyrus—whom Second Isaiah identified as Yahweh's "messiah" or "anointed one" (Isa. 45:1)—utter the last words heard in the biblical canon. Whereas the Hebrew Bible's first speaker is God—commanding the world into existence—its final speaker is a mortal, a non-Israelite leader whose decree brings the covenant community back into existence, restoring Yahweh's people to their Promised Land. A Gentile conqueror who champions the Judean cause and authorizes rebuilding the fallen Temple, the Persian emperor acts within the human realm to accomplish the divine will. Cyrus, to whom "the LORD [Yahweh], the God of heaven, has given . . . all the kingdoms of the earth," calls on Jews scattered throughout the world to reassemble in Jerusalem: "Whoever is among you of all his people, . . . Let him go up!" (2 Chron. 36:22–23).

QUESTIONS FOR DISCUSSION AND REVIEW

1. Why did a postexilic writer compose a new history of the covenant community, 1 and 2 Chronicles, that largely duplicates the material in 1 and 2 Kings? What theological goal motivated the Chronicler to produce a revised version of Judean history?

2. Describe some of the significant changes the Chronicler made in revising his primary source, the Deuteronomistic History. How did the author reinterpret the reigns of David and Solomon? What changes did he make in describing the reigns of Manasseh and Josiah?

3. From a postexilic viewpoint, what religious institution in Judea was the most important part of the partly restored covenant community? How did the Chronicler regard the transition from monarchy to priestly administration of Judah?

4. What historical figure made Judah's restoration possible? What imperial power controlled Judea between about 539 and 332 BCE?

5. After their return from Babylon, why did Yahweh not restore the covenant people to an independent political state as in the days of King David? Why was the Davidic dynasty not reestablished in fulfillment of Yahweh's unconditional promises in 2 Samuel 7 and Psalm 89? Do you think that Yahweh's purpose was better served by an administration of priests than it was by Davidic rulers?

Terms and Concepts to Remember

Chronicler
Cyrus's decree
Josiah's encounter with Pharaoh Necho

Manasseh's repentance
postexilic theocracy
revisions of Israel's history

Recommended Reading

Ackroyd, Peter R. *The Chronicler in His Age.* Sheffield, England: Sheffield Academic Press, 1991. An authoritative scholarly work.

Allen, Leslie C. "The First and Second Books of Chronicles." In *The New Interpreter's Bible,* Vol. 3, pp. 299–659. Nashville, TN: Abingdon Press, 1999. Discusses the Chronicler's revisions of his sources, such as the books of Kings.

Japhet, Sara. *The Ideology of the Book of Chronicles and Its Place in Biblical Thought,* 2nd ed. New York: Peter Lang, 1997. Important, but somewhat technical.

Kalimi, Isaac. *The Reshaping of Ancient Israelite History in Chronicles.* Winona Lake, IN: Eisenbrauns, 2004. For more advanced study.

Knoppers, Gary N. "Chronicles, the First and Second Books of." In K. D. Sakenfeld, ed., *The New Interpreter's Dictionary of the Bible,* Vol. 1, pp. 622–631. Nashville, TN: Abingdon Press, 2006. Surveys the books' main themes and contents.

CHAPTER 26

Keeping God's Law in a Hostile World

Revolt of the Maccabees and the Book of Daniel

Key Topics/Themes Although placed among the prophets in most Christian Bibles, in the Hebrew Bible, the Book of Daniel appears among the Writings, perhaps because it differs in both form and content from traditional prophetic books. Like Esther, Daniel narrates the difficulties of Jews living in the **Diaspora**—the "scattering" of Jews throughout many foreign countries following the Babylonian destruction of Jerusalem in 587 BCE—a situation in which powerful enemies often threatened the very existence of the Jewish community. Daniel also resembles Esther in taking place at a foreign court, where the title character rises to a position of promi-nence, advising kings and emperors. But where Esther focuses on human agents acting to ensure Jewish survival, Daniel emphasizes the intervention of supernatural powers that not only rescue some *torah*-observant Jews from certain death but also control the rise and fall of a series of foreign empires—including Babylon, Persia, and Greece—that dominate the covenant people. Unlike the classical prophets, the author of Daniel expresses his vision of Yahweh's purpose for Israel in apocalyptic terms, using vivid, even grotesque images to depict a cosmic struggle between good and evil that culminates in the establishment of God's kingdom.

Jews in the Diaspora

Judaism and Gentile Culture

In the Book of Esther, which resembles the Book of Daniel in dramatizing anti-Jewish intrigue at a foreign court far from Jerusalem, Haman describes the Jews to Ahasuerus, emperor of Persia: "There is a certain people scattered and separated among the peoples in all the provinces of your kingdom; their laws are different from those of every other people, and they do not keep the king's laws, so that it is not appropriate for the king to tolerate them" (Esther 3:8). In Jewish literature of the Diaspora, such as Esther and Daniel, persons hostile to Jews typically attempt to eliminate them by persuading foreign kings to issue laws or decrees calculated to destroy Judaism. Whereas Haman's plot to eradicate all Jews throughout the Persian Empire is foiled when Jews offer armed resistance, Daniel's jealous enemies convince credulous rulers to throw him into a lion's den or to incinerate his three friends in a fiery furnace, from which dangers angels miraculously rescue them. In Esther, the author

dramatizes the importance of human action to ensure Jewish survival, but in Daniel, the writer emphasizes supernatural intervention that delivers his characters from threats to both their religious integrity and their lives.

Daniel's emphasis on supernatural elements—including angelic visitations and visions of God's heavenly court—is typical of **apocalyptic literature.** A literary form bewildering to the average reader, the term derives from the Greek *apokalypsis,* which means "an unveiling, an uncovering, a stripping naked of what is normally hidden." As a literary category, an **apocalypse** is a revelation of dimensions or events ordinarily closed to human view, such as the invisible realm of heaven or the future course of human history. In the Hebrew Bible, only Daniel is a fully apocalyptic work, although there are apocalyptic elements in the visions of Yahweh's celestial council that Isaiah (6:1–12), Zechariah (3:1–10), and a few other prophets describe. The "Little Apocalypse" of Isaiah 24–27 and the obscure predictions about Israel's future redemption in Ezekiel (Ezek. 30, 37–39) and Zechariah (Zech. 9–14) also illustrate apocalyptic concerns about the ultimate fate of God's people.

Unique as it appears to some readers, Daniel belongs to a long literary tradition that produced many similar apocalyptic books. From the time the oldest parts of a noncanonical apocalypse called 1 Enoch were written in the late third century BCE through the end of the first century CE, when 2 Esdras and the Book of Revelation were composed, Jewish and Jewish-Christian authors produced a flood of apocalyptic visions. With the exceptions of Daniel and Revelation, these works (such as 1 and 2 Enoch, 2 Esdras, and 1 and 2 Baruch) were not accepted into the biblical canon (see Chapter 27). The ideas advanced in these writings, however, profoundly influenced New Testament authors, who readily adopted many apocalyptic themes and devices, particularly in Gospel forecasts of Jesus' return to earth (Mark 13; Matt. 24–25; and Luke 21); in Paul's early letters, such as 1 Thessalonians and 1 Corinthians; and in the epistles of Peter and Jude, the last of which quotes 1 Enoch as if it were Scripture (Jude 14–15; cf. 1 Enoch 1:9).

Eschatological Concerns

Apocalyptic literature typically is concerned with **eschatology**—speculations about "last things," such as the end of human history as we know it and the prophetic Day of Yahweh in which Israel's God judges the nations and vindicates his people. Besides its end-of-the-world aspects, eschatology also addresses the ultimate fate of individual persons: death, posthumous judgment, heaven, hell, and resurrection. In fact, only in apocalyptic writings do concepts of an afterlife first emerge in biblical literature, as when Daniel predicts that the "righteous" will be raised to life everlasting and the "wicked" to eternal dishonor (Dan. 12:1–3).

Judaism and Hellenism

The authors of the first two divisions of the Hebrew Bible—the Torah and the (Former) Prophets—show little interest in eschatological matters, but the situation changed radically during the last three centuries BCE, when apocalyptic speculation reached its height. Daniel's visions, for example, relate directly to the political and social upheavals of this period. Significantly, the rise of apocalyptic themes correlates closely with the introduction of Greek culture, which the conquests of Alexander the Great spread throughout the Near East and the eastern Mediterranean region during the last third of the fourth century BCE (see Figure 26.1). Known as **Hellenism** (after the Greeks' name for their country, Hellas), the widespread diffusion of Greek language, literature, philosophy, art, social customs, and religion

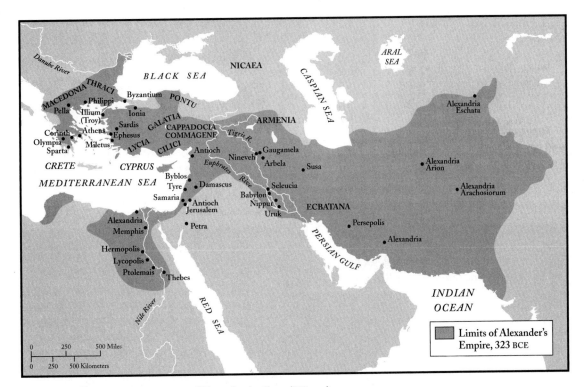

FIGURE 26.1 Map of the Empire of Alexander the Great (323 BCE).

FIGURE 26.2 This mosaic, in which Alexander of Macedonia (left) defeats the Persian Emperor Darius III (right center) at the Battle of Issus (333 BCE), pictures a decisive moment in later biblical history. Alexander's conquest of the older Near Eastern centers of power, including Egypt, Palestine, Mesopotamia, and Iran, introduced a new era in which Greek language, art, literature, science, and philosophy transformed the biblical world. By the time of Jesus, Judaism had been largely Hellenized—even in Palestine—and the New Testament was composed for a Greek-speaking audience molded by Greek ideas and culture.

transformed much of the civilized world, from Egypt and Mesopotamia to Syria and Palestine (see Figure 26.2). Following Alexander's death in 323 BCE, his vast empire—extending eastward from Greece to western India—was eventually divided among his successors, generals such as Ptolemy and Seleucus. **Palestine,** the name that Greek geographers gave Judah and its surrounding territories, was first ruled by a Greek-Egyptian dynasty that Ptolemy founded, but about 199 BCE, the Seleucid dynasty, which ruled Syria, Asia Minor, and Mesopotamia, took over the area (see Figure 26.3). For Palestinian Jews, including the author of Daniel, the consequences of this change in rulers were immense.

Under the Ptolemaic dynasty, many Jews had prospered, freely adopting the Greek way of life, giving their children Greek names, and blending Hellenistic and Judaic cultural traits. One important result of this synthesis of cultures was the gradual translation of the Hebrew Bible into Greek, the **Septuagint** edition, which Jewish scholars produced in Alexandria, Egypt, and which later became the preferred version of the Bible in the early Christian community. Like Daniel and

Mordecai, who became trusted administrators to the kings of Babylon or Persia, many upper-class, Greek-speaking Jews attained positions of responsibility and influence in Hellenistic society. With the ascent of a new Seleucid king to the Syrian throne, however, conditions for Palestinian Jews rapidly deteriorated. Unlike his predecessors, **Antiochus IV Epiphanes** (ruled 175–163 BCE) was evidently determined to make all his subjects fully Hellenized, a policy calculated to promote social unity throughout his ethnically diverse kingdom. As Haman had pointed out to Ahasuerus, the Jews—a people whose "laws are different from those of every other people, and [who] do not keep the king's laws" (Esther 3:8)—were seen as an obstacle to Antiochus's goal of national and cultural unification.

Other considerations may also have influenced Antiochus's violent persecution of Jews in **Judea,** the name by which the area surrounding Jerusalem was eventually known. His wars against Egypt had gone badly, and Antiochus needed funds, which may have triggered his assault on the Jerusalem Temple, which also functioned as the Judean state treasury. In 167 BCE, the king began

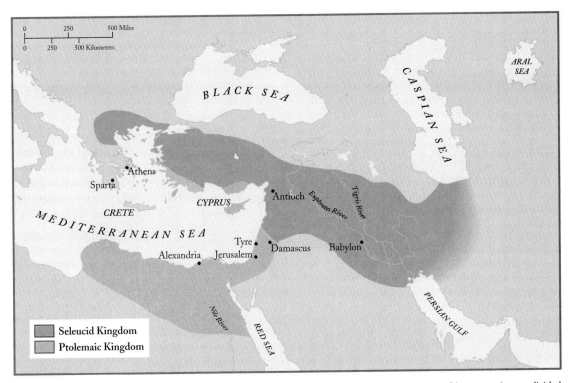

FIGURE 26.3 Map of the Seleucid and Ptolemaic Kingdoms. After Alexander's death in 323 BCE, his vast empire was divided among his military successors. General Ptolemy assumed control of Egypt, while another general, Seleucus, ruled Syria and Mesopotamia. The Ptolemaic and Seleucid dynasties repeatedly fought each other for control of Palestine.

a policy of "forced Hellenization," which included destroying copies of the Torah, barring circumcisions, preventing Jews from observing the Sabbath and other festivals, and, perhaps most importantly, seizing the Temple and its gold. According to tradition, Antiochus even erected an altar to Zeus, head of the Greek pantheon, in the Temple courts.

As recorded in the deuterocanonical books of 1 and 2 Maccabees—which provide the historical background for the Book of Daniel—Jewish response to Antiochus's "pollution" of Yahweh's sanctuary was not long in coming. In the village of Modein, not far from Jerusalem, a local priest named Mattathias and his sons killed both a royal commissioner and a Jew who had agreed to sacrifice to the Greek gods, sparking an armed Judean rebellion known as the Maccabean Revolt. Gathering an army of loyal Jews around him, Mattathias's eldest son, Judas (known as the "Maccabee" or [God's] "Hammer"), began a guerrilla-style military campaign against Antiochus's numerically superior forces. After several decisive victories, Judas was able to retake most of Jerusalem and the Temple, three years to the day (according to Jewish tradition) after Antiochus had desecrated the sanctuary. It took many more years of

fighting before the Maccabean rebels finally drove out the Seleucid troops and, eventually, established an independent Judean state in about 142 BCE, the first period of Jewish political autonomy since Nebuchadnezzar's destruction of Jerusalem more than 400 years earlier. (A more detailed discussion of the Maccabean Revolt and subsequent Jewish history appears in Chapters 27 and 28.)

Torah Loyalty, Martyrdom, and the Reward of Future Life

To many *torah*-abiding Jews, Antiochus's persecutions offered members of the covenant community a clear-cut choice between loyalty to the Mosaic tradition and surrender to the dominant political culture. For the first time in biblical history, Jews were suffering *because of their faithfulness* to Yahweh, not because Israel's God was punishing them for covenant breaking. For the first time, devout Jews were being tortured and killed because they refused to give up their ancestral faith. Whereas Deuteronomy had promised that obedience to

Yahweh's laws would bring prosperity and good fortune, during Antiochus's assault on the Jewish religion, fidelity to covenant law brought pain, loss, and death. As in the case of Job, who suffered because he was righteous, Yahweh's most loyal worshipers were singled out for intense suffering, a situation that once again raised the issue of God's justice.

The Book of 2 Maccabees paints a particularly horrific picture of faithful Jews paying for their integrity with unspeakable agony. In biblical literature's first description of religious martyrdom (dying as a "witness" to one's faith), seven young brothers, who had refused to eat pork (forbidden by *torah* commands), are subjected to fiendish torments by Antiochus's henchmen. One by one, before their mother's eyes, they are scalped, their heads flayed, their tongues cut out, and their hands and feet lopped off; then, still conscious, they are thrust into huge red-hot pans and slowly broiled alive (2 Macc. 7).

As martyrs who willingly died for their Mosaic heritage, the unnamed seven brothers not only served as models for other Jews forced to choose between life and *torah* loyalty but also voiced a belief that their sacrifice would be compensated for in a future life. Expressing his certainty that God will some day restore him to life, the second brother places his martyrdom in the light of eternity: "The King of the universe will raise us up to an everlasting renewal of life, because we have died for his laws" (2 Macc. 7:9). Partly inspired by the new phenomenon of *torah* obedience resulting in death, the author of Daniel similarly voices the Bible's first explicit promise of a resurrection to future life:

> At that time [of Antiochus's persecutions] Michael, the great prince, the protector of your people, shall arise. There shall be a time of anguish, such as has never occurred since nations first came into existence. But at that time your people shall be delivered, everyone who is found written in the book. Many of those who sleep in the dust of the earth shall awake, some to everlasting life, and some to shame and everlasting contempt. Those who are wise shall shine like the brightness of the sky, and those who lead many to righteousness, like the stars forever and ever."

(Dan. 12:1–3)

The authors of Daniel and 2 Maccabees thus present a powerful new doctrine: No longer will Sheol, the Underworld where Job hoped to end his pain in dark oblivion, claim all the dead indiscriminately. Instead, God will resurrect the wise and good to an afterlife in which they will radiate light like the stars of heaven.

Like other apocalyptic works, the Book of Daniel not only resolves the ethical problem of undeserved suffering—the righteous will eventually be awarded immortal life—but also confronts the problem of evil in human history. In the apocalyptic view, the present evil age, in which the violent and wicked too often exploit the good and the peaceful, is only temporary. It will suddenly end when God intervenes to overthrow existing empires and establish his everlasting kingdom (Dan. 2:44). In other words, the apocalyptic vision of a new age of righteousness that brings our flawed world to an abrupt conclusion actually functions as a **theodicy,** a literary defense of divine justice. The Book of Job had highlighted the ethical conflict between the concept of an all-powerful and all-good God who reigned over a morally chaotic universe, but had not reconciled this paradox. By introducing the idea that God permits evil to flourish only for a limited time and that he will (soon) overthrow wickedness and reward the righteous with new life free of pain, apocalyptic writers create a positive new scenario for human history.

 ## Characteristics of Apocalyptic Literature

Apocalyptic writing has been characterized as a literature of both "despair" and "hope." Apocalyptic writers despair because they typically see the world's condition—at least the situation of the covenant community, which is always their central concern—as so bad that human effort cannot redeem it or save it from powers seeking its destruction. At the same time, apocalyptic writers also express hope that God will soon act to accomplish what human actors cannot: permanently defeat Israel's enemies, cleanse the world of evil, and restore the cosmos to the state of goodness it possessed at creation's beginning (Gen. 1:31). A passage in Isaiah's "Little Apocalypse" anticipates this outcome:

> On this mountain the LORD of
> Hosts will make for all
> Peoples
> A feast of rich food, a feast of
> Well-aged wines, . . .
> And he will destroy on the Mountain
> The shroud that is cast over all Peoples,
> The sheet that is spread over all nations;
> He will swallow up death
> Forever.
> Then the LORD God will wipe
> Away the tears from all
> Faces,
> And the disgrace of his people he

Will take away from all
The earth . . .

(Isa. 25:6–8)

This vision of an earthly paradise—without death—is both a preview of the new world order under God's reign and a declaration of its universality. In the future, Yahweh will comfort and sustain "all peoples," not just Israel alone.

Apocalyptic writers, both Jewish and Christian, show an eagerness for God to act that borders on impatience. Israel's prophets had looked forward to the climactic "Day of Yahweh" and to the world transformation it would effect, but God's failure to intervene directly in human history—even when his people faced threats of near-extinction—encouraged both disappointment and cynicism. Historically, the indefinite postponements of Yahweh's "day of judgment" seem to have led to a skeptical attitude toward prophecy as such. In the Book of Ezekiel, Jews exiled to Babylon complain that "the days are prolonged, and every vision comes to nothing" (Ezek. 12:22). As if to reply to such doubts, the authors of Daniel, 1 Enoch, 2 Esdras, Revelation, and other apocalypses moved beyond their prophetic counterparts to insist that Yahweh would act decisively, and soon (cf. Rev. 1:3; 22:12, 20).

Apocalyptic promises of imminent deliverance plunge us into a cosmic battle between supernatural forces, a conflict in which our sense of the progression of historical time gives way to a more mythic scheme of long "ages" in which all of human history is telescoped into two opposing epochs. From the apocalyptic perspective, the present evil age is always about to give way to a new age in which God rules completely. Marked by violent upheavals, the crucial transition between the two periods is nothing less than the ultimate battle between good and evil. The finality of this struggle—the sense that time is running out and that divine patience with human error and folly is at an end—lends a note of feverish expectation to apocalyptic images of warfare in heaven and on earth, as apocalyptic authors attempt to measure the distance between the present and End time, as in Daniel's "a time, two times, and a half-time" (Dan. 7:25).

Equally characteristic of apocalyptic thought is the extraordinary passivity that these authors assign to human beings. In apocalyptic scenarios, human agents can only await the predestined catastrophes and redemptions already planned in heaven and about to be executed on earth. Understandably, when violence of cosmic proportions is about to be unleashed on the human race, mere human actions become irrelevant. Or,

as the author of Daniel 8 observes, when the evil "king of bold countenance" (presumably Antiochus IV) is at last broken, it will not be accomplished "by human hands" (Dan. 8:25). The initiative for historical change and conflict resolution lies entirely within God's hands, where, apocalyptic writers suggest, it has always been. Just as the Deity could bring a universe into being without help or opposition, so he can destroy or re-create that universe when it suits him. (Box 26.1 discusses in more detail the characteristics of apocalyptic writing.)

The Book of Daniel

The Book of Daniel was supposedly composed during the sixth century BCE, when the author was a Judean exile living successively in the Babylonian, Median, and Persian courts. Almost all scholars are convinced, however, that the book was written centuries later, between about 167 and 164 BCE, during the persecutions of Antiochus IV. One of the last-written books to enter the Hebrew Bible canon, Daniel is not a typically prophetic work but a literary creation in which stories of testing and persecution are mixed with apocalyptic visions of the distant future.

Daniel: A Literary Figure

The title character is, like the hero of the Joseph story (see Gen. 39–41), a worshiper of Yahweh transported to a foreign country where, after many trials and narrow escapes from death, he is elevated to a position of high honor. Like Joseph, too, Daniel is basically a solitary figure, facing danger alone, armed only with divinely inspired gifts to read minds, interpret dreams, and see into the future. As a boy, he studies "the literature and language of the Chaldeans," a technical term for Babylon's professional "wise men," including astrologers, magicians, and fortune-tellers. The narrator insists, however, that Daniel's famed wisdom, including his occult abilities, comes exclusively from Israel's God (1:3–7, 17). So successful is Daniel at mastering these arcane sciences that his royal patron, King Nebuchadnezzar, makes him supervisor "over all the wise men of Babylon" (2:48) and, eventually, "chief of the magicians, enchanters, Chaldeans, and diviners" (5:11; cf. 4:9).

Daniel further resembles Joseph in that God consistently favors him. Even after Babylon falls and new Median or Persian masters control the Near East, Daniel is repeatedly appointed to important positions. Supernaturally aided in his escapes from danger, most

---

BOX 26.1 Characteristics of Apocalyptic Writing

As the institution of Israelite prophecy declined during the postexilic era and prophetic inspiration became more difficult to defend to an increasingly skeptical audience, a new form of revelatory literature began to emerge, one that exhibited traits that distinguished it from both prophetic and wisdom traditions.

Universality

In contrast to prophetic oracles, which focus almost exclusively on Israel and its immediate neighbors, apocalyptic visions are universal in scope. Apocalyptic writers create visionary scenarios of global proportions, typically showing the rise and fall of great empires or portraying the fate of the entire human race. Although the writer's religious group (Israel or the Christian community) is always his central concern, he commonly surveys events both on earth and in heaven, encompassing the realms of both matter and spirit.

Cosmic Dualism

The apocalyptic worldview borrows much of its cosmology from Greek philosophical ideas about parallel worlds of matter and spirit. Accepting a dualistic "three-story universe" consisting of visible earth, Underworld (Sheol), and invisible heaven (see Figure 5.1), apocalyptic authors see human society as profoundly influenced by unseen forces, angels and demons, operating in a celestial realm. Events on earth, such as the persecution of the righteous, reflect the actions of these heavenly beings.

Chronological Dualism

Besides dividing the universe into two opposing domains of physical matter and invisible spirit, apocalyptic writers regard all history as separated into two mutually exclusive spans of time, a current wicked era and a future age of perfection. Seeing the present world situation as too thoroughly evil to reform, apocalyptists expect a sudden and violent change in which God or his Messiah will impose divine rule by force. In the apocalyptic view, there is no normal historical progression from one age to the next and no real continuity between them. Thus, Daniel portrays God's kingdom as abruptly interrupting the ordinary flow of time, shattering all worldly government with the impact of a colossal meteorite (Dan. 2:31–45).

Ethical Dualism

In the apocalyptic view, there are only two kinds of human beings, just as there are only two epochs of world history and two dimensions of existence—material and spiritual. Apocalyptic writers see humanity as divided into two opposing camps of intrinsically different ethical quality. The vast

---

notably his ordeal in the lions' den, Daniel is not an ordinary person, like the seven brothers tortured to death in 2 Maccabees. It is therefore difficult to see him as merely a role model for Diaspora Jews struggling to maintain their religious integrity in a hostile environment. Unlike the historical victims of Antiochus's persecutions, Daniel and his three Hebrew friends are miraculously shielded from all harm.

Sources of Daniel

Aside from the book bearing his name, Daniel appears nowhere else in the Hebrew Bible, nor do other writers refer to him—with one possible exception. The prophet Ezekiel twice refers to a **Danel,** who may or may not be the same figure we encounter in the Book of Daniel. Ezekiel's first reference occurs in Chapter 14, when he observes:

> Even if those three men were living there [in Israel], Noah, Danel and Job, they would save none but themselves by their righteousness.

(Ezek. 14:14)

By placing Danel (or Daniel?) alongside Noah and Job, Ezekiel appears to be holding up three ancient non-Israelites as famous examples of personal righteousness, but nowhere does he suggest that Daniel might be one of his fellow exiles. Ezekiel mentions Danel/Daniel again in Chapter 28, where he contrasts his legendary wisdom with the present folly of the king of Tyre (28:3), but the whole point of this allusion would have been lost had a sixth-century-BCE Daniel still been living.

Some commentators suggest that the primary source for the character of canonical Daniel can be found in ancient Canaanite literature. Archaeological discoveries at Ugarit (now called Ras Shamra), a Syrian city famous for its cuneiform archives, reveal the existence of a Canaanite folk hero and king named Danel. Like the biblical Solomon, Danel was revered for his extraordinary wisdom. It may be that Israelite oral traditions incorporated tales about the Canaanite sage, as they had about Job and Noah, that the author of Daniel drew upon to create the book's central figure, for dramatic purposes making him a Judean captive

majority of people walk in spiritual darkness and are doomed victims of God's wrath. Only a tiny minority—the religious group to which the writers belong and direct their message—remains faithful and receives salvation. Deeply conscious of human imperfection and despairing of humanity's ability to meet God's standards, apocalyptists take a consistently pessimistic view of society's future.

Predestination

Whereas most biblical writers emphasize that historical events are the consequences of humanity's moral choices (cf. Deut. 28–29; Josh 24; Ezek. 18), apocalyptic authors view history as progressing in a straight line toward a predetermined end. Just as the rise and fall of worldly empires occurs according to God's plan (Dan. 2, 7–8), so will history's conclusion take place at a time God has already set. Human efforts, no matter how well intended, cannot avert the coming disaster; the vast complexity of human experience means nothing in the context of the divinely prearranged schedule.

Limited Theology

Consistent with their strict division of history and people into divinely approved or disapproved units, apocalyptic writers usually show little sympathy for differing religious viewpoints or compassion for nonbelievers. All modes of life are either black or white, with no psychological or spiritual shades of gray in between. As a result of the authors' mind-set, the apocalyptic portrait of God is ethically limited. The Deity is almost invariably shown as an enthroned monarch, an omnipotent authority who brings history to a violent conclusion in order to demonstrate his sovereignty, confound his enemies, and preserve his few worshipers. The notion that God might regard all people as his children or that he might establish his kingdom by less catastrophic means does not appeal to the apocalyptic temperament or satisfy the apocalyptic yearning.

Use of Ancient Myths and Symbolic Language

Apocalyptic writers commonly adapt ancient Near Eastern "combat myths" of creation and reapply them to their visions of End time. Cosmic monsters that the gods of Babylon or Canaan defeated in order to bring the world into being—such as the "Leviathan" or "Rahab" referred to Psalms 74 and 89 or the personified "Death" (Canaanite "Mot") in Isaiah 25.7—are transformed into the serpents and dragons that Yahweh overthrows in history's final battle (Isa. 27:1; Rev. 12:7–13). Because such revelations are shared with only a chosen few, writers typically use obscure language and secretive imagery to express their understanding of past and future events. Daniel's use of animal symbolism, such as the four beasts representing Near Eastern empires (Dan. 7–8), serves not only to portray foreign governments as savage or inhuman but also to enshroud them in mystery, giving their rise and fall a mystical significance beyond that of ordinary political developments.

whose skill at interpreting dreams astonishes a series of Gentile kings.

The Organization of Daniel

Daniel divides naturally into two main sections. The first six chapters—parts of which may have been written well before Antiochus's persecutions—recount Daniel's adventures under the successive reigns of Nebuchadnezzar, Belshazzar, "Darius the Mede," and Cyrus the Persian. Except for Chapter 2, with its image of a metal statue symbolizing a sequence of Near Eastern kingdoms from the days of Babylon to the Hellenistic period, this part of the book has few apocalyptic elements. Instead, the author focuses on Daniel's strict allegiance to the laws of his God and on the conflicts with various foreign rulers that his *torah* loyalty inspires. In Chapter 1, Daniel and his Judean friends **Shadrach, Meshach,** and **Abednego** are groomed to become wise counselors at Nebuchadnezzar's court. Rather than eat forbidden foods, however, they opt for a vegetarian diet, on which they prosper, proving that it is possible to observe the biblical dietary code in a foreign land. The dangers involved in the Jewish youths' situation becomes apparent only when Nebuchadnezzar's courtiers point out to the king that Daniel's three friends do not obey his edict to worship a golden statue, prompting Nebuchadnezzar to order them thrown into a "furnace of blazing fire." After they emerge unharmed, the Babylonian ruler is represented as enthusiastically praising the Jews' "Most High God," who so miraculously protects his servants (Dan. 3:24–4:3).

In Chapter 6, it is Daniel's turn to risk martyrdom. Ordered by the "Median" king Darius* to stop offering petitions (prayers) to any god but the (divine) ruler, Daniel ignores the decree and consequently is imprisoned in a den of lions, where, as in the case of his three friends, God's angel saves him from harm. As with the

---

*"Darius the Mede" (Dan. 5:30–31), whom the author of Daniel identifies as Babylon's conqueror, is unknown to history. Other biblical writers, including Second Isaiah, Ezra, and the Chronicler, correctly state that Cyrus of Persia captured Babylon (539 BCE).

three friends' fiery ordeal, the moral lesson is clear: If people remain loyal to Israel's God, he will keep faith with them. Like Nebuchadnezzar, Darius then praises Daniel's God "who delivers and rescues" his servants (Dan. 6:16–28).

Daniel's Apocalypse: Visions of End Time

For some readers, Daniel's speculations about the arrival of End time are the book's most intriguing feature. In Chapter 2, Daniel demonstrated sensational powers of dream interpretation, first (with divine help) telling Nebuchadnezzar what his dream was and then explaining its significance. In this section, Daniel reports that the king had dreamt of a colossal statue, with head of gold, chest and arms of silver, belly and thighs of bronze, legs of iron, and feet of mixed iron and clay. Suddenly, a great stone uncut "by human hands" strikes the idol's iron-and-clay feet, causing it to disintegrate. The stone immediately grows into a mountain that fills the whole earth. In Daniel's interpretation, the various metals composing the statue symbolize a series of kingdoms—each represented by a mineral less valuable than the one before it—that rule his part of the world. Because the author lived centuries after the sequence of kingdoms he describes, he is able to present past events as if they fulfilled prophecy.

Nebuchadnezzar (Babylon) is the head of gold; and the nations that follow him—though Daniel does not identify them—are probably Media (silver), Persia (bronze), Greece (iron), and the lesser Hellenistic kingdoms of Ptolemaic Egypt and Seleucid Syria (iron combined with clay to signify the weaker successors of Alexander's ironlike empire). The gigantic meteorite represents God's kingdom, which is destined to destroy and replace all previous governments:

> In the period of those kings the God of heaven will establish a kingdom which shall never be destroyed; that kingdom shall never pass to another people; it shall shatter and make an end of all these kingdoms, while it shall itself endure for ever.

(Dan. 2:44)

When seen from a divine perspective, all earthly kingdoms, including that of Antiochus, are destined to share the fate of ancient empires that had crumbled to dust. Only the will of God, Daniel insists, shapes the outcome of all human attempts to govern the world.

In the second half of the book (Dan. 7–12), Daniel no longer interprets the dreams of a foreign ruler. Instead, he recounts four of his own dreams or visions, which collectively survey Near Eastern history from the sixth to the second centuries BCE. Writing from the viewpoint of an exile at the Babylonian or Persian court, the author—responding to the second-century-BCE crisis of Antiochus's persecutions—recasts his survey of political history in the form of prophecy. Using bizarre images of wild beasts to depict foreign nations (and thereby cloaking his meaning in mystical symbols), he can plausibly describe historical events as if they were predictions of the future. In Chapter 7, the writer disguises the Babylonian, Median, Persian, and Greek empires as wild animals: a lion with eagle's wings (Babylon), a bear with ribs in its mouth (Media), a winged leopard with four heads (Persia), and a savage beast with iron teeth and ten horns (Alexander's empire and the kingdoms of his successors, the Ptolemys of Egypt and the Seleucids of Syria). The boastful "little horn" that also turns up is probably Antiochus, who displaces three other "horns," political rivals he "uprooted" (cf. 8:9).

Daniel's parade of monsters is interrupted by a more traditional prophetic vision of the enthroned "Ancient One" (or "Ancient of Days"), who confers "glory and kingship" to "one like a human being" (or "son of man") (7:10–14). The identity of this unnamed figure—who has a human, as opposed to a "bestial," appearance and is therefore "in the image of God"—has been hotly debated. Some commentators suggest that he is a supernatural member of Yahweh's heavenly court, perhaps the celestial "prince" **Michael,**" who is the guardian patron of Israel (10:13, 21; 12:1). Although the author was probably referring either to a member of the divine assembly or to the faithful covenant people that Michael defended (7:27), later Christian writers interpreted the "son of man" concept as prophetic of Israel's Messiah. In Mark's Gospel, "Son of Man" is Jesus' preferred way of referring to himself (see Chapter 30). In Daniel, however, the author apparently uses the figure to depict a divinely appointed kingdom that will permanently replace the savage foreign nations ruling in his own day. This section closes with more veiled remarks about the "little horn" (Antiochus IV), who makes war on the "holy ones" (devout Jews), tries to "change the sacred seasons and the law" (Temple observances), and attempts to abolish the Mosaic religion altogether. Again, it is certain that when the kingdom arrives, it will destroy the persecutor (7:9–28).

The vision of Chapter 8—supposedly given when Daniel was living at Susa, the Persian capital—features a ram with two horns (the dual power of Medes and Persians) being gored by a he-goat sporting a great horn (Alexander of Macedonia), which, in turn, is broken and replaced by four smaller horns (the four divisions of Alexander's empire made after his death). From one of these lesser horns (the Seleucid dynasty of Syria) springs a small "horn" (again Antiochus) that rises "as high as the host of heaven," takes away the "regular burnt offering" (Antiochus halted approved Temple sacrifices), and sets up a "transgression that makes desolate" (Antiochus reputedly slaughtered a pig on Yahweh's altar and erected a shrine to Zeus in the sanctuary). The angel **Gabriel,** who serves as a supernatural interpreter of Daniel's dreams, clearly identifies each of the past empires while keeping vague the part about Antiochus, who represents a contemporary threat.

In Chapter 9, Daniel offers his most moving prayer, confessing his people's sins and asking God to deliver them from their enemies. For the first time in the book, he invokes the divine name, Yahweh (9:5–19). Gabriel then reinterprets Jeremiah's prophecy that Jerusalem would be restored "seventy years" after the Babylonian conquest, a prediction that had not yet been fulfilled. In revising Jeremiah's oracle, Gabriel explains that the prophet meant seventy "weeks" of years, or a span of 490 years (70 × 7 years), after which the kingdom will arrive, validating both vision and prophet. In the second century BCE, the expected fulfillment was imminent.

Chapters 10–11 sprout a thicket of prophecies about battles between "the king of the south" (the Ptolemaic dynasty of Egypt) and "the king of the north" (the Seleucid dynasty of Syria), with special reference to the ultimate fall of Antiochus. At the time these passages were written, the Maccabees apparently had not yet recaptured the Temple and restored the "regular burnt offering." The author is confident, however, that the sanctuary will be cleansed and priestly services resumed in the near future. But he is less accurate in predicting Antiochus's punishment, because the Syrian king, who "considers himself greater than any god," dies a natural death abroad, not in Palestine ("between the sea and the beautiful holy mountain") (11:21–45).

Regarding the crisis brought on by Antiochus's attack on Jewish customs as the beginning of End time, Daniel's author promises a resurrection to his faithful contemporaries who had died defending their faith against the Syrian persecutor. This explicit affirmation of life after death (12:2–3) was to be the most enduring part of his message. Daniel—who as a literary character is placed in the Persian era—is told to sleep with his ancestors until he is raised for his "reward at the end of the days" (12:13). In Daniel's End-time world, the dead as well as the living will experience judgment and redemption, and Israel's centuries-long domination by foreign powers will end gloriously. At that time, "the kingship and dominion and the greatness of the kingdoms under the whole heaven shall be given to the people of the holy ones of the Most High" (7:27). As a work of visionary hope for God's people, then, Daniel rises above history (as do virtually all apocalyptic writers) to place human events, particularly the struggle to maintain an everlasting divine–human bond, in a context of cosmic significance.

QUESTIONS FOR DISCUSSION AND REVIEW

1. As a literary category or genre, what is an apocalypse? Describe the characteristics of apocalyptic literature, including its universality, dualism, use of ancient myths, and symbolic language. How is the decline in prophecy in postexilic Judah related to the rise of apocalyptic ideas?

2. Define the term *eschatology,* and describe the eschatological interests of most apocalyptic writers, such as Daniel's author.

3. Define the term *Hellenism.* What military conquests brought Hellenism to Judean society, and what effects did it produce?

4. What were the causes and results of the Maccabean Revolt, and why do scholars think that the Book of Daniel reflects this turbulent period of Judean history? How does the author of Daniel symbolize the Near Eastern empires that sequentially dominated the covenant community?

5. Discuss the possible connections between the historical failure of Israel's political hopes and the rise of apocalyptic thought following the conquests of Alexander the Great.

6. By placing the figure of Daniel in the sixth century BCE, when Babylon was replaced by Persia as the dominant power in the Near East, how is Daniel's author—who lived during the reign of Antiochus IV of Syria—able to review past events as if they were prophecies of the future?

7. Apocalypses are commonly described as works of both hope and despair. Explain this apparent paradox. How does pessimism about the human condition lead to ideas about divine intervention in human history? What lessons about the struggle of the covenant people to maintain their religious integrity in face of hardship and persecution do we learn from Daniel?

Terms and Concepts to Remember

Antiochus IV Epiphanes	Meshach, Shadrach, and Abednego
apocalyptic literature	Michael
Danel	Nebuchadnezzar
Diaspora	Palestine
eschatology	Ptolemaic dynasty
Gabriel	resurrection
Hellenism	Seleucid dynasty
Judea	theodicy

Recommended Reading

Arnold, Bill T. "Daniel, Book of." In K. D. Sakenfeld, ed., *The New Interpreter's Dictionary of the Bible*, Vol. 2, pp. 15–26. Nashville, TN: Abingdon Press, 2007. Provides historical background and a history of the book's interpretation.

Bartlett, John R. "Maccabees, the Books of the." In B. M. Metzger and M. D. Coogan, eds., *The Oxford Companion to the Bible*. New York: Oxford UP, 1993. Reviews the Maccabean Revolt, providing background to the composition of Daniel.

Collins, John J. *The Apocalyptic Imagination: An Introduction to Jewish Apocalyptic Literature*, 2nd ed. Grand Rapids, MI: Eerdmans, 1998. A major study of biblical eschatology (visions of End time).

———. *Daniel*. Minneapolis: Fortress, 1993. Indispensable for serious study.

———. *The Encylopedia of Apocalyptism*, Vol. 1: *The Origins of Apocalypticism in Judaism and Christianity*. New York: Continuum, 2002. Contains essays describing the relationship of apocalyptic thought to Israelite prophecy and ancient Near Eastern myth.

Murphy, Frederick J. "Introduction to Apocalyptic Literature." In *The New Interpreter's Bible*, Vol. 7, pp. 1–35. Reviews the development of apocalyptic thought.

Roland, Christopher. "Apocalyptism." In K. D. Sakenfeld, ed., *The New Interpreter's Dictionary of the Bible*, Vol. 1, pp. 190–195. Nashville, TN: Abingdon Press, 2006. Surveys some characteristics of both Jewish and Christian apocalyptic writings.

Russell, D. S. *Daniel: An Active Volcano: Reflections on the Book of Daniel*. Louisville, KY: Westminster John Knox Press, 1989. A scholarly study.

Smith-Christopher, Daniel L. "The Book of Daniel." In *The New Interpreter's Bible*, Vol. 7, pp. 17–152. Nashville, TN: Abingdon Press, 1996. A useful commentary.

CHAPTER 27

The Second Canon
Books of the Apocrypha

Key Topics/Themes In finalizing the canon of the Hebrew Bible (Tanakh), Jewish editors rejected approximately fourteen documents that had been included in the Greek Septuagint edition of the Jewish Scriptures. Accepted by the early church as deuterocanonical, these books, also known as the Apocrypha, are part of Catholic and Eastern Orthodox editions of the Old Testament. Containing works of poetry, wisdom, prose fiction, and historical narrative, the Apocrypha explore important ideas in the development of Hellenistic Jewish thought that also influenced early Christianity.

 ## A Second (Later) Canon

As edited by ancient Jewish scholars, the Hebrew Bible (Tanakh) closes with the books of Chronicles, ending with the call of Cyrus, emperor of Persia, for Jews to return to their homeland. Rabbis (Jewish teachers) of the first centuries CE apparently decided not to recognize as authoritative Scripture about fourteen books—including several additions to canonical Daniel and Esther—that had been accepted into the Septuagint or other Greek editions of the Tanakh. The Christian community, however, which used Greek editions of the Hebrew Bible, eventually regarded these fourteen writings as **deuterocanonical**—as belonging to a later "second canon." In Catholic and Greek Orthodox Bibles, deuterocanonical works are interspersed among the Prophets (Nevi'im) and the Writings (Kethuvim). Following the Protestant Reformation in the sixteenth century CE, most Protestant editions of the Bible either omitted deuterocanonical books altogether or relegated them to a separate unit between the Old and New Testaments (see Table 27.1). Taking the name that the Christian scholar Jerome assigned them in the fourth century CE, these "additional" books were called the

Apocrypha (see Chapter 1). The name means "hidden," but we do not know why Jerome chose this term to describe these documents.

Most of the deuterocanonical/apocryphal books were composed in the same literary forms as those in the Writings of the Hebrew Bible: short stories (Judith and Tobit), wisdom literature (the Wisdom of Solomon and the Wisdom of Jesus Son of Sirach, also known as Ecclesiasticus), historical narratives (1 and 2 Maccabees), and an apocalypse (2 Esdras). In addition, the Septuagint edition incorporated extensive passages into Daniel and Esther that do not appear in the original Hebrew/Aramaic texts. These include long prayers highlighting Esther's obedience to *torah* rules and accounts illustrating Daniel's exceptional skills as a detective. Varied in both content and literary quality, deuterocanonical writings offer some notable milestones in the development of religious thought. These range from folklore about angels and demons (Tobit), to practical applications of wisdom (ben Sirach), to Greek ideas about the soul's immortality (Wisdom of Solomon), to the conflict between secular power and *torah* loyalty (1 Maccabees), to a belief in heavenly rewards for martyrdom (2 Maccabees). In surveying the Apocrypha, we will first examine the books of Maccabees

TABLE 27.1 Deuterocanonical (Apocryphal) Books

The Hebrew Bible (Tanakh) omits fourteen books or parts of books that some Christian churches regard as part of the Old Testament. This table presents the canonical status—the acceptance or rejection—of the deuterocanonical (apocryphal) writings by various representative groups. A dash (—) indicates that the writing is not accepted. An empty circle (O) indicates that the book is not part of the canon but is given some religious value. A dark circle (●) indicates that the writing is included in the Bible but is not equal in authority to the Old and New Testaments. A dark square (■) means that the book is accepted as part of the Old Testament.

| | | | | EASTERN ORTHODOX | |
| | | | ROMAN | | |
BOOK	JEWISH	PROTESTANT	CATHOLIC	GREEK	RUSSIAN
1 Maccabees	—	O	■	■	●
2 Maccabees	—	O	■	■	●
Additions to Daniel	—	O	■	■	●
Tobit	—	O	■	■	●
Judith	—	O	■	■	●
Additions to Esther	—	O	■	■	●
Baruch	—	O	■	■	●
Letter of Jeremiah	—	O	■	■	●
Ecclesiasticus (ben Sirach)	—	O	■	■	●
Wisdom of Solomon	—	O	■	■	●
2 Esdras	—	O	O	■	●

For additional information on deuterocanonical and extracanonical works, see James H. Charlesworth, "Biblical Literature: Apocrypha and Pseudepigrapha," in Mircea Eliade, ed., *The Encyclopedia of Religion*, Vol. 2, pp. 173–183 (New York: Macmillan, 1987).

and conclude with the Book of 2 Esdras (part of the Catholic Old Testament until 1546). Eastern Orthodox Bibles include three additional books: 3 and 4 Maccabees and Psalm 151. In addition, during the Greco-Roman period, Jewish writers produced a large body of material known as the **Pseudepigrapha,** documents ascribed to famous worthies of the past, such as Abraham, Ezra, and Enoch. Because of space limitations, we will review only a representative selection of the deuterocanonical books, particularly those documents that throw light on ideas developing between the Old and New Testament periods.

 The Book of 1 Maccabees

A vividly detailed account of Jewish struggles to defend their ancestral faith against enforced Hellenization—the adoption of Greek culture and customs—1 Maccabees

describes events in Palestine during the turbulent second century BCE. In remarkably concise, matter-of-fact prose, the book recounts a war for Jewish religious and political independence in which a particular family—the Maccabees—leads the covenant people from a state of foreign oppression to one of national independence. Emphasizing the Maccabees' crucial role in achieving Jewish freedom, the narrative opens with a description of Antiochus IV (ruled 175–163 BCE) and his attempts to impose religious conformity on his subjects by Hellenizing the entire population of his large kingdom. Antiochus's edicts forbidding Torah study, circumcision, Sabbath keeping, and observance of Kosher dietary regulations trigger an uprising led by Mattathias and his sons (Chs. 1–2), culminating in a prolonged guerrilla war conducted by **Judas Maccabeus** (Chs. 3–9). After Judas's death, his brothers Jonathan (Chs. 9–12) and Simon (Chs. 13–16) carry on the revolt and succeed in driving Syrian armies from their homeland. Simon's son, John Hyrcanus I, becomes the first king-priest of a new Maccabean dynasty, called the **Hasmonean** after Hasmon, a reputed ancestor of Mattathias.

Like the Hebrew text of Esther, 1 Maccabees narrates Jewish battles against Gentile oppression, without referring to miracles, divine intervention, or any other supernatural agency. Writing about 100 BCE, the anonymous narrator portrays his leading characters, the Maccabean family, as *torah* loyalists, but he never attributes their military or political victories to God's direct help. He does, however, imply that faithful Jews who are willing to defend their faith will achieve success.

Although widely viewed as an inspiring history of Jewish self-determination, the author probably had a specific political agenda. Recent commentators point to a passage describing the defeat of Joseph and Azariah, two Jewish patriots who fought the Syrians apart from the Maccabean family: "Thus the people suffered a great rout because, thinking to do a brave deed, they did not listen to Judas and his brothers. But they did not belong to the family of those men through whom deliverance was given to Israel" (1 Macc. 5:61–62). Without direct Maccabean leadership, the author implies, even the most heroic acts are doomed to failure, a perspective suggesting that the book was composed to validate the Hasmonean (Maccabean) dynasty.

Antiochus IV's Persecution and the Maccabean Revolt

In a brief preface, 1 Maccabees provides background for the events that follow, summarizing Alexander the Great's conquest of Persia, the spread of Greek culture, and his successors' division of Alexander's vast empire (see Figure 26.1). Palestine was first awarded to Ptolemy of Egypt but was seized by the rival Seleucids of Syria about 199 BCE. Although many Jews voluntarily embraced Greek ways, many others—known as the **Hasidim** (pious ones)—vigorously resisted what they regarded as an unacceptable compromise of their ancestral religion. Government-sponsored Hellenization greatly intensified under Antiochus IV, who met Jewish resistance by outlawing the practice of Judaism altogether, burning copies of the Torah and forbidding sacrifice to any gods but those of Greece. Mothers who had their infant boys circumcised were punished by having their babies slain, with the bodies then tied around the mothers' necks. To enforce his prohibitions, Antiochus stationed a garrison of Syrian soldiers in Jerusalem, building a massive fortress near the Temple. In a final outrage, the king erected an altar to the Olympian Zeus—and reportedly to the god's children, Athene and

Dionysus as well—in the Temple courtyard, rendering the shrine ceremonially unclean.

Mattathias Whereas some Jews, attracted by Greek culture and philosophy, willingly supported Antiochus's campaign, other reluctantly submitted, out of fear. As noted in Chapter 26, it was a village priest named Mattathias who first led the revolt against Antiochus's policies. When a fellow villager publicly swallowed a mouthful of pork, a token violation of Mosaic law, Mattathias kills both the offending Jew and an officer of the king's army. With his five sons—John, Simon, Judas, Eleazar, and Jonathan—he then flees to the neighboring hill country (1 Macc. 2).

After Syrian troops massacre 1,000 Jews who refuse to defend themselves on the Sabbath, Mattathias and his followers prudently decide that self-defense does not violate Sabbath regulations. Fighting a guerrilla war against the occupying army, Mattathias's rebels destroy numerous Greek shrines and forcibly circumcise many Jewish boys. When near death, Mattathias appoints the most capable of his sons, Judas Maccabeus (Greek, the "Hammer" [God's instrument of warfare]), as his successor to continue the fight.

Judas Maccabeus Chapters 3–9 form a tribute to the heroic service that Judas gives to the Jewish nation. Against tremendous odds, he defeats the Syrians in several decisive battles. Marching into Jerusalem in 165 or 164 BCE, he accomplishes his main religious objective: reclaiming the Temple and purifying the altar that Antiochus had polluted. Judas then institutes the joyous festival of restoration—known today as **Hanukkah** and referred to in John's Gospel as the "festival of the Dedication" (John 10:22). When Antiochus unexpectedly dies in 163 BCE, Judas concludes an armistice with the Syrians, assuring his people the right to practice their hereditary religion. When hostilities again break out three years later, Judas defeats the Syrian general Nicanor, who had threatened to burn the Jerusalem sanctuary.

Among Judas's most historically significant actions is his decision to sign a treaty of friendship with Rome, the powerful new empire then arising in the West. Writing before Roman armies took over Judea in 63 BCE, the author portrays Rome as the champion of peace and international stability, the protector of smaller states that willingly place themselves within its sphere of influence.

Jonathan After Judas falls in battle, his brother Jonathan becomes leader of the Jews (160–142 BCE). Sharing his predecessor's charismatic gifts, Jonathan rallies the people against further Syrian aggression. Alexander, the new claimant to the Syrian throne, finally concludes a peace settlement with Jonathan in 152 BCE and appoints him High Priest, by this time a political as well as religious office. This act establishes a line of Hasmonean rulers that lasts until 40 BCE, when the Romans appoint Herod I king of the Jews. During subsequent political turmoil, however, Jonathan is lured into the Syrian camp and treacherously slain (1 Macc. 9:23–12:53).

Simon The last of Mattathias's five sons, Simon now assumes military leadership and eventually the high priesthood as well. Although he marshals an army, he fights fewer battles than did his brothers. Relying more on diplomacy and guile than military force, Simon bribes Syrian troops to withdraw and secures peace for seven years. Taking advantage of the lull and of Syria's internal strife, Simon builds a series of fortresses around Judea and forms an alliance with the Syrian ruler, who confirms his appointment as High Priest and also releases the Judeans from taxation. This pact (142 BCE) effectively affirms Jewish autonomy and marks Judea's emergence, for the first time in almost 450 years, as an independent state.

John Hyrcanus In 134 BCE, however, the Syrians again attack, and many Jews are killed or imprisoned. The aged Simon commissions two of his sons, Judas and John, who lead the Jewish army victoriously against the invaders. After Simon's traitorous son-in-law murders Simon and two of his sons, Mattathias and Judas, Simon's surviving son, John (surnamed "Hyrcanus"), becomes Judah's priest-king (1 Macc. 16). This is the last event recorded in Old Testament history. (For a survey of Judean history in Roman times, see Chapter 28.)

The Book of 2 Maccabees

Written in Greek, probably in Alexandria, Egypt, after 124 BCE, 2 Maccabees is not a continuation of the history of 1 Maccabees but a revised version of events related in the first seven chapters of the earlier book. According to the compiler's preface (2:19–32), the book is an edited abridgement of a five-volume historical work (since lost) by "Jason of Cyrene," who is otherwise unknown. The period covered is approximately 176–161 BCE.

Whereas 1 Maccabees is a comparatively straightforward and plausible account of the Jewish revolt against Syria, the second book's credibility is undermined by its emphasis on exaggerated numbers, unlikely miracles, and supernatural apparitions. The writer of 2 Maccabees, who interprets the events he describes theologically, not only presents the rebellion's success as an act of God (11:13; 15:27) but repeatedly injects commentary about such matters as divine guidance and future punishment for Israel's enemies into his narrative (5:17–20; 6:12–17; 8:36; 12:40), along with the new belief in a bodily resurrection (7:9; 14:46).

Corruption, Persecution, and Martyrdom

The book opens with two letters from Palestinian Jews to their fellow Jews in Egypt, urging them to observe Hanukkah, the winter festival commemorating Judas Maccabeus's rededication of the Temple (2 Macc. 1:1–2:18). These letters are probably an editor's later addition to the compiler's original introduction (2:19–32), a review of literary sources that were probably included to establish authorial credibility. The main narrative describes the increasing corruption of two pre-Maccabean High Priests, Jason and Menelaus (Chs. 3–4); the cruelty of Antiochus IV's persecutions of faithful Jews (Chs. 5–7); the military successes of Judas Maccabeus, which culminate in his purification of the Temple (Chs. 8–10); and Judas's subsequent battles against such Syrian foes as Nicanor, chief general of Demetrius I, one of Antiochus's successors (Chs. 10–15).

Despite the doubtful historicity of some episodes, 2 Maccabees is an effectively written account, providing colorful illustrations of the greed and treachery of Jason and Menelaus, renegades who betray their own people for personal gain. Particularly memorable are the author's depictions of the tortures endured by Jews who refused to obey Antiochus's decrees that they break *torah* commands, epitomized by the eating of swine's flesh. Eleazar, ninety years old and a distinguished teacher, is bludgeoned to death. Even worse is the fate of seven brothers, who, in the sight of their mother, are systematically mutilated and slowly burned alive under Antiochus's fiendish supervision (Chs 6–7).

Emphasizing the courage and nobility of Jewish martyrs ready to die for their faith, the author offers an ingenious philosophy of suffering to account for Israel's woes. Antiochus and similar tyrants are merely God's human instruments for disciplining the covenant people. Paradoxically, the martyrs' extreme pain is a sign of divine benevolence. Whereas God allows foreign nations to multiply their crimes and guilt—implying that future retribution will be all the more severe—Israel is punished *before* its collective sins have "reached their height" (6:12–17), sparing the people greater misery in the end. Thus, the countless disasters that befall faithful Judeans constitute visible proof that their God has *not* deserted them.

The author's other distinctive views include a promised resurrection of the dead (7:9; 14:46), a belief that prayer can cleanse the dead from sin (12:43–45), a doctrine that the righteous dead can intervene on behalf of the living (15:12–16), and a concept that God created the world out of nothing (*ex nihilo*) (7:28). Although only a limited number of Hellenistic Jews may have held such beliefs, these ideas became widely accepted in Roman Catholicism, which drew on 2 Maccabees for several doctrines, including prayers for souls in purgatory and the intercessory prayers of saints.

 ## The Book of Tobit

Although the Septuagint editors placed Tobit among the historical books, along with Chronicles and Ezra-Nehemiah, it is really a work of imaginative fiction. The action is ostensibly set in the seventh century BCE when many Israelites from the northern kingdom were forcibly removed from their native land and resettled throughout the Assyrian Empire (cf. 2 Kings 17). However, the book really addresses issues of a much later period—the problems of Hellenistic Jews living in the Diaspora (scattering abroad). Probably composed during the third or second century BCE, Tobit dramatizes the conflicts that sometimes arose between devout Jews and their foreign masters. In this context, Nineveh, the Assyrian capital in which much of the story takes place, represents the kind of hostile environment in which Diaspora Jews struggled to maintain their Mosaic heritage.

A Jewish Diaspora Family

The unknown author's purpose is to encourage Jewish exiles to cultivate *torah* obedience and faithfulness to the received tradition, including family solidarity and charitable giving. Although the narrator focuses largely on a single family's everyday affairs, his narrative is designed to illustrate a larger theme. That is, Israel's God hears—and answers—the prayers of persons loyal to him, rewarding their fidelity with material success (cf. Deut.

28). This theme is dramatized in a skillfully constructed plot with three closely interwoven stories. The book's central figure is **Tobit,** an exemplary Jew who scrupulously observed all Torah requirements but who suffers the illnesses and privations of a latter-day Job. A subplot involves his kinswoman Sarah, a beautiful virgin whose seven husbands have all been killed on their wedding night by the jealous demon Asmodeus. A second subplot concerning Tobit's son Tobias, who travels to Media, drives out (exorcizes) the demon, and marries Sarah, effectively ties all the narratives together.

Tobit's story is joined to Sarah's by the Deity's hearing their simultaneous prayers for death:

> At that very moment, the prayers of both of them were heard in the glorious presence of God. So Raphael [an angel] was sent to both of them: Tobit, by removing the white film from his eyes so that he might see God's light with his eyes; and Sarah, daughter of Raguel, by giving her in marriage to Tobias and by freeing her from the wicked demon Asmodeus.

(Tob. 3:16–17)

Tobit prays to die because, in piously burying the bodies of slaughtered Israelites, he has not only incurred the wrath of the Assyrian king and been stripped of all his possessions but also been blinded by bird droppings (2:9–3:6). Sarah, unhappy that a maid has accused her of murdering her seven bridegrooms, similarly longs to end her life (3:7–15). Although God has already resolved to help them, the characters themselves must take action before the divine intervention can be accomplished. To relieve his poverty, Tobit sends his son Tobias to Ecbatana, a site in the Near Eastern country of Media (modern Iran), to claim money that Tobit entrusted to a relative, Raguel, who is also Sarah's father.

Disguised as a traveler named Azariah, the archangel **Raphael** guides young Tobias to Ecbatana, provides detailed instructions on the use of fish parts to expel Asmodeus (who flees to Egypt, where an angel binds him), and permits the union of Tobias and Sarah. Raguel, who had spent the wedding night digging a grave for his new son-in-law, is astounded the next morning when Tobias is still alive. On Tobias's triumphant return to Nineveh with the money and a new wife, Raphael also cures Tobit's blindness with fish gall (11:10–15).

A treasure trove of Hellenistic Jewish social customs and beliefs, Tobit incorporates several traditional folk motifs. Folklorists have identified two: (1) the tale of the Grateful Dead (telling of an impoverished hero who is rewarded for giving proper interment to an unburied body) and (2) the tale of the Monster in the

Bridal Chamber (describing a demon who jealously slays a new husband on the night of his marriage). In addition, Tobit includes a classic journey theme, in which a young man travels to a strange land to acquire treasure and a bride, commonly with supernatural assistance.

Combining elements of Jewish popular piety and folklore, Tobit also deals with such matters as guardian angels (5:21; 12:12–13), sacrificial obligations (1:6–7), dietary restrictions (1:10–12), personal prayers (3:2–15; 8:5–8), the importance of traditional burial (1:17–19; 2:3–8; 14:12), the power of demons and the use of fish entrails in exorcizing them (3:8; 6:6–8; 8:1–3), seven angels at the heavenly court (12:15), and the value of wise parental advice (4:3–19). Tobit's views on angels—guardian spirits who act as benign intercessors (12:12)—and demons who afflict human victims seem to reflect the influence of **Zoroastrianism,** a Persian religion that emphasizes a cosmic dualism and an ongoing battle between good and evil spirit forces.

The last chapters—Tobit's thanksgiving psalm (Ch. 13) and an epilogue recounting his advice that Tobias and Sarah leave Nineveh to escape the city's impending destruction (Ch. 14)—may be later additions. The final section, in which Tobit prophesies Nineveh's fall and Jerusalem's glorious restoration, contains a prediction notable for its universality: "the nations in the whole world will all be converted and worship God in truth" (14:6).

 # The Book of Judith

Like Tobit, the Book of Judith is a historical romance that an unknown writer composed during the Hellenistic period and set in the distant past. The book begins with a glaring historical error—asserting that Nebuchadnezzar (ruled 605–562 BCE) reigned in Babylon over the Assyrians, when in reality his father, the previous king of Babylon, had already destroyed Nineveh, the Assyrian capital, years before. This anachronism may have been intentional, to show at the outset that the book should not be mistaken for factual history. Scholars believe that the author used his Babylonian setting to address the difficulties of his own time—specifically, the Seleucid persecution of the Jews under Antiochus IV (ruled 175–163 BCE). The story's fictionalized Nebuchadnezzar, then, probably represents Antiochus, or any similar ruler who threatens the covenant people (1 Macc. 1:14–50; Dan. 3:3–15). The author

encourages Jews to rise in armed revolt against such tyrants; asserting that Israel's God will defend his people if they remain faithful (Jth. 13:11; 16:17).

A National Heroine

Judith was probably written about 100 BCE, significantly after the Maccabees had driven the Syrians from Palestine and established a Hasmonean dynasty. The heroine's name, the feminine form of "Judah," literally means "Jewess" and may be intended to symbolize the covenant community or to remind readers of Judas, its Maccabean leader. Judith embodies the traditional biblical heroism of the solitary Israelite successfully defeating a foreign superpower, as Jael killed Sisera (Judg. 4:12–24; 5:25–30), Samson slew the Philistines (Judg. 16), and David vanquished Goliath (1 Sam. 17). Judith's triumph over Holofernes, the Assyrian military commander, signifies her people's victory over their collective enemies.

The Book of Judith is divided into two parts. The first (Jth. 1–7) states that after conquering Media, Nebuchadnezzar sent Holofernes to punish countries that had not supported his campaign. After overrunning various other nations, the Assyrians lay siege to Bethulia, a fortified city that may symbolize Jerusalem, which Antiochus had sacked. When Bethulia is ready to submit, the ruler Uzziah decrees that Israel's God be given another five days to rescue his people.

In the second part (Jth. 8–15), Judith, a beautiful young widow, berates the leaders who put their God to the test and volunteers to save the city herself. After offering a prayer, she perfumes herself, dresses in her best clothes and jewelry, and enters the Assyrian camp, pretending to defect because of her admiration for Holofernes. Flattered, the commander invites the seductive woman into to his tent, where, after plying him with wine, she takes his sword and decapitates him.

Stowing the head in her travel bag, Judith and her maid convey it to Bethulia (Jerusalem?), where it is displayed on the city wall. Dispirited by their leader's death, the Assyrians withdraw, allowing the Jews to loot their camp. Judith dedicates her share of the booty to the Jerusalem Temple. In an epilogue, Judith hails her God for protecting his people (16:17). After her death at an advanced age, her compatriots honor her as a national heroine.

Although Judith was written at a time when killing an enemy could be regarded as an act of religious devotion, it is more than a nationalistic war story. Its emphasis on the power of Israel's God to rescue an obedient people echoes a theme recurrent in biblical traditions: It is not by "sword and spear" that Israel survives, but only through the will of God, who can save by the "frail hand" of a lone woman (cf. 1 Sam. 17:45–47).

 ## The Book of Baruch

Baruch is the only deuterocanonical book that resembles a traditional prophetic work. Although it purports to have been written about 582 BCE (Bar. 1:2) by the secretary and companion of the prophet Jeremiah (Jer. 36:4–10), scholars agree that it is a composite work to which at least three different writers anonymously contributed. Scholars have dated the book's four parts from about 200 BCE for the earliest passages to after 70 CE for the latest additions. Although set during the Babylonian exile, it more accurately reflects the problems of Hellenistic Jews living in the Diaspora.

The first part (1:1–3:8) contains several confusing contradictions. It states, for example, that Baruch wrote the book in Babylon five years after the Babylonians had burned Solomon's Temple (1:2). Yet it portrays the exiles asking the High Priest and his assistants in Jerusalem to offer prayers "in the house of the Lord" (1:14), which apparently is still standing. Equally confusing is the statement that Baruch "read the words of this book" to an assembly of Judean exiles living in Babylon (1:1–4), whereas the book describes events that occurred long after the date of this public reading.

The rest of this prose section (1:15–3:8), which resembles parts of Daniel (cf. Dan. 9:4–19), depicts the exiled Judeans confessing the sins that caused their nation's downfall (1:15–2:10; 2:20–26) and begging for divine mercy (2:11–19; 3:1–8). It also contains a prophecy that the scattered people will be restored to their homeland, concluding with God's vow that he "will never again remove [his] people Israel from the land that I have given them" (2:27–35).

The second part (3:9–4:4, apparently by a different author, features a hymn praising Israel's God for revealing his wisdom in the Mosaic Torah. The third section (4:5–5:9), echoing themes from Second Isaiah and Lamentations, contains poems of hope and comfort, as well as of sorrow for Jerusalem's fall. The poet realizes that Israel's exile is a punishment for its violations of covenant law but foresees a glorious future for Jerusalem and God's redeemed people.

The Letter of Jeremiah

Although some ancient manuscripts place this document after Lamentations, the Latin Vulgate and most English Bibles that include the deuterocanonical books attach it to Baruch, where it appears as Chapter 6. The New Revised Standard Version presents the Letter of Jeremiah as a separate unit immediately after Baruch. Purporting to be a report from Jeremiah to Judeans about to be deported to Babylon, the document is in fact a much later work, apparently modeled on the prophet's canonical sixth-century-BCE letter to Babylonian exiles preserved in Jeremiah 29. Estimates on the date of composition vary from 317 to about 100 BCE.

The writer's theme is the evil of idolatry, to which he devotes the most extensive attack in the Bible. Although the only foreign god specifically mentioned is Bel (Marduk) (6:4), scholars believe that he is really denouncing Zeus and other Hellenistic deities whom Diaspora Jews, for social and political reasons, might be tempted to worship. "Babylon" would then be a code name for areas outside Palestine where Jews had been dispersed. The author extends Jeremiah's prediction that the exile would last seventy years (Jer. 25:12) to "seven generations" (Bar. 6:3), which, taking a biblical generation as forty years (Num. 32:13), would mean that the Jews would remain exiled until the end of the fourth century BCE. Like the author of Daniel, the writer of this letter updates earlier biblical predictions and applies them to contemporary conditions in the Hellenistic era.

The Wisdom of Jesus Son of Sirach (Ecclesiasticus)

The longest wisdom book in either the Tanakh or the Apocrypha, the Wisdom of Jesus Son of Sirach (Ecclesiasticus) is also the only wisdom writing whose author, original translator, and date are known. The writer identifies himself as Jesus ben (son of) Sirach (50:27), a professional sage and teacher who ran a school or house of learning in Jerusalem (51:24). In a preface to the main work, ben Sirach's grandson reveals that he brought the book to Egypt, where he translated it from Hebrew into Greek at a date equivalent to 132 BCE; his grandfather had composed it in Jerusalem about 180 BCE. The book's traditional title, "Ecclesiasticus," means "church book" and may derive from its general acceptance by the early Christian church, as opposed to the Jewish community

FIGURE 27.1 Discovered at Masada, the hilltop fortress where the last important band of Jewish rebels held out against Roman armies (73 CE), this fragment of the Book of Ecclesiasticus (Wisdom of Jesus son of Sirach) is approximately 2,000 years old.

not immortal" (17:30), and all the dead, regardless of individual merit, are relegated to the permanent oblivion of Sheol (14:12–19; 38:16–23). The only forms of postmortem survival available to mortals involve the production of children and the maintenance of a good reputation (44:13–15). Avoiding apocalyptic enthusiasms, ben Sirach focuses on the benefits of wisdom applied to the art of living now.

Ben Sirach's book also resembles Proverbs and the Wisdom of Solomon in consisting mostly of poetry, chiefly pairs of parallel lines. The first forty-two chapters, containing proverbial sayings interspersed with longer discourses, offer advice and admonition on many diverse topics: from the fear of God as the basis of wisdom (1:20; 32:14–33:3), to generosity to the poor (4:1–11; 7:32–40), to the moral failings of women (25:13–36), to the human predicament and fate of the wicked (40:1–11; 41:5–16). Living in a comparatively stable era in which the wise could earn a fair share of affluence and social prestige, ben Sirach regards the world as fundamentally just, with God rewarding the righteous and punishing evildoers. Silent on the great issue of cosmic injustice dramatized in Job, he did not live to face the dilemma created when Antiochus IV tried to destroy the biblical tradition, when devout Jews suffered precisely because they were loyal to covenant principles (see the discussions of Daniel and 1 and 2 Maccabees).

that denied it a place in the Hebrew Bible canon (see Figure 27.1).

Written in the tradition of Proverbs, the Wisdom of Jesus Son of Sirach (the title preferred by contemporary scholars) is largely a collection of wise sayings, moral essays, hymns to wisdom, practical advice to the young and inexperienced, instructions in proper social and religious conduct, private meditations, and extended reflections on the human condition. Like other postexilic sages, Jesus ben Sirach perceives an ordered design in the universe and counsels others to conform their lives to it. A learned, respected, influential representative of upper-class Judaism, the author reveals a personality that is genial, pragmatic, and urbane. Writing more than a decade before the persecutions of Antiochus IV, he takes an optimistic view of life's possibilities—if one learns to behave oneself with prudence, insight, reverence for *torah*, and the right degree of rational common sense.

Wisdom and the Good Life

Firmly grounded in the biblical tradition oriented toward worthy goals of the present life, ben Sirach resembles the author of Ecclesiastes in rejecting notions of human immortality or posthumous rewards (see Chapter 23). "Human beings," he assures us, "are

A Hymn to Wisdom

Like the poet of Proverbs 8, ben Sirach personifies Wisdom as a gracious female figure who dwells with God in heaven but also communicates with humans on earth. In Chapter 24, he praises Lady Wisdom as not only God's first creation, a direct expression of eternal divinity, but also an inhabitant of earthly Zion and the source of Israel's divine teaching. Speaking before the celestial assembly, Wisdom proclaims her intimacy with God:

> I came forth from the mouth of the Most High,
> and covered the earth like a mist. . . .
> Before the ages, in the beginning, he created me,
> and for all the ages I shall not cease to be.
> In the holy tent [tabernacle] I ministered before him,
> and so I was established in Zion.
> Thus in the beloved city he gave me a resting place,
> and in Jerusalem was my domain.

(Sirach 24:3, 9–11)

Ben Sirach then adds a new dimension to Israel's developing Wisdom tradition, explicitly identifying her with the Torah, God's revelation to the covenant people:

> All this [Wisdom's speech] is the book of the covenant of the Most High God, the law [*torah*] that Moses commanded us as an inheritance for the congregation of Jacob.
>
> (Sirach 24:23; cf. 19:20)

Whereas most wisdom writers almost never refer to either the Mosaic Covenant or Israel's checkered historical experience in trying to keep it, ben Sirach at a stroke combines the Wisdom and Torah traditions, equating heavenly Wisdom with God's instructions to Moses. (The view that the Torah is eternal and existed before the world's creation also appears in the noncanonical Book of Jubilees.)

In Chapter 42, ben Sirach offers a more conventional wisdom hymn, describing the physical universe as reflecting divine glory. Like Psalm 19, the poem invites readers to discover God in the wonders of the physical cosmos (42:15–43:33). Immediately after, ben Sirach introduces the book's most famous section: "Let us now sing the praises of famous men," celebrating the exemplary faith of Israel's ancestors. A eulogy of twenty-nine biblical heroes, from Enoch and Abraham to Josiah and Nehemiah, this poetic passage reflects ben Sirach's personal viewpoint on Israel's past. He not only devotes more space to praising Aaron (Israel's first High Priest) than to Moses (Israel's foremost leader and lawgiver), he also declines even to mention Ezra, the scribe credited with assembling and editing the postexilic Torah. Many scholars believe that the omission of Ezra is deliberate—a result of ben Sirach's dislike of an emerging religious movement that claimed Ezra as a forerunner, the Pharisee party. Sirach's particular convictions, including his focus on priestly ritual and his rejection of belief in angels, demons, or a future resurrection—all of which are associated with the Pharisees—may indicate his identification with an incipient rival party, the Sadducees. (These two groups figure prominently in the New Testament; see Chapter 29).

Ben Sirach's tribute to Israelite ancestors climaxes in his praise of Simon the High Priest (c. 225–200 BCE), whom the author lauds as embodying the best of his nation's traditions (50:1–24). As intercessor between God and the covenant community, Simon was privileged to enter the Temple's Holy of Holies annually on the Day of Atonement (cf. Lev. 16) and there pronounce the divine name Yahweh, which by Hellenistic times was considered too sacred to utter publicly. The book concludes with an epilogue containing the writer's personal thanksgiving (51:1–12) and an autobiographical summary of the rewards of pursuing Wisdom (51:13–30).

The Wisdom of Solomon

A Jewish-Greek Synthesis

Although it presents itself as King Solomon's counsel to the world's rulers, this brilliant collection of poems, proverbs, and sage meditations was probably composed by an anonymous Greek-educated Jew living in Alexandria, Egypt, during the last century BCE. Like most of the deuterocanonical works, the book is directed to Jews living in the Diaspora, many of whom were moved to give up their ancestral traditions for the seemingly irresistible lure of Greek culture and philosophy, or under the pressure of social discrimination. The author's familiarity with Greek philosophical terms and concepts (Wisd. of Sol. 8:7, 19–20; 12:1), as well as his commitment to the Hebrew Bible, suggests that his work is an attempt to reconcile these two contrasting traditions by showing that the biblical revelation not only anticipates the best in Greek thought but also is superior to it.

To demonstrate Judaism's ethical and religious superiority, the author argues that his tradition offers a view of world history and divine justice that will appeal to the ethical and rational Greek. A creative synthesis of Jewish and Greek ideas, the Wisdom of Solomon makes a significant contribution to biblical theology, particularly in its visions of future immortality for the righteous and of Wisdom acting as a savior figure in human life. The book divides naturally into three parts: (1) the value of Wisdom, a divine spirit, which promises a joyous afterlife (Chs. 1–5); (2) the origin, character, and function of divine Wisdom (Chs. 6–9); and (3) God's Wisdom operating throughout world history (Chs. 10–19).

The Character and Value of Wisdom

Defining Wisdom as a "kindly spirit" emanating from an all-knowing God, the opening section vividly contrasts two views of human life. Whereas the wicked misuse reason, thinking that human existence is not only brief but also meaningless, the righteous, figuratively held "in the hand of God" (3:1), benefit from divine intelligence and receive the gift of immortality (Chs. 2–3). Confronting the problem of unmerited suffering raised in Job, the author foresees a future life that compensates for all earthly ordeals. Although evildoers may prosper on earth and oppress the good, the soul's survival in a posthumous existence guarantees that divine justice ultimately prevails. Asserting that "God created us for incorruption, and made us in the image of his own eternity" (2:23), the author assures his readers that physical death of the righteous is only an illusory defeat, for the soul transcends death to enjoy eternal communion with God (3:1–9). Skeptics may think that the good people whom they wronged will perish utterly, but their victims' suffering was merely a test to reveal their true worth, qualifying virtuous souls eventually to judge and rule over the world (3:2–8). Evil deeds are thus used for a higher good, serving to identify the righteous and ultimately to punish their oppressors (3:10).

Numerous Greek concepts appear in the second part of the book, which features "Solomon's" praise of Lady Wisdom, the bringer of immortality (cf. 6:1; 8:13). The speaker, who takes personified Wisdom as his "bride" (8:2), implies that the soul exists in heaven prior to its earthly existence (8:19–20; 9:15). This belief in an immaterial, preexistent soul that leaves the spirit realm to become incarnate (take on flesh) in an earthly body and, at death, escapes its human form to return to heaven expresses a widespread Hellenistic belief derived from the teachings of Greek philosophers such as Pythagoras, Socrates, and Plato. The author's creative association of Wisdom, the soul's temporary incarnation, and a postmortem ascent to immortal life in heaven received further development in the Gospel of John, which applies these concepts to Jesus (cf. John 1:1–14).

The influence of Greek ethical philosophy also appears in the author's celebration of the four classical virtues, which the church later adopted as the four cardinal virtues of Christian morality:

> And if anyone loves righteousness, her labors are
>   virtues;
> for she teaches self-control and prudence, justice and
>   courage;
> nothing in life is more profitable for mortals than
>   these.

(Wisd. of Sol. 8:7)

Wisdom's Role in Human History

In the third section of his book, the author presents an idealized survey of early humanity (Ch. 10) and of Israel's history (Chs. 10–19), contrasting the Deity's judgments on unbelieving Gentiles with his tender care for the covenant people, to whom Wisdom lent strength and understanding. Emphasizing God's benevolence and mercy, these passages depict Wisdom as a savior who rescues, guides, and inspires those who seek her.

Using the illustration of God's delivering the Israelites from Egypt, the writer shows that Israel benefited from the same natural elements used to inflict the ten plagues on Egypt: Whereas God, through Moses, brought water from a rock to slake the people's thirst, he made the Nile's waters undrinkable for the Egyptians by changing them to blood. Thus "one is punished by the very things by which one sins" (11:16). The author repeatedly interrupts this extended reinterpretation of the Exodus with digressions, including reflections on divine power and mercy (11:17–12:22) and a long denunciation of idolatry (13:1–15:17), reminiscent of Second Isaiah's ridicule of the Babylonian gods (cf. Isa. 40, 46). The concluding reinterpretation of biblical history may have been intended to inspire hope among Diaspora Jews that Israel's God would again intervene to aid them, as he had their distant ancestors.

In the next-to-last chapter, the author introduces a concept that was to exert a powerful influence on Christian thought. He describes Wisdom as God's "all-powerful word" leaping down "from heaven, from the royal throne," to take up residence in a "land that was doomed." Carrying "the sharp sword of [God's] authentic command," this cosmic figure "touched the heaven while standing on the earth," linking the realms of matter and spirit (18:15). Perhaps only a generation or two after the Wisdom of Solomon was written, another learned Jew living in Alexandria, Philo Judaeus, expanded on this concept of a celestial "Word" (Greek, *Logos*) to denote the principle of cosmic reason that created and sustains the universe. Philo's usage, integrating Jewish Scripture with Greek philosophy, eventually resurfaces in the Gospel of John, which adapted it to portray the prehuman Jesus, whom John identified as the "Word" active at creation (John 1:1). The Wisdom of Solomon's usefulness in formulating later Christian doctrine may explain not only why the book was widely read in Christian circles (Paul paraphrases it in his letters to the Romans and Corinthians) but also why it appears in the Muratorian Canon, a second-to-fourth-century-CE list of New Testament books its author considered authoritative.

 The Book of 2 Esdras

Written at almost the same time as the Christian Book of Revelation (c. 100 CE), 2 Esdras is the only apocalypse included in the Apocrypha. Although dropped from Catholic Bibles in the sixteenth century CE, the book now appears in several recent editions of the Old Testament, such as the Revised English Bible and the New Revised Standard Version. In its present form, 2 Esdras is a composite document; the central section (Chs. 3–14) was composed by a Jewish visionary in either Hebrew or Aramaic about thirty years after the Romans had destroyed Jerusalem in 70 CE. After the book was translated into Greek, an anonymous Christian editor added the first two chapters (c. 150 CE). Perhaps a century later, another Christian, also writing in Greek, appended Chapters 15 and 16, providing a Christian framework to this Jewish apocalypse. Composed too late to be included in the Septuagint, the book entered Christian Scripture via Old Latin translations and, eventually, later editions of the Vulgate.

The Problem of Evil in Human History

Ezra's Theodicy Attributed to Ezra, the priestly scribe credited with assembling the Mosaic Torah while exiled in Babylon (cf. Ezra 7; Neh. 8), the core chapters were actually written by an unknown Jewish author who lived more than five centuries after Ezra's time. Like his ancestors during the Babylonian exile, the author of 2 Esdras 3–14 had witnessed the humiliating overthrow of his people's holy city and Temple, a catastrophic triumph of foreign power over the covenant community that called God's justice into question. The unknown writer, who finds himself in a position similar to that of the historical Ezra, draws on the resources of apocalyptic discourse to discover some meaning or purpose in the national disaster. Chapters 3–14 present a series of seven eschatological visions, of which the first three are cast in the form of philosophical dialogues between Ezra and various angels who defend God's handling of historical events. These celestial messengers counter Ezra's repeated questions of divine ethics with attempts to justify their Deity's ways to humankind. In general, Ezra's questions are more penetrating than the conventional answers he receives.

If Babylon (Rome) is God's chosen instrument to punish his people, Ezra asks, why are Babylonians (Romans) so much worse behaved than the Jews whom they oppress? Why has God allowed an enemy nation that mocks him to destroy those who at least try to worship him (2 Esd. 3:25–32)? The angels' replies express the apocalyptic stereotype: God will dispense justice in good time. The flourishing of wickedness is only temporary; it will be terminated according to a foreordained timetable (4:27–32), and the divine schedule is not humanity's concern. As Ezra observes, however, he does not presume to inquire into heavenly

mysteries; rather, he seeks only to learn that which human intelligence is able to understand:

> To what end has the capacity for understanding been given me? For I did not mean to ask about ways above [exclusively God's domain], but about things which pass by every day, why Israel . . . whom you love [is] given to godless tribes.

(2 Esd. 4:22–23)

The wrenching disparity between the divine promises to Israel and the miserable historical reality constitutes a paradox that God does not explain.

The Afterlife Ezra is concerned about not only the earthly condition of his people but also the state of their souls after death. Reluctantly agreeing that many act wrongly while only a few are righteous, he nonetheless disputes the justice of condemning sinners to unending torment without any further chance of repentance. Chapter 7 contrasts graphic descriptions of salvation and damnation, offering the most detailed portrayal of the afterlife in the Old Testament tradition:

> Then the place of torment shall appear, and over against it the place of rest; the furnace of hell shall be displayed, and on the opposite side the paradise of delight . . . here are rest and delight, there fire and torment.

(2 Esd. 7:36–38)

As in Revelation and the parable of Lazarus and the rich man in Luke's Gospel (all written during the late first century CE), the pleasures of the blessed are enhanced by a clear view of sinners in eternal pain.

The Eschatological Future In Chapter 9, the book changes from the Job-like theodicy to a typically apocalyptic preview of the world's end. Ezra's fourth vision depicts a woman who, mourning her first son, is suddenly transformed into a thriving city. Uriel, one of the book's angelic mediators, explains that the woman is Jerusalem, her lost son the destroyed Temple, and the splendid city a future glorified Zion (Chs. 9–10; cf. Rev. 12, 21–22). In Chapters 11 and 12, the author portrays Rome as a mighty eagle that now dominates the earth but that is destined to disappear when a lion (the Messiah) appears to judge it for its persecution of the righteous (11:38–12:34). The sixth vision underscores the certainty of the Messiah's expected appearance and his righteous overthrow of unbelievers who oppress Jerusalem (Ch. 13).

The two final chapters, a Christian appendix from the third century CE, dramatize the Deity's coming vengeance on the wicked. Predicting a swarm of terrors and calamities, the book assures readers that the ungodly nation (Rome), as well as all other empires that persecute the faithful, will fall and that the guilty will be consumed by fire (Chs. 15–16).

A Book of the Pseudepigrapha: 1 Enoch

In addition to the deuterocanonical works, Hellenistic Jewish writers also produced a body of religious literature known collectively as the **Pseudepigrapha,** books that were not admitted to the canons of either the Hebrew or Greek editions of the Bible. Designated as **pseudonymous**—written in the name of famous leaders of the past, such as Enoch, Noah, Moses, or Ezra— these documents appeared between about 250 BCE and 200 CE. The Pseudepigrapha include a wide range of literary genres, but only one influential apocalypse, 1 Enoch, is discussed here.

Ascribed to **Enoch,** the man whom God apparently transported alive to heaven (Gen. 5:24), the Book of 1 Enoch is a diverse collection by many unknown authors. Composed and compiled in several stages during the Hellenistic period, it is called Ethiopic Enoch because its text has been transmitted in that language.

Following the organization of the Pentateuch, Psalms, Proverbs, and Ecclesiasticus, an editor arranged the Enoch collection into five distinct parts. Its division into 108 short chapters did not become standard until the nineteenth century. After a prefatory speech in which Enoch is shown proclaiming the ultimate destinies of the wicked and the righteous (Chs. 1–5), the first section describes the fall of the "Watchers," angels who mated with human women to produce giants and heroes (see Gen. 6:1–4) and their punishment. (Daniel, also written in the second century BCE, similarly uses the term "Watchers" to designate angels, the only book in the Bible to do so [Dan. 4:13, 17, 23].) The second part features a series of parables concerning a variety of topics, including the Messiah, the rewards of the righteous, judgment by the Son of Man, the torments of fallen angels, and similar eschatological matters (Chs. 37–71). The third section includes a presentation on astronomy—a discussion of the sun, moon, and planets and of human calendars based on them (Chs. 72–82). The fourth division recounts a sequence

of dream visions, notably a prophecy of the Flood and a panorama of world history that symbolizes the covenant people as tame animals and foreign empires as wild beasts. It begins with a portrayal of Adam as a white bull and culminates in the appearance of the Messiah as a lamb who becomes a "great animal" with black horns (Chs. 83–90).

The fifth part features Enoch's advice to his children and includes an apocalypse in which global history is divided into period of ten weeks of varying length; it then describes the blessings awaiting the righteous and woes for the godless (Chs. 91–105). The book concludes with a fragment from one of its earliest components, the Book of Noah, which describes miracles occurring at the patriarch's birth and Enoch's final words of encouragement to the pious who await their God's day of reckoning (Chs. 106–108).

From even this brief survey of its contents, it is clear that the Book of 1 Enoch—an anthology of history, astronomy, law, poetry, eschatological doctrines, and apocalyptic visions—provided a wealth of theological ideas, some of which were influential on Hellenistic Judaism. After the two disastrous wars with Rome (66–73 and 132–135 CE), however, which may have been partly inspired by apocalypse-fed expectations, the Jews largely repudiated this kind of writing. By then, Christians had taken up many of these speculations and eschatological hopes, adapting them to their own doctrinal needs.

Among some branches of early Christianity, 1 Enoch was understandably popular, although after the fourth century CE its influence declined. In time, all complete manuscripts of this work, originally composed in Hebrew and/or Aramaic, vanished. It was not until the end of the eighteenth century than an Ethiopic translation was found in Abyssinia. The first English version of the entire book appeared in 1821. In 1952, a number of Aramaic fragments of Enoch were found among the Dead Sea Scrolls, and some scholars believe the book may have originated in the Qumran community (see Chapter 28).

QUESTIONS FOR DISCUSSION AND REVIEW

1. Define the term *deuterocanonical,* and explain its application to the books discussed in this chapter. Why do Catholic and Eastern Orthodox editions of the

Old Testament contain documents not included in the Hebrew Bible (Tanakh) or Protestant Old Testament? What role did the Greek Septuagint play in the early church's acceptance of a larger canon than that of the Jewish Scriptures?

2. Summarize the historical events that 1 and 2 Maccabees describe. How did the policies of Antiochus IV affect Jews then living in Palestine? Who were the *Hasidim*, and how did they respond to enforced Hellenization?

3. What was the Maccabean Revolt, and what roles did Mattathias and Judas Maccabeus play? How did the Maccabees' efforts result in establishing an independent Jewish state under the Hasmonean dynasty?

4. How does Tobit illustrate the problems of Jews living abroad in Gentile territories? What examples of Hellenistic Jewish folklore and customs does it describe?

5. Who was Jesus Son of Sirach, and what kinds of ideas did he include in the book named after him? Why do you think that the author identified heavenly Wisdom with the Mosaic *torah*?

6. How does the author of the Wisdom of Solomon attempt to reconcile biblical revelation with Greek philosophic wisdom? What statements about heavenly Wisdom anticipate the doctrine of the Word (Logos) in the Gospel of John?

7. Briefly describe the contents of 1 Enoch, and discuss ways in which it resembles the Book of Daniel and other apocalypses. Why are angels called "Watchers" only in Enoch and Daniel? Why do you think that the New Testament letter of Jude quotes from Enoch as if it were Scripture? (Compare 1 Enoch 1:9 and Jude 14–15.)

Terms and Concepts to Remember

Antiochus IV Epiphanes	Pharisees
Apocrypha	Philo Judaeus
deuterocanonical books	Pseudepigrapha
Hanukkah	Torah loyalty in a Diaspora setting
Hasidim	Wisdom as creative Word (Logos)
Hasmonean dynasty	Wisdom as torah
Hellenization	
Judas Maccabeus	
Mattathias	

Recommended Reading

General

Albertz, Rainier. *A History of Israelite Religion in the Old Testament Period: Vol. 2: From the Exile to the Maccabees.* Trans. John Bowden. Louisville, KY: Westminster John Knox Press, 1994. Includes authoritative sociopolitical background on the period in which the Apocrypha and various noncanonical works were composed.

Cohen, Shaye J. D. *From the Maccabees to the Mishnah.* Philadelphia: Westminster Press, 1987. An informative survey of Jewish thought from 200 BCE to 200 CE.

Desilva, David A. "Apocrypha, Deuterocanonicals." In K. D. Sakenfeld, ed., *The New Interpreter's Dictionary of the Bible,* Vol. 1, pp. 195–200. Nashville, TN: Abingdon Press, 2006. A concise survey of books in the "second canon."

Stone, Michael. *Scriptures, Sects, and Visions: A Profile of Judaism from Ezra to the Jewish Revolts.* Philadelphia: Fortress Press, 1980. An accessible exposition of key developments in Jewish thought from the postexilic restoration to the uprisings against Rome.

Tobit and Baruch

Nowell, Irene. "The Book of Tobit." In *The New Interpreter's Bible,* Vol. 3, pp. 973–1071. Nashville, TN: Abingdon Press, 1999. An introduction and commentary.

Saldarini, Anthony J. "The Book of Baruch" and "The Letter of Jeremiah." In *The New Interpreter's Bible,* Vol. 6, pp. 929–1010. Nashville, TN: Abingdon Press, 1998. A clear discussion.

The Wisdom of Jesus ben Sirach (Ecclesiasticus) and the Wisdom of Solomon

Crenshaw, James L. "The Book of Sirach." In *The New Interpreter's Bible,* Vol. 5, pp. 601–867. Nashville, TN: Abingdon Press, 1997. Offers background, commentary, and analysis of this important wisdom book.

Kolarcik, Michael. "The Book of Wisdom." In *The New Interpreter's Bible,* Vol. 5, pp. 435–600. Nashville, TN: Abingdon Press, 1997. Offers thorough commentary on this Hellenistic blending of Greek and biblical ideas.

Skehan, Patrick W., and Di Lelia, Alexander A. *The Wisdom of ben Sira.* Garden City, NY: Doubleday, 1987. A fresh translation and interpretative commentary.

Winston, David. *The Wisdom of Solomon.* Anchor Bible, Vol. 43. Garden City, NY: Doubleday, 1979. A recent translation with scholarly interpretation.

1 and 2 Maccabees

Doran, Robert. "1 Maccabees." In *The New Interpreter's Bible,* Vol. 4, pp. 1–178. Nashville, TN: Abingdon Press, 1996. Provides historical background to the Maccabean Revolt and detailed annotation of the text.

———. "2 Maccabees." In *The New Interpreter's Bible,* Vol. 4, pp. 179–299. Nashville, TN: Abingdon Press, 1996. The full text, with commentary.

2 Esdras

Humphrey, Edith M. "Esdras, Second Book of." In K. D. Sakenfeld, ed., *The New Interpreter's Dictionary of the Bible*, Vol. 2, pp. 309–313. Nashville, TN: Abingdon Press, 2007. A concise introduction to this important apocalypse.

Metzger, Bruce. "The Fourth Book of Ezra [2 Esdras]." In J. Charlesworth, ed., *The Old Testament Pseudepigrapha*, Vol. 1, pp. 516–559. Garden City, NY: Anchor Books/ Doubleday, 1983. A recent translation, with critical analysis of text.

1 Enoch

Bautch, Kelly C. "Enoch, First Book of." In K. D. Sakenfeld, ed., *The New Interpreter's Dictionary of the Bible*, Vol. 2, pp. 262–265. Nashville TN: Abingdon Press, 2007. A concise evaluation of the book's origins and religious significance.

Isaac, E. "1 Enoch (Ethiopic Apocalypse of)". In J. Charlesworth, ed., *The Old Testament Pseudepigrapha*, Vol. 1, pp. 5–100. Garden City, NY: Anchor Books/Doubleday, 1983. A recent translation, with detailed commentary.

Nickelsburg, George, and Vanderkam, James. *I Enoch: A New Translation*. Minneapolis: Fortress, 2004. A scholarly edition in English.

PART THREE

The New Testament

CHAPTER 28
The World in Which Christianity Originated   265

CHAPTER 29
First-Century Judaism   282

CHAPTER 30
Telling Jesus' Story   291

CHAPTER 31
The Synoptic Problem   307

CHAPTER 32
Jesus as a Savior for "All Nations"   325

CHAPTER 33
Another Way of Telling Jesus' Story   336

CHAPTER 34
An Account of Early Christianity   350

CHAPTER 35
Paul and the Gentile Mission   363

CHAPTER 36
Continuing the Pauline Tradition   391

CHAPTER 37
General Letters on Faith and Behavior   401

CHAPTER 38
Continuing the Apocalyptic Hope   412

CHAPTER 39
Our Judeo-Christian Heritage   424

CHAPTER 28

The World in Which Christianity Originated

Roman Power, Greek Culture, and the Cult of Deified Rulers

Key Topics/Themes Three major forces largely shaped the world in which Christianity was born and developed: the Scriptures and traditions of Judaism, the political power of Rome, and the culture of Greece. These three forces represent the context in which the New Testament was written. Under control of the Roman Empire after 63 BCE, the covenant people in Palestine were successively ruled by Roman-appointed Herodian kings and a series of Roman governors, such as Pontius Pilate. Widespread political discontent erupted into a massive Jewish rebellion against Rome (66–73 CE),

which resulted in the destruction of Jerusalem and the Jewish state. Although Jesus' life (c. 4 BCE–30 CE) and teaching took place entirely within the sphere of pre-revolt Palestinian Judaism, his followers quickly spread his message abroad in the Greco-Roman world, where Greek-speaking converts interpreted him in ways that paralleled some previously existing Greek ideas and traditions. The rich diversity of Hellenistic religion and philosophy, including the Greco-Roman cult of deified rulers, provides the dynamic environment in which early Christianity grew and developed.

The Political and Social Environment in Which Christianity Originated: Roman Power and Greek Culture

The Roman Occupation of Palestine

In Jesus' day, the brutal fact of life was Rome's total control of the Promised Land. Ironically, it was a political squabble between Jewish rulers during the first century BCE that allowed Roman armies to incorporate Palestine into Rome's rapidly growing empire. As reported in Chapters 26 and 27, following the Maccabean Revolt, Jewish leaders established a politically independent Jewish kingdom ruled by the Hasmonean dynasty (142 BCE). But when two Hasmonean brothers both claimed the Judean throne, the elder, John Hyrcanus II, appealed to Rome for help in ousting his younger sibling, Aristobulus II, who had made himself both High Priest and king. Summoned as a peacekeeper, the Roman general Pompey, the great military rival of Julius

Caesar, led his legions to overthrow Aristobulus and install John Hyrcanus as High Priest (63 BCE). Instead of making Hyrcanus king, however, the Romans downgraded his rank to *ethnarch* (provincial governor), demonstrating that Hasmonean rulers were now only puppets of Rome and that the holy land was merely another province in the empire.

Herod "the Great"

After the death of John Hyrcanus in 40 BCE, the Roman Senate appointed **Herod I** king of Judea. Although he adopted a form of Judaism, Herod was not of Jewish descent; he was the son of Antipater (c. 100–43 BCE), a powerful nobleman of Idumea, the Greco-Roman name for ancient Edom, a traditional enemy of the Jewish state. Unpopular with many Jews, Herod had to overcome armed resistance to gain his throne. By 37 BCE, three years after Rome made him king, Herod had captured Jerusalem and begun a long reign (37–4 BCE) marked by a strange combination of administrative skill, cruelty, and bloodshed. Politically, Herod was remarkably successful. Enjoying Roman support, he extended the boundaries of his kingdom almost to the limits of David's biblical realm. Under Herod, the Jewish state expanded to include the districts of **Samaria** and **Galilee** (the district where Jesus grew up) and territories east of the Jordan River.

Herod's extensive building programs matched his political ambitions. He constructed monumental fortresses, the best known of which is **Masada** on the western shore of the Dead Sea. He also founded the port city Caesarea Maratima, which later became the Roman administrative capital. Herod's most famous building project, however, was renovating the Temple in Jerusalem, transforming it into one of the most magnificent sanctuaries in the ancient world. This was the Temple where Jesus and the disciples worshiped (Mark 11:27–13:2; Luke 2:22–38, 41–50; 19:47–48; Acts 2:46, etc.). Begun in 20 BCE, the Temple remodeling was not completed until about 62 CE, only eight years before the Romans destroyed it.

Despite his grandiose achievements, Herod's treachery and violence caused most of his Jewish subjects to hate him. He murdered his Hasmonean wife, Mariamne, and their two sons, Alexander and Aristobulus, as well as other family members. His fear that some conspirators might seize his crown, coupled with his ruthless elimination of any potential rival, provide the background for the Gospel story that Herod massacred Bethlehem's children (Matt. 2:16–17).

Herod's Successors

When Herod died in 4 BCE (according to modern calendars, Jesus was probably born a few years BCE), his kingdom was divided among his three surviving sons. Philip (ruled 4 BCE–34 CE) became tetrarch of the areas north and east of the Sea of Galilee; his brother **Herod Antipas** (ruled 4 BCE–39 CE) was given the territories of Galilee and Perea, a region east of the Jordan River. This is the Herod who beheaded John the Baptist (Mark 6:14–29; Matt. 14:1–12) and whom Jesus characterized as "that fox" (Luke 13:31–32). According to Luke's Gospel, Herod, as ruler of Galilee, Jesus' home district, examined Jesus at Pilate's request (Luke 23:6–12). A third brother, Herod Archelaus, inherited the southwestern portion of Herod I's dominion (Judea, Samaria, and Idumea), but the Romans removed him for incompetence. In 6 CE, the Roman Empire imposed direct rule over Judea, governing through a series of **prefects** (later **procurators**), the most famous of which was the prefect **Pontius Pilate** (governed 26–36 CE), the man who sentenced Jesus to death.

Two other members of the Herodian family, both named Herod Agrippa, play prominent roles in the New Testament. A grandson of Herod the Great, **Herod Agrippa I,** a friend of the emperor Claudius, became king of a briefly reunited Judea and Samaria (41–44 CE). According to Acts 12, after Agrippa beheaded James, one of Jesus' leading apostles, and then publicly accepted honors due a god, he quickly died a horrible death, "eaten by worms." The Romans later appointed his son, **Herod Agrippa II,** the last of the Herodian line to rule, over Philip's former territory, Galilee and Perea. When **Paul,** early Christianity's most successful missionary, was imprisoned at Caesarea Maritima, Herod Agrippa II examined him there, reportedly exclaiming that Paul almost persuaded him to become a Christian (Acts 25:13–26:32). Loyal to Rome during the Jewish Revolt, which began in 66 CE, after the rebellion was suppressed, he regained his throne with Roman help. Later moving to Rome, he died there in 93 CE.

The Jewish Revolt Against Rome

Although representatives of the Herodian dynasty and Roman governors such as Pontius Pilate are the most prominent political figures in the Gospel accounts, the real center of political power in Jesus' world lay in the person of the Roman emperor. At the time of Jesus' birth, the emperor **Augustus** (originally named Gaius Octavius, ruled 27 BCE–14 CE) reigned over an empire even larger and more diverse than Alexander's (see Figure 28.1). Rome controlled not only the Near East but also all of North Africa and most of Europe. Military conquests had reduced the Mediterranean Sea to the status of a large Roman lake (see Figure 28.2). Located at the eastern margin of the empire, the Jewish homeland was only an insignificant, though politically troublesome, part of an international colossus. After the death of Augustus in 14 CE, his stepson **Tiberius** (14–37 CE) became emperor, the ruler in power during Jesus' ministry (Luke 3:1). It was Tiberius's governmental appointee Pilate who found Jesus guilty of treason against Rome (Matt. 27:11–44; Mark 15:2–32; Luke 22:66–23:38). (Box 28.1 lists some key events that helped shape Jesus' world.)

About thirty-five years after Jesus' crucifixion, the Palestinian Jews rose in armed revolt against Rome. Whereas Jewish fighters more than two centuries earlier had succeeded in driving out foreign troops during the Maccabean uprising, the Jewish Revolt against Rome (66–73 CE) was a complete disaster for

FIGURE 28.1 This bust shows the head of Augustus (Gaius Octavius), first emperor of Rome (ruled 27 BCE–14 CE). Defeating all rivals for control of the Roman Empire, Augustus ended centuries of civil war and introduced a new era of peace and political stability.

the Jewish people. When the rebellion began in 66 CE, the emperor **Nero** sent a veteran military commander, **Vespasian,** to crush the rebels. Galilee fell easily to the Roman army, but before Vespasian could capture Jerusalem, a palace revolt in Rome drove Nero to commit suicide (68 CE). Following a year of political chaos, the Roman legions acclaimed Vespasian as emperor, a move the Senate confirmed. Leaving his son **Titus** in charge of the Jewish War, Vespasian returned to Rome. After a siege of six months, Titus broke through Jerusalem's defenses, burned the city, and ordered the Temple, a center of rebel activity, to be demolished (70 CE) (see Figure 28.3).

Our main source of information about the war is **Flavius Josephus,** a first-century Jewish historian who initially participated in the rebellion but later became a Roman ally. An eyewitness to many of the events he describes, Josephus wrote to explain and defend his countrymen's actions in revolting against Roman oppression. In *The Jewish War,* he vividly recounts the Roman capture of Jerusalem and the slaughter of many thousands of men, women, and children. While trying to evoke sympathy for his people and make their religion comprehensible to his Greek and Roman readers, Josephus also blames what he portrays as a small minority of political fanatics for their refusal to negotiate a compromise with the Romans. According to Josephus, the extreme revolutionary party, the **Zealots,** virtually forced General Titus (later emperor) to destroy the sanctuary by their refusal to surrender. Many historians doubt Josephus's sometimes self-serving interpretation of events, but his surviving works, including a history of Israel called *Antiquities of the Jews,* are an invaluable record of this turbulent period.

For three of the Gospel writers—Matthew, Mark, and Luke—Rome's destruction of the holy city and its Temple marked a turning point in world history. All three authors devote long passages to Jesus' prediction of Jerusalem's fall, which they associate with signs and portents of Jesus' return (Matt. 24–25; Mark 13; Luke 21). Until Titus sacked and burned Jerusalem in 70 CE, it also had been the center of the early church, led by Jesus' foremost disciples, Peter and John, and his "brother" James (Gal. 1–2; Acts 1–12). For Jews, Titus's demolition of the Temple brought a permanent end to Israel's long history of offering animal and other sacrifices to God as the Mosaic *torah* prescribed. With its altar and priesthood gone, the Judaism that emerged after the first revolt against Rome would focus on offering not animal sacrifice but prayer, charitable deeds, and other good works as the fruits of its covenant partnership with Yahweh.

About sixty years after Titus razed the Temple—which was never rebuilt—Palestinian Jews again revolted against Rome. This second Jewish war (132–135 CE) was led by a young man popularly known as **bar Kochba** (Son of the Star), whom many Jews believed to be the Messiah who would restore David's kingdom. When the emperor Hadrian brutally put down the revolt, he ordered a second Roman destruction of Jerusalem (135 CE) and had a Roman shrine built on the site of Herod's Temple. Hadrian also forbade Jews to enter their capital city on pain of death.

For Jews and Christians alike, Rome's destruction of Jerusalem made it the "new Babylon," the foreign power that enslaved the covenant people and desecrated the sanctuary where God had placed his "name." As a result, some New Testament documents written before and after 70 CE show marked differences in their respective authors' attitudes toward Rome. Paul, who wrote a letter to the church in Rome more than a decade before Jerusalem's fall, advises Christians to "be subject to the

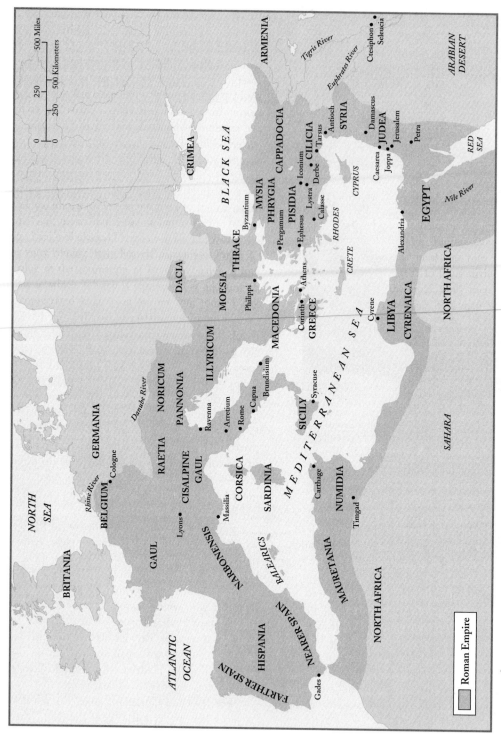

FIGURE 28.2 **Map of the Roman Empire.** By the reign of Augustus (27 BCE–14 CE), the Roman Empire controlled most of the known world.

FIGURE 28.3 This detail appears on the Arch of Titus, which the Roman Senate erected in the Forum of Rome about 100 CE. Created in honor of Titus's victories in the Jewish War, this frieze depicts Roman soldiers carrying off loot from the Jerusalem Temple, including the Menorah—the seven-branched candelabrum formerly housed in the sanctuary.

governing authorities," including their right to impose taxes, because God has appointed them to maintain civil order (Rom. 13:1–7). By contrast, the author of Revelation, writing near the end of the first century, portrays Rome as "Babylon the great, mother of whores and of earth's abominations," an empire centered at "the great city that rules over the kings of the earth" (Rev. 14:8; 17:1–18; 18:1–24; cf. 1 Peter 5:13).

The World of Greek Thought and Culture

The Influence of Hellenism

Rome was the dominant political force that put Jesus to death and destroyed the city holy to both Jews and Christians. Greek culture, however, had an equally powerful impact on the development of both Judaism and early Christianity. As discussed in Chapters 26 and 27, the military conquests of Alexander the Great (reigned 336–323 BCE) brought Hellenism—the adoption of Greek language, literature, social customs, and religious and ethical values—to the entire eastern Mediterranean region. The broad diffusion of Hellenism created a new international culture known as **Hellenistic,** a fusion of classical Greek (Hellenic) civilization with older Near Eastern culture, that produced a flowering in art, architecture, philosophy, science, literature, and religion.

Arbitrarily dated as beginning with Alexander's death (323 BCE), the Hellenistic era chronologically overlapped the period of Roman expansion and continued as a cultural force into the early centuries CE. During this creative epoch, which spanned 500 years, the last books of the Hebrew Bible, the entire New Testament, and an additional large body of noncanonical Jewish and Christian literature were composed.

Greek culture influenced not only the content of these works but also the language in which it was expressed. Both Hellenistic Jews and early Christians adopted a new form of the Greek language, the *koinē* (common) Greek spoken by Alexander's soldiers. *Koinē* became so widely spoken that the Jews of Alexandria, Egypt—the second-largest city of the Roman Empire—found it necessary to translate the Hebrew Bible into *koinē* Greek, beginning about 250 BCE with the Torah and gradually adding other books. This Greek edition, the Septuagint, was used not only by Diaspora Jews but also by the early Christian movement, which produced its own Scripture, the New Testament, in *koinē* Greek.

Among leading thinkers throughout the Greco-Roman world, Greek culture set the standard of intellectual and artistic excellence. The Greek love of learning, intense intellectual curiosity, and confidence in the power of reason to discover truth became near-universal principles shaping Hellenistic education. Archaeologists have recently discovered that even Galilee, previously

BOX 28.1 Some Representative Events That Shaped the World of Jesus and the Early Church

ALEXANDER AND HIS SUCCESSORS		THE ROMAN EMPIRE	
c. 334–323 BCE	Alexander's conquests create a new international culture, the Hellenistic, bringing Greek language, literature, ideas, and customs to the entire Near Eastern world, including Palestine. This broad diffusion of Greek philosophic and religious thought plays a major role in the development of both Judaism and Christianity.	63 BCE	Pompey's legions occupy Palestine, annexing it as part of the Roman Empire.
323–197 BCE	The Ptolemaic dynasty, established by Ptolemy I, general and one of Alexander's successors, controls Palestine. Many Jews are attracted to Greek learning and the Hellenistic way of life.	40 BCE	The Roman Senate appoints Herod (Herod the Great), a nobleman of Idumea (the ancient Edom), king of Judea.
200–197 BCE	The Seleucid dynasty of Syria, descendants of Alexander's general Seleucus, ends Ptolemaic rule over Palestine and begins a new reign over the Jews (197–142 BCE).	37–4 BCE	After laying siege to Jerusalem, Herod takes the city by force; he then lavishly rebuilds the Jerusalem Temple.
168–164 BCE	The Seleucid ruler Antiochus IV, "Epiphanes," attempts to eradicate the Jewish religion, forbidding Torah observance and erecting an altar to the Olympian Zeus in the Temple precincts ("the abomination" of Dan. 9:27). Mattathias, a Torah loyalist, and his five sons initiate the Maccabean Revolt.	27 BCE–14 CE	Gaius Octavius becomes undisputed ruler of the entire Roman Empire. Renamed Augustus by the Roman Senate, he ends the civil wars that had divided Rome for generations and establishes a long period of civil order called the Pax Romana (Roman Peace).
		THE LIFE OF JESUS	
		c. 6–4 BCE	Jesus is born to Mary and Joseph, citizens of Nazareth.
164 BCE	Led by Judas Maccabeus, a Jewish guerrilla army recaptures, purifies, and rededicates the Temple, an event later commemorated in the festival of Hanukkah.	4 BCE	After Herod the Great's death, his kingdom is divided among his three sons. Herod Antipas rules Galilee and Perea (4 BCE–39 CE); Herod Philip rules territories north and east of Galilee (4 BCE–34 CE); Herod Archelaus rules Judea, Samaria, and Idumea (4 BCE–6 CE) but is deposed. His territories henceforth are administered directly by Roman officials.
142–63 BCE	By 142 BCE, the Jews have expelled the Syrian armies and established an independent state governed by Hasmonean (Maccabean) rulers.	14–37 CE	Tiberius, stepson of Augustus, rules Rome.
		26–36 CE	Pontius Pilate, appointed by Rome, governs as prefect of Judea (26–36 CE).

thought to be a rural backwater, had a major Hellenistic city, Sepphoris, which was located only four miles from Jesus' home village of Nazareth. Although the Gospel authors depict Jesus' ministry as confined to Galilean villages and small towns, some scholars think that Jesus may have had direct experience of Hellenistic culture there. Sepphoris, which the Romans had burned to the ground following a revolt in 4 BCE, was later lavishly rebuilt by Herod Antipas, the area's Roman-appointed ruler. It is remotely possible, some historians believe, that the youthful Jesus, the son of a Nazareth carpenter, may have worked on the rebuilding project, perhaps acquiring some knowledge of Greek language and ideas.

As an anthology of Greek documents, the New Testament profoundly reflects its Hellenistic background.

c. 27–30 or 29–33 CE	Jesus conducts a public ministry. Jesus and a small band of disciples tour villages and cities in and around Galilee. A final journey to Jerusalem results in Jesus' rejection by religious authorities and his execution by Pilate on charges of treason.

THE DEVELOPMENT OF THE CHRISTIAN COMMUNITY AND ITS SCRIPTURES

c. 30 or 33 CE	A number of Jesus' followers are convinced that they have seen him risen from the dead. Gathered in Jerusalem, a commune of believers is inspired to begin carrying the oral gospel of Jesus' resurrection to Jews and (somewhat later) Gentiles. The Christian church is born.
c. 33–35 CE	Saul of Tarsus, a zealous Pharisee then persecuting Christian "heretics," experiences a vision of the risen Jesus on the road to Damascus.
c. 50–62 CE	Paul, now the preeminent Christian missionary to the Gentiles, composes a series of letters to various Christian communities in the northeastern Mediterranean region. These letters are the earliest parts of the New Testament to be written.
c. 62 CE	James, Jesus' kinsman, is killed in Jerusalem.
c. 64–65 CE	Following a major fire in Rome, the emperor Nero persecutes Christians there. According to tradition, Peter and Paul are martyred then.
c. 66–70 CE	The first account of Jesus' public ministry is written (the Gospel according to Mark).
66–73 CE	Led by the Zealot party of dedicated revolutionaries, the Palestinian Jews

revolt against Roman tyranny. Titus, son of the new emperor Vespasian, captures and destroys Jerusalem and its Temple (70 CE).

THE POSTAPOSTOLIC ERA

c. 80–85 CE	The Gospel of Matthew is written (in Antioch?).
c. 85–90 CE	Luke-Acts is published.
c. 80–100 CE	The books of James, Hebrews, and (possibly) 1 Peter are written.
c. 90 CE	Leading rabbis and Jewish scholars hold a council at Jamnia, to restructure postwar Judaism. Christians are expelled from Jewish synagogues.
c. 90 CE	The letter to the Ephesians is included among Paul's correspondence.
c. 90–100 CE	The Gospel of John is produced by the Johannine community. The letter of 1 Clement is written in Rome.
c. 95 CE	John of Patmos writes the Book of Revelation.
c. 100–110 CE	The letters of John are written.
c. 100–130 CE	The Didache, Shepherd of Hermas, and epistles of Ignatius are composed. The canonical New Testament books of 1 and 2 Timothy, Titus, and Jude appear.
132–135 CE	The bar Kochba rebellion against Rome is crushed by the emperor Hadrian (117–138 CE).
c. 130–150 CE	2 Peter is written.
367 CE	Bishop Athanasius of Alexandria publishes a list of twenty-seven New Testament books corresponding to the present New Testament canon.

In many important ways, the New Testament writers combine their Jewish biblical heritage with Greek philosophical concepts. To understand the dual legacy that the Christian Greek Scriptures transmit to us, we will review briefly some major aspects of Hellenistic philosophy and religion, a body of knowledge with which many New Testament authors—and their original audiences—would have been familiar.

Greek Philosophy

A term meaning "love of wisdom," *philosophy* is an attempt to understand human life and its place in the universe by applying rational analysis to observable facts. At first indistinguishable from primitive science, Greek **philosophy** began in the late seventh century BCE in Miletus and other Greek cities along the coast of

FIGURE 28.4   This drawing shows Phidias's Athene Parthenos (the virgin). The Parthenon in Athens was built to house a cult statue of Athene that the sculptor Phidias created in ivory and gold. As the goddess of wisdom, Athene encouraged the intellectual pursuits of Athens' democratic society.

western Asia Minor. By the fifth century BCE, Athens emerged as the intellectual center of the Greek world, home to numerous schools of thought that used the tools of logic to discredit old superstitions and to construct new theories about the universe (see Figure 28.4).

Socrates, Plato, and the Immortal Soul   Some Athenian philosophers, such as **Socrates** (c. 469–399 BCE), focused on ethical questions, particularly the mental disciplines by which one could discover and lead the "good life," a life worthy of responsible and intelligent human beings. Combining brilliant originality with an impish sense of humor, Socrates regarded human life as an ongoing quest for truth, a pilgrimage toward the unseen world of eternal spirit, the ultimate goal of the human soul. Questioning every belief that his fellow Athenians cherished as "obviously" true, Socrates good-naturedly cross-examined artisans, teachers, and politicians alike—demanding to learn how people could be so sure that their beliefs were valid. While attracting a

small circle of devoted followers, Socrates also irritated many of Athens' most influential citizens, some of whom viewed this "gadfly" and his stinging questions as a threat to conventional morality. His critics eventually placed Socrates on trial, where he was convicted and executed for introducing new gods and corrupting Athenian youth, charges that masked his adversaries' real complaint. Socrates was the only person in Athens's long history to be put to death for expressing unpopular ideas.

Many readers find suggestive parallels between the respective careers of Socrates and Jesus, both of whom followed a divine calling, advocated cultivating spiritual values and rejecting materialistic goals, and paid the supreme penalty for voicing ideas that leaders of their respective societies regarded as subversive. Although both men were sages who taught that the ultimate realities were divine powers before whom all people's conduct would be judged posthumously, their cultural differences were perhaps greater than the roughly similar patterns of their public ministries and martyrs' deaths.

Plato's Profound Influence The historical situations for Jesus and Socrates are alike in one important respect: Neither Socrates nor Jesus left anything in writing. In both cases, their teachings were reconstructed by later writers whose accounts of their subjects' lives may owe as much to editorial interpretation as they do to biographical fact. Socrates' youthful disciple **Plato** (c. 427–347 BCE) made his teacher the hero of a series of philosophical dialogues in which a saintly and humorous Socrates always outargues and outwits his opponents. Because virtually all of Plato's compositions, which he continued to produce until his death at eighty years of age, feature Socrates as the chief speaker, separating Plato's ideas from those of his mentor is difficult. New Testament scholars face a similar problem in trying to distinguish Jesus' authentic sayings from the added commentary of the Gospel writers, who wrote between forty and sixty-five years after Jesus' death (see Chapters 30–33).

Although he was a philosopher and logician, Plato strongly influenced the history of Western religion, particularly later beliefs about the immortality of the soul and the effects that decisions made in this life can have on posthumous rewards and punishments. Plato's dualistic views of reality also deeply affected subsequent religious thought. Like many later Christian theologians, he posited the existence of two distinct worlds: one the familiar physical environment of matter and sense impressions, and the other an invisible spiritual realm of perfect, eternal ideas. In this dualistic worldview, our bodies belong to the material sphere, where we are chained to the physical processes of change, decay, and death. Our souls, however, originate in the unseen spirit world and after death return to it for postmortem judgment. Education involves recognizing the superiority of the soul to the body and cultivating those qualities that prepare the soul for its immortal destiny. Hence, the person who truly loves wisdom, the genuine philosopher, will seek the knowledge of eternal truths that make real goodness possible, helping others along the way to realize that ambitions for worldly power or riches are false idols. The wise seek the perfect justice of the unseen world and, with the pure spirits of divinity, find eternal life.

Over the centuries, Plato's ideas were modified and widely disseminated until, in one form or another, they became common knowledge during the Hellenistic era. Some New Testament writers, such as the author of Hebrews, used Platonic concepts to illustrate the parallels and correspondences between the spiritual and physical worlds (Heb. 1:1–4; 9:1–14). The book's famous definition of Christian faith is primarily a confession of Platonic belief in the reality of the invisible realm (Heb. 11:1–2).

Stoicism and Stoic Endurance Another Greek philosophy that became extremely popular among the educated classes during Roman times was **Stoicism**. Founded in Athens by Zeno (c. 336–263 BCE), the Stoic school emphasized the order and moral purpose of the universe. In the Stoic view, Reason is the divine principle that gives coherence and meaning to our universe. Identified as **Logos** (a Greek term for "word" or "cosmic wisdom"), this universal mind unifies the world and makes it intelligible to the human intellect. Human souls are sparks from the divine Logos, which is symbolized by cosmic fire and sometimes associated with a supreme god.

Stoic teaching urged the individual to listen to the divine element within, to discipline both body and mind to attain a state of harmony with nature and the cosmos. Stoics rigorously practiced self-control, learning self-sufficiency and noble indifference to both pleasure and pain. The Stoic ideal was to endure either personal gain or loss with equal serenity, without any show of emotion.

Many celebrated Romans pursued the Stoic way, including the philosopher Seneca (Nero's tutor), the Greek slave Epictetus, and the emperor Marcus Aurelius (161–180 CE). The hero of Virgil's epic poem the *Aeneid*, with his rigid concept of duty toward the gods and unselfish service to the state, is intended to represent the Stoic virtues. When Paul discusses self-discipline or the ability to endure want or plenty, he echoes Stoic values that were commonplace in Greco-Roman society (Phil. 4:11–14).

Epicureanism A strikingly different philosophical outlook appears in the teachings of Epicurus (c. 342–270 BCE). Whereas the Stoics believed in the soul's immortality and a future world of rewards or penalties, Epicurus asserted that everything is completely physical or material, including the soul, which after death dissolves into nothingness along with the body. The gods may exist, but they have neither contact with nor interest in humankind. Without a cosmic intelligence to guide them, people must create their own individual purposes in life. A major goal is the avoidance of pain, which means that shrewd individuals will avoid public service or politics, where rivals may destroy them. Cultivating a private garden, the wise forgo sensual indulgences, which weaken physically and mentally. Using reason not to discover ultimate Truth, but to live well, the enlightened person, the Epicurean, seeks intellectual pleasures because mental enjoyments outlast those of the body.

Epicurus's emphasis on the material, perishable nature of both body and soul found support in the philosopher Democritus's atomic theory. Democritus (born c. 460 BCE) taught that all things are made up of tiny, invisible particles called atoms. It is the nature of atoms to move and collide, temporarily forming objects, including sentient ones like animals and humans, and then to disintegrate and re-form as other objects elsewhere. Wise or foolish, all persons are merely chance collections of atoms destined ultimately to dissolve without a trace.

Gods Offering Worshipers a Personal Relationship

The official state religion of Rome honored twelve major gods, headed by Jupiter or Jove, the Roman counterpart of the Greek Zeus, king of the gods (see Figure 28.5). Known as the Olympians, these deities were said to dwell atop Mount Olympus, the highest peak in Greece. Roman priests regularly offered animal, grain, and other sacrifices to Jupiter, his sister-wife Juno, his sister Ceres (the Roman version of Demeter, goddess of the soil's fertility and patron of the grain harvest), Mars (god of war and agriculture), and other members of the Olympian family. By the time that Augustus had assumed imperial leadership of the empire in the first century BCE, many people apparently found the traditional sky-gods increasingly remote from ordinary human concerns. Only a few deities associated with the official cult seemed to offer a satisfying personal relationship with their worshipers. Two of the most accessible figures were Asclepius and Dionysus, both of whom were born mortal and underwent suffering and death before achieving immortality, experiences that allowed them to bridge the gulf between humanity and divinity.

Asclepius, the most humane and compassionate of Greek heroes, was the son of a mortal woman and Apollo, god of music, health, and prophecy, whom the Romans also identified with the sun. Inheriting from his divine father the gift of miraculous healing, Asclepius became

FIGURE 28.5 This larger-than-life bronze (c. 460 BCE) probably represents Zeus, the king of the Olympian gods. Zeus was both a personification of storm and lightning and the heavenly enforcer of justice, lawful order, and cosmic harmony. Unlike the Judeo-Christian God, who is eternal, Zeus is the descendant of older generations of gods who ruled the universe before him.

the supreme physician, devoting his abilities to curing the sick and maimed. When his skill became so effective that he was able to raise the dead, however, Zeus killed him with a lightning bolt for disrupting the natural order. After attaining posthumous divinity, Asclepius, as the divine patron of medicine, extended his benevolence throughout the Greco-Roman world. Professional healers, known as the Sons of Asclepius, officiated at hundreds of sanctuaries, such as Epidaurus in Greece, where patients flocked to be relieved of their afflictions. Reports of miraculous cures abounded, causing Asclepius to be hailed as the "savior" and friend of humanity.

People seeking divine help at Asclepius's many shrines commonly underwent treatment that combined faith healing with the practice of scientific medicine. To create a direct relationship with the god, patients usually began their cure by spending several nights sleeping at his temple, during which time Asclepius was said to appear in their dreams, asking questions about their health and giving advice. Attending physicians then prescribed a variety of therapies, ranging from changes in diet and exercise to surgical procedures. Grateful patients commemorated their restoration to health by dedicating inscriptions and plaster replicas of their body parts that the kindly god had healed. Although Asclepius demanded strict ethical behavior of those he helped, he was also acclaimed for welcoming the poor and disadvantaged to his sanctuaries.

Dionysus of Thebes and Jesus of Nazareth

Whereas Asclepius's compassionate nature and benevolent works anticipate aspects of Jesus' ministry, the myth of **Dionysus** foreshadows some later Christian theological interpretations of Jesus' cosmic role. Although Jesus is a historical figure and Dionysus purely mythical, Dionysus's story contains events and themes—such as his divine parentage, violent death, descent into the Underworld, and subsequent resurrection to immortal life in heaven, where he sits near his father's throne—that the Christian church ultimately made part of Jesus' story.

Like Asclepius, Hercules, Perseus, and other heroes of Greco-Roman tradition, Dionysus has a divine father and human mother. The only major Olympian born to a mortal woman, he was also the only major deity to endure rejection, suffering, and death before ascending to heaven to join his divine father. The son of Zeus and Semele, a princess of Thebes, Dionysus was known as the "twice born." His first birth resulted from the jealous deceptions of Zeus's wife, Hera (Roman, Juno), who tricked Semele, then pregnant with Dionysus, into compelling Zeus to reveal himself in his true form. The resulting

blaze of lightning incinerated Semele, but Zeus snatched the unborn child from her womb and placed it in his own body, from which the infant Dionysus was born anew (see Figure 28.6). In one version of the myth, Hera released the Titans, ancient gods whom Zeus had chained in Tartarus (the dark abyss below Hades), who attacked the young Dionysus, dismembered his body, and ate it. In another tradition, the risen Dionysus descended to the Underworld to retrieve his mother, Semele, and escort her to heaven. Having experienced an agonizing death and journey to Hades' realm, Dionysus, alone among the Olympians, personally knew what it was to suffer and die.

Wine, the Beverage of Communion Between Gods and Humans As the inventor of wine-making, Dionysus bestowed upon humanity a beverage that is a two-edged sword: Wine can liberate people from their cares, temporarily giving them the freedom of a god, but its potentially negative aftereffects can also deliver a painful reminder of human limitations, the inability to assimilate a divine gift with impunity. Most authors of the Hebrew Bible similarly regard wine as a mixed blessing: Overindulgence can bring misery, but, in general, God himself provides "[the gift of] wine to gladden the human heart" (Ps. 104:15) and to "gladden [human] life" (Eccles. 10:19). Sacrificed to Yahweh in Israelite worship (Lev. 23:13; Num. 28:14), wine was also the drink to be served at the future messianic banquet celebrating God's ultimate dominion over the earth (Isa. 25:6).

Long before Jesus linked wine and bread as part of the Christian liturgy (Mark 14:22–25; Luke 22:17–30), the two tokens of divine favor were associated in the Dionysian traditions. In the *Bacchae* (worshipers of Bacchus, another name for Dionysus), the Athenian playwright Euripides (c. 485–406 BCE) has the prophet Tiresias observe that Demeter and Dionysus, respectively, gave humanity two indispensable gifts: grain or bread to sustain life and wine to make life bearable. Tiresias urges his hearers to see in Dionysus's gift of wine a beverage that brings humans into communion with the divine:

> This new God [Dionysus] whom you dismiss,
> no words of mine can attain
> the greatness of his coming power in Greece.
> Young man,
> two are the forces most precious to mankind.
> The first is Demeter, the Goddess.
> She is the Earth—or any name you wish to call her—
> and she sustains humanity with solid food.
> Next comes the son of the virgin, Dionysus,
> bringing the counterpart to bread, wine

FIGURE 28.6 Surrounded by figures associated with his ecstatic cult, the infant Dionysus emerges from his father's thigh. The second (and last) of Zeus's children to be born from their father's body (Athene emerged, fully grown, from Zeus's head), Dionysus represents the ever-changing natural world and the instinctual component of the human psyche, a counterbalance to Athene's conscious intellect. As their respective birth myths suggest, Athene and Dionysus demonstrate that reason and nonrationality spring from the same divine source.

and the blessings of life's flowing juices.
His blood, the blood of the grape,
lightens the burden of our mortal misery.
When, after their daily toils, men drink their fill,
sleep comes to them, bringing release from all
their troubles.
There is no other cure for sorrow. Though
himself a God,
it is his blood we pour out
to offer thanks to the Gods. And through him,
we are blessed. (Trans. Michael Cacoyannis)

Consumed in thanksgiving, and symbolic of the god's shed blood, wine bestows a blessing on humankind.

Emblematic of divine generosity, bread and wine were tangible evidence of the gods' care for humanity. In this context, the Gospel tradition frames Jesus' public ministry with momentous feasts involving bread and/or wine. In John's Gospel, Jesus' first miraculous act is to change water into vintage wine at a Jewish wedding, a "sign" of his divinity that seems to mimic the wine-making magic of some Dionysian priests. In the Gospels of Mark, Matthew, and Luke (but, strangely, not John), Jesus hosts a final Passover dinner with his friends at which he announces that the bread he serves is his "body" and the wine he shares is his "blood" (Mark 14). The next day, Roman soldiers execute him; his wounding and crucifixion represent a form of *sparagmos,* the ritual tearing asunder of a male sacrificial victim, a fate reminiscent of Dionysus's at the hands of the Titans.

In interpreting the theological meaning of Jesus' life to a Greco-Roman audience, New Testament authors do not present their subject as a new version of Dionysus. Nonetheless, they tell his story in ways that strikingly parallel the Dionysian tradition (see Box 28.2). The Gospel accounts of Jesus' return to Nazareth, the Galilean town where he grew up, strongly resemble the story of

---

BOX 28.2 Parallels Between Dionysus of Thebes and Jesus of Nazareth

Scholars of world religion and mythology detect numerous parallels between the stories of heroes and gods from widely different cultures and periods. Tales of mortal heroes who ultimately become gods characterize the ancient traditions of Egypt, Mesopotamia, India, Greece, and Rome, as well as the native cultures of Mesoamerica and North America. In comparing the common elements found in the world's heroic myths, scholars discern a number of repeated motifs that form a distinctive pattern. Although Jesus is a historical figure and Dionysus a mythic being, their received life stories reveal components of an archetypal pattern, including the hero's birth to a divine parent; his narrow escape from attempts to kill him as an infant; his "missing" formative years; his sudden appearance as a young adult manifesting miraculous gifts; his struggle with evil forces; his return to his place of origin, commonly resulting in rejection; his betrayal, suffering, and death; and his resurrection to divine status, followed by the establishment of a new cult honoring his name.

DIONYSUS	JESUS
Is son of Zeus, king of the Greek gods	Is Son of God (Mark 15:39)
Is son of Semele, a virgin princess of Thebes	Is son of Mary, a virgin of Nazareth (Luke 2)
Survives an attempt by Hera to kill him as an infant	Survives an attempt by King Herod to kill him as an infant (Matt. 2)
Performs miracles to inspire faith in his divinity	Performs healings and other miracles (Mark 1–2)
Battles supernatural evil in the form of Titans	Resists Satan; exorcizes demons (Mark 1–3; Matt. 4; Luke 4)
Returns to his birthplace, where he is denied and rejected by family and former neighbors	Returns to his hometown, where he is rejected and threatened with death (Mark 6; Luke 4)
Invents wine; promotes his gift to humanity throughout the world	Transforms water into wine (John 2); makes wine the sacred beverage in communion (Mark 14)
Suffers wounding and death at the hands of the Titans	Suffers wounding and crucifixion at the hands of the Romans (Mark 15; John 19)
Descends into the Underworld	Descends into the Underworld (1 Pet. 3:19; 4:6)
Rises to divine immortality, joining his father, Zeus, on Olympus	Resurrected to glory; reigns in heaven at God's right hand (Phil. 2; Acts 7:55–57)
Evangelizes the world, establishing his universal cult	Directs followers to evangelize the world (Matt. 28:19–20)
Punishes opponents who denied his divinity	Will return to pass judgement on nonbelievers (Matt. 24–25; Rev. 19–20)

(See "Dionysus" in S. Hornblower and A. Spawforth, eds., *The Oxford Classical Dictionary*, 3rd ed. [New York: Oxford UP, 1996], pp. 479–482.)

Dionysus's return to Thebes, his birthplace. In both cases, family and former neighbors fail to recognize the hero's divinity—that he is God's son—and reject him, even threatening him with death (Mark 6:1–6; Luke 4:16–30). In Euripides' drama the *Bacchae*, the unvalued god exacts a fearful revenge on those who are blind to his divine nature, whereas in the Gospel tradition, Jesus asks for forgiveness of those who reject and kill him (Luke 23:34). The author of Revelation, however, portrays the glorified Christ as behaving with Dionysian vindictiveness when he returns to punish nonbelievers (Rev. 19–20).

The Mystery Religions

In addition to the public, state-sponsored rituals honoring the principal Olympian gods, Greco-Roman society fostered a number of "underground religions" that exerted a wide influence. Known as the **mysteries** (Greek, *mysteria*) because their adherents took oaths never to reveal their secrets, these cults initiated members into the sacred rites of gods who were thought to welcome human devotees, becoming their spiritual guardians and protectors. Because Greco-Roman deities did not demand exclusive devotion, people commonly were initiated into more than one mystery religion, simultaneously cultivating a mystic bond with such diverse gods as Dionysus, Demeter, Persephone, Isis, Osiris, or Mithras (see below). Scholars question the extent to which these esoteric cults anticipated Christian rites. Nevertheless, in some cases, participants shared a communal meal in which their god was invisibly present, perhaps allowing them to absorb the divine body into themselves and thus partake of the deity's immortality.

Mithras and Mithraism

Perhaps the most rigorously organized and politically effective mystery cult in the Roman Empire was that of **Mithras,** which became Rome's official state religion in the third century CE Although Mithras, whose name means "covenant," was originally a Persian god embodying the divine power of light, his mysteries did not appear in the Greco-Roman world until the first century CE. Scholars believe that, although Mithraism uses names taken from ancient Persian mythology, it developed as a

distinct new cult in the West under the influence of Hellenistic astrology. Pictorial carvings decorating the walls of caves in which Mithraic rituals were performed show that Mithras was a solar deity who presided over the stars, planets, and other astronomical features of the zodiac. According to Mithraic tradition, he was born from a rock on December 25, then calculated as the winter solstice, the crucial turning point of the solar year when the days begin to lengthen. After shepherds visited his birthplace, Mithras went forth to slay a bull (the zodiacal sign of Taurus), from whose blood and semen new life emerged (see Figure 28.7)

Identified with the invisible forces ruling the universe, Mithras's sacrifice of a cosmic bull was a manifestation of his omnipotence. Although we do not know how Mithras's story relates to the ceremonies practiced in the small underground chambers where men were initiated into his mysteries, the initiation rites apparently involved a spiritual rebirth. Once initiated, the worshiper was a soldier of his god, committed to the principles of light and life that Mithras personified. Enormously popular among ordinary soldiers and

FIGURE 28.7 Mithras, a god of Persian origin adopted by Roman soldiers and merchants, is shown slaying a sacred bull. During the second and third centuries CE, the cult of Mithras was Christianity's chief rival throughout the Roman Empire. Men (women were excluded) initiated into the god's mysteries received a cleaning baptism with the blood of a sacrificial animal and participated in a ritual meal.

businessmen, Mithraism established sanctuaries in virtually every part of the Roman world, from Britain and Germany to Mesopotamia and Egypt.

Christianity's leading competitor during the first three centuries CE, Mithraism featured some rituals paralleling those of the church, including baptism, communal meals, and oaths of celibacy. As Christians were figuratively washed in the "blood of the Lamb" (Rev. 7:14), Mithraic initiates were sprinkled and purified with the blood flowing from a sacrificial bull. Despite the fact that it apparently fulfilled its members' emotional and spiritual needs, Mithraism had a fatal flaw: Women could not be admitted to the god's service. When the Christian church, which baptized women as well as men, overcame its chief rival, however, it retained one of Mithraism's most potent symbols, the natal day of its lord. Because the winter solstice appropriately signifies the birth of God's Son, "the light of the world" (as well as the rebirth of the Mithraic sun), the church eventually chose Mithras's birthday—December 25—as that of Jesus.

The Mother Goddesses

Other mystery religions emphasize the importance of a female figure, a mother goddess who can offer help in this life and intervene for one in the next world. By far the most popular goddess in Roman times was **Isis,** an Egyptian deity whom artists typically portrayed as a Madonna holding her infant son Horus (see Figure 28.8). Representing motherly compassion allied with divine power, Isis was the center of a mystery cult that promised initiates personal help in resolving life's problems, as well as the assurance of a happy existence after death. As an embodiment of creative intelligence and cosmic wisdom, Isis was known as the goddess of "a thousand names," a deity whom the whole world honored in one form or another. Offering the individual worshiper more comfort than the official state religions of Greece or Rome, the Isis cult found dedicated adherents throughout the Roman Empire.

In his novel *The Golden Ass,* the Roman author Apuleius (second century CE) reveals more about the mystical aspects of initiation into a mystery cult than any other ancient writer, describing his visionary experiences in which the goddess Isis became his personal savior. Like countless others before and after him, Apuleius seems to have undergone a religious awakening that transcended normal reality and bound him to a benevolent and caring deity who redeemed him from his animal nature, unveiled heavenly secrets, and imparted new meaning to this life.

FIGURE 28.8 Statuette of Isis holding the infant Horus (c. 600 BCE). Originally an Egyptian goddess, in New Testament times, Isis was worshiped throughout the Roman Empire as the embodiment of wisdom who offered worldly success and divine protection to persons initiated into her cult. Commonly pictured as a tender mother nursing her son, Isis became a prototype of the Christian Madonna and child.

The myth of Isis involved her male consort Osiris, originally a mortal ruler of ancient Egypt. Like Dionysus, Osiris suffered death by being torn to pieces but was restored to life as the god of the Underworld. Osiris owed his postmortem existence to his sister-wife Isis, who had searched throughout the world to find and reassemble the pieces of his dismembered corpse. By Greco-Roman times, the cults of Isis and Osiris, king and judge of the dead, had developed mystical rituals that promised worshipers a posthumous union with the divine.

Men Transformed into Gods

Although remaining firmly anchored in the Jewish biblical tradition, during its crucial formative years, Christianity grew and developed in a society dominated by Hellenistic ideas and values. In addition to well-known myths about mortal heroes whose re-demptive labors earned them postmortem divinity, the Hellenistic and Roman practice of awarding divine honors to exceptionally powerful rulers, such as Alexander the Great, Julius Caesar, and Augustus, also provided examples of humans being transformed into gods. The practice of honoring a great king as if he were a god reportedly began with Alexander shortly after he conquered Egypt in 331 BCE. Alexander is said to have received confirmation of his superhuman status from a priest of the god Ammon at Siwa in the Libyan desert. The priest apparently hailed Alexander, who had just been crowned king of Egypt, as the son of Amon-Ra (the chief Egyptian deity, whom the Greeks identified with Zeus), a conventional form of address traditionally accorded Egypt's pharaohs. Because the oracle of Ammon enjoyed enormous prestige, however, many Greeks seem to have taken the priest's words more literally. As conqueror of most of the known world, Alexander apparently promoted the concept of his own divinity and encouraged the establishment of a cult in his honor.

Alexander's successors, particularly the Ptolemaic and Seleucid dynasties, also found it politically useful to elicit divine honors from their subjects. Many Hellenistic cities competed with one another in acknowledging the king as their divinely empowered benefactor, offering sacrifices and practicing other rites modeled on those granted the Olympian gods. Although many Greeks opposed treating human beings as if they were gods, the practice was widely accepted and eventually adopted by the Romans.

By the fourth century BCE, Romulus, the legendary founder of Rome, had been given posthumous deification and identified with a minor Italian deity, Quirinus. After his assassination, the Roman Senate formally declared Julius Caesar (c. 100–44 BCE) henceforth a god. As Caesar's adopted son and designated heir, Octavius (the future emperor Augustus) was known as *divi filius,* "son of God." Upon his death in 14 CE, the Senate acclaimed Augustus a god in his own right. Whereas Augustus and most other emperors did not accept divine honors during their lifetimes, a few, such as Gaius Caligula and Commodus, demanded to be worshiped while still alive, a requirement that sometimes brought Christians, who held that Christ alone combined the human and divine, into conflict with the state.

As Christian missionaries carried their proclamation of Jesus' death and resurrection to heavenly power from its original, monotheistic context in Judea into the Hellenistic world, they encountered a Greco-Roman population long familiar with the concept of great persons being posthumously transformed into gods. In his *Metamorphoses,* composed around the turn of the Christian era, the Latin poet Ovid vividly describes the martyred Julius Caesar's soul ascending—like a blazing comet—to celestial glory. Jupiter (Zeus), Ovid states, guaranteed Caesar's entry into heaven "as a god," who will also "have his temples on earth."

Some emperors retained a wry sense of humor about receiving postmortem honors. When, on his deathbed, Vespasian was asked how he felt, he is said to have replied, "I fear I am becoming a god."

Although most scholars do not think that New Testament writers directly borrowed theological concepts from older religions, such as the cult of Roman emperors, their insistence that Jesus possessed superhuman status nonetheless paralleled previously existing traditions about humans undergoing posthumous deification. Operating in a thought world shaped by Greco-Roman philosophy and religion, early Christian writers, perhaps inevitably, forged their theology of Jesus in images and symbols that their Greek readers would readily comprehend.

QUESTIONS FOR DISCUSSION AND REVIEW

1. Describe the political situation in Palestine at the time of Jesus. How did Rome come to control Israel's territory? What role did Herod I and his successors play in ruling the covenant people?

2. What happened when Jewish patriots revolted against Roman rule (66–73 CE)? What happened to the Jerusalem Temple, and what did its loss signify to the Jewish people?

3. Define *Hellenism,* and explain how Greek thought, language, and culture came to dominate the eastern Mediterranean world. What effects did this have on biblical translation and the composition of the New Testament?

4. Define *philosophy,* and summarize some major ideas of Socrates and Plato about the nature of the human soul and the worlds of matter and spirit. Explain some essential differences between the Stoics and the Epicureans. What kinds of Greek philosophical concepts anticipated later teachings of Christianity?

5. Describe the "personal savior" cults of Asclepius, Dionysus, Isis, and Mithras. Why are these cults called "mystery religions"? Explain the Greco-Roman practice of elevating exceptional human rulers to the status of gods.

Terms and Concepts to Remember

Alexander the Great	Logos
Asclepius	Masada
Augustus	Mithras
bar Kochba	mysteries
Dionysus	Nero
Hellenism/Hellenistic	philosophy
Herod I (the Great)	Plato
Herod Agrippa I	Pontius Pilate
Herod Agrippa II	prefect/procurator
Herod Antipas	Stoicism
Isis	Vespasian
Galilee	Zealots
Josephus, Flavius	

Recommended Reading

Evans, Craig A., and Porter, Stanley E., eds. *Dictionary of New Testament Background.* Downers Grove, IL: Inter-Varsity Press, 2000. A wealth of information on topics relating to the historical setting and cultural environment of the Christian Scriptures.

Fox, R. L. *Pagans and Christians.* New York: Knopf, 1987. A comprehensive and insightful investigation of Greco-Roman religious life from the second to the fourth centuries CE.

Hornblower, Simon, and Spawforth, Anthony, eds. *The Oxford Companion to Classical Civilization.* New York: Oxford UP, 1998. Contains brief essays on topics from Alexander the Great to Plato to Roman history; a major tool.

Josephus, Flavius. *The Jewish War,* rev. ed. Trans. G. A. Williamson; ed. E. M. Smallwood. New York: Penguin Books, 1981. The most important contemporary source for conditions in Palestine during the first century CE, by an eyewitness of the Jewish Revolt against Rome.

Martin, Luther H. *Hellenistic Religions: An Introduction.* New York: Oxford UP, 1987. A solid introduction to the principal Greco-Roman religious movements and cults.

Parsenios, George L. "Greek Religion and Philosophy." In K. D. Sakenfeld, ed., *The New Interpreter's Dictionary of the Bible,* Vol. 2, pp. 681–698. Nashville, TN: Abingdon Press, 2007. A lucid review of Greek culture; indispensable for understanding aspects of Christianity.

Peters, F. E. *The Harvest of Hellenism: A History of the Near East from Alexander the Great to the Triumph of Christianity.* New York: Simon & Schuster, 1970. A comprehensive study of Greek and Roman history affecting Palestine.

Tuscan, Robert. *The Cults of the Roman Empire.* Trans. Antonia Nevill. Cambridge, MA: Blackwell, 1996. A lucid survey of the major cults and mystery religions that competed with early Christianity.

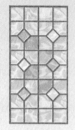

CHAPTER 29

First-Century Judaism
Diversity, Messianic Expectations, and the Birth of Christianity

---

Key Topics/Themes In Jesus' day, the Jewish faith was extremely diverse, with adherents split into numerous parties and factions, the most prominent of which included the Sadducees, Pharisees, Essenes, Samaritans, and Zealots. Although the majority of Jews did not then belong to any particular group, many held distinctively apocalyptic beliefs and hoped that Israel's Messiah would soon arrive to deliver them from their enemies. As Jewish and Christian writings of this period demonstrate, even in Palestine, Judaism was thoroughly saturated with Hellenistic ideas. The earliest surviving Christian documents, the letters of Paul, reveal that Christianity began as a messianic and apocalyptic movement within Judaism that quickly spread throughout the eastern Mediterranean world.

Reverence for the Mosaic Torah, the land, the Jerusalem Temple, and the transcendent Being whose invisible presence sanctified it were unifying aspects of first-century Judaism. Nevertheless, the Jews of Jesus' time were so deeply divided on so many different issues, both religious and political, that scholars find it almost impossible to describe the Jewish religion as a coherent whole. The more we learn about the period before 70 CE, when Roman armies destroyed Jerusalem, the more diverse Judaism appears to have been.

A Diverse First-Century Judaism

The Gospel authors and Josephus mention several distinct Jewish groups—the Sadducees, Pharisees, Herodians, Samaritans, and Zealots—but these religious parties represent only a fraction of first-century Judaism's bewildering variety. Keeping in mind that the groups discussed here represent a mere sample of Jewish pluralism, we will survey six of the best-known groups mentioned in Josephus or the New Testament. We will then briefly examine some of Paul's early letters, the oldest surviving documents of a Jewish

apocalyptic group that eventually produced a new world religion, Christianity.

The Sadducees

Because none of their writings survive, we know the **Sadducees** only through brief references in the New Testament and in other secondary sources, such as Josephus. Described as among Jesus' chief opponents, the Sadducees were typically members of the Jewish upper class, wealthy landowning aristocrats who largely controlled the priesthood and the Temple. Their name (Greek, *Saddoukaioi*, from the Hebrew, *Zaddukim* or *tsaddiqim*) means "righteous ones" and may be descriptive, or it may reflect their claim to be the spiritual heirs of Zadok, the High Priest under David and Solomon (1 Kings 1:26). Because the prophet Ezekiel had stated that only the "descendants of Zadok . . . may come near to the LORD to minister to him" (Ezek. 40:46), the Sadducees, who officiated at the Jerusalem Temple, emphasized their inherited right to this role. High Priests like **Caiaphas** (who condemned Jesus) were apparently always of their number. Along with their opponents the Pharisees, the Sadducees dominated the Great Council, or **Sanhedrin,** Judaism's highest court of religious law, where Jesus was brought to trial.

The Sadducees and the Romans Although the New Testament and Josephus give us an incomplete picture of the group, the Sadducees seem to have acted as chief mediators between the Jewish people and the occupying Roman forces. As beneficiaries of the Roman-maintained political order, the Sadducees had the most to lose from civil disorder and typically opposed any movement that might overthrow the status quo. Their adoption of Hellenistic customs and their friendship with the Romans made it possible for them to manipulate some Judean political affairs. The Sadducees' determination to preserve the uneasy accommodation with Rome is revealed in their eagerness to execute Jesus, whom they apparently regarded as a potential revolutionary and a threat to Judea's political security. Their view that rebellion against Rome would lead to total annihilation of the Jewish nation was vindicated during the Jewish Revolt (66–73 CE), when Roman troops devastated Jerusalem and Judea.

As conservative religiously as they were politically, the Sadducees practiced a literal reading of the Torah, rejecting the Pharisees' "oral law" and other interpretations of the biblical text. It is uncertain how much of the Prophets or Writings they accepted, but they apparently did not share Pharisaic beliefs about a coming judgment, resurrection, angels, or demons (Mark 12:18; Acts 23:8). As a group, the Sadducees did not survive the first century CE. Their close association with Rome, their refusal to accept developing ideas based on the Prophets, the Writings, and the Apocrypha, and their narrow focus on Temple ritual—all spelled their doom. After the Temple's destruction (70 CE), the Sadducees disappear from history. The Pharisees, emphasizing education and progressive reinterpretation of Scripture, became the leaders in formulating post-70s Judaism.

The Pharisees

The Gospels' bitter attacks on the **Pharisees,** who are shown as Jesus' leading opponents, have made the term *Pharisee* synonymous with hypocrisy and heartless legalism (Matt. 23). To the Gospel writers, the Pharisees and their associates the **scribes** are "blind guides" who perversely reject Jesus' message and thereby condemn their people to divine punishment (Matt. 22:1–14; 23:37–39; Luke 19:41–44). Modern historians recognize, however, that the Gospels' portrayal of the Pharisees is biased and unfair. According to most scholars, the Gospel writers' antagonism toward the group stems not so much from the historical Jesus' debates with the Pharisees as from the historical situation at the time the Gospels were composed. Written several decades

after Jesus' death, the Gospels reflect a period of intense ill feeling between the early Christian community and the Jewish leadership.

Hostility between church and synagogue climaxed following the Roman destruction of Jerusalem in 70 CE. In the years immediately after Jerusalem's fall, the Pharisees became the dominant force within Judaism and the chief spokesmen for the position that Jesus of Nazareth was not the expected Jewish Messiah. Although Jews and Christians had previously worshiped side by side in the Temple, following the failure of the Jewish War against Rome, Jewish-Christian relations deteriorated rapidly. After about 85 or 90 CE, some Christian Jews were expelled from the synagogues and condemned as disloyal to their Jewish heritage (see John 9). The Gospels preserve the Christian response in their angry denunciations of the Pharisees.

Strict Torah Observance Whatever their quarrel with the historical Jesus may have been, as a group, the Pharisees were completely devoted to the Mosaic Torah and its application to all the concerns of daily life. The meaning of their name is obscure, although it seems to have been derived from the Hebrew verb for "to separate." As the spiritual descendants of the Hasidim, who separated themselves from what they saw as the corrupting influence of Hellenistic culture, the Pharisees rigorously observed a code of ritual purity. They scrupulously segregated themselves from contaminating contact with anything the Torah forbade.

Many Pharisees were deeply learned in the Torah and skilled at its interpretation. Josephus states that the common people regarded them as the most authoritative interpreters of the Law. Unlike their rivals the Sadducees, the Pharisees accepted not only the written Torah but also a parallel oral law. Pharisaic oral teachings, which the Gospel of Mark calls the "tradition of the elders" (Mark 7:3), were intended to extend the laws of Temple purity to virtually every aspect of daily life, including Sabbath observance, dietary regulations, almsgiving, and prayer.

Although many scholars believe that Pharisaism evolved into the rabbi-led Judaism that eventually produced modern Judaism, the rabbis who studied and preserved their group's oral traditions never refer to themselves as Pharisees and seem to avoid the term. After the Temple's destruction, however, it was the Pharisaic emphasis on reapplication of the Torah to the Jewish people's radically changed circumstances that helped make possible the survival of their religion and distinctive way of life. As a group, the Pharisees and their rabbinical successors, however, pursued a standard of religious commitment and personal righteousness that was virtually unique in the ancient world. Even Matthew's Gospel, which contains the New Testament's most negative judgment on the Pharisees, recognizes their religious authority: "The scribes and the Pharisees sit on Moses' seat [as Torah interpreters]; therefore, do whatever they teach you and follow it . . ." (Matt. 23:2–3).

The Samaritans

Named for their capital city, Samaria, of the ancient northern kingdom of Israel, the Samaritans were a distinctive Jewish group who occupied the territory lying between Judea and Galilee. Although 2 Kings 17 depicts Samaritans as the descendants of Mesopotamians whom Assyrian conquerors settled in the area during the late eighth century BCE—and therefore not "authentic" Israelites—this picture is historically inaccurate. By the time of the Roman occupation of Palestine, Jews in Judea regarded the Samaritans as an alien people who practiced an illegitimate form of Judaism.

By contrast, New Testament writers generally portray the Samaritans favorably, offering none of the blistering denunciations they heap upon the Pharisees. The author of Luke-Acts not only shows Jesus conducting a brief ministry in Samaria (Luke 17:11–19) and making a Samaritan the hero of a famous parable (Luke 10:33–36) but also presents Samaria as the first step beyond Judea on the church's worldwide mission (Acts 1:8; 8:1–40). In John's Gospel, after Jesus holds a long discussion with a Samaritan woman about the differences between her people and the Jews of Jerusalem, she perceives that he is the Messiah and, acting as one of his first missionaries, persuades her fellow villagers to become Jesus' disciples (John 4). Some of Jesus' adversaries even label him a Samaritan (John 8:48)!

The Essenes and the Dead Sea Scrolls

A series of sensational discoveries began in 1947 that have revolutionized scholars' understanding of Judaism's complexities during the early New Testament period. According to one version of the story, in that year, a Bedouin shepherd boy, who had been idly throwing stones into the mouth of a cave near the Dead Sea, heard a sound like shattering pottery. When he climbed into the cave to investigate, he found pottery jars full of ancient manuscripts, now world famous as the **Dead Sea Scrolls.**

Some scholars recently have proposed that the Dead Sea Scrolls represent not one but a variety of Jewish groups, a collective witness to the religious diversity and apocalyptic interests of first-century Judaism. A large majority of scholars are convinced, however, that the scrolls were produced by the **Essenes,** an ascetic Jewish group that flourished in Palestine from about 140 BCE until 68 CE, when it was destroyed or dispersed by Roman armies (see Figure 29.1). First-century Jewish authors, such as Josephus and **Philo Judaeus** of Alexandria, had described some of the Essene beliefs and practices, but only after 1947 did their own extensive writings, found in eleven different caves, gradually become available.

The Qumran Library Although many Essenes lived in cities, one particularly rigorous group settled in **Qumran,** located near the northwest corner of the Dead Sea. The manuscripts that this monastic sect produced, and which they apparently hid in caves shortly before Roman armies demolished Qumran, are enormously important for biblical research. First, the manuscripts contain the oldest surviving copies of the Hebrew Bible, some fragments of which date back to the second century BCE. The complete scroll of Isaiah, which is perhaps 1,000 years older than any other previously known Isaiah manuscript, shows few variations from the Hebrew **Masoretic Text (MT),** the medieval edition of the Hebrew Bible from which most translations are made (see Chapter 2). Other Qumran copies of Scripture differ significantly from the "standard" Masoretic editions. Extensive variations between some of the Dead Sea Scrolls and later copies of the Hebrew Bible suggest that in the first century BCE, Jewish scholars had not yet adopted a universally recognized version of their sacred writings.

Second, the Qumran scrolls include copies and fragments of apocryphal and pseudepigraphal works, such as Tobit, the Wisdom of Jesus Son of Sirach, and 1 Enoch. The presence of 1 Enoch (fragments of which were also found at the nearby fortress of Masada) interspersed among canonical books indicates that the Essenes may have accepted a larger canon than that which later Jewish leaders recognized. Third, some of the most notable documents are Essene commentaries on canonical books, such as those on the prophets Habakkuk, Isaiah, Hosea, and Micah. The Habakkuk commentary is particularly illuminating because it shows that the Essenes used the same methods of interpreting biblical texts that some Christian writers later employed. Gospel authors such as Matthew regard the Hebrew Bible as a repository of prophetic texts foretelling events fulfilled in the writer's own day and in his own community. The Habakkuk commentator takes the same approach:

FIGURE 29.1 This photo shows ruins at Qumran, near the northwestern shore of the Dead Sea. Although some scholars dispute this, the majority believe that the Essenes, an apocalyptic sect that awaited Yahweh's call to battle the Romans, maintained a monastic colony here. After the Essenes had hidden their library—the Dead Sea Scrolls—in nearby caves, the Roman army destroyed Qumran (68 CE), the ruins of which have since been excavated.

The prophet's words are predictions about Essene leaders and experiences. Both Essene and New Testament writers characteristically view their own group as God's only loyal worshipers and hence the culmination of the divine plan for humanity.

Finally, besides preserving the earliest extant copies of canonical and noncanonical biblical texts and using methods of scriptural interpretation anticipating those of Christian writers, the Essenes produced numerous original writings unique to their group. Distinctive Essene documents include a "Manual of Discipline" or "Community Rule," a kind of handbook for the Essene community. The author of this document divides all humanity into mutually exclusive categories: the "children of light," who are guided by a "spirit of truth" and are ruled by a "Prince of Light," and the "children of falsehood," who walk in spiritual error under an "Angel of Darkness." This truth–error and light–dark contrast was later incorporated into John's Gospel. Another scroll, titled the "War of the Sons of Light Against the Sons of Darkness," is an Essene battle plan for the coming war between cosmic good and evil that will culminate in the establishment of God's kingdom. The Dead Sea Scrolls also include scores of other Essene manuscripts, which show that the group anticipated several Christian beliefs and

practices, ranging from communal meals, to ritual baptism, to apocalyptic expectations of God's imminent intervention into human history.

The Zealots

Known for their passionate commitment to Jewish religious and political freedom, the **Zealots** formed a party dedicated to driving the Romans from Palestine. Opposition to the Roman occupation flared repeatedly during the first century CE, including an uprising that Judas the Galilean led in 6 CE and that Roman soldiers easily crushed (Acts 5:37–39). Simon, one of Jesus' disciples, is called a "zealot" (Luke 6:15; Acts 1:13), but most scholars believe that in this case the term refers to Simon's zeal or enthusiasm for the *torah*.

Although many Jews had fought against foreign oppression since the time of the Maccabees, the Zealots did not constitute an identifiable political party until shortly after the revolt against Rome began in 66 CE. According to Josephus, the Zealots' blind nationalism launched the Judeans on a suicidal course that resulted in the destruction of the Temple and the Jewish state (see Figure 29.2). This catastrophe and the later bar Kochba rebellion of 132–135 CE discredited both the Zealot party and its apocalyptic

FIGURE 29.2 Built as a fortress retreat by King Herod, during the Jewish Revolt, Masada served as the rebels' last holdout against Roman troops. According to Josephus, in 73 CE, Masada's occupying force of 1,000, including some women and children, committed mass suicide rather than become Roman slaves.

hope of divine intervention to aid the Judean cause. Thanks to the Zealots' repeated failures, mainstream Judaism soon repudiated both armed rebellion and apocalyptic expectations.

 ## Israel's Messiah: A Jewish-Christian Debate

In Mark's Gospel, Jesus is already halfway through his public ministry before a single close disciple identifies him as "the Messiah" (Mark 8:27–29; cf. Matt. 16:13–17). In this episode, Mark assumes that *the* "Messiah" is a universally recognized concept that his audience will instantly grasp. It is not, however, a clearly defined technical term in the Hebrew Bible, early Christianity's primary authority for its messianic beliefs. Derived from the Hebrew word *mashiah*, **Messiah** means "Anointed One" and refers to the ceremony in which a priest anointed (poured oil on) the heads of various persons whom God selected and commissioned for some special undertaking. In the Hebrew Scriptures, *mashiah* is most frequently applied to the kings of ancient Israel, particularly those descended from King David (Pss. 18:50; 89:20, 38, 51; 132:10, 17). The word thus denotes a political figure, particularly a royal military leader who defends Israel against its enemies.

The Davidic Covenant

For many biblical authors, the ideal or model of God's anointed king was David, the first ruler to establish a viable Israelite state (c. 1000 BCE), a kingdom that many Jews believed foreshadowed God's reign on earth.

According to 2 Samuel 7, Yahweh concluded an "everlasting covenant" with David's "house [dynasty]," promising unconditionally to maintain a line of David's heirs on Israel's throne (see the discussion of the Davidic Covenant in Chapters 1 and 12). If some of David's royal descendants misbehaved, Yahweh would punish them, but he vowed never to overthrow them as he had King Saul (2 Sam. 7:8–17; 23:1–5; cf. Ps. 89:30–45).

After Nebuchadnezzar executed Zedekiah, the last Davidic ruler to wear Israel's crown, in 587 BCE, however, no kings of Davidic descent ever again ruled the covenant people. What, then, would become of Yahweh's sworn oath to David? In Israel's collective consciousness, Yahweh's promise meant that he would one day "remember" his covenant with David and restore the Davidic kingdom, a view that many of Israel's prophets reinforced. Isaiah of Jerusalem had envisioned a future golden age when a Davidic heir would rise to liberate Israel, defeats its enemies, and help establish God's universal rule:

> A shoot will come out from the stump of Jesse
> [David's father],
> and a branch shall grow out of his roots.
> The spirit of the LORD [Yahweh] shall rest on him,
> the spirit of wisdom and understanding,
> the spirit of counsel and might,
> the spirit of knowledge and the
> fear of the LORD . . .
> with righteousness he shall judge the poor,
> and decide with equity for the meek of the earth; . . .
> with the breath of his lips
> he shall kill the wicked.
>
> (Isa. 11:1–4)

Isaiah's vision of a future Davidic ruler who will preside over a kingdom of universal peace, when "the earth will be full of the knowledge of the LORD as the waters cover the sea" (Isa. 11:6–9; cf. Isa. 2:1–4; 9:6–7), firmly associated the Davidic royal family with Yahweh's future earthwide triumph.

All of Israel's Davidic kings were literally "messiah [*mashiah*]," "anointed of God." They reigned as Yahweh's "sons," adopted at the time of their consecration or coronation: "You are my son; today I have begotten you" (Ps. 2:7). Because the prophets had regarded these divinely adopted rulers as warrior-kings like David—God's agent in establishing an earthly government—the messianic leader was typically seen as fulfilling a military-political role. His function was to demonstrate the power of Israel's God by setting up a theocratic state whose righteous government would compel foreigners' respect for both Yahweh and his chosen people.

Psalm of Solomon 17

Only five or six decades before Jesus' birth, an unknown Jewish poet composed a striking description of Israel's expected deliverer. Ascribed to Solomon, the patron of Israel's wisdom tradition, a collection of poems known as the Psalms of Solomon envisions a noble king who will drive the hated foreigners (Roman occupational forces) from Jerusalem and establish a just sovereignty over both Jews and foreigners. Psalm of Solomon 17 is the first known work of Jewish literature to use the terms *son of David* and *Lord Messiah* (Christ) in the same sense that New Testament writers apply them to Jesus. Even more important, the psalmist portrays this messianic figure as a nonviolent leader who peacefully will subdue Israel's enemies by "the word of his mouth [his teaching]" and exercise a "compassionate" rule over "all the nations":

> See, Lord, and raise up for them [Israel] their king,
> the *son of David* [emphasis added] to rule over your
> servant Israel
> in the time known to you, O God . . .
> He will judge peoples and nations in the wisdom
> of his righteousness . . .
> And he will purge Jerusalem
> (and make it) holy as it was even from the
> beginning,
> (for) nations to come from the ends of the earth
> to see his glory,
> to bring as gifts the children who had been driven
> out, . . .
> and their king shall be the *Lord Messiah* [emphasis
> added].
> (For) he will not rely on horse and rider and bow,
> nor will he collect gold and silver for war.
> Nor will he build up hope in a multitude for a day
> of war . . .
> He shall be compassionate to all the nations
> (who) reverently stand before him . . .
> And he himself (will be) free from sin, (in order) to
> rule a great people. . . .
> This is the beauty of the king of Israel
> which God knew,
> to raise him over the house of Israel . . .
>
> (Ps of Sol. 17:21–42)

This description of a peaceful Messiah, who rejects the implements of war, is much closer to the Gospel writers' portrayal of Jesus than traditional expectations of a warrior-king like the historical David.

A Revisionist View of the Messiah

As presented in the Gospels, Jesus of Nazareth takes a view of the messianic role and the kingdom of God that many found disappointing or perplexing. Rather than liberate his people from the Roman occupation and restore David's kingdom as many expected David's true heir to do (Luke 19:11; Acts 1:6), Jesus became a victim of the Roman system, executed like a common criminal on a Roman cross. According to Luke's Gospel, even his closest followers at first were bewildered at this outcome: "We had hoped that he was the one to redeem Israel" (Luke 24:21).

In Mark's Gospel, which scholars believe was the earliest written, the author reveals his awareness that Jesus did not fulfill many popular expectations. Mark partly resolves this by emphasizing the "secret" or "hidden" quality of Jesus' messiahship (see the discussion of Mark in Chapter 30). In Mark's view, Jesus was a "suffering Messiah," with his death not a defeat but a spiritual triumph in which Jesus gave his life as "a ransom for many" (Mark 10:45). For many scripturally literate Jews, however, the manner of Jesus' humiliating death explicitly disqualified him from messianic status. According to Deuteronomy 21:

> When someone is convicted of a crime punishable by death and is executed, and you *hang him on a tree,* his corpse must not remain all night upon the tree; you shall bury him that same day, for *anyone hung on a tree is under God's curse.*
>
> (Deut. 21:23; emphasis added)

A literal reading of Deuteronomy indicates that when Jesus was officially condemned and hung on the cross—made from a tree—he was necessarily accursed (cf. Acts 5:30; 1 Cor. 1:23). Confronted with such texts, Christians reinterpreted them creatively, as offering clues to the *meaning* of Jesus' crucifixion. In Paul's letter to the Galatians, he skillfully turns a potential weakness into a strength, citing Deuteronomy and arguing that, through his execution, Jesus voluntarily accepted the Torah's curse. In his "accursed" suffering, Jesus bore the punishment that others deserved, sinners whom the Law had condemned (Gal 3:13; see Chapter 35). Some Christian writers also applied Isaiah's famous passage about a "suffering servant" to explain Jesus' alleged failure to fulfill a messianic role. Although it does not specifically refer to a Davidic messiah, Isaiah 53 describes an anonymous "servant" who willingly endures pain and humiliation for the sake of others. This concept of vicarious suffering—in which an innocent person voluntarily accepts unmerited punishment as a substitute for those who are actually guilty—became an important factor in Christian interpretations of Jesus' death.

Convinced that Jesus *was* God's anointed and that he *would*—eventually—fulfill all the biblical promises to Abraham and David, Christians soon made an enormous leap of faith. Jesus, God's *mashiah,* would make a second visit to earth to accomplish what was left unfinished at his first coming. Although the Hebrew Bible, the source of both Jewish and Christian messianic ideas, says nothing about the Messiah dividing his work into two separate installments—an initial earthly career that culminates ingloriously in a criminal's death and a second (long-delayed) reappearance as an all-powerful supernatural king—early Christianity readily embraced this belief in a two-part messianic sequence.

Paul's Apocalyptic Gospel: The Messiah's Appearance and the Inauguration of End Time

Paul, a Greek-speaking Pharisee who first persecuted Christians and then—after a "revelation (Greek, *apokalypsis*)" of the risen Jesus—became a missionary to the **Gentiles** (non-Jewish peoples) (Gal. 1:11–17; 2:1–10), was the first New Testament writer to interpret the meaning of Jesus' life, death, and resurrection. In his letters, sent to various newly founded congregations in Greece, Italy, and Asia Minor, Paul takes for granted that Jesus of Nazareth was Israel's Messiah. Unlike the author of Matthew's Gospel, he does not attempt to prove that Jesus fulfilled prophetic oracles about the Messiah (see Chapter 31) or that he was the long-awaited Davidic heir that Isaiah had foretold. In fact, Paul mentions only once that Jesus "was descended from David according to the flesh" (Rom. 1:3). Instead, Paul focuses on Jesus' theological and eschatological significance. For Paul, Jesus is **Christ** (*Christos,* the Greek term for "messiah"), and with him, God has begun the work of reconciling sinful humanity to himself. Christ's appearance therefore marks the "the ends of the ages" (1 Cor. 10:11), the crucial transition between this present "evil age" (Gal. 1:4) and the "new age" that will see the establishment of God's universal rule.

Paul's certainty that Jesus was Christ (Messiah) probably resulted from his personal experience of the risen Jesus. Writing to the house church at Corinth in the early 50s CE, Paul briefly summarized a tradition about Jesus' postresurrection appearances to prominent followers, such as Peter and Jesus' "brother" James, adding: "Last of all, as to one untimely born, he appeared also to me"

(1 Cor. 15: 8). Paul says little about the nature, duration, or form that this "revelation" took, but his communication with the risen Jesus apparently included a commission to proclaim his particular **"gospel"** (meaning "good news") to Gentiles (Gal. 1:12). As his letters reveal, Paul's "gospel" was strongly apocalyptic, emphasizing the nearness of God's final intervention into human history. (For a survey of the characteristics of apocalyptic thought, see Chapter 26, especially Box 26.1.)

Because the End—and time of judgment—are so close, Paul urges the Corinthians to abandon their ordinary pursuits:

> . . . the appointed time has grown short; from now on, let even those who have wives be as though they had none, . . . and those who buy as though they had no possessions, . . . For the present form of this world is passing away.

> (1 Cor. 7:29–31)

In one of his later letters, Paul reminds the congregation at Rome that "salvation is nearer to us now than when we became believers; the night is far gone, the day [of God's reign] is near" (Rom 13:11–12).

The Parousia

In his oldest surviving letter, 1 Thessalonians, Paul vividly describes what will happen when Jesus reappears, comparing this eschatological event to a well-known Roman custom. Paul uses the term **Parousia**—a Greek word meaning "presence" or "coming"—to denote the exalted Jesus' arrival from heaven. In using the term Parousia, Paul refers to a public ceremony—well known in his day—that accompanied the arrival of a Roman emperor or some other high official at a provincial town. As the visiting dignitary approached the city gates, a trumpet blast announced his appearance, at which sound the inhabitants were expected to drop everything they were doing and rush outside the city to greet the important visitor. Gathering along the main roadway, the crowds then followed the official inside the city. Paul's vision of Jesus' imminent Parousia, his coming in supernatural glory, makes use of the Roman practice:

> For the Lord himself, with a cry of command, with the archangel's call and with the sound of God's trumpet, will descend from heaven, and the dead in Christ will rise first. Then we who are alive, who are left, will be caught up in the clouds together with them to meet the Lord in the air, and so we will be with the Lord forever.

> (1 Thess. 4:16–17)

Jesus' followers, in joyous acclamation, will then accompany their Master—humanity's true king—as he revisits earth to begin his active rule as Israel's Messiah. After his *Parousia,* Jesus at last will reign, not only over a redeemed Israel but also over the entire cosmos.

In portraying Jesus' reappearance in the manner of an imperial entrance to a favored city, Paul is actually addressing a problem that troubled his Thessalonian audience. Many of the Thessalonians evidently thought that Jesus' coming was so near that all believers would live to witness his return. But what would happen to those who had already died? By assuring his correspondents that the faithful dead will be raised to join the cheering crowds at Jesus' Parousia, Paul quiets their anxieties, not least by alluding to "we who are [still] alive" at Christ's coming, further reassuring them of the imminence of the eschatological event. In his fullest description of the resurrection (1 Cor. 15), Paul reaffirms:

> Listen, I will tell you a mystery! We will not all die, but we will all be changed, in a moment, in the twinkling of an eye, at the last trumpet. For the trumpet will sound, and the dead will be raised imperishable, and we [the living] shall be changed . . .

> (1 Cor. 15:51–52)

By the time the earliest Gospel was written, perhaps only fifteen years after Paul's letter to the Corinthians, belief in an imminent Parousia was still strong. In Mark's account, Jesus' first words are a warning that "the time is fulfilled, and the kingdom of God has come near; repent, and believe in the good news" (Mark 1:15). Mathew's Gospel, which presents this apocalyptic warning as the initial message of both John the Baptist and Jesus (Matt. 3:2; 4:17), adopts Paul's use of *Parousia* in his prophecy of Jesus' return. Linking the Roman destruction of Jerusalem and the Temple to Jesus' "coming [*Parousia*]," Mark and Matthew assure their audience that "this generation will not pass away until all these things have taken place" (Matt. 24:34; Mark 13:30). Writing perhaps fifteen years after Mark, Matthew realizes that the Parousia did not immediately follow Jerusalem's destruction (70 CE), and he cautions readers to remember that Jesus may delay his reappearance (Matt. 25; see Chapter 31).

QUESTIONS FOR DISCUSSION AND REVIEW

1. Describe the diverse parties and religious movements in first-century Judaism. Summarize the major beliefs and attitudes of the Sadducees and Pharisees.

Which group controlled the high priesthood, the Temple services, and Jewish political arrangements with Rome? What were the major concerns of the Pharisees?

2. Who were the Samaritans, and how did they differ from the Pharisees and Sadducees?

3. Describe the Dead Sea Scrolls, and discuss their significance to the Bible's literary history and to the development of early Christianity.

4. Define the term *Messiah*. How is the term related to promises Yahweh made to the royal House of David? Discuss whether the Davidic Messiah is more a political or a spiritual leader. In what ways does the Psalm of Solomon 17 reinterpret messianic concepts?

5. In what respects does Jesus of Nazareth differ from many traditional expectations of Israel's Messiah? How did Christians defend Jesus' unusual messiahship against their critics?

6. In much Israelite tradition, the Messiah's arrival heralded God's direct intervention into human affairs, signaling the end of the present evil age and the beginning of divine rule over the earth. How do the letters of Paul, the earliest surviving Christian documents, reveal the writer's apocalyptic expectations? Describe Paul's concept of the Parousia. How soon did he expect Jesus to return to assume his rulership as Israel's Messiah?

Terms and Concepts to Remember

apocalyptic expectations	Masoretic Text (MT)
	Messiah of Israel
Caiaphas	Parousia
Davidic Covenant	Paul
Dead Sea Scrolls	Philo Judaeus
eschatology, of early Christianity	Pharisees
	Qumran
Essenes	Sadducees
Gentiles	Zealots
gospel/Gospel	
Jewish Revolt against Rome	

Recommended Reading

Abegg, Martin, Jr.; Flint, Peter; and Ulrich, Eugene. *The Dead Sea Scrolls Bible.* San Francisco: HarperOne, 1999. An English translation of the Hebrew Bible based on the Dead Sea manuscripts (many of which are fragmentary).

Allison, Dale C., Jr. "Eschatology in the New Testament." In K. D. Sakenfeld, ed., *The New Interpreter's Dictionary of the Bible,* Vol. 2, pp. 294–299. Nashville, TN: Abingdon Press, 2007. Clearly describes the intense eschatological expectations of many New Testament writers.

Brooke, George J. "Dead Sea Scrolls." In K. D. Sakenfeld, ed., *The New Interpreter's Dictionary of the Bible,* Vol. 2, pp. 52–63. Nashville, TN: Abingdon Press, 2007. An informative introduction to the scrolls and their significance.

Horsley, Richard A. "Messianic Movements in Judaism." In D. N. Freedman, ed. *Anchor Bible Dictionary,* Vol. 4, pp. 791–797. New York: Doubleday, 1992. A brief introduction to Jewish messianic expectations in the era of Jesus.

Horsley, Richard, and Hanson, John S. *Bandits, Prophets, and Messiahs: Popular Religious Movements at the Time of Jesus.* Minneapolis: Winston Press, 1985. Places Jesus' ministry in the context of other messianic claimants.

Murphy, Frederick J. *The Religious World of Jesus: An Introduction to Second Temple Palestinian Judaism.* Nashville, TN: Abingdon Press, 1991. A survey of pertinent cultural and religious groups at the time of Jesus.

Newsome, James D. *Greeks, Romans, Jews: Currents of Culture and Belief in the New Testament World.* Philadelphia: Trinity Press International, 1992. A superbly researched study of historical documents relevant to Jewish religious thought and practice at the time of Christianity's inception.

Shanks, Hershel, ed. *Understanding the Dead Sea Scrolls.* New York: Random House, 1992. A collection of popular essays from the *Biblical Archaeology Review.*

Stegemann, Ekkehard W., and Stegemann, Wolfgang. *The Jesus Movement: A Social History in Its First Century.* Trans. O. C. Dean, Jr. Minneapolis: Fortress Press, 1999. A comprehensive study of Greco-Roman sociopolitical structures in general and first-century Palestinian social environment in particular.

Vermes, Geza. *An Introduction to the Complete Dead Sea Scrolls.* Minneapolis: Fortress Press, 2000. A standard work in the field.

———. *The Complete Dead Sea Scrolls in English,* rev. ed. (Penguin Classics). New York: Penguin Books, 2004. An authoritative translation of Essene writings (but without the biblical texts) illustrating the group's conviction that they represented the true Israel and that the End of history was near.

CHAPTER 30

Telling Jesus' Story
The Gospel of Mark

Key Topics/Themes Between about 64 CE, when Nero began Rome's first official persecution of Christians, and 70 CE, when Roman armies destroyed Jerusalem (along with its Temple and the original apostolic church), the Christian community faced a series of crises that threatened its survival. Responding to the wars, revolts, and persecutions that afflicted his group, Mark composed what is probably the earliest narrative account of Jesus' public ministry. The author presents Jesus' story in a way that was directly relevant to the difficult circumstances in which his intended readers lived. Mark's "wartime" Gospel thus portrays a Jesus who faces attack on three crucial fronts: from Jewish religious leaders, local (Herodian) rulers, and Roman officials. Painting Jesus as a "hidden Messiah" whom his contemporaries devalued and misunderstood, Mark emphasizes that Jesus came to serve, to suffer, and to die—but also ultimately to triumph by submitting fully to the divine will.

 ## The Four Gospels

A New Literary Form

In the canon that the early Christian church ultimately adopted, the New Testament opens with four different accounts of Jesus' life and teachings—the Gospels "According to" Matthew, Mark, Luke, and John (for a discussion of the canon, see Chapter 2). Although Matthew appears first in the collection, a large majority of scholars believe that Mark is the earliest Gospel. In fact, Mark appears to have invented the Gospel as a new literary form: He calls his narrative "the good news [Greek, *evangelion*] of Jesus Christ" (Mark 1:1). In his letters, Paul had used the same term (*evangelion*) to describe his oral "gospel," but Mark is the first author to transform oral preaching about Jesus into the form of a written biography. As scholars have learned, however, the Gospel authors—the **Evangelists**—do not pursue the same historical goals as modern biographers, who, ideally, attempt to compile a comprehensive and objective portrait of their subject. The four Evangelists are primarily Christian believers, combining historical information with confessions of faith in Jesus through biographical narratives (John 20:31).

The earliest reference to Mark's Gospel comes from Papias, a Christian writer who was bishop of Hierapolis in Asia Minor about 130–140 CE. Papias' writings have been lost, but Eusebius, who wrote a history of the Christian church in the early fourth century, quotes him as stating that Mark had been a disciple of Peter in Rome and based his account on Peter's memories of Jesus. Papias notes that Mark "had not heard the Lord or been one of his followers" so that his Gospel lacked "a systematic arrangement of the Lord's sayings" (Eusebius, *History* 3.39). (See Box 30.1, "Mark's Order of Events.")

Papias makes two important historical observations: (1) The author of Mark was *not* an eyewitness but depended on secondhand oral preaching, and (2) Mark's version of Jesus' activities is "not in [proper chronological] order." Careful study of Mark's Gospel has convinced most scholars that it does not derive from a single apostolic source, such as Peter, but is based on a general body of oral teachings about Jesus preserved in the author's community. (A minority view arguing that Mark ultimately draws on the eyewitness testimony of first-generation Christians appears in the recent work of Richard Bauckham; see "Recommended Reading.")

BOX 30.1   Mark's Order of Events in Jesus' Life

Jesus' Ministry in Galilee

- John baptizes Jesus at the Jordan River (1:9–11).
- After withdrawing to the Judean desert, Jesus begins preaching in Galilee (1:14–15).
- Jesus recruits Galilean disciples, including Peter, Andrew, and the "sons of Zebedee" (James and John) (1:16–30).
  - Jesus performs miraculous cures and exorcisms in Capernaum and throughout Galilee (1:21–5:43).
  - Jesus returns to Nazareth, where his neighbors reject him (6:1–6).
  - Herod Antipas beheads John the Baptist (6:14–29).
  - Jesus miraculously feeds a Jewish crowd of 5,000 (6:30–44) and then a Gentile crowd (8:1–10, 14–21).
  - Peter recognizes Jesus as Israel's Messiah but misunderstands the nature of Jesus' role as suffering servant (8:22–9:1).
  - Jesus appears as a being of light to Peter, James, and John (the Transfiguration) (9:1–13) and gives his second Passion prediction (9:30–32).
  - Jesus travels south from Galilee toward Jerusalem, teaching the crowds, debating the Pharisees, and predicting his imminent crucifixion (10:1–52).

Jesus' Ministry in Jerusalem

- On Palm Sunday, Jesus enters Jerusalem, as his followers hail him in terms of the Davidic kingdom (11:1–11).

- On Monday, Jesus drives the moneychangers out of the Temple, foreshadowing its destruction by the Romans (11:15–19).
- After debating the "chief priests," Sadducees, Pharisees, and other religious leaders in the Temple precincts (11:27–12:40), Jesus predicts the Temple's destruction and the Parousia of the Son of Man (13:1–37).
- On Thursday evening, Jesus holds a Passover meal with his disciples, after which he withdraws to the Mount of Olives (Gethsemane), where, betrayed by Judas, he is arrested (14:12–52).
- Jesus faces two trials. First brought before the Jewish Great Council (Sanhedrin), Jesus is condemned by the High Priest Caiaphas for blasphemy (14:53–65); Peter denies knowing him (14:66–72). Jesus then appears before the Roman governor, Pontius Pilate, who condemns him to crucifixion (15:1–20).
- On Good Friday, Roman soldiers crucify Jesus at Golgotha, outside Jerusalem's walls, where Galilean women stand watching; Jesus' body is placed in a new tomb provided by Joseph of Arimathea (15:21–47).
- On Sunday (the first Easter), Mary Magdalene and other Galilean women find Jesus' tomb empty but are too afraid to speak of their discovery (16:1–8).

Historical Setting

Mark's author offers few hints about where or for whom he wrote, except for his insistence that following Jesus requires a willingness to suffer for one's faith. Mark's near equation of discipleship with suffering suggests that he directed his work to a group that was then undergoing severe testing and needed encouragement to remain steadfast (Mark 8:34–38; 10:38–40). This theme of "carrying one's cross" may derive from the effects of Nero's persecution (c. 64–65 CE), when numerous Roman Christians were crucified or burned alive. Papias and Iranaeus, another early church leader, agree that Mark wrote shortly after Peter's martyrdom, which, according to tradition, occurred during Nero's attack on Rome's Christian community.

Although Rome is the traditional place of composition, a growing number of scholars think it more likely that Mark wrote for an audience in Syria or Palestine.

Scholars favoring a Palestinian origin point to Mark's emphasis on the Jewish Revolt (66–73 CE) and concurrent warning to believers who were affected by the uprising (Mark 13). In Mark's view, the "tribulation" climaxing in Jerusalem's fall is the sign heralding Jesus' Parousia, his coming in heavenly glory. The association of wars and national revolts with persecutions of believers and Jesus' imminent reappearance gives an eschatological urgency to Mark's account.

Although Papias and other second-century writers ascribe the Gospel to John Mark, a companion of Peter and Paul (Philem. 24; Col. 4:10; Acts 12:12–25), the author does not identify himself in the text. The superscription—"The Gospel According to Mark"—is a later editorial addition; second-century churchmen consistently tried to connect extant writings about Jesus with apostles or their close disciples. Like many other biblical texts, the Gospel is anonymous; for convenience, we refer to the author as Mark.

BOX 30.2 **Leading Characters in Mark**

John the Baptist (1:4–9); executed (6:17–29)

Jesus introduced (1:9); final words (15:34)

Simon Peter and his brother Andrew (1:16–18; 8:27–33; 9:2–6; 14:26–32, 66–72)

The Twelve listed by name (3:13–19)

Judas Iscariot, betrayer of Jesus (14:17–21, 43–46)

Jesus' mother and other family members (3:20–21, 31–35; 6:3)

Herod Antipas, ruler of Galilee (6:17–29; 8:15)

The High Priest Caiaphas (14:53–64)

Pontius Pilate, Roman governor (15:1–15, 43–44)

Joseph of Arimathaea (15:42–46)

Mary of Magdala and other women disciples (15:40–41, 47; 16:1–8)

Mark's Controlling Irony

Unlike Matthew and Luke, Mark does not include traditions about Jesus' birth or an account of his postresurrection appearances, nor does he preserve many of Jesus' teachings (see below). Instead, he focuses primarily on Jesus' actions—his miraculous healings, his **exorcisms** (driving out evil spirits thought to possess people), and the unexpected manner of his death. In fact, Mark devotes much of his Gospel to a description of Jesus' last week on earth, the seven days from his entry into Jerusalem (traditionally known as Palm Sunday) to the women disciples' discovery of his empty tomb (the first Easter Sunday). Giving a detailed account of Jesus' last supper with his disciples, his arrest in the Garden of Gethsemane, his trials before the High Priest **Caiaphas** and before the Roman governor **Pontius Pilate,** and his crucifixion by Roman soldiers, Mark concentrates on Jesus' **Passion,** his suffering and death (Mark 11:1–15:47).

In Mark's account, Jesus' first words are a confident proclamation that "the kingdom of God has come near" (1:15), and his last a cry of despair on the cross: "My God, my God, why have you forsaken me?" (15:34). The arc of Mark's narrative thus charts a movement from eager anticipation of God's imminent rule to Jesus' apparent defeat by the Roman superpower. In arranging his material to move the reader from joy to grief, Mark produces a deeply ironic narrative. His central irony, of course, is that the forces organized against Jesus—from Roman political power to supernatural evil—only *seem* to have won the battle. From God's perspective, Jesus—who voluntarily lays down his life to redeem humanity from its oppressors, both political and spiritual—has triumphed (10:45). Far from being a defeat, as it appeared to many, Jesus'

crucifixion is part of God's plan. It also provides a model for his persecuted followers, who may also be asked to "take up their [own] cross and follow [him]" (8:34–35) (see Box 30.2).

Mark's Apocalyptic Urgency

From his opening announcement that God's rule has drawn near to his intimations that Jesus will soon return, Mark colors his Gospel with intense apocalyptic expectation. The Markan Jesus informs his followers that "there are some standing here who will not taste death until they see that the kingdom of God has come with power" (9:1). In predicting the coming destruction of Jerusalem, Jesus links the Temple's fall with "'the [eschatological] Son of Man coming in clouds' with great power and glory" (13:26). Further, he assures the disciples that "this generation will not pass away until all these things have taken place" (13:30). From Mark's perspective, both recent historical events and supernatural interventions—expected to occur in the near future—are fulfillments of ancient biblical prophecies, such as Joel's vision of astronomical chaos, in which the sun will lose its light and "the powers of the heavens will be shaken" (13:24–25; cf. Joel 2:30–31). Jesus' exorcisms, to which Mark devotes proportionately more space than any other Gospel writer, similarly testify to God's in-breaking rule. By driving out demons, the sources of disease and madness, Jesus weakens Satan's hold on humanity and prepares for God's reign. In addition, Malachi's prophecy about Elijah's long-awaited reappearance—an unmistakable sign of the last days—has already been realized in the career of John the Baptist (9:12–13). Such passages emphasizing eschatological events indicate that

Mark's community anticipated the imminent consummation of "all things," although many scholars question whether Mark's portrayal of an apocalyptic Jesus accurately represents the historical figure.

Mark's Puzzling Attitude Toward Jesus' Close Associates

Jesus' Family and Acquaintances

In composing his account of Jesus' public ministry, Mark does not seem to have regarded Jesus' relatives—or any other ordinary source a modern biographer would consult—as worthy informants. One of the author's dominant themes is his negative presentation of virtually everyone associated with the historical Jesus. From "his mother and his brothers" (3:31) to his most intimate followers, Mark portrays all of Jesus' companions as insensitive to his real nature and/or as obstacles to his work. Mark's Gospel consistently renders all Jesus' Palestinian associates as mentally slow, unable to grasp his teachings, and generally blind to his value.

The Markan picture of Jesus' closest relatives implies that they, too, failed to appreciate or support him. "When his family heard it [his drawing large crowds around him], they went out to restrain him, for people were saying, 'He has gone out of his mind,'" (3:21). (Grammatically, the Greek passage can be translated as meaning that Jesus' family thought he had lost his mind, as does the Jerusalem Bible.) When "his mother and his brothers" send a message asking for him, apparently demanding that he cease making a public spectacle of himself, Mark has Jesus declare that "whoever does the will of God is my brother and sister and mother"—a shocking rejection of his blood ties and an indication that, in Mark's view, his family was not doing the divine will (3:31–35). The force of this antifamily episode is intensified because Mark uses it to frame a controversy in which Jesus' opponents accuse him of expelling demons by the power of "Beelzebul," another name for Satan. Jesus countercharges that those who oppose his work are defying the **Holy Spirit,** the invisible power of God at work in the world (3:22–30). At this point in the narrative, Mark shows Jesus' family attempting to interrupt his ministry, thus subtly associating them with his adversaries. (See also John 7:1–10.)

Jesus' Neighbors in Nazareth

Mark also portrays Jesus' acquaintances in **Nazareth** (his hometown) as hostile to a local carpenter's unexpected career as prophet and healer, questioning his credentials as sage and teacher. "'Where did this man get all this?'" his neighbors ask. "'What is this wisdom that has been given to him? What deeds of power are being done by his hands! Is this not the carpenter, the son of Mary and brother of James and Joses and Judas and Simon, and are not his sisters here with us?' And they took offense at him" (6:2–3). In this incident of Jesus' revisiting his home turf, Mark argues that those who thought they knew Jesus best doubted not only his right to be a religious leader but also his legitimacy. The neighbors refer to Jesus as "the son of Mary," a contrast to the biblical custom of identifying a son through his male parentage even if his father is dead. The Nazarenes' refusal to see any merit in him results in a troubling decline in Jesus' power: *He could do no deed of power there . . .* except for some routine healings (6:6; emphasis added). Jesus himself is "amazed" at their refusal to trust him. Mark thus seems to exclude both family and hometown citizens as acceptable channels of biographical tradition: They all fail to trust, comprehend, or cooperate with his hero.

Mark's allusion to Jesus' "brothers" and "sisters" (see also Matt. 13:54–56) may disturb some readers. Because his Gospel does not include a tradition of Jesus' virginal conception or birth, the existence of siblings may not have been an issue with Mark's community (as it apparently was not for Paul's congregations; Paul's letters never refer to a virgin birth). Matthew, however, explicitly affirms that Jesus was virginally conceived (Matt. 1:18–25), and Luke strongly implies it (Luke 1:26–38). Some Protestant Christians believe that, following Jesus' delivery, his mother may have borne other children in the ordinary way. According to Catholic and Orthodox doctrine, however, Mary remains perpetually virgin. Jesus' "brothers" (Greek, *adelphoi*) are to be understood as male relatives, perhaps cousins or stepbrothers, sons of Mary's husband, Joseph, by a previous marriage.

Jesus' Disciples

Mark's opinion of the Galilean **disciples** whom Jesus calls to follow him (3:13–19) is distinctly unsympathetic, although these are the Twelve Apostles on whose testimony the Christian faith traditionally is founded (see Box 30.3). Almost without exception, Mark paints the **Twelve** as dull-witted, inept, unreliable, cowardly, and, in at least one case, treacherous. When Jesus stills a storm, the disciples are impressed but unaware of the act's significance (4:35–41). After his feeding of the multitudes, the disciples "did not understand about the [meaning of the miraculous] loaves" because "their hearts were hardened" (6:52).

BOX 30.3 Mark's List of the Twelve Apostles

According to Mark, Jesus recruited twelve fellow Galileans to be his chief disciples, men who witnessed his mighty works in Galilee and then accompanied him to Jerusalem. Each of the Twelve was an **apostle,** a person chosen to serve as God's special messenger: "And he appointed twelve, whom he also named apostles, to be with him, and to be sent out to proclaim the message [of the kingdom], and to have authority to cast out demons" (Mark 3:14–15). Jesus first selected two sets of brothers, **Simon,** whom he renames **Peter** (and who is also called **Cephas**), and **Andrew;** and **James** and **John,** the sons of **Zebedee** also known as **"Sons of Thunder"** (Boanerges), to form his inner circle. Later, he

adds another eight disciples to complete the Twelve, a number probably representing the twelve tribes of Israel: **Philip; Bartholomew; Matthew; Thomas; James,** son of **Alphaeus; Thaddeus; Simon** the Canaanite; and **Judas Iscariot,** the disciple who later betrays him (3:16–19). Parallel lists of apostles appear in Matthew 10:1–4, Luke 6:12–16, and Acts 1:13, although with some variations in the names included. Matthew indicates the apostles' exalted status in the Christian community: "At the renewal of all things, when the Son of Man is seated on the throne of his glory, you who have followed me will also sit on twelve thrones, judging the twelve tribes of Israel" (Matt. 19:28).

Mark's phrase here echoes the story of God's "hardening" the Egyptian pharaoh's "heart" when he refused to obey Yahweh's commands (Exod. 7:1–14; 10:1–27). Even after listening for months to Jesus' teaching, the disciples are such slow learners that they are still ignorant of "what [Jesus' reference to] this rising from the dead could mean" (9:9–10). Not only do they fail to grasp the concept of sharing in Jesus' glory (10:35–41), but even the simplest, most obvious parables escape their comprehension. As Jesus asks, "Do you not understand this parable? Then how will you understand all the parables?" (4:10–13).

Although he has "explained everything in private to his disciples" (4:33–34; cf. 8:31–32), and the disciples have presumably recognized him as Israel's Messiah (8:27–32), they desert him after his arrest (14:30). **Peter,** who had earlier acknowledged Jesus as the Messiah, three times denies knowing him (14:66–72). Almost the only character in Mark shown as recognizing the significance of Jesus' death is an unnamed Roman soldier who perceives that "truly this man was God's son" (15:39).

Mark's view that all of Jesus' original associates, including family, former neighbors, and followers, were strangely blind to his true identity and purpose carries through to the end of his Gospel. At the empty tomb, an unnamed youth in white directs a handful of women disciples not to linger in Jerusalem but to seek their risen Lord in Galilee, but they are too frightened to obey (16:1–8). The Gospel thus ends with the only disciples who had followed Jesus to the cross—a few Galilean women—inarticulate with terror, unable to cope with the news of his resurrection!

Mark's insistence that the resurrected Jesus will not be found near his burial site—Jerusalem—contrasts with the tradition in Luke's Gospel that Jesus instructed his followers to remain in Jerusalem awaiting the Holy Spirit (Luke 24:47–53; Acts 1–2). Whereas Luke makes Jerusalem the center of Christian growth and expansion, the Spirit-empowered mother church led by Peter and James, Jesus' "brother" (Acts 1:4–3:34; 15:13–21), Mark paints it as a hotbed of conniving hypocrites who scheme to murder the Son of God.

Mark's unfavorable portrayal of Jesus' closest associates and the original Jerusalem church is puzzling. Does this apparent hostility mean that the group for which Mark wrote wished to distance itself from the Jerusalem leadership, which included Jesus' closest family members, Mary and James (Acts 1:14; 12:17, etc.)? Does Mark's negative attitude suggest a power struggle between his branch of Gentile Christianity and the Jewish Christians who (until 70 CE) headed the original church?

Mark's Structure and Sequence of Events

Whatever the historicity of Mark's version of Jesus' ministry, it eventually exerted a tremendous influence on the Christian community at large, primarily through the expanded and revised editions of Mark that Matthew and Luke produced (see Chapter 31). Because both Matthew and Luke generally follow Mark's order of events in Jesus' life (see Box 30.1), it is important to understand the significance of Mark's bipolar organization. Mark arranges

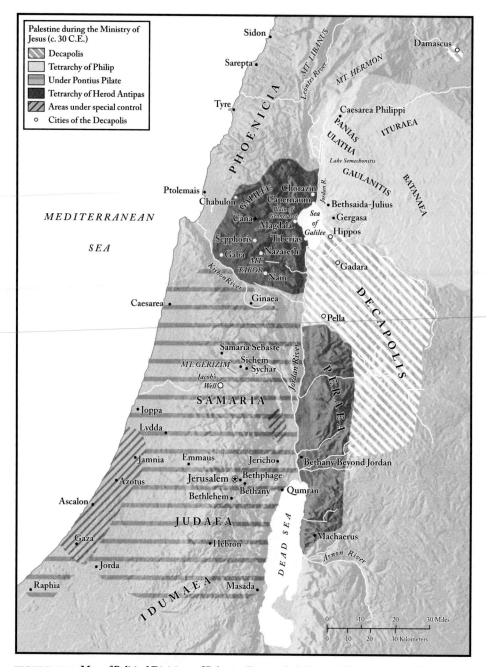

FIGURE 30.1 Map of Political Divisions of Palestine During the Ministry of Jesus (c. 30 CE). Note that Rome directly administered Judea and Samaria through its governor Pontius Pilate; Herod Antipas ruled Galilee (Jesus' home district) and Peraea; another son of Herod the Great, Philip, ruled an area to the northeast. The Decapolis was a league of ten Greek-speaking cities on the east side of the Jordan River.

his narrative around a geographical, north-south polarity (see Figure 30.1). The first half of his narrative takes place in **Galilee** and adjacent areas of northern Palestine, a largely rural area of peasant farmers and fishermen where Jesus recruits his followers (see Figure 30.2), performs numerous miracles, and—despite some opposition—enjoys considerable success. The second half (beginning at Mark 10:1) relates Jesus' fateful journey southward to Judea and Jerusalem, where he is rejected and killed. Besides setting Jesus' career in two distinct geographical

FIGURE 30.2 A sixth-century mosaic in Ravenna depicts a youthful Jesus summoning the brothers Peter and Andrew to leave their fishing boat and follow him.

areas, Mark simultaneously presents two contrasting aspects of Jesus' story. In Galilee, Jesus is a figure of power, using his supernatural gifts to expel demons, heal the sick, control natural forces, and raise the dead. The Galilean Jesus speaks and acts with tremendous authority, effortlessly refutes his critics, and affirms or invalidates the Mosaic Torah at will. Before leaving **Caesarea Philippi,** however, Jesus makes the first of three Passion predictions, warning his uncomprehending disciples that he will go to Jerusalem only to suffer humiliation and death (8:30–38; 9:31–32; cf. 10:33–34).

By using the Passion predictions as a device to link the powerful miracle worker in Galilee with the helpless figure on the cross in Judea, Mark reconciles the two seemingly irreconcilable elements in his portrait of Jesus. The authoritative Son of God who astonishes vast crowds with his miraculous works is also the vulnerable **Son of Man** who, in weakness and apparent defeat, sacrifices his life "as a ransom for many" (10:45). The author thus balances Christian traditions about his hero's remarkable deeds with a bleak picture of Jesus' sufferings, devoting his Gospel's last six chapters to a detailed account of the Passion.

Mark's Gospel can be divided into five parts:

1. Prelude to Jesus' public ministry (1:1–13)
2. The Galilean ministry: inaugurating the kingdom (1:14–9:50)
3. The journey to Jerusalem (10:1–10:52)
4. The Jerusalem ministry and Passion story (11: 1–15:47)
5. Postlude: the empty tomb (16:1–8)

Prelude to Jesus' Public Ministry

Except for informing his readers that Jesus came from the Galilean town of Nazareth (not mentioned in the Hebrew Bible), Mark offers nothing about Jesus' background or life experiences before he joins the crowds flocking to John the Baptist. Because John, conducting a campaign of religious renewal at the Jordan River, baptizes in "repentance for the forgiveness of sins," Mark perhaps implies that Jesus then viewed himself as among the repentant. (In his version of Jesus' baptism, Matthew insists that John, apparently recognizing Jesus as sinless, was reluctant to baptize him [Matt. 3:13–15].) As he rises from immersion in Jordan's waters, Jesus undergoes a life-changing experience: he sees the heavens "torn apart" and the "Spirit descending like a dove"; he also hears God speak directly to him: "You are my son, the Beloved, with you I am well pleased" (1:11). Like Israel's ancient kings at their time of their coronation, Jesus has been anointed as David's heir and thus enters into a special relationship with God (Pss. 2; 110). Empowered by the Spirit, Jesus resists Satan's temptations in the desert (1:12–13) and, through his exorcisms and healings, begins a frontal attack on the devil's dominion.

The Galilean Ministry: Inaugurating the Kingdom

Mark's Narrative Techniques At first glance, Mark's account of Jesus' miraculous deeds in his home district of Galilee seems little more than a recitation of loosely connected incidents, a series of brief, independent narratives stitched together like pearls on a string. Despite Mark's apparent simplicity as a storyteller, however, the author weaves his narrative fragments together skillfully, placing the individual episodes so that they, in effect, reflect on and interpret each other. Besides using a wealth of concrete detail to help readers visualize the scene or feel its emotional impact, Mark commonly employs the technique of *intercalation,* inserting one story inside another. This sandwiching device typically serves to make the story placed inside another story function as interpretative commentary on the framing story. In telling of Jesus' family's attempt to restrict his ministry (3:21, 31–35), for example, Mark inserts a seemingly unrelated anecdote about Jesus' critics accusing him of sorcery (3:22–30), implicitly associating his "mother and brothers" with his opponents.

Mark uses the same device of intercalation in his story about Jesus' resuscitating the daughter of **Jairus,** a synagogue official (5:21–24, 35–43). The author interrupts

---

BOX 30.4   The Synoptic Gospels' Use of the Term "Son of Man"

In the Synoptic Gospels, the phrase "Son of Man" appears almost exclusively on the lips of Jesus, who uses it to denote three important aspects of his ministry. The three categories identify Jesus as the Son of Man who serves on earth, the Son of Man who must suffer and die, and the Son of Man who will be revealed in eschatological judgment. Some representative examples appear below:

The Earthly Son of Man

Has authority to forgive sins (Mark 2:10; Matt. 9:6; Luke 5:24)

Is Lord of the Sabbath (Mark 2:27; Matt. 12:8; Luke 6:5)

The Suffering Son of Man

Must/will suffer (Mark 8:31; 9:12; Matt. 17:12; Luke 9:22)

Comes to serve and give his life (Mark 10:45; Matt. 20:28)

The Eschatological Son of Man

Comes in glory of the Father and holy angels (Mark 8:38; Matt. 16:27; Luke 9:26)

Will sit at the right hand of Power (Mark 14:62; Matt. 26:64; Luke 22:69)

---

the Jairus narrative to incorporate the anecdote about a hemorrhaging woman into the middle of the story. Pushing through the crowds surrounding him, Jesus is on his way to help Jairus's seriously ill daughter when a woman—who Mark says had suffered for twelve years from unstoppable bleeding (and was therefore ritually unclean)—suddenly grabs his cloak and, as if by force of desperate need, draws into her ailing body Jesus' curative energy. This incident is doubly unique: It is the only Gospel healing to occur without Jesus' conscious will and the Evangelists' only hint about the physical nature of Jesus' ability to heal. Mark states that Jesus can *feel* his power flow out when the woman touches him, as if he were a dynamo being drained of electrical power (5:25:34). The Markan Jesus, moreover, does not know at first who is tapping his energy.

Mark then resumes the Jairus narrative: Although a messenger reports that the girl has already died, Jesus insists that she is only "sleeping." Taking his three closest disciples into the girl's room, he commands her to "get up"—"*Talitha cum,*" an Aramaic phrase that Mark's community probably revered for its association with Jesus' authority over death (5:35–43). The author links the two stories by a single numerical device—the mature woman has been afflicted for a dozen years, and the young girl is twelve years old—and by the assertion that it is the participants' *faith* that cures them. The woman demonstrates unconditional trust in Jesus' ability to help her, and Jairus presumably accepts Jesus' advice to replace fear for his daughter's safety with "faith."

Jesus as Son of Man A phrase that appears almost exclusively in the Gospels and then always on the lips of Jesus, "Son of Man" is Mark's preferred title for Jesus in

his function as God's chief agent (see Box 30.4). For Mark, the term denotes Jesus' three essential roles: (1) an earthly figure who teaches with authority (2) a servant who embraces suffering and (3) a future eschatological judge. Although many scholars question whether the historical Jesus ever used this title, many others regard it as Jesus' favored means of self-identification.

As Mark uses it, the Son of Man concept combines both an apocalyptic ruler and a servant who must suffer and die before attaining the kind of heavenly glory that Daniel 7 and 1 Enoch attribute to him (Mark 8:30–31; 10:45; 13:26–27; 14:62). It is as the Son of Man in his earthly role that Mark's Jesus claims supreme religious authority, particularly to modify the Mosaic Torah virtually at will (2:10). Behaving as if he already reigns as world judge, Jesus forgives a paralytic's sins (2:1–12) and permits certain kinds of work on the Sabbath (3:1–5). The Torah-observant Pharisees are outraged that the Galilean presumes to revoke Moses' inspired command to forbid all labor on God's day of rest (Exod. 20:8–10; Deut. 5:12–15). As Mark presents the case, it is Jesus' flexible attitude toward Sabbath keeping that incites some Pharisees and supporters of Herod Antipas to hatch a murder plot against the Nazarene healer (3:5–6).

Mark reserves the most striking use of the Son of Man motif for his account of Jesus' final hours. At his trial before the Sanhedrin, the Jewish leaders' highest judicial council, Jesus publicly reveals his true identity for the first time: He confesses that he *is* Israel's Messiah and that Caiaphas, the High Priest, "will see the Son of Man seated at the right hand of the Power, and coming with the clouds of heaven" (14:61–62), a claim that brings him the council's condemnation.

Conflict Stories Throughout his Galilean campaign, Jesus is shown debating the Pharisees and scribes. These variously accuse him of blasphemy in daring to forgive sins (2:5), associating with "tax collectors and sinners" (2:15–17), violating Sabbath laws (2:23–28), using Satan's help to expel demons (3:22–27), and profaning tradition by neglecting to wash ritually before a meal (7:1–8). Most of Mark's conflict stories end with Jesus issuing a pronouncement on some aspect of *torah* observance: declaring all foods "clean" (7:14–23), making the Sabbath relevant to human needs (2:23–3:6), and revoking Moses' permission for men to divorce their wives (10:2–12). In each case, Jesus claims the authority to approve or invalidate both written and oral Torah.

Jesus' Use of Parables Compared to Matthew and Luke, Mark contains little of Jesus' teaching. Mark does, however, emphasize that Jesus characteristically taught in parables (4:34). The root meaning of the word **parable** is "a comparison," linking two apparently unlike objects to discover similarities between them. Jesus' simplest parables are typically **similes,** comparisons using *as* or *like* to express unsuspected resemblances between seemingly unrelated objects, actions, or ideas. Thus Jesus compares God's kingdom—which he never explicitly defines—to a number of items, including a mustard seed. Like the tiny seed, God's rule begins in an extremely small way, but eventually, like the mustard plant, it grows to an unexpectedly large size (4:30–32). Other parables take the form of brief stories that exploit familiar situations or customs to illustrate a previously unrecognized truth. In the parable of the sower, a farmer plants seeds in different kinds of ground with distinctly different results (4:2–9). The lengthy interpretation that Mark attaches to Jesus' image of sowing seeds (4:13–20) transforms what was originally a simple parable of agricultural life into an allegory. An **allegory** is a complex literary form in which each element of the narrative—persons, places, actions, even objects—has a symbolic value. Because every item in the allegory functions as a symbol of something else, the allegory's meaning can be puzzled out only by identifying what each individual feature in the story represents. Most scholars believe that Mark's elaborate allegorical interpretations, equating different kinds of soil with the different responses people have when they receive the "seed" (gospel message), do not represent Jesus' original meaning. By the time that Mark had incorporated the sower parable into his Gospel, the Christian community had already used it to explain people's contrasting reactions to Christian teaching. The reference to "persecution" (4:17)

places the allegorical factor in Mark's time rather than in the context of Jesus' personal experience in Galilee.

Jesus as Exorcist In a famous miracle story, Jesus drives a whole army of "unclean spirits" from a Gerasene madman, which he then casts into a herd of pigs—the religiously unclean animals becoming a fit home for spirits that drive people to commit unclean acts (5:1–20). The demons' name— "legion"—is an unflattering reference to the Roman legions (large military units) then occupying Palestine (and in Mark's day assaulting Jerusalem). In Mark's ironic vision, the demons recognize Jesus' identify, whereas human beings fail to do so (see Box 30.5).

In another incident involving demonic possession (3:22–30), Mark dramatizes a head-on collision between Jesus and opponents who see him as a tool of the devil. The clash occurs when Jerusalem scribes (teachers and interpreters of the Torah) accuse Jesus of using black magic to perform exorcisms. Denying that evil can produce good, Jesus countercharges that persons who attribute good works to Satan slander "the Holy Spirit," the divine force manifested in Jesus' actions.

Matthew's version of the incident explicitly links Jesus' defeat of evil spirits with the arrival of God's kingdom. The Matthean Jesus declares, "If it is by the Spirit of God that I cast out demons, then the kingdom of God has come to you" (Matt. 12:28). To both Evangelists, Jesus' successful attack on demonic control is a revelation that through his presence, God now rules. Willful refusal to accept Jesus' healings as evidence of divine power is to resist the Spirit, to blaspheme God himself.

The Existence of Demons Mark, like other New Testament authors, reflects a common Hellenistic belief in the existence of unseen entities that influence human lives. Numerous Hellenistic documents record charms to ward off demons or free one from their control. In Judaism, works like the deuterocanonical Book of Tobit reveal a belief that demons could be driven out by the correct use of magical formulas (Tob. 6:1–8; 8:1–3). Josephus, who was Mark's contemporary, relates a story about Eleazar, who allegedly exorcised a demon in the presence of the emperor Vespasian (ruled 69–79 CE), drawing the malign spirit out through its victim's nose (*Antiquities,* 8.46–49).

Jesus as a "Hidden" Messiah In Chapter 8, which forms the central pivot on which the entire Gospel turns, Mark ties together several themes that convey his essential vision of Jesus' ministry and what Jesus requires of those who would follow him. Beginning on a joyous

BOX 30.5 Mark's Identification of Jesus as "Son of God"

Although Mark's preferred title for Jesus is "Son of Man," he also identifies Jesus as "Son of God" at strategic places in his narrative. In most English editions, the phrase "Jesus Christ, the Son of God" appears in the first line of Mark's Gospel, alerting readers at once to Jesus' true identity. Some early manuscripts do not include the phrase in Mark 1:1, however, leading some scholars to suggest that the author originally intended for readers to learn of Jesus' special relationship to God at the same time he did, at his baptism. According to Mark 1:11, as Jesus rises from immersion in the River Jordan, he hears God inform him: "You are my Son, the Beloved, with you I am well pleased."

The voice coming "from heaven" paraphrases Psalm 2, a poem sung at the coronation of Israel's monarch, a royal ceremony in which Yahweh is represented as adopting the newly consecrated king: "You are my son; today I have begotten you" (Ps. 2:7). Because Mark contains no reference to Jesus' virginal conception, many scholars think that the author regards Jesus as becoming God's son by adoption, with his baptism and visitation by the Holy Spirit the equivalent of Davidic kings' being anointed with holy oil.

In an ironic counterpoint to God's voice, Mark next uses the speech of a demon to reveal Jesus' hidden identity. When driven from a man he has possessed, the demon angrily declares, "I know who you are, the Holy One of God" (1:24; cf. 3:11, 22–28; 5:7). Whereas Mark's human characters fail to recognize Jesus' true nature until after his death, supernatural creatures, including "unclean spirits" know and fear him. Emphasizing the secret or "hidden" quality of Jesus' messianic role, Mark does not have a human figure testify to Jesus' divine sonship until he hangs lifeless on the cross. Only then does a Roman soldier recognize that "truly this man was God's son" (15:39).

---

note with his account of Jesus feeding a large crowd (8:1–10), this section continues through a crisis of misunderstanding among Jesus, Peter, and the other disciples (8:11–21, 27–33) and ends with Jesus' warning (to Mark's community) that he will disown unfaithful followers (8:38). The narrative movement from joy to judgment involves the disciples' failure to understand either the significance of Jesus' miracles or the purpose of his life and death.

In contrast to John's Gospel, in which Jesus' identity is publicly proclaimed at the beginning of his ministry, no one in Mark's Gospel even hints that Jesus is Israel's Messiah until almost the close of the Galilean campaign. Then, in the town of Caesarea Philippi, Peter—as if in a flash of insight—recognizes him as such (8:29). Jesus immediately swears the disciples to secrecy, as he had earlier forbidden witnesses of his miraculous deeds to speak of them (1:23–24, 34; 3:11–12; 5:7; 7:36; 8:30; see also 9:9). Jesus' reluctance to have news of his miracles spread abroad is known as the **messianic secret,** a term that the German scholar William Wrede coined (1901).

Most scholars believe that Mark's theme of the messianic secret—his repeated emphasis on Jesus' ordering others to keep silent about his healings and exorcisms—represents the author's theological purpose. For Mark, people could not know Jesus' identity until *after* he had completed his mission. Jesus had to be unappreciated in order to be rejected and killed—to fulfill God's will that he "give his life a ransom for many" (10:45).

A Theme of Suffering A conviction that Jesus must suffer an unjust death—an atonement offering for others—to confirm and complete his messiahship is the heart of Mark's **Christology** (concepts about the nature and function of Christ) (see Box 30.5). Hence, Peter's announcement at Caesarea Philippi that Jesus is the Christ is directly followed by Jesus' first prediction that he will go to Jerusalem only to die (8:29–32). When Peter objects to this notion of a rejected and defeated messiah, Jesus calls his chief disciple "Satan." Derived from a Hebrew term meaning "obstacle" or "adversary" (see Box 23.2), the epithet *satan* labels Peter's attitude an obstacle or roadblock on Jesus' predestined path to the cross. Peter understands Jesus no better than do outsiders, regarding the Messiah as a God-empowered hero who conquers his enemies, not as a submissive victim of their brutality.

At the close of Chapter 8, Mark introduces yet another startling truth: True disciples must expect to suffer as Jesus does. In two of the three Passion predictions, Jesus emphasizes the close connection between his fate and that of those who follow him: "If any want to become my followers, let them deny themselves and take up their cross and follow me" (8:34; 10:32–45). After the third Passion prediction, the disciples still fail to grasp Jesus' meaning: James and John, sons of Zebedee, naively ask to rule with Jesus, occupying places of honor on his right and left. When Jesus explains that reigning with him means imitating his sacrifice, Mark's readers are expected to remember that when Jesus reaches Jerusalem, the positions on his right and left will be taken by the two brigands crucified next to him (15:27).

The Jerusalem Ministry

If Mark was aware of Jesus' other visits to Jerusalem (described in John's Gospel), he dismisses them as unimportant compared with the visit made during Jesus' last week on earth. When Jesus enters the city, which had been without a Davidic monarch for more than 600 years, a crowd of Galilean supporters enthusiastically welcomes him, their cries implicitly identifying Jesus as restorer of "the coming kingdom of our ancestor David" (11:1–11). For the first time in Mark's narrative, Jesus appears to accept a messianic role, one that Roman guards at the city gate could interpret as a political claim to Jewish kingship and an act of treason to Rome.

Jesus at the Temple During his few days in Jerusalem, Jesus behaves in a manner that alienates both Roman and Jewish administrations, arousing the hostility of almost every religious party and institution in official Judaism. His assault on the Temple (11:15–19)—overthrowing the moneychangers' tables and disrupting the sale of sacrificial animals—appears as a dangerous attack on the Sadducean priesthood in charge of maintaining the sanctuary, an act that probably seals his fate with the chief priests and Temple police.

In Mark 12, the author portrays Jesus scoring success after success in a series of confrontations as he moves through the Temple courts (see Figure 30.3), thronged with Passover pilgrims. The Pharisees and Herod's party attempt to trap Jesus on the controversial issue of paying taxes to Rome, a snare he eludes by suggesting that Caesar's coins be returned to their source, while God claims the rest (12:13–17). The Sadducees, who allegedly accept only the Torah and

FIGURE 30.3 King Herod I's extensive renovations of the Jerusalem Temple, begun about 20 BCE, had been completed only a few years before the Romans destroyed it in 70 CE. According to Josephus, the bejeweled curtain veiling the sanctuary's innermost room, the Holy of Holies, depicted a panorama of heaven. Visible through the main entrance (shown here in a modern scale model), the curtain is said to have been "torn in two from top to bottom" at the moment of Jesus' death (Mark 15:38). In Mark's Gospel, this event corresponds to the heavens being "torn open" at the time of Jesus' baptism (Mark 1:10).

therefore deny such doctrines as a future resurrection, fare no better. Jesus ingeniously reinterprets a passage from Exodus, where Yahweh states that he is the God of Abraham, Isaac, and Jacob, to demonstrate that "He is God not of the dead, but of the living" (12:24–27; cf. Exod. 3:6).

Interestingly, Mark closes Jesus' Temple debates with a friendly encounter in which the Galilean and a Torah scholar agree on the essence of true religion. Answering the scribe's question about the Bible's most important requirement, Jesus cites the Shema, or Jewish declaration of monotheism: There is only one God, and Israel must love him with all its force and being (Deut. 6:4–5). To this he adds a second Torah command: to love one's neighbor as oneself (Lev. 19:18). In agreement, the scribe and Jesus exchange compliments. Although not a follower, the Temple scholar sees that active love is the essence of divine rule, a perception that Jesus says makes him "not far from the kingdom of God"—a more favorable verdict than Jesus ever passes on the Twelve (12:28–34).

Jesus' Prophecy of the Temple's Fall   In Chapter 13, Mark highlights the crisis that then deeply concerned his community—Rome's imminent destruction of the holy city and its sanctuary, with all its implications for the original center of Christianity. The importance that Mark attaches to Jesus' prophecy of the Temple's fall is indicated by the fact that it is the longest continuous speech in his Gospel. Scholarly analysis of Mark 13, however, suggests that the Evangelist assembled it from a variety of sources, ranging from individual sayings of Jesus to traditional Jewish apocalyptic material. How much of the discourse on Jerusalem's destruction and the Parousia of the Son of Man originated with Jesus and how much represents interpretations by visionaries and prophets in Mark's community is unknown. Readers will notice that Mark incorporates two somewhat contradictory views of the rapidly approaching End of history. He states that a swarm of disasters and frightening astronomical phenomena will provide unmistakable "signs" that the End is near, just as the budding fig tree heralds the arrival of spring (13:8, 14–20, 24–31). Conversely, neither the Son nor his followers can know the time of Judgment Day, so one must keep constant watch because the End will occur without warning (13:32–37).

The Last Supper   On the Thursday evening after his entering Jerusalem, Jesus withdraws with his disciples to celebrate Passover, an annual observance recalling the Israelites' last night in Egypt, when the Angel of Death "passed over" their homes to slay the Egyptian firstborn (Exod. 11:1–13:16; see Chapter 6). In a ritual at the close of their meal, Jesus gives the Passover a new significance, stating that the bread is his "body" and the wine his "blood of the covenant, which is poured out for many" (14:22–24). Mark's account of this Last Supper, the origin of the Christian celebration of the **Eucharist,** or holy communion, closely resembles Paul's earlier description of the ceremony (1 Cor. 11:23–26) (see Figure 30.4). Mark, however, represents Jesus as saying that he "will never again drink of the fruit of the vine until that day when [he] drink[s] it new in the kingdom of God," a reminder of the Markan community's apocalyptic expectations (14:25).

Jesus' Passion   In describing Jesus' Passion—his final suffering and death—Mark's narrative irony reaches its height. Although the author includes many grim details of Jesus' painful execution, he intends for his readers to see the enormous disparity between the *appearance* of Jesus' vulnerability to worldly power and the actual reality of his spiritual triumph. Jesus' enemies, who believe that they are ridding Judea of a dangerous radical, are in fact making possible his saving death—all according to God's design.

Even so, Jesus is tested fully—treated with savage cruelty (14:65; 15:15–20), deserted by all his friends (14:50), and apparently abandoned by God (15:34). The agony begins in **Gethsemane,** a grove or vineyard on the Mount of Olives opposite Jerusalem to which Jesus and the disciples retreat after the Last Supper. In the Gethsemane episode (14:28–52), Mark places a dual emphasis on Jesus' fulfilling predictions in the Hebrew Bible (14:26–31, 39) and on his personal anguish. By including both these elements, Mark shows that while the Crucifixion will take place as God long ago planned (and revealed in Scripture), Jesus' part in the drama of salvation demands heroic effort. While the disciples sleep, Jesus faces the hard reality of his impending torture, feeling deeply "grieved," "distressed and agitated" (14:32–34). Although Jesus prays that God will spare him the ordeal he dreads, he forces his own will into harmony with God's, providing a model for all believers whose loyalty is tested. Even in his agony, Mark reports that Jesus addresses God as "*Abba,*" an Aramaic term of family intimacy (14:32–41).

After armed guards arrest Jesus and Peter and the other disciples forsake him, Jesus is brought before the

FIGURE 30.4 A fresco in the Catacomb of St. Domitilla in Rome shows Jesus and the apostles as beardless, with short hair, and wearing white linen tunics in the Greco-Roman fashion. Some scholars believe that this fresco depicts the Last Supper.

Sanhedrin, apparently on charges of blasphemy. Mark contrasts Peter's fearful denial that he even knew Jesus with Jesus' courageous declaration to Caiaphas that he is indeed Israel's Messiah and the appointed agent of God's future judgment (14:62). The only Gospel writer to state that Jesus explicitly claimed messianic identity at his trial, Mark may do so to underscore his theme that Jesus' messiahship is revealed primarily though service and self-denial (10:45). Like the author of Hebrews, Mark sees Jesus' divine Sonship earned and perfected through suffering and death (Heb. 2:9–11; 5:7–10).

Jesus' Crucifixion After condemning him on religious grounds, Caiaphas then sends Jesus to Pontius Pilate, the Roman governor who was in Jerusalem to maintain order during Passover week. Uninterested in the Sanhedrin's charge that Jesus is a blasphemer, Pilate focuses on Jesus' alleged political crime: claiming to be a Jewish king, a treasonous act against Rome. Because Mark re-creates much of his Passion story from passages in the Hebrew Bible, it is difficult to know if Jesus' silence before Pilate reflects his actual behavior or the author's reliance on Isaiah 53, where Israel's suffering servant does not respond to his accusers (Isa. 53:7).

Whereas Mark portrays Pilate as extremely reluctant to order Jesus' execution, the historical Pilate (prefect of Judea, 26–36 CE), whom Josephus describes, rarely hesitated to slaughter troublesome Jews (cf. *Antiquities* 18.3.1–2; *The Jewish War* 2.9.4). When a mob demands that not Jesus but a convicted terrorist named **Barabbas** be freed, Pilate is pictured as having no choice but to release Barabbas (the first person to benefit from Jesus' sacrifice) and order the Galilean's crucifixion. According to Pilate's command, Jesus' cross bears a statement of the political offense for which he is executed: aspiring to be king of the Jews, a cruelly ironic revelation of his true identity (15:22–32).

Although Mark's description of Jesus' undergoing a criminal's shameful death is almost unbearably bleak, his Passion account effectively conveys the writer's dual goals: creating a model for Christians facing a similar ordeal and showing that out of human malice and blindness the divine will is accomplished (see Figure 30.5). In Mark's report, Jesus last words are despairing: "*Eloi, Eloi, lema sabachthani?* . . . My God, my God, why have you forsaken me?" (15:34). In placing this question—a direct quotation of Psalm 22:1—on Jesus' lips, Mark emphasizes that the horror of Jesus' pain fulfills prophecy and that disciples who undergo similar martyrdoms

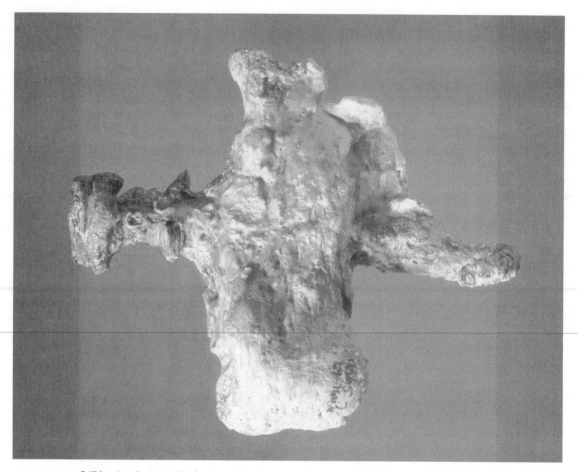

FIGURE 30.5 Still bearing the iron spike that pierced his heel bone and fastened his feet to a wooden panel on a Roman cross, this bone fragment of a crucified man was discovered in an ossuary in a Jerusalem tomb.

can also expect to share in the glory of Jesus' resurrection (see Figure 30.6).

Jesus' Burial As in all four Gospels, **Mary Magdalene** provides the key human link connecting Jesus' death and burial and the subsequent discovery that his grave is empty (15:40–41, 47; 16:1). **Joseph of Arimathea,** a mysterious figure Mark suddenly introduces into his narrative, serves a single function: to transfer Jesus' body from Roman control to that of the dead man's disciples. An acquaintance of Pilate, a member of the Sanhedrin, and yet a secret supporter of Jesus' ministry, he bridges the two opposing worlds of Jesus' enemies and friends. Not only does Joseph obtain official permission to remove Jesus' body from the cross—otherwise it would routinely be thrown into an anonymous mass grave—but he also provides a secure place of burial, a rock-hewn sepulcher that he seals by rolling a large, flat stone across the entrance (15:42–47).

When Mary Magdalene and a few other Galilean women arrive at Jesus' sepulcher early Sunday morning, they find the stone door rolled away and the crypt empty except for the presence of a young man dressed in white. (Is he the same unidentified youth who fled naked from Gethsemane in 14:50–51?) Like Jesus' absent male disciples, the women do not understand the concept of Jesus' resurrection (cf. 9:9–10). Unable to grasp the idea that Jesus has "been raised," the women flee in terror, saying "nothing to anyone" about their experience (16:8) and leaving readers to wonder how spreading the "good news" of Jesus' resurrection ever began. The Gospel thus concludes with a frightened silence, providing no account of Jesus' postressurection appearances.

Resurrection or Parousia? Mark's belief in the nearness of Jesus' Parousia may explain why the risen Jesus does not manifest himself in the earliest Gospel. Some scholars think that Mark, convinced that the political

FIGURE 30.6 *The Small Crucifixion* by Matthias Grunewald (c. 1470–1528), heightens the sense of the sufferer's physical pain and grief. Although his emphasis on Jesus' agony reflects Mark's account, Grunewald follows John's Gospel in showing Jesus' mother and the Beloved Disciple (as well as another Mary) present at the cross.

and social chos of the Jewish Revolt will soon climax in Jesus' return, refers not to a resurrection phenomenon but to the Parousia. Forty years after the Crucifixion, Mark's community may believe that their wandering through the wilderness is almost over. They are about to follow a greater Joshua across Jordan into "Galilee," Jesus' promised kingdom (16:6).

Conversely, Mark's climactic image of the empty tomb may express his wish to emphasize Jesus' *absence*: Jesus is present neither in the grave (in death) nor yet as triumphal Son of Man. Mark's Jesus lives both in memories evoked by the Gospel story and in his enduring power over the lives of his followers.

Added Conclusions Mark's inconclusiveness, his insistence on leaving his story open-ended, must have seemed as unsatisfactory to later Christian scribes as it does to many readers today. For perhaps that reason, Mark's Gospel has been heavily edited, with two different conclusions added at different times. All the oldest manuscripts of Mark end with the line reporting the women's terrified refusal to obey the young man's instruction to carry the resurrection message to Peter. In time, however, editors appended postresurrection accounts to their copies of Mark, making his Gospel more consistent with Matthew and Luke (Mark 16:8b, 9–20).

QUESTIONS FOR DISCUSSION AND REVIEW

1. Mark's account establishes an order of events in Jesus' life that two other Evangelists, Matthew and Luke, also follow. Beginning with his baptism and ending with the women's discovery of the empty tomb, briefly outline the major events in Mark's biography of Jesus. Name the two principal sections—and their respective geographical locations—into which Mark divides Jesus' story.

2. According to tradition, who wrote Mark's Gospel? Why do scholars generally regard the work as anonymous? What themes in Mark's account suggest that it was composed after the Jewish Revolt against Rome had already begun?

3. How do the three Passion Predictions serve to unite the Galilean Jesus, a powerful miracle worker, with the vulnerable Jesus whom Roman soldiers execute? Why does Mark devote so much of his Gospel to narrating Jesus' final week on earth? According to Mark 10:45, what does Jesus' death on the cross accomplish?

4. Describe the three different categories Mark assigns the Son of Man concept. How can Jesus be both a suffering servant and the eschatological judge? Why must Jesus' followers expect to suffer as he did?

5. Define *parable*, and discuss Jesus' use of the form to illustrate his vision of God's kingdom. Explain the concept of the messianic secret, and link it to Jesus' use of figurative language (see Mark 4) and to Mark's insistence that none of Jesus' associates, including his family and disciples, really understood either his teachings or his theological significance.

6. Do you think that Mark's emphasis on Jesus' exorcisms—his battle with supernatural evil—is an expression of the author's eschatology, his belief that in Jesus' activities God's kingdom has begun and the End is near? Explain your answer.

7. In your view, why does Mark end his Gospel so abruptly at 16:8? What clues do you find in Mark's narrative that the author expects Jesus' Parousia to occur imminently? In what ways could the absence of postresurrection appearances in this Gospel indicate that Mark anticipates Jesus soon reappearing in eschatological glory?

Terms and Concepts to Remember

allegory	Joseph of Arimathea
Andrew	Judas
baptism/John the Baptist	Mark's eschatological
Barabbas	urgency
Caesarea Philippi	Mary Magdalene
Capernaum	Parousia
Cephas	Paul
Christ	Peter
Christology	Sanhedrin (Great Council)
disciples	Satan
exorcism	Simon
Galilee	Son of God
Gethsemane	Son of Man
Holy Spirit	Sons of Thunder
Jairus/Jairus's daughter	Transfiguration
James	the Twelve
Jesus' family	Zebedee
John	

Recommended Reading

Bauckham, Richard. *Jesus and the Eyewitnesses: The Gospels as Eyewitness Testimony*. Grand Rapids, MI: Eerdmans, 2006. Argues that Mark and the other Gospels are based on reliable historical evidence.

Bryan, Christopher. *A Preface to Mark: Notes on the Gospel in Its Literary and Cultural Settings*. New York: Oxford UP, 1993. Links Mark with oral performance in the early Christian community.

France, R. T. *The Gospel of Mark* (New International Greek Testament Commentary). Grand Rapids, MI: Eerdmans, 2002. Analyzes Mark as a literary whole; for advanced students.

Harrington, Daniel J. "The Gospel According to Mark." In R. E. Brown, et al., eds., *The New Jerome Biblical Commentary*, pp. 596–629. Englewood Cliffs, NJ: Prentice-Hall, 1990. A helpful introduction.

Kelber, W. H. *Mark's Story of Jesus*. Philadelphia: Fortress Press, 1979. A brief but penetrating analysis of Mark's rendition of Jesus' public ministry.

Matera, Frank J. *What Are They Saying About Mark?* New York: Paulist Press, 1987. An accessible introduction for beginners.

Minor, Mitzi. "Mark, Gospel of." In K. D. Sakenfeld, ed., *The New Interpreter's Dictionary of the Bible*, Vol. 3, pp. 798–811. Nashville, TN: Abingdon Press, 2008. An up-to-date analysis of the first Gospel written.

Wrede, William. *The Messianic Secret*. Trans. J. C. G. Greig. Cambridge: Clarke, 1971. A technical but crucial study of Mark's narrative methods and theological motives, for advanced study.

CHAPTER 31

The Synoptic Problem

The Gospel of Matthew and Its Relationship to the Gospels of Mark and Luke

---

Key Topics/Themes Despite some variations in theme and emphasis, the first three Gospels are so similar that they can be placed side by side and viewed horizontally, their authors having arranged events in almost exactly the same order. Known as the Synoptic Gospels because they can be "seen together," Matthew, Mark, and Luke clearly have a close literary relationship, the resolution of which is called the Synoptic Problem. In contrast to the Gospel of John, which tells Jesus' story in a different order and presents his teachings in a distinctly different form, the Gospel of Matthew follows Mark's order closely but inserts five large blocks of teaching material that portray Jesus as a new Moses and inaugurator of a new covenant.

The Synoptic Gospels

As even casual readers of the New Testament have noticed, the first three Gospels—Matthew, Mark, and Luke—are very much alike. In fact, they have so much material in common that one can arrange their contents in parallel columns and compare their three versions of the same saying or incident in Jesus' life (see Box 31.1). Because they present Jesus' biography in approximately the same narrative order and from essentially the same viewpoint, they are called the **Synoptic Gospels** (seeing the whole together). Because the three Synoptic Gospels are so similar—in stark contrast to John's Gospel, which gives Jesus' story a different chronology and portrays his teaching in a radically different form—it appears that the first three Gospels have a literary relationship.

The Synoptic Problem

One of the Synoptic writers must have used at least one of the other Gospels as a source. Scholarly attempts to unravel the literary dependence or connection among the three is known as the **Synoptic Problem.** For reasons described here, the overwhelming majority of scholars now believe that Mark was the first Gospel written and that Matthew and Luke, independently

of each other, drew on Mark as their basic narrative source.

In analyzing the Synoptic accounts, scholars discovered a number of facts that point to Markan priority. All three Synoptics generally follow the same sequence of events, narrating Jesus' life in suggestively similar fashion. This shared narrative (and some teaching) material is known as the *triple tradition.* In addition, Matthew and Luke include a large quantity of teaching material that does not appear in Mark but that is remarkably similar in form and content. This mysterious *double tradition* includes some of Jesus' best-known sayings, such as the Lord's Prayer, the golden rule, and the Beatitudes (blessings that Jesus pronounces on the poor, the meek, and the helpless). In many cases, there is almost a word-for-word agreement on the passages, absent from Mark, that Matthew and Luke share.

In examining the order of events in the Synoptic triple tradition, scholars also noticed that either Matthew or Luke may sometimes deviate from Mark's order, but almost never do they differ from Mark in the same place and in the same way. That is, when Matthew departs from the Markan order, Luke does not; when Luke disagrees with Mark, Matthew does not. This pattern strongly suggests that Mark is the determining factor in the Synoptics' version of the principal

BOX 31.1 Parallels and Differences in the Four Gospels

In comparing the contents of the four canonical accounts of Jesus' life, it is striking that, while events in Mark generally have close parallels in Matthew and Luke, much of the material in John has no parallel in the three Synoptic Gospels. As we will discover in Chapter 33, the differences between John and the other three Gospels are even greater than appears in this chart: Even when John deals with the same events, such as Jesus' assault on the Temple and his arrest, trials, and crucifixion, he uses a different chronology and gives different descriptions of what happened.

TOPIC/EPISODE	MARK	MATTHEW	LUKE	JOHN
Jesus as eternal Word	—	—	—	1:1–14
Word made "flesh"	—	—	—	1:14
Birth story	—	1:18–2:23	1:5–2:40	—
John's baptizing work	1:9–11	3:1–17	3:1–21	1:6, 15, 19–28
Temptation by Satan	1:12–13	4:1–11	4:1–14	—
Teaching primarily or "only in parables"	4:1–24	13:3–35	8:4–18; 13:18–21	—
Teaching primarily in long, metaphysical discourses				
Conversation with Nicodemus	—	—	—	3:1–21
Conversation with Samaritan woman	—	—	—	4:1–42
"I am" speeches				
Bread of life	—	—	—	6:26–66
Good Shepherd	—	—	—	10:1–21
True vine	—	—	—	15:1–17
Farewell discourses (divine nature and return to the Father)	—	—	—	14–17
Exorcisms (casting out demons)	1:23–28; 5:1–20; etc.	8:28–34	8:26–39	—
Feeding multitudes	6:32–44; 8:1–10	14:13–21	9:10–17	6:1–13
Resuscitation of dead				
Daughter of Jairus	5:35–43	9:18–27	8:49–56	—
Lazarus	—	—	—	11:1–46
Return to Nazareth	6:1–6	13:54–58	4:16–30	—
Assault on Temple	11:15–19	21:12–17	19:45–48	2:13–27
Prediction of Jerusalem's fall	13	24–25	21	—
Crucifixion	15:21–47	27:32–66	23:26–54	19:17–42
Empty tomb	16:1–8	28:1–8	24:1–9	20:1–3
Postresurrection appearances				
In Galilee	—	28:16–20	—	21
In Jersualem	—	28:9–10	24:13–53	20:10–29

events in Jesus' story, that his Gospel is the basis for the other two.

Another factor indicating that Mark is a primary source for the other two Synoptics, rather than an abbreviation of them, is the relative amount of space each Evangelist devotes to narrating episodes that the three have in common. If Mark wished to produce a more concise account of Jesus' life by abridging Matthew and Luke, as a small minority of scholars propose, his version of events that all three share should be the shortest, a brief summary of the other two. However, the opposite is true. In almost every case, Mark's version of a specific incident is longer than the parallel version in Matthew or Luke. Whereas Mark takes ten verses to narrate Jesus' cure of the woman afflicted with a chronic hemorrhage (Mark 5:25–34), Matthew tells the same story in only three verses (Matt. 9:20–23). Similarly, Matthew reports the raising of Jairus's daughter in six verses (Matt. 9:18–19, 23–26), whereas Mark's account is almost twice as long (Mark 5:22–24, 35–43). In this and numerous other instances, Matthew appears to have abridged Mark rather than the other way around.

How, then, can we account for passages in Matthew and Luke that give an expanded account of events merely alluded to in Mark, such as Jesus' confrontation with Satan in the wilderness? Mark mentions briefly that Jesus was tempted by the devil but provides no details (Mark 1:12–13). Matthew and Luke, however, offer elaborate dramatizations of Jesus' resisting the tempter, using almost identical language (Matt. 4:1–11;

Luke 4:1–13). Most scholars agree that, although Matthew and Luke draw on Mark for a shared narrative sequence, they also incorporate other sources into their much larger Gospels.

Source criticism—the analysis of a document to discover and identify its written sources—has been particularly helpful in resolving the Synoptic Problem. After recognizing that Mark was the source for the chronological framework in Matthew and Luke, source critics also identified a second major source to account for the extensive teaching material that does not appear in Mark but that Matthew and Luke have in common. According to this theory, Matthew and Luke not only used Mark but also drew on a written collection of Jesus' sayings, including many of his parables. This hypothetical collection is called the **Q** document (from *Quelle*, the German term for "source") (see Figure 31.1).

The Q (Source) Document

Most scholars now agree that Matthew and Luke used two principal sources in composing their Gospels, Mark and Q. Although Q does not survive as a separate document—a potential weakness in the two-source theory—its contents can be reconstructed from passages that both Matthew and Luke include and that do not appear in Mark. According to this view, at a relatively early date, Christians began collecting Jesus' remembered sayings, eventually compiling them in written form between about 50 and 70 CE to produce the Q document.

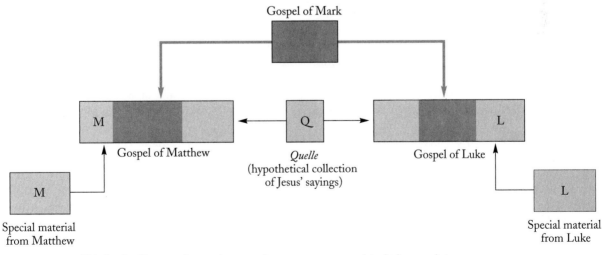

FIGURE 31.1 This drawing illustrates the two-document theory, an attempt to explain the literary relationship of the three Synoptic Gospels. Note that this theory takes Mark's Gospel as a major source for Matthew and Luke. In addition, both Matthew and Luke incorporate teaching material from Q (*Quelle*, a hypothetical collection of Jesus' sayings). Matthew also uses special material unique to his Gospel, here designated M; Luke similarly includes material found only in his account, here labeled L.

The Q passages—non-Markan material Matthew and Luke have in common—total more than 200 verses and contain some of Jesus' most memorable teachings, including much of Matthew's Sermon on the Mount (Matt. 5–7) and Luke's parallel Sermon on the Plain (Luke 6). An increasing number of scholars ascribe enormous importance to Q, for this Sayings Gospel, at least in its first edition, may preserve one of the earliest forms of Christianity. It appears to have been written, in Greek, by a community of itinerant preachers living in Galilee or western Syria who regarded Jesus as both prophet and wisdom teacher. Containing virtually no narrative, Q presents Jesus as one "greater than Solomon" (the traditional founder of Israel's wisdom school) and the last in a long line of God's prophets and sages. Q apparently included no theology interpreting Jesus' death as a saving act. Instead, it focuses almost exclusively on the living man's ethical teachings, parables, and spiritual insights. Before being assimilated into Matthew and Luke, Q was apparently a Gospel in its own right, providing the first written witness to Jesus' primary message. (See Robert Miller and John Verbin et al. in "Recommended Reading".) In addition to integrating sayings from Q into Mark's narrative framework, Matthew and Luke also used sources (perhaps from Christian oral tradition) unique to their respective Gospels (see below).

The Griesbach Theory

Although most scholars agree that the two-source theory most satisfactorily explains the literary relationship of the Synoptic Gospels, a small minority deny Markan priority. According to this view, Mark is a conflation (blending together) of the other two Synoptics. Known as the *Griesbach theory*, after Johan Griesbach (1745–1812), who first published this solution to the Synoptic Problem, this hypothesis has been revived by several contemporary scholars, notably William Farmer. These dissenting scholars emphasize the fact that a few short passages in the triple tradition (material present in all three Synoptics) show that Matthew and Luke occasionally agree while both differ from Mark in the same way. Proponents of the two-source theory, however, argue that such "minor agreements" merely suggest that both Mark and Q had some limited material in common, that in a few instances they overlapped. Other defenders of the majority theory suggest that the "minor agreements" are the result of early scribal attempts to make the Synoptic texts more consistent, "harmonizing" the verbal differences. (For a discussion of deliberate scribal changes to the ancient Gospel manuscripts, including scribal attempts to "harmonize" the Evangelists, see Ehrman in "Recommended Reading.")

More recently, several scholars have emphasized the difficulties inherent in the Q theory, questioning that it ever existed. While accepting that Mark was the first Gospel written, Mark Goodacre, E. P. Sanders, and other critics have raised serious issues about the hypothetical Q. Despite these objections, the scholarly majority still regards the two-source hypothesis as the most adequate explanation of both the general similarities and individual differences in the Synoptic Gospels. (For arguments opposing the majority view, see works by Farmer, Goodacre, and Sanders and Davies in "Recommended Reading.")

The Gospel of Matthew

Jesus as a New Moses

If the Gospel of Mark was the first Gospel written, as most scholars believe, why does Matthew's account stand first in the New Testament canon? The original editors of the Christian Scriptures probably had several reasons for assigning Matthew its premier position. Besides offering more extensive coverage of Jesus' teaching than any other Gospel, it was important to early Christian leaders because of the author's emphasis on the functioning of the *ekklesia*—the church—a term that appears only in Matthew's Gospel (10:1–42; 18:1–35). As both an instructional tool and a rudimentary guidebook to church organization, Matthew's Gospel was extremely useful.

Placing Matthew at the beginning of the New Testament is also thematically appropriate, because this Gospel forms a strong connecting link with the Hebrew Bible (Old Testament). Matthew not only opens his account with a genealogy associating Jesus with the most prominent leaders of ancient Israel, particularly Abraham and David, but also quotes more extensively from the Hebrew Bible than any other Gospel writer. Citing Jewish Scripture more than sixty times (some scholars have detected 140 or more allusions to the Tanakh), Matthew presents Jesus' life in the context of biblical law and prophecy. Nearly a dozen times, Matthew employs a literary formula that underscores the connection between ancient prophecy and specific events in Jesus' life: "All this took place to fulfill what had been spoken by the Lord through the prophet," Matthew writes, and then he quotes or paraphrases a biblical passage to support his statement (1:22–23; 2:15, 23, etc.; see Box 31.2).

Matthew is the only Evangelist who explicitly states that Jesus was "sent only to the house of Israel" (cf. 10:5–6)

> BOX 31.2 **Representative Examples of Matthew's Use of the Hebrew Bible (in a Greek Edition) to Identify Jesus as Israel's Messiah**

MATTHEW	HEBREW BIBLE

MATTHEW

"All this took place to fulfill what had been spoken by the Lord through the prophet." (Matt. 1:22):

1. "Look, the virgin shall conceive, and bear a son, and they shall name him Emmanuel." (Matt. 1:23)
2. They [the wise men] told him [Herod], "In Bethlehem of Judea; for so it has been written by the prophet:
   'And you, Bethlehem, in the land of Judah,
   are by no means least among the rulers of Judah;
   for from you shall come a ruler who is to shepherd my people Israel.'" (Matt. 2:5-6)
3. Then Joseph got up, took the child and his mother by night, and went to Egypt.
   . . . This was to fulfill what had been spoken by the Lord through the prophet, "Out of Egypt I have called my son." (Matt. 2:14–15)
4. "He will be called a Nazorean." (Matt. 2:23) [This statement does not appear in the Hebrew Bible and may be a misreading of Isaiah 11:1.]
5. He cast out the [demonic] spirits with a word, and cured all who were sick. This was to fulfill what had been spoken through the prophet Isaiah, "He took our infirmities and bore our diseases." (Matt. 8:16–17)
6. Jesus told the crowds all these things in parables; without a parable he told them nothing. This was to fulfill what had been spoken through the prophet: "I will open my mouth to speak in parables. I will proclaim what has been hidden from the foundation of the world." (Matt. 13:34–35)

HEBREW BIBLE

1. Look, the young woman is with child and shall bear a son, and shall name him Immanuel. (Isa. 7:14)
2. But you, O Bethlehem of Ephrathah, who are one of the little clans of Judah,
   from you shall come forth for me one who is to rule in Israel,
   whose origin is from of old, from ancient days. (Mic. 5:2)
3. When Israel was a child, I loved him; and out of Egypt I called my son. (Hos. 11:1)
   [Hosea refers to the Exodus from Egypt, not a future Messiah.]
4. A shoot shall come out from the stump of Jesse; and a branch [Hebrew, *nezer*] shall grow out of his roots. (Isa. 11:1)
5. Surely he [Yahweh's servant] has borne our infirmities and carried our diseases; yet we accounted him stricken, struck down by God, and afflicted. (Isa. 53:4)
6. I will open my mouth in a parable; I will utter dark sayings from of old, things that we have heard and known, that our ancestors have told us. (Ps. 78:2–3—*not* in a prophetic book)

and the only one to present Jesus as explicitly insisting on complete Torah obedience:

> Do not think that I [Jesus] have come to abolish the law or the prophets; I have come not to abolish but to fulfill. For truly I tell you, until heaven and earth pass away, not one letter, not one stoke of a letter, will pass from the law until all is accomplished. Therefore, whoever breaks one of the least of these commandments, and teaches others to do the same, will be called least in the kingdom of heaven; but whoever does them and teaches them will be called great in the kingdom of heaven . . .
>
> (Matt. 5:17–19)

As many scholars have noted, Matthew's declaration that Jesus' followers must be Torah observant may have been directed at Paul's Gentile churches. In his letters to the Galatians and Romans, Paul had argued that Christians are no longer in "bondage" to the Mosaic law but now live by "faith" in Jesus' redemptive power (see Chapter 35).

Authorship

Who was the man so deeply interested in Jesus' practice of the Jewish religion and simultaneously so fierce in his attacks on the Pharisees and other leaders of institutional Judaism (23:1–30)? As in Mark's case, the author does not identify himself, suggesting to most historians that the Gospel originated and circulated anonymously. The tradition that the author is the "publican" or tax collector mentioned in Matthew 9:9–13 (and called "Levi" in Mark 2:14) dates from the late second century CE and cannot be verified. The main problem with accepting the apostle Matthew's authorship is that the writer relies heavily on Mark as a source. It is extremely unlikely that one of the original Twelve would depend on the work of Mark, who was not an eyewitness to the events he describes.

The oldest apparent reference to the Gospel's authorship is that of Papias (c. 140 CE), whom Eusebius quotes: "Matthew compiled the Sayings [Greek, *logia*] in the Aramaic language, and everyone translated them as well as he could" (*History* 3.39.16). Whereas scholars once believed that Matthew's Gospel was first written in Aramaic by the apostle who was formerly a tax collector, modern analysts point out that we have no evidence of an earlier Aramaic version of the Gospel. Papias's use of *logia* may refer to an early collection of Jesus' sayings compiled by someone named Matthew. Or it may allude to a list of messianic prophecies from the Hebrew Bible that a Christian scribe assembled to show that Jesus' life was foretold in Scripture. Most scholars do not believe that Papias's description applies to our canonical Gospel of Matthew.

The author remains unknown (we call him Matthew to avoid confusion), but scholarly analysis of his work gives us some insight into his theological intentions and distinctive interests. Thoroughly versed in a Greek edition of the Hebrew Bible, the writer may refer to himself or to a "school" of early Christian teachers when he states: "Therefore every scribe who has been trained for the kingdom of heaven is like the master of a household who brings out of his treasure what is new [Jesus' teaching] and what is old [the Torah and Prophets]" (13:52–53). To him, Jesus' message is the legitimate outgrowth of Torah interpretation.

Date and Place of Composition

The oldest Christian document to quote what appear to be some verses from Matthew (or from an oral tradition similar to that contained in the Gospel) is a letter from Ignatius, who was bishop of **Antioch** in Syria about 110–115 CE. The Gospel text itself implies that it was written after the destruction of Jerusalem (apparently referred to in 22:7) and after the split between the synagogue and the church, which took place in the decades following 70 CE. (9:35; 10:17; 12:9; 13:54). Many scholars conclude that the Gospel was composed about 85 CE in Antioch, a major Jewish-Christian center. Of all the Evangelists, Matthew accords the highest honor to Peter (16:16–19), who had considerable influence in that city (Gal. 2:11–14; cf. Acts 11:19–26; 15:2–35).

Matthew's Structure and Themes

Using Mark as his primary source, Matthew incorporates about 90 percent of the earlier Gospel into his account. Into Mark's narrative framework, he inserts five large blocks of teaching material, the most famous of which is the Sermon on the Mount (5:1–7:29). The other four are instructions to the Twelve Apostles (10:1–42), parables on the kingdom (13:1–51), instructions to the church (Matthew's Jewish-Christian community) (18:1–35), and warnings of the Final Judgment (23:1–25:46). Matthew also frames his account of Jesus' public ministry (largely borrowed from Mark) with an introductory genealogy and narrative of Jesus' infancy (1:1–2:23) and a concluding narrative of two postresurrection appearances, the first to women near Jerusalem and the second to "eleven disciples" (minus the traitor Judas) in Galilee (28:8–20).

Like the author of Luke, Matthew draws heavily on Q, the supposed collection of Jesus' sayings that the two share but that are absent from Mark. Some of the material appearing in the five teaching sections, however, is peculiar to Matthew, such as the parables about weeds growing in a grain field (13:24–30) and the unforgiving debtor (18:23–25). Scholars label this material unique to Matthew as **M** (Matthean). M includes several parables, such as the stories about the vineyard laborers (20:1–16), and many of Jesus' kingdom pronouncements. Matthew's expression the "kingdom of heaven" means the same thing as Mark's "kingdom of God," but—following accepted Jewish tradition—Matthew avoids referring directly to God wherever possible.

Matthew's Editing of Mark

Readers can discover some of Matthew's particular theological views by observing how he edits Mark, his chief source. While retaining almost all of Mark's narrative, he modifies or omits passages that do not reflect the Torah-observant principles of his own Jewish-Christian community. He keeps Mark's story about dietary restrictions but deletes Mark's sweeping conclusion that Jesus "declared all foods clean" (Matt. 15:15–20; cf. Mark 7:14–23). Matthew also changes the absolute prohibition against divorce to permit it in cases of "unchastity [sexual misconduct]" (Matt. 5:31–32; cf. Mark 10:11–12).

Matthew further revises Mark to emphasize Jesus' ability to work miracles and to underscore the supernatural character of his mission (see Box 31.3). In his version of Jesus' return to Nazareth, Matthew changes Mark's observation that Jesus "could do no deed of power there" (Mark 6:5) to a statement that "he did not do many deeds of power there" (Matt. 13:58), eliminating the implication that Jesus had any limit to his superhuman abilities (see Figure 31.2). He similarly omits

FIGURE 31.2 In *Christ with the Sick Around Him, Receiving Little Children,* by Rembrandt (1606–1669), healing light radiates from the central figure of Jesus and creates a protective circle of illumination around those whom he cures.

Mark's definition of John's baptism as a rite performed in "repentance for the forgiveness of sins" (Matt. 3:2, 6, 11; cf. Mark 1:4), transferring the exact phrase to his account of the Last Supper (26:26–28). Matthew may have made this change to ensure that readers understood that "forgiveness of sins" comes not from John's baptism but from Jesus' redemptive death.

Matthew's editing of the Passion narrative also intensifies the supernatural element. In Gethsemane, the Matthean Jesus reminds his persecutors that he has the power to call up thousands of angels to help him (26:53), a claim absent from Mark. Matthew's Jesus allows himself to be arrested only to fulfill Scripture (26:54).

Matthew also revises Mark's crucifixion account, inserting several miracles to highlight the event's cosmic significance. To Mark's noonday darkness and the rending of the Temple curtain, Matthew adds that a Good Friday earthquake shook the earth so violently that graves opened, allowing suddenly resurrected "saints" (holy persons) to rise and walk the streets of Jerusalem (27:50–53), a spectacular phenomenon that no other Evangelist mentions. Matthew introduces yet another earthquake into his description of the first Easter morning, stating that the women disciples arrive at Jesus' tomb in time to see a divine being descend and roll away the stone blocking the tomb entrance. Mark's linen-clad youth becomes an angel before whom the Roman guards quake in terror (28:1–4). What Mark's account may only imply, Matthew typically makes explicit, ensuring that readers will not miss the hand of God in these happenings. Nor does Matthew leave the Galilean women wondering and frightened at the empty sepulcher. Instead of being too terrified to report what they have seen, in Matthew's account, the women joyously rush away to inform the male disciples (28:8; cf. Mark 16:8). In this revision, the women set the right example by immediately proclaiming the good news of Jesus' triumph over death (28:19).

BOX 31.3   Examples of Matthew's Editing of Markan Material

(Matthew's changes are printed in **boldface**.)

John Baptizes Jesus

MARK 1:9–11	MATTHEW 3:13–17
In those days Jesus came from Nazareth of Galilee and was baptized by John in the Jordan.	Then Jesus came from Galilee to John at the Jordan, to be baptized by him. **John would have prevented him, saying, "I need to be baptized by you, and do you come to me?" But Jesus answered him, "Let it be so now; for it is proper for us in this way to fulfill all righteousness." Then he consented.** And when he had been baptized, just as he came up from the water, suddenly the heavens were opened
And just as he was coming up out of the water, he saw the heavens torn apart and the Spirit descending like a dove on him. And a voice came from heaven, "You are my Son, the Beloved, with you I am well pleased."	to him and he saw the Spirit of God descending like a dove and alighting on him. And a voice from heaven said, **"This is my Son,** the Beloved, with whom I am well pleased."
In revising Mark's baptism narrative, Matthew gives John a speech emphasizing Jesus' superiority to the Baptist. By having John say that Jesus should be baptizing him, Matthew indirectly explains why Israel's Messiah submitted to John's cleansing ritual. Matthew also deletes Mark's statement that	John baptized repentant sinners (Mark 1:4), transferring the exact phrase "for the forgiveness of sins" to Jesus' lips at the Last Supper (Matt. 26:28). He also edits the heavenly voice: Instead of addressing Jesus personally ("you are"), it proclaims him publicly: *"This is* my Son."

Jesus' Neighbors Reject Him on His Return to Nazareth

MARK 6:1–6	MATTHEW 13:54–58
He . . . came to his hometown, and his disciples followed him. On the Sabbath he began to teach in the synagogue, and many who heard him were astonished. They said, "Where did this man get all this? What is this wisdom that has been given to him? What deeds of power are being done by his hands! Is this not the carpenter, the son of Mary, and brother of James and Joses and Judas and Simon, and are not his sisters here with us?" And they took offense at him. . . . And he could do no deed of power there, except that he laid hands on a few sick people and cured them. And he was amazed at their unbelief.	He came to his hometown and began to teach the people in their synagogue, so that they were astounded and said, "Where did this man get this wisdom, and these deeds of power? Is not this **the carpenter's son. Is not his mother called Mary?** And are not his brothers James and Joseph and Simon and Judas? Where then did this man get all this?" And they took offense at him. . . . **And he did not do many deeds of power there, because of their unbelief.**

The Infancy Narrative

Except for Matthew and Luke, no New Testament writers refer even briefly to the circumstances surrounding Jesus' birth. Nor do Matthew or Luke allude to Jesus' virginal conception in the main body of their Gospels. In both cases, the infancy narratives are self-contained units that act as detachable prefaces to the central account of Jesus' public ministry.

Mathew constructs his infancy narrative (1:18–2:23) with phrases from Greek versions of the Hebrew Bible. Jesus is born in Bethlehem to fulfill Micah 5:2 and to a

In editing the account of Jesus' unsatisfactory encounter with his former neighbors in Nazareth, Matthew makes several changes and deletions. Besides omitting Mark's reference to the Sabbath, to the "few" deeds Jesus performed there, and to Jesus' apparent surprise at the lack of trust shown him, he replaces the phrase "the son of Mary" with "the carpenter's son," thereby eliminating any suggestion that Jesus was illegitimate. He also changes Mark's admission that Jesus "*could do* no deed of power there" to "*did not do* many deeds of power there."

Jesus' Stilling of a Storm

MARK 6:45–52	Matthew 14:22–33
[Immediately after miraculously feeding the multitudes who had gathered to hear him preach, Jesus sends the disciples by boat across the Sea of Galilee to Bethsaida.] When he saw that they [the disciples] were straining at the oars against an adverse wind, he came toward them early in the morning, walking on the sea. But when they saw him walking on the sea, they thought it was a ghost and cried out, for they all saw him and were terrified. But immediately he spoke to them and said, "Take heart, it is I; do not be afraid." Then he got into the boat with them and the wind ceased. And they were utterly astounded, for they did not understand about the loaves, but their hearts were hardened.	When evening came, he was there [onshore] alone, but by this time the boat, battered by the waves, was far from the land, for the wind was against them. And early in the morning he came walking towards them on the sea. But when the disciples saw him walking on the sea, they were terrified, saying "It is a ghost!" And they cried out in fear. But immediately Jesus spoke to them and said, "Take heart, it is I; do not be afraid." **Peter answered him, "Lord, if it is you, command me to come to you on the water." He said, "Come." So Peter got out of the boat, started walking on the water, and came toward Jesus. But when he noticed the strong wind, he became frightened, and beginning to sink, he cried out, "Lord, save me!" Jesus immediately reached out his hand and caught him, saying to him, "You of little faith, why did you doubt?"** When they got into the boat, the wind ceased. And those in the boat **worshiped him, saying, "Truly you are the Son of God."**

Besides adding the episode involving Peter's impulsive attempts to imitate Jesus' power over nature, Matthew radically changes the disciples' reaction to their Master's miraculous control of the sea, symbol of primal chaos (Gen. 1:1–3). The Markan disciples fail to perceive Jesus' divinity in his ability to subdue wind and storm—Mark says that "their hearts were hardened," using the same expression that the Exodus writer used to describe Pharaoh's resistance to Yahweh's will (cf. Exod. 8:32). By contrast, Matthew's disciples immediately recognize Jesus as "Son of God" and "worshiped him."

virgin to fulfill the Greek translation of Isaiah 7:14. Whereas Matthew's Greek source uses the term *parthenos* (virgin), the Hebrew text of Isaiah merely states that a "young woman (*almah*)" will give birth. Foreshadowing that many non-Jews will worship the child, Matthew describes the nativity visit of foreign astrologers, "wise men" from Persia or Babylonia who apparently had concluded from a horoscope of Judah that its king was then due to appear. Roused by the news, King Herod—the Roman-appointed ruler of Judea—attempts to eliminate a potential rival by ordering the slaughter of all Bethlehem children under the age of two (2:1–18). Herod's "massacre of the innocents" is intended to parallel a similar tradition about Moses' infancy, when an Egyptian pharaoh ordered the death of newborn Hebrew boys (Exod. 1:8–2:25). Matthew also cites this incident as fulfillment of a prophecy in Jeremiah.

The holy family's flight into Egypt to escape Herod's wrath is similarly explained as a fulfillment of Hosea 11:1 ("out of Egypt I called my son"). Because Hosea's statement refers not to the Messiah's infancy but to Israel's Exodus under Moses and is clearly cited out of context, many scholars doubt the historicity of the entire Herod episode. Scholars question whether Matthew, in his eagerness to find or create analogies between Moses and Jesus, the dominant figures of the Old and New Covenants, has not invented some aspects of the infancy story. The only other Gospel account of Jesus' birth (Luke 2) does not mention either Herod's plot or the Egyptian journey, nor does Josephus or any other contemporary source refer to Herod's alleged murder of Jewish infants.

In fairness to Matthew's use of scriptural "proof texts" to validate Jesus as David's promised heir, it should be noted that biblical **exegesis**—analysis and interpretation of a written document—was in first-century Palestine a very different discipline from what it is today. Modern critics respect the integrity of a text, endeavoring to discover its primary meaning by placing it in its original social and historical setting. In Matthew's time, however, every word, sometimes even every letter, of Scripture was regarded as having an inspired meaning. In this view, a passage's original context did not matter if a single word or phrase seemed applicable to the interpreter's theological purpose. Essene scribes, for example, did not hesitate to interpret Israel's ancient prophets as foretelling events that took place in their own time and in their divinely favored community (see Chapter 29).

Matthew's Portrait of Jesus

Matthew begins his narrative of Jesus' adult life (3:1–4:25) at exactly the same point as Mark (1:1–13), giving no information about Jesus' experiences during the thirty years (Luke 3:1, 23) that separate his birth from his baptism. He does, however, greatly expand Mark's brief allusion to Jesus' temptation in the Judean desert, presenting a dialogue between Jesus and Satan that is virtually identical to that in Luke, albeit in a slightly different order (Matt. 4:1–11; Luke 4:1–13). Apparently drawing on Q, their shared source, both Matthew and Luke use the

incident to clarify the nature of Jesus' messianic role. When, in the third temptation, Satan attempts to undermine Jesus' understanding of his mission, he offers to make God's son master of all the world's kingdoms—if Jesus will but "fall down and worship" the evil one. The lure of political power—perhaps the popular concept of a Davidic messiah as conquering hero—Jesus firmly rejects. To rule as Alexander and Augustus—or King David—had ruled would inevitably entail violence and bloodshed, a use of the devil's methods that honors not God but Satan.

First Major Discourse: The Sermon on the Mount

After showing his hero rejecting some of the functions then commonly associated with a Davidic Messiah, Matthew demonstrates how radically different Jesus' concept of his messiahship is from the popular expectation of a warrior-king who will deliver Israel from its foreign oppressors. The Sermon on the Mount, which Matthew constructs from widely scattered sayings and the Q material (compare Luke's version of this speech, the Sermon on the Plain, in Luke 6:17–7:1), portrays Jesus' vision of the kingdom as the arts of peace, service, and endurance in doing good. Delivering his ethical instructions in a manner reminiscent of Moses on Mount Sinai, Jesus introduces a revolutionary concept of a "higher righteousness" that transcends a literal reading of the Mosaic Torah to achieve the ethical intent of God's revelation to Israel.

In the sermon's first section, known as the **Beatitudes,** Jesus pronounces a blessing on "the poor in spirit" and "those who hunger and thirst for righteousness" (5:3, 6). Because Luke's version of the Beatitudes applies Jesus' blessings to the literally poor and hungry (see Chapter 32), many scholars think that Matthew has modified the original import of these sayings by "spiritualizing" them. For both Evangelists, however, the Beatitudes express a stark reversal of the world's social values that will prevail in God's kingdom (which, in Matthew, is represented by the church). Whereas society presently exalts the rich, the powerful, and the successful, particularly military leaders victorious in war, Jesus reverses these common value judgments, congratulating those who seek divine justice rather than material acquisitions, as well as the "meek" and the "peacemakers" (5:5, 9). The poor and vulnerable persons whom Jesus blesses here are exactly those to whom he will direct his ministry.

For Matthew's Jewish-Christian community, Jesus' teachings did not replace the Mosaic Law; they intensified it. Rather than refuting Yahweh's Torah commandments, Jesus' explains how his disciples should obey them, emphasizing the essential core of ethical meaning that lies behind each command. Immediately after declaring the Law's unchanging validity (5:17–19), Matthew introduces a set of Jesus' sayings, known as the **antitheses,** that are found only in his Gospel. Employing a rhetorical formula, Jesus makes an initial statement (the thesis), which he then follows with an apparently opposing idea (the antithesis). In this series, he appears to contrast biblical tradition with his own authoritative opinion. As scholars have pointed out, however, Jesus does not contradict the Torah rules, but rather interprets them to reveal the human motivation that often causes them to be broken:

> You have heard that it was said to those of ancient times, "You shall not murder"; and "whoever murders shall be liable to judgment." But I say to you that if you are angry with a brother or sister, you will be liable to judgment; and if you insult a brother or sister, you will be liable to the council; and if you say, "You fool," you will be liable to the hell of fire [Gehenna].

(Matt. 5:5:21–22)

Anger, the emotion triggering murderous rage, must be rooted out, for if it leads to overt behavior, it will bring punishment both human and divine. Instead of allowing resentment to grow into rage, Jesus' followers must make every effort to reconcile with potential enemies (5:23–26).

In another antithesis, Jesus looks beyond the literal application of a Torah command to seek a more effective way to obey the principle it embodies:

> You have heard that it was said, "An eye for an eye and a tooth for a tooth." But I say to you, Do not resist an evildoer. But if anyone strikes you on the right cheek, turn the other also; and if anyone wants to sue you and take your coat, give him your cloak as well; and if anyone forces you to go one mile, go also the second mile.

(Matt. 5:38–41)

The *lex talionis,* or law of retaliation, that Jesus quotes before giving his three examples of recommended behavior is central to the Mosaic concept of justice and appears in three different Torah books (Exod. 21:23–25; Lev. 24:19–20; Deut. 19:21). Although it may seem harsh by today's standards, in ancient society, the *lex talionis* served to limit acts of revenge: Simply receiving an injury did not entitle one to kill the offending party. In the world inhabited by the generally poor and powerless members of Jesus' audience (the "you" whom he addresses), however, retaliatory actions of any kind against those who exploited them automatically led to severe punishments, including torture and death. Recognizing that the law's intent was to curb violence, Jesus goes beyond its literal application to demand that his listeners give up their traditional right to retaliate in kind.

Many commentators suggest that Jesus' main objective was probably to discover and apply the essential precepts contained in the Mosaic tradition. Matthew's version of the "golden rule" expresses this view: His Jesus asks that "in everything do to others as you would have them do to you," a principle that sums up "the law and the prophets" (7:12; cf. Luke 6:31). Similarly, after reciting the Torah injunctions to love God and neighbor wholeheartedly, Jesus declares: "On these two commandments hang all the law and the prophets" (Matt. 22:34–40; cf. Mark 12:28–34).

In Matthew's final antithesis, Jesus expands on this fundamental perception, contrasting the command to love one's neighbor (Lev. 19:18) with the apparently common assumption that it is permissible to hate an enemy (5:43–48). Again, he demands a "higher righteousness" that will imitate God's own character, revealed in the daily operation of physical nature, where he lavishes his gifts equally on both deserving and undeserving people:

> But I say to you, Love your enemies and pray for those who persecute you, so that you may be children of your Father in heaven, for he makes his sun rise on the evil and on the good, and sends rain on the righteous and the unrighteous. For if you love [only] those who love you, what reward do you have? . . . Be perfect, therefore, as your heavenly father is perfect.

(Matt. 5:44–48)

"Perfect" in loving generosity, the Father provides the supreme model for Jesus' disciples to imitate, refashioning them in his image. In seeking first "the kingdom of God and his righteousness" (6:33), they personally do not pass "judgment" on others, for judgmental attitudes blind people to their own defects (7:1–5). Instead, disciples must focus on the infinite graciousness of the Father, who endlessly gives "good things to those who ask him" (7:9–11).

The sermon ends with Jesus' parable about the advantages of building one's life firmly on the rock of his teachings (7:24–27), after which, Matthew reports, the crowds were "astounded" because, unlike the "scribes" (Torah instructors), "he taught them as one having [personal] authority" (7:28). Matthew's phrase "when Jesus had finished saying these things," or a variation thereof, marks the conclusion of each of the four other blocks of teaching material in his Gospel (11:1; 13:53; 19:1; 26:1)

BOX 31.4   **Matthew's Use of Hell: Some Biblical Concepts of the Afterlife**

Gehenna

The term that many English-language Bibles translate as "hell" is "Gehenna" (*gehinnom*). This term, which Matthew uses frequently (5:22, 29–30; 10:28; 23:15, 33), originally referred not to a place of punishment in the afterlife but to a specific geographical location, a ravine near Jerusalem. A valley bordering Israel's capital city on the southwest, Gehenna was named for the "sons of Hinnom [*ge ben(e) hinnom*]," the biblical name for an ancient Canaanite group that occupied the site before King David captured Jerusalem about 1000 BCE. Gehenna had an evil reputation as the place where humans were sacrificed and burned as offerings to false gods, a practice that the Israelite prophets strongly condemned (Jer. 7:31; 19:11; 32:35; cf. 2 Kings 23:10; 2 Chron. 28:3; 33:6).

In time, perhaps influenced by Persian ideas about fiery punishments in the next world, some Jewish writers made Hinnom's valley (Gehenna) the symbol of God's eschatological judgment, where the wicked would suffer after death (1 Enoch 26:4; 27:2–3). A potent image of alienation from God, the earthly Gehenna was eventually associated with mythic concepts of an Underworld "lake of fire," the future abode of unrepentant sinners (2 Esd. 7:36; Rev. 20).

Sheol and Hades

The concept of eternal punishment does not occur in the Hebrew Bible, which uses the term *Sheol* to designate a dismal subterranean region where the dead, good and bad alike, linger only as feeble shadows (see the discussion of Sheol in Box 23.1). When Hellenistic Jewish scribes rendered the Bible into Greek, they used the word *Hades* to translate *Sheol*, bringing a whole new mythological association to the idea of posthumous existence. In ancient Greek myth, Hades, named after the gloomy deity who ruled over it, was originally similar to the Hebrew Sheol, a dark place underground in which all the dead, regardless of individual merit, were indiscriminately housed (see Homer's *Odyssey*, Book 11). By the Hellenistic period, however, Hades had become compartmentalized into separate regions. These included Elysium, a paradise for the virtuous, and Tartarus, a place of punishment for the wicked. Influenced by philosophers such as Pythagoras and Plato and by the mystery cults (see Chapter 28), Greek religious thought eventually made a direct connection between people's behavior in this life and their destiny in the next: Good actions earned them bliss, whereas injustices brought fearful penalties.

In general, pre-Christian mythologies and other nonbiblical sources supply most of the frightening imagery for such celebrated literary works as Dante's *Inferno* and Milton's *Paradise Lost*, as well as the "hellfire" sermons of many contemporary preachers. The word *hell*, not found in the Bible, commemorates Hel, the fierce Norse goddess who reigned over the Underworld.

Second Major Discourse: Instructions to the Twelve Apostles

In his second major collection of ethical teachings, Matthew presents Jesus' instructions to his twelve chief disciples (listed by name in 10:2–4). Ordering the Twelve to preach only to fellow Israelites, Matthew's Jesus has them spread the same apocalyptic message of imminent judgment that the author ascribes to both the Baptist (3:2) and to Jesus at the outset of his career (4:17). A strong eschatological tone pervades the entire discourse. Followers are to be loyal when tested because destruction in **Gehenna** awaits the unfaithful. The New Testament name for a geographical location, the "Valley of Hinnom," Gehenna is commonly rendered as "hell" in English translations, although it is uncertain that the later Christian notion of a posthumous place of punishment accurately expresses the original meaning of Gehenna

(see Box 31.4). A site of human sacrifice in Old Testament times (Jer. 7:32; 1 Kings 11:7), the Valley of Hinnom later housed a garbage dump that was kept permanently burning, a literal place of annihilation for "both soul and body" (Matt. 10:28; 18:8; 25:30, 46).

Equally striking is the statement that the Twelve will not have completed their circuit of Palestine "before the Son of Man comes" (10:23). Writing more than half a century after the events he describes, Matthew surprisingly retains a prophecy that was not fulfilled, at least not in historical fact. The author's inclusion of this eschatological prediction indicates that he may not have understood it literally. Matthew may have regarded the "Son of Man" as already spiritually present in the missionary activity of the church. If so, this may suggest that many of Matthew's other references to "the end of the age" and Jesus' Parousia (24:1–25:46) are also to be understood metaphorically.

Third Major Discourse: Parables on the Kingdom

Matthew frames Jesus' third discourse with his version of Jesus' alienation from his family (12:46–50; cf. Mark 3:31–35) and Jesus' rejection by the citizens of Nazareth (13:54–58; Mark 6:1–6). The author divides Jesus' parable teachings into two distinct episodes, the first public and the second private (13:10–23). Although only the Twelve are initiated into the secrets of God's rule, Matthew softens Mark's explanation of Jesus' reasons for using parables in public. Instead of employing figures of speech to *prevent* understanding (Mark 4:11–12), Matthew argues that Jesus speaks metaphorically *because* most people have the wrong attitude and unconsciously shut their mental eyes and ears (13:11–15; cf. Isa. 6:9–10). Matthew's version of the parable lesson explicitly claims that the Twelve do understand Jesus' teaching, thus eliminating Mark's view of the disciples' chronic stupidity.

To Mark's original collection of kingdom parables, Matthew adds several comparisons in which the kingdom is likened to a buried treasure, a priceless pearl, a harvest of fish, and a field in which both grain and weeds grow together (13:24–30, 36–50). The last two introduce a distinctly Matthean concept: The "kingdom," which Matthew believes is manifest in the earthly church, consists of a mixture of good and bad elements that will not be separated completely until the last day. The same theme reappears in Matthew's version of the parable about ungrateful guests (22:1–13; cf. Luke 14:16–23).

One of Matthew's most celebrated additions to Mark's narrative appears in Chapter 16, where Peter recognizes Jesus' identity (16:13–29) (see Figure 31.3). Matthew's Peter not only acknowledges Jesus as Israel's Messiah but also identifies him as "Son of the living God" (a title absent in Mark). Jesus' declaration that Peter is the rock upon which Jesus will build his church appears only in Matthew, as does the promise

FIGURE 31.3 The ruins of Capernaum, a fishing village on the northwest shore of the Sea of Galilee, reveal a setting in which Jesus was said to be "at home" (Mark 2:1, 15). Sheltering about 1,500 inhabitants during the first century CE, Capernaum's houses were generally small, crudely built of rough stone blocks and roofed with thatch. Excavations of a first-century house church there, its walls bearing graffiti by Christian pilgrims, suggest that it incorporates the remnants of Peter's simple dwelling.

to award Peter spiritual powers that both heaven and earth will honor. Despite his singling Peter out as foremost among the apostles, Matthew retains Mark's tradition that Peter fundamentally misunderstands the nature of Jesus' messiahship. When Peter attempts to dissuade Jesus from a decision that will lead to his death in Jerusalem, Jesus again ironically addresses the apostle as "Satan" (16:21–23).

Fourth Major Discourse: Instructions to the Church

In Chapter 18, Matthew assembles various sayings of Jesus and applies them to the Christian community of the writer's generation. Taken together, Chapters 10 and 18 form a simple manual of instruction for the early church. The author skillfully combines numerous small literary units to achieve his intended effect. A brief glimpse of the disciples' squabbling for power (18:1–2) introduces opposing images of a powerless child and a drowning man (18:2–7), which are quickly followed by descriptions of self-blinding and the flames of Gehenna (18:8–9). The variety of literary forms gathered here makes the author's prescription for an ideal Christian community intensely vivid. The writer's devices include hyperbole (exaggeration for rhetorical effect), parable (the lost sheep and the unforgiving debtor) (18:12–14, 23–35), advice on supervising troublesome people (18:15–17), prophetic promises (18:10, 18–20), and direct commands (18:22). In Matthew's view of the church, service, humility, and endless forgiveness are the measure of leadership. Practicing the spirit of Torah mercy, the church is the earthly expression of divine rule (18:23–35), a visible manifestation of God's kingdom.

In regulating the community, Matthew gives individual congregations the right to exclude or ostracize disobedient members (18:15–17). During later centuries, this power of *excommunication* was to become a formidable weapon in controlling both belief and behavior. The same authority accorded Peter in Jesus' famous "keys of the kingdom" speech (16:16–20) is also given to individual church leaders (18:18).

Fifth Major Discourse: Warnings of Final Judgment

An Attack on Jewish Leadership   The fifth and final block of teaching material summarizes the Matthean Jesus' adverse judgment on Jerusalem, particularly its Temple and religious establishment (Chs. 23–25). It opens with a blistering denunciation of the scribes and Pharisees—professional transmitters and interpreters of the law—upon whom Jesus is pictured as heaping "seven woes," perhaps corresponding to the curses on a disobedient Israel listed in Deuteronomy 28. According to Matthew, Jesus blames the Pharisees and their associates for every guilty act—every drop of innocent blood shed—in Israel's entire history. He condemns the religious leadership to suffer for their generation's collective wrongdoing, as well as that of their distant ancestors.

Matthew implies that the Roman devastation of Jerusalem in 70 CE, an event that occurred during the author's lifetime, is tangible proof of God's wrath toward Israel (23:35–36). Matthew intensifies this theme in his version of Jesus' trial before Pilate (Ch. 27). Only in Matthew does a Jerusalem crowd, demanding Jesus' crucifixion, hysterically invite the Deity to avenge Jesus' blood upon them *and their children* (27:25). Matthew further revises Mark's Passion narrative by adding that Pilate, symbol of imperial Rome, washed his hands of responsibility for Jesus' death—even while ordering Jesus' execution (27:24). All four Gospel writers shift the blame from the Roman government to the Jewish leadership, but only Matthew extends responsibility to the Jews' as-yet-unborn descendants.

Many commentators find an ethical paradox in Matthew's vindictive attitude toward his fellow Jews who did not accept Jesus as the national Messiah. Earlier in his Gospel, Matthew presents Jesus as abolishing the ancient law of retaliation (the *lex talionis*) (5:38–40), emphasizing instead the necessity of practicing infinite forgiveness (6:12, 14–16; 18:21–35) and exercising mercy (5:7). In dealing with his church's opponents, however, Matthew judges without compassion, apparently regarding Jewish rejection of his Messiah as falling beyond the tolerable limits of charity. The author, in effect, reintroduces the old law of vengeance that Jesus himself repudiated. Historically, the consequences of New Testament writers attributing collective guilt to the Jewish people helped fuel the waves of anti-Semitism that repeatedly swept through the Western world for centuries afterward. Throughout Europe, Jews were indiscriminately persecuted as "Christ-killers," often with the blessing of church authorities.

In the Holocaust of World War II, Nazi Germany led a campaign of genocide against European Jews, killing approximately 6 million men, women, and children. Since then, a number of church leaders—Catholic, Protestant, and Eastern Orthodox—have publicly condemned the practice of anti-Semitism. In 1974, the Roman Catholic Church officially reminded Christendom that modern Jews are not responsible for Jesus' crucifixion. In the field of contemporary popular culture, however, such films as Mel Gibson's *Passion of the Christ* have helped reignite age-old prejudices.

The Fall of Jerusalem and the Parousia The second part of Jesus' fifth discourse is based largely on Mark 13, the prediction of Jerusalem's impending destruction. Whereas Mark states that the disciples asked only about when the Temple would fall (Mark 13:1–4), Matthew expands the disciples' question to include an eschatological inquiry into the "end of the age" and Jesus' Second Coming (the Parousia) (24:1–3). Jesus' reply is a good illustration of how first-century Jewish eschatology was incorporated into the Christian tradition.

Matthew's presentation of the "sign" leading to Jesus' reappearance is a complex mixture of first-century historical events, such as the Jewish uprising against Rome, and prophetic images from the Hebrew Bible, particularly Daniel, Joel, and Zechariah. All three Synoptic writers link the Jewish Revolt (66–73 CE) with supernatural portents of End time and Jesus' Parousia. Mark, the first to make this association of events, seems to have written at a time when the revolt had already begun (he refers to "wars and rumors of wars" in 13:7–8) and Jerusalem was about to fall. These cataclysmic events he called "the beginning of the birth pangs" of the end of history as we know it. Both Matthew and Luke (but not John) follow Mark's lead and connect these military and political upheavals with persecutions of believers, perhaps allusions to Nero's fiendish treatment of Roman Christians (c. 64–65 CE) or to Zealot violence against Jewish Christians who refused to support the revolt. The Synoptic authors agree that attacks on the church, then a tiny minority of the Greco-Roman population, are of critical importance. The sufferings of the Christian community will bring God's vengeance on all humanity.

Matthew follows Mark in referring to the mysterious "desolating sacrilege" as a warning to flee Judea (24:14), perhaps echoing a tradition that some Jewish Christians had escaped destruction by leaving the holy city and seeking refuge in the town of Pella, east of the Jordan River. In his version of Mark's eschatological prediction, however, Luke omits all reference to the "sacrilege" and substitutes an allusion to Roman armies besieging Jerusalem (Luke 21:20–24).

Both Mark and Matthew are aware that in the white heat of eschatological fervor there were "many" false reports of the Messiah's return (Mark 13:21–23; Matt. 24:23–27). Some Christians must have experienced crushing disappointment when their prophets' "inspired" predictions of Jesus' reappearance failed to materialize. Thus, both Evangelists caution that even "the Son" does not know the exact date of the Parousia (Mark 13:32; Matt. 24:36). Matthew adds that when the Son does return, his coming will be unmistakable in its universality, "as the lightning comes from the east and flashes as far as the west" (24:27).

Matthew preserves the "double vision" nature of the Parousia found in Mark. Jesus' "coming" will be preceded by graphic "signs" that it is near (24:21–22, 29–35); at the same time, he will come without warning and when least expected (24:42–44). Although contradictory, both concepts apparently existed concurrently in the early church, which was deeply influenced by eschatological thinking (cf. 1 Thess. 5:1–5).

Parables of Jesus' Delayed Return Although Matthew probably wrote at least fifteen years after Mark's Gospel first circulated, he retains the Markan tradition that persons who knew Jesus would live to see his predictions come true (24:34; Mark 13:30). Matthew does, however, modify the sense of imminence that Mark conveys, partly by adding a series of parables that feature delays and periods of waiting to his prophecies of Jesus' return. Beginning in 24:45, Matthew assembles a series of four parables about masters or bridegrooms who, after a prolonged absence, reappear unexpectedly. The first parable contrasts two servants, one of whom abuses his fellow employees until their master suddenly returns to punish him (24:45–51)—a clear warning to church members to treat others honorably. The parable about a bridegroom who delays his appearance until "midnight" similarly contrasts two kinds of believers: those who are alert and prepared for the wedding event and those who are not (25:1–13).

In the parable of the talents, an absent master's servants invest huge sums of money for him and are then unexpectedly called to account for their actions (25:14–30). The fourth parable, the most clearly eschatological, is a scene of cosmic judgment, in which the "Son of Man," now enthroned in "glory," appears to judge "nations." Traditionally, "nations" refers to non-Jewish peoples who are not part of the Mosaic covenant, but Matthew may intend the term to include all humanity. In this eschatological vision, Jesus separates the favored "sheep" from rejected "goats" not according to their respective religious beliefs or doctrines, but by their practice—or neglect—of charitable behavior (see Figure 31.4). Jesus praises the sheep for having fed, clothed, and ministered to people in need—"the least of these who are members of my [human] family"—and condemns the "goats" because they consistently failed to help others (25:31–46).

FIGURE 31.4 *Christ Separating Sheep from Goats,* an early-sixth-century mosaic, illustrates Matthew's parable of eschatological judgment (Matt. 25:31–46). At his Parousia (Second Coming), an enthroned Jesus, flanked by two angels, divides all humanity into two mutually exclusive groups. The sheep are gathered in the favored position at Jesus' right hand, whereas the goats, at Jesus' left, are condemned to outer darkness for their failure to help others.

By adding these four parables of delayed judgment to his expansion of Mark 13 and by linking them to "the kingdom" (25:1), Matthew shifts the apocalyptic emphasis from expectations about the Parousia to the functions and duties of the church. While awaiting his return, Jesus' followers are to remain alert and to busy themselves in good works. Whereas Matthew places the parables in the context of Jesus' delayed Parousia, Luke makes these same four narratives a part of Jesus' pre-Jerusalem ministry (cf. Matt. 24:43–44 with Luke 12:39–40; Matt. 24:45–51 with Luke 12:42–46; and Matt. 25:14–30 with Luke 19:12–27).

The Passion Story and Resurrection

Matthew retells the story of Jesus' last two days on earth (Thursday and Friday of Holy Week) with the same grave and solemn tone we find in Mark. To the Gospel writers, Jesus of Nazareth's suffering, death, and resurrection are not only the most important events in world history but also the crucial turning point in humanity's relation to God. Although Matthew's Passion narrative (26:1–28:20) closely follows Mark's sequence of events, he adds new details, probably drawn from the oral tradition of his community. He emphasizes the treachery of Judas Iscariot and links it to the fulfillment of a passage in Jeremiah, although the relevant text actually appears in Zechariah (Matt. 26:14–15; 20–25, 47–50; 27:3–10; cf. Jer. 32:6–13; Zech. 11:12–13). Matthew reintroduces the theme of a warning dream, used frequently in the birth narrative, in a brief story about Pilate's wife, who, frightened by a dream about Jesus, urges her husband to "have nothing to do with that innocent man" (27:19).

Matthew generally follows Mark's account of Jesus' burial and the women's discovery of the empty tomb, but he adds a narrative in which some Pharisees persuade

FIGURE 31.5 Located south of Jerusalem, the first-century burial cave of Midras, with its circular stone that rolls laterally to seal the tomb entrance, resembles the Gospel descriptions of Jesus' sepulcher. Several sites near Jerusalem claim to be Jesus' burial place.

Pilate to place a military guard at Jesus' sepulcher (see Figure 31.5). In Matthew's expansion of Mark, some Sadducean priests later bribe Pilate's soldiers to say that the disciples secretly removed and hid Jesus' body. These additions probably reflect the angry disputes of Matthew's day, when Christians proclaiming Jesus' resurrection quarreled with Jews who denied it (27:62–66; 28:11–15).

Postresurrection Appearances and the Great Commission. In Mark's Gospel, Jesus promises that after his death he will reappear to the disciples in Galilee (Mark 14:28; 16:7). Considering the degree to which he had emphasized the supernatural aspects of Jesus' deeds throughout his narrative, Matthew's report of the Resurrection is curiously restrained. After briefly recording the women's dawn encounter with the risen Lord, Matthew merely reports that Jesus also appeared to the Eleven at a

prearranged mountain site in Galilee. Even as the disciples "saw" him, however, "some doubted," as if mistrusting the evidence of their own senses. The author seems to imply that absolute proof of an event so contrary to ordinary human experience is impossible.

While providing no details about the nature of Jesus' postresurrection appearances, Matthew ends his Gospel with the "great commission"—Jesus' command to make new disciples throughout the Gentile world (28:16–20). Jesus' order to recruit followers from "all nations" further underscores Matthew's perception that the church has much work to do before Jesus returns. After implying that the author's tiny community had only begun what was to become a vast undertaking, Matthew closes with Jesus' assurance that he "will be with you always, to the end of the age" (28:20).

QUESTIONS FOR DISCUSSION AND REVIEW

1. Why do scholars call the first three accounts of Jesus' life (Matthew, Mark, and Luke) the "Synoptic Gospels"? Define the "Synoptic Problem."

2. Explain why most scholars favor the "two-source" hypothesis, and describe the relationship of Mark to the other two Synoptic Gospels. What was the hypothetical document called Q, and what role do scholars think it played in the composition of Matthew and Luke?

3. Define and describe the Griesbach theory. How does it differ from the two-source theory? Which of the two hypotheses do you think better explains the similarities and differences among the three Synoptic Gospels?

4. Even if Mark's Gospel is an older work, what qualities of Matthew's Gospel can account for its standing first in the New Testament canon? How does Matthew connect his account with the Hebrew Bible?

5. In adding five blocks of teaching material to Mark's narrative framework, how does Matthew emphasize Jesus' role as an interpreter of the Mosaic Torah? How does Matthew present Jesus' teachings as the standard and guide of the Christian community?

6. Although he emphasizes that Jesus' personal religion is Torah Judaism, Matthew also presents his hero as founder of the church (*ekklesia*). How "Jewish" and Torah-abiding did Matthew intend the church to be? Cite specific passages in Matthew to support your answer.

7. In the Sermon on the Mount (Matt. 5–7), Jesus delivers his most influential ethical teachings, advising his followers to love everyone and "turn the other cheek" when insulted. Explain why you think that this

counsel is primarily a "kingdom ethic"—to be observed after God has established his universal rule—or as a guide to behavior in the present. If, as Jesus advises, Christians do not resist "evil" with force, how can they survive in a violent world? Some leaders, such as Mohandas Gandhi and Martin Luther King, Jr., successfully pursued their goals of social change through nonresistance. How can Jesus' policy of nonviolence be applied to the realm of international politics?

Terms and Concepts to Remember

antitheses	M (Matthew's special
apostle	source)
Beatitudes	parousia
ekklesia	Q (*Quelle*) document
Gehenna	Sermon on the Mount
great commission	Synoptic Gospels
Griesbach theory	Synoptic Problem
lex talionis (law of	two-document (source)
retaliation)	theory

Recommended Reading

The Synoptic Problem

Farmer, W. R. *The Synoptic Problem.* New York: Macmillan, 1964. Argues for the priority of Matthew's Gospel.

Goodacre, Mark. *The Case Against Q: Studies in Markan Priority and the Synoptic Problem.* Harrisburg, PA: Trinity Press International, 2002. Questions the Q hypothesis.

Miller, Robert J., ed. *The Complete Gospels,* 3rd ed. San Francisco: HarperOne, 1994. Contains the complete texts of all known canonical and noncanonical Gospels (except for the recently discovered Gospel of Judas), plus a reconstruction of Q.

Sanders, E. P., and Davies, Margaret. *Studying the Synoptic Gospels.* Philadelphia: Trinity Press International, 1989. A thorough scholarly investigation of the Synoptic Problem, skeptical of Q's existence.

Stein, Robert H. *Studying the Synoptices: Origin and Interpretation,* 2nd ed. Grand Rapids, MI: Baker Academic, 2001. A readable argument supporting the two-document theory.

Streeter, B. H. *The Four Gospels.* London: Macmillan, 1924. A landmark study arguing that Mark is the earliest Gospel and was the principal source for Matthew and Luke.

Tuckett, C. M. "Synoptic Problem." In D. N. Freedman, ed., *The Anchor Bible Dictionary,* Vol. 6, pp. 263–270. New York: Doubleday, 1992. A clear introduction to theories about the interdependence of Mark, Matthew, and Luke

The Gospel of Matthew

Brown, Michael J. "Matthew, Gospel of." In K. D. Sakenfeld, ed., *The New Interpreter's Dictionary of the Bible,* Vol. 3, pp. 839–852. Nashville, TN: Abingdon Press, 2008. A scholarly analysis of the Gospel's probable origins, structure, and theological content.

Brown, R. E. *The Birth of the Messiah: A Commentary on the Infancy Narratives in Matthew and Luke,* 2nd ed. New York: New York: Doubleday, 1993. A thorough analysis of traditions surrounding Jesus' birth.

————. *The Death of the Messiah,* 2 Vols. New York: Doubleday, 1994. An exhaustive analysis of the Gospel accounts of Jesus' arrest, trials, and execution.

Edwards, R. A. *Matthew's Story of Jesus.* Philadelphia. Fortress Press, 1985. A readable introductory study.

Ehrman, Bart D. *Misquoting Jesus: The Story Behind Who Changed the Bible and Why.* San Francisco: HarperOne, 2007. Shows that scribes commonly changed New Testament documents to conform to evolving ideas about Jesus' divinity.

Miller, Robert J. *Born Divine: The Birth of Jesus and Other Sons of God.* Santa Rosa, CA: Polebridge Press, 2003. Compares the infancy stories of Matthew and Luke to other Greco-Roman traditions of miraculous births.

Senior, D. P. *What Are They Saying About Matthew?* New York: Paulist Press, 1983. A survey of critical approaches to interpreting Matthew; a good place to begin.

Verbin, John S.; Kloppenborg, John; and Kloppenborg, S. *Excavating Q: The History and Setting of the Sayings Gospel.* Minneapolis: Fortress Press. An authoritative study of the hypothetical Sayings source.

Wink, Walter. *The Powers That Be: Theology for a New Millennium.* New York: Galilee/Doubleday, 1998. Includes a chapter, "Jesus' Third Way" (between the extremes of violence and passivity), that perceptively interprets Matthew's Sermon on the Mount.

CHAPTER 32

Jesus as a Savior for "All Nations"

The Gospel of Luke

Key Topics/Themes The first part of a two-volume work (Luke-Acts), Luke's Gospel presents Jesus' career not only as history's most crucial event but also as the opening stage of a new historical process—the life of the Christian church—that extends indefinitely into the future (Acts 1–28). Writing for a Greco-Roman audience, Luke emphasizes that Jesus and his disciples, working under the Holy Spirit, are innocent of any crime against Rome and that their religion is a universal faith intended for all people. The parables unique to Luke's Gospel show the unexpected ways in which God's in-breaking kingdom overturns the normal social order and reverses conventional beliefs. After a formal preface and extended nativity account (1:5–2:52), Luke generally follows Mark's order in narrating the Galilean ministry (3:1–9:50). Into Mark's framework, however, he inserts a large body of teaching material, the "greater interpolation" (9:51–18:14), supposedly representing Jesus' counsel as he journeyed to Jerusalem. Luke then returns to Mark for his account of the Jerusalem ministry and Passion story (18:31–23:56). Luke's final chapter reports postresurrection appearances in or near Jerusalem (Ch. 24).

 ## The Gospel of Luke

The Preface to Luke's Gospel

Luke is the only Gospel author to offer an explicit statement about what he intended to accomplish in writing a new version of Jesus' life story. In a formal preface to his account, Luke makes clear that he did not personally know Jesus and that his work depends entirely on secondary sources, including oral traditions and previously existing Gospels:

> Since many have undertaken to set down an orderly account of the events that have been fulfilled among us, just as they were handed on to us by those who from the beginning were eyewitnesses and servants of the word, I too decided, after investigating everything carefully from the very first, to write an orderly account for you, most excellent Theophilus, so that you may know the truth concerning the things about which you have been instructed.

(Luke: 1:1–4)

Although brief, Luke's introduction outlines the general procedures he followed in compiling a Gospel that built on the labors of his predecessors. Acknowledging that "many" writers had already preceded him in documenting Christian origins—the "events" that have taken place "among us" (the Christian community)—Luke also makes clear that he stands some chronological distance from the events he describes. Living perhaps two or three generations after the original "eyewitnesses" and other (later?) "servants of the word," he must use the techniques of a researcher, "investigating everything" about Jesus and his first disciples. His goal is to create "an orderly account"—a narrative that follows accepted Hellenistic literary standards—so that his readers "may know the truth" of the oral teachings they had previously learned.

The author addresses both his Gospel and its sequel, the Book of Acts, to **Theophilus,** about whom nothing is known. Bearing a Greek name meaning "lover of God," Theophilus (whom Luke addresses as "most excellent") may have been a Greek or Roman official, perhaps a wealthy patron who underwrote the expenses of publishing Luke's compositions.

To understand Luke's intent in adding yet another Gospel to those already in existence, it is important to recognize that he was also the only Evangelist to compose an account of the early church, to follow a life of Jesus with a narrative describing what Jesus' followers accomplished after their Master's death. Aware that Christianity had undergone enormous changes during its first few decades—growing from an exclusively Palestinian Jewish movement to a largely Gentile faith in the Greco-Roman world—Luke felt the necessity of retelling Jesus' story in the light of its subsequent impact on non-Jewish society. Composing Luke-Acts as a literary unit, the author then portrays Jesus' ministry as anticipating the missionary activities of the later church (see below).

Luke's Gospel also places Jesus' ministry precisely at the center of human history, his life forming the connecting link between Israel's biblical past and the future age of a multinational Gentile church. Luke views John the Baptist, whose birth story he interweaves with that of Jesus, as both the last of Israel's prophets and the forerunner of the Messiah: "The law and the prophets were in effect until John came; since then the good news of the kingdom of God is proclaimed, and everyone tries to enter it by force" (Luke 16:16).

By making Jesus' life the central act of a three-part drama that begins with Israel and continues with the Christian church, Luke offers a philosophy of history that is important to Christianity's later understanding of its mission. Instead of an apocalyptic End, Jesus' ministry represents a new beginning that establishes a new awareness of God's intentions for humanity. Luke thus ties Jesus' resurrection to the disciples' task of proclaiming the Gospel worldwide (24:44–53; Acts 1:1–8). He creatively modifies an earlier emphasis on eschatological (End time) expectations to focus on the future work of the church. Acts thus portrays the disciples entering a new historical epoch, the age of the church, and thereby extends the new faith's operations indefinitely into the future. Acts concludes not by drawing attention to the Parousia, but by expressing Paul's resolve to concentrate on ministering to the Gentiles (28:27–28)

Authorship and Date

Like Mark, the author of Luke's Gospel did not personally hear any of Jesus' teachings or witness his miraculous deeds. In the Muratorian Canon (list) of New Testament books (compiled about the fourth century CE), a note identifies the writer as **Luke,** "the beloved" physician who accompanied Paul on some of his missionary tours. It also states that Luke did not know Jesus. Irenaeus, a second-century bishop of Lyon in Gaul (France), also refers to the author as a companion of Paul, presumably the same Luke named in several

Pauline letters (Col. 4:14; Philem. 24; cf. 2 Tim. 4:11). Most scholars, however, do not regard the writer of Luke-Acts as Paul's traveling companion, primarily because the author never alludes to Paul's letters or shows him writing to the various congregations the apostle founded. Moreover, although Paul dominates the second half of Acts, Luke only twice refers to him as an apostle, a title for which the historical Paul vigorously fought. Even though the author's identity is not conclusively settled, for convenience we call him Luke.

According to most scholars, Luke-Acts was written well after 70 CE, when Titus demolished Jerusalem (see Figure 32.1). In fact, Luke's Gospel reveals detailed knowledge of the Roman siege (21:20–24) and refers specifically to the Roman method of encircling a town, a military strategy used in the assault on Jerusalem: "Your enemies will set up ramparts and surround you, and hem you in on every side. They will crush you to the ground, you and your children within you, and they will not leave within you one stone upon another" (19:43–44). Luke-Acts apparently was composed at some point after the Jewish wars of 66–73 CE and before about

FIGURE 32.1 This bust shows the emperor Tiberius (ruled 14–37 CE). According to Luke, Jesus was "about thirty years old" when he began his Galilean campaign during the fifteenth year of Tiberius' reign (c. 27–29 CE) (Luke 3:1, 23).

90 CE, when Paul's letters were first collected and published. Many scholas place the Gospel and its sequel in the mid-to-late 80s and favor Ephesus, a Hellenistic city in Asia Minor with a relatively large Christian population, as the place of composition.

Luke's Editing of Mark

Although Luke uses less of Mark's narrative than Matthew, he nonetheless incorporates about 35 percent of Mark's text into his account and generally follows Mark's sequence of events (as opposed to John's Gospel, which has its own distinct chronology; see Chapter 33). Editing Mark more severely than did Matthew, Luke omits several large narrative sections (such as Mark 6:45–8:26 and 9:41–10:12), perhaps to delete repetitive passages and to make room for his own material. Luke's special source, known as **L,** makes up about a third of his Gospel. In addition, Luke brackets Mark's central narrative of Jesus' adult career with his own unique stories of Jesus' infancy (1:5–2:40) and postresurrection appearances (24:1–50). He also includes a distinctive genealogy that differs significantly from that in Matthew, though both writers trace Jesus' ancestry through his "supposed" father Joseph. By taking Jesus' forebears all the way back to Adam, "son of God," Luke universalizes Jesus' role, making him God's agent for all of humanity, and not Israel alone (Luke 3:23–38; cf. Matt. 1:1–18).

The Interpolations Because he produced the longest of the four Gospels and probably wished to fit his narrative onto a single scroll, Luke may have omitted some Markan material to make room for his lengthy additions, which feature two large sections devoted to Jesus' teachings. The first added section, called the "lesser interpolation" (6:20–8:3), includes Luke's version of the Sermon on the Mount, which the author transfers to level ground. Known as the Sermon on the Plain (6:20–49), this collection of sayings apparently draws from the same source that Matthew used, the hypothetical Q document. Instead of assembling Q material into long speeches as Matthew does, however, Luke scatters these sayings through his Gospel. Luke's second major insertion into the Markan framework, the "greater interpolation," is nearly ten chapters long (9:51–18:14). (He returns to the Markan sequence in 18:15.) A miscellaneous compilation of Jesus' parables and pronouncements, this interpolation supposedly represents Jesus' teaching on the road from Galilee to Jerusalem (see below).

Jesus' Return to Nazareth Because we have one of Luke's principal sources, the Gospel of Mark, it is possible to learn something of Luke's authorial intentions by examining the way in which he revises his inherited material. For example, Luke retains Mark's story about Jesus' unsatisfactory return to Nazareth, his hometown, but he rewrites it extensively. First, Luke places Jesus' rejection in Nazareth at the beginning of his ministry (Luke 4:16–30), rather than midway through it as do Mark (6:1–6) and Matthew (13:53–58). This repositioning of the Nazareth episode allows Luke to introduce themes (absent from both Mark and Matthew) that characterize not only his distinctive portrayal of a Spirit-empowered Jesus but also of Jesus' later followers in the Book of Acts. In a dramatic scene at the Nazareth synagogue, Luke shows Jesus reading aloud from a scroll of Isaiah and then declaring that Isaiah's predictions are fulfilled in his work. The "Spirit of the Lord" has "anointed" him to bring "good news to the poor, proclaim "release to the captives," grant freedom to "the oppressed," and give assurance that "the year of the Lord's favor" has at last arrived (4:16–21; cf. Isa. 61:1–4). By pointing out that both Elijah and Elisha applied their miraculous skills to healing foreigners (anticipating Acts' stories about Jewish Christians aiding Gentiles), Jesus so antagonizes his fellow Nazarenes that they try to kill him (4:28–30), an attempt that foreshadows Jesus' later fate in Jerusalem. In Luke's revision, the Nazareth episode thus functions as a model or paradigm of his entire two-volume work.

Because Luke presents Jesus' story as a prophetic model for the work of the early church, the author provides specific parallels between what happens to Jesus and events befalling the disciples in Acts, particularly in their dealings with Roman authorities. The author is aware that Christians faced potentially fatal difficulties in their relations with representatives of the Roman government, largely because their leader had been executed for sedition against Rome. Luke thus emphasizes the political innocence of both Jesus and later missionaries, such as Paul, showing that both men were unjustly prosecuted in Roman courts. In Luke-Acts, both Jesus and Paul undergo two-part trials, first before the Sanhedrin and then before a Roman governor (cf. Luke 22:66–23:25; Acts 22:25–23:19). In describing Jesus' hearing before Pilate, Luke is the only Gospel writer to include an episode in which Jesus also appears before Herod Antipas (Luke 23:6–12)—an incident that parallels and foreshadows Paul's similar hearing before another member of the Herodian dynasty, Herod Agrippa II (Acts 25:13–26:32). Just as the Roman magistrates declare Paul guiltless of any crime against the government (Acts 25:25; 26:30–32), so Pilate exonerates Jesus from the political charge of treason (Luke 23:13–15, 22). Luke's emphasis on Christians' legal innocence may explain why he changes Mark's statement about the Roman soldier's speech at the cross. Instead of perceiving Jesus' divine sonship, the centurion now simply declares: "Certainly this man was innocent" (Luke 23:47; cf. Mark 15:39; Matt. 27:54). For Luke, conscious that the church must avoid an adversarial relationship with Rome if it is to expand and prosper, a theological affirmation of Jesus' divinity is less important than a confirmation that the Master was legally blameless.

Luke's Major Themes

In both his Gospel and the Book of Acts, Luke sounds many themes that, in the emphasis and space he devotes to them, clearly distinguish his work from that of other Evangelists. In portraying Jesus' character, Luke describes him as almost always compassionate, taking a personal interest in women, the poor, social outcasts, and other powerless persons. Empowered by the Holy Spirit, Luke's Jesus forgives sinners, comforts the downtrodden, and heals the afflicted. His Jesus is particularly attentive to issues of social and economic justice. In numerous parables found only in his Gospel, Luke demonstrates that Jesus' kingdom ethic demands a radical change in society's present social and religious values. In shaping his stories of Jesus and the early church, Luke repeatedly highlights distinctive topics and themes.

The Holy Spirit Luke is convinced that Jesus' ministry and the growth of Christianity are not historical accidents, but the direct result of God's will, which is expressed through the **Holy Spirit**—an invisible force from God that guides human thought and action. Luke uses this term more often than Mark and Matthew combined (fourteen times). It is by the Spirit that Jesus is conceived and by which he is anointed after baptism. The Spirit leads him into the wilderness (4:1), and "filled with the power of the Spirit," he performs miracles throughout Galilee (4:14). Jesus receives the Spirit through prayer (4:21–22), and at death, the Lukan Jesus commits his own "spirit" to God (23:46).

The Holy Spirit reappears with overwhelming force in Acts 2 when, "like the rush of a violent wind," it sweeps upon the 120 disciples gathered in Jerusalem to observe Pentecost. Possession by the Spirit confirms God's acceptance of Gentiles into the church (Acts 11:15–18). To Luke, it is the Spirit that is responsible for the faith's rapid expansion throughout the Roman Empire. Like Paul, Luke sees the Christian community as *charismatic*, Spirit led and Spirit empowered.

The Importance of Jerusalem More than any other Gospel author, Luke links crucial events in Jesus' life with Jerusalem and the Temple. He is the only Evangelist to associate Jesus' infancy and childhood with visits to the Temple and the only one to place *all* of Jesus' postresurrection appearances in or near Jerusalem. Jerusalem is the place where his Gospel account begins (1:8–22), where Jesus' parents take their eight-day-old son for circumcision (2:31–39), and where the twelve-year-old Jesus astonishes "teachers" in the Temple with the profundity of his questions (2:41–51).

Near the conclusion of his ministry, the adult Jesus "set his face to go to Jerusalem," the city where he would endure a fatal confrontation with priestly and Roman authorities (9:51). As the Lukan Jesus insists, "It is impossible for a prophet to be killed outside of Jerusalem"— a statement that occurs only in Luke (13:33).

In Mark, the youth at Jesus' empty tomb directs the bewildered female disciples to seek their risen Lord "in Galilee" (Mark 16:7), an order that Matthew says the male disciples eventually obeyed (Matt. 28:16–20). In contrast, the Lukan Jesus commands his followers to remain in Jerusalem (24:49), where they will receive the Holy Spirit. Luke's insistence that Jerusalem and its environs—not Galilee—were the site of all Jesus' appearances after his resurrection expresses his view that Jerusalem and the Temple were central to God's plan. For Luke, Jerusalem is not only the place where Jesus dies, is buried, rises from the tomb, appears to his followers, and ascends to heaven; it is also the sacred ground on which the Christian church is founded. In Luke's theology of history, God thus fulfills his ancient promises to Israel, focusing his divine power on the holy city where King David once reigned and where David's ultimate heir inaugurates an everlasting kingdom.

Christianity as a Universal Faith The author designs Luke-Acts to show that, through Jesus and his successors, God directs human history to achieve humanity's redemption. Luke's theory of salvation history is universal in scope. That is, from its inception, Christianity was a religion intended for "all nations," especially those peoples who had hitherto lived without Israel's Torah and prophets. As the aged priest Simeon prophesies over the infant Jesus, the child is destined to become "a light for revelation to the Gentiles" (2:32). This theme also appears in Luke's genealogy, which traces Jesus' ancestors all the way back to Adam, father of the human race. In Acts, the author reports that Peter, previously wary of admitting Gentiles into the church, also came to embrace the new faith's universality: "I truly understand that God shows no partiality, but in every nation anyone who fears him and does what is right is acceptable to him" (Acts 10:34). According to Luke, the risen Jesus' final words commission his followers to bear witness about him from Jerusalem "to the ends of the earth" (Acts 1:8), conveying his message to all of Adam's descendants.

Jesus' Concern for Women From the beginning of his account, Luke makes it clear that women will play key roles in fulfilling the divine plan. **Elizabeth,** the priest Zechariah's wife, is chosen to produce and raise Israel's final prophet, John the Baptist, the one who prepares the way for Jesus. Her cousin Mary responds affirmatively to the Holy Spirit, conceiving and nurturing the world savior. During his adult ministry, Jesus accepts many female disciples, praising those who, like **Mary,** the sister of **Martha,** abandon domestic chores to take their places among the male followers—a privilege Jesus declares "will not be taken away from [them]" (10:38–42). Galilean women not only follow Jesus on the path to Jerusalem but also financially support him and his male companions (8:2–3). As in Mark, it is these Galilean women who provide the human link between Jesus' death and resurrection, witnessing the Crucifixion and receiving first the news that he has conquered death (23:49; 23:55–24:11).

Jesus' Affinity with the Unrespectable Closely linked to Jesus' concern for women, who were largely powerless in both Jewish and Greco-Roman society, is his affinity for many similarly vulnerable people on the margins of society. "A friend of tax collectors and sinners" (7:34), the Lukan Jesus openly accepts social outcasts, including publicly "sinful" women, such as an apparently notorious woman who crashes a Pharisee's dinner party and seats herself next to Jesus, bathing his feet with her tears, much to his host's indignation. Accused of being "a glutton and a drunkard," Jesus personally welcomes socially unvalued persons to share meals with him, refusing to distinguish between deserving and undeserving guests (7:29–34; 15:1–2). In Luke's version of the great banquet parable, the host's doors are thrown open indiscriminately to "the poor, the crippled, the lame, and the blind," people incapable of returning hospitality (14:12–24). To Luke, it is not the "poor in spirit" who gain divine blessing, but simply "you who are poor," the economically deprived for whom productive citizens typically show little sympathy (6:20–21; 6:24–25).

Jesus as Savior Finally, Luke presents Jesus in a way that his Greek and Roman readers will understand. Matthew had labored to prove from the Hebrew Bible that Jesus was Israel's Messiah. In his story of Jesus'

infancy, Luke also sounds the theme of prophetic fulfillment. But he is aware as well that his Gentile audience is not primarily interested in a Jewish Messiah, a figure traditionally associated with Jewish nationalism. Although Mark and Matthew declared their hero "Son of God," Luke further extends Jesus' appeal by declaring him "a mighty savior" (1:69; 2:11; Acts 3:13–15). He is the only Synoptic writer to do so. Luke's term, the Greek *soter,* was used widely in the Greco-Roman world and was applied to gods, demigods, and human rulers alike. Hellenistic peoples commonly worshiped savior deities in numerous mystery cults and hailed emperors by the title "god and savior" for the material benefits, such as peace and prosperity, that they conferred (see Figure 32.2). For Luke, Jesus is the **Savior** of repentant humanity, one who delivers believers from the consequences of sin, as the judges of ancient Israel "saved" or delivered their people from military oppressors.

Luke's Infancy Narrative

We do not know Luke's source for his story of Jesus' birth—which he links to that of John the Baptist (1:5–2:52)—but he apparently drew on a tradition that differed in many details from Matthew's account. The two writers agree that Jesus was born in Bethlehem to **Mary,** a virgin, and **Joseph,** a descendant of David. Apart from that, however, their two birth stories are difficult to harmonize.

In interweaving the birth stories of John the Baptist (the last of Israel's prophets) and Jesus (the cornerstone of a new world order), Luke subtly indicates the relative importance of the two children. He dates John's birth in King Herod's reign (1:5). In contrast, when introducing Jesus' nativity, the author connects the event not to a Judean king, but to a Roman emperor, Augustus Caesar (2:1). Luke thus places Jesus in a global (as opposed to a local Jewish) context, both suggesting the universal scope of Jesus' significance and implying his superiority to earthly rulers. For Luke and his community, Jesus—not the leader of the Roman Empire—was their true king (cf. Acts 17:7).

The Role of Mary Whereas Matthew tells his infancy story largely from Joseph's perspective, Luke emphasizes the importance of Mary's role. It is to her that God sends the angel **Gabriel** to announce that the son she is about to bear will be conceived by the Holy Spirit (1:28–33). (A Latin version of Gabriel's speech to Mary provides the text for the "Ave Maria.") Mary's prayer of exultation, the Magnificat (1:46–55), closely resembles the prayer that

FIGURE 32.2 Early Christian artists commonly pictured Jesus in the guise of earlier Greco-Roman gods or heroes, particularly Apollo, Dionysus, or Orpheus, all of whom were associated with music, inspiration, and flocks and shepherds. In this mosaic at Ravenna, Christ appears as the Good Shepherd.

Hannah recites when an angel foretells the birth of her son Samuel (1 Sam. 2:1–10). Luke implies that Mary herself became a source of traditions about Jesus' birth, noting that she reflected deeply on the unusual circumstances surrounding the event (2:19, 51). Consistent with the prominence the author gives to Mary, Luke's Gospel omits all of Mark's passages that may reflect unfavorably on Jesus' family. This means deleting the story of Jesus' "mother and brothers" trying to interfere with his ministry (Mark 3:21, 33–34) and rewriting the Markan Jesus' statement about not being respected by his "own kin and in [his] own house" (Mark 6:4; cf. Luke 4:22, 24). Unlike John, Luke does not state that Mary was present at the cross (John 19:26–27), but after the Crucifixion, he does show her gathered with the disciples and Jesus' "brothers" in Jerusalem, just before the outpouring of the Holy Spirit at Pentecost (Acts 1:14). This is the New Testament's last reference to Jesus' mother.

Jesus' Galilean Ministry

Except for the anecdote about Jesus' visit to the Temple when he was twelve years old (2:41–52), Luke tells us nothing about Jesus' boyhood or education. Like Mark, he begins his narrative of Jesus' adult life at the time of his baptism, and like Matthew, he draws on Q to report Jesus' temptation by Satan (4:1-13). Besides revising Mark's order by placing the Nazareth incident near the beginning of his career, Luke further changes Mark's sequence of events by postponing Jesus' call to the Twelve until after he had revisited his hometown (6:12–19). This transposition forms an introduction to Jesus' first public discourse, the Sermon on the Plain (6:20–49).

The Sermon on the Plain In comparing Matthew's Sermon on the Mount with Luke's version (see Figure 32.3), it is immediately apparent that Luke's beatitudes are shorter and simpler, and spoken directly to the hearer-reader—"you"! Whereas Matthew tends to spiritualize their meanings, blessing "those who hunger and thirst for righteousness," Luke's version bluntly stresses physical hunger: "Blessed are you who are hungry now, for you will be filled" (6:21). Luke's "poor" are the financially destitute, the impoverished masses for whose sake God will establish his kingdom. In a section unique to his Gospel, Luke follows the Beatitudes with a series of "woes" in which the "rich" and well-fed are condemned

FIGURE 32.3 This is the traditional site of the Sermon on the Mount. According to tradition, it was on this hill overlooking the Sea of Galilee that Jesus delivered his most famous discourse, the teachings compiled in Matthew 5–7. The Gospel of Luke, however, states that Jesus spoke to his Galilean audience on "level ground" (Luke 6:17).

to future loss and hunger. Persons who benefit unduly from the present world order that consigns many to poverty and hunger will see a total reversal of their status (6:24–26). In Luke's view, the kingdom overthrows long-accepted behaviors and customs, rewarding those who suffer want and punishing those who now enjoy good things at others' expense.

To Luke, Jesus is the model of compassionate service whom Christians are to imitate. As he tells the disciples at the Last Supper, "I am among you as one who serves" (22:27). Besides ministering to the poor and socially marginal, Jesus' service includes imparting joy to the bereaved, as when he raises a widow's "only son" from the dead (7:11–17). This miracle, found only in Luke, echoes the resuscitations that Elijah and Elisha performed for "widows," who represent the poorest classes of people in ancient Israel (cf. 1 Kings 17:17–24; 2 Kings 4:32–37).

Jesus' Teaching on the Road to Jerusalem

Whereas Mark refers only briefly to Jesus' journey from Galilee to Jerusalem (Mark 10:17, 32–33), Luke repeatedly emphasizes the importance of this final pilgrimage, devoting almost ten chapters to the trek (9:51–19:28). This restructuring of Mark's account prepares readers to see parallels to Paul's missionary journeys in Acts, underscoring the continuity between Jesus' activities and those of his later followers. While greatly expanding upon Mark's travel motif, however, Luke gives little sense of forward movement, focusing instead on the content of Jesus' teachings as he journeyed toward Jerusalem. Into this long section (the "greater interpolation"), Luke fits several of Jesus' best-known parables, most unique to his Gospel.

The Good Samaritan The narrative context into which Luke sets the parable of the good Samaritan is important to its interpretation (10:25–28). Conversing with Jesus along the road, a "lawyer" (teacher of the Torah) defines the essence of the Mosaic Law in the twin commandments to love God (Deut. 6:5) and neighbor (Lev. 19:18). Jesus then confirms that in thus practicing love a person "will live." Mark places this dialogue with the Torah instructor in the Jerusalem Temple (Mark 12: 28–34). By recasting it as an incident while Jesus is traveling near Samaritan territory, however, Luke expands Jesus' conversation with the "lawyer" to introduce a revolutionary idea about the nature and appropriate expression of compassionate love. When the Torah expert asks Jesus to explain who one's "neighbor" really is, Jesus—in typically rabbinic fashion—does not define the concept, but instead tells a story in which the questioner must find his own meaning in a specific human situation (10:29–35).

After describing a traveler whom thieves had beaten, robbed, and left for dead beside the road, Jesus states that two Torah-abiding Jews—a priest and a Levite—pass by without stopping to help the victim. Jesus' point is not that the Jewish travelers are too insensitive to help a fellow Jew (the victim had been heading toward Jerusalem), but that neither priest nor Levite (who do not know if the beaten man is alive or dead) can perform his Temple duties if he so much as touches a corpse (Num. 19:11; Lev. 21:1–11). To fulfill their Torah obligations by remaining ritually "clean," they must act uncharitably. By contrast, it is a foreigner, a Samaritan—representative of a group that Torah-observant Jews despised as apostates—who, "moved with pity," unhesitatingly aids the wounded traveler, even providing for his extended care. In this parable, Jesus not only emphasizes the role of "pity" or empathy in motivating charitable action but also insists that his hearers regard the outsider—the "apostate" Samaritan—as a moral hero, the one who embodies the Torah command to love. In typical Lukan fashion, the parable also functions to upset the accepted moral order, demanding that we, like the Samaritan, accept anyone in need as our "neighbor," regardless of social, ethnic, or religious differences (10:36–37).

Lazarus and the Rich Man Another parable of unexpected reversal found only in Luke describes the starkly different posthumous fates of two men—one a wealthy landowner who enjoys all life's good things, and the other a beggar so wretched that dogs lick the sores covering his body. In the story of Lazarus and the rich man (16:19–31)—the Gospels' only parable about the afterlife—death radically changes their respective status. After death, the poor, diseased beggar suddenly finds himself "with Abraham" (in paradise), whereas the rich man writhes "in agony" amid the "flames" of Gehenna. Emphasizing the vast "chasm" separating the places of reward and punishment, the parable appears to draw on first-century Jewish beliefs about the next world, such as the detailed description of the Underworld (Hades) in Josephus's "Discourse on Hades" (see Josephus in "Recommended Reading"). The apocryphal Book of

2 Esdras, written about 100 CE, presents a similar juxtaposition of paradise and a "lake of fire" (2 Esd. 7:36; see Chapters 27 and 39).

Interestingly, Luke charges the rich man with no specific crime and assigns Lazarus no virtue. In Luke's view, current social conditions—the existence of abject poverty and illness alongside the extravagant luxury of the rich—will be completely overthrown when the kingdom arrives. The single fault of which the rich man is implicitly guilty is his toleration of the extreme contrast between his own abundance and the miserable state of the poor. As the only Gospel writer to follow the Beatitudes with a list of "woes" to befall the rich and well-fed (6:24–26), Luke seems to believe that justice requires a sweeping reversal of the present economic system. For the author, the ideal social order is the commune that Jesus' disciples set up in Jerusalem after Pentecost, an economic arrangement in which the well-to-do believers sell their possessions, share them with the poor, and hold "all things in common" (Acts 2:42–47).

The Prodigal Son and the Forgiving Father In yet another parable unique to Luke, a wealthy man's son squanders his inheritance in wasteful living among Gentiles and "prostitutes" (15:11–30). Violating the most basic standards of Judaism, the ungrateful son not only wastes his share of his father's estate but sinks to the level of an animal groveling in a foreigner's pigpen. Even his decision to return home is based not on repentance but on a desire to improve his diet.

Yet the parable's main focus is not on the youth's unworthiness and degradation, but on the father's love for him, which causes the father to behave in a manner contrary to normal social expectations. While the prodigal (spendthrift) is "still far off," his father sees him and, forgetting his dignity, rushes to meet his returning son. The father expresses no disapproval of his son's shameful behavior, demands no admission of wrongdoing, and inflicts no punishment. Ignoring the youth's request to be hired as a servant, the parent instead orders a lavish celebration in his honor.

The narrative then switches its focus from the prodigal to the relationship between the father and his older son, who understandably complains about the partiality shown to his sibling. Acknowledging the older child's superior claim to his favor, the father attempts to explain the unlimited quality of his affection, that he loves unconditionally and makes no distinction between the deserving and undeserving recipients of his generosity. By implication, the parable expresses the same view of the divine Parent, who "is kind to the ungrateful and the wicked" alike (6:35).

Like many of Jesus' parables, this tale ends with an essential question unanswered: How will the older brother, smarting with resentment at the prodigal's unearned welcome, respond to his father's implied invitation to join the family party? As Luke views the issue, Jesus' call to sinners was remarkably successful; it is the conventionally religious who too often fail to value an invitation to the messianic banquet.

The Jerusalem Ministry

In editing Mark's account of the Jerusalem ministry, Luke subtly mutes Mark's apocalyptic urgency and reinterprets Jesus' kingdom teaching to indicate that many eschatological hopes have already been realized (18:31–21:38). While he preserves some apocalyptic traditions—warning readers to be constantly alert and prepared for the End—Luke also distances the final consummation, placing it at some unknown future time. Aware that many of Jesus' original followers assumed that his ministry would culminate in God's rule being established on earth, Luke reports that as Jesus drew "near Jerusalem," the disciples "supposed that the kingdom of God was to appear immediately" (19:11), an expectation that persisted in the early church (Acts 1:6–7). Luke counters this belief with a parable explaining that the Master must go away "to a distant country to get royal power for himself and then return" (19:12–27), indicating a delay in the Parousia. (Matthew uses this same parable for a similar purpose.)

Luke's Modifications of Apocalyptic Expectations In describing the journey toward Jerusalem, Luke deftly intermingles Markan prophecies about the appearance of the Son of Man with passages from Q and his own special material, suggesting that the kingdom is, in some sense, a present reality in the activities of Jesus. When the Pharisees accuse Jesus of exorcising demons by the power of "Beelzebul [Satan]," he answers: "If it is by the finger of God that I cast out the demons, then the kingdom of God has come to you" (11:20; cf. Matt. 12:28). The Lukan Jesus equates his disciples' success in expelling demons with Satan's fall from heaven (10:18–20), a sign that evil has been defeated and God's rule has begun. In another saying unique to Luke, Jesus tells the Pharisees: "The kingdom of God is not coming with things that can be observed; nor will they say, 'Look, here it is!' or 'There it is!' For, in fact, the kingdom of God is among you [or "in your midst"]" (17:20–21). As Luke's distinctive parables highlight the kingdom's reversal of ordinary social norms, so his kingdom statements underscore its invisible operations, not its apocalyptic violence.

The Fall of Jerusalem and the Parousia In his edited version of Mark 13, the prophecy of Jerusalem's destruction, Luke distinguishes between the historical event, which he knows took place in the recent past, and the Parousia, which belongs to an indefinite future (21:5–36). The author replaces Mark's cryptic allusion to the "desolating sacrilege" (Mark 13:14) with practical advice that urged Christians to flee the city when Roman armies began their siege (21:20–24). In Luke's modified apocalypse, a period of unknown length will occur between Jerusalem's fall in 70 CE and Jesus' reappearance. The holy city "will be trampled on by the Gentiles, until the times of the Gentiles are fulfilled" (21:24). In Luke's view, this period of "Gentile" domination will allow the Christian church to expand throughout the Roman Empire, the subject of his Book of Acts (see Chapter 34).

Luke's vision thus divides apocalyptic time into two distinct stages: events leading to Jerusalem's fall and events involving the Parousia. To describe the second phase, Luke invokes mythic and astronomical language to characterize events: Cosmic phenomena, such as "signs in the sun, the moon, and the stars" (21:25), will herald the Son of Man's presence. Luke may have regarded these cosmic "signs" as metaphorical and already fulfilled when the Holy Spirit descends upon the Christian community at Pentecost. In Acts 2, Peter's speech—interpreting the meaning of Pentecost—sees the Spirit's coming as an apocalyptic event:

> In the last days it will be, God declares, that I will pour out my Spirit upon all flesh, . . . And I will show portents in the heaven above and signs on the earth below, blood and fire, and smoky mist. The sun shall be turned to darkness and the moon to blood . . .

(Acts 2:17, 19–20).

For the Lukan Peter, prophetic images of heavenly phenomena were realized in earthly events when the same Holy Spirit that had guided Jesus was also bestowed upon his followers. After Peter's speech, Luke rarely again mentions apocalyptic expectations, nor does he show early church leaders—including Paul (and contrary to the content of Paul's own letters)—preaching about the nearness of the Parousia. Did Luke think that the figurative language of apocalypse was fulfilled primarily in symbolic events of great spiritual significance, such as the birth of the church and the establishment of a community that lived by Jesus' kingdom ethic? (For a discussion of "realized eschatology"—a belief that events usually associated with the End have already been fulfilled in Jesus' spiritual presence among his followers—see Chapter 33.)

Luke's Passion Story

Luke's Interpretation of the Passion
Although Luke's account of Jesus' last days in Jerusalem roughly parallels that of Mark, it differs in enough details to suggest that Luke may have used another source as well. In this section (22:1–23:56), Luke underscores a theme that will dominate Acts: Jesus, like his followers after him, is innocent of any sedition against Rome. More than any other Gospel writer, Luke represents Pilate as testifying to Jesus' political innocence, declaring that "he has done nothing to deserve death" (23:15) and that he found "no ground" to condemn him (23:22). Whereas the historian Josephus portrays Pilate as a ruthless tyrant contemptuous of Jewish public opinion, Luke depicts him as merely a pawn who allows himself to be manipulated by the Jerusalem leadership.

Last Words on the Cross
In both Mark and Matthew, Jesus' final words are a cry of abandonment, but Luke reports several sayings that illustrate his characteristic themes. Only in Luke's Gospel do we find Jesus' prayer to forgive his executioners because they do not understand the significance of their actions (23:34). Besides showing Jesus' heroic capacity to forgive, this prayer validates Jesus' teaching that a victim must love his enemy (6:27–38) and end the cycle of hatred and revenge that perpetuates evil in the world.

Even in personal suffering, the Lukan Jesus thinks not of himself, but of others. Carrying his cross on the road to **Calvary** (the site of public execution), he comforts the women who weep for him (23:26–31). Similarly, he consoles the man crucified next to him, promising him an immediate reward in paradise (23:43). (Readers will note that this fellow victim of Rome's laws has recognized Jesus' innocence [23:41].) In Luke, Jesus' last words address the Father whose Spirit he had received following baptism (3:31; 4:1, 14) and to whom in death he commits his own spirit (23:46–47).

Postresurrection Appearances in the Vicinity of Jerusalem

Because early manuscript copies of Mark contain no resurrection narrative, it is not surprising that Matthew and Luke, who generally adhere to Mark's order through the discovery of the empty tomb, differ widely in their reports of Jesus' postresurrection appearances. Consistent with his emphasis on Jerusalem, Luke omits the Markan tradition that Jesus would reappear in Galilee (Mark 16:7; Matt. 28:7, 16–20) and places all the disciples' experiences of their risen Lord in or near Jerusalem.

In concluding his Gospel, the author creates two detailed accounts of Jesus' posthumous teaching that serve to connect Jesus' story with that of the community of believers for whom Luke writes. The risen Jesus' words are not a final farewell, but a preparation for what follows in Luke' second volume, the Book of Acts. For Luke, the disciples' original encounter with the resurrected Jesus was qualitatively the same spiritually renewing experience that believers continued to enjoy in the Spirit-led church.

In narrating Jesus' first appearance, on the road to **Emmaus** (a few miles from Jerusalem), Luke emphasized the glorified Lord's relationship to followers left behind on earth. The two disciples, Cleopas and an unnamed companion (perhaps a woman), who encounter Jesus do not recognize him until they dine together. Only in breaking bread—symbolic of the Christian communion ritual—is Jesus' living presence discerned.

In Luke's second postresurrection account, the disciples are discussing Jesus when he suddenly appears in their midst, asking to be fed. The Lukan disciples' offering Jesus a piece of cooked fish makes several points: Their job is to care for the poor and hungry whom Jesus had also served; they have fellowship with Jesus in communal dining; and they are assured the figure standing before them is real—he eats material food—and not a hallucination. By insisting on Jesus' physicality, Luke also firmly links the heavenly Christ and the human Jesus—they are one and the same.

Perhaps most important for Luke's understanding of the way in which Jesus remains alive and present is the author's emphasis on studying the Hebrew Bible in order to discover the true meaning of Jesus' life and death. At Emmaus, Jesus explains "the things about himself in all the scriptures" (24:27), thereby setting his companions' "hearts burning within [them]" (32). In Jerusalem, he repeats these lessons in biblical exegesis, interpreting the Torah, Prophets, and Writings as Christological prophecies (24:44), an innovative practice that enabled Christians to recognize Jesus in the Mosaic revelation. Luke also connects these postresurrection teachings with the church's ongoing task: Jesus' death and resurrection, foretold in Scripture, are not history's final act but the beginning of a worldwide movement. The disciples are to remain together in Jerusalem until Jesus sends the Holy Spirit, which will empower them to proclaim God's new dispensation to "all nations" (24:46–49), a promise fulfilled in the opening chapters of Acts.

QUESTIONS FOR DISCUSSION AND REVIEW

1. In the preface to his Gospel, Luke states that he is aware that other writers (apparently including Mark) have already composed accounts of Jesus' life. Why does he wish to write another biography of Jesus?

2. A number of distinctive themes—as well as numerous parables that appear only in his work—characterize Luke's Gospel. Relate these special Lucan themes to the author's individual portrayal of Jesus' actions and teachings. In what ways do Luke's distinctive ideas color his portrait of Jesus?

3. In Luke's presentation of Jesus' message, the author emphasizes Jesus' concern for the poor, the powerless, and the socially outcast. For Luke, the kingdom's arrival will overturn and reverse commonly accepted social and economic values. How do Luke's unique parables, such as the Good Samaritan, the Prodigal Son, and Lazarus and the Rich Man, illustrate this radical reversal of conventional attitudes?

4. In what respects does Luke's account of Jesus' arrest, trial, and crucifixion differ from the other Synoptic Gospels? Why does he (contrary to Mark and Matthew) insist that Jesus' postresurrection appearances all took place, not in Galilee, but in or near Jerusalem? Why are Jerusalem and its Temple so important to Luke?

5. Discuss the importance that Luke gives to women's participation in Jesus' story. From the infancy narratives, to the Galilean ministry, to the discovery of the empty tomb on Easter morning, what crucial roles do such figures as Elizabeth, Mary (Jesus' mother), Mary Magdalene, and the sisters Mary and Martha play in Jesus' life?

Terms and Concepts to Remember

Calvary
Elizabeth and Zechariah
Emmaus
Gabriel
"greater interpolation"
Holy Spirit, role of
infancy narrative
Joseph
L (Lukan) source
"lesser interpolation"
Luke-Acts as a two-volume work
Luke's distinctive parables
Luke's major themes
Luke's modification of resurrection appearances
Mary
prophecy of Jerusalem's fall
Theophilus

Recommended Reading

Carroll, John T. "Luke, Gospel of." In K. D. Sakenfeld, ed., *The New Interpreter's Dictionary of the Bible*, Vol. 3, pp. 720–734. Nashville, TN: Abingdon Press, 2008. Surveys questions of authorship, circumstances of composition, theological issues, and recent history of critical interpretation.

Fitzmyer, J. A., ed. *The Gospel According to Luke*, 2 vols. (Anchor Bible). New York: Doubleday, 1981 and 1985. A fresh translation with helpful interpretation.

Johnson, Luke Timothy. "Luke-Acts, Book of." In D. N. Freedman, ed., *The Anchor Bible Dictionary*. New York: Doubleday, 1992. A lucid summary of scholarly studies of Luke's two-volume work.

Josephus, Flavius. "Discourse to the Greeks Concerning Hades." In *Josephus: Complete Works*. Trans. W. Whiston. Grand Rapids, MI: Kragel, 1960. Presents first-century-CE views of the afterlife similar to those appearing in Luke's Gospel and Revelation.

Karris, Robert J. "The Gospel According to Luke." In R. E. Brown et al., eds. *The New Jerome Biblical Commentary*, pp. 675–721. Englewood Cliffs, NJ: Prentice-Hall, 1990. Detailed comment on Luke's narrative themes.

Powell, M. A. *What Are They Saying About Luke?* New York: Paulist Press, 1989. A review of current scholarship on Luke's Gospel; for beginning students.

Talbert, C. H. *Reading Luke: A Literary and Theological Commentary on the Third Gospel*, rev. ed. Macon, GA: Smith & Helwyns, 2002. For more advanced study.

CHAPTER 33

Another Way of Telling Jesus' Story
The Gospel of John

Key Topics/Themes In John's Gospel, the order of events and the portrayal of Jesus and his teaching are strikingly different from those in the Synoptic accounts. Whereas the Synoptic authors depict Jesus as a healer-exorcist whose eschatological teachings deal primarily with Torah reinterpretation and an impending judgment, John describes Jesus as an embodiment of heavenly Wisdom who performs no exorcisms and whose message centers on his own divine nature. In John, Jesus is the human form of God's celestial Word, the cosmic expression of divine Wisdom by which God created the universe. As the Word incarnate (made flesh), Jesus reveals otherwise unknowable truths about God's being and purpose. To John, Jesus' crucifixion is not a humiliating ordeal (as in Mark), but a glorification that frees Jesus to return to heaven. Although John's Gospel alludes briefly to Jesus' future return, it contains no prophecies of the Second Coming comparable to those found in the Synoptics. Instead of emphasizing the Parousia, John argues that the risen Christ is eternally present in the invisible form of a surrogate—the Paraclete, or Holy Spirit, which continues to inspire and guide the believing community.

 ## A Different Gospel

The Fourth Gospel—that ascribed to John—is so different from the first three that most scholars conclude that it is fundamentally not a portrait of the historical Jesus but a profound meditation on his theological significance. The community that produced John's Gospel held a uniquely high view of Jesus' divinity, proclaiming that before descending to earth Jesus existed in heaven as the "Word [Greek, *Logos*]," the divine wisdom by which God created the universe. A mystical reflection upon Jesus' cosmic meaning and a tribute to his eternal divinity, the Fourth Gospel presents Jesus' earthly life almost exclusively in terms of his "glory," both the heavenly glory he held before birth and the splendor of his crucifixion and return to the Father.

The author clearly states that his Gospel's primary purpose is to bring readers to life-giving faith in Jesus:

Now Jesus did many other signs in the presence of his disciples, which are not written in this book. But these are written so that you may come to believe

that Jesus is the Messiah, the Son of God, and that through believing you may have life in his name.

(John 20:30–31)

This declaration follows the Gospel's climactic scene—a postresurrection appearance in which the reality of Jesus' living presence conquers the doubts of his most skeptical disciple, Thomas. Confronted with a sudden materialization of the risen Jesus, Thomas recognizes him as "My Lord and my God," a confession of faith in Jesus' divinity that the reader is intended to echo.

The Authorship of John

Since the late second century CE, the Gospel has been attributed to the apostle John, son of Zebedee and brother of James. According to one tradition, John eventually settled in Ephesus, where he lived to an exceptionally old age, composing his Gospel, three letters, and the Book of Revelation. These five works are known collectively as the Johannine literature. (Because of major differences in style, content, and theology, scholars do not believe that the same person wrote both the Gospel and Revelation.)

The tradition ascribing authorship to the son of Zebedee is relatively late. Before about 180 CE, church leaders do not even mention the Gospel's existence. After that date, opinion on its origin is divided, with some church writers accepting it as John's work and other doubting its authenticity. Some even suggested that it was written by Cerinthus, a Gnostic teacher (see the discussion of Gnosticism below).

The Beloved Disciple The Gospel itself does not mention the author's identity, stating instead that it is based on the testimony of an anonymous disciple "whom Jesus loved" (21:20–24). Some traditions identify this **Beloved Disciple** with John (whose name does not appear in the text), but scholars can find no evidence to support this claim. Jesus predicted that John would suffer a death similar to his (Mark 10:39), whereas the Gospel implies that its author, unlike Peter, James, and John, did not die a martyr's death (21:20–22). When Herod Agrippa executed James in about 41–43 CE, he may have killed his brother John as well (cf. Acts 12:1–3).

Some critics propose that another John, prominent in the church at Ephesus about 100 CE, is the author. Except that he was called "John the Elder [Greek, *presbyter*]," we know nothing that would connect him with the Johannine writings. Lacking confirmation of traditional authorship, scholars regard the work as anonymous. For convenience, we refer to the author as John.

Several verses in the final chapter associate the author with the unnamed Beloved Disciple, suggesting that at the very least, this disciple's teachings are the Gospel's primary source (21:23–24). Portrayed as enjoying an emotional intimacy with Jesus that neither Peter nor other members of the Twelve attain, this special disciple does not appear (at least as the one "Jesus loved") until the final night of Jesus' life, when we find him at the Last Supper, lying against his friend's chest (13:33). (The disciples dined in the Greco-Roman style, reclining two-by-two on benches set around the table.)

To represent the Johannine community's special knowledge of Christ, the Beloved Disciple is invariably presented in competition with Peter, who may represent the larger apostolic church from which the disciple's exclusive group is somewhat distanced. At the Last Supper, the Beloved Disciple is Peter's intermediary, transmitting to Jesus Peter's question about Judas's betrayal (13:21–29). Acquainted with the High Priest, he has access to Pilate's court, thus gaining Peter's admittance to the hearing, where Peter denies knowing Jesus (18:15–18). Whereas the Synoptic Gospels mention only women present at the Crucifixion, John's account states that the Beloved Disciple stood at the cross. His special status is indicated when Jesus instructs him to take Mary into his home, thereby becoming her "son" and hence Jesus' "brother" as well (19:26–27).

Outrunning Peter to the empty sepulcher on Easter morning, the Beloved Disciple arrives there first and is the first to believe that Jesus is risen (20:2–10). In a boat fishing with Peter on the Sea of Galilee, the disciple is the first to recognize the resurrected Jesus standing on the shore, identifying him to Peter (21:4–7). Peter, future "pillar" of the Jerusalem church, is commissioned to "feed" (spiritually nourish) Jesus' "sheep" (future followers), but Jesus has a special prophecy for the Beloved Disciple's future: He may live until the Master returns (21:20–22). (This reference to the Parousia is virtually unique in John's Gospel.) After the disciple's death, his community apparently interpreted the saying to mean that Jesus' intentions for his favorite did not involve Peter (21:21–23).

Place and Date of Composition

According to Raymond Brown's analysis of the Gospel, it may have originated in a Palestinian or Syrian locale but probably reached its present form in a Hellenistic environment. Some of the author's vocabulary parallels distinctive terms found in Essene writings, particularly the dualistic references to cosmic opposites: light–dark, good–evil, truth–lie, spirit–flesh, and children of God (the believers' community) versus the spawn of the devil (the group's critics). Some scholars once thought that John's Gospel had been composed late in the second century, when Christian authors first mention it, but tiny manuscript fragments of John discovered in the Egyptian desert have been dated at about 125 and 150 CE, making them the oldest surviving parts of a New Testament book. Allowing time for the Gospel to have circulated abroad as far as Egypt, the work could not have been composed much later than about 100 CE. John's description of believers being expelled from Jewish synagogues (9:22, 34–35)—a process of separation that began about 85–90 CE—suggests that the decisive break between church and synagogue was already in effect when the Gospel was written. Hence, the Gospel is usually dated between about 90 and 100 CE.

Differences in John's Portrait of Jesus

About ninety percent of John's Gospel has no parallel in the Synoptics (see Box 33.1). Most of Jesus' teaching

---

BOX 33.1 Representative Examples of Material Found Only in John

Doctrine of the Logos: Before coming to earth, Jesus preexisted in heaven, where he was God's mediator in creating the universe (1:1–18).

Miracle at Cana: Jesus changes water into wine (the first "sign") (2:1–12).

Doctrine of spiritual rebirth: the conversation with Nicodemus (3:1–21; see also 7:50–52; 19:39).

Conversation with the Samaritan woman (4:1–42). Jesus healing the invalid at Jerusalem's Sheep Pool (5:1–47).

The "I am" sayings: Jesus speaks as divine Wisdom revealed from above, equating himself with objects or concepts of great symbolic value, such as "the bread of life" (6:22–66) and "the resurrection and the life" (11:25).

Cure of the man born blind; debate between church and synagogue (9:1–41).

The raising of Lazarus (the seventh "sign") (11:1–12:11).

A different tradition of the Last Supper: washing the disciples' feet (13:1–20) and delivering the farewell discourses (13:31–17:26).

Resurrection appearances in or near Jerusalem to Mary Magdalene and the disciples, including Thomas (20:1–29).

Resurrection appearances in Galilee to Peter and to the Beloved Disciple (21:1–23).

---

found in Mark, Matthew, and Luke does not appear in John, and John's distinctive teaching finds little that is comparable in the Synoptics. The following list presents a dozen of the principal differences between John and the Synoptic accounts, along with brief suggestions about the author's possible reasons for omitting so many characteristic Synoptic themes:

- John has no birth story or reference to Jesus' virginal conception, perhaps because he sees Jesus as the eternal **Logos** (Word) who "became flesh" (1:1, 14) as the man from Nazareth. John's doctrine of the **Incarnation** (the spiritual Logos becoming physically human) makes the manner of Jesus' human conception irrelevant.

- John includes no report that John baptized Jesus, emphasizing Jesus' independence of and superiority to the Baptist.

- John includes no period of contemplation in the Judean desert or temptation by Satan. His Jesus possesses a vital unity with the Father that makes worldly temptation impossible.

- John never mentions Jesus' exorcisms, preferring to show Jesus overcoming evil through his personal revelations of divine truth rather than through the casting out of demons—which play so large a role in Mark's and Matthew's accounts of Jesus' miraculous deeds. Instead, opponents accuse *him* of having a demon (7:20; 8:46–52; 10:19–20).

- Although he states that some friction existed between Jesus and his brothers (7:1–6), John does not reproduce the Markan tradition that Jesus' family

thought he was mentally unbalanced or that his neighbors at Nazareth viewed him as nothing extraordinary (Mark 3:20–21; 31–35; 6:1–6). In John, Jesus meets considerable opposition, but he is always too commanding and powerful a figure to be ignored or devalued.

- John presents Jesus' teaching in a form distinctly different from that of the Synoptics. Both Mark and Matthew state that Jesus did not teach "except in parables" (Mark 4:34; Matt. 13:34), but John does not record a single parable of the Synoptic type (involving homely images of agricultural or domestic life). Instead of brief anecdotes and vivid comparisons, the Johannine Jesus delivers long philosophical speeches in which Jesus' own nature is typically the subject of discussion. In John, he speaks both publicly and privately in this manner, in Galilee and in Jerusalem.

- John includes none of Jesus' reinterpretations of the Mosaic Torah, the main topic of Jesus' Synoptic discourses. Instead of the many ethical directives about divorcing, keeping the Sabbath, ending the law of retaliation, and forgiving enemies that we find in Mark, Matthew, and Luke, John records only one "new commandment"—to love. In both the Gospel and the Johannine letters, this is Jesus' single explicit directive; in the Johannine community, mutual love among "friends" is the sole distinguishing mark of true discipleship (13:34–35; 15:9–17).

- Conspicuously absent from John's Gospel is any prediction of Jerusalem's fall, a concern that dominated

CHAPTER 33   ANOTHER WAY OF TELLING JESUS' STORY   **339**

the Synoptic writers' imagination (Mark 13; Matt. 24–25; Luke 21).

- John also deviates from the Synoptic tradition by minimizing expectations of Jesus' Second Coming, offering no prophecies of an imminent return comparable to those in Mark and Matthew. John's Gospel alludes to the tradition of Jesus' eventual return only twice. At the Last Supper, Jesus promises that he will "come again," specifically to transport his followers to their heavenly abode (perhaps at the hour of their deaths) (14:1–3). In John 21, an epilogue to the main text that may have added by a later editor, the narrator indicates that some in the Johannine community expected Jesus' reappearance (21:21–23).

  Nowhere in John's Gospel, however, are there Synoptic-style predictions of social upheavals or cosmic portents that would signal the nearness of the Parousia. John, rather, promotes the view that Jesus is already present among believers in the form of the **Paraclete,** the Holy Spirit that serves as Christians' Helper, Comforter, or Advocate (14:25–26; 16:7–15). To John, Jesus' first coming means that believers have life *now* (5:21–26; 11:25–27) and that divine judgment is a current reality, not merely a future event (3:18; cf. 9:29; 12:31). Scholars find in John a **realized eschatology,** a belief that events usually associated with the world's End, such as divine judgment and the awarding of eternal life, are even now realized or fulfilled in Jesus' spiritual presence among his followers. For John, the earthly career of Jesus, followed by the infusion of his Spirit into the disciples (20:22–23), has already accomplished God's purpose in sending the Messiah. For the Johannine community, in his hour of "glory" (crucifixion), Jesus had essentially finished his work (19:30). Just as John's doctrine of the Incarnation made the concept of virginal conception unnecessary, so his view of the Paraclete effectively replaced the expectations of the Parousia.

- Although he represents the sacramental bread and wine as life-giving symbols, John does not preserve a communion ritual or the institution of a "new covenant" between Jesus and his followers at the Last Supper. Stating that the meal took place a day before Passover, John substitutes Jesus' act of humble service—washing the disciples' feet—for the Eucharist (13:1–16).

- As his Jesus cannot be tempted, so John's Christ undergoes no agony before his arrest in the garden of Gethsemane. Unfailing poised and confident,

Jesus experiences his painful death as a glorification, his raising on the cross symbolizing his imminent ascension to heaven. Instead of Mark's cry of despair, in John, Jesus dies with a declaration that he has now "finished" his life's purpose (19:30).

Finally, it must be emphasized that John's many differences from the Synoptics are not simply the result of the author's trying to "fill in" the gaps in his predecessors' Gospels. By carefully examining John's account, we see that he does not write to supplement earlier narratives about Jesus. Rather, both his omissions and his inclusions are determined almost exclusively by the writer's theological convictions (20:30–31; 21:25). From his opening hymn praising the eternal Word to Jesus' promised reascension to heaven, every part of the Gospel is calculated to illustrate Jesus' glory as God's fullest revelation of his own ineffable Being.

Differences in the Chronology and Order of Events

Although John's essential story resembles the Synoptic version of Jesus life—a public ministry featuring healings and other miracles followed by official rejection, arrest, crucifixion, and resurrection—the Fourth Gospel presents important differences in the chronology and order of events. Significant ways in which John's narrative sequence differs from the Synoptic order include the following:

- The Synoptics show Jesus working mainly in Galilee and coming south to Jerusalem only during his last days. In contrast, John has Jesus traveling back and forth between Galilee and Jerusalem throughout the duration of his ministry.

- The Synoptics place Jesus' assault on the Temple at the end of his career, making it the incident that consolidates official hostility toward him; John sets it at the beginning (2:13–21).

- The Synoptics agree that Jesus began his ministry after Herod Antipas had put the Baptist in prison, but John states that their missions overlapped (3:23–4:3).

- The earlier Gospels mention only one Passover and imply that Jesus' career lasted only about a year; John refers to three Passovers (2:13; 6:4; 11:55), thus giving the ministry a duration of about three years.

- Unlike the Synoptics, which present the Last Supper as a Passover observance, John states that Jesus' final meal with the disciples occurred the evening before

Passover and that the Crucifixion took place on Nisan 14, the day of preparation when pascal (Passover) lambs were being sacrificed (13:1, 29; 18:28; 19:14). Many historians believe that John's chronology is more accurate in this case, for it seems improbable that Jesus' arrest, trail, and execution took place on Nisan 15, the most sacred time of the Passover celebration.

Scholars also note, however, that John's probable reason his dating of the Crucifixion is more theological than historical. Because he identifies Jesus as the "lamb of God" at the beginning of his Gospel (1:29), it is thematically appropriate for the author to coordinate the time of Jesus' death with the ritual slaying of the pascal lambs (prescribed in Exod. 12:3–10; cf. Isa. 53:7–12).

The Work of the Paraclete: Jesus and His Followers as "One"

John's Double Vision　Many commentators have noted that John's Gospel portrays Jesus not as a figure of the recent historical past, but as an immortal Being who still inhabits the author's community. In John's account, Jesus' ministry and the similar activities of his later followers—the Johannine "community" (21:23)—merge into an almost seamless whole. To express his vision that Christ and the members of his own group are "one" (17:12), John employs "double vision," creating in his Gospel a two-level drama in which Jesus of the past and believers of the present perform the same Spirit-directed work (14:12).

John is able to blend past and present in Jesus' biography through the operation of the Paraclete, a distinctively Johannine concept introduced in Jesus' farewell speeches at the Last Supper (13:31–17:26). In this long section, Jesus explains precisely why he must leave his disciples on earth when he dies and ascends to heaven. Only through his death and return to the Father can he empower his disciples with the Paraclete, the Holy Spirit, which acts as his surrogate (substitute) among them (14:12–26). Functioning as a manifestation of the postresurrection Jesus, the Paraclete inspires the Johannine community to interpret Jesus' teachings as no other group could: "The Advocate, the Holy Spirit, whom the Father will send in my name, will teach you everything, and *remind you of all that I have said to you*" (14:26, emphasis added). This Spirit, Jesus' own double, allows the author to portray Christ in his full theological glory. It also enables John's group not only to continue Jesus' miraculous work but even to surpass his deeds. He who has faith,

Jesus promises, "will also do the works that I do and, in fact, will do greater works than these, because I am going to the Father. I will do whatever you ask in my name, so that the Father may be glorified in the Son. If in my name you ask me for anything, I will do it" (14:12–14). In this vow—found only in John—the writer finds his key to understanding the continuity between the Master and his later disciples.

John's singular method of telling Jesus' story becomes especially clear in Chapter 9. In describing Jesus' restoration of sight to a man born blind (see Figure 33.1), John skillfully melds traditions of Jesus' healing miracles with the works that members of his community currently perform. John's narrative can equate the two parties—Jesus and his later disciples—because the same Paraclete operates through both. An awareness of John's method, conflating past and present, will help readers understand the historical forces at work in this episode. After Jesus cures the man's lifelong blindness, a series of confrontations and arguments ensue between the man, his parents, and officials of the local synagogue. The Jewish officials' interrogation of the man reflects circumstances prevailing not in Jesus' day but in the writer's own time. Explicit references to the expulsion of Jesus' followers from the synagogue (9:22, 34)—a process that began long after Jesus' death, during the last decades of the first century CE—are sure indicators of John's two-level approach.

John employs a similar blending of past and present in Jesus' dialogue with the Pharisee Nicodemus (3:1–21). Jesus' pretended astonishment that Nicodemus—depicted as one of Israel's most famous teachers—does not understand or experience the power of the Holy

FIGURE 33.1　This ancient mosaic in Ravenna, Italy, shows Jesus restoring sight to a blind man (John 9).

Spirit motivating the author's community could not have taken place in Jesus' lifetime. But it accords well with what John's Gospel tells us about debates between Jewish authorities and the author's group, which proclaimed the Paraclete's role in their lives. Using the first-person-plural "we" to signify the whole believing community, John affirms that his brotherhood intimately knows the Spirit's creative force, whereas "you" (the unbelievers) stubbornly refuse to credit the Johannine testimony (3:9–14). Readers will also note that in this dialogue Jesus speaks as if he has already returned to heaven (3:13), another indication that this passage reflects a perspective that developed long after the Nicodemus incident supposedly occurred.

Relation to Gnostic Ideas In addition to refuting Jewish critics offended by the Johannine community's proclamation of Jesus' divinity (viewed as an attack on Jewish monotheism) and its claim to spiritual superiority, John appears to defend his view of Jesus' nature against incipient Gnostic influences. **Gnosticism** was a complex religious/philosophical movement that developed into Christianity's first major challenge to what later became official church teaching. Whereas the church eventually embraced a doctrine that declared Jesus both fully human and fully divine, many Gnostics tended to define Jesus as pure spirit, free of human weakness. Although Gnosticism took many forms, it typically held a dualistic view of the cosmos, seeing the universe as having two mutually exclusive dimensions. The invisible world of spirit was eternal, pure, and good, whereas the physical world was inherently evil, the creation of a deeply flawed deity, which some Gnostics identified with Yahweh. According to Gnostic belief, human beings gained salvation only through special knowledge (Greek, *gnosis*), imparted to a chosen elite via communion with spiritual beings. A divine redeemer (presumably Christ) descended from the spirit realm to transmit saving knowledge to persons whose souls were sufficiently disciplined to escape the body's earthly desires. Transcending the material world's false reality, the soul could then perceive its own origins in the spirit realm and embrace its eternal truths. Salvation came from conscious knowledge (*gnosis*) that the soul was innately immortal and belonged to the higher domain of the spirit.

Gnosticism was extremely diverse and included a variety of ideas about Jesus' nature and function. One branch of Gnosticism, called **Docetism** (a name taken from the Greek verb "to seem"), argued that Christ, being good, could not also be human; he only *seemed* to have a physical body. The Docetists contended that, as God's true son, Christ was wholly spiritual, ascending to heaven while leaving another's body on the cross.

Although he sometimes uses Gnostic terms, John—despite his doctrine of Jesus' heavenly origins and divinity—avoids Gnosticism's extremism by insisting on Jesus' physical humanity (1:14). Even after the Resurrection, Jesus displays fleshly wounds and consumes ordinary food (20:24–29; 21:9–15). To show that Jesus was a mortal man who truly died, John eliminates from his Passion story Mark's tradition that Simon of Cyrene carried Jesus' cross (lest readers think that Simon might have been substituted for Jesus at the Crucifixion). John is also the only Evangelist to state that a Roman soldier pierces Jesus' side with a spear, confirming his physical vulnerability and mortality (19:34–37).

Despite its conviction that the divine Logos "became flesh" (1:14), John's Gospel was popular in many Gnostic circles (which may account for its relatively slow acceptance by the church at large). Besides the metaphysical concepts of Christ's preexistence and his inherent divinity, John contains other statements that accord with Gnostic ideas. The notion that to know "the only true God" is to gain "eternal life" (17:3); the assertion that "it is the spirit that gives life; the flesh is useless" (6:63); and the teaching that only being "born from above" can confer immortality—all found only in John—are classic Gnostic beliefs. Considering John's emphasis on Jesus' spiritual invincibility and Godlike stature, it is not surprising that the first commentaries written on John were by Gnostic Christians—or that some church leaders suspected that the author himself was a Gnostic!

 # Organization of John's Gospel

John's Gospel is framed by a prologue (1:1–51) and an epilogue (21:1–25). The main narrative (Chs. 2–20) divides naturally into two long sections: an account of Jesus' miracles and public teachings (Chs. 2–11), and an extended Passion story focusing on Jesus' private speeches to the disciples (Chs. 12–20). Because John regards Jesus' miracles as "signs"—direct evidence of his hero's supernatural power—the first section is called the Book of Signs. Many scholars believe that the author used a previously compiled collection of Jesus' miraculous works as a primary source (see below). Because it presents Christ's death as a "glorious" fulfillment of the divine will, many commentators call the second part the Book of Glory.

The Gospel can be outlined as follows:

1. Prologue: hymn to the Logos; testimony of the Baptist; call of the disciples (1:1–51)
2. The Book of Signs (2:1–11:57)
   a. The miracle at Cana (changing water into wine)
   b. The cleansing of the Temple
   c. Dialogue with Nicodemus on spiritual rebirth
   d. Conversation with the Samaritan woman
   e. Five more miraculous signs in Jerusalem and Galilee; Jesus' discourses witnessing to his divine nature
   f. The resuscitation of Lazarus (the seventh sign)
3. The Book of Glory (12:1–20:31)
   a. The plot against Jesus
   b. The Last Supper and farewell discourses
   c. The Passion story
   d. The empty tomb and postresurrection appearances to Mary Magdalene, Peter, and the Beloved Disciple
4. Epilogue: postresurrection appearances in Galilee; parting words to Peter and the Beloved Disciples (21:1–25)

Prologue: Hymn to the Word (Logos)

Greek and Jewish Background In the lyrical hymn opening his Gospel, John identifies the prehuman Jesus with the divine Word (Logos):

> In the beginning was the Word and the Word was with God, and the Word was God . . . All things came into being through him . . . What has come into being in him was life; and the life was the light of all people.
>
> (John 1:1–4)

These verses consciously echo the Genesis creation account when God's word of command—"Let there be light!"—illuminated the previously dark cosmos. The supreme irony of John's Gospel is that the very world that the Word created rejects him, preferring spiritual "darkness" to the "light" he imparts.

Logos (Word) is a Greek philosophical term, but John blends it with a parallel Jewish tradition about divine Wisdom that existed before the world began. According to the Book of Proverbs (8:22–31), Wisdom (depicted as a gracious young woman) was Yahweh's companion when he created the universe, transforming primordial chaos into a realm of order and light. As Israel's wisdom tradition developed in Hellenistic times,

Wisdom was seen as both Yahweh's agent at creation and the being who reveals the divine mind to the faithful (Sirach [Ecclus.] 24; Wisd. of Sol. 6:12–9:18; see Chapter 27).

In the writings of Philo Judaeus, a Hellenistic-Jewish scholar living in Alexandria during the first century CE, the biblical concept of heavenly Wisdom was equated with the Greek Logos, which philosophers had used to identify the principle of cosmic Reason that gives order and coherence to the world. The Logos concept had circulated among Greek thinkers since the time of the philosopher Heraclitus (born c. 540 BCE), and in John's day, it was a popular idea in Stoic philosophy. When Philo, a devout Jew, attempted to reconcile Greek rationality with biblical revelation, he employed the concept of divine Wisdom as the creative intermediary between the transcendent Creator and the material creation. However, he used the Greek term *Logos* to express Wisdom's role and function, perhaps because it is masculine in Greek, whereas Wisdom is feminine in both the Greek and Hebrew languages. Philo's interpretation can be illustrated by an allegorical reading of Genesis 1, in which God's first act is to speak—to create the Word (Logos) by which power the universe is born. In identifying the prehuman Jesus with Philo's Logos, John equates Jesus with the loftiest philosophical ideal of his age (see Figure 33.2).

Jesus' "I Am" Pronouncements

Besides identifying Jesus with the eternal Logos/Wisdom concept, John further emphasizes Jesus' inherent divinity in a series of speeches (unique to his Gospel) containing the statement "I am." These statements echo Yahweh's declaration of being to Moses at the burning bush (Exod. 3:14), in which God reveals his sacred personal name. In the Hebrew Bible, only Yahweh speaks of himself (the "I AM") in this manner. Hence, Jesus repeated assertions—"I am the bread of life" (6:35), "I am the good shepherd" (10:11), "I am the resurrection and the life" (11:25), or "I am the way, and the truth, and the life" (14:6)—express his unity with God, the eternal "I AM."

John attributes much Jewish hostility toward Jesus to their reaction against his apparent claims to divinity. When Jesus refers publicly to his prehuman existence, declaring that "before Abraham was, I am," his outraged audience attempts to stone him for blasphemy (8:56–59). Many scholars doubt that the historical Jesus really made such assertions, but in John's double-vision approach, the attempted stoning represents the later Jewish response when John's community made extraordinary claims about Jesus' divine nature.

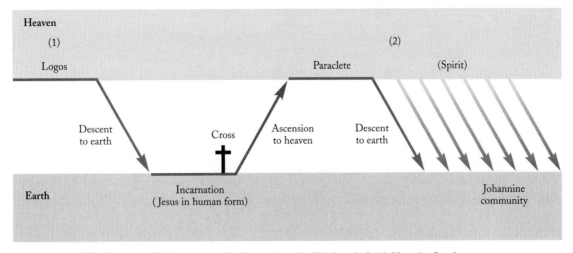

FIGURE 33.2 This chart shows John's concept of the Incarnation (the Word made flesh). Note that Jesus' ascension to heaven (return to his place of spiritual origin) is followed by a descent of the Paraclete, Jesus' Spirit—an invisible surrogate that inspires the Johannine brotherhood. Whereas Jesus' human presence on earth was brief, John implies that the Paraclete abides permanently within the believing community.

The Book of Signs

The Miracle at Cana John organizes his account of Jesus' public ministry around the performance of seven "signs"—miracles that illustrate Jesus' supernatural power—to demonstrate his divinity. The first "sign" (Greek, *semia*) takes place at the Galilean town of Cana, where Jesus, attending a wedding with his disciples and his mother, changes water into wine. Although this miracle has no parallel in the other Gospels, it is consistent with Synoptic traditions that depict Jesus eating and drinking with all kinds of people (cf. Luke 7:33–35). When informed that the host's supply of wine has run out, suggesting that the wedding guests are probably already intoxicated, Jesus adds to the party's merriment by providing an additional 180 gallons of a vintage superior to that which the guests have already consumed. According to John, Jesus' offering the celebrants the means to continue imbibing "good wine" reveals his "glory" and causes the disciples to "believe" in him (2:11), as if confirming his qualifications to host the promised messianic banquet (Isa. 25:6).

Presented as Jesus' initial "sign" that God is present in his actions, this joyous celebration of life, symbolized not only by the marriage ceremony but also by the shared enjoyment of a divinely bestowed beverage, foreshadows a more solemn moment described at the end of John's narrative—that of Jesus' "glorious" death on the cross. Using the images of water and wine—and the blood these liquids symbolize—the author thematically links the beginning of Jesus' ministry at Cana with its culmination at Golgotha, where a Roman soldier thrusts his spear into Jesus' body, releasing a flow of "blood and water" (19:34). Underscoring the connection between these two framing incidents, John has Jesus' mother present at both Cana and the Crucifixion, the only two occasions on which she appears in his Gospel (cf. 2:1–11; 19:25–27).

Assault on the Temple After showing Jesus' contributing to a joyous celebration, John next shows him in an act of public violence—the only such action any Evangelist ascribes to him. Reversing the Synoptic order, John has Jesus drive moneychangers from the Temple during a Passover at the outset of his ministry. For John, the episode represents Jesus' superiority to the Jerusalem sanctuary: The Temple is no longer sacred because the Holy Spirit now dwells in Jesus' person rather than the shrine King Herod had so elaborately reconstructed. Jesus' physical body may be destroyed, but unlike the Herodian building, he will rise again as proof that God's Spirit empowers him (2:13–25).

Conversation with the Samaritan Woman As in Luke's Gospel, John emphasizes Jesus' warm friendships with women, with whom he converses freely, teaching them on the same level as his male followers. Astonishing the disciples by ignoring social conventions that segregate the sexes, Jesus publicly discusses fine points of theology with a Samaritan woman who gives him water from Jacob's well (see Figure 33.3). Recalling the hostility then existing between Jews and

FIGURE 33.3 This Ravenna mosaic shows Jesus conversing with a Samaritan woman drawing water from Jacob's well (John 4). Both Luke and John emphasize Jesus' characteristic concern for women.

Samaritans, we understand the woman's surprise at Jesus' willingness to associate with her—not to mention her amazement when he reveals his awareness of her lurid past. As Jesus later instructs Martha in the mysteries of the Resurrection (11:17–27), so he informs the much-married Samaritan woman that the old controversy between Jews and Samaritans about the correct place to worship God—Jerusalem or at Mount Gerizim—is no longer relevant. For *now* is the time for all to worship "in spirit and in truth" (4:1–26). The woman is not merely a passive learner: When Jesus confides to her that he is the Messiah, she—the first non-Jew to receive this message—becomes his prophet, rushing to inform her fellow villagers (4:39). In this, the unnamed woman anticipates Mary Magdalene's later role as prophet to the male disciples when she brings news that their crucified Lord still lives (20:1–2, 10–18).

The Raising of Lazarus John concludes his "Book of Signs" with Jesus' seventh and most spectacular miracle, resuscitating a man who had been dead for four days (11:1–44). In John's account, the raising of Lazarus serves multiple literary and theological purposes. As a turning point in the Gospel narrative, it has the same function as the assault on the Temple in the Synoptics:

The incident provokes official hostility toward Jesus and ignites a fatal conspiracy leading to his execution. As the episode linking the Book of Signs with the Book of Glory (the story of Jesus' Passion), the Lazarus episode operates as a preview of Jesus' own death and resurrection. Like Lazarus, Jesus will be entombed in a cave from which a great stone—signifying death's finality—will be rolled away as he rises to immortal life. In the Johannine narrative, **Martha,** the sister of Mary and Lazarus, expresses her faith in Jesus (11:24–27), a confession that anticipates Thomas's more complete recognition of Jesus' true divinity (20:28).

John's Realized Eschatology The raising of Lazarus is also a good demonstration of John's distinctive doctrine of realized eschatology. Events traditionally assigned to End time, such as the dead obeying a divine summons to exit from their graves, now occur during Jesus' ministry. Earlier in the Gospel, Jesus had declared: "Indeed, just as the father raises the dead and gives them life, so also the son gives life to whomever he wishes" (5:21), adding that those who trust him *already* possess "eternal life." "Anyone who hears my word and believes him who sent me has eternal life," Jesus explains, "and does not come under judgment, but has passed from death to life" (5:24). For the Johannine community, "the hour is coming, and is now here, when the dead will hear the voice of the Son of God, and those who hear will live" (5:25; cf. 8:51). In John's view, the life-imparting final resurrection is currently taking place among believers: "I am the resurrection and the life," Jesus informs Martha, and "those who believe in me, even though they die, will live, and *everyone who lives and believes in me will never die*" (11:26, emphasis added). In thus reinterpreting the timing and nature of resurrection, the author transfers fulfillment of eschatological prophecies about eternal life from the indefinite future—the End of the world—to the concrete here and now. Instead of waiting for the Parousia to experience life everlasting, the believer can now realize it in the present.

The Book of Glory

Connecting the second part of his Gospel with the miraculous signs previously reported, John opens the Book of Glory (Chs. 12–20) by narrating a dinner party at which Jesus and his friends celebrate Lazarus's return to life. The festive scene features several important themes, looking back to Jesus' feeding of the multitudes and the resuscitation of Lazarus and looking forward to the Last Supper and Jesus' own death. Even while rejoicing in one man's escape from the tomb, the dinner guests are forewarned of their leader's imminent departure when Mary anoints Jesus' feet with expensive perfume. Jesus approves her prophetic action as preparing his body for burial, for his hour of "glory" is near at hand.

The Last Supper and Farewell Discourses John's account of the Last Supper contains no reference to Jesus' distributing the ceremonial bread and wine (the Eucharist). Instead, John dramatizes a concept found also in Luke's Gospel—that Jesus comes "like a servant" (Luke 22:27). Given the author's view that Jesus shares the nature of the omnipotent Creator (1:1), Jesus' taking the role of a domestic slave, washing his disciples' travel-stained feet, has great significance. The Master's humility both demonstrates God's loving care for the faithful and sets an example of unselfish service for the Johannine community (13:3–17).

As noted above, Jesus' care for his "friends" extends beyond his earthly service, for he will send the Paraclete to strengthen and guide them after he has reascended to the Father. Because the divine Parent dwells in him, Christ can reveal God fully—to see Jesus in his true

meaning is to see the father (14:7–11). John insists on Jesus' unique relationship to God—he and the Father "are one" (10:30), but it is a unity of spirit and purpose that also characterizes the disciples (17:20–21). Despite his close identification with the Deity, John's Jesus does not claim unequivocal equality with God. He simply states that "the Father is greater than I" (14:28).

John's Interpretation of the Passion

Crucifixion as Glorification John's Passion narrative is shaped by his high Christology—his view of Jesus' divinity—and his wish to place responsibility for Jesus' death on the Jewish leadership. Mark's Gospel had already wrestled with the problem of reconciling his portrait of Jesus as a powerful miracle worker in Galilee with the fact of Jesus' apparent helplessness before his enemies in Jerusalem (see Chapter 30). After depicting Jesus as a figure of virtually irresistible force throughout his Gospel, John faces an even greater challenge in explaining how this incarnation of divine Wisdom became his adversaries' mortal victim. John resolves the potential dilemma by affirming the paradox inherent in Jesus' circumstance: Even in Jerusalem, Jesus retains his superhuman power but voluntarily declines to use it in order to fulfill scriptural predictions that God's Son must die to save others. In John's view, by willingly submitting to a publicly shameful death, Jesus manifests a spiritual "glory" that confirms his divinity.

No Agony in Gethsemane Scholars debate whether John was familiar with the Synoptic tradition, but in his account of Jesus' last hours, John offers some clues that he may have been aware of earlier Gospels. The Johannine Jesus states: "Now my soul is troubled. And what should I say—'Father, save me from this hour'?" (John 12:27). This statement appears to be a paraphrase of Mark 14:36, in which Jesus prays for God to spare him from the coming ordeal. This concept of a grieving Jesus is one that John firmly rejects. The contrast between Mark's account of Jesus' agony in Gethsemane and John's version could not be stronger. Whereas Mark's Jesus throws himself on the ground in an agony of dread, begging that God not force him to drink the "cup" of pain and humiliation (Mark 14:32–36), John's Jesus remains calmly standing while the soldiers who come to arrest him are hurled to the ground. When the Temple police ask Jesus to identify himself, he replies, "I am he," a revelation of divinity that causes them to collapse in a heap (18:4–8). The last of Jesus' "I am" statements, this declaration echoes John's earlier association of Jesus and Yahweh, the divine "I AM" (John 8:58; cf. Exod. 3:8–16), a claim to equality with God that incites an attempt to stone Jesus. For John, enemies plotting Jesus' downfall only *seem* to be in charge: As Jesus had explained, he alone makes the decision to give up his life (10:17–18). Pilate, representative of Roman imperial power, is explicitly informed that his role as judge is only illusory (19:9–10).

An Innocent Pilate John's version of Jesus' appearance before Pontius Pilate seems to mirror his community's hostility toward the Jewish establishment. Only John states that Pharisees, as well as Temple priests, are involved in Jesus' indictment before the Roman governor. Presenting events in a strangely implausible way, John shows a frightened and harried Pilate dashing back and forth between a Jewish crowd outside his palace and the accused prisoner inside. (John explains that Jewish priests could not enter a Gentile's quarters because such contact would make them ritually unclean for the upcoming Passover.) In his desire to foster good relations with Rome, Luke had depicted a Pilate technically innocent of arranging Jesus' death (Luke 23:1–25), but John goes even further. His Pilate is literally run ragged shuttling between accommodation of the priests who demand Jesus' execution and his sympathetic support of the "king" whom they wish to kill (18:28–19:16). In John's account, Pilate makes no fewer than *eight* attempts to persuade Jesus' priestly accusers (John indiscriminately labels them collectively as "Jews," as if Jesus and the disciples did not belong to the same group) that Jesus is guilty of no crime (18:31, 38–39; 19:4–6, 12, 14–16). Only after the crowd threatens to accuse Pilate himself of sedition against Rome for championing Jesus' cause (19:12) and insists that their nation has no ruler but the Roman emperor (19:15–16) does Pilate reluctantly submit and turn Jesus over for crucifixion. John also has Pilate symbolically vindicate Jesus' claim to be the rightful Jewish king by refusing to revise a public notice of the crime for which Jesus is executed (19:19–22). (See Box 33.2.)

Postresurrection Appearances in Jerusalem

Although John apparently follows a tradition similar to what Luke used, placing Jesus' postresurrection appearances in and around Jerusalem (instead of Galilee as in Mark and Matthew), he modifies the story to illustrate his characteristic themes. On the first Easter morning,

FIGURE 33.4 In this Ravenna mosaic, Thomas kneels before the risen Jesus. Having doubted reports of Jesus' resurrection, Thomas now confesses Jesus as "my lord and my God" (John 20:26–28).

Mary Magdalene is alone when she discovers that Jesus' corpse has vanished from Joseph of Arimathea's garden tomb, where it had been placed late the previous Friday. Prophet of her Lord's resurrection, she is the first to report the empty sepulcher and the first to see the risen Jesus, announcing these glad tiding to the male disciples (20:1–2, 10–18). When, on Sunday evening, Jesus appears to the male followers, he breathes into the them Holy Spirit, the first manifestation of the Paraclete. After describing Jesus' last Jerusalem appearance, to "doubting" Thomas, the narrative concludes with its frank statement of purpose, to inspire life-giving faith (20:8–9, 26–29) (see Figure 33.4).

Epilogue: Postresurrection Appearances in Galilee

Most scholars believe that a later editor added the twenty-first chapter of John, incorporating both the tradition of Jesus' appearances in Galilee and final thoughts on the contrasting roles of Peter and the Beloved Disciple. When Jesus suddenly appears to share an early-morning breakfast of bread and fish (again demonstrating that the risen Christ is not a ghost or other disembodied spirit), he questions Peter about the depth of his commitment. Using three different Greek verbs for "love," Jesus emphasizes that love for him means feeding his "sheep." Thus, Peter and the church he represents are to provide spiritual and other care for future believers, the "other sheep" (10:16), including Gentiles, who will soon join the apostolic fold (21:4–17). Jesus then predicts contrasting fates for Peter, who will suffer martyrdom (21:18–19), and for the Beloved Disciple, who will have a long life (21:20–23).

BOX 33.2 Jesus' Last Words: A Summary of the Evangelists' Beliefs About Him

Jesus' final utterances, compiled from the four different Gospel accounts of his crucifixion, are traditionally known as the "seven last words on the cross." Whereas Mark and Matthew agree that Jesus is almost entirely silent during his agony, crying out only once—in Aramaic—to ask why God has deserted him, Luke and John ascribe several short speeches to their dying hero, showing him in full control of his final hours. The particular statements that each Evangelist has Jesus voice represent that author's individual understanding of Jesus' nature and the meaning of his death.

MARK (15:34)

Eli, Eli, lema sabachthani?

(My God, my God, why have you forsaken me?)

MATTHEW (27:46)

Eli, Eli, lema sabachthani?

(My God, my God, why have you forsaken me?)

LUKE (23:34, 43, 46)

Father, forgive them [Roman executioners]; they do not know what they are doing.

Truly I tell you: today you [the sympathetic felon next to him] will be with me in Paradise.

Father, into your hands I commit my spirit.

JOHN (19:26-27, 28, 30)

Mother, there is your son. . . . There is your mother [placing Mary (the church) in the future care of the Beloved Disciple (the Johannine community)].

I am thirsty [to fulfill Scripture].

It is accomplished!

Writing to a vulnerable group then undergoing hardship and suffering, Mark devotes much of his Gospel to a bleak description of Jesus' Passion, emphasizing that, if God permitted his son to endure pain and humiliation, the disciples may expect no better fate. Jesus' cry of despair anticipates his persecuted followers' sense of similarly being abandoned by God. Although Matthew modifies the Passion story to underscore its fulfillment of biblical prophecy, he retains Mark's emphasis on Jesus' solitary and extreme anguish.

Luke, who presents Jesus as a model of self-sacrificing service to others, edits the Passion narrative to highlight Jesus' innocence of any crime against Rome and to illustrate the themes of forgiveness and spirituality that color his portrait of Jesus. Contrary to Mark's account, in which Jesus appears almost numb with shock at his brutal treatment, Luke's Jesus is neither silent nor despairing: He speaks repeatedly and confidently, as if he were already enthroned as eschatological judge. He pardons his Roman tormentors, absolving them of responsibility for his execution, and comforts the felon crucified next to him, granting him a posthumous reward in paradise. Because

Luke presents Jesus as led by the Holy Spirit throughout his earthly ministry, it is thematically appropriate for him to show, at the end, Jesus calmly relinquishing his own spirit to God.

Consistent with his picture of Jesus as fully aware of his divine nature, including his prehuman existence in heaven, John paints a Jesus absolutely untroubled by doubt or dejection. Acting out the purpose for which he descended to earth, John's Jesus remains in complete charge of his destiny, allowing soldiers to capture him only to fulfill the divine will (John 18: 4–9). The Johannine Jesus thus undergoes no agony in Gethsemane or despair on the cross. In contrast to Mark's picture of lonely abandonment, John shows Jesus accompanied by his mother and his favorite disciple, whose future lives together he arranges. When he says he thirsts, it is not because he experiences ordinary human suffering, but only to fulfill prophecy. His moment of death is simultaneously his "hour of glory," when he can announce that he has accomplished all the Father sent him to do. In his serene omniscience, the Johannine Jesus seems altogether a different being from Mark's Son of Man.

John's Historical Significance

The Gospel of John closes with the editor's reflection on the vast body of oral tradition surrounding Jesus (most not included in John's account). If Jesus' entire career were to be recorded in detail, the writer supposes, "the world itself could not contain the books that would be written" (20:25). By making his theologically oriented selection from the Jesus tradition (20:30–31), the author resolves many of the issues that must have troubled Christian thinkers at the end of the first century CE. Believers concerned about the long delay in the Parousia are reassured that Jesus' "second self"—the Paraclete—is already present to comfort, guide, and instruct the community of faith. Inspired by the Spirit, Jesus' followers have already passed from death to eternal life. God has, in the present, given them his favorable judgment.

The Paraclete's abiding presence in the Johannine community not only empowers believers to accomplish "greater" deeds than those of the earthly Jesus, it also fully reveals the "glory" and splendor of Jesus' First Coming. Inspired by the Paraclete, John's author gives Jesus unparalleled cosmic stature, portraying a figure so exalted that he can have no rivals, even in heaven. More than any single book in the New Testament, the Gospel of John lays the foundations for later theological interpretations of Christ's divine nature. John's distinctive portrayal of Jesus' divinity eventually exerted a tremendous influence on Christine doctrine. In post–New Testament times, Christian theologians came to see Jesus as the Second Person in the Trinity (a term that does not appear in canonical Scripture). For orthodox believers, Jesus is co-equal, consubstantial, and co-eternal with the Father. Although the Johannine writings do not articulate so formal a dogma, historically, John's high Christology profoundly influenced official Christianity's eventual understanding of its Master.

QUESTIONS FOR DISCUSSION AND REVIEW

1. Discuss the role of the Beloved Disciple in John's version of Jesus' story. Why does this unnamed disciple appear as "the one Jesus loved" only at the Last Supper? Why is he the only male follower to stand beside Jesus at the cross?

2. List a dozen specific ways in which John's Gospel differs from the Synoptic accounts. In the Synoptics, Jesus teaches primarily in short speeches and parables, whereas in John he almost always speaks in long, philosophical discourses, both privately and in public. How do you explain this difference in teaching method? Why does John change the subject of Jesus' message from God's dawning kingdom to Jesus' own divine nature?

3. John's Gospel contains almost no traditional apocalyptic teaching and has no prediction of Jesus' Second Coming comparable to that in the Synoptics. How does Jesus' instruction about the Advocate, or Paraclete, deal with the problem of Jesus' delayed return? Remember that John was probably written almost seventy years after Jesus' death.

4. Name several of the "signs" or miracles that Jesus performs to demonstrate his divinity. How does the seventh sign—the raising of Lazarus—lead to Jesus' death?

5. Jesus delivers "I am" speeches only in John's Gospel. How do such statements relate Jesus to heavenly Wisdom? And to God?

6. Define the concept of *realized eschatology,* and discuss the Johannine Jesus' final statement: "It is finished." Does this mean that Jesus has accomplished his divine purpose at his first coming? Explain how these factors may account for John's decision to omit Synoptic-type prophecies of the Parousia.

Terms and Concepts to Remember

Beloved Disciple
Book of Glory
Book of Signs
Christology, John's high
Gnosticism/Docetism
Incarnation
John's differences from the Synoptics
Lazarus
Logos, hymn to
Mary and Martha
Paraclete (the Advocate)
Philo Judaeus
transubstantiation
realized eschatology
Wisdom

Recommended Reading

Brown, R. E. *The Community of the Beloved Disciple.* New York: Paulist Press, 1979. A readable and insightful study of the Christian group that produced the Gospel and letters of John.

Conway, Colleen M. "John, Gospel of." In K. D. Sakenfeld, ed., *The New Interpreter's Dictionary of the Bible*, Vol. 3, pp. 356–370. Nashville, TN: Abingdon Press, 2009. Surveys distinctive qualities of the Gospel's portrait of Jesus including its socio-historical setting and theological meaning.

Fortna, R. T. *The Fourth Gospel and Its Predecessor: From Narrative Source to Present Gospel.* Philadelphia: Fortress Press, 1988. The definitive analysis of the hypothetical Signs source underlying John's Gospel.

Kysar, Robert. *John, the Maverick Gospel*, 3rd ed. Louisville, KY: Westminster John Knox Press, 2007. A superb guide for the beginning student.

————. *Voyages with John: Charting the Fourth Gospel.* Waco, TX: Baylor UP, 2006. Traces the history of critical interpretation to the present; for advanced students.

Martyn, J. L. *History and Theology in the Fourth Gospel,* 3rd ed. (New Testament Library). Louisville, KY: Westminster John Knox, 2003. A brilliant interpretation of John's literary method, focusing on the author's "double vision" of John 9.

Perkins, Pheme. "The Gospel According to John." In R. E. Brown et al., eds. *The New Jerome Biblical Commentary,* pp. 942–985. Englewood Cliffs, NJ: Prentice-Hall, 1990. A perceptive commentary on the Gospel; for beginning study.

Sloyan, Gerard S. *What Are They Saying About John?* New York: Paulist Press, 1991. An accessible introduction to contemporary scholarship on John's Gospel.

CHAPTER 34

An Account of Early Christianity

The Book of Acts

Key Topics/Themes In the Book of Acts, Luke continues his two-part narrative of Christian origins, portraying characters who, like Jesus, are models of Christian behavior and service. This theologically shaped account of the early church emphasizes many of the same themes that dominated Luke's Gospel. As the Holy Spirit inspired Jesus' teachings and miracles, so the same Spirit guides his followers, who are to carry Jesus' message "to the ends of the earth" (1:8). The first half of Luke's narrative focuses on the Jerusalem church and activities of Palestinian-Jewish Christians. After describing the Spirit's descent upon 120 disciples at Pentecost, the author depicts Christianity's numerical growth and geographical expansion as a step-by-step process,

beginning in Jerusalem and then moving into Samaria and Syria (8:1–12:25). The milestone events of this section are the conversions of Paul, a Pharisee (9:1–31), and Cornelius, a Roman soldier, the first Gentile anointed by the Holy Spirit (10:1–11:18). In the second part of Acts (13:1–28:31), Luke focuses almost exclusively on the travels of Paul, who leads a successful mission to the Gentiles in Asia Minor and then carries "the new way" to Europe, arriving in Rome about 60 CE. Arguing that Christianity is a natural extension of Judaism that offers no threat to the Roman state, Luke designs his narrative to show that the church's task is to create an international and ethnically diverse community, a work that extends indefinitely into the future (28:28).

Luke's Purpose in the Book of Acts

A continuation of Luke's Gospel, the Book of Acts is an idealized account of Christian beginnings. Addressing his second volume to the same (otherwise unknown) Theophilus, the author creates a linear narrative tracing early Christianity's progression from a Jewish apocalyptic movement to a largely Gentile faith destined to hold an honorable place in the Greco-Roman world. A vigorous defense of "the new way" (9:2), Acts presents Christianity as a law-abiding religion that does not threaten the Roman government, dramatically staging a series of courtroom scenes in which Roman magistrates and governors find Christians innocent of any illegal activity. At the same time, Luke structures his narrative to demonstrate that the new faith's rapid transition from

a Jewish to a mostly Gentile phenomenon directly fulfills God's will. The book opens in Jerusalem, where Galilean disciples and members of Jesus' family lead the church, but ends in Rome, where Paul, an advocate of Hellenistic Christianity, vows to devote himself entirely to converting Gentiles. By emphasizing the geographical movement from Jerusalem to Rome, capital of the vast Roman Empire, the author illustrates his conviction that, from the beginning, it was God's purpose to bring people of all nationalities into relationship with him (10:34–48).

In composing his narrative, the author (whom we call Luke) is highly selective in his use of the oral traditions and "eyewitness" reports on which Acts presumably is based (cf. Luke 1:1–4). Although he lists the names of the original eleven apostles (1:13), Luke tells us almost nothing about most of them. Instead, he focuses on only a few figures, using them to represent crucial stages in early Christianity's swift transition from a Jewish to a largely Gentile movement. The apostle Peter, representing Palestinian–Jewish Christianity and the original Jerusalem church, presides over the first half of Acts (Chs. 1–12). Paul, exemplifying Hellenistic Christianity's mission to the non-Jewish peoples, dominates the second half (Chs. 13–28). Except for brief references to James and John, the sons of Zebedee (3:1–4:22; 12:1–3; cf. Gal. 2:6–10), Luke rarely mentions Jesus' Galilean disciples or their activities. Whatever anecdotes about other apostles the author may have heard, he does not include them in his narrative. Nor does he explain how some major churches, such as that at Rome, were founded. More important, although Paul is Luke's heroic exemplar of true Christianity, the author does not actually portray him as Paul reveals himself in his letters, omitting controversial Pauline ideas and even contradicting some of Paul's own versions of events.

In looking at maps depicting Paul's missionary journeys (see below), we see immediately that Luke is interested in only one trajectory of Christianity's geographical expansion—that which resulted in the founding of Pauline churches in Asia Minor and Greece and in Paul's preaching in Rome. Concentrating entirely on the northeastern Mediterranean region, Luke says nothing about other large areas where churches were concurrently being established, such as those in Egypt, Cyrene, and other locations in North Africa. Although we cannot be sure why Luke ignores the southern Mediterranean churches, his silence may result from a strong preference for Pauline Christianity, a branch of the faith that historically came to dominate the Western church.

The Divine Plan of Humanity's Salvation

The incidents about early Christian leaders that Luke chooses to include in Acts are arranged to express the author's overarching theme: the Spirit-directed growth of the church and its expansion westward, from Judea to Italy. In general, the narrative advances chronologically, showing the religion's incremental spread into new territories. Luke's organizing principle appears in Acts 1:8, in which the risen Jesus gives the disciples his final command: They are to be his "witnesses in Jerusalem, in all Judea and Samaria, and to the ends of the earth." Acts thus begins in Jerusalem (1:1–7:60), records a mission to Samaria (8:1–40), gives a detailed account of

Paul's three missionary journeys throughout Asia Minor and Greece, and concludes with Paul's arrival in Rome, perhaps representing, from a Christian perspective, "the ends of the earth" (see Box 34.1).

God's Spirit Operating in Human History

In tracing Christianity's growth from its Palestinian roots to Gentile flowering, Luke illustrates the manner in which God has kept his biblical promises to Israel. Jesus and his Jewish followers are the fulfillment of Israel's prophetic goals, a demonstration of God's faithfulness that will reassure Theophilus and other Gentiles who join their ranks. At the end of his Gospel and the beginning of Acts, Luke takes pains to remind readers of Israel's hopes for a Davidic king. The disciples approaching Jerusalem wonder if the kingdom is at last about to materialize (Luke 19:11), a question they reformulate to Jesus immediately before his ascension to heaven: "Lord, is this the time when you will restore the kingdom to Israel?" (Acts 1:6). Jesus' answer, that they must remain in Jerusalem to "receive power" from above and then carry his message worldwide—implies a positive response to their question. In Luke's view, God indeed reestablishes his rule over true citizens of Israel, the Jewish disciples of Jesus who represent the covenant people.

Luke further highlights the theme of Israel's restoration when the Eleven elect a replacement for Judas Iscariot (who dies soon after betraying Jesus), thus re-creating a leadership of Twelve, symbolic of Israel's twelve tribes (1:23–26). Once this continuity between Israel and the Christian community has been affirmed, however, Luke never again refers to the replacement (Mattathias) or to any of the Twelve except for Peter and, briefly, John. (James, John's brother, is mentioned only when Herod Agrippa I has him beheaded [12:2].) In Luke's thematic strategy, the Twelve are the Israelite foundation of the Christian church, a cornerstone on which Gentiles will build the superstructure.

At Pentecost, when the Lukan Peter states that God's eschatological promise of Israel's Spirit-anointing is fulfilled (2:14–36), 3,000 Jews join the Galilean disciples (2:37–41). Throughout both his Gospel and Acts, Luke is careful to distinguish the Jewish people, many of whom accept Jesus as the national Messiah, from the small group of their priestly leaders who had advocated Jesus' execution. Not only had the Jews as a whole—including their "rulers"—"acted in ignorance" of Jesus' identity, but it was also God's foreordained will that the Messiah *had* to suffer—no human action could have prevented it (3:17–24).

BOX 34.1   Major Milestones in the Book of Acts

According to Acts' version of Christian origins, the new faith began at a particular moment in time—at the Jewish Feast of Pentecost, in Jerusalem, when the Holy Spirit descended upon a gathering of Jesus' Galilean disciples (Acts 2). In Luke's carefully structured presentation, Christianity's growth in adherents and geographical expansion are marked by significant milestones, crucial events at which Christianity enters into a new stage of development. Each step along the path from a Palestinian-Jewish sect to a largely Gentile faith preached throughout the Greco-Roman world is indicated by a representative episode, headlining the author's "good news" bulletins.

1. The Christian church is born in Jerusalem—the Holy Spirit anoints 120 disciples at Pentecost, followed by mass conversions to the new Jesus movement (2:1–47).
2. Peter performs the first miraculous cure "in Jesus' name" (3:1–10), continuing Jesus' work.
3. Stephen, a "Hellenist" Jew, becomes the first Christian martyr (6:8–7:60).
4. Another Hellenist, Philip, makes the first non-Jewish converts—a Samaritan sorcerer and an African eunuch (8:4–40).
5. Saul (Paul) of Tarsus, while fiercely persecuting "the way," is suddenly converted by a vision of the risen Jesus on the road to Damascus (9:1–30; cf. 22:6–11; 26:12–19).

6. Peter converts the Roman centurion Cornelius, who becomes the first non-Jew to receive the Holy Spirit (10:1–42).
7. Believers in Jesus are first called "Christians" in Antioch, Syria, which becomes the second major center of Christianity (11:19–26).
8. James, the son of Zebedee and brother of John, becomes the first member of the Twelve to suffer martyrdom (12:1–3).
9. Paul, following Barnabas, makes his first missionary journey from Antioch to Asia Minor (modern Turkey) (13:1–14:28), carrying Pauline Christianity to the Greek-speaking world.
10. The first church council, held at Jerusalem to discuss whether Gentile converts must observe Mosaic Law, decides in favor of admitting uncircumcised males, opening "the way" to all nationalities (15:1–35).
11. Carrying the faith from western Asia to Europe, Paul makes his first missionary tour of Greece, founding churches at Philippi, Thessalonica, and Corinth (16:9–18:23).
12. In Jerusalem, Paul is arrested by a Roman officer (21:15–22:29). After two years in a Caesarean prison, Paul appears before Governor Festus and Herod Agrippa II (25:6–32), fulfilling the risen Jesus' prediction that Paul will testify "before kings" (9:15).
13. Exercising his right as a Roman citizen, Paul is sent to Rome for trial. Under house arrest in Rome, Paul vows to focus exclusively on recruiting Gentiles (28:16–30).

In his second Jerusalem speech, Peter insists that he and his fellow Jews "are the descendants of the prophets and of the covenant that God gave to your ancestors," the means by which God's blessing "for all the families of the earth" is accomplished (3:25–26). As Luke presents his history of salvation, Jerusalem and its Temple—where Pharisees and Jewish Christians worship side by side—are the focal point of God's redemptive acts for all humanity.

Luke's Use of Speeches

Like other historians of his day, Luke ascribes long, elaborate speeches to his leading characters, such as Peter, Stephen, James, and Paul. But whoever the speaker, most of the speeches sound much alike in both style and thought. This similarity among Acts' many discourses, as well as the fact that they seem to reflect attitudes prevalent in the author's time rather than the era of the historical figures he describes, suggests to most scholars that they are largely Luke's own compositions. In the absence of exact transcriptions of apostolic speeches, many of which were delivered amid noisy and unruly crowds, Luke apparently follows the standard practice of Greco-Roman authors by supplementing what was remembered with material of his own creation. Ancient historians and biographers like Thucydides, Livy, Tacitus, and Plutarch commonly enlivened their narratives with speeches put in the mouths of historical figures. The classical writer composed such discourses based on his conception of the speaker's character and major concerns at the time the speech was given. He was not expected to reproduce a particular speech exactly as it was delivered. Thucydides explains the historian's method clearly and briefly:

> I have found it difficult to remember the precise words used in the speeches which I listened to myself and my various informants have experienced the same difficulty; so my method has been, while keeping as closely as possible to the general sense of the words that were actually used, to make the speaker say what, in my opinion, was called for by each occasion. (*The Peloponnesian War* 1.22)

In short, while attempting to reproduce the "general sense" of what people said, Thucydides created their speeches according to his understanding of what "was called for" in a particular situation. We cannot know the extent to which Luke's speeches reflect ideas expressed in generations before his time.

Organization of the Book of Acts

Luke arranges his narrative in ten major sections:

1. Prologue and account of Jesus' ascension (1:1–11)
2. Founding of the Jerusalem church (1:12–2:47)
3. The work of Peter and the Galilean apostles (3:1–5:42)
4. Persecutions of the "Hellenist" Jewish Christians and the first missions (6:1–8:40)
5. Preparation for the Gentile mission: the conversions of Paul and Cornelius (9:1–12:25)
6. The first missionary journey of Barnabas and Paul: the Jerusalem conference (13:1–15:35)
7. Paul's second missionary journey: founding the first congregations in Greece (16:1–18:21)
8. Paul's third missionary journey: revisiting Asia Minor and Greece (18:22–20:38)
9. Paul's arrest in Jerusalem and imprisonment in Caesarea (21:1–26:32)
10. Paul's journey to Rome and his preaching to Diaspora Jews (27:1–28:31)

Prologue and Account of Jesus' Ascension

Luke is the only New Testament writer to state that Jesus' postresurrection appearances (all in or near Jerusalem) spanned a period of forty days, a symbolic time reminiscent of that Moses spent with Yahweh on Mount Sinai and that Jesus passed in the wilderness. Although

his account of the risen Jesus is tantalizingly brief, Luke uses it for a characteristic purpose: to show that God's plan does not involve the literal restoration of the Jewish state that the disciples had anticipated (Luke 19:11; Acts 1:3, 6–7). Contrary to apocalyptic expectations, God's rule expands gradually as the Christian message slowly penetrates Greco-Roman society. The historical process must begin in Jerusalem, to fulfill God's ancient promises to Israel, but the Spirit will energize believers to impart their faith to Gentiles everywhere. In describing Jesus' ascent to the spirit realm, Luke portrays it as a physical movement skyward, culminating in Jesus' disappearance into the clouds, symbolic of the divine presence (cf. Exod. 40:34–35); 1 Kings 8:10; Dan. 7:13). Luke also makes this peaceful ascension, which only a few observe, a prophetic model of Jesus' quiet return at the Parousia (1:9–11).

Founding the Jerusalem Church: The Role of the Holy Spirit

The first two chapters emphasize the divine power that transforms the Jerusalem church from a group of about 120 persons (1:15) to several thousand worshipers, including some priests (2:41; 4:4; 5:14–16; 6:1, 7). Symbolically rendered as wind and flame, the Holy Spirit enables the disciples to speak in foreign tongues—representing the multinational nature of Christianity (see Figure 34.1). In a long speech, Peter interprets this ecstatic phenomenon, known as *glossolalia*, as the fulfillment of Joel's prediction that in the last days men and women, young and old, would prophesy (2:1–24; cf. Joel 2:28–32). Peter thus equates the disciples' religious ecstasy with Joel's vision of cosmic "portents," such as the sun's eclipse and the moon's turning to "blood." While implying a metaphorical fulfillment of apocalyptic visions, Luke's main point is that God has anointed his church, appointing its members to teach in every known tongue, the many languages of Pentecost representing the universality of the Christian mission.

Repeating a theme prominent in his Gospel, the author connects the Spirit's presence with its recipients' revolutionary way of life, particularly in creating an ideal community without rich or poor. Luke reports that the faithful sold their possessions so that money and goods could be distributed according to individual members' needs. Holding "all things in common," (2:43–45; 4:32–35), the Jerusalem community meets Jesus' challenge to sacrifice material possessions to attain true discipleship (Luke 18:18–30). As a result of establishing the kingdom's economic ethic as its

FIGURE 34.1 In *The Descent of the Holy Spirit at Pentecost*, El Greco (1541–1614) depicts the Holy Spirit as a radiant dove and as tongues of flame playing above the disciples' heads. This miraculous anointing of Jesus' followers at Pentecost parallels Luke's version of Jesus' receiving the Holy Spirit after his baptism.

standard, however, the Jerusalem church apparently soon had to depend on financial help from Paul's Gentile churches to sustain its ideal (Gal. 2:10; Rom. 15:25–28).

The Work of Peter and the Apostles

In the next section (3:1–5:42), Luke presents a series of dramatic confrontations between the apostles and the Jerusalem authorities. He attributes much of the church's trouble to the Sadducee party, whose priests control the Temple (4:1–6; 5:17–18). By contrast, many Pharisees tend to tolerate or even champion some Christian activities (5:34–40; 23:6–9). During Peter's second hearing before the Sanhedrin, the Pharisee **Gamaliel,** a famous first-century rabbinical scholar, is represented as protecting the infant church.

Persecution of the Hellenists

In the following section (6:1–8:40), Sadducean hostility focuses on **Stephen,** a leading Hellenist, or Greek-speaking Jew of the Diaspora. The episode culminates in Stephen's impassioned speech to the Jews, who stone him for blasphemy (6:8–7:60). The execution of this first Christian **martyr** (Greek, "witness") and the persecution that follows have the unintended effect of fueling the church's growth. Scattered throughout Judea and Samaria, Hellenist Christians carry "the new way" to new populations, making such diverse converts as **Simon Magus,** a sorcerer, and an Ethiopian eunuch, treasurer of Queen Candace (8:26–40).

Conversions of Paul and Cornelius

Luke represents the progress of Christianity from a Messianic Jewish sect to its (hoped-for) status as a world religion in two additional conversion stories of monumental importance. In the first, **Saul of Tarsus,** a Pharisaic persecutor of the church is suddenly recruited to the new faith when the glorified Jesus appears to him on the road to Damascus. Henceforth, Saul will be known by his Roman name, **Paul,** whom God will make his principal instrument in transforming Christianity into a mostly Gentile religion. The author regards Paul's Damascus experience as so crucial that he gives no fewer than three separate accounts of the incident (9:3–8; 22:6–11; 26:12–19).

Luke devotes the next two chapters (10:1–11:30) to the second landmark conversion, that of **Cornelius,** a Roman centurion, and his household. Although Peter generally represents a Torah-conservative position in the Jerusalem community, the author here shows him as the agent who first opens the church's doors to non-Jews. Initially, Peter receives a vision implying that all foods, as well as the Gentiles who eat them, are now "clean" and acceptable to God (10:9–16). Following the vision, a delegation brings Peter to Cornelius's house, where Peter, directed by the Holy Spirit, baptizes the entire family (10:1–8, 17–48). Underscoring his view that the Spirit's presence validates a religious decision, Luke shows Cornelius and his household speaking in tongues exactly as the Jewish Christians had at Pentecost. Peter then interprets the incident's religious meaning: that people formerly excluded from Yahweh's covenant can now become the people of God (10:34). Luke also depicts Peter as instrumental in persuading the "circumcised believers" in Jerusalem to agree that God now accepts non-Jews as his own (11:1–18). On what terms the Gentiles may join the church, however, remains unresolved.

First Missionary Journey of Barnabas and Paul

When Gentiles flock to the church at **Antioch** in Syria, the Jerusalem apostles dispatch **Barnabas,** a Greek-speaking Jewish Christian from Cyprus to report on the situation. Impressed by the converts' zeal, Barnabas imports Paul, who had returned to Tarsus, to help instruct them (11:19–30). Barnabas and Paul are remarkably successful in converting Gentiles not only in Antioch but throughout Asia Minor (modern Turkey) (13:1–14:28) (see Figure 34.2). Their missionary tour is interrupted, however, when controversy breaks out between Gentile and Jewish Christians over obedience to the Mosaic Torah. Among other requirements, some Jewish Christians insist that Gentile converts must be circumcised and observe Jewish dietary laws.

The Jerusalem Conference According to Acts 15, the first church council in history takes place at Jerusalem, where the apostles and "elders" gather to debate whether a believer must first become a Jew in order to be a Christian. Christian Pharisees demand that the entire Torah be kept. But Peter reportedly opposes this (15:10) and, citing his own key role in bringing uncircumcised Gentiles into the church (15:7–11), thereby silences the opposition.

This dispute between Torah-keeping Christians who advocated circumcision and their opponents who denied its necessity bitterly divided the early church. Writing many years after the issue had been settled in favor of admitting uncircumcised Gentiles, Luke does not attempt to reproduce the hostilities that then prevailed. His purpose is to create a model for dealing peacefully with such internal conflicts. In describing the Jerusalem conference held about 49 CE to resolve

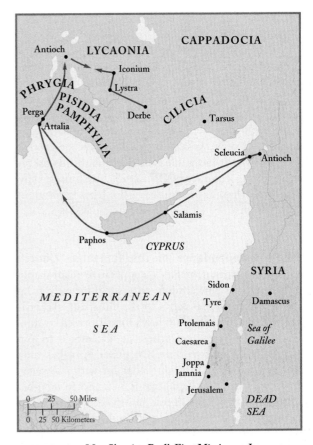

FIGURE 34.2 Map Showing Paul's First Missionary Journey. According to Acts, Paul made three major tours through the northeastern Mediterranean region. Although the account in Acts may oversimplify Paul's complex travel itineraries, it correctly shows him focusing his efforts on major urban centers in Asia Minor (modern Turkey).

the Torah issue, Luke presents an ideal of orderly procedure in which delegates from Antioch and Christian Pharisees agree unanimously on a compromise solution. After Peter advises against laying the Torah "yoke" upon converts, Barnabas and Paul plead their case for the Gentiles' freedom from the Torah's legal burdens.

According to Luke, the deciding voice is that of **James** (Jesus' "brother" or kinsman), the person who later succeeds Peter as head of the Jerusalem church. Although Paul's letter paints James as a strongly conservative advocate of circumcision (see Gal. 2), the Lukan James is a "moderate" who imposes only limited Torah regulations. James's dietary restrictions are based on rules from Leviticus, according to which both Jews and Israel's foreign residents are forbidden to eat meat that has not been drained of blood (15:13–21; Lev. 17–18).

The author completes his ideal example of church procedures by illustrating the manner in which James's recommendation is carried out. Themes of unity and cooperation shape Luke's account: The "whole church" decides to send "unanimously" elected delegates back to Antioch with a letter containing the Jerusalem leadership's directive. Characteristically, Luke notes that the Holy Spirit has guided the decision of this precedent-setting conference (15:22–29). In Luke's view, when the church's Jewish leadership agrees to admit Gentiles on an equal footing, the divine will is accomplished.

Paul's Independence of the Jerusalem Church

Luke's description of Paul's cooperative relationship with the Jerusalem leaders differs significantly from the account in Paul's letter to the Galatians. According to Luke, shortly after Jesus first appeared to him, Paul went to Jerusalem, where he "attempted to join the disciples," but was rebuffed. After Barnabas took this zealous new Christian under his wing, however, Luke indicates that Paul became an accepted member of Jerusalem's Christian community (9:26–30). In his own version of events, however, Paul categorically denies that he had early contact with the Jerusalem church or that his teaching about Jesus owed anything to his apostolic predecessors. After his private "revelation" of the risen Jesus, Paul states: "I did not confer with any human being, nor did I go up to Jerusalem to those who were already apostles before me, but I went away at once into Arabia, and afterwards I returned to Damascus" (Gal. 1:16–17). Three years later, Paul says, he did travel to Jerusalem "to visit Cephas [Peter] and stayed with him fifteen days, but I did not see any other apostle except James the Lord's brother" (Gal. 1:18–19). When Paul immediately adds, "In what I am writing to you, before God, I do not lie!" (Gal. 1:20), he clearly rejects any suggestion that he was ever under the influence or authority of the Jerusalem leadership.

Given Luke's policy of depicting Paul as a cooperative churchman, willingly subject to apostolic decrees, it is not surprising that Acts' description of the Jerusalem conference contrasts markedly with Paul's eyewitness report (Gal. 2:1–10). Whereas Acts shows the Gentile–Torah issue peacefully and unanimously settled, Paul declares that he "did not submit to them [advocates of Torah obedience] even for a moment" (2:5). As Paul recalls his "private" meeting with "James and Cephas [Peter] and John," the three "acknowledged pillars" of the church, he successfully insists that Gentile Christians be permitted to live absolutely "free" of Torah obligations. According to Galatians, Paul accepted no restrictions, whereas Acts states that he unhesitatingly agreed to James' four Torah prohibitions. In addition, Paul reveals an attitude toward eating meat sacrificed to Greco-Roman gods that differs from that Acts ascribes to him (1 Cor. 8:8; 10:27).

Some historians suggest that the apostolic decree involving dietary matters may have been issued at a subsequent Jerusalem conference, one that Paul did not attend. Later in Acts, the author seems aware that Paul did not know about the Jerusalem church's decision regarding Torah-forbidden meats. During Paul's final Jerusalem visit, James is shown speaking about the dietary restrictions as if they were news to Paul (21:25).

Paul's Second Missionary Journey: Bringing the Word to Greece

Shortly after the Jerusalem conference, Paul and Barnabas separate. Acts attributes this parting to a quarrel over John Mark's alleged unreliability, but in Galatians, Paul states that he and Barnabas differed over the question of Torah observance, Barnabas having been "led astray" by Torah-keeping Christians (whose views Paul labels "hypocrisy") (Gal. 2:13). As a result, Paul takes Silas with him to visit the newly founded churches of Syria and Asia Minor; a vision then directs Paul into Macedonia (northern Greece) (15:40–16:10) (see Figure 34.3). Here Luke shows Paul following his usual pattern of preaching in local synagogues until Jewish leaders evict him (16:11–17:15).

Driven from the Macedonian cities of Philippi, Thessalonica, and Beroea, Paul finds unusual tolerance in **Athens,** the center of Greek philosophy, where he is invited to speak before an intellectually curious group at the Areopagus (highest public council) (17:16–34) (see Figure 34.4). After making few converts among the sophisticated Athenians, Paul enjoys greater success in **Corinth,** a prosperous Greek seaport, where he founds a thriving church. Paul's letters to the Corinthians contain some of his most vivid writing (see Chapter 35).

Paul's Third Missionary Journey: Revisiting Asia Minor and Greece

A third missionary tour, in which Paul revisits the churches of Greece and Asia Minor (18:1–21:10),

FIGURE 34.3 Map Showing Paul's Second Missionary Journey. As Acts depicts it, this journey brought
Christianity to Europe, with new Christian congregations established in Philippi, Thessalonica, and Corinth.
Note that Antioch in Syria serves as Paul's missionary headquarters.

culminates in **Ephesus,** a large and prosperous city in
what is now western Turkey (see Figure 34.5). Luke
frames Paul's adventures in Ephesus with intimations
of the apostle's final journey—to Rome. As Luke had
portrayed Jesus turning his face resolutely toward
Jerusalem and the prophet's death that awaited him
there (Luke 9:51), so the author shows Paul determined to complete his last tour and head for the imperial capital (19:21–22). After summoning Ephesian
church leaders to Miletus, an ancient Greek city on
the Aegean, Paul delivers a farewell speech, predicting
his imminent imprisonment and possible martyrdom
(20:17–38).

The remainder of Acts concentrates on Paul's legal
difficulties with the Roman government. Reinforcing
his theme that Christianity poses no danger to Roman
security, Luke takes pains to demonstrate that Paul
is charged with sedition only because his religious
competitors stir up trouble against him. Roman officials
repeatedly testify that he is guilty of no punishable
action. When some Corinthian Jews charge him with
defaming God, the Roman proconsul **Gallio** throws the
case out of court (18:12–17). (For the importance of
Gallio's administration in dating Paul's career, see
Chapter 35.) Similarly, when the Greek silversmiths of
Ephesus, who fashion images of the goddess Artemis

FIGURE 34.4   This model shows a reconstruction of the Athenian Acropolis. According to Acts 17, Athenian philosophers invited Paul to explain his new religion at the Areopagus (Hill of Ares), a public forum located on a spur of the Acropolis. Named for Athene, goddess of wisdom, Athens was celebrated for encouraging freedom of thought and speech.

(Diana) for sale to tourists, try to force Paul to stop his anti-idolatry campaign, local authorities argue that they have no legal cause to do so (19:23–41) (see Figures 34.6 and 34.7).

Paul's Arrest in Jerusalem and Imprisonment in Caesarea

On Paul's return to Jerusalem, Jewish resistance to his association with Gentiles reaches a climax when some Diaspora Jews accuse him of blasphemy and of profaning the Temple. When a mob attacks him, Roman soldiers intervene and conduct him to the Sanhedrin. Disclosing that he is a Pharisee, Paul succeeds in dividing the council so that scribes of his party call for his release while the Sadducees and others denounce him (21:27–23:10). The divine plan operating through Paul's suffering is now revealed: He must proclaim the Christian witness in Rome as he has in Jerusalem (23:11).

After a Roman army commander, Lysias, takes him into protective custody, Paul is imprisoned for two years at Caesarea under Governor **Antonius Felix,** who apparently has no plans to release his troublesome prisoner without receiving the customary bribe. Under Felix's successor, **Porcius Festus,** Paul exercises his legal rights as a Roman citizen and "appeal[s] to the emperor" (25:11), demanding to be tried in Rome. Luke's detailed narration of Paul's defense before Festus, King **Herod Agrippa II,** and his sister Bernice (25:8–26:32) is intended to demonstrate his innocence of any religious or political crimes. Paul's long defense (26:1–29) is a vivid summary of his career as depicted in Acts, including a third account of Jesus' first appearance to him. The author's main purpose in this courtroom scene is to establish Christianity's potentially friendly relationship to the Roman Empire. Echoing Pilate's opinion of Jesus, Governor Festus admits that "this man is doing nothing to deserve death or imprisonment." King Agrippa drives home the point: Paul could have been set free "if he had not appealed to the emperor" (26:30–32). In Luke's introduction of the Christian church to his Greco-Roman audience, he makes clear

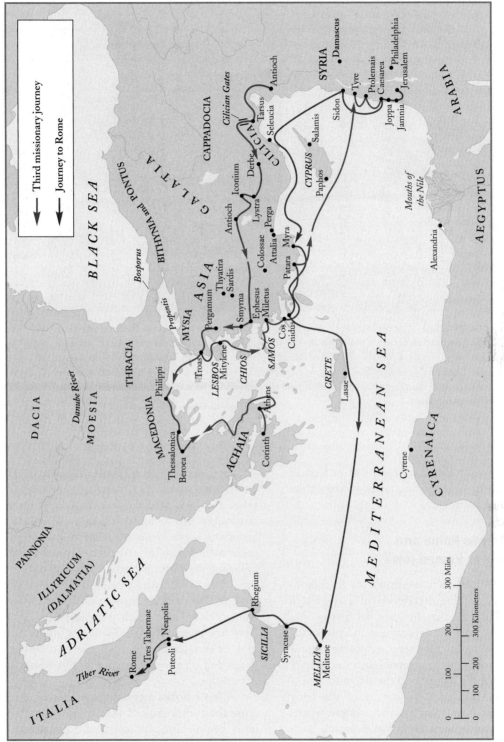

FIGURE 34.5 Map Showing Paul's Third Missionary Journey. According to Acts, this journey ended with his arrest in Jerusalem and two-year imprisonment in Caesarea. The bottom line shows the route of Paul's sea voyage to Rome, where he was taken to be tried in the imperial courts.

FIGURE 34.6 This photo shows the amphitheater at Ephesus. A wealthy Greco-Roman seaport in Asia Minor (western Turkey), Ephesus was the site of one of the Seven Wonders of the Ancient World, the lavish marble Temple of Artemis (the Roman Diana). According to Acts 19, Ephesian silversmiths staged a riot in the amphitheater when Paul's Christian message threatened to subvert the worship of Artemis—and the prosperity of the silversmiths, who profited from selling miniature silver replicas of the goddess's statue and shrine to tourists.

that missionaries like Paul are prosecuted in Roman courts only through officials' misunderstanding or the malice of false accusers.

Paul's Journey to Rome and His Preaching to Roman Jews

Luke begins his final section—Paul's sea journey to Rome—with an exciting description of a shipwreck (27:1–18:31). Here the narrator uses the first person, one of several "we" passages appearing in this part of the book. Scholars are unsure whether these passages represent an eyewitness report or merely use the literary device to heighten the vividness of the account.

The author concludes his survey of the early Christian movement with Paul's arrival in Rome, where, although under house arrest, he is free to preach "with all boldness and without [legal] hindrance" (28:31). This final statement is probably a reminder to Roman authorities that Paul's case established a legal precedent. Awaiting trial, and with full knowledge of his captors, Christianity's most famous missionary continued to proclaim his gospel to the Roman population.

Luke does not reveal Paul's ultimate fate. One tradition states that, after remaining in the capital for two years, Paul was released and carried out his planned missionary trip to Spain (cf. Rom. 15:24, 28). Most historians, however, believe that Paul's first Roman imprisonment led to his execution, perhaps about 62 CE, following the emperor Nero's order to impose the death penalty on anyone who spoke or behaved in a way that appeared to criticize his supreme authority. Other scholars date Paul's death at about 64 or 65 CE, when Nero first persecuted Christians as a group. According to a brief reference in 1 Clement (c. 96 CE), both Peter and Paul suffered martyrdom during Nero's persecution.

A few scholars suggest that Acts ends abruptly because the author did not wish to admit that Paul, like Jesus before him, was executed for sedition against Rome, a fact contrary to his theme of cooperation with the imperial government. The majority, however, believe that Acts concludes as it does because Luke regards Paul's preaching in Rome as the fulfillment of Jesus' commission to testify about him "to the ends of the earth." Paul's last words are a vow that henceforth he will minister only to Gentiles, because "they will listen," a prediction that charts the future course of Luke's Gentile community.

QUESTIONS FOR DISCUSSION AND REVIEW

1. A sequel to Luke's Gospel, the Book of Acts continues the story of Christian origins. Which of the same themes that appear in the Gospel are also found in Acts? Compare the account of Jesus' trial before Pilate and that of Paul before Pilate's successors, Felix and Festus.

2. How does Luke organize his account of Christianity's birth and early growth? Identify the leaders of the Jerusalem church and the missionaries who helped carry "the new way" into the large world beyond the Jewish capital.

3. In what ways do the events at Pentecost show that Christianity is a universal religion—led by the Holy Spirit and destined for peoples of all nations?

4. How does the Jerusalem commune put into operation the social and economic principles that Jesus advocates in Luke's Gospel? How does the early church "equalize" wealth and poverty?

5. The conversions of an Ethiopian eunuch, a Pharisee, and a Roman centurion are milestones in Christianity's transformation from an apocalyptic Jewish sect into an international religion in which Gentiles dominated. Explain how this process of ethnic change led to problems in the believing community. According to Acts 15, how is the problem resolved at the first church conference in Jerusalem? What roles do Peter, James, and Paul play?

6. In contrast to the author of Revelation, Luke includes no condemnation of the Roman Empire or predictions of its cataclysmic fall. Given Luke's universalism and concern for social justice, how do you think he envisions Christianity's goals and obligations in its ongoing role in secular society?

FIGURE 34.7 This cult statue of Diana of Ephesus, where the world's largest temple was erected in the goddess' honor, emphasizes her function as giver of fertility. Although the Romans identified Diana with Artemis, the Greek virgin goddess of wild creatures and the hunt, the Ephesian Diana bears a greater resemblance to older Near Eastern fertility deities such as Ishtar and Astarte. Acts records a confrontation between Paul and the silversmiths of Ephesus, whose livelihood making silver figurines of Diana was threatened by the apostle's monotheistic gospel (Acts 19:23–41).

Terms and Concepts to Remember

Ascension, the	Holy Spirit, role of in Acts
Athens	Jerusalem conference
Barnabas	Jesus' postresurrection
Corinth	commission to the
Gamaliel	apostles
glossolalia	Paul/Saul of Tarsus
Hellenists	Stephen

Recommended Reading

Arlandson, James M. *Women, Class, and Society in Early Christianity: Models from Luke-Acts.* Peabody, MA: Hendrickson, 1997. Applies social theory to the role of women in ancient society and the church.

Dunn, James D. G. *The Acts of the Apostles* (Narrative Commentary Series). Philadelphia: Trinity Press International, 1997. Examines the nature of history writing in the first century CE and Act's narrative structure; for advanced study.

Gaventa, Beverly Roberts. "Act of the Apostles." In K. D. Sakenfeld, ed., *The New Interpreter's Dictionary of the Bible,* Vol. 1, pp. 33–47. Nashville, TN: Abingdon Press, 2006. Surveys contents and themes of Acts; helpful to beginning students.

Levine, Amy-Jill, and Blickenstaff, Marianne, eds. *Feminist Companion to the Book of Acts* (Feminist Companion to the New Testament and Early Christian Writings). Cleveland: Pilgrim Press, 2005. A collection of scholarly essays offering women's perspectives on Christian origins.

Powell, M. A. *What Are They Saying About Acts?* New York: Paulist Press, 1991. A helpful review of current scholarship on Acts.

Wall, Robert W. "The Acts of the Apostles." In *The New Interpreter's Bible,* Vol. 10, pp. 3–368. Nashville, TN: Abingdon Press, 2002. Offers extensive historical and literary analysis.

Paul and the Gentile Mission

Letters to Churches at Thessalonica, Corinth, Galatia, Rome, Philippi, and Colossae

---

Key Topics/Themes Paul is second only to Jesus in his contribution to the development of Christianity. Although Paul apparently never knew the living Jesus and once persecuted his disciples, he experienced an *apokalypsis* (revelation) of the risen Jesus that transformed his life. Becoming a missionary to the Gentiles, Paul created and disseminated a view of Jesus' cosmic significance that profoundly shaped the future course of Christian thought. In a series of letters to newly founded congregations in Greece, Asia Minor, and Rome, Paul argues that Christians are free of Torah obligations and that faith in Christ makes them Abraham's spiritual descendants and therefore in a saving relationship with God. Viewing Jesus' resurrection and exaltation to heaven as the dawning of a new age, Paul warns his recipients to live ethically because Jesus' Parousia is imminent.

Paul's Contribution to the New Testament

Paul, former Pharisee and persecutor of the church who later pioneered Christianity's mission to the Gentiles, dominates the second half of Acts. To an incalculable degree, he also dominates the later history of Christian thought. His letters, which form a crucial part of the New Testament, represent the religion's first—and in many ways most lasting—attempt to interpret the meaning of Jesus' sacrificial death and its significance for human salvation. Paul's starting point is that Jesus' crucifixion and resurrection introduced a radically different relationship between God and all humanity—both Jews and Gentiles. In his letters to the Romans and Galatians, Paul outlines a theology of redemption through faith that has become central to Christianity's self-understanding. Later theologians as diverse as the Roman church father Augustine (354–430 CE) and Martin Luther (1483–1546), the German monk who ignited the Protestant Reformation, derived many of their doctrines from Paul's letters.

A Direct Voice

In contrast to Jesus, who apparently wrote nothing, Paul speaks directly to us through his letters, permitting us to compare what he says about himself with what later writers, such as Luke, say about him. Paul's position in the canon is unique: He is the only historical personage who is both a major character in a New Testament book and the author of New Testament books himself. Church tradition ascribes no fewer than a dozen canonical letters to Paul, in total length nearly one-third of the New Testament. Most scholars regard only seven as genuinely Pauline, but the presence of additional works attributed to him shows in what high esteem he was held. His ideas and personality so captured the imagination of later Christian authors that they paid tribute to the great apostle by writing in his name and perpetuating his teachings for new generations. (The map in Figure 35.1 hints at the extent of Paul's influence even in his own time.)

Although our most reliable source for details about Paul's life is his letters, they do not offer enough information to form a real biography. The letters are silent on

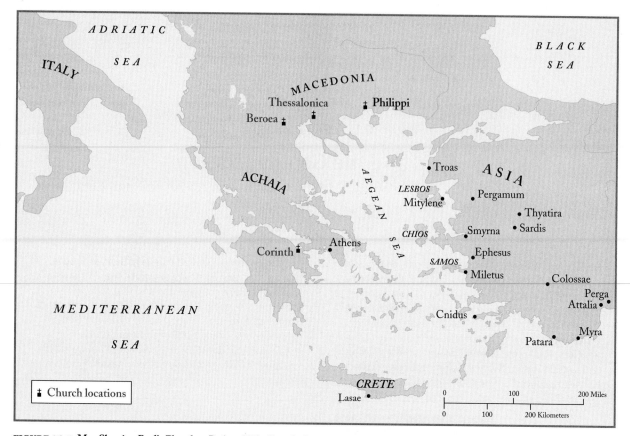

FIGURE 35.1 Map Showing Paul's Churches. Paul established largely Gentile churches in the northeastern Mediterranean at Philippi, Thessalonica, Beroea, and Corinth. Paul's teaching was also influential in the Asia Minor city of Ephesus, where he lived for at least two years. The sites of some other prominent Christian centers are also given.

such matters as his birthplace, parentage, education, and other essentials of his formative years, as well as on the later sequence of his travels as a Christian missionary. Paul tends to mention biographical details only when they are useful in supporting his theological arguments, particularly in controversies with fellow Jews. In defending his qualifications as a formerly observant Jew, Paul states that he is "a member of the people of Israel, of the tribe of Benjamin, a Hebrew born of Hebrews; as to the law, a Pharisee, as to zeal, a persecutor of the church; as to righteousness under the law, blameless" (Phil. 3:5–6). In his "earlier life in Judaism," Paul states, "I advanced in Judaism beyond many among my people of the same age, for I was far more zealous for the traditions of my ancestors" (Gal. 1:13–14). For Paul, his Jewishness and ability to interpret Torah are important to his qualifications as an apostle.

Acts offers biographical data that Paul never mentions, such as his birth in Tarsus, capital city of Cilicia (southeastern Turkey), and the belief that Paul's family possessed Roman citizenship. These and

other traditions—such as Paul's originally being named Saul, his studying at the feet of Rabbi Gamaliel (the leading Pharisee scholar of his day), and his supporting himself by tent making—are never referred to in Pauline letters, so we have no way of verifying their historical accuracy. (Box 35.1 summarizes some differences between Acts and Paul's letters.)

Luke fits all of Paul's missionary activities into three separate journeys, which take him from Syria to Greece. Although Paul does not confirm Acts' three-part itinerary, his letters prove that he traveled to most of the major cities in the northeastern Mediterranean. Paul's stamina—even today duplicating his journeys would exhaust most healthy people—is matched by the strength of his feelings. The letters reveal their author's emotional intensity, ranging from paternal tenderness to biting sarcasm (see Figure 35.2). Writing to the Galatians, he insults his readers' intelligence and suggests that some of their advisors castrate themselves (Gal. 3:1; 5:12). In other letters, he reacts to criticism with threats, wild boasting, and wounding

BOX 35.1 Some Differences Between Acts and Paul's Letters

ACCORDING TO ACTS	ACCORDING TO PAUL'S LETTERS
Is named Saul and raised in Tarsus	Is not mentioned (but was born to the tribe of Benjamin, whose first king was Saul (Phil. 3:5))
Studies under Rabbi Gamaliel	Is not mentioned
Belongs to the Pharisee party	Is confirmed in Philippians 3:6
Experiences a vision of Jesus on the road to Damascus	Receives a "revelation" of Jesus (Gal. 1:12, 16)
Following his call, goes immediately to Damascus, where he preaches in synagogues	Goes immediately to "Arabia" for an unspecified period (Gal. 1:17)
Is initially shunned by the Jerusalem disciples but is later introduced to the apostles (9:26–30)	Does not go to Jerusalem until three years after his return from "Arabia," and meets only Peter and James (Gal. 1:17–20)
Receives the Holy Spirit after Ananias baptizes and lays hands upon him	Asserts that he owes his gospel and apostolic commission to no one; never refers to his baptism (Gal. 1:11–12, 16–17)
Attends an apostolic conference on his third Jerusalem visit	Attends the conference on his second Jerusalem visit (Gal. 2:1–10)
Agrees to impose Torah dietary restrictions on Gentile converts	Refuses to accept any legal restrictions (Gal. 2:5)
Agrees to forbid eating meat sacrificed to idols	Regards eating such meat as nondefiling (1 Cor. 8; 10:27; Rom. 14:13–15:6)

FIGURE 35.2 In this ancient Christian mosaic portrait of Paul, the apostle stares directly at the viewer, the intensity of his gaze suggesting a passionate commitment to his mission. Although no one knows what any New Testament figure looked like, later Christian artists commonly depicted Paul as physically unimpressive.

anger (2 Cor. 10–13). In still others, he expresses profound affection and gentle tact (1 Cor. 13; Phil. 1:3–9; 2:1–4; 4:2–3).

Paul's conviction that Jesus had privately revealed to him the one true gospel (Gal. 1–2) isolated the apostle from many fellow believers. Acts and the letters agree that Paul quarreled with many of his intimate companions (Acts 15:37–39; Gal. 2:11–14), as well with entire groups (Gal. 1–5; 2 Cor. 10–13). This sense of unique vision, one not shared by most other Christians, may have shaped Paul's admitted preference for preaching in territories where no Christian had preceded him. The more distant his missionary field from competing evangelizers, the better it suited him. Paul's desire to impress his individual gospel upon new converts may have influenced his plan to work in areas as far removed from established churches as possible (Rom. 15:20–23).

Paul's Letters

The Genuine Letters The large majority of scholars accept seven canonical letters as genuinely Pauline: Romans, 1 and 2 Corinthians, Galatians, Philippians, 1 Thessalonians, and Philemon. Many also accept 2 Thessalonians and Colossians. But the majority doubt that Paul wrote Ephesians and are virtually unanimous in denying Paul's authorship to 1 and 2 Timothy and Titus, which scholars believe were composed by a disciple after Paul's death.

Although scholars debate the exact order in which Paul wrote his letters, they generally agree that 1 Thessalonians was written first (c. 50 CE) and is thus the oldest Christian document in existence. If Paul also wrote 2 Thessalonians, it also dates from about 50 CE. First and Second Corinthians were probably composed in the early-to-mid-50s, and the more theologically mature letters, such as Romans and Philippians, a few years later. Four letters—Colossians, Philippians, Philemon, and possibly Ephesians—are commonly known as the "captivity letters," all supposedly written while Paul was in prison. Unfortunately, Paul does not reveal where he was imprisoned, so we do not know whether he composed them at Ephesus, Caesarea, or Rome—all cities in which he was kept prisoner. The canonical letters (others have been lost) were probably all written during a relatively brief time, between about 50 and 60 CE.

Paul's Use of the Letter Form Paul is aware that his letters are persuasive documents, describing them as "weighty and strong," a contrast to his unimpressive physical appearance and limitations as a public speaker

(2 Cor. 10:9–11). The apostle may exaggerate his shortcomings for rhetorical effect, but he is right about his letters, a literary form that later New Testament writers deliberately imitated. Twenty-one of the twenty-seven canonical books are (at least theoretically) letters. Even the writer of Revelation uses this form to transmit Jesus' messages to the seven churches of Asia Minor (Rev. 2–3).

Hellenistic Letters In general, Paul follows the accepted Hellenistic literary form in his correspondence, modifying it somewhat to express his peculiarly Christian interests. Much Greco-Roman correspondence, both personal and business, has survived from early Christian times, allowing us to compare Paul's letters with those of his contemporaries. The Hellenistic letter writer typically begins with a prescript, identifying the writer and the recipient, and a greeting, wishing good fortune to the reader and commonly invoking the blessing of a god. Paul varies this formula by mentioning the Christian allegiance of the writer and his recipients, substituting "grace" and "peace" for the customary greetings, and typically including an associate's name—such as Timothy or Titus—in the salutation. He also elaborates on the Hellenistic custom by giving praise, thanks, or prayers for the welfare of his readers.

Paul also modifies his letters' prescripts according to his attitude toward the church he is addressing. Paul's missive to his trusted friends at Philippi opens with an effusive outpouring of affection and praise for the Philippians (Phil. 1:1–11). By contrast, when he writes to the churches in Galatia, he is furious with the recipients and includes no warm or approving salutation (Gal. 1:1–5).

After stating the letter's principal message, the Hellenistic writer closes with additional greetings, commonly including greetings from other people and sometimes adding a request that the recipient(s) convey the sender's respects to mutual acquaintances. Paul often expands this custom to include a summary statement of faith and a benediction, as well as a list of fellow Christians to be greeted (Rom. 16; 1 Cor. 16:10–21; Col. 4:7–18).

The Role of Dictation As was customary in Greco-Roman correspondence, Paul apparently dictated all his letters to a secretary or scribe, occasionally adding a signature or a few other words in his own hand. In antiquity, secretaries or scribes ordinarily did not record the precise words of those dictating, but paraphrased the gist of what was said (Rom. 16:21–22; Gal. 6:11; Col. 4:18; Philem. v. 19; 2 Thess. 3:17), a practice that helps to explain the spontaneous quality of Paul's genuine letters.

Circumstances of Writing Most of Paul's letters were composed under the pressure of meeting an emergency in a given church. With the exception of Romans, which is addressed to a congregation that he had not yet visited, every Pauline letter is directed to a particular group, most members of which the writer knows personally. Because Paul's letters are *occasional*—dealing with a specific occasion, issue, or crisis—scholars caution that they do not represent a complete or systematic exposition of Paul's beliefs. When Paul make a theological statement, he does so primarily to support the counsel he applies to a troublesome situation in an individual congregation. For instance, in his first letter to the Thessalonians, he outlines his beliefs about the future resurrection of persons who die before the Parousia only because some believers at Thessalonica were worried that the Christian dead would miss out on their reward (1 Thess. 4:13–5:11). When writing to the church at Corinth, he passes on the traditions he received about Jesus at the Last Supper primarily because some Corinthians were behaving improperly at the sacramental meal (1 Cor. 11:17–34). If there had been no misconduct, Paul would have had no occasion to mention the tradition, and we would have been deprived of one of the few passages in which Paul cites a teaching from Jesus. In no letter, with the partial exception of Romans, does Paul set out a comprehensive statement of his theology. The occasional nature of his correspondence means that we have only partial glimpses of Pauline doctrines. In addition, on some topics, Paul's thoughts seem to change and develop from one letter to another (see below).

Some of Paul's Theological Beliefs

Mysticism and Eschatology Although Paul's letters present his theology in fragmental form, some of his distinctive beliefs are clearly expressed. Because of limited space, here we will explore only three of his major theological preoccupations: his mysticism, his eschatology, and his unique doctrine that believers receive salvation through faith in Christ. Understanding Paul's "gospel" means recognizing his sense of the spiritual power that inspires his apostolic career. As noted previously, Paul bases his authority as a Christian leader and the validity of his distinctive gospel on an *apokalypsis,* a private revelation of the postresurrection Jesus (Gal. 1:11–12, 15–17). Paul's understanding of Christ, which he insists he received as a direct heavenly communication and not from any apostolic predecessor, informs Paul that Jesus now exists in two separate but related dimensions. Following his ascension to heaven, Jesus has been made

ruler of both the macrocosm (great world) of God's spiritual domain and the microcosm (little world) of human consciousness. This **dualism,** characteristic of apocalyptic thought (see Chapters 26 and 38), expresses Paul's conviction that Christ possesses both an objective and a subjective reality. Christ is at once a cosmic figure who will soon return to judge the world and a being who mysteriously dwells within the individual believer. The tension between the transcendent and the immanent Christ, one who is simultaneously universal and yet intimately experienced by the faithful, appears in almost every letter Paul wrote.

Paul's mysticism—his powerful sense of union with an unseen spiritual reality—is an important component of his worldview. Indeed, some scholars suggest that even before his ecstatic encounter with Christ, Paul may have belonged to an apocalyptic branch of Pharisaism that included mystical beliefs and practices. In 2 Corinthians, he describes being "caught up to the third heaven," "into paradise," where he "heard things that are not to be told, that no mortal is permitted to repeat" (2 Cor. 12:1–4). The "visions and revelations of the Lord," which undoubtedly played their part in sustaining Paul through the many dangers and hardships he endured, may not have occurred as often as he would have liked. He adds that to prevent him "from being too elated" by "the exceptional character of the revelations," he was given "a thorn . . . in the flesh," a human "weakness" in which God's "power" is made manifest (12:5–10). (For a discussion of Paul's eschatological urgency, including his belief that he would survive to witness the Parousia, see Chapter 29.)

Justification by Faith Historically, perhaps Paul's most influential concept was his understanding of the moral logic by which a perfectly righteous God can accept or "justify" human beings whose unrighteous behavior makes them veritable "slaves" to sin. Does God, who sits as Judge over the universe, compromise his ethical standards by granting salvation to sinful humans? Paul's personal experience of divine mercy, expressed in a "revelation" of Jesus, convinced him that in Christ he had been justified or "made right" before God. This conviction—that faith in Christ had delivered him from sin more effectively than had obedience to the Mosaic Torah—placed Paul on a collision course with his native Judaism, as well as with many Jewish Christians who saw no reason to abandon their Mosaic heritage. For Jewish Christians of the first century CE (probably including Jesus' "brother" James), to accept Jesus as Israel's Messiah (Christ) was to follow the same Torah obligations that Jesus had.

For observant Jews, the Torah provided a God-given—and fully adequate—means of atoning for sin and maintaining a right relationship with the Deity. Mosaic Law prescribed detailed rituals by which genuinely repentant sinners could express their desire to make peace with God. (As many scholars have noted, Torah statutes involving "sin offerings" and other sacrifices to effect forgiveness presupposed that petitioners had already experienced appropriate sorrow and remorse for their errors.) Both personal contrition and sacrificial rites were part of the biblical arrangement for restoring harmony between Israel's God and his worshipers (see Chapter 7).

Although Paul claimed that "as to righteousness under the law" he had been "blameless" (Phil. 3:6), at some point after his encounter with the risen Jesus, he came to believe that the Mosaic Covenant was no longer the means by which God reconciled imperfect humanity to himself. In two of his most theologically important letters, Galatians and Romans, Paul argues that the Torah serves only to expose the universal reality of human sin, which it justly condemns. By his sacrificial death on the cross, however, Jesus paid for *everyone* the Law's penalty for human sin, effectively canceling the Torah's authority. Through spiritual union with Christ, who is now God's sole instrument of human redemption, believers share in the benefits of Jesus' self-sacrifice and freely receive the divine favor that grants them eternal life. For Paul, the Torah can no longer confer forgiveness, a function that in God's new arrangement belongs exclusively to Christ.

In Paul's view, it is God's *grace*—his undeserved kindness and mercy—that opens the way to salvation for Jews and Gentiles alike, graciously assigning them the capacity to accept and believe in Jesus. Believers are thus justified before God only through their faith—complete trust—in Jesus' power to save those with whom he is spiritually united. (For more on Paul's ideas about faith in Christ replacing Torah obedience, see the discussions of Galatians and Romans below.)

During the sixteenth century CE, European Christians were bitterly divided over the interpretation of Paul's doctrine of justification by faith. Martin Luther, the Protestant reformer, held that it was through faith alone that believers were saved, whereas the Catholic Church maintained that salvation also came through deeds, particularly observance of such sacraments as baptism, confession, and absolution. It was not until the close of the twentieth century that Catholics and Protestants reached an accord on Paul's teaching. In 1999, on the 482nd anniversary of Luther's posting his protests against church practices on the door of Castle Church

in Wittenberg, Germany—an act that ignited the Protestant Reformation—leaders of the Catholic and Lutheran churches signed a historic agreement stating that faith is essential to salvation. According to this joint Catholic–Lutheran declaration, "By grace alone, in faith in Christ's saving work and not because of any merit on our part, we are adopted by God and receive the Holy Spirit, who renews our hearts while equipping and calling us to good works."

First Thessalonians

Paul's oldest surviving letter, to the recently founded congregation at Thessalonica, Greece, reveals how thoroughly apocalyptic his message was. Probably written in Corinth about 50 CE, 1 Thessalonians refers to the Parousia in no fewer than six different passages, at least once in each of the letter's five brief chapters. Composed a scant twenty years after the Crucifixion, Paul makes the imminence of Jesus' return his central message (1:10; 2:19; 3:13; 4:13–18; 5:1–11).

Because the Second Coming is so near, the Thessalonians must reform their typically lenient Gentile attitudes toward sexual activity. They have already made progress in living "to please God," but they can do better, abstaining from "fornication," avoiding "lustful passion," and cultivating their capacity to "love" selflessly and to "quietly" "mind [their] own affairs" (4:1–12). Convinced that all will soon be brought to judgment, Paul strives to bring his new converts to an ethically pure life, a "holy" state that Christ will approve when he appears.

The Thessalonians, Paul writes, have already become a shining example to other Greek churches because they have

> turned to God from idols, to serve a living and true God, and to wait for his Son from heaven, whom he raised from the dead—Jesus, who rescues us from the wrath that is coming.

(1 Thess. 1:10)

This passage may, in fact, summarize the principal themes of Paul's oral "gospel," the message he preached in urban marketplaces, shops, and private homes. In general content, it resembles the more elaborate speech that Luke placed on Paul's lips when he spoke to the Athenians (Acts 17:22-31). Urging the Greeks to forsake lifeless idols for Israel's "living God," Paul presents Jesus' resurrection as introducing history's climactic moment: his impending descent from heaven to rescue his followers from God's righteous anger at the sinful world.

The Parousia and the Resurrection

After the long introductory section (1:1–4:12), Paul arrives at his main reason for sending the letter—a clarification of his teaching about End time (4:13–5:11). Apparently, some Thessalonians thought that the Parousia would occur so swiftly that all persons converted to Christianity would live to see Jesus return. That belief was shaken when some believers died before Jesus had reappeared. What would become of them? Had the dead missed their opportunity to join Christ in ruling over the world?

Paul explains that the recently dead are not lost but will share in the glory of Christ's return. Revealing a conviction that he will personally witness the Parousia, Paul declares that "we who are alive, who are left until the coming of the Lord, will by no means precede those who have died" (4:15). Implicitly comparing Jesus' triumphal reappearance to a Roman emperor's parousia, his official public entry into a city, Paul states that all Christians, both alive and dead, will rush to greet their Lord's arrival. When the trumpet call of Final Judgment sounds, the Christian dead will rise first. Simultaneously, Christians who are still alive—Paul and his fellow believers—will be lifted from earth into the air to join the resurrected saints, presumably to accompany Jesus as he returns to earth, beginning his rule as Israel's Messiah. (See Chapter 29 for Roman parallels to the Parousia concept; see also 1 Corinthians 15 for Paul's more complete description of the resurrection.)

On Not Calculating "Times and Seasons" Although he expects that Jesus will soon reappear, Paul has no patience with believers who try to predict the exact date of the Parousia. He discourages speculation, noting that calculating "the times and the seasons" is futile because the last day will come as quietly as "a thief in the night." Emphasizing the unexpectedness of the Parousia, Paul states that it will occur while leaders proclaim "peace and security" (a common political slogan in Roman times as well as today). Disaster will strike the nations suddenly, as labor pains strike a pregnant woman without warning (5:1–3).

In the Hebrew Bible, the "Day of the Lord" was the time of Yahweh's intervention into human history, his visitation of earth to judge all nations and to impose his universal rule (Amos 5:18–20; Joel 2:14–15). In Paul's apocalyptic vision, Jesus is the divinely appointed agent who brings ordinary history to a close. As the eschatological Judge, Jesus serves a double function: He brings punishment to the disobedient (the divine "wrath that is coming") but vindication and deliverance to the faithful.

Paul's cosmic Jesus is paradoxical: He dies to save believers from the negative judgment that his return will impose on disobedient humanity. Returning to his main theme, Paul concludes that "whether we are awake [living] or asleep [dead]" all the faithful live in permanent association with Christ (5:4–11).

The Role of the Spirit With anticipation of Jesus' speedy return a vital reality, Paul reminds the Thessalonians that the Holy Spirit's visible activity among them is also evidence of the world's approaching transformation. As noted in Acts, the Spirit motivating believers to prophesy, heal, or speak in tongues was taken as evidence of God's active presence. Thus, Paul tells his readers not to "quench the Spirit" or otherwise discourage believers from prophesying. Christian prophets, inspired by the Spirit, play a significant role in Pauline churches, but Paul is aware that enthusiastic visionaries can cause trouble. Believers are to "test" prophetic utterances, presumably to see if they are consistent with Paul's teachings. Besides providing evidence that the End is near, the Spirit's presence also validates the Christian message (cf. Joel 2:28–32; 1 Cor. 2:9–16; 12–14). (A disputed letter, 2 Thessalonians, is discussed in Chapter 36.)

First Letter to the Corinthians

According to Acts (17:1–18:7), after establishing churches at Philippi, Thessalonica, and Beroea (all in northern Greece), Paul briefly visited Athens and then journeyed to Corinth, where he remained for a year and a half (c. 50–52 CE). Accompanied by Prisca (Priscilla) and Aquila, Jewish Christians exiled from Rome, he subsequently sailed to Ephesus, from which city he addressed several letters to the Corinthians. The first letter has been lost (1 Cor. 5:9), but the documents presently numbered 1 and 2 Corinthians embody the most voluminous correspondence with any single church group in the New Testament.

Paul's communication with the Corinthian church was not a one-way affair, for the Corinthians wrote to the apostle as well (1 Cor. 7:1). Delegations from Corinth also kept Paul in touch with the group (1:11; 16:15–18; 2 Cor. 7:5–7, 13). A diverse assortment of Jews and Gentiles, slaves and landowners, rich and poor, educated and unlettered, the Corinthian group was apparently divided by class distinctions and educational differences as well as by diverse religious opinions. Even in observing the communion ritual, members' consciousness of inequality in wealth and social status threatened to splinter the membership (1 Cor. 11:17–34). Paul faced the almost impossible challenge of bringing this divisive and quarrelsome group into a working harmony of belief and purpose. In reading Paul's letters to Corinth, we must remember that he is struggling to communicate his vision of union with Christ to an infant church that has apparently only begun to grasp the basic principles of Christian life.

The Necessity of Christian Unity

In the first six chapters, Paul's chief objective is to halt the rivalries that divide the Corinthians. Like all early Christian congregations, that at Corinth met in a private house large enough to accommodate the entire group. Although membership was limited to perhaps 50–100 persons, the group was broken into several factions. Some members placed undue importance on the particular leader who had converted or baptized them and competed with one another over the prestige of their respective mentors (1:10–17).

A more serious cause of division may have been the members' unequal social and educational backgrounds. As in any group, modern or ancient, some individuals believed that they were demonstrably superior to their neighbors (see Figure 35.3). Examining Chapter 1

FIGURE 35.3 In this painting of a Roman couple, uncovered at Pompeii (buried by an eruption of Mount Vesuvius in 79 CE), Terentius Neo and his wife proudly display the pen and wax tablets that advertise their literary skills. Similar young Roman couples of the professional classes undoubtedly were among the members of Paul's newly founded churches in Corinth and other Greco-Roman cities.

carefully, readers will see that Paul's attack on false "wisdom" is really an attempt to discourage human competitiveness. In Paul's view, all believers are fundamentally equal: "There is no longer Jew or Greek, there is no longer slave or free, there is no longer male and female; for all of you are one in Christ Jesus" (Gal. 3:28). This assumption of equality in Christ underlies Paul's concept of Christian life. When he reminds the Corinthians that he taught them his message as simply as possible, he does so to show that the new faith is essentially incompatible with individual pride or competitiveness. Thus, with almost brutal directness, he proclaims "Christ crucified, a stumbling block to Jews [who look for a victorious conqueror, not an executed criminal] and foolishness to Gentiles [who seek rational explanations]" (1:23). Paul's relative lack of success in debating philosophers in Athens just before coming to Corinth (Acts 17) may have influenced his decision to preach henceforth without any intellectual pretensions.

Paul's argument against "the wise" (1:17–2:5) is sometimes misapplied to justify an anti-intellectual approach to religion, in which reason and faith are treated as if they were mutually exclusive. The apostle's attack on "wisdom" is not directed against human reason, however. It is aimed instead at individual Corinthians who boasted of possessing special insights that gave them a "deeper" understanding than that granted their fellow Christians. Such elitism led some persons to cultivate a false sense of superiority that devalued believers who were less "spiritual" or less well educated, fragmenting the congregation into groups of the "wise" and the "foolish."

Seeking to place all believers on an equal footing, Paul reminds the Corinthians that human reason by itself is not sufficient to know God, but that God revealed his saving purpose through Christ as a free gift (1:21). No one merits or earns the Christian revelation, which comes through God's unforeseen grace, not through human effort. Because all are equally recipients of the divine benefits, no believer has the right to boast (1:21–31).

Paul does, however, teach a previously hidden wisdom to persons mature enough to appreciate it. This wisdom is God's revelation through the Spirit that now dwells in the Christian community. The hitherto unknown "mind of God"—the ultimate reality that philosophers make the object of their search—is unveiled through Christ (2:6–16). The divine mystery, although inaccessible to rational inquiry, is finally made clear in the "weakness" and obedient suffering of Christ, the means by which God reconciles humanity to himself.

Answering Questions from the Congregation

Marriage, Divorce, and Celibacy In Chapters 7–15, Paul responds to a letter from the Corinthians, answering their questions on several crucial topics. The first item concerns human sexuality (7:1–40), a subject in which the writer takes a distant but practical interest. Earlier in the letter, Paul had already pronounced a severe judgment on a church member's sexual misconduct, ordering the congregation to expel a young man who created a public scandal by living with his stepmother (5:1–13). After quoting a statement from the Corinthians—"it is well for a man not to touch a woman"—Paul reaffirms the traditional Jewish view of married life, in which husbands and wives both have "conjugal rights." "This I say," Paul writes, "by way of concession, not of command. I wish all were as I myself am [unmarried and celibate]" (7:1–7). Marriage not only causes "distress in this life" but also tends to interfere with full commitment to "the Lord" (7:32–35). As a general rule, Paul believes, people should remain in the state—married or single, slave or free—in which they were first "called" to Christ. Although aware of Jesus' command forbidding divorce, he concedes that a legal separation is acceptable when a non-Christian wishes to leave a Christian mate (7:10–24).

Paul makes clear that his apocalyptic expectations determine his views on human sexuality: "In view of the impending crisis," he warns, people are better off if they imitate his celibate example. "The appointed time has grown short . . . and the present form of this world is passing away" (7:26–31). What advice Paul would have given had he realized that, almost 2,000 years after his time, the Parousia still lay in the future, we cannot know.

The Importance of Women in the Church
In recent decades, many Christians have become increasingly critical of Paul's regulations about women's roles in the church. Because we know so little of very early Christian practices, it is difficult to establish to what degree women originally shared in church leadership. Jesus numbered many women among his most loyal disciples, and Paul refers to several women as "co-workers" (Phil. 4:3). In the last chapter of Romans, in which Paul lists the missionary Prisca (Priscilla) ahead of her husband, Aquila, the apostle asks his recipients to support **Phoebe,** a "deacon" of the Cenchreae church, in discharging her administrative duties (Rom. 16:1–6).

In Corinthians, however, Paul seems to impose restrictions on women's participation in church services. His insistence that women cover their heads with veils (11:3–16) is open to a variety of interpretations. Is it the writer's concession to the existing Jewish and Greco-Roman custom of secluding women, an attempt to avoid offending patriarchal prejudices? If women unveil their physical attractiveness, does this distract male onlookers or even sexually tempt "angels," such as those who, prior to the Flood, desired mortal women (Gen. 6:1–4)? Conversely, is the veil a symbol of women's religious authority, to be worn when prophesying before the congregation?

Paul's argument for relegating women to a subordinate position in church strikes many readers as labored and illogical. (Some scholars think that this passage [11:2–26] was inserted by a later editor, who wished to make Corinthians agree with the non-Pauline instruction in 1 Timothy 2:8–15.) Paul grants women an active role, praying and prophesying during worship, but he argues as well that the female is a secondary creation, made from man, whom God directly created. The apostle uses the second Genesis version of human origins to support his view of a sexual hierarchy, but he could as easily have cited the first creation account, in which male and female are created simultaneously, both in the "image of God" (Gen. 1:27). Given Paul's revelation that Christian equality transcends all distinctions among believers, including those of sex, class, and nationality (Gal. 3:28), many commentators see the writer's choice of a Genesis precedent as decidedly arbitrary.

Communion (the Lord's Supper, or Eucharist)
Christianity's most solemn ritual, the reenactment of Jesus' last meal with his disciples, represents the mystic communion between the risen Lord and his followers. Meeting in private homes to commemorate the event, however, the Corinthians have turned the service into a riotous drinking party. Instead of a celebration of Christian unity, it has become another source of division. Wealthy participants come early and consume all the delicacies of the communion dinner before the working poor arrive, thus leaving their social inferiors both hungry and humiliated (11:17–22). (In Paul's day, the Christian "love feast" included a full dinner, as well as the ceremonial bread and wine.)

Paul contrasts this misbehavior with the tradition coming directly from Jesus himself. Reporting Jesus' sacramental distribution of bread and wine, he insists that the ceremony is to be decorously repeated in memory of Christ's death until he returns. This allusion to the nearness of Jesus' reappearance reminds the Corinthians of the seriousness with which they must observe the Last Supper (11:23–34).

Gifts of the Spirit Led by the Holy Spirit, the early Christian community included many persons who possessed supernatural gifts (Greek, *charisma*). Some charismatic believers had the gift of prophecy; others were apostles, teachers, healers, miracle workers, or speakers in tongues. In Corinth, these individual gifts, and the rivalries among those possessing them, were yet another cause of division. Reminding the Corinthians that one indivisible Spirit grants all these different abilities, Paul employs a favorite metaphor in which he compares the church to the human body, with its many differently functioning parts. Each Christian gift is to be used to benefit the whole body, the church.

The Gift of Love (Agape) In the history of world religion, perhaps the most revolutionary aspect of early Christianity was its commitment to the practice of unconditional love. The Synoptic Gospels show Jesus summarizing the entire Torah in two essential commands: to love both God and neighbor (Mark 12:28–34). Most astoundingly, Jesus also instructs his followers to love their "enemies," thereby imitating the Creator's unlimited generosity (Matt. 5:44–48). In John's Gospel, Jesus gives but a single directive: to love, stating that Jesus' followers will be identified by their ability to express love to each other (John 13:34–35; 15:12). Elevating the quality of love even higher, a writer in the Johannine community declares that God himself "is love" (1 John 4:8, 16).

Paul's contribution to the Christian concept of *agape* (selfless love) appears in 1 Corinthians 13, where he argues that love is not only the highest "spiritual gift" but also the fundamental basis of a truly Christian life. In perhaps the most-quoted passage he ever wrote, Paul applies the principle of *agape* to human relationships, describing not God's love but the expression of human love that brings harmony and peace to human interaction. Listing the most highly prized charismatic abilities—prophecy, knowledge, power, and self-sacrifice—Paul declares that without "love" these gifts are meaningless. Calling it "the more excellent way," Paul emphasizes love's practical application: Love is patient, kind, forgiving; it is neither envious nor boastful, and it keeps no record of offenses. Its capacity for selfless devotion is infinite: "Love never ends" (13:8). Love once given is never withdrawn. Whereas other spiritual gifts are merely partial reflections of the divine reality and will be rendered obsolete in the perfect world to come, the supreme trio of Christian virtues—faith, hope, and love—endures forever (12:31–14:1).

Although he gives love top priority, Paul also acknowledges the value of other spiritual gifts, especially prophecy, which involves rational communication. "Speaking in tongues" (*glossolalia*) may be emotionally satisfying to the speaker, but it does not "build up" the congregation as do teaching and prophecy. Although he does not prohibit *glossolalia* (Paul states that he is better at it than any Corinthian), the apostle ranks it as the least useful spiritual gift (14:1–40).

The Eschatological Hope: Resurrection of the Dead

Paul's last major topic—his eschatological vision of resurrection of the dead (15:1–57)—is theologically the most important. Apparently, some Corinthians challenged Paul's teaching about the afterlife. One group may have questioned the necessity of a future bodily resurrection because members believed that at baptism (and upon receiving the Spirit) they had already achieved eternal life. (This view resembles the "realized eschatology" in John's Gospel; see Chapter 33.) Others may have denied Paul's concept of resurrection because they shared the Greek philosophical view that a future existence is purely spiritual: In the afterlife, an immaterial soul requires no physical body. According to Socrates, Plato, and numerous mystery religions, death occurs when the immortal soul escapes from the perishable body. The soul does not need a body when it enters the invisible spirit realm. To believers in the soul's inherent immortality, Paul's Hebrew belief in the physical body's resurrection was grotesque and irrelevant.

The Historical Reality of Jesus' Resurrection To demonstrate that bodily resurrection is a reality, Paul calls on the Corinthians to remember that Jesus rose from the dead. Preserving the earliest tradition of Jesus' postresurrection appearances, Paul notes that the risen Lord appeared to as many as 500 believers at once, as well as to Paul (15:3–8) (see Box 35.2). Paul uses his opponents' denial against them and argues that if there is no resurrection, then Christ was not raised and Christians hope in vain. He trusts, not in the Greek concept of innate human immortality, but in the Judeo-Christian faith in God's ability to raise the faithful dead. Without Christ's resurrection, Paul states, there is no afterlife, and of all people, Christians are the most pitiable (15:12–19).

Paul now invokes two archetypal figures to illustrate the means by which human death and its opposite, eternal life, entered the world. Citing the second Genesis creation account, Paul declares that the "first man," Adam (God's first earthly son), brought death to the human race, but Christ (Adam's "heavenly" counterpart, a new

BOX 35.2 Resurrection Traditions in Paul and the Gospels

The oldest surviving account of Jesus' postresurrection appearances occurs in Paul's first letter to the Corinthians, which contains a tradition "handed on" to Paul from earlier Christians. None of the Gospels' resurrection narratives, written fifteen to forty years after the date of Paul's letter, refers to Jesus' manifestations to his kinsman James or to the "over 500 brothers" who simultaneously beheld him (cf. 1 Cor. 15:3–8.)

PAUL (C. 54 CE)	MARK (C. 66–70 CE)	MATTHEW (C. 85 CE)	LUKE (C. 85–90 CE)	JOHN (C. 90–100 CE)
Jesus appears to Cephas (Peter) to "the Twelve" to "over 500" to James (Jesus' "brother") to "all the Apostles" to Paul (as an *apokalypsis,* or "revelation" [Gal. 1:15–16])	No postresurrection account in original text (Two accounts were added later: Mark 16:8b and 16:9–19, in which Jesus appears first to Mary Magdalene and then to the Eleven.)	No parallels Jesus appears to "the eleven disciples" (minus Judas Iscariot) "in Galilee"	Reference to "Simon [Peter]" to "the Eleven" (in Jerusalem) Jesus appears to "Cleopas" and an unnamed disciple on the road to Emmaus (near Jerusalem)	No parallels Jesus appears to Mary Magdalene (in Jerusalem) to "the disciples," particularly Thomas (in Jerusalem) to "the sons of Zebedee," Simon Peter, and the "Beloved Disciple" (in Galilee)

creation) brings life. The coming resurrection (and perhaps salvation as well) is universal: "for as all die in Adam, so all will be made alive in Christ" (15:22). Reaping the "first fruits" of the resurrection harvest, Christ will return to raise the obedient dead and defeat all enemies, including death itself. Christ subjects the entire universe to his rule but himself remains subordinate to God, "so that God may be all in all" (15:20–28). Noting that the Corinthians practice baptism of their dead (posthumously initiating them into the church?), Paul insists that this ritual presupposes the resurrection's reality (15:29).

Paul next responds to the skeptics' demand to know what possible form bodily resurrection might take. Although he admits that "flesh and blood cannot inherit the kingdom of God," Paul retains his Hebraic conviction that human beings cannot exist without some kind of body. First, he uses analogies from the natural world, demonstrating that life grows from buried seeds and that existence takes different forms. As heavenly bodies surpass earthly objects in "glory," so the resurrection body will outshine the physical body: "What is sown is perishable, what is raised is imperishable. It is sown in dishonor, it is raised in glory . . . It is sown a physical body, it is raised a spiritual body" (15:42–45). Paul describes

here a supernatural transformation of the human essence, a process that creates a paradox, a contradiction in terms—a material body that is also spirit (15:35–44).

Impressing his readers with the nearness of the impending transformation, Paul concludes by unveiling a "mystery": "We will not all die, but we will be changed, in a moment, in the twinkling of an eye, at the last trumpet." When the Parousia occurs, Paul and other living Christians will be instantly transformed and clothed with an imperishable, immortal existence. In the universal restoration, death itself will perish, consumed in Christ's life-giving victory (15:51–57).

Nurturing a Spiritual Body Paul's thoughts on the nature of resurrection and the acquiring of immortality seem to have developed over time. In his second letter to the Corinthians, he writes as if believers are already growing a spiritual body that they will assume at the moment of death. God, Paul states, has prepared for each Christian an eternal form, a "heavenly dwelling," that endows the bearer with immortality. Yearning to avoid human death, he envisions receiving that heavenly form now, putting it on like a garment over the physical body, "so that what is mortal may be swallowed up by life." The presence of the Spirit, he concludes, is visible evidence that God intends this process of spiritual transformation to take place during the current lifetime (2 Cor. 5:1–5). United with Christ, the believer thus will become a new creation (2 Cor. 5:11–17).

When discussing the afterlife in 1 Corinthians 15, Paul says little about the Christian's state of being or consciousness during the interim period between death and the future resurrection. In 2 Corinthians 5, however, he appears to state that death immediately will bring believers into closer association with Christ: "We would rather be away from the body and at home with the Lord" (2 Cor. 5:6–8). Paul expresses a similar view in Philippians, where he weighs the relative benefits of remaining alive to help others or dying to be with the Lord:

> For to me, living is Christ and dying is gain. . . . I am hard pressed between the two: *my desire is to depart and be with Christ,* for that is far better, but to remain in the flesh is more necessary for you.

(Phil. 1:21–24, emphasis added)

Dying in order to be "with Christ" implies that Paul assumes a continuity of consciousness that death does not interrupt, a view that the believer's soul survives physical mortality and is instantly united in the spiritual realm with Christ. Paul does not explain the apparent contradiction between the necessity of resurrection to attain eternal life and the believer's instantaneous transition "away from the body" to be "at home with the Lord." The later church, however, resolved the difficulty by adopting both the biblical concept of bodily resurrection *and* the Greek doctrine of the soul's inborn immortality. In the church's official teaching, at death the immortal soul departs immediately for posthumous rewards or punishments. At the Last Judgment, the body will be raised to be reunited with the soul.

Closing Remarks Paul closes his first surviving letter to the Corinthians by switching abruptly from his cosmic vision of human destiny back to earthly themes. He reminds his recipients of their previous agreement to give financial help to the Jerusalem church. The Corinthians are to contribute money every Sunday, an obligation Paul had assumed for his Gentile churches when he met with the Jerusalem leadership (Gal. 2:9–10).

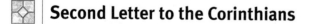 **Second Letter to the Corinthians**

Whereas 1 Corinthians is a unified document, 2 Corinthians seems to be a compilation of several letters or letter fragments that Paul wrote at different times to settle a series of conflicts with the Corinthian church. Even casual readers will note the contrast between the harsh, sarcastic tone of Chapters 10–13 and the generally friendlier, more conciliatory tone of the earlier chapters. As many scholars believe, Chapters 10–13 represent a letter Paul refers to in 2 Corinthians 2:3–4, a communication he wrote "with much distress and anguish of heart." In this view, Chapters 1–9 were composed after the section that now appears in Chapters 10–13. Some commentators find as many as six or more fragments of different letters in 2 Corinthians, but for our purposes, we concentrate on the work's two main divisions (Chs. 10–13 and 1–9), taking them in the order in which scholars believe they were composed.

Underlying the writing of 2 Corinthians is a dramatic conflict between Paul and the church he had founded. After he had dispatched 1 Corinthians, several events took place that strained his relationship with the church almost to the breaking point. New opponents, whom Paul satirizes as "super-apostles" (11:5), infiltrated the congregation and rapidly gained positions of influence. Paul then made a brief "painful visit" to Corinth, only to suffer public humiliation (2:1–5; 7:12). His visit a failure, he returned to Ephesus, where he wrote the Corinthians a severe reprimand, part of which is preserved in Chapters 10–13. Having carried the "severe letter" to Corinth, his associate **Titus** then rejoins Paul in Macedonia, bringing the welcome news that the Corinthians are sorry for their behavior and now support the apostle (7:5–7). Paul subsequently writes a joyful letter of reconciliation, included in Chapters 1–9. Although this reconstruction of events is conjectural, it accounts for the sequences of alienation, hostility, and reconciliation found in this composite document.

The Severe Letter: Paul's Defense of His Apostolic Authority

In the last four chapters of 2 Corinthians, Paul writes a passionate, almost brutal defense of his apostolic authority. A masterpiece of savage irony, Chapters 10–13 show Paul boasting "as a fool" (11:17, 21), using every device of rhetoric to demolish his opponents' pretensions to superiority. We do not know the identity of these opponents, except that they were Jewish Christians whom Paul accuses of proclaiming "another Jesus" and imparting a "spirit" different from that Paul introduced in *his* "gospel" (11:4–5). The label "super-apostles" suggests that these competitors enjoyed unusual prestige, perhaps as representatives from the Jerusalem church. They may have been representatives from James, "the Lord's brother," similar to those who drove a wedge between Peter and Paul in Antioch. In both cases, Paul describes their "gospel" as differing from his (Gal. 2:11–15).

Although Paul's bitter sarcasm may offend some readers, we must realize that this unattractive quality represents the reverse side of his intense emotional commitment to the Corinthians' welfare. Behind the writer's "boasting" and threats (10:2–6; 11:16–21; 13:3, 10) lies the sting of unrequited affection. The nature of love that Paul had so confidently defined in his earlier letter (1 Cor. 13) is now profoundly tested.

It is not certain that the "super-apostles" (11:5) who question his teaching are the same as the "false apostles" (11:13) whom Paul accuses of being Satan's agents (11:12–15). Whoever they were, these unnamed opponents apparently base their authority at least partly on their ability to command supernatural visions and revelations. Paul responds by telling some of his own mystical experiences, in which he was carried—"whether in the body or out of the body I do not know" as far as the "third heaven," where he "heard things . . . that no mortal is permitted to repeat" (12:1–13).

The Letter of Reconciliation

After Titus left to carry the disciplinary letter from Ephesus to Corinth, Paul began a journey to Macedonia. When Titus caught up with Paul, he brought the good news that the Corinthians had disavowed their divisive leaders and now gave Paul their full support, acknowledging him as a genuine apostle who had treated them honorably (2 Cor. 7:2–16).

Despite the reconciliation, Paul refers again to his competitors (the "super-apostles"?), dismissing them as mere "peddlers of God's word" and asking if he must begin all over again proving his apostolic credentials (2:17; 3:1). Placing the responsibility for recognizing true apostolic leadership squarely on the Corinthians, Paul reminds them that *they* are his living letters of recommendation. Echoing Jeremiah 31:31, Paul contrasts the Mosaic Covenant—inscribed on stone tablets—with the new covenant written on human hearts. Inhabited by the Holy Spirit, the Christian reflects God's image more splendidly than Moses (3:2–28).

In the most theologically intriguing portion of this letter, Paul elaborates on the concept of a "spiritual body" that he had outlined in 1 Corinthians 15. In this passage, he expresses a hope that he will receive his transformed body—"a building from God"—before he has to give up his physical body—"the earthly tent we live in" (see above for a discussion of Paul's concept of resurrection). For Paul, the Parousia, with its spiritual transformation of believers, is so near that he expects it to occur while he is still alive.

Because the Holy Spirit is presently active among believers, God is even now inspiring a spiritual renewal that reconciles humanity to himself. As Christ's ambassador, Paul advances the work of reconciliation; his many sufferings are an act of love for them (5:18–6:13). Imploring the Corinthians to return his affection, Paul ends his defense of the apostolic purpose with a warm but somewhat tentative expression of confidence in their restored loyalty (7:2–16).

Chapters 8 and 9, which concern Paul's collection for the Jerusalem poor, seem repetitive and may have originated as separate notes before an editor combined them. Citing the generosity of Macedonia's churches, Paul reminds the Corinthians that "God loves a cheerful giver" (9:7).

Letter to the Galatians

Asserting his own independence of the Jerusalem apostolic church, Paul writes an angry declaration of believers' freedom from Torah requirements and a vigorous defense of his unique "gospel": It is faith in Christ's power to save, not obedience to the Mosaic Law, that makes believers "righteous" before God.

A Furious Paul to the "Foolish Galatians"

Perhaps written at about the same time he was battling the "super-apostles" at Corinth (2 Cor. 10–13), Paul's Galatian letter contains a similarly impassioned defense of his apostolic authority and teaching. Apparently, almost everywhere Paul founded new churches, troublemakers infiltrated the congregation, asserting that Christians must keep at least some provisions of the Mosaic Law. Perhaps influenced by representatives from the Jerusalem church or other advocates of Torah obedience, the Galatians had abandoned Paul's gospel (1:6) and now urged all male converts to undergo circumcision (5:2-3; 6:12–13), the physical sign of belonging to Yahweh's covenant community (Gen. 17).

The Identity of Paul's Recipients and Opponents
The identity of the Galatian churches Paul addresses is uncertain. In Paul's time, two different geographical areas could be designated "Galatia." The first was a territory in north-central Asia Minor inhabited by descendants of Celtic tribes that had invaded the

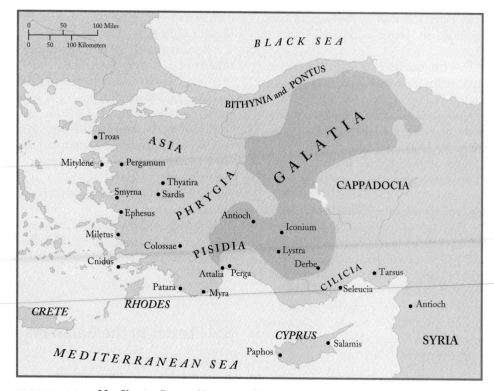

FIGURE 35.4 Map Showing Potential Locations of Paul's Galatian Churches. The identity of Paul's Galatians is uncertain. The letter may have been directed to churches in the north-central plateau region of Asia Minor (near present-day Ankara, Turkey) or to churches in the southern coastal area of east-central Asia Minor (also in modern Turkey). Many scholars believe that the Galatians were Christians living in Iconium, Lystra, Derbe, and other nearby cities that Paul had visited on his first missionary journey.

region during the third to first centuries BCE. Brief references to Galacia in Acts (16:6; 18:23) suggest that Paul may have traveled there, but this is not certain.

The other possibility, as many historians suggest, is that Paul was writing to Christians in the Roman province of Galatia. The southern portion of this province included the cities of Iconium, Lystra, and Derbe, places where the apostle had established churches (Acts 14). If the "southern Galatia theory" is correct, it helps to explain the presence of Jewish Christians advocating circumcision, for the Roman province was much closer to Jewish-Christian centers at Antioch and at Jerusalem than was the northern, Celtic territory (see Figure 35.4).

Some commentators identify Paul's opponents as emissaries of the Jerusalem church, such as those whom James apparently sent to inspect the congregation at Antioch (2:12). It seems improbable, however, that Jewish Christians from Jerusalem would have been unaware that requiring circumcision meant keeping all the other Torah regulations as well (5:2–3). Paul's opponents appear to combine aspects of Greco-Roman cult worship, such as honoring "elemental spirits of the world," with observance of Jewish holy days (4:1–10). This **syncretism**—mixing together aspects of two or more different religions to create a new doctrine—suggests that the opponents are Galatian Gentiles. In Paul's view, their attempt to infuse Jewish and pagan elements into Christianity fails to recognize the supreme importance of Christ, who alone reconciles both Jews and Gentiles to God.

Purpose and Contents

Writing from Corinth or Ephesus about 56 CE, Paul has a twofold purpose: (1) to prove that he is a true apostle, possessing rights equal to those of the Jerusalem "pillars" (1:6–2:21), and (2) to demonstrate the validity of his gospel that Christian faith replaces works of Torah, including circumcision. The letter can be divided into five parts:

1. A biographical defense of Paul's autonomy and his relationship to the Jerusalem leadership (1:1–2:14)
2. An exposition of Paul's unique gospel: justification through faith (2:15–3:29)
3. An argument that by imitating Abraham's faith Gentiles become Abraham's heirs and therefore children of God (4:1–31)
4. An assertion that freedom from Torah liberates Christians to cultivate ethical responsibility (5:1–6:10)
5. A final summary of his distinctive gospel (6:11–18)

Paul's Freedom from Institutional Authority

Largely dispensing with his usual greetings and thanksgiving, Paul opens the letter with a vigorous defense of his personal independence from church authority. His apostolic rank derives neither from "human commission nor from human authorities" but directly from God (1:1–5). Similarly, his message does not depend upon information learned from any "human source"—including "those who were already apostles before [him]"—but from a "revelation of Jesus Christ" (1:12; cf. 1:17). Because he regards his gospel of faith as a divine communication, Paul sees no need to consult other church leaders, such as the apostles Peter and John, about the correctness of his policies (1:15–17).

In Acts, the author portrays Paul as a cooperative churchman, but in Galatians, Paul presents himself as essentially independent of the parent church in Jerusalem. Nevertheless, he apparently recognizes the desirability of having his work among the Gentiles endorsed by the Palestinian leadership. His visit with the Jerusalem "pillars"—Peter (Cephas), John, and James—is probably the same conference described in Acts 15. According to Paul, the pillars (a term he uses sarcastically) agree to recognize the legitimacy of his Gentile mission. Imposing no Torah restriction on Gentile converts, the Jerusalem trio ask only that Paul's congregations contribute financially to the mother church, a charitable project Paul gladly undertakes (2:1–10; cf. Paul's appeals for donations in 2 Cor. 8–9 and Rom. 15).

After the Jerusalem conference, Paul meets Peter again at Antioch, an encounter that shows how far the Jewish-Gentile issue is from being resolved. Paul charges that Jesus' premier disciple is still ambivalent about associating with uncircumcised believers. When James sends emissaries to see if Antioch's Jewish Christians are properly observing Mosaic dietary laws, Peter stops partaking in communal meals with Gentiles. Apparently, Peter fears James's disapproval. Although Paul denounces Peter's action as hypocrisy, claiming that Peter privately does not keep Torah regulations, we cannot be sure of Peter's motives. As chief apostle to his fellow Jews, he may have wished not to offend his Torah-observant fellow Israelites and behaved as he did out of respect for others' consciences, a policy Paul himself advocates (1 Cor. 8:1–13).

Justification by Faith

Paul's strangely negative attitude toward the Mosaic Law has puzzled many scholars. Why does a Pharisee trained to regard the Torah as God's revelation of ultimate wisdom so forcefully reject this divine guide to righteous living? Is it because of a personal consciousness that (for him) the Law no longer has power to validate his existence before God? In both Galatians and Romans, Paul closely examines his own psychological state, attempting to show how the experience of the risen Christ achieves for him what the Law failed to do—assure him of God's love and acceptance.

Replacing Law with Faith In Paul's interpretation of the Crucifixion, Jesus' voluntary death pays the Torah's penalty for all lawbreakers (3:13–14). Thus, Paul can say that "through the law I died to the law." He escaped the punishments the Torah prescribes through a mystical identification with Israel's Messiah whose sacrificial death atones for believers' sins. Vicariously experiencing Jesus' crucifixion, Paul now shares in Christ's new life, which enables him to receive God's grace as never before (2:17–21).

Paul also appeals to the Galatians' experience of Christ, reminding them that they received the Spirit only when they believed his gospel, not when they obeyed the Mosaic Law (3:1–5). If they think that they can be judged righteous through Torah observance, then Christ's sacrifice was in vain (2:21). Following a typical rabbinic custom, Paul reinforces his argument by finding a precedent in the Hebrew Bible that anticipates his formula of "faith equals righteousness [right standing before God]." He quotes a line from Genesis: "He [Abraham] believed the Lord, and the Lord reckoned it to him as righteousness" (Gen. 15:6). Because Abraham's spontaneous belief (trust) that God would fulfill his vow made him "righteous" in God's eyes, Paul reasons that persons who imitate Abraham's faith are his spiritual children, the very descendants whom God promised to bless (3:6–10). Faith, then, not obedience to Law, is the key to divine approval.

In support of his appeal to biblical authority, Paul finds only one additional relevant text, Habakkuk 2:4: "The righteous live by their faith." Paul interprets the Habakkuk text as prophetic of the messianic era and contrasts its emphasis on faith with the Mosaic Law's focus on action (3:11–12). The faith Habakkuk commended comes to the lawless Gentiles because Christ, suffering a criminal's execution, accepted the Law's curse on unlawful people and thus allowed them to become reconciled to God (3:13–14).

The Role of the Mosaic Torah in Human Salvation If, as Paul repeatedly asserts, the Torah cannot really help anyone, why was it given? Paul's answer is that the Mosaic Law is a temporary device intended to teach humans that they are unavoidably lawbreakers, sinners whose most conscientious efforts cannot earn divine favor. Using an analogy from Roman society, Paul compares the Law to a tutor—a man appointed to guide and protect youths until they attain legal adulthood. Like a tutor imposing discipline, the Law makes its adherents aware of their moral inadequacy and their need for a power beyond themselves to achieve righteousness. That person is Christ. Having served its purpose of preparing Abraham's children for Christ, the Torah is now obsolete and irrelevant (3:19–25).

The Equality of All Believers In declaring that faith in Christ's power to save has replaced the Mosaic Law as the means to a right relationship with God, Paul abolishes the legal barrier that had for centuries separated Jew from Gentile. In his vision of a people of God united under Christ, Paul asserts the absolute equality of all believers, regardless of their nationality, social class, or sex. Among people of faith, "there is no longer Jew or Greek, there is no longer slave or free, there is no longer male and female, for all of you are one in Christ Jesus" (3:28). This bold proclamation of total equality is one of Paul's most enduring contributions to human freedom.

Believers as Heirs of Abraham

Because Jesus purchased Christians' freedom from slavery to the Torah's yoke, all are now God's adopted heirs. As such, they are entitled to claim the Deity as "*Abba*" (Aramaic, "father," or "daddy") and to receive the Abrahamic promises. Paul emphasizes the contrast between the church and Jewish keepers of Torah by interpreting the Genesis story of Abraham's two wives as an **allegory,** a narrative in which the characters and their actions symbolize some higher truth. Hagar, Abraham's Egyptian slave girl, is earthly Jerusalem, controlled by Rome. Sarah, the patriarch's free wife, symbolizes the "heavenly Jerusalem," the spiritual church whose members are also free (4:21–31).

Responsibilities of Freedom

What does freedom from Torah regulations mean? Aware that some Galatians used their liberty as an excuse to indulge any desire or appetite (a practice called **antinomianism**), Paul interprets his doctrine as freedom to practice neighborly love without external restrictions. Quoting lists of vices and virtues typical of Stoic ethical teaching, the apostle notes that the Spirit will enable believers to transcend their natural selfishness and to act generously (5:13–26).

Paul's exasperation with the Galatians' failure to understand that Jesus' death and resurrection are God's complete and all-sufficient means of human salvation inspires his most brutal insult. With savage irony, he suggests that men who insist on circumcision finish the job by emasculating themselves (5:7–12). Paul's remark may refer to an infamous practice among male adherents of the goddess Cybele, some of whom mutilated themselves in a religious frenzy. This oblique allusion to a pagan cult also implies that Paul's opponents were practicing syncretism, blending Jewish observances with non-Jewish rituals.

A Final Summary

In closing his letter, Paul seizes the pen from his secretary to write a final appeal to the Galatians in his own hand. Accusing his opponents of advocating circumcision only to escape persecution, presumably from Torah-abiding Jews, Paul summarizes his position: Torah obedience is meaningless because it implies that God's revelation through Jesus is not sufficient. Contrary to his opponents' limited view, Paul asserts that Jesus alone makes possible the new creation that unites humanity with its Creator. Paul's closing words are as abrupt and self-directed as his opening complaint (1:6): "From now on, let no one make trouble for me" (6:17).

Letter to the Romans

In Romans, Paul offers the most comprehensive statement of his doctrine of salvation through faith: All humanity, both Jewish and Gentile, imitates Adam's disobedience and is therefore enslaved to sin and alienated from God; the Torah serves only to increase an awareness of human imperfection and to condemn the lawbreaker. Only God's undeserved love expressed through Christ and accepted through faith can reconcile humankind to the Creator. In Paul's view, the Jewish refusal to accept Jesus as Israel's Messiah is only temporary, a historical necessity that allows believing Gentiles also to become God's people.

Paul's Gospel of Freedom from Torah and Justification by Faith

Paul wrote Galatians in the white heat of exasperation; his letter to the Romans is a more calmly reasoned presentation of his "gospel" that salvation comes through faith. Written about 56–57 CE, when he had not yet visited Rome but hoped to make it his departure point for a pioneering mission to Spain, Romans offers Paul's most thoughtful exploration of an issue central to all monotheistic religions: how to bridge the gap between God and humankind, to reconcile imperfect, sinful humanity to a pure and righteous Deity. As a Jew, Paul is painfully aware of the immense disparity between mortals and the immaculate holiness of Israel's God, whose justice cannot tolerate human wrongdoing. Paul's "good news" is that these seemingly irreconcilable difference between God and humanity are overcome in Christ, the Son who closes the gulf between perfect father and fallible children. In Paul's view, God himself takes the initiative by re-creating a deeply flawed humanity in his own transcendent image.

Form and Organization

In form, Romans resembles a theological essay or sermon rather than an ordinary letter, lacking the kind of specific problem-solving advice that characterizes most Pauline correspondence. Some commentators regard Romans as a circular letter, a document intended to explain Paul's teachings to various Christian groups who may at that time have held distorted views of the apostle's position on controversial subjects. Most scholars view Chapter 16, which contains greetings to twenty-six different persons—more than the writer is likely to have known personally in a city he had never visited—as a separate missive. This section originally may have been a letter of recommendation for Phoebe, who was a deacon of the church at Cenchreae, the port of Corinth.

The longest and most complex of Paul's letters, Romans can be divided into nine thematically related parts:

1. Introduction (1:1–15)
2. A statement of themes (1:16–17) and survey of humanity's sad predicament (1:18–3:31)
3. Abraham's example as the model of faith (4:1–25)
4. Faith in Christ as God's means of deliverance from sins and death (5:1–7:25)
5. Renewed life in the Spirit (8:1–39)
6. The causes and results of Israel's disbelief (9:1–11:36)
7. Behavior in the church and the world (12:1–15:13)
8. Paul's future plans and greetings (15:14–33)
9. Appendix: letter recommending Phoebe (16:1–27)

Humanity's Need for Redemption

The Human Predicament After an introductory greeting that affirms his apostolic authority (1:1–15), Paul reviews the human predicament (1:18–3–20), a sorry condition in which all people, Jews and Gentiles alike, are incapable of justifying their existence before God. He announces his main theme by citing Habakkuk 2:4, the same verse proclaiming that the "righteous will live by faith" that he had earlier quoted to the Galatians (1:17; Gal. 3:11). Paul's goal is to show that faith in Christ is humanity's only way to escape God's just anger and its own deserved punishment.

The Gentiles' Error Paul continues with a thorough indictment of the entire human race, using ammunition borrowed from the arsenal of Hellenistic Judaism. He echoes passages from the Wisdom of Solomon, a deuterocanonical work (see Chapter 27), as well as the concepts of "natural" and "unnatural" from the philosophies of Aristotle and the Stoics, to denounce everyone who fails to recognize and worship the one true God. God's qualities, he argues, can be deduced from the physical world of nature. The wisdom and power of God, as well as his grand design, are evident in the cosmic order. Persons who worship the images of Greco-Roman gods have perverted natural law; they honor created things in human or animal form instead of the One God who created them (1:18–23).

Turning their backs on the Creator, humans fall into ethical and sexual errors as well (see Wisd. of Sol. 14:11–31). In this controversial passage, Paul attributes the homosexual love affairs that characterized Hellenistic society to the Gentile practice of idolatry. Paul describes homosexual acts as a deliberate or willful turning away from a person's natural state, apparently assuming that same-sex attraction is a matter of conscious moral choice (rather than culturally or genetically determined). How this attitude relates to Paul's doctrine of human freedom and his principle of conscience he does not explain (1:14–2:16).

The Jews as Equally Guilty Although God provided the Jews with the Torah to guide them in righteousness, a fact that gives them an initial advantage over Gentiles, they have not, Paul asserts, lived up to the Mosaic Law's high standards. As a result, Jews have not achieved justification before God any more than Gentiles have. Paul reiterates his argument to the Galatians that the Torah fails to effect a right relationship between God and the law-keeper; it serves only to make one conscious of sin (2:17–3:20).

All humanity, then, is in the same sinking boat, incapable of saving itself. No one can earn through his or her own efforts the right to enjoy divine approval. Paul now goes on to show how God—whose just nature does not permit him to absolve the unjust sinner—works to rescue undeserving humanity.

Abraham as the Model of One "Justified" by Faith

Paul realizes that if his doctrine is to convince Jewish Christians, it must find support in the Hebrew Bible. He therefore argues that God's plan of rescuing sinners through faith began with Abraham, foremost ancestor of the Jewish people. As in Galatians, he cites Genesis 15:6: Abraham's faith "was reckoned to him as righteousness" (4:3). Therefore, Gentiles who follow Abraham's example—trusting that God will do what he has promised—are also heirs of the divine promises given in Genesis. Without compromising his impartiality, God succeeds in justifying both Jew and Gentile, encompassing previously distinct groups in an act of redemptive grace. As Abraham proved his faith by obediently responding to God's voice, so must the faithful now respond to God's new summons through Christ (4:15–25). "Justified by faith" in Jesus' sacrificial death, a demonstration of divine love, believers are now reconciled to God (5:1–11).

In using Abraham's example to support his thesis that "a person is justified by faith apart from works prescribed by the law" (3:28; cf. 4:1–25), Paul selects only one verse (Gen. 15:6) from the thirteen chapters that Genesis devotes to Abraham's story. Another New Testament letter—traditionally ascribed to James, Jesus' Torah-keeping "brother"—cites a different part of the Genesis narrative to argue that it was not Abraham's faith in itself but his faith expressed in *action* that pleased God. Insisting that "faith without works . . . is dead," the author of James interprets Abraham's significance as that of a person who demonstrates his faith through his deeds, such as his (almost) offering his son Isaac as a human sacrifice (James 2:14–26; for a discussion of James's position on faith expressed through action, see Chapter 37).

Faith in Christ Ensuring Deliverance from Sin and Death

The Roles of Adam and Christ At the outset of his letter (1:5), Paul declares that he tried to bring the whole world to a state of obedient faith. In Chapter 5, he outlines a theory of history in which God uses these two qualities—obedience and faith—to achieve human salvation. God's intervention into human affairs becomes necessary when the first human, Adam (whose name means "humankind"), disobeyed the Creator. Through this act, Adam alienated not only himself but all of his descendants from their Maker (see Box 35.3). Like other Jewish teachers of the first century CE, Paul interprets the Genesis story of Adam's disobedience as a tragic **Fall** from grace, a cosmic disaster that introduces sin and death into the world. Paul's word for "sin"—*hamartia*—is a Greek archery term that means "missing the mark" or "falling short of a desired goal." Aristotle used the same term to denote the "fatal flaw" of the tragic hero in Greek drama. *Hamartia,* in fact, commonly refers to an error of judgment, rather than an expression of inborn human wickedness. In Paul's moral scheme, all of Adam's descendants (the entire human race) fail to hit the target of union with God, thus condemning humanity to death—permanent separation from the Source of life.

In Paul's view, obedience to the Torah cannot save because Mosaic Law merely defines errors and assigns legal penalties. It is God himself who overcomes the hopelessness of the human predicament. He does this by sending his Son, whose perfect obedience and self-effacing death provide a saving counterweight to Adam's sin. Just as all Adam's children share his mortal punishment, so all will share the reward of Christ's resurrection to life. It is the believer's faith in the saving power of Christ that makes him or her "righteous," enabling the just Deity to accept persons trustfully responding to his call (5:12–21).

Some later theologians used Romans 5 to formulate a doctrine of **original sin,** which states that all human beings inherit an unavoidable tendency to do wrong and are innately corrupt. From Augustine to Calvin, such theologians had a deeply pessimistic view of human nature, in some cases regarding the majority of people as inherently depraved and justly damned.

Paul, however, emphasizes the joyful aspects of God's reconciliation to humanity. It is the Deity who initiates the process, and God's "grace"—his gracious will to love and to give life—far exceeds the measure of human failings. So powerful is God's determination to redeem humankind, Paul implies, that he may ultimately save all people:

BOX 35.3 **Paul's Views on the Origin of Sin and Death**

In Romans 5, Paul attributes the existence of sin and death to the first man's deliberate disobedience of a divine command, that which prohibited Adam and Eve from eating the fruit of the tree of knowledge (Rom. 5:12–23; cf. Gen. 3). According to orthodox interpretations of Paul's thought, particularly Augustine's doctrine of original sin, the first couple's error resulted in a death sentence not only for them but also for their descendants, all of whom are born under divine condemnation. In scrutinizing Genesis 3, however, readers will notice that most of the terms commonly used to describe the tale of Adam's and Eve's alienation from Yahweh are entirely absent. The Genesis narrator makes no reference to sin, evil, rebellion, disobedience, punishment, damnation, or a fall from grace—all are interpretative terms supplied by later theologians. The narrator, moreover, does not present the talking serpent who persuades Eve to taste the forbidden fruit as "bad," but only as "subtle" or "shrewd." Interestingly, after Genesis 3, no writer in the canonical Hebrew Bible (Tanakh) ever again refers to this Genesis episode or accords it any theological significance.

It was not until shortly before Paul's day that Hellenistic Jewish writers began to reinterpret the events related in Genesis 3. During the first century BCE, a Hellenistic Jew in Alexandria, Egypt, composed the Wisdom of Solomon, a book that integrated Greek philosophy with the Hebraic biblical tradition. (Excluded from the Tanakh, the Wisdom of Solomon was part of the Septuagint Apocrypha and is included in Catholic and Orthodox editions of the Old Testament.) According to this source, the devil was responsible for introducing death into human experience: "God created man for immortality, and made him the image of his own eternal self; it was the devil's spite that brought death into the world" (Wisd. of Sol. 2:23–24). Other extrabiblical traditions that it was the devil, speaking through the serpent, who tempted Eve to sin were eventually incorporated into the noncanonical Life of Adam and Eve, a Hellenistic work that imaginatively dramatizes Satan's role in corrupting the first humans. Whether directly influenced by this work or by the oral traditions underlying it, Paul evidently adopts the book's Hellenistic view that Adam and Eve are the sources of sin and death (Rom. 5:12–21; 2 Cor. 11:3; cf. 1 Tim. 2:4). (A Jewish apocalyptic work, 2 Esdras [c. 100 CE], also explores the concept of original sin.)

Therefore just as one man's trespass [Adam's disobedience] led to condemnation for all, so one man's act of righteousness [Christ's obedience unto death] leads to justification and life for all. For just as by the one man's disobedience the many were made sinners, so by the one man's obedience the many will be made righteous.

(Rom. 5:18–19; see Paul's similar declaration in 1 Cor. 15:21–23)

This passage, in which Paul optimistically seems to envision a universally redeemed humanity, must be balanced against his more negative evaluation of human sinfulness in Romans 8. In this chapter, he contrasts two different ways of life that produce opposite results. People who submit to the "things of the flesh [their "lower nature"]" make themselves God's enemies and earn "death"; those united with Christ, however, live on a higher plane, embracing the "things of the spirit [their "higher nature"]," which produces "life and peace" (8:5–13).

A Distortion of Paul's Teaching on Freedom In Chapter 6, Paul seems to be refuting misconceptions of his doctrine on Christian freedom. As in Galatia, some persons apparently were acting as if liberty from the Torah entitled them to behave irresponsibly. In some cases, they concluded that "sinning" was good because it allowed God's grace more opportunity to show itself. Paul reminds such dissidents that sin is a cruel tyrant who pays wages of death. In contrast, Christ treats his servants generously, bestowing the gift of everlasting life (6:1–23).

The Law's Holiness and Human Perversity Paul makes one final attempt to place the Torah in the context of salvation history and to account for its failure to produce human righteousness. In Galatians, Paul describes the Mosaic Law harshly, referring to it as slavery, bondage, and death. Writing more temperately in Romans, he judges the Law "holy . . . and just and good" (7:12). If it is, why does it not serve to bring its practitioners into a saving relationship with God?

In this instance, Paul answers that the fault lies not in the Torah, but in human nature. The Torah is "spiritual," but human beings are "of the flesh" and enslaved by sin. Throughout this long passage (7:7–25), Paul uses the first person, as if he were analyzing his own nature and then projecting his self-admitted defects onto the rest of humanity. His "I," however, should probably read "we"—for he means to describe fallible human nature collectively. Laws not only define crimes, he asserts, but create an awareness of lawbreaking that does not exist in their absence. Thus, the Torah makes sin come alive in the human consciousness (7:7–11).

Speaking as if sin were an animate force inside himself, Paul articulates the classic statement of ethical frustration—the opposition between the "good" he wishes to do and the "evil" he actually performs. As he confronts the huge gap between his conscious will and his imperfect actions, Paul can only conclude that it is not the real "he" who produces the moral failure, but rather "the sin that dwells within [him]" (7:14–20).

With his higher reason delighting in the Torah but his lower nature fighting against it, he finds that he incurs the Law's punishment—death. He bursts with the desire to attain God's approval but always "misses the mark." In agony over his fate, he seeks some power to rescue him from an unsatisfying existence that can end only in death (7:21–25). Paul may be accused of attributing his personal sense of moral imperfection to everyone else, but his despairing self-examination illustrates why he believes that the Law is unable to deliver one from the lethal attributes of imperfect human nature (8:3).

Renewed Life in the Spirit

Paul then tries to show how God accomplishes his rescue mission through Christ (8:1–39). By sharing humanity's imperfect nature and by dying in God's grace, Jesus "condemned sin in the flesh so that the just requirement of the law might be fulfilled." Christ thus transfers the Torah's punishments to sin itself, condemning it and not the human nature in which it exists (8:3–4). Because Christ's Spirit now dwells within believers, sin no longer exerts its former control, and new life can flourish in each Christian's body. By this means, Christians escape their imperfection, having put it to death with Christ on the cross. No longer sin's slaves, they become God's children, joint heirs with Christ (8:5–17).

Paul uses mystical language to describe not only human nature but also the physical cosmos itself, as it struggles to shake off the chains of mortality. During this period of cosmic renewal, the whole universe wails as if in labor pains. Believers now hope for a saving rebirth, but the reality is still ahead. Then they will be fully reshaped in the Son's image, the pattern of a new humanity reconciled to God (8:18–30):

> For I am convinced that neither death, nor life, nor angels, nor rulers, nor things present, nor things to come, nor powers, nor height, nor depth, nor

anything else in all creation, will be able to separate us from the love of God in Christ Jesus, our Lord.

(Rom. 8:38–39)

The Causes and Results of Israel's Disbelief

In Romans 9–11, Paul discusses Israel's continuing role as God's chosen people, even though most have not accepted Jesus of Nazareth as the national Messiah. Like many of his fellow Christian Jews, Paul has pondered the meaning of this historical puzzle: How is it that the people to whom God granted his covenants, Torah, Temple, and promises have, as a group, failed to recognize Jesus as the Christ? Paul offers an ingenious solution to this puzzle.

First, Paul argues that God never intended all Israelites to receive his promises; they were meant for only a faithful remnant, represented in Paul's day by Christian Jews (9:1–9). Second, Paul tries to show that Israel's present unbelief is part of God's long-range plan to redeem all of humanity. In a long discourse echoing phrases from the Hebrew Bible, Paul makes several important assumptions about God's nature and the manner in which the Deity controls human destiny. Assuming that God's will is irresistible, Paul implies that humans' freedom of choice is therefore severely limited. Citing the Exodus story, Paul reminds his readers that Yahweh manipulated the Egyptian king— "hardening" his heart—in order to demonstrate God's power over human events (Exod. 9:15–16). Because God is all-powerful and enjoys total freedom, he can choose to extend favor or cruelty to whomever he pleases. Paul compares the Deity's arbitrariness to that of a potter who can assign one clay pot an honorable use and smash another if it displeases him. Implying that might makes right, Paul declares that no human can justly challenge the supreme Potter's authority to favor one person and not another (9:10–21; 10:7–10).

In this difficult passage, Paul appears to state that the Creator predetermines the human ability to believe or disbelieve, thus foreordaining an individual's eternal destiny. This assumption troubles many believers for its apparent repudiation of free will, although some churches have embraced it. Later theologians such as Augustine and Calvin formulated a doctrine of **predestination,** in which God, prior to the world's creation, decreed everyone's fate, selecting a few to enjoy heavenly bliss and relegating the large majority to damnation.

Paul, however, emphasizes the positive aspects of God's apparent intervention into the human decision-making process. In God's long-range plan, Jewish refusal to recognize Jesus as Israel's Messiah allows Gentiles to receive the gospel message; thus, nations previously ignorant of God can achieve redemption. In a famous analogy, Paul likens Gentile believers to wild olive branches that have been grafted onto a cultivated olive trunk, which signifies Israel. If some of the old branches from the domesticated tree had not been lopped off, there would have been no room for the new (11:16–18). For humanity's universal benefit, God has taken advantage of Israel's unresponsiveness to produce a greater good.

Paul also states that the creation of churches in which Greeks and Romans now worship Israel's God will incite a healthy envy among Jews, kindling a desire to share the churches' spiritual favor. Furthermore, Israel's disbelief is only temporary. When all Gentiles become believers, then the original branches will be regrafted onto God's olive tree, with the result that "all Israel will be saved" (11:19–27).

Paul does not explain why both Israelites and Gentiles could not have been "saved" simultaneously, but he remains absolutely certain that the Jews are still God's chosen people. Writing more than ten years before Rome destroyed the Jewish state (in 70 CE), Paul

does not predict divine vengeance upon Israel. He affirms instead that God's own integrity ensures that he will honor his promises to the covenant community. For Paul, Israel continues to play a crucial role in the divinely ordered drama of human salvation (11:1–36).

Behavior in the Church and the World

Paul's ethical instruction (Rom. 12–15) is again closely tied to his sense of apocalyptic urgency. Because the New Age is about to dawn, believers must conduct themselves with special care. Their rescue from the present evil age is extremely near—closer now than it was when they first believed: "For salvation is nearer to us now than when we became believers; the night is far gone, the day is near" (13:11–12). Paul remains convinced that the Parousia will occur in his day (see the discussions of 1 Thessalonians and 1 Corinthians 15 above).

Paul's advice, written before his imprisonment and prosecution in Rome, extends to behavior outside the church and includes a program of cooperation with government authorities (see Figure 35.5). Echoing the

FIGURE 35.5 Remarkably well preserved, this streetside restaurant in Ostia, the seaport of Rome, offered convenient meals to busy passersby. Such "fast food" establishments were common in Roman cities and a familiar sight to Paul and other early Christians.

Stoic view that the state exists to maintain public order and punish wrongdoing, Paul implies that the Roman Empire was "instituted by God" (13:1–3)—an opinion conflicting with his earlier view that the present world is ruled by demonic forces (2 Cor. 4:4).

Although he emphasizes the Christian's duty to pay taxes and submit to legally constituted authority, Paul does not consider the ethical problem of a citizen's duty to resist illegal or unethical acts by the state. He does not advise believers to expend energy trying to change the present social system, perhaps because he sees it as so near its end (13:1–12). Paul's acceptance of the state parallels his acceptance of slavery as a social institution (see the discussion of Philemon below).

When Paul recommends voluntary cooperation with Rome, he could not have known that he would soon be among the first victims of government persecution. Following Emperor Nero's execution of many Roman Christians (c. 64–65 CE), some New Testament authors came to regard the state as Satan's earthly instrument to afflict God's people. After Rome destroyed Jerusalem (along with the original church there) in 70 CE, the empire became a "new Babylon" in the eyes of many believers. The author of Revelation pictures Rome as a beast and predicts its fall as a cause for universal rejoicing (Rev. 17–19). At the time Paul wrote, however, the adversarial relationship between church and state was still in the future.

Letter to the Philippians

Although it contains some sharp criticism of his opponents, Paul's letter to the church at Philippi is particularly warm and friendly. Urging cooperation for the mutual benefit of all believers, Paul cites an early hymn that depicts Jesus as the opposite of Adam—a humbly obedient son whose self-emptying leads to his heavenly exaltation. He also provides some important biographical material (3:4–8). In this short letter, Paul expresses special affection for the church at Philippi, the first in Europe, which he and his associate Timothy had founded (Acts 16:11–40). Paul's unusual intimacy with the Philippians appears in the warmth of his greetings (1:1–11) and by the fact that they were the only group from whom he would accept financial support (4:15–16). Further, in welcome contrast to the "boasting" and threats that characterize the letters to Corinth and Galatia, Philippians contains no impassioned defense of his authority (his friends in Philippi did not question it).

Paul instead expresses a more kindly and loving aspect of his personality. Like all genuinely Pauline letters, however, Philippians reveals the author's quick changes of mood, ranging from a thoughtful meditation on the meaning of his impending death to a brief but savage attack on his opponents. The letter features so many abrupt changes of subject and shifts in emotion that many analysts believe it to be, like 2 Corinthians, a composite work, containing parts of three or four different missives. The letter may be a literary unity, however, for Paul commonly leaps from topic to topic, registering different emotional responses to different problems in the course of a single letter.

Place of Origin

According to an early church tradition, Philippians is one of four canonical letters—including Philemon, Colossians, and Ephesians—that Paul wrote while imprisoned in Rome. Scholarly analysis of the four works, however, has raised serious questions about the time and place of their composition, as well as the authorship of two of them. Whereas scholars accept Philippians and Philemon as genuine Pauline documents, a majority challenge Paul's authorship of Colossians, and most doubt that he wrote Ephesians (see below).

If Philippians was not composed during Paul's house arrest in Rome (cf. Acts 28), it may have originated in a prison at Ephesus. The letter implies that Paul's friends made four journeys between Philippi and Paul's place of imprisonment and that a fifth trip was planned (2:25-26). Because the distance between Philippi and Rome (almost 800 miles) seems too great for such frequent shuttling back and forth, some historians propose that he wrote the letter in Ephesus, which is only about ten days' travel time from Philippi. Philippians' reference to the "imperial guard," the Roman emperor's personal militia (1:13), and the "emperor's household" does not necessarily mean that the letter originated in Rome. Ancient inscriptions recently discovered in Ephesus show that members of the Praetorian Guard and other imperial officials were stationed in the Roman province of Asia, where Ephesus and Colossae are located.

Although many scholars support the "Ephesian theory," others suggest that Paul wrote from Caesarea, where he spent two years in prison (cf. Acts 23–25). Still other critics point out that we lack proof that Paul was actually jailed in Ephesus and claim that the difficulties in traveling between Macedonia and Rome have been overstated (see Figure 35.6 for the relative distances

FIGURE 35.6 **Map Showing Potential Sites Where Paul Wrote His "Prison Letters."** Paul may have written these letters in Rome (in the far west on this map), in Ephesus (on the coast of present-day Turkey), or in Caesarea (in the far eastern Mediterranean). Note that Ephesus is much closer to Philippi than either of the other two cities.

between Rome, Philippi, Ephesus, and Caesarea). Where Paul was imprisoned remains an open question, although many commentators uphold the traditional view that Paul's "captivity letters" originated in the Roman capital.

The Significance of Paul's Imprisonment

Paul gives a surprisingly mellow response to his prison experience, courageously underscoring its positive results. Apparently widely talked about, his case gives other believers the opportunity to witness publicly for Christ. Unfortunately, not all of Paul's fellow Christians support him; some use his incarceration as a means of stirring up new troubles for the prisoner. Paul does not identify those Christians whose personal jealousies complicate his already difficult situation, but they may have been connected with the advocates of circumcision he denounces in Philippians 3:2–4. In Acts' account of Paul's arrest, imprisonment in Caesarea, and transportation to Rome under armed guard,

the Jerusalem church leadership is conspicuously absent from his defense. Perhaps those who shared James's adherence to Torah obligations were in some degree pleased to see Paul and his questionable views put under legal restraint.

Paul's attitude toward his troublesome rivals is far milder than in Galatians. Determined to find positive results even in his opponents' activities, he concludes that their motives, whether sincere or hypocritical, are finally irrelevant. They successfully proclaim the Christian message (1:12–18).

The Hymn to Christ

Philippians 2 contains the letter's most important theological concept. Urging the Philippians to place others' welfare before their own, Paul cites Jesus' behavior as the supreme example of humble service to others. To encourage his readers to emulate the same self-denying attitude that Jesus displayed, he recites a hymn that illustrates his point. The rhythmic and poetic qualities of this passage, as well as the absence of typically Pauline ideas and vocabulary, suggest that it is a pre-Pauline composition. The first stanza reads:

> Who, though he was in the form of God,
> Did not regard equality with God
> A thing to be grasped,
> But emptied himself,
> Taking the form of a servant,
> Being born in the likeness of men.
> And being found in human form,
> He humbled himself
> And became obedient unto death.

(Phil. 2:6–8, Revised Standard Version)

The hymn's second stanza (2:9–11) describes how God rewards Jesus' selfless obedience by granting him universal lordship and elevating him to heaven, thereby glorifying "God the father."

In this famous poem, which has been translated in various ways to highlight different theories about Christ's divinity, Jesus' relation to the Father is ambiguously stated. Since the fourth century CE, when the church officially adopted the doctrine of the Trinity, it has commonly been assumed that the hymn refers to Jesus' prehuman existence and affirms the Son's co-eternity and co-equality with the Father.

Remembering Paul's explicit subordination of Jesus to God in 1 Corinthians (15:24–28), many readers will be cautious about attributing post–New Testament ideas to the apostle. A growing number of scholars believe that Paul employs the hymn in order to contrast two "sons" of God—Adam (Luke 3:38) and Jesus. The Adam–Christ contrast figures prominently in both 1 Corinthians (15:21-23, 45–49) and Romans (5:12–19). Paul's use of the term "form" (Greek, *morphe*) refers to the divine image that both Adam and Jesus reflect (cf. Gen. 1:26–28). But whereas Adam tried to seize God-like status (Gen. 3:5), Jesus takes the form of a slave. Instead of rebelling against the Creator, he is fully obedient, undergoing the agony of the cross.

Finally, Adam's disobedience brings shame and death, but Jesus' total surrender to the divine will brings glory and exaltation. Jesus' self-emptying earns him the fullness of God's reward, the bestowal of "the name that is above every name," to whom all creation submits. In accordance with his usual method of using theology to offer instruction in proper behavior, Paul implicitly compares the reward given to Jesus for his humility with that in store for humbly obedient Christians. Now shining like "stars" in a dark world, they will inherit a future life similar to that which Jesus now enjoys (2:14–18).

Recommendations of Timothy and Epaphroditus

The references to Timothy and Epaphroditus, two of his favorite companions, suggest Paul's capacity for loyal friendships. Timothy, whose name appears as courtesy co-author of this letter (1:1), is one of Paul's most reliable assistants. Unlike Barnabas and John Mark, with whom Paul quarreled, Timothy (whose father was Greek and mother Jewish) shares Paul's positive attitude toward Gentile converts. In the apostle's absence, Paul trusts him to act as he would (2:19–24).

Epaphroditus, whom the Philippians had sent to assist Paul in prison, has apparently touched Paul by the depth of his personal devotion. Epaphroditus's dangerous illness, which delayed his return to Philippi, may have resulted from his helping the prisoner. Paul indicates his gratitude when urging the Philippians to give Epaphroditus an appreciative welcome home (2:25–3:1a).

Paul's concern for individual believers in Philippi is also apparent in his personal message for two estranged women, Euodia and Syntyche. Pleading with sensitivity and tact for their reconciliation, he ranks the two women as co-workers who aid his efforts to promote the gospel (4:2–3).

Attacking Advocates of Circumcision

In Chapter 3, flashes of Paul's old fire give his words a glowing edge. This section (3:1b–20), which may have originated as a separate memorandum, attacks believers who insist on circumcising Gentile converts, calling them "dogs" and "evil-doers . . . who mutilate the flesh" (3:2). In a reprise of his "boasting" to the Corinthians, Paul then cites his own superior claims as an exemplary Jew: From the tribe of Benjamin, he was "circumcised" as an infant, grew up to become a Pharisee (and a "persecutor of the church"), and "under the law" was "blameless" (3:5–6). Yet all his advantages in Judaism, both inherited and acquired by talent and labor, he dismisses as "loss" when compared to "the surpassing value of knowing Christ Jesus my Lord" (3:8).

Although he faces the possibility of imminent death (1:21–26), Paul remains convinced that "the Lord is near" and that the glorified Jesus will soon return "from heaven":

> and it is from there that we are expecting a Savior,
> the Lord Jesus Christ. He will transform the body
> of our humiliation that it may be conformed to the
> body of his glory, by the power that also enables
> him to make all things subject to himself.

(Phil. 3:20–21)

Letter to Philemon

Consisting of a single chapter, Philemon is a short letter dealing with a large topic—the relationship of Christian slaveholders to their human property. Contemporary readers are typically shocked that Paul, who had proclaimed the essential equality of all believers united in Christ (Gal. 3:28), does not use this occasion to denounce the institution of slavery as totally incompatible with Christian faith. Although Paul does not condemn the practice of buying and selling human beings—probably because he believes that the Greco-Roman world order will soon end—he does argue persuasively for a new relationship between master and slave. He asks the slave-owner, **Philemon,** to accept his runaway slave, **Onesimus,** as a "beloved brother," thereby establishing a new bond of kinship humanely linking Christian owners and their human chattel.

Unfortunately for enslaved persons, the divine intervention into human history that Paul expected to occur in his own day did not happen. Israel's Messiah did not reappear to overthrow unjust governments and set up a divinely empowered kingdom in which transformed believers would enjoy the full social and racial equality that Paul had envisioned. To the contrary, as late as the pre–Civil War United States (1860), southern clergymen and slaveholders continued to cite Paul's letter to Philemon as scriptural justification for their "peculiar institution" of legally sanctioned slave labor. The historical consequences of Paul's brief missive to his friend Philemon give this personal note an extraordinary importance.

The Question of Slavery

In seeking out Paul's purpose in writing this letter, it is helpful to realize that it is addressed not only to Philemon but also to "Apphia our sister, to Archippus our fellow soldier, and to the church in your house" in the town of Colossae (v. 2; because Philemon has only one chapter, all citations refer to verse numbers). Although the letter's main body (vv. 4–24) speaks directly to Philemon (the Greek pronoun "you" is singular throughout this section), the text clearly was intended to be read aloud to the whole congregation meeting in Philemon's house. (Apphia may have been the host's wife, and Archippus their son.)

Because the exact circumstances that prompted Paul to write this letter are not clear, scholars differ in their reconstruction of the situation involving Onesimus and his master. According to one plausible interpretation, Onesimus had stolen money or other property from Philemon. Somehow he then made his way from Colossae to Rome or Ephesus (if that is where Paul was imprisoned), where the apostle converted him to Christianity. Paul therefore speaks of Onesimus as "my child, . . . whose father I have become" (by imparting to him the life-giving faith in Christ) (v. 10). Some recent commentators, however, think it highly unlikely that Onesimus happened to encounter Paul by pure chance. More likely, they suggest, Onesimus—after having displeased his master—deliberately set out to find Paul and enlist his aid in reconciling with Philemon, whom the apostle had earlier converted to the faith. According to widely accepted Roman legal practice, a third party could settle disputes between masters and slaves, and Paul may have filled that role. Punning on the meaning of Onesimus's name (Greek, "useful"), Paul writes to Philemon that "formerly he [the slave] was useless to you, but now he is indeed useful both to you and to me" (v. 11).

Although Onesimus has made himself almost indispensable to the imprisoned apostle, Paul—perhaps compelled by Roman law—decides to send the slave back to his master. Maintaining a fine balance between exercising his apostolic authority and appealing to the equality existing among all Christians, Paul asks Philemon to receive Onesimus back, treating him "no longer as a slave, but more than a slave, a beloved brother—especially to me but how much more to you" (v. 16). We do not know if Paul is thereby requesting the master to free Onesimus, granting him legal and social status to match his Christian freedom, but the writer clearly underscores the slave's human value. Paul writes that Onesimus is "my own heart" and that Philemon should welcome him as he would the apostle himself (vv. 12, 17).

Paul also gives his guarantee to reimburse Philemon for any debt Onesimus may have incurred, or perhaps, money he may have embezzled or stolen (vv. 18–20). Appealing to Philemon's reputation for showing love to his fellow Christians (vv. 4–6), Paul gently pressures the slaveholder to be generous, anticipating that Philemon "will do even more than I say" (vv. 20–21). Is Paul asking Philemon, in a not-too-subtle way, to free Onesimus in order for him to remain in Paul's service?

Having invoked his apostolic authority and addressed his letter so that it will be read before the entire congregation at Colossae (which will expect Philemon to live up to his saintly reputation and give Onesimus a loving welcome?), Paul adds a final element of persuasion at the letter's close. As if penning an afterthought, Paul says that he now expects to be freed from his prison and will pay Philemon a personal visit (v. 22), an apostolic parousia ensuring that his requests will be honored.

He concludes with greetings from, among others, Mark and Luke, traditional authors of the two Gospels bearing their respective names.

Slavery in Context

Most readers today are deeply disappointed that Paul does not reject slavery outright as an intolerable evil. Instead, he advises slaves "not [to] be concerned" about their status, advising them to remain in whatever social "condition" they had when they first became Christians (1 Cor. 7:17–24). Paul's reasons for accepting the slave–master arrangement even in Christian society probably derive from his expectation that Jesus will soon return.

But other factors also influenced Paul's lack of interest in abolishing slavery or reforming other unjust social customs. In its acceptance of slavery, the Hebrew Bible differs little from the Greco-Roman society in which Paul lived. The Torah does, however, distinguish between Gentile slaves captured in battle and native-born Israelites who sold themselves or their children to pay off financial depts. In a passage known as the "Book of the Covenant," Mosaic Law decrees that after six years' servitude a male Hebrew slave is to be set free. Any children born to him and one of his master's female slaves, however, are to remain the master's property. If at the end of six years' time the freed man wishes to remain with his wife and family, he must submit to a mutilation of his ear (the organ of obedience) and remain a slave for life (Exod. 21:2–6). This legal statute clearly favors slaveholders' "rights."

Following Torah regulations—and the institutions of Greco-Roman society at large—New Testament writers neither condemn slavery nor predict its abolition. Only after the scientific Enlightenment of the eighteenth century CE was the persistence of slavery seen as inconsistent with the ethical principles of Christian freedom and with the innate worth of all humans as "images" of God. In American history, both pro- and antislavery parties used the New Testament to support their conflicting views. Slavery's proponents argued that biblical writers, including Paul, accepted the institution as a "natural" condition. Focusing on Paul's doctrines of freedom and Christian equality (Gal. 3:28), slavery's opponents eventually persuaded the Western world to grant a corresponding social and legal freedom to all people.

QUESTIONS FOR DISCUSSION AND REVIEW

1. Summarize what we know of Paul's biography from his letters. How did Paul's experience of the risen Jesus change his life purpose? In what respects does the biographical information contained in Acts differ from that found in Paul's correspondence?

2. Which passages in 1 Thessalonians and 1 Corinthians indicate that Paul believed that Jesus' Parousia was very near? In what ways does this belief affect his ethical advice to Christians, such as his preference to remain unmarried?

3. Explain Paul's doctrine of love as the essential quality of Christian life. How does he describe love (*agape*) in 1 Corinthians 13? How does his own way of life manifest love for others?

4. Why do some Corinthians disagree with Paul's belief in the future resurrection of the body? Explain the difference between belief in the inborn immortality of the soul and the concept of receiving eternal life through resurrection. Why does Paul argue that Jesus' resurrection is absolutely indispensable if Christians are to hope for an afterlife? What does Paul mean by a "resurrection body"?

5. If Paul was wrong when he preached that the Parousia would occur during his lifetime, to what extent does that mistaken view affect readers' confidence in his teachings? Which of Paul's teachings were most influenced by customs of the Jewish and Greco-Roman worlds?

6. Describe Paul's "gospel" of justification by faith as he presents it in Galatians and Romans. Why does Paul contrast Torah-observance with trust in Christ's power—and willingness—to save? What passages from the Hebrew Bible does Paul cite to show that God always intended to have a relationship with humans based on trust?

7. How do you think Paul's ideas about submission to governmental authority (Rom. 13) should be modified to reflect post-Enlightenment principles of freedom and individual rights? If the framers of the Declaration of Independence had followed Paul's advice in Romans 13, would the United States have broken free of Great Britain? Would there have been an American Revolution?

8. Analyze the hymn to Christ in Philippians 2 and compare it with Paul's contrast (in 1 Corinthians 15 and Romans 5) between an obedient Jesus and a disobedient Adam. In Genesis, Adam apparently tries to be "like God" in acquiring divine knowledge (Gen. 3:5, 22). According to Philippians, does Jesus attempt to win equality with God? Who is responsible for Jesus' posthumous exaltation? Summarize the arguments for and against different interpretations of this passage.

9. Identify Philemon and Onesimus and their association with Paul. Why do you think that Paul does not condemn human slavery as an evil institution, particularly among Christians? Does Paul's attitude toward slavery show that he sometimes thinks in terms of commonly accepted social practices of his time and place?

10. If Paul were alive today—and fully aware of the past 1,900 years of human history—do you think that he would revise his opinions on such topics as master–slave relationships, the position of women in the church, same-sex attachments, and unquestioning submission to governmental authorities? Cite passages that may indicate that Paul was sometimes open to changing the status quo.

Terms and Concepts to Remember

Adam and Christ, Paul's association of
antinomianism
Apostle to the Gentiles
Christ, cosmic role of
circumcision
dualism
eschatology, Paul's emphasis on
Fall (of humanity)
hymn to Christ (Philippians)
justification by faith, Paul's doctrine of

law, works of
letter form, Paul's use of
love (*agape*)
Paul's major theological concerns
original sin
Philemon/Onesimus
Phoebe
resurrection
slavery, as a Christian issue
Timothy and Titus
Torah, Paul's attitude toward
women, ministry of

Recommended Reading

Paul (General)

Beker, J. C. *Paul the Apostle: The Triumph of God in Life and Thought*. Philadelphia: Fortress Press, 1980. A thoughtful examination of Paul's apocalyptic message and its effects on his theology.

Dunn, James D. G. *The Theology of Paul the Apostle*. Grand Rapids, MI: Eerdmans, 1998. An authoritative study of Paul's views on God's actions in Christ; for more advanced study.

Fitzmyer, Joseph. *Paul and His Theology: A Brief Sketch*, 2nd ed. Englewood Cliffs, NJ: Prentice-Hall, 1989. A concise discussion of Paul's central teachings; useful for beginners.

Hawthorne, Gerald F.; Martin, Ralph P.; and Reid, D. G., eds. *Dictionary of Paul and His Letters*. Downers Grove, IL: InterVarsity Press, 1993. Argues for the authenticity of all letters traditionally ascribed to Paul, including the pastorals.

Keck, Leander E., and Furnish, Victor P. *The Pauline Letters*. Nashville, TN: Abingdon Press, 1984. A good place to begin studying Paul's thought.

Levine, Amy-Jill, ed. *A Feminist Companion to Paul*. Cleveland: Pilgrim, 2004. Ten scholarly essays analyzing Paul's writings on women in their original social/cultural context.

Malina, Bruce J., and Pilch, John J. *Social-Science Commentary on the Letters of Paul*. Minneapolis: Fortress Press, 2006. Except for the mistaken claim that Paul's mission was to Hellenized Jews rather than Gentiles, provides important insights into the cultural context of Paul's thought and writings.

Murphy-O'Connor, Jerome. *Paul: A Critical Life*. New York: Clarendon, 1996. Explores psychological motivation for Paul's persecution of Christians, his Pharisaic background, and his missionary tours.

Neyrey, Jerome H. *Paul in Other Words: A Cultural Reading of His Letters*. Louisville, KY: Westminster John Knox Press, 1990. An analysis of first-century-CE social, cultural, and religious assumptions that shaped Paul's worldview.

Sanders, E. P. *Paul: A Very Short Introduction*. New York: Oxford UP, 1991. A concise, clearly-written explanation of Paul's main theological beliefs; an excellent place to begin studying the apostle's essential message.

———. *Paul, the Law, and the Jewish People*. Philadelphia: Fortress Press, 1983. An influential study of Paul's attitudes toward the Torah and his Jewish heritage.

Wall, Robert W. "Introduction to Epistolary Literature." In *The New Interpreter's Bible*, Vol. 10, pp. 369–391. Nashville, TN: Abingdon Press, 2002. A brief introduction to Paul and his letters.

Witherup, Ronald D. *101 Questions and Answers of Paul*. New York: Paulist Press, 2003. A good introduction to Paul's life and theological concerns.

1 Thessalonians

Beker, J. C. *Paul's Apocalyptic Gospel: The Coming Triumph of God*. Philadelphia: Fortress Press, 1982. Describes the eschatological assumptions on which Paul based his interpretation of Jesus' significance.

Collins, R. F. "The First Letter to the Thessalonians." In R. E. Brown, et al., eds. *The New Jerome Biblical Commentary*, pp. 772–779. Englewood Cliffs, NJ: Prentice-Hall, 1990.

Krentz, Edgar M. "Thessalonians, First and Second Epistles to the." In D. N. Freedman, ed., *The Anchor Bible Dictionary*, Vol. 6, pp. 515–523. New York: Doubleday, 1992.

Malherbe, Abraham J. *The Letters to the Thessalonians: A New Translation with Introduction and Commentary* (Anchor Bible, Vol. 32B). New York: Doubleday, 2000. Provides the full text, with commentary.

First and Second Corinthians

Hays, Richard B. *Interpretation: First Corinthians*. Louisville, KY: Westminster John Knox Press, 1997. Examines Paul's theological response to socioeconomic problems at Corinth.

Meeks, Wayne. *The First Urban Christians: The Social World of the Apostle Paul*, 2nd ed. New Haven, CT: Yale University Press, 2003. An influential investigation into the socioeconomic status of the earliest Gentile Christians.

Sampley, J. Paul. "The First Letter to the Corinthians." In *The New Interpreter's Bible*, Vol. 10, pp. 773–1003. Contains the full text of the letter, with interpretative commentary.

Theissen, Gerd. *The Social Setting of Pauline Christianity: Essays on Corinth.* Ed. and trans., and with an introduction by, J. H. Schutz. Philadelphia: Fortress Press, 1982. Examines the social dynamics operating in early Christianity.

Thiselton, Anthony C. "Corinthians, First Letter to." In K.D. Sakenfeld, ed., *The New Interpreter's Dictionary of the Bible,* Vol. 1, pp. 735–744. Nashville, TN: Abingdon Press, 2006. A helpful introductory survey of the letter's contents and theology.

Towner, Philip. "Corinthians, Second Letter to." In K. D. Sakenfeld, ed., *The New Interpreter's Dictionary of the Bible,* Vol. 1, pp. 744–751. Nashville, TN: Abingdon Press, 2006. Surveys the letter's main themes and theological significance.

Galatians

Barclay, J. M. G. *Obeying the Truth: Paul's Ethics in Galatians.* Minneapolis: Fortress Press, 1991.

Koperski, Veronica. *What Are They Saying About Paul and the Law?* Mahwah, NJ: Paulist Press, 2001. Essays on current interpretations of Paul's complex views on the Torah.

Martyn, J. Louis. *Galatians* (Anchor Yale Bible Commentaries). New Haven, CT: Yale UP, 2004. A thorough, scholarly commentary.

Soards, Marion. "Galatians, Letter to the." In K. D. Sakenfeld, ed., *The New Interpreter's Dictionary of the Bible,* Vol. 2, pp. 508–514. Nashville, TN: Abington Press, 2007. An informative introduction.

Romans

Dunn, James G. *Paul and the Mosaic Law.* Grand Rapids, MI: Eerdmans, 2001. Scholarly essays exploring Paul's attitude toward the Torah and its relationship to his doctrine of salvation through faith in Christ; for advanced students.

Gorman, Michael J. *Apostle of the Crucified Lord: A Theological Introduction to Paul and His Letters.* Grand Rapids, MI: Eerdmans, 2004. Explores Paul's doctrine of justification by faith.

Sanders, E. P. *Paul and Palestinian Judaism.* Philadelphia: Fortress Press, 1978. An important scholarly study of Paul's relationship to his native Judaism.

Westerholm, Stephen. *Perspectives Old and New on Paul: The "Lutheran" Paul and His Critics.* Grand Rapids, MI: Eerdmans, 2004. Surveys the history of interpretation of Paul's doctrine of faith versus works of the law.

Witherington, Ben II, and Hyatt, Darlene. *Paul's Letter to the Romans: A Socio-Rhetorical Commentary.* Grand Rapids, MI: Eerdmans, 2004. For advanced study.

Wright, N. T. "The Letter to the Romans." *The New Interpreter's Bible,* Vol. 10, pp. 395–770. Contains the full text, with thorough commentary.

Philippians and Philemon

Byrne, Brendan. "The Letter to the Philippians." In R. E. Brown, et al., eds. *The New Jerome Biblical Commentary,* 2nd ed. Englewood Cliffs, NJ: Prentice-Hall, 1990.

Fitzmyer, Joseph. *The Letter to Philemon: A New Translation with Introduction and Commentary* (Anchor Bible). New York: Doubleday, 2000. A detailed analysis by a major scholar.

Lohse, Eduard. *Colossians and Philemon* (Hermeneria). Philadelphia: Fortress Press, 1971. A scholarly analysis concluding that Colossians is by a Pauline disciple.

Martin, R. P. *Philippians* (New Century Bible Commentary). Grand Rapids, MI: Eerdmans, 1983.

Silva, Moises. *Philippians* (Baker Exegetical Commentary of the New Testament). Grand Rapids, MI: Baker Academic, 2005.

Stendahl, K., ed. *Romans, Galatians, and Philippians* (Anchor Bible, Vol. 33). Garden City, NY: Doubleday, 1978. An editor's translation with commentary.

CHAPTER 36

Continuing the Pauline Tradition
Second Thessalonians, Colossians, Ephesians, and the Pastoral Epistles

Key Topics/Themes Paul's continuing influence on the church was so great that for years after his death, various Pauline disciples composed letters honoring his name and spirit. Whereas numerous documents claiming Pauline authorship, such as the noncanonical Acts of Paul, were rejected by the church, several others were accepted into the New Testament canon. Since the eighteenth century, scholars have increasingly doubted Paul's responsibility for six canonical letters attributed to him. The large majority of scholars now agree that three—1 and 2 Timothy, and Titus—do not come from his hand, and most question the authenticity of Ephesians as well. Paul's authorship of two—2 Thessalonians and Colossians—is still vigorously debated.

 ## The Problem of Pseudonymity

The author of 2 Thessalonians tells his readers not to become overly excited if they receive a letter falsely bearing Paul's name, indicating that the practice of circulating forged documents purportedly by apostolic writers had already begun (2 Thess. 2:1–3). To some modern readers, the notion that unknown Christians wrote in Paul's name is ethically unacceptable on the grounds that such "forgeries" could not be part of the New Testament. In the ancient world, however, twenty-first-century ideas about authorship would have been irrelevant, for it was then common for disciples of great thinkers to compose works perpetuating their masters' thoughts. They wrote about contemporary issues as they believed their leader would have if he were still alive.

This practice of creating new works under the identity of a well-known but deceased personage is called **pseudonymity.** Intending to honor an esteemed figure of the past rather than necessarily to deceive the reading public, both Jews and early Christians produced a large body of pseudonymous literature. In an attempt to apply the teachings of a dead prophet or spiritual mentor to current situations, Hellenistic Jewish authors wrote books ascribed to such revered biblical figures as Daniel, Enoch, Noah, David, Isaiah, Ezra, and Moses. Some, such as the

Book of Daniel, were accepted into the Hebrew Bible canon (see Chapter 26); others, such as 1 Enoch (quoted as scripture in the letter of Jude [see Chapter 38]), were not. Still others, including the apocalyptic 2 Esdras, became part of the Apocrypha (see Chapter 27).

The precise motives inspiring pseudonymous writers are unknown, but some may have wished to obtain a respectful hearing for their views that only a work purportedly by Paul, Peter, or another authority in the early church could command. During the first three centuries CE, numerous works, including gospels, apostolic acts, letters, and apocalypses, appeared in the name of Peter, John, James, Barnabas, and Paul (see Chapters 2 and 38). Some of these pseudonymous books conveyed a message persuasive enough to gain them a place in the New Testament. For many Christians, it is not the author but the spiritual content of a disputed work that gives it religious value.

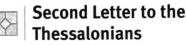 ## Second Letter to the Thessalonians

Repeating themes from Paul's genuine letter to the church at Thessalonica, 2 Thessalonians reinterprets Paul's original eschatology, asserting that a number of

traditional apocalyptic "signs" must precede the End. An increasing number of scholars, however, are skeptical about the genuineness of 2 Thessalonians. If Paul actually composed it, why does he repeat—almost word for word—so much of what he had already just written to the same congregation? More seriously, why does the author present an eschatology so different from that found in the first letter? In 1 Thessalonians, Paul states that the Parousia will come stealthily, "like a thief in the night." In 2 Thessalonians, however, a number of apocalyptic "signs" must occur first. In contrast to the first letter's sense of urgency, the author of 2 Thessalonians insists that a whole series of predestined events must precede the End, thus postponing the Parousia to some distant time in the future.

Scholars defending Pauline authorship advance several theories to explain the writer's apparent change of attitude toward the Parousia. In the first letter, Paul highlights the tension between the shortness of time the world has left and the necessity of believers' vigilance and ethical purity as they await the Second Coming. In the second missive, Paul writes to correct the Thessalonians' misconceptions about or abuses of his early emphasis on the nearness of End time.

If Paul is in fact the author, he probably wrote 2 Thessalonians within a few months of his earlier letter. Some converts, claiming that "the day of the Lord is already here" (2:2), were upsetting others with their otherworldly enthusiasms. In their state of apocalyptic fervor, some even scorned everyday occupations and refused to work or support themselves. It is possible that the visionary Spirit of prophecy that Paul encouraged the Thessalonians to cultivate (1 Thess. 5:19–22) had come back to haunt him. Empowered by private revelations, a few Christian prophets may have interpreted the Spirit's presence—made possible by Jesus' resurrection and ascension to heaven—as a mystical fulfillment of the Parousia. According to this belief in a presently realized eschatology, the Lord's Day is *now*. Paul, however, consistently emphasizes that Jesus' resurrection and the Spirit's coming are only the first stage in God's plan of cosmic renewal. God's purpose can be completed only at the final consummation of history.

Placing the Second Coming in Perspective

In 2 Thessalonians, Paul (or a follower building on his thought) takes on the difficult task of urging Christians to be ever alert and prepared for the Lord's return and at the same time to remember that specific events must take place before Jesus' reappearance. The writer achieves this delicate balance partly by insisting on a rational and

practical approach to life during the unknown interval between his writing and the Parousia.

In introducing his apocalyptic theme, the author invokes a vivid image of the Final Judgment to imprint its powerful reality on his readers' consciousness. He paraphrases images from the Hebrew prophets to imply that persons now persecuting Christians will soon suffer God's wrath. Christ will be revealed from heaven amid blazing fire, overthrowing those who disobey Jesus' gospel or fail to honor the one God (1:1–12).

Having assured the Thessalonians that God will surely punish their persecutors, Paul (or a disciple) now admonishes them not to assume that the punishment will happen immediately. Believers are not to run wild over some visionary's claim that the End is already here. Individual prophetic revelations declaring that Jesus is now invisibly present were apparently strengthened when a letter—supposedly from Paul—conveyed the same or a similar message. (This reference to a pseudo-Pauline letter indicates that the practice of composing documents in Paul's name had begun at a very early date.) Speculations founded on private revelations or forged letters, the author points out, are doomed to disappoint persons who fall for them (2:1–3).

Traditional (Non-Pauline?) Signs of the End

As mentioned previously, one of the strongest arguments against Paul's authorship of 2 Thessalonians is the letter's insistence that a whole series of eschatological events must unfold before the End arrives. Although the writer admits that the Parousia is imminent (1:6–10), he also argues that it cannot happen until specific developments characteristic of Jewish apocalyptic thought have occurred. At this point, 2 Thessalonians reverts to the cryptic and veiled language typical of apocalyptic discourse, referring to mysterious personages and events that may have been understood by the letter's original recipients but that are largely incomprehensible to modern readers. The End cannot come before the final rebellion against God's rule, when evil is revealed in human form as a demonic enemy who pollutes the Temple and claims divinity for himself. In this passage, the terminology resembles that of Daniel, a Jewish apocalyptic work denouncing Antiochus IV, a Greek-Syrian king who profaned the Jerusalem Temple and tried to destroy the Jewish religion (see Chapter 26).

Some commentators suggest that the author regards the Roman emperor, whose near-absolute power gave him virtually unlimited potential for inflicting evil on humankind, as a latter-day counterpart of Antiochus. Paul's explicitly stated view of the Roman government, however, is positive (Rom. 13), so readers must look elsewhere to identify the doomed figure.

Reminding the Thessalonians that he had previously informed them orally of these apocalyptic developments, the author states that the mysterious enemy's identity will not be disclosed until the appointed time. This is an allusion to the common apocalyptic belief that all history is predestined: Events cannot occur before their divinely predetermined hour. Evil forces are already at work, however, secretly gathering strength until "the one who now restrains it [the "lawless" egomaniac who claims divine honors] is removed." Only then will the hidden identity of the evil ruler be revealed (2:3–12).

In this passage, the writer paints a typically apocalyptic worldview, a moral dualism in which the opposing powers of good and evil have their respective agents at work on earth. The enemy figure is Satan's agent; his opposite is Christ. As Jesus is God's representative working in human history, so the "lawless" rebel is the devil's tool. Operating on a cosmic scope, the conflict between good and evil culminates in Christ's victory over his enemy, who has deceived the mass of humanity into believing his "lying wonders." This deception, perhaps, is the false belief that any being other than God is the source of humanity's ultimate welfare. An evil parody of the Messiah, the unnamed satanic dupe functions as an **anti-Christ,** God's ultimate human enemy (cf. 1 John 4:2–3; 2 John).

The writer's language is specific enough to arouse speculation about the probable identifies of the enigmatic "lawless one" and the equally mysterious one who temporarily "restrains" the former's malign influence. It is also vague enough to preclude connecting any known historical figures with these eschatological roles. In typical apocalyptic fashion, the figures are mythic archetypes that belong to a realm beyond the reach of historical investigation.

A Disputed Letter to the Colossians

In Colossians, a Pauline disciple (or perhaps Paul himself) emphasizes Jesus' identification with the cosmic power and Wisdom by and for which the universe was created. The divine "mystery" is revealed as Christ's life-giving Spirit now dwelling in the believer.

If Paul is the author of Colossians, as many scholars believe, he had not yet visited the city when he wrote this theologically important letter. A small town in the Roman province of Asia, Colossae was located about 100 miles east of Ephesus, the provincial capital (see Figure 34.5). Epaphras, one of Paul's missionary associates, apparently had founded the church a relatively short time before the letter was written.

If genuine, Colossians was probably composed at about the same time as Philemon, to which it is closely related. In both letters, the author writes from prison, including his friend Timothy in the salutations (1:1) and adding greetings from many of the same persons—such as Onesimus, Archippus, Aristarchus, Epaphras, Mark, and Luke—cited in the earlier missive (4:9–18). If Philemon hosted the house church at Colossae, it is strange that the writer does not mention him. Nevertheless, his absence from the letter does not discredit Pauline authorship.

Purpose and Organization

Although it was not one of his churches, Paul (or a later disciple) writes to the Colossae congregation to correct some false teachings prevalent there. These beliefs apparently involved cults that inappropriately gave honor to angels or other inhabitants of the invisible world. A few commentators suggest that some Colossians may have attempted to worship supernatural beings that the angels themselves worshiped. Paul refutes such "empty deceit," born only of "human tradition" (2:8), by emphasizing Christ's uniqueness and supremacy. Christ alone is the channel to spiritual reality; lesser spirits—the "elemental spirits of the universe"—are now his captives, over whom he has triumphed (2:15).

The letter's purpose is to ensure that the Colossians clearly recognize who Christ really is and make him the sole channel to God. The author highlights two principal themes: (1) Christ is supreme because God's power now manifested in him was the same power that created the entire universe, including those invisible entities the false teachers mistakenly worship; and (2) when they realize Christ's supremacy and experience his indwelling Spirit, the Colossians are initiated into his mystery cult, voluntarily harmonizing their lives with the cosmic unity he embodies.

Christ—The Source of Cosmic Unity

In the opinion of some interpreters, both the complex nature of the false teachings, which seem to blend Greco-Roman and marginally Jewish ideas into an eclectic synthesis, and the **Christology** of Colossians seem too "advanced" for the letter to have originated in Paul's day. Other critics point out that, if the letter was composed late in Paul's career to meet a situation significantly different from ones he had earlier encountered, it could well have stimulated the apostle to produce a more fully developed expression about his concept of Christ's nature and function.

Jesus as the Mediator of Creation As in Philippians 2, the author seems to adapt an older Christian hymn to illustrate his vision of the exalted Jesus' cosmic role:

> He is the image of the invisible God, the firstborn of all creation; for in him all things in heaven and on earth were created, things visible and invisible, whether thrones or dominions or rulers or powers— all things have been created through him and for him. He himself is before all things, and in him all things hold together. He is the head of the body, the church; he is the beginning, the firstborn from the dead, so that he might come to have first place in everything. For in him all the fullness of God was pleased to dwell, and through him God was pleased to reconcile himself all things, whether on earth or in heaven, by making peace through the blood of his cross.

(Col. 1:15–20)

Like the prologue to John's Gospel, this beautiful poem is modeled on biblical and Hellenistic Jewish concepts of divine Wisdom (Prov. 8:22–31; Ecclus. 24:1–22; see also the discussion of John's usage of Logos [Word] in Chapter 33). Hellenistic Jews had created a rich lore of speculative thought in which God's chief attribute, his infinite Wisdom, is the source of all creation and the means by which he communicates his purposes to humanity. Many historians believe that early Christian thinkers adopted these ready-made wisdom traditions and applied them to Jesus.

Like the Philippians hymn, the Colossian poem is traditionally seen as proclaiming Jesus' heavenly preexistence and his personal role as mediator in creation. More recently, many scholars—recognizing the hymn's use of wisdom language—view it as a declaration that the same divine Presence and Power that created the universe now operates in the glorified Christ. The personified Wisdom which God employed as his agent in fashioning the cosmos is now fully revealed in Christ, the agent through whom God redeems his human creation.

The phrase "image" [*eikon*] of the invisible God" (1:15) may correspond to the phrase "form [*morphe*] of God" that Paul uses in Philippians 2:6. In both cases, the term echoes the words of Genesis 1, in which God creates the first humans in his own "image" (Gen. 1:16–27). In harmony with this interpretation, the author of Colossians also describes his fellow believers as bearing the divine "image" (3:10). Rather than asserting that the prehuman Jesus was literally present at creation, the hymn may affirm that he is the ultimate goal toward which God's world trends.

Whatever Christology he advances, the writer's main purpose is to demonstrate Christ's present superiority to all rival beings in the cosmos. The "thrones," "dominions," "principalities," and "authorities" mentioned (1:16) probably represent the Jewish hierarchy of angels, the "sons of God" who serve at the heavenly court. Christ's perfect obedience, vindicating God's image in humanity, and his ascension to heaven have rendered these lesser beings irrelevant and powerless. By his triumph, Christ leads them captive, just as a Roman emperor leads a public procession of conquered enemies (2:9–15).

Moving from Christ's supremacy to his own role in the divine plan, Paul (or his disciple) states that his task is to deliver God's message of reconciliation. He is the agent chosen to reveal the "mystery that has been hidden throughout the ages" but is now revealed: The risen Christ presently dwells within believers, spiritually reuniting the Christian with God. Christians thus form Christ's visible body, here identified with the church (1:21–2:8).

The Mystical Initiation into Christ Employing the rather obscure language of Greek mystery religions (see Chapter 28), the author compares the Christian's baptism to a vicarious experience of Christ's death and resurrection (2:12, 20; 3:1). It is also the Christian equivalent of circumcision, the ritual sign that identifies one as belonging to God's people, and the rite of initiation into Christ's "body" (2:12–14). Raised to new life, initiated believers are liberated from religious obligations sponsored by those lesser spirits, who, the author claims, were the actual conveyers of the Torah revelation to Moses.

Empowered by Christ's Spirit, the Colossians should not be intimidated by self-styled authorities who mortify the body and piously forbid partaking of certain food and drink, for Christ's death ended all such legal requirements. Although the author declares the equality of all believers, regardless of nationality or social class, he omits the unity of the sexes that Paul included in Galatians 3:28 (2:20–3:11). As with many Greco-Roman mystery religions, initiation into Christ's "body" gives the initiates both social and religious equality.

Consistent with Paul's custom, the author concludes by underlining the ethical implications of his theology. Because Christians experience the indwelling Christ, they must live exceptionally pure and upright lives. The list of vices (3:5–9) and virtues (3:12–25) is typical of other Hellenistic teachers of ethics, but the writer adds a distinctively Christian note: Believers behave well because they are re-created in Christ's nature and "image" (3:10).

Letter to the Ephesians

Authorship, Date, and Context

Echoing ideas and phrases from Colossians, Ephesians appears to revise and update Pauline concepts about God's universal plan of salvation for both Jews and Gentiles and about believers' spiritual warfare against supernatural evil. Whereas many scholars challenge Paul's authorship of Colossians, most deny that he wrote Ephesians. Although it closely resembles Colossians in phrasing and thought, Ephesians differs from the undisputed Pauline letters in (1) vocabulary (containing over ninety words not found elsewhere in Paul's genuine writings), (2) literary style (written in extremely long, convoluted sentences, in contrast to Paul's usually direct, forceful statements), and (3) theology (lacking typically Pauline doctrines such as justification by faith, freedom from Torah observance, and the nearness of Christ's return).

Despite its similarity to Colossians (75 of Ephesians' 155 verses parallel passages in Colossians), it presents a different view of the sacred secret or "mystery" revealed in Christ. In Colossians, God's long-hidden "mystery" is Christ's mystical union with those initiated into the faith (Col. 1:27), but in Ephesians, it is the union of Jew and Gentile in one church (Eph. 3:6).

More than any other disputed letter (except those to Timothy and Titus), Ephesians seems to reflect a time in church history significantly later than Paul's day. References to the church being "built on the foundation of the apostles and prophets" (2:20; 3:5) imply that these figures are from the past, not the author's generation. The Gentiles' equality in Christian fellowship is no longer a controversial issue but an accomplished fact; this strongly suggests that the letter originated after the church membership had become largely non-Jewish (2:11–22). Opponents no longer question Paul's stand on circumcision, again indicating that the work was composed after Jerusalem's destruction had largely eliminated the influence of the Jewish parent church. If Ephesians was written by Paul, it probably originated from his Roman prison (early 60s CE). But if it was penned by a later Pauline disciple, as many scholars believe, Ephesians was probably written about the time Paul's letters first circulated as a unit, perhaps about 90 CE.

When Paul uses the term "church" (*ekklesia*), he always refers to a single congregation (Gal. 1:2; 1 Cor. 11:16; 16:19, etc.). In contrast, Ephesians' author speaks of the "church" collectively, a universal institution encompassing all individual groups. This view of the church as a worldwide entity also points to a time after the apostolic period.

The cumulative evidence convinces most scholars that Ephesians is a deutero-Pauline document, a post-apostolic work that an admirer thoroughly familiar with Paul's thought and theology composed in his name. The close parallels to Colossians, as well as the use of phrases taken from Romans, Philemon, and other letters, indicate that, unlike the author of Acts, this writer had access to Paul's correspondence. Some scholars propose that Ephesians was written as a kind of "cover letter" or essay to accompany an early collection of Paul's letters. The phrase "in Ephesus" (1:1), identifying the recipients, does not appear in any of the oldest manuscripts. That fact, plus the absence of any specific issue or problem being addressed in a particular congregation, reinforces the notion that Ephesians was intended to circulate among several churches in Asia Minor. In summarizing some of Paul's ideas and updating others to fit the changing needs of a largely Gentile church, the pseudonymous author creates a tribute to Paul's enduring influence.

Despite its long and sometimes awkward sentence structures (reorganized into shorter units in most English translations), Ephesians is a masterpiece of devotional literature. Unlike Paul's undisputed letters, it has a generally quiet and meditative tone, with no temperamental outbursts or attacks on the writer's opponents. Although it imitates the letter form by including a brief salutation (1:1–2) and a final greeting (6:21–24), Ephesians is really a highly sophisticated tract.

God's Plan of Salvation Through the United Body of Christ

The author's main theme is the union of all creation with Christ, manifested on earth by the church's international unity (1:10–14). Echoing Romans' concept of predestination, the writer states that before the world's foundation God selected Christ's future adopted "children" (composing the church) to be redeemed by Jesus' blood, a sacrifice through which the chosen ones' sins are forgiven. According to his preordained plan, God has placed Christ as head of the church, which is his body. The Spirit of Christ now fills the church as fully as God dwells in Christ (1:22–23). This mystical union of the human and the divine is God's unforeseen gift, his grace that saves those who trust him (2:1–10).

The Divine Mystery God's long-kept secret is that Gentiles, previously under divine condemnation, can now share in the biblical promises made to Israel. This divine purpose to unite Jew and Gentile in equal grace— "the plan of the mystery hidden for ages"—is the special message that Paul is commissioned to preach (3:1–21).

For most scholars, the writer's assumption that Gentile converts are fully acknowledged as Christ's heirs indicates a situation that did not develop until considerably after Paul's generation.

Instructions for Living in the World In the second part of his letter (4:1–6:20), the author explores four areas in which the Spirit imparts unity. The first area is life in the church, where all believers are called to "one Lord, one faith, one baptism, one God and Father of all" (4:4–5). The second area is the outside world (4:17–5:20), where ignorance leads unbelievers to "practice every kind of impurity"; by contrast, Christians abandon such unseemly pursuits "to be renewed in the spirit of [their] minds," enabling them to be recreated "in the likeness of God" (4:17–24). In the third area, the Spirit permeates family life so that husbands, wives, children, and slaves show mutual love and self-control (5:21-6–9)

Heavenly Armor In Ephesians' most famous passage, the Pauline analogy of Christians armed like Roman soldiers is vividly elaborated (see Figure 36.1). In 1 Thessalonians (5:8), Paul urges believers to imitate armed sentries who stay awake on guard duty, for Christians must remain similarly alert for Jesus' return. Ephesians' author discards the eschatological context of Paul's metaphor, however, and instead presents an ongoing battle between good and evil with no end in sight. In the genuine Pauline letters, the apostle foresees evil demolished at the Parousia. By contrast, the writer here paints a picture of cosmic conflict reminiscent of **Zoroastrianism**—the Persian religion in which the world is viewed as a battlefield between invisible forces of light and dark, good and evil.

In Zoroastrian terms, the Ephesian Paul describes two levels of "cosmic powers"—the earthly rulers of "this present darkness" and the invisible forces in heaven (6:10–12). Like Mark, the author apparently senses the reality of an evil so powerful that mere human wickedness cannot explain it. As Walter Wink has observed, the unseen "powers" include entrenched social attitudes, deep-seated prejudices, and benighted mental states that resist God's healing Spirit (see Wink in "Recommended Reading"). Instead of despairing at these "dark" forces, however, the writer rejoices that God provides ammunition with which to defeat even supernatural evil. Each article of protection is a Christian virtue:

> For our struggle is not against enemies of blood and flesh, but against the rulers, against the authorities, against the cosmic powers of this present darkness, against the spiritual forces of evil in the heavenly places. Therefore take up the whole armor of

FIGURE 36.1 This bas-relief shows Roman soldiers. The Book of Ephesians' famous description of a Christian's spiritual defenses against evil is based on the armor and other military equipment that Roman soldiers used (Eph. 6:13–17).

> God, . . . fasten the belt of truth around your waist, and put on the breastplate of righteousness. As shoes for your feet put on whatever will make you ready to proclaim the gospel of peace. With all of these, take the shield of faith, with which you will be able to quench all the flaming arrows of the evil one. Take the helmet of salvation, and the sword of the Spirit, which is the word of God.

(Eph. 6:12–17)

Rich in spiritual insight, Ephesians is a creative summary of some major Pauline concepts. Even if not by Paul, it is nevertheless a significant celebration of Christian ideals, an achievement worthy of the great apostle himself.

 ## The Pastorals: Letters to Timothy and Titus

The three letters addressed to Paul's young missionary companions, Timothy and Titus, are known as the **pastoral epistles** (from the English word *pastor*, the "shepherd" of a flock). The Pauline authorship of 1 and 2 Timothy and Titus, however, has been under critical attack for more than two centuries, with a large scholarly consensus that Paul did not write them. Besides the fact that they do not appear in early lists of Paul's letters, the pastoral epistles (or pastorals) seem to reflect conditions that prevailed long after Paul's day. Their views of church offices—"bishops," "elders," and "deacons"—mirror the more tightly organized church of the late first or early second century CE, in which such offices had far more specialized functions than in Paul's time.

Lacking Paul's characteristic ideas about Christ's indwelling Spirit or justification by faith, the pastorals are also un-Pauline in their flat style and different vocabulary (containing 306 words not found in Paul's undisputed letters). Scholars believe that a single Pauline follower—who shows little of his master's fire or originality—wrote all three, between about 90 and 120 CE. Known for convenience as "the Pastor," the pseudonymous author writes to preserve an inherited doctrinal tradition and to bolster the authority of an increasingly well-organized church.

In the pastoral epistles, Timothy and Titus—Paul's trusted missionary companions—are less real historical characters than literary symbols. They represent a new generation of believers to whom the task of guarding apostolic truths and combating false teachings is assigned.

First Letter to Timothy

Writing to Timothy as representing a postapostolic generation of Christians, the Pastor warns his readers against false teachers and recommends the standards necessary for ensuring proper order and discipline within the church.

Establishing Orthodoxy and Institutional Order

The writer's primary goal is to combat "doctrines" that differ from orthodox (correct) teachings (1:3) then circulating among the church membership. As Christianity spread among diverse Gentile groups, some converts apparently brought ideas from older Greco-Roman religions and philosophies, which they subsequently tried to integrate into the Christian proclamation. Because the Pastor does not offer a rational criticism of his opponents' errors, we do not know the exact nature of the beliefs attacked. Some commentators suggest that the false teachers practiced an early form of **Gnosticism** (from the Greek *gnosis,* meaning "knowledge"), a movement in which believers cultivated a spiritual enlightenment making them aware of their souls' heavenly origins. Other critics note that the Pastor offers too little information to confirm that the alleged **heretics** (teachers of doctrinal error) were Gnostics.

According to the Pastor, the false teachings involved "myths and endless genealogies that promote speculations rather than divine training" (orthodox doctrines). Their practitioners apparently included people who tried to observe Torah statutes (1:7–9), as well as puritans who "forbid marriage and demand abstinence from foods" (4:1–4). Timothy, and the leadership he represents, must correct this misguided self-denial by transmitting the correct Pauline teaching (4:11), thereby saving himself as well as those who obey him (4:16).

Qualifications for Church Offices

The Pastor's second concern is to outline the qualifications for leaders aspiring to church offices (3:1–13). Invoking Paul's authority to establish a stable church organization, the writer lists credentials for "bishops" (overseers), "deacons" (assistants), and "elders," all of which implies a more rigid hierarchy than was the case in Paul's day. Paul had once used the terms "bishop" and "deacon" (Phil. 1:1), but apparently to describe areas of service rather than the kinds of church positions elaborated here. According to the Pastor, candidates must demonstrate all the virtues typical of Hellenistic ethical philosophy: They are to be "above reproach, married only once, temperate, sensible, respectable," with their households in good order and their children properly "submissive" to paternal authority (3:2–23). Rather than requiring the spiritual gifts—the abilities to prophesy, teach, interpret the "Spirit," or otherwise strengthen the congregation—that Paul valued, the Pastor merely lists some standards of ordinary social respectability. His descriptions of church leadership indicate an increasingly institutionalized community that is closer to Roman standards of organization than to the loosely structured, Spirit-led congregations that Paul nurtured. As many commentators have remarked, the historical Jesus—an unmarried, itinerant prophet who stirred controversy and public criticism even in his hometown—would seem to be excluded from holding office in the Pastor's church. Nor would Paul himself, an unmarried and frequently jailed man with no permanent residence or family properly held in subjection to husbandly control, meet the Pastor's organizational requirements.

The Pastor regards the institution of the church—rather than the Spirit of Christ dwelling in believers—as "the pillar and bulwark of the truth" (3:15). In the writer's generation, a tightly organized church structure administered by right-thinking leaders replaces the dynamic and charismatic fellowship of the Pauline congregations. The Pastor's church's stratified membership also reflects the social order of the larger Greco-Roman society. Bishops, deacons, and elders govern a mixed group composed of different social classes, including heads of households, masters, slaves, wives, widows, and children (all of whom are commanded to submit to their respective superiors).

Women's Roles Whereas Paul recognizes women as prophets and speakers (1 Cor. 11:5), the Pastor permits "no woman to teach or to have authority over a man; she is to keep silent" (2:12). His reason for denying all women a teaching position derives from a male-oriented interpretation of the second Genesis creation story, in which he sees Eve, the first woman, as having been "deceived" by the serpent and thus tempting her husband into sin (2:8–15). The detailed instruction concerning women's dress and conduct probably applies to public worship and parallels the restricted positions that Greco-Roman society assigned women. A reflection of then-current social customs, it is not necessarily a timeless prescription limiting women's roles in Christian life.

In his discussion of the church's treatment of widows, the Pastor distinguishes between women who are "really widows" who demonstrate their worth by good deeds and women who are unqualified for that status because of their youth or inappropriate conduct. Following Jewish law (Exod. 22:22; Deut. 24:17–24), the church early assumed responsibility for supporting destitute widows (Acts 6:1), but the author stipulates that widows must be sixty years old before they can qualify for financial assistance. Relatives must support underage women who have lost their husbands (5:3–16). The author seems uninterested in the fate of young widows who have no family to help them.

Final Thoughts As Christians are to pray for government rulers (2:1–3), so slaves are to recognize their duties to masters and obey them (6:1–2). Yet the rich and influential are reminded to share their wealth (6:17–19). People who are ambitious to acquire riches are told that "the love of money is a root of all kinds of evil, and in their eagerness to be rich some have wandered away from the faith and pierced themselves with many pains" (6:10).

The author concludes by instructing Timothy to guard the apostolic legacy given him. Anyone who disagrees with the Pastor's updated interpretation of Paul's teachings is both "conceited" and a troublemaker (6:3).

Second Letter to Timothy

In a style more closely resembling that of Paul than the other pastoral epistles, 2 Timothy counsels against various false teachings. Of the three pastorals, 2 Timothy most successfully captures elements of Paul's genuine

style. Although the letter is similarly concerned with refuting false teachings, its tone is more intimate and personal. Especially moving are several passages in which the author describes himself as abandoned by former companions and languishing alone except for the company of Luke (1:15; 4:9–11, 16). These sections—along with other flashes of Paul's characteristic vigor and emotional fire (4:6–8, 17–18)—lead some scholars to speculate that the work contains fragments of otherwise lost Pauline letters. Such theories, however, are not widely accepted.

The part of 2 Timothy with the best claim to Pauline authorship is the section ending the letter (4:6–22), in which the writer reproduces the fluctuations between lofty thoughts and mundane practicalities so typical of the apostle. In the first part, he compares himself to a runner winning the athlete's coveted prize—not the Greek competitor's laurel crown, but "the crown of righteousness" that God will award him on Judgment Day (4:6–8). Switching abruptly to practical matters, the author asks the recipient to remember to bring his books when he visits Paul. In another quick change of subject, he complains that during his court hearing nobody appeared in his defense and that the testimony of one "Alexander the coppersmith" seriously damaged his case. Then, in a seemingly contradictory about-face, the writer states that he has (metaphorically) escaped "the lion's mouth" and that God will "save" him for the "heavenly kingdom" (4:13–18). Although such rapid changes of subject and shifts from gloom to optimism characterize Paul's genuine correspondence, most scholars believe that the entire document is the Pastor's work. The more vivid passages are simply the writer's most effective homage to the apostle.

In describing the false teachings within the church that he identifies as signs of the last days, the Pastor reveals he is using Paul to predict conditions taking place in the writer's own time. During the world's last days, hypocrites insinuate their way into Christians' homes, corrupting their occupants. Those intruders typically prey upon women because, in the Pastor's insulting opinion, even when eager to learn, women lack the ability to understand true doctrine (3:1–8). Instead of the false teachings being punished at the Parousia, the Pastor implies, the mere passage of time will expose their errors (3:9).

As in 1 Timothy, the Pastor does not refute the false teachers with logical argument but merely calls them names and lists their vices (3:1–6, 13; 4:3–4), duplicating the catalogues of misbehavior common in Hellenistic philosophical schools. Even believers do not adhere to healthy doctrines, but instead tolerate leaders who flatter them with what they want to hear.

Whereas the church is the stronghold of faith in 1 Timothy, in 2 Timothy, the Hebrew Bible is the standard of religious orthodoxy (correct teaching), confounding error and directing believers to salvation. Scripture also provides the mental discipline necessary to equip the believer for right action (3:15–17). Concluding with his memorable picture of the apostle courageously facing martyrdom, the Pastor graciously includes all the faithful in Christ's promised deliverance—not only Paul but "all who have longed for [Jesus'] appearing," the day of his Parousia (4:6–8).

Letter to Titus

The letter to Titus, who represents the postapostolic church leadership, urges him to preserve the Pauline traditions and sets forth the requirements and duties of elders and biships. Although the shortest of the pastorals, Titus has the longest salutation, a wordy review of Paul's credentials and the recipient's significance (1:1–4). This highly formal introduction would be inappropriate in a personal letter from Paul to his friend and fellow missionary, but it is understandable as the Pastor's way of officially transmitting Paul's authoritative instruction to an apostolic successor.

The historical **Titus**, a Greek youth whom Paul refused to have circumcised (Gal. 2), accompanied the apostle on his missionary tours of Greece, acting as Paul's emissary to reconcile the rebellious Corinthians (Gal. 2:1, 3, 10; 2 Cor. 8:6, 16–23). Like the "Timothy" of the other pastorals, however, "Titus" also represents the postapostolic church leadership, the prototype of those preserving the Pauline traditions. Consequently, the commission of "Titus" is to establish an orthodox and qualified ministry. The letter's chief purpose is to outline the requirements and some of the duties of church elders and overseers (bishops).

Qualifications for the Christian Ministry The writer states that he left "Titus" in Crete, an ancient island center of Greek civilization, to install church assistants (elders) in every town (1:5). Such persons must be completely respectable married men who keep their children under strict parental control (1:6). Besides possessing these domestic credentials, bishops (church overseers) must also have a reputation for devotion, self-control, and hospitality (1:7–8). Again, the writer says nothing about the leaders' intellectual or charismatic gifts, so highly prized in the Pauline churches (2 Cor. 11–14). Instead, one of the bishop's primary functions is to guard the received religion, adhering to established beliefs and correcting any persons who deviate from inherited

tradition (1:7–9). Titus is the only book in the New Testament that used the term **heretic** (3:10), which at the time of writing (late first to early second century CE) probably meant a person who held opinions of which the proto-orthodox leadership disapproved. Heretics are to be warned twice and then ignored (excluded from church fellowship?) if they fail to change their ways (3:10–11).

Christian Behavior in an Ungodly World The pastor reminds his readers that, because they are Christians in a disbelieving world, they must live exemplary lives of obedience and submission to governmental authorities (3:1). Men and women, old and young, slaves and masters—all are to behave in a way that publicly reflects well on their religion (2:1–10). Christians must preserve an ethically pure community while awaiting Christ's return (2:13–14).

In a moving passage, the author contrasts the negative personality traits that many believers had before their conversion with the grace and hope for eternal life that they now possess (3:3–8). In counsel similar to that in the letter of James, he urges believers to show their faith in admirable and useful deeds and to refrain from "stupid controversies, genealogies, dissensions, and quarrels about the law, for they are unprofitable and worthless" (3:9–10).

The Pastor's Contribution

Although compared to Paul's the Pastor's style is generally weak and colorless (except for some passages in 2 Timothy), the Pastor successfully promotes Paul's continuing authority in the church. His insistence that Paul's teaching (as he understood it) be followed and that church leaders actively employ apostolic doctrines to refute false teachings helped to ensure that the international Christian community would build its future on an apostolic foundation.

The Pastor values continuity, but he does not seem to show an equal regard for continuing the individual revelations and ecstatic experiences of Christ's Spirit that characterized individual congregations that Paul himself founded. Regarding the "laying on of . . . hands" as the correct means of conferring authority (2 Tim. 1:6), he would probably not welcome another like Paul who insisted that his private experience of Jesus—not ordination by apostolic predecessors—validated his teachings. Using Scripture, inherited doctrines, and the institutional church as guarantors of orthodoxy, the Pastor sees the Christian revelation as already complete, a static legacy from the past. He ignores Paul's advice not to "quench the Spirit" or "despise the words of [church] prophets" (1 Thess. 5:19–20); his intense conservatism allows little room for future enlightenment.

QUESTIONS FOR DISCUSSION AND REVIEW

1. Define the term *pseudonymity,* and describe its practice among Hellenistic Jewish and early Christian writers. Which books of the New Testament do many scholars think are pseudonymous?

2. In what specific ways concerning Jesus' return does 2 Thessalonians differ from Paul's first letter to the Thessalonians? What elements in the second letter lead scholars to suspect that it was written after Paul's day? Describe the conventional apocalyptic "signs" that the writer says must occur before the End.

3. Summarize the arguments for and against Paul's authorship of Colossians. Describe the book's *Christology*—its theological portrayal of Christ's nature and cosmic function.

4. Why do most scholars suspect that Paul did not write Ephesians? In this document, how are Christ and his church united, and what does this union mean for believers? Explain the significance of the author's vision of continuing warfare with unseen powers.

5. What factors cause most scholars to deny Pauline authorship of the pastoral epistles? In what particular ways do the pastorals reflect church organization and administration that are different from those existing in Paul's time? Why are these letters so concerned about holding to tradition and fighting "heresy"?

6. Discuss the Pastor's views on women, children, and slaves. How does his prescription for internal church order reflect the hierarchical organization of contemporary Greco-Roman society? Would the historical Jesus, an unmarried prophet who had no settled residence and who raised considerable controversy, have met the Pastor's standards for qualifying for church leadership?

Terms and Concepts to Remember

anti-Christ
apocalyptic "signs"
bishop, qualifications of
Christology (Colossians)
deutero-Pauline
disputed Pauline letters
Epaphras
Ephesians' "sacred secret"
Gnosticism
heresy, heretic
Jesus as "image of God"
Pastor, the
pastoral epistles
pseudonymity
Timothy
Titus
women, role of
Zoroastrianism

Recommended Reading

Second Thessalonians

Krentz, Edgar M. "Thessalonians, First and Second Epistles to the." In D. N. Freedman, ed., *The Anchor Bible Dictionary,* Vol. 6, pp. 515–523. New York: Doubleday, 1992. A helpful introduction to Paul's letters and eschatological expectations.
Malherbe, Abraham J. *The Letters to the Thessalonians: A New Translation with Introduction and Commentary* (Anchor Bible, Vol. 32b). New York: Doubleday, 2000. Defends Pauline authorship of 2 Thessalonians.

Colossians

Dunn, James D. G. "Colossians, Letter to." In K. D. Sakenfeld, ed., *The New Interpreter's Dictionary of the Bible,* Vol. 1, pp. 702–706. Nashville, TN: Abingdon Press, 2006. A good introductory analysis that does not rule out Pauline authorship.
Schweizer, Eduard. *The Letter to the Colossians: A Commentary.* Minneapolis: Augsburg, 1982. A lucid introduction, suggesting that Timothy played a role in writing Colossians.

Ephesians

Barth, Markus, ed. *Ephesians* (Anchor Bible, Vols 34 and 34a). Garden City, NY: Doubleday, 1974. An extensive commentary defending Pauline authorship.
Turner, Max. "Ephesians, Letter to." In K. D. Sakenfeld, ed., *The New Interpreter's Bible,* Vol. 2, pp. 269–276. Nashville, TN: Abingdon Press, 2007. Argues that Paul wrote both Colossians and Ephesians.
Wink, Walter. *The Powers That Be: Theology for a New Millennium.* New York: Galilee (Doubleday), 1998. Interprets traditional biblical imagery about supernatural forces (as Ephesians refers to) as social/cultural assumptions and practices that inhibit God's redemptive role in human society.

The Pastorals

Johnson, L. T. *The First and Second Letters to Timothy: A New Translation with Introduction and Commentary* (Anchor Bible). Garden City, NY: Doubleday, 2001. Advocates the minority opinion that Paul wrote the pastoral epistles.
Quinn, J. D., ed. "Timothy and Titus, Epistles to." In D. N. Freedman, ed., *The Anchor Bible Dictionary,* Vol. 6, pp. 560–571. New York: Doubleday, 1992. An introductory discussion.

CHAPTER 37

General Letters on Faith and Behavior

Hebrews and the Catholic Epistles

Key Topics/Themes Grouped together to form a third unit of the New Testament canon, the books of Hebrews and the catholic (general) epistles emphasize the concept that God's revelation through Jesus Christ is now final and complete. Addressed to churches scattered throughout the Roman Empire, six of the documents in this collection—most in letter form—are ascribed to revered leaders of the Jerusalem church: James, Peter, and John (cf. Gal. 2). In contrast, the anonymous Hebrews resembles an elaborate sermon rather than a true letter and is the only canonical work to present Jesus as both a Davidic king and God's heavenly High Priest. Probably the last-written document to be included in the New Testament canon, 2 Peter reaffirms the early Christian hope for an imminent Parousia, which will transform the world into "new heavens and a new earth."

 ## Use of the Letter Form

As noted in Chapter 36, Paul's extensive use of the letter form influenced many later New Testament writers. Besides the authors who wrote in Paul's name, other early Christian writers imitated the apostle by composing "letters" to instruct and encourage the faithful. Unlike Paul's genuine correspondence, these later documents commonly are not addressed to individual congregations but are directed to the Christian community as a whole. This group of eight canonical writings, headed by the Book of Hebrews, forms a discrete unit between the collection of letters traditionally ascribed to Paul and the Book of Revelation, which closes the New Testament canon.

Because of their general nature, seven of these writings are known collectively as the **catholic epistles** ("catholic" referring to their "universal" scope and "epistle" being another term for a letter). The seven—James; 1 and 2 Peter; 1, 2, and 3 John; and Jude—differ from Paul's correspondence in that most are not addressed to a specific congregation known to the writer but are intended for the church at large.

Even the term *epistle* does not adequately describe the diverse literary forms characterizing these works. Of the three traditionally ascribed to John, for example, the first is actually a sermon or tract, the second a warning letter to an unidentified group, and the third a private note. Although some catholic epistles, such as James and 1 Peter, superficially resemble letters, they in fact belong to different categories of religious literature (see below).

Besides their debatable classification as epistles, another significant factor links these seven documents: All are attributed to prominent leaders of the original Jerusalem church. Six are ascribed to the three Jerusalem "pillars"—James, Peter, and John (Gal. 2:6–9)—while the seventh, Jude, was supposedly written by James's brother.

With the possible exception of 1 Peter, most of the catholic epistles are also linked by the fact that, collectively, they are the last documents to be accepted into the New Testament canon. As late as the fourth century CE, Eusebius classified several as "doubtful" and noted that many churches did not accept them (*History* 3:3; 3:24.1; 3.24.18; 3.25.4; 3.39.6). Church leaders do not even mention most of these epistles until almost 200 CE, and Jude, James, 2 Peter, and 3 John are typically absent from early lists of canonical books.

In discussing these general works on faith and behavior, we begin with two commonly associated with Jewish Christianity—Hebrews and James—followed by the epistles attributed to Peter, Jude, and John. Despite their diverse contents, these works are thematically united by their authors' profound commitment to prescribing an ethical way of life appropriate for believers living at the End of time. Probably the last-written book in the canon, 2 Peter marks a fervent reaffirmation of early Christianity's apocalyptic expectations. However long the Parousia is delayed, Christians must live as if Jesus will return at any moment to judge the unbelieving world, as well as the conduct of the faithful (2 Pet. 3:1–5).

 ## The Book of Hebrews

Although its author is unknown, the Book of Hebrews clearly was written by an early Christian scholar equally well acquainted with a Greek edition of the Hebrew Bible and with Greek philosophical concepts. An elegant exercise in rhetoric (the art of speaking or writing effectively), the book is really a complex sermon, despite the letterlike closing paragraphs with their reference to Paul's companion Timothy (13:18–25). Scholars suggest that this final section may originally have belonged to another document, which a later editor added to make Hebrews seem more like a genuine letter. Because the text itself does not contain the phrase "to the Hebrews" or otherwise identify its intended audience, scholars are also unsure of where it was written or to whom it was addressed. Some commentators favor Rome as its place of composition; others think it originated in Alexandria or Palestine. The date of composition is equally uncertain, with estimates ranging from about 80 to 100 CE.

Hebrews' Intellectual Challenge

Warning his readers that he has "much to say that is hard to explain" (5:11), the author presents a dualistic view of the universe in which earthly events and human institutions are seen as reflections of invisible heavenly realities. Employing a popular form of Platonic thought (see Chapter 28), he assumes the existence of two parallel worlds: (1) the eternal, perfect realm of spirit above and (2) the inferior, constantly changing world below. Alone among New Testament writers, he attempts to show how Christ's sacrificial death links the two opposing realms of perishable matter and immortal spirit. He is the only biblical writer to portray Jesus as a heavenly priest who serves as an everlasting mediator between God and humanity.

The author states his central thesis boldly: Through Jesus, God has given his final and complete revelation to humanity. Using typical Hellenistic Jewish methods of scriptural analysis and interpretation, the writer examines selected passages from the Hebrew Bible—principally Genesis 14:18–20 and Psalm 110:4—to demonstrate Christ's unique role in the universe. In the author's view, biblical texts can be understood only in the light of Christ's death and ascension into heaven. He thus gives the Jewish Bible a strictly Christological interpretation, explaining biblical characters and Torah regulations as prophetic "types" or models of Jesus' theological significance. Like Philo Judaeus and other Greek-educated Jewish scholars in Alexandria, Egypt, the author gives biblical texts an allegorical interpretation—earthly events and persons are to be viewed as symbols of realities in heaven. Israelite religious practices, such as animal sacrifices offered on the Day of Atonement (cf. Lev. 16), are thus explained as symbolic prophecies of Jesus' crucifixion, when God's son gave up his life as a perfect and unrepeatable gift (see below).

Christ—A Priest like Melchizedek

Of special importance to the author is the Genesis figure of **Melchizedek,** a mysterious king-priest of Canaanite Salem to whom the patriarch Abraham gave a tenth of the goods he had captured in war (Gen. 14:18–20). According to the writer, Melchizedek is a type or prophetic symbol of Jesus, who is both a king (Davidic Messiah) and a priest (like Melchizedek). In this interpretation, Melchizedek's dual function serves to prefigure Jesus' royal priesthood.

Emphasizing his conviction that Christ is superior to all other beings, human or divine, the author begins Hebrews by contrasting earlier biblical revelations with that made in the last days through the person of Jesus. Whereas God formerly conveyed his message in fragmentary form through the Hebrew prophets, in Jesus he discloses a complete revelation of his essential nature and purpose. As in Colossians and the prologue to John's Gospel, Jesus is the agent (or ultimate goal) of God's creative design and a perfect reflection of the divine being (1:1–4).

Echoing Paul's assertion that Jesus attained heavenly glory through obedient humility (Phil. 2), the writer states that Jesus was perfected through suffering. As a perfectly obedient Son, he is greater than Moses, leading his followers, not to an earthly destination, but to God's celestial throne (3:1–4:16). Through him, God grants believers a vision of hitherto unknown realities.

Asking his listeners to move beyond basic ideas and to advance in understanding (5:11–6:3), the author introduces his unparalleled interpretation of Jesus as an eternal High Priest, one whom the mysterious figure of Melchizedek foreshadowed. To show that Christ's priesthood is superior to that of Aaron, Israel's first High Priest, and the Levite priests who assisted him at the Tabernacle, Hebrews cites the Genesis narrative in which Abraham pays tithes (a tenth of his captured wealth) to Melchizedek (Gen. 14:18–20). Because Melchizedek blessed Abraham and accepted offerings from him, the writer argues, the king-priest of Salem was Abraham's superior. Furthermore, Abraham's descendants, the Levitical and Aaronic priests of Israel, also shared in Abraham's homage to Melchizedek. Present in his ancestor's "loins" when Abraham honored Melchizedek, Aaron and all his priestly offspring, though yet unborn, implicitly confessed their inferiority to the Canaanite king-priest (7:1–10). Melchizedek is thus acknowledged as superior to Israel's priesthood by virtue of his priority in time and the eternal duration of his office.

After Genesis, the Bible refers to Melchizedek only once, in Psalm 110, which the author now adds to his interpretation of the king-priest's (previously unsuspected) significance. He notes that Yahweh swore that Israel's king, or "messiah," is both God's son and an everlasting priest like Melchizedek (Ps. 110:4). Because the Scriptures do not mention either ancestors or descendants for Melchizedek, the writer argues, this absence of human connections (past or future) must mean that Melchizedek is without either beginning or end—an eternal priest. The symbolic everlastingness of Melchizedek's priesthood is thus the prototype of Christ, who similarly remains a priest for all time (7:3, 21–24).

In biblical times, a priest's main function was to offer animal sacrifices to atone for the people's sins and to win God's forgiveness for those sins, a rite of **expiation,** the appeasement of divine wrath. According to Hebrews, Jesus is both the priest and the sacrifice. In this view, the Torah's elaborate program prescribing animal sacrifice is actually prophetic of Jesus' sacrificial death on the cross. By offering his life to cleanse believers of sin, Jesus fulfills the reality of the Torah's required sacrifice, but he is also superior to the old system because his life was perfected through suffering (5:8–9). Unlike the sacrifices offered regularly at Israel's Tabernacle or Temple, which had to be repeated endlessly to ensure divine approval, Jesus' sacrifice is made only once. It remains eternally effective and brings forgiveness and salvation to those accepting its spiritual power (7:26–28).

Earthly Copy and Heavenly Reality

Hebrews adopts the Platonic view that the universe is composed of two dimensions; a lower physical realm and a higher, unseen spirit world. The author envisions Israel's earthly ceremonies of sacrifice and worship as reflections, or copies, that parallel or correspond to invisible realities in heaven (8:5) (see Figure 37.1). He then cites the solemn ritual of the Day of Atonement—the one time of the year that the High Priest was permitted to enter the Tabernacle's innermost room, the Holy of Holies, where God's glory was believed to dwell. Interpreting the atonement ritual allegorically, the author states that the priest's annual entry into God's presence foreshadowed Christ's ascension to heaven itself. There, his life stands as an eternally powerful sacrifice, making redeemed humanity forever "at one" with God (8:1–6; 9:1–14; see the discussion of the Day of Atonement in Chapter 7).

Because his sacrifice surpasses those decreed under the old Mosaic Covenant, Jesus inaugurates a New Covenant with his shed blood. He acts as a permanent mediator, always pleading for humankind's forgiveness (7:24–25; 9:15–22). The writer repeatedly emphasizes that neither the Mosaic Tabernacle nor Herod's Temple in Jerusalem was intended to be permanent. Both sanctuaries are only pale imitations of heavenly realities (9:23), "only a shadow of the good things to come and not the true form of these realities"—Christ's supreme priestly sacrifice (10:1–25).

Exhortation to Remain Faithful

Because Christ's singular death is God's final method of redeeming humanity, Hebrews argues that believers who "willfully persist in sin after having received the knowledge of the truth" will have no second chance at eternal life—the only canonical book to deny Christians who sin the grace of repentance (10:26–31). The author is also the only New Testament writer to define faith, and he does so in terms of his belief in two parallel worlds. The book's most famous passage, Hebrews 11 expresses Plato's classic view of an eternal realm superior to the world of physical matter: "Faith is the assurance of things hoped for, the conviction of things not seen," a belief that the material world "was made from things that are not visible" (11:1–3). Unlike Paul, who always associates faith with a living trust in Jesus' power to save, the author of Hebrews defines faith without mentioning Christ.

In Hebrews, the faithful are thus armed with a conviction that invisible realities include an eternal High Priest whose perfect sacrifice provides a potentially

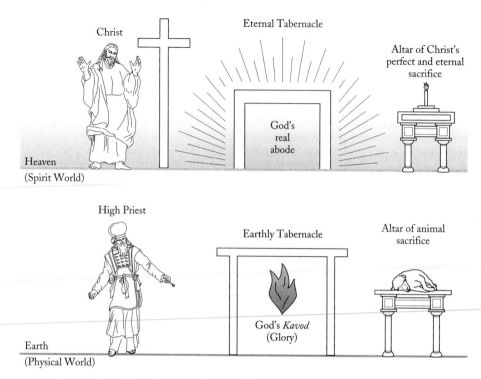

Christ

Eternal Tabernacle

Altar of Christ's
perfect and eternal
sacrifice

God's
real
abode

Heaven
(Spirit World)

High Priest

Earthly Tabernacle

Altar of animal
sacrifice

God's *Kavod*
(Glory)

Earth
(Physical World)

FIGURE 37.1 According to the Book of Hebrews' theory of correspondences, reality exists in two separate but parallel dimensions—the spirit world (heaven) and the physical world (earth). Material objects and customs on earth are temporary replicas, or shadows, of eternal realities in heaven. The author's notion that Jesus' "perfect" sacrifice has rendered Jewish worship obsolete is clearly partisan and represents a claim that many scholars find highly unacceptable.

ceaseless forgiveness and union with God. Christians must maintain their faith while awaiting the inevitable Day of Judgment (10:36–39). Characters in the Hebrew Bible, such as Abel, Noah, Abraham, Moses, and Rahab (the Canaanite prostitute who hospitably welcomed Israelite spies), proved their loyalty when they had only a dim preview of heavenly realities. Believers now possess a complete vision of God's purpose and must behave accordingly. Just as God introduced the Mosaic Covenant amid blazing fire, earthquakes, and other frightening signs, Jesus' New Covenant embodies even more awe-inspiring phenomena, not on earthly Mount Sinai, but in heavenly Jerusalem. If the Israelites who disobeyed the Mosaic Law were punished by death, how much more severe will be the punishment of those who fail to keep faith in the new dispensation (12:1–29).

Urging believers to lead blameless lives of active good deeds, the author reminds them that Jesus Christ is "the same yesterday and today and forever." This is another powerful reason to regard this world, with all its temptations and troubles, as a temporary trial resolved

only in the light of eternity (13:1–9). Christians have no permanent home on earth, but they may seek the unseen and perfect city above as their life's goal (13:14).

The Letter of James

Although relatively late church tradition ascribes this epistle to **James,** whom Paul called "the Lord's brother" (Gal. 1:19), most scholars question this claim. The writer reveals no personal knowledge of either Jesus' life or his specific teachings, as a family member would be expected to do. According to Josephus, James was illegally executed in about 60–62 CE (*Antiquities* 20.9.1), yet this document refers to a Christian community in which some members had already grown rich and complacent (2:1–17; 4:13–5:6), a condition that did not prevail during the faith's early years (cf. Acts 2:43–47). Scholars generally regard the work as a compilation of Jewish-Christian ethical advice put together between about 80 and 100 CE. The Western and Syrian churches only reluctantly accepted James into the canon, perhaps because the author appears to attack Paul's doctrine of salvation by faith (see below). (For a defense of the author's relationship to Jesus, see Johnson in "Recommended Reading.")

A Religion of Active Compassion

The writer addresses his book to "the twelve tribes in the Dispersion [Diaspora]," but he is probably referring not to Israelites living outside Palestine but to Christians scattered throughout the eastern Mediterranean region. Lacking most characteristics of a letter, including salutations, greetings, and a complimentary close, James resembles a sermon more than an epistle. Commentators typically compare James to a Hebrew wisdom book, with topics ranging from the character of God, to the evils of gossip, to the misuse of wealth. Because the author does not arrange his material around a central theme—casually jumping from subject to subject with no apparent connection between them—it is difficult to find a unifying principle in the book. For many commentators, James's controlling purpose is best expressed in his definition of religion, the only one given in the entire New Testament: "Religion that is pure and undefiled before God, the Father, is this: to care for orphans and widows in their distress and to keep oneself unstained by the world" (1:26–27). In James's two-part definition, the "orphans and widows" are Judaism's classic examples of the poor and defenseless whom God makes his special concern, and "the world" represents a society that honors neither God nor human compassion. Thoroughly Jewish in its practical emphasis on charitable good works, James's "pure" religion cannot be formulated into doctrines, creeds, or rituals (cf. Matt. 25:31–46).

Sin and Suffering

In his introductory section (1:2–27), James puts his practical counsel into theological perspective. Facing the twin problems of external suffering and internal temptations to do wrong, the author asks us to consider God's reasons for permitting evil to afflict even the faithful. "Trials" (presumably including loss and pain), James argues, are really beneficial because they allow believers the opportunity to build faith and fortitude, qualities that God will amply reward. To help Christians endure such ordeals, God grants insight to persons who pray for it single-mindedly and never doubt that God, who is always present, will provide the strength necessary to maintain faith.

James vigorously opposes the view that God tests people by giving them opportunities to do wrong, "for God cannot be tempted by evil and he himself tempts no one." Instead, people are motivated by their own hidden desires, which can lead them to commit errors that bring spiritual death. By contrast, God—"in whom there is no variation or shadow due to change"— generously provides a way to escape both the act and the consequences of wrongdoing (1:12–17). If believers resist evil, God grants them the power to drive away even the devil (4:7–8).

Addressing a social problem that plagues almost every group, whether religious or secular, James denounces all forms of snobbery. Christians must make the poor feel as welcome in their midst as the rich and powerful (2:1–13). Noting that it is the wealthy who commonly oppress the church, James reminds his audience that the poor will inherit "the kingdom" and that insulting them is an offense against God. Interestingly, the author does not cite Jesus' teaching to emphasize God's gracious intentions toward the poor, but instead quotes from the Hebrew Bible. If believers do not love their fellow humans (Lev. 19:18), they break all of God's laws, for to fail to keep one precept is to disobey the entire Torah (2:10).

Humanitarian Action as the True Measure of Faith

In James's most famous passage (2:14–26), the writer exposes the futility of persons who claim to have faith but who do not follow the practical religion of good works. To James, belief that fails to inspire right action is "dead." Only "works"—serving the "orphans and widows" and others suffering comparable need—can demonstrate the reality of faith.

Many interpreters see this section as an attack on Paul's doctrine of salvation through faith (the apostle's rejection of "works" of Torah obedience in favor of trust in God's saving purpose in Christ). Like Paul, James cites the Genesis example of Abraham to prove his point, but he gives it a strikingly different interpretation. James asserts that it was Abraham's *action*—his willingness to sacrifice his son Isaac—that justified him before God. The writer's conclusion is distinctively un-Pauline: "You see that a person is justified by works and not by faith alone" (2:24). With its implication that one can win divine approval through compassionate service to others, this conclusion seems to contradict Paul's doctrine that salvation comes only through God's grace, accepted on trust (see the discussions of Galatians and Romans in Chapter 35).

James's pronouncement that faith without "works" is as "dead" as a corpse without breath (2:26) may seem a rejection of Paul's viewpoint, but many scholars see it as merely correcting an abuse of Paul's gospel. Apparently, some Christians of James's day misinterpreted Paul's teaching on faith (trust), misusing it as an excuse to avoid the work and expense of helping the less fortunate. For James, however, genuine faith manifests itself in positive action, which includes feeding, clothing, and sheltering the destitute (2:14–17).

Denouncing the Abuse of Wealth

In another memorable passage (4:15–5:6), James offers the New Testament's most severe criticism of the rich. Even more passionately than Luke, he denounces Christian businessmen and landowners who use their wealth and power not to help the laboring poor, but to exploit them. Without conscience or compassion, employers have defrauded their workers, delaying payment of wages on which laborers and their families depend to survive. Such injustice outrages the Creator, who views the luxury-loving exploiters as overfed animals ripe for slaughter.

Reminding his audience that the Lord will return (5:7), presumably to judge those who economically murder the defenseless (5:6), James ends his sermon on a positive note for any who have strayed from the right path. Sinners and others who are "sick" (perhaps spiritually as well as physically) can hope for recovery. God's healing grace operates through congregational prayer for the afflicted. A faithful person's prayer has the power to rescue a sinner from death and to erase countless sins (5:13–20).

◇ | First Peter

Like James, 1 Peter is ascribed to one of the three Jerusalem "pillars" and is addressed to "exiles of the Dispersion," Christians scattered throughout the Roman Empire. The two epistles have other points in common as well, including a conviction that "love covers a multitude of sins" (James 5:20; 1 Pet. 4:8). Both also refer to believers enduring social discrimination, and even persecution (James 1:2–8; 5:7–11; 1 Pet. 1: 6–7; 4:12–19). Both urge believers to submit peacefully and patiently when undergoing trials and suffering.

Although James refers to Christ's return, implying that it is imminent, Peter emphasizes the Parousia more forcefully. Believers who endure faithfully will be rewarded "when Jesus Christ is revealed" (1:7, repeated in v. 13). Like Paul, the author believes that Christians now live "at the end of the ages" (1:20), for "the end of all things is near" (4:7). The writer also echoes Paul in urging that believers follow a high standard of behavior so that, when Christ appears, he will find them worthy of sharing his "glory" (1:3–9, 13–25). If persecutions afflict the church, it is because God's judgment of the world has already begun, starting with "the household of God" (4:14–19).

Perhaps because he believes that God will soon overthrow all existing governments, the author also echoes Paul in advising his recipients to "accept the authority of every human institution, whether of the emperor as supreme, or of governors, as sent by him" (2:13–15; cf. Paul's similar counsel in Rom. 13). For perhaps the same reason, he commands Christian slaves to submit to their masters, even those who seriously abuse them (2:18–25). Similarly, wives must submit to their husbands, who are to treat their mates kindly "as the weaker sex" (3:1–7). Convinced that God will soon reward the faithful, including those who suffer unjustly, the author does not anticipate a need to change the social or political status quo.

Authorship and Date

The majority of scholars agree that 1 Peter, like James and the pastoral epistles, is pseudonymous, the work of a later Christian writing in Peter's name. This consensus is based on several factors, ranging from the elegant Greek style in which the epistle is composed to the particular social circumstances it describes. As an Aramaic-speaking Galilean fisherman who had little formal education (Acts 4:13), the historical Peter seems unlikely to have produced the work's exceptionally fine Greek prose. Critics defending Peter's authorship note that the epistle was written "through Silvanus [Silas]" (5:12), perhaps the same Silvanus who accompanied Paul on some of his missionary travels (Acts 15:22) and who presumably was skilled in preaching to Hellenistic audiences. According to the minority theory, Silvanus acted as Peter's secretary, transforming his Aramaic dictation into sophisticated Greek.

Regarding the argument that Peter used a highly literate secretary as unverifiable, most scholars conclude that too many other factors combine to cast doubt on Peter's authorship. If Peter—a member of Jesus' inner circle—was the author, why does he not reveal personal knowledge of Jesus' teachings, as an apostle would do? If Peter wrote the work shortly before he fell victim to Nero's persecution in Rome (mid-60s CE), as defenders of the work's genuineness maintain, why does he address the letter to churches in Asia Minor (modern Turkey) (1:1)? The reference to his recipients' "fiery ordeal" (4:12) suggests that Christians living in that faraway region were then undergoing persecution. Scholars can find no evidence, however, that Nero's attacks on Roman believers extended beyond the imperial capital.

According to nonbiblical sources, Christians of Asia Minor were indeed persecuted, but not until the reigns of later emperors, such as Domitian (c. 95 CE) and Trajan (c. 112 CE). When Pliny the Younger, then governor of Bithynia, one of the provinces of Asia Minor, wrote to Trajan, he asked for official advice on how to treat Christians. The conditions Pliny describes seem to match the circumstances outlined in 1 Peter (Pliny, *Letters* 97) (see Figure 37.2). For that reason, many scholars believe that the epistle was written in the early second century, though no consensus exists.

A date after 70 CE is indicated because the author refers to "your sister church in Babylon" (5:15). "Babylon" became the Christian code name for Rome after Titus destroyed Jerusalem, thus duplicating the Babylonians' demolition of the holy city in 587 BCE. As a model or archetype of the ungodly nation, "Babylon" is also Revelation's symbol of Rome (Rev. 14:8; 18:2). Most critics assume that 1 Peter originated in the capital, the traditional site of Peter's martyrdom.

Jude

Placed last among the general epistles, Jude is less a letter than a tract denouncing an unidentified group of heretics. Its primary intent is to persuade the (also unidentified) recipients to join the writer in defending orthodox Christian traditions (v. 3). (Because the book has only one chapter, all references are to verse numbers.) Rather than specify his opponents' doctrinal errors or refute their arguments, the writer threatens the heretics with eschatological punishment drawn from both biblical and nonbiblical sources.

Authorship, Date, and Style

The author describes himself as "a servant of Jesus Christ and brother of James" (v. 1), and thus probably also a kinsman of Jesus (cf. Mark 6:3; Matt. 13:55). Scholars, however, agree that Jude is not the work of Jesus' "brother" but rather is a pseudonymous writing that entered the canon because of its presumed association with Christ's family. Like James, the author shows no personal familiarity with Jesus and cites none of his characteristic teachings. He refers to Christianity as a fixed body of beliefs that the faithful already possess—"that was once for all entrusted to the saints" (v. 3)—and to the apostles as prophets of a former age (vv. 17–18). These assumptions suggest that the book was composed significantly after the historical Jude's time. Most scholars propose a date in the first quarter of the second century CE.

In literary style, Jude represents a kind of rhetoric known as *invective*—an argument characterized by verbal abuse and insult. Rather than specify his opponents' errors or logically refute their claims, the author merely calls them names. They are "irrational animals" who "pervert" Christian teaching into "licentiousness," and "intruders" who cause "blemishes on your love feasts" (referring to the early Christian custom of sharing a full dinner when celebrating communion) (vv. 4, 12). Like Old Testament villains such as Cain, Balaam, and Korah, they are doomed to suffer God's wrath.

Besides its vituperation, Jude is notable for citing at least two nonbiblical works as religiously authoritative.

FIGURE 37.2 This bust shows the emperor Trajan (98–117 CE). Under Trajan, the Roman Empire reached its greatest geographical extent, stretching from Britain in the northwest to Mesopotamia (Iraq) in the east. Pliny the Younger wrote to Trajan about the proper method of handling Christians. The emperor replied that he opposed anonymous accusations and ordered that accused persons who demonstrated their loyalty to the state by making traditional sacrifices should not be prosecuted.

In verses 14–15, the author quotes directly from the noncanonical Book of 1 Enoch (cf. Enoch 1:9). He also alludes to a postbiblical legend about the archangel Michael's contending with the devil for Moses' body (v. 9), a tradition that may have been preserved in the noncanonical Assumption of Moses (sections of which have been lost). To balance its largely vindictive tone, Jude closes with a beautifully lyrical prayer praising God and Christ.

Second Peter

Like Jude—parts of which it incorporates into its second chapter—2 Peter was written for the double purpose of condemning false teachers and warning of the imminent world judgment. Theologically, its importance lies in the author's attempt to explain why God allows evil to continue and to reassert the early Christian belief that Jesus' Second Coming is near (3:1–15). Offering a theory that human history is divided into three distinct chronological epochs, or "worlds," 2 Peter is the only New Testament book to insist that the present world is destined to be consumed by fire.

Authorship and Date

Whereas some scholars defend Petrine authorship of 1 Peter, virtually none believe that Jesus' chief disciple wrote 2 Peter. The unknown author takes pains to claim Peter's identity (1:1), asserting that he was present at Jesus' transfiguration (1:17–18) and that he wrote an earlier letter, presumably the canonical 1 Peter (3:1). Under the Galilean fisherman's name, he writes to reaffirm his concept of the true apostolic teaching in the face of heretical distortion of it. Portraying Peter as about to face death, the writer offers this epistle as the apostle's last will and testament, a final plea to cherish the apostolic faith.

Scholars do not find these authorial claims convincing, however, because 2 Peter contains too many indications that it was written long after Peter's death in about 64–65 CE. The pseudonymous author's main intent—to reestablish the early Christian anticipation of an imminent Parousia—shows that the writer is addressing a group that lived long enough after the original apostles' day to have given up believing that Christ would return soon. The author's opponents deny the Parousia doctrine because the promised Second Coming has not materialized, even though the "ancestors" (first-generation disciples) have long since passed away. In addition, the writer makes use of Jude, itself an early-second-century-CE document, incorporating most of it into his text.

Second Peter also refers to Paul's letters as Scripture (3:16), a status they did not achieve until long after Peter's martyrdom. A late date is also indicated when the author insists on divinely inspired Scripture as the principal authority for belief (1:20–21). This tendency to substitute a fixed written text for the early church's Spirit-led faith expressed through oral preaching also appears in the Pastor's letters (2 Tim. 3:15–16), which are probably also products of the second century.

Finally, many early church leaders doubted 2 Peter's apostolic credentials, resulting in the epistle's absence from numerous lists of "approved" books in the Christian canon. Not only was 2 Peter one of the last works to gain entrance into the New Testament, but scholars believe that it was also the last canonical book written. Composed at some point after 100 CE, it may not have appeared until as late as about 140–150 CE.

The Delayed Parousia

Chapter 2, which borrows heavily from Jude, is devoted to invective. The author attacks unidentified false teachers, comparing them to dogs that eat their own vomit (2:1–22). Like the authors of Jude and John, the writer seems unaware of any contradiction between the teaching of Christian love the one one hand and the savage abuse of fellow believers who disagree with him on the other. To him, dissenters have no more claim to respect than wild beasts that are born only to be trapped and slaughtered (2:12).

The writer does not make clear whether the false teachers he berates in Chapter 2 are the same skeptics who deny the Parousia in Chapter 3. To rekindle his audience's apocalyptic expectations, he reminds them that one world has already perished under a divine judgment—the world drowned in Noah's Flood (3:5–6). For the present "heavens and earth," God has in reserve a different natural element, a cosmic fire that will incinerate all unbelievers, presumably including his opponents.

In predicting a universal conflagration, the author apparently adopts the Stoic philosophers' theory that the cosmos undergoes cycles of destruction and renewal. Employing Stoic images and vocabulary, 2 Peter states that the world's "elements will be dissolved in fire," exposing all earth's secrets (3:10). Because the entire universe is destined to fall apart in a cosmic catastrophe, the author warns believers to prepare for an inescapable judgment. He also urges Christians to work hard to hurry it along, implying that correct human behavior will influence God to accelerate his schedule for the

End (3:11–12). Citing either Revelation's vision (21:1–3) or the Isaiah passages on which it is based (Isa. 65:17; 66:22), the writer promises that a third world will replace the two previously destroyed, respectively, by water and fire. A "new heavens and a new earth" will then provide a "home" for true justice, the eschatological kingdom of God (3:13).

The author is aware that some Christians doubt the Parousia because God, despite the arrival, death, and ascension to heaven of the Messiah, has not acted to conquer evil. God's seeming delay, however, has a saving purpose. Holding back judgment, the Deity allows time for more people to repent and be spared the coming holocaust (3:9, 15). Although exercising his kindly patience in the realm of human time, God himself dwells in eternity, where "a thousand years is like one day." From his vantage point, the Parousia is not delayed; God's apparent slowness to act is really a manifestation of his will to save all people (3:8–9).

 ## Letters from the Community of the Beloved Disciple

The three letters traditionally ascribed to the apostle John give us some important insights into the community that produced and used John's Gospel as its standard of belief. Whereas 1 John is anonymous, the author of 2 and 3 John identifies himself as "the elder" (Greek, *presbyteros*). Most scholars believe that the same person wrote all three documents but that he is not to be identified with either the apostle John or the author of the Gospel. Although some critics link him with the editor who added Chapter 21 to the Gospel, most commentators view the letter writer as a separate party, albeit an influential member of the Johannine family (John 21:23). The majority of scholars date the letters to about 100–110 CE, a period when Gnostic Christianity began to be viewed as a threat to what eventually became Christian orthodoxy (correct teaching; see below).

First John

The opponents whom 1 John denounces were apparently proto-Gnostics who taught that Christ was pure spirit, a cosmic being who only *seemed* to have a physical body. (For a discussion of possible Gnostic influences in John's Gospel, see Chapter 33.) Known as **Docetism** (from the Greek verb meaning "to seem"), this brand of Gnosticism regarded Jesus as a heavenly Revealer who temporarily appeared as an ordinary human and who

escaped physical death by returning to his original home in the spirit realm. In refuting this extreme position, 1 John's author decisively set the limits to which the Fourth Gospel could be interpreted spiritually (or Gnostically). By insisting that "Jesus Christ has come *in the flesh*" (4:2, emphasis added), the writer affirms that the Jesus who died on the cross and the exalted heavenly Christ are one and the same. The divine Logos, "the word of life," assumed physical humanity in the person of Jesus (1:1–4; 4:2). Many scholars believe that 1 John's clear assertion of the Incarnation—the celestial Word (Logos) becoming "flesh"—interpreted John's Gospel in a way that made it acceptable to the mainstream church. Jesus was "Son of God" and divine, but on earth, he was definitely a material human.

Setting Standards for Belief and Behavior Writing at a time when internal disagreements within an individual Christian community could not be resolved by appealing to an established central authority, the author of 1 John provided an important means of settling doctrinal controversies. In the absence of an international church structure that could define and enforce orthodoxy (correct belief), the Johannine writer is the first to propose standards by which believers can distinguish "the spirit of truth [from] the spirit of error" (1 John 4:6). Decades earlier, Paul had faced a similar situation in which believers on both sides of a controversy had claimed spiritual inspiration for their beliefs. While emphasizing that Christians must "not quench the spirit," Paul offered only general advice: "test everything" and "hold fast to what is good" (1 Thess. 5:19–21).

In 1 John, however, the author makes specific proposals to "test the spirits and see whether they are from God" (4:1). Essentially, he offers two areas of testing—in matters of belief and of behavior. Accordingly, he divides his sermon into two parts, the first beginning with his declaration of the Johannine community's primary teaching: "This is the message we have heard from [Christ] and proclaim to you, that God is light" (1:5). The divine light illuminates doctrinal truths, particularly the correct understanding of Jesus' nature. In the introductory passage, which resembles the Gospel's Hymn to the Logos, the writer affirms that his group possesses a direct, sensory experience of Jesus' true humanity. The divine Word, manifest in the man Jesus, was visible and physical; he could be seen and touched. Yet the author's opponents—who have apparently abandoned the community—seem to deny Christ's full humanity. For the writer, real faith is to believe in the Incarnation, to believe that the heavenly Word became the earthly Jesus. Those who deny this "light" now walk in "darkness" (1:1–7).

Besides the Incarnation test—that Jesus came "in the flesh"—the author offers a test of behavior: True disciples of Jesus, obeying his supreme commandment, genuinely love their fellow Christians, who are "brothers and sisters," members of God's family. He thus begins the second part of his discourse with a statement paralleling his first declaration: "For this is the message you have heard from the beginning, that we should love one another" (3:11). Like Cain, who murdered his brother, Abel, those who have withdrawn from the group fail to show love for their spiritual kinfolk. In his most quoted passage, the author declares that people who do not love cannot know God because "God is love" (4:8–9). Pointing out that divine love is expressed through human affection, the author reminds us that to love God is also to cherish God's human creation (4:19–21).

Finally, the writer implies that his opponents not only fail to love but also neglect Christian ethics, for believers must live as Jesus did and keep his commandments (2:6; 5:5). The only commandment that the author can cite, however—"the old commandment you have heard from the beginning"—is the single commandment that John's Gospel ascribes to Jesus: the instruction to love (John 13:34–35; 15:12, 17). Unlike the Synoptic tradition, that treasured in the Johannine community is the law of love; all other ethical obligations and behaviors are encompassed in that unique command.

Second John

Although containing only thirteen verses, 2 John is a true letter. Identifying himself only as "the elder," the writer addresses it to "the elect lady and her children, whom I love" (v. 1)—the congregation or house church that belongs to the Johannine community. As in 1 John, the author's purpose is to warn of the anti-Christ, the deceiver who falsely teaches that Jesus did not live as a material human being (v. 7). He urges his recipients not to welcome such apostate Christians into the believers' houses or otherwise encourage them (vv. 10–11). As before, the author can prepare against his opponents' attacks by citing only one cardinal rule—the love that is their community's sole guide (vv. 5–6).

Third John

In a private note to his friend Gaius, the elder asks him to extend hospitality to some Johannine missionaries led by Demetrius (otherwise unknown). The writer asks Gaius to receive these travelers kindly, honoring their church's tradition of supporting those who labor to spread their understanding of "the truth" (v. 8). By contrast, one Diotrephes, apparently a rival church leader, offends the elder not only by refusing hospitality to members of the elder's group but also by expelling from the congregation any persons who try to help them. We do not know if the spiteful charges Diotrephes brings against the elder relate to the opponents denounced in 1 John. Although Diotrephes may not be one of the "anti-Christ" faction, his malice and lack of charity suggest that he does not practice the Johannine community's essential commandment.

Some scholars have noted that the elder's disapproval of Diotrephes may result from the latter's acting with undue authority. Whereas the Johannine community seems to have operated with little formal structure, Diotrephes behaves as if he has the power, in effect, to excommunicate a member of the elder's group. In exercising this kind of power, Diotrephes anticipates the actions of some authoritarian bishops in the more strictly organized church of later centuries.

QUESTIONS FOR DISCUSSION AND REVIEW

1. Define the term *catholic epistles,* and describe their general nature and major themes. According to tradition, who were the authors of these seven documents, and what was the authors' relationship to the Jerusalem church?

2. Identify and summarize the principal themes in the Book of Hebrews. How does the author's belief in a dualistic universe—an unseen spirit world that parallels the visible cosmos—affect his teaching about Jesus as an eternal High Priest officiating in heaven?

3. Almost every book in this unit of the New Testament—Hebrews and the catholic epistles—contains a theme or concept not generally found in any other canonical document. For example, only Hebrews presents Jesus as a celestial High Priest foreshadowed by Melchizedek; it is also unique in being the only New Testament work to define faith (11:1). Indicate which of the catholic epistles contains the following definitions or statements:

    a. A definition of religion

    b. A belief that Jesus descended into Hades (the Underworld) and preached to spirits imprisoned there

    c. A definition of God's essential nature

    d. A set of standards by which to determine the truth of religious teachings

    e. An argument that actions are more important than faith

f. A concept that human history is divided into three separate stages, or "worlds"

g. A defense of the early apocalyptic hope involving Jesus' Second Coming (the Parousia)

h. Citations from noncanonical books as if they had the authority of Scripture

i. The New Testament's most severe condemnation of the rich

Terms and Concepts to Remember

Aaron	Incarnation (Jesus in the
Book of 1 Enoch	flesh)
catholic epistles	invective
cosmic fire	James
definition of faith	Jesus as both sacrifice and
(Hebrews)	High Priest
definition of God	Jesus' descent into Hades
(1 John)	Johannine community
definition of religion	Jude
(James)	Levitical priesthood
delayed Parousia	Melchizedek
epistle	2 Peter, date of
Gnosticism/Docetism	2 Peter's three "worlds"

Recommended Reading

Hebrews

Attridge, Harold W. *The Epistle to the Hebrews*. Philadelphia: Fortress Press, 1989. An authoritative analysis of the book's origin and theology; for more advanced study.

Desilva, David A. "Hebrews, Letter to the." In K. D. Sakenfeld, ed., *The New Interpreter's Dictionary of the Bible*, Vol. 2, pp. 779–786. Nashville, TN: Abingdon Press, 2007. A helpful introduction to this complex sermon.

Donelson, Lewis. *From Hebrews to Revelation: A Theological Introduction*. Louisville, KY: Westminster John Knox, 2000. Surveys the final units of the New Testament canon and their theological functions.

Kasemann, E. *The Wandering People of God: An Investigation of the Letter to the Hebrews*. Minneapolis: Augsburg, 1984. An influential study; for more advanced students.

James

Johnson, L. T. *The Letter of James: A New Translation with Introduction and Commentary* (Anchor Bible, Vol. 37a). New York: Doubleday, 1995. Argues that the author was Jesus' brother.

Leahy, Thomas W. "The Epistle of James." In R. E. Brown, et al., eds., *The New Jerome Biblical Commentary*, 2nd ed., pp. 909–916. Englewood Cliffs, NJ: Prentice-Hall, 1990. Surveys the book's main themes.

1 and 2 Peter and Jude

Brown, R. E.; Donfried, K.; and Reumann, J., eds. *Peter in the New Testament: A Collaborative Assessment by Protestant and Roman Catholic Scholars*. Minneapolis: Augsburg, 1973. An informative study of Peter's role in New Testament tradition and literature.

Dalton, William J. "The First Epistle of Peter." In R. E. Brown, et al., eds. *The New Jerome Commentary on the Bible*, 2nd ed., pp. 903–908. Englewood Cliffs, NJ: Prentice-Hall, 1990.

Elliott, J. H. *A Home for the Homeless: A Sociological Exegesis of 1 Peter, Its Situation and Strategy*. Philadelphia: Fortress Press, 1981. A critical analysis of the historical conditions that prompted the composition of 1 Peter.

Neyrey, Jerome H. "The Epistle of Jude." In R. E. Brown, et al., eds. *The New Jerome Biblical Commentary*, 2nd ed., pp. 917–919. Englewood Cliffs, NJ: Prentice-Hall, 1990.

1, 2, and 3 John

Brown, R. E. *The Community of the Beloved Disciple*. New York: Paulist Press, 1979. An insightful analysis of the Johannine group that produced the Gospel and letters of John.

———. *The Churches the Apostles Left Behind*. New York: Paulist Press, 1984. A concise study of several different Christian communities at the end of the first century CE.

———. *The Epistles of John* (Anchor Bible, Vol. 30). Garden City, NY: Doubleday, 1982. A scholarly translation and commentary on the letters of John.

Mitchell, Margaret M. "John, Letters of." *The New Interpreter's Dictionary of the Bible*, Vol. 3, pp. 370–374. Nashville, TN: Abingdon Press, 2008. A concise discussion of the Johannine epistles..

CHAPTER 38

Continuing the Apocalyptic Hope
The Book of Revelation

Key Topics/Themes Revelation vividly illustrates Christianity's original expectation that God would soon transform the world, bringing an end to evil and the establishment of divine rule on earth. Like similar apocalyptic writings, Revelation presents its visions of heaven and of future history in highly symbolic language. Using images of dragons, beasts, and other monsters to depict forces such as tyrannical governments and corrupt leaders, the author asks readers to view oppressive societies as God sees them—repellent distortions of his original intentions for humanity. Placing Rome's imperial power in a cosmic perspective, this *apokalypsis* (unveiling of unseen realities) invites us to look beyond present evils to discover God's ultimate purpose: the cleansing, renewal, and salvation of the universe.

 Revelation's Place in the Apocalyptic Tradition

Although Revelation was not the last New Testament book written, its position at the end of the canon is thematically appropriate. The first Christians believed that their generation would witness the end of the present wicked age and the establishment of God's kingdom. Revelation expresses that eschatological hope more powerfully than any other Christian document. Looking forward to "new heavens and a new earth" (21:1), the book envisions the glorious completion of God's creative work begun in the first book of the Bible. In this sense, it provides the *omega* (the last letter of the Greek alphabet) to the *alpha* (the first letter) of Genesis.

Jesus' Cosmic Role

Revelation's climactic placement is also fitting because it reintroduces Jesus as a major character. Its portrayal of an all-powerful heavenly Jesus provides a counterweight to the Gospels' depiction of the human Jesus'

earthly career. In Revelation, Jesus is no longer Mark's suffering servant or John's gracious embodiment of divine Wisdom. Revelation's Jesus is the Messiah of popular expectations, a conquering warrior-king who slays his enemies and proves beyond all doubt his right to universal rule. In striking contrast to the Gospel portraits, the Jesus of Revelation comes not to forgive sinners and instruct them in a higher righteousness but to inflict a wrathful punishment upon his enemies (19:11–21).

Revelation's portrayal of Jesus' character and function, qualitatively different from that presented in the Gospels, derives partly from the author's apocalyptic view of human history. Like the authors of Jude and 2 Peter, the writer perceives a sharp contrast between the present world, which he regards as hopelessly wicked, and God's planned future world, a realm of ideal purity. In the author's opinion, the righteous new order can be realized only through God's direct intervention in human affairs, an event that requires Jesus to act as God's Judge and Destroyer of the world as we know it.

To understand Revelation's emphasis on violence and destruction, with its correspondingly harsher picture of Jesus' cosmic role, we must remember that the author belongs to a particular branch of the Jewish and Christian apocalyptic movement. (For a discussion of the characteristics of apocalyptic writing, see Chapters 26 and 27). In the two centuries prior to the beginning of the Christian era, and for at least a century after, Jewish writers composed numerous apocalyptic works, ascribing their authorship to such venerated figures as Enoch, Moses, Daniel, Baruch, and Ezra. Only the Book of Daniel was admitted to the Hebrew Bible canon, but other apocalypses—including 1 Enoch, 2 Esdras, and 2 Baruch—significantly influenced Jewish and (later) Christian thought.

Authorship and Date

During the early centuries CE, many Christian authors contributed to the apocalyptic genre. We have already discussed the apocalyptic elements in the Gospels, especially Mark 13 and its parallels in Matthew 24 and Luke 21, as well as Paul's eschatological concerns in his letters to the Thessalonians and the Corinthians (see Chapters 30–32 and 35). Besides these canonical works, other Christian writers produced apocalyptic books, typically attributing them to prominent apostles, including Peter, John, James, Thomas, and Paul. The canonical Revelation is unique in being ascribed, not to a figure of the distant past, but to a contemporary member of the first-century church. The work is also unique in being the only surviving document by a Christian prophet (Rev. 1:3), which was a common function or office in the early church (Acts 2:15–17; 1 Thess. 5:19–21; 1 Cor. 12:10; 14:22, 24–25, 31–33).

Who was the writer who created the bedazzling images found in Revelation? According to some late-second-century traditions, he is the apostle John, the same person who wrote the Gospel and letters of John. However, other early Christian sources recognized the immense differences in thought, language, and theology between Revelation and the Fourth Gospel and concluded that they could not have originated with the same author. Eusebius suggests that another John, known only as the "Elder," a leader of the late-first-century church at Ephesus, may have written the Apocalypse (*History* 3.29.1–11).

Virtually all modern scholars agree that the Gospel and Revelation are the products of different authors. A few accept Eusebius's theory about John the Elder of Ephesus, but the scholarly majority notes that we have no evidence to link the book with that obscure figure. Most scholars prefer to accept no more than the writer's own self-identification: He simply calls himself John, a "servant" of Jesus Christ (1:2). Because he does not assert apostolic authority and never claims to have known the earthly Jesus, most analysts conclude that he was not one of the Twelve, whom he classifies as different from himself. In the author's day, the apostles had already departed earth to become the "twelve foundations" of the heavenly Temple (21:14). Exiled to the island of Patmos in the eastern Aegean Sea, where he received his visions (1:9), the author perhaps is best described as John of Patmos, a mystic who regarded himself as a Christian prophet and his book as a highly symbolic preview of future events (1:1–3; 22:7–10).

By studying the contents of his work, scholars can infer something of John's background. He is intimately familiar with internal conditions in the seven churches addressed (2:1–3:23), even though he seems to belong to none of them (see Figure 38.1). To some commentators, this indicates that John was an itinerant Christian prophet who traveled among widely scattered churches. Although he evidently held no congregational office, his recognized stature as a mystic and visionary gave him considerable influence in the communities to which he directed his apocalypse.

Because he writes Greek as if it were a second language, phrasing his sentences in a Semitic style, most scholars believe that John was a native of Palestine, or at least had spent much time there. Whereas the Evangelist writes in a generally correct, smooth style, John of Patmos typically phrases his Greek awkwardly. He may, however, have had some connection with the Johannine community. In referring to Christ, he employs some typical Johannine terms, such as Logos (Word), Lamb, Witness, Shepherd, Judge, and Temple. Both Revelation and the Gospel also express a duality of spirit and matter, good and evil, God and Satan. Both regard Christ as present in the church's liturgy, and both view his death as a saving victory. By contrast, their respective theologies are worlds apart: Whereas the Gospel presents God's love as his primary motive in dealing with humanity (John 3:15–16), Revelation mentions divine love only once. The Johannine Jesus' supreme commandment—to love—is conspicuously absent from Revelation.

Writing about 180 CE, the church leader Irenaeus stated that Revelation was composed late in the reign of Domitian, who was emperor of Rome from 81 to 96 CE. Internal references to government hostility toward Christians (1:9; 2:10, 13; 6:9–11; 14:12; 16:6), consistent with Domitian's policies toward Christians, support Irenaeus's statement. Most scholars date the work to about 95 or 96 CE.

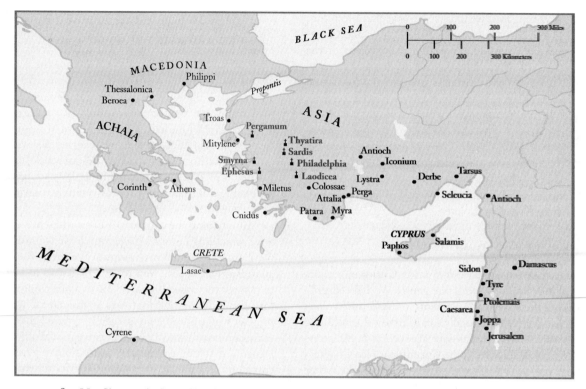

FIGURE 38.1   Map Showing the Seven Churches in Asia Minor (Western Turkey) Addressed in Revelation 1–3. These sites (marked by small crosses) include Ephesus, one of the major seaports of the Roman Empire, and Sardis, once capital of the older Lydian Empire (sixth century BCE). John pictures the heavenly Christ dictating letters to seven angels who act as invisible guardians of the individual churches. With this image, John reminds his audience that the tiny groups of Christians scattered throughout the Roman Empire do not stand alone. Although seemingly weak and insignificant, they are part of God's mighty empire of the spirit and are destined to triumph over their earthly oppressors.

The Sociopolitical Context: The Emperor Cult and the Persecution of Christians

Domitian was the son of Vespasian and the younger brother of Titus, the general who had successfully crushed the Jewish Revolt against Rome and destroyed the Jerusalem Temple. After Titus's brief reign (79–81 CE), Domitian inherited the imperial throne, accepting divine honors offered him and allowing himself to be worshiped as a god in various parts of the empire. We have no solid evidence that Domitian personally enforced an emperor cult, but in specific areas—especially Asia Minor—some governors and other local officials demanded public participation in the cult as evidence of citizens' loyalty and patriotism (see Figure 38.2). During this period, persecution of

Christians for refusing to honor the national leader seems to have been local and sporadic. Despite the lack of a concentrated official assault on the faith, however, John clearly feels a growing tension between church and state, a sense of impending conflict that makes him regard Rome as a new Babylon, destroyer of God's people.

Because Rome had recognized their religion's monotheism, Jews were generally exempted from the emperor cult. Jewish and Gentile Christians, however, were not. To most Romans, their "stubborn" refusal to honor any of the many Greco-Roman gods or deified emperors was not only unpatriotic but also likely to bring the gods' wrath upon the whole community. Early Christians denied the existence of the Hellenistic deities and rejected offers to participate in Roman religious festivals and other communal events. They became known as antisocial "atheists" and

FIGURE 38.2 Vespasian's younger son, Domitian, during whose reign John wrote Revelation. Domitian reputedly demanded worship as "lord and god." In John's view, the spiritual battle between good and evil will culminate in the fall of imperial Rome (Rev. 17:1–19:2).

"haters of humankind." Rumors spread that they met secretly to drink blood and perform cannibalistic rites (an apparent distortion of the sacramental ingesting of Jesus' blood and body). Labeled as a seditious underground sect dangerous to the general welfare, early Christian groups endured social rejection and hostility. When they also refused to pledge their allegiance to the emperor as a symbol of the Roman state, many local governors and other magistrates had them arrested, imprisoned, tortured, and, in some cases, killed.

About seventeen years after John composed Revelation, Pliny the Younger, a Roman governor of Bithynia (located in the same general region as Revelation's seven churches), wrote to the emperor Trajan inquiring about the government's official policy toward Christians. Pliny's description of the situation as it was about 112 CE may also apply to John's slightly earlier time.

Although a humane and sophisticated thinker, Pliny reports that he did not hesitate to torture two slave women, "deacons" of a local church, and to execute other believers. If Christians held Roman citizenship, he sent them to Rome for trial. Trajan replied that, although his governors were not to hunt Christians or accept anonymous accusations, self-confessed believers were to be punished. Both the emperor and Pliny clearly regarded Christians as a threat to the empire's security. (Pliny, *Letters* 10.96–97).

Revelation's Purpose and Organization

The Christians for whom John wrote were experiencing a real crisis. They were faced with Jewish hostility, public suspicion, and sporadic governmental persecution. Many believers must have been tempted to deny Christ, as Pliny asked his prisoners to do, and conform to the norms of Roman society. Recognizing that the costs of remaining Christian were overwhelmingly high, John recorded his visions of cosmic conflict to strengthen those whose faith wavered, assuring them that death is not defeat but victory. In the light of eternity, Rome's power was insignificant, but its victims, slaughtered for their fidelity, gained everlasting life and the power to judge the fates of their former persecutors.

Despite its complexities, we can outline Revelation as follows:

1. Prologue: the author's self-identification and the basis for his authority—divine revelation (1:1–20)

2. Jesus' letters to the seven churches of Asia Minor (2:1–3:22)

3. Visions from heaven: a scroll with seven seals; seven trumpets (4:1–11:19)

4. Signs in heaven: visions of the woman, the Dragon, the beast, the Lamb, and the seven plagues (12:1–16:21)

5. Visions of Rome as the "great whore" and the fall of Babylon (Rome) (17:1–18:24)

6. Visions of heavenly rejoicing, the warrior Messiah, the imprisonment of the beast and Satan, judgment of the dead, and the final defeat of evil (19:1–20:15)

7. Visions of the "new heavens and a new earth" and the descent of a new Jerusalem to earth (21:1–22:5)

8. Epilogue: the authenticity of the author's prophetic visions and the nearness of their fulfillment (22:6–21)

From this outline, we observe that John begins his work in the real world of exile and suffering (1:1–10) and then takes his readers on a visionary tour of the spirit world—including a vivid dramatization of the imminent fall of worldly governments and the ultimate triumph of Christ. At the book's close, he returns to earth and gives final instructions to his contemporary audience (22:6–21). The book's structure thus resembles a vast circle starting and ending in physical reality but encompassing a panorama of the unseen regions of heaven and the future.

Alone among New Testament writers, John claims divine inspiration for his work. He reports that on "the Lord's day [Sunday]" he was "in the spirit," permitting him to hear and see heaven's unimaginable splendors (1:9). His message derives from God's direct revelation to Jesus Christ, who in turn transmits it through an angel to him (1:1–2). John's visions generate a sense of intense urgency, for they reveal the immediate future (1:1). Visionary previews of Jesus' impending return convince the author that what he sees is about to happen (1:3). This warning is repeated at the book's conclusion when Jesus proclaims that his arrival is imminent (22:7, 10, 13).

John's Use of Symbols

Revelation's opening chapter gives a representative example of John's writing style. It shows how profoundly the Hebrew Bible influenced him and how he utilizes its vivid images to construct his fantastic symbols. Without ever citing specific biblical books, John fills his sentences with metaphors and phrases borrowed from all parts of the Hebrew Scriptures. Scholars have counted approximately 500 such verbal allusions. (The Jerusalem Bible helps readers recognize John's rephrasing of biblical passages by printing them in italics.)

A Heavenly Being   In his first symbolic depiction of a heavenly being (1:12–16), John describes a male figure with snow-white hair, flaming eyes, incandescent brass feet, and a sharp sword protruding from his mouth. These images derive largely from Daniel (Chs. 7 and 10). To universalize this figure, John adds astronomical features to his biblical symbols. Like a Greek mythological hero transformed into a stellar constellation, the figure holds seven stars in his hand and shines with the brilliance of the sun.

The next verses (1:17–19) reveal the figure's identity: As "the first and the last" who died but now is "alive forever," he is the crucified and risen Christ. The author's purpose in combining biblical and Greco-Roman imagery is now clear: In strength and splendor, the glorified Christ surpasses rival deities such as Mithras, Apollo, Helios, Amon-Ra, and other solar gods worshiped through the Roman Empire.

John further explains his symbols: Christ identifies the stars as angels and the lamp stands standing nearby as the seven churches of John's home territory. This identification reassures the author that his familiar earthly congregations do not exist solely on a material plane but are part of a larger visible/invisible duality in which angelic spirits protectively oversee Christian

gatherings. The symbols also serve John's characteristic purpose in uncovering the spiritual reality behind physical appearances. To John, the seven churches—small and despised as they may be by the general public—are as precious as the golden candelabrum that once stood in the Temple's Holy of Holies. Like the eternal stars above, they shed Christ's light on a dark world.

The Lamb and the Dragon   In asking readers to view the universe as God sees it, John challenges us to respond emotionally and intuitively, as well as intellectually, to his symbols. Thus, he depicts invisible forces of good and evil in images that evoke an instinctively positive or negative response. Using a tradition also found in the Fourth Gospel, the author portrays Christ as the Lamb of God, whose death removes the world's sins (John 1:29, 36; Rev. 4:7–14; 5:6; 7:10, 14). Harmless and vulnerable, the Lamb is appealing; his polar opposite, the "great red **Dragon**," elicits feelings of fear and revulsion. A reptilian monster with seven heads and ten horns, the Dragon is equated with "that ancient serpent, who is called Devil and Satan, the deceiver of the whole world" (12:3, 9). In depicting the archangel Michael battling the Dragon, John here updates an ancient Mesopotamian myth in which a creator god slays a seven-headed dragon, symbolizing the chaos that must be defeated before a harmonious world order can come into being (see Figure 23.3). As for John's identification of the Eden serpent (Gen. 3) with Satan and the devil, that connection does not appear in Genesis (the serpent is "crafty," not evil). The serpent–Satan link does not enter the biblical tradition until the first century BCE, when the author of the Wisdom of Solomon identifies "the devil's envy" as the origin of human death (Wisd. of Sol. 2:24).

To unspiritual eyes, the Lamb—tiny and weak—might appear a ridiculously helpless opponent of the monstrous Dragon, particularly because John views Satan as possessing immense power on earth as he wages war against the Lamb's people, the church (12:13–17). Although nations that the Dragon controls, figuratively called Sodom and Egypt (11:8), have already slain the Lamb (when Rome crucified Jesus), God uses this apparent weakness to eliminate evil in both heaven and earth. John wishes his readers to draw comfort from this seeming contradiction: Christ's sacrificial death guarantees his ultimate victory over the Dragon and all he represents.

The Lamb's death and rebirth to immortal power also delivers his persecuted followers. The church will overcome the seemingly invincible strength of its oppressors; the blood of its faithful martyrs confirms that God will preserve it (6:9–11; 7:13–17). Although politically and socially as weak as a lamb, the tiny Christian communities embody a potential strength that their enemies fail to recognize. John expresses this conviction in the image of an angel carrying a golden censer, an incense burner used in Jewish and Christian worship services. He interprets the censer's symbolism very simply: Smoke rising upward from the burning incense represents Christians' prayers ascending to heaven, where they have an astonishing effect. In the next image, the angel throws the censer to earth, causing thunder and an earthquake. This image makes clear that the prayers of the faithful can figuratively shake the world (8:3–5). Throughout Revelation, John gives many of his most obscure or grotesque symbols a comparably down-to-earth meaning.

Jesus' Letters to the Seven Churches

Having validated his prophetic authority through the divine source of his visions, John now surveys the spiritual health of the seven churches of Asia Minor. Like the contemporary author of 2 Esdras (14:22–48), John presents himself as a secretary recording the dictation of a divine voice, conveying the directions of a higher power.

Christ's letters to the seven congregations all follow the same pattern. After he commands John to write, Jesus identifies himself as the sender and then employs the formula "I know," followed by a description of the church's strengths or weaknesses. A second formula, "but I have this against you," then introduces a summary of the church's particular defects. Each letter also makes a call for repentance, a promise that the Parousia will occur soon, an encouragement to maintain integrity, a directive to "listen," and a final pledge to reward the victorious.

After reading Jesus' messages to Ephesus (2:1–7), Smyrna (2:8–11), Pergamum (2:12–17), Thyatira (2:18–29), Sardis (3:1–6), Philadelphia (3:7–13), and Laodicea (3:14–22), we have a good idea of John's method. Church conditions in each of these cities are rendered in images that represent the spiritual reality underlying those conditions. Thus, Pergamum is labeled the site of Satan's throne (2:13), perhaps because of its elaborately decorated altar to Zeus (Jupiter) or its "idolatrous" veneration of the emperor. For John, any worldly ruler who claims divine honors is an agent of Satan and hence an anti-Christ, the enemy of Jesus.

Visions from Heaven

Limited space allows us to discuss here only a few of John's most significant visions. We focus on those in which he pictures the cosmic tension between good and

evil, light and dark, Christ and Satan. After John sees an open "door" to heaven, the Spirit carries him to God's throne, where he is shown images of events about to take place (4:1–2). In considering the meaning of the symbolic scrolls, seals, trumpets, and other images, it is important to remember that John's purpose is not primarily to predict specific future events, but to remove the material veil that shrouds heavenly realities and to allow his readers to see that God retains full control of the universe. The visions that follow are intended to reassure Christians that their sufferings are temporary and their deliverance is certain.

Breaking the Seven Seals John conveys this assurance in two series of seven visions involving seven seals and seven trumpets. Seen from the perspective of God's heavenly throne (which the author describes in images borrowed from Isaiah 6 and Ezekiel 1 and 10), the opening of the seven seals reveals that the future course of events has already been recorded on a heavenly scroll. (For a description of scrolls and their uses, see Box 2.2.) Important communications from kings or other officials were commonly sealed with hot wax, which was imprinted while still soft with the sender's identifying seal. Because the scroll could not be opened without breaking the seal, the wax imprint effectively prevented anyone from knowing the scroll's contents until the intended recipient opened it.

In John's vision, the Lamb opens each of the seven seals in sequence, disclosing either a predestined future event or God's viewpoint on some important matter. (Breaking the seventh seal is an exception, producing only an ominous silence in heaven—the calm preceding the Lord's Final Judgment [8:1].) Breaking the first four seals unleashes four horses and riders—the famous Four Horsemen of the Apocalypse—representing, respectively, conquest, war, food shortages (including monetary inflation), and the "pale green horse" whose "rider's name was Death," followed closely by Hades (the subterranean abode of the dead) (6:1–8).

Breaking the fifth seal makes visible the souls of persons executed for their Christian "testimony." While crying for divine vengeance, "they were each given a white robe" and told to rest until the full number of predestined martyrs had been killed (6:9–11). In such scenes, John suggests that believers' willingness to die for their faith earns them the white garment of spiritual purity—and that God will act soon to avenge their deaths.

Showing how terrifying the great day of God's vengeance will be, John portrays it in terms of astronomical catastrophes. Apparently borrowing from the same apocalyptic tradition the Synoptic Gospel writers used to predict Jesus' Second Coming (Mark 13; Matt. 24–25; Luke 21), the author predicts that the sun will turn black, the moon will turn a bloody red, and the stars will fall to earth as the sky vanishes into nothingness (6:12–14). As he clothes Jesus in astronomical images, so John also paints the End in livid colors of cosmic dissolution.

As the earth's population hides in fear, angels appear with God's distinctive seal to mark believers on the forehead, an apocalyptic device taken from Ezekiel 9. The symbolic number of those marked for salvation is 144,000 (a multiple of 12), the number representing the traditional twelve tribes of Israel. This marking suggests that John sees his fellow Jews redeemed at End time (cf. Paul's view in Rom. 9:25–27). In Revelation 14, the 144,000 are designated the first ingathering of God's harvest (14:1–5). Accompanying this group is a huge crowd from every nation on earth, probably signifying the multitudes of Gentile Christians. Both groups wear white robes and stand before God's throne. (In contrast, see John's description of those marked by the demonic "beast" [13:16–17].)

Sounding the Seven Trumpets As if answering the churches' prayers (symbolized by the censer in 8:4–5), seven angels blow seven trumpets of doom. The first six announce catastrophes reminiscent of the ten plagues on Egypt. The initial trumpet blast triggers a hail of fire and blood, causing a third of the earth to burn (8:6–7). The second causes a fire-spewing mountain to be hurled into the sea, perhaps a reference to the volcanic island of Thera, which was visible from Patmos (8:8–9). Devastating volcanic eruptions like that of Mount Vesuvius in 79 CE were commonly regarded as expressions of divine judgment.

The third and fourth trumpets introduce more astronomical disasters, including a blazing comet or meteorite, called Wormwood (perhaps representing Satan's fall from heaven) and causing the sun, moon, and stars to lose a third of their light (8:10–12). After the fifth trumpet blast, the fallen star opens the abyss, releasing columns of smoke that produce a plague of locusts, similar to those described in Exodus (10:12–15) and Joel (1:4; 2:10). Persons not angelically marked are tormented with unbearable agonies but are unable to die and so end their pain (9:1–6). These disasters, in which the locusts may represent foreign soldiers invading the Roman Empire (9:7–11), are equivalent to the first disaster predicted (8:13; 9:12).

Despite the unleashing of further hordes as the sixth trumpet sounds (9:14–19), John does not indicate that such afflictions will change human behavior. People who survive the plagues will continue committing crimes and practicing false religions (9:20–21). In fact,

John presents the world's suffering as gratuitous and essentially without moral purpose. Revelation's plagues intensity human misery, but they fail to enlighten their victims about the divine nature or to produce a single act of regret or repentance.

Eating the Scroll As he had borrowed the device of marking the saved from Ezekiel 9, John now draws upon the same prophet to describe the symbolic eating of a little scroll that tastes like honey but turns bitter in the stomach (Ezek. 2:8–3:3). The scroll represents the dual nature of John's message: sweet to the faithful but sour to the disobedient (10:8–11).

In the next section, John is told to measure the Jerusalem Temple, which will continue under Gentile domination for forty-two months. In the meantime, two witnesses are appointed to prophesy for 1,260 days—the traditional period of persecution or tribulation established in Daniel (7:25; 9:27; 12:7). The witnesses are killed and, after three and a half days, resurrected and transported to heaven. (The executed prophets may refer to Moses and Elijah, to Peter and Paul, or, collectively, to all Christian martyrs whose testimony caused their deaths.) After the martyrs' ascension, an earthquake kills 7,000 inhabitants of the great city—Rome—whose ethical reality is represented by Sodom and Egypt, a city and nation that suffered divine judgment. Sodom, guilty of violence and inhospitality, was consumed by fire from heaven; Egypt, which enslaved God's people, was devastated by ten plagues. So Rome, the tyrannical state that executed Jesus and persecutes his disciples (11:1–13), suffers deserved punishment.

The seventh trumpet does not introduce a specific calamity, but rather proclaims God's sovereignty and the eternal reign of his Christ. With the Messiah invisibly reigning in the midst of his enemies (cf. Ps. 2:1–12), God's heavenly sanctuary opens to view amid awesome phenomena recalling Yahweh's presence in Solomon's Temple (1 Kings 8:1–6).

Conflict in Heaven and on Earth

Revelation 12 introduces a series of unnumbered visions dramatizing the cosmic battle between the Lamb and the Dragon. In this section (12:1–16:21), John links unseen events in heaven with their consequences on earth. The opening war in the spirit realm (12:1–12) finds its earthly counterpart in the climactic battle of **Armageddon** (16:12–16). Between these two parallel conflicts, John mixes inspirational visions of the Lamb's domain with warnings about "the beast" and God's negative judgment upon disobedient humanity.

The Celestial Woman, the Dragon, and the Beast from the Sea This section's first astronomical sign reveals a woman dressed in the sun, moon, and stars—resembling Hellenistic portraits of the Egyptian goddess Isis. Despite its nonbiblical astrological features, however, John probably means the figure to symbolize Israel, historically the parent of Christ. Arrayed in "twelve stars" suggesting the traditional twelve tribes, the woman labors painfully to give birth to the Messiah. John's fellow first-century apocalyptic writer, the author of 2 Esdras, similarly depicted Israel's holy city, Jerusalem, the mother of all believers, as a persecuted woman (2 Esd. 9:38–10:54). Like most of John's symbols, this figure can be interpreted in many ways, including the view that it represents the Virgin.

The Dragon, whom the archangel **Michael** hurls down from heaven, wages war against the women's children, identified as the faithful who witness to Jesus' sovereignty (12:13–17). Lest they despair, however, John has already informed his audience that this satanic attack on the church is really a sign of the Dragon's last days. His expulsion from heaven and his wrathful aggression on earth signify that Christ has already begun to rule. Satan can no longer accuse the faithful of unworthiness to God as he did in Job's time (Job 1–2). In John's mystic vision, the Lamb's sacrificial death and believers' testimony about it have conquered the Dragon and overthrown evil (12:10–12).

His activities now limited to human society, the Dragon appears in the form of a "beast," a monster with ten horns and seven heads. The reversed number of heads and horns shows the beast's kinship with the Dragon, who gives him his power (13:1–4). As scholars have pointed out, John's symbol of the "beast"—along with the "great whore" who rides it (17:3)—represents a twin-pronged attack on the power of Rome, a deliberate rejection of Roman political propaganda that presented the empire as sustained by heaven's highest gods and as a benefactor of humankind. John asks his readers to see the "beast" as it appears from heaven—a government that builds its power through brutal conquest and maintains its supremacy through violence and intimidation of its subject peoples. The beast is "blasphemous" because it promotes itself as humanity's political savior, an ugly falsification of God's kingdom.

Whereas the beast represents political tyranny, the "whore" of Chapters 17–18, who is closely associated with the beast, symbolizes Rome's greedy exploitation of the world economy (see Figure 38.3). This burdensome system benefits the wealthy ruling class but condemns the majority to unending poverty. Although the "kings of the earth" revel in the "wine" of her economic prosperity, the whore is doomed to public exposure and disgrace because she piled up enormous riches with no thought for the poor (17:9–18:20). Like the man wallowing in luxury who ignored the beggar Lazarus (Luke 16:19–31), the prostitute's excessive possessions—unshared with the destitute—reveal her to be no friend to God (cf. James 5:1–6).

In interpreting the beast's "death-blow" or "mortal wound [that] had been healed" (13:3–4), one scholar suggests that it refers to political events that followed the emperor Nero's suicide in 68 CE. (see Richard Bauckham in "Recommended Reading"). After Nero's death, several contenders vied for the throne, bringing widespread political disorder that represented a potential "death-blow" to the imperial system and threatened to plunge the state into chaos. When Vespasian finally became emperor a year later and founded a new dynasty, the Flavian, however, the imperial rulership was reborn, resuscitating Rome's "monstrous" tyranny—as well as the practice of deifying emperors.

A second beast then emerges, not from the sea like the first, but from the earth to work miracles and promote public worship of the first beast. This duplicate monster, also called the "false prophet" (16:13; 19:20), proceeds to enforce the imperial cult by erecting an "image" of the beast. According to one interpretation, this perverse ascribing of godlike qualities to an idol probably signifies the policies of the state priests who encouraged emperor worship in the cities of Asia Minor, including those to which John wrote (see Bauckham). In a parody of the angelic sealing, the earth-monster allows no one to conduct business unless he bears the beast's mark. John then offers a "key" to unlock this bestial riddle: The beast's number is "the number of a person": the infamous "six hundred sixty-six" (13:14–18).

John's Numerical Symbols John's hint that the beast's cryptic number applies to a specific person has inspired speculation from his day to the present. Assuming that the beast is a real figure who will appear bearing a numerical identity during End time, apocalyptists have repeatedly tried to label some man or institution of their own generation as the person about whom John prophesied. In contrast, most New Testament scholars believe that the author (or an older source he employs) refers to an historical personage of his own era, a figure known to his original audience. In trying to discover which mystically numbered person John had in mind, scholars note that in the author's day all numbers, whether in Hebrew, Aramaic, or Greek, were represented by letters of the alphabet. Thus, each letter in a name was also a number. By adding up the sum of all

FIGURE 38.3   This scale model of imperial Rome shows the Flavian Amphitheater (the Colosseum), built in the late first century CE, at the center. Whereas Luke-Acts promotes an accommodating relationship with Rome, the author of Revelation envisions the Roman government as a "beast" and "whore," a new Babylon that is doomed to fall (Rev. 17:1–19:2).

letters in a given name, we arrive at its "numerical value." Because the name "Nero Caesar"—in Aramaic—has a numerical value of 666, some commentators think that Nero, who staged Rome's first official persecution of Christians, was John's intended target.

Although identifying Nero as the bearer of "the number of the beast" is a common presumption, we have no evidence that the author intended readers to use Aramaic letters in computing the name's mystical significance. As noted above, the battles following Nero's death threatened to undermine the imperial system (a potential "mortal wound"), and Vespasian's subsequent restoration of public order may have been what John meant when he wrote that "the first beast['s] . . . mortal wound had been healed" (13:12). Other scholars suggest that Nero was figuratively reborn in Domitian, his vicious spirit ascending "from the bottomless pit" (17:8) to torment Christians in a new

human form. Still others observe that we do not have enough solid information about John's intentions to resolve the issue.

As readers know, every age—like John's at the time of the Roman Empire—has its beast, a distortion of the divine image in which God created humanity. A human leader who somehow gains the power to inflict evil on a large scale, the beast is a figure of continuing relevance. In many societies, then as now, there is always someone who fills the role.

Methods of Interpretation

Our brief examination of John's mysterious beast illustrates the more general challenge of trying to find a reliable method of interpreting Revelation's complex system of symbols. We have already touched on an approach, favored by scholars, that assumes that John

FIGURE 38.4 Nero, the first emperor to persecute Jesus' followers, executed the apostles Peter and Paul in the mid-60s CE.

recorded his visions for an audience of the first century CE, people presumably familiar with apocalyptic imagery, and that his chief purpose was to give an eschatological interpretation of then-current events. Reasoning that the book could not have been written or understood well enough to have been preserved if it had not had considerable immediate significance to its first readers, many scholars look to contemporary Roman society to supply the primary meaning of John's symbols.

Another interpretative method recognizes that John's visions have an emotional vitality that transcends any particular historical period or place. John's lasting achievement lies in the universality of his symbols and dramatic visions. His images continue to appeal, not because they apply explicitly to Rome of the past or to some particular time of the future, but because they reflect some of the deepest hopes and terrors of the human imagination. As long as the dread of evil and the longing for justice and peace motivate humans, Revelation's promise of the ultimate triumph of divine rule over chaos will be relevant.

John's arrangement of his visions also emphasizes that the struggle against evil in both human actions and social institutions does not end with a single victory but is a battle that must be fought over and over again. After the seventh trumpet blast, we are told that Jesus has won and now reigns as King over the world (11:15). Another battle ensues, however, in Chapter 12, after which John declares that Christ has now achieved total victory (12:10). Yet, still another conflict follows—the Battle of Armageddon (16:13–16)—after

which the angel repeats, "It is done!" (16:18). But it is not finished, for Satan's earthly domain—Babylon—has yet to fall (Chs. 17–18). When Babylon does collapse and a fourth victory is proclaimed (19:1–3), the empowered Christ must repeat his conquest again (19:11–21). In John's cyclic visions, evil does not stay defeated but always rises in a new form and must be resisted time after time. Similarly, human life is a continual battleground in which the contestants must be prepared to defend previous victories and combat the same enemies in new guises.

Visions of the Final Triumph

In contrast to the cyclic repetitions of earlier sections, after Chapter 20, John apparently (we cannot be sure) pursues a linear narration, presenting a chronological sequence of events. In this final eschatological vision (20:1–22:5), events come thick and fast. An angel hurls the Dragon into the abyss, the primordial "deep" that existed before God created the world (20:1–3; cf. Gen. 1:1–3). With the Dragon temporarily imprisoned, Christ's reign at last begins. Known as the **millennium** because it will last 1,000 years, even this triumph is impermanent because at its conclusion Satan is again released to wage war on the faithful. The only New Testament writer to present a 1,000-year prelude to Christ's kingdom, John states that during the millennium the martyrs who resisted the beast's influence will be resurrected to rule with Christ (20:4–6).

The Dragon's release and subsequent attack on the faithful (based on Ezekiel's prophetic drama involving the mythical God and Magog, symbols of Israel's enemies [Ezek. 38–39]), ends with fire from heaven consuming the attackers. A resurrection of all the dead follows. Released from the control of death and Hades (the Underworld), they are judged according to their deeds (20:7–13).

The Lake of Fire John's eschatology includes a place of punishment represented by a lake of fire, an image drawn from popular Jewish beliefs about punishment in the afterlife (see Josephus's Discourse on Hades in Whiston's edition). Defined as the "second death" (20:15), it receives a number of symbolic figures, including death, Hades, the beast, the false prophet, and persons (or negative human qualities) not listed in God's book of life (19:20; 20:14–15). Earlier, John implied that persons bearing the beast's fatal mark would be tormented permanently amid burning sulphur (14:9–11), a fate similar to that described for the rich man in Luke (17:19–31).

John's fiery lake also parallels that depicted in 2 Esdras (written about 100 CE):

> Then the place of torment shall appear, and over against it is the place of rest; the furnace of hell shall be displayed, and on the opposite side the paradise of delight . . . here are rest and delight, there fire and torments.

(2 Esd. 7:36–38)

Although John uses his image of torture to encourage loyalty to Christ, his metaphor of hell invites many commentators to question the author's understanding of divine love.

The Wedding of the Lamb and the Holy City John's primary goal is to demonstrate the truth of a divine power great enough to vanquish evil for all time and create the renewed universe described in Revelation 21–22. The author combines images from Isaiah and other Israelite prophets to portray an oasis of peace contrasting with the violent and bloody battlefields of his previous visions. Borrowing again from ancient myth, in which epics of conflict commonly end with a union of supernatural entities, John describes a sacred marriage of the Lamb with the holy city that descends from heaven to earth.

The wedding of a city to the Lamb may strike readers as a strange metaphor, but John attains great heights of poetic inspiration describing the union. The brilliance of the heavenly Jerusalem is rendered in terms of gold and precious stones, the jewel-like city illuminated by the radiance of God himself. John draws again on Ezekiel's vision of a restored Jerusalem sanctuary to describe a crystal stream flowing from God's throne to water the tree of life Whereas Genesis shows Yahweh preventing the first humans from partaking of the "tree of life" and thus gaining God-like immortality (Gen. 3:22–24), John makes the tree accessible to all: Its "leaves are for the healing of the nations" (22:2). Growing in a new Eden, the tree's products restore humanity to full health. The renewed and purified faithful can now look directly upon God (21:1–22:5). With his dazzling view of the heavenly city, portrayed in the earthy images of the Hebrew prophets (Isa. 11, 65, 66), John completes his picture of a renewed and completed creation. God's will is finally done on earth as it is in heaven.

In contrast to the prophet Daniel, who was instructed to seal his vision until End time (Dan. 12:4), John is told not "seal up the words of the prophecy of this book" because its contents will soon be fulfilled. He then adds a curse upon anyone who tampers with his manuscript (22:6, 10, 18–19). In his final address to the reader, the author again invokes Jesus' speedy return, a reminder of the intense fervor with which many early Christians—generations after Jesus' death—awaited their Master's Second Coming.

QUESTIONS FOR DISCUSSION AND REVIEW

1. To what branch of prophetic/apocalyptic writing does the Book of Revelation belong? Name some similar works by other Jewish or Christian apocalyptic writers. What qualities and themes characterize apocalyptic literature?

2. Describe John's attitude toward the Roman Empire and its religious and economic policies. State John's purpose in composing Revelation, and explain the book's significance to its original late-first-century-CE audience.

3. Discuss John's use of symbols and figurative language. Why does he disguise his meaning by referring to Rome as "Babylon" and to Roman oppression as the work of a "beast"? What meaning would this have to first-century Christians?

4. The Protestant reformer Martin Luther thought that Revelation did not truly reveal the nature of God and Christ. Discuss the ethical strengths and religious limitations of John's portrayal of the Deity and the divine interaction with humanity.

5. Although their suggestions were later condemned by the church, some early Christian thinkers, such as Origen, believed that God's limitless love would eventually result in the redemption of all human souls. If God desires the salvation of all people, how do you think he would accomplish this objective? How would Origen's doctrine of universal salvation work to enhance human reverence of the divine glory?

Terms and Concepts to Remember

abyss (bottomless pit)
apokalypsis
apocalypse (literary form)
apocalyptic literature
apocalyptic dualism
Armageddon
astrological images
authorship of Revelation
the beast
Domitian
the Dragon
Four Horsemen of the Apocalypse
heavenly Jerusalem
heavenly woman
the Lamb
lake of fire
means by which the Lamb conquers the Dragon
methods of interpreting apocalyptic literature
Michael

millennium

Nero

numerical values (of
names)

Revelation's abiding
significance

seven seals

seven trumpets

war in heaven

wedding of the Lamb and
glorified Jerusalem

Recommended Reading

Aune, David. *Prophecy in Early Christianity and the Ancient Mediterranean World.* Grand Rapids, MI: Eerdmans, 1983. Places Christian apocalypticism in historical perspective.

Barr, David L., ed. *Reading the Book of Revelation: A Resource for Students.* Atlanta: Society of Biblical Literature, 2003. A collection of essays analyzing Revelation in its historical and social context.

Batto, Bernard F. *Slaying the Dragon: Mythmaking in the Biblical Tradition.* Louisville, KY: Westminster John Knox Press, 1992. Show how ancient myths are used to express the role of Christ in overcoming cosmic evil.

Bauckham, Richard. *The Theology of the Book of Revelation.* New York: Cambridge UP, 1993. Offers a rational interpretation of John's visions, correlating them to conditions in the early Christian community and the Roman Empire.

Collins, A. Y. *Crisis and Catharsis: The Power of the Apocalypse.* Philadelphia: Westminster Press, 1984. A carefully researched and clearly written analysis of of the sociopolitical and theological forces affecting the composition of John's visions.

Josephus, Flavius. "Josephus' Discourse to the Greeks Concerning Hades." In *Josephus: Complete Works,* trans. William Whiston. Grand Rapids, MI: Kregel, 1960. Presents first-century Jewish views of the afterlife similar to those postulated in the Synoptic Gospels and Revelation.

Osborne, Grant O. *Revelation.* Grand Rapids, MI: Baker, 2002. Argues that the apostle John wrote Revelation and that the book is a prophecy of future events, views different from those presented in our text.

Perkins, Pheme. *The Book of Revelation.* Collegeville, MN: Liturgical Press, 1983. A brief and readable introduction oriented toward undergraduate students.

Rowland, Christopher. "Apocalypticism." In K. D. Sakenfeld, ed., *The Interpreter's Dictionary of the Bible,* Vol. 1, pp. 190–195. Nashville, TN: Abingdon Press, 2006. A concise introduction to the types and qualities of apocalyptic literature.

Schüssler Fiorenza, Elizabeth. *The Book of Revelation: Justice and Judgment.* Philadelphia: Fortress Press, 1985. A theological interpretation of Revelation's symbols.

CHAPTER 39

Our Judeo-Christian Heritage
The Biblical Concept of God

Key Topics/Themes The biblical God is not the God of philosophical abstractions, a divine first principle whose nature manifests perfect serenity and logical consistency. Instead, different biblical writers commonly portray God as an almost humanlike personality, a cosmic authority figure manifesting character traits and behaviors of bewildering variety: He is creator and king, warrior and executioner. Whereas some authors associate God with love, generosity, compassion, and mercy, others emphasize his anger and violence. From Genesis to Revelation, God is portrayed as eager to save his human creation and as equally eager to destroy those who offend him. The Bible thus offers a complex, even contradictory, portrait of God, a composite portrayal that results partly from the writers' differing historical circumstances and conflicting experiences of the divine. Ancient Israel, repeatedly trampled by invading Near Eastern armies, saw revealed a God of righteous judgment. The early Christian community, threatened by the power of imperial Rome, looked to their Messiah, the Son of God, to deliver them from a world of suffering. Some biblical writers, in both the Old and New Testaments, recognized the unfailing presence of God in their midst and experienced the transforming power of divine grace.

The Bible's Composite Portrait of God

In Revelation, the climactic moment in human history arrives when John sees "the holy city, new Jerusalem, coming down out of heaven from God." At last, a heavenly voice proclaims, "the home of God is among mortals" (Rev. 21:3). With God's presence on earth now a living reality, all creation is transformed: All the old human afflictions—including sorrow and death—are no more. In a sense, the conditions of Eden before the first human couple disobeyed Yahweh are restored, and God's original intent for the divine–human relationship is fulfilled. The heavenly Jerusalem, descended to earth, has no specific place of worship because "the Lord God the Almighty and the Lamb" sanctify the entire city by their glorious presence.

When John promises his readers that redeemed humanity "will see [God's] face" (Rev. 22:4; cf. Exod. 24:9–11), readers may wonder what aspects of divinity humans will perceive. What kind of God will be revealed? As we have learned in studying the various portrayals of God in the Torah, the Prophets, the Writings, and the New Testament, different biblical writers ascribe a dazzling variety of personal qualities, intentions, and roles to the Judeo-Christian God. From the all-powerful creator (Genesis 1), to the warrior Yahweh who rescues his people from Egyptian slavery (Exod. 1–19), to the stern Judge who makes Babylon his instrument in destroying Israel for its covenant disobedience (Jer.; 2 Kings 25), to the lofty Intelligence that directs the universe while seeming to ignore human ideas of justice (Job 9; 38–42), to the heavenly Father whose dawning kingdom Jesus proclaims, the biblical Deity reveals a character of profound complexity.

Scholars have long recognized that human attempts to describe God must necessarily rely on the use of analogies. Because human language cannot hope to depict an infinite, transcendent Being whose nature is ultimately unknowable, biblical authors commonly portray God metaphorically, comparing the Deity to figures of power and authority in human society, such as king, warrior, or judge. To understand the kind of God whom John may envision reigning over an eschatologically renewed universe, we will survey some biblical texts that offer glimpses of the divine character. Besides reviewing some of the historical developments that contributed to the Bible's composite portrait, we will also examine some crucial passages that express ethically problematical concepts of God. Limited space permits us to investigate only a few of the many roles and functions biblical writers assign God, ranging from creator and destroyer, to ruler of the heavenly council, to champion of the poor and powerless, to loving parent, to the grantor of mercy and grace. As we shall discover, some of the biblical God's conflicting behaviors—impulses to create or to destroy, to bring joy or to inflict mass suffering—seem to result from the fact that biblical writers, who collectively span a period of 1,100 years—experienced sometimes radically different aspects of the divine presence.

 ## God as Creator and Destroyer

The first eight chapters of Genesis, in which God first creates life and then exterminates it, establish a tension between the Deity's creative and destructive tendencies that characterize his behavior throughout most of the Bible. The Bible begins its composite portrait with a narrative celebrating God's creative might. In Genesis 1, Elohim first appears as the originator of light, methodically transforming the sterile darkness of primal chaos into a life-filled cosmos in which light and dark alternate. Surveying his completed work, Elohim pronounces the harmonious world order he has fashioned, including the human images of his divinity, "very good" (Gen. 1:31). Only five chapters later, however, Yahweh reverses his optimistic evaluation of humanity: "And the LORD was sorry that he had made humankind on the earth, and it grieved him to his heart. So the LORD said, 'I will blot out from the earth the human beings I have created—people together with animals and creeping things and birds of the air, for I am sorry that I have made them'" (Gen. 6:6–8). Repelled by humankind's "wickedness," Yahweh then drowns all of earth's creatures, both human and animal, except for the few that he preserves in Noah's ark.

The seeming paradox (a concept that embraces two contradictory truths) of God as both creator and destroyer of life stems in part from conflicting traditions about divine beings that Israel inherited from older Near Eastern cultures. As noted in Chapter 3, part of the biblical God's wide range of personal qualities and behaviors results from the fact that biblical authors commonly incorporated diverse traits of Mesopotamian gods in their portrayal of the "LORD God [Yahweh Elohim]" (see Boxes 3.1 and 3.2). When the Genesis authors composed their narratives of creation and a prehistoric flood, they assigned to Israel's God the personalities and actions of no fewer than three different Mesopotamian deities (see Box 5.1). In the Babylonian tradition, the god Marduk is both a warrior who defeats the primal dragon of chaos (Tiamat) and a creator who fashions the cosmos from her dismembered body. According to the Babylonian creation epic, the *Enuma Elish*, he then assigns his father, Ea, god of wisdom, the task of creating humankind. It is neither Marduk nor Ea, however, who brings the catastrophic flood that drowns most of humanity: It is Enlil, god of chaotic winds, who takes the role of destroyer. Ea, who cares for humankind, plays the part of savior, warning Utnapishtim to build an ark in which the seed of humanity and other living creatures will be preserved.

To exalt Israel's God, the Genesis writers boldly transformed older Mesopotamian traditions by assigning the actions of all three gods—Marduk, Enlil, and Ea—to a single divine Being. By blending the traits and behaviors of three very different divine personalities into one all-powerful God, however, the Genesis authors created a deity who seems to possess conflicting emotions and motivations. While gracious and compassionate, he is also violent and destructive, even vindictive.

God's Self-Description

Acutely aware of the biblical God's dual nature, Paul reminds Roman Christians of "the kindness and the severity of God" (Rom. 11:22). The apostle warns believers that unless they "continue in his kindness," they will experience the same "severity [as] those who have fallen." In this passage, Paul evokes Yahweh's self-description to Moses at Mount Sinai/Horeb, where God declares that he is "slow to anger, and abounding in steadfast love" (Exod. 34:5). Although "merciful and gracious," however, he "by no means [clears] the guilty, but [visits] the iniquity of the parents upon the children and the children's children, to the third and the fourth generation" (Exod. 34:5–7). Yahweh's resolve to punish any generation of Israel for the sins of its ancestors expresses his divine sovereignty—a function of his omnipotence and absolute moral freedom. It is this unlimited independence that allows God to employ any means he wishes to accomplish his goals. As he informs Job, Yahweh is not subject to human standards of fairness or ethical responsibility (Job 38–41). God can "harden" Pharaoh's heart in order to make his power recognized throughout the earth (Exod. 9:16), or command a "lying spirit" to lure Ahab to his death (1 Kings 22:19–22), or send an "evil spirit" to torment King Saul (1 Sam. 16:14–23).

As Paul recognizes, God is accountable to no one for his actions: "I will have mercy on whom I have mercy, and I will have compassion on whom I have compassion" (Rom. 9:15, citing Exod. 33:19). In emphasizing divine freedom from human concepts of justice, Paul concludes that God "has mercy on whomever he chooses, and he hardens the heart of whomever he chooses" (Rom. 9:17–18). In this passage, Paul refers to God's unexpected extension of mercy to whole groups of people—non-Israelites—with whom he did not have a prior covenant relationship. The divine right to behave generously, even to those whom the righteous may consider unworthy of mercy, expresses a major principle of divine conduct. As Jesus demonstrated in his parable about the father who unconditionally loves both obedient and prodigal sons, God is free to embrace individuals whom the pious are likely to condemn (Luke 15:11–32).

Ezekiel's Modification of a Mosaic Principle

In time, some biblical writers modified the Torah principle that Yahweh would discipline the entire covenant community for errors their ancestors committed. During the Babylonian exile (sixth century BCE), Yahweh declares to the prophet Ezekiel that henceforth the Israelites will not be made to suffer for their forebears' mistakes. Having punished Israel so thoroughly that it was virtually annihilated, Yahweh states that in the future he will deal with each new generation individually: A son will not be punished for his father's sins, nor a father for his child's misdeeds. Moreover, the sinner who repents will be forgiven, whereas the formerly righteous person who falls into sin will not escape retribution. Under this revised code of divine justice, which honors free will, "A child shall not suffer for the iniquity of a parent, nor a parent suffer for the iniquity of a child; the righteousness of the righteous shall be his own, and the wickedness of the wicked shall be his own" (Ezek. 18:20). Yahweh has "no pleasure in the death of anyone" but invites all to turn from their evil behavior and "live" (Ezek. 18:1–32).

Addressing a more perplexing aspect of Israel's God, Ezekiel also reveals that Yahweh sometimes gave his people laws that "were not good" and "by which they could not live," ordinances that "defiled" those who obeyed them (Ezek. 20:24–26). The prophet's claim that God's instructions to the covenant community included a requirement to sacrifice firstborn males (cf. Exod. 13:2) shocks contemporary readers, but it is part of the history of biblical ideas about God. When Yahweh declares that "the firstborn of your sons you shall give [sacrifice] to me" (Exod. 22:29b–30; cf. 13:2; 34:20), many Israelites—according to Ezekiel—took the command literally, an act of obedience Yahweh used to "horrify" them (but see prohibitions of human sacrifice in Micah 6:6–8 and Jer. 19:5–6) The story of Abraham's near-offering of his son, Isaac, may have served to illustrate that Yahweh would also accept an animal sacrifice in lieu of a human firstborn (see Gen. 22; Exod. 13:13 allows Israelites to "redeem" their sons, presumably by substituting an animal). (See the discussion of Abraham in Chapter 5, and Levenson in "Recommended Reading.")

From the perspective of twenty-first-century Jewish and Christian ethics, Deuteronomy's commands to slaughter the entire Canaanite population may also fit Ezekiel's category of laws that "defile." In Deuteronomy, God places all Canaanites under the "ban"—a provision of holy war in which conquered victims are dedicated to Yahweh. Invading Israelites are to kill "without mercy" every inhabitant of the land, from newborns to the elderly (Deut. 7:2–4). They must "not let anything that breathes remain alive" (Deut. 20:16–18; cf. Josh. 10:30–40; 11:11–14) In the Deuteronomistic authors' view, Israel's enemies are God's enemies, and Yahweh—a divine executioner—does not hesitate to employ genocide against them (see Chapter 8).

Deuteronomy's rationale for the mass slaughter of Canaan's native population is that the Canaanite religions—particularly the worship of Baal—will tempt the Israelites to betray Yahweh by honoring other gods (Deut. 7:2–4). For Yahweh, "whose name is Jealous, is a jealous God" (Exod. 34:14; cf. Exod. 20:5), a quality that distinguishes him from all other deities in the ancient world. Israel's God is unique in his inflexible demand to be worshiped exclusively. Yahweh is also unique in his refusal to permit any artistic representation of himself or of his material creation (Exod. 20:3–6). Because the biblical God cannot be limited by any image the human imagination devises for him, his unknowable nature can be experienced not through works of art but only through his actions, his spiritual presence, and his words of command.

God's Heavenly Court

When John accepts an angel's invitation to enter heaven through an open "door," he suddenly finds himself in God's throne room (Rev. 4:1–2). Around God's throne are twenty-four lesser thrones occupied by twenty-four "elders, dressed in white robes, with golden crowns on their heads," as well as four mysterious "living creatures" (Rev. 4:2–11). In addition, John sees countless thousands of angels "surrounding the throne and the living creatures and the elders" (Rev. 5:11). John's vision of the heavenly multitudes echoes similar scenes in the Hebrew Bible, in which several writers show Yahweh presiding over a divine council, a celestial assembly of supernatural beings. Most readers assume that all the beings who surround God's throne are the familiar figures of "angels" (from the Greek *angelos,* meaning "messenger"), but the author of Job calls them *bene ha elohim* (which may be translated as "sons of God" or "sons of the gods") (Job 1:6–12; 2:1–6). The presence of these unnamed divine "sons" reminds us that the biblical God incorporates yet another aspect of Mesopotamian tradition: He is the leader of a divine council.

An ancient Near Eastern concept that appears in the Bible, the *Epic of Gilgamesh,* and the *Enuma Elish,* the divine council was apparently modeled on the practice of kings and emperors holding conferences with high-ranking advisors (see Box 3.2). In Mesopotamian mythology, the gods typically assemble to discuss issues relating to humankind, such as bringing punishment for blasphemy or disobedience. In biblical parallels, such as Psalm 89, Yahweh similarly holds court over the "assembly of holy ones," where he is distinguished by his unique "faithfulness":

> For who in the skies can be compared to the LORD
>   [Yahweh]?
> Who among the heavenly beings is like the LORD,
> a God feared in the council of the holy ones,
> great and awesome above all that are around him?

(Ps. 89:6–7)

As other psalmists noted, "the LORD is a great God, and a great king above all gods" (Ps. 95:3); he is "exalted far above all gods" (Ps. 97:9).

God's Ethical Superiority

The biblical God's superiority to older Near Eastern concepts of divinity lies in his ethical nature, particularly his unusual concern for humanity's poor and downtrodden.

According to Psalm 82, God implicitly contrasts his passion for social justice with the other gods' misguided support of economic oppression. Although the biblical Deity is free to ignore humanly instituted ethics, throughout both the Old and New Testaments he consistently sides against the rich and powerful on behalf of society's have-nots:

> God has taken his place in the divine council,
> in the midst of the gods he holds judgment:
> "How long will you [the other gods] judge unjustly
> and show partiality to the wicked?
> Give justice to the weak and the orphan;
> maintain the right of the lowly and the destitute.
> Rescue the weak and needy;
> deliver them from the hand of the wicked."

(Ps. 82:1–4)

Because other members of the council lack Yahweh's insight and compassion, "they have neither knowledge nor understanding," causing them to blunder about "in darkness," undermining the "foundations" of justice on which the moral universe is based (Ps. 82:5). Without the capacity for ethical growth, the lesser deities are doomed to extinction, a prediction that forms the poem's climax:

> I say, "You are gods, children of the Most High
>   [Elyon], all of you;
> nevertheless, you shall die like mortals, and fall like
>   any prince."

(Ps. 82:7)

Empowered by his incomparable wisdom and ethical superiority, Yahweh is eventually seen as reigning supreme over other council members, the "sons of God [or, "the gods"]," who become his servants. It is presumably these divine beings whom God addresses at creation when he proposes, "let us make humankind in our image, according to our likeness" (Gen. 1:26; cf. 3:22). God's associates in creation are also identified as the "morning stars" and "heavenly beings" who joyfully acclaim the universe's formation (Job 38:7). Yahweh's heavenly courtiers include cherubim—hybrid creatures combining the features of humans, animals, and birds—who surround his throne (Ezek. 1). Like the cherubim, John's "four living creatures" combine animal, bird, and human characteristics and, like the fiery seraphim of Isaiah 6, they praise God's holiness (Rev. 4:6–9).

God's Associates in Cosmic Rule

Some biblical writers indicate that selected members of the heavenly assembly assist God in his governance of the world. According to an old poem incorporated into Deuteronomy, when the "Most High [Elyon]" first assigned nations and people "according to the number of the gods," giving each deity a particular group to rule, Yahweh (who in this context is probably distinct from the "Most High"), received Israel as his "portion" or "allotted share" (Deut. 32:8–9). This ancient tradition also probably lies behind the Book of Daniel's portrayal of different heavenly beings directing the activities of various nations. The only canonical book in the Hebrew Bible to provide names for individual divine beings, Daniel states that individual spirit "princes" act as guardians of particular countries, such as the divine patrons of imperial Persia and ancient Greece (Dan. 10:4–21). Wars between nations on earth correspond to conflicts in heaven as Michael—the "protector" of Israel—defends the covenant people against their enemies (Dan. 10:13, 21; 12:1).

Paul may refer to these spirit rulers when he states that, before coming to Christ, "we were enslaved to the elementary spirits of the world" (Gal. 4:3), whom he also calls "weak and beggarly elemental spirits" (Gal. 4:9). In Colossians, Paul (or a close Pauline disciple) declares that Christ, by his resurrection and ascension to heaven, totally "disarmed the [heavenly] rulers and authorities and made a public example of them, triumphing over them in it" (Col. 2:15; cf. 1:15–16). Like a victorious emperor celebrating a public triumph in which defeated rulers were paraded in chains through Rome, the risen Christ demonstrates his superiority to all other spiritual beings and claims his right to sit beside God's throne.

God's Wisdom a Heavenly Figure

According to Colossians, the triumphant Christ who subdues other (rival?) members of the divine council is also "the firstborn of all creation," whom God from the beginning destined to rule over "things visible or invisible, whether thrones or dominions or rulers or powers [of the celestial court]" (Col. 1:15–17). Interestingly, earlier biblical writers assigned this distinction of being God's "firstborn" to a female companion of Yahweh, holy Wisdom. (A feminine noun in both Hebrew [Hochmah] and Greek [Sophia], Wisdom is appropriately referred to as she; see Chapters 23 and 33.) In Proverbs 8, a poet personifies (gives human qualities to) God's chief attribute, the wisdom by which he creates and sustains the universe. In this poem, Lady Wisdom is not only God's first creation but also his main channel of communication with his human creation:

To you, O people, I call, and my cry is to all that live . . .
Hear, for I will speak noble things,
and from my lips will come what is right;
for my mouth will utter truth; . . .
by me kings reign,
and rulers decree what is just; . . .
I love those who love me,
and those who seek me diligently find me . . .

Wisdom, personified as God's constant companion, is "the first of his acts":

The LORD created me at the beginning of his work,
the first of his acts of long ago.
Ages ago I was set up,
as the first, before the beginning of the earth . . .
then I was beside him, like a master worker;
and I was daily his delight,
rejoicing before him always,
. . . and delighting in the human race.

(Prov. 8:4–6, 15, 17, 22–23, 30–31)

"The Satan": A Member of the Heavenly Court

In contrast to Lady Wisdom, who "loves" and "delights in" God's human creation, "the Satan," another of Yahweh's celestial companions, acts as humanity's bitter enemy. Counted among the "sons of God" who make up the divine council, "the Satan" serves as God's prosecuting attorney, tirelessly seeking to demonstrate that humankind is unworthy of divine blessings (see Box 23.1). In fact, God's relationship to the Satan figure is both fascinating and ethically ambiguous, a strangely intimate relationship that biblical writers developed in different ways over time. The Hebrew Bible includes three memorable scenes of the heavenly court in which "the Satan" (meaning "Adversary" or "Accuser") plays a prominent role. In the Book of Zechariah, he appears before Yahweh "accusing" Joshua, the High Priest of former exiles who have recently returned from Babylon to Jerusalem. On this occasion, Yahweh speaks through an angel who defends Joshua from "the Satan's" charges (which are not specified). Ignoring his prosecutor's advice, God decides in favor of the accused priest, ordering that his "filthy" garments be exchanged for clean "festal apparel," symbolizing his restoration to divine favor (Zech. 3:1–10).

In the prologue to Job, which dramatizes two sessions of the divine council, "the Satan" again appears (Job. 1–2). As in Zechariah's account, "the Satan" is primarily a functionary whose job, like that of the secret police of an ancient Near Eastern emperor, involves patrolling the earth to find and expose potentially disloyal subjects. Serving as the appointed officer through whom Yahweh identifies and punishes human misconduct, "the Satan" not only introduces distrust of humanity into the council proceedings but also tempts God to doubt the integrity of his human creation. In contrast to his validation of Joshua the High Priest, in this case Yahweh accepts Satan's challenge, stripping Job of all he holds dear, including his children, reputation, wealth, and confidence in God's justice (see Chapter 23). In a second consultation with the Adversary, Yahweh admits that he torments Job "for no reason," but nonetheless permits Satan to destroy Job's health as well, afflicting him with a painfully disfiguring disease (Job 2:3–7). The author of Job does not explain why God allows Satan to persuade him to perform an ethically unjustifiable act, subjecting a faithful worshiper to undeserved suffering. (Commentators typically cite God's authority to act as he pleases, Job's exercise of free will to remain faithful, or the rewards Yahweh finally bestows on Job—including ten new children—at the book's end. Job's slain children, however, are not returned to him.)

By contrast, the author of James categorically denies that God can be influenced, by Satan or any other heavenly being, "for God cannot be tempted by evil and he himself tempts no one" (James 1:13). James, in spite of biblical evidence to the contrary, argues that "the Father of lights" is utterly unchanging, for in God "there is no variation or shadow due to change" (James 1:17).

Satan's Expulsion from the Divine Assembly

According to John of Patmos, God introduces a major change in the divine environment when Michael, Israel's heavenly champion (Dan. 12:1), expels humanity's chief enemy from heaven (Rev. 12:3–12). Satan takes with him "a third of the stars of heaven," presumably including such mysterious entities as the "lying spirit" and the "evil spirit," which had formerly served in Yahweh's heavenly court (1 Kings 22:19–22; 1 Sam. 16:14–15, 23), as well as the "beggarly elementary spirits" to which Paul refers. At this decisive point in biblical history, God appears to repudiate the negative forces he had previously tolerated in his heavenly council, an event that John praises as a triumph of divine sovereignty:

Now have come the salvation and the power
and the kingdom of our God
and the authority of his Messiah,
for the accuser of our comrades
has been thrown down,
who accuses them day and night
before our God.

(Rev. 12:10)

John thus interprets Satan's ejection from the celestial assembly as the beginning of God's universal rule, "the kingdom of our God." With the permanent removal of "the Satan," who had successfully tempted Yahweh to persecute Job and who subsequently "accused" all the faithful, heaven is cleansed of a malign influence, and God is free to develop a closer relationship with humankind (see below). John's vision of Satan's fall and the inauguration of God's kingdom thus marks the symbolic culmination of a lengthy historical process in which the biblical concept of divinity is significantly redefined. In this process, biblical authors gradually attribute negative qualities formerly associated with God to Satan, who subsequently becomes a figure of pure evil. As historians such as Jeffrey Russell have shown, manifestations of divine violence or cruelty—the unacknowledged "shadow" of the divine personality—are ultimately transferred to the Satan figure (see Russell in "Recommended Reading"). Space permits only one example of this monumental change in the theological evolution of the biblical concept of God—the two accounts of David's census. In the older narrative, probably written during the time of the monarchy, Yahweh puts it into David's head to sin by taking a census of Israel. David's census-taking angers God, who then punishes not the king who ordered it but the people at large, sending a plague that kills thousands of Israelites (2 Sam. 24:1–25). In the second version of this episode, written hundreds of years later, it is not Yahweh who inspires David's census, but "the Satan"; Yahweh only punishes (1 Chron. 21:1–30). The centuries that elapse between the composition of these two parallel accounts had apparently witnessed a significant shift in the biblical viewpoint. It is no longer possible to see Yahweh as both the *cause of sin* and the righteous God who punishes it. The contradictory actions that Samuel's author had ascribed to God, the writer of Chronicles now separates, assigning the evil motive to "the Satan."

In John's vision of heavenly battles, Satan becomes not merely humanity's Adversary, but a cosmic opponent of God himself. By identifying Satan with the Greek concept of evil—"the Devil"—John makes him the embodiment of cosmic disorder, the monster of primordial chaos whom God must defeat to bring peace and order to the world. (Figure 23.3 shows an ancient Mesopotamian image of the seven-headed dragon, an image that Revelation's author revives to depict Satan.)

After his fall from heaven, Satan, his schemes now confined to earth, intensifies his attack on God's people (Rev. 12:13–17). Accordingly, he empowers "a beast" and the "whore of Babylon," symbolizing the world's oppressive governments that abuse the people of God (Rev. 13:1–17:18) and that God eventually overthrows (Rev. 18). Following the defeat of Satan's imperial system, an angel casts him into "the bottomless pit," thrusting the Dragon of Chaos into the primal abyss that had preceded God's creation of the world (Rev. 20:1–3; cf. Gen. 1:1–3). Released after a thousand-year imprisonment. Satan again tempts "the nations" until God destroys his former counselor once and for all, consigning him to "the lake of fire and sulfur" (20:7–10)—"which is the second death" (21:8). If, as some theologians believe, Revelation's fiery lake—which already contains the metaphorical "beast," "false prophet," "death," and "Hades"—symbolizes total extinction, God at last purges his world (and himself) of all "Satanic" qualities, including divine doubts about the intrinsic worth of his human creation.

 God as Loving Parent

Revelation's visions highlight God's omnipotence—an irresistible power that easily overcomes all opposition in heaven and on earth—but offer little insight into other divine qualities, such as God's love. For many believers, the author of 1 John provides the most essential—and the most concise—concept of divinity: "God is light" (1:5) and "God is love" (4:8, 16). In the Gospel and letters of John, the writers consistently emphasize God's infinite love and compassion for humanity (John 3:16), insisting that love is the defining quality of Christian life (John 13:34–35). When Jesus commands his followers to love even their "enemies" (Matt. 5:44), it is because God himself embraces all people, however worthy or unworthy, in his universal love:

> Love your enemies . . . so that you may be children of your Father in heaven, for he makes his sun rise on the evil and on the good, and sends rain on the righteous and on the unrighteous.

(Matt. 5:44–45)

Living in a way that imitates God's defining attribute, his disciples will be "perfect"—expressing a God-like completeness by manifesting an all-encompassing love (Matt. 5:48). Similarly, Paul declares that love (*agape*) is the supreme motivator in Christians' interaction with each other and with the world (1 Cor. 13).

Yet the same God in whose infinite love Jesus expressed such confidence is also the Deity who rejects Jesus' prayer to "remove the cup" of suffering he must drink (Mark 14:35–36). Enduring the agony of crucifixion, Jesus keenly feels God's absence: "My God, my God, why have you forsaken me?" (Mark 15:35; Matt. 27:46). In their accounts of Jesus' death, Luke and John delete this despairing cry and replace it with more hopeful final words, giving Jesus a serene death and implying that he did not feel that the Father had abandoned him (Luke 23:46; John 19:30; see Box 33.2). For Luke and John, who provide more extensive narratives of Jesus' postresurrection appearances than the other Evangelists, Jesus' suffering is followed by resurrection, vindication, and eternal life. For these Gospel writers, the evil of Good Friday is transformed by the radiance of the first Easter and the arrival of the Holy Spirit that infuses Jesus' disciples with renewed hope (Acts 2; John 20:21–23). Out of human failure to recognize Jesus' value—which leads to his rejection and unjust execution—God brings the promise of universal renewal.

A few biblical passages depict God's love as opposing his other qualities, such as his sense of justice. In Hosea 11, the prophet envisions Yahweh as a devoted father who grieves over his disobedient son, Israel. Providing a rare glimpse into God's thought processes—an inner debate between the conflicting emotions of righteous anger and "tender" compassion—Hosea shows God's *hesed* (steadfast love) winning out over his wrath:

> When Israel was a child, I loved him
> and out of Egypt I called my son.
> The more I called them, the more they went
>   from me;
> they kept sacrificing to the Baals,
> and offering incense to idols . . .
> How can I give you up, Ephraim [Israel]?
> My heart recoils within me;
> my compassion grows warm and tender.
> I will not execute my fierce anger;
> I will not again destroy Ephraim;
> for I am God and no mortal;
> the Holy One in your midst;
> and I will not come in wrath.

(Hos. 11:1–3, 8–9)

In this argument with himself, Yahweh decides to spare his people because he is "God" and not a fallible "mortal" who reasons according to merely human standards of retributive justice.

But Yahweh eventually did "come in wrath" against Israel, bringing Assyrian armies to destroy the northern kingdom so completely that the nation ceased to exist (721 BCE; 1 Kings 17). Only two chapters after Hosea's portrayal of God as loving father who can not bear to inflict punishment on his disobedient son, we find the same prophet delivering oracles in which God compares himself to a wild beast savagely attacking his offending child:

> So I [Yahweh] will become like a lion to them [Israel].
> like a leopard I will lurk beside the way.
> I will fall upon them like a bear robbed of her cubs,
> and will tear open the covering of their heart, . . .
> as a wild animal would mangle them.
>
> (Hos. 13:7–8)

Like a ravenous predator, Yahweh abandons his fatherly *hesed*, devouring Israel so that the nation vanishes from history.

 ## God and Eternal Punishment

The harshness of God's punishment of the covenant people under Assyria, Babylon, and Rome is troubling, occasionally even to God (Jer. 42:10). Several New Testament writers introduce an even more unsettling aspect of divine judgment, however: the concept of an afterlife of eternal torment. Whereas most Tanakh authors envision a bleak posthumous existence in Sheol for good and evil persons alike (Job 3; Eccles. 9:5, 10, etc.), the first three Evangelists (but not John) show Jesus warning of a postmortem punishment in Gehenna, which Luke depicts as a flaming hell (Luke 16:19–31; cf. Mark 9:43–48; Matt. 5:29–30; 10:38). Although virtually absent from the Hebrew Bible, in later Greco-Roman times, a belief developed that sinners would be condemned to a place of everlasting pain—a concept that the Pharisees and some other parties of first-century Judaism adopted. Josephus, for example, vividly describes an underworld "lake of fire" in his "Discourse to the Greeks on Hades," and the author of 2 Esdras depicts a "furnace" in which the wicked burn in full view of the redeemed: "The pit of torment shall appear, and opposite it shall be the place of rest; and the furnace of hell shall be disclosed, and opposite it the paradise of delight" (2 Esd. 7:36).

John of Patmos, who wrote Revelation at almost exactly the same time that 2 Esdras was composed, offers an even more horrific description: Condemned souls "will be tormented with fire and sulfur in the presence of the holy angels and in the presence of the Lamb. And the smoke of their torment goes up forever and ever" (Rev. 14:10–11). These unfortunates include "the cowardly, the faithless, the polluted, . . . and all liars, their place will be in the lake that burns with fire and sulfur, which is the second death" (Rev. 21:8). John's assumption that the sufferings of the damned and the bliss of the redeemed will co-exist in plain sight of each other was apparently a common belief in the first century CE, a belief shared by such diverse writers as Josephus and the authors of Luke and 2 Esdras.

To some Christian writers, the Roman practice of burning martyrs alive invited divine retaliation, in which the persecutors would suffer the same kinds of torture, with the difference that their suffering would not end at death. Tertullian, a Christian theologian of the late second and early third centuries CE, looked forward to an eschatological reversal in which familiar figures from Roman society would soon be writhing in hellish misery, providing an entertaining spectacle for the souls of their former victims. Anticipating the Day of Judgment, Tertullian states that he will not know whether to "laugh" or "applaud" at the sight of Roman administrators who had ordered Christians burnt at the stake now "melting in flames fiercer than those they had kindled for brave Christians." He delights in the prospect of "philosophers and their students" (promoters of rival beliefs) burning together, while tragic actors who had enraptured audiences in Roman theaters will bellow their lines in genuine anguish (see Turner in "Recommended Reading"). Offering better entertainment than any of Rome's circuses or athletic events, Tertullian's fantasy makes observing the pain of the damned one of the major rewards of the faithful.

In the noncanonical Apocalypse of Peter (second century CE), the pseudonymous author paints early Christianity's most lurid images of hell, where those who have displeased God are condemned to feel maximum pain with no hope of release, to endure the highest pitch of agony imaginable for all eternity. Although John does not question the ethical value of such a doctrine, his fellow apocalyptist, the author of 2 Esdras, is appalled at the divine sadism: "What does it profit us [humans]," he asks, "that we shall be preserved alive [in the next world] but cruelly tormented?" Surely, he concludes, it would be better simply to perish, to vanish into nothingness (2 Esd. 67–69). Recognizing that the notion of eternal punishment is profoundly incompatible with the nature of a merciful and loving God, many contemporary theologians reject traditional concepts of hell.

God Revealed in the Johannine Jesus

Except for the deceased rich man who begs for a drop of water to cool his burning tongue (Luke 16:23–24), biblical writers rarely articulate the thoughts or feelings of persons assigned to Gehenna. The writer who most forcefully expresses the effects of God's negative judgment on human lives is the author of Job. Feeling like one whom Yahweh cruelly persecutes (Job 10:16–20), Job asks God to reflect on what it is like to be a suffering human: "Do you have eyes of flesh? Do you see as humans see?" (10:4). Suggesting that Yahweh learn empathy—the capacity to understand and share the sufferings of mortal humanity—Job demands that God develop sympathy for human pain. In his speeches to Job, however, Yahweh reveals that he is too absorbed in the divine attributes of irresistible power, omniscience, and immortality to identify empathetically with the human predicament (38-41).

As if to meet Job's challenge, the author of John's Gospel portrays God—or his eternal attribute, the Word—as descending to earth to become the man Jesus of Nazareth (John 1:1–17). When he declares that the Word "became flesh and lived among us" (1:14), John makes the New Testament's most explicit statement of the Incarnation, in which the divine becomes human, and thus vulnerable to suffering and death. For John, Jesus is cosmic Wisdom incarnate (visible in human form), which allows Jesus' disciples to see "[God's] glory, the glory as of a father's only son, full of grace and truth" (1:14). Alone among the Gospel writers, John portrays Jesus as having a prehuman existence in heaven, which permits him to reveal the Father fully: "Whoever has seen me has seen the Father" (14:9). "The Father and I," Jesus asserts, "are one" (10:30). Only in John's Gospel do opponents accuse him of claiming equality with the Father (5:18; cf. 8:54–59). Although John emphasizes Jesus' divinity more than any other Evangelist, he seems to stop short of completely identifying Jesus with God. "The Father," Jesus observes, "is greater than I am" (14:28; cf. 5:30). His unity with the Father is not unique, but resembles the spiritual unity of his disciples: "The glory that you have given me I have given to them, so that they are one as we are one" (17:22). The Johannine Jesus also observes that his followers will accomplish even greater deeds than he (14:12) (see Chapter 33). Nonetheless, John's Gospel, more than any other New Testament document, illustrates Paul's conviction that the "glory of God" shines brightest in "the face of Jesus Christ" (2 Cor. 4:6).

Because his earthly ministry is merely a brief interlude in the eternity of his heavenly existence, the Johannine Jesus repeatedly emphasizes his unique connection to the celestial realm. "No man has ascended into heaven," he states, "except the one who descended from heaven, the Son of Man" (John 3:13). In contrast to the Synoptic Gospels, John's Jesus almost never speaks of his return to earth (the Parousia), but instead emphasizes his return to the Father in heaven—the principal topic of his Farewell Discourse to the disciples (John 13–17). Before he ascends to the Father, the Johannine Jesus has only one commandment for his followers: "that you love one another as I have loved you" (15:12; cf. 13:34–35). Love, both human and divine, is the incarnate Word's essential message. In revealing the Father, John's Jesus reveals a God of love.

God as Guarantor of Social Justice

"No one has greater love than this," Jesus explains to his disciples, "to lay down one's life for one's friends" (John 13:13). Although often overlooked in discussions of the biblical God's requirements for his human creation, behaving generously to one's fellow human beings is no less important than worshiping one God alone. As the poet of Psalm 82 noted, the biblical God is distinguished from rival concepts of divinity by his firm commitment to "the weak and the needy," to whose plight he pays special attention (Ps. 82:3–4). In both Old and New Testaments, God demands not only that people love him but also that they love their "neighbor" (Deut. 6:4–5; Lev. 19:18)—directives that Jesus pronounces the "greatest" of all commandments (Mark 12:28–34). In biblical usage, to "love" means much more than cultivating warm feelings toward other people. Biblical love is an active force that works in a very concrete way to help others in the business of life. When an Israelite master frees the slave who has worked off his debt, Deuteronomy is specific about the former owner's obligation to take care of the slave's material needs, "lavishly" bestowing upon him material means of support (Deut. 15:13–15). The Torah makes specific provisions for the poor, mandating that they are entitled to the same legal rights in court as the rich (Deut. 16:19). Torah statutes also require that no interest be charged for loans made to the poor (Lev. 23:35–37) and that their debts be cancelled every seventh year (Deut. 15:1–2). In addition, landowners are not to cut the wheat growing in the corners of their fields, but are to leave it for the poor to harvest, a stipulation that plays a major role in the Book of Ruth (see Chapter 24). When he offers the Bible's only definition of religion, the author of James gives care of society's defenseless members top priority:

> Religion that is pure and undefiled before God, the Father, is this: to care for orphans and widows in their distress, and to keep oneself unstained by the world.

(Jas. 1:27)

Despite such humanitarian principles and the social customs they reflect, in both ancient Israel and the later Christian community, some privileged members found ways to increase their wealth by exploiting the poor, a practice that the prophets consistently denounce as hateful to God. Although commonly ignored today, one of the major reasons the prophets give for divine anger is economic injustice—the painfully unequal distribution of material possessions in Israelite society. Prophets such as Amos, Micah, and Isaiah of Jerusalem repeatedly point out that Yahweh champions the poor and "lowly," and that he despises the ruling classes' practice of gaining riches at the expense of the poor. Amos declares that God regards social justice as an indispensable aspect of loyalty to him (see Chapter 15). Similarly, Isaiah condemns wealthy landowners who ruthlessly acquired other people's property, perhaps foreclosing on loans during time of drought or famine:

> Ah, you who join house to house, who add field to field,
> until there is room for no one but you,
> and you are left to live alone in the midst of the land!

(Isa. 5:8; cf. 10:1–2; Micah 2:1–2)

Jesus' parables of the greedy "fool" who obsessively accumulates possessions (Luke 12:16–20) and of the "rich man" who apparently ignores the starving beggar at his door (Luke 16:19–31) make the same point: Wealth that is unshared with the needy brings divine condemnation because "you cannot serve God and wealth" (Luke 16:13). When focused exclusively on gaining wealth, particularly at others' expense, the rich will have as much chance of entering God's kingdom as a camel does of squeezing through the eye of a needle (Mark 10:25).

In Luke's Gospel, Jesus promises the "kingdom of God" to "you who are poor" and future blessings to "you who are hungry now" (Luke 6:20–21). Because he sees the kingdom as totally reversing ordinary economic standards, Luke—the only Evangelist to do so—pronounces a series of "woes" on "you who are rich" or "full now" of good things (Luke 6:24–26). When the kingdom arrives, persons who benefited from the injustices of the present system—in Isaiah's words, "grinding the face of the poor"

(Isa. 3:15)—will learn the consequences of economic injustice. (For more positive biblical views on wealth, see the list of secular blessings promised a faithful Israel in Deuteronomy 28:1–14; cf. Proverbs 3:16; 10:22.)

Closely linked to God's special interest in society's marginalized people, to whom the successful typically show little respect, is Jesus' refusal to exclude from his followers persons usually categorized as "sinners." Even when conventionally respectable people accuse him of being "a glutton and a drunkard, a friend of tax collectors and sinners" (Luke 7:35), Jesus continues to "eat and drink" with socially or morally "unacceptable" persons, including lepers, prostitutes, and other social outcasts. True to his understanding of a divine Father who showers his gifts indiscriminately on all humans, regardless of their individual merits, Jesus practices a hospitable inclusiveness that astonishes his contemporaries (cf. Luke 7:33–50).

Because his God hears the cries of the oppressed and devalued, Jesus—like Israel's prophets—insists that just and generous treatment of other people, particularly in matters of economic fairness, is essential to a healthy divine–human relationship. In one of his most awe-inspiring parables, Jesus depicts the eschatological Son of Man presiding over the Final Judgment—a universal judgment in which the sole criterion for divine favor is humanitarian action. When the "Son of Man comes in his glory," Matthew states, "all the nations will be gathered before him, and he will separate people one from another as a shepherd separates the sheep from the goats." In this apocalyptic scene, the divine judge grants his "kingdom" to "sheep" because of their generous help to those in need:

> for I was hungry and you gave me food; I was thirsty and you gave me something to drink, I was a stranger and you welcomed me, I was naked and you gave me clothing, I was sick and you took care of me, I was in prison and you visited me.

(Matt. 25:31–32, 35–36)

Significantly, this parable says nothing about a test of correct belief or doctrinal orthodoxy; the only persons consigned to "everlasting punishment" are those who have made no effort to relieve human suffering and thereby please God. As the cosmic judge explains, "Just as you did it to one of the least of these who are members of my family, you did it to me" (25:40). To worship God acceptably, Matthew implies, is to care for his human image. In the Sermon on the Mount, Jesus makes clear that only by imitating God's generosity to both "the righteous and . . . the unrighteous" can believers hope to approach the "completeness" expected of his earthly "children" (Matt. 5:44–48).

The Postmillennium God

To contrast the present world order with the eschatological kingdom of God, John of Patmos employs images of two strikingly different cities, Rome and "the new Jerusalem." The socially, economically, and politically dominant power of his day, Rome is represented as "the great whore . . . with whom the kings of the earth have committed fornication" (Rev. 17:1–2). Gorgeously "adorned with gold and jewels and pearls," this imperial city, destroyer of earthly Jerusalem, has symbolically become "Babylon the great, the mother of whores" (Rev. 17:4–5). As the new "Babylon," Rome not only persecutes "the witnesses to Jesus," she also fosters an economic system that rewards greed and corruption: "the merchants of the earth have grown rich from the power of her luxury" (Rev. 18:3). When God overthrows her,

> . . . the merchants of the earth [will] weep and mourn for her, since no one buys their cargo anymore, cargo of gold, silver, jewels and pearls, fine linen, purple, silk and scarlet, . . . all articles of ivory, cattle and sheep, horses and chariots, slaves—and human lives.

(Rev. 18:11–13)

In stark contrast to the Roman Empire's exploitation of "human lives" is the heavenly Jerusalem that descends to earth, bringing peace and justice to human society. In John's vision, Jerusalem, its streets paved with gold, is the true cosmic capital and source of priceless treasure that Rome falsely claimed to be. Unlike Rome, which built its architectural magnificence on the economic oppression of subject peoples, the new Jerusalem's splendor is a divine gift. The city is radiant with jewels and gold, but the gold is "transparent as glass" (Rev. 21:9–21), manifesting a quality utterly different from the precious metals that Roman conquerors and merchants fought to possess. Capital of "a new heaven and a new earth," the city has no need of sun or moon because "the glory of God is its light, and its lamp . . . the Lamb" (Rev. 21:23). Whereas God's first creation alternated night and day, and light and dark (Gen. 1:4–5; 8:22), in the transformed cosmos, night never dims the new Jerusalem; its golden buildings—perfectly transparent—cast no shadows. The God whose first command brought light to primal darkness (Gen. 1:3) now sheds his radiance uniformly over redeemed humanity (cf. 1 John 1:5).

Totally secure, the city keeps its twelve gates (formed of lustrous pearl) continuously open, ready to receive "the glory and the honor of the nations" that "people will bring into it" (Rev. 21:25–26). Despite the global devastations and the thousand-year reign of Christ that John had previously narrated, in the postmillennial world human ethnic and political distinctions apparently continue to exist. These "people"—unidentified outsiders—whom God draws into his eternal presence he also invites to eat of "the tree of life," the leaves of which "are for the healing of the nations" (Rev. 22:2). In Genesis, Yahweh posted cherubim to keep the first humans from this "tree" because tasting its fruits would make them "live forever" (Gen. 3:22–24). Now, his relationship to humanity permanently changed, God allows humankind to share his immortality.

In his description of nations flocking to Jerusalem, John explicitly echoes earlier visions of Isaiah, who prophesies that one day Israel's capital will be exalted above all competing cities and that "all the nations shall stream to it" (Isa. 2:2). For Isaiah, foreign multitudes travel to Jerusalem because Yahweh will "teach [them] his ways," a divine instruction that will result in universal peace:

> They [all nations] shall beat their swords into plowshares, and their spears into pruning hooks; nation shall not lift up sword against nation, neither shall they learn war any more.

(Isa. 2:3–4)

Later prophets, who added their oracles to the Book of Isaiah (see Chapter 19), expand on Isaiah's original vision, adding vivid details of God's peaceable kingdom:

> The wolf and the lamb shall feed together,
> the lion shall eat straw like the ox;
> but the serpent—its food shall be dust!
> They shall not hurt or destroy on all my holy mountain,
> says the LORD.

(Isa. 65:25)

With the symbolic "serpent" who had ceaselessly disturbed heaven with his accusations against humanity now expelled forever from the divine presence (Rev. 12), the divine–human bond is healed and restored. (For John, the defeat of cosmic evil was ensured by the life-giving power of Jesus' sacrificial blood [Rev. 19].) As he refashions the world into "new heavens and a new earth," God assures us that humanity's "former troubles are forgotten and hidden from [his] sight" (Isa. 65:16–17). By wiping memory's slate clean, voluntarily refusing to recall humanity's defects and crimes, God enters into a fresh relationship with his formerly mortal image. Deeply influenced by these ancient prophetic anticipations of his visions, John of Patmos suggests the kind of God whose "face" restored humanity "will see" (Rev. 22:4)—a God of grace. A gracious willingness to grant favor, help, and renewal to humans who have—at last—learned to trust in him, divine grace permits God's love to transcend all other attributes.

QUESTIONS FOR DISCUSSION AND REVIEW

1. The Judeo-Christian concept of a God who is both all-powerful and all-good is the Bible's most important contribution to world religion. In reviewing the different scriptural passages discussed in this chapter, which aspects or qualities of the biblical God do you find most attractive? Which biblical writers do you think show the most religious or ethical maturity in their portrayals of God?

2. To many people, the ethically problematic passages discussed above do not reflect their personal views of God, whom most believers regard as gracious, merciful, infinitely loving, and ever faithful to his word. In order to maintain this concept of a completely good and just Deity, which specific biblical passages would you use to support your view? Which specific passages would you choose to reject or ignore?

3. According to some biblical authors, we can most acceptably worship God by exercising love toward our fellow humans. How does the biblical concept of love translate into effective action? In Matthew's parable of the Final Judgment (Matt. 25), what standard does the Son of Man employ in separating favored "sheep" from rejected "goats"?

4. Discuss the biblical prophecies, from Isaiah to Revelation, that predict an ultimate reconciliation between God and humanity and an era of eternal world peace. What elements in both human nature—and in our human concepts of the divine nature—must be eliminated or changed before this cosmic transformation can take place?

5. In the historical development of biblical concepts of God, what does it mean when God finally expels "the Satan"—and all that he stands for—from heaven (Rev. 12; cf. Luke 10:18)? According to Job 1–2, what traditional function in the divine council did "the Satan" have? What influence did he exert on God? Speculate about the theological consequences—for both the nature of God and for humanity—of permanently removing this figure from the divine presence. Why does John of Patmos equate "the salvation and the power and the kingdom of our God and the authority of his Messiah" (Rev. 12:10) with Satan's fall?

6. In post–New Testament times, the Christian church articulated a doctrine in which Jesus is proclaimed not only Son of God but God himself. Only in John's Gospel, the account that most emphasizes Jesus' divinity, do we find Jesus making such statements as "whoever has seen me has seen the Father" (John 14:9). In what respects does John's portrayal of Jesus most reveal God? What specific divine qualities, actions, and intentions toward humankind does the Johannine Jesus manifest?

Terms and Concepts to Remember

angels
aspects of the divine character
conflicting qualities of God
the divine assembly
divine ethics
divine grace
eternal punishment
Gehenna and the "lake of fire"
God and social justice
God and the Word (Logos)
God as creator and destroyer
God as both "kind" and "severe"
God's love in human society
heavenly Jerusalem
heavenly Wisdom
Johannine Jesus, the
members of the heavenly court
Michael (archangel)
Satan, significance of his expulsion from heaven
sons of God

Recommended Reading

Armstrong, Karen. *A History of God: The 4,000-Year Quest of Judaism, Christianity, and Islam.* New York: Knopf, 1994. Traces developing concepts of God from ancient Israel to contemporary Western science.

Brueggemann, Walter. *Theology of the Old Testament: Testimony, Dispute, Advocacy.* Minneapolis: Fortress Press, 1977. A rewarding study of the biblical God, for thoughtful students.

Ehrman, Bart D. *God's Problem: How the Bible Fails to Answer Our Most Important Question—Why We Suffer.* San Francisco: HarperOne, 2008. An analytical survey of different biblical responses to God's relationship to the problem of evil and undeserved suffering.

Friethem, Terence E. "God, Old Testament View of." In K. D. Sakenfeld, ed., *The New Interpreter's Dictionary of the Bible,* Vol. 2, pp. 603–618. Nashville, TN: Abingdon Press, 2007. Examines the diverse cultural sources and the evolution of biblical concepts of God.

Levenson, Jon D. *The Death and Resurrection of the Beloved Son: The Transformation of Child Sacrifice in Judaism and Christianity.* New Haven, CT.: Yale UP, 1993. An important investigation of the biblical concept of God, approached though God's demand that Abraham sacrifice Isaac and the divine Father's own sacrifice of his son, Jesus.

Miles, Jack. *Christ: A Crisis in the Life of God.* New York: Knopf, 2001. Examines God as incarnate in Christ.

———. *God: A Biography.* New York: Knopf, 1995. Analyzes the Israelite God as a literary character in the Hebrew Bible.

Miller, Patrick D. *The Religion of Ancient Israel.* Louisville, KY: Westminster John Knox Press, 2000. Analyzes the growth of Israel's God concept, emphasizing parallels to other ancient Near Eastern views of divinity.

Richardson, Neil G. "God, New Testament View of." In K. D. Sakenfeld, ed., *The New Interpreter's Dictionary of the Bible*, Vol. 2, pp. 595–603. Nashville, TN: Abingdon Press, 2007. Because God rarely appears in New Testament documents, surveys Christian writers' assumptions about God and his revelation through Jesus.

Russell, Jeffrey B. *The Devil: Perceptions of Evil from Antiquity to Primitive Christianity.* Ithaca, NY: Cornell University Press, 1978. Examines the historical process by which negative qualities earlier ascribed to God are eventually transferred to humanity's enemy, "the Satan."

Smith, Mark S. *The Memoirs of God: History, Memory, and the Experience of the Divine in Ancient Israel.* Minneapolis: Fortress Press, 2004. A scholarly analysis of biblical ideas about God as they evolved in a Near Eastern context.

Stackhouse, John G., Jr. *Can God Be Trusted? Faith and the Challenge of Evil.* New York: Oxford UP, 1998. Defends traditional concepts of divine justice.

Turner, Alice. *The History of Hell.* New York: Harcourt Brace, 1993. Describes the social and legal environment of Rome in the second century CE that provided a context for Christian ideas about hell.

Glossary

Aaron Brother of Moses and Miriam, Israel's first High Priest.

Aaronites Priestly descendants of Aaron.

Abel The second son of Adam and Eve and brother of Cain, who murdered him.

Abimelech In Genesis, (1) a king of Gerar at whose court Abraham presented his wife Sarah as his sister; (2) a Philistine king at Gerar to whom Isaac passed off his wife Rebekah as his sister. (3) In Judges, the son of Gideon who made himself king at Shechem.

Abraham First called "Abram," meaning "exalted father"; in Genesis 12–24, the chief ancestor of Israel through his son Isaac. See also **patriarch.**

Abraham's bosom In Luke's parable of Lazarus and the rich man, a term designating a position of divine favor in the afterlife.

Abrahamic Covenant The series of unconditional promises that Yahweh makes to Abraham, including vows to give his descendants the territory of Canaan, the divine presence, and a line of kings, and to make them a source of universal blessing.

Absalom In 2 Samuel, the son of David who leads an uprising against his father but who is killed by David's general Joab.

abyss In Genesis, the term used to describe the precreation watery chaos out of which God created the universe. In the New Testament, the abode of evil forces and the subterranean prison where the devil is confined for 1,000 years.

acrostic In Hebrew poetry, a series of lines or verses of which the first words begin with consecutive letters of the Hebrew alphabet, as in Psalm. 119.

Adam In Genesis, Yahweh's first human creation, an "earthling" composed of clay and animated by the divine breath. In Romans 5 and 1 Corinthians 15, Paul contrasts Adam, a symbol of mortality, with Christ, through whom God grants eternal life.

Adonai A Hebrew word (meaning "Lord") applied to Israel's God, commonly as a substitute for the divine name "Yahweh."

Ahasuerus In Esther, the name for the Persian emperor, thought to refer to Xerxes I (reigned 486–465 BCE).

Ahaz King of Judah (c. 735–716 BCE) and father of Hezekiah, who succeeded him.

Ai A name meaning "ruin," a Canaanite city that Joshua supposedly conquered, but that archaeologists found was already an abandoned site in the thirteenth century BCE when the Israelites allegedly invaded Palestine.

Akenaton The name of the pharaoh Amenhotep IV (reigned 1364–1347 BCE), adopted when he made the sun god Aton (Aten) Egypt's only officially recognized god. See also henotheism.

Akkad (Accad) The area of Mesopotamia lying north of Sumer, center of the world's first empire under Sargon I (c. 2334–2279 BCE).

Akkadian (Accadian) (1) The period when the Semitic dynasty that Sargon I established dominated Mesopotamia (twenty-fourth to twenty-second centuries BCE). (2) The Akkadian language, a Semitic tongue (written in cuneiform script) spoken in Mesopotamia from about the twenty-eighth to the first centuries BCE.

Alexander the Great Son of King Philip of Macedonia who conquered most of the known world from Greece to western India, introducing Greek language and culture (Hellenism) to the entire Near East, including Egypt and Palestine (reigned 336–323 BCE).

Alexandria Major city that Alexander founded on the Egyptian coast, home to a large Jewish colony that produced the Septuagint, a Greek edition of the Tanakh.

allegory A literary narrative in which persons, places, and events have a symbolic meaning. In the Hellenistic era, Jewish scholars such as Philo of Alexandria interpreted the Hebrew Bible allegorically, as does Paul in Galatians 4.

alpha The first letter of the Greek alphabet. See also **omega.**

Amalekites Nomadic tribes, supposedly descended from Esau, with whom the early Israelites repeatedly were at war.

Amarna Age Term describing the reign of Amenhotep IV (Akhenaton), who built a new capital at Amarna, Egypt.

amen Derived from a Hebrew word, it signifies agreement ("so be it").

Ammon A tribal state located northeast of the Dead Sea; a traditional enemy of Israel.

Ammonites A Semitic group supposedly descended from Abraham's nephew Lot that frequently harassed the Israelites (Gen. 19:38).

Amorites A Semitic people (called "Westerners" or "highlanders"), who founded the cities of Babylon and Mari about 2000 BCE; Hammurabi was their most famous ruler.

Amos A shepherd and arborist from Judea who proclaimed Yahweh's words condemning practices in the northern kingdom of Israel, the earliest prophet to have his oracles collected under his name.

Andrew A Galilean fisherman who, with his brother Peter (Cephas), formed part of Jesus' inner circle of disciples.

angel From a Greek word meaning "messenger," a member of Yahweh's heavenly council, typically conveying God's messages to human recipients. The Tanakh and New Testament name only two angels, Michael and Gabriel, although the Apocrypha lists others, such as Uriel and Raphael.

Annas A former High Priest and father-in-law to Caiaphas, at whose residence Jesus was brought to trial, an incident appearing only in John's Gospel.

Annunciation A term describing Gabriel's announcement to Mary of Nazareth that she is to bear a son, Jesus, who would inherit David's throne.

anointed The literal meaning of the Hebrew word *mashiah,* a term applied to Davidic kings who were consecrated in office by the ritual pouring of holy oil on their heads. See **Messiah.**

anthropomorphism The practice of attributing human qualities to something not human, particularly the ascribing of human shape and form to a deity.

anti-Christ The ultimate enemy of Jesus Christ who appears during End time (2 and 3 John).

antinomianism A term (meaning "opponents of law") applied to some early Christian groups who argued that faith in Jesus freed them from obeying traditional legal or ethical restraints.

Antioch (1) In Syria, the capital of Seleucid kings; under Roman rule, the city where Jesus' followers were first called Christians (Acts 11:26) and where Paul had his missionary headquarters. (2) Pisidian Antioch, a major city in Galatia (Asia Minor), where Paul founded a church.

Antiochus The name of several Seleucid kings, the most notorious of whom was Antiochus IV (175–163 BCE), whose attempt to destroy the Jewish religion triggered the Maccabean Revolt.

antitheses The term scholars apply to the section of Matthew's Sermon on the Mount in which Jesus contrasts selected provisions of the Mosaic Law with his own ethical directions (Matt. 5:21–48).

Antonius Felix See **Felix, Antonius.**

Anu The head of the older generation of Mesopotamian gods, the Babylonian version of the Sumerian sky god An, whose name means "heaven."

aphorism A brief, memorable statement that expresses a (commonly ignored) truth about human experience, a favorite rhetorical device of Jesus.

'Apiru The Egyptian version of the term *Habiru.*

apocalypse From the Greek *apokalypsis,* meaning to "uncover" or to "reveal"; refers to a special kind of prophetic writing that claims to unveil otherwise hidden realities of the spirit realm and/or to disclose future events, typically of an eschatological nature.

apocalyptic literature A branch of prophetic writing that flourished in Judaism from about 200 BCE to 140 CE and that greatly influenced Christianity. Jewish apocalyptic works include the canonical Daniel and the noncanonical 1 and 2 Enoch, 2 and 3 Baruch, and 2 Esdras. Revelation is the only full-fledged apocalypse in the New Testament canon, but many apocalyptic themes appear in Paul's letters and the Synoptic Gospels.

Apocrypha A Greek term meaning "hidden things"; refers to deuterocanonical books such as Tobit and 1 Maccabees that were included in the Septuagint but not in the Hebrew Bible (Tanakh).

apodictic law Also called "absolute law"; refers to legal commands cast in unconditional form and without qualifying phrases, such as the Exodus command to honor no god but Yahweh.

apokalypsis The English transliteration of the Greek term meaning a "revelation"; typically an unveiling of future history or the invisible heavenly realm.

Apollos A Christian Jew from Alexandria, Egypt, noted for his eloquence; an associate of Paul in Corinth.

apostasy The act of abandoning or rejecting a previously held religious belief; from a Greek term meaning "to revolt." Persons who criticize or reject doctrines of their religious groups are commonly labeled apostates.

apostle In the New Testament, a person "sent" or commissioned to represent Jesus and his teachings, such as (but not restricted to) the twelve disciples listed in the Synoptic Gospels. According to Acts 1, an apostle was one who had accompanied Jesus during his earthly ministry and who also had seen the risen Lord, a definition that excludes persons such as Paul, who had not known Jesus in life but who vigorously maintained his right to be recognized as an apostle.

Aquilla With his wife Priscilla, an associate of Paul.

Aram (1) In Genesis, the son of Shem and grandson of Noah; (2) the territory north and east of Palestine, corresponding to the modern area of northern Syrian and northwestern Iraq, a region settled by some of Abraham's descendants from which Isaac and Jacob took their wives.

Aramaic A west Semitic language closely related to Hebrew that became the official language of the Persian Empire after about 500 BCE; the tongue commonly spoken by Jews after the exile and the language in which several late books of the Hebrew Bible were composed. Jesus probably spoke a Galilean dialect of Aramaic.

archetype The primal form or original pattern from which all other things of a like nature are descended; refers to characters, ideas, or actions that represent the supreme and/or essential examples of a universal type, as Moses is the archetypal model of prophet and lawgiver and David of a kingly ruler.

ark The rectangular wooden houseboat that Noah built to contain his family and pairs of all animals during the Genesis Flood.

Ark of the Covenant The portable wooden shrine, covered in gold leaf, that the Israelites built and carried with them during their journey through the Sinai wilderness. Guarded by golden images of cherubim, it was later kept in the Jerusalem Temple. Its fate is unknown.

Armageddon A Greek transliteration of the Hebrew place-name *Har-Megiddon* or "Mountain of Megiddo," a famous battlefield in ancient Israel; symbolizes the site of the ultimate battle between good and evil (Rev. 16:16).

Artaxerxes The emperor of Persia who commissioned his Jewish courtier Nehemiah to go to Jerusalem to rebuild its defensive walls.

Ascension A term denoting the risen Jesus' ascent to heaven (Acts 1:6–11).

Asclepius A human son of the god Apollo and a moral women; allegedly the first physician. Granted posthumous immortality, he became a patron of medicine and healing who was worshiped throughout the Greco-Roman world.

Asherah The Hebrew name for the Canaanite goddess Asherat, "Lady of the Sea," a consort of El, Canaan's chief god, whom some Israelites apparently included in their worship of Yahweh.

Ashurbanipal IV King of Assyria (c. 668–627 BCE) and grandson of Sennacherib, who made a large collection of cuneiform texts at Nineveh, including copies of the Gilgamesh epic.

Assur (Asshur) (1) King of the Assyrian gods and patron of war; (2) Assyria's first capital city; (3) the name of the country from which the Assyrians took their name.

Assyria A large territory centered along the upper Tigris River in Mesopotamia; (2) the empire that dominated the Near East from the eleventh to the seventh centuries BCE; it destroyed the state of Israel (721 BCE) but was overthrown by a coalition of Babylonians and Medes in 612 BCE.

Assyrians The "people of Assur" (god of war), who controlled most of the Near East from about 1100 to 612 BCE; although they failed to capture Jerusalem, they destroyed Israel and imposed ruinous taxes on Judean kings.

Athaliah The only woman (and non-Davidic ruler) to head the state of Judah; reigned in Jerusalem from 842 to 837 BCE, when Temple priests murdered her.

Athanasius A bishop of Alexandria; the first Christian leader to list the present order and contents of the New Testament canon (367 CE).

Athens A leading city and cultural center in Greece, virtually the only place where Paul was neither mobbed nor imprisoned but was invited to speak at a public forum about his new religious message (Acts 17).

Aton (Aten) The Egyptian sun god whom Akhenaton proclaimed the sole deity worthy of national worship.

Atonement, Day of (Yom Kippur) The annual fall ceremony at which Israel's High Priest offered animal sacrifices for the people's collective sins in order to reconcile them to God (Lev. 16). See also **scapegoat.**

Atrahasis A phrase meaning "extra-wise," applied to Utnapishtim, hero of the Mesopotamian flood story.

Augustus The first emperor of Rome (27 BCE–14 CE); brought an end to civil war and established the *pax romana* (Roman peace). In official inscriptions, he was commonly described as "son of a god."

Azazel In Leviticus, the unidentified place or demon to which a sacrificial goat was sent on the Day of Atonement.

Baal A Canaanite-Phoenician term meaning "lord" or "master," the son of El and god of storm and rain that gives life to growing things. Before the exile to Babylon, he was Yahweh's chief rival for Israel's worship.

Babel A term meaning the "gate of God." The "tower of Babel" was a ziggurat (Gen. 11).

Babylon An ancient city on the Euphrates River, the capital of both the Old and Neo-Babylonian empires. Under Nebuchadnezzar II (reigned 605–562 BCE), it destroyed Jerusalem and its Temple (587 BCE) and deported the Judean ruling classes to Mesopotamia. In Revelation, it is the code word for Rome, which also destroyed Yahweh's sanctuary.

Babylonian exile The period between 587 and 538 BCE when Judah's upper classes were held captive in Babylon. An earlier deportation of Jewish leaders in 597 BCE included the prophet Ezekiel.

Balaam A fortune-teller whom Balak, king of Moab, hired to curse the Israelites, but whom Yahweh caused to pronounce a blessing on Israel instead (Num. 22–24).

ban The practice of holy war in which all defeated peoples are killed in God's name. According to Deuteronomy, the Israelites were to place all Canaanites under the ban.

baptism From the Greek word meaning "to immerse," a rite of initiation into the Christian community that Paul interprets as a symbolic dying (submersion in water) and rising with Christ. As John practiced it, baptism was a ritual cleansing from sin in preparation for the arrival of God's kingdom (Mark 1:4; Matt. 3:5–12).

Barak An early Israelite judge (military leader), apparently subordinate to the prophet Deborah.

bar An Aramaic word meaning "son of."

bar Kochba Simeon bar Kosiba (nicknamed bar Kochba, "son of a Star"), the messianic leader of a Jewish revolt against Rome (132–135 CE), which culminated in a second destruction of Jerusalem.

Barabbas A condemned murderer whom Pontius Pilate released in place of Jesus.

Barnabas A prominent leader of the Christian community in Jerusalem and Antioch, and a mentor to Paul.

Baruch A friend and secretary to the prophet Jeremiah, supposed author of the deuterocanonical book bearing his name.

Bathsheba The wife of Uriah, a Hittite soldier whom David employed and whose death David arranged in order to marry her; she became the mother of Solomon.

Beatitudes The list of blessings upon the poor and merciful that begins Jesus' Sermon on the Mount (Matt. 5:3–12; cf. Luke 6:20–23).

Beersheba A site marking the traditional southern boundary of ancient Israel.

Behemoth A mysterious beast probably derived from Mesopotamian myth, but sometimes identified with the hippopotamus. See also **Leviathan.**

Bel The Babylonian-Assyrian version of Baal and a common name for Marduk, the chief Babylonian deity.

Belshazzar In Daniel, a son of Nebuchadnezzar and the last king of Babylon. Archaeological discoveries indicate that he was instead a son of Nabonidus who acted as his father's regent at the time of Babylon's fall to Cyrus the Great (539 BCE).

Beltshazzar The name his Babylonian supervisors gave to Daniel.

bene ha Elohim A Hebrew phrase commonly translated as "sons of God," although it can also mean "sons of the gods [plural]"; describes members of Yahweh's heavenly council (Job 1–2).

Benjamin The twelfth and last son of Jacob, second son of Jacob's wife Rachel and the full brother of Joseph, traditional founder of the tribe of Benjamin, which became part of the southern kingdom of Judah.

Bethel An ancient site (meaning "house of God") where Abraham and Jacob established shrines and that, under Jeroboam I, became an important sanctuary in the northern kingdom of Israel.

Bethlehem A village about five miles south of Jerusalem, the birthplace of David and the traditional site of the Messiah's birth (Micah 5:2; Matt. 2; Luke 2).

Bible From the Greek *biblia*, meaning "little books," a collection of Jewish and Christian sacred writings commonly divided into two main sections—the Hebrew Bible (Old Testament) and the later Christian Greek Scriptures (New Testament).

Bildad One of Job's three friends who defend traditional concepts of divine justice.

bishop From the Greek *episcopes*, meaning "overseer," the supervisor or presiding officer of a church.

Bithynia A Roman province in northern Asia Minor (modern Turkey) along the Black Sea coast, the location of several Christian churches.

blasphemy Speech that allegedly offends God and/or his representatives.

Boanegeres "Sons of Thunder," a phrase Jesus uses to describe the brothers James and John (Mark 3:17).

Boaz A wealthy landowner in Bethlehem who married the Moabite Ruth and became an ancestor of David.

Book of the Covenant A collection of ancient laws that now appears in Exodus 20:23–23:33; the code takes its name from Exodus 24:7.

Caesar A hereditary name by which the Roman emperors commemorated Gaius Julius Caesar, great-uncle of Augustus, the first emperor.

Caesarea The port city that Herod built on the Mediterranean coast about sixty-four miles northwest of Jerusalem; Paul was imprisoned there for two years.

Caesarea Philippi An inland city located north of the Sea of Galilee, the site of Peter's recognition that Jesus was Israel's Messiah.

Caiaphas Joseph Caiaphas, High Priest of Jerusalem during the reign of the emperor Tiberius (14–37 CE), the leader who turned Jesus over to the Roman governor Pilate.

Cain The first son of Adam and Eve, who killed his younger brother Abel; Yahweh gave him a special mark that protected him from his enemies.

Caleb With Joshua, one of the two Israelite leaders of his generation that Yahweh allowed to enter the Promised Land.

Calvary From the Latin word *calveria* (a translation of the Greek *kranion,* meaning "skull"), the site of Jesus' crucifixion outside Jerusalem's walls; Calvary was also called Golgotha, derived from the Aramaic term for "skull."

Canaan The Tanakh name for the territory of Palestine west of the Jordan River, from Egypt in the south to Syria in the north; according to Genesis, the land promised to Abraham's descendants.

canon From the Greek *kanon*, a list of books that a religious community honors as sacred and authoritative. See also **deuterocanon.**

Capernaum A small port on the northwestern shore of the Sea of Galilee that Jesus used as headquarters for his Galilean ministry.

Carchemish A Hittite city in northern Syria where Nebuchadnezzar defeated the Egyptian forces of Pharaoh Necho II (605 BCE), thereby making Babylon master of the Near East.

Carmel From a word meaning "garden" or "orchard," a heavily vegetated area extending from the hills of Samaria to the Mediterranean Sea. Sacred to Baal, Mount Carmel was the site of a contest between the prophet Elijah and the priests of Baal.

case law Law expressed in conditional terms: If such an act is committed, then such must be the punishment, a legal form characteristic of Mesopotamian and biblical law.

catholic epistles A collection of seven letters and letter-like documents placed in the New Testament between letters ascribed to Paul and the Book of Revelation. They are "catholic" in the sense of being general or "universal," addressed to the church as a whole.

centurion A Roman army officer in charge of a "century," or division of about 100 men.

Cephas A name meaning "stone" that Jesus bestowed on his disciple Simon Peter.

Chaldea A Mesopotamian region occupied by the Neo-Babylonian Empire; the Chaldeans were famous for their "wisdom," particularly in astronomy and astrology.

chaos The Greek term designating the original chasm or abyss that predated the world's creation; in the ancient Near East, it was typically portrayed as a vast, dark waste of boundless sea, out of which the cosmos emerged. See also **cosmos.**

Chemosh The national god of Moab, to whom children were sometimes sacrificed.

cherub, cherubim (pl.) Supernatural beings derived from Mesopotamian myth; hybrid creatures part bird, part human, and part animal (cf. Ezek. 1), golden images of which protected the Ark of the Covenant in the Jerusalem Temple.

Christ From the Greek *Christos,* a translation of the Hebrew *mashiah* (messiah, or "anointed one"). The term derives from the Israelite practice of anointing (pouring holy oil) on the heads of kings at the time of their coronation to designate their status as God's representative (cf. 2 Sam. 7; Ps. 2). Greek-speaking Christians applied the term to Jesus to denote his role as God's chosen agent.

Christology Theological interpretation of the nature and function of Christ, particularly doctrines about his divinity, relationship to God, prehuman existence, and role in creating the universe.

church From the Greek *ekklesia,* meaning "assembly of ones called out"; the term Matthew, Paul, and other New Testament writers used to denote the Christian community, the "people of God."

circumcision An ancient Semitic operation performed to remove the foreskin of the male organ; in Israel, the physical sign of belonging to the covenant community (Gen. 17). According to Acts and Paul's letters, the question of whether to circumcise Gentile converts to Christianity was an important source of controversy.

Claudius The fourth Roman emperor (reigned 41–54 CE), who reputedly expelled Jews from Rome (Acts 11:28; 18:2).

codex A manuscript book consisting of leaves bound together, a format that Christians commonly used to replace the more cumbersome scroll.

conquest of Canaan According to Joshua, the Israelites' military invasion of Canaan (Palestine) about 1200 BCE, a tradition that archaeology does not seem to support.

Constantine The first Christian emperor of Rome (reigned 306–337 CE), who began state support of the church and presided over the Council of Nicaea (325 CE), where churchmen debated the nature of Jesus' divinity and relationship to the Father.

Coptic A late form of the Egyptian language that, in Hellenistic times, was written using the Greek alphabet; the term also refers to the Copts, a people reputedly descended from the ancient Egyptians who preserved an early form of Christianity. The collection of texts found at Nag Hammadi in 1945 (including the Gospel of Thomas) was written in Coptic, as was the more recently discovered Gospel of Judas.

Corinth A large and prosperous port in Greece that the Romans made capital of the province called Achaia (Greece); Paul founded an important church there about 50 CE.

Cornelius According to Acts 10–11, a Roman centurion whom Peter made the first Gentile convert to Christianity.

cosmogony A theory or tradition about the origin or birth of the universe (cosmos).

cosmology A theory describing the natural order or structure of the universe.

cosmos The Greek term denoting the universe, viewed as an ordered system characterized by structure, stability, balance, and harmony. See also **chaos, cosmogony,** and **cosmology.**

Court History Also called the Succession Narrative; refers to the hypothetical document underlying the story of David's reign and Solomon's succession to Israel's throne, the source for the present account found in 2 Samuel 9–24 and 1 Kings 1–2.

covenant (1) An agreement or compact between individuals, such as Abraham and Abimelech (Gen. 21:27) or David and Jonathan (1 Sam. 18:3); (2) a vow or promise that Yahweh makes to selected people, such as Noah (Gen. 9:13) and Abraham (Gen. 15:18–21; 17:4–14); (3) a legal bond Yahweh forms with a chosen group, such as Israel, and the demands he makes for exclusive worship in return. In Christian tradition, Jesus introduced a "New Covenant (New Testament)" with his disciples (Mark 14:22–25; Matt. 26:26–29).

Covenant Code See **Book of the Covenant.**

cult The formalized practices of a religious group, particularly its system of sacrifice, worship, and public (or secret) rites.

cuneiform A system of writing featuring wedge-shaped symbols that originated in ancient Sumer about 3200 BCE and spread throughout Mesopotamia.

Cyrus the Great The founder of the Persian Empire and conqueror of Babylon (539 BCE) who liberated the Jews from captivity and encouraged their return to Jerusalem, the person Second Isaiah calls Yahweh's "messiah" (Isa. 45:1).

D See **Deuteronomists.**

Dagon The Canaanite agricultural deity that the Philistines worshiped at Ashdod and Gaza; according to Judges 16, Samson destroyed the Gaza temple.

Damascus The capital of Syria and terminus of ancient caravan routes in the Fertile Crescent, the site of Paul's experience of the risen Christ.

Dan (1) The son of Jacob and Rachel's servant, Bilhah; (2) one of the northern tribes of Israel; (3) a Danite city where Jeroboam established a cult center. The phrase "from Dan to Beersheba" (Judg. 20:1; 1 Kings 4:25, etc.) refers to the north-south extent of Israel's territory.

Danel (Daniel) An ancient king whose name (Danel) appears in the epics of Ugarit and whom Ezekiel cites, along with Noah and Job, as an example of righteousness (Ezek. 14:14, 20; cf. 28:3). He is not the same as the literary character in the Book of Daniel.

Darius The name of several Persian rulers mentioned in the Hebrew Bible: (1) Darius I, who continued Cyrus the

Great's favorable treatment of Jews (Ezra 5–6); (2) Darius "the Mede," alleged to have thrown Daniel into a lion's den, is unknown to history (Dan. 5:31; 6:7–26).

David The second king of a united twelve-tribe Israel (c. 1000–961 BCE) and founder of the Davidic dynasty. After the death of David's son Solomon, the ten northern tribes seceded from the union to form the state of Israel, although Davidic heirs continued to reign over the southern territory of Judah until Babylonian armies destroyed Jerusalem and ended the dynasty in 587 BCE.

Davidic Covenant (Royal Covenant) The idea that, according to Yahweh's sworn oath (2 Sam. 7:8–17), David's descendants were to rule over Israel "forever," an unconditional vow that was later modified to make the divine promise dependent on the Davidic rulers' obedience (1 Kings 8:25–26). After Nebuchadnezzar permanently ended the Davidic dynasty, the poet of Psalm 89 questioned the fidelity of Yahweh's word (Ps. 89:38–51).

Day of Atonement (Yom Kippur) See **Atonement, Day of.**

Day of Judgment See **Judgment, Day of.**

deacon A church office in early Christianity; one who serves or ministers.

Dead Sea Scrolls A collection of ancient Jewish manuscripts found preserved in caves near Qumran on the northwestern shore of the Dead Sea. Beginning in 1947, scholars recovered copies (most in fragmental form) of every book of the Tanakh (except Esther), as well as copies of works from the Apocrypha and Pseudepigrapha. Among the noncanonical documents were commentaries and other writings assumed to be the work of Essenes. See also **Essenes.**

Deborah A woman judge and prophet who, with Barak, helped lead the Israelites to a victory over Canaanite enemies (Judg. 4–5).

Decalogue From the Greek meaning "ten words," the Ten Commandments (Exod. 20; Deut. 5).

Delilah The woman whom the Philistines bribed to discover and betray the secret of Samson's strength (Judg. 16).

deuterocanon From the Greek meaning "second canon," refers to the fourteen books or parts of books included in the Septuagint edition but not in the Hebrew Bible (Tanakh). Deuterocanonical works include Judith, Tobit, and the Wisdom of Solomon.

Deutero-Isaiah See **Second Isaiah.**

Deuteronomist (D) The term scholars use to denote the unknown scribe(s) who compiled and edited the present Book of Deuteronomy.

Deuteronomistic History (DH) The scholarly term for the books of the Former Prophets, the historical narratives of Joshua through 2 Kings, that apply the principles of Deuteronomy to Israel's rise and fall.

devil The English word commonly used to translate two Greek words with different meanings: (1) *diabolos*, "the accuser" (John 8:44), and (2) *daimonion*, one of the many evil spirits believed to inhabit the world and to cause disease,

madness, and other afflictions. Revelation 12:9 identifies the Greek *diabolos* with the Hebrew Satan and the serpent of Genesis 3.

Diana of the Ephesians The Near Eastern form of the Greek Artemis, goddess of wild animals and the hunt (identified with the Roman Diana).

Diaspora Literally, a "scattering." The term refers to the distribution of Jews outside their Palestinian homeland, such as the many Jewish communities established throughout the Greco-Roman world.

Dionysus Born to Zeus, king of the Olympian gods, and Semele, a mortal woman; the Greek god of wine, ecstasy, and emotional liberation. The only Olympian to suffer death and resurrection to immortality, he also descended into the Underworld (Hades) before ascending to heaven. Also known as Bacchus, the Romans called him Liber.

disciple From the Greek for "learner," the follower of a religious figure such as Moses (John 9:28), the Baptist (Luke 11:1), the Pharisees (Mark 2:18), or Jesus (Matt. 14:26). A disciple is "taught," whereas an apostle is "sent." See also **apostle.**

Docetism From a Greek verb meaning "to seem," a belief—commonly associated with Gnostic Christianity—that Jesus only appeared to be physically human, but was really a pure spirit.

Domitian Roman emperor (reigned 81–96 CE), younger son of Vespasian, during whose reign the Book of Revelation was probably composed (c. 95 CE).

documentary hypothesis A scholarly theory that the Pentateuch is not the work of one author, such as Moses, but the product of many generations of anonymous scribes and editors; the hypothetical four main sources are known as J (the Yahwist), E (the Elohist), D (the Deuteronomist), and P (the priestly writer(s)).

doxology In a religious writing or service, the formal concluding expression of praise ascribing glory to God.

Dragon The image that Revelation 12 applies to Satan, portrayed as the embodiment of chaotic evil that opposes God and his purpose in the world. Whereas the dragon figure was originally a Near Eastern symbol of the forces of disorder that preceded creation, apocalyptic writers later transformed it into a supernatural monster to be defeated at End time.

dualism A philosophic or religious system that posits the existence of two parallel worlds, one of physical matter and the other of invisible spirit. Moral dualism, held by most apocalyptic writers, views the universe as divided between powers good and evil, and light and dark, which contend for human allegiance.

E See **Elohist.**

Ea The Babylonian god of wisdom and benefactor to humanity who warned Utnapishtim (the Babylonian Noah) of a coming deluge and instructed him to build an ark.

Edom In Hebrew Bible times, a region or country extending southward from the Dead Sea to the Gulf of ʿAqaba, bordered on the north by Moab, the northwest by Judah, and the southeast by the Sinai Peninsula. It was also called "Seir"; its inhabitants supposedly descended from Jacob's twin brother Esau (Gen. 36:1).

Edomites According to Genesis, the descendants of Esau, a Semitic people who occupied the territory southeast of Judah and were among Israel's bitterest enemies, participating in the Babylonian sack of Jerusalem (Ps. 137).

Egypt The world's first nation-state, centered along the Nile River, where Abraham's descendants settled and where they became enslaved until led to freedom by Moses in the Exodus (c. 1280–1250 BCE). Several Davidic kings made alliances with Egypt to defend them against aggressive Mesopotamian states, such as Assyria and Babylon.

El, Elohim (pl.) A Semitic term for a divine being; in the Canaanite religion, El was the chief god, father of lesser deities such as Baal. Hebrew Bible writers commonly associate El with Yahweh (Exod. 3; 6; cf. Gen. 14:18–23). Early Israelites saw themselves as the people of El (Gen. 33:20). See also **El Shaddai.**

Elihu In Job, a young man who condemned Job's alleged self-righteousness.

Elijah A name meaning "Yahweh is my God"; was a prophet from the northern kingdom who led attacks on King Ahab's tolerance of cults of Baal (ninth century BCE). He was reportedly carried to heaven in a fiery chariot (2 Kings 2) and was expected to reappear at End time (Mal. 4:5–6). The Synoptic Gospels identify John the Baptist as the returned Elijah (Mark 9:12–13; Luke 1:17); along with Moses, he appears at Jesus' Transfiguration (Mark 9:4; Matt. 17:3).

Eliphaz The most moderate and restrained of Job's critics.

Elisha The prophetic successor to Elijah, famous for his miracles, who anointed Jehu to replace Ahab as king of Israel (ninth century BCE).

Elizabeth The wife of the Levite priest Zechariah and mother of John the Baptist.

Elohim Plural form of El, the generic term for God, commonly used for Israel's God.

Elohist (E) The scholarly term designating the anonymous scribe responsible for the E material (probably oral traditions from the northern kingdom) incorporated into the Pentateuch to supplement the Yahwist (J) narrative, so named because he used *Elohim* rather than "Yahweh" to denote Israel's God.

El Shaddai A Hebrew phrase commonly translated "God Almighty," although scholars believe it probably means "God of the Mountain," referring to the concept of a cosmic mountain inhabited by divine beings. Yahweh is associated with Mount Sinai/Horeb.

Emmaus A village near Jerusalem (site unknown) where the risen Jesus appeared to two disciples (Luke 24:13–32).

Enoch A son of Cain (Gen. 4:17) or Jared (Gen. 5:18) and father of Methuselah (Gen. 5:21), whom God apparently transported to heaven. Several noncanonical books, such as 1 Enoch (quoted as Scripture in the letter of Jude), are ascribed to him.

Enuma Elish The Babylonain creation epic that takes its name from the opening phrase (in Akkadian) "when above." It depicts the God Marduk creating the world from an original watery chaos by a process of separation and division.

Ephraim (1) A son of Joseph whom Jacob adopted; (2) the Israelite territory that the tribe of Ephraim occupied. Because of this tribe's political dominance, Israel was commonly called "Ephraim" (Hos. 11).

Ephesus A wealthy Hellenistic city, in New Testament times the capital of the Roman province of Asia, site of the famous temple of Artemis (Diana); Paul probably composed his letters to the Corinthians from there.

Epicureanism A Greco-Roman philosophy founded by Epicurus that advocated avoiding pain and pursuing intellectual rather than sensual pleasures. Epicurus taught that the universe is entirely physical, including the human soul, which perishes at death.

epiphany An appearance or manifestation, particularly of a divine being, typically sudden and accompanied by dramatic natural effects (Exod. 3; 6; 19; 24; Job 38–42).

epistle A formal letter intended to be read publicly.

eponym The person from whom a people or group is reported to have taken its name.

Esau The firstborn son of Isaac and Rebekah, twin brother of Jacob, who gave up his birthright to his cleverer sibling; the eponymous ancestor of the Edomites.

eschatology From the Greek, meaning a "study of last things," the scholarly term for beliefs about events at End time, including tribulations leading to God's final victory over evil, universal judgment, and the ultimate fate of individuals.

Essenes According to Josephus, one of the three major religious parties of first-century Judaism, an apocalyptic group that apparently formed during the Maccabean period and that most scholars believe produced the Dead Sea Scrolls. See also **Qumran.**

Esther The heroine of the canonical book bearing her name, cousin and adopted daughter of Mordecai, queen of Persia under Xerxes.

etiology A statement of causes or origins; in literary terms, a narrative created to explain the origin or meaning of a social practice, topographical feature, ritual, or other factor that arouses the storyteller's interest.

Eucharist From the Greek word meaning "gratitude" or "thanksgiving," the Christian ceremony of consecrated bread and wine that Jesus initiated at the Last Supper (Mark 14:22–25; 1 Cor. 11:23–26).

Euphrates River The longest river of southwest Asia, along which the earliest Mesopotamian cities were built; listed as one of the four rivers of Eden (Gen. 2:14).

Eusebius A Christian scholar (c. 260–339 CE) who composed the *History of the Church* (through about 323 CE) and forty other works, including a biography of Constantine, the first Christian emperor.

Evangelist From the Greek *evangelion*, meaning "good news"; the author of a Gospel.

Eve The first woman, wife of Adam, who derived her name from the Hebrew verb "to live," "because she was the mother of all living" (Gen. 3:30).

exegesis The close analysis and interpretation of a literary text to discover the original author's intended meaning and/or purpose in writing. After that, other interpretations consistent with the text are possible.

exile The period during which upper-class Jews were held captive in Babylon (587–538 BCE); the beginning of the Jewish Diaspora (dispersion outside the Palestinian homeland).

exogamy The act or practice of marrying outside of one's tribe or ethnic group; its opposite is endogamy.

exorcism The act or practice of expelling a demon or evil spirit from a person or place, a prominent aspect of Jesus' ministry in the Synoptic Gospels but not mentioned in John.

expiation In religious terms, the act of making atonement for sin, usually by offering a sacrifice to appease divine wrath (Lev. 16; Heb. 9).

Exodus From a Greek word meaning a "going out" or "departure," referring to the escape of Israelite slaves from Egypt under Moses' leadership (c. 1280–1250 BCE).

Ezekiel A major prophet of the sixth century BCE, exiled to Babylon, who was distinguished by his strange visions and priestly interests. The name means "God strengthens."

Ezra (Esdras) A postexilic Jewish priest who returned to Jerusalem from Babylon during the reign of the Persian emperor Artaxeres to proclaim and enforce obedience to the Mosaic Torah in the partly restored Jerusalem community (Neh. 8–10; Ezra 7–10).

Fall, the A belief that when Adam disobeyed God by eating forbidden fruit, the effects of his sin passed to all humanity, which collectively "fell" from a position of divine grace. See also **original sin.**

Felix, Antonius The Roman procurator of Judea (52–59 CE) before whom Paul was tried at Caesarea.

Fertile Crescent The semicircular or crescent-shaped slice of land that curves from the head of the Persian Gulf on the northeast to Egypt on the southwest and including Mesopotamia, Syria, and Palestine.

Festus, Porcius The procurator of Judea (c. 59–62 CE) whom Nero appointed to succeed Felix and through whom Paul appealed to be tried by Caesar's court in Rome.

firmament The biblical term for the vault or arch of the sky that separated the earthly oceans from the heavenly ocean of rain-giving clouds and in which Elohim placed the sun, moon, and stars (Gen. 1; 7:11).

Flavius Josephus See **Josephus, Flavius.**

Flood, the The global deluge of Noah's day (Gen. 6–8), apparently based on ancient Mesopotamian flood traditions akin to that found in the Gilgamesh epic; a catastrophe used as a prototype of later world judgment (Matt. 24:36–42; 2 Pet. 2:5; 3:5–7).

form criticism The English translation of the German *Formsgeschicte*, a method of biblical criticism that attempts to identify, classify, and analyze individual units or characteristic forms contained in a literary text and to find the probable preliterary form of these units before their incorporation into the written text, including the "life-setting" in which they originated. Torah narratives and the Gospels feature many self-contained individual units that probably circulated independently in oral form before being included in longer written narratives. See also **pericope.**

Fourth Gospel The Gospel of John, so-called to emphasize its differences in form and content from the first three Gospels (the Synoptics).

fundamentalism A largely North American Protestant movement, beginning about 1900, that insists on the literal factuality of all biblical statements; a rejection of post-Enlightenment questioning of biblical infallibility.

Gabriel In Daniel and Luke, an archangel who conveys God's decrees to human agents; with Michael, one of the two named angels in canonical Scripture.

Galatia A region in the interior of Asia Minor (Turkey), settled by Gauls; a Roman province that Paul visited. Paul's letter to a Galatian church outlines his doctrine of salvation by faith.

Galilee The region of northern Palestine lying west of the Jordan River, where Jesus grew up and conducted much of his public ministry.

Galilee, Sea of The largest body of fresh water in northern Palestine, source of livelihood to many Galilean fishermen, such as Peter, Andrew, James, and John (Matt. 4).

Gallio A procounsul of Achaia (the Roman province of Greece) who dismissed the Corinthians' charges against Paul (Acts 18). Appointed to his office about 50–51 CE (he did not serve a full two-year term), the time of Gallio's tenure offers one of the few solid dates in fixing Paul's chronology.

Gamaliel A leading first-century-CE Pharisee and scholar, the reputed teacher of Paul (Acts 5:34–40).

Gehenna The New Testament name for the "Valley of the Sons [or Children] of Hinnom," a topographical depression bordering Jerusalem on the south and west; the site of human sacrifices (Jer. 7:32), it later became a visible symbol of punishment in the afterlife (Matt. 10:28–29; 18:8; 25:30, 46) and is commonly rendered as "hell" in English translations.

genealogy A minihistory of descent, either for an individual or a group, listing a succession of fathers and sons; biblical writers commonly use such lists as linking devices between narrative units.

Gentile Someone who is not a Jew; an uncircumcised person; one belonging to the (non-Israelite) nations, with whom God had no formal covenant (Ps. 9:17; Isa. 2:2; cf. Acts 10–11, 15).

Gethsemane The site of a garden or orchard on the Mount of Olives near Jerusalem where Jesus took his disciples after the Last Supper; the place where he was arrested (Mark 14).

Gideon Also called *Jerubbaal,* meaning "let Baal contend," a reluctant judge (military leader) who delivered Israel from the Midianites (Judg. 6–8).

Gilgamesh, Epic of The ancient Sumero-Babylonian narrative about the adventures of Gilgamesh, legendary king of Uruk, fragments of which date from shortly after 3000 BCE; it is celebrated for its account of a global deluge, from which only Utnapishtim and his family are saved.

gnosis The Greek word for "knowledge."

Gnosticism A widespread and extremely diverse movement in early Christianity that apparently emphasized the supreme importance of the individual soul and its origin in heaven; only special knowledge (*gnosis*) of one's spiritual origins—revealed by a savior figure such as Jesus—would allow the soul to recover its immortal destiny.

Gog The term Ezekiel uses to depict a future leader of Israel's enemies (Ezek. 38), whose attack on Jerusalem will bring about Yahweh's intervention and the ultimate destruction of the wicked (Rev. 20:8).

golden calf (1) An image that some Israelites fashioned out of gold jewelry and other treasures taken from Egypt and that, under Aaron's direction, they worshiped as their deliverer from slavery (Exod. 32:1–6); (2) two calf images that Jeroboam I set up at Bethel and Dan as rivals to the Jerusalem Temple. Such images were probably regarded as visible pedestals for the invisibly enthroned Yahweh.

Goliath The Philistine giant from Gath whom the young David defeated with a slingshot (1 Sam. 17).

Gomer The unfaithful wife of the prophet Hosea, perhaps a symbol of Israel's disloyalty to Yahweh.

Gospel When capitalized, a literary narrative about Jesus (and/or a collection of his teachings); when uncapitalized, it refers to the Christian message, literally meaning "good news."

Habakkuk A prophet of the late seventh or early sixth century BCE whose oracles concern Babylon's imminent threat to Judah.

Hades The Greek god of the Underworld, which was named after him; the term Septuagint editors used to translate the Hebrew *Sheol,* the subterranean abode of the dead (cf. Rev. 1:18; 20:14). See also **Sheol.**

Hagar Sarah's Egyptian slave, who bore Abraham's son Ishmael and whom Yahweh rescued after Sarah jealously expelled her from Abraham's household (Gen. 16, 21).

haggadah Jewish narrative writings dating from the early centuries CE that illustrate and interpret the nonlegal portions of the Torah.

Haggai A postexilic prophet who, with his contemporary Zechariah, urged the partly restored community of Jerusalem to rebuild the Temple (c. 520 BCE).

Haibru An ancient Near Eastern term designating people or clans who were outside the urban social and legal structure; they appear to have been nomads who raided settled populations during the Amarna period (fourteenth century BCE); although scholars once believed that the biblical Hebrews may have been related to these groups, they recently abandoned this theory.

halakah A collection of Jewish interpretations and applications of the Mosaic Law dating from the early centuries CE; the core of the legal sections of the Talmud.

Ham A son of Noah and the father of Canaan; considered the ancestor of various nations in Africa, Phoenicia, and west Arabia (Gen. 6, 7, 9).

Haman An official at Ahasuerus's (Xerxes') court who plotted a massacre of Jews throughout the Persian Empire (Esther 3, 7).

Hammurabi The sixth king of Babylon's First Dynasty (1792–1750 BCE) and founder of the first Amorite Empire in Mesopotamia; his famous law code was inscribed in Akkadian cuneiform, using legal forms anticipating those of biblical covenant law. See also **Code of Hammurabi.**

Hannah The wife of Elkanah and mother of the priest-prophet Samuel (1 Sam. 1–2).

Haran An ancient trade center on the Euphrates River in northwestern Mesopotamia, the site of Yahweh's first call to Abraham (Gen. 12). Later the last refuge of the Assyrians, the Medes destroyed it about 606 BCE.

Hasidim The term describing devout Jews who refused to forsake their ancestral faith when Antiochus IV attempted to destroy the Mosaic religion (second century BCE).

Hasmodians The Jewish royal dynasty that the Maccabees founded (mid-second century BCE), named for Hasmon, an ancestor of Mattathias. The Roman conquest of Palestine in 63 BCE brought Hasmonean rulership and Jewish independence to an end.

Hebrew (1) A member or descendant of one of a group of northwestern Semitic peoples, including the Israelites, Edomites, and Moabites (Gen. 10); biblical writers commonly use the term to describe the covenant people before their settlement in Canaan; (2) the west Semitic language spoken by the Israelites and in which most of the Hebrew Bible is written.

Hebrew Bible Also known as the Tanakh for its three-fold division into Torah (divine teaching), Nevi'im (Prophets), and Kethuvim (Writings); the collection of documents in Hebrew and/or Aramaic known to Christians as the Old Testament (referring to God's "testaments" or covenants with Israel). Catholic and Eastern Orthodox editions include deutero-canonical works (the Apocrypha) excluded from the Tanakh.

Hebron An ancient town nineteen miles southwest of Jerusalem, located near the site where Yahweh announced that Abraham would soon have a son (Isaac).

Hellenism The influence and adoption of Greek language, thought, values, and customs that began with Alexander's conquest of the Persian Empire (fourth century BCE).

Hellenistic Greek-like, pertaining to the historical period following Alexander's death in 323 BCE during which Greek language and culture permeated the eastern Mediterranean region, as well as most of the Near East.

Hellenization The diffusion of Greek language and culture (Hellenism) throughout the Mediterranean region, beginning with Alexander's conquests (fourth century BCE) and continuing into the period of Roman dominance. The Maccabean Revolt was partly a rejection of Hellenization among Palestinian Jews.

henotheism The worship of a single god while conceding that other gods may also exist (Pss. 95:3; 97:9).

herem In holy war, the practice of dedicating conquered populations and their possessions to the victors' deity and offering them as a mass sacrifice (Deut. 13:12–17; Josh. 6:15–21; 1 Sam. 5:1–22).

heresy Holding an opinion contrary to that officially endorsed by religious authorities or persons in power. Applied to early Christianity by its detractors (Acts 24:14), the term was not generally used in its modern sense during New Testament times except in the pastoral epistles (1 Tim. 1:1; Titus 3:10).

Herod The name of seven Palestinian rulers: (1) Herod I (the Great), the Idumean Roman-appointed ruler of Palestine (37–4 BCE) when Jesus was born, who lavishly rebuilt the Jerusalem Temple; (2) Herod Antipas, son of Herod I, tetrarch of Galilee and Perea (4 BCE–39 CE), who had John the Baptist beheaded; (3) Herod Archaelus, son of Herod I, who so misruled Judea that the Romans removed him and appointed a governor (prefect) instead; (4) Herod, a son of Herod the Great and half-brother to Herod Antipas; (5) Herod Philip II, son of Herod I and half-brother of Herod Antipas, who ruled parts of northeastern Palestine; (6) Herod Agrippa I, grandson of Herod I, whom the emperor Claudius made king over most of Palestine (41–44 CE) (Acts 12); (7) Herod Agrippa II, son of Herod Agrippa I, the ruler (with his sister Bernice) before whom Paul appeared at Caesarea (Acts 25–26).

Hezekiah Fourteenth king of Judah (c. 715–686 BCE); ruled during the Assyrian crisis when first Sargon II and then Sennacherib overran Palestine (2 Kings 18–20). The DH commends him for his religious reforms.

hieroglyphics The ancient Egyptian system of writing in pictorial script.

higher criticism The branch of biblical scholarship that attempts to analyze biblical texts for the purpose of determining their origins, their literary history, and their author's apparent purpose in writing; it explores the religious, political, and historical forces that produced a given document. Lower criticism confines itself to studying the written texts.

Hinnom, Valley of A topographical depression lying south and west of Jerusalem; called Gehenna in the New Testament it became a symbol of posthumous punishment.

Hiram (1) The name of a series of rulers of Tyre, an ancient Phoenician seaport, with whom David and Solomon made treaties; (2) a half-Tyrian, half-Israelite architect and craftsman whom King Hiram sent from Tyre to help build Solomon's Temple (1 Kings 7).

historical criticism The scholarly analysis of a written work to determine its original historical setting, authorship, date of composition, relationship to historical events, and literary redaction (editing).

Hittites A non-Semitic Indo-European people that formed an older kingdom (c. 1700–1400 BCE), as well as a later kingdom (c. 1400–1200 BCE) centered in Asia Minor (modern Turkey); Hittite influence extended into Mesopotamia, Syria, and Palestine, where biblical writers list them as occupants of Canaan.

Holiness Code The name given to the body of laws and rituals in Leviticus 17–26; derives from the code's emphasis on holiness (separateness, religious purity) of behavior, which was to distinguish Israel from other nations.

Holy of Holies In Hebrew, a superlative referring to the Most Holy Place, the innermost room of the Tabernacle and Temple, where Yahweh was believed to be invisibly present.

Holy Spirit The presence of God active in human life, a concept most explicitly set forth in John 14 and in the Pentecost miracle depicted in Acts 2. In post–New Testament times, the Holy Spirit was defined as the Third Person in the Trinity.

Horeb The name that the E and D traditions give to Yahweh's mountain where Moses received the Torah. Called Sinai in the J and P sources, its exact location is unknown.

Hosea An eighth-century prophet active in the northern kingdom (c. 750 BCE) until shortly before its fall to Assyria (721 BCE).

Huldah A woman prophet associated with Josiah's royal court in Jerusalem who pronounced on the authenticity of a "book of the law," probably an early edition of Deuteronomy.

Hyksos From an Egyptian term (perhaps meaning "rulers of foreign lands"); refers to a largely Semitic group that infiltrated and finally controlled Egypt about 1720–1570 BCE, establishing the Fifteenth and Sixteenth dynasties; they were expelled by Theban kings who founded the Eighteenth Dynasty. Some scholars believe that the Hebrews (Jacob and his family) entered Egypt during the Hyksos era.

Idumea A word meaning "pertaining to Edom," the name that Greeks and Romans applied to the former territory of Edom, Judah's southern neighbor; Herod I was an Idumean prince.

immanence The divine quality denoting God's active presence in the material world, including human society and history

Immanuel The name (meaning "God is with us") that Isaiah gave to a child whose birth he predicted as a sign to

King Ahaz (late eighth century BCE). Matthew interpreted it as a messianic prophecy (Matt. 1:22–23).

Incarnation The Christian doctrine that the Word of God (the Logos) became flesh, the man Jesus of Nazareth (John 1:1–18, especially 1:14).

Isaac The son of Abraham and Sarah, through whom the Israelites traced their descent; Yahweh first demanded that Isaac be sacrificed but later rescinded the command (Gen. 22). Isaac and his wife Rebekah bore twin sons, Esau and Jacob.

Isaiah A major prophet and counselor of Judean kings (eighth century BCE); during the Assyrian threat, Isaiah of Jerusalem produced oracles concerning the Davidic dynasty and the sanctity of the Temple, now preserved in Isaiah 1–39.

Ishmael The son of Abraham and Sarah's slave Hagar (Gen. 16); the eponymous ancestor of twelve princes, later regarded as the father of the Arab peoples.

Ishmaelites The name the J writer applies to caravan merchants trading with Egypt, but whom the E tradition calls Midianites (Gen. 37).

Isis An ancient Egyptian goddess, wife of Osiris and mother of Horus, who was worshiped from prehistoric to Roman times.

Ishtar The Assyrian and Babylonian goddess of love and war; the divine patron of Gilgamesh's city of Uruk.

Israel (1) The name given Jacob by an unnamed being (Gen. 32:28, J source) and by El Shaddai at Bethel (Gen. 35:10–11, P source); although interpreted as "he has been strong against God" (Gen. 32:28), it probably means "may God show his strength" or "may God rule." (2) The Israelite nation descended from the twelve sons of Jacob (Israel), Yahweh's covenant people. (3) The northern kingdom as opposed to the southern kingdom of Judah during the period of the divided monarchies (922–721 BCE).

itinerary An ancient literary genre dealing with geographical locations and features that mark the stages of a journey narrative, such as the accounts of the patriarchs' wanderings in Genesis and the Israelites' trek through the Sinai wilderness in Exodus-Numbers.

J See **Yahwist.**

Jacob The younger of twin sons born to Isaac and Rebekkah, famous for his quick wit and opportunism, as when he tricked his brother Esau out of his birthright and then deceived his dying father (Gen. 25–27). When fleeing to Mesopotamia (where he married his two principal wives, Leah and Rachel), he encountered God (El Shaddai), who changed his name to Israel. Father of twelve sons, eponymous ancestors of Israel's twelve tribes (Gen. 46), he pronounced deathbed evaluations of his sons' respective characters (Gen. 49).

Jael The wife of Heber the Kenite who killed Sisera, the Canaanite general, thus becoming a national heroine in Israel (Judg. 4–5).

Jairus The head of a synagogue in Galilee whose unnamed daughter Jesus resuscitated (Mark 5:35–43).

James (1) Son of Zebedee, brother of John, and one of the Twelve Apostles, who was beheaded by Herod Agrippa I (Acts 12); (2) James, son of Alphaeus and Mary, one of the Twelve; (3) James, the eldest of Jesus' four named "brothers" (or close male relatives) (Mark 6), who experienced the risen Jesus (1 Cor. 15:7), and later became head of the Jerusalem church (Gal. 1:18–2:12; Acts 15; 21); he was martyred about 62 CE.

Jamnia, Academy of According to tradition, an assembly of leading Palestinian rabbis held about 90 CE in the coastal village of Jamnia (Yavneh) to define and guide Judaism after the Roman destruction of Jerusalem and its Temple.

Japheth One of Noah's three sons, the eponymous ancestor of various Indo-European nations, especially Aegean Sea Peoples, including the Greeks and Philistines (Gen. 10).

Jashar, Book of Apparently, a collection of Hebrew poetry (since lost), quoted in Joshua 20, 2 Samuel 1, and 1 Kings 8.

JE The designation scholars give the hypothetical document uniting J's (the Yahwist's) account of Israel's beginnings with E's (the Elohist's) parallel (but probably oral) narrative. A Judean scribe supposedly combined the two traditions at some point after the Assyrians destroyed the northern kingdom of Israel in 721 BCE, when refugees carrying northern traditions migrated to Judah.

Jehoiachin The young king of Judah, son and successor of Jehoiakim, whom Nebuchadnezzar deposed and exiled to Babylon; his release from prison in 562 BCE is the last recorded event in the Deuteronomistic History (2 Kings 25).

Jehoiakim The second son of Josiah, made king of Judah about 609 BCE, when Pharaoh Necho of Egypt placed him on Judah's throne; he rebelled against Babylonian control but died before Nebuchadnezzar attacked Jerusalem and exiled many of the ruling class to Babylon (the first deportation, 597 BCE).

Jehovah An English rendering of the divine name artificially created by adding the vowels of *Elohim* and *Adonai* to the four consonants (YHWH) of the Tetragrammaton; scholars believe that "Yahweh" is a more accurate rendition of the name.

Jehu A son of Jehoshaphat (not the king of Judah) whom the prophet Elisha anointed king of Israel and who then slaughtered Ahab's family and all connected with it; his long reign (842–815 BCE) was distinguished by the loss of Israel's territory and the enforced payment of tribute to Assyrian overlords.

Jephthah A judge (military leader) of early Israel, best known for his vow that—if Yahweh gave him victory—he would sacrifice the first person he met after the battle; that person was his unnamed daughter (Judg. 11).

Jeremiah A major prophet of the late seventh and early sixth centuries BCE) who warned Judah's leaders that the Babylonian threat was Yahweh's punishment for covenant breaking. He also prophesied the destruction of the Temple (Jer. 7, 26) but added that God would eventually make a "new covenant" with his people (Jer. 31).

Jericho One of the world's oldest cities, whose ruins lie near an oasis on the west side of the south Jordan River valley. Although supposedly a heavily fortified city during Joshua's conquest of Canaan (c. 1250 BCE), archaeologists can find no evidence that the site was occupied at that time (cf. Josh. 2, 5).

Jeroboam Name of two important kings of Israel: (1) Jeroboam I, who led the ten northern tribes' secession from the Davidic monarchy and became first ruler (922–901 BCE) of the northern kingdom, where he established cult sites at Bethel and Dan (the infamous "golden calves" on which Yahweh was invisibly enthroned) (1 Kings 11–12); (2) Jeroboam II (786–746 BCE), who greatly expanded Israel's territory in a generally prosperous reign, though the prophets Amos and Hosea denounced the nation's economic injustices (2 Kings 14).

Jerome An eminent Christian scholar (347–419/420 CE) known for his translation of the Bible into Latin. See also **Vulgate.**

Jerusalem An ancient Palestinian holy city, sometimes identified with the Salem of Genesis 14:17–20 but more often with Jebus, the stronghold of a Canaanite tribe (Josh. 18:28; Judg. 19:10). Jerusalem became King David's capital after he captured it from the Jebusites (c. 1000 BCE). The city suffered three major destructions: in 587 BCE, when the Babylonians razed Solomon's Temple; in 70 CE, when Roman armies burned it and tore down the Temple Herod had built; and in 135 CE, when the Romans again obliterated the town and forbade Jews, on pain of death, to enter it.

Jesse The son of Obed and grandson of Ruth and Boaz, he was a Judean shepherd and father of David (1 Sam. 16; cf. Isa. 11:1, 10).

Jesus The English form of a Latin name derived from the Greek *Iesous,* which translated the Hebrew name *Jeshua,* a later version of *Jehoshua* or *Joshua,* meaning "Yahweh is salvation." The name was borne by several biblical figures, including Joshua, leader of the conquest of Canaan. It was also the name of the author of the Wisdom of Jesus ben Sirach (also called Ecclesiasticus).

Jesus Christ The name and title given to Jesus of Nazareth, the firstborn son of Mary and Joseph (the child's legal father), the one whom Christians regard as the Spirit-begotten Son of God and Savior of the world (Matt. 1:21; Luke 1:31). The term *Christ* is not a proper name but the English version of the Greek *Christos,* a translation of the Aramaic *meshiha* and the Hebrew *mashiah* (messiah, meaning "the anointed one").

Jethro A shepherd and priest of the Kenites, a Midianite tribe of coppersmiths, with whom Moses took refuge during his flight from Egypt and whose daughter Zipporah he married (Exod. 2, 18).

Jew Originally a member of the tribe or kingdom of Judah (2 Kings 16:6; 25:25). The term later referred to anyone of Israelite descent who returned from Babylonian captivity and finally encompassed all members of the covenant community scattered throughout the world.

Jezebel The daughter of King Ethbaal of Tyre and wife of Ahab, king of Israel, who promoted the worship of Baal and persecuted the prophet Elijah; under Jehu's orders, her body was thrown out to be eaten by dogs (1 Kings 21; 2 Kings 9).

Joab A commander of David's armies, who managed the capture of Jerusalem and defeated Israel's enemies, including the Syrians, Ammonites, and Edomites (2 Sam. 12). He murdered Abner, general of the northern tribes under Saul's heir, Ishbaal; arranged for Uriah's death; and reconciled David and Absalom (but later killed the rebellious son). He also supported Solomon's rival for Israel's throne, for which, on the dying David's advice, Solomon executed him (1 Kings 2)

Job A name, apparently dating from the second millennium BCE, that may mean "one who comes back to God," a penitent, or that may derive from the Hebrew *ayah,* "to be hostile," denoting one whom God makes his enemy. A legendary example of righteousness (Ezek. 14:14, 20), he became the central character in the Book of Job.

Johanan ben Zakkai A rabbinic scholar of the first century CE who, according to tradition, presided over the Academy of Jamnia (Yavneh) following the Roman destruction of Jerusalem (70 CE).

Joel A prophet of postexilic Judah (c. 350 BCE); his name means "Yahweh is God."

John A common New Testament name, borne by (1) John the Apostle, son of Zebedee and brother of the apostle James; (2) John the Baptist, son of Zechariah and Elizabeth, and relative of Jesus, whom he baptized in the Jordan River; (3) John of Patmos, author of the Book of Revelation.

Jonah The central figure in the Book of Jonah, whom Yahweh sent to warn Nineveh, capital of Assyria, of impending judgment and who was outraged when God spared the city.

Jonathan The son and heir of King Saul, famous for his selfless devotion to David, and whom the Philistines killed at the Battle of Gilgoa (1 Sam. 18–21).

Jordan River The main river of Palestine connecting the Sea of Galilee in the north with the Dead Sea in the south, a distance of about sixty-five miles. It was the last barrier that Israelites crossed before entering Canaan and the site of John's baptizing campaign.

Joseph The name of several biblical figures, borne by (1) the son of Jacob and Rachel, the interpreter of dreams, who rose from the status of a slave to become the Egyptian pharaoh's chief advisor (Gen. 37–50); (2) a descendant of David, the husband of Mary and legal father of Jesus (Matt. 1–2); (3) Joseph of Arimathea, a wealthy member of the Sanhedrin, who claimed Jesus' body from Pilate for burial in his private garden tomb (Mark 15:43–46).

Josephus, Flavius A Jewish historian (c. 37–100 CE) whose two major works—*Antiquities of the Jews* and *The Jewish War* (describing the revolt against Rome, 66–73 CE)—provide invaluable background material for first-century Judaism and the early Christian period.

Joshua (1) A name meaning "Yahweh is salvation"; the successor to Moses who, according to the book named after him, led the Israelites on their military conquest of Canaan; (2) following the Judeans' return from Babylon, the High Priest of Jerusalem during the governorship of Zerubbabel (c. 520 BCE) (Zech. 3).

Josiah King of Judah (640–609 BCE), who led a major religious reform apparently based on the principles articulated in Deuteronomy, for which the Deuteronomistic historian accorded him the highest praise of any ruler since David (1 Kings 22–23). His reconquest of the former territories of Israel were cut short when Pharaoh Necho killed him.

Jubilee Derived from the Hebrew word for "ram's horn" or "trumpet"; refers to the sabbatical year (every fifty years) described in Leviticus 25, when all debts were to be canceled and private property returned to its original owners.

Judaeus, Philo See **Philo Judaeus.**

Judah (1) The fourth son of Jacob and Leah, the eponymous founder of the tribe of Judah; (2) the kingdom of Judah, the southern kingdom of the divided monarchy, composed chiefly of the tribes of Judah and Benjamin, which supported the Davidic dynasty after the ten northern tribes withdrew to form the kingdom of Israel (922 BCE). As an independent state, Judah ended when the Babylonians destroyed it (587 BCE).

Judaism The name applied to the religion of the people of Judah (Judeans, or Jews) after the northern kingdom of Israel fell to Assyria (721 BCE) and particularly after the Babylonian exile (587–538 BCE). Modern Judaism developed in the centuries following the Roman destruction of Jerusalem (70 CE).

Judas (1) Judas Maccabeus, the third of five sons of the village priest Mattathias, who led a successful uprising against the Syrian king Antiochus IV (1 Macc.); (2) Judas the Galilean, a Jewish revolutionary who led an abortive revolt against Roman occupation of Palestine (6 or 7 CE; Acts 5:27); (3) the brother or kinsman of Jesus (also called Jude); (4) Judas Iscariot (Judas the man of Kerioth), son of Simon Iscariot, the apostle who betrayed Jesus to the chief priests and Romans, the central figure of the recently discovered Gospel of Judas.

Jude The English version of the name *Judah* or *Judas,* one of Jesus "brothers" (Mark 6:3; Matt. 13:55), traditional author of the epistle of Jude.

Judea The name given to territory comprising the old kingdom of Judah. It first appears in Ezra 5:8, when the Persians made Judea a province in their empire. In the time of Jesus, Judea was the southernmost of the three divisions of the Roman province of western Palestine, the other two of which were Samaria and Galilee.

judges In the Book of Judges, charismatic (spirit-filled) men and women who led Israelite tribes or clans, primarily in military battles with Israel's close neighbors, such as the Moabites or Philistines.

Judgment, Day of A theological concept derived from the ancient Israelite belief that on a future day Yahweh would judge all nations in the earth. The prophet Amos insisted that Yahweh would also judge Israel severely for its covenant breaking and other sins.

Jupiter The Latin name of the chief Roman god, counterpart of the Greek Zeus, king of the Olympian gods, for whom some men of Lycaonia mistook Paul's companion Barnabas (Acts 14).

kavod A Hebrew term commonly translated as "glory" or "splendor" and denoting Yahweh's presence in the Jerusalem Temple.

Kenite hypothesis A hypothesis that Yahweh was originally the tribal god of the Kenite clan from which Moses and his Israelite followers borrowed and adopted their religion (Exod. 2–3, 18).

Kenites A Midianite clan of nomadic coppersmiths and metalworkers to which Jethro, Moses' father-in-law, belonged (Exod. 18).

kerygma A Greek word meaning "proclamation," the act of publicly preaching the Christian message.

Kethuvim (Ketubim, or Kethubim) The Hebrew term designating the Writings, the third division of the Hebrew Bible (Tanakh), which includes poetical and wisdom books, as well as late histories, such as Ezra and Chronicles.

kingdom of God From a Greek phrase *basileia tou theu,* the rule or dominion of God in human affairs, which Jesus preached as soon to replace all human governments.

KJV Abbreviation for the King James Version of the Bible, authorized by England's James I and published in 1611.

koine A commonly spoken form of Greek (as opposed to the formal Greek of the classical writers), introduced through Alexander's conquests; the language of both the Septuagint edition of the Hebrew Bible and the New Testament.

Laban The brother of Rebekkah, father of Leah and Rachel, and thus father-in-law of Jacob (Gen. 24–31).

Lachish A major fortified city in Judah, about thirty miles southwest of Jerusalem and twenty miles from the Mediterranean coast.

Laodicea A commercial city on the Lycrus River in Asia Minor and one of the seven churches of Asia (Gal. 4; Rev. 3).

Last Supper Jesus' final meal with his disciples, presented as a Passover observance in the Synoptic Gospels at which Jesus initiated a "New Covenant" with his disciples and inaugurated the ceremony of bread and wine, the Eucharist or Holy Communion (Mark 14:12–26; 1 Cor. 11:23–26).

Latter Prophets The books of Isaiah, Jeremiah, Ezekiel, and the twelve minor prophets—the second part of the Nevi'im in the Tanakh.

Law The common term for the Torah, the Bible's first five books (the Pentateuch), that contain divine instruction or teaching.

Lazarus (1) The brother of Mary and Martha, whom Jesus resuscitated (John 11); (2) the beggar in Jesus' parable of the afterlife (Luke 16).

Leah Laban's oldest daughter, whom he married to Jacob by trickery after the latter had worked seven years for her younger sister, Rachel (Gen. 29–30); she bore him six sons—Reuben, Simeon, Levi, Judah, Issachar, and Zebulun—and a daughter, Dinah.

legal procedures Also known as case law, or casuistic law; refers to legal decrees phrased in a qualifying manner, commonly in the form "If this happens, then that must be done." See also **apodictic law, case law,** and **policy law.**

legend A term describing unverifiable stories or narrative traditions about celebrated people or places of the past. Legends grow as the popular oral literature of a people, their purpose being not to provide historical data but to entertain and to illustrate treasured beliefs and ethical principles.

Levi The third son of Jacob and Leah, and the eponymous ancestor of the tribe of Levi to which Moses, Aaron, and Miriam belonged. See also **Levites.**

Leviathan A mythical sea monster, the ancient Near Eastern Dragon of Chaos and symbol of evil that Yahweh defeated in creating the universe (Ps. 74:14; Isa. 27:1; Job 41:1–14; Rev. 12:3; 13:1–8).

Levites The Israelite tribe descended from Levi that was given hereditary priestly duties (Deut. 18). Only descendants of Aaron could be high priests; in the postexilic period, the Levites functioned as secondary Temple priests.

lex talionis The ancient Near Eastern law of retaliation that appears in the Code of Hammurabi and also in the Torah, which prescribed "eye for eye, life for life" (Exod. 21:23–25; Lev. 24:19–20; Deut. 19:21), a principle of vengeance that Jesus rejected in the Sermon on the Mount (Matt. 5:38–42).

literary criticism A form of literary analysis that attempts to isolate and define literary types, the sources behind them, the stages of composition from oral to written form (with their characteristic rhetorical features), and the stages and degree of redaction (editing) of a text.

liturgy A body of formal rites, including both actions and spoken words, used in public worship, such as the sacrifices, prayers, and other rituals performed at the Jerusalem Temple, or the ceremony of the Eucharist (Holy Communion) celebrated in Christian churches.

Logos A Greek term, meaning either "word" or "reason," that Greco-Roman philosophers used to denote the principle of divine intelligence that shapes and sustains the universe. Philo Judaeus of Alexandria, Egypt (c. 20 BCE–50 CE), used the term to represent the mediator between God and humanity, the "word" that God spoke to create the material world (Gen. 1); the author of John's Gospel used it to denote Jesus in his prehuman existence (John 1:1–14).

Lot The nephew of Abraham whom Yahweh's angels rescued from doomed Sodom, and who then fathered (by his daughters) the eponymous ancestors of two nations, Moab and Ammon (Gen. 19).

Lucifer A term meaning "light bearer" and referring to the planet Venus when it is the morning star; the English "Lucifer" translates the Hebrew word for "shining one"

(Isa. 14:12). An epithet applied to the king of Babylon, it was later mistakenly taken as a name for Satan before his expulsion from heaven.

Luke A Christian physician and traveling companion of Paul to whom a second-century-CE tradition ascribes the Gospel of Luke and the Book of Acts.

LXX A common abbreviation for the Septuagint, the Greek translation of the Hebrew Bible made in Alexandria, Egypt, during the last three centuries BCE; it is the edition of the Bible that most New Testament writers quote.

Lystra A city in the Roman province of Galatia where Paul and Barnabas performed such successful healings that they were identified as Hermes and Zeus (Mercury and Jupiter) (Acts 14:6–19; 16:1).

M The scholarly term for material found only in Matthew's Gospel.

Maat An ancient Egyptian goddess of truth and justice.

Maccabees The name given a family that won (second-century BCE) religious and political independence for the Jews from their Greek-Syrian oppressors. Judas, called *Maccabeus* (meaning "[God's] hammer"), son of the village priest Mattathias, led his brothers and other faithful Jews against the armies of Antiochus IV. See also **Hasmonian.**

Macedonia The large mountainous region in northern Greece ruled by Philip of Macedon (359–336 BCE). Philip's son, Alexander the Great (ruled 356–323 BCE) extended the Macedonian Empire over the former Persian Empire as far east as western India.

Malachi The title of the last book of the Minor Prophets; the word means "my messenger" and is not a proper name.

Mamre A plain near what later became the city of Hebron in southern Palestine, the site where Yahweh visited Abraham to promise the birth of his son Isaac (Gen. 18).

Manasseh (1) The elder son of Joseph; (2) one of Israel's twelve tribes, divided into two parts and occupying land east and west of the Jordan River; (3) the king of Judah (c. 687–642 BCE) whom the Deuteronomistic History blamed for Judah's fall to Babylon (2 Kings 23:26–27).

manna The food miraculously supplied the Israelites during their wanderings in the Sinai wilderness (Exod. 16).

Marcion A Gnostic Christian who attempted to establish a Christian Scripture distinct from the Hebrew Bible, which he rejected for its portrayal of a violent deity.

Marduk The patron god of Babylon, hero of the creation epic *Enuma Elish,* in which he defeated the monster Tiamat and created the cosmos from her bifurcated corpse.

Mark (John Mark) The son of Mary, a Jerusalem Jew who accompanied Barnabas (his cousin) and Paul on an early missionary journey (Acts 12–13) but later left them.

Martha The sister of Mary and Lazarus of Bethany (Luke 10:38–42; John 11:1–12:2), whose home Jesus frequently visited.

martyr A "witness" for Israel's God who prefers to die rather and to give up his or her faith (cf. 2 Macc.); Stephen was the first Christian martyr (Acts 7; 22:20).

Mary From the Latin and Greek *Maria* and the Hebrew *Miryam* (Miriam), a name borne by several women in the New Testament: (1) Mary the Virgin, wife of Joseph and mother of Jesus (Matt. 1; Luke 1–2; Acts 1:13–14); in John's Gospel, she is present at Jesus' first miracle and at the cross (2:1–12; 19:25–27). (2) Mary Magdalene, a woman from Magdala in Galilee who became Jesus' disciple, following him to the cross and to his empty tomb; in John 20, she is one of the first to see her risen Lord. (3) Mary, sister of Lazarus and Martha (Luke 10:38–43; John 11). (4) Mary, wife of Clopas, mother of James the Less and Joseph (Joses), a witness to Jesus' crucifixion, burial, and resurrection (Matt. 27:56–61; Mark 15:40, 47; 16:1). (5) Mary, sister of Barnabas and mother of John Mark (Acts 12:12).

Massada A stronghold that Herod the Great built on a fortified plateau 800 feet above the Dead Sea. Captured by Zealots during the revolt against Rome (66 CE), it fell to a Roman military siege in 73 CE. According to Josephus, its Jewish defenders committed mass suicide rather than become Roman slaves.

Masoretes From a Hebrew term meaning "transmitters," the name applied to medieval Jewish scholars who copied, annotated, and added vowels to the text of the Hebrew Bible.

Masoretic Text (MT) The standard text of the Hebrew Bible as given final form by the Masoretes in the seventh through ninth centuries CE. It differs in many respects from the older biblical texts found among the Dead Sea Scrolls.

Mattathias A Jewish village priest who, with his sons, John, Simon, Judas, Eleazar, and Jonathan, led a revolt against the oppressions of Antiochus IV (c. 168–167 BCE).

Matthew A Jewish tax collector working for Rome whom Jesus called to be one of the Twelve Apostles (Matt. 9:9; Mark 2:13–17); the traditional author of the Gospel bearing his name, a claim most scholars dispute.

Matthias The disciple elected to replace Judas among the Twelve, about whom nothing else is known (Acts 1:23–26).

Medes An ancient Indo-European people occupying the mountainous area south of the Caspian Sea who established a kingdom that by 600 BCE extended from the Persian Gulf to the Black Sea. In 612 BCE, they joined the Babylonians and Scythians to destroy Nineveh, and they were later absorbed into the Persian Empire.

Megiddo An ancient Palestinian city overlooking the Valley of Jezreel, the site of many decisive battles in biblical history and the symbolic location of Armageddon (Rev. 16:16).

Megillot A Hebrew word meaning "scrolls"; the five biblical books—Song of Songs, Ruth, Lamentations, Ecclesiastes, and Esther—each of which was read publicly at one of Israel's annual religious festivals.

Melchizedek The king-priest of Canaanite Salem (probably the site of Jerusalem) to whom Abraham paid a tenth of the spoils of war (Gen. 14:17–20), whom the author of

Hebrews cited as foreshadowing Jesus Christ (Ps. 110:4; Heb. 5:6–10; 7:1–25)

Mercury The Roman name for Hermes, Greek god of persuasion, business, and travel, and the messenger of Zeus, for whom Paul was mistaken in Lystra (Acts 14:12).

Merneptah The Egyptian pharaoh (c. 1224–1211 BCE), son and successor of Rameses II, whose victory stele commemorated his military conquests in Canaan, including his defeat of Israel—the oldest nonbiblical reference to Israel's existence.

Mesopotamia The region between the Euphrates and Tigris rivers at the head of the Persian Gulf (modern Iraq); cradle of the Sumerian, Akkadian, Assyrian, and Neo-Babylonian civilizations.

messiah/Messiah A Hebrew term (*mashiah*) meaning "anointed one," referring to an Israelite king or priest who had been consecrated by ritually pouring holy oil on his head. King David was the model of Yahweh's anointed ruler; Christians believe that Jesus of Nazareth was David's anointed heir (Mark 8:27–30). See also **Christ.**

metaphor A figure of speech in which one object is used to describe the quality of another; an implied comparison of one thing to another, inferring that the second has an unrecognized likeness to the first. Biblical poets, for example, call Yahweh a "shepherd" because he guides and protects Israel, his "flock," and a "rock," because he is solid and reliable.

Methuselah According to Genesis 5:21–27, a pre-Flood patriarch who attained an age of 969 years.

Micah A Judean prophet (late eighth century BCE) who denounced the corruptions of urban life and predicted Jerusalem's fall (Mic. 3:12; cited in Jer. 26:18–19).

Michael The angel whom the Book of Daniel represented as the spirit prince, guardian, and protector of Israel (Dan. 10:13, 21; 12:1). In Revelation, he cast Satan from heaven (Rev. 12:7). His name means "who is like God."

Michal A daughter of King Saul whom David married (1 Sam. 18–19).

Midian An ancient tribal territory, the exact location and extent of which is unknown, that lay in the northwestern Arabian desert, east of the Gulf of 'Aqaba and south of Moab.

Midianites A nomadic or seminomadic group of shepherds and traders with whom Moses took refuge after his flight from Egypt and from whom he took his wife, the daughter of the Midianite priest Jethro (Ruel) (Exod. 2:15–3:1; 18). The Midianites are later portrayed as enemies of Israel (Judg. 3:12–20; Ezek 28:8–11).

midrash From a Hebrew word meaning "to search out," refers to a commentary on or interpretation of Scripture.

Millennium A 1,000-year-long period, particularly the period of Christ's universal reign (Rev. 20:1–8), during which Satan will be chained and the dead resurrected.

Minor Prophets Twelve prophetic books short enough to be recorded together on a single scroll, including the oracles of Hosea, Joel, Amos, Obadiah, Micah, Nahum, Habakkuk, Zephaniah, Haggai, Zechariah, and Malachi.

Miriam The elder sister of Aaron and Moses and a prophet of Yahweh (Exod. 2:4–8; 15:20–21; Micah 6:4).

Mishnah From the Hebrew verb "to repeat," a collection of traditional interpretations of the Torah (c. 200 CE).

Mithras A Persian savior god who killed a celestial bull and was worshiped in mystery cults throughout the Roman Empire.

Moab An ancient neighbor-state of Israel located in the Jordan highlands east of the Dead Sea and north of Edom. Although supposedly related to Israel (Gen. 19:30–38), the Moabites were traditional enemies of Israel. David's ancestors included the Moabite Ruth (Ruth 4:13–22). Chemosh was the national god of Moab.

Molech (Moloch) The patron god of Ammon whose worship typically involved human sacrifice.

money An imprinted piece of metal generally accepted as a medium of exchange. In early biblical times, before coins were first minted, value in business transactions was determined by weighing quantities of precious metals. In the early period, the term *shekel* referred not to a coin but to a certain weight of silver. The use of coinage was introduced in Palestine during the Persian era, when the daric or dram, named for Darius I, appeared. In New Testament times, Greek and Roman coinage became standard, including the silver drachma. The talent (Matt 18:24) was not a coin, but money on account, and was worth many thousands of dollars. The denarius (Matt. 18:28), the basic unit of the period, was a silver coin, the day's wage of a rural laborer (Matt. 20:20).

monotheism The belief in the existence of one God, a central theme of Second Isaiah (Isa. 40–55).

Mordecai A name derived from *Marduk* or *Merodach* (the chief Babylonian god); the cousin and foster father of Esther, who, according to the book bearing her name, was married to Ahasuerus, emperor of Persia. Mordecai outwitted Haman, who had persuaded the emperor to order the extermination of all Jews in his empire.

Mosaic Covenant An agreement between Yahweh and the nation of Israel that was mediated by Moses. According to the terms of the pact, Israel swore to keep all the laws enumerated in the Torah. Failure to do so would result in suffering all the curses listed in Leviticus 26 and Deuteronomy 28–29.

Moses The great Hebrew lawgiver, religious leader, and central figure of the Pentateuch; he was reportedly adopted by a daughter of the Egyptian pharaoh but later fled Egypt and settled in Midian among the Kenites, where Yahweh appeared to him at a burning bush (Exod. 2–3). Following God's orders, Moses returned to Egypt and demanded that pharaoh release his Israelite slaves. He then led the Israelites to the mountain (Sinai or Horeb) where Yahweh had appeared and mediated a covenant between God and his people. After forty years of wandering through the Sinai wilderness, Moses died before he could enter the Promised Land (Deut. 34).

Muratorian Canon A fragmentary document in which an unknown author listed books of the New Testament he regarded as canonical. Although written in Latin during the eighth century CE, the fragment was a translation of a much older Greek work, which may date to the late second century CE or, as scholars recently proposed, to the early fourth century CE.

mystery Derived from a Greek word meaning "to initiate" or "to shut the eyes or mouth," probably referring to the secrets of Hellenistic "mystery religions," and used variously by New Testament writers. Jesus speaks at least once of the "mystery" of the kingdom (Mark 4:11), but Paul employs the term frequently, as if the profounder aspects of Christianity were a sacred secret into which the Spirit-directed believer becomes initiated (Rom. 11:5; 16;25; 1 Cor. 2:7; 4:1; 15:51; Col. 1:26; 2:2; 4:3, etc.).

myth From the Greek *mythos* (story), referring to a narrative expressing a profound psychological or religious truth that cannot be verified by historical inquiry or other scientific means. Myths typically involve the actions of supernatural beings in the remote past, such as the creation of the world, or the interaction between gods and a particular people's distant ancestors, such as the Greek heroes who fought at Troy or Israel's forebears in Genesis and Exodus.

mythology A system or cycle of myths, such as those featuring the deities of ancient Sumer, Greece, or Rome. Once the embodiment of living religious beliefs, Babylonian or Greco-Roman mythologies are now seen as expressions of perceptions and intuitions about the interaction of spiritual hopes and physical limitations that characterize the human unconsciousness.

Nabonidus The father of Belshazzar and the last ruler of the Neo-Babylonian Empire (556–539 BCE).

Naboth The owner of a vineyard that King Ahab of Israel coveted and whom Queen Jezebel had stoned for blasphemy, an injustice that the prophet Elijah used to help overthrow Ahab's dynasty (1 Kings 21; 2 Kings 9–10).

Nahum A prophet who rejoiced in the fall of Nineveh, Assyria's capital (c. 612 BCE).

Naomi The wife of Elimelech of Bethlehem and mother-in-law of Ruth, whose marriage she encouraged to her Jewish kinsman Boaz. Her name means "my pleasantness" (Ruth 1–4).

Naphtali (1) The son of Jacob and Rachel's handmaid Bilah, the eponymous ancestor one of Israel's twelve tribes; (2) the tribe of Naphtali held territory north of Megiddo along the upper Jordan River valley and the western shore of the Sea of Galilee. It was dispersed when the Assyrians destroyed Israel in 722/721 BCE.

Narim-Sin A grandson of Sargon I, creator of the world's first empire (c. 2260–2223 BCE), and a famed military leader who campaigned throughout Mesopotamia and Iran.

narrative A literary composition that tells a story, arranging the characters and events in a sequential order.

Most of the Bible's first eleven books are theologically oriented narratives illustrating the origin, nature, and consequences of Israel's covenant relationship with Yahweh (Gen.–2 Kings).

Nathan (1) A son of David; (2) a prophet and political counselor at David's court who conveyed the terms of God's covenant to David and his dynasty (2 Sam. 7), denounced David for arranging the murder of Bathsheba's husband Uriah (2 Sam. 12), and helped Solomon succeed to David's throne (1 Kings 1).

national epic The term scholars use to describe the long narrative of Israel's origins, rise to political independence, and eventual fall to Babylon (Gen. 12–2 Kings 25).

navi (nabi) The Hebrew word for "prophet," a spokesperson for Yahweh who delivered God's judgments on contemporary society and expressed his intentions toward the world (Deut. 18:9–22).

Nazareth A town in Lower Galilee above the Plain of Esdraelon (Megiddo) where Jesus spent his youth and began his ministry (Luke 1:26; 4:16; John 1:46). Early Christians were sometimes called *Nazarenes* (Acts 24:5).

Nazirites From the Hebrew *nazar*, meaning "to dedicate," referring to a group in ancient Israel known for their rigorous way of life, including a refusal to drink wine, cut their hair, come in contact with the dead, or eat religiously "unclean" food (Num. 6).

Nebuchadnezzar The son of Nabopolassar and the most powerful ruler of the Neo-Babylonian Empire (reigned 605–562 BCE) who defeated Pharaoh Necho at the Battle of Carchemish (605 BCE) and brought the Near East under his control. He attacked Judah and deported many of the upper class to Mesopotamia in 598–597 BCE; when King Zedekiah of Judah rebelled, he destroyed Jerusalem (587 BCE) and exiled its leading families to Babylon.

Necho Pharaoh Necho II, second king of the Twenty-Sixth Egyptian Dynasty (610–594 BCE), who defeated and killed King Josiah of Judah at Megiddo (609 BCE), thus ending Josiah's religious reforms. Nebuchadnezzar's forces however, defeated Necho's army at the Battle of Carchemish (605 BCE), making Babylon master of the Near East.

Nehemiah A Jewish court official (cupbearer) living at the Persian capital in Susa who persuaded the emperor Artaxerxes I (465–423 BCE) to send him to go to Judah, where he rebuilt Jerusalem's walls and, with the priest Ezra, implemented numerous social and religious reforms (Neh. 8–13).

nephesh In biblical Hebrew, the term for "living being" or "animate creatures" that applies to both humans and animals. A physical body infused with God's *ruah* ("breath" or "spirit"), the first human is created a *nephesh* (Gen. 2:7), a mortal unity of clay and spirit. In Greek editions of the Hebrew Bible, *nephesh* was commonly translated as *psyche*, the Greek word for "soul" that had connotations of immortality absent in the Hebrew text.

Nero Emperor of Rome (54–68 CE), the Caesar by whom Paul wished to be tried in Acts 25:11 and under whose persecution Paul was probably beheaded (c. 64–65 CE).

Nevi'im (Prophets) The Hebrew term for the second major division of the three-part Hebrew Bible (Tanakh).

New Year (Rosh Hashanah) Also called the Feast of Trumpets (Lev. 23:23–25), an annual ceremony marking a time when work ceased and the Israelites assembled (Num. 29). Prior to the exile (587–538 BCE), the Jews observed the festival in the autumn, but afterward they adopted the Babylon custom of observing the new year in the spring, the first day of the month of Nisan (March-April).

Nicodemus A leading Pharisee and member of the Sanhedrin who discussed spiritual rebirth with Jesus (John 3) and defended him against other Pharisees (John 7:45–52) and, with Joseph of Arimathea, helped entomb his body (John 19:38–42).

Nimrod The great-grandson of Noah, grandson of Ham, son of Cush, and a legendary hunter and founder of cities in Mesopotamia (Gen. 10:8–12).

Nineveh The last capital of the Assyrian Empire, located on the east bank of the Tigris River, whose rulers imposed heavy tribute on Israel and Judah. Assyria's last major ruler, Ashurbanipal (668–627 BCE), collected thousands of literary works, inscribed on clay tablets, for Nineveh's royal library. A coalition that included the Medes and Babylonians destroyed the city in 612 BCE.

Noah The son of Lamech and father of Ham, Shem, and Japheth, whom Yahweh chose to build a wooden houseboat containing pairs of all living creatures to survive the Flood (Gen. 6–8) and with whom God made an "everlasting" covenant.

Obadiah The otherwise unknown prophet whose oracles appear in the book named after him, the fourth and shortest collection among the Minor Prophets

Obed The son of Ruth and Boaz, and father of Jesse, father of David (Ruth 4).

Olives, Mount of A mile-long limestone ridge with several distinct summits paralleling the eastern section of Jerusalem, from which it is separated by the narrow Kidron Valley; the site where Yahweh will stand at the final eschatological battle (Zech. 14:3–5), the location of Jesus' prophecy of Jerusalem's fall (Mark 13; Matt. 24), and the place where he was arrested (Mark 14:26).

omega The last letter in the Greek alphabet, used with the first letter (alpha) as a symbol of the eternity of God (Rev. 1:8; 21:6) and of Jesus (Rev. 1:17; 22:13), probably echoing Second Isaiah's description of Yahweh as "the first and . . . the last" (Isa. 44:6; 48:12).

Omri The sixth ruler of the northern kingdom (876–869 BCE), one of Israel's most militarily successful kings whose achievements the Deuteronomistic authors largely ignore (2 Kings 16:23–28).

Onesimus The runaway slave of Philemon of Colossae whom Paul apparently converted to Christianity and reconciled to his master (Philem. 8–21).

oracle (1) A divine message or utterance, such as the messages that Yahweh gave to his prophets; (2) the supposedly inspired words of a priest or priestess at such shrines as Delphi in ancient Greece.

oral tradition Material passed from generation to generation by word of mouth before finding written form. Scholars believe that much of Israel's early history, customs, and beliefs about its origins, such as tales about Abraham in Genesis and Moses in Exodus, were orally transmitted before being incorporated into a written text.

original sin The theological concept of humanity's inborn corruption, a doctrine holding that the entire human race has inherited from the first man (Adam) an irresistible tendency to sin, thereby bringing God's condemnation. Not part of the Jewish tradition, this pessimistic view of human nature was formulated by the early Christian theologian Augustine, who formulated an extremist view of Paul's comments on Adam (Rom. 5:12).

orthodoxy Literally, "correct teaching," holding beliefs or doctrines established by a religious or political authority, such as a church leadership.

Osiris The ancient Egyptian god of fertility and also of the Underworld.

P See **priestly document.**

Palestine A strip of land bordering the eastern Mediterranean Sea, lying south of Syria, north of the Sinai Peninsula, and west of the Arabian Desert. Also known as Canaan, this region was named for the Philistines.

pantheon The accepted list or roster of a people's chief gods, such as the Olympian family of gods worshiped in classical Greece. It is also the name of a famous domed temple in Rome, the house of "all the gods."

parable From the Greek *parabole,* meaning "a placing beside"; commonly fictional narratives comparing something familiar to an unexpected spiritual value. In the Synoptic Gospels, Jesus typically uses a commonplace object or action to illustrate a religious or psychological insight into the nature of the divine–human relationship.

Paraclete A Greek term meaning "an advocate" that John's Gospel uses to denote the abiding spiritual presence of the risen Jesus. Paraclete, a manifestation of God's Holy Spirit, is variously translated as "Comforter," "Helper," "Advocate," or "Spirit of Truth."

paradise Literally, a "park" or walled garden, the name applied to Eden (Gen. 2:8–17) and in post–Hebrew Bible times to the abode of the righteous dead, of which the lower part housed souls awaiting resurrection and the higher was the permanent home of the just. Jesus may have referred to the lower realm when he promised paradise to a fellow victim of crucifixion (Luke 23:43). Paul mystically visited "paradise" when "caught up" to the "third heaven" (2 Cor. 12:2–5).

parallelism A structural feature typical of Hebrew poetry, consisting of the repetition of similar or antithetical thoughts in similar phrasing, such as "The wicked will not stand firm when Judgment comes nor sinner when the virtuous assemble" (Ps. 1:5).

Parousia From a Greek word meaning "being by" or "being near"; refers to Jesus' Second Coming or reappearance, commonly regarded as his return to judge the world, punish the wicked, and redeem the faithful (Matt. 24–25; Mark 13; 1 and 2 Thess.).

Passion The term commonly used to denote Jesus' suffering and death (Acts 1:3).

Passover An annual Jewish observance commemorating Israel's last night of bondage in Egypt when the Angel of Death "passed over" Israelite homes marked with the blood of a sacrificial lamb to destroy the first-born of every Egyptian household (Exod. 12). Beginning the seven-day Feast of Unleavened Bread, it is a ritual meal eaten on Nisan 14 (March–April) that traditionally includes roast lamb, unleavened bread, and bitter herbs. According to the Synoptics, Jesus' final dinner with his disciples was a Passover celebration (Mark 14; Matt. 26) and the model for Christian communion (the Eucharist) (1 Cor. 11:17–27).

pastoral epistles The New Testament books of 1 and 2 Timothy and Titus, supposedly written by Paul to his fellow ministers (pastors). Most scholars deny Pauline authorship of these works, which seem to represent a more highly organized church than that in Paul's day.

Patmos A small Aegean island off the coast of Asia Minor (modern Turkey) where John, author of Revelation, was exiled about 95 CE.

patriarch The male head (father) of an ancient family line, a venerable tribal founder or leader, especially (1) the early ancestors of humanity listed in Genesis 4–5, known as the "antediluvian patriarchs"; (2) prominent "fathers" living after the Flood in the time of Abraham (Gen. 11); (3) the immediate ancestors of the Israelites, particularly Abraham, Isaac, and Jacob (Gen. 12–50).

Paul The most influential apostle and missionary of the mid-first-century Christian movement, the author of at least seven (or nine) New Testament letters. According to Acts, he was named Saul of Tarsus and held Roman citizenship; after the risen Jesus was revealed to him on the road to Damascus, Paul (his Roman name) led three missionary tours, founding new congregations in Asia Minor and Greece before being arrested and sent to Rome for trial, where he was probably martyred under Nero (c. 64–65 CE).

Pella A Gentile city in Palestine east of the Jordan River, to which tradition says that Jesus' family and other Jewish Christians fled during the Jewish Revolt against Rome (66–73 CE).

Peniel A site on the Jabbok River (in modern Jordan) where Jacob wrestled with El (God) and thereby won a blessing and a name change to Israel (Gen. 32:22–33).

Pentateuch From a Greek word meaning "five scrolls"; denotes the first five books of the Hebrew Bible, the Torah.

Pentecost (1) Also known as the Feast of Weeks, the Feast of Harvest, and the Day of the First Fruits, a one-day celebration held fifty days after Passover at the juncture of May and June; (2) the occasion when the Holy Spirit was poured out on Jesus' disciples (Acts 2), regarded as the spiritual baptism of the Christian movement.

Peraea (Perea) A name the historian Josephus gave the area that the Hebrew Bible called the land "beyond" or "across" (east of) the Jordan River.

pericope A term used in form criticism to describe a literary unit (a saying, anecdote, parable, or brief narrative) that forms a complete entity in itself and is attached to its context by later editorial commentary. Jesus' parables probably circulated independently and orally before they were incorporated into the Gospel narratives.

Persepolis A capital of the Persian Empire established by Darius I (522–486 BCE) and burned by Alexander the Great (330 BCE).

Persia A large Asian territory southeast of Elam inhabited by Indo-European peoples that became an empire under Cyrus the Great, who united Media and Persia (549 BCE) and conquered Lydia (546 BCE) and Babylon (539 BCE), including its former dominion, Palestine. Under the emperor Darius I (522–486), the Jerusalem Temple was rebuilt (Ezra 3–6). Scholars believe that many of the biblical texts were revised and edited under Persian rule.

personification A literary term denoting the attribution of personal qualities to an object or abstraction, such as the biblical practice of portraying the divine attribute of Wisdom (Hebrew, *hochmah*; Greek, *sophia*) as a heavenly companion of Yahweh who assisted the Deity at creation and acted as his mediator between divinity and humanity (Prov. 8; Ecclus. 24; Wisd. of Sol. 7:22–9:18).

Peter The most prominent of Jesus' twelve chief disciples, also known as Simon (probably his surname), Simeon (Symeon), and Cephas (the Aramaic equivalent of *petros*, meaning "rock" or "stone"). The son of Jonas or John, brother of the apostle Andrew and a native of Bethsaida, a fishing village on the Sea of Galilee, he was the first to recognize Jesus as Israel's Messiah (Mark 8:27–30), although he later three times denied knowing Jesus (Mark 14:66–72). In the first part of Acts, Peter leads the Jerusalem church and is instrumental in bringing the first Gentiles into the Christian fold (Acts 10–11). He was probably martyred under Nero about 64–65 CE.

pharaoh The title of Egypt's king; none of the pharaohs mentioned in Genesis or Exodus are named, making it difficult to find a historical context for the events narrated there. Only after Solomon's death, when Pharaoh Shishak (Sheshonk I) stole "everything" from the Jerusalem Temple (c. 922–915 BCE), are Egyptian rulers identified by name. Pharaoh Necho killed Judah's reforming King Josiah at Megiddo (609 BCE) but was later defeated by Nebuchadnezzar.

Pharisees A leading religious movement or sect in Judaism during the last two centuries BCE and the two first centuries CE. The Pharisees were probably descendants of the Hasidim (Torah loyalists) who opposed Antiochus IV's attempts to destroy the Mosaic tradition. Although the New Testament typically presents them as Jesus' opponents

(Matt. 23), their views on resurrection and the afterlife anticipated Christian teachings.

Philemon A citizen of Colossae whose runaway slave, Onesimus, Paul converted to Christianity.

Philip (1) King of Macedonia (359–336 BCE) and father of Alexander the Great; (2) one of Jesus' twelve apostles, a man of Bethsaida in Galilee (Mark 3:18; John 1:43–49; 12:21–22); (3) a leading figure of the Jerusalem church who was an administrator and preacher, and the converter of Simon the sorcerer and of an Ethiopian eunuch (Acts 8).

Philippi A city in eastern Macedonia, the first European center to receive the Christian message (Acts 16:10–40). Philippi became the apostle Paul's favorite church and the one to which his letter to the Philippians is addressed.

Philistines A people from the Aegean Sea islands (called Caphtor in Amos 9:7) who settled along the southern coast of Palestine during the twelfth century BCE to become the Israelites' chief rivals during the period of the judges and early monarchy (1200–1000 BCE). Samson destroyed their shrine to Dagon, and David eventually subdued them.

Philo Judaeus The most influential philosopher of Hellenistic Judaism, a Greek-educated Jew living in Alexandria, Egypt (c. 20 BCE–50 CE), who promoted a method of interpreting the Hebrew Bible allegorically. Philo's doctrine of the Logos (the divine Word) anticipated the opening hymn to the Logos in John's Gospel.

Phoebe A servant or deacon of the church of Cenchrae, a port of Corinth, whose good works Paul commends in Romans 16:1–2.

Phoenicia A narrow coastal territory along the northeast Mediterranean, lying between the Lebanon range on the east and the sea on the west. It included the ports of Tyre and Sidon.

phylactery One of the two small leather pouches containing copies of four Torah passages, worn on the left arm and forehead by Jewish men during weekday prayers (Matt. 23:5).

Pilate, Pontius See **Pontius Pilate.**

Plato The Athenian philosopher (427–347 BCE) who taught that the material world is only a flawed reflection of a perfect spiritual realm, from which the human soul descends to be born in a mortal body and to which it returns for judgment after death.

policy law Also known as *apodictic*, or *absolute* law, refers to laws stated unconditionally, such as the Ten Commandments (Decalogue). See also **apodictic law.**

polytheism The belief in more than one god, the most common form of religion in the ancient world.

Pompey A leading Roman general and rival of Julius Caesar, with whom he established a temporary political alliance known as the First Triumvirate. Pompey (106–49 BCE) conquered much of the eastern Mediterranean region for Rome, including Syria and Judea (63 BCE).

Porcius Festus See **Festus, Porcius.**

Potiphar In Genesis, the head of Pharaoh's bodyguard who placed Joseph in charge of his household but later threw him in prison when the Hebrew slave was accused of seducing Potiphar's wife.

predestination The act of foreordaining or predetermining by divine decree the ultimate destiny of an individual or a people; a theological doctrine asserting the absolute, irresistible power and control of God. In some biblical traditions, particularly in apocalyptic literature, both divine predeterminism of events and the individual's freedom of choice seem to operate simultaneously.

prefect See **procurator.**

priestly document The parts of the Torah composed by a priestly writer or school, known as P. Scholars believe that Israel's priestly class also performed the final shaping and editing of the Torah, probably during and after the exile (587–450 BCE).

Prisca (Pricilla) The wife of Aquila and a leading member of the early church (Acts 18:18; Rom. 16:3).

proconsul A Roman governor or administrator of a province or territory, such as Gallio, proconsul of Achaia (Greece), before whom Paul appeared (Acts 18:2).

procurator The Roman title of the governor of a region before it became an administrative province. During the reigns of Augustus and Tiberius, Judea was governed by a prefect, the most famous of whom was Pontius Pilate. The office was upgraded to the level of procurator under Claudius.

Promised Land The popular term for the territory of Canaan that Yahweh vowed to give Abraham's heirs in perpetuity (Gen. 15:5–21; 17:1–8), traditionally the land area occupied by David's kingdom.

prophet One who preaches or proclaims the word or will of his or her Deity (Amos 3:7–8; Deut. 18:9–22). A true prophet in Israel was regarded as divinely inspired.

proverb A brief saying that memorably expresses a familiar or useful bit of folk wisdom, usually of a practical nature.

Providence A quasi-religious concept in which God is viewed as the force sustaining and guiding human destiny. It assumes that events occur as part of a divine plan or purpose working for the ultimate triumph of good.

psalm A sacred song or poem used in praise or worship of God, particularly the lyrics collected in the Book of Psalms.

Pseudepigrapha (1) Literally, books falsely ascribed to eminent biblical figures of the past, such as Enoch, Noah, Moses, or Isaiah; (2) a collection of religious books outside the Hebrew Bible canon or Apocrypha that were composed in Hebrew, Aramaic, or Greek from about 300 BCE to 200 CE.

pseudonymity A literary practice, common among Hellenistic-Jewish and early Christian writers, of writing or publishing a book in the name of a famous religious figure of the past. Thus, an anonymous author of about 168 BCE ascribed his work to Daniel, who supposedly lived during the sixth century BCE. The pastoral epistles, 2 Peter, James, and Jude are thought to be pseudonymous books

written in the early or mid-second century CE but attributed to eminent disciples connected with the first-century Jerusalem church.

psyche The Greek word for "soul," which philosophers like Socrates and Plato taught was the invisible center of rational consciousness and personality that survived bodily death to experience rewards or penalties in the afterlife.

Ptolemy (1) Ptolemy I (323–285 BCE), a Macedonian general who assumed rulership of Egypt after the death of Alexander the Great; the Ptolemaic dynasty controlled Egypt and its dominions until 31 BCE, when the Romans came to power; (2) Ptolemy II (285–246 BCE), who supposedly authorized the translation of the Hebrew Bible into Greek, the Septuagint edition.

publican In the New Testament, petty tax collectors for Rome, despised by the Jews, from whom they typically extorted money (Matt. 9:10–13; 21:31). Jesus often dined with these sinners and called one, Levi (Matthew), to apostleship.

Purim A Jewish nationalistic festival held on the fourteenth and fifteenth days of Adar (February–March) and based on events in the Book of Esther.

purity laws Rules defining the nature, cause, or state of physical, ritual, or moral contamination. According to Leviticus and other parts of the Torah, ritual impurity results from a variety of activities, including consumption of forbidden foods such as shellfish and physical contact with impure persons or objects, such as a corpse, a leper, or a menstruating woman, all of which render violators "unclean" and hence religiously unacceptable. The Torah also prescribes elaborate purification rites to restore ritually impure persons to participation in the community, a practice that the Essenes emphasized in their communities.

Q An abbreviation for *Quelle*, the German word for "source," a hypothetical document that many scholars believe contained a collection of Jesus' sayings. The theory of its existence was formed to explain material common to both Matthew and Luke but absent from Mark's Gospel.

Queen of Heaven A Semitic goddess of love and fertility worshiped in various forms throughout the ancient Near East. Known as Ishtar to the Babylonians, she was denounced by Jeremiah but worshiped by Jewish refuges in Egypt after the fall of Jerusalem (Jer. 7:18; 44:17–19, 25).

Qumran An archaeological site containing the ruins of what most scholars assume to have been an Essene monastic community located in the northwestern corner of the Dead Sea, near which the Dead Sea Scrolls were hidden in caves.

rabbi A Jewish title, meaning "master" or "teacher," given to scholars learned in the Torah.

Rachel The daughter of Laban, second and favorite wife of Jacob, and mother of Joseph and Benjamin (Gen. 29–31), who became a symbol of all Israelite mothers (Jer. 31:15).

Rahab (1) A prostitute of Jericho who hid Israelite spies and was spared her city's destruction (Josh. 2); (2) a mythological sea monster, the Dragon of Chaos, whom Yahweh subdued before creating the universe (Ps. 89:10); also a symbol of Egypt (Isa. 30:7).

Rameses II A powerful ruler of Egypt (c. 1290–1224 BCE) whom many scholars think was the pharaoh of the Exodus.

Ras Shamra See **Ugarit.**

realized eschatology A belief that events usually associated with the *eschaton* (world's End), such as divine judgment and resurrection to eternal life, are even now realized or fulfilled by Jesus' spiritual presence among believers (John 5:24–25; 11:26; 14:12–21; 16:7–14).

Rebekah (Rebecca) The wife of Isaac and mother of the twins Esau and Jacob; preferring Jacob, she helped him deceive Isaac into giving the younger son the paternal blessing (Gen. 25:21–28; 27:5–30).

redaction criticism A method of analyzing written texts that tries to define the purpose and literary procedures of redactors (editors) who compile and revise older documents, such as the scribes who collected the oracles of the prophets into their present canonical form.

redactor An editor. See **redaction criticism.**

Rehoboam A son of Solomon and the last ruler of the united kingdom (922–915 BCE); his harsh policies spurred the northern ten tribes to secede from the union and form the northern state of Israel (1 Kings 12:1–24; 14:21–31).

rephaim The Hebrew term for the shades of the dead, which had a grim, joyless posthumous quaisi-existence in the depths of Sheol (Ps. 88:10). The term is also applied to the pre-Israelite inhabitants of Transjordan (Deut. 2:10–11) and to the Philistine giants (2 Sam. 21: 16, 18, 20). The connection between these diverse usages of *rephaim* is unknown.

resurrection The returning of the dead to life, a later Hebrew Bible belief (Isa. 26:19; Dan. 12:2–3, 13) that first became prevalent in Judaism during the time of the Maccabees (after 168 BCE) and eventually became part of the Pharisees' teaching. Like the prophets Elijah and Elisha, Jesus performed several temporal resuscitations, including Lazarus (John 11). Unlike these persons, Jesus ascended to heaven after his own resurrection (Acts 1). Paul offers the New Testament's most complete discussion of the resurrection concept (1 Thess. 4; 1 Cor. 15).

Reuben (1) The son of Jacob and Leah, eldest of his father's twelve sons; (2) the northern Israelite tribe supposedly descended from Reuben (Num. 32) that along with Gad settled in the highlands east of the Jordan River.

rhetorical criticism A method of textual analysis that studies not only the form and structure of a given literary work but the distinctive style of the author.

Roman Empire The international, interracial government centered in Rome, that conquered and administered the entire Mediterranean region from Gaul (France and southern Germany) in the northwest to Egypt in the southeast and that ruled the Jews of Palestine from 63 BCE until Hadrian's destruction of Jerusalem during the second Jewish Revolt

(132–135 CE). In the late fourth century CE, emperors made Christianity Rome's state religion.

Rosetta Stone A granite block bearing the same message inscribed in three linguistic forms: Greek, ancient Egyptian hieroglyphics, and demotic, which used Greek letters to write a later form of the Egyptian language. This trilingual inscription enabled scholars for the first time to begin translating ancient hieroglyphic texts.

ruah A Hebrew word meaning "wind," "breath," or "spirit" (Gen. 1:2). It can be interpreted as the mysterious power or presence of God operating in nature and human society, implementing the divine will and inspiring individuals or communities to carry out the divine purpose. Yahweh created the first human by animating "dust" with *ruah* (Gen. 2:7).

Ruth A young widow from Moab who married Boaz of Bethlehem and became an ancestor of King David (Ruth 4:17).

Sabbath The seventh day of the Jewish week, sacred to Yahweh and dedicated to rest and worship (Exod. 20:8–11; Deut. 5:12–15; cf. Mark 2:23–28).

Sabbatical Year According to the Torah, the idea that every seventh year was to be a Sabbath among years, a time when fields were left fallow, native-born slaves freed, and outstanding debts canceled (Exod. 21:2–6; Lev. 25:1–19).

sacrifice In ancient religion, something precious—usually an unblemished animal, fruit, or grain—offered to a god and thereby made sacred. The Mosaic Torah required the regular ritual slaughter of sacrificial animals and birds (Lev. 1–7, 16–17).

Sadducees A conservative Jewish party of the first century BCE and first century CE composed largely of wealthy and politically influential landowners. An aristocracy controlling the priesthood and Temple, they cooperated with the Roman rulers of Palestine, a collusion that made them unpopular wit the common people (Matt. 3:7; 16:1; Mark 12:18; Acts 4:1; 5:17).

saints Holy persons of exceptional virtue and sanctity; believers outstandingly faithful despite persecution (Dan. 7:18–21; Acts 9:13; 1 Thess. 3:13; Rev. 13:7–10).

Salem The Canaanite settlement ruled by the king-priest Melchizedek (Gen. 14:18), later identified with Jerusalem (Ps. 76:2).

Salome (1) The daughter of Herodias and Herod (son of Herod the Great) and niece of Herod Antipas, before whom she danced to secure the head of John the Baptist (Mark 6:17–28). She is anonymous in the New Testament; her name is given by Josephus (*Antiquities* 18.5.4). (2) A woman present at Jesus' crucifixion (Mark 15:40) and at the empty tomb (Mark 16:1).

Samaria The Capital of the northern kingdom (Israel), Samaria was founded by Omri (c. 876–869 BCE) (1 Kings 16:24–25) and destroyed by the Assyrians in 721 BCE (2 Kings 17).

Samaritans Inhabitants of the city or territory of Samaria, the central region of Palestine lying west of the Jordan

River. Separated from the rest of Judaism after about 400 BCE, they had a Bible consisting of their own edition of the Torah and a temple on Mount Gerizim (destroyed 138 BCE). Jesus discussed correct worship with a Samaritan woman (John 4) and made a "good Samaritan" the hero of a famous parable (Luke 10:29–37).

Samson The son of Manoah of the tribe of Dan and a Nazirite judge of Israel famous for his exceptional strength, love affair with Delilah, and destruction of the Philistine temple of Dagon (Judg. 13–16).

Samuel The son of Hannah and Elkanah, and Israel's last judge (1 Sam. 7:15), a prophet and seer (1 Sam. 9:9), who performed priestly functions (1 Sam. 2; 7:9–12); an influential kingmaker, he first anointed Saul as Israel's ruler but later rejected him in favor of David (1 Sam. 13, 15).

sanctuary A holy place dedicated to the worship of a god and commonly believed to confer personal security to those who take refuge in it. Yahweh's Temple on Mount Zion in Jerusalem was such a sacred edifice.

Sanhedrin The supreme judicial council of the Jews (also called the "Great Council") from about the third century BCE until the Romans destroyed Jerusalem in 70 CE. Jesus was tried before the Sanhedrin and condemned on charges of blasphemy (Matt. 26:59; Mark 14:55; Luke 22:66). Peter, John, and other disciples appeared before its court (Acts 4:5–21; 5:17:41), as did Paul (Acts 22).

Sarah The wife and half-sister of Abraham, who traveled with her husband from Ur to Haran to Egypt, ultimately settling in Canaan; after many years of childlessness, she bore Abraham a single son, Isaac (Gen. 18, 21). Paul contrasts the free-born Sarah with her slave Hagar (Gal. 4:22–31).

Sardis The capital of the kingdom of Lydia (modern Turkey), captured by Cyrus the Great (546 BCE); later part of the Roman province of Asia and the site of a cult of Cybele, a pagan fertility goddess (Rev. 3:1–6).

Sargon I The Semitic founder of a Mesopotamian empire incorporating ancient Sumer and Akkad and extending from Elam to the Mediterranean Sea (c. 2360 BCE).

Sargon II The successor of Shalmaneser V and king of Assyria (722–705 BCE) who completed his predecessor's three-year siege of Samaria and captured the city, bringing the northern kingdom (Israel) to an end in 722/721 BCE (2 Kings 17).

Satan In the Hebrew Bible, initially a prosecutor among the "sons of God" in the heavenly council (Job 1–2; Zech. 3) and only later a tempter (1 Chron. 21:1; cf. 2 Sam. 24:1). In the Synoptic Gospels, Satan tries but fails to tempt Jesus (Matt. 4; Luke 4); Revelation identifies him as the "devil" and the primordial serpent who deceived Eve (Rev. 12:9).

Saul From the tribe of Benjamin and Israel's first king (c. 1020–1000 BCE), anointed by Samuel to meet the Philistine crisis. After losing Samuel's support, he and his heir Jonathan were killed at the Battle of Gilboa, after which David became king (1 Sam 9–11, 18–24, 31).

Saul of Tarsus See **Paul.**

Savior One who saves from danger or destruction, a term applied to Yahweh in the Hebrew Bible (Ps. 106:21; Isa. 43:1–13; 63:9) and to Jesus in the New Testament (Luke 2:11; John 4:42; Acts 5:31).

scapegoat In Leviticus 16, a sacrificial goat upon whose head Israel's High Priest placed the people's collective sins on the Day of Atonement, after which the goat was sent into the desert to Azazel (probably a demon). The term has come to signify anyone who bears the blame for others (cf. Isa. 53).

scribes Professional copyists who recorded commercial, royal, and religious texts and served as clerks, secretaries, and archivists at Israel's royal court and Temple (2 Kings 12:10; 19:2; Ezra 4:8; Jer. 36:18). After the Babylonian exile, scribes or "wise men" preserved, expanded upon, and interpreted the Mosaic Torah (Ezra 7:6; Neh. 7:73–8:18). Matthew links scribes with Pharisees as Jesus' opponents (7:29; 23:2, 13), although some became his followers (Matt. 8:19; cf. Acts 6:12; 23:9).

scroll A roll of papyrus, leather, or parchment such as those on which the Hebrew Bible and New Testament were written. The rolls were made of sheets about 9 to 11 inches high and 5 to 6 inches wide, sewed together to make a strip up to 25 to 30 feet long, which was wound around a stick and unrolled when read (Jer. 36, Rev. 6:14).

Sea of Reeds A body of water or swampland bordering the Red Sea that the Israelites miraculously crossed (or into which their Egyptian pursuers sank) during their flight from Egypt (Exod. 14–15).

Second Coming The return of the risen Jesus to earth; also called the Parousia, from the Greek *parousia* (a standing by). Both Paul and the Synoptic authors used this term to denote Jesus' supernatural reappearance to establish the kingdom of God (Matt. 24; Mark 13; Luke 21; 1 Thess.).

Second Isaiah Also known as Deutero-Isaiah, the name scholars assign to the anonymous prophet responsible for Chapters 40–55 of the Book of Isaiah and to the work itself.

Second Temple period The span of Judean history from the rebuilding of the Jerusalem Temple about 515 BCE to the Temple's destruction by the Romans in 70 CE, a period in which Judea was consecutively occupied by Persians, Greeks, and Romans.

seer A clairvoyant or diviner who experiences ecstatic visions (1 Sam. 9:9–11), forerunner of the prophets.

Seir A mountain range extending through Edom almost to the Gulf of 'Aqaba, through which the Israelites passed during their desert wanderings and which was regarded as the home of the Esau tribes; it was an early name for Edom.

Seleucids The Macedonian Greek dynasty founded by Alexander's general Seleucus I (ruled 312–280 BCE), centered in Syria with Antioch as its capital. After defeating the Ptolemies of Egypt, the Seleucids controlled Palestine from 198 to 165 BCE. Maccabean guerrilla fighters defeated the forces of Antiochus IV and eventually drove the Seleucids from Judea (142 BCE).

Semites According to Genesis 10, peoples descended from Noah's son Shem; in modern usage, the term applies to linguistic rather than to ethnic groups, such as those who employ one of a common family of inflectional languages, including Akkadian, Hebrew, Aramaic, and Arabic.

Sennacherib The son of Sargon II and king of Assyria (704–681 BCE). In 701 BCE, Sennacherib devastated Tyre and besieged Jerusalem; although he failed to capture the city, he levied a heavy tribute upon Hezekiah (2 Kings 18).

Septuagint (LXX) A Greek edition of the Hebrew Bible traditionally attributed to about seventy Palestinian scholars during the reign of Ptolemy II (285–246 BCE), but actually the work of several generations of Jewish translators living in Alexandria, Egypt, beginning about 250 BCE and extending into the first century CE. This Greek edition included several documents not accepted into the Hebrew canon (the Apocrypha).

seraphim Heavenly beings, usually depicted with six wings (Isa. 6), who attend the throne of Yahweh.

serpent A common symbol in Near Eastern fertility cults, the original temper of humanity (Gen. 3–4), and a symbol of Assyria, Babylon (Isa. 27:1), and the Israelite tribe of Dan (Gen. 49:17). A bronze image of a snake that was used to heal the Israelites during a plague of snakes in the wilderness (Num. 21:4–9) was later destroyed by King Hezekiah (2 Kings 18:4). Some Christians later identified the Eden serpent with Satan and the devil (Rev. 12:9).

Seth The third son of Adam and Eve (Gen. 4:25–26; 5:2–8), cited as the first man to invoke Yahweh's personal name.

Shalmaneser The names of five Assyrian kings, two of whom appear in the Hebrew Bible: (1) Shalmaneser II (859–824 BCE), who defeated a coalition of Syrian and Palestinian states (including King Ahab's army) (2 Kings 8); (2) Shalmaneser V (726–722 BCE), who laid siege to Israel's capital, Samaria, for three years but died before he could take the city (2 Kings 17).

Shamash The Babylonian sun god associated with justice and prophecy; the Akkadian counterpart of the Sumerian Utu.

Sharon, Plain of The most fertile part of the coastal plain of Palestine, extending about fifty miles north to the headland of Mount Carmel; belonged to the northern kingdom after 922 BCE.

Shechem (1) The son of Hamor (a Canaanite) who wished to marry Jacob's daughter Dinah but whom Jacob's sons Simon and Levi killed (Gen. 33-34); (2) an ancient Canaanite city located about forty miles north of Jerusalem and later allocated to the tribe of Ephraim; the site of Joshua's covenant renewal ceremony (Josh. 24) and of Abimelech's attempt to make himself king (Judg. 9). Solomon's son Rehoboam came to be crowned there, only to be divested of his northern territories by Jeroboam I, who made Shechem his capital (Kings 12).

Shem Noah's oldest son, brother of Ham and Japheth, the eponymous ancestor of the Semites, including the Akkadians, Hebrews, and Arabs (Gen. 9:21–27; 10:1).

Shema Judaism's supreme declaration of covenant faith, expressed in Deuteronomy 6:4–9, beginning: "Listen [Hebrew *shema*, "hear"], Israel: Yahweh our God is the one Yahweh." It also includes Deuteronomy 11:13–21 and Numbers 14:37–41.

Sheol According to the Hebrew Bible, the subterranean region to which the "shades" of all the dead descended, a place of intense gloom and virtual unconsciousness (Eccles. 9:5, 10). In the Greek Septuagint, the term was translated as *Hades* and was commonly regarded as the abode of the dead awaiting resurrection. It is not the same theological concept as hell. See also **Gehenna.**

Shiloh A religious center in the highlands of Ephraim where Joshua assigned Israel's tribes their allotted territories (Josh. 18) and where the Ark of the Covenant was kept until Israel's war with the Philistines (1 Sam. 4), who may have destroyed Shiloh (Jer. 7:12–15; 26:6–9).

Shishak An Egyptian pharaoh (Sheshonk or Sheshonq I) (935–914 BCE) who invaded Judah after Solomon's death and stripped the Temple of its treasures (1 Kings 14:25–28).

shrine A sacred place or altar at which a god is worshiped, usually with ritual sacrifices. According to the Judeans' interpretation of Deuteronomy 12, Yahweh would accept sacrifice only at the Jerusalem Temple, inspiring King Josiah's destruction of all other Israelite shrines (2 Kings 22–23).

Sidon A wealthy Phoenician port city that suffered repeated destructions during the Assyrian, Babylonian, and Persian periods but was rebuilt in Hellenistic times. *Siddonians* is a common term for Phoenicians.

Silas The Semitic, perhaps Aramean, name of an early Christian prophet (Acts 15:32), otherwise called Silvanus, who accompanied Barnabas and Paul to Antioch and joined Paul on his second missionary journey (Acts 16–18); 1 Thess. 1:1). He may have helped write 1 Peter (1 Pet. 5:12).

Simeon (1) Another name for Simon Peter (Acts 15:14; 2 Pet. 1:1); (2) the devout old man who recognized the infant Jesus as the promised Messiah (Luke 2: 22–34).

simile A comparison using "as" or "like," usually to illustrate an unexpected resemblance between a familiar object and a new idea. Jesus' parables about the kingdom of God are typically cast as similes (Matt. 13:31–35, 44–50; Mark 4:26–32; Luke 13:18–19).

Simon The name of several New Testament figures: (1) Simon Peter (Matt. 4:18; 10:2); (2) Simon the Zealot, one of the Twelve (Matt. 10:4; Mark 3:18); (3) one of Jesus' named "brothers" (Matt. 13:55; Mark 6:3); (4) a leper whom Jesus cured (Mark 14:3–9); (5) a man from Cyrene in North Africa who was forced to carry Jesus' cross (Mark 14:3–9); (6) a Pharisee who entertained Jesus in his home (Luke 7:36–50).

Simon Magus A Samaritan sorcerer ("magus") who tried to buy the power of the Holy Spirit from Peter (Acts 8:9–24).

Sinai (Horeb) The sacred mountain where Yahweh appeared to Moses (Exod. 3, 6) and to which he led the Israelites after their flight from Egypt; the site of Yahweh's revelation of his instruction (*torah*). In the J and P traditions, the mountain is called *Sinai*, whereas E and D call it *Horeb*. See also **documentary hypothesis.**

Sisera The Canaanite leader whose forces Deborah and Barak defeated and whom Jael, wife of Heber the Kenite, murdered in her tent (Judg. 4–5).

Socrates The Athenian philosopher (c. 469–399 BCE) and mentor of Plato who taught that life's purpose was to seek the good and prepare the soul for immortality in the afterlife. After being executed for questioning accepted ideas about the gods, he became the subject of his disciples' memoirs, including very different accounts by Plato and Xenophon.

Sodom A city near the shores of the Dead Sea destroyed by a great cataclysm attributed to Yahweh (Gen. 19).

Solomon The son of David and Bathsheba, and Israel's third king (c. 961–922 BCE), famous for his wisdom, who built Yahweh's Temple in Jerusalem, but whose policies reportedly exhausted Israel's resources, eventually triggering a disastrous split between Israel's twelve tribes (1 Kings 1–12).

Son of Man (1) A Hebrew Bible phrase used to denote a human being (Ps. 8:4; 80:17), as it is throughout the Book of Ezekiel, where it commonly describes the prophet himself; (2) a mysterious figure, "one like a son of man," in the Book of Daniel; (3) In the Gospels, the phrase by which Jesus typically refers to himself.

Sons of Thunder See **Thunder, Sons of.**

soul In Hebrew, *nephesh* (breath), applied to both humans and animals as living beings (Gen. 1:20; 2:7; 2:19; Exod. 1:5). It was translated *psyche* in the Greek Septuagint, the same term used for "life" rather than the immortal personality in the New Testament (Matt. 10:28; 16:26; Phil. 1:27; Rev. 20:4).

source criticism Analysis of a biblical document to discover the sources, written or oral, that the author(s) incorporated into it.

stele (stela) An upright slab or pillar inscribed with a commemorative message, such as that bearing the Code of Hammurabi or that of King Mesha of Moab, who commemorated his victory over Israel following Jehu's revolution.

Stephen A Hellenistic Jew whom a Jerusalem mob stoned for his Christian preaching (Acts 6), thus becoming the first martyr of the early church.

Stoicism A Greek philosophy that became popular among the upper classes in Roman times. Stoicism emphasized duty, endurance, self-control, and service to the gods, the family, and the state. Paul debated with Stoics in Athens (Acts 17:18–34).

Succession Narrative The account of David's rise to kingship and his succession by Solomon that many scholars believe underlies the narrative in 2 Samuel 9–24 and 1 Kings 1–2. It is also known as the Court History.

Succoth (Sukkoth) A Hebrew Bible term meaning "booths," commonly referring to an autumn festival of thanksgiving commemorating Israel's wilderness journey from Egypt to Canaan, when the people lived in booths, improvised shelters.

Sumer The region at the head of the Persian Gulf between the Tigris and Euphrates rivers, site of the oldest literate urban civilization in the ancient Near East and the traditional homeland of Abraham and his ancestors.

Sumerians The inhabitants of ancient Sumer, who first emerged as a distinctive people in the late fourth millennium BCE.

symbol From the Greek *symbolon*, a "token" or "sign," and *symballein*, to "throw together" or "compare." In its broadest usage, it means anything that stands for something else, as the Star of David signifies Judaism and the cross represents Christianity. The authors of both Daniel and Revelation use highly symbolic language.

synagogue In Judaism, a gathering of no fewer than ten adult males assembled for worship, scriptural instruction, and administration of local Jewish affairs. Synagogues probably began forming during the Babylonian exile, when the Jerusalem Temple no longer existed.

syncretism The blending of different religions, a term biblical scholars typically apply to the mingling of Canaanite rites and customs with the Israelites' Mosaic traditions.

Synoptic Gospels The first three Gospels—Matthew, Mark, and Luke—so named because they share a large quantity of material in common, allowing their texts to be viewed together "with one eye."

Synoptic Problem A term referring to scholars' attempts to discover the literary relationship among the three strikingly similar Synoptic Gospels; in John, the Fourth Gospel, Jesus' teaching differs in both form and content from the Synoptic traditions.

Syria (1) The territory extending from the upper Euphrates River to northern Palestine; (2) the kingdom of Aram, with its capital at Damascus.

Tabernacle The portable tent-shrine, elaborately decorated, that housed the Ark of the Covenant (Exod. 25–31) from the Exodus to the building of Solomon's Temple (1 Kings 6–8). As a symbol of God "tenting" with his people, it expressed Yahweh's presence in Israel.

Tables (Tablets) of the Law The stone slabs on which the Ten Commandments were inscribed (Exod. 24:12; 32:15–20).

Talmud A huge collection of Jewish religious traditions containing two parts: (1) the Mishnah (written editions of ancient oral interpretations of the Torah) (c. 220 BCE) and (2) the Gemara, extensive commentaries on the Mishnah. The Palestinian version of the Talmud, which is incomplete, was produced about 450 CE; the Babylonian Talmud, nearly four times as long, was finished about 500 CE. Both editions contain the Mishnah and Gemara.

Tamar (1) The wife of Er, son of Judah, who, when widowed, posed as a prostitute to trick her father-in-law into begetting children (Gen. 38); (2) Absalom's sister, who was raped by her half-brother Amnon, whom Absalom latter killed (2 Sam. 13).

Tanakh A comparatively modern name for the Hebrew Bible, an acronym consisting of the consonants that represent the three major divisions of the Bible: the *Torah* (divine teaching), the *Nevi'im* (Prophets), and the *Kethuvim* (Writings).

Tarsus The capital of the Roman province of Cilicia (southwestern Turkey) and birthplace of Paul (Saul) (Acts 9:11; 11:25).

tel Flat-topped artificial mounds consisting of the superimposed ruins of ancient cities that dot the landscape of Mesopotamia, Syria, and Palestine.

Temple (1) The imposing sanctuary that King Solomon built on Mount Zion in Jerusalem to house the Ark of the Covenant in its innermost room (the Holy of Holies) (1 Kings 5:15–9:25). Later recognized as the only authorized center for sacrifice to Yahweh, it was destroyed by Nebuchadnezzar in 587 BCE (2 Kings 25:8–17). (2) The Second Temple, which exiles returned from Babylon rebuilt about 515 BCE; was extensively renovated by King Herod; Roman armies destroyed it in 70 CE, thus permanently ending the system of sacrifice mandated by the Mosaic Torah.

Ten Commandments (Decalogue) The set of ten religious and moral laws that Yahweh inscribed on stone tablets and gave to Moses (Exod. 20; Deut 5).

Tent of Meeting See **Tabernacle.**

teraphim Small figurines representing household gods or possibly a family's guardian spirit or ancestors. Rachel stole and hid her father's teraphim, presumably to enhance Jacob's status as their possessor (Gen. 31:30–35); King Josiah outlawed them (2 Kings 23:24).

testament From the Latin for "covenant," the term used for the two main divisions of the Bible—the Old Testament (canonical Hebrew Scriptures) and the New Testament (Christian Greek Scriptures).

Tetragrammaton The four Hebrew consonants ("YHWH" is the English equivalent) representing the personal name *Yahweh*, the God of Israel. Although the sacred name appears almost 7,000 times in the Hebrew Bible, most contemporary translators continue the traditional Jewish practice of inaccurately rendering it as "the LORD."

Tetrateuch A scholarly term for the first four books of the Bible, Genesis through Numbers; Deuteronomy, the fifth Torah volume, is written in a different style that links it to the narrative histories that follow it (Joshua–2 Kings).

textual criticism The comparison and analysis of ancient manuscripts to discover copyists' errors and, if possible, to reconstruct the probable original form of the document; also known as "lower criticism."

Thaddeus One of the most obscure of Jesus' apostles, listed among the Twelve in Matthew 10:3 and Mark 3:18, but not in Luke 7:16 or Acts 1:13.

theocracy Literally, a "rule by God"; typically a society or state in which priests or other religious authorities govern in the name of a deity, such as in ancient Israel. The Vatican and contemporary Iran are modern examples.

theodicy From the Greek term combining "god" and "justice"; denotes a literary attempt to explain how an all-good, all-powerful God can permit the existence of evil and undeserved suffering.

theology The study and interpretation of concepts about God's nature, purpose, attributes, and relationship with humanity; from the Greek *theos* (god) and *logos* (word, or rational discourse).

theophany From the Greek, meaning an appearance of a god to a person, as when El wrestled with Jacob (Gen. 32:26–32), Yahweh appeared to Moses (Exod. 3:1–4:17; 6:2–13) and the elders of Israel (Exod. 24:9–11), and the risen Jesus revealed himself to Thomas (John 20:24–29) and Paul (Acts 9:3–9).

Theophilus The otherwise unknown man to whom the Gospel of Luke and the Book of Acts are addressed. He may have been a Roman official who became a Christian.

Thessalonica A major Macedonian city where Paul and Silas converted many of the local citizens, both Jews and Greeks; Paul wrote 1 (and possibly 2) Thessalonians to the congregation there.

Third Isaiah See **Isaiah.**

Thomas One of the Twelve Apostles (Matt. 10:3; Mark 3:18), seldom mentioned in the Synoptics but relatively prominent in the Fourth Gospel, where he is called Didymus (twin) (John 11:16; 20:24). Thomas doubted the other disciples' report of Jesus' resurrection, but when suddenly confronted with the risen Jesus, he pronounces the strongest confession of faith in the Gospel (John 20:24–29).

Thunder, Sons of A phrase (Greek, Boanerges) that Jesus applied to the apostles James and John (Mark 3:17), possibly because of their impulsive temperaments (Luke 9:52–56).

Tiberius Stepson of Augustus and second emperor of Rome (14–37 CE). According to Luke 3:1, Jesus came to John for baptism in the fifteenth year of Tiberius's reign. Except for in Luke 2:1, he is the Caesar referred to in the Gospels.

Tiglath-Pileser II The emperor of Assyria (745–727 BCE) and the biblical "Pul" (2 Kings 15:19) who captured Damascus in 732 BCE and imposed tribute from Israel and Judah (2 Kings 16).

Tigris River According to Genesis 2:14 (where it is called the Hiddekel), the third of four rivers that watered Eden. Approximately 1,146 miles long, it forms the eastern boundary of Mesopotamia, where the Assyrians built the cities of Nineveh and Asshur.

Timothy The younger friend and fellow missionary of Paul, and the son of a Greek father and a devout Jewish mother (Acts 16:1; 2 Tim. 1:5). The portrayal of Timothy in the pastoral epistles seems irreconcilable with what is known of him from Acts and Paul's genuine letters.

tithe The payment of a tenth of one's income in money, crops, or animals to support a government or religion. In ancient Israel, upkeep of the High Priest, Levites, and Temple was supported by required tithing (Luke 11:42; 18:12).

Titus (1) The son of and successor to Vespasian, and emperor of Rome (79–81 CE), he directed the siege of Jerusalem, burned the city, and ordered his army to tear down Herod's Temple. His carrying of the Temple treasures to Rome is portrayed in the triumphal Arch of Titus that still stands in the Roman Forum. (2) A Greek whom Paul converted and who became a companion on his missionary journeys (2 Cor. 8:23; Gal. 2:1–3). A post-Pauline writer made him a model of the Christian pastor (Titus 1–3).

Torah A Hebrew term commonly translated "law," "instruction," or "teaching"; refers primarily to the Pentateuch, the first five books of the Hebrew Bible, and in a general sense to all the canonical writings, which are traditionally regarded as a direct oracle or revelation from Yahweh. In lowercase, *torah* refers to the teaching content of the Pentateuch.

tradition (1) Collections of stories and interpretations transmitted orally from generation to generation and embodying the religious history and beliefs of a people or community, such as the contents of the Yahwist or Priestly components of the Torah; (2) oral explanations, interpretations, and applications of the written Torah (1 Chron. 4:22; Mark 7:5; Matt. 15:2; Gal. 1:15); (3) in the New Testament, orally transmitted stories about Jesus circulated in the Christian community before finding written form in the Gospels.

tradition criticism The analysis of the origin and development of specific biblical stories and themes—such as the Exodus motif in the Hebrew Bible and the eschatology of the kingdom of God in the New Testament—as presented by different biblical writers. In some cases, tradition criticism emphasizes the early and oral stages of development.

Trajan The emperor of Rome (98–117 CE) who brought the Roman Empire to its greatest geographical extent and who may have persecuted some Christians, although he wrote to Pliny the Younger, governor of Bithynia, that Christians were not to be sought out or denounced anonymously.

transcendence The quality of God expressing his inherent limitlessness and surpassing of all physical and cosmic boundaries.

Transfiguration A supernatural transformation of the human Jesus into a being of light, which Jesus' three closest disciples—Peter, James, and John—witnessed on an isolated mountaintop (Matt. 17:1–13; Mark 9:2–13; Luke 9:28–36).

Transjordan The rugged plateau area east of the Jordan River, a region Joshua assigned to the tribes of Reuben, Gad, and half of Manasseh (Josh. 13) but which they failed to wrest from other Semites living there.

tree of life An ancient Mesopotamian symbol of rejuvenation or immortality, which the Genesis author places in the Garden of Eden (Gen. 2:9; 3:22–24); its leaves are reserved for the "healing" of nations (Rev. 2:7; 22:2, 24).

Trinity The post–New Testament doctrine that God exists as three divine Persons in One—father, Son, and Holy Spirit—and that was formally affirmed at the Council of Nicaea (325 CE), although not accepted by the entire Christian community until centuries later.

Trumpets, Feast of A festival, assembly, and sacrifice held on the first day of the seventh (sabbatical) month (Lev. 13:23–25; Num. 29:1–7).

Twelve, the The twelve Apostles whom Jesus specifically chose to follow him. Different names appear in different New Testament lists of the Twelve (Matt. 10:1–5; Mark 3:16–19; Luke 6:12–16; Acts 1:13–14).

Twelve Tribes of Israel Traditionally descended from the twelve sons of Jacob (Israel) (Gen. 49); the tribes were Reuben, Simeon, Levi, Judah, Issachar, Zebulun, Joseph (later divided into the tribes of Ephraim and Manasseh), Gad, Asher, Dan, Naphtali, and Benjamin (cf. Josh 13–19). Simeon disappears early from the biblical record.

Tyre An ancient Phoenician seaport famous for its commerce and wealth, built on a small island about twenty-five miles south of Sidon (Ezek. 26–28); Alexander sacked the city in 332 BCE, although it was later rebuilt.

Ugarit An ancient Canaanite city (Arabic Ras Shamra) in modern Syria where cuneiform archives preserve prebiblical myths about El and Baal, some of which anticipate traditions later associated with Yahweh.

Ur One of the world's oldest cities, in Sumer, and Abraham's ancestral homeland, from which his family migrated to Haran (Gen. 11:28–31). Archaeologists have excavated a well-preserved ziggurat there, as well as richly appointed royal tombs.

Uriah A Hittite soldier whose wife, Bathsheba, King David seduced, causing him to arrange for Uriah's death in battle (2 Sam. 11–12). Bathsheba then became the mother of Solomon, David's heir to the throne.

Urim and Thummin Undescribed objects (whose names may mean "oracle" and "truth") that were used by Israel's priests in casting lots to determine Yahweh's will on a specific matters.

Uruk One of Mesopotamia's oldest cities, the capital of Gilgamesh.

Utnapishtim The Babylonian Noah, the only man (with his wife and servants) to survive the Flood and the only mortal on whom the gods conferred immortality. Warned of the coming deluge, he built an ark, stocked it with animals, and, when the flood waters retreated, offered sacrifice to the gods.

Uz Job's unidentified homeland, which various scholars have suggested was Edom, Arabia, or a location east of the Jordan River.

Uzziah (Azariah) The king of Judah (783–742 BCE), and a contemporary of King Jeroboam II of Israel (786–746 BCE), who defeated the Philistines, Ammonites, and Arabs, and greatly extended Judah's political jurisdiction.

Vashti The empress of Persia (unknown to history) who refused to exhibit herself to the male friends of her husband, Ahasureus (Xerxes I), and whom Esther replaced as queen (Esther 1:9–2:18).

veil The elaborately decorated curtain separating the Holy Place from the Most Holy Place in the Tabernacle and (later) in the Jerusalem Temple (Mark 15:30; cf. Heb. 9–10).

Vespasian The emperor of Rome (69–79 CE) who earlier, as a general under Nero, led Roman legions into Judea during the Jewish Revolt (66–73 CE); when he became emperor, he left the capture of Jerusalem to his son Titus.

Vulgate Bible Jerome's Latin translation of the Bible (late fourth century CE), to which the Apocrypha was later added and which became the official edition of Roman Catholicism.

Wisdom A personification of the divine attribute of creative intelligence, portrayed in the form of a gracious woman who mediates between God and humanity (Prov. 1:20–33; 8:1–31; Ecclus. 24). In John's Gospel, Wisdom's speeches appear to be the model for Jesus' discourses.

wisdom literature Biblical works dealing primarily with practical and ethical behavior, as well as ultimate religious questions, such as divine justice and the problem of evil: Proverbs, Job, Ecclesiastes, the Wisdom of Jesus Son of Sirach (Ecclesiasticus), and the Wisdom of Solomon. The New Testament Book of James also has characteristics of wisdom writing.

Word, the (1) The "word" or "oracle" of Yahweh, a phrase characteristic of Israel's prophets, typically referring to a divine pronouncement, judgment, or statement of purpose that the prophet delivers in his God's name; (2) the Word (Logos), the philosophical term that John uses to denote Jesus in his prehuman form (John 1:1–18).

Writings See **Kethuvim.**

Xerxes I Thought to be the biblical Ahasuerus, emperor of Persia (486–465 BCE) (Esther; Ezra 4:6).

Yahweh A translation of the sacred name of Israel's God, represented almost 7,000 times in the Hebrew Bible by four consonants of the Tetragrammaton (YHWH) (Exod. 3; 6; cf. Gen. 4:26).

Yahwist The name scholars give the anonymous scribe or compiler who produced the J document, the oldest literary strand in the Pentateuch, so called for the author's use of the name Yahweh throughout.

YHWH English letters transliterating the four Hebrew consonants (the Tetragrammaton) denoting the personal name of Israel's God, Yahweh.

Yom Kippur See **Day of Atonement.**

Zadok A priest officiating during the reigns of David and Solomon who supported the latter's claim to the throne and was rewarded by being made chief priest at the Temple. Ezekiel regarded Zadok's descendants as the only legitimate priests (Ezek. 40–46).

Zealots A fiercely nationalistic Jewish party dedicated to freeing Judea from foreign domination that coalesced about 67–68 CE during the great rebellion against Rome (66–73 CE).

Zebedee A Galilean fisherman, husband of Salome, and father of the apostles James and John (Mark 1:19–20; 14:33).

Zebulun (1) The sixth son of Jacob and Leah; (2) the tribe of Zebulun, represented in Jacob's blessing as a seagoing group located near the Phoenician port of Sidon, but actually settled in a landlocked farming area of northern Palestine (Josh. 19).

Zechariah A Judean prophet whose message is contained in the book of the Minor Prophets bearing his name. A contemporary of Haggai (c. 520–515), he urged the returned exiles to rebuild Yahweh's Temple in Jerusalem. The final chapters of the book bearing his name are thought to be the work of a later author (Zech. 9–14).

Zedekiah The last king of Judah (c. 597–587 BCE), who reigned as a tribute-paying vassal of Nebuchadnezzar and who rebelled against the Babylonian king, who then destroyed Jerusalem and blinded him (2 Kings 24–25; cf. Jer. 21:1–7; 27:12:22; 38:7–28).

Zephaniah A seventh-century-BCE Judean prophet whose oracles of judgment are collected in the book bearing his name.

Zerubbabel A grandson of Jehoiachin, the king of Judah imprisoned in Babylon (1 Chron. 3:17), and therefore a legitimate heir to the Judean throne, who served as Persia's governor of the partly restored Judean community in Jerusalem (Ezra 3; Hag. 1:1, 14) but who later disappeared from history. His name means "begotten in Babylon."

Zeus In Greek myth, the king of the Olympian gods and patron of civic order. A personification of storms and other heavenly forces, he ruled by wielding the lightning bolt. The Romans identified him with Jupiter (Jove).

ziggurat A characteristic architectural form of the Sumerian and Babylonian temples; a multileveled tower resembling a stepped or recessed pyramid consisting of successively smaller platforms built one atop the other. At its top was a chapel dedicated to a major civic god (cf. Gen. 11:1–9).

Zion A word probably meaning "citadel," originally a Jebusite hilltop fortress that David captured and on which he built his palace and housed the Ark of the Covenant (2 Sam. 5–6). In time, the term came to refer either to the hill on which Solomon built Yahweh's Temple or to the surrounding city of Jerusalem.

Zipporah A daughter of Jethro, a Midianite shepherd and priest, who became Moses' wife (Exod. 2:11–22) and who bore him at least two sons, Gershom and Eliezer, saving the latter from Yahweh's wrath by circumcising him with a flint knife (Exod. 4:18–26).

Zoroastrianism The official religion of imperial Persia, founded by the east Iranian prophet Zoroaster, who taught that the universe is composed of parallel worlds of matter and spirit in which legions of good and evil spirits contend. In a final cosmic battle, Ahura Mazda, god of light and righteousness, will totally defeat Ahriman, embodiment of darkness and chaos. Historians believe that many biblical concepts of angelology and demonology, including the character of Satan, ultimately derive from Zoroastrian influence.

Index

Aaron, 88, 91, 206, 257, 403
Aaronites, 91
Abba, 378
Abel, 70, 404, 410
Abimelech, 59, 115, 117, 118
Abraham, 12, 35, 45, 63, 65, 123, 145, 332,
   403, 404, 405
   believers as heirs of, 378
   God's call to, 4, 52, 71, 82
   Isaac/Ishmael as son of, 72
   as justification by faith model, 380
   theophany of, 71–72
   Ur birthplace of, 31, 33, 71, 214
   Yahweh and, 55, 71
Abrahamic Covenant, 15, 55, 65, 71–73
   circumcision and, 72
   as unconditional, 16
Absalom, 123, 125, 127, 235
abyss (bottomless pit), 421, 430
acrostic, 229
Acts, 12, 325, 350–362
   Gentile mission in, 353
   God's spirit operating in human history
      in, 351–352
   "Hellenist" Jewish Christians persecutions in,
      353, 354
   Holy Spirit in, 328
   humanity's salvation, divine plan for in, 351–352
   Jerusalem church founding in, 353–354
   Jerusalem Conference in, 355
   Jesus' ascension in, 353
   Luke's use of speeches in, 352–353
   organization of, 353–361
   Paul/Cornelius conversions in, 353, 354–355
   Paul's arrest/imprisonment in, 266, 353,
      358, 360
   Paul's letters *vs.*, 365
   Paul's missionary journey in, 266, 331, 353–359
   Paul's preaching to Diaspora Jews in, 353,
      360–361
   Pentecost and, 333
Adam, 39, 69–70
   Paul's association with Christ with, 372–373,
      380–381, 386
Adonai, 14
Advocate. *See* Paraclete
afterlife, 210, 259, 318, 374
agape love, 372, 430
Ahab (king), 134–135, 425
   Elijah confrontation with, 146
   Jehu's massacre of dynasty of, 137–138
Ahasurerus (Xerxes I), 230, 238, 240
Ahaz (king), 147, 161
Ahijah (prophet), 134, 146
Ai, 106, 108–109
Akhenaton, 45
Akkadians, 34–35
Alexander the Great, 44, 231, 239, 240,
   246–247, 251, 269, 270, 280
allegory, 202, 228, 299, 378
alpha, 412
Amalekites, 124, 125
Amarna Age, 45
Ammon, 123, 127
Amorites, 35, 41

Amos, 8, 144, 153, 433
   Assyrian Crisis and, 148
   Day of Yahweh and, 154–155
   on human suffering indifference, 154
   visions of, 155
   Yahweh's demand for economic justice in, 154
Ancient Near East, 31–50
   Akkadians and, 34–35
   Bible and, 31–32
   Biblical world prologue and, 33–35
   Code of Hammurabi, 41–44
   Egypt, 31, 44–46, 77, 78, 79, 81, 82, 161–162,
      171–172, 337
   Epic of Gilgamesh and, 35–40, 57–58, 71,
      221, 427
   Mesopotamian underworld, 40–41
   Sumerians in, 33–34
Andrew, 293, 295, 297
angel, 254, 260
   Gabriel, 247, 329
   in God's heavenly court, 427
   Jacob wrestling with, 73–74
   Michael, 100, 246, 416, 419, 428
Angel of Death, 91, 128
   Assyrians and, 141, 163
   death of firstborn and, 80
anointed rulers, 206
anointing
   of Davidic kings, 287
   ritual of, 122, 123
anthropomorphism
   in Exodus, 93
   J portrayal of, 98
   in Torah, 85
anti-Christ, 393
antinomianism, 378
Antioch, 312, 355
Antiochus IV, 231, 241, 242, 243, 382
   persecutions of, 246, 251–252, 254, 256
Antiquities of the Jews (Josephus), 267
antithetical parallelism, 202
Anu, 33–34
apocalypse, 150, 194, 238, 249, 413
   of 2 Esdras, 258
   2 Thessalonians on, 391–393
   Gospel of Luke on expectations
      of, 333
Apocalypse of Peter, 24, 431
apocalyptic literature, 150–151, 238,
   412–413
   ancient myths/symbolic language in, 245
   characteristics of, 242–243
   chronological dualism of, 244
   cosmic destruction in, 243
   cosmic dualism in, 244
   ethical dualism in, 244–245
   Gospel of Mark as, 293–294
   Gospel of Matthew and, 289
   predestination in, 245
Apocrypha, 24, 199, 249, 381, 391
   of Catholic Bible, 4
   Prayer of Manasseh in, 236
   Tanakh/NIV lack of, 27
Apocryphal books, 249–262
   1 Maccabees, 11, 250–252

2 Maccabees, 11, 241, 242, 244, 250,
   252–253
   additions to Daniel/Esther, 250
   Baruch, 102, 168, 239, 250, 255
   Ecclesiasticus, 250, 255–257
   Judith, 250, 254–255
   Letter of Jeremiah, 250, 255
   Tobit, 250, 252–254, 284, 299
apokalypsis, 367, 412
apostasy, 99, 235
   in DH, 103
   in Hosea, 155
   of Israelites, 92, 135
apostle, 295
Aquilla, 360, 371
Ark of the Covenant, 46, 55, 98, 104, 106, 125, 235
   cherubim on, 70, 86, 177
   in Jerusalem Temple, 130
   Philistine capture of, 123
Armageddon *(Har-Megiddo)*, 44, 47, 418
Artaxerxes (emperor), 22, 197, 198
Asa, 236
ascension, of Jesus, 353
Asclepius, 274–275
Asherah, 112, 139, 172
Ashubanipal IV, 35
Asia Minor
   Christians persecuted in, 406
   Paul's missionary journey to, 356–358
   seven churches in, 414
Assyria
   Ashurbanipal IV as ruler of, 35
   decline of, 148–149
   Israel invasion of, 49, 139, 162–163
   map of, 159
Assyrian Crisis
   Amos/Hosea/Isaiah/Micah and, 148
   prophets of, 158–167
Assyrian Empire, 166, 253
Assyrians, 254–255
   Angel of Death and, 141
   Empire of, 137
   Israel conquering by, 95
   Manasseh removal by, 236
   Samaria destruction by, 153
Athanasius (bishop)
   canon of, 25
   New Testament and, 22
Athens, 356, 369
Aton, as Egyptian sun god, 47
Atonement, Day of (Yom Kippur), 89, 257,
   402, 403
Augustus (Gaius Octavius), 266, 267, 280
Azazel, 89

Baal, 92, 99, 111, 112, 116, 156
   Elijah's challenge to, 147
   Gideon as follower of, 114
   Jezebel as worshiper of, 134
   Yahweh contest with, 134–135
Babel, Tower of, 34, 71
Babylon, 4
   Amorite dynasty in, 41
   Cyrus the Great capture of, 181
   exile to, 95

fall of, 130, 163, 181
Jerusalem demolished by, 8, 54, 127
Judah conquest by, 103, 169, 214
Marduk and, 34
Nebuchadnezzar and, 170
rise of, 148–149
scale model of, 180
threat of, 173
Babylonian Exile, 203
Israel's last prophets after, 184–191
Judah's religious mission reinterpretation after, 192–193
prophets of, 149, 168–175
wisdom literature absence of, 209
Balaam, 92
bar Kochba rebellion, 267, 285–286
Barabbas, 303
Barak (king), 92
Barnabas, 353, 355–356
1 Baruch, 239
Jeremiah writing of, 168
Letter of Jeremiah in, 250, 255
2 Baruch, 239
Bathsheba, 127, 130, 146, 234, 235
beast, in Revelation, 419
Beatitudes, 307, 330, 332
Behemoth, 218
Belchazzar, 245
Beloved Disciple, John as, 337
ben Sirach. *See* Wisdom of Jesus Son of Sirach
bene ha Elohim, 39, 214–215, 427
Benjamin, 119
Bethel, 34, 73, 74, 130
Bethlehem, 226
Bible. *See also* New Testament; Old Testament
abbreviations of books of, 26
analytical reading of, 27–28
German translation of, 25
social viewpoints and, 29
Bible, creation of, 18–30
analytical reading of, 27–29
canon within canon in, 29–30
Hebrew Bible, canon of, 22
New Testament, canon of, 22–27
text transmission in, 18–22
Bible, overview of, 3–17
contents of, 4–7
God, encountering in, 12–14
reasons for reading, 3–4
Septuagint/Christian Bible, 10–11
topic/location in, 7
Yahweh/Lord of Covenant in, 14–16
Bildad, 216
bishop, qualifications of, 386
Boaz, 224–226
Book of Glory. *See* Gospel of John
Book of Signs. *See also* Gospel of John
Jesus' discourses of divine nature, 342
Lazarus raising in, 342, 344
miracle at Cana in, 342, 343
of Nicodemus spiritual rebirth, 342
of Samaritan woman conversation, 342, 343–344
of Temple cleansing, 342, 343
Book of the Covenant, 42, 388
Moses and, 58, 83
at Mount Sinai, 84
Bronze Age, 35, 108, 109, 112

Caesar, Julius, 265, 280
Caesarea, Paul's imprisonment in, 358, 360, 384–385
Caesarea Philippi, 297
Caiaphas, 282, 293, 298, 303
Cain, 70, 410
Caleb, 91
Calvary, 334
Canaan, 237. *See also* Palestine
Egypt's military fortresses in, 44

Israelite's conquest/occupation of, 4, 8, 15, 95, 103, 106–111, 426
Israelites travel to, 56
map of, 140
Moses, forbidden to enter, 95
Pentateuch promise of, 55
canon
of Athanasius, 25
within canon, 29–30
Luther on, 30
of New Testament, 22–27
Canticles. *See* Song of Songs
captivity letters, Colossians/Philippians/Philemon/Ephesians as, 366
Catholic Bible, 4, 11, 249
catholic epistles
James, 401, 404–406
1 John, 401, 409–410
2 John, 401, 410
3 John, 401, 410
Jude, 401, 407–408
1Peter, 401, 406–408
2 Peter, 22, 401, 408–409
Cephas, 295
Chaldea, 173
chaos, 13, 67
Chemosh, 138
cherubim, 41
on Ark of the Covenant, 70, 86, 177
at Eden, 70
Christ, 428. *See also* Jesus
cosmic role of, 367
as cosmic unity source, 393–394
glorified, 416
hymn to, in Philippians, 385–386
as Lamb of God, 416
Melchizedek *vs.*, 402–403
Paul's association of Adam with, 372–373, 380–381, 386
Romans on faith in, 380–382
supremacy of, 393–394
united body of, 395–396
Christianity
events that shaped, 270
Gnosticism as heretical by, 24
Herod I and, 265–266
Jewish Revolt against Rome and, 266–269, 283, 292, 305, 321, 414
origination of, 265–281
Roman occupation of Palestine and, 265
as universal faith, 328–329
Christians
Asia Minor persecution of, 406
ministry qualifications of, 399
persecution of, 414–415
unity necessity of, 370
Christology, 300, 348, 393
Chronicler
authorship of, 233
on David/Solomon/Hezekiah/Manasseh, 234
DH reliance by, 234
on Judah, 235–236
1 Chronicles, 8, 234–235
Chronicler of, 233
David's reign in, 122
genealogy in, 234
Judah/Israel kings in, 104
Temple rituals in, 194
2 Chronicles, 8, 10, 235–237
Chronicler of, 233
on Manasseh, 141, 236–237
from Solomon to Hezekiah on, 236
Temple rituals in, 194
church
instructions to, 312, 320
offices of, 397

circumcision, 46
Abrahamic Covenant and, 72
James as advocate of, 355
P on, 65
Paul attacking advocates of, 386
1 Clement, 23, 360
Code of Hammurabi, 41–44
codex, 18, 20
Colossians, 366, 393
communion. *See* Eucharist
Constantine, 18–19
Coptic translation, of Gospel of Judas, 23
Corinth, 356, 369
1 Corinthians, 366, 369–374
on afterlife, 374
on agape love, 372
on Christian unity necessity, 370
on Eucharist, 371
on gifts of the spirit, 372
on resurrection of dead, 372–374
on spiritual body, nurturing of, 373–374
on women's ministry, 371
2 Corinthians, 366, 374–375
Cornelius, conversions of, 353, 354–355
cosmic destruction
in apocalyptic literature, 243
in Revelation, 415
cosmic rule, God's associates in, 427–428
cosmic unity, Christ as source of, 393–394
cosmos, 13, 67, 69
Court History (Succession Narrative), in 2 Samuel, 104
covenant. *See also* Abrahamic Covenant; Ark of the Covenant; Book of the Covenant; Davidic Covenant; Fifth Covenant; Mosaic Covenant; Noachan Covenant
Canaan conquest as fulfillment of, 106–110
Israel's breaking of, 15, 54
Joshua renewal of, 111
Malachi messenger of, 188–189
Pentateuch promise of, 55
renewal, in Deuteronomy, 97–99, 102
territorial dimension of, 110–111
Covenant Code. *See* Book of the Covenant
creation, 57
Egypt myths of, 47
Jesus as mediator of, 394
second version of, 68–70
crucifixion, of Jesus, 288, 303–304, 313, 340, 345
cult, 86
cuneiform
on Bronze Age, 35
Sumerian system of writing of, 33
Cyrus the Great, 10, 22, 96, 159, 186, 196, 231, 245
Babylon capture by, 181, 184
decree of, 235

D. *See* Deuteronomist
Dagon, Samson and, 118
Damascus, 354
Daniel (Danel), 8, 39–40, 70, 150, 209, 231, 238, 243–247, 255, 298, 392, 422
apocalyptic work of, 194, 242, 246–247, 250
on death, 40
in Ezekiel, 244–245
Joseph resemblance of, 243–244
literary figure of, 243–244
Nebuchadnezzar and, 243, 246
organization of, 245–246
prayer of, 247
sources of, 244–245
Darius (king), 185, 197, 240, 245–246
David (king), 4, 8, 49, 92, 103, 121, 125, 126, 234
anointing ritual for, 122, 123
census taking of, 215, 429

David (king) (*continued*)
    Goliath and, 124
    as idealized priest-king, 234–235
    J narrative on, 62–63
    Messiah as descendant of, 11
    Philistine refuge for, 124
    Psalms authorship by, 203
    rise to power of, 104, 124–125
    Yahweh's presence and, 55
Davidic Covenant (Royal Covenant), 16, 127,
    193–194, 206, 286–287
Day of Atonement. *See* Atonement, Day of
Day of Judgment. *See* Judgment, Day of
Day of Yahweh, 154–155, 164–165, 174,
    188, 239, 243
Dead Sea Scrolls, 18, 19–22, 27, 38, 260, 284, 285
Deborah, 114, 117, 145
Decalogue. *See* Ten Commandments
Delilah, Samson and, 119
deuterocanonical books, 4, 249
Deutero-Isaiah. *See* Second Isaiah
Deuteronomist (D), 63, 64–65, 96
Deuteronomistic History (DH), 97–98, 119, 150, 234
    apostasy in, 103
    David as pivotal character in, 121
    of Deuteronomy/Joshua/Judges/
        Samuel/Kings, 96
    Former Prophets as, 101
    on Hezekiah, 139
    on Judah's collapse, 235
    major events/meaning in, 103–104
    on Manasseh, 141, 236
    on Omri, 138
    two editions of, 102–103, 129–130
Deuteronomy, 3, 8, 64, 83, 94–100, 193–194
    Canaan slaughter in, 426
    covenant renewal/national restoration in,
        97–99, 102
    on Jesus crucifixion, 288
    Josiah and, 95–96
    Moses and, 59, 96–97, 100, 103
    prophecy in, 99
    on religious purity, 99
    revised Ten Commandments in, 96–97
    on Sabbath, 68, 96
    slaves/marginalized groups in, 97
    Torah law in, 53–54, 59
    transcendence, 98–99
    war/conquest/genocide in, 99
devil. *See* Satan
DH. *See* Deuteronomistic History
Diana of Ephesus, 361
Diaspora, 192, 197, 253–254, 405
    Jews in, 238–241, 354
    Paul's preaching to Jews of, 360–361
    survival in, 231
Dionysus of Thebes, 147, 275–277, 279
    Jesus of Nazareth *vs.*, 275, 277
    as wine-making inventor, 275–276
disciples, 294
"Discourse on Hades" (Josephus), 332
divine council, 427
    prose prologue for, 214–216
    Psalms on, 38
    Satan expulsion from, 429–430
divine promises, in Pentateuch, 54–55
Docetism, 341, 409
documentary hypothesis, of Torah, 62–65
    D, Deuteronomist of, 63, 64–65
    E, Elohist of, 63–64
    J, Yahwist of, 62–63
    P, priestly writer of, 63, 65
    recent challenges to, 65
Domitian, 407, 414, 420
Dragon, in Revelation, 416, 419
Dragon of Chaos. *See* Leviathan
dualism, 367

E. *See* Elohist
Ea, 37, 40, 425
Ecclesiastes, 8, 151, 171, 194, 208, 219–222, 256
    allegory in, 202
    contradictory wisdom in, 222
    cycle of nature in, 219
    death finality in, 220–221
    pessimism in, 209
Ecclesiasticus. *See* Wisdom of Jesus Son
    of Sirach
Eden, 31, 40, 70, 424
Edom, 79, 116, 174, 206
Egypt
    circumcision in, 46
    Eighteenth Dynasty of, 45
    Gospel of John circulation in, 337
    Hezekiah alliance with, 161–162
    hieroglyphics of, 44–45
    Hyksos rule of, 45
    Israel in, 78
    Israel reference of, 45
    Israel religious traditions and, 31, 45–46
    Israelite escape from, 77, 81, 82
    Jeremiah in, 171–172
    Maat concept of, 46
    Moses flight from, 79
    myths of creation by, 47
    Nineteenth Dynasty of, 78
El, 13, 56, 79, 86, 111. *See also* El Shaddai; Elohim
El Shaddai, 27, 62, 79
Elihu, 217
Elijah, 171, 293, 327, 331
    in 2 Samuel/1 Kings, 104
    death, lack of experience of, 40
    return to earth of, 11, 189
    theophany of, 146
    Yahweh/Baal contest of, 134–135, 146
Eliphaz, 216
Elisha, 104, 327, 331
Elizabeth, 329
Elohim, 59, 62, 63, 79, 425
Elohist (E), 63–64. *See also* JE Epic
Emmaus, Jesus' postresurrection appearance at, 334
End time, 321, 339, 369, 422
    apocalyptic signs preceding, 392
    Gospel of Luke and, 326
    Paul on, 289
    traditional signs of, 392–393
Enoch, 40, 188, 260
1 Enoch, 239, 243, 260, 284, 298, 391, 408
2 Enoch, 239
enthronement psalms, 206–207
Enuma Elish, 35, 37, 38, 57, 68, 425, 427
Ephesians, 366
    authorship/date/context of, 395
    God's salvation plan in, 395–396
    heavenly armor in, 396
    sacred secret in, 395
    on women's roles, 398
Ephesus, 357, 360, 369, 413
    Jesus letter to church of, 417
    Paul imprisonment in, 384
Ephraim, 64, 117
Epic of Gilgamesh, 35–40, 57–58, 71, 221, 427
epicureanism, 273–274
Epicurus, 221, 273
epistle, 401
eponymous (name-giving), 71
Esau, 73, 116, 174
eschatology, 239, 372–374
    Ezra on future of, 259–260
    Paul emphasis on, 367
    Zechariah focus on, 186
2 Esdras, 199, 239, 243, 258–260, 332, 417, 419, 431
Essenes, 20, 284–285. *See also* Qumran
Esther, 8, 74, 194, 229–231, 238, 250
    Feast of Purim recitation of, 228

history to fiction in, 230–231
    melodrama in, 230
etiology, 58, 70
Eucharist (Holy Communion), 302, 371
Euphrates River, 31, 71, 79, 176
Eusebius, 291, 312, 401, 413
Evangelists, 291, 328, 431, 432
Eve, 39, 69–70, 381
excommunication, 320
exegesis, *316*
Exodus, 3, 8, 42, 77–86, 382
    anthropomorphism in, 93
    Canaan promise in, 55
    circumcision in, 72
    golden calf in, 54, 56, 84–85
    historical evidence for, 78
    Israelites and, 77, 78, 81
    Mosaic Covenant in, 15, 83
    Moses and, 79–80
    on Sabbath, 68, 96
    Tabernacle/Ark of Covenant in,
        55, 85–86
    Ten Commandments in, 57
    ten plagues in, 80
    theophany in, 79–80, 82–86
    wisdom literature absence of, 209
    Yahweh and, 53, 62, 78–79, 80–81
exorcisms, 293, 299
expiation, 403
Ezekiel, 8, 10, 144, 208, 213–214, 238, 243
    Babylonian Exile/Judah Restoration
        in, 149
    Danel and, 244–245
    false prophets denouncement by, 151
    future Israel and, 180–181
    on Jerusalem, 422
    legal material in, 90
    Mosaic principle modification by, 426
    oracles against foreign nations in, 178–179
    strange behavior of, 147
    Torah revision in, 178
    visions of, 176–179
    Yahweh's abandonment of
        Jerusalem and, 178
    on Zadok, 282
Ezra, 8, 31, 194, 233, 257
    on afterlife, 259
    eschatological future of, 259–260
    on Judah, postexile, 24
    mission of, 197–198
    as proclaimer of Torah, 199–200
    Temple rebuilding in, 196–197
    theodicy of, 259
    visions of, 259–260

faith, 401–411, 405–406
fall. *See also* original sin
    of Adam/Eve, 39, 69–70
    of Babylon, 130, 163, 181
    of Jerusalem, 267–269, 302, 321, 333, 338–339
    of Nineveh, 166
    of Samaria, 139
    of Satan, 429–430
Fast of the Ninth of Av, 225, 228
Feast of Booths. *See* Feast of Tabernacles
Feast of Pentecost, 224, 225, 332, 333
Feast of Purim, 225, 229, 230
Feast of Tabernacles (Feast of Booths), 225
Felix, Antonius, 358
Fertile Crescent, 32, 33, 35, 71
Festival Scrolls. *See* Megillot
Festivals
    Fast of the Ninth of Av, 225, 228
    Feast of Purim, 225, 229, 230
    Feast of Tabernacles, 225
    Passover, 80–81, 225, 228, 301, 339
    Pentecost, 224, 225, 332, 333

Festus, Porcius, 358
Fifth Covenant, 16
Final Judgment, 312, 369, 392, 433
    in Gospel of Matthew, 320–323
    Jewish leadership attack, 320–322
flood
    Genesis account of, 59, 60–61, 70–71
    Noah and, 14–15, 37, 40, 59, 408, 425
    two versions of story of, 60–61
Former Prophets, of Nevi'im, 150, 193
    as DH, 101
    Joshua, 8, 10, 72, 83, 91, 95, 96, 102, 103,
        106–113, 116, 121, 184, 185, 197, 429
    Judges, 8, 10, 96, 103, 114, 115–119, 121
    1 Kings, 8, 96, 103, 104, 121, 130–135
    2 Kings, 4, 8, 15, 31, 59, 67, 96, 103, 104, 121,
        135–143
    1 Samuel, 8, 96, 103, 104, 121–128, 215
    2 Samuel, 8, 16, 96, 103, 104,
        125–128, 127
Four Horsemen of the Apocalypse, 417

Gabriel, 247, 329
Gaius Octavius. *See* Augustus
Galatia, 375–376
Galatians, 364, 366, 375–378
    on believers as Abraham's heirs, 378
    on human salvation, Torah role, 378
    identity of recipients/opponents in, 375–376
    on justification by faith, 377–378
    Paul to "foolish," 375–376
    Paul's freedom from institutional authority
        in, 377
    purpose/contents of, 376–377
    on responsibilities of freedom, 378
Galilean ministry, of Jesus, 49, 292, 297–301,
    330–331
Galilee, 266, 296, 346
Galilee, Sea of, 108
Gallio, 357
Gamaliel, 354, 364
Gehenna, 318, 332, 431
genealogy
    in 1 Chronicles, 234
    in Genesis, 58
    in Gospel of Luke, 328
Genesis, 67–76
    through 2 Kings, 4, 15, 31, 67
    Abrahamic Covenant in, 15, 55, 71–73
    on circumcision, 46
    creation account in, 4, 47, 59, 67–68
    creation second version in, 68–70
    divine presence in, 55
    divine promise to Abraham in, 54–55, 67
    etiologies/genealogies in, 58
    God as creator in, 425
    Israel's ancestor stories in, 71–75
    Noachan Covenant in, 14–15
    Noah's Flood in, 59, 60–61, 70–71
    Peniel theophany in, 73–74
    primeval history in, 67–71
    serpent in, 70
    universal blessing in, 55
    Yahweh Elohim in, 59
genocide, in Deuteronomy, 99
Gentiles, 12, 192, 288, 353
    culture, Judaism and, 238–239
    Paul on error of, 379
Gethsemane, 302, 313
Gideon, 114
    Baal worship by, 116, 117
Gilgamesh, 33, 79
    epic of, 35–40, 57–58, 71, 221, 427
glossolalia, 353
Gnosticism, 397
    Gospel of John and, 341
    New Testament canon and, 24–25

God, 13, 53, 64, 351–352. *See also* Adonai; El; El
    Shaddai; Elohim; Greek Gods; Yahweh
    Abraham's call from, 4, 52, 71, 82
    as Accuser/Judge, 213
    Bible's composite portrait of, 424–425
    Biblical concept of, 424–436
    chaos/cosmos transformation by, 67
    cosmic rule associates of, 427–428
    dual nature of, 98, 425–426
    encountering, 12–14
    eternal punishment and, 431
    ethical superiority of, 427
    fidelity to His Word, 28
    heavenly court of, 427–429
    Jesus as image of, 394
    of Judah, 181–182
    as loving parent, 430–431
    Mount Sinai physical visibility of, 85
    Numbers conception of, 92–93
    postmillennium, 434
    promise of, 144
    salvation plan of, 395–396
    self-description of, 425–426
    as social justice guarantor, 432–433
    transcendence of, 12
Gog, 179
golden calf, 56
    Jeroboam and, 130, 137
    at Mount Sinai, 84–85
    worship of, 54
Goliath, David and, 124
Gomer, 156
Gospel, 3, 22, 289
    historical setting of, 292
    new literary form of, 291
    of New Testament, 11, 23
    parallels/differences in, 308
    Pharisees portrayal in, 283
    rejection of, 23
    resurrection traditions in, 373
    on Satan, 215
Gospel of John, 258, 336–349
    authorship of, 336–337
    chronology/order of events in, 339–340
    crucifixion as glorification in, 345
    double vision of, 340–341
    Gethsemane and, 345–346
    Gnostic ideas related to, 341
    historical significance of, 348
    Jesus "I Am" pronouncements in, 3, 342
    Jesus' last words in, 347
    Jesus portrait by, 337–339
    on Jesus' postresurrection experiences, 346
    Last Supper in, 345
    Lazurus raising of dead in, 344
    Logos doctrine in, 338
    miracle at Cana in, 343
    organization of, 341–346
    paraclete work in, 340–341
    Passion interpretation by, 345–346
    on Pontius Pilate, 346
    realized eschatology in, 344–345
    Samaritan woman conversation in, 343–344
    spiritual rebirth doctrine in, 338
    Synoptic Gospels difference of, 337
    Temple assault in, 343
Gospel of Luke, 10, 288, 295, 307, 325–335,
    352–353. *See also* Luke-Acts
    authorship/date of, 326–327
    Christianity as universal faith in, 328–329
    Galilean ministry, of Jesus in, 330–331
    Holy Spirit in, 328
    infancy narrative in, 329–330
    interpolations in, 327
    Jerusalem importance in, 328
    Jesus in, 329, 331–333, 334. 347
    on John the Baptist, 326

    major themes of, 328–329
    Mark editing by, 327–328
    Passion story in, 334
    postresurrection appearances in, 334
    preface to, 325–326
Gospel of Mark, 246, 284, 291–306, 307
    apocalyptic urgency of, 293–294
    controlling irony in, 293
    disciples in, 294–295
    divisions of, 297
    editing of, 305–306
    Jerusalem ministry in, 301–306
    Jesus in, 288, 293, 294, 297, 300, 347
    leading characters in, 293
    Luke editing of, 327–328
    Matthew editing of, 312–313, 314
    structure/sequence of events in, 295–306
    Twelve Apostles in, 293, 294–295
Gospel of Matthew, 44, 310–324
    apocalyptic warning in, 289
    authorship of, 311–312
    church, instructions to, 320
    date/place of composition of, 312
    Final Judgment warnings in, 320–323
    Gehenna/Sheol/Hades in, 318
    infancy narrative in, 314–316
    Jerusalem fall in, 321
    Jesus in, 310–311, 316–323, 347
    kingdom parables in, 319–320
    Mark editing by, 312–313, 314
    Parousia in, 321
    Passion Story/Resurrection in, 322–323
    Sermon on the Mount in, 316–318
    structure/themes in, 312
    Twelve Apostles instruction in, 312, 318
Great Council. *See* Sanhedrin
"greater interpolation," 327
Greek culture/philosophy
    epicureanism in, 273–274
    gods in, 274–277
    Hellenism influence on, 269–274
    intellectual/artistic excellence of, 269
    koine as language of, 269
    mysteries in, 277–280
    New Testament and, 270–271
    philosophy in, 271–274
    Plato influence on, 273
    Socrates/Plato/Immortal Soul and, 272
    Stoicism/Stoic endurance and, 273
Greek Gods
    Asclepius, 274–275
    Dionysus of Thebes, 275–277
    on Mount Olympus, 274
    Zeus, 274–275
Greek Orthodox Bible, 11, 249
Griesbach Theory, 310

Habakkuk, 8, 144, 148, 173–174, 284, 378
Hades, 318, 421, 430, 431
Hagar, 72
Haggai, 149, 151, 184–185
Ham, as eponymous ancestor of Egyptians, 71
Haman, 230, 238, 240
Hammurabi (king), 41, 44. *See also* Code of
    Hammurabi
Hannah, 122–123, 330
Har Megiddo. See Armageddon
Haran, 71
Hasidim, 251, 283
Hasmonean dynasty, 206, 251, 254, 265
Hazor, 108, 109, 112, 153
heavenly court, Satan as member of, 428–429
heavenly Jerusalem, 422, 434
Hebrew Bible, 7–10, 229, 311. *See also* Tanakh
    canon of, 22
    Chronicles placement in, 237
    cuneiform literature and, 33

Hebrew Bible (*continued*)
 Daniel as apocalyptic work in, 194, 238, 242, 246–247, 250
 Day of the Lord in, 369
 divine council in, 38–39
 as First Testament, 16
 Obadiah as shortest book of, 174
 Pentateuch of, 22
 poetry of, 201–202
 portrayal of God, 13
 Yahweh in, 38
Hebrew Poetry
 parallelism in, 202
 personification in, 202
 simile/metaphor/allegory in, 201–202
Hebrews, 12, 402–406
Hebron, 125, 235
Hellenism
 on Adam/Eve, 381
 Greek culture/philosophy influence by, 269–274
 Jewish social customs/beliefs and, 253–254
 Judaism and, 239–241
 Paul's letters and, 366
Hellenistic culture, 269
Hellenistic writer, 210
Hellenists, persecution of, 353, 354
henotheism, 45, 83–84
herem, 99, 108–109
heresy, 397, 399
Herod Agrippa I, 266, 337
Herod Agrippa II, 266, 327, 358
Herod Antipas, 266, 270, 283, 298, 327, 339
Herod Archelaus, 255
Herod I (king), 252, 265–266, 301
Herod the Great. *See* Herod I (king)
Herodotus, 141, 231
hesed, 156, 190, 225, 226, 430, 431
Hezekiah (king), 95, 103, 130, 141, 181, 236
 Chronicler on, 234
 DH on, 139
 Egypt alliance by, 161–162
 Isaiah's advice to, 158
 JE narratives and, 64
hieroglyphics, 44–45
High Priest
 Aaron as first, 88, 257
 Caiphas as, 282
 Eleazar as, 90
 Hasmoneans over, 206
 Jesus as, 403
 John Hyrcanus as, 265
 Jonathan as, 252
 Joshua as, 184, 185, 429
 Menelaus, 252
 Simon as, 252
 Zadok as, 282
Hiram of Tyre
 David's treaty with, 125
 Jerusalem Temple and, 131
historical narratives, 8, 249
History (Herodotus), 231
Holiness Code, 90
Holy Communion. *See* Eucharist
Holy of Holies, 46, 257, 301, 403, 416
Holy Spirit, 294, 339. *See also* Paraclete
 gifts of, 372
 Jerusalem Conference and, 356
 Jesus conception by, 329
 Jesus empowered by, 328
 at Pentecost, 333
 role of, 328, 353–354, 369
Holy War, 107–110
Horeb. *See* Mount Sinai
Hosea, 8, 144, 146, 153, 155–157, 284, 431
 apostasy in, 155
 Assyrian Crisis and, 148
 biblical canon of, 155

 disastrous marriage of, 155–156
 Yahweh, lack of commitment to, 153
Huldah, as prophetess, 145
human frailty, consequences of, 70–71
Hyksos, Egypt rule by, 45, 78
hymns, 203–204

"I Am" pronouncements, of Jesus, 338, 342, 346
immanence, 12
Incarnation
 Gospel of John's doctrine of, 338, 343
 of Jesus, 410
infancy narrative
 in Gospel of Luke, 329–330
 in Gospel of Matthew, 314–316
 Mary role in, 329–330
intermarriage, 92
 Ezra on, 197
 historical setting for, 224–225
 Ruth on, 198
invective literary style, 407
Irenaeus, 326, 413
Isaac, 15, 35, 55, 64, 72–73
Isaiah, 8, 10, 144, 153, 158–163, 238, 284, 287, 433.
  See also Second Isaiah;
  Third Isaiah
 Assyrian Crisis and, 148
 David heir in, 145
 divine judgment/restoration in, 159
 on Jesus as suffering servant, 288
 Jesus reading of scroll of, 327
 "Little Apocalypse" in, 163, 242–243
 scapegoat in, 89
 strange behavior of, 147
Isaiah of Jerusalem, 158–159, 160–163
 Assyria's assault on Jerusalem in, 162–163
 fates in, 160–161
 Hezekiah's alliance with Egypt in, 161–162
 oracles structure in, 160
Ishmael, 55, 72
Ishra-il, 35
Ishtar, goddess of love/war, 39
Isis, 279, 419
Israel, 4, 8, 78, 104, 108
 ancestor stories of, 71–75, 101–105
 Assyrians destruction of, 49, 144
 autonomy of, 46–47
 breakup of, 132
 Canaan possession by, 15
 conquest model for origin of, 112
 covenant breaking of, 15, 54
 Egypt and, 31, 45–46
 Ezekiel on future of, 180–181
 Genesis on epic of, 67
 geographical location of, 46–49
 infiltration model for origin of, 112
 map of, 9, 136
 Mesopotamia ancestors of, 31
 Moses as chief instrument in creation of, 78–79
 north/south tensions in, 49
 prophetic divination in, 147
 prosperity of, 130–131
 secession of, 132
 social revolution model for origin of, 112
 twelve tribes of, 74, 83
 Yahweh and, 55–56, 98, 150, 156, 228
Israelites, 56, 115
 apostasy of, 92, 135
 ben Sirach's tribute to, 257
 circumcision of, 46
 escape from Egypt, 77, 81, 82
 faith of, 77
 J/P on, 81
 Moses speaking to, 97
 numbering of, 90
itinerary, 58

J. *See* Yahwist
Jacob, 15, 35, 65, 123
 Bethel and, 34
 El altar of, 111
 Esau reconciliation with, 74
 Israel name change of, 74
 ladder dream of, 34, 73
 Odysseus *vs.*, 73
 twelve sons of, 45
 wrestling with angel by, 73–74
Jael, 117
Jairus, 297–298
James, 337, 377
 as Jerusalem church head, 355–356
 Josephus on, 404
 rejection of, 23
 as Twelve Apostle, 295
James, letter of, 401, 404–406
Japheth, 71
Jashar, Book of, 104
JE Epic, 64
Jehoash (king), 138
Jehoiachin (king), 142, 177, 231
Jehoiakim (king), 142, 168
Jehoshaphat, valley of, 188, 236
Jehovah. *See* Yahweh
Jehu, 137–138
Jephthah, 115, 118
Jeremiah, 142, 144, 168–174, 208
 attempts to kill, 171
 confessions of, 171
 in Egypt, 171–172
 strange behavior of, 147
 Zedekiah and, 171
Jeremiah, book of, 8, 10, 95, 168, 250, 255
 Babylonian Exile/Judah Restoration in, 149
 Book of Consolation and, 172
 covenant in, 16
 Lamentations and, 229
 map during time of, 169
 MT version of, 20, 21–22
 structure of, 168–171
Jericho, 33, 107, 108
Jeroboam I (king), 130, 146, 235
 golden calves of, 137
 revolt against Davidic dynasty by, 132–133
Jeroboam II (king), 139, 153, 155, 189
Jerome, 25, 234, 249
Jerusalem, 229. *See also* heavenly Jerusalem
 Assyria's assault on, 162–163
 destruction of, 4, 8, 22, 127, 267–268, 384
 Ezekiel's vision of restoration of, 179
 fall of, 267–269, 321, 338–339
 Herod I capture of, 265
 importance of, 328
 Jesus' ministry in, 292, 301–306, 333
 Jesus' postresurrection appearances near, 334, 346
 Nebuchadnezzar capture of, 141, 142, 241
 Paul's arrest in, 358, 360
 prophecy of fall of, 302, 333
 road, Jesus teaching on, 331–332
 wedding of Lamb with glorified, 422
 Yahweh's abandonment of, 178
Jerusalem Church
 founding of, 353–354
 Paul and, 376
 Paul's independence from, 356
Jerusalem Conference, 377
 Barnabas/Paul missionary journey and, 355
 Holy Spirit and, 356
Jerusalem Temple, 46, 55, 59, 64, 98, 128, 130, 139, 203, 209, 234, 240–241, 254, 301, 331, 418
 dedication of, 131–132

Herod I renovation of, 266
lament over destruction of, 205
Nebuchadnezzar destruction of, 144
rebuilding of, 10
sacrificial rituals at, 90
Sadducees officiating at, 282
Yahweh acceptance of, 132
Jesus, 284, 294, 315, 330, 331–333, 353, 394, 403, 409. *See also* Christ
    affinity with unrespectable, 329
    on biblical faith, 29
    crucifixion of, 288, 303–304, 313, 340, 345
    as David's heir, 145
    Dionysus of Thebes *vs.*, 275, 277
    on equality, 29
    exorcisms of, 293, 299, 338
    Gabriel announcement of birth of, 329
    Galilean ministry of, 49, 297–301, 330–331
    Gospel of John portrait of, 337–339
    as heavenly priest, 402
    Holy Spirit empowering of, 328
    "I Am" pronouncements of, 342, 346
    Isaiah scroll reading by, 327
    Jerusalem ministry of, 301–306, 333
    Johannine, 432
    last words of, 347
    life of, 270–271
    as Messiah, 11, 293, 299–300, 311, 412
    parable use by, 299
    Parousia and, 289, 304–305
    Passion of, 293
    perfection through suffering of, 402
    Peter and, 16, 295
    postressurection appearances of, 334, 338, 346
    prophecy of Temple's fall by, 302
    resurrection of, 304–305
    Satan temptation of, 297, 330, 338
    Second Coming of, 339
    as suffering servant, 412, 430
    Temple assault by, 339
    Torah interpretation by, 338
    women concern by, 329
Jesus ben Sirach, 256–257
Jewish Revolt against Rome, 266–269, 283, 292, 305, 321, 414
The Jewish War (Josephus), 267
Jews, 4, 251, 380
    Diaspora in, 192, 197, 231
    genocide against, 320
    Greek synthesis and, 257
    identity of, 22
    martyrdom of, 241–242
Jezebel (queen), 134, 135, 137, 146
Joab, 125, 127
Job, 8, 9, 171, 194–195, 213–219, 242, 244, 257, 428–429
Joel, 149, 187–188
Johannine community, 409, 413
Johannine Jesus, 432
Johannine letters, 338, 348
John. *See also* Gospel of John
    as Beloved Disciple, 337
    Jesus' postresurrection appearance to, 346
    as John the Elder, 337
    as Twelve Apostle, 295
John the Baptist, 11, 266, 293, 297, 313, 314, 326, 329, 338
1 John, 401, 409–410
2 John, 401, 410
3 John, 401, 410
Jonah, 149, 189–190
Jonathan, 124, 251–252
Jordan River, 49, 59, 106, 108, 266, 297, 321
Joseph, 65, 123, 209, 329
    Daniel resemblance of, 243–244
    defeat of, 251
    in Pharaoh's court, 74–75

as prophet, 145
sons as tribes of Israel, 74
story of, 74–75
Josephus, Flavius, 153, 267, 284, 332
Joshua, 8, 10, 91, 96, 106–113
    Canaan and, 95, 103, 116
    circumcision in, 72
    covenant renewal of, 102, 111, 116
    as David's story prologue, 121
    as High Priest, 184, 185, 429
    military/religious exploits of, 102
    as Moses' successor, 83, 106–107
    temple rebuilding and, 197
Josiah (king), 59, 65, 95–96, 130, 141–142, 165, 168, 172, 236
    reforms of, 102, 103, 129, 141
Judaeus, Philo, 213, 284, 342, 402
Judah, 31, 74, 100, 104, 138, 139–141
    all-powerful God of, 181–182
    Babylon conquest of, 103, 214
    Chronicler on, 235–236
    covenant violations of, 142
    David governing of, 49
    destruction of, 95, 139, 162, 169
    DH on collapse of, 235
    Edom's revenge by, 174
    Ezra on postexile, 24
    incomplete restoration of, 149
    J focus on, 63
    last days of, 142
    map of kingdom of, 136
    religious mission after Babylonian Exile, 192–193
    restoration of, 149, 192
    Sennacherib invasion of, 139–140
    survival of, 132
    tribe of, 235
    Zerubbabel as governor of, 184–185
Judaism, 238–241
    First-Century, 282–290
Judas Iscariot, 293, 295, 322
Judas Maccabeus, 250, 251, 252
Jude, 401, 407–408
Judea, 192, 240
    province of, 186
    Roman Empire rule of, 266
Judeans, 235, 255
Judges, 8, 10, 96
    Abimelech, 115
    as David's story prologue, 121
    Deborah/Gideon/Samson as major, 114
    downward spiral in, 115–119
    tribal disunity in, 103
Judgment, Day of, 155, 404, 431
Judith, book of, 250, 254–255
justification by faith, 367–368, 377–380

kavod (glory), 177, 185
Kethuvim. *See* Writings
King James Version (KJV), 25, 27, 178
kingdom parables, 312, 319–320
1 Kings, 8, 96, 103, 130–135
    Ahab/Elijah in, 134–135
    Court History in, 104
    on David's successors, 121
    Elijah/Elisha traditions in, 104
    Solomon reign in, 130–132
2 Kings, 8, 59, 96, 103, 135–143
    Assyrian invasion in, 139
    on David's successors, 121
    Elijah/Elisha traditions in, 104
    Genesis through, 4, 15, 31, 67
    Jehu's bloody purges in, 137–138
    Josiah in, 141–142
    Judah in, 139–141
KJV. *See* King James Version
Koheleth, as Ecclesiastes writer, 219
koine, 10, 269

L. *See* Lukan source
Lachish, 104, 162
Lady Wisdom, 202, 212, 256, 428
lake of fire, 421–422, 430
Lamb of God, 416
Lamentations, 8, 194, 201, 228–229
laments, 205–206, 216
Laodicea, Jesus letter to church of, 417
Last Supper, 16, 302, 313, 331, 337, 339–340, 367
Latin Vulgate. *See* Vulgate Bible, Latin
Latter Prophets, of Nevi'im, 150, 193. *See also* Major Prophets, of Latter Prophets; Minor Prophets, of Latter Prophets
    Ezekiel, 8, 10, 90, 144, 147, 149, 151, 176–181, 208, 213–214, 238, 243, 244–245, 282, 422, 426
    Isaiah, 8, 10, 89, 144, 145, 147, 148, 153, 158–163, 238, 242–243, 284, 287, 288, 327, 433
    Jeremiah, 8, 10, 16, 20, 21–22, 95, 149, 168–171, 172, 229, 250, 255
Law of Instruction. *See* Torah
Lazurus, 332, 338
Leah, as Jacob's wife, 73
"lesser interpolation," 327
letter form
    of Paul's letters, 366
    Paul's use of, 401–402
Letter of Jeremiah, 250, 255
Levi, 100
Leviathan (Dragon of Chaos), 216, 218–219
Levirate Law, 226
Levites, 235
Levitical priesthood, 403
Leviticus, 8, 88–90
    circumcision in, 72
    Holiness Code in, 90
    Mosaic Covenant in, 83
    priestly functions/concerns in, 88–89
    rituals of atonement in, 89
    sacrifice offering in, 89
    Yahweh's instructions in, 53
lex talionis, 43–44, 320
"Little Apocalypse," in Isaiah, 163, 242–243
Logos (Word), 213, 257, 273, 394, 413, 432
    Jesus as, 336, 338, 341, 342, 409
Lord's Prayer, 307
Lord's Supper. *See* Eucharist
Lot, 72
Lucifer. *See* Satan
Lukan source (L), 327
Luke, as beloved physician, 326, 334, 352–353. *See also* Gospel of Luke; Luke-Acts
Luke-Acts, 327–328, 334, 420
Luther, Martin, 25, 30, 363, 368
LXX. *See* Septuagint

M. *See* Matthean
Maat concept, of Egypt, 46
Maccabean Revolt, 195, 206, 241, 251–252, 265, 266
1 Maccabee, 11, 250–252
2 Maccabee, 11, 241, 242, 244, 250, 252–253
3 Maccabee, 11
Magog, 179, 421
Major Prophets, of Latter Prophets
    Ezekiel, 8, 10, 90, 144, 147, 149, 151, 176–181, 208, 213–214, 238, 243, 244–245, 282, 422, 426
    Isaiah, 8, 10, 89, 144, 145, 147, 148, 153, 158–163, 238, 242–243, 284, 287, 288, 327, 433
    Jeremiah, 8, 10, 16, 20, 21–22, 95, 149, 168–171, 172, 229, 250, 255
Malachi, 8, 149, 150, 151, 188–189, 293
Manasseh (king), 103, 141, 214, 234, 236–237
manna, 56, 91
Marcion, 24

Marduk, 34, 37, 38, 179, 204, 231, 425
Martha, 329, 344, 345
martyr, 354, 418, 431
martyrdom, 241–242, 245, 252–253, 292, 354, 408
Mary Magdalene, 293, 304, 338, 344, 346
Mary, mother of Jesus, 329–330
Masada, 256, 266, 286
Masoretic Text (MT), 18–21, 284–285
Mattathias, 250, 251
Matthean (M), Gospel of Matthew source, 312
Matthew, 295. See also Gospel of Matthew
Medes, conquer of, 254
Megiddo, 47, 49
Megillot (Festival Scrolls), 194, 224–234
Melchizedek, 206, 402–403
Merneptah, 45, 46
Mesopotamia, 30, 46, 71, 176, 425
    Amorite invasion of, 35
    cylinder seal in, 39
    invasion of, 44
    Israel's ancestor origination in, 31
    underworld of, 40–41
Messiah, 235, 246
    Davidic Covenant and, 286–287
    Jesus as, 11, 145, 299–300
    Jewish-Christian debate on, 286–288
    Parousia and, 289
    Psalm of Solomon 17, 287
    revisionist view of, 288
metaphor, 201
Micah, 8, 144, 148, 163–166, 284, 433
Michael, archangel, 100, 246, 416, 419, 428
Midian, 79
Midianites, 92, 117–118
millennium, 421
Minor Prophets, of Latter Prophets
    Amos, 8, 144, 148, 153, 154–155, 433
    Hosea, 8, 144, 146, 148, 153, 155–157, 284, 431
    Malachi, 8, 149, 150, 151, 188–189, 293
    Micah, 8, 144, 148, 163–166, 284, 433
Miriam, 91, 145
Mithras, 278–279
Moabites, 92, 138, 224
monotheism, 32, 37, 45, 183, 302
Mordecai, 230, 231, 240
Mosaic Covenant, 15, 31, 57, 83, 116, 127, 209, 257, 368, 375, 403, 404
Mosaic Law, 8, 22, 135, 375, 377, 381–382, 388, 404
Mosaic Torah. See Torah
Moses, 3, 8, 12, 15, 45, 54, 59, 91, 96–97, 103, 123, 171, 203, 260, 404, 425
    Book of the Covenant and, 58, 83
    burning bush experience of, 79–80
    Canaan, forbidden to enter, 95, 100
    death of, 59, 100
    God's self-disclosure to, 14
    infancy/flight from Egypt, 79
    as Israel's chief instrument of creation, 78–79
    Jesus as new, 310–311
    Joshua as successor of, 83, 106–107
    as prophet, 145
    Yahweh and, 55, 78–79, 146
Mount of Olives, 302
Mount Sinai, 15, 57, 64, 77, 425
    Book of the Covenant, 84
    God's physical visibility at, 85
    golden calf at, 54, 56, 84–85
    Tabernacle, 85–86
    Ten Commandments, 82–84
    theophany at, 82–86, 145
    Yahweh's appearance at, 53
MT. See Masoretic Text
Muratorian Canon, 23–24, 326
mystery, 277–280, 394

Naboth, 135, 146
Nahum, 148, 166, 188
Naomi, 224
Naram-Sin, Elba destruction by, 34–35
narratives, as Pentateuch literary form, 57
Nathan, 122, 127, 130, 146
navi (nabi), 145
Nazareth, 294, 314, 327
Nazarite, Samson as, 118
Near East. See Ancient Near East
Nebuchadnezzar (king), 142, 168, 176, 196, 229, 231, 235, 245, 254, 287
    Babylon at time of, 170
    Daniel and, 243, 246
    Jerusalem capture by, 141, 144, 168–171, 241
    Tyre overthrown by, 179
Necho II (pharaoh), 141–142, 166, 236
Nehemiah, 8, 194, 198–200, 233
Nero, 267, 292, 321, 360, 384, 421
Nevi'im. See Prophets
New Revised Standard Version Bible (NRSV), 16, 20–21, 27, 178, 219, 255, 259
New Testament, 11–12, 25
    Athanasius and, 23
    canon of, 22–27
    copying of, 18
    copyist changes to, 19
    Matthew at beginning of, 310
    Paul contribution to, 363–369
New Testament, canon of
    English traditions of, 25, 27
    Gnosticism/Muratorian Canon and, 24–25
    growth process of, 23
    KJV and, 27
    Latin Vulgate and, 25
    Marcion and, 24
    Modern English/American translations, 27
Nicodemus, spiritual rebirth doctrine and, 338, 340–341
Nile River, 44, 45, 71
Nimrod. See Satan
Nineveh, 35, 104, 142, 166, 189, 254
Noachan Covenant, 14–16
Noah, 213, 244, 260, 404. See also Noachan Covenant
    covenant with, 14–16
    flood and, 14–15, 37, 40, 59, 408, 425
    Ham/Shem/Japheth, sons of, 71
NRSV. See New Revised Standard Version Bible
Numbers, 8, 59, 83, 90–93

Obadiah, 149, 174
Obed, Ruth's birth of, 227
Odysseus, Jacob vs. ., 73
Old Testament, 4, 7–10, 25
    Christian Bible division of, 11
    order of books in, 5–6
omega, 412
Omri (king), 134, 138
Onesimus, 387, 393
oracle, 8, 145
    against foreign nations, 178–179
    of Habakkuk, 173–174
    during Josiah/Jehoiakim/Zedekiah reign, 168
    of Second Isaiah, 181–183
    of Third Isaiah, 186–187
original sin, 217, 380, 381
Orpheus, 147
orthodoxy, 397, 399

P. See priestly document
Palestine, 240, 251. See also Canaan
    archaeology at, 109
    geography of, 47, 48
    during Jesus' ministry, 296
    occupation of, 47, 265
parable, 299, 321

Paraclete (Advocate), 339, 340–341, 346, 348
parallelism, 202
Parousia, 304–305, 321, 333, 348, 368–369, 373, 392–393, 417
    delayed, 408–409
    on Jesus arrival from Heaven, 289
    Peter emphasis on, 406
Passion, of Jesus, 293, 300, 302–303, 313, 322–323, 334
    crucifixion as glorification, 345
    Gospel of John's interpretation of, 345–346
Passover, 80–81, 225, 228, 301, 339
Pastor, 397–399, 408
pastoral epistles, Timothy/Titus letters in, 396–399
patriarch, 62
Paul, 29, 327, 365, 377–378
    apocalyptic gospel of, 288–289
    apostolic authority of, 374–375
    arrest/imprisonment of, 266, 353, 358, 360
    on Christ association with Adam, 372–373, 380–381, 386
    churches of, 364, 376
    on circumcision advocates, 386
    conversions of, 353, 354–355
    Diaspora Jews preaching by, 353, 360–361
    direct voice of, 363–364, 366
    on Jerusalem's fall, 267, 269
    on Jesus as Messiah, 288
    on justification by faith, 367–368
    missionary journey of, 355–359
    mysticism/eschatology of, 367
    New Testament contribution by, 363–369
    theological beliefs of, 367–368
    on women, 29
Paul, letters of, 11–12, 23, 363–390
    circumstances of writing, 367
    Colossians, 366, 393
    1 Corinthians, 366, 369–374
    2 Corinthians, 366, 374–375
    Galatians, 364, 366, 375–378
    Hellenistic, 366
    letter form of, 366
    Philemon, 366, 387–388
    Philippians, 366, 384–386
    resurrection traditions in, 373
    role of dictation in, 366–367
    Romans, 366, 378–385
    1 Thessalonians, 366, 368–369
    2 Thessalonians, 366, 391–393
    1 Timothy question of authorship by, 366
    2 Timothy questions of authorship by, 366
    Titus question of authorship by, 366
Peniel (Penuel), 73–74
Pentateuch, 8, 22, 62–63
    authorship of, traditional view of, 58–59
    Deuteronomy, 8, 53–54, 59, 64, 68, 83, 94–100, 102, 103, 193–194, 288, 426
    divine promises in, 54–55
    Exodus, 3, 8, 15, 42, 53, 54, 55, 56, 57, 62, 68, 72, 77–86, 93, 96, 209, 382
    Genesis, 4, 8, 14–15, 15, 31, 46, 47, 54–55, 58, 59, 60–61, 67–76, 425
    God's creation of world in, 53
    Leviticus, 8, 53, 72, 83, 88–89, 90
    literary forms in, 57–58
    major themes of, 54–55
    Mosaic authorship of, problems with, 59–62
    Numbers, 8, 59, 83, 90–93
    Yahweh's promises in, 54
Pentecost. See Feast of Pentecost
Penuel. See Peniel
Persia, 196–197
Peter, 337, 355. See also Simon Peter
    covenant in, 16
    denial of Jesus by, 295
    as Jesus chief disciple, 16
    Jesus' resurrection appearance to, 338, 346
    martyrdom of, 292, 408
    work of, 354

1 Peter, 401, 406–408
2 Peter, 22, 401, 408–409
Pharaoh, 80–81, 236, 425
Pharisees, 283–284, 298, 301, 333
Philemon, 366, 387–388
Philip, 295
Philippians, 366, 384–386
Philistines, 108, 118
    Ark of the Covenant capture by, 123
    David's refuge in, 124
    Palestine occupation by, 47
Phoebe, 371
Plato, 24, 258, 272, 273, 372, 403
Pliny the Younger, 407, 415
polytheism, 32
Pompey, 265
Pontius Pilate, 266, 293, 303, 322, 327, 346
poor, 163, 164, 432–433
Potiphar, 74–75
Prayer of Manasseh, 236
predestination, Paul on, 382–383
prefects. See procurators
priest, 88–91, 180, 193. See also High Priest
priestly document (P), 63, 65, 81
primeval history, of Genesis, 67–71
Priscilla, 369, 371
procurators, 266
Promised Land. See Canaan
prophecy, 99, 148–151
    burden of, 149–150
    forms/characteristics of, 146–147
    of Jerusalem's fall, 302, 333
    monarchs and, 146
    against nations, 168
    as performance art, 178
    of redemption/restoration, 168
prophet, 22, 144–146, 147, 164
    of Assyrian Crisis, 158–167
    of Babylonian Exile, 168–175, 176–183
    Israel's last, after Babylonian Exile, 184–191
Prophets (Nevi'im), 3, 7. See also Latter Prophets,
    of Nevi'im
    appearance order of, 148–149
    Former Prophets subsection of, 8
    Joshua, 8, 10, 72, 83, 91, 95, 96, 102, 103,
        106–113, 116, 121, 184, 185, 197, 429
    Judges, 8, 10, 96, 103, 114, 115–119, 121
Protestant Reformation, 25, 249, 368
Proverbs, 8, 208, 211–213, 256
Psalm of Solomon 17, 287
Psalms, 8, 10, 193, 194, 203–207
    Davidic authorship of, 203
    on divine council, 38
    enthronement, 206–207
    Melchizedek in, 403
    religious power of, 207
psalms, categories of, 203–207
psalms of instruction, 207
psalms of thanksgiving, 204
psalms of wisdom, 207
Pseudepigrapha, 250, 260
pseudonymity, 260, 391, 406
Ptolemaic dynasty, 240, 241, 246, 280
Ptolemy I, 44, 240

Q (Quelle) (Source) Document, 309–310, 327, 333
Qinoth, 229
Queen of Heaven, 172
Quelle. See Q Document
Qumran, 20, 284–285

rabbi, 22, 249
Rachel, 55, 73, 110
Rahab, 204, 218, 404
Rameses I, 45
Rameses II, 45, 78
Rameses III, 112
realized eschatology, 339, 344–345, 372

Rebekah, as Isaac's wife, 73
Red Sea, 81
redemption, 187–188, 379–380
Rehoboam (king), 132, 235
resurrection
    of dead, 179, 372–374
    of Jesus, 304–305, 322–323, 372–373
Revelation, 4, 12, 23, 239, 243, 259, 336, 412–423
Revised English Bible, 16, 27, 259
Roman Catholic Church, 25, 252, 368
Roman Empire, 25, 266, 268, 270, 329, 333, 358, 406
Romans, letter to, 366, 378–385
Rosetta Stone, 45
Royal Covenant. See Davidic Covenant
royal psalms, 206
ruah Elohim, 147
Ruel, 79
Ruth, 8, 74, 194, 229
Ruth, book of, 8, 194, 198, 224–227

Sabbath, 68, 84
sacrifices, 89–90, 99, 130, 131, 163, 403
Sadducees, 257, 282–283
salvation, 351–352
Samaria, 137, 139, 154, 158, 266
    Assyrian destruction of, 95, 153
    fall of, 139
Samaritans, 49, 139, 197, 284
Samson, 114, 115, 118–119
Samuel, 122–124, 330
1 Samuel, 8, 96, 103, 122–125
    Ark of the Covenant in, 104
    David rise to power in, 104, 121–128
    Saul narrative in, 104, 123–124, 215
2 Samuel, 8, 16, 96, 103, 125–128
    appendices in, 127–128
    Court History in, 104
    David/Bathsheba in, 127
Sanhedrin (Great Council), 282, 298, 303, 327, 354
Sarah, 55, 59, 72, 253
Sardis, Jesus letter to church of, 417
Sargon I, 34, 41, 79
Sargon II, 139, 158
Satan, 235, 300, 333, 416
    divine assembly expulsion of, 429–430
    Gospel accounts on, 215
    as heavenly court member, 428–429
    Jesus resistance to temptation of, 297
    Job and, 39, 214–216, 429
Saul (king), 8, 119, 235
    in 1 Samuel, 104, 123–124, 215
    anointing ritual for, 122
    Jonathan as son of, 124
    map of kingdom of, 126
    Michal as daughter of, 124
    Yahweh's spirit possession of, 147
Saul of Tarsus. See Paul
Savior. See Jesus
scapegoat, 89, 182
scribes, 18, 283
scroll, 20
Sea of Reeds. See Red Sea
Second Coming, 368, 392, 408, 418
Second Isaiah (Deutero-Isaiah), 159, 237, 258
    Babylonian Exile/Judah Restoration in, 149
    Cyrus the Great in, 181
    oracles of, 181–183
    Servant Songs in, 182–183
Second Temple, 184, 185, 192, 194
    rededication of, 188
    Yahweh's appearance at, 189, 193
seer, 147, 163
Seleucid dynasty, 240, 241, 246, 254, 280
Sennacherib, 139–140, 158, 162
Septuagint (LXX), 24, 88, 240, 269, 381
    Christian Bible and, 10–11
    Esther in, 230
    Ruth placement in, 224

Sermon on the Mount, 29, 44, 310, 316–318, 327,
    330, 331, 433
Sermon on the Plain, 310, 327
serpent, 70, 434
Servant Songs, 182–183
Shalmaneser III, 137–138
Shalmaneser V, 158
Shamash, 44, 58
Shechem, 106, 111, 115, 118, 130
Shem, 71
Shema, 97, 302
Sheol, 40, 204, 209–210, 216, 242, 256, 318. See also
    Underworld
Shiloh, kidnap of women of, 119
Shishak (pharaoh), 236
simile, 201, 299
Simon Magus, 354
Simon Peter (Simon the Canaanite), 252, 293,
    295, 297
Sisera, 117
slavery, 29, 44, 97, 387–388
Socrates, 258, 272, 372
Sodom, 58, 72, 155
Solomon (king), 8, 146, 203, 234, 236. See also
    Jerusalem Temple
    Adonijah murder by, 130
    division after death of, 49, 130
    Ecclesiastes and, 208, 219
    economic policies of, 132
    Proverbs of, 208, 212–213, 256
    reign of, 130–132
    Song of Songs and, 8, 194, 201, 208, 227–228
Solomon's Temple. See Jerusalem Temple
Son of God, 297, 300, 329, 409
Son of Man, 297, 298, 321, 333, 433
Song of Solomon. See Song of Songs
Song of Songs, 8, 194, 201, 208, 227–228
songs of praise, 203–204
source criticism, 309
speculative wisdom, 194
stele, 44, 46
Stephen, 354
Stoicism, 221, 273, 383–384, 408
Succession Narrative. See Court History
Suffering Servant, 182, 412
Sumer, Akkadian invasion of, 34–35
Sumerians, 30, 33–34
symbolic parallelism, 202
syncretism, 114, 376
synonymous parallelism, 202
Synoptic Gospels, 307–310, 432
    double/triple tradition, 307
    Gospel of John and, 337, 339–340
    Griesbach Theory in, 310
    Jesus' Torah interpretation in, 338
    Johannine community and, 410
    Q in, 309–310
Synoptic Problem, 307, 309

Tabernacle
    Aaronite males direct access to, 91
    Deuteronomy view of, 98–99
    in Exodus, 55, 85–86
    priests and, 88
    Tent of Meeting at, 89
    Yahweh entering of, 86
Tables of the Law. See Ten Commandments
Tamar, Ammon rape of, 127
Tanakh (Torah), 3, 7–10, 27, 40, 193, 215
    deuterocanonical books of, 250
    Greek translation of, 10–11
    Lamentations in, 8, 194, 201, 228–229
    order of books in, 5–6
    theodicy of, 213
tel, Jericho's ruins of, 33
Temple of Solomon. See Jerusalem Temple
Ten Commandments (Decalogue), 3, 57,
    82–84, 96–97

Tent of Meeting, 89
Tertullian, 431
Tetragrammaton (YHWH), 14
Thaddeus, 295
theocracy, 77, 193
theodicy, 173, 242
    of Ezra, 259
    of Job, 194–195, 213, 259
theophany
    of Abraham, 71–72
    first/second, in Exodus, 79–80, 82–86
    at Mount Sinai, 82–86
Theophilus, 325
1 Thessalonians, 366, 368–369
2 Thessalonians, 366, 391–393
Third Isaiah, 159
    incomplete Judah Restoration in, 149
    oracles of, 186–187
Thomas, 295, 346
thummim, 147
Tiberius, 266, 326
Tiglath-Pileser III, 158
Tigris River, 31, 35
Timothy, Paul recommendations by, 386
1 Timothy, 366
    church office qualifications in, 397–398
    orthodoxy/institutional order in, 397
Titus, 266, 267–268, 326, 366, 374, 399, 414
Tobias, 253
Tobit, book of, 250, 252–254, 284, 299
Torah, 3, 7, 22, 43, 53–76, 192–193, 231, 255, 338.
    See also Mosaic Law; Tanakh
    anthropomorphic imagery, of God, 85
    on atonement of sins, 368
    on circumcision, 72
    documentary hypothesis of, 62–65
    Ezra as proclaimer of, 199–200
    lex talionis in, 43–44, 320
    loyalty, 241–242
    obedience, 253, 405
    Paul's attitude toward, 367–368
    Pharisees strict observance of, 283–284
    on poor, 164
    regulations in, 77
    revision in Ezekiel, 178
    on sacrifices, 403
    Sadducees literal reading of, 283
    salvation role of, 378
    Samaritan edition of, 49
    on slavery/women, 29, 388
Trajan, 407
transcendence, of God, 12
Transfiguration, of Jesus, 408
Transjordan, 49
transmission, of Biblical text, 18–22
tree of life, 39, 40, 70
Twelve Apostles, 295, 318
Twelve Tribes of Israel, 83, 103
Tyre, 178–179, 244

Ugarit, 244
Underworld, 40–41, 332

Ur, 31, 33, 71, 214
Uriah, 127, 146, 234, 235
urim, 147
Utnapishtim, 37, 40, 71
Uzziah, of Judah, 153, 254

Vespasian, 267
visionary speculations, 8, 246–247
visions
    of Amos, 155
    of Ezekiel, 176–179
    of Ezra, 259–260
    of Joshua, 185
    in Revelation, 417–418
Vulgate Bible, Latin, 88, 259
    Jerome as translator of, 25, 234

wine, 275–276
Wisdom as creative Word, 342, 428
    character/value of, 257–258
    human history role of, 258
    Jesus as, 412
wisdom literature, 208–223, 249
    Babylonian Exile absence in, 209
    on cosmic balance of good/evil, 209
    Exodus absence in, 209
    introduction to, 208–210
    Job, 8, 9, 171, 194–195, 213–219, 242, 244, 257, 428–429
    Mosaic Covenant absence in, 209
    order in, 209
    Proverbs, 8, 208, 211–213, 256
Wisdom of Jesus Son of Sirach (Ecclesiasticus), 22, 250, 255–257, 284
Wisdom of Solomon, 209, 210, 220–221, 256, 257, 379, 381, 416
women, 62, 89, 119
    Bible perspective of, 29
    Jesus concern for, 329
    ministry of, 371
    prophetic roles of, 145
    roles of, 398
    women and, 279
Words of Solomon, 208
Writings (Kethuvim), 3, 7, 192–195. *See also* wisdom literature
    brief survey of, 193–195
    canonization of, 22
    1 Chronicles, 8, 104, 122, 194, 233, 234–235
    2 Chronicles, 8, 10, 141, 194, 233, 235–237
    Daniel, 8, 39–40, 70, 150, 194, 209, 231, 238, 242, 243–247, 250, 255, 298, 392, 422
    Ecclesiastes, 8, 151, 171, 194, 202, 208, 209, 219–222, 256
    Esther, 8, 74, 194, 228, 229–231, 238, 250
    Ezra, 8, 9, 194
    historical narratives of, 8
    Job, 8, 9, 171, 194–195, 213–219, 242, 244, 257, 428–429
    Lamentations, 8, 194, 201, 228–229
    Nehemiah, 8, 9, 194
    poetry of, 8

Proverbs, 8, 208, 211–213, 256
Psalms, 8, 10, 38, 193, 194, 203–207, 403
Ruth, 8, 194, 198, 224–227
short stories of, 8
Song of Songs, 8, 194, 201, 208, 227–228
visionary speculations of, 8

Xerxes I. *See* Ahasurerus

Yahweh, 24, 27, 38, 39, 52, 62, 64, 71, 86, 90, 103, 123, 142, 169, 170, 188, 204, 236, 424.
    See also Adonai; El; El Shaddai; Elohim; God
    anointed of, 206
    Baal contest with, 134–135
    Canaan worship of, 116
    cosmic justice of, 15
    David and, 55, 234
    Davidic Covenant rejection by, 193–194, 286–287
    earthling placement by, 68–70
    economic justice demand of, 154
    forgiveness, 98
    glory of, 130, 131
    heavenly court of, 214–215
    Israel's bond by, 55–56, 98, 156, 228
    jealousy of, 45, 56, 111, 112, 114, 116
    Jerusalem abandonment by, 178
    Jerusalem Temple acceptance by, 132
    Jews faithfulness to, 241–242
    justice/compassion of, 56
    on Leviathan's role, 218–219
    as Lord of the Covenant, 14–16
    Moses and, 55, 78–79, 146
    Mount Sinai appearance by, 53
    Pentateuch promises in, 54
    revelation of His universe, 217–219
    sanctuary, priest presiding over, 88
    Second Temple appearance of, 189, 193
    transcendence/immanence of, 182
    war against Pharaoh, 80–81

Yahwist (J), 62–63. *See also* JE Epic
    anthropomorphic portrayal of, 98
    on Israelite escape from Egypt, 81
YHWH. *See* Tetragrammaton
Yom Kippur. *See* Atonement, Day of

Zadok, 180, 282
Zealots, 267, 285–286
Zebedee, 295, 336
Zechariah, 149, 150, 185–186, 238, 322, 329
Zedekiah (king), 142, 168, 171, 287
Zephaniah, 148, 164–166
Zerubbabel, 184–185, 197, 198
Zeus, 274–275
ziggurat, 34
Zion, 204
Zipporah, 91, 92
Zoroastrianism, 254, 396